1 MONTH OF
FREE
READING

at
www.ForgottenBooks.com

By purchasing this book you are eligible for one month membership to ForgottenBooks.com, giving you unlimited access to our entire collection of over 1,000,000 titles via our web site and mobile apps.

To claim your free month visit:
www.forgottenbooks.com/free867812

ISBN 978-0-265-56713-5
PIBN 10867812

BYE-GONES,

RELATING TO

WALES AND THE BORDER COUNTIES.

1880-1.

MRS. HARDCASTLE.—Ay, *your* times were fine times, indeed. . . I hate such old-fashioned trumpery.

MR. HARDCASTLE.—And I love it. I love everything that's old : old friends, old times, old manners, old books, old wine.

OSWESTRY:

PRINTED AT THE CAXTON WORKS, OSWALD ROAD.

———

(Only one hundred and fifty Copies printed.)

BYE-GONES—INDEX, 1880-1.

BYE-GONES FOR 1880.

NOTES, QUERIES, and REPLIES, on subjects interesting to Wales and the Borders, must be addressed to "ASKEW ROBERTS, Croeswylan, Oswestry." Real names and addresses must be given, in confidence, and MSS. must be written legibly, on one side of the paper only.

OSWESTRY ADVERTIZER, JANUARY 7, 1880.

NOTES.

RICHARD EDWARDES OF TREVONNEN, p: Oswestry, gent.—Will 1647-8 (28 Essex) wife Elinor house in Soughton (wh. came to me from my mother) for life. House etc. in Sweeney to Nephew Peirce Edwardes and Susanna Edwardes, my sisters children. . . . Nephew John E. eldest brother of said Peirce and Susanna. . . . Chief mansion house in Trevonnen to Elinor my wife for life—remainder to John Edwardes sonne of my Nephew,Samuell E. . . . House called the plassey in Soughton and lands "to the use of the poore of the parishes of Oswestrye and Llansillin and for two Sermons heareafter in and by these presents expressed equally to bee devided betweene them for ever." . . . . "Cozine" Thomas Williams sonne of my Aunt Owen-howar. . . . "Item I give and bequeath the somme of sixe shillinges and eight pence to the viccar of the parish of Llansillin...Denbigh to be payd yearely to the viccar of Llansillin aforesaid for ever for a lecture Sermon to be preached in the parish Church of Llansillin uppon the ffive and Twentyeth day of December yearely for ever"—bequest in same terms to Vicar of Oswestry. . . Son in law Robert Muttrom daughter in law Ruth, wife of the said Samuell Edwards. . . . Son in law William Muttrome. . . . Nephews John Jones and Samuell Jones. . . . Cousins Roger Evans of Sweeney, gent and Ric. Davyes of Kewhinva, Montgomery, gent.
Sentence "Johannem Edwards, Davidem Jones, nepotes ex fratre." J.C.C.S.

A LADY'S IMPRESSIONS OF WALES
A CENTURY AGO.

Sometime between the years 1765 and 1771, probably during the latter year, a Shropshire lady made an excursion into Merionethshire, and stayed for a month at Peniarth. Seven letters, giving an account of this journey, are preserved at Hatton Grange by Mrs. Kenyon-Slaney; and there are copies at Peniarth, from which, by the kindness of Mr. W. W. E. Wynne, we are able to give readers of *Bye-gones* the benefit of them.
The writer was Elizabeth, wife of Thomas Presland, Esq., of Walford Hall, near Baschurch, and daughter of Robert Aglionby Slaney, Esq., of Hatton Grange, near Shiffnal, (who was born in 1693) by Frances Theresa his wife, daughter of William Plowden of Plowden, Esq., also of Shropshire.
The letters are curious, as describing parts of Merionethshire and Montgomeryshire, and the habits of society there, amongst the upper class of the gentry, in the latter half of the eighteenth century. As was usual in the writings of ladies of that day" the letters are badly spelt.
ED.

Dear Sister,—After we had bid edieu to Walford we proceeded to Elsemere, drank tea at Mr. Moretons, see the green, from whence their is a very fine view. We then set out for Orton [Overton], on the road see many pleasing prospects, but why the shoud call the Church yard one of the seven wonders, I cant tell, for exapt the Old Yew trees, I see nothing to be admired, so on we whent to Wrexham, where the out side of the Church, and one monument is noble, but the Town we see little of, for it raind so violent for three days we coud not stir, and did Little Else, but eat drink, and pick our fingers, at neither hearing nor seeing Miss Williamsis, without whom we ventured an others days journey, and was highly pleasd with seeing the Vale of Cluen, [Clwyd] and many other things worth notice, we stopd at a little Inn upon the road to refresh our horses, but exapt Mr. P. and I coud have eat some hangd veal and drank some ginn there was no food for us, so on we rode to Ballow [Bala] where the told us there had bin a dreadful fever, and what shoud I see on a Bench at the Ale house door, with a pipe in his mouth, but their Doctor as fat as a pig, his face as red as the hung veal, the woman offerd me, his nose purple, his cloths if well sold, not worth half a crown, and this was the man, who attended near three hundred of a putrid fever, most of which I need not tell you dy'd, the account sunk my spirits, but upon hearing Miss Williams was within an hours ride the rise, but a monstar of a Dog had likd to have fetchd them down, for he catchd hold of my jacket, and the woman desired I woud lett him conduct me to her pantry, where she gave me some oat bread, desired I wud present it to the Dog, who woud then become my friend, and loose me, and so he did and I never bestow'd any thing with greater pleasure. I then askd what meat was in the house, she said some fissh, and a leg of mutton, I bid her roast it, yess good Bless you I will take it out of the pot, and put it down directly, for it has not boild an hour, I said no more and roasted it came to table, but I eat none but got a good

---

* "Dr. Johnson was talking to her ('Mrs. Thrale) and Sir Philip Jennings, of the amazing progress made of late years in literature by the women. He said he was astonished at it, and told them that he well remembered when a woman who could spell a common letter was all accomplished; but now they vied with the men in everything."—*Diary of Madame D'Arblay* Vol. I., p. 227. The remark was made by Dr. Johnson in 1779.

bed and slept till morning. We then set out for a Mr.
Vaughns of Hangwood [Hengwrt] and whent close by the
side of Ballow pool, which is many miles long, the driving
rode close to the edge of it, and truly thankfull I was when
past.   we stop'd at an Inn to regale ourselves, but such a
house, and entertainment I never met with, it is a house
many gentlemen meet at once a year, in the parlour was
two small windows cover'd with Ivy, fac'ing the door a
little house, and pigsty, in the room a large old fashiond
bread and cheese cubard, within two . . . . , usd I
do suppose the last meeting, but stunk most shamefully,
in came dinner mutton chops swiming with gress, and a
veal pye, which the woman assured Miss Williams had
bin kept for her above a fortnight, which by their eating
I supose the thought a perfection, but to my shame I say
it, I was forcd to take drops, say I was sick, for fear the
shoud think me more nice then wise, farewell for ever
hopes I, and in to the Coach we whent, we soon got
to Mr. Vaughns where we met with an excellent
entertainment, of which I eat not a Little, his House is a
good one, the situation romantick, and pretty, it looks
upon an arm of the sea, on the other side of which is a
Little Village, a neat Church on ariseing ground,
[Llanelltyd] mixed with wood, on the back of the house, a
good garden with walks cascade, and shrubs, and near by
some Beautyfull medows, and a hanging wood, at one side
of the house a very high green Hill, from the top of which
you see a charming Country. some milles after we left
Mr. Vaughns, we drove for milles between too long high
black mountains, with rocks all along them, on one rock
is a peice of white Rock, exactly the shape of a woman,
which affords some odd storry, but I coud not hear what,
no sooner out of this confind ride, but we mount up, and
down many high mountains, from the highest I see
Ballmouth [Barmouth] and the mean Ocean, what an amaze-
ing sight, the milles off it, but down the Hill we go . . . .
no more, but the guid tells me by . . . . will show me a
wonder full sight. . . . . . shud it be, but a stone Bridg,
such . . . . . . every day in England, which he seemd
surprizd I did not more admire, but we proceed across a
long common to a narrow lean which takes us up to Peniart,
where the family if sincere, are not a Little glad to see
me, and I rejoiced to arive safe at a place so much talkd of,
and will in my next tell you how I like it, till then remain
with only adding Mr. Freslands love to mine,   your ever
aff sister   E Pres   Peniarth July ye 10
[Addressed to "Miss Slaney, Shrewsbury."]

QUERIES.

LLANYMYNECH AND TRAFALGAR.—I was
told the other day that there was a movement set on foot
after the battle of Trafalgar to erect a "Nelson's Pillar"
on Llanymynech Hill which should rival "Rodney's
Pillar" on The Breidden.   Can any of your readers tell
how far the project advanced.   H.B.

THUNDER ON THE ORGAN.—Some years
ago an old Shrewsbury man told me that in his younger
days a very clever performer astonished the good folks of
that town with his imitations of thunder on the organ.
Do any of your readers know anything about this individual?   WYLE COP.

BWLCH-Y-PAWL.—Mr. C. W. W. Wynn, in
his address to the Archæologists last August, mentions
the above as "the established place of arbitration by the
princes of Powys in any dispute that arose between
Gwynedd and Dyfed." It is on the border of Powysland
on the old road from Bala to Machynlleth. I ask if this
has any connection with Paulinus or Pawl Hen, whose

epitaph is said by Camden and others to have finished with
the words, "Cultor pientissimus æqui," though these
words are not now to be seen on the celebrated stone at
Dolaucothy. The stone was found at Pantypolion.
                                          CAEAWC.-

SHROPSHIRE GRAMMAR SCHOOLS.—You
would do good service in your pages, I think, if you were
to invite correspondents to send you the names, and any
records, of men in any way of mark, who have been
educated in the public schools of Shropshire. Anyone
who has access to old newspapers would be able to find
plenty of material, I apprehend. After doing duty in
your columns these notes ought to be woven into an
interesting paper for the Shropshire Archæological
Society's Transactions.   AN OLD SALOPIAN.

A WELSH PROVERB.—In a report (in the
Cambrian News) of an Eisteddfod held at Llanfihangel-y-
Creuddyn, the following proverb was given out as a theme
for an extempore speech, "O'i phen y mae godro buwch,"
literally translated would read, "From out of her head a
cow is to be milked." This proverb, in Merionethshire,
is understood to convey the following meaning, that a
good milcher is to be known by her horn and her nose, and
a mistress in speaking to a servant maid about the quantity
of milk given by a cow, says, "If you want the cow to
give milk you must look to put something in her head
[mouth]," that is upon what, and how, you feed her with.
The proverb is also varied in the same county, "Wrth
ei phen y mae prynu buwch," i.e., "By her head you
should select a cow." I should like to know what meaning
is attached to this proverb in Cardiganshire.   T.W.H.

MONTGOMERYSHIRE ENCLOSURE ACTS,—
From the abstracts of Enclosure Acts in the interesting
paper by "M.C.J." in the No. of *Montgomeryshire Collections* for October, 1879, it appears that by the two first
Acts of 1761 and 1788, no account whatever was made of
the right of the poor to pasturage, &c., on the Commons
specified, and in the subsequent Acts of 1796, 1800, 1801,
1810, while some compensation was made to poor persons
who had erected cottages by the grant of a lease for 20
years, or by payment of a sum to be determined by the
arbitrary will of the Commissioner, none whatever was
made to the poor for the loss of their property in pasturage, &c., unless, indeed, in the single case of Caer-
einion Uchcoed Manor, "allotments to be made
for public stone quarries and for public tur-
baries," are to be considered as such.   The
effrontery with which the entire property in
these commons is declared, by statutes of which the
spoliators were themselves the framers, to be vested chiefly
in the Earl of Powis, and other territorial magnates of
the Church of England, would probably fail of its object
from the enlightened resistance it would encounter, if
attempted now, instead of in the last century. The
aggression, however, bears a marked resemblance to the
wholesale enclosures of commons in England, whereby the
rights of the poor in their commonage and recreation
grounds were confiscated to the use of the rich by means
of similar legislative enactments, passed for their own
benefit by the latter, during the period which intervened
between the Wars of the Roses, and the assumption by
the Sovereign of the title, hitherto unheard of, of
"Supreme Head under God of the Church of England."
The confiscation of the property of the poor in commonage
and pasturage was followed immediately by that of the
property of the Church, which became the bribe of the
confiscators for their assent to the usurpation of the
spiritual supremacy by the secular power. The connection
of the two confiscations will readily reveal itself to a

thoughtful enquirer into the historical bearings of the
subject. The communication of any information would
be interesting that would show whether the poor in North
Wales, and particularly in Montgomeryshire, are still in
possession of any portion of their ancient rights in
commonage and pasturage, or whether they have become
wholly extinct.   H.W.L.

AN OLD OSWESTRY ROBBERY.— Years ago,
I have heard the late Mr. Abraham Morgan relate the
particulars of a daring robbery effected on the premises of
Messrs. Croxon and Lucas, drapers, Cross-street, Oswestry, in the year 1820. As far as I recollect the particulars,
they were as follows :—The shop in question was that now
occupied by Mr. Weaver, chemist, and Mr. Morgan, who
lived opposite, one night, as he was going to bed, noticed
a light through the fanlight of Messrs. Croxon and Lucas's
shop ; on which he remarked to his wife that their neighbours must be going to have a funeral to supply the next
day, or they would not be so late in their shop. The next
morning one of the assistants came across and told Mr.
Morgan that their shop had been robbed, but they wished
the matter kept as quiet as possible ; on which Mr. Morgan
told him what he had seen. This being communicated to
Mr. Croxon, he came across and told Mr. Morgan that
there must have been more than one engaged, for the goods
not taken had all been neatly arranged again on the
shelves. Some time afterwards, a piece of print was
brought to the shop to be matched, the party having
it saying she had not quite enough to make a dress. Mr.
Lucas at once identified the pattern as being one like a
print that had been amongst the goods stolen. Further
enquiry elicited the fact that a man named Lewis, who
was a tenant of Mr. Croxon's at a house in Beatrice-street,
had given the print to a child whose parents resided
on the Bailey Head, to whom he had stood godfather.
Lewis was apprehended, and other goods stolen were
traced. He was afterwards tried and condemned, and
was executed at Shrewsbury. Mr. Croxon visited him in
gaol when he admitted the fairness of the trial, and stated
that when engaged in the robbery he noticed one of the
female servants of the house (through a pane in the door
looking from the shop to the house) come down the stairs];
she fortunately did not turn her head towards the place
where he was or he would have shot her. He also said he
had noticed Mr. Morgan in his night shirt at his window.
I believe only four days before the robbery Lewis had
taken the Plough Inn. Is there any report of the trial
extant?   AN OLD OSWESTRIAN.

————

STRAY NOTES.

The following amongst other anecdotes about judges'
lodgings is told in the *Leisure Hour* for December :—"In
a small Welsh guide in our possession under date of
1734 we find a presentment made by the grand jury at
Beaumaris that the judges' lodgings of that town "ought
to be improved," and the curious facts are stated that such
lodgings are so "poore and straight that the judge eateth
and sleepeth in rooms with earth floors where fowls and
other unseemly things do congregate, and noteth his
arrival in the town by a flag fixed to a prop which is
posted up through the chimney of the house."

The Fireside for December says :—Until as late as the
former part of the last century the southern counties had
a flourishing iron trade, the smelting furnaces having been
fed with wood which abounded in neighbouring forests.
The railings of St. Paul's Cathedral are a specimen of old
English iron-work before the experiment was tried of
smelting the ore with coal. When the trade was

gradually coming to an end in the last century for want
of fuel, the manufacturers were not aware that coal would
serve as a substitute for wood until the experiment was
successfully tried by the Darby family, who set up their
works at Coalbrookdale, in Shropshire.

The following extract from a letter by Mrs. Stanley,
the wife of the Bishop of Norwich and mother of Dean
Stanley, shows the singular popularity of Lord Hill at
the time of the visit of the Allied Sovereigns in 1814.
"The mob got hold of Lord Hill in the Park at the
review, and did literally pull his coat and his belt to pieces.
He snatched off his Order of the Bath and gave it to
Major Churchill, who put it in the holster of his saddle,
where he preserved it from the mob only by drawing his
sword and declaring he would cut any man's hand off who
touched it. Some kissed his sword, his boots, his spurs,
anything they could touch ; they pulled hair out of his
horse's tail ; and one butcher's boy who arrived at the
happiness of shaking his hand they chaired, exclaiming
'This is the man who has shaken hands with Lord
Hill !'"

IN WREXHAM CHURCHYARD.
Here lies interr'd beneath these stones,
The beard, the flesh, and eke the bones
Of Wrexham's clerk, old David Jones.

————

AN EPITHALAMIUM OF THE 15TH CENTURY

On the marriage of Robert Whitney of Whitney, in the
county of Hereford, to Alice, daughter of Sir Thomas
ap Sir Roger Vaughan, Lord of Herast, or Hergest, in
Herefordshire, who was beheaded at Banbury in 1469,
and great-grand-daughter of Sir David Gam. (From
the Welsh of Lewis Glyn Cothi, Works, p. 27.)

1.
Is there one on the banks of the Wye has the humour,
 Of Squire Robert Whitney, whom God ever bless?
Of the cross-figured mansion how staunch is the eagle !
 From Trysel he takes his descent, and no less.

2.
His bridal descent—not a thought it needs further,
 —Thomas Roger's own daughter is her pedigree :
'Tis enough—if he choose Mistress Alice to marry,
 Of a sun among stars his selection will be.

3.
Of the Court every Courser with stars is bespangled,
 The liquor and viands there harbour would fill ;
Past the strong tow'rs of Robert whene'er I've to travel,
 His watch and his ward make my blood to run chill.

4.
This master of mine's in the Tow'rs of his father ;
 Newgate holds not the money about him in coin ;
The parish can't number his men in plate-armour,
 And his steeds, and his spearmen, the battle to join.

5.
There sits Mistress Alice, all retired in her bower
 With her money and treasures, so grandly array'd :
On a Monday she puts on a fine robe of damask,
 Of camlet, like velvet, with pattern displayed.

6.
O'er her cheek and her temple of gold her attire is,
 She wears garlands, and scarlet, in dignity great ;
For the salmon's own life-time (a) she'll call upon Jesus,
 For nine lives of a man shall she bear her estate.

7.
All Elvael's invited, so lavish is Robert,
 Of his store he gives freely to me, nor afraid,
As a Justice, is he to deliver just sentence,
 When sitting in judgment on some Master Cade. (b)

————

(a) The salmon is often referred to by the Welsh Bards as a
long-lived animal. 'Nine lives' is also a common expression with
them.   (b). i.e. traitor, like Jack Cade.

8.
There breathes not the man who shall prove in him treason,
  While there lives boat or ship with an anchor at sea :
Permit it he will not—he'll never give reason—
  While the moon night illumine, or blue the sky be.

9.
As all the world knows, in my Lord's lordly mansion,
  Are huntsmen and yeomen—that none will deny :
In its stalls stand the coursers, all gilded and neighing,
  Bows for battle, and horns, and the stag's bleating cry.

10.
In Whitney are greyhounds, of hounds, too, a hundred,
  There are huntsmen in plenty, all ready to start ;
With kitchens for Christmas (c), and buttery, and cellars,
  And while workmen chatter, many cooks play their part.

11.
From the Mansion is carried loud laughter of peasants,
  From the Tow'r that of many an unbidden guest :
From the Bridegroom bring progeny, offspring, descendants ;
  From the Bride bring a blossom,—a line to be blest.

12.
Amen ! I say too, may her children content her,
  And gladden the bosom of Whitney's brave lord :
May they grow in their Mansion, in lieu of good liquor,
  And in their white Tower, where riches are stored.

13.
My Lady's free Mansion, my lord's goodly mansion,
  Is the wretches' asylum, so holy is she :
Tower fairer to us than the White Tow'r of London,
  Is Whitney's, so bounteous and gentle is he !

14.
What mansion, save that on the headland of Alice,
  Like Sandwich, is fashion'd like five on the dice !
More lofty than Joseph's, or Sisera's palace,
  The fortress on Wye will grow ever in size.

15.
Not dearer to me are the Houses for Charity
  By Lazarus built, nor Nudd's own on the strand,
Than Whitney's, as peerless for wine and hilarity,
  As flowers from the South are to ev'ry far land.

16.
From the one and the other more lavish the gifts are,
  Than the flow of the stream to the guileless and meek ;
So the Wise Men gave Mary the gold from their coffers,
  From far when they travell'd their Saviour to seek.

17.
Of their gold-ore and mead, goods of both and of either,
  I shall ne'er be denied by this well wedded pair ;
Their land, too, will revenue bring me, and raiment,
  Divers herbs, and, of feasts, too, ne'er fail me a share.

18.
Divers dainties shall reach us from plain and from mountain,
  Divers birds, too, and fishes fresh out of the sea ;
He is Arthur himself, so he will not o'erlook me,
  His Queen, too, Gwenhwyvar,—like-minded is she.

19.
Woe, woe to the Saxon who loves not their Castle,
  Of the Welshman who scorns them be told a sad tale ;
Nor Non, Daniel, Denis, Cedwyn, them to cherish,
  David, Dwynwen, Elias, nor Hilary fail !

20.
May they live the long life both of Nöe and Moses,
  Of two trees, the oak female and male be their age ;
Late let them be parted, when Death their course closes,
  With health, Mary, start it, make happy its stage !

21.
Yes, late be their parting, the length of their life-time,
  From Whitney to Monmouth, the oldest defy :
To bestow, with their links of pure gold many collars,
  And with wine crown the bowl on the bank of the Wye.
                                 H.W.L.

(c). The Welsh is 'Ystwyll,' literally, Epiphany. Dr. Owen Pughe derives this word from Yst and Gwyll, "that exists in the gloom." It appears to me to be compounded rather of ys, and twyll, or ys and tywyll—ex dolo (Diaboli), or ex obscuro.

JANUARY 14, 1880.

NOTES.

AN INTERESTING REMINISCENCE.—In the *Life-and Correspondence of Mrs. Delany,* vol. II., page 131, appears the following letter, from Lady Elizabeth Cavendish Bentinck (eldest daughter of William, 2nd Duke of Portland) to Mrs. Dewes :—

                       Bulstrode, 23 Nov., 1740.

DEAR PIP,
  I love you with all my heart. Mrs. Elstob gives her service to you. I thank you for the pretty letter you sent me by Penny. I learn very well the Common Prayer-book and Bible, and have almost got by heart the Turtle and Sparrow. Papa and mama's best compliments to you. I have learnt Molly Mog of the Rose, and am learning now the English grammar. I should be very glad to see you, and am
         My dear Pip, your affectionate friend
              ELIZABETH CAVENDISH BENTINCK.

About the year 1823, I went to breakfast at the house of the above lady—she was then Marchioness Dowager of Bath, and resided in Charles Street, or Hill-street, Berkeley Square, I think the former. Of the party were two of Lady Bath's grand-nieces, the Misses Cotes, and a Miss Arbuthnot. After breakfast, we went to a review in Hyde Park, where, in the crowd, Miss Arbuthnot lost her shoe, for which we had a difficult search. We afterwards adjourned to Lady Stamford's, Lady Bath's sister, for luncheon. So I, who am alive and in health upon 2nd Jan., 1880, visited at the house of a lady who wrote a letter upon 23 Nov. 1740.   W.

WELSH MEMBERS OF PARLIAMENT.
  Mr. Breese, in his *Kalendars of Gwynedd* (quoting Mr. Wynne of Peniarth) gives the following names of persons chosen to represent Merionethshire in Parliament 15 Edw. II. :—Eignion Vachan, Jevan, ap Gurgenn (Gurgeneu), Llewelyn ap David Vaughan, and Griffith ap Madoc.
  A Blue Book, "Return of Members of Parliament," has just been issued by Government in which the following is the first record for Wales :—
         20 Edw. II. (1326-7)
  By Writ, dated Kenilworth, 8 Jan. 1326-7, the Justiciary of North Wales is ordered to send Twenty-four Men from those parts, as well English as Welsh—the following were Returned :—
  Anglesey County : Howel ap Griffuyth, David ap Howel, Tuder Duy, Tuder ap Lewelyn, Lewelyn Vaghan, Howel ap Tuder.
  Beaumaris Borough : Petrus Russel, Willielmus Saleman.
  Carnarvon County : Jorwerd ap Griff', Griffuyth ap Howel, Howel ap Jevan, David ap Ada, Howel ap Madoc, Griffuyth ap David.
  Carnarvon Borough : Ricardus de Monte Gomeri, Ricardus de Middleton.
  Conway Borough : Henricus Som', Ricardus de Heywode.
  Merioneth County : Eygu' Vaghan, Eygu' Vaghan (sic), Jevan ap Gurgen, Lewelyn ap David Vaughan, Griffiuus ap Madoc'.
  In future issues we hope to give a complete list from this Government Return, for the whole of Wales and Shropshire, with, probably, the other Border Counties.
                             ED.

QUERIES.

OLD CUSTOMS.—There are a good many of us who have no objections to old customs when they are carried within reasonable limits, and have the proper ring about them ; but when the singing of "Wissel wassel, bread and possel " is kept up for three or four nights, and is varied with such foreign importations as "Mary came weeping, and drew the stone away " (as it was at several Oswestry doors last November) it is time to protest. Then at Christmas, too, there is no reason why—morning, noon, and night—discordant noises should be uttered at your doors for the space of a week, under the pretence that the good old Christmas feeling is being kept up ! But it was not merely to expostulate that I took up my pen, but to put a query. In Oswestry, year after year, we have howled before our houses a tune something like a polka gone demented, which I am able to present in the Tonic Sol-Fa notation, thus :—

Key G.

d | m.m : m : r | d.d : d ‖ r | m.s : f : m | r : — ‖
f | m.m : m : l | s.s : s ‖ d | s.f : m : r | d : — ‖

In years gone by, I believe, this tune (under the name of "Arlington") was in use by Church and Chapel choirs, but I am not aware that it is usual elsewhere to sing it at all, or at any rate to the exclusion of everything else, during the Christmas week. I should like to know whether this is so or not ? The favourite carol to it is " When Angels Watch, &c."   JARCO.

CAMBRIAN INSTITUTIONS.

I should be glad if your correspondents would supplement the following list of Institutions founded at various times for the benefit or delectation of Wales and Welshmen. Also if they would give fuller information as to such as I have enumerated :—

Society of Ancient Britons. This Society met in London, on Mar. 1, 1820, to celebrate its 106th anniversary. There was a service at St. Martins in the Fields, and afterwards a dinner, at which Lord Bute presided. It was announced that the subscriptions on the occasion amounted to £1,341 13s., which included a hundred guineas from George IV. on his accession to the throne. The money was raised for the Welsh Charity School. Who founded this society ?

The Cycle; mentioned in *Bye-gones* June 18, 1873. A list of the members of this society in 1723, is given in the *Cam. Quar. Mag.* Vol. 1, p. 212, and it existed as a social club in 1829, the date at which the magazine was issued. When was it originated, and when did it die out ?

Old Cymmrodorion Society. This was established in London in 1751, under the patronage of the Prince of Wales, for the cultivation of the Welsh language. When did it cease ? I observe it was revived in 1820, with the additional title " or, Metropolitan Cambrian Institution." Sir Watkin Wynn, Mr. Charles Wynn, Lord Dynevor, and others, attended the meeting. When did the Society finally disappear ?

Gwyneddigion Society. This was founded in 1771 by Mr. Owen Jones, a native of Llanfihangel-Glyn-y-Myfyr, in Denbighshire, who early went to London, where it is said of him he became so much excited at a theatre, during the performance of Shakespeare's Henry V., that, when Fluelen compelled Pistol to eat the leek, he clapped his hands and called out "That's right ! that's right." Mr. Owen Jones, "Myfyr," was the father of Mr. Owen Jones, architect. How long did this institution exist ?

The Caractacusian Society. The *Gents : Mag :* 1755 records the annual meeting of this society on Tuesday, August 5, 1755, and adds, "It was held upon that memorable mount Caer Caradoc, in the lordship of Cardington; which name was derived from Caractacus, that heroic British prince, who made a noble resistance

upon the summit of this hill, against Ostorius, proprætor of the Romans, A.D. 53, and whose kingly virtues shone forth in native pomp even when a captive in chains, before Claudius seated on his tribunal at Rome." What was the ' object' of this society, and how long did it exist ?

Cymreigyddion Society. This was established in 1792 for debating subjects in the Welsh tongue, and preserving the language. It was also a charitable institution, and at all meetings a board bearing the words "Elusengarwch" was displayed. It had its rise in North Wales. Where ? and how did it dispose of the money ? and when did it die ?

Welsh Bardic Society. This is mentioned in the Memoirs of Richard Roberts Jones (Dick o Aberdaron) as existing in London in 1810, it being an "association of his countrymen," to whom he applied for relief. What more is known of it ?

I hope to give another instalment next week.

      N. W. S.

REPLIES.

THUNDER ON THE ORGAN. (Jan. 7, 1880.)—We are told in the *Salopian Journal* of the period, that on Mar. 27, 1805, in answer to an advertisement for an organist at Whitchurch, Salop, three only out of the candidates who attended ventured to attempt reading the pieces selected for the occasion by Mr. Vickery of Oxford, the umpire appointed. The choice fell upon Mr. Charles Saxton of Shrewsbury. A month later we find a paragraph in the same paper stating that " Mr. Weston's performances of Sacred Music at St. Chad's Church (Shrewsbury) on Sunday last (Apr. 27) were much admired, particularly his imitation of Thunder, introduced into the Voluntary after Divine Service, both morning and afternoon. The collections for the benefit of the Sunday Schools of that parish amounted to upwards of £24." It would appear that instead of the usual "Charity Sermon," the method for "raising the wind" for the benefit of the Schools, was out of the organ. A fortnight later it was announced that "Mr. Weston, whose astonishing performances on the organ at St. Chad's" had been previously recorded, had " consented to repeat them at St. Mary's and St. Julian's, for the benefit of the Sunday Schools of those parishes ; also of St. Alkmond and the Abbey ;" this being "positively the last time of his performing in public." The performance was again to be on a Sunday. In a later issue of the paper I gather that Mr. D. Parkes, one of the churchwardens, prohibited the performance at St. Mary's—that Mr. Weston was a candidate, though not a competitor, for the office of organist at Whitchurch—and that a libel lawsuit in connection with some remarks made upon him in another paper, loomed in the future. These I will again refer to ; meanwhile I should like to know how such a genius ever came to offer himself for so subordinate a post as organist at Whitchurch.   J.?.R.

IN TAIBACH CHURCHYARD, SOUTH WALES.
    Hurrah, my boys ! at the Parson's fall,
    For if he'd liv'd he'd a-buried us all.

IN LLANFLANTWTHYL CHURCHYARD.
Under this stone lies Meredith Morgan,
Who blew the bellows of our church organ ;
Tobacco he hated—to smoke most unwilling,
Yet never so pleased as when pipes he was filling ;
No reflection on him for rude speech could be cast.
Tho' he gave our old organist many a blast.
      No puffer was he,
        Though a capital blower ;
      He could fill double G,
        And now lies a note lower.

ELEGY BY IEUAN DEULWYN

On Sir Richard Herbert of Colebrook, near Abergavenny, Knight, brother of Sir William Herbert, Knight, afterwards Earl of Pembroke, sons of Sir William ab Thomas (Y Marchog Glas o Went), by his second wife Gwladus, daughter of Sir David Gam, Knight Banneret of Agincourt. The two brothers were taken and beheaded by the Lancastrian party after the battle of Banbury, or Danesmore, A.D. 1469.

Cut short hath been the fair, well-rounded neck,
Of Herbert tall—the best of Christians he.
The very world itself is all extinct,
And, since Sir Richard's death, the month's an age.
For our betrayal God caused, unawares,
Of treasons greatest that at Banbury's fight.
Like that of Christ our Lord, beside the Cross,
Is my affecting tale, anent a Knight.
'Twere hard for me to pardon even one,
Since not one there would yield to spare his life.
Had there been left a hope of this, belike,
Wrath would not now be roused in either Gwent.
A wretched town Trefenni (a) is become !
No town at all, save when and while he lived.
They cozen'd us at first but one was slain ;
Less were our plaint had all been slain but he.
T' avenge his death will be no easy thing ;
Not one the land hath left to quit the deed,
Appear what pow'r there may of belted knights ;
What boots it all, when stunted is the neck !
Surrender'd all shall be the forest now,
Since he is dead, who was its doughtiest Tree !
Thorns will be sown throughout the Island's length,
And, from her Oaks, a harvest reap'd of chaff.
Bright-red the boughs are, by St. James' Feast !
Where'er they grow, o'er all our country round.
Dead is our cause indeed in Cymru's vales,
The head cut off, that whilom was our stay.
Belike the bodies twain thus headless made
Will bring to us beheading of our sports.
Long shall we be without another Earl,
Or—greater acquisition still—a Knight !
Ne'er was our noble blood more null than now,
Since first our being was, now he's entombed.
From dignity primeval Adam fell,
And now his low estate is even ours.
The pains of some began with summer's dawn,
And with S. James' vigil came their worst.
One Sunday lay the South in all her pride,
The Thursday after, too, whom Alice (b) ruled ;
But, on the Monday next, the Kingdom's rib
Was shatter'd, to my simple intellect ;
When that fell Summer founder'd to its fall,
The very World seem'd waning to its end.
That day a hideous cry uprose to Heav'n,
For th' Earl, and for the Knight his brother, both ;
That they were far away made greater grief.
We yet in memory bear a Prince (c) of yore,
As these at Banbury, so cut off at Buillt.
Low had we pitch'd the keynote of our cry,
Had they, not he, been shorter by the head ;
His end, for that, in sooth were well enough,
Had edge of English axe not hewn him down.
The keenness that hath cleft that lofty neck,
With thud our hearts that froze, may Warwick feel !
                                        H.W.L.

(a) Probably for Abergavenny. Tref 'Fenni, the town on the Gavenni, near which Colebrook is situated.
(b) A cant term for the English, probably from Alis Rhonwen or Rowena, daughter of the Saxon Hengist, espoused by the traitor, Vortigern.—See *Enwogion*, s. v. Gwrtheyrn.
(c) Llewelyn ab Gruffydd.

A MONSTER OAK TREE.—The *Gents: Mag:* for June 1820 says, at p. 555: "C. H. Leigh, Esq., has upon a farm of his, near Pontypool, a very large hollow oak-tree ; in the cavity of which his tenant, Mr. Williams, has, during the winter, fed six or seven calves. Two gentlemen on horseback lately rode into it, one of whom turned his horse round, and came out again without dismounting."

SIR WATKIN AND HIS FOXHOUNDS.—"Llangedwin, Sep. 1843. My cousin is now here, and has brought over nearly two hundred hounds to hunt some wretched foxes which are supposed to be in the woods. I proposed to him to take a gun and shoot them in order to save time, but he was quite horrified at the idea, so the whole valley has been disturbed this morning by the howling and screeching of these beasts, and the glorious result has been three little foxes, to accomplish which he had to be out at four o'clock in the morning."—(*Memorials of Charlotte Williams-Wynn.*)

A SHREWSBURY SWARM OF BEES 60 YEARS AGO.—A large swarm of bees lately visited the Market Square at Shrewsbury, and many of them settled on the head of one of the dealers in vegetables. A sergeant of militia immediately procured a broom which he hoisted on his halbert, whilst a female sounded the usual music on such occasions ; and in about half an hour the whole of the swarm were collected on the broom—to the great joy of the market people—and hived. A dispute then arose between the sergeant and the woman, respecting which had a right to the new colony, and the latter in a passion upset the whole, in consequence of which many of the bees were killed, but fortunately no person was stung. The sergeant again, with other assistance, restored the bees to the hive ; after which it was taken to the Mayor, the Rev. H. Owen, by the contending parties ; when it was claimed by his worship, Lord of the Manor of the town, to the mutual disappointment of the sergeant and his opponent.—*Gents: Mag:* 1820, page 630.

DEAN SWIFT AND THE CURATE.—The eccentric Dean Swift, in the course of one of those journeys to Holyhead which it is well known he several times performed on foot, was travelling through Church Stretton, Shropshire, when he put up at the sign of the Crown, and finding the host to be a communicative, good-humoured man, enquired if there was any agreeable person in the town with whom he might partake of a dinner (as he had desired him to provide one), and that such a person should have nothing to pay. The landlord immediately replied that the Curate was a very agreeable, companionable man, and would not, he supposed, have any objection to spend a few hours with a gentleman of his appearance. The Dean directed him to wait on Mr. Jones with his compliments, and to say that a traveller would be glad to be favoured with his company at the Crown, if it was agreeable. When the Dean had dined, and the glass began to circulate, the Curate made an apology for an occasional absence, saying that at three o'clock he had to read prayers and preach at the church. Upon this intimation the Dean replied that he should also attend prayers. Service being ended, and the two gentlemen having resumed their station at the Crown, the Dean began to compliment Mr. Jones upon his delivery of a very appropriate sermon, and remarked that it must have cost him (Mr. Jones) some time and attention to compose such a one. Mr. Jones observed that his duty was rather laborious, as he served another parish church at a distance, which, with the Sunday and weekly service at Church Stretton, straitened him much with respect to the time necessary for the composition of sermons, so that when the subjects pressed he could only devote a few nights and days to that purpose. "Well," says the Dean, "it is well for you to have such a talent; for my part, the very sermon you preached this afternoon cost me some months in the composing." On this observation Mr. Jones began to look very gloomy, and to recognize his companion. "However," rejoined the Dean, "don't you be alarmed; you have so good a talent at delivery that I hereby declare you have done more honour to my sermon this day than I could myself; and by way of compromising the matter you must accept of this half guinea for the justice you have done in the delivery of it."

LEVYING THE INCOME TAX.—The *Chester Chronicle,* in one of its issues for 1807, is responsible for the following:—"A collector of the income tax lately called upon his neighbour for the sum levied upon him, agreeably to the Act of Parliament, which he obstinately refusing to pay, the officer took the extraordinary method of recovering it by stripping him from top to toe, leaving him to enjoy the cooling breezes of our happy climate in the dress of an African negro."

SURGERY AT CARNARVON.—The papers of Nov. 1820 narrate the circumstances connected with the loss of a nose by a man in an affray at Carnarvon. When he came into court to seek damages he was so handsome looking a fellow that no one knew him. The secret was that a clever Carnarvon surgeon had, out of the integuments of the forehead, formed a new nose of such comely proportions as completely to have eclipsed the old one in beauty. So uncommon was such an operation sixty years ago, that it attracted the attention of some of the London magazines.

TRAVELLING IN WALES.—The great route through Wales to Holyhead was in such a state that, in 1685, a viceroy, going to Ireland, was five hours in travelling fourteen miles, from Saint Asaph to Conway. Between Conway and Beaumaris he was forced to walk a great part of the way; and his lady was carried in a litter. His coach was, with great difficulty, and by the help of many hands, brought after him entire. In general, carriages were taken to pieces at Conway, and borne, on the shoulders of stout Welsh peasants, to the Menai Straits. See *Thoresby's Diary,* Dec., 1708, quoted in *Macaulay's England,* vol. 1, p. 373, 8vo edition.

JANUARY 21, 1880.

NOTES.

PARLIAMENT OF ENGLAND (Jan. 14, 1880). As space is with us an object we only give the year in which the Parliament was summoned, and the names of the members. The following are the earliest representatives for Shropshire and Shrewsbury:—

COUNTY OF SALOP.

1290 Robertus Corbet; Johannes fil' Aer'
1295 Ditto; Rogerus Sprughos'
1298 Willielmus de Hodenit; Petrus de Eyton
1299 Ricardus de Harleye; Thomas de Roshale
1300 Thomas de Rossele; Petrus de Ayton
1302 Thomas de Rochale; Walterus de Beysyn
1304 Ricardus de Harleye; Johannes le Estraunge de Erkalowe.
1306 Ricardus de Harley; Johannes le Estraunge de Ercalewe

1307 Ricardus de Harleye; Johannes de Dene
1307 Willielmus de Lodelowe, Miles; Johannes **Extraneus** de Erkalewe
1309 Rogerus Corbet; ditto
1311 Ditto; Ricardus de Harleye
1312 Rogerus de Baskervill'; Henricus de Mortuo Mari
1313 Thomas de Tytteleye, or de Tuttele, Miles; Ricardus de Leighton', or de Letton, Miles.
1313 Ricardus de Leyghton,'; Thomas de Tittele
1314 Ditto; Thomas de Tyttenleye
1315 Ricardus de Harleye; Walterus de Hugeford
1316 Ditto; Thomas de Rossale
1316 Ricardus de Leyghton'; Willielmus de Forcer
1316 Johannes de Forcer; Walturus Haket
1318 Ricardus de Leyghton'; Rogerus Corbet de Caus.
1319 Thomas de Rosbale; Andreas de Kendale
1320 Willielmus de Soutford'
1321 Rogerus Corbet; Andreas de Kendale
1322 Walterus de Hugeford'; Fulco de Penebrugg'.
1322 Johannes du Lee; Thomas de Roshall.
1323 Rogerus Corbet, de Caus, miles; Willielmus de Ercalewe, miles
1324 Rogerus Corbet, de Hadleye; Willielmus de Walley
1325 Rogerus Corbet, de Caus, miles; Willielmus de Ercalewe, miles
1326 Rogerus de Cheigne; Willielmus de Ercalewe

BOROUGH OF SHREWSBURY.

1295 Ricardus Sturye; Galfridus Rondolfe
1298 Ricardus Pryde; Galfridus Roundulf.
1300 Ricardus Stury; Johnnes de Ludelowe
1302 Galfridus Rondulf'; Thomas Champeneys
1304 Willielmus Yaghan; Thomas de Byketon'
1306 Galfridus Rondolf; Ricardus Pride
1307 Thomas de Bykedon'; Rogerus de Staunton'
1307 Galfridus Rondulf; Simon de Stafford
1309 Ditto; Thomas de Bykedon
1311 Nicholaus le Spicer, de Salop'; Ricardus Pryde
1311 Hughe Gregory; Ricardus de Westbury.
1312 Hugo Gregori; Rogerus Pryde
1313 Johannes de Lodelowe; Ricardus Stury.
1313 Hugo, fil' Roberti de Dunfowe; Rogerus Pride, clericus
1314 Galfridus Randolf; Nicholaus fil' Nicholai, de Salop.
1316 Nicholas le Spicer; Willielmus de Golden'
1318 Galfridus Rondulf'; Willielmus Rondulf'
1319 Johannes Rayner; Willielmus de Lodelowe
1321 Rogerus Pryde; Johannes fil' Johannis
1322 Willielmus de Skynnere; Rogerus Pryde
1322 Rogerus Pryde, clericus; Ricardus de Staunton.'
1323 Thomas le Formon, de Salop; Johannes Reyner, de Salop.'
1325 Rogerus Pryde; Laurencius Prykett
1326 Johannes Reyner; Rogerus Pryde.

This brings our list down to the end of the reign of Edw. II., and the period when the four and twenty Welshmen were summoned as recorded Jan. 7. In the Blue Book we extract from, in several instances the records are said to be torn or lost; to such years we do not refer.

CAUS CASTLE.—There was a Campus Gaus on the R. Forth where Cadwallawn is supposed by Skene (*Anc. Books,* I. 178) to have fought. A little before he had attacked Iudeu, an island in the same River. In the Welsh poem (qu. Ib. I. 433, II. 227) he is said to have encamped on "Yddon" and also beyond "Caer Kaew" which Rev. D. S. Evans in notes identifies with Caio in Carmarthenshire. This last is generally supposed to be called after a Roman Caius. It is Cair Caiau in *Lib. Landav.* In the

Gododin poems a leader is called Caeawc, and thus distinguished as the lowland chief from Mynydawc the highland chief. Skene (Ib. II. 365) says the first syllable of Catraeth is from a root signifying an enclosure. (Comp. *cau* and *cae*.) I would suggest that all these names are cognate.

C.C.

QUERIES.

GWIBERNANT.—Mr. Hancock announced some time since, that he purposed publishing a life of that incomparable man, William Morgan, who filled the sees of Llandaff and St. Asaph at one time. Looking back to some of the early reprints of *Bye-gones*, I see that the old property which once belonged to the Morgans, is now vested in Lord Penrhyn; but the old home in which the Bishop was born, and where some of his descendants afterwards dwelt, is said to be standing even now. I remember seeing a drawing of it, and also of Plas Isa, Llanrwst, at an eisteddfod held in the latter place. Could we not manage to get these old dwellings engraved? Mr. Hancock should know of them, for no work upon Bishop Morgan can be perfect without a reference to his friend, William Salesbury, and, I might almost add, without some descriptions of the old homes, where, as lads, they dwelt.

CADWGAN.

DOLWYDDELAN.—It is a matter of controversy whether this place was called after a saint or a queen. If the former, is there another instance of a Welsh town or village called after a saint, with other prefix than "Llan"? If there is not, will this fact not rather strengthen the theory that the place derives its name from Ellen and not from Gwyddelan?

N.W.S.

WILLIAM ROOS.—I have several small things painted by this artist, and should be glad if some of your readers could give me an account of him; whence he came from, what he did, when and where he died. He painted *and engraved* likenesses of the late Revs. John Elias, Christmas Evans, and John Hughes (of Liverpool); the engravings are very good specimens of his art. He was excellent in water colours, and I have a very beautiful drawing of his, in that style, of Carnarvon Castle. A friend tells me that he was of the same family as the Rooses of Amlwch; but another friend says he derived from the Rooses of Flintshire, one of whom lived in the early days of the present century at Gadlys, near Holywell.

MORTIMER.

REPLIES.

LLANYMYNECH AND TRAFALGAR (Jan. 7, 1880.)—At the beginning of Nov. 1805, when rumours of the Naval Engagement fought in the Bay of Trafalgar, on the 21st Oct., began to be rife in the rural districts of England, although the nation mourned the death of its hero Nelson the rejoicings were loud and enthusiastic. The local papers of the period put the following down to the credit of Llanymynech, near Oswestry:—

We hear the inhabitants of Llanymynech, ever ready to testify their loyalty to the best of Kings and the best of Governments, and in imitation of the example shown by the kingdom in general, on the most glorious naval victory ever obtained in the annals of history by that much lamented friend of Britain, the late Lord Nelson, assembled at the Cross Keys on the 28 Nov., being joined by great concourse of persons of the neighbouring country. On a small hill, well situated in front of the lime rock, the Dyddwr, and part of the Oswestry Volunteers took their station at 3 o'clock; the rock extending near half a mile, was charged in front of the Volunteers, and divided into four batteries, and kept up at intervals a correspondent fire for the space of an hour. The Volunteers under their respective officers behaved in the most orderly

manner. Four sheep were roasted, two of which were distributed on the hill to the populace; another was carried down to the village, preceded by the Oswestry Band, and followed by the Volunteers, on which they feasted, and were regaled with plenty of strong beer, after which they fired several regular [vollies] and feu-de-jois. Night coming on fireworks were put off with great ingenuity, and had a very pretty effect, giving much satisfaction to numerous spectators. Immediately on the fire-works ceasing the illuminations began, and almost in an instant became general—the village and the houses round seemed to vie with each other in the splendor of their lights, and several mottoes and transparencies were exhibited, expressive of the valour of our naval heroes.

Then came the inevitable dinner. The Rev. Mr. Howell was called to the chair, at 9 o'clock, and the subscribers partook of the remaining sheep, and after several toasts had been duly honoured, *it was decided to erect an obelisk on Llanymynech Hill to the memory of Lord Nelson*. Mr. Howell, Mr. Dovaston, and Mr. Broughton, were appointed a committee to carry this out, and "solicit subscriptions thereto." The memory of Lord Nelson has not been so fortunate as that of Lord Rodney in that district, for the monument was never erected.

G.G.

BWLCH Y PAWL. (Jan. 7, 1880.)—Bwlch y Pawl is generally stated to be in Mawddwy; but such is not strictly the case. Mawddwy consists of the whole of the parish of Llan ym Mawddwy, and of as much of the parish of Mallwyd as lies in Merionethshire, that is, seven out of the eight townships into which the parish is divided. In the *Iolo MSS.* (p. 30, trans. p. 405) the place is said to be on the banks of the Dovey, which is still somewhat further from the mark. The passage runs thus:—" If contention arise between the provinces of Dinevwr and Aberffraw, in Anglesey, the seat of arbitration shall be at Bwlch y Pawl, on Dovey-side; the King of Powys being the juridical and judicial president." Bwlch y Pawl is at a place where the parishes of Llanuwchllyn, in Merionethshire (Gwynedd), and Llanwddyn, in Montgomeryshire (Powys), meet, and is at least a full mile from the nearest point of the parish of Llan ym Mawddwy, with which the district of Mawddwy in this direction is co-extensive. These three parishes meet at the turning of the water on the top of Bwlch y Groes. One stream, taking the direction of Llanwddyn, contributes to form the Severn, and falls eventually into the Bristol Channel; the other turns towards Llanuwchllyn, and passing through Llyn Tegid, enters the sea as the Dee below Chester; while the third, forming the Dovey, flows down the valley of Mawddwy, and falls into the sea at Aberdovey. About a mile, or a little more, from this place of divergence is the pass known as Bwlch y Pawl. I may also mention that it is at some distance from the old road (by Llan ym Mawddwy and Dinas Mawddwy) from Bala to Machynlleth. Local tradition does not connect Bwlch y Pawl with St. Paulinus or Pawl Hen, but a very different origin is ascribed to the name. In the olden time there lived a fair lady at Llwyn Gweru (now a farm house) in the parish of Llanuwchllyn, and within sight of the pass under notice. She was greatly admired by a worthy young man of the neighbourhood, of about her own age, but slightly below her in position. To prove his fidelity and to test the strength of his affections, she hit upon a somewhat original ordeal; which was that he should in this cold and exposed place pass a winter night *in naturalibus*. The spot on that bright moonlight night could be plainly seen from the lady's bedroom window, where she stationed herself in order to ascertain whether the conditions on which he was to obtain her hand were carried out to the letter. To that lonely place he proceeded at the appointed time; and to keep up his heat during the tedious hours he was to spend there, he took up a *pawl* (a pole or stake) from a hedge close by; and with that, cheered by the taper light at the lady's window, and inspired by the knowledge that she was observing his movements, he exercised himself so energetically that he managed to keep up his warmth until the dawn relieved him from his painful position. Having successfully passed the strange ordeal, his faithfulness was never doubted, he obtained the hand which he so much coveted, and, for anything that is stated to the contrary, "they lived happy together ever after." From this circumstance the place obtained the designation of *Bwlch y Pawl*, which it retains to this day.

DYVNIG.

JANUARY 28, 1880.

NOTES.

SUGGESTED MEMENTO TO THE PRINCES OF WALES.

I observe in the *Times* of the 19th inst. a paragraph with the above heading, quoting a suggestion* from a correspondent of the *Carnarvon Herald.* May I ask what this writer means by "the compact which was entered into on behalf of the Welsh nation, when they accepted the first Prince of Wales?" Is there any one possessing a knowledge of Welsh History who has a doubt that Wales was as much conquered by Edw. I., as the French were at the battle of Waterloo?

But I shall be expected to give my authorities. I will. In the early "Ministers' Accounts," in the Public Record Office in London, there are allusions to what took place when the King held the Principality of Wales—"tempore Regis." In the same repository is a letter from Edward of Carnarvon to Walter Reynald, stating that the King had, in the 29th year of his reign, granted to the Prince the land of Wales. But, beyond all this, the enrolment of the Letters Patent, conferring upon young Edward the Principality of Wales, is in the Public Record Office. They give him the whole of Wales, excepting that part which had been granted to the Queen in jointure, and the reversion of that.

Edward of Carnarvon was then in his 17th year !

With regard to the "loyal manner in which it [the compact, but there never was one] has been kept," what shall we say to the Welsh outbreak in 1293-4, or to the Rebellion of Glyndwr?

W.

PRINCE RUPERT AND THE COUNTY OF SALOP.

A copy of Rupert's Commission to the loyal men and soldiers of the county of Salop exists among some other MSS. at Sandford, and I have ventured to transcribe it for the pages of *Bye-gones.*

PRINCE RUPERT, Count Palatine of the Rhyne, Duke of Bavaria, Knight of the most nobell order of the Garter, and Generall vnder his ma'tie of all his ma'ties forces of horse. FFOR as much as his ma'ties great, and vrgent affaires will frequently require my personall apeareance in severall parts of his ma'ties dominions, for the more effectuall accomplishing the same, wheareby I shall be vnabell immediately to perform thos his ma'ties locall and perticuler services, to and for which I am obliged and authorised by his ma'ties Commission vnder the Greate Seale of England, to mee directed, as Captaine Generall vnder his ma'tie of all his ma'ties forces raysed or beinge in, or to be raysed or brought into his ma'ties Counties of Worcester, Salopp, Chester, Lancaster, and the Six Northern Counties of his ma'ties dominion of Wales,

* The suggestion was that a stone tablet, on which should be inscribed the names of the 17 Princes who have already enjoyed the title, (with room to add to the number) should be embedded in the walls of Carnarvon Castle. Of course the old fable of the birth in the Castle was assumed as true !—ED.

5

I haue therefore thought fitt by vertue of that his ma'ties sayd Commission, to Constitute ordaine and authorise you the heare vnder named Gentelmen to be ioynt Commissioners in my absence, for the effectinge all such his ma'ties services in and for his ma'ties Countie of Salopp, as I am obliged enabelled and authorised to doe by his ma'ties sayd Commission. Which that you may be the better able to performe, I doe hereby enable and endue you (in and dureinge my absence from the sayd Countie) with the selfe same power wheare with his ma'tie hath invested and Authorised mee as Captaine Generall vnder his ma'tie as aforesayd : and that yeu may fully vnderstand and know the latitude and limitt of my sayd power, you shall heare-with receiue a true and perfect Copie of his ma'ties sayd Commission vnder my hand for your directions in the prociutio' and performance of his ma'ties sayd services Commited to your Charge and execution according to this my Com'ission for the same heare by given vnto you.

Willinge and Commandinge all and singular such persons what soever as are by vertue of his ma'ties sayd Commission to mee subordinate to be obedient, aydinge, and assistinge to all such orders, directions, and instructions as they and every of them shall receiue from you or any seven of you for his ma'ties service, and on his ma'ties behalfe in and for the sayd Countie. And you your selves and every of you in like man'er to follow and accomplish all such matters and affaires as you shall be en-abelled and authorised to vnder take and doe by vertue of his ma'ties sayd Commission to mee directed. And by vertue of this my Commission directed vnto you and every of you . . . . and Instructions as you shall from time to time receiue from my selfe and not otherwise, wheare of you and every of you, or any Seven of you are duely and Constantly to meete, advise and Consult, at some such Convenient place as you shall by agreement apoynt twise every weeke at the least, and oftener if occasion shall require, And in the Agrement appoynt twise every weeke att the least, or oftener if occasion shall require. And in the agitation of his ma'ties sayd affaires and service to beare, Governe, and acquite your selves accordinge to your duties and my speciall trust and Confidence reposed in you and every of you heare vnder named touchinge your loyalties and good affections to his Sacred ma'tie and his p'sent Cause.

In Considerac'on wheare of I haue nominated and appoynted you and every of you, Commissioners as aforesayd by this my Commission to you and every of you directed vnder my hand and seale att armes this tennth day of March, In the nienetenth yeare of the Raine of our soveraine lorde Charles, by the Grace of god of England, Scootland, france and Ireland, Kinge, defender of the faith &c.

RUPERT.

John lo : Biron, ffeild marshall generall.
S'r William Belenden, kn't, Comisary generall.
Will' Legge, Governor of Chester.
S'r John Vrrin, Sergaent maior Generall of horse.
S'r Richard Cranne, Collonell.
S'r John Mennes
The Governor of Shrewsbury
S'r Richard Lloyd, his ma'ties Attorney
S'r Lewis Kirke, governor of Bridgnorth
Doctor Lewin, Advocate Generall
John Ball, Tresurer at warrs
Arthure Trevor, esq'r.   Dudley Wyatt, esq'r.
S'r Paule Harries, Knight and Barronett
S'r Vincett Corbett, Knight and Baronett
Thomas Edwards, esq'r, high sherriff
S'r John Weild, Knight
S'r Thomas Eyton, Knight.   Somersett fox, esq'r
Edward Kinastone, esq'r.   Lawrance Benball, esq'r
Mr. Chanceler Littelton, esq'r
the maior of Shrewsbury
Thomas . . . . . er, esq. towne Clerk
ffra's Thornes, esq'r.   fra : Smith.
Thes followinge w'th the princes owne hand
at [apparently " Pelto !"] the 16 : of May.
The Lord Newport
S'r Richard Lee, Knight Bar :
S'r Richard Leveson, knigh. of Bar
S'r ffrancis Ottley.   fra : Sandford, esq'r
James La . . . .
Raph Good . . . .

On the flyleaf of this historic document is the followingr scrap, in the same hand, but having no connection with, the body of the Commission :—

2

"The 18: of this moneth, Mongomery Castell was releiued by Sʳ Willia' Brerereton, Sʳ Thomas Middleton,and Sʳ William ffairefax, whoe was slaine theare. the next day the rebells marched of and faced the Red Castell."

The King's Commission to Prince Rupert, a copy of which also remains among the evidences at Sandford, bears date at Oxford, 8 Jan., 1643 ; and the Instructions given to him for carrying out the said Commission were dated 5 Feb., 1643.

Chester. T. HUGHES.

QUERIES.

CAMBRIAN INSTITUTIONS (Jan. 14, 1880.)— I now resume my list, reserving for another week a last instalment:—

The Cambrian Society. On Friday, July 9, 1819, there was a contest on the harp at "the first meeting of the Cambrian Society" at Caermarthen. Thomas Blayney and Henry Humphreys, both of Montgomeryshire, were the competitors, and the former was victorious. The Society was established Oct. 28-9, 1818. Was this the "Cambrian Society in Dyved?"

Cymmrodorion Society in Powys. This institution was to North Wales what the Cambrian Society was in the South, and was designed to act in concert with it. It was established at a Wrexham meeting, Oct. 6, 1819, at which were present Sir Watkin W. Wynn, Sir E. Pryce Lloyd, &c. The Rev. J. Jones, of St. Asaph, was appointed secretary. At a committee meeting held at Welshpool, Oct. 16, 1821, it was resolved to co-operate with the London and Provincial Societies. How far did they co-operate ?

Jesus College Association. This was composed of Welshmen who had been educated at Jesus Coll : Oxon, and the first meeting was held at Dolgelley, Aug. 4, 1819. "It was attended by Sir R. W. Vaughan, Col. Vaughan, the Principal, and several of the Fellows of the College, with many other individuals of the first respectability." The chief object of this Society was to cultivate the Welsh language amongst the Collegians destined for the Church. Did it ever accomplish its mission ?

Central Society in London. Established with the object of the cultivation of Welsh Literature, in 1820, under the auspices of the Bishop of St. David's and Sir Watkin W. Wynn. I have only seen a notice that it was to be established. Did it float ?

The Welsh Club held its annual dinner at the Thatched House Tavern, London, on Saturday, June 10, 1820. The Marquis of Anglesey presided, supported by the Duke of Beaufort and Mr. Charles Wynn. Viscount Bulkeley, Lord Dynevor, Sir R. W. Vaughan, Gen. Gascoyne, Sir Charles Morgan, and others, were present. Had the Club any special mission ?

Welsh Dispensary in London.—A meeting of the friends of this institution was held in the Freemasons' Tavern on May 20, 1820, Sir W. W. Wynn in the chair. The report stated that from Mar. 1819 to Mar. 1820 medical relief had been administered to 560 patients, natives of Wales. The subscriptions for the year amounted to £119, and the King (under whose auspices when Prince of Wales it had been established) sent a letter, through Sir Benjamin Bloomfield, announcing his continued patronage. Is this Dispensary in operation yet? N.W.S.

REPLIES.

THUNDER ON THE ORGAN (Jan. 14, 1880).— To resume my narrative concerning Mr. Weston and his performances. It was on the 15th of May, 1805, that the *Salopian Journal* stated that it gave the editor "peculiar pleasure to inform the inhabitants of Shrewsbury," that Mr. Weston would repeat his "astonishing performances" on the following Sunday. A fortnight had elapsed since the first performance, which netted £24 for the funds of St. Chad's Sunday School, had been given ; so I presume no objection had been made in the town to such Sunday exhibitions. The second performance, as I have already stated, was announced to take place in two churches, and for the benefit of four schools ; and the day came—the performer was ready—and the audience was assembled ; when at the last moment a churchwarden stepped in and prohibited the performance ! Whereupon Mr. Weston wrote to the *Journal* of May 22 a letter full of wrath, italics and small capitals, from which I take the following passage :—

Not my *Imitations* of *Thunder*, no—not even the Thunderbolt of HEAVEN (I sincerely believe), could produce a greater SHOCK than that which I felt, when the worthy and ingenious Mr. PARKES (one of the churchwardens), informed me, at ten o'clock last Sunday, that I was not permitted to perform on the organ at St. Mary's : I was absolutely *petrified.*

No reason is given in Mr. Weston's letter why the performance was prohibited, and he goes on to say :—

That a thousand of the most respectable inhabitants of Shropshire were disappointed of a promised, and consequently expected gratification (for St. Mary's Church, on Sunday morning, was crammed almost to suffocation, numbers having come, in spite of the very unfortunate weather, from remote distances), I deeply lament ; but you, Sir, and many others know that I was not to blame ; and that the Sunday Schools of four parishes in this respectable town were deprived, in all probability, of two hundred pounds, at least, I still more deeply lament ; but the fault was not mine. It was, in truth, a combination of unfortunate circumstances, which human wisdom could not foresee, nor human power control.

What the "petrified" organist means by this, except to hint that the prohibition was the result of supernatural agency, it is hard to say. He had evidently great faith in the generosity of the thousand nearly suffocated Salopians, for although only £24 was collected at St. Chad's, he anticipated more than £200 at St. Mary's! However, as he very justly goes on to say, "Whining lamentation is useless ;" and he consoles himself by "discharging a duty ;" which is no more nor less than writing an elegy to the memory of a departed friend, and sending it to the *Journal* for publication ! This I will not transcribe ; and will leave for another week, Mr. Weston's grievance in connection with the Whitchurch organship, the *Shrewsbury Chronicle*, and another paper. J.?.R.

CURRENT NOTES.

THE GROAT.

A few months ago a man, by name William Oliver, employed in making a road somewhere in the parish of Yspytty Ystwyth, was fortunate enough to discover a [number of old coins concealed in a square hole cut out of clay-slate, cropping up near the surface. I am unaware whether or not the whole or any of these coins have yet been identified. I have one in my possession, and have been able to identify it with the groat of Henry VI.'s reign (i.e., 1422-1461).

The following is a description of the coin :—

Obverse side—(cross) Henric. (rose) Di. (rose) Gra. (rose) Rex (lozenge) Angl. (rose) & (rose) Franc. In the centre there is a youthful face, crowned, with long flowing hair.

Reverse side—(cross) Posvi (rose) Deum (two quatrefoils) Adintore' (two quatrefoils) Meum. Inner circle : Vil (lozenge) la (two quatrefoils) Calisie (rose). There is also a large cross on the reverse side.

This coin is well figured and described in Ruding's great work on British Coinage.[*]

When Edward III. took Calais he made it a staple of, among other things, lead and tin[†]. In Henry V.'s reign an Act was passed to erect a mint in that town[‡]. However, the words "Villa Calisie" appear on coins of Edward III., showing that coins were struck there in that reign.

The groat of Henry VI. is certainly not pure silver, but may be stated to be an alloy of silver and lead. The value of the groat is usually said to be fourpence. But in 1460 it was enacted that the gross of London, York, and Calais, not clipped within the extreme circle, should be fivepence, the demygross and denier in proportion. The gross clipped was valued at fourpence, and the others at an equal rate.

Although Henry VI. was the only Monarch of England ever actually crowned King of France in France, the words "Rex Angl. & Franc." occur on coins of Edward III. of the value of twopence, and on coins of Henry V. This was a very simple method of king-making, though the fact might possibly be open for the reigning French Monarch to dispute.

I believe the words "Posui, &c.," "I have made God my helper," first occur on groats of Edward III.'s reign. My specimen of groat is only about one-fortieth of an inch in thickness, and weighs 3.783 grammes.

Strata Florida.   E. HALSE, A.R.S.M.

FEBRUARY 4, 1880.

NOTES.

ENGLAND SAVED BY HODNET !—"Oh! Jemmy Thompson, Jemmy Thompson, Oh!" What a lot you have to answer for! Had you not written your vain-glorious song, Hodnet would not in 1803 have rivalled the "Three Tailors" by such an effusion as the following :—

HODNET VOLUNTEERS.
TUNE—*Rule Britannia.*

Bellona spreads her dire alarms,
And calls the HODNET men to arms,
  With eager haste behold them fly,
  Resolv'd to conquer or to die.
Arouse, free born Britons, at your country's call,
Join your bold leader and your foe shall fall.

With joy the glorious call obey,
For glory points to them the way,
  Undaunted they with British heart,
  Will join to conquer Bonaparte.
Arouse, free born Britons, at your country's call,
Join your bold leader and your foe shall fall.

Let dastard souls be aw'd by fear,
And tremble when no danger's near,
  The gallant heart no danger knows,
  But pants to meet great George's foes.
HODNET's brave sons in loyal bands unite,
BOULT cheers their valour and directs their might.

Britannia rais'd her drooping head,
And smiling thus the Goddess said,
  "My sons the glorious task pursue,
  Maintain your rights and France subdue."
HODNET's brave sons, in loyal hands unite,
BOULT cheers their valour and directs their might.

Who the party with the ominous name of "Boult" was, I cannot say. The name does not appear in the list of

[*] "Annals of the Coinage of Great Britain, &c.," by the Rev. Rogers Ruding, 1840.
[†] Hume's History of England, chap. XV.
[‡] "Miscellaneous Views of the Coins struck by British Princes in France," &c., Thos. Snelling, 1769.

Salopian officers a year or two later. The lines I have quoted appeared in the *Salopian Journal* for Oct. 12, 1803, with the following request :—"*To the Printers.* You are desired to insert the following Song in your Paper, and you will much oblige the Hodnet Volunteers."   J.?.R.

A LADY'S IMPRESSIONS OF WALES. [LETTER IL]
(Jan. 7, 1880.)

From Mrs. Presland (of Walford Hall, Salop) at Peniarth, Merionethshire, to her sister Miss Slaney, at Shrewsbury :—

I promised in my last to tell my Dear Sister how I likd Peniart. very well, but am unfortunate in the weather. and this situation is low, and damp, constant fogs, which is owing in some measure to ten Acres of Gardening being so full of wood, bowers, walks coverd with trees, it is romantick, and if it was layd open to the river, which runs close up to it, and layd in a Lawn and Shrubery it woud be more beautyfull and healthfull; and by that means get a full view of some medows, and a pretty Hill planted with trees, amongst which a gothick, or any Building woud have a pretty effict to the eye, on the back of the House is a steep mountain coverd with trees, near the bottom a small hill, at top of which is a Summer House, from it a View of the sea, a Caskade below, a cottage in the view of a small raget rock, with gloomy walks, and some shrubs, in the front windows, you see one very high rock, and the highest mountain in North Wales cald Cadridrous, which nombers go to see, but when they get to the top are quite lost in clouds except it be by chance, and them from it the view is said to be wonderfull beyand description but you may go twenty times and not see it, which chance we intended to have took, if the weather had not bin so bad. Peniarth House, as in it a dale of room, bad-rooms backwards, four good ones, but not large to the front of the House, the furniture old but good, the tea drinking room, is fitted up quite in taste with a large India Cabinet, wherein is many valuable trinkets, at top some fin old china our table consists of nine, and are move, thirty Sallmon at a time catchd out of the river at bottom of the garden, the family seems friendly without form, but the weather has bin so bad, no body coud come, but tenants and the lower kind of neighbours, with eggs, butter, fowl, Ducks, &c., which the all present at their coming in to the country, where their stables and housekeeping must be very expencive, I went yesterday to the Sea but when I heard it rore, see the Breakers and so many naked men and wemen half drownded my spirits sunk, my eyes weepd and upon my horse I got, disparing of ever geting courage to go in, but the next day I did, but still think the appearance of the Sea, a pleasing melloncholy sight, there was twelve small ships sailing, the tide quite out, the breakers very high, and the thoughts of being under mountains of water, had a second time like to have got the better of me, but away with the reflection. We ride out every day the Views are uncommon, and surprizing, we rode to day near four miles along some medows on each side rocks wood, and rivulets purling by, at last we came to a prodigious perpendicular rock, all over Little holes, out of which at the smack of a wip, came thousands of birds of different kinds, which made a pleasing consert, we then went up to the Rock, and heard something within so like human voices that I coud not help saying it was another world, and they inhabitants by their mirth and jolity Welch, whos spirits and merry lives, is not to be outdone, Cotillions are here danced every night, musick at meals ramping, or walking all morning, tea drinkinhing at

Summer Houses, suping at Coteges or such like at night and yesterday we all whent to see the mountibanks at Towen, and mob'd it on a bench in the street, but it set a raining, and I with a Captain took into an Ale house, but upon looking up to the top of the parlour, what shoud I see but, through the board, a great fat woman steping out of bed, away run I, and so did the Captain as soon as he coud for laughing. on Sunday I went to Church, but wheither to hear the parson scold or pray I coud not determin so will go no more. I have inquired about Aberystwyth, where the Sea is very rough, and no Apothecary near, and most ignorant people in regard to illness, which they are so happy to know nothing of, as the Sea is their ownly Physition. I think the Sea fogs very unwholesom, but dare not say so, as they are for ever talking of the purity of their air, which I don't allow, but will agree that constant exsersize chearfull company, and different amusements may contribute to their health, and if the English instead of going to Birmingham to be ground young, woud take a trip into Weals they woud teach them how to live long and merry, but if the fear the Itch lett them stay a way, but from the nomber of children &c:c that have it here, one woud supose it was a desireable complaint, or the woud try to cure it, may I never want a remedy for that disorder amongst mine, is the sincere wish of your ever   aff sister E PRES
                      Peniart July ye 18

QUERIES.

TRINITY CHURCH, OSWESTRY. — During the month of August, 1836, a bazaar was held at the Wynnstay Hotel for the benefit of the funds of this church, then in course of erection. In an account of the proceedings we are told that "all eagerly pressed forward to obtain a sight of the articles sent by Her Majesty." Through whose influence was Queen Adelaide interested in the affair—what were the articles Her Majesty sent—and who purchased them?   JARCO.

CAMBRIAN INSTITUTIONS (Jan. 28, 1880).— With the following I conclude my list :—

Cambrian Society in Gwent. A meeting was held Dec. 5, 1821, in the Town Hall, Brecon, in order to form a society in the district for the preservation of the remains of Ancient British Literature, and the encouragement of Poetry and Music in Wales. In the absence of Sir Charles Morgan, Major Price presided. The Rev. W. J. Rees, M.A., delivered an address on the objects of Cambrian Societies. On the 6th an adjourned meeting was held of the newly-formed Committee, including Sir E. P. Lloyd, Bart., Mr. C. W. W. Wynn, Archdeacon of Cardigan, &c., to arrange about an eisteddfod to be held at Brecon.

Cambrian Society in Dyved. On the 10th of January, 1822, a meeting of the Committee of this Society was held at Carmarthen, the Bishop of St. David's presiding, at which certain communications from and to the 'Cymmrodorion in Powys' and the 'Cambrian Society in Gwent' were read or adopted.

Cymmrodorion in Gwynedd. The first Eisteddvod under the auspices of this society was held at Carnarvon in September 1821.

Literary Society of Wales. This was projected in 1829, at a meeting presided over by the Rev. R. B. Clough. The Rev. R. Newcome, Warden of Ruthin, was appointed treasurer, and the Rev. R. Richards, rector of Caerwys, secretary. Did anything come of it?

The Welsh MSS. Society, for publishing valuable Welsh Literature was in operation as recently as 1846. Did it publish much?

In addition to the foregoing I have seen notices of the *Cymreigyddion in Liverpool.* At the meeting in the Castle Inn, Jan. 1, 1821, Mr. O. Williams presided, and a learned address in Welsh was delivered by the Rev. John Richards of Anglesey, critic to the Society. Then in 1822 an effort was made to establish a *Cymmrodorion in Chester.* I suppose these societies would be branches of the larger ones? I have also seen a notice of an *Historic Institute of Wales,* of the probable date of 1852. Did this ever float, and what was the intention of its promoters?

A complete list in *Bye-gones* of all the general and local institutions that have been attempted in Wales would be interesting, and also such as remain. Under what auspices have the National Eisteddfodau of recent years been conducted? How long has the Cambrian Archæological Society been in existence? And are there other local societies doing similar work to that of the Powysland Club?   N.W.S.

REPLIES.

THUNDER ON THE ORGAN (Jan. 28, 1880).— I now come to Mr. Weston's grievances with the news-papers respecting the Whitchurch competition, &c. In the *Journal* of June 5, 1805, he writes a long letter, dated May 29, in which he says :—

A Mr. W. Hawkes having thought proper to sign his Name to a Statement entitled "A Trial of Skill," which found Insertion in the Shrewsbury Chronicle, and in Aris's Birmingham Gazette, about eight or nine weeks since ;—which Statement reflected on the Conduct of the Whitchurch Committee who regulated the Business for the Election of an Organist—I undertook to vindicate those respectable Gentlemen ; and, in the Opinion of every Person possessed of common Sense and common Candour, succeeded. My answer was *reluctantly* printed in the Shrews-bury Chronicle, on the Friday following that on which the Libel appeared ; which Libel (by the way) was refused Admission by the ingenious and upright Editor of the Birmingham Commercial Herald, as "a Disgrace to his Columns."

Mr. Weston is rather obscure in his statement of the nature of the libel complained of. He goes to say that "EDWARD LORD ELLENBOROUGH will, in *due Time,* and in *proper Form,* reward [Mr. Hawkes] and his Publisher according to *their Deserts.*" Not having access to the file of papers in which the Libel appeared I can only guess at its character from the following further passage in Mr. Weston's letter :—

It may not be amiss to examine how far the following Assertions are founded—viz. "that the Committee would not suffer ME to play (on the Organ) on any Terms ;"—that, "in their Opinion, I was not *fit* for a Candidate,"—and that they said, "We do not *want* you for an Organist. Here are your Expenses."

To show how unjust all this is, Mr. Weston publishes a letter sent to him at Solihull, Birmingham, on the 27th of the previous March, by Mr. James Horseman, chairman of the Whitchurch Committee, in which that gentleman says that his committee "being apprehensive that a return of the Complaints with which he [Mr. Weston] has been afflicted for so many Years, may again disable him from performing the Duties of his Office, they hope he will decline his Intention of being a Candidate, &c." With this polite note the chairman enclosed £5 to cover Mr. Weston's expenses. It is scarcely worth while following Mr. Weston's rigmarole any further. He concludes by stating that all Mr. Hawkes's statement should be answered in a Memoir of his life he was going to add to a work he had in the press, entitled "Philotoxi Ardenæ— The Woodman of Arden."   J.?.R.

NOTES.

YSPRYD LLANEGRYN.

A few days ago, as a farmer and his shepherd were together in a field, near Towyn, Merionethshire, looking after a large flock of sheep, a peculiar crackling, rustling sound caused them to lift up their heads, when, to their great astonishment, they perceived the stacks and sheaves in an adjoining wheat field being whirled about by some invisible agency in the direction where the flock of sheep were quietly grazing. With a rushing sound, what proved to be a whirlwind was soon upon them, and in a few seconds, to the intense alarm and consternation of the farmer and his shepherd, scattered the flock about like chaff. One of the sheep was lifted by the force of the whirlwind a tremendous height into the air, and fell to the ground dead. The wind passed quickly away in a westwardly direction, without further damage. There is no record of, neither do the oldest people of the locality remember, so singular an occurrence,—*Newspaper paragraph*, Sep., 1879.

A gentleman told me many years ago that he recollected " the laying" of a ghost by the then curate of the parish, Mr. Williams. He also used to relate some of the doings of that celebrated ghost, from which it appears it used to do very much in those days as the whirlwind mentioned above did in the adjoining parish of Towyn in September last. In the case of the ghost, upon one occasion when the people of the farmhouse had left the fields for their mid-day meal, they also left the sheaves of corn standing, everywhere ready to be carried, but when they returned in about an hour every sheaf had been scattered broadcast. This ghost was finally laid by a religious service, in Latin, held at night, the minister being alone, with twelve great candles burning before him (" efo deuddeg Canwyllau'r Eglwys"). My informant said, " I was a boy at the time and staying at the house, and I and some other boys got up secretly from our beds in the night, and through some cracks in a panel beheld there the clergyman reading to himself aloud, and ' laying the ghost,' and the ghost was not known to be troublesome afterwards," showing that the good and worthy divine knew his work well, and so quieted many minds in those bye-gone days about Llanegryn.   W.P.
Southsea.

PARLIAMENT OF ENGLAND (Jan. 14, 1880).

Our instalment this week commences with the reign of Edward the Third, which want of space will prevent our completing this week :—

COUNTY OF SALOP.

1327	Thomas de Roshale, miles; Johannes du Lee, miles.
1328	Rogerus de Cheyne; Willielmus de la Hulle
1328	Ditto; Rogerus Corbet', de Leighe
1328	Laurencius de Lodelowe, miles; Walterus de Beysin, miles
1329	Rogerus de Cheyne; Rogerus Corbet', Leighe
1330	Johannes de Hynkele; Willielmus de Mokleston
1330	Willielmus de Ercalewe; Rogerus Corbet, de Caus
1331	Ditto; Ditto
1332	Ditto; Willielmus de Leversete
1332	Ditto; Rogerus Corbet, de Caus
1332	Henricus de Bisshebur'; Walterus Buffry
1333	Ricardus de Peshale; Willielmus de Leversete
1334	Willielmus de Ercalewe; Griffinas de Lee
1335	Johannes de Hynkeley; Willielmus de Hopton
1336	Johannes de Hinkeleye; Willielmus de Caynton
1336	Willielmus de Botiller; Simon de Ruggeleye
1337	No returns found (1)
1337	Walterus de Hopton', miles; Rogerus Corbet, de Caus, miles

1338	Robertus de Harleye; Willielmus de Ercalewe
1338	Ditto; Rogerus Corbet (2)
1339	Walterus de Hopton'; Willielmus de Kayton'
1339	Willielmus de Ercalewe; Robertus de Harleye
1340	Ditto; Walterus de Hopton'
1340	Griffunis de Lee; Simon de Ruggeley
1340	Nicholaus Deverus (3)

BOROUGH OF SHREWSBURY.

1327	Johannes Reyner; Rogerus Pryde.
1328	Thomas de Formon; Ditto
1328	Rogerus Pryde, clericus; Johannes de Wetenhull'
1328	Johannes Reyner; Rogerus Pryde
1329	Ditto; Thomas Colle
1330	Johannes de Weston'; Rogerus Pryde
1330	Ricardus de Walleford'; Ditto.
1332	Willielmus le Skynner'; Johannes Reynor.
1332	Thomas Colle; Rogerus Pryde
1333	Willielmus le Skynnere; Johannes de Weston'
1334	Johannes de Watenhull'
1336	Willielmus le Skynnere, senior; Willielmus le Skynnere, junior
1336	Willielmus le Skynnere; Thomas Gamel
1337	No returns found
1337	Thomas Colle, junior; Johannes de Weston'
1338	Ditto; Willielmus Pryde
1338	Ricardus Russel; Robertus de Upton'
1339	Willielmus Pryde; Ricardus Russel
1339	Willielmus le Skynnere; Willielmus de Bromleye
1340	Ditto; Willielmus de Bromley
1340	Johannes de Weston'; Ricardus de Weston'

(1) By writ dated at Westminster 18 Aug. 11 Edw. III, summonses directing the attention of persons to advise with the King on special matters at Councils and in Parliament, were issued. From Salop county, Rogerus Corbet, de Caus; Johannes de Huggeford'; and Robertus Corbet, de Whetelburgh', are named. From Shrewsbury, Thomas Colle, Johannes de Weston', and Ricardus de Weston'. (2) A similar writ was issued, dated Ipswich, 16 July 12 Edw. III, but no names from Shropshire are given. (3) Similar summonses were issued by writ dated Kensington 27 July 1340; when the following were chosen :—Salop County, Willielmus de la Hulle, Johannes de Crouk' de Bruge, Adam de la Home, Johannes de Shrosebury, de Lodelowe; and from Shrewsbury, Thomas Colle, Johannes de Weston', and Willielmus de Bromelye.   ED.

QUERIES.

FIRST SUNDAY SCHOOL IN OSWESTRY.— It is believed, but there are no written records of the fact, that the first Sunday School in Oswestry was in existence in 1782, and that it was commenced by Dr. Williams, the minister of the Old Chapel; his daughters teaching in it. On what grounds is this belief founded ?
PURITAN.

A MERIONETHSHIRE MARTYR. — Bishop Challoner, in his *Memoirs of Missionary Priests*, gives an account, of which the following is an imperfect abstract, of the death of the Rev. John Roberts, O.S.B., who, he informs us, "was born in Merionethshire of Wales, from whence he was called in religion Father John de Mervinîâ. In what school or college he had his first education I have not found; though I find one of that name in the Douay Diary, sent from Rheims to Rome in 1583. If so, he must afterwards have gone from Rome to Spain : for this Mr. Roberts was afterwards an *alumnus* of the English Seminary of Valladolid; and from thence betook himself to the Spanish congregation of Valladolid of the venerable order of S. Benedict; amongst whom he entered in the

year 1595 ; and having not long after received the holy
order of priesthood in 1600, he was that same year sent
upon the English mission."
"He was a man of admirable zeal, courage, and
constancy,'who, during his ten years' labours in the mission,
was four times apprehended and committed to prison ; and
as often sent into banishment ; but still returned again
to the work of his Master, upon the first favourable
opportunity. His extraordinary charity evidently showed
itself during the time of a great plague in London ; where
he assisted great numbers of the infected ; and was instrumental in the conversion of many souls from their
former errors and vices. He was apprehended for the 5th
time at Mass, on the 1st Sunday of Advent, 1610, and
hurried away in his vestments, and thrust into a dark
dungeon, from whence he was quickly after brought out
to his trial ; and condemned to die barely for his priestly
character. His life, however, was offered him, if he would
have taken the new oath, which he constantly refused."
Being drawn to the place of execution, in company with
the Rev. Thomas Somers, alias Wilson, who suffered at
the same time and place, so great was the multitude of
gentry and others that they were forced to walk, when
within 18 yards of the place of execution, to the cart, in
which stood 16 condemned men with their ropes about
their necks and tied to the gallows. Taking notice that
he was to be hung among thieves, he was reminded by an
officer "that his Master was so served." When seated in
the cart he turned towards the poor condemned prisoners,
and displaying his hands and blessing them, said :—
"We are all come hither to die, from which there
is no hope of escape, and if you die in the religion now
professed in England, you shall undoubtedly perish ever-
lastingly ; let me, therefore, for the love of our Blessed
Saviour, entreat you that we may all die in one Faith : in
testimony whereof let me beseech you to pronounce
with me those words, 'I BELIEVE THE HOLY CATHOLIC
CHURCH,' protesting your desires to die members of the
same, as also your sorrowfulness for having led so naughty
and wicked lives, whereby you have offended our sweet
and merciful Saviour : which, if you will truly and constantly profess, I will pronounce absolution, and then my
soul for yours." Afterwards he said :—'I am condemned
to die for that, being a priest, I came into England contrary to a statute made in the 27th year of the late Queen's
reign.' To the objection that he came into England without due authority, he replied that he was sent into England by the same authority by which St. Augustine, the
Apostle of England, was sent, whose disciple he was, being
of the same Order, and living under the same rule in which
he lived ; and that for the profession and teaching of that
religion, which St. Augustine planted in England, he was
now condemned to die. For his last farewell he entreated
them to return to the unity of the Catholic Church, praying them to take certain notice that, 'Extra Ecclesiam
nulla salus,' the English whereof he enforced himself to deliver with a most strong voice, saying :—'Unto this end
I will not cease to pray for you all during my life, and
after my death I shall have greater ability to perform the
same.' Embracing and blessing each other for the last
time with manacled hands, Mr. Roberts said "All ye
Saints of God, intercede for me," and Mr. Wilson, "Into
Thy hands, O Lord, I commend my spirit." They were
suffered to hang till they were quite dead (a permission by
no means universally conceded), then cut down, bowelled,
beheaded, and quartered. Their entrails being burnt,
their quarters were buried in the pit prepared for the 16
malefactors, all of whose bodies were cast upon them.
Their quarters were, however, afterwards dug up at midnight, and carried away. An arm of F. Roberts was sent

to Compostella in Spain, and a portion of his remains to
Douai in France.
It would seem probable that some additional records
should be extant of so remarkable a man in his native
county or elsewhere. The publication of any information
tending to the discovery of his family, birthplace, or
original place of education would be valuable. H.W.L.

REPLIES.

A WELSH PROVERB (Jan. 7, 1880).—The proverb, "O'i phen y mae godro buwch," is very generally
used in Cardiganshire, and has the same meaning as in
Merionethshire, viz., that if you want a cow to give a
large quantity of milk, you must feed her accordingly. I
have never heard the variation alluded to, "O'i phen y
mae prynu buwch," used in this county.   CARDI.
The proverb, "O'i phen y mae godro buwch,"
simply means that you must feed a cow well if you wish
to have much milk from her. Abundance of food will
produce abundance of milk, and vice versa.
                                             CEREDIG.

SHROPSHIRE GRAMMAR SCHOOLS (Jan. 7,
1880).—As a contribution to the historical notices AN OLD
SALOPIAN asks for, I send the following from the Salopian
Journal of Mar. 11, 1835 :—"At the late Cambridge Examinations Mr. Francis Proctor, of Catherine Hall, was
30th Wrangler ; Mr. George Frederick Harris, of Trinity
College, was 3rd on the 1st class of Classical Tripos ; and
Mr. John Cooper, of Trinity College, was 7th in the same
class. And at the examination for the Pitt University
Scholarship, Mr. W. G. Humphry, of Trinity College,
was elected Pitt Scholar. All these gentlemen were
educated at Shrewsbury School."   READER.
In an autobiographical sketch of the Bishop of Manchester sent by request for a biography in the forthcoming
number of the Manchester Magazine, Dr. Fraser says : "In
1832 I was sent to Bridgnorth School, then under Dr.
Rowley ; and in 1834, my mother, wishing to give me every
advantage possible, placed me at Shrewsbury, where I
spent two years under Drs. Butler and Kennedy." E.

CURRENT NOTES.

In an article on Civic Maces in the Feb. No. of
The Antiquary, Mr. Lambert, F.S.A., says :—The only
mace of lead that I know of is at Llanidloes, in Wales.
At Laugharne are two maces of wood which were replaced
by brass. At Bridgnorth and at Carlisle the crown on
the mace unscrews, so as to form a drinking cup.
At the meeting of the British Archæological Society,
Jan. 21st, Mr. Irvine exhibited a photograph of an
engraved sepulchral slab, of much beauty, found during
the recent works at Bangor Cathedral. The engraving
represents a lady clad in the costume of the middle of the
14th century, with the peculiar headdress of the period,
and a curious side purse hanging from the waist.

THE LATE CANON OAKELEY.—Canon Oakeley, the well-
known Catholic writer, whose death is announced, was
born in the Abbey House, Shrewsbury, on the 5th of September, 1802. His early education was received from his
mother, a most accomplished lady, from whom he inherited his love of music. So great was his proficiency in
this art that at the age of four he was able to reproduce
simple airs on the pianoforte which had made an impression on his ear ; and at eight years of age the organist of
Lichfield Cathedral was wont to allow him to play the
chant on week days. At this time his parents removed

to the Episcopal Palace of Lichfield, and he describes the delight with which he used to assist at the services at the cathedral, and the impression that noble edifice made on his young mind. At 15 years of age he was placed under the care of the Rev. C. R. Sumner, afterwards Bishop of Winchester, for whom he retained a life-long affection. Passing to the University of Oxford, in 1827, he won a Chaplain Fellowship, and, ten years after, he was appointed Oxford Preacher at Whitehall. It was here that he went more to the Tractarians, and in 1839, when he became minister of Margaret Chapel, he was the first clergyman in London to introduce that form of external worship which is now popularly known by the name of Ritualism, although the most startling of the changes which he introduced were moderation itself compared with those which are now tolerated. In 1845 Mr. Oakeley was received into the Roman Catholic Church, and in 1852 he was appointed Canon of Westminster. He was a frequent contributor to the *Contemporary*, and the author of several religious works.

AN INTERESTING CHAPTER IN OSWESTRY HISTORY.

The first part of the third volume of the *Transactions* of the Shropshire Archæological Society, which has just been published, although the matter it contains is of undoubted interest to the more educated classes in the county generally; is still of peculiar interest to Oswestry readers, but, we regret to say, there are not more than a dozen residents of the borough who are members of the Society, and of these only three who are members of the Corporation. The matter contained in the number that makes it so valuable to Oswestry is the long instalment devoted by Mr. Stanley Leighton to our Corporation Records. Space will not allow of our presenting our readers with anything like a comprehensive idea of what these records include, but such notice of them as we are able to give will, we trust, induce some of our readers to become subscribers to the Club, and, as such, recipients of its publications.

Mr. Stanley Leighton begins the present chapter with the Muringer's Accounts for 1560. In those days this official was a man of importance, second only to the Bailiffs in the borough; he had charge of the repairs of the walls and gates, and the general handling of the public money. The account is curious, coming as it does the year after a plague had visited Oswestry. Rents and tolls from native tradesmen, and "foreguers" who sold "clothe by the Crose," "pynes and glases," on market days, &c., were collected by "Towlers," and in the year in question many of these rents had to be abated, the entries against the names being stated in this way:—"It'm the sayde accomptaunt alowance for a qr Rent vato (here follow names) apsent in tyme of the plage." "Fled" or "Dead" is attached to other names, and the account altogether points to a sad state of affairs in the borough.

Another of the Documents given is the "Book of Constitutions," defining the rights of our ancestors in 1582. Under its provisions, some of the powers of the Muringer were transferred to the Bailiffs, and every Burgess was liable to serve as Bailiff once in seven years, if elected, under a penalty of forty shillings. Even so far back as three centuries ago, it would appear that there was rivalry in business matters between Oswestry and the county town, for one of the enactments was that no Shrewsbury man was to be made a burgess unless he resided in Oswestry.

Next we have a "Quo Warranto" of 1600, under the "Rights and Preveleges" of which there were "Punishments of pillory, tumbrel, and stake." A Pillory on the Bailey Head would draw a pretty large crowd in the present day, although we many of us remember the Stocks being set up there; and some of us think it would be no harm to revive it as the compulsory punishment for drunkenness.

Another interesting document is a "Declaration of the Burgesses" arising out of a dispute with the Earl of Suffolk in 1603, to which is attached a large number of names. This dispute was caused by a real or fancied abridgment of their "auncient priveleges," which the burgesses seem to have resented highly. In a few years these disputes ended in a Royal Charter granted by James I. This Mr. Leighton gives in full, and in so doing has added greatly to the interest of his paper, for our local histories pass over this charter with a very bald notice, and Mr. Cathrall, who probably never saw it, falls in consequence into the error of calling a succeeding Charter of Charles II., "the Magna Charta of Oswestry," &c., &c. Whereas (as we shewed in *Bye-gones*, June 30, 1875,) the latter was little more than a repetition of the one James granted, only giving us Mayors instead of Bailiffs.

Another subject contained in Mr. Leighton's paper will interest Shrewsbury as greatly as Oswestry, for it refers to the Welsh Cloth Trade, formerly done in both towns, and the many disputes as to which should monopolize it. And, lastly, we have, for the first time, the official document relating to the trick General Mytton played the county when he stole a march on the electors by nominating a candidate at Alberbury when (as Sheriff) he had fixed the election to take place at Oswestry.

The part, we should say, contains other interesting papers, of which, however, this is not the time to speak.

FEBRUARY 18, 1880.

NOTES.

EMBANKMENTS WITH BUTTRESSES. — Near Caio, Carmarthen, there is a long embankment, half a mile, along a marshy flat of valley. Where least disturbed it is 5 feet high, 23 feet wide, and has several well-marked "buttresses" or bastions with regular intervals of 18 feet between them. They project 27 feet and are 23 feet wide, sloping from the height of the embankment to about a foot high at their extremities. At this spot it is composed chiefly of peat, and therefore could hardly have been a road. It may, perhaps, have been the artificial foundation of dwellings, whose defence was aided by surrounding marsh—as Irish Crannoges were. See Lubbock's *Prehist. Times*, 181-2.   CAEAWC.

PHILLIPS' HISTORY OF SHREWSBURY, 1769.—The real author of this book was Mr. James Bowen, herald painter, of Shrewsbury, the grandfather of the late John Bowen, and son of the John Bowen who published the four prints of Shrewsbury (known as "Bowen's Views"). James Bowen was employed by Mr. William Mytton of Halston to make the manuscript collection for the proposed History of the County of Salop, and having in consequence obtained sufficient information he simply made use of Phillips' name. Phillips was a grocer in Shrewsbury.   W. H. SP.

THE FIRST SIR WATKIN'S DAUGHTER.— In a notice of *Wynnstay and the Wynns* in *Local Gleanings*, published at Manchester, and edited by Mr. J. P. Earwaker, M.A., F.S.A., the writer says it would appear that the first Sir Watkin had an only daughter who died young, although the fact is not stated in the book. This daughter, he continues, is alluded to in the following lines. They are from a MS. volume of poems, written by Amos Meredith of Henbury Hall, near Macclesfield, Esq., and are dated 1735 :—

> "Look up to Watkin, eminently blest,
> Of noble fortune, nobler heart possest,
> Dreaded by all the bad, the good carest,—
> Then see his only child in beauteous pride,
> Panting, expiring by her father's side.
> Think of the thrilling pangs of that despair,
> The swelling tear, the throb, the fervent prayer.
> Impartial Crito, tell me, would'st thou choose
> To gain his fortune and thy children lose?
> There nature suffers in her tenderest part,
> A wound not felt but in a parent's heart."

"The child to whom these verses refer, was, I think," writes Mr. W. W. E. Wynne, "Mary, daughter of the first Sir Watkin Williams Wynn, by his first wife, the heiress of Llangedwin. She died at the age of 17. There were other children of that marriage who probably died young. There is a portrait of her at Llangedwin, and some beautiful table linen spun by, or which belonged to her."
A.R.

A LADY'S IMPRESSIONS OF WALES. [LETTER III.]
(Feb. 4, 1880.)

From Mrs. Presland (of Walford Hall, Salop) at Peniarth, Merionethshire, to her sister Miss Slaney, at Shrewsbury :—

Dear Sister   Peniarth July ye 26 [1771?]

I receivd yours, and am very happy in hearing you are all well, we have had a sad wet week, and for this time of year very tempestous, but thank God the Sun shines, the Sea calm and to morrow I hope to take a dip, for I am gone quite coragious it is seven mile from Peniarth, I ride single and after Bathing, am in such spirits, I never think of being tired, not that the views are so amuseing here as some other parts of the country, but not without beautys, one is the Little white stone Cotages, which have a pert look on the outside, but misarable within, and the people very poor, no wonder youll say, for the sell fine chickings at threepence a couple, Ducks a groat &c:c and yet be in nature generous, and hospitable, but frugall, for to save their shoes, and stockings. when wet, they pull them off, and walk without. Mutton is here delightful and cheap, veal very indiferent, Beef so scarse that if there is one kild within ten mile they send to lett you know what brave doings if you like a peice. We was yesterday at a Sea port calld Aberdove we went four miles in Miss Williams Boat, had a Duke to steer it, a Generall to command it, we landed near Towen and then mounted twenty horses, and Gallop along the Sands for Aberdove Seaport where there is about thirty houses built on the side of a Rock which in front commands a large arm of the Sea, over against it Aberystwyth, on the side of a very Beautyfull Rock, on one side the Alehouse, you see the mean Ocean, on the other side eight different valleys, intermixd with craggy rocks woods houses medows not forgeting a large Park between to Hills, which in these parts is a very uncommon thing. in the room was to dine, in came a girl, and removd off I cant say how many stinking stockings, Dirty shirts Breechis, and swept out our room, which by the cobwebs dust &c:c I do supose had not bin cleand of months, no matter for that, down we sat at the window you may be sure for the sake of fressh air, and to see the Sea hemty itself into a Beautyfull Serpentine river, at the begining of which lay ten ships at harbour, one of which, (the while our Turbets Soulls, &c:c was cooking) we whent on board, and very neatly

papperd and fitted up the caben was, after we returud to shore, all the men run up the masts and gave severall huzeas, and desended quick as lightning, so pretty a sight I never see. after dinner we had severall excelent songs, Duke Wynn* sings well, but the Governour better than Beard himself, we drunk tea on the Beech and had round us a hundred people, all Amazement. we then took horse, and in coming home, see eight or nine ships in full sail, running Races, which the tell me they sometimes do for large summs, how shockingly doth the spirit of gambling prevail, both by land and Sea we got home before ten, as soon as I came in the inform'd me the hot day had brought out whole regements of adders, and sneaks in the Gardens for which reason I shall never more visit any of the privet-walks, but some time I hear they chose to take a peep at us in the Hall, where they told me I had like to have set my foot on one, thank fortune I did not seet, if I had, do beleive I shoud not have injoyd myself so much as I have done. but it is now time to conclude, and hope you will acknowlede me very good in sparing time to write such long Letters to you, whos I am with love and great affection E Pres say all thats kind from me to mine

QUERIES.

THE WELSH CROWN JEWELS.—In Williams's *Ancient and Modern Denbigh*, there is a note stating that " a portion of the Welsh Crown Jewels was discovered, a few years back, at Maesmynan, where Prince Llywelyn resided." It would be interesting to know who is the present possessor of these "relics," and where may they be seen, and a description given of them. Who will reply?
T.W.H.

[See *History of Anglesey*, by Angharad Lloyd, pages 115, 311. Query if true?—ED.]

TOPOGRAPHICAL NAMES.—Can any of your readers assist me in ascertaining the meanings of the following :—*Guas* or *Geias* (a hill), *Buga* or *Biga* (a tributary), *Mamhilad, Pontnewynydd* (ecclesiastical districts in Monmouthshire), *Bod-aioch* and *Pen roryn*, farms in the parish of Trefeglwys?
IDLOES.

Corris.—Can any reader give the derivation, or refer me to any article that treats on the word *Corris?*
J.

Dimbeth : the name of hills near Montgomery, Cowbridge, and Caio in N. Carmarthenshire. It is, I think, the softened form of Din-byd, as under the last in a hollow we have still "Pwll-din-byd." The last also shows faint traces of fortification, hence the well known *din :* but what in the world "byd" may be I know not—perhaps some relation of Denbigh.
C.C.

SHROPSHIRE'S "TWELVE APOSTLES."—What was the origin of the term "Lord Clive's Twelve Apostles" applied to the members of parliament for Shropshire? In the *Shrewsbury Chronicle* for July 28, 1837, in a notice of the recent elections, the editor congratulated the county on being no more represented by "the 'Twelve Tools' of the Lord Lieutenant, Lord Powis, whose ancestor was a Whig;" and the article went on to say, "The 'Twelve Tools' have in various publications, been called by the Lord Lieutenant, his 'Twelve Apostles.'" On what occasion did Lord Powis thus speak or write about the twelve Conservative members of the county?
SCROBBES BYRIG.

* Wm. Wynne of Wern, Esq., married soon after this time to Miss Williams of Peniarth.

SEDAN CHAIRS.—When were Sedan chairs abandoned in the district, and how were they formerly supplied? Were there regular hirers of them? As it took two men to carry each, I presume they were not often owned by private individuals. BATH CHAIR.

REPLIES.

WILLIAM ROOS (Jan. 21, 1880).—This wandering artist paid at least two visits to Oswestry; one between thirty and forty years ago, and the other within the last ten years. On his first visit he painted, in oils, several portraits, and I have observed in some of these (notably one of the late Mr. Sabine, sen.), a tendency to make the face very long in comparison with the body. He generally hit off a likeness successfully. On his last visit he coloured (in water-colours I think) pictures of the west front of the Old Church, taken by a peripatetic photographer of the name of Peters, which enhanced their sale value to the amount of a few shillings. JARCO.

THUNDER ON THE ORGAN (Feb. 4, 1880).—I have just one more word to say about Mr. Weston, whose imitations of Thunder on the Organ enlivened the Sundays, and whose letters to the newspapers, the week days of our Salopian ancestors at the beginning of this century. On the 13th of June, 1805, he announced for publication a volume of original songs which had "not only 'made time steal away on downy pinions' at *private* Parties, but also *enraptured* the Theatres Royal of &c., &c." The first song of the collection was to be a brand new one; "Our *old* FRIEND and *New* MEMBER—JOHN HILL." Mr. Hill had been returned M.P. for Shrewsbury, in the room of Sir W. Pulteney, deceased, on June 10, that year. In a subsequent paper Mr. Weston published some of the Testimonials to his own excellent qualities; amongst others one from the inhabitants of Solihull, Birmingham (where he had been organist before his "disorders"), to the Churchwardens of Whitchurch. Mr. Weston seems to have been irrepressible in the newspapers. After his manifestoes, in which, as your readers have seen, Small capitals and Italics occupied so conspicuous a position, he seems to have subsided for a few weeks; but from a paper of July 24, we discover that "severe indisposition" was the cause of this, and he turned up again in quite a new character, for, it is recorded, that at 11 o'clock of the night of the 22nd of July somebody knocked him down as he was going along the street at the bottom of Claremont Hill, and then ran away. J.?.R.

FIRST ENGLISH PRINCE OF WALES (Jan. 28, 1880).—It appears that the first Prince was created in the year 1244, that is forty years before the royal birth at Carnarvon Castle, April 25th, 1284. I copy the following from Bridgman's *Princes of South Wales* :—"In the year 1244 Rees Mechyll, otherwise called Rhys Vychan, son of Rhys Grug, died (see *Brut y Tywysogion*). And in that same year before the end of April Griffith ap Llewelyn broke his neck in attempting to escape from the king's prison in London. Whereupon the King (Henry III.) gave to his eldest son Edward the title of Prince of Wales; a measure which so exasperated Prince David that he took up arms again at once. He was joined by all the Welsh Princes except Griffith ap Madoc, &c., &c., who were afterwards compelled to join the confederacy." Undoubtedly the son of Edward, born at Carnarvon, was the first Prince of Wales acknowledged as such by the Welsh people. JESSIE H.

5

CURRENT NOTES.

If Mr T. Rought Jones is right, we must no longer look for Mediolanum in Wales, but at Bearstone, Shropshire, near Market Drayton. Dating from the District Bank, Market Drayton, Mr. Jones writes to the *Athenæum* :—"In Horseley's 'Britannia Romana' he ends a discourse on this station by observing that 'if Mediolanum be placed anywhere near Draiton, we can then go on in our route with ease and success.' I have to announce that the anticipation of this antiquary has been realized, and I have the gratification to inform those interested in Roman remains of the discovery of an hitherto unknown and unnoticed Roman camp, close to the old road from London to Chester, at Bearstone, Salop, on the north bank of the Tern, about four and a half miles to the north-east of this town. The camp is on the estate of E. F. Coulson, Esq., of Bellaport, Salop, who, with considerate courtesy, has given me permission to make what examination I think necessary. A superficial inspection has revealed the remains of a smelting-place and some rude pottery. If any reader wishes a key to the position of the camp, let him consult the second and tenth Itineraries of Antoninus, and at Condate (Middlewich), at Rutunium (Bury Walls), at Bovio (Tiverton)—for there appears to be a consensus of opinions on these stations—describe on an Ordnance map at each place a circle of the radius, in Roman miles, to Mediolanum, as given by Antoninus; the intersection of the three circumferences will be a very short distance from the Bearstone Camp. This will be a somewhat different process from the straining and cramping of the distances to force this long-lost station at Chesterton. I hope in other communications to fully and fairly establish my claim to having solved the riddle of Mediolanum."

ANCIENT MONUMENTS.—The following are amongst the objects which Sir John Lubbock proposes to include in his Bill for the Preservation of Ancient National Monuments :—In Anglesey, the tumulus and dolmen, Plas Newydd, Llandudwen; in Glamorganshire, Arthur's Quoit, Gower; in Pembrokeshire, the Pentre Evan Cromlech, at Nevern.

The only antiquities in North Wales, apparently, which Sir John Lubbock proposes to include in his Ancient Monuments Bill are the tumulus and dolmen at Plas Newydd, Anglesey. It is not easy to understand why these alone have been selected. The stone circle above Penmaenmawr, though not so large as the one on Castle Rigg, near Keswick, which is included in the Bill, is also worth treasuring as a most impressive memorial of remote times; and it would be an irreparable loss if, through any freak, the remains of Tre'r Ceiri, a few miles from Pwllheli, or Tomen-y-Mur, near Festiniog, not to mention many others, were destroyed. The last-mentioned, we happen to know, is in exceedingly good hands at present, but if ancient monuments are to be preserved by law, all eventualities of future possession should be guarded against. The Rev. Edmund Venables of Lincoln writes to the *Times* :—"Sir, May I be permitted, in the interests of archæology, to express my hope that the schedule appended to Sir John Lubbock's Bill for the Preservation of Ancient Monuments, printed in the *Times* of to-day, is representative, and not exhaustive? But under any view of its character it is somewhat surprising to read a list of ancient monuments which it is desired to preserve from mutilation or destruction, which does not include a single example from the two districts most fruitful in pre-historic remains— the county of Cornwall and Merionethshire. The Land's-End district and the vicinity of Barmouth can show more-

3

cromlechs than all the rest of the island collectively, while both districts are abundant in so-called 'British villages,' often in a wonderful state of preservation, early fortifications both of stone and earth, stone circles, and other priceless memorials of the earlier races."

ST. CADVAN'S CHURCH, TOWYN.

The restoration of this most interesting, but in its architecture, rude old church, has been commenced in earnest. The two remaining ones of the arches which supported the western tower, which fell in 1692, have been taken down. Their state was dilapidated, and the masonry very bad; but we wish they were to be restored precisely in their former style, of course with good masonry. The state of the church to one who knows nothing of "construction" appears most formidable, but we hope that it will not be necessary to destroy and rebuild the venerable fabric. Some very interesting fragments of good filleted "Early English" mouldings have been dug up, far better than any part of the church as it now is. They are probably portions of a window in the central tower, or of an east window, removed when the present, not bad, but dilapidated "perpendicular" one was inserted. There has also been found a very perfect little bell, excepting that it wants its "clapper"—probably it was the "Sanctus bell"—and a fragment of a very curious and early vessel, very small, of black-glazed pottery, with three handles, close to the base. We hope that the architect will be summoned immediately, and should have preferred to see the church restored in its present rude style, without the introduction of certainly beautiful arches and windows, but as it appears to us out of character with the old building. However, the gentleman employed was the skilful architect in the restoration of Llandaff Cathedral, and but little fault can be found with what has been done there.   W.

STRAY NOTES.

Mr. Joseph Hughes of Hodnet, near the seat of Lord Hill at Hawkstone, Shropshire, has at this time [June, 1820] an extraordinary cow, which is fed on grass only, that gives every day 24 quarts of milk, which as regularly produces 21lbs. of butter every week.—*Gents: Mag:* Vol. 90, p.629.

The papers of Nov. 1833, say :—"That rare bird the Immer, or Great Doucker, otherwise called the Ember Goose was taken a few days ago near the mouth of the river Ystwyth near Aberystwyth, in a net, at night, in company with a fine salmon. This is the Colymbus Immer of Linnæus, or Le Grand Plougeon of Buffon, and was never before seen in these parts."

The newspapers of June 1820 published the following tale of Love and Adventure :—"In the neighbourhood of Denbigh, the following extraordinary circumstance occurred; and the parties concerned are, or lately were, living. A young man married a young woman of suitable age, and after a few years of conjugal felicity he enlisted as a soldier in the militia, and from the militia he volunteered into the regulars. His wife, hearing nothing of him during a long period, and being impatient of a cheerless bed, married again. The husband, influenced by similar feelings, married a buxom English damsel. Years rolled on, when death stepped in and separated these happy pairs. The husband again became a widower and the wife a widow. The regiment was disbanded, he returned home, and was welcomed with joy into the embraces of his former and earlier spouse."

Mr. Shaw of Shrewsbury (says a newspaper for Jan. 25, 1837) has in his possession a beautiful specimen of that variety of Wild Swan, lately added to the British Fauna, called Bewick's Swan *(Cygnus Bewickii, Yarrell.)* It was shot near Aberystwyth by Capt. Powell of Laura Place.

FEBRUARY 25, 1880.

NOTES.

CAVE-HUNTING.—There is a cave on the Berwyn above Dolydd Ceiriog, and about four miles from Corwen, known as *Ogof Ceryg Oedog*, and has never been explored. There are many tales and legends in connection therewith, with which I shall not at present trouble you, but the meaning of "Ogof Ceryg Oedog" is "The Cave of Ancient Stones," and very probably stone and flint instruments may be found there, for it is rarely ever that Welsh names of places prove misleading in matters of history and archæology. If any of your readers, prompted by the suggestive and insinuative name, or by any other attractions, should ever visit the spot, let them take with them a couple of labourers equipped with picks and spades, for the mouth of the cave has fallen in, about thirty years ago, and there are but one or two of the old shepherds who know the exact spot. The writer can give their names and further particulars if necessary.   J.C.H.

PARLIAMENT OF ENGLAND (Feb, 11, 1880). This week we continue the list to the end of the reign of Edward the Third.

COUNTY OF SALOP.

1341	Robertus de Harleye ; Rogerus Corbet, de Caus
1343	Thomas de Swynnerton'; Walterus de Hopton'
1344	Johannes de Aston'; Willielmus Bannastre, de Yorton'
1346	Philippus de Bourghton', or de Broghton' ; Willielmus Banastre
1347	Hamo Lestrange ; Willielmus de Caynton'
1348	Johannes de Burghton; Willielmus de Banastre, de Yorton'
1350	Willielmus Banastre, de Hadenhale ; Johannes de Upton'
1351	Johannes de Botiller ; Edwardus Bumel
1352	Robertus de Penybrugge
1353	Johannes de Westhope
1354	Walterus de Hopton'; Johannes de Burton
1355	Johannes de Borghton'; Willielmus Banastr', de Hadenale
1357	Johannes de Burghton' ; Willielmus Banastre
1358	Johannes de Lodelowe ; Willielmus Banastre, de Hadenhale
1360	Robertus Corbet, de Morton' ; Willielmus Banastre, de Hadenale
1361	Johannes de Lodelowe ; Ditto
1362	Johannes le Manter ; Johannes de Coxhale (1)
1363	Walterus de Hopton'; Johannes de Stoke
1365	Hugo de Moutuo Mari ; Rogerus Cheyne
1366	Johannes de Lodelowe, chivaler; Willielmus Banastr', de Hadenhale
1369	Willielmus Carles, chivaler ; Brianus Cornewaill, chivaler
1370	Robertus de Kendale ; Robertus Corbet
1371	Robertus de Kendale
1372	Robertus Corbet, miles ; Robertus de Kendale, miles
1373	Johannes de Lodelowe, chivaler ; Adam de Peshale
1375	Ditto ; Robertus de Kendale, chivaler
1376	Brianus de Cornewaille, chivaler ; Willielmus de Chetewynde, de Calwynton'

BOROUGH OF SHREWSBURY.

1341 Johannes Stury ; Thomas Colle
1344 Petrus Gerard ; Johannes de Ardeston'
1346 Johannes de Foryate ; Thomas de Lodelowe
1347 Ricardus de Weston'; Reginaldus Perle
1348 Thomas de Lodelowe ; Johannes Pryde
1350 Johannes Stury ; Johannes de Caumpedene
1353 Johannes Scury ; Robertus Reyner
1354 Johannes de Foryate ; .... de Mutton'
1358 Johannes Stury ; Robertus de Thornes
1360 Ditto Ditto
1361 Ditto ; Reginaldus Perle
1362 Ditto ; Johannes de Caumpeden
1363 Willielmus de Longenolre ; Johannes Gaffreye
1365 Johannes Soury ; Robertus de Thornes
1366 Thomas de Mutton' ; Johannes de Caumpeden'
1369 Rogerus atte Yate ; Johannes Geffrey
1371 Thomas le Skynnere (2)
1372 Ditto ; Philippus Godberd
1373 Ricardus Pontesburi ; Reginaldus de Mutton'
1375 Willielmus de Longenolre ; Thomas Skynner, de
            Salop
1376 Willielmus de Wytheford ; Rogerus atte Yate
                                                  ED.

(1) The enrolment of the Writ de Expensis gives
Johannes le Mounter and Willielmus Banastr'.
(2) The same name is also given as one of the members
for Bridgnorth. "Thomas Skynner" also represents
Bridgnorth in the Parliament of 1375-6.

QUERIES.

MORWYNION GLAN MEIRIONYDD.—The
newspapers of 1804 announce the death, at an advanced
age, of Mrs. Parry, the widow of the Rev. the Warden of
Ruthin, who had died a week previously. "This was the
lady whose personal charms in early life drew forth from
the discriminatory pen of Lord Littleton, the appellation
of 'The Fair Maid of Bala.'" What was Mrs. Parry's
maiden name, and who was her father ? NEMO.

DAVID HOLBACHE.—Amongst the members of
Parliament summoned to meet at Coventry 15 Feb.
1405-6, is given the name of David Holbache, as one of
the representatives of Salop County. He is also in the list
of members summoned to attend the Parliament at Gloucester 20 Oct. 1407, and at Westminster 27 Jan. 1409.
Another name takes his place in the Parliament assembling at Westminster 3 Nov. 1411, but in 1413 we have
him as one of the representatives of the borough of Shrewsbury ; and in two or three Parliaments, extending up to
1417 his name is given as representing sometimes the
County and at others the County town. All this I glean
from the new Blue Book. I presume this is the David
Holbatche who founded a "Free Grammar School" in
Oswestry (whatever that may mean). Leland, who travelled in these parts in the time of Henry VIII., referring
to the School, says it was "founded by one Davy Holbeche, a lawyer, steward of the towne and lordship, who
gave xli land to it." Stowe says " Owen Glyndwr was
pardoned at the intercession of David Holbetche, esq."
In Cotton's Records by Prynne, we are told that "David
Holbetch was made a denizen, or free citizen of England,
in the reign of Henry IV." Extracts from the Wills of
Old Oswestrians have come to light in *Bye-gones* that have
helped to clear away doubts connected with the history of our parish church ; would it be unreasonable to
hope that Holbache's may some day turn up, by which
this generation may learn what was meant four centuries
ago, by a "Free School ?" JARCO.

REPLIES.

FIRST ENGLISH PRINCE OF WALES (Feb.
18, 1880).—It is not generally known that Edw. III. was
never Prince of Wales. He is said to have been so created
in a Parliament at York, in 1322, but this is perfectly
incorrect. Anyone who will examine the Ministers
Accounts for Wales, in the Public Record Office, will be
convinced at once that he never held the Principality till
he became king. On his seal in 1325 he is styled *Edwardus
Primogenitus Regis Anglie Dux Aquitanie Comes Cestrie.
Pontivi et Montistrolli.* W.

BWLCH Y PAWL (Jan. 21, 1880).—It appears
certain that the Bwlch y Pawl referred to by CAEAWG and
DYVNIG is not the pass appointed by the Prince Rhodri
Mawr as the place of arbitration, to decide peaceably any
dispute that might arise between the province of Aberffraw and the province of Dinefwr. But the position of
that historical pass lies in the neighbourhood of Pennal,
in Merionethshire, for there is a spot on the mountain
in that district which bears the name Bwlch y Pawl (or,
perhaps, in common parlance, Bwlch Pawl), and at a
distance of some three miles from the river Dovey. And
the proximity, comparatively speaking, of the spot to the
banks of that river is such that it may be taken as corresponding with the description of its position given in the
Iolo MSS., where it is said to be "on the banks of the
Dovey," which proves that the Bwlch y Pawl, in the
vicinity of Pennal, is the one appointed by the said Prince
as the place for arbitration to decide and settle any dispute
that might arise between the two provinces before named.
He similarly appointed Rhyd yr Helig on the Wye as the
place of arbitration for deciding quarrels between the
province of Mathrafal and that of Dinefwr ; and Dol yr
Hunedd in Iâl for the like purpose in case of a dispute
between the provinces of Mathrafal and Aberffraw.
Tradition has brought this pass also into notice in connection with a love affair ; but the legend reflects in this case
much more credit on the conduct of the lady than in the
one narrated in *Bye-gones* in connection with the Bwlch
y Pawl situate near Bwlch y Groes. In "Yr Amser
Gynt " in the columns of the *Goleuad* some two years
ago, it is stated that it was the father of the young lady,
and not the lady herself, who compelled the young man to
undergo the terrible ordeal narrated. But to leave that,
the tradition respecting Bwlch y Pawl in the neighbourhood of Pennal runs to this effect :—The daughter of Cefn
Caer had placed her affections upon a young man that her
father did not at all approve of ; but her lover fully reciprocated her affection, so much so that he had risked his
life to win her. The father feared that nothing but the
death of one of the young people would prevent their being
joined together in matrimony, if by any means they could
manage to have the marriage ceremony accomplished. He
therefore placed before the young man a condition by
which he should become possessed of the one he loved,
which was both extremely difficult to comply with, and
inhuman in the extreme. There is no doubt that the
father intended to compass the death of the young man,
and at the same time keep himself clear of a charge
of murder under the plea of an agreement.
Notwithstanding the severity of the ordeal, and
the improbability of his ever being able to survive
it, he cast away all thoughts of the difficulty and danger
for the sake of his beloved one. The terms upon which
her father would consent to the union were, that the
young man should remain out all night naked on Bwlch
Pawl, probably on a night of the father's own selection,
when perchance the snow covered the hills and the banks
of the Dovey, the lakes and rivulets were locked in the

stern grip of the severe frost; a threatening redness spread over the horizon across the Estuary, and the piercing frost-wind blew across the country. The young man divested himself of all clothing at nightfall, and braved the fierceness of the night in the strength of his love, his devotedness, and courage. He ascended the mountain taking with him a stake (Pawl) and a mallet; and, alone on that inhospitable pass, he spent the weary night, striving hard to keep up the circulation of his blood, and so preserve his life, by driving the stake into the ground with the mallet, and when the iron became heated by the continuous blows he would place it on his heart to assist it in sending the blood forth through his veins. At last the welcome dawn broke on the distant horizon and he was alive to hail it, and could now claim as his wife the one for whom he had suffered so much. His beloved one was true to him during all his troubles, and on that memorable night she remained all night at her window holding in her hand a light to cheer him and encourage him to persevere in the terrible ordeal he had to undergo.

It appears that afterwards the young woman was taunted by her parents for having assisted her lover in his trial by holding the light in the window for him all night; for it is related that, some time afterwards, she was told by her parents, one Sunday morning, when they were going to church, to roast a goose for dinner. Instead of performing that culinary operation in the ordinary way, she took a candle and placed it at one end of the house, and the goose at the other. When her worthy parents returned from church and remonstrated with her for not having roasted the goose, she curtly answered them that it was as easy for the goose to be roasted by the heat of the candle at one end of the house as it was for her lover to live on that cold night on Bwlch Pawl by the light of her taper held at the window. It is said that the legend just narrated gave to this pass the name of Bwlch Pawl.   ROBYN FRYCH.

Dolgelley.   [Translated by BONWM.

UNREFORMED CORPORATIONS.

The report of the Commissioners appointed to inquire into Municipal Corporations not subject to the Municipal Corporations Acts (other than the City of London) has been issued. It is a Blue Book of 160 pages, and contains the report of the Commissioners, special reports respecting eighty-six places into which enquiry has been made, and some correspondence and schedules. The Commissioners conclude their report with the following recommendations as to the manner in which they think it expedient Parliament should deal with the Corporations which were the subject of their inquiry :—"It appears to us that it is not expedient that any of these Corporations which are municipal in their character should continue in their present state and condition. We are, however, of opinion that in many of the boroughs municipal institutions might usefully be retained, and that the best mode of dealing with them would be to subject them to the provisions of the Municipal Corporations Acts, placing them, as nearly as may be, in the position of the boroughs included in Schedule B of the Act of 1835." Amongst the Boroughs which it appears to them may be so dealt with are Kidwelly, Llanfyllin, Montgomery, and Radnor. The Commissioners state that in making this selection they have been "guided generally by the number of the population, its increase or decrease since the former report, the value of the property possessed by the corporations, and the nature and extent of the municipal and magisterial functions now exercised by them, rather than by any one of these con-

siderations in particular. We have also kept in view the importance of the boroughs relatively to the surrounding districts, and the difficulty or otherwise of obtaining the assistance of the justices of the county. In case the general body of the inhabitants of any of the boroughs to which our recommendation applies should not desire to retain municipal institutions, effect can be given to their wishes by omitting them from the list of boroughs to be dealt with in this way. On the other hand, if the majority of the inhabitants of any boroughs not included in the list should desire to retain these institutions, it would be easy, if it were thought expedient, to add them to it. It seems to us desirable that in all boroughs within our commission in which it may be thought right to preserve municipal institutions, their corporations should, as far as possible, be dealt with on a uniform plan, and be constituted in the manner provided by the Municipal Corporations Acts, and be made subject to their provisions. The effect of so dealing with them would be that the existing magisterial, judicial, and licensing jurisdiction of the officers and members of the present corporations would be superseded. With regard to the remaining boroughs with which we have to deal, it appears to us that by reason of the smallness of their population and corporate property, and the nature of the duties now performed by their corporations, it is not expedient that those bodies should retain municipal functions, or the magisterial powers (including those of coroner) exercised by their members or persons elected or appointed by them. The effect of abolishing the separate jurisdictions within these boroughs would, of course, be that they would for all purposes fall into the body of the counties in which they are situate." The following reports are added :—

LLANFYLLIN.

We could obtain no information as to the correctness of the Report of 1835, but it was stated to us that no alteration had been made in the constitution of the borough since that time, and that the title remains the same.

The governing charter is the 25 Car. 2 (1685).

There are two bailiffs, who are elected annually out of the capital burgesses for a year, one by the common burgesses and the other by the steward of Lord Powis, who is lord of the manor; one is termed the burgesses' bailiff, and the other the lord's bailiff. They are sworn in before the outgoing bailiffs and the steward. They are the chief officers of the corporation, and act as magistrates within the borough. One of them is the returning officer at Parliamentary elections. They have no salary, but they receive the tolls from the market hall and from a small sheep fair, which amount to about £20 a year. Formerly the bailiffs applied these tolls to their own private purposes, but for the last 12 years they have been devoted to the repair of the market hall, or to any other public purpose which the bailiffs may have deemed expedient.

The bailiffs keep an account of their receipts and expenditure, which they produce when called upon by any burgess at the annual court leet. Permission to see the books has never been refused to any burgess, although the bailiffs believe that they are entitled to use the money received by them and to apply it to their own purposes.

There is still a bellman or yeoman, who receives yearly a suit of clothes in lieu of the £1 5s. salary mentioned in the former report.

There are serjeants-at-mace; their duties are nominal and they have no salary.

There are at present 15 capital burgesses, the full number required by the charter. When a vacancy occurs a capital burgess nominates a common burgess, and his nomination being seconded by a capital burgess, the question is put to the court. The election is for life. The duties of the capital burgesses are to attend the court leet, and to serve as bailiff when elected.

There are at present 45 common burgesses. They are proposed and seconded by a capital burgess, and elected at the court by a majority of votes. They pay a fee of half a guinea on appointment to the deputy steward. They pay no stamp duty on election. Llanfyllin is one of the Montgomery boroughs.

The bailiffs sit as magistrates at petty sessions once a month, and are always assisted by a professional clerk. One of the present bailiffs is a retired draper, and the other is an auctioneer. The retired draper is a county magistrate. All ordinary petty sessions business is conducted by the bailiffs, and they grant licences for public houses. One of the public houses is owned by one of the bailiffs. We heard no complaint as to the administration of justice, and the magistrates never interfere in granting licences where either is interested, but the case is sent to the county magistrates. It was stated to us that the corporation had power to hold quarter sessions, but that in practice it has never done so. Prisoners committed for trial are sent to the county gaol at Montgomery ; the quarter sessions are held at Welshpool or at Newtown.

There is a recorder who, as well as the steward, is a justice of the peace, though they never act. These two officers, in conjunction with the bailiffs, have power to make bye-laws and to levy rates for the administration of the borough.

There is no longer a coroner for the borough. Inquests are held by the county coroner.

The population of the parliamentary borough is 1,000, that of the municipal borough is 2,000.

The only land now owned by the corporation is an eighth of an acre, which is occasionally used for the sheep fair.

It has been alleged that during last year the corporation allowed an inhabitant of the town to make an encroachment on the street. We were, however, informed that it was decided at a public meeting held for the purpose, that the land in question could not be considered corporation property.

No part of the corporation funds is expended in entertainments. Each of the bailiffs gives a sovereign out of his own pocket for an annual dinner, and the deputy steward of Lord Powis pays the remainder.

MONTGOMERY.

The Report of 1835 is believed to have been correct at the time it was written, and with a few slight exceptions is applicable to the present state of things.

The title of the corporation is the bailiffs and burgesses of the borough of Montgomery.

The municipal officers are the two bailiffs, the high steward, the recorder and town clerk, and the two serjeants-at-mace.

The bailiffs act as magistrates during their year of office, and hold petty sessions once a month. There is no non-intromittant clause, and the county magistrates occasionally act within the borough.

Prisoners convicted at petty sessions, or committed for trial, are sent to the county gaol.

The borough magistrates grant licences for public houses.

There are now eight public houses within the borough. The population is about 1,200.

It was stated that the bailiffs are of a class quite capable of acting efficiently as magistrates.

Each bailiff has power to appoint a deputy, but the deputy bailiff cannot act as a magistrate. The bailiffs have not of late years been appointed aldermen after their year of office, and there are now no aldermen.

The same person is recorder, town clerk, and coroner. He is elected in common hall by the burgesses. He has no duty to perform as recorder and has no salary as such.

The deputy town clerk receives a salary of £10, £5 of which is paid by the Earl of Powis and £5 by the borough magistrates.

The present coroner is not a professional man. On holding inquests the deputy town clerk generally sits with him and takes an active part in the proceedings. The coroner is paid a salary of £5 a year by the county, which he hands over to the deputy town clerk.

There are two serjeants-at-mace, who each receive £1 a year. There is a seal with the arms of the borough upon it. The serjeants-at-mace act as constables occasionally, but the duties of keeping the peace are discharged by the county police.

There are 51 burgesses, 47 of whom are resident within the borough. All the sons of burgesses have a right to take up their freedom. Formerly on admission a stamp was required, but since 1871 the office of Inland Revenue has ceased to require a stamp. Neither marriage nor apprenticeship confer a right to the freedom. There are no honorary burgesses or burgesses by election.

There are markets, but no tolls are levied in respect of produce coming into the town. There are small sums paid for the privilege of standing under shelter in the town hall, but no account is kept of the amounts paid, and they are retained by the town serjeant as his own perquisite.

The corporation owns the town hall and 89 acres of land, 14 acres of which is arable, the remainder is pasture. They also own a small piece of land called the bailiff's patch, for which a rent of 12s. a year is paid.

A perpetual rentcharge of 20 guineas annually is payable by the Cambrian Railway Company for land taken by them, over which the burgesses had formerly a right of common.

The corporation has held the portion of land called the "Flos" from time immemorial. Formerly the produce of this land was divided among the whole body of the burgesses and widows of deceased burgesses, the bailiffs each receiving an extra share. This land produced from 30s. to £2 for each of the burgesses and widows of burgesses. There were between 40 and 50 persons entitled either as burgesses or widows of burgesses. The lands are now let, and as a compensation for the extra share of the produce, an additional guinea is paid to the bailiffs.

The burgesses formerly had the right of common over certain land belonging to Lord Powis, and in the year 1783 arbitrators were appointed to estimate the value of this land, and to allot land to be taken in exchange from Lord Powis for this right of common. The arbitrators allotted land adjoining the Flos, and this land, together with the "Flos," constitutes the 89 acres above mentioned.

These two properties have been let since 1873 as a whole to Mr. Wm. Davies Bryan at a rent of £210. The properties were let by auction, and such has been the custom of letting which has prevailed in the borough during several years.

The rent of the land occupied by Mr. Bryan and all other moneys received for the corporation are paid to the town clerk, who keeps an account of them which he produces twice a year to the burgesses in common hall.

After the accounts are examined, audited, and passed, the balance remaining in the hands of the town clerk after payment of expenses is divided amongst the resident burgesses and widows, in number during the last three years from 48 to 52.

We went through the accounts of the year 1873-74, and found them properly kept.

The details of the account will be found in the Appendix. No money of the corporation is spent in dinners.

The effect of placing Llanfyllin and Montgomery in Schedule B of the Act of 1835 is to give them a Mayor and Corporation like Welshpool and Oswestry; in fact to put them in the position of ordinary municipal boroughs, except that they will not have a separate commission of the peace, unless it is asked for, in which case it may be granted.

OVERTON.

The Report of 1835 is supposed to be correct, except that it mentions as a charter what is really only a grant of a market in the 7th year of Edward I., and omits the operative charter of the 20th year of the same reign.

This charter, which has since the date of that Report been discovered at the Record Office, provides, among other things, that Overton should be a free borough; that the burgesses were to elect three upright men as bailiffs, and that the King's bailiff of Mailor hundred was to select one of the three as the bailiff of the town.

There are at present no bailiffs or other officers, no municipal or judicial functions, and no property. The magistrates of the county act within the borough, and grant the licences to public houses.

Overton is still one of the Flint boroughs.

The population in 1871 was 1,324, and seems to be diminishing.

RUYTON.

The following letters are appended:—

6, Town Walls, Shrewsbury, June 24, 1879.

Sir,—I believe the printed report on the borough of Ruyton, Salop, so far as I know, to be correct. A court leet was regularly held by the late John Edwards, Esq., of Great Ness, lord of the manor, up to the time of his death. His son Rowland, in the absence of his elder brother, in India, who is the present lord of the manor, held one court leet after his father's death, and that was the last held.

The last bailiffs elected were the late Samuel Harman, Esq., and my brother, Thomas Roden Comberbach, who is now living, Edward Ralphs was the last serjeant-at-mace. I myself delivered the mace into the keeping of the present vicar, who keeps it with the church plate.

I bought the lock-up from Rowland Edwards, Esq., and took it down and sold the grounds to the township for the nominal sum of £1. I believe the freeholders still possess the right of common over the Cliffe, but I feel sure there has been no perambulation for the last 10 years.

. . . .

I am, &c., J. S. COMBERBACH.

A. G. C. Liddell, Esq.

6, Town Walls, Shrewsbury, July 10, 1879.

Sir,—The last election of bailiffs was made at the court leet held on October 20, 1851, which was the last held.

The lock-up was purchased on the 30th June, 1854.

So long a time having elapsed since the customs and privileges under the Corporation Act of the borough of Ruyton were carried out, and having myself left the neighbourhood for some time, I have had a little trouble in obtaining the information you required.

Messrs. Peele and Peele, town clerk of Shrewsbury, hold the court rolls of the borough, and may give any information required.

I am, &c., J. S. COMBERBACH.

A. G. C. Liddell, Esq.

The following letter is also appended with reference to Machynlleth:—

Machynlleth, April 18, 1877.

Sir,—In reply to your letter of the 3rd instant, addressed to the town clerk of Machynlleth, inquiring whether any municipal institutions exist at Machynlleth, I beg to state that there are not any.

I am, &c., LEWIS WILLIAMS,

A. G. C. Liddell, Esq. Assistant Overseer.

Through the kindness of Lady Williams Wynn we are able to publish the following beautiful threnody by Sir F. Doyle on the death of Captain Arthur Watkin Williams Wynn:—

TO THE MEMORY
OF THE LATE
CAPTAIN ARTHUR WATKIN WILLIAMS WYNN,
OF THE
23RD ROYAL WELSH FUSILEERS, WHO FELL AT ALMA.

"There lay Col: CHESTER, and four of his gallant Officers, with their faces to the sky."—Morning paper.

"He had gone right up to the gun."—Private letter.

I.

When, from grim Alma's blood-stained height,
  There came the sound of woe
And, in the first and latest fight,
  That noble head was low,
Fond hearts, that writhed beneath the blow,
  Were tortured with keen thirst to know
How, ere their loved and lost one bled,
  By Fate's cold hand, the gloomy thread
    Of that last hour was spun :
And yearnings, from thine English home,
  Bounded across the ocean foam,—
" Where did ye find my son ? "
The answer, from that fatal ground,
Came pealing with a trumpet sound,—
  " Close to the Russian gun !
With many a gallant friend around him,
In one proud death "—'twas thus we found him.

II.

"His look, though soft, was calm and high,
  His face was gazing on the sky,
As if he said,—' Man cannot die,
  Though all below be done.'
Thus was it that we saw him lie,
  Beneath the Russian gun.
Right up the hill our soldiers sped,
No hurrying in their earnest tread ;
The iron thunder broke in storms,
  Again, and yet again,—
On their firm ranks and stately forms
  It did but break in vain.
Though yet untrained by war to bear
  The battle's deadly brunt,
The ancient heart of Wales was there,
  Still rushing to the front ! "
Their blood flowed fast along those steeps,
  But the proud goal was won ;
And the moon shone on silent heaps,
  Beyond the Russian gun :
'Twas thus, with friends he loved around him,
Among the foremost dead they found him.

III.

Oh ! there are bitter tears for thee,
  Young sleeper by the Eastern sea ;
Grief that thy glory cannot tame,
  It will not cease to ache,
And anguish beyond any name,
  In hearts that fain would break.

Still, thy brave bearing on that day
Lends those pale lips its strength to pray,
"Thy will, oh God ! be done !
We bow before Thy living throne,
And thank Thee for the mercy shewn,
E'en when Thy summons dread was thrown
  Forth from the Russian gun."
No agony that gasps for breath,
Lengthened his hopeless hours of death ;
No fevered longing woke in vain,
For those he ne'er could see again :
By noble thoughts and hopes befriended,
By honour to the last attended,
His haughty step the hill ascended.
At once !—his brain and hand reposed,
At once !—his dauntless life was closed ;
One mystic whirl of mighty change—
One sea-like rush of blackness strange,—
And all the roaring tumult dim
Was cold, and dark, and still for him ;
No pain could rack, no fever parch,
  That form whose course was run ;
So ended his majestic march
  Up to the Russian gun,
For there, with friends he loved around him,
Serene as sleep, the searchers found him.

IV.
And still, for ever fresh and young,
  His honoured memory shall shine,
A light that never sets, among
  The trophies of his ancient line—
Yea—though the sword may seem to kill,
Each noble name is living still,
  A ray of glory's sun ;
And children of a future day,
Each, in his time, shall proudly say,
  "I bear the name of one,
Who in that first great fight of our's
Against the lawless Tyrant's powers,
Upon the red Crimean sod,
Went down, for Liberty and God,
  Close by the Russian gun !"
For there, with friends he loved around him,
Among the *free-born* dead they found him.
11th October, 1854.   F. H. DOYLE.

MARCH 3, 1880.

NOTES.

A LADY'S IMPRESSIONS OF WALES. [LETTER IV.]
(Feb. 18, 1880.)

From Mrs. Presland (of Walford Hall, Salop) at
Peniarth, Merionethshire, to her sister Miss Slaney, at
Shrewsbury :—

Dear Sister,. We continue to spend our time very
lovelly, no less then sixteen horses just set out for Towen,
fourteen Left us yesterday, more exspected to night, it is
well they can make in the House, and out building eighty
beds, and that whole calvs sheep Lambs &c:c are still
presented, the weather continues bad. Miss Bett† last post
had a Letter from a lady in Paris, she says the weather is

† Elizabeth, second daughter of Edw. Williams, Esq., and
Jane, Viscountess Bulkeley, of Peniarth ; she died 5 May, 1830.

as bad there, I coud not help saying, that consideration
alone, must make it acceptable to every other nation, as
nothing here is approv'd of but the Beaumond, exapt the
Welch goats, and your humble servant, who when full
dress'd woud do honour to a Dukes table, oh ; when shoud
I received such acompliment in England, but I do now
and then discover a Little flatery. I was a few days
since to see a Mr. Williams, he comes from London, but
cant help describing his country House at Peniritha,
which I think woud nearly stand in our Market House, if
square. the parlour, and best chamber is fitted up, most
Eligantly, the way to the House is up a steep, with trees
on each side, which you desend till you come to a Little
murmering Brook just before the House, beyand which
his a high Rocky Hill, on one side a riseing orchard within
a Rural walk. in face of some medows, and high Rocks,
with here and there Busshy trees, on the other
side of the House a garden upon riseing ground,
till you come to a cover'd seat from whence you look down
a romantick vail, at the hend of which appears the Sea, near
to it a Church and steeple and if the Gentleman cuts down
the orchard and lays it in to a Lawn, I think he may
challenge Nort Wales, for situation. the day after we
dind at a Mr. Owens of Carbuthlen, where I was highly
entertaind with a Misers feast, and the old Butler biding
us eat hartily, as much as to say, such doings dont come
often, all tho is master a man of good fortune. the house
is new, not fitted up scrounded with high hils, one of
which is very long and high, where the trees are planted
in great taste, here and there a short Aveneu, a speace of
ground, and then a round patch, between bits of ground
with a beautyfull verdure then comes a square patch all
down the side of it, and from the top a very extensive
vieu but it rains and we retire, I lementing more then
ever my not attending in my youthfull days, to quick
writing, and good spelling, for if I had I coud have communicated to you a much more just, and entertaining
account of Wales, then it is now, I bluss to say in my
power to do, I wish I coud give you an Idea of the Droll
figures, I have the honour of being dayly intreduce to,
my lips are sore with kissing, and if Idye dont fancy that
it is the Sea that drowns me, but the stifeling of laughter,
and if I continue to behave as well as I have done, I
shall think I have the wisdome of Solaman. I wish you
coud seet the face and figure of a young gentleman aged
twenty, with an imbroderd coat, waistcoat & cue
wig &c:c, to whom I have took care to intreduce all the
old wemen, he begs, prays, stars, and dont know how to
look, but I tell him he must comply, as I have done before
him, but when he talks of his Phaeton, Chariot, dutches
of such a one, my Lord and Lady, and so forth. they
people eye him from head to foot, and wonder weither he
is man or monkey, such a contrast is he to the youths of
this Country, that it is no wonder they are all surprise,
who I supose he takes for stentots. as one set of company
goes out, others come in strange faces every day, ye very
strange, one woud think the whole kingdom coud scarsely
supply the consumption of this family, and friends, belonging to their own house upwards of forty, three good
hands to play on the musick, one on the flute, an other
the fidle, and a charming harper, which in our walking
tea drinking often attend us, we went on friday to ride on
the sands, till we came to a kave in a Rock within a few
yards of the Sea,‡ it is very romantick and high, at top
the stones hang over, and look as it cut in large squars,
seemingly lose and nothing to prevent their droping on
your head, and when the tide is out you appear to be in
the Sea and the tell you up the kave, you may go milles,

‡ Glyndwr's Cave, near Llangelynin, in Welsh, *Ogof Owain*.

that some yards up it, you hear constant musick, and they Welch who are very superstitious, tell you it is haunted, but I heard nothing. in the mouth of it is a large square stone, where some Ladys chose to play at Cards, and by not attending to the tide coming in, was all finely wet; and very much frighted, as the breakers often fling above the top some yards, here I pickd up a few shells, and some weeds for Dear Fan, who with Mr. P. and your selves I long to see, till that happy moment adieu Dr Sister belive me yours with great affection
Peniarth, Aug. ye 11 [1771 ?]
[Addressed " Miss Slaney, Shrewsbury."]

QUERIES.

WELSH WEBS.—A newspaper of Mar. 17, 1837, states that an order for Welsh Webs, amounting in value to £20,000, had been received at Dolgelley. Were there at that period mills in that district capable of executing such an order in anything like reasonable time ? G.G.

SIR JOHN BRIDGEMAN.—There is a monument, I believe, to Sir John and his lady, in Ludlow Church. He was Lord President of the Marches. It is said that one Ralph Gittins wrote the following epitaph on Sir John :—
" Here lies Sir John Bridgeman, clad in his clay,
God said to the Devil, sirrah, take him away ! "
Who was Ralph Gittins, and what was his quarrel with the Lord President ?   TELL.

OLD PARR.—In the Water Poet's Life of Old Parr, which professes to be founded on—
"——— Records and true certificate
From Shropshire late———"
mention is made of his drinking cyder at wakes and fairs, and hearing the nightingale from his Salopian home. Was cyder ever a Shropshire beverage, and was the nightingale ever a Shropshire bird? The Glyn, where Parr lived, is under the shadow of The Breidden-hills, a few miles from Welshpool. And let me take this opportunity of asking your readers to record in your columns description of paintings and engravings of Old Parr, and notices of his life, they may have met with, so as to form a complete record of this notable old Salopian.   H.B.

OSWESTRY CHURCH.—*The Yale Monument.*— Hugh Yale's name is appended to a Corporation document as lately as 1603, and he was unquestionably dead in 1616, but according to Pennant's reading of the inscription on the monument in St. Oswald's Church, in the thirteen years that elapsed between these dates, Yale must have died, and been buried in a chancel—the chancel destroyed in war—and the monument erected in the north aisle. This view, I notice, is adopted, by the Vicar, the Rev. Howell Evans, in an interesting paper he read in Aug. last before the members of the Cambrian Arch. Scy, and published in the last vol. of *Arch : Camb :* it is also endorsed by Mr.Stanley Leighton in a note on page 90, vol. 3, Sh. Arch. So. *Trans.* We have vague references in Oswestry history to " Incursions of the Welsh," but nothing so late as the 17th century. What then were " the late wars" the inscription refers to, if the monument was erected in 1616?   JARCO.

REPLIES.

DOLWYDDELAN *V.* DOLYDDELEN (Jan. 21, 1880).—There are several places named after saints with other prefixes than " Llan," viz., Caergybi, Rhosbeirio, Bodedern, Llechylched and Llechynfarwy in Anglesey.

Maentwrog, Maenafon, Garthbeibio, Dolanog, Delgadfan, and I believe there is a place called Dolbadarn near Llanberis, in Carnarvonshire. Then why not Dol-wyddelan? If this place is named after a Queen, why is the prefix in the plural (Dolydd)? This is the only instance of a plural prefix that I can think of. May not this go far to settle the orthography of Dolwyddelan ?   W.D.W.

SEDAN CHAIRS (Feb. 18, 1880).—I well remember Sedan Chairs' being used in Shrewsbury when I was a boy, about a quarter of a century ago. Several times, I can recollect, invalids were carried to chapel in them from my home.   E.

They were generally hired, and some persons owned several, men being employed to stand in some conspicuous places with them until called for. In Chester the common stand was along the walls of St. Peter's Church, in the centre of the city. I believe in Welshpool several private individuals owned "chairs."   LLERTWEF.

I recollect an old lady named Jenkins being regularly carried to Wrexham Church on a Sunday in one of the above conveniences—it usually waited for her in front of the Town Hall. I am not certain as to the date ; it would, however, be from 1828 to 1832, as near as I can judge. I believe it was her own property, but am not certain of it.   LANDWOR.

I remember one Sedan Chair in Oswestry, half a century ago, that I fancy must have been a joint-stock affair. The bearers (of whom William Edwards, the gardener, was one) were dressed in a plain livery. It was in great demand on wet Sundays, on which days it was carried several times into the Church, first with one and then with another. It also paid many a visit to the Theatre. I remember Mrs. Withers, who lived where Mrs. Smale's shop now is, often making use of it.
BEN STARCH.

FIRST SUNDAY SCHOOL IN OSWESTRY (Feb. 11, 1880).—There can be no question that a Sunday School was held at the Old Chapel in Dr. Williams's time, for he mentions the fact in a letter, dated "Oswestry, May 14, 1789," addressed to " H. Thornton, Esq., M.P., London ;" and by the wording of the letter we are led to infer that it had been for some time established. At the date when he wrote he regretted that the number in attendance had been " lessened through the carelessness of parents " (see *Life* by Gilbert, p. 288). Possibly the students of Dr. Williams' " Academy" were the teachers : his daughters (if he had any at that period) would have been too young, for he was only married in 1777. The Life of Dr. W. does not give the date when the school was established ; but it was not until May, 1782, that the Academy was removed to Oswestry ; although for twelve months before he had the charge of two young men. Dr. Williams was also the means of establishing Sunday schools at Denbigh, Llanfyllin, Bala, Carnarvon, Machynlleth, and other places, and the work seems to have been done by paid teachers.   JARCO.

On Christmas Day, 1855, Mr. G. Clement Davies read a history of the Old Chapel Sunday School. The following is an extract :—" There exists very little doubt of the fact that there was a Sabbath School here in the very same year that Robert Raikes commenced his at Gloucester, for we find that William Hughes was in the school as a boy 8 years old in the year 1785, and he states as his belief that it had been established three or four years previous to that time, thus giving the year 1782 or 1781 the very date of the first establishment of the school

at Gloucester, the jubilee of which was celebrated in 1831.'
William Hughes died on 26 September, 1865, aged 87
years, so that he was born in 1778.

Betty Hughes of Tynycoed, Llanforda, was reading a
Tract one day when I called in to see her. I asked her
how she learnt to read, and she replied that when she was
10 years of age the Miss Williams's daughters of the
Minister of the Old Chapel, Oswestry, taught her in the
Sunday School that they kept there. Betty Hughes died
on 5th February, 1851, aged 80 years; she was therefore
born in 1771, and was 10 years of age in 1781, the very
year in which we say our school was established, and in
which Robert Raikes commenced his school. T.M.

MARCH 10, 1880.

NOTES.

DR. JOHN DEE. — In *Local Gleanings* (an
archæological magazine relating chiefly to Lancashire and
Cheshire) edited by Mr. Earwaker, M.A., F.S.A., Mr.
J. E. Bailey has published the Diary of this famous
astrologer during the period that he was Warden of Manchester. Dr. Dee was proud of his Welsh descent, and
traced his genealogy from Roderick the Great. His
father belonged to a Radnorshire family, and by the
extracts we give from the Diary; it will be seen that Dee
kept up his connection with the Principality :—

1595. June 29, Mr. John Blayney of Over Kingesham
in Radnorshyre, and Mr. Richard Baldwyn of Duddlebury
in Shropsire, visited me at Mortlak. The great grandfather of the sayd John, and my great grandmother by
the father side, were brother and sister,

July 7, Mr. Morgan Jones my cosen cam to me at
Mistres Walls twise

July 15, I gave Mr. Morgan Traharn his bill to Mr.
Harbert.

Aug. 2' At Mr. Cosener his table at Grenewich ; I spake
that was greatly liked, Mr. Sergeant Oliver Lloyd ;
wold have disputed against, &c.

[In the Ashm. MSS. No. 847 is a book containing chiefly Welsh
history and descents, in which this memorandum occurs: "This
Booke was given to Mr. J. D. of Mortlake by his cousyn Mr.
Oliver Lloyd of the Welsh Pole. 1575. Mense Novembris die
12. At Mortlake."]

July 9, I sent Roger Kay of Manchester with my letters
into Wales.

[Kay was perhaps a carrier into Wales. The letters were for
Dee's relations at 'Llanydloes.']

Aug. 10, Mr Thomas Jones of Tregarron cam to me to
Manchester and rode toward Wales bak agayn. 13 day
to meet the catall coming.

Aug. 13, I rid toward York, Halifax, and Mr. Thomas
Jones rode toward Wales.

Sep 5, 17 hed of cattell from my kinsfolk in Wales by
the curteous Griffith David, nephew to Mr. Thomas
Griffith, browght, &c.

1597. Feb. 7, John Morryce came to Manchester.

[He seems to have been a Welsh carrier]

Feb. 14, John Morryce went toward Mountgomeryshire.
This Monday John Morrice went with my letters to Mr.
John Gwyn of Llandles and twelve more in Montgomery-
shyre, esquyers.

[Llandles, which appears in the form of Llanydles on July 1st,
is the town of Llanidloes, in that part of Montgomeryshire
which adjoins Radnorshire. Hereabouts Dee's connections
resided.]

July 1, I sent Roger Kay to Llanydles for cattall.

Oct. 22, John Fletcher of Manchester went with my
letters to Llanydlos this Sunday morning.

5

1598. Jan. 17, My brother Arnold to Chester and
Llandlos.

[He had come from London to Manchester on 15 Dec. preceding.]

1600. Sep. 16, Mr. Hanmer and Mr. Davis gentlemen
of Flyntshire, within four or five mile of Harden Castle,
did viset me.

NEMO.

PARLIAMENT OF ENGLAND (Feb. 25, 1880).
From the first year of Richard II.

COUNTY OF SALOP.

1377	Johannes de Lodelowe, chivaler ; Robertus de Kendale, chivaler
1378	Hugo Cheyne ; Edwardus de Acton
1379	Brianus de Cornewaill ; Hugo Cheyne
1380	Ricardus de Peshale, chivaler ; Thomas Neuport
1380	Petrus de Careswell ; Thomas le Younge
1381	Brianus de Cornewaille, chivaler ; Robertus de Kendale, chivaler de Kenlet
1382	Ditto ; Ditto.
1382	Petrus de Careswall', chivaler ; Edwardus de Acton
1383	Rogerus Corbet, chivaler ; Brianus de Cornewayle, chivaler, de Kenlet
1383	Ditto ; Thomas le Younge
1384	Petrus de Careswell' ; Edwardus de Acton
1384	Robertus Cuyne ; Ditto
1385	Willielmus Huggeford', chivaler ; Thomas de Lee
1386	Hamo de Peshale, chivaler ; Edwardus de Acton'
1387	Ricardus de Lodelowe, chivaler ; Willielmus Huggeford', chivaler
1388	Hugo Cheyne, chivaler ; Edwardus de Acton'
1389	Ricardus de Lodelowe. miles ; Thomas de la Lee
1390	Ricardus de Ludlowe ; Thomas de Whitton'
1391	Rogerus Corbet, chivaler ; Hugo Cheyne, chivaler
1393	Willielmus Huggeford' ; Johannes Darrus
1394	Adam Peshale ; Willielmus Hugeford'
1395	Thomas Youge ; Johannes Longford'
1397	Fulco Sprenghose ; Willielmus de Lee
1398	Fulco de Pembrugge, chivaler ; Ricardus Chelmeswyk'

BOROUGH OF SHREWSBURY.

1377	Willielmus de Longnoire ; Reginaldus Mutton'
1378	Johannes Gefferey ; Thomas Pryde
1379	Thomas Skynner, Willielmus Beorton'
1380	Ricardus Beorton'; Thomas Skynnere
1380	Ditto ; Ditto
1381	Willielmus di Boerton'; Ditto
1382	Ditto ; Ditto
1382	Willielmus de Beorton'; Robertus Thornes, junior
1382	Willielmus de Burton'; Ditto
1383	Willielmus de Beorton'; Ditto
1384	Willielmus de Birtton'; Thomas Skynnere
1384	Willielmus de Beorton'; Ditto
1385	Thomas Skinner ; Thomas Pryde
1386	Robertus de Grafton'; Hugo Wygan'
1387	Robertus Thornes ; Ditto
1388	Robertus de Graffton' ; Hugo Wygan
1389	Robertus de Grafton; Thomas Pryde
1391	Hugo Wygan ; Ditto
1393	Thomas Gamull'; Ditto
1395	Ricardus Aldescote ; Rogerus de Thornes
1397	Thomas Skynnere ; Johannes Geoffrey

The Parliament 21 Rich. II., summoned to meet at
Westminster 17 Sep. 1397, was continued by Adjourn-
ment at *Shrewsbury* 27 Jan. 1398. The last Parliament
in the reign of Rich : II. was summoned to meet at Westminster on 30 Sep. 1399; but the King abdicating the
previous day it did not meet. No return of members for
this Parliament is given. ED.

4

QUERIES.

WELCH CONJURORS.—Can any one give information as to the history of Savage, of Llangurig; Roberts, of Llanbremair; Harries, of Cwrt Cadno, and Roberts, Caergybi, Astrologer?　PROSPERO.

TOPOGRAPHICAL NAMES.—Can any reader of *Bye-gones* give a good derivation of *Llwyntidman* and *Treprenal*, townships in the parish of Llanymynech. I have never heard the meaning of "tidman," and feel inclined to think it may be a proper name.　Treprenal I have seen spelt Treprenhol in old records. I shall be thankful if someone can help me with these derivations?　LLERTWEF.

Bailey : usually derived from Med. Latin *vallium*=a small fort. D. S. Evans, *Dicty.* s. v., says "mound" is beili in Welsh. In ancient Gaelic baile is a town according to Skene. The mounds at Oswestry and Mold favour the first interpretation. In Carmarthenshire at Llansawel we have "Pen y bailey" at the head of the village : also near "Bailey-tew" : but I wish to call attention to "Bailey Vicar," a large farm in same parish, and same name also according to an old map occurs on the mountain of Mallaen, at present uninhabited. Neither has, I am sorry to say, any connection with the present Vicarage; nor in ancient times do I think the name could be given from an ecclesiastical source, as this would probably be the better known "offeiriad" (priest). I find, however, that in Gaelic "baile betagh"=township. "There were thirty townships or baile betaghs in a barony . . . and a brughaidh [officer] over every baile." Skene, *Celt. Scotland* I. 209 n. In the neighbouring parish of Llanegwad there is a manor called "Brunus." *Arch. Camb.* 1879, p. 171, 182. I suggest "bailey Vicar" as a survival of the Gadhelic occupation of these parts.
C.C.

["Lewes ap David alias the Fryhr late Bayly of the towne of Oswester," who died in 1547, left property in "the baylif streete." In a deed dated more than a century ago, property is mentioned as situated in "Bailey street, otherwise Bailiffs street." It is still usual for illiterate people to speak of Bailiffs as Bayleys. ED.]

REPLIES.

OLD CAMBRIAN INSTITUTIONS.
(Feb. 4, 1880.)

Society of Ancient Britons. The birthday of Caroline, Princess of Wales, was the same as that of the tutelar saint of the Principality; and some influential Welshmen, anxious to testify their attachment to the Hanoverian dynasty and commemorate the memory of St. David, formed themselves into a society. The *London Gazette* of Feb. 9, 1714-15, announced that on the 1st of March, the service and sermon at St. Paul's, Covent Garden, would be in Welsh, and desired all those who were willing to join in establishing a society in honour of the Princess's birthday, and of the Principality of Wales, to dine with Viscount Lisburne, the Bishop of Bangor, and the rest of the nobility, gentry, and clergy of Wales, in order to choose a president, stewards, &c., and to continue the service on every St. David's Day for the future. The sermon was preached by Mr. George Lewis, a native of the Principality of Wales; the dinner was held at Harberdashers' Hall, in Maiden Lane (now Gresham Street West, near the Post-office), where at least two of the Society's festivals were held. On the 24th of March the Princess of Wales recognized the body as the "Most Honourable and Loyal Society of Ancient Britons," a name which it has never abandoned. From that time the Society devoted itself to the task of educating the children of necessitous Welshmen; and in 1854, finding the existing accommodation inadequate to their purpose, they proceeded to build a school at Ashford, Middlesex, where a large number are educated.　TAFFY.

The Cycle. "Wynnstay, Dec. 5, 1843. I am suffering under a bad headache to-day, the consequence of a terribly hot dinner of thirty people last night, when a club called 'The Cycle' held one of its annual meetings. It was a Jacobite Association, set on foot the day that Prince Charles Edward was born. The Sir Watkin of the day was always the President, and his wife the only lady allowed to dine with them. The health of the Pretender was drunk with great solemnities, and I believe altogether the club did much to keep up the old Jacobite feeling; now, it has dwindled into a dinner with no meaning in it, but they still cling to the garb, though the spirit that once gave it life is gone, and I suffer, therefore"—(*Diary of Charlotte Williams-Wynn.*)

A correspondent of the *Cheshire Sheaf* gives the following list of Members' names of "The Cycle for 1795."

Lady Patroness for the year ;	Dowager Williams Wynn
Rt. Hon. Earl Grosvenor	Frederick Phillipse, Esq
T. B. S. Boycott, Esq	Sir Foster Cunliffe, Bart
Lord Belgrave	Samuel Riley, Esq
J. Humberston Cawley, Esq	Rev. Ph. Puleston, D.D
Wm. H. C. Floyer, Esq	Gwyllym Wardle, Esq
Chas. W. W. Wynn, Esq	Henry E. Boates, Esq
Edwd. W. Lloyd, Esq	Rev. W. Whitehall Davies
William Leche, Esq	Rev. H. W. Eyton
Sir Thomas Hanmer, Bart	Edwd. Morgan, Esq
Watkin Williams, Esq	Thos. Tarleton, Esq
Thos. Boycott, Scnr., Esq	Thos. Cummings, Esq
Thomas Crewe Dod, Esq	John Leche, Esq
Peter W. Davies, Esq	Richd. Puleston, Esq
Richd. Aldersey, Esq	John Hill, Esq
Philip H. Fletcher, Esq	John Kynaston, Esq
Thos. Apperley, Esq	John Wynne, Esq
Sir Watkin W. Wynn, Bart	

These names were copied from a memorandum belonging to the grandfather of the party who supplied them.
NEMO.

The most recent announcement in connection with *The Cycle* I have met with is the following from the "Salopian Journal" of Nov. 22, 1837 :—"Mr. Kynaston's Cycle will take place at Hardwick on Monday Dec. 11th."
JARCO.

STRAY NOTES.

The *Athenæum* says—In a treatise entitled "Old Breton Glosses," and privately printed at Calcutta, Mr. Whitley Stokes has published some very old and undoubtedly Breton glosses, and has elucidated them with his usual philological learning. The peculiar value of those glosses is that they are all from MSS. earlier than A.D. 1100. They illustrate the possibility of distinguishing even at that period between the work of old Welsh, Cornish, and Breton scribes.

ANOTHER NOTABLE TREE.—There is the following reference to a fine ash tree in an account of Llansaintffraid, published nine years ago in *Mont. Coll.*: "A notable ash tree on the Finnant Farm, belonging to William Evans, Esq., well merits the title of 'Brenhin Bren' of the parish; it is computed to contain 210 cubic feet of good clefty timber, knotless and faultless. The trunk, twenty-seven feet long by thirty inches girth, is a magnificent piece of timber, straight, and without branch or fault."

UNREFORMED CORPORATIONS.
(Feb. 25, 1880).

We continue our extracts from the report of the Royal ommissioners :—

BISHOP'S CASTLE.

The Report of 1835 is said to have been at that time ubstantially correct, and to be applicable generally to the resent condition of the borough.

The bailiff acts as a magistrate ; he has an allowance of 0s. per annum. He sits at petty sessions in the borough ssisted by the bailiff of the preceding year, who is called he justice, and by the recorder.

He acts as coroner within the borough.

The recorder is now elected annually from the body of 5 capital burgesses. He is not required to be a person of egal education, nor are the bailiff or justice.

The clerk to the justices is a solicitor, and now receives '10 per annum, besides fees, according to the county table, he present bailiff is a tanner and farmer, Mr. Samuel orton. The office of recorder, owing to the death of Mr. akeley, who was a county magistrate, was at the time of ur inquiry vacant.

The justice is a brother of the bailiff and by trade a utcher.

The borough justices license the public-houses without he intervention of county magistrates, excepting in the ase of confirmation of new licences.

The number of cases tried at petty sessions is said to verage 120 or 130 annually.

The county police act within the borough.

The court of quarter sessions is still holden, but prac-'cally no business is done.

The income of the borough arises mainly from the rent f land called Moat Hill, which in the former report is escribed as a common containing from 90 to 100 acres, on rhich the burgesses had then a right of common without tint.

With reference to this common, it seems that encroach-aents or enclosures began some 150 years ago, on which ents have been only recently paid. About the year 1850 transaction took place which appears to us to have been f a very questionable character. The resident burgesses rere entitled to common over a tract of sheep walk called 'Moat Hill." It seems that portions of the common land ad been recently enclosed and were in course of enclosure y burgesses who held these lands and deprived other bur-esses of their rights. Ejectments seem to have been rought by the corporation to recover the lands, which re-alted in an arrangement by which the ejectments served pon these burgesses were discontinued on payment of the osts of the action and their acknowledging themselves anants to the corporation. It was further settled that ae enclosures already made on the Moat Hill might, on pplication by the burgesses who have enclosed the same, e let on lease to them for the term of sixty years, renew-ble for ever on payment of a fine of five pounds, and at ae annual rent of 5s. an acre, and in proportion for a less uantity, with a further rent of 2s. 6d. for every cottage, ad should any burgess now or hereafter possess a greater uantity than an acre, he should pay for every additional uantity after the rate of 7s. 6d. per acre.

After this arrangement further enclosures were made nd leases granted by the corporation to different burgesses t 5s. or 7s. 6d. per acre, according to the terms of the asolution. In the result nearly the whole of Moat Hill, 'hich was common, has been enclosed, and the burgesses 'ho enclosed and who were the lessees have in many in-tances assigned the leases for valuable consideration ; and t the present time the town clerk is the holder of more than 40 acres of the former common, obtained by assign-ments from different lessees. This land has increased in value and was stated to be worth from £1 to £1 5s. per acre annual rent, and from £40 to £60 an acre to sell.

About this year 1850 Lord Powis, a landowner in the immediate neighbourhood, enclosed several acres of open land by the side of the turnpike road adjoining his en-closed land without any remonstrance from the corpora-tion. The corporation claim this as part of their common, but have taken no steps to recover it. On the part of Lord Powis it was contended that he was within his right, and he appears to have held the land as his own ever since its enclosure without paying any rent or acknowledgment.

There is now practically no common left to those who might be otherwise entitled to it.

Whether the leases above referred to were valid or not we do not pretend to decide, but the granting of them under the circumstances appears to us to have been a grave abuse of the powers of the corporation.

The rents of these enclosures together with other lands and houses amount to £65 1s. 10d. The other sums are £4 for stallage in the market, and between £2 and £3 for the use of the town hall, making the total income of the corporation average between £70 and £80 per annum.

The accounts, which are kept by the chamberlain, are audited and signed by the bailiff, but not published or cir-culated. The balance sheet for the year 1873-74 will be found in the Appendix.

The conduit mentioned in these accounts has since been handed over to the sanitary authorities.

About £10 or £11 of the income of the corporation ap-pears to be expended in refreshments, and the rest in salaries and repairs.

There seems to be considerable dissatisfaction amongst the inhabitants who are not members of the corporation at the way the money is spent.

A statement was also made that although the number of public-houses had been diminished it was still excessive, there being 13 public-houses to 2,000 inhabitants, but this could hardly be the fault of the authorities, who cannot take away existing licences for such a cause.

Dissatisfaction was expressed at the administration of justice in the borough and at the class from which the justices were appointed, but it was stated that there was no wish to substitute the county for the borough magis-trates, but that what was really wanted was that the borough and parish which are not conterminous should be united in a municipal borough.

One particular instance of the maladministration of jus-tice was given by a witness, Mr. Newill. The Home Secretary was written to on the subject, and we obtained the papers from the Home Office, including a petition by the accused asking for a remission of the fine. On receiving this petition the Home Office had applied to the magis-trates for their version of the case, and an answer was sent by them. Upon receipt of the answer a letter was written to the accused, informing him that the question was one of law, and that if he was dissatisfied with the magistrates' decision, his remedy was by asking for a case to be stated for the opinion of the Court of Queen's Bench, which he had, for reasons which he stated, purposely omitted to do.

We have not thought it necessary to set out the docu-ments relating to this case in the Appendix, but we believe we have given the substance of them with sufficient ac-curacy.

DINAS.

The history of this remote place is given in the report of Mr. Hogg of 1835. Mr. John Jones, recorder of the borough, who since 1842 has been steward of the manor of Mowddwy, and has known the place nearly all his life, considers that the report was substantially accurate at the date at which it was written, and in the main is applicable to the existing state of things.

No charter of incorporation has been discovered, but Mr. Jones produced a translation of a charter, the original of which is in Latin, which purported to have been granted by James I., giving to the Lord of the Manor certain fairs which the witness said were held within the borough.

The Mayor has, in recent years at least, been elected by the burgesses and not by the steward of the Lord of the Manor.

Burgesses are at times elected at what is called the borough court. At the time of the former report, the Lord of the Manor within which the borough is situate, and who seems to have felt "his dignity increased" by maintaining the corporation, was mainly instrumental in getting these burgesses appointed. The appointment was duly recorded on parchment, signed by jurats, and to the admission of each burgess was affixed a stamp of £3, which was paid out of the pocket of the Lord of the Manor. Of late years, it seems that the appointment and admission of a burgess are performed in a more economical manner. The ceremony of paying for the stamp and affixing it to the admission has, without the assent, as far as we know, of the Legislature, been entirely discontinued.

It is stated in the former report that the Mayor "acted as justice of the peace within the borough" jointly with county magistrates, that he quelled disturbances at the fairs, and sat with the county magistrates to grant licences to public houses.

From the statement of the witness called before us upon this point we infer that the Mayor did sometimes act as a magistrate within the borough, but his acts then were very irregular even supposing he had any jurisdiction as a magistrate.

Mr. Jones states that for some years after he was connected officially with the borough, the Mayor used to sign the public-house licences, and then send them to Dolgelley for a county magistrate to sign. Since the Licencing Act this practice has been altogether discontinued. The Mayor no longer acts as a magistrate, and the county magistrates sitting beyond the borough exercise jurisdiction in granting licences within the borough.

The following questions were put to the witness :—
"In point of fact, the corporation have no revenue of any sort or kind ?—No.
"And they do nothing ?—They do nothing.
"They exercise no control of any sort or kind within the borough ?—Nothing whatever."

There is no town hall in the borough. The population amounts to 500. There is some building going on in the village. Slate works have been opened in the neighbourhood, and have given employment to the neighbouring inhabitants.

LAMPETER.

Several changes have taken place in the state of the borough since the report of 1835.

The Corporation at the present time consists of a portreeve, a town clerk, a beadle, and one burgess. Since the year 1832 no burgess has been admitted.

The portreeve and beadle are presented to the steward of the manor by the jury of the court leet, and sworn in by that officer.

The portreeve no longer acts as a magistrate for the borough, within which the justices of the peace for the county exercise exclusive jurisdiction.

The town clerk is in practice always the same person as the steward of the manor, and is appointed by the Lord of the Manor ; he has now no emoluments.

The common over which the burgesses were said to have had rights of common in 1835 was enclosed under an award of the Inclosure Commissioners, dated the 21st October, 1858 ; and a portion of it thereby invested in the churchwardens and overseers of the parish as a public garden and recreation ground.

All tolls have ceased to be levied within the borough.

The corporation have no property of any kind, and apparently exercise no municipal functions.

The sanitary administration of the place is in the hands of a local board.

The population of the borough in 1871 was 1,225.

HARLECH.

No report.
The following letters are given :—

Peniarth, Towyn-Merioneth,
April 12, 1877.

Sir,—Your letter of the 3rd instant, addressed to the "Town Clerk of Harlech," has been forwarded to me.

By the Letters Patent of 22nd Nov. 13, Edward I., to the corporation of Harlech, I, as constable of the castle, am ex-officio mayor of the town. I think the same Letters Patent empower the burgesses to elect annually two bailiffs. These are all the municipal officers I ever heard of, but the Letters Patent of Her present Majesty appointing me constable of the castle empower me to hold a court of "Pied Poudre." The Letters Patent of Edward I. are enrolled in the Public Record Office in London.

I am, &c.,
(Signed)   WM. W. E. WYNNE.

Peniarth, Towyn-Merioneth,
April 14, 1877.

Sir,—There was formerly property belonging to the corporation of Harlech, but I do not know if they possess any now. I am not aware that I have any jurisdiction as a magistrate there, beyond that of a county magistrate. Perhaps the Queen's Letters Patent authorising me to hold a court of "Pied poudre," may be considered in a magisterial light. My salary as constable of the castle and mayor of the town is paid by the Crown. There are many grants by the corporation in existence, with their seal attached to them.

I am, &c.,
(Signed)   WM. W. E. WYNNE.

I have referred to the Queen's Letters Patent, they grant to me "All that land called the Castle Yard, and all that land called the Castle Green, with all fees, wages, profits, emoluments, &c., &c.," and the privilege of "holding one market every Thursday in the town of Harlech," and "one fair on the Feast of St. Andrew, and on the eve before and the morrow after the said feast." They also grant all "tolls, stallage, piccage, fines," &c , &c., "during the time of the said fair," and exonerate me from receiving the judges of assize in the castle. The Letters Patent bear date June 9, 37th of Her present Majesty.

CURRENT NOTES.

Mr. W. Thompson Watkin, who recently contributed a paper on "Roman Shropshire" to the *Shropshire Archæological Society's Transactions*, writing in the current number of the *Athenæum*, disputes the grounds upon which Mr. T. Rought Jones of Market Drayton identifies Bearstone as Mediolanum. The second Iter of Antoninus, says Mr. Watkin, who believes Chesterton is the site of Mediolanum, makes Mediolanum to be at a distance of thirty miles from Chester, with an intermediate station, Bovium, at ten miles distance from the latter. Now we have a fine Roman road connecting Chester with Chesterton (the *viâ Devana*), the distance between the two places is just thirty miles, and at Tiverton, ten miles from Chester, along the Roman road, there has been a small station. I cannot see that there is "straining or cramping of the distances" here, as Mr. Jones asserts. Again in the Tenth Iter of Antoninus, Mediolanum is placed at thirty-six (or thirty-seven, for MSS. differ) miles from Manchester *viâ* Condate. The distance from Manchester to

Chesterton *viâ* Kinderton, along fine Roman roads, is almost exactly the same. Again, I repeat this is not "cramping or straining the distances." If Mr. Jones admits that Bovium is represented by Tiverton, and Mediolanum by Bearstone, where is the road connecting the two stations? Again, there can be no doubt that, like all the *castra* which formed the starting-points or termini of the Itinera of Antonine, Mediolanum would be a walled station. Is this the case at Bearstone? At Chesterton we have this evidence. It is one thing for Mr. Jones to assert that "the intersection of the three circumferences" of the circles which he draws "will be a very short distance from the Bearstone camp," and another to find a large walled station, with a Roman road connecting it with Tiverton and with other stations. There are vestiges of several camps, generally from their conformation supposed to be Roman, in North Shropshire, which might with equal reason be supposed to represent Mediolanum. [See *Current Notes*, page 17.]

CYMMRODORION SOCIETY.

A lecture, being one of the course promoted by this Society, was delivered on Friday evening, Feb. 20, at the Freemasons' Tavern, by Professor F. W. Rudler, the title of which was

"PREHISTORIC TIMES IN WALES."

The lecture was admirably illustrated by large well-drawn diagrams and specimens, exhibiting ancient British Ethnography, and other remains, in skulls, bones, weapons of supposed different ages, pottery, internal views of tumuli, or barrows, caves, with geological views exhibiting the glacial period in a series of ideal views of the Vale of Llanberis, according to Professor Ramsay's theories. The Lecturer said it required no apology for introducing an archæological subject before that Society, as all Welshmen were interested in tracing the past history of their race. He himself could not sympathize with that class of persons who say, "Here we are in a fair world what matters about our origin, or, how we came or who we are." When the parent of this Society was established, some century and a half ago, a lecture on the prehistoric times of this country would have been an impossibility. Tradition, a sort of will o' the wisp, was uncertain and misleading. The term "prehistoric" was first introduced by Dr. Wilson in 1851, who published a work called "The Prehistoric Annals of Scotland." The title in itself was a contradiction, a solecism, for annals supposed history. But anything like authentic history in this country could not be traced back beyond 2,000 years. It truly commences with the Roman invasion. The prehistoric has no absolute chronological signification; for the prehistoric events of one country may have been contemporaneous with events coming within the historic period of another country. Everything in this island which happened more than two thousand years ago might undoubtedly be termed prehistoric. But Rome and Greece, the centres of classical culture, were enjoying at that time the benefits of civilization, and Egypt and other oriental nations were at far earlier times existing under the full blaze of historical light. The practice of burying the dead in barrows, tumuli, or cairns, has been of great advantage to the student of prehistoric archæology. The variety of skeletons therein found, with the manner of their burial, aided science in determining variety of race in the island with their comparative antiquity and peculiarities with very high probable accuracy. The burial of the ashes of the dead, and their preservation in pottery, the weapons and implements found in the graves with the skeletons or with the ashes, illustrate the man-

ners, customs, and arts of those times. Sometimes the ashes of the dead were preserved in urns, of rude pottery, at other times the ashes, or so much as could be recovered after the fire, were collected together on a stone and the urn turned with its mouth down over it. The interments are in some cases associated with other vessels, more or less enigmatical in their use, and known variously as drinking-cups, food vessels, incense cups, and immolation urns. Implements of bronze are occasionally found deposited with the calcined bones, and these give an insight into the metallurgical industries of some of the people who raised these barrows or tumuli. The bronze chisel or axe-shaped implements called celts being composed of copper and tin were of British manufacture, for the very moulds used for their casting have been discovered in Wales. Before bronze was generally used for implements and weapons such objects had been made of stone. Hence most antiquaries believe that the race in passing from a savage state to civilized progression went through three stages of culture, represented by what are called the stone-age, the bronze-age, and the iron-age. The stone-age is divided into epochs, exhibited in the rough cut stone implement, and the smooth or polished stone implement. The men who lived in this country during the later stone using period generally buried their dead in long barrows, and not in round barrows, or they used as sepulchres large stone chambers and even caverns. The men who buried in such chambers and even caverns—some of which have been discovered in Denbighshire—had the peculiarity of having flat-shins; these are termed platycnemism. The same men who buried in these tombs, and who used stone weapons, probably reared the dolmens and other megalithic monuments. The lecturer spoke strongly in favour of Sir John Lubbock's Ancient Monuments Bill. He hoped that a large addition would be made to the schedule, which as yet contained a very meagre representation of remains in Wales, to be preserved. Noticing the subject of caves, the lecturer explained that while in some cases there were contained remains of the later stone-age, others contained relics of an evident earlier period. The older stonge-age is termed the palæolithic, and the later the neolithic. The earliest trace of man yet found in Wales is of the neolithic age. The country was then inhabited by a race short in stature, and having long skulls, a dolichocephalic, who were ignorant of metals, and who built long barrows. They may be identified with the Silures of Tacitus, represented, typically, by the short swarthy oval faced Welshmen. These neolithic people were probably invaded by a still later race, having shorter skulls and a rounder cast of head, and which are termed brachycephalic folk. These knew the use of bronze, they also generally burnt their dead and built round barrows to inter in. These are probably the men who survive at the present time in the taller light-complectioned element in Wales. Before our authentic history commences, a fusion of the two races had probably occurred. The earlier race, however, were still dominant in the west, while in the south-east of the country the iron-using Belgæ, who came hither from the Continent, had obtained a footing. Such probably was the distribution of races in this island when the curtain rises and the light of history shines forth. The lecturer urged the desirableness of collecting all prehistoric antiquities, as celts, urns, &c., and depositing them in well ordered museums, and expressed the hope that when the British Association visited Swansea in the autumn of the present year they would find collections which gave them new prehistoric revelations of Wales, that were not known when it had met in Wales thirty years ago.

Mr. STEPHEN EVANS, in proposing a vote of thanks to the lecturer, said that he felt the removal of Professor Rudler was a great loss to the University College of Wales, but what was a loss to them was a gain to him.

The chair was ably occupied by Dr. Isambard Owen, a member of the Council, who stated that it was now looking up again. The Council had cut out some new work, and were reviving old points of interest. Endeavours were to be made to obtain rooms for the Society, and the formation of a Welsh library and reading-room and museum for the benefit of the members. The .death of the late lamented editor of the *Cymmrodor*, the Rev. Robert Jones, vicar of Rotherhithe, who had been so much the life and soul of the Society, had created some temporary derangement, and his loss was yet greatly felt amongst them; but he was glad to say there was now a programme before them that promised a pleasant and useful future.

The following gentlemen took part in proposing and supporting votes of thanks to the lecturer and the chairman: Mr. Stephen Evans, Mr. Brinley Richards, Mr. John Thomas (Pencerdd), and Mr. David Lewis. The next lecture, to take place in course of the month of March, will be by Mr. Hugh Owen, upon "Eisteddfodau," to be followed by a discussion.

MARCH 17, 1880.

NOTES.

A LADY'S IMPRESSIONS OF WALES. [LETTER V.]
(March 3, 1880.)

From Mrs. Presland (of Walford Hall, Salop) at Peniarth, Merionethshire, to her sister Miss Slaney, at Shrewsbury:—

Oh; Breave Wales, no less than sixteen yesterday set out for the Seaport of Ballmouth, about 12 mile from here up the Mountains we whent, and varitity of pleasing prospects, a good mile before we cross the Arm of the Sea, we assended a precepice, frightful beyand description, on one side us was the highest ragget Rock I have seen, they stones to appearance lose, and look as if just droping on your heads, some of which have fell a few years ago, the Precepice down to the mean Ocean not less than thirty yards, and us travelers not a yard from the side of it, where the waves dash, and tide rores till it made me tremble, but sweet Balmouth appeared across the arm of the sea with many ships lying at Anchor. the Town is small, most of the Houses Built on the side of a very high Rock, one above another for half a mile up, over the tops of all the house still rises higher, and higher, more rocks, at the top of which I got up upon my legs, but when I got there, I cannot tell you how I was pleasd at the wonderfull views, and how terefied at the precipice below that I was to get down, which I did on my hands and knees, for I coud stand no longer, and much Bleamd for going so high, but what will not a womans curiosity do. when I came down I discoverd on one side across the river, some fine green medows, on the side of a long high Rock, coverd with hanging wood down which run severall small pistles of water, which we had the missfortune to see in great perfection, for just as we got in to the boat to cross the Arm of the Sea, it set a thundring, raining, and lightning to a great degree, which gave me an opertunity of seeing fire works in the greatest perfection, for the Beauty of the lightning Darting on the waves is beyand discription. before I got in to the Boat we drank tea and from the part of the room where I sat, I see nothing but the mean ocean, not a house tree or land. I then rose up, not a little rejoicd to see the shore,

for I must own to you I shoud not like to travell by water no; no poor Old England for me. the while they company was puting on their hats &c:c I whent with Mr. Vaughn† on board a ship, dureing which time, they sent for the Captain, and woud fain have prevaild on him to have orderd me searchd, but he said no, he woud never fright a sissnes Lady, meaning English, after I had seen the Ship, he took me into a shop presented me with ribena a sailors wigh [wig] with one round curl, made of jersey after we had crossd the river we got on horse back, and was obligd to out Gallop the tide, which by the gentlemens looks I perceevd approachd us to near. we then mounted the precipice, which is worse going then coming, as in the front, the rock seemd tumbling on us and if we turnd our heads I expected to fall backwards in to the Sea, so was truely thankfull when off this tremendous precipice, at the end of which upon the Sea appeard the setting Sun, how beautyfull. stop I did; and admired the wonderfull works of him, who made both Sea and land, a little further on they shewd me the Island of Gernsay Gersay, [Bardsey] and Snowden Mountain (which is recond the second highest in North Wales) and many other pleasing objects, but it gets near ten, and we approach the house, where supper Bellrings, no unpleasing hearing after such a days excersise, which wanted nothing to add to the pleasure of it, but Mr. P: company yours, and my Dear Fans, who I long to see, and not withstanding I have spent my time so agreeably, with pleasure reflect it wont be long before we meet. till then adieu, from yours with great affection Eliz. Presland

[No address]   Peniarth Aug. ye 4 [1771?]

LORD HILL'S SWORD.—There is not much dignity attaching to the title of Knight, when it is conferred on a man who happens by chance to be the mayor of a borough when some auspicious event happens; and at times the reflected title of "My lady" adopted by the good "dame," his wife, is excessively amusing to her circle of acquaintances. There was one Shropshire man on whom the honour was conferred, who could boast that in conferring it an additional honour was imparted! The Knight in question was Sir John Bickerton Williams, Mayor of Shrewsbury in 1837, and the circumstance I allude to was a topic for some of the after-dinner speeches at a banquet the Mayor gave at the end of Oct., 1837. In proposing the health of Lord Hill, Sir John said, "You all know that, unworthy as I am, I received a while ago a mark of the Royal favour. I am proud to say it was arranged with, and consented to by, our late most excellent Majesty, without my knowledge. The melancholy event which bereaved the nation of its father deprived me of so receiving the honour. When I knelt before our most gracious Queen, the Court was in mourning for the calamity to which I have alluded. Sombre as were my reflections, I must state that joy relieved the gloom when I saw the noble lord who now graces this entertainment with his presence, draw *his* sword, and hand it to her Majesty. Nor, gentlemen, was that all; my joy approached as near perfection as possible when that very hand which wielded that sword as it glittered on the plains of Waterloo carried it across my shoulder." Lord Hill, in giving the health of the Mayor, said, "I own myself to be exceedingly gratified with anything which can add to the dignity of my native place; and feel that the compliment paid by!Her Majesty to Sir John Bickerton Williams was an honour conferred, not only on his learning and talents, but on the town of

† Hugh Vaughan, of Hengwrt, Esq., eldest brother of the first Sir Robert Vaughan, Bart.

which he is the chief magistrate. I recollect well the circumstance which the Mayor has alluded to respecting my sword having been used by the Queen in conferring the honour he received, and few events in my life have afforded me more pleasure than in having assisted in that ceremony."   SCROBBES BYRIG.

QUERIES.

TOPOGRAPHICAL NAMES (Mar. 10, 1880). *Morton or Moreton.*—Which is the correct way of spelling the name of this village near Oswestry, and is there any reason why the "e" has been omitted or added as the case may be?   DNALWOR.

Pimblemere.—Can any of your readers inform me when and how Bala lake—Llyn Tegid—acquired the name of Pimblemere? It has occurred to me, and I offer the suggestion with great diffidence, that the name has been derived in the following manner :—It is known to nearly all your readers that the parishes which adjoin the lake are called the five parishes of Penllyn. At some remote period, the lake must have been called "The Lake of the Five Parishes," or Llyn y Pump plwy, just as the lake of Lucerne is called the lake of the four forest Cantons (Vierwaldstattersee). Llyn y pump plwy, which became corrupted into Llyn y pum'blwy, and this Anglicized would give Pimblemere. I should be glad if any light can be thrown upon the subject.   TEGID.

[The definition is an old one ; see *Cambrian Travellers' Guide,* &c.—ED.]

A CAERNARVONSHIRE MARTYR.—The following curious relation is given in Williams' *History of Aberconwy.* Like many others which have survived only through the medium of oral tradition, circumstances derived from imagination and prejudice appear to have got mixed up with the facts. The hole in which arms for a hundred men were said to have been concealed, and the notion of a wholesale massacre of the Protestant inhabitants of Creiddyn may have been derived from some confused memories of an episode in the Civil War of Charles I. In the fact of a Catholic priest and Chaplain to a private Catholic family being hunted down, and hanged (?), drawn, and quartered for his faith, the mere profession of which was made high treason by statute law in the reign of Elizabeth, and so continued for three centuries afterwards, there is nothing so uncommon as to need any such adventitious particulars to add to its credibility :—

At a short distance from the house (Penrhyn Creiddyn, the seat of the extinct, but ancient family of Pugh, descended from Ednyfed Vychan) is the family chapel, now desecrated into a stable ; it is about 25 feet long, by 15 wide ; the altar table of stone is recollected by several now living ; by a grant of Pope Nicholas three-fourths of the tithe of Penrhyn were attached to this chapel, and the same is now vested in the estate. The family for a long period after the Reformation professed the Roman Catholic religion, and they kept a priest, who officiated in this chapel for themselves, and a few Catholic neighbours ; in connexion with this circumstance is the following anecdote, which is current in the neighbourhood. It is said that a plot was formed here to put to death all the Protestants in Creiddyn, and for the accomplishment of this deed a body of men was to arrive at a certain time of the night ; previously to their coming great preparations were made in preparing provisions, and a servant of Gloddaith, who paid his addresses to a woman in the service of the family, finding her engaged at an unseasonable hour, obtained by his urgent enquiries a knowledge of the conspiracy ; he immediately hastened home, and disclosed what he had heard to his master, who with the greatest despatch procured a troop of horse, and invested Penrhyn. This speedy intervention frustrated their designs, and some of the inmates escaped, while others were taken ; but the priest, who was supposed to be the contriver of the plot, for some time eluded the strict search made for him : it happened however that some persons, being in a boat out at sea, observed smoke ascending from Rhiwleden rock, which circumstance exciting their curiosity, they hastened there, and, in a small cave called *Ty yn y graig,* (the house in the rock), which is about 90 feet from the summit, and the approach to which is extremely difficult, the priest was discovered ; he was drawn and quartered in a field below the house, and his name, Sir William Guy, is even preserved : there was a hole behind the house called *Twll arfau cant o wyr,*[†] where it was supposed that the arms were concealed; and, after the departure of the Pughs to Coytmor, among other things left behind, was an old trunk, which the tenants and some of their neighbours opened, and found therein a withered hand, which is supposed to have been one of the members of this same priest.

The statement is doubtful that Sir William Guy was "drawn and quartered" only, instead of being, as the sentence for high treason required, as the law stood until repealed by 54 Geo. III. c. 146, "hanged, but taken down alive, and then have his bowels taken out (which is what is meant by drawn) and burnt before his face." It would seem to convey the idea that the whole proceeding was the result of mob violence, and not of regular legal process. If the latter, are there any legal records extant to prove it? The first Act of the first year of Elizabeth (1 Eliz. cap. 1), prescribed this penalty for the third offence "for any one who should, by writing, printing, teaching, preaching, express words, deed, or act, affirm or defend the authority or jurisdiction, spiritual or ecclesiastical, of any foreign prelate heretofore claimed or used within the realm," which, with the next Act (1 Eliz. cap. 2), prohibiting every where the sacrifice of the mass under pain of forfeiture of goods and perpetual imprisonment, was tantamount to doing away by force with the Catholic religion in Englahd.   H.W.L.

REPLIES.

CHURCH BELLS (Dec. 24, 1879).—The Bells of *Berrington* Church, Co. Salop, were cast by Thomas Mears of London in 1796, and bear the following inscriptions :—

     Tenor.—Chaunt praise to God above.
     Fifth.—Sound cheers to wedded love.
     Fourth.—Obey each happy call.
     Third.—In harmony join all.
     Second.—Unite while joy surrounds.
     Treble.—Follow with joyful sounds.

Hordley. One of the Bells at Hordley Church, Shropshire, has inscribed on it the novel invocation "Sancta Trinitas Ora Pro Nobis." When this was first stated in *Bye-gones,* Nov. 5, 1879, two or three writers in *Notes and Queries,* doubted the accuracy of the transcriber, but it since transpires that there are similar inscriptions on bells in the churches of Stoke Hammond, Bucks, and Stoke Charity, Hants.   NEMO.

WILLIAM ROOSE (Feb. 18, 1880).—He was born at Bodgadfa, near Amlwch, in 1808, and died at the latter place somewhat suddenly on the 4th July, 1878. His ancestors settled in that part of the principality some time in the early part of the last century. As regards his works, he painted some few first class original pictures (although his *forte* was more in the portrait and landscape than in historical paintings), notably amongst them being "The death of Llewelyn," which gained a first prize at an eisteddfod at Carmarthen ; also a portrait of a young lady named Miss Harris, which gained several prizes at public exhibitions, in addition to numerous others. As an artist he excelled in oil, water-colour, or crayon ; whilst as an engraver, I think I can

† The Hole of the Arms of 100 men.

safely aver that there were few (if any) in the principality that would bear favourable comparison with him. In addition to the engravings which MORTIMER enumerates, he published a splendid portrait of "Talhaiarn," the noted Welsh Bard, very few copies of which are now in existence, and which displayed far more skill than any of his former productions in that branch. His other achievements in the art may be found in almost every part of the country; and, altogether, he was undoubtedly (considering the disadvantages he laboured under in the earlier part of his career, which were very great) one of the cleverest men in his particular line that the principality has ever produced, although he died in comparative obscurity.   J.H.R.

ON TWO SEPULCHRAL EFFIGIES IN MONTGOMERY CHURCH.

The following notes by Mr. M. H. Bloxam, the well-known antiquary, upon the remarkable effigies in Montgomery Church, which the courtesy of the Rector of Montgomery enables us to publish, will interest many of our readers :—

It is in the south transept of Montgomery Church, wherein an altar formerly existed, the usual appendage to which, a piscina, still remains in the eastern part of the south wall, are two sepulchral effigies in armour placed on the pavement, and apparently removed from high tombs either formerly existing in this church, or perchance moved, which I think likely, hither from tombs in the neighbouring conventual church of Chirbury, some two miles distant, on the suppression of that religious establishment.

The most ancient of these represents a Knight, or one of higher grade, on whose head appears a vizored basinet, of unusual design, encircled by a wreath or orle of rosettes, so as to counteract the pressure of the tilting helme with its crest, on which the head reposes. The vizor of the basinet is raised. Attached to the basinet is a camail or tippet of mail covering the neck, breast and shoulders. The face, which is exposed, exhibits the moustache worn over the upper lip. Flexible epauliers appear beneath the camail protecting the shoulders, whilst the upper and lower arms are incased in rerebraces and vambraces, and the elbows in coudes, all of plate.

The defensive armour of the body is covered with an emblazoned jupon, no doubt formerly painted with the proper charges, though the colours no longer remain. Round the skirts of the jupon and about the loins is a horizontal bawdrick or belt, rich in detail and buckled in front, and below this appears the escalloped skirt of the jupon. The thighs, knees, legs, and feet are incased in cuisses, genouilleres, jambs, and sollerets, all of plate except the insteps, which are protected by gussets of mail. The straps of the spurs alone are visible. The hands are conjoined on the breast as in prayer, and on the right side a fragment only of the sword is left. I should assign this effigy to the close of the fourteenth century, or reign of Richard the Second, circa A.D. 1395—1400.

Since writing the above I have read the late Mr. Boutell's notes on this effigy—published in part XIII. Collections, Historical and Archæological, relating to Montgomeryshire—wherein he describes the tilting helme as surmounted by a panache or upright rest of feathers rising from a crest coronet, a cognizance of the Mortimers, as appears from the seal of Edward de Mortimer, Earl of March, A.D. 1400. Mr. Boutell also remarks that the armorial insignia displayed on the jupon of this effigy are unquestionably those of the Mortimers, Earls of March.

The second effigy is one more recent in date, and this I would ascribe to the latter part or the fifteenth century, circa A.D. 1480. The personage represented appears bare-headed with long untrimmed flowing locks of hair, his head reposes on a tilting helme, and his face is close shaven. Covering his neck is a collar of gorget of mail and beneath that a collar of roses. Square plates or pallettes appear in front of the armpits, the shoulders are defended by epaulieres of flexible plates, the arms and elbows by rerebraces, vambraces, and coudes, all of plate. The hands are bare and conjoined on the breast as in prayer, and on the fingers are many rings. The breast plate is globular with taces escalloped upwards, and to these angular shaped tuilles are attached. From the right hip to the left thigh is a sword belt disposed diagonally, and beneath the taces

appears an apron of mail. Cuisses, genouilleres and jambs protect the thighs, knees, and legs, and laminated sollerets the feet, which rest against a dog. Spur leathers appear in front of the insteps.

Mr. Boutell places this effigy to about A.D. 1460—1470, and states that about the neck is the Yorkist collar of Suns and roses sustaining the White Lion of the house of March.

Mr. Planché, Lancaster Herald, states that the collar is the family one of Edward IV., with the White Lion of March appendant, and consequently gives the probable date to A.D. 1461 —1483.

The White Lion of the house of March would indicate I think this effigy to be, like the former, that of a Mortimer.

I conjecture it to be not only possible but probable that both these effigies were removed to the place they now occupy from the neighbouring conventual church of Chirbury, for in the destruction of the conventual churches many sepulchral effigies were removed thence to neighbouring churches.

It is a matter of inquiry, which I cannot answer, whether the Mortimers had any connection with Chirbury, and I have not by me "Eyton's History of Shropshire" to consult. The account of Chirbury in the Monasticon is very short, and throws no light on this matter, one well deserving of further investigation.

Rugby, 23rd December, 1879.   MATT. H. BLOXAM.

CURRENT NOTES.

THE LATE REV. T. JAMES'S LIBRARY.

The Library of the late Rev. T. James, L.L.D., F.S.A., (LLALLAWG) Vicar of Netherthong, Huddersfield, was sold in London last week ; when the following prices were realized for works interesting to Wales and the borders :— Archæologia Cambrensis from the commencement in 1846 to 1879, £22 10s. (Quarrich) ; Y Beirniad : 1860 to 1879, £2 10s. ; Borrow's Wild Wales, original edition, 3 vols., £2 2s. ; Cambrian Journal, 1854 to 1863, £4 13s. (Breese) ; Cambrian Quarterly Magazine, 5 vols., £2 8s. (Ridler) ; Cambrian Register, 3 vols. £2 16s. (Ridler) ; another copy, £1 19s. (Quarrich) ; Cambro Briton, 3 vols., £1 14s. (Quarrich) ; Yr Haul, 1835 to 1878, £1 10s. (Clark) ; Bye-gones, 1871 to 1875, £1 2s. (Smith) ; Coxe's Tour in Monmouthshire, £1 12s. (George) ; History of the Gwydir Family, (Oswestry edit., 1878), 17s. (Smith) ; Giraldus' Itinerary through Wales, £1 17s. (George); Gough's Camden, £4 6s. (Mullany) ; Edw. Llwyd's Archæologia Britannica, 1 vol., all published, £1 15s. (Wilson) ; Llyfr Gweddi Gyffredin, "ending with sheet Cccc, and with title reprinted within old woodcut border (sold with all its faults), first folio edition, 1664," £5 (Quarrich) ; Aneurin Owen's Ancient Laws of Wales, £1 8s. (Steble) ; Montgomeryshire Collections, vols. 1 to 8, £6 7s. 6d. (Breese) ; Ditto, vols. 9 to 11 and part of 12, 17s. (Smith) ; Myvyrian Archæology, Denbigh, 1870, £1 15s. (Wilson) ; Pennant's Tours in Wales, large paper, 3 vols. 8vo, 1810, 17s. (Ridler) ; The Reliquary, 1860 to 1879, £8 (Smith) ; Transactions of Shropshire Archæological Society, vol. 1 and parts 1 and 2 of vol. 2, 19s. (Quarrich) ; Williams's Eminent Welshmen, 7s. (George) ; Williams's Y Seint Greal, 14s. (Quarrich) ; Jones and Freeman's History of St. David's, £1 17s. (Wilson) ; Meyrick's Cardigan, £2 11s. (Wilson) ; Meyrick's Heraldic Visitations of Wales and Part of the Marches between 1586 and 1613, £9 15s. (Ellis) ; Phillips and Hulbert, History of Shrewsbury and Shropshire, two vols. in one, £1 10s. (Scutet) ; Pugh's Cambria Depicta, tinted views, 17s. (George) ; Westwood's Lapidarium Walliæ, £2 10s. (George) ; Wood's Principal Rivers in Wales, large paper, £3 (Breese) ; Williams's Monmouthshire, £1 12s. (Breese) ; Williams's Lexicon Cornu Britannicum, £1 5s. (Quarrich) ; Wyndhams's Monmouthshire, £1 10s. (Breese) ; Wynnstay and the Wynns, and another book, 14s. (Smith) ; Yorke's Royal Tribes, with (additional) portrait of the author, £1 1s. (Ridler) ; Thomas's History of the Diocese of St. Asaph, half morocco, 10s. (Ridler).

MARCH 24, 1880.

NOTES.

MONTGOMERY AND TRAFALGAR.—I have already (Jan. 21) given the proceedings at Llanymynech when the nation rejoiced over the victory at Trafalgar and mourned the death of Nelson. The manner of acting the double part at Montgomery was at least ingenious. On Thanksgiving Day (Dec. 5, 1805), the Magistrates and Volunteers proceeded to Church, "the ensigns of office being covered with crape, the bells and drums muffled, and the music playing a solemn march." Having heard "a pious and affecting discourse" they returned, the music playing that inevitable manifesto of British Bounce, 'Rule Britannia,' and "the bells ringing a merry peal." On the previous evening there was a ball,—"after an excellent dinner at Reid's" for the gentlemen,—when "the fair belles wore laurel, with black feathers."

                          G.G.

FIRST CHAPEL IN OSWESTRY.—In *Bye-gones* for Oct. 1, 1879, I gave the statement of accounts of James Felton, for sundry alterations in the first "Meeting-House" the Nonconformists used in Oswestry; a building (now the Butchers' Arms) which they rented in 1692, (when their "Church" was removed from Sweeney to Oswestry) and purchased in 1715. In 1749 the Nonconformists worshipping in this place desired to erect a chapel, and issued the following circular with their reasons for so doing :—

To the ministers of Christ, & all other Charitable & well disposed Christians to whom these presents shall come.

WE whose names are under written members of ye Protestant Dissenting Congregation at Oswestry in ye county of Salop do hereby Certify, yt for many years past, we have labour'd under great disadvantages on ye account of ye inconvenience of our present place of Worship, & its being so unhappily situated as to be expos'd to ye noise of Passengers & Children in two adjoining streets ; and not only so but it is now gone to decay & ready to fall. We therefore think it advisable, & indeed necessary to build another in a more commodious place ; & have accordingly purchas'd a spot of ground for yt purpose. The proposed Building together with ye purchase of ye Ground amounts to upwards of £200. And as we are poor, and few in number, we are oblig'd to apply to our Christian friends for assistance ; and we hope those who are able will lend us a helping hand to compleat our Design ; as we believe it will tend to ye Glory of God & ye support of Religion among us ; and we doubt not but ye Lord will reward their Labour of Love at the resurrection of ye Just.

Tho. Morgan
John Felton
John Bickerton
John Jackson
Jer : Paye*
Wm : Bickerton
Saml : Bickerton
Saml : Jackson
David Price
Edw : Paye*
Edwd : Edwards
(In ye name of all ye rest)

WE whose names are hereunto subscrib'd Ministers of ye Gospel are well assur'd of ye truth of what is above certified concerning ye meeting place at Oswestry and ye circumstances of ye people assembling there ; and therefore recommend ye case as highly deserving ye countenance and assistance of our fellow Christians.

Job Orton
Joseph Fownes
Ebenezer Keay
Jen : Jenkins
Joseph Baker

* It is impossible to say whether this name is Paye or Page.

5

Mr. Thomas Morgan, whose name appears first to the appeal, was the minister, and Mr. John Felton was son of the James Felton whose account for fitting up the first "Meeting-house" I have already referred to. The Rev. Job Orton, who signs first as recommending the appeal, was a well-known Nonconformist minister, and a native of the county. The site referred to as secured is the one in Arthur Street on which stands the present Old Chapel (erected 1829, and converted into Sunday School Rooms when Christchurch was built on the site of the Borough Gaol), was then known as the "Baily Molt Mill." The chapel Mr. Morgan asks subscriptions for was opened in 1750, under the following "licence" from the Court of Quarter Sessions :—

"SHROPSHIRE *To Wit.*
"At the General Quarter Sessions of the Peace of our Sovereign Lord the King, held at the Guildhall in Shrewsbury, in and for the County of Salop, on Tuesday in the week next after the Translation of Saint Thomas the Martyr (to wit) the tenth day of July in the twenty-fourth year of the reign of our Sovereign Lord George the Second, by the Grace of God King of Great Britain, France, and Ireland, King, Defender of the Faith and so forth, and in the year of our Lord 1750, before Sir Henry Edwardes and Sir Richard Corbett, Baronets, John Walcot, Richard Lyster, Andrew Hill, Esqrs., and others, His Majesty's Justices assigned to keep the peace in this county aforesaid, and also to hear and determine divers Felonies, Trespasses, and other Misdeeds in the said county done and committed, and which are there to be heard and determined.
"It is ordered by this Court that the new Chappel situate in Street Arthur in Oswestry in this county be recorded as a place of religious worship for his Majesty's Protestant subjects dissenting from the Church of England.
          "By the Court,
"RICHARD BALDWYN, *Clerk of the Peace for the County of Salop.*"

It will be seen by all this that the "Old Chapel" has existed, in one form or other, in Arthur-street—at the bottom ; in the centre, and at the top—for a couple of centuries !
                         JARCO.

PARLIAMENT OF ENGLAND (Mar. 10, 1880)
Reign of Henry IV. and Henry V.

COUNTY OF SALOP.

1399	Thomas Yonge ; Johannes Burley.
1400	Hugo Cheyne ; Johannes Boerle.
1402	Johannes de Cornewaylle, chivaler ; Adam de Peshale, chivaler.
1403	Johannes Borley ; Georgius de Hankeston'.
1404	Ditto ; Johannes Daras.
1405	David Holbache ; Thomas de Whitton'.
1407	Johannes Cornewayll', chivaler ; David Holbache.
1409	Johannes Boerley ; David Holbache.
1411	Adam de Pishale, chivaler ; Johannes Boerleye.
1413	Robertus Corbet ; Ricardus Laken.
1413	David Holbache ; Johannes Wele.
1414	David Holbach' ; Ricardus Laken'.
1415	Hugo Burght ; Georgius Haukeston'.
1417	Willielmus Boerley, or Bromcroft ; Ricardus Fox.
1419	Robertus Corbet ; Willielmus Boerley.
1420	Willielmus Boerley ; Johannes Wynnesbury.
1421	Hugo Burgh' ; Willielmus Boerley.
1421	Ricardus Laken, chivaler ; Johannes Stepulton'.

BOROUGH OF SHREWSBURY.

1399	Nicholaus Jerard' ; Thomas Berwyk'
1402	Rogerus Thornes ; Thomas Pride.
1403	Simon Tour ; Thomas Pryte.
1405	Robertus Thornes ; Johannes Perle
1407	Johannes Scryven ; Thomas Pryde.
1409	Robertus Thornes ; . . . . Thornes
1411	Thomas Pryde ; Johannes Wythyford'
1413	David Holbache ; Urianus Seintpier
1414	Robertus Horseley ; Willielmus Hord'.

6

1415 Johannes Shotton'; ditto.
1417 David Holbache ; ditto.
1419 Rogerus Corbet ; David Rathebon'.
1420 Robertus Whitcombe ; Ricardus Bentley.
1421 Robertus Whitcoumbe ; Urianus Seyntpere.
1421 Willielmus Horde ; Robertus Wytcombe

QUERIES.

CHAPEL OF THE RED HAIRED.—In *Bye-gones* for Oct. 29, 1879, a correspondent mentioned that the chapel of the Anglo-Norman garrison at Brecon formerly went by this name, and remarked on the fact that red hair was not uncommon in South Wales at the present day. When I lived in Denbighshire, some twenty years ago, a labourer's family, many of whom were red-haired, were commonly called "Red-headed Danes." Has this anything to do with Anglo-Norman descent? The tradition, I believe, in the neighbourhood was that some of the Danish invaders of England had at some time penetrated thus far into Wales. Red hair, I should say, was not at all common in that part of Wales. W.T.

CYFRAITH PLWYF.—I have an imperfect copy of *Cyfraith Plwyf* (Parish Law) by Edward Jones, mentioned in *Llyfryddiaeth y Cymry*, s.a. 1794, No. 46, Can any one supply me with the full title of the work?—apparently a rare work, for I never met with but one copy of it, and that in a dilapidated condition. The author of the *Llyfryddiaeth* appears never to have seen the book, the notice alluded to, which does not give the full title, being supplied by the editor. UST.

REPLIES.

DAVID HOLBACHE (Feb. 28, 1880).—Lest any one should hope to find the Will of David Holbache at London, I may as well say, I have searched for it there, without success. S.

TOPOGRAPHICAL NAMES (March 17, 1880.) *Corris.* As a preliminary towards arriving at the meaning of the name usually of late written *Corris*, it may perhaps be of some use to give the correct or popular name of this village, the ordinary orthography being misleading. At the place itself, and in the country around we never hear of *Corris* (with a short *o* and an *i* for the last vowel) but always *Corus*, or (which is the same as regards pronunciation) *Corys*, the *o* being long, as in *coron*, *pori*, and the like, and the last vowel *u*, not *i*. The name of the village is properly *Aber Corus*, which is descriptive of its situation on the confluence of the Corus and the Dulas, the united stream of which falls into the Dovey from the right or north bank at a short distance above Machynlleth Railway Station, and nearly opposite the outfall of another Dulas, called Dulas Cyfeiliog. As to the meaning of *Corus*, I am hardly prepared to hazard an opinion ; but I may mention that Dr. Owen Pughe, in a paper on the names of places in Merionethshire printed in the *Cambrian Register* for 1795, p. 295, has the following note on the name :—"Corus, a rivulet, so called from its making round excavations in the angles of its banks." I am not sufficiently acquainted with the course of the stream to enable me to express an opinion as to the accuracy of this description. So far as I know this Merionethshire stream is the only one in the Principality which bears the name of *Corus*. If there is another I shall be glad to know of it. DYVNIG.

Cwrt. Generally this word is the equivalent of English "Court" from Latin Curia. Mr. G. T. Clarke shows *Arch. Camb.*, 1877, p. 251) that in one instance at least it

is the modern Welsh form of Castrum or Caer. "Caerpile, or Castrum Bulœum, *now* Cwrt y Bela, near Newport." There is "Cwrt-y-Cadno" in North Carmarthenshire, in the valley of the Cothy. If the fox (caduo) were deprived of his tail, it would then be Cwrt y gad, or fort of the army. C.C.

Meifod. The learned Vicar, (*Hist. Dio. St. Asaph* p. 774) derives the name from "Mai-fod—Summer Residence." This is an unusual use of the month of May—and it should have been the common *Haf*-fod. There is an ancient Welsh word appearing under different forms which will better explain the name. In Taliessin we have "tra maeu"=beyond the plains (D.S.E's transl. in *Anc. Books*). Dr. O. Pughe gives Mai as a "plain, a field." In Carmarthenshire we find Maes Moy the present name of a farm—and the adjectival form of the same word in Brynmeuog (the last is mentioned in Lewis Morris's *Celtic Remains*.) In early times it would, I suspect be given to a settlement which made an opening in the uncleared country. OLIM INCOLA.

Lwyn-tyd-man, an unbroken Copse or Wood.

Tre-penal, the head or chief district. The name of this place is thus written on the ordnance survey, but locally is written and spoken as *Tre-pren-al*. A homestead in a very woody district. There is a residence near to the above place called "Argoed." Many places from their being situated amidst woods are called "Argoed." The whole of the low level country south-west of Llanymynech was at one time thickly wooded, and at the present day, when viewed from the summits of the Montgomeryshire Hills presents to the eye an immense forest of wood, with here and there an opening. Names of other places also testify to the fact that this district abounded with wood, for instance, we have Llwyn y Groes, Llwyn y go, Gwern y ddan bwll. The Woods, and most likely the names of fields would also give the same testimony. GYPT.

MARCH 31, 1880.

NOTES.

CAPT. ARTHUR WATKIN WILLIAMS WYNN (Feb. 25, 1880).—The following Inscription, on a monument in Nant-y-belan Tower, Wynnstay, is by the late Milnes Gaskill, Esq., M.P. :—

TO THE HONOURED AND LAMENTED MEMORY OF ARTHUR WATKIN, SECOND SON OF THE RIGHT HONOURABLE SIR H. W. WILLIAMS WYNN, K.C.B., G.C.H., Captain and Acting Major in the Royal Welsh Fusiliers. BORN 21st APRIL, 1819 ; DIED 20th SEPTEMBER, 1854.

HE fell, mortally wounded, in the front of his gallant Corps, while storming a Russian Battery on the Heights of Alma, with an ardour and self devotion worthy of his name and race, and with that dauntless courage which has ever characterized the Noble Regiment in which he served.

This is not the only record of the bravery of Welshmen preserved in Nant-y-belan. N.W.S.

EASTER CUSTOM AT CLUNGUNFORD.—From the State Papers in the Record Office, vol. CCCLXij, no. 57, cal. p. 247, the following Petition of the Inhabitants of Clungunford, co Salop, dated 27 June 1637, is extracted. It is addressed to Archbishop Laud, who in his new position began to remedy many Church abuses. The Petitioners say that their parish is spacious having many old inhabitants therein, where there has been an ancient custom

that at the feast of Easter, and upon Easter Day, after
Evening Prayer, the parson of the parish always provided
a church-feast, in the church, of bread & cheese and ale or
beer, for refreshing those ancient people that repaired
thither to Evening Prayer, having received the Sacrament
the same day in the morning, and also for the relief of
divers poor people of the parish. About 50 years since it was
then ordered by the then Archbishop of Canterbury that
this feast should be kept in the parsonage-house, where it
has been ever since kept till Easter last; but then Samuel
Barkeley, who is Rector at present, detained the same
from the Inhabitants, and will not let them have their
ancient custom, neither in the church or parsonage house.
Their suit is that you will restore this ancient custom, and
settle it again in the parsonage house.

[Underwritten in Laud's hand.]

I shall not go about to break this custom, so it be done
in the parsonage-house in a neighbourly and decent way,
but I cannot approve of the continuance of it in the
church; and if ever I hear it be so done again, I will not
fail to call the offenders into the High Commission Court.
—June 27, 1637.	W. Cant.	J.E.B.

MERIONETHSHIRE ELECTIONS.—The fol-
lowing particulars of the election of 1774 are copied from
a card published at the time:—

"November 11, 1774: An Exact Copy of the Numbers
who voted at the Merionethshire Election, with the Nature
of their Freeholds; Carefully extracted from the original
Poll-Books."

	For Mr. Vaughan.	For Mr. Corbet.	Maj. for Vaughan.	Maj. for Corbet.
Freeholders	244	208	36	0
Clergy	9	10	0	1
Parish Clerks	5	7	0	2
Schoolmaster	1	0	1	0
Lactuals & Tyths	0	1	0	1
Annuitants	5	12	0	7
Leases	78	20	58	0
	342	258	95	11

Deduct Corbet's 258 342

Maj. for Vaughan 84 Total 600

"Tra rhetto Dw'r, Cyflwr cu,
Daliwn wrth'r hên Deulu.
Edernion lân dirion Lu
Ai Gwyr oll a geir fellu."
	A.R.P.

Amongst some old papers collected by a Morgan
Davies, who was either butler or personal attendant on
Sir R. W. Vaughan of Nannau, I find the following:—
Voted for Mr. Vaughan of Corsygedol, 342; for Mr.
Corbet, 258; majority for Mr. Vaughan, 84. The Motto on
Mr. Vaughan's flag by T. Edwards of Nant and Mr.
Rice Jones of Blaeneu:—

Tra rhetto dwr cyflwr cu,
Daliwn at yr hên Deulu.—T.E.
Edernion lan dirion lu
Au gwyr oll a geir felly.—R. JONES.

The "T. Edwards" was the celebrated "Twm o'r Nant."
	CYFFIN.

LLYNCLYS LEGEND.—In vol. 12, page 406, of
Mont: Coll: reference is made to the Legend of Llynclys,
near Oswestry, and the author quotes the late Mr.
Dovaston for the story of King Alaric. In a foot-note
he also quotes the legend from Bye-gones, as told by
Humphrey Lloyd. In doing this, however, he makes one

important omission. I have referred to Bye-gones, Jan. 1,
1879 (not Dec. 18, 1878, as Mr. Fewtrell states), and find
it there stated that the words "Rex Powisiæ" are given in
a side note to the passage in the original work. The
legend doubtless was one of Powysland when the Princes
of Powys were paramont; and I never heard of an
"Alaric" amongst their number. A story of love would
suit the erratic pen of a genius like Mr. Dovaston, better
than one of God's judgments on infidelity, but his romance
would have run better in the foot note, and that of the
dry antiquary, Llwyd, in the text of an archæological
paper like the organ of Powysland Club.
	POWYSLANDER.

MUTINY AT THE NORE.—In one of Mr.
Kingston's stories he tells of the "San Fiorenzo" ship,
whose men were so faithful and loyal at this trying time,
that "it was intended to raise a sum in every seaport
town in England to present to them. For some reason,
however, the Government put a stop to it, and the only
subscription received was from Ludlow, in Shropshire,
from whence the authorities sent £500 to Sir Harry Neale
[the captain], which he distributed to the ship's company
on the quarter-deck." How much truth is there in this?
	N.W.T.

THE LATE MR. JOHN FRAIL.—It is many
years since I last saw the late John Frail of Shrewsbury,
and it was on the stand at Shrewsbury races we met and
had a chat. He had then "soft, glossy hair," "retaining
firmly the curl." This recollection has come over me in
reading an advertisement he put into the Salopian Journal
of May 13, 1835, in which he says:—

JOHN FRAIL, in recommending his celebrated Oil of Orange
to the public, assures them that this regenerative fluid is pre-
eminently successful in producing a soft, glossy and luxuriant
appearance of the Hair, and is much admired for its nourishing,
strengthening, and cleansing qualities, also for retaining firmly
the curl, promoting the growth of Hair, and preventing its falling off from illness, &c.

Did he use it I wonder? Mr. Frail also describes himself
as "from McLean's, 20, Lowther Arcade," and boasts in the
making of perukes of the "superiority of his system over
that of his contemporaries, on Principles which defy the
closest Scrutiny." Mr. Frail very soon applied his
"Principles" to "systems" more intricate than those of
wig making !	JARCO.

OLD CAMBRIAN INSTITUTIONS.
(Mar. 10, 1880.)

The Cambrian Society.—The following paragraph
refers to the origin of this society:—Oct 28, 1818. A
meeting was held at the White Lion, Carmarthen, which
formed itself into a society for the preservation of the remains of Ancient British Literature, political, historical
antiquarian, sacred and moral; and for the encouragement
of the National Music; by the name of the Cambrian
Society, under the patronage of the Duke of Beaufort, the
Earl of Powis, the Bishops of Bangor, St. David's, St.
Asaph and Llandaff; Lord Dynevor, Lord Kenyon, Lord
Cawdor, Lord Clive, Sir Watkin Williams Wynn, Sir
Thomas Mostyn, Sir Robert Vaughan, Sir Charles
Morgan, and C. W. W. Wynn, Esq, M.P.	G. G.

A writer in the Gents: Mag: of Nov. 1820, refers
to the first meeting of the Cambrian Society, which
he states was held at Carmarthen on the 5th and
6th of July, 1819. Bishop Burgess, he says, in the
obsence of Lord Dynevor, presided. The Rev. Walter

Davies of Manafon was honoured with the Bardic Chair, in which he was placed by Mr. Edward Williams, the Senior Bard. "The Secretary was the Rev. David Rowland, curate of Caermarthen, whose decease, as well as that of the Rev. Eliezer Williams, the following winter, the friends of the Society have cause to deplore."
                                                      TAFFY.

The *Cymmrodorion Society* was established, as stated, in 1751, as "The Honourable Society of Cymmrodorion," but hardly attained its majority when it broke up. The Society in supposed pursuance of its programme undertook to publish Pennant's *British Zoology* : this was not its legitimate groove, and the Society owing to this burden then dissolved. On the 24th June, 1820, it was again brought to existence, starting with about 50 members, under the presidency of Sir W. W. Wynn, and through the exertions of Dr. O. Pughe and others, and with a very comprehensive programme. This Society was the means of promoting the largest and most successful Eisteddfodau ever held in Wales, viz., at Wrexham and Welshpool, and offered medals and money prizes at subsequent ones. It seems to have reached its meridian in 1833 when a meeting was held in London, and which developed into an Eisteddfod. From this time the Society appears to have faded, until in 1843, at a meeting of its members, it was resolved to send all its papers and transactions to the British Museum for safe custody, where they now are. One name must be mentioned in connection with the Society, "Gwrgant," who was then the Librarian, and is now the only surviving member. The year 1873 was a Red letter year with Welsh Musicians, the South Wales Choral Union having carried off the prize trophy at the Crystal Palace, valued at a Thousand Guineas : A Committee was formed in London to aid the Union with funds, and when the Committee had completed its labours, "Gohebydd" alluded to the good offices of the Cymmrodorion Society, and proposed "That the then Musical Prize Fund Committee should be a nucleus of a Society for the encouragement of Literature and the Fine Arts in Wales." This was unanimously carried, and a revival of the Cymmrodorion resolved upon on the 10th Nov., 1873, the proposal receiving the cordial approval of Welshmen in general. On the last named date a meeting was held at the Freemasons' Tavern, at which our esteemed countryman, Mr. Hugh Owen, presided, and the late lamented Rev. R. Jones and "Gohebydd" spoke. I must refer to *Y Cymmrodor*, the journal of the Society, for further particulars.   ST. J.H.

Cymmrodorion Society in Powys.—I see in some of the local papers of 1820 that early in that year "this truly patriotic institution was daily acquiring an accession of patronage and support." And in an advertisement dated "Wrexham, Oct. 6, 1819," the list of subscribers included "Sir W. W. Wynn, Sir Edw. Pryce Lloyd, Sir Thomas Mostyn, Foster Cunliffe, Esq., Sir John Evans, Knight," and other names from Denbighshire; also in March, 1820, the names of "Lord Viscount Clive, C. W. Williams Wynn, Esq., William Owen, Esq., Panton Corbett, Esq., Humphrey R. Jones, Esq., Rev. R. J. Davies, Richard Mytton, Esq., Lord Kenyon, Lord Bagot, John Edwards, Esq., David Pugh, Esq.," and others, as a Welshpool list.   G. G.

The first Bardic Sessions of the *Cymmrodorion Society for Powys*, which was held at Wrexham on Sep. 13 and 14, under the presidency of Sir Watkin Wynn, is referred to in a letter on page 400 of the *Gents : Mag :* for Nov. 1820. Mr. Robert Davies of Nantglyn was awarded premium for Ode on the death of George III., and placed in the Bardic Chair. The Rev. D. Richards vicar of Llansilin, near Oswestry, acted as secretary, and there were ten competitors for the honour of the Silver Harp, which was awarded "by the King's Bard" to R. Roberts, a blind man from Carnarvon. The Rev. Walter Davies and Mr. Charles W. W. Wynn took part in the proceedings.   TAFFY.

CURRENT NOTES.

CRICKETING IN AUSTRALIA.

The *Adelaide Observer* for January 17, 1880, contains the following notice of the retirement of an amateur cricketer that will interest some of our readers. William Oswald Whitridge is the eldest son of the late Mr. William Whitridge Roberts, of Oswestry (the originator of the *Oswestry Advertizer*), who assumed as a surname his mother's maiden name when he emigrated thirty years ago :—

Mr. W. O. Whitridge's retirement from the cricketfield, on account of ill-health is an event of considerable importance to the South Australian Cricketing Association as well as to the Norwood club, of which he has so long been a leading member. There is no man whom Adelaide cricketers could so ill afford to lose at the present time, perhaps excepting Jarvis, the wicket-keeper, and it can safely be said that no man has more earnestly striven to merit the large measure of success and of popularity that has fallen to his lot. But Mr. Whitridge now retires finally from the field on the strong recommendation of his medical adviser. I use the word "finally" because I hear a rumour has been current during the week that he may play in the match against Hindmarsh next Saturday or against the North Adelaides on the following week. His club may need him sorely then ; but I have his own assurance that his retirement from active cricket is absolute. And now that a remarkably useful cricketing career is closed, I am glad to say I am in a position to give a few particulars concerning it. I feel sure they will be read with interest by thousands of South Australian players or cricket-admirers to whom Mr. Whitridge's name has become a household word. Mr. Whitridge retires while the laurels he has won are still fresh. Indeed he now holds the position of premier bowler of the colony, which he earned during the last two years, while in the season before that he ranked second only to his club companion, Giffen. Since the first South Australian Challenge Cup was established in 1874 no bowler has taken as many wickets, and few have bowled more balls in first-class matches. In Cup matches only he has bowled 4,973 balls for 1,373 runs, 262 maidens, and 262 wickets ; his average during the whole of that time being only a trifle over five runs per wicket. His best bowling performance—which brought him a great deal of praise at the time—was 8 wickets for 10 runs for South Australia against the Victorian Eleven, who played on the Adelaide Oval in 1875. Bowling seems always to have been a strong passion with him, and the "record" he has now completed is one in which he may well take pride as he resigns the leathern sphere into the hands of those who have looked up to him as their premier bowler. In all the matches he has played—Association, Norwood, Press and country—he has bowled 13,461 balls for 1,851 runs, 738 maidens, and 633 wickets ! "Noble six hundred !" As a batsman, Mr. Whitridge was formerly a "sticker" rather than a free player ; but of late he has shown a little more dash, and his defence has always been good. Some of my readers will no doubt be surprised to find that in the Cup matches played during the last five years Mr. Whitridge's batting average has been over 20 runs per innings. The fact will be seen from the following figures :—64 innings, 1,190 runs, five times not out. In 1876-7 Mr. Whitridge was highest aggregate and average scorer in the colony, and in the following year he had a still better average (27), though it was surpassed by two or three other batsmen. During the present season his batting has been as good, if not better, than before, he having twice exceeded 40 runs per innings—against the premier club's most dangerous rivals. But he has never once reached the century, his best performances having been 92 not out for the Registers against East Adelaide, 84 run out for Norwood against Kensington, 76 for Norwood against the South Australians, and 64 against the South Adelaides. I have on previous occasions expressed my conviction that Mr. Whitridge was the best all-round cricketer in the colony. The above "record," I think, proves the point if proof were needed. A genial fellow, and a thorough cricketer, he has borne his honours modestly ; and now that illness has obliged him to give up active play he, I am sure, leaves the field with the heartiest good wishes of all who love the good old game and who appreciate sterling worth, whether in friend or foe.

The *South Australian Register* of Feb. 21, says that the Australian eleven who are to visit England this season, are negociating with Jervis (mentioned in the foregoing) as they want South Australia to be represented.

APRIL 7, 1880.

NOTES.

DAVID JONES A LONDON WELSHMAN.— The Golden Torque at Wynnstay, as we know, was found by some gentlemen when grouse-shooting on Cader Idris in the year 1823. In his account of it, published in *Arch : Camb :* Vol. 1, p. 242, the late Dr. W. Owen Pughe says the finder "gave it to Mr. David Jones of the House of Commons, with a View of ascertaining what it might be, not supposing it to be valuable." It could not have been submitted to a better authority, for this Mr. Jones was an enthusiastic Welshman. For many years he held a responsible situation in the Engrossing Office of the House of Commons. He was a native of Towyn, and lived nearly all his lifetime in London. Everything connected with his native country had a charm for him, and when he died, in 1837, at his residence in the Adelphi, he was said to possess the best library of Welsh books in the Metropolis. He was 68 years of age when he died.

N.W.S.

SHROPSHIRE WORDS.—Miss Jackson in the first instalment of her *Shropshire Word Book* gives the following words as being in partial use in the county, but in naming the localities in which they are used, omits to note that they are known in the Oswestry district :— Abide, achern, adland, afterclap, aftermath, agwine, ashen-plant, askal, bake-hus, banter, base-child, beestings, behappen, bespattle, blether, battin, bugabo, bowl, brat, buft, bullyrag, burrow, bytack, careyn, cats-gallows, chance-child, cofer, coodle, corncrake, cuckoos's-meat, dash-boards, dinge, dolly, dog's-leave, dreep, dresser, driblets, dribble, dubbin. In the second instalment, just published, the following may be stated as used quite as commonly in the Oswestry district as in the places named :—Easings, easement, earnest, egg, flag, flen, gaby, gaffer, happen, harnish, haulier, hike, hod, ill-contrived, in-lieu, keffel, lag-end, lewn, mizzle. I also note that where Miss Jackson gives words as being in use in certain localities, and adds, "Qy. Com.," these words are almost invariably in use in the Oswestry district.

OLD OSWESTRY.

Badgers.—Miss Jackson gives "Badger, a middle-man between the wholesale selling farmer and the town-retailer of farm produce," as connected with the localities of Shrewsbury, Pulverbatch, Bridgnorth, and Clun. In the *Salopian Journal* for Aug. 27, 1800, the following paragraph appears :—"At Worcester, Kidderminster, Birmingham, and most other large towns, the magistrates have exerted themselves with the utmost vigilance to detect and prosecute Badgers, Forestallers, and Regraters, both in and out of the markets ; and the inhabitants have entered into associations and formed committees for the same laudable purpose."

JARCO.

Bonkie.—In the first part of Miss Jackson's admirable *Shropshire Word Book* she has "honkie" as a term applied to a girl occupied on the bank of a colliery. We had once in Oswestry an eccentric character known as "Miss Bonkie." Why was she so called? OSWALD.

Belter.—In some parts of Shropshire a "Belter" means a liar, and such an individual is said to "wear the belt" if notorious for his untruthfulness. Miss Jackson's meaning of the word is "anything of an extraordinary size."

W.F.

Dhu Stones.—In connection with this term Miss Jackson offers the following explanation :—

DHU-STONE [deu'stone *and* joo'stwun] *sb.* basalt, of a black or very dark colour, quarried at Titterstone Clee. *Dhu*—the local spelling—is a mistake. *Dhu*= W. *du,* black ; sable.

In *Bye-gones,* July, 1873, "An Old Inhabitant of Ludlow" wrote on this subject, and said :—

The hard basaltic rock on the top of the Titterstone is still called Jew (not, I believe, Jews) stone. Three reasons are given : 1, Because they have a peculiar power of condensing the dew ; and therefore should be called Dew-Stones. 2, Because they are basalt, and therefore should be called Dhu-Stones. 3, Because they are as hard to deal with as a Jew.

This explanation was called forth by a previous query in which the following passage was quoted from an old book of travels :—"We were very much incommoded [on the Titterstone] by large stones, called from their hardness Jews Stones."

N.W.S.

Welsh Words.—Mr. Walter White, in *All Round the Wrekin,* says: "It is noteworthy that scarcely a Welsh word has been adopted in the common speech of the people on the English side of the boundary line." Surely this is a rash assertion, and one Miss Jackson will be able to disprove in the course of her valuable work.

CYMRO.

Nobbler.—I have just received part 2 of Miss Jackson's valuable *Shropshire Word Book,* which includes the letter "N." I observe she does not give the word "Nobbler," which, when I was resident at Shrewsbury, was commonly used to describe a bricklayer who was handy at the performance of odd jobs, and who did not work under any regular master.

FAR AWAY.

A LADY'S IMPRESSIONS OF WALES. [LETTER VI.]
(Mar. 17, 1880.)

From Mrs. Presland (of Walford Hall, Salop) at Peniarth, Merionethshire, to her sister Miss Slaney, at Shrewsbury :—

Dear Sister, I receiv'd yours, was much shokd At the account you give me, of the dreadfull storm, and much concernd to hear the thunder Boult fell so near, but shall ever with great thankfullness acknowledg the mercy of it not falling nearer. I fear my dear girl, and all of you was much frighted, no wonder, it was here shocking and I supose Louder amongst so many mountains their in any

open Country, the lightning was so great and constant, that out of these windows, the walks and trees in the Garden appeard all in fire, the whole family so frighted that except my self, not one durst stir, the begd for Prayrs, but the ownly devine in the House, was I am sorry to say, so drunk he coud do nothing but talk prophain, and make a joke, I wishd him Dumb, and at last they took him up stars, and lockd him in his room, the next day he came down no body spoke to him and away he took himself, we hear of no lives being lost, which is surprising, for.there is dosens of Gentlemen grousing on the Hills, from whence we are supplyed with game of all sorts, some of the Baux [beaus] cald here and yesterday we had Miss Williamsis Markee pitchd upon ariseing hill, in full view of the Sea, at the hend of a sweet vail, we drunk tea, eat sillybub under the cow, had the three musicianers, and three good singers, who entertain us highly, we then walkd for a stumack to our suppers, where we had grous, soulls, Turbet, prawns, Lobsters, &c:c. and how am to bring myself to an English two dish table of plaint meat I cant tell, but flatter myself the joy of meeting with my dr husband, child and Sister will reconsile me to the loss of so luxurious a table, where I have great reason to think I am welcom, but home, is home, and I long to see it, and with pleasure reflect how near the time draws, our hours are very unlike what mine us'd to be, ten a clock breakfast, three dinner, ten supper, 12 bed time, who coud have thought these hours, and me coud ever have agreed, with every thing but my skin, and that is turnd brown and yellow, a pleasing mixture, and now I can with pleasure inform you Mr P: is arrivd safe and well and to morrow by five, we start I intend as I go a long, to take a dip in the Sea, and then bid adieu to Meryonethshire, where I shou'd be ungreatfull not to say I had spent my time very agreeably, and for mirth and jollety, shall say Wales, for ever, how cou'd you call your last stupid, did it not bring me the agreeable nows of you my Dear Girl and all friends being well, till I meet with whom say all thats kind from.   Your aff sister,
              Peniarth Aug ye 18 [1771?]
[Addressed " Miss Slaney, Shrewsbury."]

QUERIES.

TALHAIARN.—A Correspondent replying to a query about William Roose, Mar. 17, says that he engraved a portrait of "Talhaiarn," the noted Welsh bard, which has now become scarce." I am curious to know from what source he copied his picture? 1 don't know much about Welsh Bards, and less of the language in which they wrote, but I should very much doubt the authenticity of a picture said to be a likeness of one who existed a dozen centuries ago!   DUBIOUS.

CALICO PRINTING IN SHROPSHIRE.—In reference to this important branch of art and industry—carried on somewhat extensively, I believe in the neighbourhood of Oswestry in the early part of the present century—perhaps some of your readers may be able to give us some historical account of this business, or fuller information than is now generally known. For instance what extent, and where established, the origin, when declined and by what cause? I may observe that such an establishment was certainly in operation there up to about the year 1816 or 1818, inasmuch as an Uncle of mine at that time was a leading Block printer, and another Uncle an apprentice boy of 12; and also I remember two other gentlemen who were my former Sunday School Superintendents, &c., had been respectively engraver and printer there up to that time.   LANCASTRIAN.

REPLIES.

THE YALE MONUMENT (Mar. 3, 1880).—JARCO is wrong in saying that Mr. Stanley Leighton endorses Pennant's opinion to the effect that this monument in Oswestry Church was put up in 1616. I am aware that on page 90, vol. 3 (Sh. Arch. So. Trans.), Mr. Leighton says that to the Yales "a handsome monument remains in St. Oswald's Church, of the date 1616 ;" but that (no doubt like Pennant) he has recorded hastily, may be gathered from the fact that on page 104 of the same volume Mr. Leighton says that Hugh Yale "was an alderman, and died in 1616." The Vicar, however, in his paper, as it appears in the Reprint of Bye-gones, dates the monument at 1618, on what grounds I am at a loss to say. Is Yale's death not recorded in the parish register?
                                            OSWALD.

SEDAN CHAIRS (March 3, 1880.)—Fifty years ago Mrs. Hatchett of Ellesmere, grandmother to the Rev. T. M. B. Owen of Tedsmore, kept a sedan chair in which she was carried to church on Sundays if the weather was at all unfavourable. In it she had a footstool constructed so as to hold hot water, which on her arrival at Church was transferred to her pew. Forty years ago sedan chairs were in common use in the city of Chester, and I have many times seen a row of them with their bearers waiting outside the houses of Nicholas-street, which was then the fashionable street, at which parties were being held. They were kept for hire by the keepers of livery stables and others.   ELGO.

TOPOGRAPHICAL NAMES (Mar. 17, 1880.)—Mallaen: an extensive mountain in North Carmarthen. Mullagh in Irish is a summit, and this may be another vestige of the Gael.

Trafle. Traver occurs frequently in Scotland, as in Traverquair, now Traquair, but Skene (Celt. Scot. I. 215) says "it does not occur in Wales." He says it is properly "treabhar," a naked side. Trafle is a place on a naked hill side in N. Carmarthen. Theo. Jones, in History of Brecknock mentions a Walter de Travelya : (comp. Trevelyan), and I think Skene is wrong.

Telych. This name occurs in Cefn Bryntalch, in Montgomery and Cefntelych in Carmarthen. In the ancient Life of St. Brynach it is the name of a monk. In the Life of St. Gwynllyw the derivation is given. Gwynllyw at a certain place met a white ox with a black spot on its forehead, "wherefore he gave the name Dutelych to the territory, from the blackness of the forehead of the ox which met him." Rees's Camb. Br. SS., 453.' (Du, black ; tal, forehead ; ych, ox.) This is an instance how names were given in olden time, as now among Red Indians, from fanciful animal resemblances. St. Thomas Aquinas was known as the "great dumb ox of Sicily."
                                            C.C.

BORDER NAMES.—Ikin, Deakin, Gittins, Shone. In reply to a friend I drop a line into Bye-gones to say that I always considered the above names emanating from the Borders of Wales. At one time they were either pet appellations or nicknames of :—

    Isaac, or Heicyn, Ike and Ikin.
    David, or Dei, Deio, and Deicyn.
    Griffith, or Gutto and Guttyn.
    John, or Jack, Sionyn and Sion.

Some of the Ikins are spelt Eykin, Akin, and Atkin. The Deakins vary into Dyke, Dakin, Deakin, and Dickens, and the Gittins into Gittens and Gittings.
                                            MRS. MALAPROP.

GENERAL ELECTION, 1880.

[The figures in brackets that follow the name of the constituency indicate the number of members. The other figures show the number of voters on the register. The new members elected are marked by a †.]

NORTH SHROPSHIRE (2).　7,716.

Viscount Newport, C...	...	... }	Unopposed.
Stanley Leighton, C ...	...	... }	

In 1868 the numbers were—

J. R. Ormsby Gore, C	...	...	3603
Viscount Newport, C	...	...	3402
R. G. Jebb, L	...	...	2410

SOUTH SHROPSHIRE (2).　5,741.

Sir B. Leighton, C	...	...	...	2491
Capt. Severne, C	...	...	...	2216
Jasper More, L ..	...	...	...	2149
H. Davenport, L	...	...	...	1634

In 1868 the numbers were—

Gen. P. E. Herbert, C	...	...	2703
Col. Corbett, C...	...	...	2514
R. Jasper More, L	...	...	2161

SHREWSBURY (2).　3,891.

C. C. Cotes, L ...	...	...	...	1945
H. Robertson, L	...	...	...	1884
A. Scoble, C	...	...	...	1622
Viscount Newry, C	...	...	...	1568

In 1874 the numbers were—

C. C. Cotes, L	...	...	1672
H. Robertson, L	...	...	1561
J. Figgins, C	...	...	1388
D. Straight, C	...	...	1326

NORTH WALES.

ANGLESEA (1).　3,147.

R. Davies, L	...	...	...	1394
P. Rayner, C	...	...	...	1085

In 1874 the numbers were—

R. Davies, L	...	...	1630
Capt. Bulkeley, C...	...	...	793

ANGLESEA BOROUGHS (1).　2,575.

Morgan Lloyd, L ... ...Unopposed.
Mr. Fanning Evans (L) began a canvass, but withdrew.
In 1874 the seat was contested, with the following result—

M. Lloyd, L	...	...	947
H. Lewis, C	...	...	341
Capt. Verney, L	...	...	255

CARNARVONSHIRE (1).　6,387.

†Watkin Williams, L ...	...	...	...	3303
G. Douglas-Pennant, C	..	...	...	2206

In 1874 the numbers were—

Pennant, C	...	...	2750
L. Jones-Parry, L	...	...	2318

Mr. Watkin Williams sat in the last Parliament for Denbigh Boroughs.

CARNARVON BOROUGHS (1).　4,080.

W. Bulkeley Hughes, L ... ...Unopposed
Mr. Sorton Parry (L) began a canvass, but withdrew.
At the last contest, in 1868, the numbers were—

Hughes, L ...	...	...	1601
Wynn, C ...	...	...	1051

FLINTSHIRE (1).　4,170.

Lord R. Grosvenor, L ... ...Unopposed
There has been no contest since 1861, when the numbers were—

Grosvenor, L	...	...	1168
Hughes, L.C.	...	...	868

FLINT BOROUGHS (1).　3,766.

J. Roberts, L	...	...	...	...	2039
P. P. Pennant, C	...	...	...	...	1468

At a by election in 1878 the numbers were—

Roberts, L ...	...	...	1636
Pennant, C...	...	...	1511

DENBIGHSHIRE (2).　7,409.

Sir W. W. Wynn, C }		
G. Osborne Morgan, L }		.........Unopposed

At the last contest in 1868 the numbers were—

Wynn, C ...	...	...	3355
Morgan, L ...	...	...	2720
Biddulph, L	...	...	2412

There had been no previous contest since 1852.

DENBIGH BOROUGHS (1).　3,013.

†Sir R. Cunliffe, L	...	...	...	1424
Hon. G. T. Kenyon, C	...	...	...	1409

In 1874 the numbers were—

W. Williams, L	...	...	1238
G. Kenyon, C	...	...	1208

Sir R. Cunliffe represented the Flint Boroughs from 1872 to 1874.

MERIONETHSHIRE (1).　3,469.

S. Holland, L	...	...	...	1860
A. M. Dunlop, C	...	...	...	1074

At the last contest, in 1870, the numbers were—

Holland, L	...	...	1610
Tottenham, C	...	...	963

MONTGOMERYSHIRE (1).　5,212.

†Rendel, L	...	...	...	2232
Wynn, C	...	...	...	2041

The last contest was in 1862, when the numbers were—

C. Wynn, C	...	...	1269
S. C. Hanbury Tracy, L	...	...	959

The county had been represented by three Wynns in succession since 1799.

MONTGOMERY BOROUGHS (1).　3,111.

Hon. F. Hanbury Tracy, L ...	...	...	...	1572
Pryce Jones, C ...	...	...	...	1211

At a by-election in 1877, the numbers were—

Tracy, L	...	...	1447
Lord Castlereagh, C	...	...	1118

SOUTH WALES.

CARDIGANSHIRE (1).　4,763.

†L. Pugh Pugh, L	...	...	...	2406
T. E. Lloyd, C	...	...	...	1605

In 1874 the numbers were—

Lloyd, C,	...	...	1850
Richards, L...	...	...	1605

CARDIGAN BOROUGHS (1).　2,110.

David Davies, L ... ...Unopposed.
At the last contest, in 1855, the numbers were—

J. L. Davies, C	...	...	298
Evans, L	...	...	286

Col. Pryse, L, succeeded in 1857 without a contest.

CARMARTHENSHIRE (2). 8,172.

†Powell, L...	4101
Lord Emlyn, C	3030
J. Jones, C	2712

In 1874 the numbers were—

Emlyn, C	3389
J. Jones, C	3261
W. Powell, L	2799
E. J. Sartoris, L	2331

CARMARTHEN BOROUGHS (1). 4,865.

B. T. Williams, L	1935
J. Jones Jenkins, L	1825

In 1874 the numbers were—

Nevill, C	1654
Stepney, L	1481

In 1876 Mr. Nevill retired, and Stepney was returned without a contest. In 1878 Stepney retired, and Williams was returned without a contest.

PEMBROKESHIRE (1). 5,029.

†W. Davies, L	2185
C. E. G. Phillips, C	1737

At a by-election in 1876 the numbers were—

Bowen, C	1882
W. Davies, L	1608

Mr. Davies is the first Liberal who has sat for the county since 1832.

HAVERFORDWEST (1). 1,388.

Lord Kensington, L	636
E. D. T. Cropper, C	522

At the last contest in 1873 the numbers were—

Kensington, L	610
Peel, C	558

PEMBROKE (1). 3,438.

†H. G. Allen, L...	1462
T. C. Meyrick, C	1429

In 1874 the numbers were—

Reed, L	1339
Meyrick, C...	1310

GLAMORGANSHIRE (2). 12,785.

C. R. M. Talbot, L } Unopposed.	
H. H. Vivian, L }	

In 1874 the numbers were—

Vivian, L	4100
Talbot, L	4040
Guest, C	3353

There had been no contest before since 1857.

CARDIFF (1). 8,081.

†Reed, L...	3831
Guest, C...	3483

In 1874 the numbers were—

Stuart, L	2780
Giffard, C	2771

Mr. Reed sat in the last Parliament for Pembroke.

MERTHYR TYDFIL (2). 14,242.

H. Richard, L	8035
†C. H. James, L	7526
W. T. Lewis, C	4445

There had been no contest with a Conservative since 1859, when there was only one member, and Mr. Bruce beat Mr. Elderton by 800 to 106.

SWANSEA (1). 14,311.

L. L. Dillwyn, L ... ... Unopposed.	

In 1874 the numbers were—

Dillwyn, L...	5215
Bath, C	2708

BRECONSHIRE (1). 4,402.

W. F. Maitland, L	1810
A. Morgan, C	1550

At a by-election in 1875 the numbers were—

Maitland, L	1703
Gwyn, C	1600

BRECON (1). 843.

†Cyril Flower, L	438
J. P. G. Holford, C...	379

In 1874 the numbers were—

Holford, C	374
Morgan, L	353

With the exception of a short interval in 1869-70 no Liberal had sat for Brecon since 1866.

RADNORSHIRE (1). 2,389.

†Sir R. Green-Price, L	1137
B. Mynors, C	800

In 1874 the numbers were—

Walsh, C	889
Price, L	832
Haig, L	100

A Conservative had previously sat for the county since 1840.

RADNOR BOROUGHS (1). 989.

Marquis of Hartington. ... ... Unopposed.	

In 1874 the numbers were—

Hartington, L	612
Cockburn, C	162

A Liberal has sat for the Boroughs since 1855. Sir (then Mr.) R. Green-Price retired in 1869, when the Marquis of Hartington was elected.

PARLIAMENTARY POLL BOOK.
1832 TO 1879.

In the following lists (which we take from a little book under the above title) compiled by Mr. McCalmont of the Inner Temple, the abbreviations are C. conservative, L. liberal, L.C. liberal-conservative, P. protectionist, C.H. Chiltern Hundreds. The names of unsuccessful candidates are printed in italics :—

NORTH SHROPSHIRE

Population : 1831—119,681. 1861—146,410. 1871—120,285.
Electors : 1832— 4,682. 1868— 7,611. 1874— 7,445.
1832—Dec. Sir R. Hill, C, 2,981 ; John Cotes, L, 2,117 ; *Wm. Ormsby Gore, C*, 2,045.
1835—Jan. Sir R. Hill, C. W. Ormsby̦Gore, C.
1837—Aug. Ditto, ditto
1841—July Ditto, ditto
     Sir Rowland Hill created a peer.
1843—Jan. Viscount Clive, C.
1847—Aug. W. Ormsby Gore, P. Viscount Clive, P.
     Viscount Clive succeeded to peerage.
1848—Feb. J. Whitehall Dod, P.
1852—July. W. Ormsby Gore, C. J. Whitehall Dod, C.
1857—March. J. Whitehall Dod, C. Hon. R. C. Hill, C.
1859—April. Hon. R. C. Hill, C. J. R. Ormsby Gore, C.
1865—July. J. R. Ormsby Gore, C. Hon. C. F. Cust, C.
     Capt. Cust accepts C.H.
1866—Aug. Hon. A. W. Cust, C.
     Mr. Cust succeeded to peerage.
1867—March. Viscount Newport, C.
1868—Nov. J. R. Ormsby Gore, C, 3,603 ; Viscount Newport, C, 3,402 ; *R. G. Jebb, L*, 2,410.
1874—Feb. J. R. Ormsby Gore, C. Visc. Newport, C.
     Mr. Ormsby Gore created a peer.
1876—Jan. Stanley Leighton, C, 2,737 ; *Salusbury Kynaston Mainwaring, C*, 2,700.

SOUTH SHROPSHIRE.

Population : 1831—102,822. 1861—104,549. 1871—69,811.
Electors : 1832— 2,791. 1868— 5,847. 1874— 5,717.
1832—Dec. Earl of Darlington, C, 642; Hon. R. H. Clive, C, 573; *Thomas Whitmore*, C, 20.
1835—Jan. Darlington, C. Clive, C.
1837—Aug. ditto ditto.
Earl of Darlington succeeded to peerage.
1842—Mar. Viscount Newport, C.
1847—Aug. Clive, LC, Newport, P.
Viscount Newport appointed Vice Chamberlain.
1852—Mar. Viscount Newport, C.
1852—July. Clive, L.C, Newport, C.
Mr. Clive died.
1854—Jan. Hon. R. W. Clive, C.
1857—Mar. Newport, C. Clive, C.
1859—Apl. Ditto ditto.
Mr. Clive died.
1859—Sep. Sir Baldwin Leighton, Bart., L.C.
1865—July. R. Jasper More, L, 1,837; *General Percy Herbert, C.*, 1,678; *Sir B. Leighton, L.C*, 1,399.
1868—Nov. General Herbert, C, 2,703; Colonel Corbett, C, 2,514; *Jasper More*, L, 2,161.
1874—Feb. Herbert, C, Corbett, C.
Sir Percy Herbert died.
1876—Nov. Lieut.-Col. Severne, C.

SHREWSBURY.

Population : 1831—16,055. 1861—22,163. 1871—23,406.
Electors : 1832— 1,714. 1868— 3,381. 1874— 3,675.
1832—Dec. Sir J. Hanmer, Bart., C, 808; R. A. Slaney, L, 797; *J. C. Pelham*, C, 634.
1835—Jan. Hanmer, C, 760; Pelham, C, 627; *Slaney*, L, 584.
1837—Aug. R. Jenkins, C, 700; Slaney, L, 697; *Pelham*, C, 655; *F. Dashwood*, L, 537.
1841—June. G. Tomline, C,793; B. Disraeli, C, 785; *Sir L. P. J. Parry*, L, 605; *Christopher Temple*, L, 578.
1847—Aug. E. H. Baldock, P, 769; Slaney, L, 743; *Tomline*, L, 732.
1852—July. Tomline, L, 1,164; Baldock, C, 745; *Augustin Robinson*, L, 440.
1857—Mar. Tomline, L, 706; Slaney, L, 695; *J. W. Huddleston*, C, 548; *Major Phibbs*, C, 484.
1859—Apr. Tomline, L, Slaney, L.
Mr. Slaney died.
1862—Feb. Henry Robertson, L, 671; *R. Banner Oakley*, C, 361; *Henry Atkins*, 10.
1865—July. Tomline, L.; W. J. Clement, L.
1868—Nov. Clement, L, 1,840; Alderman Figgins, C, 1,751; *R. Crawford*, L, 685.
Mr. Clement died.
1870—Sep. Douglas Straight, C, 1,291; *C. C. Cotes*, L, 1,253.
1874—Feb. Cotes, L, 1,672; Robertson, L, 1,561; *Figgins*, C, 1,388; *Straight*, C, 1,326.

MONTGOMERY (COUNTY.)

Population : 1831—66,485. 1861—66,919. 1871—48,946.
Electors : 1832— 2,523. 1868— 4,803. 1874— 5,034.
1832—Dec. Right Hon. C. Williams Wynn, C.
1835—Jan. Ditto. 1837—Aug. ditto.
1841—July Ditto. 1847—Aug. ditto, L.C.
Mr. Wynn died.
1850—Oct. Col. Herbert W. Williams Wynn, C.
1852—July Ditto. 1857—Mar. ditto.
1859—Apr. Ditto.
Col. Wynn died.
1862—June. Charles W. Williams Wynn, C. 1,269; *Hon. S. C. G. Hanbury Tracy*, L. 959.
1865—July C. W. W. Wynn, C.
1868—Nov. Ditto. 1874—Feb. ditto.

MONTGOMERY (BOROUGHS).

Population : 1831—18,680. 1861—18,036. 1871—18,677.
Electors : 1832— 723. 1868— 2,559. 1874— 2,836.
1832—Dec. David Pugh, C, 335; *Col. Edwards*, L, 321. [Election declared void.]
1833—Apr. Edwards, L, 331; *Panton Corbet*, C, 321.
1835—Jan. Col. Edwards, L.
1837—Aug. Edwards, L, 472; Corbet, C, 443.

1841—July. Hon. H. Cholmondeley, C, 464; *Sir John Edwards*, L, 437.
1847—Aug. David Pugh, P, 389; *Hon. H. Cholmondeley, L.C*, 389. (Mr. Cholmondeley declined to defend the seat.)
1852—July. David Pugh, P, 435; *G. H. Whalley*, L, 300.
1857—March. D. Pugh, LC. 1859—Apr. D. Pugh, L.C.
Mr. Pugh died.
1861—Apr. Capt. Willes Johnson, L.C.
Capt. Johnson died.
1863—July. Hon. C. Hanbury Tracy, L, 439. *Major C. V. Pugh, L.C, 330.*
1865—July. Tracy, L, 437; *Capt. Hampton*, C, 372.
1868—Nov. Tracy, L. 1874—Feb. Tracy, L.
Hon. C. H. Tracy succeeded to peerage.
1877—May. Hon. Frederick Hanbury Tracy, L, 1,447; *Viscount Castlereagh*, C, 1,118.

DENBIGHSHIRE (COUNTY.)

Population : 1831—83,167. 1861—100,778.
Electors : 1832— 3,401. 1868— 7,623.
1832—Dec. Sir Watkin Williams Wynn, C, 2,528; R. Myddelton Biddulph, L, 1,479; *Hon. Lloyd Kenyon*, C, 1,291.
1835—Jan. Sir W. W. Wynn, C, 2,378; Hon. W. Bagot, C, 1,512; *R. M. Biddulph, L, 1,256.*
1837—Aug. Sir W. W. Wynn, C.; Hon. W. Bagot, C.
Sir Watkin died.
1840—Jan. Hon. H. Cholmondeley, C.
1841—July. Bagot, C.; Sir W. W. Wynn, C.
1847—Aug. Sir W. W. Wynn, C, 2,055; Hon. W. Bagot, C. 1,530; *Col. R. M. Biddulph, L. 1,394.*
1852—July. Sir W. W. Wynn, C, 2,135; Biddulph, L. 1,611; *Bagot, C. 1,532.*
1857—Mar. Sir W. W. Wynn, C. Col. Biddulph, L.
1859—Apr. Ditto ditto. 1865—July ditto ditto
1868—Nov. Sir W. W. Wynn, C. 3,355; *G. Osborne Morgan* L. 2,720; *Col. Biddulph, L. 2,412.*
1874—Feb. Sir W. W. Wynn, C. G. O. Morgan, L.

DENBIGH (BOROUGHS).

Population : 1831—14,245. 1861—17,888. 1871—20,224.
Electors : 1832— 1,131. 1868— 2,785. 1874— 2,907.
1832—Dec. John Maddocks, L.
1835—Jan. Wilson Jones, C, 490; *Maddocks*, L, 242.
1837—Aug. W. Jones, C, 411; *Capt. T. M. Biddulph*, L, 338.
1841—July. Townshend Mainwaring, C, 442; *Capt. T. M Biddulph*, L, 416
1847—Aug. R. Frederick West, L.C.
1852—July. West, C, 362; *Langford Foulkes*, L, 288.
1857—Mar. T. Mainwaring. C. 364; *James Maurice*, L, 302.
1859—Apl. Mainwaring, C. 1865—July. Mainwaring, C.
1868—Nov. Watkin Williams, L, 1,318; *Townshend Mainwaring*, C, 944.
1874—Feb. Watkin Williams, L, 1,238; *Hon. G. T. Kenyon*, C, 1,208.

MERIONETHSHIRE.

Population : 1831—35,609. 1861—38,963. 1871—46,598.
Electors : 1832— 580. 1868— 3,185. 1874— 3,861.
1832—Dec. Sir R. W. Vaughan, C. 1835—Jan. Vaughan, C.
Sir R. W. Vaughan accepts the C.H.
1836—June R. Richards, C, 501; *Sir W. Wynn*, L, 150.
1837—Aug. Richards, C. 1841—July. Richards, C.
1847—Aug. Ditto C. 1852—July. W. W. E. Wynne, P.
1857—Mar. W. W. E. Wynne, C.
1859—Ap. Ditto C, 390; *D. Williams*, L, 350.
1865—July W. R. M. Wynne, C, 610; *D. Williams*, L, 579.
Mr. Williams died.
1870—Jan. S. Holland, L, 1,610; *Col. Tottenham*, C, 963.
1874—Feb. S. Holland, L.

CARNARVONSHIRE (COUNTY).

Population : 1831—65,753. 1861—95,694. 1871—78,581.
Electors : 1832— 1,688. 1868— 4,852. 1874— 6,478.
1832—Dec. T. Assheton Smith, C. 1835—Jan. Smith, C.
1837—Aug. J. R. Ormsby Gore, C.

1841—July.   Hon. Douglas-Pennant, P. 1847—Aug. Pennant, P.
1852—July.   Ditto, C   1857—March.   Ditto, C.
1859—April   Ditto, C   1865—July.   Ditto, C.
          Col. Douglas-Pennant raised to Peerage.
1866—Aug.   Hon. C. Douglas-Pennant, C.
1868—Nov.   Love Jones-Parry, L, 1,963 ; *Pennant*, C, 1,815.
1874—Feb.   Pennant, C, 2,750 ; *Parry*, L, 2,313.

CARNARVONSHIRE (BOROUGHS).
Population : 1831—7,642. 1861—22,907. 1871—27,340.
Electors :   1832— 855. 1868— 3,376. 1874 — 3,909.
1832—Dec. Sir Charles Paget, L., 410 ; *Major O. J. E. Nanney*,
           C., 363. [A petition was lodged, but eventually Sir
           Charles was declared the sitting member.]
1835—Jan. Col. Love P. Jones-Parry, L, 378 ; *Major Nanney*,
           C, 350.
1837—Aug. W. Bulkeley Hughes, C, 405 ; *Capt. Charles Paget*,
           L, 385.
1841—July. Hughes, C, 416 ; *Lord George Paget*, L, 337.
1847—Aug. W. Bulkeley Hughes, L.C.
1852—July. Ditto, L.C., 396 ; *R. Davies*, L, 276.
1857—March. W. Bulkeley Hughes, L.C.
1859—Apr. Charles Wynne, L.C., 380 ; *W. B. Hughes*, L, 328.
1865—July. W. Bulkeley Hughes, L.
1868—Nov. Ditto L, 1,601 ; *Hon. T. J. Wynn*, C, 1,051.
1874—Feb. W Bulkeley Hughes, L.

FLINTSHIRE (COUNTY).
Population : 1831—60,012. 1861—69,737. 1871—52,347.
Electors :   1832— 1,271. 1868 — 4,150. 1874 — 3,864.
1832—Dec. Hon. E. Lloyd Mostyn, L. 1835—Jan. Mostyn, L.
1837—Aug. Sir S. R. Glynne, Bart., L C, 945 ; *Hon. E. Lloyd
           Mostyn*, L, 905.
1841—July. Mostyn, L, 1,234 ; *Glynne*, L C, 1,192 [On petition
           Mostyn unseated].
1842—May. Sir S. R. Glynne, L C.
1847—Aug. Hon. E. Lloyd Mostyn, L C.
1852—July. Ditto,   L, 1,276 ; *Edmund Peel*, C, 910.
           Mr. Mostyn succeeded to peerage.
1854—May. Hon. T. Lloyd Mostyn, L.
1857—March. Ditto, L, 1,171 ; *Sir S. Glynne*, L C, 876.
1859—April. Hon. T. Lloyd Mostyn, L.
           Mr. Mostyn died.
1861—May. Lord Richard Grosvenor, L, 1,168 ; *H. R.
           Hughes*, L C, 868.
1865—July. Grosvenor, L. 1868—Nov. Grosvenor, L. 1874—
           Feb. Grosvenor, L.

FLINTSHIRE (BOROUGHS.)
Population : 1831—31,327. 1861—18,845. 1874—22,989.
Electors :   1832— 1,279. 1868— 3,280. 1874 — 3,670.
1832—Dec. Sir S. R. Glynne, L. 1835—Jan. Glynne, L.C.
1837—Aug. Capt. Dundas, L, 625 ; *R. J. Mostyn*, C, 446.
1841—June Sir R. Bulkeley, L. 1847—Aug. Sir J. Hanmer,
           L.C.
1852—July. Sir J. Hanmer, L, 386 ; *R. P. Warren*, C, 267.
1857—March. Ditto,   L. 1859—April. Hanmer, L.
1865—July.   Ditto,   L. 1868—Nov. Ditto, L*
1874—P. Ellis Eyton, L, 1,076 ; *C. R. Conwy*, C, 1,072 ; *Sir
           Robert Cunliffe, Bart*, L, 772.
           Mr. Eyton died.
1878—July. J. Roberts, L, 1,636 ; *P. P. Pennant*, C, 1,511.
  * The authority we quote omits to state that Sir John
Hanmer was raised to the Peerage in 1872, and Sir R. Cunliffe
returned unopposed.

ANGLESEA (COUNTY).
Population : 1831—48,323. 1861—54,609. 1871—37,368.
Electors :   1832—1,187. 1868—3,195. 1874—3,355.
1832—Dec. Sir R. Bulkeley, Bart., L. 1835—Jan. Bulkeley, L.
           Sir R. Bulkeley accepts the C.H.
1838—Feb. Hon. W. O. Stanley, L, 693 ; *F. Meyrick*, C, 586.
1837—Aug.   Ditto   1841—July, Stanley, L.
1847—Aug. Sir R. Bulkeley, L. 1852—July, Bulkeley, L.
1857—Mar.   Ditto   L. 1859—Apr. Ditto, L. 1865—
           July, Ditto, L.
1868—Nov. R. Davies, L.
1874—Feb.   Ditto   L, 1,630 ; *Capt. Bulkeley*, C, 793.

ANGLESEA (BOROUGHS).
Population : 1831—10,817. 1861—13,275. 1871—13,672.
Electors :   1832— 329. 1868— 1,944. 1874— 2,354.
1832—Dec. Capt. F. Paget, L. 1835—Jan. Paget, L. 1837—
           Aug. Paget, L.
1841—June Lt. Col. F. Paget, L.
1847—Aug. Lord G. A. F. Paget, L. 1852—July Lord Paget, L..
1857—Mar. Hon. W. O. Stanley, L. 1859—Apr. Stanley, L.
1865—July. Stanley, L.
1868—Nov. Hon. W. O. Stanley, L., 941 ; *Morgan Lloyd*, L., 651.
1874—Feb. Morgan Lloyd, L., 947 ; *Capt. Hampton Lewis*, C.,
           841 ; *Captain Verney*, L, 255.

NEW MEMBERS OF PARLIAMENT.

CHEETHAM, JOHN FREDERICK (North Derbyshire) (L),
of Eastwood, near Staleybridge, Cheshire, is the eldest
son of Mr. John Cheetham, of Staleybridge, who represented South Lancashire from 1852 till 1859, and Salford
from 1865 till 1868, by Emma, daughter of the late Mr.
Thomas Rayner, of Ashton-under-Lyne. He was born
in 1834, and is a magistrate for the counties of Chester
and Lancaster. He is a brother of Mrs. James Barnes's,
of Brookside, near Oswestry.

CUNLIFFE, SIR ROBERT.—Sir Robert Alfred Cunliffe,
(Denbigh District) (L), of Acton Park, Denbighshire, who
takes the seat formerly occupied for twelve years by Mr.
Watkin Williams, is the eldest son of the late Mr. Robert
Ellis Cunliffe, of the Honourable East India Company's
service, by Charlotte, eldest daughter of Mr. Iltid Howell.
He was born in 1839, was educated at Eton, succeeded his
grandfather in the title as fifth baronet in 1859, and
married in 1869 Eleanor Sophia Egerton, only daughter of
the late Colonel Egerton Leigh, M.P., of High Leigh,
Cheshire. Sir Robert Cunliffe, who is a justice of the
peace and deputy-lieutenant for the county of Denbigh,
of which county he was high sheriff in 1868, and
lieutenant colonel commandant of the Royal Denbigh
Militia from 1872, was formerly a captain in the Scots
Guards. He is not new to parliamentary life, as he represented the Flint Boroughs from 1872 till 1874, at the
general election of which year he was defeated by Mr.
Peter Ellis Eyton, who polled 1,076 to Sir Robert's 772.

FLOWER, C. (Brecknock.)—Mr. Cyril Flower, of Aston
Clinton, near Tring, Buckinghamshire, and of Hyde Park-
place, London, elected as a Liberal, in the room of Mr.
James P. W. Gwynne Holford, is the eldest son of the late
Mr. Philip William Flower, of Furze Down-park, Streat-
ham, Surrey, by his marriage with Mary, daughter of
Mr. Jonathan Flower. He was born in the year 1843,
and was educated at Harrow School. He was called to
the Bar at the Inner Temple in Easter Term, 1870, and
practises as a special pleader. He is also a commissioner
of lieutenancy for the city of London, and a lieutenant
in the Royal Buckinghamshire Yeomanry. Mr. Flower
married, in 1878, Miss Constance de Rothschild, daughter
of the late Sir Anthony de Rothschild.

DUCKHAM, T. (Herefordshire.)—Mr. Thomas Duckham,
of Baysham-court, near Ross, elected as a Liberal, in the
place of Mr. Daniel Peploe, is the eldest son of the late
Mr. John Duckham, of Shirehampton, near Bristol. He
was born in the year 1816, and was educated at private
schools at Bristol and Hereford. He married in 1845.
He is a tenant farmer in the neighbourhood of Ross.
His name appears in the Modern Domesday Return as
the owner of 113 freehold acres, with a rental of £243.
He is returned as a strong supporter of the agricultural
interest.

HUDSON, CHARLES DONALDSON (Newcastle-under-Lyme) (C), of Cheswardine, Shropshire, is the younger and only surviving son of the late Mr. J. Donaldson of Wigton, Cumberland, by Catherine, daughter of Mr. Anthony Halliley. He was born in 1840, was educated at Merton College, Oxford, and succeeded his great uncle, Mr. Thos. Hudson, M.P. of Cheswardine, whose surname he assumed by Royal licence. Mr. Donaldson-Hudson, who married in 1870 Sarah Marie, only daughter of the late Major Robert Streatfeild, of the 52ud Foot, is a magistrate for the counties of Stafford and Salop, and was on the roll for High Sheriff of the latter county for the present year.

LAWLEY, HON. BEILBY (Chester), (L), is the eldest son of Beilby, second Lord Wenlock, by his marriage with Lady Elizabeth, daughter of Richard, second Marquis of Westminster. He was born in 1849, and educated at Eton and at Trinity College, Cambridge. Mr. Lawley, who married, in 1872, Lady Constance Mary, eldest daughter of Henry, fourth Earl of Harewood, is a magistrate for the North and East Ridings of Yorkshire, and has been a captain in the Yorkshire Hussar Yeomanry since 1874. He is heir to the barony of Wenlock.

McINTYRE, Æ. J. (Worcester.).—Mr. Æneas John McIntyre, Q.C., LL.D., of Brick-court, Temple, and of Park-squarewest, Regent's Park, elected as a Liberal, in the place of Mr. John Derby Allcroft, is the eldest son of the late Dr. Æneas McIntyre, of King's College, Aberdeen, by his marriage with Charlotte Susanna, daughter of Mr. William Thomson, of Kingston, Jamaica. He was born in the year 1821. He was called to the Bar at the Middle Temple in Michaelmas Term, 1846, and practised for some years as a special pleader. He goes the North Wales, Chester, and Glamorganshire Circuits, attending also the Cheshire and Knutsford Sessions. He was nominated a Queen's Counsel in 1872. Mr. McIntyre married, in 1854, Miss Eleanor Corbett, daughter of Mr. George Corbett.

POWELL, W. R. H. (Carmarthenshire).—Mr. Walter Rice Howell Powell, of Maesgwynne, near Whitland, Carmarthenshire, elected as a Liberal, in the place of Mr. John Jones, is the eldest son of the late Mr. Walter Rice Howell Powell, of Maesgwynne, by his marriage with Mary, daughter of Mr. Joshua Powell, of Brislington, Somerset. He was born in the year 1819, and graduated at Christ Church, Oxford. He is a magistrate and deputy-lieutenant for the counties of Pembroke and Carmarthen, and served the office of High Sheriff for the latter county in 1849. Mr. Powell, who has for upwards of forty years been a master of foxhounds in South Wales, married first, in 1840, Miss Emily Anne Skrine, second daughter of Mr. Henry Skrine, of Stubbings, Berkshire, and of Warleigh Manor, near Bath; and, secondly, in 1851, Catherine Anne, second daughter of Mr. Grismond Philipps, of Cwmgwilly, Carmarthenshire.

PRICE, SIR R. GREEN- (Radnorshire.)—Sir Richard Green-Price, of Norton Manor, Radnorshire, elected as a Liberal, in the place of the Hon. Arthur Walsh, is the eldest surviving son of the late Mr. George Green, of Cannon-bridge, Radnorshire, by his marriage with Margaret, daughter of the late Mr. Richard Price, of Knighton, in that county, whose name he has assumed in addition to his patronymic. He was born in the year 1803, and was for many years a member of the legal profession. He is a magistrate and deputy-lieutenant for Radnorshire, and also a magistrate for Herefordshire, and he served as High Sheriff of the former county in 1876. He is not new to Parliamentary life, having represented the Radnor district of boroughs from 1863 to 1869, when he retired, and

Lord Hartington was elected in his place. He was an unsuccessful candidate for this constituency at the general election in 1874, when he was defeated by Mr. A. Walsh, whom he now displaces. Sir Richard, who was created a baronet in 1874, has been twice married—first in 1837 to Frances Milborough, eldest daughter of Mr. Dansey Richard Dansey, of Easton-court, Herefordshire; and, secondly, in 1844, to Laura, third daughter of Mr. Richard Henry King, M.D., of Mortlake, Surrey.

PUGH, LEWIS PUGH, (Cardiganshire) (L), of Abermaide, in that county, is the eldest son of Mr. John Evans, of Lovesgrove, Cardiganshire, by Eliza, daughter of Mr. Lewis Pugh. He was born in 1837, and was educated at Winchester and at Corpus Christi College, Oxford, where he graduated B.A. in 1859, taking his M.A. degree in 1862, and being called to the bar at Lincoln's-Inn the same year. Mr. Pugh, who married in 1864 Veronica Harriet, daughter of Mr. James Hills, of Neechindeepore, Bengal, East Indies, assumed the name of Pugh by royal licence, under the will of his late uncle, Mr. Lewis Pugh, in 1868. He is a magistrate for the county of Cardigan.

RENDEL, S. (Montgomeryshire).—Mr. Stuart Rendel, of Plas Dinam, Montgomeryshire, and Palace-gardens, Kensington, elected as a Liberal, in the place of Mr. C. W. Williams Wynn, is the third son of the late eminent engineer, Mr. James Meadows Rendel, F.R.S., and was born in the year 1834. He was educated at Eton and at Oriel College, Oxford, where he took his Bachelor's degree in 1857. He was called to the Bar at the Inner Temple in Trinity term, 1861, and nominally joined the Home (now the South-Eastern) Circuit, but has never practised, having become a member of Sir William Armstrong's engineering firm and its managing partner in London. Mr. Rendel married, in 1857, the daughter of Mr. William Egerton Hubbard, of Leonardsdale, near Horsham, Sussex.

WOODALL, W. (Stoke-on-Trent).—Mr. Wm. Woodall, Bleakhouse, Burslem, Staffordshire, elected as a Liberal, in the place of Mr. Robert Heath, was born in the year 1832 at Shrewsbury, and was educated at the Crescent Schools, Liverpool. He is a magistrate for the county of Stafford, and a manufacturer at Burslem, being a member of the firm of Messrs. James Macintyre and Co. He is also chairman of the Burslem School Board. Mr. Woodall married, in 1862, Miss Evelyn Macintyre, daughter of the late Mr. James Macintyre of Burslem.

APRIL 14, 1880.

NOTES.

FRENCH PRISONERS IN SHROPSHIRE.—A paper was forwarded to me from Yorkshire containing the following paragraph. As it bears upon a point of local interest, I send it to *Bye-gones*. H.W.W.

Passing through a little town near Lille, I was invited to see an old woman, over 100 years of age, of English extraction. I went, and found, in a most wretched hovel, living with her youngest daughter, a hale and hearty old body, able to walk about as if only sixty years old. Addressing her in English, although she had not heard the sound of her native tongue for many and many years, I arrived with the help of some papers, at the following facts, and I may at once say that she spelt her name to me in the most perfect and clear manner possible:—Her maiden name was Charlotte Brookfield, youngest daughter of Richard Brookfield, farmer, at Hanmer, Flintshire. According to her own statement, she was 100 years old last 20th October, but I believe she is 103 years old. She was married to a French officer called Mesnier, at Whitekirk, [Whitchurch?] Shropshire, when twenty-eight years old, he being about thirty-five and representing himself to be a very rich man (so I was told by her daughter). Mesnier served under Napoleon I.; he was an officer, and was pensioned in 1817. His pension certificate I have had in my hands; it states that Mesnier was born on the 20th of May. 1769, and he drew until his death, which occurred forty years ago, 500 francs per annum as pension. If Charlotte Brookfield was seven years younger than Mesnier when she married him, she must be in her 104th year. She had eleven children, now all dead but one—her youngest daughter, who is forty-nine years of age, and upon special enquiry made I was told that this daughter was born to her when in her fifty-second year. I promised the old woman, who wrote for me in the clearest possible manner the name of her native village, "Hanmer," with chalk on a piece of board, to make inquiries after any relatives. A few francs for snuff were gratefully received. Can I send any message from a descendant of Richard Brookfield, of Hanmer, to the centenarian Charlotte Brookfield?

Dewsbury.	F. W. REUSS.

A LADY'S IMPRESSIONS OF WALES. LETTER VII.
(April 7, 1880.)

We now come to the last of the interesting letters from Mrs. Presland to her sister, Miss Slaney, written, probably, in 1771. The former letters have all been addressed from Peniarth, but the last of the series is penned at Walford Manor, Baschurch, and describes very graphically the lady's journey home through Merionethshire and Montgomeryshire :—

Dear Sister according to my design which I mentioned in my last, I left Peniarth on thursday, much entertaind with severall waves on the journey, one Caskeadon [cascade on] the rode side, out of a rock, I shoud suppose Lord Littleton woud, to get in his pleasure ground not think thousands to much to give, we got to Tallgarth by dinner, was jenteely receivd by Mr, and Mrs Edwards, and sat down to a very handsom dinner, walkd drank tea and set to dance eight couple. the house is very old, and aukward, it stands on a green Bank, below sweet medows, and a fine broad serpentine river [The Dovey] with severall small brigs Sailing on the other side the river, some slitting mills and small houses, above them a sloping mountain, with some rocks and wood in plenty, back part of his house a Little Village, with a neat small new church, on one side of the house some pretty vallys and round high cops of trees, near to them runs in face of the house, a long steep mountain, with shady walks up it, off the top of which you see the Sea, and variety of diferent prospects, to which situation it is not my power to do justice. we stayd here three days. I got up one mourning by five a clock, to see a place calld the devels . . . (how indelicate) but it rain so hard I coud not go, but as discribd to me you have it. but one rode to the house behind which is a mountain, at one hend and in the face of it ragget high rocks, intermixd with wood down from the top of which powers severall Kaskeades into a murmering Brook, on each side a green medow, over this Brook is built a Little house which poor Dick Loyd, had occation to visit one rainy day, just as he had . . . . the Brook rose, wind blew, water rored, and in short he so frighted for Dear self, that out he runs, into the parlour full of company he goes, never reolecting his . . . . which I am assurd the was, and now with a song equell to Governor Gynns, do I take my leave of Meryonethshire and proceed to Montgomeryshire, where I have found the whole country up to Mr Hughes of Cemiss a perfect Garden, this house is very bad, a pretty hanging wood and river faceing it, but nothing to what I have seen, Mrs Hughes is very friendly, sensible and agreeable as three sweet children, free from Scabs, which is not the case with some I have seen. Mr. Hughes was so good the third day, to bring us at least ten miles, and persuaded us to go some miles out of the way to see a

veiw which we approachd up a long narrow rode, that I do suppose the Sun had never shon, upon at the hend of it, we rode up asteep hill at the top of it, in full front, at the hend of a swet vally was a high Rock, down which fell a beautyfull Caskaid in to a turning Brook, charming green medows, on each side, five different Hills, with vails between each, and wood sufficient to make the view exceeding fine, to which there is but one rode, as Mr. Hughes informs me, he conducted us back into the mean rode, and then we came on to Mr. Davises of Truwellin, before I reachd it was wet to the skin, and am a Little hoarse, but if no sour sause, comes after sweet meat shall think my self well off, and to morrow Mrs. Davis and I set out in her chaise, fulldressd to dongey. we got there about one a clock, was receivd upon the green)by Mr. and Mrs. Loyd(where they musick playd, and company walkd till dinner, then we proceeded a Gentleman, and a Lady to dinner, where there mas a most Eligant entertainment in the parlour, and another set out upon tables in the garden which came up to the parlour window, where is two large casements, so wide that when open from a large looking glass at the top of the parlour, it appeard all one company, as soon as dinner was over we filld up our glasses, and drank Mr Loyds health and happyness with three huzaes to Beat of drum, in the same manner, Mrs and Miss Loyds, upon which they returd thanks to all their friends, and did them the honour to rejoice on the occasion, and that was a great many. there was sheep rosted, Bells ringing, and Bonny fires all round the neighbour hood, as soon as all the toasts was Drank we whent to the green, which is parted from the common by a sunk fence, upon the common was long tables, set with meat drink &c:c for the lower people, which by the help of a plank we got to, and drank their healths, with loud huzeas. we then returnd upon the green daue'd several dances and then came on a very well dressd set in maskqurade, which they lower company, agreed was the prettyest morice dancers they had ever seen, as soon as the mask whent off, across the plank, scips all the Gentlemen and each took out it his lass, and danc'd a good hour, they then returnd to the House, and took out the Ladys, dancd till ten, then set. out to view the bonfires, some on Hills, some in vallys, and very pretty the lookd, when we came in we all sat down to a very handsom cold supper jenteely set out,. and well got, after being very chearfull for an hour, we set to dance till five, then retired, and the next day after dinner, when the company was going to dance, we took our leave, and set out for Walford, where I am now arrivd, and propose myself as much pleasure in eating old winger Beans with my dear old friends and family as ever I have done Turbet with the inchanting musick of the Welch harp, I beg my best respects to all friends and to morrow hope you will not fail to shake hands with your ever aff Sister

Walford Aug ye 27	E P
[Addressed " Miss Slaney, Shrewsbury."]

QUERIES.

POST-OFFICE LOSSES AT WREXHAM.—I have recently copied from a newspaper of Jan. 16, 1805, the following paragraph :—"A meeting of the principal inhabitants of Wrexham was held last week, in consequence of the recent losses sustained by several tradesmen of that town, remitting bills by the post, which have not been received by their correspondents." If a meeting was called one must suppose the losses were many and serious. Was the loss confined to Wrexham, or did other towns have cause to complain? And was the cause of the irregularity discovered?	H.B.

ALMS HOUSES AT OSWESTRY.—In the *Gents: Mag:* for Feb. 1821, in a "Compendium of Shropshire history," Oswestry is stated to contain Alms-houses erected by William Adams in 1656. What has become of them?

                               FITZ-OSWALD.

REPLIES.

OLD PARR'S PORTRAITS (Mar. 3, 1880).—As a contribution to the list of portraits "H.B." asks for, let me instance the following engravings:—

The picture by Dobson (?) of feeble old man, blind, seated in a large chair; and beneath the inscription "The olde, old, very olde" &c. Published by I. Caulfield, 1794. Demy 8vo. plate.

The same, from Burton's *Admirable Curiosities of Great Britain*, 1811. Demy 8vo. wood.

The same, but without the inscription; published by Allex. Hogg, Paternoster Row, Oct. 1, 1802. Demy 8vo. plate.

The same head, but with the eyes open. "Neele, sc. Strand," small 8vo. lithograph.

The same likeness as that given on the Parr's Life Pill Boxes, with flowing wig, &c. (said to be by Rubens). Engraved by R. Page, no date, demy 8vo. plate.

Then I have seen a portrait of "Young Parr" "sold by I. Herbert, Pall Mall." I think there is one of these hanging in Old Parr's Cottage at Winnington; also one of Old Parr himself, quite different from any I have described above: a wide-awake man apparently in the prime of life. Small 4to.

                               D.

On June 1, 1878, Messrs. Christie sold for 180 guineas a picture of Old Parr by Rubens: Lot 94 of the Novar Collection. It was thus described in the Catalogue :—

     RUBENS, *Portrait of Thomas Parr.* "Old Parr," born 1483, died 1635. 24 in. by 18½ in. Painted when the artist was Ambassador from the Archduchess to King Charles I. See back. From the Collection of Sir Robert Price. Exhibited at the British Institution, 1846.

I did not catch the name of the purchaser. Crosswood.

                         J. H. HEYWARD.

At the North Wales Exhibition, held in Wrexham in 1876, the portrait by Dobson was exhibited by Mr. R. Cholmondeley. Parr is represented as blind, and the inscription "The old, olde," &c., is in a scroll at the top corner, and not underneath as in numerous engravings:—See one in *Bye-gones* in Nov., 1876, from Cassell's *World of Wonders*. Another likeness (artist unknown) was also exhibited by the Earl of Powis, in which Parr is depicted as a vigorous man, staff in hand, crossing the fields.

                         WREXHAMITE.

Sir Baldwyn Leighton, M.P., in a little almanack published in Alberbury parish in 1874, sketched the life of Old Parr, and, in connection with the likeness of him says :—

There are pictures of the old man known to be extant at 'the following places, some of which are duplicates of a picture probably by Dobson. 1. The Ashmolean. 2. The Dresden Gallery. 3. Belvoir Castle. 4. Moor Park, Ludlow. 5. Condover Hall, Salop. 6. Rowton Castle. 7. Loton. Park, Salop. There are prints of some of the portraits by Vosterman, G. White, T. Grainger.

To No. 6 of this list Sir Baldwyn appends the following note :—"This portrait, painted by Vandyke, was originally in the collection of Charles I. Soon after his execution it was sent to Paris with many others of his pictures. It was afterwards brought back to England,

and became, by purchase, the property of the late Earl of Warwick, who presented it to its present owner, Lady Charlotte Lyster." Elsewhere Sir Baldwyn describes this picture as "a half-length of the *school of Vandyke*," and "one of the best likenesses extant." Has this ever been engraved? As regards the so-called portraits by Dobson and Rubens, nothing can be more dissimilar. That by the latter, which it may be assumed was taken when Parr was in London (where he died after a short sojourn) represents him as a particularly wide-awake and hale man; that by Dobson as blind and decrepit!

                         JARCO.

APRIL 21, 1880.

NOTES.

PARLIAMENT OF ENGLAND (Mar. 24, 1880.) From the commencement of the reign of Henry VI. :—

COUNTY OF SALOP.

1422	Hugo Burgh'; Willielmus Boerley.
1423	Ricardus Laken', miles et chivaler; Thomas Corbet de Lye
1425	Willielmus Boerley; Hugo Burgh'
1426	Georgius de Haukeston'; Johannes Brugge'
1427	Willielmus Boerley, de Bromcroft; Willielmus Ludlowe
1429	Ditto; Rogerus Corbet, de Culseys
1431	Ricardus Laken', chivaler; Willielmus Boerley, de Bromcrofte
1432	Willielmus Boerley; Johannes Wynnesbury
1433	Ricardus Laken', miles; Willielmus Boerley
1435	Thomas Corbet, de Morton'; Ditto.
1437	Hugo Cresset; Ditto
1442	Christoforus Talbot, miles; Ditto
1447	Rogerus Corbet; Hugo Cresset
1448	Nicholaus Eyton', armiger; Ricardus Banastre
1449	Willielmus Boerley, de Bromcrofte; Willielmus Laken'
1450	Ditto; Ditto
1453	Johannes Burgh', miles, filius et heres Hugonis Burgh de Watl.........
1455	Willielmus Boerley, de Bromcroft, armiger; Thomas Hourde, armiger
1459	Thomas Hoord', armiger et homo generosus; Thomas Acton', armiger et homo generosus.

BOROUGH OF SHREWSBURY.

1422	Johannes Pearle; Robertus Whitcoumbe
1423	Ditto; Uriauus Sempyer
1425	Rogerus Corbet; Johannes Gamull'
1426	Willielmus Foster; Urianus Semper
1427	Willielmus Boerley, de Salop; Willielmus Horde, de Salop
1429	Ricardus Benteley; Johannes Colle, junior
1431	Willielmus Horde; Robertus Whitcombe
1432	Ditto; Ditto
1433	Ditto; Ditto
1435	Robertus Thornes; Willielmus Bastard'
1437	Thomas Thornes, de Salop'; Willielmus Boerley, de Salop'
1442	Robertus Whitcoumbe; Willielmus Bastard
1447	Thomas Beget; Ditto
1448	Johannes Horde; Ditto
1449	Ditto; Johannes Luyt
1450	Thomas Luyt; Willielmus Bastard'
1453	Thomas.........; ....
1455	Rogerus Eyton,' armiger; Johannes Hourde
1459	Johannes Trentham; Edwardes Esthope

QUERIES.

THE TOWYN VOLUNTEERS.—On the 24th of June, 1795, as I gather from a newspaper of the period, Edward Corbet was appointed captain ; Lewis Edwards, gent., lieutenant ; and Rice Edwards, gent., ensign ; in the Towyn company of Volunteers. In *Bye-gones* of Apr. 2, 1879 (see p. 194 of Reprint), you say "the first movement in Merionethshire to form a little Volunteer army seems to have been in the autumn of 1803." What, then, was this earlier Towyn movement? Was it strangled in the birth, or did it grow awhile ?   G.G.

METHODISM IN OSWESTRY.—I note that on the 25th of June 1820, two sermons were preached in the "Methodist Chapel, Salop Road, Oswestry," by the Rev. Minshall Claxton of Shrewsbury, "Chairman of the district." Was Oswestry in the Shrewsbury 'Circuit' then? Up to a recent period I believe it was allied to Wrexham. Now it is the head of a Circuit itself. I also note that the worshippers fifty years ago called themselves by the good old name of *Methodists*, not 'Wesleyans.'—"The Rev. Mr. Jones, Willow Street," was at that time the Oswestry minister. According to Cathrall's *History of Oswestry*, the Salop Road Chapel was built in 1813. I have been told that previous to its erection the Methodists worshipped in the room now used as a Guildhall, and that a notice was placed at the doors asking the ladies to take off their pattens before entering. When was Methodism established in Oswestry, and by whom? It is pretty certain that John Wesley once preached in the Old Chapel.   JARCO.

REPLIES.

MUTINY AT THE NORE (Mar. 31, 1880).— In reply to the query of "N.W.T.," I am able to say, on the authority of the *Salopian Journal* of the time, that there was some truth in Mr. Kingston's story, only, as is too often the case, the matter is exaggerated. The following is an abstract of the newspaper account :—" June 5, 1797. The King's birthday kept at Ludlow, when amongst other toasts at the dinner was that of the health of the officers and sailors of the St. Fiorenzo. A meeting was held the following day, when a vote of thanks to the crew was passed for carrying help through a mutinous fleet, at the imminent peril of their lives. A sum of £132 8s. was collected, and sent to the captain, Sir Harry B. Neale, for distribution amongst the crew, for so nobly separating that ship from the flag of mutiny." A large sum, truly ; as large, perhaps, as would now-a-days be subscribed for Indian Famine or Irish Distress. UNCLE.

WELSH CONJURERS (Mar. 10, 1880).—Your correspondent will find all that can be said about "Old Savage, the Llangurig Conjurer," in the Folk Lore chapter of Mr. Hamer's papers on the Parochial History of Llangurig, in *Mont: Coll:* (see Vol. 3, p. 266). He was born in 1759, resided at Felin Fawr, and subsequently at Troed-y-lon. He was a small farmer, a herb doctor, and gun-smith, but derived his chief source of income from his more superstitious fellow-mortals, who made pilgrimages to Llangurig from the neighbouring counties for his advice. He prided himself on his skill in discovering stolen goods, and was himself made a victim by some wags, who stole his bacon ! He died in 1849, aged 90, and his wife survived him one year, dying at the age of 85. Both lie buried in Llangurig Churchyard, where a head-stone marks their graves. Mr. Hamer also outlines the history of other conjurors in the district, notably that of a curate "Sir David Llwyd," one of the olden time.
POWYSLANDER,

LLYNCLYS LEGEND (Mar. 31, 1880).—In the preface to the ballad "Llunck Llys," alluded to in Vol. xii. *Mont: Coll:* I find the following passage—"The name in the Welsh signifies Sunk Palace, and the vulgar have a firmly believed superstition (in which this neighbourhood abounds) corresponding with the catastrophe of this ballad." The reference in my paper contributed to the *Mont: Coll:* was simply to show the connection of the ballad with the Ogof Cave upon Llanymynech Hill, and this is stated at p. 404 vol. xii. It is very evident from the poet's preface, erratic though his pen may have been, that the legend which he had heard, and the ballad, are substantially the same. I am inclined to think that the version by Llwyd and the one known by Dovaston were not the same ; the use of the name "Alaric" seems to bear this out, as POWYSLANDER cannot find the name among the Princes of Powis. I gave Llwyd's account to show there was another legend extant, but as it had no reference to the text of the paper it was inserted as a footnote, consequently there was no necessity to add the words "Rex Powisiæ" which are only found as a side note, I presume, in Davies's MSS. account.
Llanymynech.   J. FEWTRELL.

CAPT. ARTHUR WATKIN WILLIAMS-WYNN. (Mar. 31, 1880).—The following extract of a letter relative to the death of the above gallant soldier will be worth preserving with the other records in *Bye-gones*. It is written by the late Miss Charlotte Williams-Wynn, and addressed to "Bn. V. von Ense" :—

On our arrival we were met by the news of the death of my cousin Arthur Williams-Wynn, in that fearful battle. For two others we were also in mourning, though they were not such near relatives. My poor Uncle, Sir Henry, has been quite overwhelmed by his loss—his favourite son, and the one whom he trusted was coming home to marry and live with him ! Every alleviation that the case admitted of they have. The poor (?) boy had a presentiment he should fall, and wrote the day before to take leave of his father and sister, expressing his last wishes. The next evening he was found surrounded by his brother-officers close to the Russian gun, lying sword in hand, the ball having passed through his forehead. He evidently had died instantaneously, and for this exemption from suffering we are most thankful, for the thought of the long agony that the wounded went through is a horrible one. In truth, one never realized before what war is ; *you* all know it well, and our fathers knew it ! I do not think, if I had a dozen brothers there, I could feel more anxiety.
The letter is dated "London, Nov. 1, 1854." The writer had only landed at Dover on the 13th October.
JARCO.

TALHAIARN (Apr. 7, 1880).—Probably your correspondent DUBIOUS was only joking when he assumed the likeness Mr. Roose engraved to have been that of the original *Talhaiarn* who was supposed to exist some centuries ago. You have already published a very interesting memoir of the modern *Talhaiarn* (Ap. 4, 1877), and it was his portrait Roose engraved. I am not going to defend our Welsh Bards in thus adopting names already famous ; and I can conceive how strange such a custom must seem to an Englishman, who would doubtless make merry over any modern poet, clever as he might be, who called himself Spencer, Shakespeare, Jonson, or Milton ; but it must be borne in mind that the bards whose names we adopt did not leave printed volumes behind them, to be read by the masses, so we merely take a name when we call ourselves after the ancients. This, I submit, is a different matter from an Englishman calling himself "Chaucer."   CYMRO.

It was, of course, the modern, not the ancient, *Talhaiarn* the late Mr. Roose painted. He was a surveyor by profession, and in the office of the late Mr. Penson of

Oswestry. By the way, when did the practice first arise for modern Welsh Bards to adopt the names of those of the olden time? All the examples I can call to mind have lived in the present century. Are there any instances where more than one modern poet has appropriated the same name? In the event of such a catastrophe what court would decide the rival claims?　　　N.W.S.

SHROPSHIRE WORDS. (April 7, 1880.)—If Old Oswestry will kindly refer to the Introduction to my *Shropshire Word-Book* (p. xv.), he will see that I have endeavoured to guard against the error of supposing that because words are assigned to certain localities they are therefore only in partial use in the county. I would ask the students of the Glossary to bear in mind the substance of the opening paragraphs of the Introduction, as they give the key to the right understanding of the scheme of the work. I have omitted nothing that I knew, but it has been quite impossible to ascertain the range of a considerable number of the many hundreds of words I have recorded as being used in the county. "Qy. com." leaves the question open. I have done what I could. A note from Far Away in *Bye-gones* shortly after the publication of Pt. I. of the *Shropshire Word-Book*, drawing attention to the fact that the Oswestry district was not so fully represented as some others, called forth a reply from me which was the means of obtaining—through the courtesy of one whom I know only as "A distant Powys-Lander" —a copious list of Oswestry words, many of which will be found in Pt. II., just published. I am extremely obliged to my unknown friends, and I shall be grateful for any further help for the concluding section of my work. I would venture to recommend to those who have copies of my *Word-Book* that they should interleave them for the greater convenience of annotating the text. My labours might be most usefully supplemented by additions and corrections thus made, and when the time comes for the great "English Dialect Dictionary" to be compiled, the work for Shropshire will be found, through such agencies, fairly complete.　　　Georgina F. Jackson.
13, Whitefriars, Chester.

CURRENT NOTES.

Death of Mr. John Robert Kenyon, Q.C.
(From the *Oswestry Advertizer*).

It is with feelings of no little regret that we this week announce the death of Mr. John Robert Kenyon, Q.C., D.C.L., Recorder of Oswestry, and Chairman of the Shropshire Sessions. Mr. Kenyon, as our Oswestry readers will remember, presided at our Quarter Sessions on Friday, the 2nd of April, and, we believe, was only ill a few days—of bronchitis; but the attack was a severe one, and he died on Saturday evening last, at his residence at Pradoe, at the ripe age of seventy-three.

Mr. J. R. Kenyon was born in 1807, and was the third, but oldest surviving son of the late Hon. Thomas Kenyon (who died 1851) by Louisa Charlotte, second daughter of the late Rev. John Robert Lloyd (grandfather of the present Col. Lloyd) of Aston, and grandson of the eminent lawyer, Lord Kenyon. He married, in 1846, Mary Eliza, only daughter of Edward Hawkins, Esq., F.R.S., F.S.A., &c., at that time holding the important position of Keeper of Antiquities in the British Museum. Mr. Kenyon was Vinerian Professor of Law in the University of Oxford, and was formerly Judge and Assessor of the Chancellor's Court in the same University.

Mr. Kenyon was educated at the Charterhouse under Dr. Russell, and afterwards entered at Christ Church,

Oxford, where he took his Bachelor's degree in 1828. In the same year he was chosen a Fellow of All Souls, at which college he took his degrees of B.C.L. and D.C.L. In 1834 he was called to the Bar at the Middle Temple, and in 1862 he was appointed a Queen's Counsel, and was elected a Bencher of his Inn, of which in 1874 he held the Treasurership.

By the Municipal Corporations Act of 1835 we lost our right of holding Quarter Sessions, which we enjoyed under the provisions of our old Charters; and in 1842 this right was restored to the borough, Mr. Kenyon being appointed Recorder; and from that date to the present month, we believe, Mr. Kenyon has never failed to perform his duties in person.

The first Sessions at which Mr. Kenyon presided was held in what was then the Guildhall—an upper chamber of the front Powis Hall—and he was supported on the bench by Mr. Hayward, mayor; Mr. Penson, ex-mayor; his honoured father, the Hon. Thomas Kenyon (under the old regime "Steward" of the borough, and under the new Act one of the first permanent justices), Messrs. H. P. T. Aubrey of Broomhall, T. N. Parker of Sweeney-hall, and John Jones of Brook-street, also permanent justices. There were two cases for trial, in which Mr. N. Minshall, sen., and Mr. J. Jones Thomas appeared as advocates. Mr. Jones, ironmonger, was foreman of the Grand Jury. Now that Mr. Kenyon is dead there is not one left of those we have named, the rest having passed away years ago; and we imagine there are but few left who were in attendance in the court on that occasion.

In 1846 Mr. Kenyon was married, and on Oct. 2 of that year the Corporation and other inhabitants of Oswestry commemorated the event by a presentation to the learned gentleman in the room over the Town Clerk's Offices. The day selected was that of the Quarter Sessions, and at eleven o'clock the Mayor (T. Rogers, Esq.), attended by the Recorder, the Hon. T. Kenyon, the Rev. Orlando Kenyon, and other gentlemen of the town and neighbourhood, entered the room, in which a number of ladies had previously assembled to witness the presentation. The presentation was made by the Mayor, and consisted of a salver of chaste and elegant workmanship, weighing 164 ounces, and measuring across 24 inches. On it was inscribed as follows:—"To John Robert Kenyon, B.C.L., on his marriage, from the Corporation and inhabitants of the town and neighbourhood of Oswestry, in testimony of the respect in which he is held as Recorder of this Borough, and of the grateful feelings entertained for his liberal support of the different charitable institutions connected with the town."

The Hon. Thomas Kenyon occupied the post of Chairman of County Sessions from 1830 to 1850. In 1855 the late Sir B. Leighton was appointed chairman, and Mr. J. R. Kenyon, vice-chairman; and on the death of Sir B. Leighton Mr. J. R. Kenyon was chosen to succeed him. The election took place on Mar. 13, 1871. After passing a just and merited compliment to the memory of Sir Baldwin, Viscount Hill proposed Mr. J. R. Kenyon as his successor, and this was seconded by the Earl of Bradford, and carried unanimously. Thus the two offices, of Chairman of the Quarter Sessions of the County, and of the Borough of Oswestry, have been held by father and son; for the Hon. Thomas Kenyon, as High Steward of the Borough, presided far oftener at our Local Sessions than did the Recorder of that day, the Right Hon. C. W. Williams Wynn.

Though always a kindly man, when first appointed to the office of Judge in our local Court, Mr. Kenyon got the reputation of severity; but of late years all this has passed away, and more than one criminal who has stood in the dock

before him, has received less than he deserved. As a speaker
Mr. Kenyon was undoubtedly somewhat tedious ; but
here, again, we have, during late years, noticed a change :
his charges to the Grand Jury have been much shorter
than formerly, and therefore more interesting. Mr. Kenyon's death will be deplored by a very large circle of
friends in Shropshire, and also in the metropolis, where
he was a contributor to many of the charities. The
learned gentleman leaves a widow and a large family.
His eldest son, Mr. Robert Lloyd Kenyon, was born in
1848.

JACOBITE CORRESPONDENCE IN 1696.

Hampstead, March, 1880.

Among the correspondence and papers of John Ellis,
Under-Secretary of State, from 1695 to 1705, lately in the
hands of Lord Macclesfield, and brought to light by the
Historical Records Commission in 1870, is a thin folio
volume of a hundred pages, consisting of letters written
from abroad, addressed to persons in England, lettered on
the back "Intercepted Jacobite Letters, A.D. 1696." It
consists of two sets of letters, the first from Jacobites
chiefly residing at St. Germain, and the second from nuns
in a convent apparently at Gravelines. Among the former
are five letters relating to the death and will of William
Herbert, first Marquis of Powis, who died at St. Germain,
June 2nd, 1696. The first of these letters is merely a short
note, dated Nov. 21st, 1696, unsigned, but written by
John Daniel, a servant of Lord Powis, to the eldest
daughter of his master, Mary, second wife of Francis
Browne, fourth Viscount Montagu, of Cowdray, near Mid-
hurst, in Sussex, and begging her to give the enclosed
letters to her brother, William Herbert, Viscount Montgomery, afterwards second Marquis of Powis, whom he
calls by the pseudonym of Mr. William Sibson. The
envelope bears the private seal of Queen Mary Beatrice,
wife of James II. The second letter is from the same J.
Daniel to his young master, of the same date as No. 1, and
addressed to Mr. Sibson. It speaks of the viscount's ill
health and of the late marquis as Mr. Lucas, and ends by
an allusion to his youngest sister, Lady Lucy Herbert, a
nun at Bruges. The third epistle is a holograph one, but
unsigned, from Queen Mary Beatrice herself to Lord
Montgomery, and, having never been published, is of great
interest. It is as follows :—

Nou : the 14.

It has not been without a great deel of constraint to myself
that i haue thus long forboren writting to you. Nothing but
the fear of doing you harme could haue kept me from doing it,
at a time, when nor then euer you deserue it of me and that indeed should keep me still : but "that" hearing that seuerall l'rs
haue gott safe to you this way, i do hope this will haue the
same good fortune, and therfor i uenture to tell you, that my
partner and i haue been, and are still in the greatest concerne
imaginable for your sickness, and tho wee are in hopes that the
remedys you take, will keep you out of danger, yett wee can not
be at ease, nor free from fears, when wee think of your condition, nor is ther anything wee would not do to mend it, wee haue
also shared with you in the losse of your father, in whom my
partner has lost a most honest zealous seruant and i a most
faithfull friend ; i haue seen with som trouble a l're from you
upon this subiect, in which you seem to beleeue that you haue
been forgott and euen iniured in your affaires hear, but i hope
that has been only a flying thought, for if otherways i must call
it a wrong iudgment and you will find it so, when you are truly
informed of all that has passt, which no man can do so well as
your father's ghostly father, which is the same that my partner
has, and who's word upon whom you may take, i haue therfor
desired him to giue you an account of what matters of fact he
knows and the rest will be giuen you by others next post. i send
his l're enclosed with this, and i hope it will gett safe to you, in
the meane time i coniure you to beleeue, that wherouer i am i shall
suffer no w,ong to be don to you, but shall euer procure you all
the good i can, as to the personal estate your father left it is all

in the hands you desired it should be kept whicch my partner
and i had ordered euen befor wee heard you desired it, excepting a few things your sister has borrowed to make use of in the
conuent wher she now liues, whicch i am sure you would not
haue refused her had you been hear yourself, and the twoo wills
are in the ghostly father's bands as yeur father himself desired,
wher i can assure you, they are as safe, as in your owne ; i haue
taken the peines to enter in this detaille, to remooue any
iealousy that you might haue had of your friends hear, whicch i
think are all uery trew and sincere to you ; i am sure i can
answer for myself, that i haue all the esteem, and friendship for
you that you can desire, and that you haue so well deserued
from me, i can answer as much for my partner. i putt this note
in the long l're, and seale with the little seale that i beleeue you
will remember.

The fourth letter, addressed to Mr. Sibson, and dated
Nov. 14th, 1696, is signed "ff. Long." It appears to be
from the father confessor of James II. to Lord Montgomery. It consists wholly of a vindication of his conduct with regard to the will of Lord Powis and its dispositions in favour of Lady Lucy Herbert, his youngest
daughter, the nun at Bruges. The fifth and last of the enclosures, dated Nov. 16th and unsigned, but written by
Mrs. Grif, housekeeper to the late marquis, has no address, but is evidently intended for Lord Montgomery.
It informs him that she had allowed his last letter to be
read by the ex-queen and her husband, who had read it to
their father confessor, and that the said father confessed
he had the marquis's two wills, and would furnish copies
for her to send. She then proceeds to give him a brief
inventory of the plate, jewels, household linen, and books
left by his father, and furnishes him with an account of
his father's last illness and place of burial, and his desire
to see his heir. The present condition of his domestics is
alluded to, and the wish of James II. that the young lord
should visit him ; and the letter concludes with the account of the sums of money left to the Church by his
father for the repose of his soul. The second set of letters
spoken of above, viz., those from nuns at Gravelines to
their relations in England, give details of their daily life
and pursuits, and are especially interesting for their allusions to the confessional and their father confessors.
—*Athenæum.* EDWARD SCOTT.

VOLUNTEER ARMY OF 1803-4.

THE *MONTGOMERYSHIRE COLLECTIONS* OF
THE POWYS-LAND CLUB.

Notwithstanding the Powys-land Club has been in
existence a dozen years, Mr. Morris Charles Jones, the
able secretary and editor, manages not only to fill a goodly
volume of nearly 500 pages every year, but, in some res-
peets, offers to subscribers matter of greater variety as the
work advances with age. When the Club was established
many were the prognostications that half-a-dozen years, at
most, would be its duration ; by that time the Montgomeryshire mine would be exhausted, and the Company
would be wound up. Instead of which now lodes are
being continually tapped, and so far the prospect of ex-
haustion seems very remote.

The first part of Vol. 13, which has recently been issued,
opens with a paper by Mr. Charles Williams-Wynn, on
the Rise and Progress of the Voluntcers in Montgomeryshire, early in the century, when the alarm of a French
Invasion was so great that almost every able-bodied man
was in some shape a soldier ! The readers of the *Collections* have already been told (Vol. 11., p. 273), how
during a similar panic in 1798, Montgomeryshire Patriotism
subscribed vast sums, in common with the rest of the
nation, for the defence of our shores. In the present
paper Mr. Wynn begins with 1803, and confines his nar-

rative to the results of the martial notes of the fife and drum, and the marchings and countermarchings of the amateur soldiery. In some of the issues of *Bye-gones* we have given the names of officers connected with the volunteer regiments of other counties at the same period; and as our sources of information have been different from Mr. Wynn's, it will be no harm here to copy from them some of the statistics connected with Montgomeryshire. In a Return made in December, 1803, the "Montgomery-shire Legion" is stated to have consisted of 1,560 infantry and 120 cavalry. A much larger number volunteered, but only this number was accepted. The following is the War Office Return of Officers, dated October 1804. Mr. Charles Watkin Williams Wynn (the father of the present Mr. C. Wynn) commanded the whole force; but the colonels were attached to the yeomanry and the majors to the infantry:—

MONTGOMERY LEGION.

Lt. Col. Commandant : Charles W. W. Wynne—2 Nov. 1803.

Lt. Cols.: Charles Hanbury Tracy, John Edwards—2 Nov. 1803.

Majors : John Winder, John Humphreys, Price Jones— 2 Nov. 1803.

Cavalry.

Captains : Arthur David Owens, John Williams—2 Nov. 1803 ; John Price—24 Nov. 1803.

Lieutenants : Matthew Jones, Richard Price, Edward Farmer—2 Nov. 1803.

Cornets : John Meredith Williams, John Williams, Arthur David Jones—2 Nov. 1803.

Chaplain : Edward Jones—2 Nov. 1803.

Adjutant : Francis Deakin—2 Nov. 1803.

Surgeon : William Owen—24 Jan. 1804.

Infantry.

Captains : Thomas Colley, John Davies, John Owen Herbert, Thomas Jones, Humphrey Rowland Jones, Maurice Jones, Thomas Kinsey, David Lloyd, Maurice Lloyd, Thomas Edward Marsh, John Morris, Edward Price, Evan Stephens, Christopher Temple, John Williams, William Williams—2 Nov. 1803; John Davies—24 Nov. 1803 ; Robert Price, John Jones, Richard Mytton—3 Jan. 1804.

Lieutenants : Edward Baugh, Leonard Baugh, George Colley, Edward Evans, David Evans, George Gould, Lewis Griffiths, James Hamer, John Hill, William Hughes, William Jones, Thomas Marsh, Edward Morgan, Edward Pritchard, Lewis Vaughan, Edward Wilson—2 Nov. 1803 ; Christopher Brees Hall, Richard Lloyd—3 Jan. 1804 ; Devereux Mytton—19 Jan. 1804.

Ensigns : Francis Allen, John Asterley, Edward Baugh, Joseph Davies, Thomas Lloyd Dicken, Maurice Evans, William Howell, Thomas Hughes, William Hughes, Thomas Jones (adjutant), Hugh Owen, Edward Powell, John Stephens, William Tilsley, George Williams—2 Nov. 1803 ; Matthew Powell, John Brees, Henry Evans—3 Jan. 1804 ; John Jones—19 May, 1804.

Chaplain : Evan Jones—2 Nov. 1803.

Adjutants : Richard Farmer—24 Jan. 1804 ; Thomas Jones.

Surgeons :—Edward Jones, John Ford—24 Jan. 1804.

The dates given after the foregoing names relate to the time the respective officers were gazetted. From other sources we are able to add one or two more whose names appear on earlier, and unofficial lists. Thus in Jan., 1804, there was William Browne, (omitted by Mr. Wynn), lieut. of infantry ; and the name of Thomas Jones appears as fellow-surgeon with Ford. John Jones, who figures as a captain in the official list, was previously a lieutenant,

and took the place of Mr. Mytton, who resigned. At the same time (May 1804) Ensign Richard Lloyd was promoted to the rank of lieutenant vice Thomas Jones, who became adjutant.

From a Diagram published in 1806 we find the total strength of the force at that period set down at 1,743. In the *Cambrian Quarterly Magazine* for Jan., 1829, we are told that on the 17th of the previous October ; "The Montgomeryshire Volunteer Cavalry assembled at head quarters, Welsh Pool, previous to their final disbandment." (Mr. Charles Wynn states that as far back as 1808 the Infantry had been transferred to the Militia.) The Magazine we quote goes on to say that on the occasion of the disbandment of the cavalry, "The Right Hon. C. W. Williams Wynn, colonel of the regiment, gave a farewell dinner to the corps. Lord Clive (Colonel of the Ludlow Yeomanry) (1) together with the resident officers of the Montgomeryshire Militia, honoured the assembly with their company. The long room in the Town Hall was completely filled. In addition to the noble baron of beef of Old England, was to be seen our own native delicacies, not forgetting the *gwyniad* and giant pike of Llyn tegid. The Right Honourable gentleman, after commanding twenty-five years, took leave of his Yeomanry in a very emphatic speech."

This was in 1828 : during the spring of 1831 the regiment was resuscitated, as the following "Commissions signed by the Lord Lieutenant of the County of Montgomery" will show :—

MONTGOMERYSHIRE YEOMANRY CAVALRY.

Lt. Col. Commandant : C. W. W. Wynn, esq.

Major : David Pugh, esq.

Captains : Henry Adolphus Proctor, Pryce Buckley Williames, John Davies Corrie, Robert Bonnor Maurice, esquires.

Lieutenants : Edward Williames, Thomas Beck, David Hamer, gents.

Cornets : Edward Conroy, John Buckley Williames, jun. Evan Stephens, John Robinson Jones, gents.

Paymaster : Richard Griffithes, esq.

Chaplain : (Rev.) Richard John Davies.

Surgeon : Maurice Lloyd Jones, gent.

Veterinary-Surgeon : John Gwyn, gent.

The Right Hon. Charles Wynn finally retired from the command in 1844, and was succeeded by Sir Watkin, who in 1877 resigned in consequence of ill-health. Mr. Charles Wynn the writer of the paper in *Mont. Coll.*, who was major at that period, then assumed the command, and retained it until relieved of the duties, in 1878, by Sir W. G. Williams, Bart.

Further notice of this interesting instalment of *Mont. Coll.* we must leave until another week, when we hope to call attention, also, to the contents of the new number of the *Transactions* of the sister society, the "Shropshire Archæological."

THE NEW LORD TREVOR.

Lord Arthur Edwin Hill-Trevor of Brynkinallt, who represented County Down as a Conservative up to the dissolution of Parliament in March, has been called to the Upper House under the title of Baron Trevor.

It was only two or three weeks ago that we recorded the death of the Viscountess Dungannon, widow of the 3rd

(1) On Oct. 5, 1804, "Two elegant standards and a pair of colours" were presented to the Ludlow and Bishop's Castle Yeomanry Cavalry, and the Ludlow and Cleobury Loyal Volunteers, by Lady Powis and her daughters Ladies Charlotte and Harriet Clive.

Viscount, who was well known to many of our readers. The late Lord Dungannon died in 1862, and was succeeded at Brynkinallt by Lord Arthur Edwin Hill-Trevor, the new peer, third son of Arthur, third Marquis of Downshire.

The common ancestor of the Marquis of Downshire and the late Viscount Dungannon was Michael Hill, Esq., of Hillsborough, Ireland, who succeeded to the estates in 1693, and married Ann, daughter and co-heir of Sir John Trevor of Brynkinallt, Master of the Rolls in England, Speaker of the House of Commons, and First Lord-Commissioner of the Great Seal. Mr. Michael Hill had two sons, Trevor, who succeeded him at Hillsborough, and whose son was created Marquis of Downshire, and was the great-grandfather of the new Lord Trevor; and Arthur, who, succeeding to the estates of his maternal grandfather, was created Viscount Dungannon, and was great-grandfather of the late Viscount.

According to Burke the family is of Norman extraction and was originally called De la Montagne. By the reign of Edward III. the name had been anglicized and the members of the family were called Hill alias De la Montagne; and in succeeding ages the Hill alone was retained. Sir Moyses Hill, Knight, went over to Ireland as a military officer with the Earl of Essex in 1573, to suppress O'Neil's rebellion, and was subsequently appointed governor of Alderfleet Castle. He represented the County of Antrim in Parliament in 1613, and was the great grandfather of the Michael Hill already mentioned.

Lord Arthur Edwin Hill-Trevor is the third son of Arthur third Marquis of Downshire, by his union with Lady Maria Windsor, eldest daughter of the fifth Earl of Plymouth. He was born in November, 1819, and educated at Eton and at Balliol College, Oxford, where he graduated B.A. in 1841. He was appointed lieut.-colonel of the South Down Militia in 1845, lieutenant in the South Notts Yeomanry cavalry in 1848, and major in the North Salop Yeomanry cavalry in 1863. He is a justice of the peace, and deputy-lieutenant for the counties of Denbigh, Down, Notts, and Salop, patron of three livings, and was for some time a gentleman of the bedchamber to the Lord-Lieutenant of Ireland, but resigned that office in 1845. The new peer represented the county of Down from April, 1845, till the late dissolution, and assumed the name of Trevor on succeeding to the estates of Lord Dungannon in 1867. He has been twice married—firstly, in 1848 to Mary Emily, eldest daughter of the late Sir Richard Sutton, Bart., she dying in 1855; secondly, in 1858, to the Hon. Mary Catherine, youngest daughter of the late Hon. and Rev. Alfred Curzon, and sister to the fourth Lord Scarsdale. The heir to the title is the Hon. Arthur William Hill-Trevor, only son by his first wife, who was born in November, 1852, and entered the 1st Life Guards in 1875.

BARON ROWTON OF ROWTON CASTLE.

Mr. Montagu Corry, Lord Beaconsfield's private secretary, has been elevated to the peerage as Baron Rowton, of Rowton Castle, in the county of Salop. Mr. Montagu William Lowry-Corry, C.B., is the younger son of the late Right Hon. Henry Thomas Lowry-Corry, many years M.P. for county Tyrone, and some time First Lord of the Admiralty, by his marriage with Lady Harriet Anne Ashley-Cooper, second daughter of Cropley, sixth Earl of Shaftesbury, and nephew of Lady Charlotte Barbara Lyster of Rowton Castle, Alberbury, Shrewsbury. He was born in October, 1838, and was educated at Trinity College, Cambridge, where he took his Bachelor's degree

in 1861. He was called to the Bar at Lincoln's inn in Trinity Term, 1863, and joined the Oxford Circuit. Having held for some years a clerkship in the Treasury, in 1873 he was appointed private secretary to the Prime Minister, Lord Beaconsfield, whom he accompanied on his mission to the Congress at Berlin in 1878, as acting secretary of Embassy. Mr. Montagu Corry, who is a deputy-lieutenant for the county of Salop, was nominated a Companion of the Order of the Bath, in reward for his diplomatic services abroad, in 1878. He is unmarried.

BARON WIMBORNE.

Sir Ivor Bertie Guest., Bart., of Dowlais, Glamorgan, of Canford Manor, Wimborne, Dorset, and of Auchnashellach, Ross-shire, who will be made Baron Wimborne, is the great grandson of Mr. John Guest, who migrated from Shropshire in the first half of the 18th century, and established the Dowlais Iron Works, now the oldest and most extensive in South Wales. His father, Sir Josiah John Guest, the first Baronet, first sat for the borough of Honiton, and subsequently represented Merthyr Tydvil for twenty years—viz., from the date of its enfranchisement to that of his death in 1852. On the female side he is descended from the Baroness Willoughby de Eresby and the Earls of Lindsey through his mother, the Lady Charlotte Elizabeth Bertie, daughter of Albemarle, 9th Earl of Lindsey, and sister of the present peer. Besides being the sole proprietor of the Dowlais Iron Works, Sir Ivor owns large landed estates in England, Scotland, and Wales. He was born in 1835, and educated at Harrow and at Trinity Coll-ge, Cambridge, where he took his M.A. degree in 1856, having already succeeded his father as second baronet in 1852. He is a deputy-lieutenant and a magistrate for Dorsetshire; a magistrate for Glamorganshire, of which county he was High Sheriff in 1862; an officer of the Dorsetshire Yeomanry Cavalry from 1850 to 1867; and patron of seven livings in Monmouthshire, Glamorganshire, and Dorsetshire. The new peer, who married in 1868 the Lady Cornelia Henrietta Maria Spencer Churchill, eldest daughter of the sixth Duke of Marlborough, unsuccessfully contested Glamorganshire in the Conservative interest in February, 1874; Poole, May of the same year, when he was defeated by the narrow majority of nine; and Bristol in 1878, and again at the present general election. The heir to the peerage is his eldest son, Ivor Churchill Guest, who was born in January, 1873.

APRIL 28, 1880.

NOTES.

FLINTSHIRE TOKENS.—Minshull the Printer, a well-known character in Oswestry half a century ago, at one period of his erratic career attended the services at the Old Chapel in Street Arthur. On one occasion he put on the collecting plate twelve Flintshire pennies wrapped up in a piece of paper, on which was written —

"These Flints are better than hard stones,
For they will pass with Thomas Jones;
Excuse such cash, for I've a store
That fills a pot, and something more."

Mr. Thomas Jones ("of Siamber Garreg," as he was called to distinguish him from other Joueses) was a grocer, and his shop, at the bottom of Willow Street, was the last place in Oswestry at which these Tokens were current.
JARCO.

THE FIRST SIR WATKIN (Feb. 18, 1880.)—
On Feb. 15, 1745, at the annual meeting of the Inde-
pendent Electors of Westminster, Sir Watkin Williams
Wynn was chosen one of the stewards for the succeeding
year. Amongst the toasts were "Great Britain un-
Germaniz'd"; "That the Fleet of England may be the
Terror of Europe;" "To the re-establishment of publick
confidence, by a speedy punishment of publick offenders;"
"That German measures may never get the better of
English liberty," &c., &c.　　　　　　　　　　　　H.B.

SOME OLD SALOPIAN LETTERS.

A hundred and twenty-five years ago, Samuel Savage
(a descendant of Philip Henry's), finding himself "prettily
fixt" in Chiswell-street as a glover, bestowed his affections
on a relative, one Sarah Roe, then visiting in London, and
who came from that part of Shropshire which would
doubtless be well known to Mr. Savage as the district in
which his distinguished Nonconformist ancestor had lived
and laboured. Miss Roe's affections, most likely, had
already been given to the London tradesman, but her
hand was, very properly, subject to her father's approval;
so to the father the lover wrote, and this was his
letter :—

"Coz Roe. S'r haveing had ye Pleasure of your
Daughters company—has created in me a Vast Esteem for
Her. But notwithstanding that great regard am not
willing to Pay any further Respects without your consent
or approbation. As being now Prettily fixt in Business
& well assured its in my Power to maintane Her
handsomely for tho I have not been long at House keeping
yet I have done Business for myself some Time so yt I
am fully satisfyed it will answer.——It may Perhaps be
thought Vanity in me to [ask that] you should Immediately
give Consent to my request. But excuse me S'r if I
tell you the Industrous Honest Man as I hope I may call
myself is Esteem'd here prefferable to ye man of Fortune
that is not Indefatigable in Trade & give me leave to
add that other Gentlemen have readily Consented &
thought there Children & Fortunes wellbestow'd on my
Brother who have had No better a Beginning then I Na
even Brother Rich'd has already had three Hundred
Pounds with his wife & a Promis of a good Dele more.—
Coz Sally is now at Mrs. Hamonds of Hackney is very
well and desires her Duty to you both hopeing you'll
write soon & excuse this liberty taken by your Affectionate
kinsman & Hu'ble Serv't　　　　　　" SAML. SAVAGE."
" S'r. if you and Please you may direct to me Glover in
Chiswell Street London Sept. 25, 1753
" Please to favour me with Suitable Compliment to your
Spouse"

This latter was duly addressed "To Mr. Roe, Tallow
Chandler, Whitchurch, Shropshire," and I presume, very
speedily elicited a favourable answer, for three years later
we find Miss Molly Roe of Whitchurch visiting her
married sister in Chiswell Street, who by that time had
become a happy mother. All this is to be gathered from
the following letter addressed by Mrs. Roe of Whitchurch
to "Miss Moly Roe, London :"—

"Whitchurch, November ye 24, 1756
"Dear Child. wee rec'd yours with pleasure & have
sent you a paire of Stocking & your Sister nancy will knit
you another pair as quick as shee can. I have sent you my
blue silk gown with linlia(sic) to line it you may have it
maid up when your sister thinks proper and besure you have
it maid as large as you can, as you are growing fast if your
bit of Lace is too little for a mob you send it in a franck
sum time yt I may may mack it for you—but my
Dear Child bee not proud of your Clothes for
God vexeth ye proud but giveth Grace to ye Humble—

bee strickly just as you will awnser att ye great day & as
strickly modest is to flee from ye aperances of evell
rembering yt a yong womans carickter is as a piece of
righting paper, yt one blot makes a great aperince on it
—remember ye Sabothday to keep it Holy—& strive to
excell in evry good qality & then may you hope for a
Blesing from God wich is beter then great riches—endever
to be as usfull as you can to your sister & very careful
of ye Baby—bee delegent all waye to impruve your time
to ye best I have not forgot ye hamoek quilt but as ye
nights are could thought ye baby wold ly with mam'ma &
when ye days are longer can make it up beter— I have
found a bit of ye same as your work caleco when it is
made whiter will make pleats for ye back of it—pray my
best compliments to Mr. & Mrs. Persell (qy.) & ten
thousand thanks for all favors to mee & expeshall those
theay bestow on your sister. . . . . . if done to my
self—my complements to Mrs. Savage wishing her a happy
moment if shee hath not had it— my comp'm to mr.
Savage'is— & Mr. Harles—Mrs. Alioge (qy.) desire her
kind love to you & your sister & wishing her much comfort of ye baby. Mr. William Alige (qy.) has sent your
sister a pair of tea toungs of his one making—Your
Father & I Humbly Des'r yt God allmightey wold Bless
& presev you from all Hurt & harm. I remain your
affekshnate mother　　　　　　　　　" SARAH ROE."

"Your sisters desire theire love to you. When you right
next to us [send] a letter to your Grandmother who desire
her kind love to you & Blessing "

Readers of this must not be prejudiced against Mrs. Roe
on account of her bad spelling. As late as Dr. Johnson's
time it was notorious that even ladies of quality and title
were but imperfectly educated. It will be noted that the
mother speaks of Molly as a growing girl, but the next
letter, from the father "Richard Roe of Whitchurch," to
"Miss Molly Roe, att Mr. Savages in Chiswell Street,
London," written six years later, shews that the young
lady at that period considered herself no longer a child ;
for she wants to be married, and in answer to her application for her father's approval, gets the following sensible
letter :—

"Daughter Mary I rc'd a Letter from you last Saturday but am at a loss what answer to make to it, Son Savage
told me of a marraige like to be betwixt you & Mr.
Mathew Whitton & further said as I take it his Father
and Mr. Crane would let him have two Hundred pounds
he paying the interest for his Father & mothers life but
to Return a part of it Back at their Death, but how much
I am not Certain, & as it is not like te be without
interest untill their Death I think it ought to be made sure
how much of it he must have then, and that would
be ameans to prevent uneasyness hereafter, upon ye above
I think I told him what I intended to do as I heard he
had a very good charecter and like to behave well, but in
my oppinion it is too soon for you to think of marrying
yet, however as you have been always very good and dis-
creet & think of a very great prospect your Brother being
so good to lett you come in partners in Trade, I leave it
to your own judgement praying God to direct you for the
Best. I sent ye paper parcill to Chester as directed, tell
your Brother I shall send to Namptwich Directly about
ye Bill it being due now, My Love & Blessing to your
Brother, Sisters your self & their children, & am your
affectionate Father
　　　　　　　　　　　　　　　　　" RICH'D ROE"
"Whitechurch June ye 16, 1762."

Let us hope Molly was happily married, and that her
husband permanently retained a goodly portion of the Two-
hundred pounds.　　　　　　　　　　　　　　　　J.?.R.

OSWESTRY SCHOOL ENTERTAINMENTS.—
The young gentlemen of Oswestry School now-a-day give
Concerts—and very pleasant Concerts they are. Do any
of the older Oswestrians remember "The *Andria* of
Terence performed by the Scholars of Oswestry School
before a numerous assembly" in Dec. 1837? The *cast* included "Messrs. Bartley, Archer, Turner, Roberts,
Nicholls, Moore, Vesey, and Parry." Have any of these
"old boys" made names for themselves in the theatre of
life?   JARCO.

RICHARD PRYCE OF TREWYLLAN.—This
Montgomeryshire worthy and J.P. for the county during
the reign of Queen Anne, is said to have had such a respect for her Majesty that he desired to be buried as near
her effigy in St. Paul's Churchyard as possible, "which
was done." At least, so says the *Gents: Mag.* Was Mr.
Pryce in any way noted? Talking about this same effigy;
where is it stated that Her Majesty has her back to the
church and her eye on a gin shop?   LUD.

THE LIVING OF MORTON.—I was once told
by an old lady that formerly there was a board in Morton
Church which stated that there was a living at that place
for a single man as long as the sun shone and water ran;
by which she inferred that no married man would be happy
as the clergyman. There is generally some foundation for
old wives' tales; what is the origin of this?   NEMO.

SHROPSHIRE WORDS (Apr. 21, 1880).—Miss
JACKSON must not suppose I wrote in any carping spirit;
for I think her work is performed most admirably. I am
not a subscriber to it myself, but have had the opportunity
of seeing the two parts whilst on a visit to a friend. All
I wished to convey was the fact that certain words given
as being in use in certain localities are (or used to be in
my time) known in the Oswestry district; and that many
of the words placed to the credit of certain localities, with
"Qy. Com." attached to them, were also used in the
Oswestry district. I submit that no perusal of the
"Introduction" will alter this fact; and it is one I would
suggest that those should "make a note of" who adopt
Miss JACKSON's very sensible recommendation of inter-
leaving their copies of the *Word Book.* Such notes as
mine, I take it, will help to make those leaves more than
blank paper. Miss J. asks for the very information I
have given when she writes "Qy. Com."
                                             OLD OSWESTRY.

LLYNCLYS LEGEND (Apr. 21, 1880).—Mr.
FEWTRELL may, of course, be right, but I much question
whether there were ever two legends of Llynclys. The
connection of the lake with the ogof was, doubtless,
wholly Mr. Dovaston's fancy. And if "Rex Powisiæ"
is merely a supposition of Davies's (which, by the way, it
is not) what princes but those of Powys had possession of
the palace supposed to have sunk into a bottomless pit?
I fancy Mr. FEWTRELL will find a difficulty in tracing
Mr. Dovaston's clever story to an earlier period than
the publication of Mr. Dovaston's rhymes, recent as that
is!   POWYSLANDER.

"Alaric" was doubtless entirely a creation of
Dovaston's; as was the story of the lady who renewed her
youth in her weekly interviews with the devil. His in-
ventive genius merely attempted to weave together the
remarkable stone at "Croeswylan;" the lake "Llynclys"
and the "Ogof;" a thing nobody had ever done before.
Such a tradition was never current; any more than was

the lively one from the same pen, about the devil's doings
with the Breidden! I have not seen the periodical in
which your correspondent's contribution has appeared;
but I am not surprised to see his statement challenged.
                                                      T.O.D.

Allow me to call Mr. FEWTRELL's attention to the
fact that the late Mr. Dovaston did not himself attempt
to make his readers suppose that his "Llunck-Llys" ballad
was anything more than a fancy of his own, put on paper
hastily, to amuse a fishing party. He says in his introduction that "the vulgar have a firmly-believed
superstition . . . *corresponding with the catastrophe of
the ballad.*" I remember the lake before the ballad was
published; and all the common people said was that there
was no bottom to it, and that in fine weather the chimneys
of a palace were to be seen in its depths. For the
Tradition we must look to a far older source; viz., Llwyd.
                                             OLD OSWESTRY.

THE NEW RECORDER OF OSWESTRY.
Mr. Charles Watkin Williams-Wynn has been appointed Recorder of Oswestry in the room of John Robert
Kenyon, Esq., Q.C., deceased.
We are not quite sure when Oswestry first enjoyed the
privileges of a Court of its own. Mr. Stanley Leighton,
M.P., in the *Journal* of the Sh. Arch: Society has given
the text of a Charter granted by Henry the Fourth in
which it was provided that "Cases within the borough
should be tried before the Steward and Bailiffs;" and in
the reign of Elizabeth a "Book of Constitutions" expressly mentions a Borough Court, a deputy-steward,
learned in the law, and four attorneys to practise in the
town court.
In the Charter granted by James the First, in 1617, a
Recorder is named—Sir H. Towneshend—who, with the
Steward and Bailiffs, were to have "authority to enquire
into all manner of felonyes, murders, homicides, poyson-
yngs, inchantments, witchcraft, arte magick, trespasses,
forestallers, regrators, ingrossers, and extortions whatever" within the borough; and their Court of Record
was to be held weekly. Under the same Charter Burgesses
of Oswestry were exempt from sitting on juries beyond
the limits of the Borough. The same privileges were renewed by the Charter of Charles the Second, in 1674;
and it was under that Charter that the Rt. Hon. C. W.
Williams-Wynn acted up to the passing of the Municipal
Corporations Act in 1834.
Mr. C. W. Williams-Wynn, our new Recorder, will, we
believe, be the third of the family who has held the office.
Robert Williams, Esq., the Recorder, who died in 1763, was
a brother of the first Sir Watkin Williams-Wynn, and
the second son of Sir William Williams of Llanvorda;
and he was also M.P. for Montgomeryshire. When the
Rt. Hon. C. W. Williams-Wynn was appointed we are
not sure, but as early as 1809 a very handsome service of
plate was presented to him by the Corporation of Oswestry,
accompanied by the thanks of that body for "voting independently in the case of the late Duke of York, period than
his strict attention to parliamentary duties."
Amongst others who have held the office of Recorder
between the years 1635 and 1764, the names are preserved
of John Davies of Middleton (who wrote a history of the
Borough), Morgan Wynne, Thomas Powell, Robert Williams, and Richard Hill Waring of the Hays.
Mr. Charles Watkin Williams-Wynn, now appointed, is
the only surviving son of the late Rt. Hon. C. W. Williams-
Wynn, M.P., by Mary, eldest daughter of the late Sir
Foster Cunliffe, Bart. He was born in 1822, and in 1853

married the Lady Annora Charlotte, younger daughter of Charles, second Earl Manvers. He was educated at Westminster· and Christ Church, Oxford (B.A. 1843; M.A. 1845). Mr. Wynn was for many years attached to the Montgomeryshire Yeomanry Cavalry, and resigned his appointment of Commander in 1878. He sat for the County of Montgomery in Parliament from 1862 to 1880, and is Deputy-Chairman of the Quarter Sessions of that County.

CONGREGATIONALISM AT WELSHPOOL.

The Independents of Welshpool during the past week have been celebrating their centenary. In the days when a Church of Nonconformists was first formed in that town it would appear that there, as elsewhere in the district, Oswestry was the centre of operations, and the Rev. Edward Williams (afterwards Dr. Williams) was the "Bishop!" From 1777 to 1792 he was minister of the Old Chapel, Oswestry, and at the head of a Nonconformist "Academy" (as it was then called), for the training of Congregational Ministers; and by means of his students he was able to set going and keep alive small Nonconformist Churches that otherwise would scarcely have existed at so early a period. Welshpool was one of these; and in the same county Aberhafesp was another; whilst on the other side of the border may be mentioned Ellesmere and Ruyton-of-the-Eleven Towns. Documents are still preserved amongst the muniments of the Old Chapel, Oswestry, which indicate this, and one, (as follows) was published in the *Montgomeryshire Collections* of the Powysland Club, in 1878 :—

"To the right Rev'd Father in God, Jonathan, Lord Bishop of St. Asaph :—
"WE whose names are hereunto subscribed being Protestant Dissenters called Presbyterians, do hereby certify to your Lordship that a New erected Chapel in the Town of Welshpool in the above said Diocess is intended to be a place of Meeting for religious Worship. Therefore We require that this our Certificate may be recorded at your Court according to an Act of Parliament in that case made and provided in the Reign of King William and Queen Mary, called the Toleration Act.
"July the 11, 1783, signed by us,
"John James, minister
"Bonner Hughes
"Heth Hughes
"Edward Morris
"Edward Hughes
"Joseph Jones."

"Entered and recorded amongst the Archives in the publick episcopal Registry of Saint Asaph pursuant to an Act of Parliam't in this case made and provided. The 30th of July 1783 "by John Jones, Dep: Reg'r."

In this document the people call themselves "Presbyterians ;"—that, we believe, was a common name at the period, and scarcely meant more than that there was an association of ministers for counsel and assistance. In a MS. history of the Old Chapel at Oswestry, written by the Rev. William Reeve, who was minister there 1836-43, it is stated that it was probably when Dr. Williams was the minister that "the church assumed the Independent, or Congregational form of Government." Earlier than this, Nonconformists on the borders were pretty generally called merely "Protestant Dissenters," occasionally Presbyterian or Independent being added.

A few years later than the period to which we have been referring the Welshpool Nonconformists performed an act that proved they were "Independents" in their form of government; for they invited a minister to preside over their church, without the action of any Board or Presbytery. A letter is preserved amongst the papers belonging to the Independent Chapel at Sarney, written

by the Rev. J. Griffiths from Abergavenny, in 1787, in which the following passage occurs :—"I find that the people at Welsh Pool are still without a minister, and they have writ a Call to me to come among them, promising to subscribe thirty pounds; but I cannot comply with their wishes at this time." This letter was addressed "Mr. Edward Ashley, near New Chapel, to be left at Mr. Thos. Evans, mercer, Welsh Pool, Montgomeryshire." Mr. Griffiths had previously been an Independent Minister at Llanfyllin, and, at the same time, at Sarney. What the Welshpool Independents or Presbyterians did between the years 1787 and 1794 we cannot say. We write all this without reference to the proceedings at the Centenary services recently held ; the report of which has not yet reached us : but in 1794, as we gather from *Mont : Coll :* 1878, p. 8, and elsewhere that Mr. Thomas Evans, and Grace, his wife (whose maiden name was Sugden), with six others, signed a memorandum in the Minute Book of the Chapel (19 Dec. 1794), forming themselves into a "Church on the Independent plan" ; the "Thomas Evans" mentioned being, we presume, the same as the one to whose care the letter of Mr. Griffiths was addressed in 1787. There is a tablet to his memory in the chapel at Welshpool ; and some of our older Oswestry readers may remember him, for he died in Oswestry in 1829, and a daughter of his still lives in Castle Buildings.

It is stated in *Mont : Coll :* that the Minute Book referred to has been mislaid. It was in the possession of the late Mr. G. Parker a few years ago, so it is to be hoped it may yet be found.

MAY 5, 1880.

NOTES.

INSCRIPTIONS IN NANT-Y-BELAN TOWER.
In addition to the Tablet to the memory of Captain Arthur Williams Wynn in Nant-y-Belan (inscription on which was given in *Bye-gones*, Mar. 31, 1880), there is also a monument to the memory of all those who belonged to the Royal Welsh Fusiliers who fell in the Battle of the Alma, 20 Sep., 1854. The following is a copy of the Inscription :—

ALMA
To the Memory of
LIEUT:COLONEL ; Harry George Chester.
CAPTAINS : Arthur Watkin Williams Wynn ; Francis Edward Evans ; William Pitcairn Campbell ; John Charles Conolly.
LIEUTENANTS : Frederick Peter Delmé Radcliffe ; Sir William Norris Young, bart. ; Henry Anstruther ; Joseph Henry Butler.
SERGEANT-MAJOR : H. Jones. COLOUR SERGEANT : R. Hitchcock.
SERGEANT : F. Edwards. DRUMMER : J. Collins.

PRIVATES :—

G. Dobson.	T. Owens.	J. Powell.
J. Handrahan.	J. Knightley.	J. Williams.
L. Kelly.	J. Fry.	T. Spiller.
H. Marsh.	D. Povey.	J. Evans.
J. Harrington.	Js. Fry.	C. Barnett.
J. Hall.	G. Lowman.	H. Hine.
W. Martin.	G. Evans.	T. Lynch.
J. Stevens.	J. Wells.	J. Badcock.
H. Goddard.	M. Clack.	T. Seymour.
T. Conroy.	E. Jones.	W. Lines.
T. Maloney.	E. Williams.	T. Randall.
J. Grooms.	P. Peterson.	S. Draper.
J. Lynch.	H. Husband.	R. Walters.

Of the Royal Welsh Fusiliers, who fell 20th Sept., 1854.
Another week I will give the oldest Inscription of all in the Nant-y-Belan mausoleum—to the memory of those of the Ancient British Fencibles who fell in the service of their country during the Irish Rebellion.   N.W.S.

THE COMING-OF-AGE OF A WELSH LADY, 119 YEARS AGO.

Miss Jones, the writer of the following letter, was a daughter of the Rev. Thomas Jones, Master of the Free School at Llanegryn, in Merionethshire, and at the time it was written, she was living as companion to Viscountess Bulkeley of Peniarth, in that county. The young lady, of the celebration of whose coming-of-age she gives the details, was Jane,* eldest daughter of Edward Williams, Esq., and Lady Bulkeley, his wife, above-mentioned. Miss Williams was afterwards married to Wm. Wynne, Esq., of Wern, in Carnarvonshire. The letter was written in May, 1761·

W.

"*A copy of a letter from Miss Cath. Jones of Peniarth to Mr. Edward Lloyd at Mr. Barnstone's Wine Merchant in Chesr.*

"Sr. I'm sensible ye trouble you had in so proper a Discharge of Lady Bulkeley's Commission, merited an earlier return of thanks, & possibly her Ladyship may be condemn'd for the omission when I alone am Culpable, loath to dedicate any time [to] the Sedentary employ of writeing amidst those Sprightly Scenes of amusements yt. wholely engross'd my thoughts for some days past, which being come to a Period, I have leisure to rally my Scatterd senses, and be myself again, I suppose you'll expect I should insert some extracts of our late Jubille but lest I should be lost in so agreeable a retrospect, I'll first execute Lady Bulkeley's commands, viz. informing you that the sweatmeats &c. were well chose, your thought concerning the Glasses approved of, your kind present acceptable, your expedience seasonable, your congratulation graciously received, and everything you did worthy the thanks I'm desired to send you'. As for the money you were so obligeing to expend, her Ladyship will remit agreeable to any order you shall please to send, or leave them unpaid till your Merionethshire excursion. We fully expected to see you the 17th. a Day that was celebrated in great Pomp I assure you'. There was the greatest resort of Company I ever saw in the County the Morning was ushered in by the firing of Cannons, Ringing of Bells in the Neighbouring Steeples and the greatest acclamations of Joy that could be shown on the like occasion, ye Days Entertainment was closed with a very sumptuous cold collation in the Garden at night, Now fform to yourself an idea of our Assembling in Numbers to ye Covert of a long walk arch'd over with Luxurient Branches of Odourifferous Limes,† the Verdant Canopy giveing Lustre to the Glimmering rays of 200 Lamps ranged into two rows, on each side, in one End an Ambrocial Arbour fronted with the Initial Letters of the young Lady's Name ffigured out in Lamps, in the centre a venerable Oak displaying her declining branches bespangled with the same fiery pendants, her body the receptacle of a good band of Music consisting of Welch Harps, Violins, ffrench Horns, Trumpets, German fflutes, & Drums‡, Whose exalted sound reached the most distant parts of the Garden, the meandring stream of gentle sunny‖ adding softness to the Melody made it per-

*In Evans's *Specimens of the Poetry of the Antient Welsh Bards*, pages 14,161, a poem is dedicated to her.
†The avenue, still remaining at Peniarth.
‡ This tree, still known as the "Fiddler's Oak," a remarkably fine one, is yet standing, and was probably as large in 1761, as it is now. It is impossible to say what may not be the age of a great oak like it.
‖ The river Dysynni. This is a different description of it to that of the great poet David ap Gwilym;
"Dysynni tame thy furious tide,
Fixed at thy source, in peace abide,
She comes, oh, greet her with a smile,
The charmer of sweet Mona's Isle."

fectly Harmonious and decending from above seemed the Music of the Spheres, here our Banquet was laid on which having regal'd our appetites we formed a set of Country Dances in Number about 50 Couple, our Spacious Ballroom was lin'd with Idle Spectators, in Short nothing was wanting to Compleat the Rural Scene and this delightful Landship could be compared to nothing but a piece of inchanted Ground, plan'd out by the Deities—(*ye La. their representatives*§) whose native Beauty, and unaffected innocence appear'd with double Lustre through the unstudy'd negligence of a genteel Disabille *which they were array'd in for the better enjoyment of this nocturnal Scene* our Ball Broke up at four when our gallant Partners escorted us to the House where Tea, & Coffee was ready for our reception; the time insensibly elapsed during this agreeable hour of refreshment; nor should we have thought any other necessary, had not ye sight of Phœbus Scimming the Horizon in his firery Carr summond us to our respective apartments, where the fatigue of the Preceeding day proved a most-powerful Opium, wrap'd in ye soft embrase of Lethe; we did not quit the Down till noon, and rally'd again to Breakfast which at an End ye remaining part of the declining day was dedicated to the various turns of our different dispositions, at night (to varyfy the Scene) we resorted to a Ranelagh in miniature opening from the Garden, this room was very magnificently illuminated with Lamps, the Same initial Letters burning at the upper end divided by a Starr in the Centre, a Good Music Gallary erected on the opposite end, the room so well adorn'd with lights and the more Splendid appearance of the Company ; Conspired to render it a very brilliant Assembly, who continued in the mazy dance till the rosy morn eclipsed the sable curtain of the night and the usual hour of recreation expired; we repaired to our Downy habitations, Thus in a Series of the most pleasing amusements ended our Joyous Festivals' and wishing all the dispersed Celebrators well at their repective abodes, I shall close the tedious narrative whose length is an encroachment upon your patience, nay you may leave a Side reading it if you please ; all this family Join in Compts. to you with

"Sr. your obliged Humble Servant
"Cath : Jones."

"Mr. Williams & Lady Bulkeley present Compts. to Mr. & Mrs. Barnstone Please to make mine acceptable to the Doctr. ¶ & Miss Vaughan. . . . ."

QUERIES.

ELLESMERE ASSOCIATION.—At a meeting held at the Royal Oak Inn, Ellesmere, on Aug. 14, 1805, Sir Thomas Hanmer, Bt. in the chair, an Association was formed for the prosecution of poachers, and unqualified persons ; and for preserving the Game and Fish within a circuit of twelve miles. The following gentlemen were appointed a committee of management :—Sir T. Hanmer, the Hon. T. Kenyon, John Kynaston Powell, Philip Lloyd Fletcher, Edward Dymock, Lewis Cooke, Edward Kynaston, Owen Roberts, Robert Clarke, John Burlton, and Charles Garland Greenwollers, esquires ; Richard Hilton and Edward Meeson, clerks. Mr. Peter Pritchard and Mr. Francis Lee, joint solicitors ; and Francis Lloyd, Esq., treasurer. How long did the Association exist?

E. C.

§ There were three young Ladies.
¶ Afterwards Sir Robert Howel Vaughan, of Nannau, and Hengwrt, the first Baronet of his family. During the lifetime of his eldest brother, Hugh Vaughan, of Hengwrt, Esq., he practised medicine, at Chester.

CATHRALL'S *HISTORY OF OSWESTRY*.— Who was Mr. Cathrall, the author, or rather compiler, of this book? I am aware that more than thirty years before Mr. G. Lewis issued it Mr. C. had been a printer in Oswestry, and from 1820 to 1823 published a newspaper called the *Oswestry Herald*. But where was he a native of, and what first brought him into these parts? I have been told he was a son of the author of a history of Wales; but he, I think, spelt his name Catheral. I have also been told he was a native of Chester; but Mr. Salisbury would have mentioned it had such been the case.

OSWALD.

OWAIN GLYNDWR AT MACHYNLLETH.— Does the following, from a newspaper of June 1838, contain any more than Penny-a-lining guesswork?—"Some workmen in building a kitchen to Col. Edwards's mansion, Greenfields, Machyalleth, suddenly fell through into a cavity or vault, that was unknown to anyone living. On the minds of many intelligent persons there is no doubt that this vault entered a dungeon used by Owen Glendower for the imprisonment of captives, as Machynlleth was the seat of his assumed royalty, and the site of one of his fortresses was where Greenfields stands."

G.G.

OLD CANOE AT ELLESMERE.—Whilst taking a quiet ramble upon the banks of the Mere at Ellesmere four or five years ago, I met with an ancient Canoe formed out of the trunk of a single tree. It was raised upon trestles or frame work. Is there any history attached to it?

LANDWOR.

REPLIES.

TALHAIARN (Apr. 21, 1880.)—No doubt many of our ancient Bards were myths, but such scanty biographies of them as we have present them as men of power and genius! Then does it not seem just a trifle "cheeky" (as my son would say were he writing this paragraph) for "John Jones"—clever though he may be—to call himself after a bard said to have written superlative verses! It may be that "John Jones" is the cleverer of the two, and that if his prototype had left behind him a "printed volume" the "masses" CYMRO talks about, would be sensible enough not to waste their time in reading them.

JONES.

CURRENT NOTES.

One of the curious beliefs which still linger amongst the "residuum" is that there is "no law on election day." At Chester last week a man named John Bithell was charged with assaulting his wife on the 12th April. According to the evidence he threatened to hit the complainant with a poker, "as there was no law for that day," and Mr. Mason, solicitor, who appeared for the wife, said there was a general impression about that there was no law on election day! The case was adjourned.

On Thursday, April 22, the fine old parish church of St. Dyfrog, Llanrhaiadr, in the Vale of Clwyd, was re-opened after complete restoration at a cost of nearly £3,000. The contractor was Mr. Williams, St. Asaph, and the architect Mr. Arthur Baker, London. The original church was of 13th century date. The eastern window, which has now been restored, was erected in the 14th century; the present edifice, with its fine perpendicular windows and magnificently carved oak roof (all of which have been restored) is 15th century work. The preachers at the opening services were the Bishop of Bangor, the Bishop of St. Asaph, and the Rev. Canon Howell of Wrexham.

SIR THOMAS MEYRICK, BART.—Mr. Thomas Meyrick of Bush, Pembrokeshire, and of Apley Castle, Shropshire, who has been made a Baronet, is the second son of the late Mr. St. John Chiverton Charlton, of Apley Castle, by his marriage with Jane Sophia, only daughter and heiress of the late Mr. Thomas Meyrick, of Bush. He was born in the year 1836, and was educated at Eton. He is a magistrate and deputy-lieutenant for Pembrokeshire, of which county he served as High Sheriff in 1877. He also holds a commission as major in the Shropshire Militia. He sat in the Conservative interest as M.P. for the Pembroke Boroughs from 1868 down to the General Election of 1874, when he was defeated by Mr. E. J. Reed. Mr. Meyrick married, in 1860, Miss Mary Rhode Hill, daughter of Colonel Frederick Hill and niece of Rowland, late Viscount Hill.

DEATH OF MR. WILLIAM DICAS.—The *Sportsman* says: "With deep regret we announce the death of Mr. William Dicas, which took place at his residence, York-street, Covent Garden, London, on Wednesday evening, April 21. The deceased gentleman, who was in his 68th year, was the head of the firm of Dicas and Paddon, wine merchants, and had for years been known as a lover of sport of all descriptions. He was the son of a London solicitor, but early in life took to coaching, and was part proprietor of the well appointed equipages which ran from Bangor to Holyhead, and from Chester to Llandudno. Mr. Dicas was a grand whip, and though contemporaneous with 'Dick Castle,' was admitted to be one of the smartest of the Welsh coachmen. The deceased was intimately associated with the Messrs. Topham in their management of the Liverpool and Chester meetings; and, though, we believe, he never personally owned any racehorses, he was a constant subscriber to the various handicaps in the north of England. Mr. Dicas had been in business in London some twelve years, was a member of the sporting clubs, and about as genial and good-hearted a soul as could be met with in a day's march." Mr. Dicas resided for some years at Llangollen, and married the daughter of Mrs. Phillips, the respected landlady of the Hand Hotel in that town.

MAY 12, 1880.

NOTES.

FORETOKENS OF DEATH.—The superstitious place great importance on certain "signs," which are said to prognosticate death in the family. A goose flying over the house. The clock coming to a sudden stand. The hen laying a small egg and crowing like a cock; to avert the evils, in first case care is taken to throw the egg over the roof of the house, and cut the "crowing hen's" head off at once. The cockerels crowing after midday, and especially previous to midnight, is a terror to many.

BORDERER.

VERACITY OF THE WELSH PEASANTRY.—As new vicar of a Welsh parish I soon found out who was, of all my parishioners, some said of all men, the least distinguished for accuracy of statement. After expressing official and becoming concern in his behalf I ventured to inquire how he had fallen behind his fellows in this accomplishment, and found that for years he had been in the habit of relating to the gaping rustics the deeds and sights of Sinbad the Sailor. He had probably read these and other histories in a book, and therefore his conscience was clear in respect of them; but like other too brilliant plagiarists he forgot to give his authority—hence his unenviable notoriety. From this I may remark, archæologically, that the ignorance of his audience shows that the Arabian Nights' tales do not seem to be much known among the Welsh peasantry, and that much of the folk lore, common to them, and the Aryan authors of these Tales has gone out as Puritanism came in.　HYFAIDD HIR.

EXTINCT ANIMALS IN WALES.

FALCONS. In the Vale of the Cothy, Carmarthenshire, a gamekeeper found one caught in a trap in 1822. Another was found dead in 1868. Are they more frequently found in other parts of Wales and the borders? Giraldus Cambrensis (Itin. I. 207 Ed. Hoare) says he "ought not to omit mentioning the falcons of these parts (Pembroke) which are of a large and generous kind, and exercise a most severe tyranny over the river and land birds."

BITTERN. One was caught near Talley Lake, in Carmarthenshire, in 1858. It was said to bark like a dog and frighten the whole neighbourhood.

WILD CATS. The real wild cat lingered in parts of Wales till recent times. They were striped like the tiger, and the male had a brush on the end of the tail just like a lion. The male was of the size of an ordinary sheepdog, with shorter legs; the female being markedly smaller. They seem to have been frequent in the dense covers of the vale of the Cothy. Old inhabitants say that in their youth old people spoke of them just as we would of foxes now. The last two known were killed in the year 1822, or the following. One ran before a pack of hounds, near Merthyr Tydfil, and secreted itself in the fork of a tree, and so tore the face of the huntsman who climbed up and attempted to dislodge it, that he died in the course of three days. This was about the beginning of the century.

RAVENS were common a few years ago in the Vale of the Cothy, and the people seem to have regarded their inaccessible nests with some superstition, as it was supposed there was a pot of gold, "crochan aur," somewhere near. A party, recently, tried to find it but were scared away by thunder and lightning, which are the natural guardians of such treasures here, whether placed under ancient tumuli or ravens' nests.

KITES. The forktailed, short-tailed, ginger, and whitetailed (Aderyn Sion Silyn) Kites were common in N, Carmarthenshire thirty years ago, the first only now surviving.　CAEAWC.

THE REV. DR. WILLIAMS.—I have just had for perusal a letter, dated from Wrexham in 1792, and addressed to the "Rev. Dr. Williams, Oswestry," which is thus endorsed by a more modern hand:—"From the students under the care of Dr. W. at Oswestry, in acknowledgment (probably) of the dedication of the sermon in answer to Belsham." This probability is an error, but before I give my reasons for saying so, I transcribe the letter :—

Rev. and Dear Sir. We embrace this opportunity of acknowledging our obligations to you for the notice you have publickly taken of us, the affection you have testified both to the public and ourselves that you have for us. The discourse which with pleasure we have heard from the pulpit, and with profit we read from the press, is received as a token of continuing affection, and abiding regard. As we have for some time attended your instructions with pleasure and profit, we hope we shall be enabled to *Hold fast the profession of our faith without wavering*, and live and die joining the Apostle and you in exclaiming, *God forbid that I should glory save in* THE CROSS *of our Lord Jesus Christ.*

(Signed) Lewis Williams, Joseph Gronow, David Francis, John Williams, William Evans, John Roberts, Jonah Lewis, Thomas Picton, Wm. Morgan, Arthur Clegg.

Wrexham, signed at our meeting, April 27, 1792.

The Rev. Edward Williams became the minister of the Old Chapel, Arthur-street, Oswestry, in 1777 – the precise date is not given by Canon Williams in his *Eminent Welshmen*—and in 1782, the Nonconformist College (or "Academy" as it was called in those days) was removed from Abergavenny to Oswestry to be under his care. His sermon in refutation of the famous. Unitarian, Mr. Belsham, was preached in 1791 (before Mr. Williams received his diploma from Edinburgh), and was printed the same year by Messrs. Eddowes of Shrewsbury. It has no dedication. On the 18th of Dec., 1791, Mr. Williams preached his farewell sermon in Oswestry from the text quoted by the students in the letter I have given ; and this, too, was printed by J. & W. Eddowes, in 1792. It bears on the title-page "By Edward Williams, D.D.," and from his *Life* by Gilbert, I gather that he received his diploma whilst engaged in the preparation of the sermon. In its printed form there is a dedication—which comprehends the congregation he bid farewell to at Oswestry, the one he became minister of in Birmingham, and the students recently under his charge. Probably Dr. Williams was in Oswestry at the date of the students' letter (Apr. 1792) for the purpose of removing his family to Birmingham, as I find they were left behind for awhile when he went to Birmingham in the previous January. The "Academy" had in the meanwhile been removed to Wrexham, to the care of the Rev. Jenkin Lewis.　JARCO.

PARLIAMENT OF ENGLAND. (Apr. 21, 1880.) Commencing with reign of Edw. IV., in which several are missing ; also in subsequent reigns :—

COUNTY OF SALOP.

1461	No returns found until
1472	Thomas Horde, armiger ; Johannes Leghton, armiger
1477	Willielmus Younge, miles ; Ditto
1529	Thomas Co[r]nwall, miles ; Johannes Blount, armiger ("mortuus" against his name)
1547	Georgius Blunte, miles ; Ricardus Newport, armiger
1552	Ricardus Mytton, armiger ; Thomas Vernon, junior, armiger
1553	Ditto ; Edwardus Leyghton, armiger
1554	Willielmus Chorlton, armiger ; Franciscus Kenaston, armiger
1554	Ricardus Mytton ; Willielmus Gatagre
1555	Andreas Corbett, miles ; Henricus Stafforde, miles
1557	Ricardus Corbett, armiger ; Thomas Fermer, armiger

BOROUGH OF SHREWSBURY.

1461	No returns found until
1472	Thomas Mitton ; Johannes Horde
1477	Robertus Beyneon ; Johannes Gyttons
1529	Robertus Dudeley ; Adam Mitton
1547	Riginaldus Corbett, armiger ; Johannes Jevans, generosus
1552	Nicholaus Pursell, aldermannus ; Georgius Lye, mercator, stapule ville Calicie
1553	Reginaldus Corbett, armiger ; Nicholaus Pursell, aldermannus
1554	Ricardus Mytton, armiger ; Ditto
1554	Thomas Mytton ; Georgius Lye
1555	Reginaldus Corbett, armiger ; Nicholaus Pursell, armiger
1557	Nicholaus Pursell, aldermannus ; Georgius Lye, generosus

QUERIES.

MR. EVANS'S SEVEN CEDARS.—In a very interesting parochial history of Llanfyllin, published by the Rector in the third volume of *Montgomeryshire Collections*, he says there is a remarkably fine cedar in front of the mansion at Llwyn ; "one of seven trees, raised from the seeds of a cone which John Evans, the publisher of the Map of Wales, and the grandfather of the Ven. Archdeacon Wilson Evans, author of *Tales of the Early British Church*, bought in London for half-a-guinea, about a century ago." In his Salopian history the late Mr. Hulbert alludes to some of these trees: He says:—

A little distance from Llanymynech is Llwynygroes, the beautiful villa residence of Dr. Evans, an eminent physician, author of a poem called *The Bees*, &c. I have seldom experienced greater delight, than I did Aug. 24, 1834, during my interview with this venerable sire of many excellent sons, including the amiable and talented author of *The Rectory of Vale Head*; nearly twenty years had elapsed since our last interview, I remembered all the kindness and medical skill he manifested, while resident in Shrewsbury, at a period when fever had nearly destroyed my existence. The hour I stayed with him, was indeed a short one, he kindly pointed out to me in the grove near his house, a stately Cedar of Lebanon, which he denominated a younger brother.

I give this extract in full to supply the omission of one generation of the Evanses in the passage by the Rector of Llanfyllin. Mr. Hulbert has something more to say about these cedars, for he adds in a note, "Mr. J. F. M. Dovaston informed me, the great Cedar of Lebanon at West Felton, that at Llwynygroes, and that at Llandrinio, were all seeds out of the same cone, and sown by his late father, in 1765." We have thus four out of the seven cedars accounted for. In *Bye-gones* as far back as Sep. 19, 1877, it was stated that :—

The late Dr. Evans of Llwynygroes, long prior to the year 1838 when calling at Pentreheylin Hall, Maesbrook, informed the late Mr. Richard Croxon that the cedars at Llwynygroes and Llandrinio—and also one at Pentreheylin Hall—were planted at the same time, the cones having been purchased at half-a-guinea each by Mr. Clopton Pryse of Llandrinio Hall. The one at Pentreheylin was an old tree, and in perfection, at the beginning of the present century. The tree at Llwynygroes was planted either by Dr. Evans's father or grandfather. Dr. Evans's father was a great botanist, and wrote a good deal about trees and shrubs.

This will bring up the number of trees to five, viz., Llwynygroes, West Felton, Llandrinio, Llwyn, and Pentreheylin. Can any of your readers trace the other two, and tell us any thing about the grandfather of Dr. Evans, a name not, I think, alluded to in local histories ? G.G.

AN ORIGINAL CADER IDRIS GUIDE.—I have been told that early in this century there lived at Dolgelley one Robert Edwards, a Guide-General to Cader Idris and the Waterfalls, who was a little man and a great boaster, and had an address printed for distribution amongst his patrons. Can any of your readers give us an account of the man, or a copy of the address ? T.

REPLIES.

SEDAN CHAIRS (Apr. 7, 1880).—Turning over the pages of *The Stranger in Shrewsbury* at a book-stall the other day, I found in a chapter of "Miscellaneous Notices and References" the following :—

HACKNEY CHAIRMEN.

Hackney Chairs, or as they are sometimes called *Sedans*, are to be had for conveyance within the town at a moderate rate.

This application of the term "Hackney" is new to me. The date of the book, I think, was 1815 or thereabouts.
H.B.

CAMBRIAN INSTITUTIONS (Mar. 31, 1880). *Canorion.*—In a supplement to *Y Cymmrodor*, p. xvii., issed in 1877, I find the following paragraph :—" A society was now (? 1820) formed, branching from the Cymmrodorion, called the *Canorion*, for the cultivation of

Pennillion singing. Its meetings were held at the Freemasons' Tavern, and, for a period, were highly successful, giving considerable delight to the lovers of Welsh music." A few further particulars of the doings of this Society would be interesting. How are we to account for the fact that very few are at present skilled in this delightful style of song ? St. J. H.

On the 1st of March, 1714, we are told, a new Society calling themselves *The Antient Britons* went in a body to St. Paul's, Covent Garden, where a sermon was preached, "in the British language by the Rev. Mr. Lewis," from Gal. vi., 10. Says the enthusiastic first secretary, in his "Rise and Progress" of the Society—

But, there being 4,000 of these Sermons printed, some whereof I have sent, and the rest are to be sent into the Country, to be dispersed amongst the Common People for whose Good it was intended, that they might be instructed in the Duties of Brotherly Love, and of Loyalty to their King in their own Language, I beg leave to refer you to them for your better Satisfaction.

Are there any copies of this sermon in existence ? It was not the only one, I believe, issued by the Society in its early days. CYMRO.

Who and what was "Thomas Jones of Lincoln's Inn, Esq.," the original secretary of this Society, who was knighted on the occasion of the presentation of a very fulsome address to George I. on the failure of the Pretender ? G.G.

MAY 19, 1880.

NOTES.

BURIAL OF SUICIDES IN WALES.—The writer lately found (in Carmarthenshire) a round earth mound on the north side of a hill, about 18 feet in diameter and 3 feet high, and supposed it to be an ancient Tumulus. Tradition, however, says it is the grave of a woman who lived at a neighbouring farm, and having committed suicide was buried here, not so very long ago. CAEAWC.

THE SWEENEY GRAVES.—There is one inscription amongst those at the Nonconformist burial ground at Sweeney, near Oswestry, that, so far as I know, has never been printed. It is written in Roman letters on a small copper plate fastened in the flat stone of the grave ; and reads as follows :—

Here lyeth the body of A blessed saint
exercised all her dayes in mortification &c
Self denial strong loves to God and the
most spiritual saints zeal to his glory
and the most tender to her husband
honest Jane ye wife of Ambrose Mostin
deceased July 26th 1651
Witness Walter Cradock with all
the saints that knew her.

There is a reference to this lady in Calamy's *Nonconformists' Memorial*. Her husband was Vicar of Wrexham before the Restoration, "when he gave way to the sequestered minister." Previously he had "preached for some time at Redcastle in Montgomeryshire, in connection with Mr. Powel." He was the "son of Dr. Mostyn, of an ancient and honourable family at Greenfield in Flintshire." Calamy says "his last wife, (daughter of Sir. E. Broughton, Bart.) tho' eminent for piety, was exercised with great trouble of mind, in which he was a successful comforter." Walter Cradock (the "witness") was also connected with Wrexham, as a Curate, before he became famous as an associate of Vavasour Powel, described in Green's *Short History of the English People*, as "the Apostle of Wales." JARCO.

THE "CONVENTION" OF 1739.—In conse-
quence of the atrocities of the Spaniards to the English
merchant vessels, our Government in Jan. 1739 demanded
compensation from the King of Spain, who consequently
signed a Convention by which he agreed to give £95,000
by way of indemnification. The following is the result of
the parliamentary division on the subject in June that
year, as far as the districts covered by *Bye-gones* is concerned :—

For the Convention : William Corbet, Montgomery ;
John Griffiths, Carnarvonshire ; Gray James Grove,
Bridgnorth ; Hon. Arthur Herbert, Ludlow ; Sir
Humphrey Hawarth, Radnorshire ; William Kinaston,
Shrewsbury ; Thomas Lewis, Radnor ; Walter Lewis,
Cardiganshire (Attorney General in Wales) ; Richard
Lloyd, Cardigan ; Hon. John Talbot, Brecon ; Thomas
Wynn, Carnarvon.

Against the Convention : Sir John Astley, Salop ;
Nicholas Bayley, Anglesea ; Charles Cholmondeley,
Cheshire ; John Crewe, Cheshire ; Hon. Pryce Devereaux,
Montgomeryshire ; Corbet Kynaston, Salop ; Edward
Kynaston, Bishop's Castle ; Sir Thomas Mostyn, Flint-
shire ; John Myddelton, Denbigh ; William Vaughan,
Merionethshire ; Thomas Whitmore, Bridgnorth (absent);
Lord Bulkeley, Beaumaris ; Sir Charles Banbury,
Cheshire ; Sir Richard Corbet, Shrewsbury ; William
Forester, Brook Forester (father and son), Wenlock ;
Richard Herbert, Ludlow ; Robert More, Bishop's
Castle.

The sum offered was not considered by the country an
adequate compensation, and, as the money was not paid
on the appointed day, Walpole yielded to the popular
feeling and prepared for war, which was declared 19th
Oct. 1739. J.?.R.

WILD DEER IN WALES.

The following extracts from the original record of a
Trial between the celebrated Robert Dudley, Earl of
Leicester, and Robert ap Howel ap Owen, of Cefn, in
Eivionydd (a gentleman of old family, and landed property
in that part of Carnarvonshire) will show how common,
even so late as the reign of Elizabeth, Red Deer, in a wild
state, were in the more mountainous parts of North
Wales :—

Extract from the evidence of Richard Owen ap Res
Vachan, of Neygolf, in the county of Carnarvon, gentleman, of the age of 38 or thereabouts, taken at Llanystyndwy, on 23 May 1586 :—" And (he) knoweth furthior
that certayne acres of encrochments weare found amonge
others vppone Hoell ap Owen in a place called Gwern
Viriagle and knoweth also that the most p'te of the said
Gwerne Viriagle was moore and wast and hard say that
redd deere did vse to resorte thether for refuge."

Extract from the depositions of "Mores ap Res ap d'd
Ove of Gest" in the same county. He is described as of
the age of 69 years or thereabouts, from the same authority :—" and (he) sayeth further that he hard say and
sawe redd deere resort to the said Gweru viriagle for
refuge."

Extract from the evidence of Wm. Maurice of Clenenney,
Esq., of the age of 46 years or thereabouts :—" he re-
membreth to see Mr. doctor El[lis] prys and others chas-
singe redd deere out of th . . . . . moore w'th a great
company of men that had mu[ch a]dooe to drive them
out."

Griffith ap Rhys Griffith of Llanarmon (who is described as of the age of "fyvescore and iiii yeres") also
says :—" that he sawe redd deere resorting thether and
chased them out himself diverse tymes." This was in
reply to the interrogatory, "Dyd not yo'u knowe or have
hard the said moore of gwern viriagle to be wast and

comone and that the redd deer Resorted thether for reffuge
because of the wildernes of hit."

Gwern Viriagle is in Penyved, or Rhwyngdwyfor a
dwyfach, in the vicinity of Penmorva and Llanystyndwy.
W.

QUERIES.

ABERDOVEY LIFE BOAT.—On June 7, 1837,
a meeting was held at Aberdovey, Capt. Thruston, R.N.,
in the chair, for the purpose of establishing a Life Boat
at that port. About £40 was subscribed at the meeting,
and a letter was read from Sir John Conroy, in which he
said that the Duchess of Kent and the Princess Victoria,
in grateful recollection of their reception in Montgomeryshire, the first Welsh county they entered in the Principality, had forwarded a subscription of £10, the Duchess
adding a request that the Boat should be called after the
Princess Victoria. Was this ever done? G. G.

OSWESTRY RACES.—The following account,
which I to-day met with in the *Chester Courant* for Oct.
3, 1803, is so gushing in style and withal so descriptive of
the Shropshire and Denbighshire belles of three-quarters
of a century ago, that I venture to offer it for the adorn-
ment of *Bye-gones* :—

OSWESTRY, Sept. 29, 1803.
Our Races, which ended on Wednesday last, were never
better attended. The assemblage of the neighbouring nobility
and gentry was crowded beyond all example, and their expecta-
tions gratified by a display of beauty, wit, and elegance, by a
profusion of delicacies and an exhibition of amusements such
as few countries, few tables, and few races can boast.
The sport on the two first days was good, and on the last was
of superior excellence. If the well-contested rivalry of the noble
animals, if the joyous hearts of a collected multitude, and the
splendid display of brilliant equipages could add to the magnificence of resplendent days and extensive prospects, then might
it be said that the gladdened face of nature had condescended
to seek embellishment from the vicinity of Oswestry.
Our elegant Lady Patroness, Miss Charlotte Williams Wynn,
shone with peculiar lustre, and diffused a spirit of gaiety that
was caught and confirmed by the concordant feelings of the
whole company. There might one see love and beauty com-
mingling in the mystic dance, to brighten every eye and gladden
every heart.* Amongst the numerous contributors to this con-
stellation of wit and beauty, we noticed the lovely and bewitch-
ing Lady Dungannon and her festive Lord ; the amiable and
sprightly Misses Cunliffe, with their lively and accomplished
friend, the sweetly pretty Miss H. Williams Wynn ; the fair and
elegant daughter of our respected Steward, Owen Ormsby, Esq.;
the gaily blooming Miss Jodrell ; the charming and fascinating
Mrs. R. Wingfield ; with the much admired Misses Lloyd of
Aston ; the Kynastons, Bevans, Warringtons, Mytton, Herberts,
Venables, Dobb, and other beauties too numerous to be enumerated and too excellent to be described.
For the ensuing year were named Lord Dungannon, and the
Hon. T. Kenyon, as our Stewards ; and it was with peculiar
pleasure that we heard the interesting Miss Owen, of Wood-
house, announced as the succeeding Lady Patroness, more
especially when we reflect on the alarming accident that had
very nearly snatched her from us, together with her chearful
and engaging sister, and had almost deprived us of the valuable
lives of their brother and the fashionable Mr. E. Davenport ;
for, on returning from the Ball of Monday last, their carriage
was overturned into the Canal, and themselves with difficulty
rescued from a watery grave, by the timely exertion and intre-
pidity of a passing pig man.

This accident was just the sort of event likely to be
turned to account in verse. I wonder if any local bard of
the period chanted the praises of the "passing pig man?"
Chester. T. HUGHES."

[* The same account, signed "Veritas," appeared in the *Salopian
Journal* for Oct. 5, 1803, with the addition of the following paragraph at this point :—" It is difficult to avoid the language of
bombast in using terms that are barely adequate to the splendour
of the *spectacle* and the festivities of the meeting."—ED.]

OSWESTRY WATCHMAKERS (Dec. 10, 1879).
A friend has just informed me that he has recently seen
an old clock, with a brass face on which was engraved
the name of *Wickstead*. Amongst the names of Oswestry
burgesses elected under the Charter of Charles the Second
is the following: "Charles Wickstead of Oswestry Watchmaker 2s. 0d. June 6, 1732," so the clock face, bearing
his name, must be venerable.   JARCO.

[The Oswestry Watchmakers previously mentioned, were
Campbell and Highfield or Hyffield. The latter dated back as
far as 1777.—ED.]

CAMBRIAN INSTITUTIONS (May 5, 1880).
Welsh Manuscript Society.—In a newspaper dated
May 23, 1838, a paragraph appears which said it was
stated at a late meeting of the Royal Society of Litera-
ture, that the late Dr. Richards, formerly rector of St.
Martin's, and one of the earliest friends of the Welsh
Manuscript Society, had bequeathed £5,000 to its funds,
the interest of which was to be applied to the publication of
old MSS. The same paper stated that the Duke of New-
castle was deeply interested in the progress of the Ancient
British Manuscript Society, and with the Marquis of
Bute, Lords Dynevor and Mostyn, Sir Charles Morgan,
Bart., and other parties, had commenced enquiries that
were likely to lead to satisfactory results.

Metropolitan Cambrian Institution.—In the *Gent's.
Mag.* for May 1821, there is a letter addressed to Sir W.
W. Wynn, as president of this "Society formed in London." The writer, who signs himself "D. W.," calls
Sir Watkin's attention to the fact that the Welsh language
was falling gradually into disuse, owing to the rapid strides
the English was making in the Principality; and he urges
that the plan of the Society is faulty, because it will tend
to arrest the progress of English. In the first place, it
would drive the Welsh more than ever into the hands of
the sectaries, and next, would interfere with the course of
justice. The writer thinks Welsh should be cultivated
only as a dead language. In the same magazine for Aug.
1821, "Caradoc" defends the Welsh as a living language,
also in a letter to Sir Watkin, and denounces "D. W.,"
and denies his facts!   TAFFY.

THE GWYNEDDIGION SOCIETY announced
its intention, in May, 1820, of holding an Eisteddfod at
St. Asaph in the following September. Some of the
leading prizes were announced.   H.B.

EPITAPHS (Jan. 7, 1880).—Referring to page 3,
reprint of *Bye-gones*, January, 1880, I noticed an epitaph
stated to be in Wrexham Churchyard; as this is
erroneous I wish to correct the same. The tablet upon
which the lines are inscribed is inside the Parish Church
and reads thus—

Daniel Jones dy'd ye 13th day of Feby, 1668.

Here lies interr'd beneath these stones,
The beard, ye flesh, and eke ye bones
Of Wrexham Clerk, old Daniel Jones.

Upon the same tablet is inscribed—

Philip Jones his Son succeeded him, and was interred ye 18th
of March, 1720.

Upon another tablet below the above is inscribed—

William Jones, Clerk, Son of Phillip Jones, Clerk, died Jany
10th, 1735, aged 39.

Thus, there were three generations of the same family,
who successively filled the office of Parish Clerk. There
is a lady now residing in Wrexham who is a direct lineal
descendant of the above.   LANDWOR.

RESTORATION OF BANGOR CATHEDRAL.

After a further restoration, which has occupied a little
more than a year in execution, Bangor Cathedral was
re-opened on Tuesday, May 11. The present work, which
is due in a marked degree to the zeal and energy of Dean
Edwards and the munificence of the Lord-Lieutenant of
Carnarvonshire and Mr. Assheton Smith, who have contributed nearly a moiety of the outlay, is a continuation
of the partial restoration which was effected in May, 1873,
and includes the thorough renovation and beautifying of
the nave and aisles, which have hitherto presented a cold,
cheerless, and unsightly appearance, and the erection of a
new chapter house and muniment room on the north side.
The old roof remains, and it has been cased in both nave
and aisles with panelled oak intersected with carved bosses,
which appears to give it the higher pitch suggested by the
late Sir Gilbert Scott, from whose designs the restoration
has been carried out under the direction of his son, Mr.
J. Oldrid Scott. The concrete floor has been laid with
encaustic tiles; the baptistry has been slightly raised and
tiled; and, in the nave and transepts, oaken open seats
have been provided for the congregation in lieu of chairs.
Before the work of renovation was commenced, the windows presented a great variety of architectural features,
but they have now been made uniform, the style being
14th century Decorated. In Bishop Skeffington's tower
and the two other windows at the west end have been
placed portions of the stained glass window which was
erected in 1838, out of a testimonial fund subscribed
by the inhabitants of Bangor to mark the preferment of the late Dean Cotton from the Vicarage
to the deanery of the cathedral city. The Caen
stone pulpit, recently placed in the cathedral as a
memorial to the late Rev. Morris Williams, rector of
Llanrhyddlad, familar to Welshmen as "Nicander," has
been removed to the north transept, and a carved oak
movable pulpit occupies its site. The six arches on each
side of the nave have been cleaned, and the fragment of a
respond of an earlier arcade which was discovered has been
left open to view. Additional accommodation has been
provided for the choristers under the great tower; an
organ screen has been erected in the north transept; and
the chancel stalls, including those of the dean and sub-
dean, have been handsomely canopied. The curious
carved slab which was found under the old chapter room,
and is supposed to have been erected in the 14th century
as a memorial to a female member of the Penrhyn family,
occupies a conspicuous position near the west door in a
corner which has been laid with the old green encaustic
tiles that were disinterred from the same spot. The new
gas coronæ were supplied by Messrs. Skidmore of Coventry,
and the nave is heated by two of Musgrave's large patent
stoves. Mainly through the efforts of Mr. Wm. Jarvis,
the I.P.M. of St. David's Lodge, the Freemasons of the
Province of North Wales and Shropshire have subscribed
the funds for a bishop's throne, the masonic emblems upon
which were designed by Mr. Hathaway, C.E., which was
on Tuesday formally presented to Bishop Campbell. A
pair of massive candlesticks, purchased by a subscription
initiated by Mrs. Vincent Williams, were on Tuesday
placed on the super altar. Externally the edifice has
undergone great renovation, and one appreciable improvement has been the leveling of the burial ground, which
has been tastefully laid out under the superintendence of Mr. H. W. Humphreys, of the Bangor nursery
gardens. The cost of the works, which have been well
and expeditiously carried out by Messrs. Thompson, of
Peterborough, is slightly in excess of £8,000, the principal

subscribers to the building fund being the Lord-Lieutenant and Mr. Assheton Smith, who each contributed £2,000 ; the Bishop of Bangor and Mr. R. Bamford Hesketh, who were donors of £500 each ; Mr. T. Warner, a subscriber of £400 ; and Mr. H. Kneeshaw and the Dean of Bangor, who each gave £250. As previously stated, the restoration has been carried out under the direction of Mr. J. Oldrid Scott—Mr. Wills, who has been appointed to a similar position in connection with the new cathedral to be erected at Newfoundland, having acted as clerk of the works. Mr. Philip Jones, High-street, Bangor, was the contractor for the gasfitting and plumbing department, and the ironwork was executed by Mr. John Owen, Menai Foundry. Although within the last ten years not much less than £35,000 raised by voluntary effort—the Dean and Chapter having no available corporate estate or property, and no grant having been received from the Ecclesiastical Commissioners—has been expended upon the Cathedral, which dates as a foundation from the sixth century, its restoration is far from complete. The "dignified reredos and the noble open screen" included in the original designs of the architect are still conspicuous by their absence ; and the insufficiency of funds at present prevents the erection of the proposed Lady Chapel on the south side of the choir, and bars the completion of the tower and spire—works which will necessitate a further outlay of some £5,000. Tuesday's services were prefaced by an early choral celebration of the holy communion, the Bishop and Dean of Bangor being the celebrants. Prior to the commencement of the morning service, the Freemasons of the province, the choirs, and clergy of the Diocese assembled at the Penrhyn Hall, and formed a procession to meet the Bishop at the Palace. They entered the Church by the west door, the Freemasons in their regalia preceding the choirs and taking up a position in the chancel. "Onward, Christian Soldiers," was sung as the processional hymn, the choirs being followed by 106 surpliced clergymen, for whom seats were provided in the chancel, the south transept being reserved for the Masonic body. When the Bishop of Bangor arrived at the chancel, he was conducted to the throne, which is on the south side of the choir, by Bro. D. Cameron, the W.M. of St. David's, Bangor, the Lodge which has taken the initiative in the presentation and has successfully carried it through. His Lordship was also presented with a handsomely bound volume containing the names of the subscribers. The prayers were intoned by the Minor Canons, the Revs. Foulkes Jones and Owen Evans ; Canon Evan Lewis (the canon in residence), and the Dean read the lessons ; and an eloquent sermon, based upon 2 Thessalonians i, 1, was preached by Dr. Alexander, Bishop of Derry and Raphoe. In the course of his remarks, the preacher drew attention to the great antiquity of the edifice, whose foundation went back something more than 1,200 years. The present building was not an innovation but a renovation, and was a fitting memorial to hand down to ages to come of the zeal, loyalty, and liberality of the Churchmen of the diocese. He trusted that the funds still needed to fully complete the restoration would soon be forthcoming, and that a third ceremonial such as the present one would take place at an early date in celebration of the finishing of the tower and spire. The congregation was a very large one, and the offertory, which amounted to £146, was collected, amongst others, by the Marquess of Londonderry, Lord Penrhyn, the high sheriff of Anglesey (Major Platt), Colonel the Hon. W. E. Sackville West, Mr. H. J. Ellis-Nanney, Captain F. Mansel Morgan, Mr. Nicholls Jones (Penrhos), Mr. John Lloyd (Bodhyfryd), and Mr. W. Pughe.

The musical portion of the service, which was under the direction of Dr. Roland Rogers, the cathedral organist, was very effective, the ordinary choir being largely augmented by representatives of the cathedral choirs of Chester, Hereford, and St. Asaph, the Rev. W. Morton, of the latter Cathedral, acting as precentor. Stainer's service was used ; the psalms were sung to a setting by Dr. Roland Rogers, and the anthems—Ouseley's "It came even to pass," and Sullivan's "Sing, O Heavens," —were rendered with telling effect. About sixty Freemasons took part in the ceremony of presenting the throne, the following lodges being represented :—St. David's, Royal Leek, Bangor; St. Tudno, Llandudno ; St. Eleth, Amlwch ; Anglesey, Llangefni ; Mariners', Liverpool; Caradoc ; St. Cybi, Holyhead; Segontium, Carnarvon ; and Equality. Owing to prior engagements the W.P.G.M. (Sir W. W. Wynn, Bart., M.P.) and his deputy (Mr. Bulkeley Hughes, M.P.) both of whom were liberal subscribers, were unavoidably absent. The Rev. R. W. Forrest, D.D., vicar of St. Jude's, Kensington, preached in the afternoon. Stainer's service was again sung, the Hallelujah chorus from "The Messiah" being the anthem. The closing service was in Welsh, the Ven. Archdeacon Griffith, rector of Neath, occupying the pulpit. The other preachers announced to take part in the octave of services, which will be closed on Whit-Sunday, are the Revs. D. Howell, Wrexham, D. Roberts, Llandyrnog, George Body, vicar of Kirbury, Misperton, and W. Barker, vicar of St. Mary's, Cowes.

In emulation of the example recently offered in connection with the restoration of Chester Cathedral, a musical festival took place on Wednesday, May 12, at Bangor, in continuation of the re-opening services. The proposal, when first mooted, was regarded with so little favour that the formation of a guarantee fund was deemed necessary ; but, judging from the congregation, representative of all parts of the diocese, and including a great number of Nonconformists, which thronged the nave and aisles of the restored cathedral, so far from any call being made upon the guarantors who so generously proffered their assistance, there is every likelihood that the restoration fund will be substantially benefited. In every respect, financially as well as artistically, the festival—a novelty in Wales—was an unmistakable success, and the favour with which the movement has been supported encourages the hope that a venture of the same character, although perhaps on a less extensive scale, may be an annual institution in the diocese. The programme, which occupied about two hours in performance, was judiciously chosen. Fittingly opening with the "Hallelujah" chorus from Beethoven's "Mount of Olives," it included some of the best known morceaux from Mendelssohn's "Hymn of Praise," together with half a dozen selections, including a chorale from "Prayer and Praise," the cantata composed three or four years ago by Dr. Roland Rogers, the cathedral organist, as his Mus. Doc. composition at Oxford. Interest attached chiefly to the latter composition, which occupied the place of honour in the programme. Dr. Roland Rogers enjoys a well-earned popularity in the diocese, and has done much to advance the standard of high-class musical culture in North Wales ; and, although his cantata has been rendered in an occasional and fragmentary form through the medium of the well-trained choir under his control, this was the first occasion of its performance in the Principality with full orchestral accompaniment. Its reception was most favourable, amply justifying the high anticipations that had been formed of it, and well meriting the hearty and numerous congratulations which were subsequently showered upon the composer. The tenor solos were rendered with pathos and sympathy by Mr. Joseph Maas, whose perfect vocalisation created a noticeable impression, a remark which applies with equal force to Mrs. Osgood, who did ample justice to the soprano music. Madame Louise Mills was the second soprano, and, although suffering by comparison with such a star as Mrs. Osgood, she acquitted herself admirably. An instrumental prelude, *in memoriam* to the composer's father, and written since the publication, was included in the programme. The Liverpool Philharmonic orchestra, under the leadership of Mr. E. W. Thomas, were the instrumentalists, and their assistance contributed in a material degree towards the success of the performance. The choruses were admirably sung by a united choir of about 150 voices, the cathedral staff being augmented by members of those belonging to Chester, St. Asaph and Hereford Cathedrals. The choir of Christ Church, Carnarvon, which enjoys the reputation of being the best trained in the diocese, together with a portion of the choral union belonging to the same town, also took part in the programme. In the opening chorus the orchestra was too strong for the voices, but this defect was subsequently remedied, and the performance was gone through in a manner which reflected great credit upon all engaged in it. Dr. Rogers, who wore the robes and hood of a doctor of music, conducted, his place at the organ being ably filled by Mr. Bennett Jones. Prior to the commencement of the programme, the Dean of Bangor conducted a brief service, and at its close the benediction was pronounced. There was a large and efficient body of stewards, and the general arrangements were excellently carried out by a committee, of which Colonel the Hon. Sackville West was chairman, Mr. W. Jarvis a hard-working and energetic honorary secretary, and Messrs. H. Barber, Davies, J. W. Hughes, J. H. A. Hall, J. Lloyd, J. Pritchard, W. Rowlands J. Thomas, W. H. Phillips, Dr. Hughes, with the Rev. Foulkes Jones and Owen Evans prominent members. The performers were placed on a temporary orchestra erected under the central tower. Mr. W. Jarvis, the acting honorary secretary, Lord and Lady Penrhyn, the Marquess of Londonderry, the Bishop of Bangor and Mrs. Campbell, the High Sheriff of Anglesey (Major Platt) and Mrs. Platt, Mr. and Mrs. Ellis Nanney, the Mayor of Carnarvon, (Alderman Lewis Lewis), Colonel the Hon. and Mrs. Sackville West, Mr. Kneeshaw (the late High Sheriff of Carnarvonshire), and Colonel Humberston were amongst the occupants of the reserved seats.

At night, a second performance attracted an immense audience. In the general musical arrangements in connection with the re-opening of the cathedral great assistance has been given by the Rev. W. Morton and the Rev. C. Hilton Stewart, the precentors of St. Asaph and Chester Cathedrals.

The octave of services in connection with the re-opening services was closed on Sunday, the Revs. George Body, rector of Kirby Misperton, and W. Barker, vicar of St. Mary's, Cowes, preaching in English ; and the Rev. D. Roberts, rector of Llandyrnog, in Welsh.

MAY 26, 1880.

NOTES.

"DYING IN HIS SHOES."—In Oct. 1837 an inquest was held at the Cross Guns, near Llanymynech, on the body of a man who had hung himself. It was stated that "to prevent the disgrace of 'dying in his shoes' he had carefully taken them off."   H.B.

5

INSCRIPTIONS IN NANT-Y-BELAN TOWER

(May 5, 1880).—I now give the promised copy of the monument to the memory of the Ancient British Fencibles who fell in Ireland (serving under Sir Watkin) at the time of the Rebellion :—

To the Memory of

CAPTAIN John Burganey
LIEUTENANT Adolphus Giffard
CORNET and ADJUTANT John Davies
QUARTER MASTERS Joseph Golsby, John Davies
CORPORALS Edward Roberts, Joseph Tilstone, John Bellis, George Chalener, Ambrose Tarling
TRUMPETERS Edward Edwards, Anthony King

[PRIVATES]

Peter Clarke	Edward Jackson	John Hughes
Thomas Edwards	William Leadbeater	Robert Mathews
Robert Griffiths	John Parry	George Owens
John Powell	John Parry	Richard Williams
Randle Roberts	William Roberts	John Davies
Robert Roberts	David Roberts	Thomas Davies
Samuel Dunn	Robert Jones	Thomas Lee
Hugh Davies	Michael Bellis	William Lucas
Boas Roberts	David Burgess	John Parish
James Hughson	Thomas Chadwick	Edward Jones
William Jones	Edward Jones	James Patterson

of the Ancient British Fencible Cavalry.

Thus lives the soldier's name who fought and fell
Thus Cambria to her latest sons shall tell
How her own Bands her ancient Britons bore
Her dragon Banner to Ierne's shore
By courage zeal and diciphne maintained
The ancient glory which their sires had gained
And true to Honour and their country's cause
Sealed with their blood the triumph of her laws.

Several references to the Ancient British Fencibles have appeared in the issues of *Bye-gones*.   N.W.S.

OSWESTRY IN THE 14TH CENTURY.—In the *Arch : Camb :* for 1852 is given the translations of sundry old Latin Deeds relating to Oswestry and the neighbourhood. A transcript of some of these will be interesting to the readers of *Bye-gones*. Here is a specimen :—

William son of Richard le Saltere de Ossewaldistr' gives to Alexander de M'Channton, a burgage with its appurtenances in Ossewaldistr : to wit, in Midelstret, between the house of Isolde le Saltere, my mother, and the house of John Merlor. To have, &c. Yeilding therefor to his head lord, lord of the county, a pair of gloves [cirotecar :] of the value of 1d. and to me 12s. yearly rent, viz. 6s. at the feast of St. Michael, and 6s. at the feast of the Annunciation of the Blessed Mary, for secular services, &c. Witnesses: Roger de Chene, then temporary Steward, William English, or the Englishman [Anglico], Roger son of Roger, John the Roter, John Merlor, John Lombard, Richard L'Estrange [extraneus] and others many.

Oswestry has been destroyed by fire more than once since this deed was in force, and where Middle Street was we can only guess. The Salter family still exists. "The name 'extraneus,' in the original Latin rendered ' L'Estrange,' was the family name of the Lords Strange of Knockin, near Oswestry." John the Roter, was doubtless a "minstrel who played on the rote, a kind of hurdygurdy."   M.C.A.S.

PARLIAMENT OF ENGLAND (May 12, 1880). Commencing and ending the reign of Elizabeth :—

COUNTY OF SALOP.

1558 S r Andrew Corbet, Knt ; Sir Arthur Maneryng, iKnt
1562 Richard Corbett, esq.; Edward Leighton, esq.
1572 George Bromley, esq., (Attorney of the Court of the Duchy of Lancaster) ; George Manwayring, esq., son and heir apparent of Sir Arthur Manwayring, Knt.
1584 Walter Leveson, esq.; Francis Bromley, esq.

10

1586   Richard Corbett, esq., of Mooreton Corbett ; Walter
            Leveson, esq.
1588   Sir Walter Leveson, Knt.; Richard Leveson, esq.
1592   Francis Newporte, esq.; Robert Nedham, jun. esq.
1597   (Writ only found).
1601   John Egerton, esq.; Roger Owen, esq.

BOROUGH OF SHREWSBURY.

1562   Robert Ireland, jun., esq.; Richard Pursell, esq.
1572   George Lighe (or Leighe), esq.; Richard Purcell,
            esq.
1584   Thomas Owen, esq., of Lincoln's Inn ; Richard
            Barker, esq.
1586   Reginald Scryven, esq.; Thomas Harris, esq., of
            Lincoln's Inn.
1588   Andrew Newport . . . . R . . . .
1592   Reginald Scriven, esq.; Robert Wrighte, esq.
1597   Roger Owen, gent; Reginald Scriven, gent.
1601   John Barker, esq.; Reginald Screven, esq.

QUERIES.

THE SWEENEY GRAVES (May 19, 1880).—
The fact has never been explained why there ever should
have been a burial-place formed in front of the Mansion
of Sweeney. It would be interesting to know too, whether
the common people amongst the Puritan party found a
last home there.   Only three inscriptions seem to have
been preserved, and two of these are over the graves of
baronets' daughters ; the third on that of an ex-M.P.
Who was Sir Richard Chetwood, and why was his daughter
buried at Sweeney ?   And who Sir J. Broughton ?   It
does not appear that his daughter ever lived in the immediate neighbourhood.   PURITAN.

BOY OR GIRL?—In the Second Volume of
Notes and Queries, p. 600, " M.E.F." related a curious
mode of discovering the sex of an infant previous to birth,
in a *Denbighshire* family.   An old dame, attached to the
household of the writer, held the blade-bone of a shoulder
of mutton to the fire till it was scorched, so as to permit
her to force her thumbs through the thin part.   Through
the holes thus made she passed a string, and having
knotted the ends together, she drove in a nail over the
back door and left the house, giving strict injunctions to
the servants to hang the bone up in that place the last
thing at night.   Then they were carefully to observe who
should first enter that door on the following morning,
exclusive of the members of the household, and the sex
of the child would be that of the first comer.   The first
comer proved to be a man, and in a few weeks a boy was
born !   Of course the old woman's reputation was established.   Is the custom at all known, or peculiar to Denbighshire?   H.B.

REPLIES.

CAMBRIAN INSTITUTIONS (May 12, 1880).—
It was announced in the papers of Jan. 1837, that the
King had graciously been pleased to testify "his entire
approbation of the objects of the committee named at the
last anniversary of the *Abergavenny Cymreigyddion Society*
for the purpose of forming a society for perpetuating, by
publication, the numerous Welsh MSS. which yet exist in
the Principality."   His Majesty also signified his acceptance of the position of patron of the Society.   The
Duchess of Kent and the Princess Victoria were also announced as patronesses.

In reporting the St. David's Day proceedings of 1837, a
London correspondent of one of the country newspapers
points out what he considers to be the " advantage of employing a Drill Corporal to discipline the boys " of the

Welsh Charity School, "a custom for some years discontinued."   He thought, were it resumed, "what capital
recruits the school would then produce for the 41st Royal
Welsh Regiment of Foot, or for the 23d. Welsh Fusiliers."   CYMRO.

EPITAPHS (May 19, 1880). —Quaint epitaph in
Wrexham Church :—
            " Here lyes a Church Warden
            A choyce Flower in that Garden
            Joseph Critchley by name
            Who liued in good fame
            Being gone to his Rest
            Without doubt he is blest.

   " Hee dyed the 10th of March 167¾ { Age 37
   " Dauid Yale, Edw Jeffreys, Jo : Nichols, yt yeare his
   Fellow Wardens."
                                                      LANDWOR.

SHROPSHIRE SCHOOLS (Feb. 11, 1880).—My
note does not refer to any particular man of note who was
educated at a Salopian School, but it is none the less
interesting as a contribution to a history of the Schools
of Shropshire.   I take from the *Shrewsbury Chronicle* of
Mar. 31, 1837, the following extract from a paragraph
alluding to a false report of the death of the Bishop of
Lichfield :—"The *Courier* said with truth that the loss of
such a man would be a public calamity.   The science of
Education was raised by his efforts to such a height that
when the *best* scholars from other parts of the kingdom
competed for the high prizes at our Universities, they
never felt disgraced in being defeated by a *Shrewsbury
Boy*."   SCROBBES BYRIG.

Mr. George Augustus May of Magdalene College,
Cambridge, and late of Shrewsbury School, is elected
Bell Scholar of that University.—*Salopian Journal*, Ap.
8, 1835.

Mr. Osborne Gordon, student of Christ Church, Oxford,
who has just been declared the successful candidate for
the Oxford University Scholarship, on Dean Ireland's
Foundation, was educated under Dr. Rowley at Bridgnorth School.—*Ibid.*, Ap. 15, 1835.   H.B.

AN ORIGINAL CADER IDRIS GUIDE (May
12, 1880).—A writer in the *Gents: Mag:* for Jan., 1820,
says :—" A few years ago there lived at Dolgelley in Merionethshire an individual who, although moving in a low
sphere of life, was extremely tenacious of the celebrity of
his illustrious progenitors.   This was Robin Edwards,
'Guide General to Cader Idris and the Waterfalls,' whose
character will be further exemplified by the following copy
of a paper, delivered by him to such strangers as visited
his neighbourhood for the purpose of viewing its numerous beauties :—

    " ' ROBERT EDWARDS, second son of the celebrated Tanner,
William Edwards, ap Griffith, ap Morgan, ap David, ap Owen,
ap Llewelyn, ap Cadwaladr, great-great-great grandson of an
illegitimate daughter of that illustrious hero—no less famed for
his irresistible prowess when mildly approaching under the
velvet standards of the lovely Venus, than when he sternly advanced with the terrific banner of the bloody Mars—and Sir
Rice Ap Thomas, who was the son of Anne, alias Catharine,
daughter of Howel ap Jenkyn of Ynys-y-Maengwyn, thirteenth
in descent from Cadwgan, a lineal descendant of Bleddyn ap
Cynfin, Prince of Powis.   Since his nativity full four and eighty
times hath the sun rolled to his summer solstice.   Fifty
years was he host of the Hen and Chickens, Pen-y-Front,
twenty of which he was Apparitor to the late Right Reverend
Father in God, John, Lord Bishop of Bangor, and his predecessors ; by chance made a glover, by genius a fly-dresser and
angler ; is now, by the all-divine assistance, conductor to and
over the most tremendous mountain Cader Idris ; to the
stupendous cataracts of the Cayne and the Mowddach ; and to
the enchanting cascades of Dol-y-Melynllyn, with all its beauti-

fully romantic scenery: Guide-General and magnificent expounder of all the natural and artificial curiosities of North Wales; professor of grand and bombastical lexicographical words, Knight of the most anomalous, whimsical, yet perhaps happy, order of hair-brained inexplicables.'

"Poor Robin, with all his eccentricities, is now gathered to those fathers he so enthusiastically venerated. I remember him well, and am greatly indebted to him for many an hour's amusement during my boyish days: he was a famous story-teller, and abounded in all the traditionary tales known in Merioneth, and almost every other shire in North Wales; the rehearsal of which afforded him great delight and gave full scope to the garulity and circumstantiality for which he was noted . . . Arrayed in his best suit, his head decorated with a large equilateral cocked-hat, and his diminutive person bestriding a poney as dwarfish as himself, he proudly led the way . . . He was a harmless, and, in his way, a very interesting personage, and his memory will not speedily be forgotten." The writer goes on to say that Edwards died in 1810 or 1811, and that his "address" quoted, was printed in 1806, when he was eighty-four years old. We are not told who wrote it, or whether it was done in joke or not.   N.W.S.

CURRENT NOTES.

MR. C. E. WILLIAMS, M.P.—Mr. Samuel Charles Evans Williams, of Bryntirion, Radnorshire, who has been [elected as a Liberal for the Radnor district of boroughs in the place of the Marquis of Hartington, is the eldest son of the late Rev. John Williams, of Bryntirion, formerly student and Censor of Christ Church, Oxford, by his marriage with Mary Charlotte, widow of Mr. John Patterson, of Devonshire. He was born in the year, 1842, and was educated at Westminster School and at Christ Church, Oxford, where he took his bachelor's degree in 1864, and proceeded M.A. in 1877. He qualified to be called to the bar at Lincoln's Inn in 1870. Mr. Williams is a magistrate for Radnorshire, and was appointed High Sheriff of that county for the present year. He is also master of the Radnorshire Harriers, and chairman of the Rhayader Highway Board. Mr. Williams, who has never before sat in the House of Commons, is the fourth new member returned to St. Stephen's since the commencement of the present Parliament. He married, in 1867, Mary Caroline, daughter of the Rev. Henry William R. Luttman-Johnson (formerly Michell), of Binderton House, Sussex.

VICTORIA REGINA.—Amongst the oil paintings in the Royal Academy this year, and in Gallery No. 3, there is a picture by H. T. Wells, R.A., numbered 217 in the catalogue, which was inspired by the following passage from the *Diaries of a Lady of Quality*, (Miss Frances Williams Wynn):—"On Tuesday, at 2¼ a.m., the scene closed [death of William the Fourth at Windsor Castle], and in a very short time the Archbishop of Canterbury and Lord Conyngham, the Chamberlain, set out to announce the event to their young sovereign. They reached Kensington Palace about five; they knocked, they rang, they thumped for a considerable time before they could rouse the porter at the gates; they were again kept waiting in the Court-yard, then turned into one of the lower rooms, where they seemed forgotten by everybody. They rang the bell, and desired that the attendant of the Princess Victoria might be sent to inform H. R. H. that they requested an audience on business of importance. After another delay and another ringing to enquire the cause, the attendant was summoned, who stated that the Princess was in such a sweet sleep, she could not venture to disturb her.   Then they said, 'We are come to the *Queen* on business of State,

and even sleep must give way to that.' It did, and to prove that *she* did not keep them waiting, in a few minutes she came into the room in a loose white nightgown and shawl, her nightcap thrown off, her hair falling upon her shoulders, her feet in slippers, tears in her eyes, but perfectly collected and dignified." The lady whose diary is here quoted was the sister of the Right Hon. Charles W. Williams-Wynn, and consequently the aunt of the Miss Charlotte Williams-Wynn whose journal and correspondence have been more recently published.

JUNE 2, 1880.

NOTES.

JUDICATURE IN WALES. — The following members of Parliament were appointed, in 1820, to enquire into the Judicature of Wales :—Hon. John Frederick Campbell, Lord J. Russell, Sir J. Mackintosh, Mr. Allen, Mr. Chetwynd, Sir W. W. Wynn, Mr. Berkeley Paget, Sir T. Mostyn, Col. Wood, Mr. C. W. Wynn, Mr. Henry Clive, Mr. Wilkins, Chancellor of the Exchequer, Attorney General, Sir James Nicholl, Mr. Abercrombie, Mr. E. Barham, Mr. Wrottesley, Sir John Owen, Mr. Davenport, Mr. W. Courtenay, Mr. J. Macdonald, Mr. P. Pryse, Mr. P. Corbet.   G.G.

KYNASTON'S CAVE.

The inhabitant of this cave, to whom it owes its name, was Humphrey Kynaston, usually called "The Wild"; son of Sir Roger Kynaston, Knight, of Hordley, by Lady Elizabeth, daughter of Henry Grey, Earl of Tankerville, his second wife. By his first wife (daughter of Lord Cobham and widow of Lord Strange) Sir Roger had a son who died without issue. During the life of his elder brother, Humphrey lived at Middle Castle. The character of the reign in which Humphrey was born and of that in which he suffered outlawry will fairly account for the bent of his, and the issue of his fortunes. His father was in favor in the time, and at the Court of Edward the 4th, and the son, though not quite a cotemporary with the young monarch, was a man of some fashion, and an imitator of the Court :—

> Now Edward was indeed the glass
> Wherein the noble youth did dress themselves.

Adopting such manners and habits he would be splendid with little prudence, brave with little moderation; addicted to pleasure but capable of activity in great emergencies,—precisely the character to produce an outlaw of some eminenee. Heartily attached to the Court of the House of York, in which he had enjoyed the pleasures of his youth; and where he was a favourite through the honoured period of his early manhood. How far he had been imprudent in the time of the Impostor Lambert Simnel, in 1487, the second year of Henry 7th, is not known, but his outlawry took place in 1491; six years after the death of Edward the 4th; when Perkin Warbeck, the second Impostor, assuming the character of the heir of the House of York, was supported in the Netherlands by the Duchess of Burgundy, mother-in-law of Henry the 7th; who, besides the Flemish troops she sent over to Ireland, assisted Perkin to fit out a naval expedition, with a mixed collection of outlaws, pirates, robbers, &c., of every description, to the amount of about 600 :—

> Of all the unsettled humours of the land,
> Rash, inconsiderate, fiery voluntaries :
> Bearing their birthright proudly on their backs,
> To make a hazard of new fortunes;
> In brief, a rasher choice of dauntless spirits
> Did never float upon the swelling tide.

Whether debt was the real or pretended cause; it is not to be wondered at that a Prince so cautious as Henry kept a watchful eye over such an adventurer as Humphrey: he was, however, pardoned two years afterwards.

This cave was certainly his retreat, at that time much overgrown with wood. Among many reports, is one that his mother lived at Ruyton, and each Sunday took him his dinner, &c., that day being, as now, a kind of sanctuary for civil freedom.

Both mother and son were in pecuniary distress. In the Corporation books of Shrewsbury there is a Register (under the law called 'Statute Merchant') of a joint Bond of Twenty pounds.

Being a man of enterprise, he became the wild hero of popular romance, and was the Robin Hood of his day. Once being on the eastern side of Montford's Bridge, over which he must needs return, the under sheriff came with his posse to the bridge, which consisted of planks laid upon stone pillars, and made such a breach as he thought no horse could pass over, and then lay in ambush; when Wild Humphrey returned and entered upon the bridge they pursued to apprehend him, which he perceiving put spurs to his horse and cleared the breach : the measure of this leap was cut out afterwards on Knockin Heath with H.——K. at each end of it.

When the Lordships of Middle and Knockin descended from Lord Strange to the Derby family, the Constable or Castle keeper (third in succession) was this Wild Humphrey.

He died in the year 1534 at the memorable era of the Reformation, rendered eminently remarkable by the death of Cardinal Wolsey, the rise of Cranmer, and the marriage of Anna Buleyne, in the reign of Henry the eighth.

N.B. The greater part of this account, as far as it relates to Humphrey's pedigree &c., I was favoured with by Col. Kynaston Powell of Hardwick, near Ellesmere, a descendant of Sir R. Kynaston, Knight.

[Mr. Rowland Hunt, who penned the foregoing was a prolific writer and publisher of pamphlets. He was the grandfather of the late Right Hon. Ward Hunt, First Lord of the Admiralty, and died in 1811. He was an active magistrate for the county of Salop ; and, Mr. Salisbury says in his *Border Counties Worthies* "dedicated his time and talents to the superintendence of the building of the new county gaol in Shrewsbury in accordance with Howard's humane plans." It was stated in *Bye-gones*, Apr. 7, 1875, that Mr. Hunt was, with another gentleman, instrumental in placing a bust of Howard (by Bacon) over the entrance to the gaol. We hope another week to give an extract from Gough's *History of Middle*, about Kynaston; also Dovaston's ballad.—Ed.]

OSWESTRY NOTES.—I send you a few desultory notes ; if I only had the leisure, they deserve some annotations, and would repay the trouble. For the convenience of modern readers I have translated some passages from the Latin. I have given references to White Minster in my *English Minsters* (Chatto and Windus).

NEW HUNDREDS.—27 Henry viii. Places assigned to the sheeretoune adjecte to Salop. *Oswestre* Whetington Masbroke (Mosa forsan Marsle) Knocking Ellesmere, Downe and Cherbury hundreds.

That the lordshippes of *Oswestre* Whitington Masbroke and Knocking with their membre shalle be knowen by the name of the hundred of *Oswestre*, that the lordship of the Ellesmere with the membres of the same be annexed to the hundred of Pymhille, that the lordship of Downe with the membres to the hundrede of Chyrbyri. *(Leland Coll. II. 453.)* [I. Will. I.] Alane Fleilsone had gyven to him *Oswaldestre (Leland Coll. I. 231).*

OSWESTRY.—Of Henry's expedition to *White Minster* and his losses owing to floods of rain ; and of beseigers slain. Anno. *1211* the King at White Minster, with a large

army mustered, marched into Wales *(III. 336.)* S. Oswald was killed by Penda, King of Mercia, at Maserfield, it adjoins the Marches of Wales, and is distant about 7 miles from Shrowesbyri ; on the domain which belongs to the Abbot of that town ; *White Church* was built in honour of S. Oswald. Hard by is the spring which the country folk call *S. Oswald's Well*, and on the bank a vast tree throws its pleasant shadow across the water ; and it is close to this spot that the head and hands of S. Oswald were impaled during a whole year. *(Leland Coll. II. 367.)* We took our way to White Minster, and thence to Oswalstree, where as it lies on the Powysland, the noble Prince of Powis, Griffin Madoc's son, Elisset, and others, met us. We passed the night at Oswalstreae, where William Fitzalan, a young man of generous temper, pressed us heartily to partake of a banquet after the English fashion, of sumptuous entertainment, far too splendid and lavishly set out. (Giraldus in *Leland Coll. III. 105.*)

                              MACKENZIE E. C. WALCOTT.

QUERIES.

PARISH LAW LAST CENTURY (Jan. 8, 1879). Recently I found amongst some old papers a scroll, of which the enclosed is a true copy. The writing is very elaborate, and distinct. The signatures are very neat, notably that of J. C. Maurice and Hump. Kynaston. Opposite the signatures of the Churchwardens (E. Lloyd and W. Waller) are two seals (black wax), but the seal impression is indistinct. It seems to be a certificate from one parish acknowledging Tho. Joseph to be a parishioner. The system before the Poor Law and Unions. Perhaps you may think the copy worth inserting in *Bye-gones*, and may be some light may be thrown on it ?

The Glyn.   T. A. H.

To the Churchwardens and Overseers of ye Poore of ye Parish of Llansanfrayd Glan Keiriog in the County of Denbigh and to any or eithr of them.

MONTGOM'Y

We Edward Griffith Churchwarden for that part of ye Parish of Llansanfrayde-y-mechin, w'ch lyes in ye Hundred of Poole in ye said County and William Waller Overseer of ye Poor for ye same doe hereby own and acknowledge Thomas Joseph now an Infant to be an Inhabitant legally settled w'thin the s'd parishe. In witness whereof wee have hereunto set our hands and seals this twentieth day of January in ye fourth year of Her now mat' Reign Anne of great Britaine Qeen Defender of ye ffaith er'rg. in the year of our Lord God 1709.

Attested By   signed
John Lloyde   Geo : Reynolds   E Griffiths (seal)
                   Vior of Llansanfraid William   Waller
Ic : Maurice   y mechin   (seal)
Joseph Griffiths

We whose names are und'r writen being two of her Mat'js Justices of ye Peace for ye said County of Mountgom'y doe allow of the Certificate above writen witness our hands this 22d day of March 1709-10

                              Lumley Williams
                              Hump Kynaston

The back of the parchment bears this inscription :—
" A Certificate from Llansauffrayd in Mechain
to indemnefye   . . Parish from Thos. Jones
son of John Jones "

THE BATTLE OF CHIRK BRIDGE. — The Oswestry correspondent of the *Salopian Journal* of Nov. 1, 1837, in reporting a chase after a thief, and his capture in Aston covers, adds, "he turns out to be an old fox, a deserter of the artillery, of whom a description has been

in the Oswestry police office for the last four years, sent down by that artillery-man who looked so well and distinguished himself so nobly at the ever memorable battle of Chirk Bridge, and who ever after that event was known to say, *he thought they could do something at Oswestry !* Now anything bearing upon the colliery riots of 1831 is interesting to the borders, so I should be gl d to glean some particulars about "that artillery-man" and his performances?
                                     CLINKER.

REPLIES.

THE REV. DR. WILLIAMS (May 12, 1880).— Amongst the list of students at the Oswestry 'Academy' given at this date was that of "William Evans." A record of his future career may be found in a work entitled *Nonconformity in Cheshire*, published in 1864. You will, perhaps, not be inclined to publish more than an outline of the life of Mr. Evans, so I will condense the information into a paragraph. He was born at Bala in 1773, and when quite a boy—so much was his opinion valued—he was selected by Mr. Robert Hughes, "an aged poet who was appointed judge" at an Eisteddfod, as his assistant in the adjudication. In Jan. 1791 he became one of Dr. Williams's students at Oswestry ; and after a short residence as Congregational Minister, at Lane Delph, in the Potteries, he settled at Bridgnorth, where he remained two or three years, when he removed to Stockport. As Minister of Orchard-street Chapel in that place he interested himself in the plan of sending out lay preachers to the villages ; a course which led to the formation of the Cheshire Union for the support of Itinerant Preachers. Of this Society he became secretary, and in 1806 prepared its first report. He died in 1814 at the age of 42. His congregation at Stockport at his death subscribed a sum whereby £40 a year was paid to the widow for her life ; and at her death the principal was divided amongst his children. Perhaps some of your readers will be able to trace the career of other students mentioned in the document you have published.   WREXHAMITE.

STRAY NOTES.

RICHARD ROBERTS OF LLANYMYNECH AND THE CONWAY TUBULAR BRIDGE.—"In connection with the subject of railways, we may allude in passing," says Mr. Smiles in his *Self Help*, p. 271, "to Mr. Roberts's invention of the Jacquard punching machine—a self-acting tool of great power, used for punching any required number of holes, of any pitch and to any pattern, with mathematical accuracy, in bridge or boiler plates. The origin of this invention was something similar to that of the self-acting mule. The contractors for the Conway Tubular Bridge while under construction, in 1848, were greatly hampered by combinations amongst the workmen, and they despaired of being able to finish the girders within the time specified in the contract. The punching of the iron plates by hand was a tedious and expensive, as well as inaccurate process ; and the work was proceeding so slowly that the contractors found it absolutely necessary to adopt some new method of punching if they were to finish the work in time. In their emergency they appealed to Mr. Roberts, and endeavoured to persuade him to take the matter up. He at length consented to do so, and evolved the machine in question during his evening's leisure—for the most part while quietly sipping his tea. The machine was produced, the contractors were enabled to proceed with the punching of the plates, independent of the refractory men, and the work was executed with a despatch, accuracy and excellence, that would not otherwise have been possible."

THE RECORDER OF OSWESTRY IN 1644.

Now that we have so recently undergone a change in the Recordership of Oswestry, it will interest some of our readers to peruse the following "Opinion" written by Sir Sampson Eure (*) in 1644. The borough was then governed by the Charter of James the First ; and the choice of local magistrates—Steward, Recorder, and Bailiffs— was in the hands of the burgesses.

"Mr. Bayliffs/ I haue receaued . . . . . . the 3d of Aprill wch . . . . . to my hands till the . . . . . . Touching the elecc'on of the Record' it must be within the moneth of the vacancy, but he may be sworne at any time before he take on him the execuc'on of the place, therefore you are mistaken in yor l're. I com'end yor care in the choice of yor Recorder ; that he showld be learned in the lawes yor charter requireth and I aduise you to choose a man not onely learned but of grauity & worth that may honor the place, and not disparage it. Sr Henry Townsend a graue man and a Judge in Wales and one of the Councell in the Marches of Wales was yor Recorder and yor steward or deputy steward, you may bethink yor selues of a fitt man ; I shall name none to you, nor take excepc'on to him whose name you menc'on, because I know him not. I am not pleased wth yor elecc'on of Forrein Burgesses, wthout my app'bac'on, (wherein p'aduenture you haue forfeited yor charter) I expect & doe require you that they receiue noe benefitt or priuiledge as Burgenses till they haue my approbac'on according to yor charter ; wherein if there be any opposic'on I expect to be speedily certified thereof ; and if y charter appoint that they showld not be sworne before, or wthout my consent, I expect that be allsoe p'formed. And soe wth my very hearty co'mendac'ons to yor selves and the rest of that Corporac'on, I rest
             "Yor very loueing Friend
                   "SAMP: EURE.

"Lincoln Colledg
"Aprill the 13th 1644.
"I haue sent you my opinion to yor questions inclosed ; and wish you to p'ceed to the elecc'on of yor Recorder wthin the time p'fixed by yor ch're."
[Addressed :] "To the worll my very loueing Friende
           Francis Smallman and Siluanus Jones gent.
           Bayliffs of the Town and Libertye of
           Oswestry in the County of Salop,"

(Extract from Charter and Bailiffs' Questions).

"'And o'r will and pleasure is that as often as the said place or office of Recordershipp shall happen to become void that then yt shall and may be lawfull to and for the said Bayliffes and Burgesses and their successors wthin one moneth re . . . . after such tyme or tymes as the said office shall become voyd and notice thereof by them had to assemble themsel . . . . together in the said Guildhall or any other place convenient wthin the said Borough or the Lib'ties thereof, and then and there as often as the said office shalbe void yt shall & may be lawfull to & for the said Bayliffs and burgesses and their successors and the greater parte of them, then and there to elect & choose out one honest and discreate man and learned in the lawes of our Realme of England to be Recorder of the said Borough. And we will and graunt That eu'ie p'son and p'sons soe elected shalbe Recorder of the said towne duringe his life and shall take his oathe before the Bayliffes of the said Borough honestlie and truelie to execute his said place./'

(*) Sir Sampson Eure was of the family of Ralph, the 3d. Lt Eure, who was King's lieutenant in the Principality of Wales in 1608. Sir Francis Eure, brother to the above, married Ellin, elder dau. and coheir of William Maurice, of Clenenny, the son by Margaret dau. and heir of John Lacon, of Porkington, of Sir William Maurice, Kt., of Clenenny. The Eures were thus connected with the neighbourhood of Oswestry. The Barony of Eure became extinct in 1698.

"These above written are the verie woordes coppied from the Charter of o'r graunt & warrant to choose o'r Recorder/ And also we desier yor advise vpon these woordes of o'r Charter vnderwritten whether the ould Bayliffs may sweare the new bayliffes wthout havinge the Steward or Recorder to ioyne wth them, or not : viz And we further will that they after they shalbe soe chosen and no'iated shall before they or any of them may dee or execute any thinge by vertue of there Bayliffshipps take their corporall oath before the ould Bayliffes and the Steward or Recorder, of the sayd towne or one of them to doe &c.

Also whether yor Deputie Steward may supplie & serve in place of the Steward to sweare the new bailiffs.

Our Steward, Recorder, & Bayliffs by o'r charter are seu'all Justices of the peace wthin o'r towne & lib'ties"

[Addressed :] "For the right woo'll Sr Sampson Eure Knight this p'sent at Linckoln Colledge."

(Sir Sampson Eure's Opinion.)

"1. Thowgh by the charter the Recorder must be chosen wthin one moneth after the place becomes void, yet he may be sworne at any conuenient time before he take vpon him the execuc'on of that office, For there is noe time limitted for the taking of his oath, as is supposed in ye Baylieff's I're.

"2. I conceiue the ould Bayliffs may sweare the new Bayliefs wthout the Steward or Recorder joyneing wth them, And soe may the Steward or Recorder alone sweare them, otherwise these words (or one of them) would signifie noething & be meerely sup'fluous. For these words (before the ould Bayliefs and the Steward or Recorder, or one of them) carry the same sence (as I take it) as if the words were, (before the ould Bayliefs, Steward, or Recorder) For the words or one of them, make the whole clause disiunctiue, & giue a seu'all awthority in that p'ticuler to the Bayliefs, Steward or Recorder. And I think the Bayliefs alone haue vsed to doe it, wch is somewhat considerable, but whatsoeuer the vsage hath bene, I take the Lawe to be as I haue here expressed myself.

"3. The Deputy Steward hath noe authority to sweare any of the Bayliefs.

"SAMP : EURE Bo. Aprilis, 1644."

We copy the foregoing from Mr. Stanley Leighton's interesting chapter on the "Oswestry Corporation Records," published in the "Transactions of the Shropshire Archæological Society," to which we refer our more intelligent Oswestry readers who are not yet subscribers to that publication.

SHREWSBURY SCHOOL.—The Porson prize, which is given annually at Cambridge to such resident undergraduates as shall make the best translation of a proposed passage in Shakspeare, or some other English dramatist, into Greek verse, has been awarded this year to Mr. Garland of St. John's College, and Mr. Inge of King's College (equal). The passage selected is from "Timon of Athens," Act 3, Scene 5, "I am a humble suitor . . . Weigh but the crime with this." Mr. Garland left Shrewsbury School in July, 1877, having previously obtained the Clasical Minor Scholarship at St. John's College. This is the 24th Porson [prize (including five brackets) which has been gained by a Shrewsbury man since 1848. The Browne Medals, which are offered annually at Cambridge for the best Greek ode in imitation of Sappho, and the best Latin ode in imitation of Horace, have been adjudged this year to Mr. J. C. Moss of St. John's College. The subject of the Greek ode is "Sicilia." The subject of the Latin ode is "Cyprus." Mr. Moss, who left Shrewsbury in July, 1878, obtained the same distinctions last year.

OSWESTRY AND WELSHPOOL NATURALISTS' FIELD CLUB.—The second excursion for 1880 took place on Thursday. After meeting at Buttington Station the party proceeded to explore the volcanic range, which stands in front of the Long Mountain. Moel y Golfa was first ascended, and the labour of climbing the steep sides is well repaid by the magnificent panorama stretched out beneath you. As the View on the Welsh side was very clear, Cader Idris, Plynlimon, and the Arans were distinctly visible. The camp on the neighbouring hill of Cefn y Castell was very plain. It is said by some to have been the camp of Caractacus, and that he was defeated on Moel y Golfa by the Romans. The party then crossed the intermediate valley to the Breidden, and thence made their way to Pool Quay Vicarage, where they were very hospitably invited to tea. There were present Major and Mrs. Barnes, Mr. T. St. J. Oswell, and Miss Oswell, Mr. G. Humphrys, the Revs. A. Field and O. M. Feilden, &c. Amongst the plants found were Saxifragia Granulata, Sedum Forsterianum, Geranium Sanguineum, Lychnis Viscari, Helianthemum Vulgare, and Oak Fern. The day was very fine, and the excursion was a most pleasant one.

JUNE 9, 1880.

NOTES.

THE FATHER OF THE REV. JOB ORTON.—Mr. Salisbury, in his *Worthies* (see Reprint of *Bye-gones*, 1876, page 53) gives a short notice of the Rev. Job Orton. "He was born" we are told by the *Salopian Magazine* for Nov. 1815, "on the seite on which stands Messrs. Beck and Co.'s bank. His father was a respectable grocer, of honest and upright principles, and one of the most industrious habits. Such was the attention of Mr. Orton to his business, that it became a provincial proverb, and nothing was more generally introduced, as a sort of appeal in the confirmation of a circumstance or narrative, than—*It's as sure as that Job Orton is in his shop!*" The son, the Rev. Job Orton, died on July 19, 1783.

SCROBBES BYRIG.

BURNING OF FRIAR FOREST.—Some account of the image of Derfel Gadarn, and the martyrdom of Friar Forest is given in the *Gossiping Guide to Wales*, but there are some incidents connected therewith related by Froude (*History of England*, Vol. 3, pp. 296-7) that I have not met with elsewhere. The author says :—

"An accidental coincidence contributed to the dramatic effect of his (Forest's) execution. In a chapel at Llan Dderfel, in North Wales, there had stood a figure of an ancient Welsh Saint, called Dderfel Gadern. The figure was a general favourite. The Welsh people 'came daily in pilgrimage to him, some with kyne, some with oxen and horses, and the rest with money, insomuch' (I quote a letter of Ellis Price, the Merionethshire Visitor) 'that there were five or six hundred, to a man's estimation, that offered to the said image the fifth day of this month of April. The innocent people hath been sore allured and enticed to worship, insomuch that there is a common saying amongst them that, whosoever will offer anything to the image of Dderfel Gadern, he hath power to fetch him or them that so offer, out of hell.'"

This letter of the "Visitor" Price, was one addressed to Thomas Lord Cromwell, and he went on to enquire what he was to do with the image, and received orders to despatch the thing at once to London. "The parishioners offered to subscribe forty pounds to preserve their profitable possession, but in vain—Cromwell was ruthless. The image was sent to the same destination with the rest of his kind ; and arriving opportunely, it was hewn into fuel to form the pile where the victim of the new heresy court was to suffer."

Mr. Froude quotes "MS. Cotton, Cleopatra, E 4" for the letter of Ellis Price, and "MS. State Paper Office, second series, vol. 34," for the reluctance of the Welshmen to part with the image.   N.W.S.

KNIGHTS OF THE ROYAL OAK (Nov. 1, 1876.)—The *Camb: Quar: Mag:* v. 2, p. 165-6, gives a list of the Knights of the Royal Oak, an Order invested by Charles II, as a reward to several of his followers, but which Order was soon laid aside, lest it might create heats and animosities. The following is the list for North Wales :—

ANGLESEY.	£
John Robinson, esq.	800
William Bould, esq.	1000
Thomas Wood, esq.	600
— Bodden, esq.	1000
Pierce Lloyd, esq.	1000

CARNARVON.	
Sir John Owen's heire	1500

DENBIGH.	
Charles Salisburie, esq.	1300
Huscall Thelwall, esq.	600
Foulke Middleton, esq.	600
John Wynn, esq	600
Sir Thomas Middleton, knt. (of Chirk Castle, of Westminster after, spent most of his estate)	600
Bevis Lloyd, esq.	600
John Lloyd, esq.	800

FLINTSHIRE.	
Sir Roger Mostyn, knt,, of Mostyn, bart.	4000
Sir Edward Mostyn, knt.	1500
— Salisbury of Hegragge, esq.	600

	£
Robert Davis, esq.	2000
John Puliston, esq.	2500
John Hanmer, knt., bart.	3000
William Hanmer, esq.	1500

MERIONETH.	
William Salisbury, esq.	800
William Price, esq.	1500
William Vaughan, esq.	1200
Howell Vaughan, esq.	800
— Attwyll, of Palke, esq.	1500
Lewis Owen, esq.	600
John Lloyd, esq.	600

MONTGOMERY.	
William Morgan, esq.	4000
William Jones, of Lanarthe, esq.	1000
Thomas Lewis, esq.	1000
Charles Vann, esq.	800
Walter Rumsey, esq.	600
William Jones, of Llantrishent, esq.	600
— Milbourne, esq.	800

The foregoing list, which is of those deemed "fit and qualified to be made Knights," with "the value of their estates," Anno Dom. 1660, is "taken from a MS. by Peter le Neve, esq." They were to wear a medal pendant to a ribbon, on which was to be a device of the King in the oak; but we are not told that the medals were ever executed.			M.C.A.S.

PARLIAMENT OF ENGLAND (May 26, 1880). Reign of James the First to accession of Charles II.

COUNTY OF SALOP.

1603	Sir Richard Liveson, Knt. ; Sir Robert Needham, Knt.
1614	No returns found.
1620	Sir Robert Vernon, Knt. ; Sir Francis Kynaston, Knt.
1623	Sir Richard Newport, Knt. ; Sir Andrew Corbett, Knt.
1625	Ditto	Ditto
1626	Sir Roland Cotton, Knt. ; Richard Leveson, Esq.
1627	Sir Richard Newporte, Knt. ; Sir Andrew Corbett, Knt.
1640	No returns found.
1640	Sir Richard Lee, bart. ; Sir John Corbett, bart. [This was the "Long Parliament." Sir Richard Lee was afterwards disabled to sit; and Humphrey Edwards, Esq., was elected. See *Sh. Arch. Trans.* Vol. 3, p. 143.]
1654	[Humphrey Mackworth, sen., gent. [Writ torn. The writ directs that four Knights shall be elected.]
1656	Samuel Moore, esq ; Andrew Lloyd, esq. [The other two names torn.]
1658	No returns found.

BOROUGH OF SHREWSBURY.

1603	Richard Barker, esq. ; Francis Tate, esq. [This election having been declared void, another took place when the same parties were re-elected ; Mr. Barker being described as the Recorder of Shrewsbury.]

1614	No returns found.
1620	Sir Richard Newport, Knt. ; Francis Barckeley, esq.
1623	Thomas Owen, esq. ; Francis Barkley, esq.
1625	Ditto ;	Sir William Owen, Knt.
1626	Ditto ;	Ditto.
1627	Ditto ;	Ditto.
1640	Ditto ;	Francis Newport, esq.
1640	William Spurstowe, merchant ; Ditto. ["Long Parliament." Francis Newport was "disabled" and Spurstowe "deceased." Thomas Hunte, esq, and William Masham, esq, were elected.]
1654	Richard Cheshire, gent ; Humphrey Mackworth, jun, gent.

QUERIES.

SIR PHILIP SIDNEY.—In *Bye-gones,* Dec. 25, 1878, you published (from Mr. Arbor's *English Garner*) a letter written by Sir Henry Sidney to his son Philip at Shrewsbury School, in 1564. A version of the same letter appears in *Shreds and Patches* for May 5, which contains the following clause, not included in Mr. Arbor's reprint :—

"If you hear a wise sentence, or an apt phrase, commit it to your memory, with respect to the circumstance when you shall speak it. Let never oath be heard come out of your mouth, nor word of ribaldry : detest it in others, so shall custom make to yourself a law against it in yourself."

The correspondent of *Shreds and Patches* does not say so, but I gather that his version of the letter is taken (probably at second hand) from "the original at Penshurst." If so, how has Mr. Arbor omitted the passage ?
							J.?.R.

MINERAL SPRINGS IN WALES.—In a newspaper for Nov. 1804, I find a long extract on this subject from Campbell's *Political Survey.* The writer seems to be of opinion that many "salubrious springs" exist were only some trouble taken to discover them, and he goes on thus to enumerate those already known :—"There are, however, instances enough to encourage such a search. A very good chalybeate spring has been found in the garden belonging to the episcopal palace at Bangor, in Carnarvonshire. At Caergwrle, in Flintshire, there are two salt springs, one of which is in great credit for curing obstinate scurvies, and even leprosies, by drinking the water and washing with it. Llandrindod, in the county of Radnor, is of late years become famous for several chalybeate and other springs, which have done extraordinary cures in a variety of chronic distempers. At Llanrwst, in Denbighshire, there is a spring which the country people have found by experience to have very salutary effects in scrophulous and scorbutic cases ; and, if some accounts that have been given of it be true, it certainly deserves to be more carefully examined, when perhaps it will be found of a very singular nature. In the road, about a quarter of a mile north of Ruthin, in the same county, in the way to Denbigh, there is a very fine medicinal spring called St. Peter's Well, which was secured by a wall built round it, and a basin placed to receive the water; but these having been decayed, the spring is disregarded. On Troesellyne hill (or Tresylwin hills, for there are two of that name) in the north part of the island of Anglesey, there rises a medicinal spring, the waters of which have a very pleasing acidity, and are found to be of very great service in agues, in dropsies, at the beginning of consumptions, and also in a jaundice. At Swansea, in Glamorganshire, mineral waters have been discovered which resemble those of Shadwell, and have done great cures in palsies, rheumatisms, and consumptions, but are particularly remarkable for restraining hemorrhages, and stopping fluxes of all kinds." Llandrindod and Trefriw springs, as we all know, are still celebrated. Have any of the others ever been developed ? G.G.

REPLIES.

CORRIS (Mar. 24, 1880).—The general way of spelling this place is *Corris*; but it seems that this modern custom of spelling it is quite erroneous; and that it ought to be spelled *Corus*. In the "Sketch of the History of Merionethshire, by Mr. Robert Vaughan of Hengwrt" (*Camb : Reg* : for 1796) it is written *Corys*; the *y* bearing similar sound to that in *erys*, or the *u* in *melus*. Probably the first place which had its name from the confluence of the river Corus was a farm house called *Aber Corus*. But as to the derivation of the name of the river, it may be added to the quotation given by DYVNIG, that the *Darlundraith o Fachynleth* &c ; says that it is supposed its meaning is, the sheep steps (Grisiau defaid). The late J. A. Owen ("Bardd Meirion") was of that opinion, as it is said ; who probably suggested that meaning at first ; taking *cor* for dafad or defaid, and *ris* for step. But in doing so he must have followed the present style of spelling the word. As for myself I do not think that either of these suggestions will account for the name of the river, but that it simply bears the name of some person called *Corus*. To prop up this suggestion with facts bearing on the subject, I may say that there are two persons of historical note of the name of *Corus*. The one was a monk from Brittany (Llydaw), who came over to Wales with Padarn about the year 516. The other was a son of Cynedd Wledig, as it is sta'.ed. It is rather probable the river had its name from one of these; but it may be it had it from some other person whose memory has been preserved only in the name of this river. As to the meaning of the word *Corus* in itself I must leave it to etymologists. But if my suggestion is right, whatever its etymological meaning may be, that has nothing to do with the name of the river, as it would be called *Corus* from the name of a person, and not from any thing in the river itself, neither in its bed, or vicinity. It seems that the letter *o* in *Corus* does not bear the long sound as the word is generally pronounced ; on the contrary it has the short sound.

Dolgelley. ROBYN FRYCH.

THE CYMMRODORION SOCIETY.—LECTURE ON CELTIC ART.

A lecture on Celtic Art was delivered by Mr. St. John Hancock, on Wednesday evening, May 26. The chair was taken by Mr. Henry Jenner, of the British Museum, in the unavoidable absence of the Rev. John Davies, M.A., F.S.A.

The Lecturer explained that although advertised as a lecture on "Celtic Art," his remarks would specially refer, on this occasion, to Celtic Ornament, or the Decorative Art. The civilization of a nation being known by its progress in the Arts, and its first expression of feeling would be found in what is termed the Fine Arts. Mounds and cairns were only certain records of the history of a people, which ultimately gave way to the more complete expression of language and literature. The lecturer traced the characteristics and contrasts of the four great building races of mankind, viz., the Turanian, the Semitic, the Celtic, and the Aryan. While in literature the Celtic races gave good account of themselves, there was—though latent—a power for discovering, appreciating, and executing works of art of the highest order, and in support of this the lecturer quoted the opinion of an eminent authority, Professor Ferguson, who says—"The true glory of the Celt in Europe is his artistic eminence. It is not, perhaps, too much to assert that without his intervention we should not have possessed in modern times a Church worthy of admiration, or a picture, or statue, we could look at without shame," &c. And Mr. Gladstone, in an address delivered before the Society at the London Institution, on the "Potter's Art in Britain," ascribed to the Celt, "a very strong natural sense of beauty." To trace the history and influence of Celtic Art comprehensively, it would be necessary to trace the history of civilization in Europe, for which reason the lecturer confined himself to the peculiarities of some forms of art in these islands, and he expressed a hope that the whole subject would be undertaken by a competent person. In Europe three influences were traceable in the arts—the influence of Rome, and of Byzantium, thirdly the supervening influence traceable to a Celtic source, the main-spring of which lay in these islands, and more especially in Ireland, which enjoyed much of the privileges of Byzantium, and from whence art sallied forth in those "dark ages," from the fifth to the ninth centuries. After referring to the stone, bronze, and iron age classification of mankind, the lecturer said that the chief art remains of the Bronze-age, corresponded with the period of Celtic predominance in that prehistoric time and were principally in Pottery, some of it of a highly ornamental character —diagrams and illustrations of which were exhibited— betraying sound ideas, in the mind of the artist, of the true principles of Ornament, the styles of which were not superseded but developed and applied to other forms by their conquerors. By the aid of diagrams the lecturer illustrated the characteristics of the stone monuments of these islands—the sepulchral remains possessing great beauty of proportion, and, in ornament and sculpture, high artistic talent. Referring to the work of the early painters in Britain an examination of the illustrations (which were handed round the room) would show that the style was characterized by excessive elaboration of ornament, and in colour presented chromatic effects of great beauty, and that while in Italy and Greece from the fifth to the eighth centuries, pictorial art was all but extinct, and outside those countries it scarcely existed, there flourished a style of art in the British Isles which had been originated, cultivated, and brought to a high state of perfection, and distinct from anything which preceded it. After referring to the commercial value of the cultivation of art, the lecturer expressed a hope that the "Welsh Eisteddfod" would be made a means of encouraging its study, and he trusted that the Hon. Society of Cymmrodorion, which he believed represented the talent and intelligence of the Celt in Wales, would be a means of fostering, aiding, and encouraging the Art energies of our fellow-countrymen, and directing that flood of artistic feeling which they undoubtedly possessed into useful and profitable channels.

Mr. Jenner being obliged to leave the meeting soon after the close of the lecture, Mr. Bernard Quaritch presided during the remainder of the meeting, and added some interesting remarks on European and Celtic Art, after which a discussion followed, sustained by Mr. R. Charles, Mr. Howel W. Lloyd, M. A.,Mr. T. W. Hancock, and Professor Rudler. Mr. Quaritch lent some of the very valuable illustrations exhibited.

Death of Mr. Wynne of Peniarth.

(From the *Oswestry Advertizer.*)

" Died, at his residence, Peniarth, Towyn-Merioneth, June 9, 1880, William Watkin Edward Wynne, Esq., in the 79th year of his age."

By the death of this accomplished gentleman Welsh archæology and genealogy have lost their best exponent. For the last generation no single person has done so much to illustrate the antiquities and family histories of Wales. In ecclesiology Mr. Wynne was especially learned. Under his unerring guidance, so wisely invoked by the Rector in preference to that of a professional architect, the beautiful parish church of Llanaber (Barmouth) was restored some twenty years ago in a manner which makes it one of the glories of early English church architecture in this country. His contributions to archæological journals and other papers are numerous, and especially valuable from a genealogical point of view. His memory was an extraordinary storehouse of family history and a perfect register of the devolution of estates in Caernarvonshire and Merionethshire. It is a matter for profound regret—a regret which he often expressed himself—that he could not bring himself to face the laborious task of writing a history of Merionethshire. For such a work he had qualifications and materials which no other living person possesses. In the year 1859 the last Sir Robert Williames Vaughan of Nannau dying without issue left his distant kinsman, Mr. Wynne, one of the executors and trustees of his will, and bequeathed to him the splendid collection of MSS. known as the "Hengwrt Collection." This historical library was formed by Robert Vaughan of Hengwrt—known as the Antiquary—in the 17th century. He was himself a distinguished Welsh litterateur, and acquired a large number of rare and early Welsh MSS., and transcribed a still larger number of others. He was the contemporary and intimate friend of another great literary Welshman and collector, John Jones of Gelli Lyfdy. The two friends made a bargain that whichever should die first should leave to the other his collection. John Jones predeceased Robert Vaughan and faithfully carried out the compact. Thus the already good collection of the Antiquary Vaughan was immensely enriched, and through two centuries it remained in the possession of his descendants at Hengwrt, near Dolgelley, until in 1859, it found a worthy home and an enthusiastic custodian at Peniarth. Among some of its most famous treasures are two of the "Four Ancient Books of Wales," edited by Mr. Skene (Edinb., 1868), viz., "Y Llyfr Du o Gaerfyrddin" (Black Book of Caermarthen), said to be written by Cynddelw Brydydd Mawr in the twelfth century, and the "Llyfr Taliesin," written in the thirteenth century. A version of "Chaucer's Canterbury Tales," published in 1868 by the Chaucer Society, and " The Greal " and other prose works now being published and translated by Mr. Wynne's old and learned friend, Canon Williams (late of Rhydycroesau, and now rector of Culmington, Salop) are some amongst the many priceless works of this unrivalled collection. One of the versions of the "Ancient Laws and Institutes of Wales," published by the late Aneurin Owen, by order of the Record Commissioners in 1841, is from the MSS. at Peniarth, no less than twelve different copies of the various codes being referred to by the editor as forming part of "the splendid Hengwrt Collection." Some years ago Mr. Wynne published in the *Archæologia Cambrensis* an exhaustive catalogue of his collection, which in amplitude of description, may be almost classed amongst catalogues raisonnés. (See *Arch : Camb :* III. Series, Vol. XV.; and IV. Series, Vols. I. and II.) In 1874, on the death of the Hon. T. Pryce Lloyd, Mr. Wynne was appointed Constable of Harlech Castle in his stead. In 1872 he was elected a

Fellow of the Society of Antiquaries, and was at the time of his death one of the Secretaries for North Wales. Two years ago he, in conjunction with his friend Mr. Clark of Dowlais, published an interesting account of the castle, which is now the standard guide book to the old ruins. In 1873 he contributed to "Kalendars of Gwynedd," a work compiled by Mr. E. Breese, very copious notes of great genealogical value and interest. He also did the same for Sir Samuel Rush Meyrick, when the latter, in 1846, edited for the Welsh MSS. Society the Heraldic Visitations of Lewis Dwnn, and his notes in that important work are very illustrative. Sir Henry Ellis, the editor of "The Record of Caernarvon," published in 1838 under the direction of the Commissioners of Public Records, also acknowledges in the introduction the assistance he had received from Mr. Wynne. Two of his latest contributions to literature were a history of his own parish of Llanegryn, published in the *Arch : Camb :* last year—and notes to a new edition of the "History of the Gwydir Family," published by Mr. Askew Roberts in 1878. He was a constant contributor to *Bye-gones*, and the familiar and well-known signature, "W.," will be sadly missed by the readers and writers of that collection of antiquarian notes.

Mr. Wynne may well be called the Mæcenas of Welsh literature. Although he had only a very slight conversational proficiency in the language of his native country, he was well acquainted with it from a literary point of view, and was thoroughly well versed in the Welsh MSS. which are the glory of his collection. His house and its ample hospitality were open "nocte atque die" to men of letters and students of our country's literature without reference to social rank, or differences of creed or politics. No trouble appeared too much, no application for assistance appeared too frequent, to this most perfect host and courteous gentleman in showing and explaining to his guests the treasures of his library. No one who has had the privilege of being entertained by him at Peniarth (and the number of those living must be large) can forget the grace and simplicity of his courtly manners, or the charm of his companionship. A polished and conspicuous beacon amongst Welsh scholars, he has slowly disappeared through the valley of the shadows. But the light he has left behind him is not gone, and its gentle rays will illuminate the hearts of his surviving friends as long as they live, and will serve in the future as a guide to that Cambrian literature which he loved so well, and which he did so much to illustrate and perpetuate. He died full of years and full of honour, and no better motto could be applied to him than the old legend of the Vaughans of Llwydiarth—

" Hwy pery clod na hoedl."

The family of Wynne of Peniarth may in antiquity of lineage vie with the oldest in the kingdom. They trace their descent from Gerald de Windsor, constable of the castle of Pembroke, who married Nesta, daughter of Rees ap Tudor, Prince of South Wales, living in 1108. His son, Maurice Fitz Gerald, accompanied Richard Strongbow to Ireland, in 1168, in the conquest of that country. Osborn, a descendant of Maurice, is said to have been accompanied from Ireland to Wales by his kinsman Griffith, son of the famous Ednevet Vychan ; probably before the middle of the thirteenth century. Einion ap Griffith, fourth in descent from Osborn, in the reign of Richard II., was commander of certain men at arms and archers in the King's service from the county of Merioneth. The descendants of Einion have always been known by the Welsh bards and heralds as Tylwyth Einion=the Family of Einion, which is one of the mottoes of the House of Peniarth. David ap Ievan ap

Einion is celebrated in the "Life of Lord Herbert of Chirbury" for his brave defence of Harlech Castle for the House of Lancaster in 1468. In the reign of Queen Elizabeth the family adopted the name of Wyn. Robert Wyn ap John of Glyn, Esq., married, about 1544, the daughter of Ellis ap Maurice of Clenenney whose father, Sir Wm. Maurice, was owner of Porkington, and ancestor of Lord Harlech. Robert Wynne, in the reign of Charles I., married Katherine, eldest daughter and heir of Robert Owen, Esq., of Ystymkegid, lineally descended from Owen Gwynedd, sovereign Prince of North Wales. William Wynne of Wern, Esq., and of Peniarth, jure uxoris, in 1771, married Jane, daughter of Edward Williams, Esq., grandson of Sir William Williams, Speaker of the House of Commons in the reign of Charles II. By this marriage the family became connected with the Houses of Wynnstay and Bodelwyddan. Miss Williams was representative, through her mother, Jane, Dowager Viscountess Bulkeley, of the ancient family of Owen of Peniarth, long seated at that place, but which became extinct at the death of Lewis Owen, Esq., Custos Rotulorum for the county of Merioneth in 1729. Of this family was the Puritan Dean of Christ Church, Dr. John Owen. By the marriage of William Wynne of Wern, Esq., there was issue—William, the eldest son and heir of Peniarth, born 1774, and who married the daughter and heiress of the Rev. Philip Puleston, D.D., of Pickhill Hall, Denbighshire. He was High Sheriff of Merioneth in 1812, and sold Wern to a Captain Barlow, who resold it to the famous Col. Wardle. One of his sisters was married to Col. Apperley, the well-known "Nimrod." Mr. Wynne, Mr. Apperley, and Mr. Wardle were all officers in Sir Watkin's "Ancient British Fencibles" in the Irish Rebellion. William Watkin Edward Wynne, Esq., whose lamented death we this week record, was the eldest son of William Wynne, Esq., and Elizabeth, daughter of Dr. Puleston.

Mr. W. W. E. Wynne was born at Pickhill Hall, Denbighshire, on Dec. 23, 1801, so was not a native of Merioneth as is generally supposed. He was educated at Westminster School, and Jesus College, Oxford ; and was married on May 8, 1839, at Baschurch, Salop, to Mary, second of the three daughters and co-heiresses of Robert Aglionby Slaney of Walford Manor and Hatton Grange, Esq., in the same county, and M.P., for Shrewsbury. Mr. Wynne went then to reside at Ruyton Hall (where his two sons were born) and afterwards removed to Mount Sion, Oswestry, and whilst a resident there was an active magistrate for the borough of Oswestry, to which office he was appointed in 1850. He was also a magistrate for the county of Salop. After leaving the neighbourhood of Oswestry Mr. Wynne resided for some years at Aberamffra, Barmouth, before he finally settled down at Peniarth. He did not serve the office of High Sheriff of Merionethshire until 1867, although he was, when he died, the eldest Deputy Lieutenant, and the oldest magistrate but one in the county, having qualified in 1832. He represented Merioneth in Parliament from 1852 to 1865, being thrice elected.

Mr. Wynne died, as we have stated, at his family residence, Peniarth, a place he himself thus described in the pages of the *Arch: Camb:* in 1879, in his paper, on the Parish of Llanegryn :—

"This place, formerly called Maes Peniarth and Plas Peniarth, was obtained in pledge or mortgage ("in pridâ") by Griffith ap Aron (a lineal descendant from Ednowain ap Bradwen, called Lord of Merioneth) in the fifth year of Henry V. It continued for many generations in his direct descendants, till, in the reign of Elizabeth, it passed by settlement from William David Lloyd, Esq., to his nephew, Lewis Owen, grandson of Lewis Owen, Baron of the Exchequer of Carnarvon, Custos Rotulorum and M.P. for Merionethshire, who was murdered near Dinas Mawddwy in Oct., 1555. From these Owens it passed by marriage to another family of the same name, of Morben, near Machynlleth, and from them, through the Williamses, a branch of the Wynnstay and Bodelwyddan families, to the Wynnes, its present owners."

This ancient seat of the Wynne family is situated on the north bank of the river Dysynni. The present house was built in 1700, and underwent alterations in 1812. What life was in the old mansion a century ago, was very vividly described in the letters of Mrs. Presland, published in the *Oswestry Advertizer* during the months of Jan. — May, of this year. Those letters, which are well worth preserving, have been reprinted in permanent form.

To revert, in conclusion, to Mr. Wynne's literary labours. With the exception of short Notes for *Bye-gones* (which we received from him as lately as the last week in April), the last paper of any length he published was the one on the Parish of Llanegryn, previously alluded to, but we gather from the following extract of a letter dated Mar. 1, 1880, he had another one prepared for the press :—"I am enabled to complete the Maesmochnant pedigree, but it is in tabular form, so would not fit in to 'Bye-gones.' However, you shall have one of the copies which I shall have from the 'Arch: Camb;,' to which I have sent it." He had also in contemplation—if not actually in progress—yet another contribution to Merionethshire County history. In a letter to the editor of *Bye-gones*, dated Oct. 3, 1879, he says :—"I hope that now the 'Gwydir Family' is finished, you will undertake a reprint of 'Davies's Display of Heraldry ;' but I am rather inclined to differ from Canon Williams that extracts from 'Reynolds's Book of Pedigrees' should be added to it. Should my life and intellect be spared—I am now in my 78th year—I would give you any assistance in my power, in the way of annotations. I am now beginning, for the 'Arch: Camb:,' a History of Towyn parish, like that of Llanegryn. It will, I fear, be a troublesome job."

In 1878 Mr. Wynne most kindly offered to revise the "Gossiping Guide to Wales," previous to the issue of a new edition. An interleaved copy was supplied to him for the purpose, and this he enriched with a number of interesting notes, in addition to the corrections intended for the press. We need scarcely say that this copy is highly prized by the author of the book !

The reference to his age in the letter just quoted brings to mind one of Mr. Wynne's more recent contributions to *Bye-gones*. In January last we published "An Interesting Reminiscence" from his pen, in which, quoting the "Life and Correspondence of Mrs. Delany," he gives a letter written in 1740, from the little daughter of the Duke of Portland to Mrs. Dewes. He adds :—"About the year 1823, I went to breakfast at the house of this lady—she was then Marchioness Dowager of Bath, and resided in Charles-street, or Hill-street, Berkeley Square, I think the former. Of the party were two of Lady Bath's grandnieces, the Misses Cotes, and a Miss Arbuthnot. After breakfast, we went to a review in Hyde Park, where, in the crowd, Miss Arbuthnot lost her shoe, for which we had a difficult search. We afterwards adjourned to Lady Stamford's, Lady Bath's sister, for luncheon. So I, who am alive and in health upon 2nd Jan., 1880, visited at the house of a lady who wrote a letter upon 23 Nov. 1740."

This was published on the 14th of January. Soon after we hear of a "troublesome cold ;" then a return to better health ; too soon to be followed by the bronchial attack which began to assume serious proportions early in May, and ended fatally on the 9th of June.

JUNE 16, 1880.

NOTES.

OSWESTRY.—The following variations in the way in which the name of your town has been spelt at times "whereof the memory of man runneth not to the contrary" (to use a phrase in one of your Royal Charters), is curious, some of these variations have already been pointed out in *Bye-gones* but not all of them :—

Oswestry	Oswaldestr	Osestry·
Oswalstree	Oswaldestre	· Oswestr
Oswalstrie	Osewastre	Osestree
Oswester	Oswaldstree	Ossewaldistr
Oswestrey	Oswestre	Osewaldestr
Osestre	Oswestrye	
Oswestree	Oswestrie	

The common people, also, have their own unauthorized ways of pronouncing the name ; such as

Odestry	Orswestry	Hodgestry
Odgestry	Hodgistry	Oswastry
Orestry	Odgester	Osistry

Your Welsh neighbours, not to be behind hand, have the following varieties :—

Croesoswallt	Suswallt	Cosuswallt
Crysuswallt	Crysyswallt	Maesuswallt
Croesuswallt		

Will some of your other contributors try and add to the list? G.A.

THE BUSHOPRICK OF CHESTER, &c.—The Rowland Whyte, whose name is attached to this, was of Fryars, near Beaumaris. "I have no doubt" (wrote the late Mr. Wynne of Peniarth, in contributing this to *Byegones*) "that he is the same person as is mentioned in Mackintosh's *History of England*, as a correspondent of Sir Robert Sidney (see Vol. 4, pp. 76, 80)." A.R.P.

"My deere Lord. At my cominge to London I found a straunge alterac'on. The earle of Somersett comitted to the dean of Westm'rs and S'r oliuer S'r John apointed to be his keaper. The La : somersett confined to the L. Knolly's howse, great w'th child and neare her tyme. mrs. Turner a gentlewoman of the La : Somersetts comitted to the Sheriff of londons, Whiteackres a gentlman of the c. of Somersets comitted. Weston a fellow preferred by mrs. Turners meanes to the liffetenant of the Towre, was apointed to waite on Sir Tho : overburie when he liued a prisoner in the Towre, this man was examined and confesses to haue receaued by the bandes of some of the above named 3 or 4 seuerall sortes of poison w'ch he gaue ourbury, of w'ch he died, and had for his reward 200*l.* This fellow is indited for the poisoning of hym and vpon his arrainment stands mute, and refuses the o'dinar triall. Tyme will discover more.

"Here is mallory and massy competitors for the Bushoprick of chester. Massy is to strong, and hath taken a better way. I find malloryes huisnes slubred, yet I will doe my best indeuer to make yt faire againe, w'ch I feare much wilbe a great and a difficult worke.

"By Rowland ap Robert yo'r lo : shall riceue yo'r scarlett. Comend my loue to my cosen mrs. Rowland, to yo'r dean, Archdecon and chancelor. I am yo'r lo : "Row : WHITE"

"23 october, 1615 "

[Addressed]—"To the right Reuerend father in god and my very good Lord the L : Bishop of Bangor."
(From the original at Brogyntyn.)

KYNASTON'S CAVE (June 2, 1880). — The following is given in Gough's *History of Middle* (Shrewsbury : Adnitt and Naunton) under the heading "Inhabitants of Myddle Castle" :—Wee have a tradition that Lord Strange, whilst hee was Lord of Myddle, did live part of the yeare at Myddle Castle, and part of the yeare at Knockin Castle. But after these Lordships descended to the Darbys, then there was a Constable, or Castle Keeper of this Castle. The first that I read of in antient deeds was Will Dod, Constable of the castle of Myddle, after him Sir Roger Kinaston, of *Hordley*, was, by comission, made Castle Keeper of Middle Castle and Knocking. After his decease his younger son, Humphry Kinaston (who for his dissolute and ryotous liveing was called the wild Humphry), was tenant of this castle. Hee had two wives, but both of soe meane, birth, that they could not lay claime to any Coat of Armes, as appeares by the card of Kinaston's Armes, which Mr. Edward Kinaston of Oateley, shewed mee not long before his death. I have not heard of any children which wild Humphry had but I have heard of much debt that hee had contracted ; and beeing outlawed in debt, he left Myddle Castle (which hee had suffered to grow ruinous, for want of repaire), and went and sheltered himself in a Cave neare to Nescliffe ; which, to this day, is called Kinaston's Cave, and of him the people tell almost as many romantick storyes, as of the great outlawe Robin Whood. Yet one thing I must remember that on a time when hee was gott over Monford's Bridge, and was on the that side Severne which is next Shrewsbury, and must needs returne over that bridge, the under shiriffe came with a considerable company of men to the bridge, (which then was made with stone pillars and wooden planks), and haveing taken up severall plankes, and made such a breadth as they thought noe horse was able to leape over, they laid themselves in ambush ; and when wild Humphry returned, and was about to enter upon the bridge, they rose up to apprehend him, which he perceiving, put spurrs to his horse, and rideing full speed, leaped clearely over the breadth. The measure of this leape was afterwards marked out upon Knockin Heath, upon a greene plott by the way-side that leads from Knockin towards Nescliffe, with an H and a K cut in the ground att the ends of the leape. The letters were about an elne long, and were a spade graff broad and a spade graff deep. These letters were usually repaired yearely by Mr. Kinaston, of Ruyton. I confesse I have seen the letters, but did not take the measure of the distance. After wild Humphry's time, this castle [Myddle] was never inhabited, but went utterly to ruine. R.

[Gough wrote in 1700, so, if the practice had been kept up, there must have been a constant renewing of the letters on the turf for nearly two centuries !—ED.]

In the MS. account of Humphrey Kynaston by Mr. Hunt, recently quoted, he is said to have died in 1534. The well-known inscription in the cave ("H. K. 1564 ") would therefore appear to be fictitious, although I have never heard it called in question. Can anyone explain the discrepancy? The person who has charge of the cave shews visitors an old drawing, said to be a portrait of the famous outlaw. Has this picture any history? and is there any reason to suppose it to be more than an imaginary likeness? SAXON.

[In Nightingale's *Shropshire* ("Beauties of England and Wales") it is stated that "Kynaston's will bears date 1534."—ED.]

QUERIES.

THE ESTABLISHED CHURCH IN WALES.—Nearly half a century ago sundry Welsh clergymen and laymen sent a lengthy memorial to Sir Robert Peel, First

Lord of the Treasury, asking, that in his contemplated measures for Church Reform, provision should be made to secure Welsh-speaking Bishops, "that the Apostle's declaration may no more be verified in the Welsh Churches—'If I know not the meaning of the voice, I shall be to him that speaketh a barbarian, and he that speaketh shall be a barbarian to me.'" Can any of your readers tell me who prepared this memorial, which I am told is historically interesting, and whether it has been published anywhere save in the newspapers of the time?

CHURCHMAN.

CALAMITY AT CHIRK, IN WALES.—Under this heading I find the following "extract from a letter" in the *Annual Register* for 1816, under the date of Dec.:—

"It is not without strong feelings of regret that I communicate an account of the destruction of the extensive collieries at Chirk, in Denbighshire. On Saturday evening, the 28th ult., owing, as it is supposed, to inattention in the servants of the Ellesmere Canal Company, the stop-gates, plugs, &c., for regulating the quantity of water on that part of the canal which is embanked up to Chirk aqueduct, were neglected. The fatal consequence was that the embankment, being overpowered by the great weight of superfluous water, gave way, and falling down a precipice, completely dammed up the river Ceiriog, which flows below it, and over which the canal is continued by an aqueduct. The water being thus impeded, quickly found its way in another direction, and in half an hour every pit belonging to the colliery was filled with water, earth, gravel, &c. The machinery was torn in pieces by the tremendous force of the current, and very considerable damage done to the surrounding country. Had it not been for the judicious and timely interference of Mr. Ed. Davies, engineer to the Chirk Colliery, in stopping the wickets or stop-gates of the canal, the whole of the water, increased by the overflowing of the Dee river—which is received by a feeder into the canal—must have swept away Chirk mills and everything in the valley into one general destruction. Most providentially this was the only night in which, for several years past, the workmen were absent from the pits. They had been allowed a little time to collect Christmas bounties, &c. ; and thus this dreadful calamity is not aggravated by the loss of so many valuable lives as must have been otherwise inevitably sacrificed. All the horses employed in the works were instantly drowned. The immediate loss to the proprietors is immense ; and the destruction of so valuable a colliery, which has for a long series of years produced fuel for the country and employment for its poor, is, as a public calamity, irretrievable."

From this it would seem that the valley between Chirk and Glyn was once upon a time as much at the mercy of careless watermen as was Cantrev y Gwaelod when it was flooded by the drunkard Seithenyn! What is there known, locally, of the Chirk inundation? And what were the special Christmas bounties to be collected in 1816, that we may presume were uncollected "for several years past" if the men got no holiday? Was the colliery ever pumped dry again? N.W.S.

REPLIES.

JUDICATURE IN WALES (June 2, 1880.)—On the 10th May, 1820, a meeting was held at Carmarthen to deliberate on the propriety of petitioning Parliament for some amendment in the system of Judicature in Wales. Amongst other alterations suggested were pensions to Welsh Judges, securities for monies paid into court, compulsory attendance of witnesses without the jurisdiction of Courts of Great Session, &c. Another meeting was held at Pembroke on May 20, when it was resolved to petition for the abolition of Welsh Judicature altogether, if legislative permission could be made for emendation. They asked to have an efficient Court of Equity, to which all Chancery business should be brought, and that the judges should change their circuits as in England. Several irregularities in the manner of conducting business were pointed out, and complaints were made of the manner of appointment of Welsh Judges, by the Treasury instead of by the Lord Chancellor. H.B.

OLD FOLKS (July 16, 1879).—It is pretty well for the old magazines and newspapers to try and make us believe that in their day centenarians were as thick on the ground as peas in a pod ; it is too much to suppose we can take in the following, which I extract from the *Gents: Mag:* for 1809 :—May 23. Died, "aged 103, Richard Williams of Bodewran, in the parish of Honeglwys, co. Angelsea : who had been blind upwards of six years, but whose sight was restored a short time before his death ; and he had also four new teeth." On the next page of the volume is recorded the death, at 101, of Mrs. Gwilliam of Bishops Castle, "who retained her faculties until a few days of her death." She is described as being "formerly of the Nag's Head Inn of that town." Again, on the next page, there is the death announced of a Mr. Wilson, of Lydbury North, Salop, at the age of 108 ; but he seems to have been an ordinary individual. Another record, in the vol. for 1811, would almost suggest that the parents when they named their child were inspired, for it publishes the death of "Methusalem Williams, a butcher at Llanfadwanen, Llanharnge, aged 104." CAMBRO-BRITON.

STRAY NOTES.

The Hon. G. Lascelles, in an article in *Time* upon Otter Hunting, says that foremost among the packs of the Otter Hounds comes the well-bred, well-managed, well-hunted pack of the Hon. R. C. Hill, or the H.O.H., whose neat blue and red flannel dress is known in most counties of England and Ireland, and in almost every corner of Wales. Perhaps this pack is one of the oldest in existence. For years the late Lord Hill, father of the present master, hunted the otter in the country around his home. On giving up his pack, very many years ago, the hounds were bought by Lord Londonderry. The present Lord Hill, when Mr. Rowland Hill, revived the family pack, which he brought to perfection, and showed with them great sport in Wales, Shropshire, and in Yorkshire, where he had some capital days on the Wharfe and Derwent. It is more than ten years since Mr. Rowland Hill, finding the duties of master of foxhounds and of otter hounds also press too hardly upon him, resigned the pack of otter hounds into the able hands of his brother, the present master, who has gone on from year to year with increasing sport and popularity, as the testimonial picture and piece of plate recently presented to him at Builth, the centre of the Welsh country, will attest. And when I state that in 1873 this pack accounted for no less than thirty-nine otters, while the score in 1874 reached the astonishing number of fifty-two, my readers will have no doubts left as to the fact of there being good fun in the shape of hunting, to be seen and enjoyed in summer as well as in winter, or of the exercise of consummate judgment and care in the breed and care of such a pack.

MAD DOGS IN OSWESTRY.—The good people of our town during the hot season of 1820 seem to have been badly "bitten" with fears of hydrophobia ; and magisterial orders were given for the destruction of all dogs found on the streets not under control. It would seem that there was cause for alarm, and dogs belonging to Mr. Judson, butcher, Church-street, Mr. Jennings of Peny-lan, and Mr. Warren of Weston, were declared to be un-doubtedly mad. On Aug. 13, a farmer named Roberts, residing at Selattyn, who had been bitten by a dog twelve weeks previous, died in great agony, from evident hydrophobia; and on the 22nd of the same month Mr. Cockerill, surgeon, cut away the poisoned flesh from the thigh of a collier named Morris, who was "bitten by a mad dog" in Church-street.

JUNE 23, 1880.

NOTES.

TEST AND CORPORATIONS ACT.—The com-paratively recent jubilee in London to commemorate the abolition of the obnoxious Test and Corporations Act has made additionally interesting to Nonconformists any re-cords of the good work done by Lord John Russell fifty years ago. A document has been preserved in Oswestry, in the form of a letter addressed to the Rev. T. W. Jenkyn, minister of the Old Chapel, and bearing post mark Sep. 10, 1830, in which an appeal is made by Mr. Apsley Pellatt of the Falcon Glass Works, on behalf of a London Committee who desire the friends of Religious Liberty in the country to help them with funds to secure the return of Lord John Russell as member for Southwark. On the back of the appeal the names of the following subscribers in Oswestry are given :—T. W. Jenkyn, Nath: Minshall, David Thomas, Saml. Roberts, Jonathan Francis, J. Davies (draper), J. Jones (grocer), J. Lacon, J. Morris, Bickerton(Salop-road), Mrs. Bishop, Mrs. Hayward, Mrs. Roberts (chandler), Jones (hatter), Warren, Jones (paper maker), Cooper and Lewis (Llwynymaen), T. Minett (Morda), E. Davies (Llwynymapsis), C. Sabine, S. Bickerton, R. Minshull, D. Edwards, J. Vaughan, J. Randles, J. Oliver, C. J. Hanmer, and W. Bolas.

PURITAN.

ARMS OF WALES.—In a work entitled *Historical Anecdotes of Heraldry and Chivalry* (Worcester 1795) p. 309, the following passage occurs :—

"The Ancient Arms of the Princes of Wales, while they were Sovereigns, were *quarterly gules and or, four lions passant counterchanged.* 'Brute gave Camber,' his third son, Cambria, with these arms :—*argent, three lions passant reguardant gules* which his offspring used for a long time, until the country was divided into three distinct principal-ities.'"

On page 306 there is as follows :—

"The device of Henry VII. was a red dragon, on a silk pendant, painted green and white. Sir William Brandon, father to the famous Charles Brandon, was his standard bearer. Henry claimed this ensign by his descent from Cadwallader, who had his green shield from Brutus II. who was surnamed Greenshield from a shield of that colour which he used in battle.

> Brute Greenshield ; to whose name we providence impute
> Divinely to *revive*, the land's first conqueror, Brute.
>   *Drayton.*

> How oft that day did sad Brunchieldis (a) see,
> The greenshield dyde in dolorous Vermeile,
> That not *Scuith guirdth*, it mote seeme to bee,
> But rather *y Scuith goch*, scine of sad crueltye.
>   *Spencer.*

Henry VII. sent into Wales purposely to enquire into the pedigree of Owen Tudor, his grandfather ; which was traced up to Belin the Great, alias Hely ; the Britains

(a) Brunchield was Prince of Henault, where the war being, caused these lines.

call him *Beli Mawr*, that is Beli, or Belinus the Great ; because thence, quite up to Æneas, the pedigree of the Britains is sufficiently known and allowed (see Borlase, p. 363). The pedigree is printed in the appendix to Wynne's *History of Wales*, 8vo., 1702."

The name of the author of this work, which abounds in curious information, does not appear. ZETA.

PARLIAMENT OF ENGLAND (June 9, 1880).—Reigns of Charles II., James II., William and Mary, William III., to first Parliament of Anne ; where for the present the Blue Book stops.

COUNTY OF SALOP.

1660	No Returns found
1661	Sir Francis Lawley, bart.; Sir Richard Oakeley, knt. [Nov. 17, 1670, Richard Newport, esq., *vice* Sir Richard Oakeley, knt, deceased]
1678	Richard Newport, esq.; Sir Vincent Corbett, bart.
1679	Ditto ;　　　　　　　　　　　　　ditto.
1680	Ditto ;　　　　　William Leveson Gower, esq.
1685	Edward Kinaston, esq., of Otley ; John Walcott, esq., of Walcott
1688	No Returns found *
1689	Hon. Richard Newport, of Eyton-on-Severn ; Ed-ward Kynaston of Oatley
1695	Richard Lord Newport ; Edward Kynaston, esq.
1698	Sir Edward Leighton, bart.;　　　　ditto.
1700	Sir Humphrey Briggs, bart., of Haughton, county Salop ; Robert Lloyd, esq., of Aston, county Salop
1701	Richard Corbet, esq., of Moreton Corbet, county Salop ; Robert Lloyd, esq., of Aston, county Salop
1702	Roger Owen, esq., of Cundover, county Salop; Rich-ard Corbett, esq., of Moreton Corbett, county Salop

BOROUGH OF SHREWSBURY.

1660	Samuel Jones, esq., of Berwicke, county Salop ; Thomas Jones, esq., of Shrewsbury
1661	Robert Leighton, esq. ; Thomas Jones, esq. [Mar. 17, 1676-7, Sir Richard Corbett, bart., *vice* Thomas Jones, esq.. appointed a Puisne Justice of the King's Bench]
1678	Sir Richard Corbett, bart. ; Edward Kinaston, esq.
1679	Ditto　　　　　　　　　　　　Ditto
1680	Edward Kynaston, esq., of Albright Lee ; Sir Richard Corbett, bart.
1685	Edward Kynaston, esq. ; Sir Francis Edwards, bart.
1688	Andrew Newport, esq. ; Sir Francis Edwardes, bart.*
1689	Hon. Andrew Newport, esq. ; Richard Mytton, esq.
1695	Andrew Newport, esq. ; John Kynaston, esq., of Acton Reignold, within the liberty of the town of Shrewsbury
1698	John Kynaston, esq., of Hordley, county Salop ; Richard Mitton, esq., of Horlston, county Salop
1700	Ditto ;　　　　ditto
1701	John Kynaston, esq., of Hordley, county Salop ; Richard Mytton, esq., of Hallston, county Salop
1702	Ditto ;　　　Richard Mytton, esq., of Halston.

* Parliament (Convention) of England, summoned 22 Jan., 1688-9, dissolved 6 Feb., 1689-90.

DICK OF ABERDARON:—Mr. William Bates, B.A., of Birmingham, writes to "N. & Q" of May 29, in reply to some queries respecting the etchings of Mrs. Dawson Turner, and in course of his remarks gives some inter-esting details in connection with the life of the singular being whose sobriquet heads my note. Mr. Bates says he possesses "a slender volume of considerable interest, entitled *Memoir of Richard Robert Jones, of Aberdaron, in the county of Carnarvon, in North Wales ; exhibiting a Remarkable Instance of a Partial Power and Cultivation of Intellect*, London, Cadell, &c., 1822, 8vo., pp. 50. This, though published anonymously, for the benefit of the extraordinary character who was the subject of the memoir, was the production of William Roscoe, of Liverpool, the historian of the Medici, and is thus alluded to by his son" :—

Many are the singular and amusing anecdotes recorded of Richard in this Memoir, which concludes with a short comparison between the subject of it and the famous Moses Mendelsohn and the learned Magliabechi. The portrait of Richard prefixed to it is from a drawing by Williamson, formerly a portrait painter at Liverpool, of considerable ability. The plate is etched by Mrs. Dawson Turner of Yarmouth, whose efforts in this branch of art have excited so much admiration among her friends.—*Life of William Roscoe*, ii. 289.

Mr. Bates adds some further allusions to the portrait of Jones, from a letter written by Roscoe to Mr. Dawson Turner :—

I had the pleasure of receiving your kind favour of the 18th July, enclosing an impression of the etching of my Welsh friend by Mrs. Turner, for which I cannot sufficiently express my thanks. The likeness is admirable, so that it is impossible that any person who has seen this should not immediately recognize it ; and the execution of it is beautiful beyond what I could have thought it was in the power of the needle to produce, so that it may be ranked amongst the happiest of Mrs. Turner's works. This etching has confirmed me in the idea, in which I hope Mrs. Turner will agree with me, that there is a character of apostolic simplicity in the countenance which is highly interesting, and which, I am certain, will attract the attention of the public, and be the chief cause of any advantage which this poor child of adversity may derive from the memoir.

With respect to the inscription to be placed under it I must give you a singular anecdote. A day or two after I received the etching Richard called, as he is in the frequent habit of doing, and I showed it to him and asked him if he knew it, when, after some strange turns of his head from side to side, he said 'it is my portrait.' I then told him I wished him to give me an inscription of his name, &c., to put under it, when, suddenly opening his waistcoat, he began to unwind from around his body a piece of white calico, at least five or six feet long by three broad, at the top of which there appeared, in large letters inscribed by himself, 'Verbum Dei Libertas,' and towards the bottom the following inscription, 'R. Johannis, Caernarvonensis, Linguæ Hebraæ (*sic*) professor, Rabbi Nathan unus e Discipulis, et veritatis libertatisque indignissimus Martyr.'

This seemed to me the more extraordinary as he had not the least idea of his head being engraved or any such inscription wanted, nor am I satisfied that it would be proper to adopt the above ; but on this you shall hear again from me.—*Ibid*, p. 289.

Canon Williams, I think, does not mention "Dick of Aberdaron" in his dictionary ?

                 R. ROSSE TEWK, B.A.

QUERIES.

A ROYAL COBBLER.—It is stated in *Chambers's Journal* for Sep. 28, 1850, in an article on Decay of Royal Families, that "The great great grandson of Margaret Plantagenet, daughter and heiress of George, Duke of Clarence, followed the craft of a cobbler at Newport, Salop, in 1637." Is this fact mentioned in any of our local histories?   N.W.T.

THE CAPEL CURIG ROAD.—In *Bye-gones*, May 8, 1878, in some references to Evans's maps of North Wales, mention was made of "The Capel Cerrig and Bangor Road Bill," which had received the Royal Assent on Aug. 7, 1802. It was said that the promoters hoped to complete their work in three months, " whereby the distance between Shrewsbury and Holyhead will be shortened at least nine miles, avoiding the dangerous Ferry of Conway, &c." In the newspapers at the end of July, 1805 (just three years later) I read—" Lord Penrhyn

has at length opened his new road through the mountains of North Wales, by which cut ten miles are saved to the traveller on his way to Holyhead, besides the avoidance of that terrible nuisance, Conway Ferry. The new road, which is uncommonly picturesque and romantic, turns off at Kernioge, thro' Capel Cerrig, where an admirable inn is erected near Mount Snowdon, and thence by Lord Penrhyn's slate mines to Bangor Ferry." Can any one shortly explain the relative routes of the two roads mentioned here?   TELL.

HAIL STORM IN MERIONETHSHIRE.—The newspapers of the time reported a hail storm at Bala such as, fortunately, is not of every day occurrence. It took place on June 29, 1820, and some of the hailstones that fell are said to have weighed upwards of a pound each ! "The storm came from the south-west, and passed by Bala : at Rhiwlas in particular it did great damage to the windows, and to the greenhouses ; at Cerrig-y-Drudion the parsonage house suffered severely, and on the upland farm of Nant-dedwydd our informant saw at ten o'clock the following day about two cart loads of hail stones, lying nearly together, of the size of large eggs, when they must have been considerably reduced : the corn has in many places been wholly destroyed." Such a storm as this ought to have left some local records. Has it?   G.G.

REPLIES.

SHROPSHIRE SCHOOLS (May 26, 1880).—At Trin : Coll : Cam : the Latin Declamation prizes this year have been adjudged to Augustus Macdonald Hopper and J. M. Neale ; and at Queen's Coll : the Latin Declamation prizes have been adjudged to John Thomas, of this town, and Francis Simpson. Messrs. Hopper, Thomas and Simpson were educated at the Shrewsbury School.—*Shrewsbury Chronicle*, Nov. 3, 1837.

Mr. Edward Rowland Dukes, son of Thomas Farmer Dukes, Esq., of Shrewsbury, was, this Michaelmas term, elected to a studentship of Christ Church, Oxford, by Dr. Pusey, Regius Professor, on the recommendation of the Dean and Censors of the said College. Mr. Dukes obtained also, at the commencement of term, a scholarship on the foundation of Dr. Fell. He was educated at Shrewsbury School.—*Salopian Journal*, Dec. 20, 1837.

                 SCROBBES BYRIG.

OLD PARR'S PORTRAITS. (Ap. 14, 1880.)—Your correspondent " D" mentions a Demy 8vo. portrait of Parr published by I. Caulfield in 1794. During the same year " James Caulfield, No. 6, Clare Court" issued a reprint of Taylor's *Life of Parr* in small octavo, the bastard title page of which is headed "Caulfield's Edition of Curious Tracts." It was illustrated with " seven elegant prints, from the designs of Anthonio Van Assen."

                 H.B.C.

JUNE 30, 1880.

NOTES.

JESUS COLLEGE, OXFORD, 1599.—From the original at Brogyntyn. The entering of a young gentleman at Oxford, in these days, costs somewhat more than the sums specified in the account beneath.   A.R.P.

            Jesus.

Wor'll S'r I rec'd l'res and xls in money by the handes of this bearer, and I have sent here Inclosed the Particularies of his expences hitherto, w'ch must be discharged quarterlye, and by half yeares, according to the custome, order, and many wantes of our towne, in regard whereof I am instantly to desire y'u to furnish vs w'th all such necessaries, rather befor' the time then any waye afte'r; the youth will doe well I doubte not, by the grace and assistance of the Almightie, to whose blessed tuition I hartiely recom'end y'r wor : as also mr. and m'resse Brynkir

Junii 11 [or 17] 1599
Your Worr : most readie
C. [or G.] Owens.

(Addressed)   To the Wor'll mr. William Maurice, Esquire, at the Clenenne, give these

Sm'a recept .... vijli 10s
Soluta
Imprimis fo'r his admission .... iiijs xd
Ite' to buy bookes .... iiij
Ite' for shoes........ .... xxd
Ite' to ride to my L. Bishop........................ ijs
Ite' his studie chamb'r & teachng .... xxs
Ite' the stuffe and makenge of his hose ...... xviijs
Ite' his landr'es .... xxd
Ite' his batt'es .... lixs vd
Sm'a solutu' est .... vli xjs id.
(Endorsed)   "William Brynkirs note of expences,"

THE MANOR OF WENLOCK.—Mr. Watkin Williams, who on the death of Sir John Wynn of Wynnstay, in Jan. 1719, took the surname of Wynn and possession of the estates his aged relative had willed to him ; in Oct. the same year exercised his right as Lord of the Manor of Wenlock, as set forth in the following document :—

A Deputation from Watkin Williams Wynne, Esq., to Hen : Sprott, Esq., ffor the Mannor of Wenlock.
To all . . . to whom these p'esents shall come I Watkin Williams Wynn, of Wynnstay in the County of Denbigh, Esq., Lord of the Mannr. of Wenlock, in the County of Salop, send greeting. Know yee that I the s'd Watkin Williams Wynn for diverse good causes and considerations me thereunto moveing have given and granted and by these p'esents doo give and grant unto my trusty and well beloved friend Henry Sprott, of the Marsh, in the County of Salop, afores'd Esq., full power absolute authority free liberty and licence to Hunt, Course, Sett, Hawk, Fish, and Fowl from time to time and at all times hereafter at the will and pleasure of the s'd Henry Sprott in upon and within my said Mann'r of Wenlock aforesaid, and in and upon all and singuler the lands, grounds, rivers, and woods thereof in as free, full, large, ample, and benediciall Mann'r as I my self may or can doe in any respect w'tsoever without any hinderance of me w'tsoever. And moreover I the said Watkin Williams Wynn doe hereby for me my heirs Exec't'rs & adm'rs coven't and agree (soe far as by law I can or may) to and with the s'd Henry Sprott that it shall and may be lawfull to and for the s'd Henry Sprott from time to time and at all times hereafter (as often as occasion shall require) to seize detaine and keep to his own use or otherwise to destroy (as p'hibited to be kept by p'sons unqualifyed by law) as well all and every the guns, cross bows, tunnells, Low bells, Hare pipes Quail pipes and snares, as alsoe all the gray hounds, spanialls, setting dogs, coney dogs, or lurchers of any p'scn or p'sons w'tsoever that shall at any time or times hereafter hawk, hunt, fish, or fowl within the s'd Mann'r or within any parte or portion thereof. In Witness whereof I have hereunto sett my hand and seal this fifteenth day of October, Anno Dni. 1719.
Sealed and deliv'd in the p'esence of }
us the paper being first legally stampt } WAT : WMS : WYNN.
Randle Jones.
Tho : Greene.

I copy the document at second hand, pretty nearly ver.batim, from the *Salopian and West-Midland Journal*, a magazine published in Madeley ; so have not compared it with the original.   N.W.S.

SUNDAY VESTRY-MEETINGS.—Either be.cause "the better the day the better the deed," or because our fathers and grandfathers were very busy all the week : the fact seems to have been that vestry-meetings in Oswes-

try early in this century generally took place on Sundays. In June, 1820, one was held to take into consideration the desirability of "reinstating the venerable decorations of the old tower of the Church ;" and a few weeks later (July 16, 1820) one " numerously attended " was held to " consider the propriety of appointing a permanent overseer for the town." It was agreed that an Overseer should be appointed on the next Sunday week.   JARCO.

QUERIES.

MONUMENT IN LLANDDWYWE CHURCH.—Reading the curious inscription on the monument in Llan-ddwywe Church, on which are sculptured the kneeling effigies of Mr. and Mrs. Vaughan, their two sons and four daughters, by the dim light of a misty day I made out that one of the daughters was given in marriage to Mr. Hooks or Hookes. The date on the monument was 1606 ; and I wondered whether this was the wonderful Mr. Hookes who had so many brothers and sisters and so many children, and who was buried at Conway in 1637. Can any of your readers tell me?   E.

OSWESTRY MANUFACTORIES. — Whether Flannel and Woollen Manufactories ever existed in Oswestry has been doubted, and some reference to the subject appeared Sep. 4 and Oct 9, 1872. But from a report of the Shropshire Spring Assizes, 1796, it may be inferred that at least one manufactory existed in the town at that date, because it is stated that " Edward Jones for stealing woollen yarn from the manufactory of Mr. Slade of Oswestry was sentenced to seven years' transportation." Can anyone say who Mr. Slade was and where his mill stood ?   FITZOSWALD.

EDWARD MEREDITH.—Can any reader of *Bye-gones* give any information respecting Edward Meredith, who was famous as a public singer about ninety years ago, in this neighbourhood and in Liverpool ? He was father of Mrs. Parry, who kept a large boarding school at Brynyffynnon, Wrexham, sixty years ago. His sister was grandmother of the present Mr. Meredith Jones, of Wrexham. He is said to have been much patronized by Sir Watkin. In the *Life of William Hazlitt* published by Bentley 1867, the following passage occurs under date of 1790, " I was very much pleased at the concert, but I think Meredith's singing was worth all the rest." It is believed his portrait was published. I shall be glad to hear of anyone having a copy.   E.M.J.
Wrexham.

REPLIES.

SOCIETY OF ANCIENT BRITONS.
(May 26, 1880.)

The enthusiastic secretary,—the first secretary and treasurer of the " Most Honourable and Loyal Society of Antient Britons,"—wrote what he called " The Rise and Progress " of the institution, but as the rise dates 1714–5, and the book was issued in 1717, not much progress is reported. This original officer seems to have been so full of patriotism and loyalty that I fear in this degenerate age we shall some of us be inclined to think that he, in common with sundry of the Antient Britons who came after him, was just a trifle snobbish in his devotion to their Royal Highnesses, the Georges, Kings of England, Princes of Wales, Defenders of the Faith, and Patrons of the Antient Britons.

The secretary in question was " Thomas Jones of Lincolns Inn, Esq.," when the Society was established, but speedily to be raised to the honour of knighthood on the presentation of an exceedingly loyal address presented by the new Society to Majesty on the fall of the Pretender. Sir Thomas calls his book, as I have said, " The Rise and Progress" of the Society, and it takes the form of " a Letter to his Countrymen of the Principality of Wales ;" and it was " printed by W. Williams for W. Taylor, at the Ship in Pater-Noster-Row."

The book is dedicated to His Royal Higness George, Prince of Wales, and President of the Antient Britons, also to " The Right Hon. Talbot, Lord Viscount Longueville and Baron of Ruthin ; Sir Robert Cotton, Bart.; Sir John Austen, Bart.; Sir Humfrey Howarth, Bart.; Sherrington Davenport, Esq., Major-General of his Majesty's Forces ; Samuel Mollyneux, Esq., Secretary to his Royal Highness, and one of the Members of the Honourable House of Commons ; Thomas Wynne, Esq., Equerry to his Royal Highness, and one of the Members of the Honourable House of Commons ; John Roberts, Esq., one of the Members of the Honourable House of Commons ; Charles Greenwood, Esq., one of the Commissioners of His Majesty's Duties arising from Wines ; and Edward Hughes, Esq., Judge-Advocate."

The dedication completed the author addresses himself to his countrymen in the following strain :—

The glorious and happy Accession of his Majesty to the Throne of his Royal Ancestors in spight (sic) of all the Secret Designs and Contrivances of the Enemies of our happy Constitution in Church and State who were, designing to deprive him of his just and undoubted Right ; This, and the safe Arrival of their Royal Highnesses the Prince and Princess, and Three of their most illustrious and beautiful Offspring, in these Kingdoms, were such Blessings and of so inestimable a Value, as required, from all true Lovers of their Country, the most sincere and grateful Returns of thanks and Acknowledgments to Heaven for them.

Hence arose the loyal Welshmen of London to form themselves into a

Regular Society, which they resolved to establish, both in Honour of the Day which gave Birth to that Most Excellent Princess her Royal Highness, as also by appropriating it to the Memory of St. David, the Tutelar Saint of their Antient Country.

Our author then goes on to prove that St. David was " a Person every way adorned with Honour and Dignity," so that by allying his name with Carolina of Anspach they were not contaminating her by an association with a vulgar plebeian. It is said of St. George of England that he dealt in bacon, and cheated : not so St. David; he was " of Blood Royal, and Uncle to the great King Arthur, and a son of a Prince of Wales," and an Archbishop to boot ; which, if you doubt it, consult Bishop Godwin's Lives of the Bishops, and you will be satisfied.

Here then we have, as the newly-created knight states, "Heaven," showing a "previous and peculiar regard " for Welshmen, by causing the Princess of Wales to be born on the first of March ;—a " providential coincidence that her birthday should be the very same with that on which the Antient Britons have so long celebrated the Festival of their Tutelar Saint." Sir Thomas has no doubt about it, and he further tells us that because St. David did such great good to their Religion and Country—the benefits of which they enjoy to this day, . . . with a sensible Pleasure and a becoming Pride, they distinguish themselves and their dear Country, by wearing a Leek, wherever they reside in any Part of the World.

Sir Thomas intrenches himself behind Bishop Godwin for his reasons why Welshmen wear leeks, and he further informs us tnat so ancient was the custom, that " even our own Histories are silent about its rise, and only give us leave to conjecture," so he conjectures with a vengeance, and presumes that this—

Perpetuates the Memory of an abstemious Saint, who lived a rigid Eremetick Life, feeding only on Herbs (of which perhaps Leeks were a principal Part) and drinking nothing but Water.

We will not throw cold water on the theory, further than to say that there have been Welsh heretics who have affirmed that the patron Saint of Wales belonged to the family of which the late lamented Mrs. Harris—the guide, philosopher and friend of Mrs. Gamp—was so illustrious a member ; and that the Welsh people in the Principality up to the end of last century, showed no more affection for St. David's food than they did for his beverage. But let this pass. At least Leeks and Welshmen were associated in London as far back as Shakespeare's time ; and that was enough for Sir Thomas Jones.

(To be continued.)

LOCAL LITERATURE.

TRANSACTIONS OF THE SHROPSHIRE ARCHÆOLOGICAL SOCIETY. Pt. II. Vol. 3. Shrewsbury : Adnitt and Naunton ; Oswestry : Woodall and Venables.

THE new part of the Transactions of this Society contains a paper on Oswestry Ecclesiastical History, illustrated with a very beautiful photo-lith of the south side of the Old Church, showing the new windows, also a copy of a rough photograph of the interior of the church as it was previous to restoration, drawn on stone. In the article itself mention is made of a plan that was proposed half a century ago, to take the roof off the church, in order to raise the walls and build galleries all round ; and we are told that this would have been carried out, only fears were entertained that the strain on the voices of the officiating clergymen would be too great ; so it was decided instead to build a new church. Another circumstance connected with Oswestry church history, mentioned in the paper, will be new to our readers, viz., that in all probability some of the lead stript off the Abbey, Shrewsbury, at the time of the dissolution, came to Oswestry to roof St. Oswald's. The part also contains a list of those who voted at the Shrewsbury election of 1747, and the rejected votes, with the reasons why such were refused. This curious old MS. has been preserved by Mr. W. Hughes, to whom the Society is indebted for it. Lastly, the part contains the first instalment of what is well known, by name, to Shropshire antiquarians, viz., "Taylor's Manuscript," which is preserved in the Shrewsbury School Library. This valuable MS. abounds with matter interesting to Salopians, and the Society, in the acquisition of the modernized copy of it, owes yet another debt of gratitude to the Rev. W. Allport Leighton, whose papers have enriched each succeeding volume of the Society's Transactions. We hope another week to give some extracts from this quaint old diary.

SHROPSHIRE WORD BOOK : a Glossary of Archaic and Provincial Words used in the County. By Georgina F. Jackson. Part II. (Trubner and Co.)

WHEN the late Rev. C. H. Hartshorne issued his Salopia Antiqua—the interest of which centres in the list of archaic words of Shropshire, with examples of their use— he fixed the price at 16s. At best it is an imperfect book, but the last copy we saw offered for sale fetched no less a sum than 45s., so scarce has it become in the market. In our Bye-gones column attention has repeatedly been called to the Shropshire Word Book, compiled by Miss G. F. Jackson. The first part, published some months back (containing A to D), shewed how thoroughly the task had been executed, and in calling attention to it a writer in our columns advised such as were interested to enter their names as subscribers at once. Those who did so will not regret having taken the advice. The second part is, if possible, an improvement on the first ; that is to say, the illustrations of the use of various words are gathered from a wider range. As we hope when the work is completed to give a fuller notice of it, we will content ourselves here with the following extract from " N. & Q." of June 19, relative to the part now before us:—Part II. shows no falling off, and is equally full of things good and useful. The numerous examples of the folk-speech exhibit the same raciness, and come home to all who have lived long enough in the county to feel their truth. As the present part ends with "now just," which, by the way, is extremely characteristic as a Salopian formula, we have not yet been informed that oonts (wants) are moles ; but we are introduced to the old plural flen for "fleas," as used by Chaucer : " Old Munslow of the Thresholds was wont to say 'as God made the oonts, but the devil made the rots and flen.'" And again, " I couldna sleep for the *flen* ; I wuz scroutin' at 'em all night." There is a creepy suggestiveness about the verb *to scrout*. "A parish clerk of Cound (Salop) gave notice—during the time of Divine Service—of a vestry meeting, in the following terms : ' This is to give you all notice that theer'll be a meetin' in the vestry nex' Toosd'y wik—'ould, I'm wrung—nex' Toosd'y as ever comes I mane—to fettle the pews and so forth'." We admire the honesty of his self-correction. The following sentence, such as may be heard at Ellesmere, would puzzle a stranger : " M'appen 'er met, an' m'appen 'er metna." The solution is, Perhaps she will (might), and perhaps she won't, expressive of the usual difficulty of predicting what a woman will do under special circumstances. The relative depth of Kettlemere and Blackmere has been decided to be as follows : " Kettle-mar, it's no bottom to it, and the t'other's deeper till that." Since the foregoing was in type we learn that another grant from the Civil List has been accorded to Miss Jackson.

JULY 7, 1880.

NOTES.

ENORMOUS GOOSEBERRIES. — Under this heading JARCO on Oct. 15, 1879, referring to "Oswestry Gooseberry Show" in 1833, said that Mr. Abraham Morgan had berries weighing as much as "20 dwts. 4 grs." I have just seen in *The Young Gentleman's Book*, published in 1832 by Baldwin and Cradock, London, the following:— "The four heaviest gooseberries grown in England in 1831 are as follows—Red Roaring Lion, 27 dwts. 6 grs., Mr. Davies, Oswestry meeting: Yellow Leader, 26 dwts. 17 grs., Richard Riley, at Nantwich : Green Peacock, 23 dwts. 15 grs., John Pisher, Rockwood meeting : White Eagle, 25 dwts. 18 grs., James Dean, Chester meeting".

N.W.T.

TERMING.—The distinguished topographer, Mr. Pennant, was by no means an abstemious man in his younger days, and in his old age when he wrote his book about Whiteford his stories of the drinking customs of his father's time are not accompanied with any regret or apology. The custom of "Terming," related by him at page 23 of the work I have referred to, is new to me, and it may be so to many of your readers. Mr. Pennant says :—" In those days [a hundred and fifty years ago] the neighbors were much addicted to *terming*, i.e, brewing a barrel of ale at some favorite ale-house, and staying there till it was all drunk out. They never went to bed, even should the *term* last a week ; they either slept in their chairs or on the floor, as it happened, then awoke and resumed their jollity. At length, when the barrel was exhausted, they reeled away, and the hero of this Bacchanalian rout always carried the spiggot in triumph. Coursing was very frequently the occasion of these *terms ;* each gentleman brought his gre-hound, and often made matches, more for the glory of producing the best dog, than for the value of the bet."

N.W.S.

CENTENARY OF SUNDAY SCHOOLS.—Anything of a local nature bearing on Sunday Schools will be readable just now, so I offer no apology for introducing some extracts from a Personal Diary kept in 1830-1 by the Rev. T. W. Jenkyn, when he was minister of the Old Chapel, Oswestry. Under date Dec. 28, 1830, he writes :— Went to the Theatre to Mr. Lloyd's second Astronomical lecture. There were about 50 present. The lecturer when praising Galileo's triumph over superstition, made some remarks on the march of intellect in our days, and said that he had been expecting it for the last 30 years—that " mistaken benevolence had instituted Sunday Schools, and Sunday Schools would unhinge the State"! This coming from an itinerent lecturer going about to diffuse knowledge came with a very bad grace— but thanks to the Schoolmaster, this sentiment concerning Sunday Schools comes at least fifty years too late. I was very much displeased with him.

The very fact that such an utterance should form part of the stock-in-trade of a peripatetic lecturer was ominous. It must have found approvers or it would not have found a place in a hacknied oration. On the 31 Dec. the lecturer called on Mr. Jenkyn, and the interview is thus recorded :—

Mr. Lloyd, the Astronomer, called to be paid for his lectures : I reminded him of his observation on Sunday Schools : he declared that what he said then was his deliberate opinion. He said the children were taught by respectable ladies and gentlemen whose manners and dress the children would naturally imitate ; and consequently, if taught at all should be taught by old women. The children, he said, learnt to read, and then they read "The Age of Reason" or the Bible (sic) and this would unsettle their submission and loyalty. Sunday Schools, he said, were the cause of all the infidelity in the land, and of the present disturbances in the kingdom. He said that he knew Mr. Raikes of Gloucester personally, and a greater knave and scoundrel never existed ! I asked him if Sunday Schools were the cause of Infidelity in France ? were Sunday Schools the cause of the insurrections in Belgium and Poland ? why should the infidelity of our country be ascribed to Sunday Schools any more than to the National Schools ? I remarked also that if there was any state not founded in knowledge the sooner that state was unhinged the better. Mr. Lloyd is ultra loyal, and a warm defender of Taxes and Pensions.

The foul libel on Mr. Raikes goes far to disarm the power of Mr. Lloyd's other opinions. JARCO.

THE CANTLIN STONE NEAR KERRY.—In the current number of *Arch : Camb :* the Earl of Powis writes to point out some errors in Mr. Westwood's recently published work on the Sculptured Stones of Wales. The letter refers to the following passage :—

THE CANTLIN STONE.—This stone, at the southern extremity of the county of Montgomery, is marked in the Ordnance Map between Kerry Hill and Clun Forest, and was stated, in a letter addressed to me by S. W. Williams, Esq. of Pennallay House, Rhayader, as being a large upright cross covered with interlaced work and ornamental designs After several vain attempts to find this stone made by George E. Robinson, Esq., one of the secretaries of the Cambrian Archæological Association, he succeeded, in October 1878, in finding it one-and-a-half miles away from the spot marked on the Ordnance Survey, and he informs me that it is a cross with pseudo-druidic embellishments of twining serpents, eggs, and seeds, erected about two-and-twenty years ago to mark the grave of some eccentric benefactor of the neighbourhood, and at its foot is a slab bearing the following inscription :—

"W C BURIED HERE 1691. DIED AT BETUS."

It is difficult of approach, and not less than 2,500 feet high up the mountain.

The errors in the foregoing Lord Powis describes as follows, his lordship's letter being dated from Powis Castle, March 22, 1880 :—

The description of the Cantlin Stone in Mr. Westwood's *Lapidarium Walliæ,* p. 155, is almost wholly erroneous. The original Cantlin Stone is that of which he speaks as "a slab." " W.C." was a pauper from a distance, who died on the hill there, and the two parishes of Mainstone and Bettws disputed which was to go to the cost of burying him. At last Bettws buried him, and was rewarded some years ago, as this was taken in evidence as to the disputed boundary, that the spot was in Bettws parish. The modern Cross was erected by the late Beriah Botfield, Esq., M.P., the owner of the land. It is not difficult of access, as it lies only a few yards off a hill-road from Bishop's Castle to Kerry.

It is well the Earl of Powis "minds the biggin o' it," or the error would have been perpetuated. M.C.A.S.

QUERIES.

GENERAL THOMAS MYTTON.—In his second instalment of Oswestry Corporation Documents (communicated to the *Transactions* of the Shropshire Archæological Society), Mr. Stanley Leighton gives a copy of the

Petition presented against the return of Mr. Humphrey Edwards, as Knight of the Shire, on the displacement of Sir Richard Lee, in 1646. General Mytton was the Parliamentary Sheriff, and in that capacity fixed the election for Oswestry on Aug. 17 of that year, but secretly stole away with a few chosen followers to Alberbury, where the election was held. The petition was signed in the interests of Andrew Lloyd; and Mr. Stanley Leighton expresses his surprise that Mytton should have acted "hostile to his neighbour Col. Andrew Lloyd of Aston, who was engaged on the same side as himself," and adds, that of the successful candidate, Edwards, he has been unable to obtain any account. In Price's *History of Oswestry*, p. 59, the editor (the Rev. Peter Roberts) in reference to this matter observes that Mr. Humphrey Edwards was a relative of Mytton's. This would in some measure account for the conduct of the Sheriff. Perhaps some reader of this will be able to say in what way the parties were related?
JARCO.

LEWIS DWNN'S VISITATIONS.—Could any one inform me 'if Sir Sam. Meyrick's edition of *Lewis Dwnn's Visitations* is the only book in existence recording these Visitations, or if the Peniarth Library has any MSS. relating to them unprinted, or where such books or MSS. might be examined?
L.L.

WYNNS OF WYNNSTAY.—What is the origin of the Eagle bearing the arms of this distinguished family? "The paternal arms of Grenville, Lord Lansdown, *upon the breast of the Roman Eagle*, were borne in that manner on account of a Hungarian Enterprize. Charles Grenville, second Baron Lansdown, and thirty-first of Grenville, serving during his father's life-time in Hungary against the Turks, was created Count of the Holy Roman Empire, and permitted to wear his arms on the Imperial Eagle." (*Anecdotes of Heraldry and Chivalry*, p. 105.) Had the supporting Eagle of the Wynn arms a similar origin? The Wynns are connected with a family of Grenville's.
ZETA.

RICHARD ROBERTS.—Mr. Smiles in his *Self Help*, p. 264, says "Richard Roberts was born in 1789, at Carreghova, in the parish of Llanymynech. His father was by trade a shoemaker, to which he occasionally added the occupation of toll-keeper. The house in which Richard was born stood upon the border line which then divided the counties of Salop and Montgomery : the front door opening in the one county, and the back door in the other." In which county was the room that gave birth to this famous engineer? Was he an "Eminent Welshman" or a "Border Counties Worthy"?
ROATH.

REPLIES.

JUDICATURE IN WALES (June 16, 1880).— The popular feeling in 1820 and in 1828 seems to have been different. On Dec. 2 of the latter year we are told in the newspapers a meeting was held at Llangefni, Anglesey, to take the sense of the country on the propriety of "retaining our judicature." The Chairman of Quarter Sessions, Mr. John Williams, presided. He was of opinion that the introduction of English judges; and including Wales in the circuits of fourteen judges, was a measure disadvantageous to Wales, inasmuch as all actions tried in Wales were comparatively tried with small expense. He moved that "The principal objections to our Judicature arise from having the same judges continually on one circuit : that their appointment proceeds from political interest. The proposed remedy is that the circuits should be alternately visited by all the Welsh Judges, or, if possible, that the introduction of English

Judges should be adopted, provided our Judicature be not changed." Meetings were also held in Ruthin, Haverfordwest, and other places in North and South Wales a few months later to consider "the first report of His Majesty's Commissioners of the Superior Courts of Common Law."
NEMO.

ARMS OF WALES (June 23, 1880).—In an article on Heraldry by G. T. Clark, Esq. (of Dowlais), a very able writer, in the new edition (9th) of the *Encyclopœdia Britannica*, it is stated—
"There is no authority of any standing for a Coat of Arms for the whole of the Principality of Wales, but the coat usually attributed to it is *quarterly azure and gules, 4 lions passant gardant, counterchanged*. The ancient princes of Wales would scarcely have adopted the lions of England. Moreover, this coat was never used by any leading chief in either *middle* or *south* Wales."
From the words which we have italicized we should infer that Mr. G. T. Clark confines the use of this coat to the Princes of *North* Wales.
BETA.

SEDAN CHAIRS (May 12, 1880).—My earliest recollection of Sedans is, seeing infirm old ladies carried to church in them, and others going in full dress to evening parties. They were very common in Shrewsbury until the introduction of "Flys," and even then the enterprising proprietor, Yeomans, brought out a covered Bath chair for the use of those who could not trust themselves behind a horse and yet preferred wheels. I cannot say when the use of Sedans was discontinued, but as the name of "Thomas Yeomans, Sedan chairman, Claremont Hill," appears in the poll book of 1852, and not in that of 1857, it is presumable that their discontinuance took place between those dates. A singular incident occurred in the Christmas time of 1844-5, when on returning from a festive ball given by the then Mayor of Shrewsbury, a certain gentleman availed himself of one of these antiquated vehicles to help him home. It had not proceeded far, when the bottom of the Sedan fell out, and the inmate found himself compelled to use his feet to keep pace with his carriers, until by bawling "Murder" at the top of his voice they released him from his unpleasant situation.
WHAFS.

[The "Fly" mentioned here was the successor of the "Sedan." Dr. Brewer, in his *Dictionary of Phrase and Fable*, says "Fly," as applied to a hackney coach, was a contraction of "Fly-by-Night" as "Sedan chairs on wheels used to be called in the Regency."—ED.]

THE NEW RECORDER OF OSWESTRY.
(Apr. 28, 1880).

The Quarter Sessions held on Tuesday, June 29, were of more than usual interest to the borough from the fact that our new Recorder, Mr. Charles Watkin Williams-Wynn, sat for the first time. On such an occasion as this it was only to be expected that the Recorder should be received by more than the usual officials. Accordingly, there were gathered in waiting at the Savings Bank the following representative gentlemen :—Aldermen E. Wynne Thomas, J.P., and George Owen, J.P.; Messrs. Benjamin Roberts, J.P., Askew Roberts, J.P.; Councillors T. P. Parry, J.P., E. Shaw, J.P., Spaull, J.P., Saunders, and C. W. Owen (ex-Mayors); Mr. Bull, Clerk of the Peace; Mr. Jackson, Deputy Town Clerk, &c., &c.
The appointment of Mr. Charles W. Williams-Wynn restores to Oswestry a family connection that existed more or less from 1728 to 1835. In the first-mentioned year "the Honour'd Mr. Watkin Williams-Wynn" (who had

only adopted the additional surname a few years earlier) became our chief magistrate. In those days, and under the Royal Charter, the office of Mayor meant more than it does in the present age, and was often filled by a neighbouring gentleman, the work being `done by deputy. In 1735 Mr. Robert Williams of Erbistock, brother of the gentleman just named, was chosen .Mayor, and in a few years afterwards he became our Recorder. Mr. Robert Williams was second son of the second Sir William Williams of Llanvorda, and grandson of "The Speaker." In 1747 Mr. Richard Williams of Penbedw (a younger brother of the Recorder) was appointed mayor, and in 1770 the office was filled by Mr. Watkin Williams of Penbedw, the son of this Mr. Richard Williams. Mr. Robert Williams, the Recorder, represented Montgomeryshire in Parliament ; and Mr. Richard Williams, and his son Mr. Watkin Williams after him, the Flint Boroughs. "The Honoured" Mr. Watkin Williams-Wynn, previously mentioned, did not become "Sir Watkin" until the death of his father, Sir William Williams, in 1740, and he died in 1749. In 1774 Sir Watkin Williams Wynn, his son, was made mayor ; and he dying in 1789, a third "Sir Watkin" became lord of Wynnstay. This member of the family was also mayor of Oswestry, filling the office in 1800 and again in 1831. And yet another of the family occupied the post of chief-magistrate of the borough, viz. : —Henry Watkin Williams-Wynn, Esq. (afterwards Sir Henry), who was elected in 1819. We have recently alluded to the fact that the father of the new Recorder filled the same office (under the Charter of Charles II.) from an early period in the century up to 1835, when the Municipal Corporations Act for a time deprived us of the Local Court we had enjoyed, in one form or other, from the time when the Fitzalans were the feudal lords of Oswestry. In these early days the Steward was the Judge of the Local Court.† The first Recorder of which we have mention is Sir Henry Townshend, appointed in 1616 under the Charter of James I.

When Mr. Wynn arrived, shortly before eleven o'clock, he was escorted (preceded by the macebearers) into Court, where Mr. G. Owen, in the absence of the Mayor, and at the wish of his brother Magistrates, addressed a few congratulatory words to the newly appointed judge.

Alderman OWEN said—Your Honour,—In the absence of the Mayor and ex-Mayor, the pleasing duty has devolved upon me, of congratulating you upon the occasion of your taking your seat for the first time as the Recorder of this ancient borough, and I may use the word "ancient" advisedly, for our first charter dates from the time of Henry II. This charter was renewed from time to time, but it was not until the year 1673, in the reign of Charles II., that any mention was made of a Recorder, and in that document we find that the Mayor, Recorder, and Steward, or any two of them may hold a Court of Record, and, strange to say, sir, one bearing in part your own name, a Morgan Wynne, was the first Recorder ; but on the passing of the Municipal Reform Act, Oswestry was left out in the cold, and its claims ignored, until 1842. When Robert Peel being then in office, the Quarter Sessions were re-established, and our late lamented Recorder, Mr. John Robert Kenyon, was appointed, which office he continued to hold until his death ; and of him I may say, in passing, he was an upright judge, a courteous country gentleman, and a sincere friend, and though he has lately passed from among us, I am sure he will long live in our memories. His mantle, sir, has worthily fallen upon you, and I am sure it will be worthily worn, and, although many may say, " What's in a name," I think there is often a good deal in a name, and there is this singular fact in connection with the respected name you

bear, that three of your ancestors have been mayors of this town, and another three of your ancestors have also been recorders, making six persons in all who have been intimately connected with the borough. I am sure, sir, I am repeating the sentiments of my brother magistrates in saying—whether looking back at these facts, or whether looking at the way in which you have conducted the business of the Court when acting in a similar capacity in an adjoining county—we congratulate ourselves upon the appointment, and have no doubt you will conduct the business here in a way that will redound to the credit of the Court, and I was going to say, to the satisfaction of all concerned, but I suppose in this I must omit those who will be brought before you as prisoners. Sir, I once again offer you our warmest congratulations.

The RECORDER, in reply, said—Mr. Owen and gentlemen,—When her Majesty was graciously pleased to offer me the appointment of Recorder of your ancient and honourable borough, I had some hesitation in accepting office, fearing it might clash with another position I held, that of Deputy Chairman of the Quarter Sessions of the County of Montgomery. But when I found that the one office would not interfere with the other, it was with peculiar pleasure that I accepted this ; for there is not a borough in England or Wales where such an appointment could afford me equal pleasure. It is known to most of you that my father was Recorder of Oswestry for, I think, more than thirty years, and up to the time when the Municipal Corporations Act was passed. His numerous political and parliamentary avocations often prevented his taking his place at your Sessions; but when in the country he always made a point of attending ; and his services were recognized by your Corporation by the presentation of a piece of plate, which I am proud to say now stands on my table. By the passing of the Municipal Corporations Act Oswestry lost its Charter, and the right of holding Quarter Sessions. I was a mere boy at the time, but I remember being invited to the first dinner given by the Mayor (I think it was Mr. Penson) that took place after the Court was restored, and your late Recorder, Mr. J. R. Kenyon, was appointed. I feel it is a difficult thing to follow in the footsteps of so worthy a man. During the long period in which he so ably and honourably filled the office, I believe he was never absent from a single sessions. I will do my best to follow his good example, and I trust to the satisfaction of the Borough of Oswestry. I thank you for the cordial reception you have given me, and Mr. Owen for his kind wishes.

<hr>

There are one or two historical notices in Alderman Owen's graceful little speech of congratulation to the new Recorder that it will be well to amend. Led astray no doubt by the loose statements in Cathrall's *History of Oswestry*, Mr. Owen said that the first mention of a Recorder for Oswestry was in the charter of Charles II, granted in 1673, when Morgan Wynne was appointed. Cathrall seems to have been ignorant of the fact that under the charter of James I, granted in 1616, Sir Henry Townshend was nominated Recorder. In passing, I may say, that it has never been stated in any historical notices of Oswestry, who the Morgan Wynne referred to was? The Williamses of Llanvorda did not become Wynns until half a century after the appointment of this Morgan Wynne to the office of Recorder ; and I have never heard that there was any relationship between them.

Then Mr Owen stated that three of Mr. Charles Wynn's ancestors had been Recorders of Oswestry. Strictly speaking there has only been one, viz., the Right Hon. Charles Wynn, his father. The only other member of the family who filled the office being Mr. Robert Williams, a brother of Mr. Charles Wynn's great-great-grandfather—the first Sir Watkin.

In addition to the "three ancestors" of Mr. Charles Wynn's, "who have been mayors of the town," Mr. Owen might have mentioned Sir Henry Williams Wynn (father of the present Lady Williams Wynn) who resided at Llanvorda, and three of the Williamses; two brothers, and one nephew of the first Sir Watkin.

There is one other matter in connection with Mr. Owen's address I will just mention; and it is his observation that "in the absence of the Mayor and Ex-Mayor" it devolved upon him to perform the pleasing duty. Again, "strictly speaking," the ex-mayor (unless he is a "permanent justice") ranks as junior on the Bench, and if chosen to perform the task would not be called upon as ex-mayor, but, as Mr. Owen was called upon, by the wish of his brother magistrates. JARCO.

In your introductory remarks on the reception of the new Recorder, you say that Sir Henry Townshend, who is mentioned in the Charter of James I., is the first known to have held the office. This was in 1616. You have recently mentioned "John Davies, Recorder in 1635," who left a MS. history of Oswestry; and still more recently you have published an interesting extract from Mr. Stanley Leighton's contributions to the Shropshire Archæological Society, in which the election of a Recorder in 1644 is referred to. Morgan Wynne, Mr. Alderman Owen referred to in his speech, was Recorder under the Charter of Charles II., granted in 1673. Is it known whether he acted under the previous charter? And what was the name of the Recorder elected in 1644, who I presume succeeded Mr. Davies? And before I lay down my pen allow me to amend a slip of the pen of the writer in your columns of June 2, who said that the election of Steward was in the hands of the Burgesses. The Lord of the Lordship or Manor always appointed the Steward, and the last that ever was appointed (the Hon. T. Kenyon) was nominated by Lord Clive, in 1823.
OSWALD.

STRAY NOTES.

THE RIGHT HON. C. W. WYNN'S POLITICS.—In reference to the allusion by Mr. Bright (mentioned in our last) to the politics of the Right Hon. C. W. Wynn, "Alfred B. Beaven, Preston," writes thus in Friday's *Times*: —"Mr. Bright having occasion in his speech last night to refer to the late Right Hon. C. W. W. Wynn (whose remarkable knowledge of Parliamentary precedent gained him the sobriquet of 'Small-journal Wynn'), spoke of him as 'a leading and influential member of the Conservative party,' whereupon some hon. member interrupted him with a cry of 'Whig.' Mr. Bright was quite correct. Mr. Wynn had never been in the strict sense of the word a Whig; but he was a prominent member of the small party known as the Grenville connexion which supported Catholic emancipation but opposed Parliamentary reform. Having voted in the majority against the Wellington Administration, he accepted the Secretaryship for War under Earl Grey, but retained office for only a few months, resigning on account of his opposition to the Reform Bill. From that time he was a consistent supporter of Sir R. Peel, and filled the office of Chancellor of the Duchy of Lancaster in his first Administration. It may be worth mentioning that Mr. Wynn was one of the many distinguished politicians who began their Parliamentary careers as member for Old Sarum, where he was elected in succession to the Marquis Wellesley on the latter's appointment to the Governor Generalship of India (1797), and that at his death he was the 'father' of the House of Commons, having sat for the county of Montgomery during the long period of more than fifty-one years (March, 1799, to September, 1850)."

VALUE OF MILKING COWS SEVENTY YEARS AGO.—Each milch cow, belonging to Mr. Thomas Jackson, late of Rhos y lan, in the parish of St. Martins, near Oswestry, was averaged to produce one thousand quarts of milk per annum, from the month of July 1809 to the same month in the year 1814, and the value of each gallon of milk was estimated at 1s., or £50 a year for each cow. This was proved upon oath before a Commission directed by the Court of Exchequer, on the 29th October 1817, and confirmed by the Report of the Deputy Remembrancer. It appears from the case of the appellants (just published) now pending in the House of Lords, that the Commission was founded on a claim for the tithe of milk, and that the annual value of each cow's milk was estimated at £50 over and above what had been used for the suckling of calves, and the feeding of the cows upon dry fodder, turnips, after-pasture, stubble, &c., which paid tythes in another manner.—*Oswestry Herald*, Aug. 1, 1820.

WYNNSTAY AGRICULTURAL SOCIETY.—At the "annual shew" of 1820 Sir Watkin Williams Wynn offered the following amongst other prizes:—"A Piece of Plate to the person who shall produce a Swing-Plough, with two horses abreast and one man to attend it, which shall plough half an acre of ground in four hours, in the best and most husband-like manner." A prize was also offered to "the Ploughman holding the same." Then there was "A Premium of Ten Guineas to any person who shall invent, and produce at Wynnstay Shew, 1820, the best Agricultural Implement, the cost of which shall not exceed £25; simplicity and cheapness of construction being deemed essential parts of its merit." When the show came off the Ten-guinea prize for the "best implement invented and produced," was awarded to John Copner Williams, Esq., of Chirk, and consisted of a "new contrivance for gearing two horses abreast to a strong common cart, whereby the horses, although of different sizes, were made to bear an equal share both of the draught and of the weight on the shafts." This implement and its appendages were made (under Mr. Williams's direction) by Mr. Edwards, Wheelright, of Chirk; and "although not strictly coming within the terms of the advertisement, were recommended to the favour of Sir Watkin by the judges (Viscount Clive and T. N. Parker, Esq.) as an ingenious and useful method of applying the power of two horses in conveying heavily laden carts up and down steep ascents and descents."

OSWESTRY AND WELSHPOOL NATURALISTS' FIELD CLUB AND ARCHÆOLOGICAL SOCIETY.—The third excursion took place on Friday, June 25. After meeting at Welshpool the party proceeded by carriage to the Golfa Hill, the top of which commands a most extensive and beautiful view, Cader Idris and other high peaks being easily seen in the distance. The line of ancient entrenchments are just visible on the hill, and immediately opposite is Pen-y-Voel, once probably the stronghold of King Einion, which gave its name to the village of Castle Caer Einion, and the surrounding district. Thence they proceeded to the village of Llangynyw. There is a handsome carved oak rood-screen in the church, and some very fine old yew trees in the churchyard. A heavy thunder shower, which soon after overtook the party prevented their exploring Pen-y-Castell, but from a point on the road just beyond a fine view of the Vernyw Valley was obtained. They then went on to Llanfair, which is prettily situated on the banks of the Einion. The church was rebuilt some years ago, but the fine old doorway arch was retained, and there is a stone effigy of a knight in armour. On their return to Welshpool the party partook of an excellent tea, provided by Mr. Roberts, of the Bull. The excursion was a very pleasant one, and there were present Mrs. J. R. Barnes and a friend, Miss Oswell, the Revs. D. P. Lewis, G. G. Monck, and O. M. Feilden, and Messrs. Barrett, Wilding, and Baker, &c.

WELSH BOOKS PRINTED ABROAD.

CYMMRODORION SOCIETY.

On Wednesday, the 30th June, a paper was read before the Cymmrodorion Society, by Mr. Howel W. Lloyd, M.A., on "Welsh Books Printed Abroad in the 16th and 17th centuries, and their Authors." Mr. Lloyd commenced his paper by relating the manner in which Prince L. L. Bonaparte became the purchaser from M. Marcel, the learned publisher and bibliographer in Paris, in the reign of Napoleon I., of his Highess' unique copy of the "Athrawaeth Cristionogawl," which was exhibited to the Prince by that gentleman, under the impression that it was written in the Cornish language. It is now being printed in facsimile by the Cymmrodorion Society. After some observations on the peculiarities of orthography and punctuation adopted in the work, which was printed in Milan by the learned Dr. Griffith Roberts, the author of the celebrated Welsh Grammar, and commenting on the proof furnished by the words "O Fylen, noswyl Sant Nicolas" in the colophon at the end of the preface, that the grammar, imprinted according to the title *Mediolani*, at Mediolanum, must also have been printed at Milan, and not at any place in Wales, as maintained by the late Sir A. Panizzi, Librarian of the British Museum, Mr. Lloyd proceeded to show from the preface, written by Dr. Roberts, that the work itself was composed by Dr. Maurice Clynog, the first Rector of the English College at Rome, to whom the preface is addressed. He then proceeded to comment upon another work by Dr. Roberts, "Y Drych Cristionogawl," which consisted of three parts, but of which the first part only appears to have been printed at Rouen by his friend and admirer, Dr. Roger Smyth, of S. Asaph, who followed the example set by Dr. M. Clynog and Dr. Griffith Roberts, in the attempt to provide books of religious instruction and devotion for the use of their persecuted Catholic brethren in Wales. Another work, by Dr. Roger Smyth, was a translation of the "Opus Catechisticum" of F. Peter Canisius, S.J., printed at Paris, under the patronage, and probably also at the cost of Cardinal Perron, in 1611, which was followed by one of the "Theatre du Monde," composed in French and Latin, by Peter Boaystuan, a Breton, and in English by John Alday, printed in London in 1574. The title of the Welsh work is "Theater du Mond, sef iw Gorsedd y Byd, lle i gellir gweled trueni a llaseni Dyn o ran y Corph ai Odidawgrwydd o ran yr Enaid, a Sgrifenwyd gynt yn y Frangaeg, ag a gyfieithwyd i'r Gymraeg drwy lafyr Rosier Smyth o Dref Lan Elwy Athraw o Theologydiaeth." This work appears to have been seen by Rowlands, who speaks in "Llyfryddiaeth y Cymry" of having had an imperfect copy of it under his hand, but Mr. Lloyd could not say whether that, or any other copy of the work, was known to be still in existence. The next work referred to was "Eglurhad Helaethlawn o'r Athrawiaeth Gristnogawl, a gyfansodhwyd y tro cyntaf yn Italaeg, trwy Waith yr Ardderchoccaf a'r Hybarchaf Gardinal Rhobert Bellarmine, O Gymdeithas yr Iesu. Ag o'r Italaeg a gymreigwyd er budh ysprydol i'r Cymru, drwy ddiwydrwydh a dyfal gymhorth y pendefig canmoladwy V. R.", being a translation of the Larger Catechism of Card. Bellarmine printed in 1618 at St. Omer by Father John Salisbury, S.J., a short biographical account of whom was given by the reader of the paper. The last Welsh work referred to was "Allwydd, neu Agoriad Paradwys i'r Cymrv. Hynny yw, Gweddiau, Devotionau, Cynghorion ac Athrawiaethau tra duwiol ac angenrheidiol i bob Cristion yn mynnu agoryd y Porth a myned i mewn i'r Nef. Wed eu cynnull o amryw lyfrau duwiol, a'i cytieithu yn Gymraeg: neu wedi eu cyfansoddi, gan J. H. Yn Luyck. Imprintiwyd yn y Flwyddyn MDCLXX. [12 plyg bychan]." "A Key or Opening of Paradise to the Cymru. That is, Prayers, Devotions, Counsels, and Instructions, very godly and necessary for every Christian desiring to open the Gate, and enter into Heaven. Gathered out of several godly books, and translated into Welsh: or composed by J. H. At Luick. Printed in the year 1670 [small 12mo]." The reader referred to the opinion of the Rev. D. S. Evans that the author was one of the Havards of Devynog, in Brecknockshire, and that Luick, where the work was printed, is to be identified with Liège; an opinion corroborated afterwards by the assent of several competent authorities present. We refrain from giving a fuller account of the paper, as we understand that it is intended to appear in its full substance in the forthcoming number of the "Cymmrodor." A conversation followed, in which the reader of the paper was complimented on the success which he had achieved in imparting interest and pleasure to what had promised to be a dry and unattractive subject. Prince Lucien favoured the Society with remarks in which he showed that the orthography of the "Athrawaeth" tended in some respects to prove that the book could only have been printed by an Italian, the division of some syllables being in accordance with the Italian style of pronunciation, in which the *s* is not separated from the *t* as in the northern languages of Europe. After some interesting observations by Mr. Wyman on the difficulties with which printers are beset in calculating the proportions of the different "sorts" requisite for putting works in a foreign language into type, and by other speakers on the dotting of letters in mediæval MSS., the meeting was brought to a close with a vote of thanks to the reader of the paper, moved by the Rev. J. Davies, the learned author of "The Celtic element of the English People" in the "Archæologia Cambrensis," and seconded by Mr. Miller, of the British Museum.

A WELSH M.P. EXPELLED THE HOUSE.

Amongst the precedents given in the Report of the Bradlaugh Committee is the following, taken from the Commons Journal, Vol. 18, p. 260 ; 8th August, 1715.

The House was called over according to order.

And the names of such as made default to appear were taken down.

Ordered that the names of such as made default be now called over.

And they were called over accordingly.

And several of them appeared, and others were excused upon account of their being ill, some in the country, some in town; and others upon account of their being in the country upon extraordinary occasions; and some as being upon the road.

Upon calling over the names of * * * Lewis Price, Esquire, * * * they were not excused.

Several members sent for.

Ordered, that Lewis Price, Esquire, be sent for, in custody of the Serjeant at Arms attending this House.

The Serjeant at Arms being called upon to give the House an account of what he had done in relation to Lewis Pryse, Esquire, who was, the 8th of August last, ordered to be sent for in custody for not attending the Service of the House; he acquainted the House, that the messenger he sent to bring up Mr. Pryse, had been at his house at Gargathen [Gogerddan], but that he was not there; nor could the messenger have any intelligence where he was.

Ordered, that Lewis Pryse, Esquire, do surrender himself into the custody of the Serjeant at Arms attending this House, by this day month at the farthest, upon pain of occurring the farther displeasure of this House, and of being proceeded against with the utmost severity.

The Order of the 2nd of February last being read, requiring Lewis Pryse, Esquire, to surrender himself into the custody of the Serjeant at Arms attending this House by that day month at farthest ;

The Serjeant was called upon to know whether he had heard from the said Mr. Pryse, and he acquainted the House, that he had not heard from him.

Mr. Speaker acquainted the House, that he had received a letter from the said Mr. Pryse, and he delivered the same to the Clerk to be read ; and the same was read accordingly, and is as follows, viz :—

"Sir,—'Tis with pleasure that I embrace every opportunity of returning you my acknowledgments for the good offices you have done me, as often as the case of my unavoidable absence has come under debate in the House. The repeated experience I have had of your friendship in this point, encourages me to hope for the continuance of them, which I shall not offer to desire longer than the reasonableness of my case shall appear to deserve them.

"I beg leave once more to represent it to you; and through your assistance to the honourable House ; whose displeasure as it is a very sensible affliction to me, I should be glad by any means in my power to remove. That as it is impracticable for me to attend by the time appointed, because of a very severe fit of the gout which I am now afflicted with, and thereby give satisfaction to the House in the method they have insisted on ; I hope they will accept of such as is in my power, and give me a favourable hearing when I represent to them, that I was chose knight of the shire of Cardigan when I was at 100 miles distant from it, and had been absent thence for ten months before the time of my election ; which I was so far from seeking, that I never asked a vote for it, and was chose even against my inclinations.

"I know not how far a man is obliged to stand to the choice a county makes of him. Sure I am that I have reason to complain of a force that has administered the occasion of my disobliging the Honourable House, by an absence caused by infirmities, under which I laboured at the time of my choice, and which have continued upon me ever since with the greatest severity, and with little or no intermission.

"In these circumstances I would fain hope that the honourable House will rather blame the country's choice, than him who has been unwillingly forced into a post, and lies under the misfortune (for I flatter myself 'twill not be thought a crime) of not being able to attend the business of it : and will therefore lay aside their displeasure, and remit the sentence ordered against me.

"And I am the rather encouraged to hope this, because Mr. Prynne, in his comment on the fourth book of Sir Edward Coke's Institutes, shows from various records, that incurable distempers have been constantly allowed by the House for a just excuse of non-attendance ; and upon debates in such cases, no other punishment has been inflicted than excusing the service of the House, and ordering a new writ for electing a person duly qualified, and capable of attending the business of the House. This being the course of Parliamentary proceedings in such cases as mine, which I have now truly represented to you, and can produce hundreds of witnesses to confirm. I hope that the unhappy incapacity I am under of attending the service of the House, will be thought to deserve no severer treatment than has been usual in the like cases ; and that my ready submission to the honourable House's pleasure in this point will be a means to restore me to their favourable opinion, and engage you to promote the request of

"Your most obliged and obedient humble servant,
"Aberllefenny, 18 February, 1715."   LE PRYSE."

"I know not how far the House in their last order about me, might be influenced by any report of the messenger who came down to my house ; but to prevent misrepresentation, I think it proper to assure you, that within three days after a very dangerous fit of the gout suffered me to come downstairs, I came from thence hither to my father-in-law's, 18 miles in my way to London. But the motion of even so small a journey brought another fit upon me immediately, with which I have been laid up here ever since, and not having been yet so much as able to return to my own house."

Then the journal of the * day of May, 1689, in the case of Mr. Cholmondley, was read.
(House interrupted—Conference.)
The House resumed the consideration of the matter relating to Mr. Pryse.

Resolved, that Lewis Pryse, Esquire, a Member of this House, having been sent for in custody of the Serjeant at Arms attending this House, the 8th day of August last, for not attending the service of this House, and having never qualified himself as a Member of this House, by taking the oaths at the table, be forthwith brought up in custody.

The messenger gives the House an account of what he had done pursuant to the order of the House.

Resolved, that Lewis Pryse, Esquire, a Member of this House, having been sent for in custody of the Serjeant at Arms attending this House, the 8th day of August last, for not attending the service of this House, and having never qualified himself as a member of this House by taking the oaths at the table ; and having been on the 2nd of February last, summoned to surrender himself into custody of the Serjeant at Arms, upon pain of being proceeded against with the utmost severity, and he having absconded, and peremptorily refused to surrender himself into custody, be, for the said contempt, expelled this House.

JULY 14, 1880.

NOTES.

CENTENARY OF SUNDAY SCHOOLS (July 7, 1880).—In the same MS. Diary kept by the Rev. J. W. Jenkyn at Oswestry I find the following allusion to Sunday Schools. The date is Nov. 1831, and reference is made to the "Jubilee of Sunday Schools" recently celebrated. A Mr. Wilson, a "Sunday School Missionary" sent about by the Sunday School Union, visits Oswestry, and speaks at a Wesleyan Missionary Meeting which happened to be held when he was in the town. After the meeting several of the persons engaged in it (including Messrs. McNicoll and Osborne of Liverpool, the Deputation) met at Mr. Hillmore's, cabinet-maker, to supper. Mr. Jenkyn writes :—

At supper as Mr. Wilson was with us we talked about the origin of Sunday Schools as some had attributed them to Cardinal Boromeo whose schools at Milan are noticed in Daniel Wilson's "Letters from an Absent Brother." Mr. Wilson, of course, advocated the claims of Robert Raikes of Gloucester. Mr. Osborne said that the fact was that Mr. Raikes of Gloucester had only carried into fuller execution the plan of a man of the mame of Webb who lived in Stroud, who was a *Wesleyan*, and had a Sunday School for some time at his house !

Mr. Wilson's visit to Oswestry seems to have been to try and form a "Sunday School Union between the Independents, Wesleyans, and Baptists." The use of the Old Chapel was allowed him to address the children of the schools, and also to hold a meeting to detail his plans of Sunday School instruction.   JARCO.

A SALOPIAN MISER. –In Jan., 1840, one William Jones, aged 60, was discharged from the Salop Infirmary incurable. When in the infirmary he pleaded poverty, but on the usual examination to see that his linen was clean some silver fell from his pocket, and from his coat thirty sovereigns. He was conveyed in a "fly" to his residence at Bayston Hill, near Shrewsbury, where he died on the following Monday. Shortly before his death he told some persons where in his cottage they would find some money, and he died in making an effort to grasp it. On a further examination of his cottage—in which there was scarcely an article of furniture—cash to the amount of £240, and securities amounting to £500 were found, and besides this it was discovered that he owned the cottage and other premises. In his house, in odd corners, had been accumulated a large number of pocket knives, about a score of pewter pots, quantities of old shoes and books, &c. Jones had accumulated his wealth by begging and selling vegetables. He left a brother and sister—the former had been an inmate of Atcham Union, and the latter was a widow residing near Newtown, Montgomeryshire—who inherited his savings.

SCROBBES BYRIG.

QUERIES.

THE BEDDGELERT PINT.—A writer in the Apr. part of the *Arch: Camb:* asks for information as to the once celebrated Beddgelert Pint, mentioned by Mr. Williams of Llandegai in his *Observations on the Snowdon Mountains*, published in 1802. Speaking of an old house near the church, which Mr. W. thought may have been that of the Prior, he remarks that it contained the vessel in question,—an old pewter mug, that might have held two quarts. "Any one who could hold it in one hand, and drink the contents in ale at one draft, was entitled to the liquor gratis, the tenant charging the value of it as part payment of rent."   G.G.

POWYSLAND HORSES.—It appears that the breeding of horses in this principality received very early attention, and the effect of this early care may be still perceptible. Giraldus, writing in the year 1188, when an acute observer, he travelled through the whole of Wales in company with Archbishop Baldwin, says (*Itin.* ii. 173, Ed. Sir R. C. Hoare):—"In this third district of Wales, called Powys, there are most excellent studs set apart for breeding and deriving their origin from some fine Spanish horses, which Robert de Belesme, Earl of Shrewsbury, brought into this country; on which account the horses sent from hence are remarkable for their majestic proportions, and astonishing fleetness." Probably these had some of the well-known Moorish or Arab blood, and it was new to me, as it may be to many of your readers, to find that this fine strain had been introduced into this country at such an early period.   CAEAWC.

SALOPIAN LITERATURE.—Mr. Thoms, the gentleman to whom the world of letters is indebted for *Notes and Queries*, writes to that publication on July 3, to solicit the loan of the first number of the *Albion Magazine*, edited by Mr. J. B. Revis of Ludlow, in 1829 or 1830, and published, Mr. Thoms thinks, in Liverpool. If this was the John Brookes Revis who commenced a magazine called the *Shropshire and North Wales Standard* in 1839, he was then a bookseller in Shrewsbury, and his name appears on the Magazine as its printer, though its execution is better than the usual country printing of that day. The magazine was Conservative in politics, and had as a contributor the well-known sporting writer "Nimrod." The first part (2s.) contained a portrait of the Hon. T. Kenyon, and the second was announced to have one of the Earl of Powis. Can any reader of this give further information respecting this Mr. Revis and his Salopian serials?   JARCO.

REPLIES.

SHROPSHIRE WORDS (Apr. 28, 1880.)—*Dark.* The following notice of death appears in the *Oswestry Herald* for Aug. 1, 1820 :—"Lately, at Bridgnorth, Mr. Thomas Curtis, formerly a hairdresser, in the 88th year of his age ; he had supported throughout life the character of a peaceable, honest man ; he had been dark for the last 17 years."   SALOPIAN.

BURNING OF FRIAR FOREST (June 9, 1880.)—Your correspondent "N.W.S." has evidently not seen in the *Arch: Camb:* Vol. 5, p. 152, a paper on the subject of Dervael Gadarn in which the

letters of Ellis Price and the account of the burning of Katharine of Arragon's Confessor are given in extenso. In the same Vol. p. 252 is a letter on the subject from our able countryman Mr. Howel Lloyd whose susceptibilities the writer of the article had very unintentionally hurt. The trunk of the horse, known as Ceffyl Dervael, and a portion of the spear supposed to have been held by the wooden Saint are still, or were very recently, in the porch of Llandderfel Church near Bala.   E.B.

SOCIETY OF ANCIENT BRITONS.
(June 30, 1880.)

Again to follow the Secretary's narrative. Another allusion to "the surprizing Coincidence of our most glorious Princess' Birth-Day, with that of the Festival of St. *David*," and he goes on to inform his countrymen how "this propitious Opportunity was piously embraced by the true Zeal of the Antient *Britons*, for which they have ever been so famous." To show their "gratitude to God and Man for this Day's *double* production, they publish'd an Advertisement in the *Gazette* on the 9th of February, 1714," announcing service and sermon in the "Antient British *Language*," at St. Paul's, Covent Garden, for the 1st of March following. All loyal Welshmen were invited to accompany Lord Lisburne, the Bishop of Bangor, and others, to attend Divine service, and afterwards to dinner at the Haberdasher's Hall ; after which President and Stewards were to be appointed in order to keep up the practice. Accordingly on the day of the "surprising coincidence" service was read by the Rev. Mr. Phillips, and a sermon was preached by the Rev. Mr. Lewis, and a "splendid entertainment" was prepared at Haberdasher's Hall, where "two Chairs were provided for *both* their Royal Highnesses." It does not appear that these [four!] chairs were occupied, but they "were attended by Lord Lysburne and Lord-Almoner to the Prince, two *Welch* Gentlemen." The sermon, which was from Gal. vi., 10., was ordered to be printed, and 4,000 copies were to be sent to "be dispersed among the Common People for whose Good it was intended," a large proportion of these coming into Wales.

After "the usual solemnities were over" (i.e., the Toast List drunk !) the diners proceeded to elect their Stewards, and the choice fell upon the following :—Lord Lysburne ; Sir Walter Younge, First Commissioner of the Customs ; The Honourable Sydney Godolphin, Esq., Auditor of Wales ; Sir John Sabine, Commander of the Welsh Fuziliers ; The Honourable Brigadier Henry Grove ; Roger Jones, Esq., M.P., Charles Allenson, Esq., M.P., William Price, Esq., William Wynn, Esq., John Lloyd, Esq. The name of the Society was then agreed upon, and it was also resolved that "all Charity Money which shall be given to the said Society," should be vested in the Bishop of Bangor, his Royal Highness' Almoner, in conjunction with the Stewards, for the benefit of the Welsh nation. Our author, Mr. Thomas Jones, was appointed Secretary, and the Rev. Mr. Phillips, vicar of Devenock, was "declared chaplain." These matters satisfactorily arranged,—

the Stewards marched in Procession, each having a golden Cup carried before him, the Musick playing before them round the Hall ; and when they returned to the Table where the Chairs were prepared for their Royal Highnesses, the Secretary aloud proclaimed the said Rules.

After this there was shouting, and loud huzzas for King, Prince, and the Princess—who had so obligingly been born on the first of March—and the rest of the royal family. Then came a song, "performed by Mr. Durfey, and of his own composing." When Mr. Banting of ponderous memory offered a prize, in our own day, at an Eisteddfod, Mr. Edmund Yates, his appointed adjudicator

objected to the effusions that were sent in, and was hypercritical enough to toss on one side such as were so
common-place as to contain rhymes to "Wales." Judged
by such criticism, Mr. Durfey's composition would be out
of court, albeit, Sir Thomas Jones considered it was one,
"being designedly plain and the Tune easy and natural,"
every "honest Briton's voice could readily resound the
Loyal Sentiments of his Heart." Here are the first two
verses, as a sample of the six of which it is comprised :—

As far as the glittering God of Day
    Extends his Radient Light,
Old *Britain* her Glory will display,
    In every Action bright ;
The *Fleur de Lis* and *English* Rose
    May boast of their Antique Tales,
But the *Leek* with the greatest Honour grows,
    For the lasting Renown of Wales.

In vain all our musical Bards did seek
    To know whence this Glory sprung,
For Time, without Date, has this famous *Leek*
    In tuneful Verse been sung
By the *Teutons* allowed, and Victorious Rome,
    And the brave *Black Prince* ne'er fails
The Battle of old by this Signal o'ercome
    To exalt the renown of Wales.*

The "Solemnity of the Day" over, a meeting of the
Stewards was arranged to be held on the 6th of March at
the Secretary's house, and it was, of course, resolved to
ask the Prince who had married the Princess with the
"surprising" birthday, to be the president. Some preliminaries had to be arranged before the Stewards could
be admitted into The Presence, but at length it was
effected, when, after agreeing to their request, His Royal
Highness—
    With great Goodness, assured them, THAT HE WOULD DO ANY
THING WITH PLEASURE TO COUNTENANCE AND ENCOURAGE HIS
COUNTRYMEN ; and as a token thereof, gave them the Honour to
kiss his Hand.
The Prince, our readers will observe, is made to speak
in what printers call "small caps." The Princess, into
whose presence the Stewards next entered, seems only to
have replied in "Italics," her Royal Highness declaring :—
    That the Society was very acceptable to her. And as such gave
them the Honour to kiss her Hand.
It will be needless to follow the writer in all his details
of the after proceedings. On the 2nd of April a meeting
was held, at which resolutions were passed, thanking the
Prince, for his condescension ; the Duke of Argyle, for
introducing them to Royalty, &c.; and also arranging for
an account of the Royal interview for the *Gazette*. The
account is short, but it contains the Prince's assurance—
again in Capital letters. It was gazetted by order of the
principal Secretary of State, on April 9, 1715, and the
society was established.

(To be continued.)

CURRENT NOTES.

Dr. Edward M. Boykin of Camden, South Carolina,
has written to the Mayor of Carnarvon to ask if there
are any traces of the Boykin family in the county of Carnarvon. The tradition is that Edward Boykin went to
Virginia in 1685.

An Eisteddfod is about to be held in Hyde Park,
Schuylkill county, Pennsylvania, at which General Garfield, the Republican candidate for the Presidency, is expected to preside. The States are evidently well disposed
towards Welshmen. The present President speaks of the
Welsh as the best immigrants. The probably future
President presides over an Eisteddfod.

* This is in allusion to a popular notion that "the Welshmen
in commemoration of the Great Fight by the Black Prince of
Wales, do wear Leeks." (*Royal Apophthegms* of James I).

At the last meeting of the Cymmrodorion Society, Mr·
Quaritch suggested that a full and correct Bibliography
could easily be obtained if every collector of Welsh books·
would furnish a minute copy of the title page of the works
in his possession. These could afterwards be collated, and ·
in the course of time a full, correct Welsh Bibliography
obtained. He (Mr. Quaritch) did not propose that this
should be carried down any later than say 1850.

On Thursday, July 1, the tower and north and south
transepts of the church of Llanbadarn-fawr were re-
opened by the Lord Bishop of St. David's, after having
been thoroughly restored at a cost of nearly £3,000. The
tower has been re-pointed externally, and the woodwork of
the interior has been strengthened so as to make it possible to
ring the fine-toned bells without danger of bringing down
the timber. The chief work of restoration, and the most
striking because it is the most visible, is in the remodel-
ling of the north and south transepts, the floors of which
have been laid with oak taken from the old woodwork and
mosaics. A stone pulpit has replaced the old oaken one.
It is beautifully carved, and two recesses contain the
figures, sculptured in Caen stone, of the Apostles Peter
and John. The pulpit is the gift of the Bishop of St.
David's, in memory of his mother. A tablet bears the
following inscription :—" Ad majorem evangelii æterni-
profectum necnon in piam memoriam Matris suæ Janæ,
uxoris Gulielmi Tilsley Jones, de Gwynfryn, in Provincia
Ceretica Arm. Hunc abonem construendum curavit·
Gulielmus Basilius Episcopus Menevensis, ob. ilia Xmo.
Die Mensis Dec, A. S. MDCCCXXII." On the opposite
side is a handsome lectern, the gift of the builders,
Messrs. Roderick Williams and Son. The architect is
Mr. J. P. Seddon, London. The chancel yet remains to
be restored.

A writer in the *St. James's Gazette* charges the Eisteddfod with having left undone those things which it ought to·
have done, and with having done those things which there
was no necessity or advantage in doing. Well, the Eisteddfod is a human institution, and at the worst stands
charged with the failing which humanity pleads guilty to·
every Sunday in church. But the writer makes a very
common mistake, and forgets that if the promoters of the
Eisteddfod shot over the heads of the people, by neglecting·
their tastes and inclinations, and inviting them to a feast·
which had no attractions for their literary palate, the
"national institution" would soon come to an end. It is
a means of amusement, and if it is not much more nobody
has a right to complain. At the same time we join heart
and soul with the critic in lamenting that more is not done
to cultivate a higher literary faculty, a love for writers like
DAVYDD AP GWILYM, and an interest in the legends and
traditions, and archæological remains, of the Principality.
The pleasure of a visit to Wales is vastly increased by an
acquaintance, even if it is only elementary, with
the archæology of the country, covered as it is
with traces of ancient and prehistoric inhabitants.
Amongst the mountains of Merionethshire and Carnarvonshire it is almost impossible to take a walk of three or
four miles without coming upon a cromlech, or a barrow,
a venerable church, or a sacred well, the traces of a rude
encampment, or the remains of an ancient town. The
people are surrounded with these monuments of the past,
and it is possible, we believe, to excite an interest in them,
and by means of the Eisteddfod to collect fresh and valuable information concerning the antiquities of Wales and
the legends which still linger amongst the inhabitants.
The taste of the people must not be handled too roughly.
They may still write their odes to the sea, to time, to
silence; and we have no desire to stop the flow of essays on
the subject of "kindness to animals," for that is a topic

which still requires a large amount of elucidation. But to all this something can be added, and a determined and persistent attempt made to encourage study and investigation in the direction we have indicated. There is a good opportunity for the Presidents of the approaching Eisteddfod at Carnarvon to do a real service to the institution itself and to the study of archæology and of the best Welsh poetry. Let them make the archæological riches of Wales, with its legends and traditions, and the records of its greater poets, the subject of their addresses, and finish by offering handsome prizes to encourage students and collectors. One result may be the spread of enlightenment amongst English critics, and then future writers in the *St. James's Gazette* will not refer to Saint Tudno as "a river!"

MAYORAL CHAIN FOR BRIDGNORTH.—Messrs. T. and J. Bragg have just completed the maufacture of a Mayoral chain for the Corporation of Bridgnorth. The chain has thirty-two shields at intervals, engraved successively with the names and dates of service of all mayors since the Municipal Reform Act, leaving sufficient space to insert the names of future mayors for the next twenty-four years. On either side the centre link, which is richly enamelled, are facsimiles in miniature of the borough maces. The large shield, azure, bears-the castle, with portcullis, turrets, and bomb-proof centre tower, standing upon green, daisy-covered hills, heraldically displayed in enamel. The arms of St. George of England and the Royal arms of France and England, shown in one of the early charters, are placed above. Below is the motto, in gold letters, on a crimson riband, *Fidelitas urbis, salus regis.*

JULY 21, 1880.

NOTES.

OSWESTRY IN THE 14TH CENTURY (May 26, 1880).—The following, which relates to a Court of Record in Oswestry as early as 1393, is taken from *Arch : Camb :* 1852, p. 43 :—

At the Court for the Vill of Oswestry, held at the same place, the 7th May, 16th Richard II. [1393] it was granted to Thomas Salter and Matilda his wife, and their heirs male and female, &c, that they should possess and enjoy all that land and tenement which Richard the son of Thomas Salter gave to him by his charters in the Vills of Oswestry, Weston, Swyney, Llanvorda, Llenelyde, Mersbury, Grucketh, Treforclauthe and Coton, as well of the lands of a certain John Lloit as of the lands of him Richard the son of Thomas in the towns before named . . . . For which the said Thomas and Matilda, before the grant, gave a fine of £10. Paying at the feasts of St. Matthew [Sep. 21], the Annunciation of the Blessed Mary [Mar. 25] and St. Matthew next afterwards. Pledges [sureties] David ap Jonnorth Vaughan and Madewyn ap David Gothyn. In testimony whereof this present capias is enrolled. John Boerley, steward of the same, has set his seal. Given at Oswestry the day and year above written.

"The seal has an etoile of five points in the centre: legend in old English small letters, 'Sigillum Thome Boerleie.'" It has already been remarked in *Bye-gones* that David Holbach, the steward of Oswestry (and founder of the Grammar School) represented the county in Parliament. In 1409 we have the name of "Johannes Boerleye" as his fellow member. M.C.A.S.

GENERAL ELECTION, 1820.—In March, 1820, there was a general election caused by the death of George III. In Wales the result was as follows :—Anglesey, Earl of Uxbridge ; Brecon, Thomas Wood ; Cardigan, W. E. Powell ; Carnarvon, Sir Robert Williams, Bart.; Denbigh, Sir Watkin Williams-Wynn, Bart.; Flint, Sir

Thomas Mostyn, Bart.; Merioneth, Sir R. W. Vaughan, Bart.; Montgomery, C. W. Williams Wynn. Of these all were re-elections save Anglesey, and were uncontested. The Boroughs returned members as follows :—Beaumaris, T. Frankland Lewis ; Cardigan, Pryse Pryse ; Carnarvon, Hon. C. Paget ; Denbigh, J. W. Griffith ; Flint, Sir E. P. Lloyd ; Montgomery, Hon. Henry Clive. In the Boroughs all returned were old members ; and there was only one contest—at Denbigh, where F. R. West was the defeated candidate. H.B.

A WELSHPOOL TOAST.—The *Gents : Mag :* for Jan. 1856 contained a notice of Panton Corbett, Esq., who died on Nov. 22, of the previous year, at his residence, Longnor Hall, Salop. Mr. Corbett thrice contested Shrewsbury, once successfully ; but on the last occasion of his doing so was defeated. This was in 1830. The notice I am referring to says that :—

He then retired to his house and estate at Leighton Hall, near Welshpool ; where he enjoyed social relaxation and cultivated the amenities and friendship of a large circle of the surrounding gentry. He likewise further engaged himself in those duties which pertained to a magistrate for Montgomeryshire, endeavouring to conciliate whenever practicable any differences that might occur among litigant parties ; and in promoting the unanimity and welfare of his neighbours, for whose happiness on all occasions his warm heart and diffusive sympathies manifested a becoming concern, especially in acts of benevolence to the humbler classes. For many years previous to the passing of the Municipal Act, he was the High Steward of the borough of Welshpool, and when, after the death of his father, the Leighton estate was sold, and he became resident at the family mansion of Longnor, the inhabitants of Welshpool on most festive gatherings indulged the reminiscent sentiment :— "Though lost to sight to memory dear—our late respected neighbour Panton Corbett, Esq."

Mr. Corbett was the second son of Archdeacon Plymley, who took the name of Corbett in 1806.

BLACKPOOL.

CYMRU FU.
"Cara Bardd yr Encilion."

COED Y FRON.—The inhabitants of Edeyrnion are well acquainted with Coed y Fron, a plantation surrounding Rûg Hall, the ancient seat of the Vaughans of Nannau. There is a tradition in the neighbourhood alluding to two brothers, one residing at Rûg, and the other at Ucheldref. The brother at Ucheldref was not so wealthy as the one at Rûg. One evening he said to his brother, "My brother, you have enough, and could well afford to give me the Fron in addition to my resources." The wealthy brother was not very willing, but at last he muttered, "You shall have it for three crops, but remember it comes back to me after you have finished gathering the last crop." The brother of Ucheldref afterwards went and sowed the Fron with acorns, saying that neither he nor his family would give it up until they had finished reaping three crops of ancient oaks from the place.

RÛG.—There is another tradition connected with Rûg. It is believed amongst the mass, especially the old people, that whenever the field before the front door is ploughed, the heir to the estate will die the following year. There is a small farm belonging to the estate named Penygryglyn, the rent of which for generations was a young goose. The tenant was obliged to take it to Rûg annually on the night before Christmas Day.

CYNWYD.—On Foel Hafod Bleddyn, above this hamlet, there is a large granite stone, which the inhabitants call "The Stone of Jesus Christ." It is believed that the stone broke in two when the Saviour was suffering.

OWEN SHON ADAM'S STILE.—This stile is situated under Penyllwyn, near Llanfyllin. About one hundred years ago a butcher named Lewis, from the lower part of the parish of Llanfihangel, who had been attending Llanfyllin market, where he had received a large amount of money, at the Swan public-house, where Brook Side is situated, on his way towards home, indulged himself too freely with strong beer. The butcher left the Swan late at night, it being very dark, and as he was approaching the stile, which was in a lonesome place, at the nearest end of the present large plantation to the town, he was struck across the head with a heavy pole, which felled him to the ground, and he died instantaneously. His money was taken from his pockets, and Lewis's body was found the following morning smeared with blood. One Owen Shon Adam, who was drinking freely with Lewis, and who had left the Swan before the butcher had started for his home, was apprehended and committed for trial to the assizes on the capital charge. It is related that by some means or other, through the influence of the Llwyn family, the Humphreyses, his sentence was mitigated. He was imprisoned at Montgomery gaol, and on his release he was branded with hot iron in the arm. Adam was buried in Llanfyllin churchyard, where a common slab was to be seen above his remains until lately, and the stile where he committed the murder has been called ever since " Camfa Owen Shon Adam."

Pant-y-pwdin.   LLYWARCH HEN.

QUERIES.

TREES ON THE ASTON ESTATE. — In Plymley's "General View of the Agriculture of Shropshire," published under the auspices of the Board of Agriculture in 1803, the Rev. J. R. Lloyd of Aston contributes, amongst other items, something about Plantations, in the course of which he observes that "a singular custom prevails in this county (Salop) which tends wonderfully to the consumption of oak timber, few persons consenting to bury their relations in coffins of any other wood ; and not content with this, the best possible pieces of timber are selected for the purpose. If the legislature thought it once necessary to enact a law to oblige the use of woollen in funerals, to encourage a *manufacture*, there can be no doubt of the propriety of prohibiting the use of oak upon such occasions, when the bulwark of the nation is in want of it. As farmers are frequently in want of small wood, it may be proper to appropriate an acre and a half to be planted with ash and spring coppice-wood, that a quarter of an acre may be cut every year, which would supply handles for spades, and other such implements, and the tenant would then have no excuse for lopping the trees upon his farm." Archdeacon Plymley adds to this the following note :—"Mr. Lloyd has planted extensively, and twice obtained a premium from the Society of Arts : he had one medal for a plantation of oaks exceeding 50,000." This fact has been mentioned in *Bye-gones*, I believe, but does not the author here understate the number of trees planted by Mr. Lloyd ?   H.B.

WELL AT WOOLSTON.—Nineteen out of every twenty Oswestrians probably are unaware that within half a dozen miles of them exists the remains of a well that at one day no doubt was famous, although now its history is "veiled in obscurity." The well is situated in the parish of West Felton, about half a mile from Maesbury. Over the spring, which issues out of the Woolston bank, and which makes a good sized stream there, has been built a well and bath—cruciform in shape—of the red sandstone of the district ; together with a timbered house, the roof of which might lead one to suppose that it had been more than a bath-house—probably a chapel. No one, so far as I am aware, has fixed a date for this well ; but Mr. Hulbert, in his history of the county, in a vague way refers to it as "dedicated to St. Winifred." Another

supposition is that the spot was one of the resting-places for the bones of St. Winifred on their way from Gwytherin to Shrewsbury Abbey. The other day a gentleman who visited the well for the first time made a suggestion that deserves consideration. Whence does the hamlet in the vicinity of the well get its name "Woolston"? In the time of the Conqueror "St. Wulston" was Bishop of Worcester. Had he any connection with this district, and can the well be traced to him? The only notice of St. Wulston I have read is in Alban Butler's *Lives of the Saints*, where the notices are necessarily short. It may be that the more complete biographies that have been published would afford a clue ; if some of our readers who can readily do so would kindly refer to them.   JARCO.

KERRY SUNDAY SCHOOL.—I recently saw an old book, on the inside of the cover of which was pasted a printed slip, of which the following is a copy :—"The gift of the Institution of the Kerry Sunday School, in Montgomeryshire, North Wales, on the Black-Hall foundation, Established at Kerry, by a descendant of the Black-Hall family. The fourth of March, 1787." Now that the centenary of Sunday Schools is being celebrated, it would be interesting to know somewhat of the history of this early Montgomeryshire School.   GORORFAB.

REPLIES.

DICK OF ABERDARON (June 23, 1880).—Mr. Salisbury of Glan-Aber, Chester, has in his collection a pen and ink miniature of "Richard Robert Jones (Dick Aberdaron) taken from life by Mrs. Dawson Turner, Norwich," and which was presented to him by Mr. William Wallace Currie of Liverpool, some forty-two years ago. It is a very admirable likeness of this strange character, as he appeared when taken ; but, so far as my recollection goes, it is not the one from which the etched plate referred to by Mr. TEWK was produced. I remember Dick well, and have had many conversations with him about books ; but, linguist though he undoubtedly was, he knew very little about the history of Welsh literature, and often mixed up his authorities in a curious and very laughable manner. There are several specimens of his handwriting in the Glan-Aber collection, and some of them beautifully done, with headings of harps and other musical instruments in pen and ink.   CURIG.

Mr. TEWK will not find this eccentric character in the literary Valhalla of Welsh Worthies erected by Canon Williams. He can not be called "an eminent Welshman." He was a half-witted, restless wanderer, and with the true spirit of a nomad resented any attempt to make him amenable to either the restraints or the comforts of a civilized life. He had a natural aptitude for acquiring an imperfect knowledge of languages—but he had neither sufficient brain-power nor ratiocination to follow up the smattering he acquired of various tongues. I have his own copy of the memoir written by Mr. Roscoe—with his signature on the title page, and Our Lord's Prayer written by him in Hebrew, Greek, and English, on the fly-leaf. I have also a small vol. of MS. Greek exercises in his handwriting. The natives of Aberdaron have always been, and are to this day called "gwirioniaid Aberdaron," or the simple folk of Aberdaron. The place is a parish and village at the extremity of the promontory of Lleyn, in Carnarvonshire, opposite Bardsey Island.
                                        E.B.

HAIL STORM IN MERIONETHSHIRE. (June 23, 1880).—The storm referred to by "G.G." must have been a disastrous event in the county. From another account of it I gather the following particulars. The weather had been intensely hot during the latter part of June 1820, and on the 29th the storm burst near Bala, about 3 o'clock in the afternoon. " All of a sudden the hills and plains within range were white from the hail as if in the depth of winter. The hail in some places lay on the ground from one to three feet deep : the difference being in places where it had rolled down declivities of the hills. Some of the hailstones measured nearly eight inches in circumference. They were round masses of solid ice, mostly of an oval form; but some were of very irregular and angular shape. In many of them was observed a kind of nucleus, like hail of the size of a large pea, which was incrusted over with ice, not unlike a bullock's eye." The farmers had a terrible loss, not only in crops, but in stock—sheep, pigs, lambs, and geese being killed. A relief committee was formed to solicit subscriptions for the sufferers.   N.W.S.

CATHRALL'S *HISTORY OF OSWESTRY*, (May 5, 1880).—I always thought it was the same " W. Cathrall" who published the *Oswestry Herald* who was also the author of the *History of North Wales*, and, thirty years later, the compiler of a *History of Oswestry*. At least OSWALD is wrong in saying they spelt their names differently. I have just seen in the newspaper I have alluded to, under the date Dec. 5, 1820, an advertisement of Pt. 3 of the Welsh history, in which " W. Cathrall" says he is " assisted by several gentlemen of Literary Distinction."   N.W.S.

RICHARD ROBERTS (July 7, 1880).—The house in which this great inventor and engineer was born is still in existence, and is known as the " Old Carreghova Gate." It stands on the north side of the canal bridge, Llanymynech. There are two rooms on the ground floor, and two bedrooms above. When the canal was made, the road was raised about eight feet, and consequently one of the bedrooms was converted into a kitchen, and a doorway made in the wall of the room. This alteration limited the accommodation to a kitchen and one bedroom, with a cellar beneath. In this bedroom Richard Roberts was born 22nd April, 1789. In common with many houses of this village, the gate-house is built upon Offa's Dyke, which forms in this parish the boundary between England and Wales. It can plainly be seen by examining the fence north and south of the house, noting that the house projects into the roadway, that it stands exactly upon the boundary line. From the shape of the room it is almost certain that Richard was born on the Shropshire side of the line. In the parish registers the house is entered as being in the township of Llwyntidman, which is in Shropshire. He may thus be claimed as a " Border Counties Worthy." At the same time there is a claim as an " Eminent Welshman," seeing that his father, William Roberts, was a Welshman, and his mother was formerly Mary Jones of the parish of Meifod.   J. FEWTRELL. Llanymynech.

STRAY NOTES.

MARTIN CAT, &c.—In Nov. 1838 a remarkably fine specimen of that rare animal the Yellow-breasted Martin Cat *(La Marte,* Buffon) was captured in a pine coppice, near Walcot. It measured from the nose to the end of the tail 2ft. 6in. The Earl of Powis had it preserved by Mr. Shaw of Shrewsbury. In September of the same year Mr. Shaw received a *White Swallow* for preservation, from Mr. Hunter of Mount Severn, Llanidloes. And yet another rara avis was reported as captured in Nov. 1838, viz., a *Sea Frog,* measuring 4ft. 6in., at Llanfair P.G., Anglesey.

TREE AT COWBRIDGE.—In 1838 an experiment was made, to ascertain the capacity of a hollow elm tree on a farm belonging to Capt. Howell, half a mile from Cowbridge, Glamorganshire, when it was found that thirty-three persons could find room in it with ease, and it was thought that three more could have been accommodated had they been at hand.

OSWESTRY AGRICULTURAL SOCIETY, — At the annual meeting of this Society held Dec. 2, 1820, the ploughing matches came off on Mr. Hunt's farm at Weston Cotton. Nine teams started for the prize, and four for the sweepstakes. The following were the candidates for the prize:—W. Lloyd, Esq , Aston ; W. Ormsby Gore, Esq., Porkington ; Mr. Barrett, Pentrepant ; Mr. Jackson, Pont re Wern ; Mr. Jones, Ty Coch ; Mr. R. Menlove, Hisland ; Mr. Poynton, Weston Mill ; Mr. Williams, Tyn y Celyn. For the sweepstakes :—W. Ormsby Gore, Esq.; John Mytton, Esq., Halston ; the Rev. G. N. K. Lloyd, Selattyn ; Mr. Roger Evans, Halton. The prize was won by Mr. Poynton, and the sweepstakes by the Rev. G. Lloyd. It was stated that the Society showed signs of decay, partly caused by the establishment of a similar one in Shrewsbury.

DOING HONOUR TO SIR WATKIN.—Every now and then a monster banquet at Wynnstay, when the grandfather of the present Sir Watkin came of age, crops up in the newspapers ; but we have never seen the following account of how one Welshman ate at a Sir Watkin banquet, save in the *Oswestry Herald* for Dec. 19, 1820. We give the account entire :—

A short time since an honest yeoman of the parish of Machynlleth, Montgomeryshire, at a public dinner at that town, given by the friends of Sir Watkin Williams Wynn, at once to celebrate the baronet's birthday and the christening of his son, devoured the following trifling articles :—

About half a pound of salmon and *apple sauce !*
About half a pound of roast beef, with *cabbage and custard !*
Leg of a goose ; and of a turkey, with an appropriate quantity of potatoes.
Half of a pigeon pie, consisting of four pigeons, with *oyster sauce !*
N.B. Nothing disliked but the oyster sauce.
Three jellies and above a pound of pudding !
Finished with a quantity of bread and cheese and celery. After, seeing biscuits amongst the desserts, he called for a plate of butter (conceiving that they were not to be eaten without it) and devoured no less than 17.

Perhaps the good man thought that as the dinner commemorated a double event, he was only doing his duty in thus consuming viands.

PORKINGTON FORESTERS.—In 1839 a gentleman near Oswestry made an experiment with a local potato known by this name. He selected a fine specimen and divided it into fifty sets, and from them were taken up 2½ bushels of 90lbs. to the bushel ! The " Porkington Foresters" were described as " of a long form, abounding in eyes, in colour a fine crimson red."

EDUCATION IN OSWESTRY.—The *Shrewsbury Chronicle* of Jan. 25, 1839, says that one of the Town Council of " the borough of O——y," in sending a woman to the Poor House, wrote the following note to the master, " Mr. Phillps—Ples to admitt the Barrar into the Hous."

AN OSWESTRY CAT.—It was recorded in the local papers that after the funeral of " Mrs. Roberts of Salop-road, Oswestry," in Jan. 1839, a cat that had belonged to her was " taken in a basket to the house of Mr. Francis of Penrhos (son-in-law of deceased) a distance of ten miles, the road to which is over the river Verniew." In less than three weeks puss was found in her old quarters.

NOTES.

LAUNCH OF VESSELS AT BARMOUTH.—
The 8th of August 1838 was quite a gala day at Barmouth.
Two fine schooners were launched from its Building Yards
amidst a large concourse of visitors. Miss Williams Wynn
christened one, which was called the "Ann and
Elizabeth." and Miss Ricketts the other, the "Maria and
Ellen." Sir Watkin Williams Wynn, Sir Robert
Williams Vaughan, and other distinguished visitors were
present. The Maria and Ellen was built by Mr. Jones
for Capt. R. Barnett, son of Mr. Barnett of the Corsygedol
Arms, at whose house a good substantial dinner was provided for upwards of forty guests. The Ann and
Elizabeth was built by Mr. G. Thomas for Capt. Edward
Roberts son of Hugh Roberts, Esq., at whose house, also,
a large party was entertained. The Bardd Tecwyn
commemorated the one event and the Bardd Mawddach
the other, and their effusions were published.
                                        MAWDDACH.

VOLUNTEER ARMY OF 1803-4 (Apr. 21, 1880.)
We have already given some of the lists of officers connected with the volunteer army of Wales at the period
when fears of invasion animated every breast, and
every other able-bodied man in the nation became a
soldier. This week we give *Anglesey.*

LOYAL ANGLESEA, First Battalion.

Colonel : Warren Viscount Bulkeley—12 Oct. 1803.
Lieut. Col.: Owen Pulland Meyrick—12 Oct. 1803.
Major : Robert Williams, Bart.—12 Oct. 1803.
Captains : John Williams, Rowland Williams, William
    Sparrow, William Bulkeley Hughes, Knight—12 Oct.
    1803; John Jones (adjutant)—13 Dec. 1803 ; Augustine
    Elliott Fuller—12 Oct. 1803.
Lieutenants : William Williams, John Jones, William
    Williams, William Meyrick, Griffith Roberts, John Jones,
    William Hughes, Owen Roberts, William Price—12
    Oct. 1803 ; William Thomas—13 Dec. 1803.
Ensigns : Richard Lewis, John Lloyd, Hugh Lloyd,
    Henry Hughes—12 Oct. 1803; R. Lewis—13 Dec. 1803.
Chaplain : John Williams—19 Nov. 1803.
Adjutant : John Jones—12 Oct. 1803 (Captain 13 Dec.
    1803).
Quarter Master : William Toone—19 Nov. 1803.

LOYAL ANGLESEA, Second Battalion.

Colonel : Warren Viscount Bulkeley—12 Oct. 1803.
Lieut.-Col. Paul Panton—12 Oct. 1803.
Major : Bodychen Sparrow—12 Oct. 1803.
Captains : John Griffith Lewis, John Price, William
    Hughes—12 Oct. 1803 ; John Roberts, Jared Jackson—
    28 Ap. 1804.
Lieutenants : James Webster, John Evans, Stephen Roose,
    Robert Bulkeley, John Paynter, John Owen, William
    Williams, Robert Pritchard, Pierce Thomas—12 Oct.
    1803 ; Thomas Lewes, Peter Webster—28 Apr. 1804.
Ensigns : Thomas Jones, Evan Richards—12 Oct. 1803 ;
    William Owen, James Fisher—28 Ap. 1804.
Chaplain : Evan Lloyd—19 Nov. 1803.
Adjutant : Theophilus Jones, 12 Oct. 1803.
Quarter-Master : John Parry—28 Apr. 1804.
Surgeons : Owen Titley, David Jones—19 Nov. 1803.

The foregoing are copied—without any attempt to correct the spelling—from the War Office List of 1 Oct.
1804. Our next instalment will be *Cardiganshire.*
                                                ED.

PROPHECY RECORDED IN SHROPSHIRE.
This prophecy was found in the eves of a house in Shropshire 1616 :—
                The Gipsies Prophecy.
    The English like Heroicke Elves
    Shall bee the ruine of themselves
    . . . . is the cause by which they are
    The propagators of a warre
    They force away theyr sacred king
    Which shall on them destruction bring
    The auncient Scotts and Picts shall joyne
    One thousand six hundred forty-nine
    And overrunne this Brittish Isle
    Which by Rebellion is made vile
    London shall flame with fire like hell
    to shew that there the Divells dwell
    when crosses and church decays
    Observe well what the Gipsis sayes.
                    Subscribed by H : W : Gipsir.
[Add. MSS. 14,898.]   Z.

MINSHUL OF MINSHUL, CHESHIRE.—"The
Crusade of Richard gave rise to more Crusadial bearings
than any other." Amongst many instances the following
may be given :—"Michael Minshul of Minshul, in
Cheshire, had given him the crescent and star for his arms,
and his family have ever since borne them ; and for a crest
two lion's paws holding a half moon. In a patent, July
4th, 1642, by the Earl Marshal to Sir Richard Minshul of
Buckinghamshire, a descendant of the Cheshire family, he
is allowed to change his coat for distinction, to a Sultan
kneeling and holding a crescent."—(*Anecdotes of Heraldry
and Chivalry*, p. 86.)   ZETA.

QUERIES.

MERIONETHSHIRE CYDER.—Mr. Thomas
Payne of Cowbridge, writing to *Notes and Queries* of July
3, says that forty years ago, when a boy in Merionethshire, he was told by an old lady who lived at Traws-
vynydd that a rough kind of drink was made from the
berries of the mountain ash. Is such cyder manufactured
now-a-days?   G.G.

WILLIAM OWEN PUGHE.—Southey, "in a
letter to Wynne in 1823," says of this well-known Welshman, that he was "full of Welsh information . . but
a muddier-minded man he never met with." Who was
the Wynne mentioned here? I have also seen it stated
that Edward Williams ("Iolo Morganwg") who was
associated with William Owen Pughe in the publication
of an edition of the *Myvyrian Archaiology of Wales*, said
of him that he "ruined everything he took in hand : in
his Dictionary and Grammar he has introduced into a
most horrid cacophony of pronunciation a most barbarous
orthography." Williams also says that in the *Cambrian
Biography* by the same author, "more than half the
articles are erroneous." Are these severe strictures on
William Owen Pughe endorsed by Welsh scholars of the
present age?   R. ROSSE TEWK, B.A.

SPRINGS IN WALES.—I was ascending Diphwys
a few days ago with a native of the district, when we
came to a well called Ffynnon Goledd, three miles or so
from Barmouth, and about a mile from Sylfaen farm.
The well was large enough to bathe in, and steps led
down into the water. My companion told me that within
his recollection patients afflicted with rheumatism came
from far and near to bathe in Ffynuon Goledd, and he
well remembered one instance in which a friend of his,

mounting the hillside to the well with much difficulty, because of his stiffened joints, returned home with a lighter step and a lighter heart. Near Llanfachreth is a well called Ffynnon Capel, supposed to be good for sore eyes and much resorted to a few years ago.　　E.

REPLIES.

OSWESTRY MANUFACTORIES (June 30, 1880).—Mr. Thomas, sen., of Penylan Lane; whose memory of Oswestry affairs dates back perhaps further than any other inhabitant; informs me that he has heard his father say that Mr. Slade, the manufacturer, lived in the original house where the Wynnstay Hotel now stands. Whether it was then an inn or not he cannot say, but it was enlarged at the time of the Union with Ireland (1800) to meet the demand for increased traffic—Oswestry being on the high road between London and Ireland. The mark where the additional building commences, Mr. Thomas says, is observable on the front of the house. Mr. Slade, he thinks, carried on his manufacture on the premises, and on one occasion a stack of flax he had in Maesylan, opposite the Grammar School, took fire and was destroyed. "The Union" was a notable event in Oswestry, and the party who looked after the roads called a block of houses he erected in the lower part of Beatrice street, "Union Place," a name they are known by to this day.　　JARCO.

[According to the query, June 30, Mr. Slade's manufactory was in working order in 1796; and by reference to *Bye-gones*, Mar. 26, 1879, it will be seen that the Wynnstay Arms (or Cross Foxes as it was sometimes called, and sometimes Bowling Green Inn) was in existence as an inn as early as 1800. It probably never was more than an ordinary public house until Mr. Leigh came in possession in 1802; when it (as well as the Cross Keys) was advertised as a house on the road to Ireland. (See *Bye-gones*, Mar. 12, 26, 1879.)—ED.]

EDWARD MEREDITH (June 30, 1880).—I enclose a newspaper cutting which I met with some time back, it relates to the Edward Meredith, "E.M.J." inquires about.　　LANDWOR.

The *North Wales Chronicle* tells the following story, for the truth of which it vouches—Some seventy years ago, as the Sir Watkin Williams Wynn of those days was riding in the neighbourhood of Wrexham, he heard a man singing in a cooper's workshop, with whose voice he was much struck. It was a person of the name of Meredith, who possessed a splendid bass voice. Sir Watkin had him instructed, and he became celebrated as a singer of sacred music. He was engaged at the ancient concerts, oratorios, &c., but he resided chiefly at Liverpool. Having heard that a parish clerk of a village in the Vale of Clwyd, of the name of Griffiths, could sing down to double C, Meredith was determined to visit him. He accordingly started, and walked about forty miles. When he arrived in the village he inquired for Griffiths. A very little fellow, digging potatoes in a garden, was pointed out to him. "What," thought Meredith, "that shrimp of a thing to sing lower than I can? Impossible!" Meredith, it is said, was a fine, tall man, upwards of six feet high. He walked around the garden, eyeing poor Griffiths disdainfully; at length he said, upon low G, "Good day to you, sir." Griffiths, resting on his spade, replied on double low C (five notes lower), "Good day to you, sir." Upon which, Meredith marched off with double C ringing in his ear, all the way to Liverpool.

SAMUEL SAVAGE (April 28, 1880).—Your correspondent "J.?.R." alludes to Samuel Savage as "a descendant of Philip Henry." Some friends of mine have since written to me to suggest that this is a mistake, because as they say "John Savage of Wrenbury Wood, had but one

son, *Philip*, by Sarah Henry his wife, and he died unmarried." True enough, but their second daughter Katharine married a John Savage in 1717, and it was their son Samuel Savage who married Sarah Roe, and he was great grandson therefore to Philip Henry. So far as I can make out they had a son Richard (of Chiswick-street, London), who married Susan Jones, and who died in 1840 leaving no issue; also a son Samuel who married Mary Wellum, and he left no issue at his death: but there were three daughters; Sarah, Mary, and Elizabeth, and Philip Henry's descendants in that particular line, must be looked for in their issue. SARAH married John Kenrick in 1781, and the Kenricks of Wynn Hall, Denbighshire, derive from them. MARY in 1789 married Z. Bunnell, and several of their descendants, Bunnells, Mays, and Lewises, flourished in the present century. ELIZABETH married William Woollatt, and their descendants, Woollatts and Greenhows are still flourishing. It is remarkable, however, that no descendants of Philip Henry *in the male line* remain, for his only son, the celebrated MATTHEW HENRY, had but one son, PHILIP, born in 1700, and who upon the death of his maternal grandfather—George Warburton—took his name, and was elected M.P. for Chester in 1742 as PHILIP HENRY WARBURTON. He died single, so that of the very numerous descendants of the saintly Philip Henry now living, they one and all descend from his daughters SARAH (who married Savage), KATHARINE (who married Tylston), ELEANOR (who married Radford), and ANN (who married Hulton); but so loyal have they all been to the sacred memory of their great ancestor that there is hardly a branch of the house remaining who does not boast of a PHILIP HENRY. This applies not only to his English and Welsh descendants, but also to the Americans, who take a pride in their descent from him, and thus the great name of the best of men lives honoured to this day, and has become a household treasure on the two continents where the English language is the mother tongue.　　A DESCENDANT OF THE HENRYS.

CURRENT NOTES.

THE LATE MR. W. W. E. WYNNE.—We are glad to learn that a memoir of the late Mr. Wynne of Peniarth will appear in the forthcoming number of the *Archæologia Cambrensis*; and trust the Council at the head of affairs in connection with the Cambrian Archæological Association will see the fitness of giving with the paper a portrait of the deceased gentleman. Such a course would commend itself to every member of the Society.

CARNARVON CASTLE.—A massive slate tablet bearing the names of the nineteen princes of Wales, together with the dates of their birth, has been placed in Carnarvon Castle, near the chamber in which Edward II. was at one time supposed to have been born, though the tradition is now exploded. The cost has been borne by Mr. R. Sorton Parry, who was High Sheriff of the county when the Prince of Wales last visited Carnarvon Castle.

SCHOLARSHIP SCHEME FOR WALES.—The *Liverpool Mercury* says—"The practicability of bridging over the wide gulf between the elementary schools and the universities has been so fully demonstrated by the successful operations of the Liverpool Council of Education that our Welsh neighbours are invited to extend the system to the schools of the Principality. The Liverpool Council provide a fund out of which certain scholarships, tenable for three years, are awarded to clever lads attending elementary schools who figure conspicuously in competitive examinations. These scholarships are connected with the Liverpool College and the Liverpool Institute, and if the boys continue their successes in those primary schools they are passed on to the universities. A correspondent suggests a similar scheme for Wales. Captain Verney has offered £100 to the necessary fund, and Mr. John Roberts, M.P., has promised a similar amount on condition that Flintshire is included in the proposal. The scheme, as carried out by the Liverpool Council of Education, is so simple and so effective that our Welsh friends need be under no apprehension as to its practicability. All that is wanted is a fund to provide for the scholarships. Wales is justly proud of the moral virtues and educational acquirements of her sons, and she will certainly give a great impetus to the efficiency of her elementary schools by adopting a scheme similar to that which is working so admirably in Liverpool."

THE SCHOOLS OF THE SOCIETY OF ANCIENT BRITONS.

A scheme has been issued for the "reconstruction and amendment of the regulations of the Welsh Charity Schools in connection with the most honourable and loyal society of Ancient Britons and defining and declaring the objects of the bounty of the Society submitted by the Sub-Committee for the approval of the Governors of the Society." The Society of Ancient Britons possesses a school at Ashford capable of accommodating about 200 boys and girls, and invested funds amounting to nearly £50,000. As at present constituted, the school is a mixed one, and at the date of the last report there were within its walls 90 boys, of whom 46 were pay boys, that is, boys who pay for their education, and 55 girls, of whom 22 were pay girls. Under the provisions of the new scheme the character of the school is to be changed. The new scheme, after providing that the school shall be called "The School of the Society of Ancient Britons," states that the future object of the school will be to provide board and education for girls of the Welsh middle class, preference being given to orphans who have lost their father; mother or father of applicants for admission must have been a native of the Principality of Wales, the county of Monmouth, or the parishes of Oswestry, Selattyn, and Llanymynech in the county of Salop. Rules are then laid down for the constitution of the governing body and for the election of committee and officers, as also for the keeping of books of account. After specifying that the school should be a boarding school, and be established in the building at Ashford, several rules are given for the election, and as to the duties of the mistress. It is then provided that the scholars shall be girls only, divided into foundation scholars, whose board and education would be provided entirely free, half-pay scholars and full-pay scholars. Of the foundation scholars two are to be nominated by the Queen, one by the Prince of Wales, and one by the President of the Society's Festival held annually on St. David's Day. No girl is to be admitted under eight or over twelve years of age, or be allowed to remain in the school after attaining the age of seventeen years. After several rules as to sanitary regulations, such as vaccination, &c., "Rule 45" declares that "the religious instruction shall be in accordance with the principles of the Church of England."

THE BISHOP OF MANCHESTER ON WELSH BOYS AND EDUCATION.

In presenting the prizes at Beaumaris Grammar School on Thursday, the Bishop of Manchester said—He did not know perhaps as much as he ought to do—certainly not as much as the Dean of Bangor, who sat on his left, or the everend prelate (the Bishop of Bangor) who occupied the rhair—of the educational requirements and appliances for high-class education in the Principality of Wales, but he imagined that the Beaumaris Grammar School occupied one of the foremost, if not the foremost, place in schools which were providing for what he might term the higher class education in Wales. And its work, he was glad to find, was not limited to Welsh boys, but English boys also formed a large number of its scholars, many of them being sent there for health, and others because their parents found from experience that they were receiving an education which was the most useful for their sons. (Hear, hear.) He found, further, that about half the boys were boarders, and half were day scholars —a circumstance which indicated pretty well what the school was doing for the immediate district in which it was planted. The Welsh, he thought, were a people possessing quite an average amount of intelligence. He was at the Old Edwardian School of Shrewsbury, which, as they were aware, lay on the Marches of the Principality, and attracted a considerable number of boys from Wales, who were amongst those possessing the quickest parts, and subsequently distinguished themselves at the universities. As regarded such establishments as the present, it was certainly desirable that good schools of the higher grade should be placed within the reach of the populations inhabiting our great towns, and if the Government had ruled that efficient and sufficient elementary schools should be placed within easy distance of every family in the land, it was hardly of less importance that the upper and middle classes should also be within easy distance of schools which would give their children an education enabling them to play their proper part in life. (Hear, hear.) There was at the present moment a conflict between intelligent minds as to the best and wisest course of education to be given to the rising generation, and there had been a debate in the House of Lords—a debate, which, in the opinion of his own metropolitan, was "an ignominious one"—whether the subjects included in the fourth schedule were a wise and proper development of the system of elementary education to be imparted in this country. He did not share in the opinion that the debate was "ignominious," seeing that the Bishop of Exeter was heard on one side, whilst the brother-in-law of the Bishop of Bangor (Lord Aberdare) was matched against him. The question at issue was what was best—quantity or quality—a larger surface slightly scratched over, or a smaller surface thoroughly and efficiently cultivated—(hear, hear)—and the difficulty which had presented itself for the consideration of thoughtful minds was to know where to draw the limit now that knowledge was advancing so rapidly. This question had to be fought out, and the sooner it was decided the better it would be. If he were educated again he should certainly not care to have the subject-matter of his early education very materially changed, and yet at the same time, he agreed fully with those who thought the curriculum of study was then unduly narrow and that it had been wisely widened. (Hear, hear.) The subjects taught at Beaumaris were neither too wide nor too large for the faculties of the boys who were being educated there, although they were considerably in advance of what he had been taught—which included Latin and Greek, a little mathematics, a very little Hebrew, together with a modest amount of geography. That was the programme at Shrewsbury School when it was under the care of Dr. Butler, and his successor, Dr. Kennedy. He quite admitted that greater liberty and latitude to such a programme were necessary, but whether they were not now in danger of running to another extreme by introducing a much larger range of subjects for a young man's mind was a subject deserving of very serious consideration. He did not see his way to vote on the question when it was discussed by the House of Lords, as he had no wish to embarrass the new president of the council by seeming to throw cold water upon his scheme, but the speech of the Bishop of Exeter did tell with effect upon his mind, for he liked thoroughness and accuracy better than surface scraping. (Hear, hear.) In America he had seen the result of taking up a new subject, then dropping it to take up another, and how the boy or girl left school without a thorough and complete knowledge of any one subject but with a smattering of many, and he feared lest a similar system should arise in England, and that the thoroughness and accuracy of the boys and girls should be squandered over many subjects, instead of being concentrated on a few. (Hear, hear.)

AUGUST 4, 1880.

NOTES.

SIR WILLIAM MAURICE OF CLENENNEY.
(Oct. 15, 1879).

Extract of a letter from William ap William to Sir Wm. Maurice of Clenenney, dated at London upon Nov. 7, (1615). From the original at Brogyntyn :—

"I haue no other newes to writt to yo'r worr' but what mr Brynkir and myself haue written to yo'r worr' befor, but that my L. chamberlayne is comited to the towr, and S'r Thomas hawart to the fleet, for some speeches he vttered. S'r Georg moor is leavitenant of the towr, and my L. of pembrook as men thinketh shalbe L. chamber-layne, and my L. of Essex m'r of his ma'ts horsses. this is the rumor I knowe not howe it will fall &c. . . . . and wher yo'r worr' do writt to me to knowe the price of Spices they ar Risen both pepper and suger. pepper is at ijs viijd a pound & sugeer at xviijd or xviijd * . . . . the sherifs names are these, John Lloyd of Rhiwedog for m'ioneth, mr willm gruffith, of Caeru, & hugh lewis ap hoell ap Ierwerth, p' Anglesea."　　　　　　　　　　A.R.P.

* or xviiijd

OSWESTRY INSTITUTIONS. — Oswestry has always been a progressive town and in the van of improvements. We are told in Cathrall's History that Oswestry originated Societies for the Prosecution of Felons ; and in Bye-gones we have seen how the Nonconformists of the borough originated Sunday Schools as early as Raikes' time, and Day Schools before the controversies of Bell and Lancaster. I have accidentally seen in a copy of the Oswestry Herald for Aug. 13, 1820, that so well known and approved was the "Oswestry Society for Bettering the Condition of the Poor," that the Earl of Hardwick, chairman of a kindred institution in London, stated publicly that there "could not be a better model" to form a country society by, when the town of Carnarvon applied to him for advice. His lordship, as chairman of the Metropolitan institution, also caused the seventh report of the Oswestry Society (supposed to have been written by the Rev. G. N. K. Lloyd) to be sent to chairmen of Quarter Sessions, with a view of getting such institutions generally established.　　　　　　　　　　OSWALD.

QUERIES.

JOHN EVANS OF LLWYNYGROES.—It was stated in Bye-gones, Sep. 17, 1877, and again quoted at a later date, that "Dr. Evans's father was a great botanist, and wrote a good deal about trees and shrubs." The person referred to would be John Evans of Llwyny-groes, publisher of the map of North Wales, and an antiquarian. What authority is there for the statement that he was a "great botanist"? From some family letters before me, I find Dr. Evans was a great botanist, and his poem upon "Bees" has a large number of notes relating to botany, showing that he was well acquainted with the subject. Is it not possible that the statement alluded to should refer to the son, and not to the father? If John Evans wrote upon botany, where are his writings to be found?　　　　　　　　　　LLERTWEF.

THE WELSH COAST.—In a newspaper of forty years ago, in extolling the men and manners, scenery and attractions, of Aberystwyth, the writer pictures the Londoner leaving the metropolis behind him, and "like our great moralist"

Resolved at length from vice and London far
　To breathe in distant fields a purer air ;
　- And fix on Cambria's solitary shore,
　Give to St. David one true Briton more.

By "our great moralist" I presume Dr. Johnson meant. Where, in his works, do the lines appear, and to what part of Wales do they refer ?　　　　TAFFY.

REMARKABLE TREES.—There are three within a dozen miles of Oswestry that are little known and have found no place in Bye-gones. 1.—Situated on the road side near Penybont Fawr, and which consists of the trunk of an oak with a birch growing out of it, and both living. Perhaps some reader of this will supply fuller information. 2.—An oak tree at Tyn-y-Llwyn, near Meifod. All I know about this is that five and forty years ago there was a lithograph published of it, in which it was thus described :—"Girth 24 feet ; extreme girth round the roots 50 feet. Height 83 feet ; to set off of highest branches 62 feet. Girth when the bark was on was about 29 feet. The tree has had neither bark nor leaves for at least 25 years. Pigeons frequent the branches. Oct. 10, 1836." The tree was described as "the property of Sir Robert Williames Vaughan, bart." Can any of your readers say if it is still standing. 3.—An "Oak tree at Cil Cychwyn in the lower valley of Glyn near Llangollen, North Wales. Girth 41 feet 3 inches at one yard from the ground. 44 feet 8 inches at the ground." This discription I take from a lithograph published more than half a century ago. A gentleman who saw the tree a short time ago informs me that he was told in the neighbourhood that it was "said to be 60 feet in circumference," but I am not aware that it has recently been measured. It is situated five minutes walk from Pont-fadog, at a place locally called, I believe, "Cil cochwyn."　　　　JARCO.

REPLIES.

SOCIETY OF ANCIENT BRITONS.
(July 7, 1880.)

Very soon did our Antient Britons have an opportunity of shewing their loyalty ; "for the Popish Pretender to his Majesty's Dominions offering to invade this Kingdom," they penned an address, which was signed by "above 200 Persons of the best Quality in the Principality of Wales." This was presented by Lord Lysburne and the other stewards, and Mr. Thomas Jones, on Sept. 20, to the King himself, who graciously held out his hand to be kissed, and who made a Knight of Mr. Jones on the spot. In one of Mr. Dickens's novels there is a Mr. Dick who never can keep King Charles's head out of a petition. It would seem that these Antient Britons, or at least Mr. Thomas Jones, could not put pen to paper without dragging in the "extraordinary coincidence." And here it is again in the address. After referring to the "Hand of Heaven" which gave "Blessing" to his Majesty's labour for "the good of Mankind," there comes the inevitable allusion to the "auspicious Day" that gave birth to the Princess and St. David.

For the first anniversary meeting of the Society great preparations were made. "Favours" were prepared, to be worn in honour of the day, "made of good silver ribbon, with the motto *Carolina and St. David.*" Each steward, too, was to bear a green staff, with the arms of Wales on it, and an ode for the occasion, "by the ingenious Mr. Hughes, and set to Musick by the famous Dr. Pepuch," was prepared. The day arrived in due course, the Rev. Mr. Lewis read the service, and the Rev. Mr. Phillips preached. The dinner was enjoyed, and the music was performed—the ode being for two voices—by Mrs. Margaretta and Mrs. Barbier. Stewards for the year to come were appointed; and these included, Lord Talbot, Sir R. Cotton, Sir John Aysten, Sir Humfry Howarth, Barts., Sherrington Davenport, Esq., Samuel Mollyneux, Esq., M.P., Thomas Wynne, Esq., M.P., John Roberts, Esq., M.P., Charles Greenwood, Esq., and Edw. Hughes, Esq. Whether it was that Mr. Phillips's sermon was not up to the mark, or that the "Common People" had not benefitted as they ought to have done, by the 4,000 copies distributed amongst them on the previous year, or that they had so greatly benefitted that so many copies were not needed, it is hard to say ; at least only 2,000 copies of the sermon were ordered on this occasion,

At a meeting held May 9, 1716, all the stewards being present, and also "the Right Reverend Father in God *Benjamin,* Lord Bishop of *Bangor,* Almoner to his Royal Highness the Prince "—(our author dearly loves to parade the full titles of everyone) : at this meeting it was resolved " that two *Welsh* Boys be put out Apprentices to Trades, and that one be of that part called *North-Wales,* and the other of that part called *South-Wales,* and that 10*l.* be given with each Boy ; and that the Secretary do find out Masters, and Report them to the Board for Approbation.

Pursuant to this resolution masters were found, and the boys apprenticed, and "several other charities given to other poor Persons, Natives of the Principality."

At the May meeting just alluded to it was arranged that the stewards should meet once a month at the house of the secretary "to consider the Good of the Society."

Thus the Society was fairly afloat. The narrator, by his silly inflated style ; aided, perhaps, by a trifle too much veneration for royalty on the part of his fellows ; has cast a somewhat ludicrous air over the formation of it ; but the increasing prosperity of 164 years has pretty well tested its usefulness ; and we Welshmen of 1880 are justly proud of an association formed in 1714.

We have not quite done, however, with Sir Thomas Jones and his record. During the early months of the Society's existence it was invaded on all sides by poets. The effusions of a couple we have already mentioned, and "several Poems in Honour of the Day," we are told, were received ; amongst others one from "Mr. *John Morgan,* eldest Son of *John Morgan* of *Tredegar,* Esq : " who, " tho' a very young Gentleman and then at School at *Monmouth* ;" was honoured by having his effusion read at one of the meetings, and published in Sir Thomas's book. Here is a sample :—

Thrice happy Day, shine forth with Beams of Mirth,
From you our gracious Princess dates her Birth ;
August all o'er, endu'd with every Grace,
She seems as born of more than mortal Race.

This promising boy must have been a poet after the worthy knight's own heart ! And after the hearts of others too ; for at the meeting where it was read, thanks were voted to "Mr. John Morgan, for his excellent Poem."

Thus endeth Sir Thomas's narrative, but not so his letter to his Countrymen. There are several pages of reflections appended ; and even these are worthy a hasty perusal by any one with the slightest sense of humour. After congratulating the Society on such a Patron (!) as St. David, the writer again goes into rhapsodies on the "providential coincidence." He cannot forget it. That the birthday of the Princess "should be the very *same* with that on which the Antient *Britons* have so long *celebrated* the Festival of their Tutelar Saint !" He thinks it is "a fair Indication that Heaven it self had it in view."

Then Sir Thomas rambles off into an elaborate proof that George and George alone has a right to the throne of England ; and then he descends to a defence of dinners. "This is the *best way* of promoting publick and diffusive Charities." For why ? "The Joy and Pleasure that attends such Festivals raises Men, as it were, above their ordinary selves ; the Spirits grow exalted, and the Mind enlarged, and they then laudably strive to rival and out-do each other in Beneficence, Bounty, and Generosity." However although "Leeks is goot," and St. David, as he before told us, lived on them ; washed down with water ; it by no means follows that the Haberdasher's Hall banquets were to be of the same quality. Solomon, and not St. David, is here the authority, and the passage reads as if the knight had incorporated part of an after-dinner speech into his letter :—

Whence these glorious Aims and Ends therefore, Gentlemen ! sanctify Feasting and publick Entertainments : I may say to every honest *Briton,* in the Words of Solomon, *Go thy way, eat thy Bread with joy, and drink thy Wine with a merry Heart ; for God now accepteth thy Works ;* Eccles.; ix. 7.

Next we have wonder expressed that such a society had not been established long before. For a moment Sir Thomas seems to have forgotten the "providential coincidence ;" but only for a moment ; and he pulls up with, "But whither am I going ?" and again falls back on the "double Festival."

With this Sir Thomas's yarn is nearly spun out. The "worthy Lord Longueville . . who for many years hath born the Title of Baron of Ruthin, a place within the Principality of Wales" comes in for eulogy, and so does Lord Lysburne—and his ancestors too. Nor does "the Right Reverend Father in God Benjamin" (whose titles are again fully rehearsed) escape flattery ; but shortly all merges in the Great Idea, with which the letter closes —: "St David's Day 1714 . . being the first *Birth-Day* of the Princess after her Arrival in *England,* and the Birth-Day also of the *first* which hath born the Name of Princess of WALES for these many Years past, I would not omit the Opportunity of paying a proper Complement to my Countrymen, because I hope it would not be unpleasing to them."   CYMRO AM BYTH.

STRAY NOTES.

CRICKETING IN AUSTRALIA.—Under this heading we gave an extract from the *South Australian Register* a few months back, reporting the cricketing career of Mr. William Oswald Whitridge (nephew of Mr. Askew Roberts of Croeswylan), whose late father emigrated from Oswestry thirty years ago. The same paper of June 16, gives the account of a presentation to Mr. Whitridge by the members of the Norwood Club. There was a dinner at which the Mayor of the city of Adelaide (Mr. E. T. Smith, M.P.), presided, the vice-chair being filled by Mr. C Peacock, M.P. In making the presentation the mayor said : "He was sure that he was not overstating it when he said that Mr. Whitridge had unquestionably been the best cricketer that South Australia had ever produced.

If they looked at his analysis from the time he started cricket they would find that he stood unequalled. The loss that the Norwood Club had sustained was very great indeed. He believed that if Mr. Whitridge had remained with the club it would still hold the premier position. He deeply regretted his retirement, and he thought all present did. Mr. Smith then presented to Mr. Whitridge a fine walnut piano, to which was attached a silver plate with the following inscription :—'Presented to Mr. W. O. Whitridge by members and friends of the Norwood Cricket Club, in recognition of his valuable qualities and gentlemanly conduct as a cricketer during the past fifteen years.—Adelaide, June, 1880.' Mr. Whitridge suitably responded, and said no one felt more than himself his retirement from the game. He had been in the club some years, and the members had always worked harmoniously and peacefully together."

PROTECTION OF SEA FOWL.—Notwithstanding the scarcity of sea fowl on the Merionethshire Coast in 1839, the papers stated that one gentleman, a temporary resident at Towyn, by his " exertion and experience" was able to bag more than a hundred brace !

APRIL FOOL DAY IN MONTGOMERYSHIRE.—On the First of April, 1839, a wag successfully hoaxed the good people of Welshpool, Newtown, and Llanidloes, by spreading the news that "the brave Forty-Second Regiment" would march through those towns on their way from Brecon to Liverpool. The preparations made to receive the guests were great, and much money was spent in laying in store of provisions, but the soldiers never came.

AUGUST 11, 1880.

NOTES.

DOING PENANCE AT WELLINGTON.—The *Shrewsbury Chronicle* of Aug. 17, 1838, says that between two and three thousand persons congregated in Wellington on the previous Sunday to see a woman " doing penance." The paragraph is headed " Burdon v. Pool," and it was stated that the punishment was in accordance with a decree from the Consistory Court of Lichfield. The punishment was to have taken place in Wellington Church, but owing to some informality in the sentence the " performance of the 'fair penitent' did not take place," to the " great chagrin and disappointment of the assembled noodles."   SCROBBES BYRIG.

SHROPSHIRE WORTHIES. — Mr. Salisbury, when he completed his second series of " Border Counties Worthies" requested contributors to *Bye-gones*, when they found anything about worthies unmentioned by him, to make a note of the fact. A case in point occurs in the " Salopian Shreds and Patches" of May 12, taken from Shaw's *Staffordshire* ; the worthy being one · John Baddeley, who was born at Tong, Sep. 21, 1727 ; brought up a blacksmith, and afterwards became a watchmaker. About 1752 he turned his attention to optics, and constructed reflecting telescopes of uncommon excellence. In 1801 he was living at Albrighton, and was joint proprietor of Smethwick manor. The column I take this from gives a "worthy" or two nearly every week ; but (with the foregoing exception) I invariably find Mr. Salisbury has booked them.
                                        SCROBBES BYRIG.

LEIGHTON OF PLAISH.—The following singular fact which gives some notoriety to the Mansion of Plaish is upon record, which tradition and general belief support as being well founded. When this place belonged

to Mr. Justice Leighton, one of the Council of the Marches, he reconstructed and repaired the mansion. At the period of the Chief Justice's reparations, he was presiding at an assizes for the trial of prisoners at Shrewsbury or in Wales. The anecdote is thus related :—

He took occasion to enquire of the High Sheriff, whether there happened to be in these parts any man who could undertake the building of ornamental chimneys ? when the Sheriff replied that the only person he knew of that was capable of the performance was the very man that his Lordship had just then tried for a capital offence, and had sentenced to be hung ; where-upon the judge said, " He shall go and do my chimneys first." The sentence thus passed on the convict was respited and his execution deferred. This poor unfortunate man was then commissioned to erect the ornamental chimneys at Plaish Hall, and was forwarded to that place under the escort of Sheriff's officers to complete the undertaking, which he satisfactorily performed, and according to the traditionary and generally believed opinion this miserable operative was remanded again to prison and finally suffered the sentence so passed upon him.

British *Archæological Journal*, 1848 (Gloucester Congress), p. 312.   ZETA.

QUERIES.

THE GOLDEN FARMER.—In the *Salopian Journal* of Aug. 8, 1804, there is the following announcement of death :—" On Thursday last, Mr. John Thomas of Llandregynwyn, Llandisilio, usually denominated, on account of his supposed wealth, The Golden Farmer." Which Llandisilio is referred to here ? Was Mr. Thomas " a character," and is he still remembered in farm-house talk in the district where he resided?   TELL.

" FRIENDS " IN OSWESTRY.—One of your *Bye-gones* contributors in an interesting paper on Nonconformity in Meifod, published in the eleventh volume of *Montgomeryshire Collections*, quotes from the Minute Book of the Quakers, under the date of 1707, an entry stating that " the dwelling-house of Ed. Reese called Queen's Head, in Oswestry, was recorded for a meeting-place." Was this in the town of Oswestry or in the hamlet known as " The Queen's-head " ?   NONCON.

ROBINSON OF BRITHDIR. (Feb. 16, 1876.)—A curious Will dated in 1720 is given in *Bye-gones* of Jane Robinson, wife of George Robinson of Brithdir. She seems to have been a sister of Edward Fowler. In Llanfyllin Church there is a monumental tablet to " George Robinson of Brithdir, Attorney at law," who died in 1769, aged 57, and of his widow Mary Robinson, who died in 1788, aged 72. The latter George Robinson would, it is presumed, be the son of the first named. Could any of your contributors refer to a pedigree of the Robinson family shewing its connection with the present family that owns Brithdir, which preserves the name Robinson as a Christian name ?   T.

SAM. JARVIS THE CHESTER RIBBONER.—I happened to be turning up a vast collection of old rubbish the other day, when my eye fell upon the words I have quoted for the heading of this scrap. Who could Samuel Jarvis, the Chester Ribboner be, was the very natural enquiry to make under the circumstances ; and after some research I found he had served the offices of Sheriff of Chester in 1724, and the still higher office of Mayor in 1742. Hemingway, the Chester historian, says he was a ribbon weaver, who at one time kept a small shop in Shoemaker's Row (Northgate-street), but resided in a little house adjoining an old inn called the Falcon ; and that suddenly emerging from poverty and obscurity, to a position of respectability and affluence, his neighbours, wondering at his luck, found out (or manufactured) the following facts in relation to him—

5   14

A banker's clerk in London had absconded with a large amount of his employers' money, and made his way to Chester, taking up his domicile at the Falcon Inn aforesaid. He was pursued and traced to his hiding place, whereupon he threw his money bags into the area of Jarvis's "little house," and then went to bed again, from whence he was taken into custody, and conveyed back to London; but being minus the money, his prosecutors failed to convict him, and he was accordingly discharged. Sam Jarvis finding the money bags in his area next morning, took possession of them, adventured his suddenly obtained wealth in trade, throve, made a fortune, became Mayor of Chester, and died in the very year when he was pricked for high sheriff of his county! Can any sane man believe that story? Is it at all likely that the London detectives would have left Chester without a search for the lost money; or that the jade rumour, who saw Sam Jarvis growing rich all of a sudden, could have kept the story of his ill gotten wealth so snugly that no trace of it could be conveyed to London, in time to secure a remand of the prisoner "for further enquiries"? Not a word is said by Hemingway of Jarvis's having filled the office of Sheriff in 1724; and as we may fairly assume that he was even then a person of some consequence in the city, I should like to know when his great luck befell him, and why he was allowed to keep this money if he had really found it as stated above; and, above all, how the proud Cestrians could have stomach'd such a man for Sheriff or Mayor; or the authorities could have dared to prick him for the then dignified office of High Sheriff of his county? May I ask you to allow me to call the attention of your excellent correspondent THOMAS HUGHES (of Chester) to this little story? If there is a grain of truth in it, he can—if anyone can—give us a clue to the evidence upon which it found its way to a standard historical work; or if he cannot do that, he may, perchance, be able to tell us something more about the Ribboner than I can find in Hemingway; for within his vast store of Cestrian lore, are so many things new and old, that I would fain hope he can produce some scrap or other that can solve the doubts, I have ventured to suggest, upon the truth of the narrative. I even doubt if Sam Jarvis, the Ribbonman, was the person who filled the Civic Offices alluded to, but in any case the story needs correction before it can be accepted as fact, notwithstanding that Hemingway has conveyed it to us as such.   GLENCOE.

REMARKABLE STORM AT OSWESTRY.— The papers of Jan. 1839 give lengthy accounts of a tremendous hurricane that swept over some parts of the country on Sunday the 6th of that month. One writer calls attention to its novel effects at Oswestry. He says—

Observing as soon as I awoke in the morning [Monday] that my windows had a white incrustation upon them of rather an unusual appearance, I suspected what it was, and on applying it with a wet finger to my tongue, my suspicions were at once confirmed;—it was salt! . . . The incrustation remained unaltered all day, notwithstanding the influence of the sun. But on Tuesday, when the salt had been dissolved by the moisture of the atmosphere, it was still plainly visible upon all the lower panes of the windows, on which it appeared in broad white milky bands, and which had still a saline taste.

The writer goes on to say that the phenomenon is of usual occurrence near the coast, and comments on the remarkable fact of its occurring fifty miles from the nearest point of ocean—Cardigan Bay. The writer then goes on to speculate on the effect all this deposit of salt would have on vegetation. Living, as I do, on that side of Oswestry facing south west, I have often fancied there was a saline taste in the breezes when of more than ordinary duration. I should be glad to know whether any "observations" have been made by others?   JARCO.

REPLIES.

A WELSHPOOL TOAST (July 21, 1880).—Mr. Panton Corbett was the eldest son of the Archdeacon. The second son was Mr. Uvedale Corbett, for many years judge of the County Court of Shropshire.   W.H.

THE REV. DR. WILLIAMS (June 2, 1880). Died, Aug. 23, 1838, in his 80th year, the Rev. Emanuel Davies, of Hanover, near Abergavenny. "He was educated for the ministry at Oswestry, under the late Dr. Edward Williams, and was a preacher of the gospel for upwards of half a century." Mr. Davies was no doubt a student at an earlier period than that referred to June 2, and his name does not appear amongst the number who addressed the letter to Dr. Williams on his removal to Birmingham.   PURITAN.

WELL AT WOOLSTON (July 21, 1880).—A writer in Salopian Shreds and Patches for Aug. 5, 1874, in reference to this well said, "'Oostan's Well' at West Felton is said to be called after a man to whom the field, in which the stream gushed forth, belonged. Like Cause Castle, which is the Norman Caux, this name seems to be French too—'St. Goustan's' (Murray's France, p. 168) seems the original name. It is said to be dedicated to St. Winefred, and it probably is, as the cottage above it is evidently a chapel, where those who derived benefit from the waters returned thanks, and is borrowed from the beautiful chapel above St. Winefred's Well, in Holywell, Flintshire."   NEMO.

RICHARD ROBERTS (July 21, 1880).—He was a powerful, heavily-made man, of above 6 feet in height. The writer had the honour of his company at a St. David's Day dinner, at the Waterloo Hotel, Manchester, some twenty years ago. He was very patriotic and proud of his country and countrymen. Said, "I am bred and born at Llanymynech, and though I do not join you here every St. David's Day, daru fi ddim anghofio Cymraeg." He then spoke Welsh with all round and bade good bye. His Welsh was a llediaith fain, and his English pronunciation very Welshified. There was a large room in the Peel Park Museum containing models of his numerous inventions. He was second only to Arkwright in making Lancashire millionaires by the score. He was once partner in Sharp Stewart's Locomotive Works. Firm then was Sharp and Roberts. A prize of £100 for the life of Richard Roberts and Owen, the founder of Owen's College (now Victoria University) would be an appropriate offer from the commercial travellers of Manchester to the committee of the next National Eisteddfod, 1881. Owen, I am told, was a Conway man.   VERNWYON.

SHROPSHIRE WORDS (July 14, 1880.)—Cross-Winded. Miss Jackson, I see, only gives "Cross-waund," =ill-tempered; and Mr. Hartshorne "Crosswind"= crooked, twisted. Boy and man in the Oswestry district I have often heard the complaint of such and such a one, that he "was such a cross-wine-ded chap nobody could live along with him." Halliwell, has "Cross-wind"=to warp, to twist; as a North country word.   OSWALD.

CURRENT NOTES.

The Standard, in an article on the extirpation of wild flowers and ferns says that "all over Wales, which is the great home of the fern tribe in our island, there are not only hundreds of tourists each intent on carrying off a few roots, but numberless working men, who make it their trade to hunt through the unfrequented mountain paths, and bring back the choicer ferns to stand it pots round their doors in the villages till some traveller thinks fit to purchase them. Even beyond these, there would appear to be regular fern-factors somewhere in England, to whom are sent, by their agents, cart-loads and waggon-loads of roots. One of these—a waggon entirely filled with *Osmunda*—was recently seen borne away from a well-known district in Merioneth, where formerly the royal fern grew abundantly, but where now a single root is rarely to be met with in a long day's walk. The beech-fern and the oak-fern have similarly become rare in Wales." An Act has been passed for the protection of wild birds. Could not an Act be passed for the protection of wild flowers and ferns ?

On Tuesday, August 3, the Dowager Lady Margaret Willoughby de Broke died at her residence, Plas Newydd, Anglesey. Her ladyship was the widow of Henry Verney, eighth Baron Willoughby de Broke of Compton Verney, Warwickshire, to whom she was married in 1829, and who died in 1852. She was the daughter of the late Sir John Williams, of Bodelwyddan, by Margaret, daughter and heiress of Mr. Hugh Williams, Tyfry, Anglesey. She held a lease for life of Plas Newydd, which now reverts to the Marquis of Anglesey.

PORTRAIT OF THE LATE MR. W. W. E. WYNNE.—It was recently stated in these columns that a memoir of the late Mr. Wynne of Peniarth would appear in the forth-coming number of the *Archæologia Cambrensis*, and a hope was expressed that it would be accompanied by a likeness of the deceased gentleman. We understand that there is no precedent for such a course in the annals of the Cambrian Archæological Association, but so favourably has the idea of a portrait been received that a private subscription has been set on foot to defray the cost, and the work has been placed in the hands of the well-known firm of Maclure and Macdonald, who will reproduce from a photograph by Mr. Maclardy of Oswestry a picture in crayons, suitable for binding up with the memoir in the Magazine. Some of our readers will remember that an autotype portrait of the Hon. Thomas Kenyon (the result of private subscription) was given with his memoir in the last volume of the *Transactions* of the Shropshire Archæological Society. We cannot help thinking that the more frequent publication of memoirs and portraits (especially if they are subscribed for by friends) would form an interesting feature in the annals of Societies like the Cambrian Archæological, the Shropshire, the Powysland, &c. May we suggest to the Cymmrodorion one of the late Rev. Robert Jones of Rotherhithe ?

THE DARWIN PRIZE.—The Midland Union of Natural History Societies, which consists of twenty-three of the leading scientific societies (including the Shropshire Archæological and Natural History Society and the Oswestry Field Club) in the central counties, is about to issue the details of a scheme formulated by them, the object of which is to encourage and reward original research among the members, who are 3,000 in number. An annual prize of the value of £10 (including a gold or bronze medal, at the option of the successful candidate), and by permission of Mr. Charles Darwin, F.R.S., to be called "The Darwin Prize," will be offered for the best paper contributed during twelve months, ending March 31 each year, to the Journal of the Union (the *Midland Naturalist*), on the subject of the year, which for 1881 is geology, and 1882 biology. The scheme is so framed as to allow, within specified limits, absolute freedom in selecting the subject of research, in order that original workers in science may be as little hampered as possible. On the obverse of the "Darwin Medal" will be a profile portrait of Mr. Darwin, after a well-known photograph by Rejlander. We also understand that the President of the Union (Sir Herewald Wake, Bart.) has offered to

the members a prize, to be called " The President's Prize," of the value of £5 in books, for the best original essay on the life-history of any one genus of insects indigenous to the Midland Counties. The essays are to be sent in not later than the 1st of May, 1881, and will be submitted to some eminent naturalist chosen by the President, whose award will be made known at the annual meeting of the Union, which will be held at Cheltenham in June next.

AUGUST 18, 1880.

NOTES.

THE OLD COACHING DAYS.—The *Carmar- then Journal*, in one of its issues of October, 1838, singing the praises of Aberystwyth as a watering-place, says—"When we state that the roads are excellent, it will follow that travelling is expeditious and secure. To instance only the Aberystwyth and London Royal Mail, that runs every day throughout the year ;—you pay your £2 2. 0. in London and in 24 hours, almost to the minute, you are at Aberystwyth !" This was, certainly, not bad travelling, and in one thing, viz., punctuality, will make modern travellers sigh for the good old times.
　　　　　　　　　　　　　　　　　　　　TALLY HO.

WILL SOMMERS.—I recently copied the follow-ing lines from a Scrap Book :—

Will Sommers borne in Shropshire, as some say,
Was brought to Greenwich on a holy day,
Presented to the King, which foole disdayn'd,
To shake him by the hand, or else asham'd,
Howe're it was, as ancient people say,
With much adoe was wonne to it that day.
Leane he was, hollow-eyde, as all report,
And stoope he did too ; yet in all the Court
Few men were more belov'd than was this foole,
Whose merry prate kept with the King much rule.
When he was sad, the King and he would rime,
Thus Will exil'd sadness many a time.
I could describe him, as I did the rest,
But in my mind I doe not think it best ;
My reason this, howe're I doe descry him,
So many know him, that I may belye him,
Therefore to please all people one by one,
I hold it best to let that paines alone.
Only thus much, he was a poore man's friend,
And helpt the widow often in the end :
The King would ever graunt what he did crave,
For well he knew Will no exacting knave ;
But wisht the King to doe good deeds great store,
Which caus'd the court to love him more and more.

Can any of your readers say who wrote the above ? And perhaps something more about this Salopian Celebrity may be acceptable to your readers. 　　　　W.E.M.

[Mr. Salisbury, of course, gives a notice of Sommers, and it will be found on page 335 of Reprint of *Bye-gones* for 1878-9. Still there is room for more about so singular a being. The lines appeared in Arnim's *Nest of Ninnies*, 1608, referred to in *Bye-gones*, June 28, 1876, in a note about Sommers.—ED.]

A PANIC AT LLANRWST.—Some of the news-papers of the period record what might have been a very serious affair—but for the presence of mind of John Elias, the famous preacher—at the Welsh Calvinistic Associa-tion at Llanrwst on Christmas Day, 1818. It was esti-mated that 12,000 persons had assembled in the town for the meetings, and a vast crowd packed one of the chapels when the door of a seat in the gallery gave way with a loud crack. The alarm was great, and, as is too often the case, a rush was made to the doors. Mr. Elias called out in a loud voice that there was no danger, and gave out a hymn to sing, which had the effect of tranquilizing the minds of the people. There were none injured.
　　　　　　　　　　　　　　　　　　　　SASSIWN.

OUTCAST NEAR ELLESMERE.—In a Shrewsbury paper of Feb. 1839 the death is recorded of "Mr. Edward Harrison of Outcast, near Ellesmere, aged 72." Whence so singular a name for a house? PHIL.

HOPS IN MONTGOMERYSHIRE.—Were hops ever grown with profit in this county? I have seen it stated that forty-two years ago there was a plantation in the neighbourhood of Welshpool, which looked flourishingly until the middle of August, and then became suddenly blighted. Whose crop was this, and for how long a period were hops grown in the locality? H.B.

COAL AT OSWESTRY.—Forty years ago we were "Oswestry near Maesbury," as we are now "Oswestry near Gobowen!" In those days goods from the centres of industry were consigned hither by canal, and the junction was at Maesbury. It would seem by a paragraph I have recently cut from a Shrewsbury paper of April, 1839, that an attempt was contemplated to bring Maesbury and Oswestry nearer together by means of a tramway; the Company projecting the scheme having also in hand the prosecution of a new colliery near the Gallows Tree Gate at the junction of the Shrewsbury and Maesbury roads. The tram was to carry coals to Maesbury wharf, and to bring back Liverpool and Manchester goods. What came of the   m ? JARCO.e

THE DIAL IN LLANFECHAIN CHURCHYARD.—This dial is one of more than ordinary interest. It gives the time of day in six latitudes including Greenwich, the other five being, Pekin in China, Plymouth in New England, Jerusalem, Barbadoes, and Rome. On the face is engraved—"Ex dono Humph. Kynaston, Armig. Anno, 1697." Above that are the words, "Fran. Cleaton in Salop made it. Lattitude 52. 46." On it are minute divisions between 3·40 a.m. and 8·40 p.m. The upright is not quite perpendicular, and therefore the time is not recorded correctly. I have referred to the paper on Llanfechain parish in *Mont: Coll:* to find something about this Sun-dial, but the writer passes it over with a mere record of its existence, and says it is dated 1710. (See vol. 5, p. 236.) C.A.D.

OSWESTRY QUARTER SESSIONS.—You have had a good deal on this subject in your columns of late, but there is one question I should like solved. As I understand it, under the provisions of the Charter of Charles II., the Mayor, the ex-Mayor (who became Coroner, and was so designated), the Steward, and the Recorder were the magistrates who presided at Quarter Sessions; and any two could act provided the mayor was one. In those days the mayor often chose a deputy. Well, the Quarter Sessions holden on Friday, Oct. 20, 1820 (as I read in the *Oswestry Herald*), was held " before Richard Salisbury, Esq., deputy mayor; Thomas N. Parker, Esq., and Mr. Alderman Jones." I find by Cathrall's *History* that H. Watkin Williams Wynn, Esq., was mayor that year, and Mr. Salisbury his deputy; Mr. Parker was ex-mayor. This accounts for his presence on the bench. But by what right was "Alderman Jones" present? Was he "deputy ex-mayor and coroner?" But if so, he would, I take it, have no place on the bench when his chief (Mr. Parker) was present? CIVIS.

WILLIAM OWEN PUGHE (July 28, 1880.)—Most Welsh scholars of the present day agree that the indefatigable William Owen Pughe was, linguistically considered, a person full of crotchets; but few among them will, I think, be found prepared to endorse Iolo Morganwg's violent strictures upon him. In private life he was, I am told, very amiable and unassuming; but rather dull in conversation. "Old Iolo" could not express himself in anything like moderate terms when he referred to anyone who differed from him on any point in matters of literature, religion, or politics. Theoretically he was a most liberal-minded man, but practically he was one of the most illiberal and narrow-minded men in Christendom. Whoever dared entertain an opinion different from his, was denounced not only as an arrant fool, but also as utterly devoid of any honest principle. Witness not only his opinion of Dr. W. O. Pughe, as quoted by Mr. TEWK, but also his violent attacks upon Lewis Morris, Owain Myfyr, Theophilus Jones (the historian of Brecknockshire), and others. According to him their writings were trash of the most worthless kind, and there was not a single bright spot in their personal character. His opponents, or supposed opponents, were not only heretics but "scoundrels." Inability to look at things in the same light that he viewed them, was always with him synonymous with moral obliquity; and it does not appear that it ever occurred to him that views opposed to his own could by any possibility be right, or that persons holding such opinions could in any way be honest men. There are plenty of passages in the published and unpublished writings of Iolo Morganwg to justify these somewhat adverse remarks. CHWARE TEG.

I am not able to reply to the query respecting this gentleman, but I am enabled to record a hurried visit he once paid to Oswestry: my information being gleaned from the MS. Personal Diary (previously quoted) kept by the Rev. T. W. Jenkyn when minister of the Old Chapel: —"Oct. 30, 1829 : This morning before I was down stairs Mrs. Jenkyn came up to say that an old gentleman was in the house who would not give his name, because he wished to take me by surprise. Of course I hurried down, and I found my old friend Dr. Wm. Owen Pughe, the famous Welsh lexicographer. He had been through South Wales on a literary tour with his son, Aneurin Pughe, Esq., of Denbigh, who is employed by Government to collate all the Welsh manuscripts down to the Conquest. My old friend looked very well, and pressed me to take breakfast with him at the Cross Keys Inn, which I did." JARCO.

SALOPIAN LITERATURE (July 14, 1880).— The *Salopian Journal* for Oct. 24, 1838, contains the following advertisement:—

BRITISH AND FOREIGN PUBLIC SUBSCRIPTION LIBRARY, HIGH STREET, SHREWSBURY.

MR. J. BROOKES REVIS (of Ludlow) has the honour to announce that the above establishment will be opened in the early part of the ensuing month, prospectuses of which are in the press, and will be ready for distribution in the course of a few days. The entire Library consists of near 50,000 Volumes, in all languages and classes of Literature, to which the *new works* are constantly added immediately on publication. *Shrewsbury*, Oct., 1838.

Mr. Revis did not commence his Magazine, "The Shropshire and North Wales Standard," until July, 1839, but soon after he began business in Shrewsbury he advertised a newspaper to be called the *Shropshire Mail*, the first number to appear on Dec. 1, 1838. The wording of the advertisement is ambiguous, for it is called "a new weekly paper, of Tory politics, which will be published for the first time in Shrewsbury, on &c., &c. ;" implying that it was either, or had been, published at other places. Whether this paper made its appearance or not I cannot say. A few months later there were two now papers announced for the county—the *Shrewsbury Times*, by Mr. Matthews; and the *Shropshire Mercury* by Mr. Ouseley.

Mr. Revis seems to have been a go-a-head tradesman, for in one of his announcements he says he has made arrangements that "Subscribers of the first and second classes [to his library] residing in any of the principal towns and villages throughout the County of Salop, or within a circuit of fifty miles, will have their parcels delivered free of charge." Mr. Revis also commenced a Musical Library. Mr. James Heaton advertised himself as Mr. Revis's successor at Ludlow, and as continuing the book Library there; whether in conjunction with Mr. Revis or not I cannot say.

Enterprising as he was, Mr. Revis did not succeed, and in one short twelvemonth an ominous advertisement appears in the papers relating to his assignment; and requesting parties who had books out of his library to return them. In Oct. 1839 Mr. G. Matthews of 10, High-St., Shrewsbury, announces that he has purchased Mr. Revis's Library, and intends to add to it. What became of the Magazine I cannot say, nor do I know how many numbers appeared. I have Nos. 1 and 3, but have never met with a fourth.

The Mr. Matthews mentioned in the foregoing paragraph is the same man who advertised the *Shrewsbury Times* in July 1839, and in the announcement he says "the Proprietors feel called upon to state . . . that Mr. J. Brookes Revis . . . has no connection whatever with the undertaking." Why this emphatic declaration it is hard to say; for Mr. Revis was a good Conservative as will be seen on reference to the *Salopian Journal* of Mar. 13, 1839, where the presentation of a silver tankard to him at Ludlow, "for his exertions in the good of the town, and more especially in the advancement of Conservatism" is recorded.

So far I have been able to reply to my own query, and should be glad if any reader of this could supplement it. A man of Mr. Revis's mark must be well remembered at Ludlow.   JARCO.

STRAY NOTES.

AN OLD MARRIAGE ANNOUNCEMENT.—Editors did not charge for marriage announcements half a century ago, or we should not have such a one as the following, which is taken from the *Oswestry Herald* of Dec. 5, 1820:—SUMMER AND WINTER!—On Tuesday last, at St. Martin's, near this town, after a "lingering" courtship, Mr. Thos. Jones of the Glyn, aged *eighty*, to Miss Martha Parry, aged *twenty-three*!

The CORNHILL MAGAZINE, in a paper on "The Sweating Sickness," states that in the summers of 1506, 1517, and 1528, this curious epidemic broke out in Shrewsbury—from whence it spread all over the country. It also raged in our county town in 1551. Its first appearance in England was a few days before the battle of Bosworth:—

In the year of our Lord 1485 (writes a Dr. Caius, a Welsh physician, who had made the disease his special study), shortly after the seventh day of August, at which time King Henry VII. arrived at Milford, in Wales, out of France, and in the first year of his reign, there chanced a disease among the people, lasting the rest of that month and all September, which for the sudden sharpness and unwont cruelness passed the pestilence. For this commonly giveth in four, often seven, sometime nine, sometime eleven, and sometime fourteen days, respite to whom it vexeth. But that immediately killed some in opening their windows, some in playing with children in their street doors; some in one hour, many in two, it destroyed; and, at the longest, to them that merrily dined it gave a sorrowful supper. As it found them, so it took them; some in sleep, some in wake, some in mirth, some in care, some fasting, and some full, some busy and some idle; and in one house sometime three, sometime five, sometime more, sometime all; of the which if the half in every town escaped, it was thought great favour. This disease, because it most did stand in sweating from the beginning until the ending, was called *The Sweating Sickness*; and because it first began in England, it was named in other countries "The English Sweat."

CURIOUS LETTER ADDRESSES.—Under this heading Mr. T. Hughes sends the following to the *Cheshire Sheaf*;—On the 23 June 1859, there was posted at the Chester Post Office (fortunately, or it might never have reached its destination) a letter with the following address :—

> "Mistralling es is
> eagen too is
> Iodchep
> edclinston chaser."

This was a puzzle for a long while to our old "sorter," but it seems he spelt it out at last to read thus :—

> "Mr. Allen, as is
> Agent to his Lordship,
> Eccleston, Cheshire."

Judging by the direction alone, the letter itself must have been a perfect phonetic study !

DEPARTURE OF THE ROYAL WELSH FUSILIERS FOR INDIA.

PRESENTATION OF COLOURS BY THE PRINCE OF WALES.

At the embarkation of none of the reinforcements for India has there been such a demonstration as that with which the 1st battalion of the 23rd Royal Welsh Fusiliers were greeted at Portsmouth on Monday. The regiment, consisting of twenty-five officers, and 880 non-commissioned officers and men, arrived in the Dockyard by special train from Woolwich, about half-past ten o'clock, under the command by Lieut.-Col. Elgee, who, until recently was in command of the brigade depôt at Wrexham, from whence, during the last two weeks, upwards of 150 men have been sent to strengthen the battalion.

The presentation took place on the military recreation grounds, and was witnessed by thousands of persons. The ground was kept by the 69th and 108th Regiments, and a detachment of the 5th Dragoon Guards from Hilsea. The men marched to the recreation ground, headed by their admirable band and their no less famous Royal Goat Billy, who was presented by the Queen in 1872, and is supposed to have attained the venerable age of thirteen, having remained with the battalion longer than any other pet. The men appeared in light marching order, with white helmets. On entering the ground they formed single line two deep along the whole length of the green, with their faces towards the Royal tent, and thus awaited the arrival of His Royal Highness. At half-past twelve the Royal carriage, containing the Prince and Princess of Wales, the Duke of Edinburgh, and His Serene Highness Prince Edward of Saxe-Weimar, drove up to the pavilion. After a Royal salute, the Prince of Wales, with Colonel Elgee and other officials, inspected the regiment. The band, headed by the goat, passed along the line in slow time from right to left, repassing in quick time. The trooping of the old colours followed. The band, with the first company of the regiment, passed along the line with the colour party bearing the old colours, and in retiring they passed between the line, the band meanwhile playing "Auld Lang Syne," &c. The old colours were then conveyed to the rear. Three sides of a square having been formed, with a pyramid of drums in the centre, the new colours were uncased. The Royal party advanced, and the Rev. Assheton Craven, the senior chaplain of the garrison, read the consecration service. Four officers of the regiment advanced, and Major Tilby, one of the four, presented the Queen's colour to the Prince of Wales, who handed it to Lieutenant Carey, the latter receiving it on bended knee. Major Williamson presented the regimental colour, and the Prince handed it to Lieutenant Evans, who was also kneeling. His Royal Highness then addressed the regiment in the following terms :—

Colonel Elgee, officers, non-commissioned officers, and men of the Royal Welsh Fusiliers,—I consider it a very great privilege to have been asked to present your regiment with new colours on the eve of its departure for India. It occurs to me in presenting these colours that they are to replace those which were given to you about thirty-one years ago by my late lamented father, and which during three campaigns your regiment has carried with honour and success. You will in a few years celebrate your two hundredth anniversary. During that time your regiment has served in nearly every quarter of the globe, and has seen as much or more service than any regiment in the army. You have served in Egypt, at Corunna, Salamanca, in the Peninsula, at Waterloo, Alma, Inkerman, Sebastopol, Lucknow; and, coming down to more modern times, in Ashantee. I feel sure that there will always be the same emulation among those who serve in your ranks as there has been in the past, and that the good name of your regiment will always be maintained as prominently as it is now. You are now on the eve of departure for India, and nobody wishes you "God speed" more sincerely than I do. I feel sure that whatever your services may be, they will be such as will bring credit to your regiment, and will add additional proof of the valour for which it is so justly celebrated.

Col. Elgee, having thanked his Royal Highness for making the presentation, the colours were saluted by the whole regiment, the officers bearing them facing the line, and the band playing the National Anthem. After a march past the whole of the officers were presented to the Prince by Colonel Elgee. The Royal party then, amid loud cheering, left the ground, driving to the dockyard, and proceeding to the Royal yacht Osborne, on board which a numerous party were entertained at luncheon.

The Royal Welsh Fusiliers were raised in Wales, and received their title in 1714, in honour of the Prince of Wales, and their nationality is further betokened by the Prince of Wales's plume, with the motto "Ich dien," which, together with the Rising Sun, the Red Dragon, the White Horse, and the Sphinx they bear on their colours. The regiment is one of the oldest and most famous in the army, and the proud words "Nec aspera terrent," which are emblazoned on its regimental silk, it has amply justified by its gallant conduct from the battle of the Boyne in 1690 to the Indian Mutiny in 1858, including Egypt, Corunna, Martinique, Albuera, Badajoz, Salamanca, the Pyrenees, Nivelle, Orthes, Toulouse, Waterloo, Alma, Inkerman, Sebastopol, and forty-eight other engagements which are not recorded on its colours.

The colours with which the regiment parted on Monday have a glorious history. They were presented to the regiment in 1849 by the late Prince Consort at Winchester, and the first campaign in which they were borne was that of the Crimea at the battle of the Alma. They were in the first attempt to storm the heights carried by Lieutenant Anstruther and Lieutenant Butler. The latter, while crossing the river, was shot dead. Lieutenant Anstruther, closely followed by Sergeant O'Connor, made his way up the heights, but the sergeant on looking back discovered that the regiment was not following, and he intimated to the lieutenant

that it was impossible for them to advance. Within a few seconds both were shot, the sergeant in the breast, Anstruther through the heart. O'Connor seized the Queen's colour, and though bleeding profusely from his wound, he succeeded in crawling up the redoubt. With his right arm he held aloft the Queen's colour, a feat which had the effect of rallying the regiment, which by this time was getting dispirited. Under Codrington and Brown, the 23rd dashed up the heights, and succeeded in capturing the redoubt. For this valorous deed O'Connor received the Victoria Cross (he was, indeed, one of the first recipients of that honour) and a commission, and he has since attained the rank of colonel. The gallant officer's appearance on Tuesday evoked immense enthusiasm. It had been originally intended that the old colours should be deposited in the church at Wrexham, but having, as already stated, been originally presented to the regiment by the Prince's father, they have been given to his Royal Highness, who will have them deposited in Marlborough House. After luncheon on board the Osborne the Royal party proceeded on board the Malabar and spent three-quarters of an hour in inspecting the ship. Everything was now in readiness for a start, and on their Royal Highnesses' leaving, the Malabar got under way, the band of the Royal Marine Artillery playing "The March of the Men of Harlech." The crews of the neighbouring ships and the spectators on the jetty cheered enthusiastically, the greeting being no less warmly returned from on board the trooper. About forty officers from various other corps go out in the Malabar.

AUGUST 25, 1880.

NOTES.

VOLUNTEER ARMY OF 1803-4 (July 28, 1880). According to promise, we this week give the list of officers in *Cardiganshire.*

ROYAL CLARENCE, OR CARDIGAN.
Lt.-Col. Comm.: Owen Lloyd—12 July, 1803.
Lt.-Col.: William Davies—6 Dec. 1803.
Major : George Price—6 Dec., 1803.
Captains : John Vaughan, James James, Thomas Lewis, Morgan Davies, Richard Dickens, John Griffith, Evan Jones—12 July, 1803 ; Thomas Howells—11 Feb., 1804.
Capt.-Lieut. and Capt.: Thomas Bowen—12 July, 1803.
First Lieuts.: William Mitchell, Henry Peach, Thomaa Propert—12 July, 1803 ; David Lewis, Griffith Jenkins,' Thomas Makeig—11 Feb., 1804.
Second Lieuts.: Edward Troy, David Thomas, John Edwards, Richard Steele, John Morgan—12 July, 1803 ; Alban Williams, Evan Evans, David Evans, Isaac Noot—11 Feb., 1804 ; William Jones, David Evans.
Chaplain : John Nelson—11 Feb., 1804.
Adjutant : John Williams—12 July, 1803.
Surgeon : Thomas Noot—6 Dec., 1803.

TIVY (Upper).
Lt.-Col. Comm. : John Lloyd—24 Oct. 1803.
Lt.-Col. : Edward Warren Jones—24 Oct., 1803.
Major : William Caleb Gilbertson—24 Oct., 1803.
Captains : Isaac Bonsall, Thomas Jones, Alban Thomas, David Evans, William Poole, John Jordan Jones, Thomas Pelham Hopley, Lewis Morris—24 Oct., 1803.
Lieutenants : John Lloyd, Edward Evans, William Herbert, Job Sheldon, James Morgan, Walter Jones, James Morris, William Morris—24 Oct., 1803.

Ensigns : Richard Lloyd Hughes, Rowland Parry, James
Hughes, — Strick, Evan Morgan, John Jones, Joseph
Francis—24 Oct., 1803.
Adjutant : David Jones—24 Oct., 1803.
Quarter Master : Surgeon : Joseph Francis—24 Oct.,
1803.
In this company there seem to have been no changes
from the time of appointment of officers to the date of our
list—Oct. 1, 1804.   Ed.

OSWESTRY IN THE 14th CENTURY (July
21, 1880).—Another of the documents published in the
vol. of *Arch. Camb.* for 1852, is as follows :—
Richard de Sontbache and Cristiana his wife give to John
Loyt and E'me his wife 6s. yearly rent in the town of Oswaldestre, viz. 5s. arising out of the tenement which William Haston
holds of us in the street of Wyhastret, which tenement lies
between the tenement of Thomas le Rotour and the tenement
of Ævys de Brugge and extends from the highway to the wall
of the town, and twelvepence arising out of a tenement which
Jan. ap Thomas holds of us in the same street, which tenement lies
between the tenement of a certain Richard de Caula and the
tenement of William Haston, and extends from the highway to
the fosse of the town. To Have &c. for ever. For this, before
the gift, the said John and Emma give us £4 sterling in hand.
Witnesses : G'ffino de Glyndeuerdo, then Steward, Roger the
Rotour, and Richard Dangleys [English], bailiffs of the town,
John Haston, Howel ap Thomas, Richard, son of William the
Salter, and others many. Given at Oswaldestr, on Saturday
next before the feast of the Circumcision of the Lord, [Jan. 1.]
in the 20th year of Edward III. [1347.]
Here again we have a burnt-out street ; and names pro-
bably not known to this generation.   M.C.A.S.

TRIAL OF THE QUEEN.—When it was known
in *Oswestry* that the Bill of Pains and Penalties against
the Queen (Caroline) in Nov. 1820, was withdrawn, the
satisfaction of some of the inhabitants seems to have
taken a rough form. The illuminations were not general,
for, of course, people " took sides " on that question as
they do on every other. On the streets the "rejoicing"
was, as I have hinted, boisterous, and we are told that " a
young woman, daughter of Mr. Lloyd, shoemaker,
Church-street, was dreadfully injured, by the contents of
a pistol being discharged in her face." A dinner took
place at the Queen's Head, under the presidency of
Richard Salisbury, Esq., at which " from sixty to seventy
gentlemen, tradesmen, and respectable farmers of the
town and neighbourhood attended." Mr. Salisbury was
Deputy Mayor that year. At *Wem* every inhabited
house in the town, save one, was illuminated, and sheep
were roasted, and distributed to more than three hundred
families. A sweep, personifying the Devil, and carrying
a Green Bag (which he finally consigned to a bonfire)
paraded the streets. Lord Kenyon passing through the
town was escorted out of it amidst the enthusiastic cheers
of the inhabitants. The Earl of Bridgewater, who had
voted against the Queen, was mobbed at Watford. At
Llanymynech, near Oswestry, the illuminations were
general, and here, again, the Green Bag was conspicuous,
being hung on a gallows over a bonfire. At *Llanfihangel
Glyn*, on Nov. 11, the inhabitants were terrified at a late
hour by a strange light in the sky, but they were calmed
" by the Schoolmaster, who, assuring them that the
object of their terror was merely a flying globe, declared
it portended the acquittal of the Queen !" It was, really, a
fire-balloon—a novelty in those parts, that had been let off
eleven miles away to celebrate the Baptism of the heir of Talgarth ! At *Aberystwyth* the illuminations were brilliant and
general. " A large party of gentlemen, friends to the King,
Queen, and Constitution, partook of an excellent dinner at
the Gogerddan Arms, George Bonsall, Esq., of Glanrhidol,
in the chair." On the 28 Nov. " the triumph of the Queen"

was celebrated at the house of Mr. S. Davies of the Frood,
near *Wrexham*, " when a respectable company of fifty
gentlemen sat down to an excellent supper." It was
stated in your pages on Dec. 16, 1874, that some fine
Brawn was sent to Her Majesty as a congratulatory
present from *Shrewsbury*, and that " some females received
a subscription to enable them to present the Queen with a
' Simnel' weighing 70 lbs."   P.D.

QUERIES.

THE DOLGELLEY WORKHOUSE.—In June,
1838, the Dolgelley Guardians applied to the Assistant
Poor Law Commissioner for advice in consequence of the
numerous applications for relief by able-bodied men ; and
were told they must either build a workhouse, or find
work for the applicants. A vestry was called for the 3rd
of July to consider the question ; between 60 and 70
parishioners attended, and every one voted against having
a workhouse. The objections to it were various ; such as
the enforced separation of man and wife ; the probability
that in a thinly-populated district it would be no benefit
to debar the able-bodied from out-door relief ; the rigid
prison system and dietary of workhouses, &c. It was
stated that there had only been thirty applications from
able-bodied persons for six months. When was the workhouse built, and how were these objections overruled ?
                                   NEMO.

LADY PENRHYN'S WILL.—When did the
Lady Penrhyn die whose legacies to old servants, and dogs,
formed the subject of newspaper paragraphs ? In an old
scrap book I find a paragraph containing the following
account of the legacies :—Mrs. Furey (who had been her
ladyship's companion for nearly half a century) £10,000
(sic) Ann Lough, Lady Penrhyn's maid, the wardrobe and
£900, with an annuity of £100 for life, and £40 per annum
to each of three pug dogs for their lives, they to be under
the care of Ann Lough. To Elizabeth Kent, her ladyship's secretary, who had been with her 15 years, £900 ;
to Mary Harris, who had been housekeeper 30 years,
£300 ; to John Mann, butler 25 years, £400 ; Margaret
Lough, housekeeper 30 years, £500 ; Margaret Goulden,
housekeeper in London 29 years, £300 ; Charles James,
footman, 16 years, £200 ; George Moore, do., 19 years,
£300 ; James Linstead, under butler, £100 ; William
Gatcliff, coachman 20 years, £300 ; John Capper, groom
40 years, £300, with the care of seven horses and seven
dogs—for each horse £45 per annum, and for each dog £25 ;
Joseph Wilkinson, groom 16 years, £300 ; William Nichols,
gardener, £300, with an additional £100 for his eldest
daughter ; Mary Bowyer, a girl her ladyship had brought
up, £20 a year for life ; George Goody (Sir Peter
Warburton's late coachman) who once lived with Lady
Penrhyn, £200. In addition to these every servant had
one year's wages, handsome mourning, and £10 for second
mourning, and Benjamin Wiatt and James Greenfield,
Esq., had each £1,000. The length of service of twelve of
the servants added together amounted to 267 years.
                                   O's S.B.

REPLIES.

SHROPSHIRE WORTHIES (Aug. 11, 1880).—
Since I wrote *Shreds and Patches* has called attention to
another " Worthy" not mentioned by Mr. Salisbury viz.,
Samuel Lawrence, " an artist of great ability, born in
Wem about 1813." Early in life he went to London,
where he painted portraits of Carlyle, Tennyson, and
others ; and then emigrated to America, his work being
" too stern and truthful " for England ! It will be seen

on page 131 of the first series of *Border Counties Worthies* (also on page 273 of *Bye-gones* for 1874-5) that Mr. Salisbury gives a memoir of a Samuel Lawrence, son of William Lawrence, who was born in Wem in 1661. Was the Samuel Lawrence now referred to of the same family ?
SCROBBES BYRIG.

AN ORIGINAL CADER IDRIS GUIDE (May 26, 1880).—A more recent guide than Robin Edwards may fairly be called original. I allude to lt. Pugh who died a few years ago. In Aug. 1838 a Salopian tourist wrote in a Visitors' Book Pugh kept the following lines :—

I walked o'er the Simplon, and noble I found it,
　　I slept on the Ostler Spitz drear,
In moonlight's pale beams St. Gotherd's I crossed,
　　But ne'er found such a guide as is here.

The Sneighbergh I mounted, enveloped in snow,
　　All the Thalenberg's wonders I view'd,
Helenor's broad pass I clambered along,
　　But ne'er was so thoroughly "Pugh'd."

On the Tyrol's bleak wonders I wander'd full oft,
　　And reposed in its rime covered dells,
'Midst Styria's woods I moodily sat,
　　And quaffed from its excellent wells.

Through Austria's land I in solitude wandered,
　　And dreamed that its natives were free,
On the Saltzer's green waters my fly has been cast,
　　I have shot o'er the wild Thoenigg lee.

Carriola's dark caves I keenly explored,
　　And bathed in Dalmatia's sea,
The Danube's swift current I glided along,
　　But ne'er met such a guide, "Pugh," as thee.

Pugh is said to have been a very amusing companion. If he got up for recitation on the heights a few such verses as these, he might well be deemed a descendant of the party Mrs. Hemans wrote about in her poem on Cader Idris, which gives the fate of the man who sleeps on its rock !   G.G.

THE CONWAY PEARLS (Nov. 13, 1878).— The river Conway in North Wales was noted for producing pearls in the time of Camden ; and it is said that Sir Richard Wynn of Gwydir, Chamberlain to Catherine, queen of Charles II., presented her Majesty with one taken from that river, which is to this day honoured with a place in the Royal crown. The pearls found at the mouth of the river are generally very small, of a dirty white, or sometimes blue colour, and the shell from which they are taken is the common mussel. Near Llanrwst they have been found as large as a moderate-sized pea, and they were sold at a guinea a couple, but the search is very precarious, and good pearls are rarely found. The shells in which these latter pearls were found is the *Alasmadon margaritiferus* ; the Welsh call them "Cregin y Dylu," or shells of the flood. (*Chambers's Miscellany*, No. 167.)
NORTH.

THE GOLDEN FARMER (Aug. 11, 1880).—I suppose there have been two "Golden Farmers." The one TELL enquires about was by name Thomas, and lived early in this century. The one I am going to write about flourished in the time of Charles II., and was William Davies. Both were Welshmen. My hero was a highwayman, and acquired his nick-name from his custom of paying any considerable sum in gold. He left North Wales at an early period in life, for Sudbury in Gloucestershire, where he took a farm, and married the daughter of an innkeeper, by whom he had eighteen children. Under the guise of a farmer he was a robber for forty-two years. Amongst other exploits he robbed the Duchess of Albemarle, having to fight and subdue her grace's two

footmen, coachman, and a postilion before he could reach her carriage. In Johnson's *Lives of Highwaymen* several of his exploits are narrated, and we are told "Many a hue and cry was sent after him, and conspired to his overthrow. He was seized, imprisoned, tried, and condemned. A violent death terminated his wicked course."
ARGUS.

CURRENT NOTES.

A brass plate, bearing the following inscription, has been placed on the base of the marble pulpit lately placed in the nave of Bangor Cathedral :—"In memory of the Rev. Morris Williams, M.A. (Nicander), late Rector of Llanrhyddlad and Rural Dean. An eminent Welsh scholar, poet, and divine. Born August 24, 1810 ; died Jan. 4, 1874."

The *British Architect*, apropos of the revival of the art of modelling in wax, reminds us that Hulbert, in his "Memoirs," records some of the eccentric doings of a gentleman of the name of Moss, who resided at Ringway Outwood, Cheshire, in the early part of this century. "This gentleman, to make up for want of society, made several wax figures, which were elegantly and fashionably attired, one of which it was said he called Mrs. Moss, and at dinner she was placed at the head of the table, the other figures being guests. After dinner they were seated opposite the window, as if observing the passers-by, and many a countryman's bow did these ladies receive, with which Mr. Moss was greatly delighted."

THE 23RD ROYAL WELSH FUSILIERS. — In a letter addressed to the editor of the *Liverpool Mercury*, Mr. P. H. Salusbury, of Glan Aber, writes :—I notice that in one of the leading articles the 23rd Royal Welsh Fusiliers is stated to be "the one regiment of the service which is identified with the Principality." But there are other regiments which claim connection in some way or other with Wales. The 41st are called "The Welsh," and, besides the Prince's plume, bear on their appointments the motto "Gwell Angeu na Chywilydd." This regiment, one of the finest in the Queen's service, greatly distinguished itself at Detroit, Queenstown, Miami, Niagara, Ava, Candahar, Ghuznee, Cabul 1842, Alma, Inkerman, and Sevastopol. The 82nd regiment, known as "The Prince of Wales's Volunteers," wear emblazoned on their colours the following distinctions :—The Prince's Plume, Roleia, Vimiera. Vittoria, Pyrenees, Nivelle, Orthes, Peninsula, Niagara, Sevastopol, and Lucknow. It must not be supposed because the 82nd and other regiments are called "volunteers" that they were volunteers in the sense of the word at the present time. The corps of the line termed "volunteers" were, as a rule, given that name because they were originally militia regiments which had volunteered for service in the regular army. In the cavalry there are a few regiments connected by name with the Principality, viz., the 3rd Dragoon Guards, 10th Hussars, and 12th Lancers. So that, proud as Welshmen undoubtedly are of the 23rd Royal Welsh Fusiliers, yet they have a wider interest in the army, and can be also proud of other regiments.

LLANYCIL CHURCH RESTORATION AND RE-OPENING.

Llanycil Church, the old parish church of Bala, was re-opened on Wednesday, August 18, by the BISHOP OF ST. ASAPH after a complete restoration. The church, which is dedicated to ST. BEUNO, is connected by a chain of tradition with the ninth century, and its more modern associations are of great interest to the inhabitants of the Principality.

The churchyard has been called the "Bunhill Fields of Wales," from the number of eminent Nonconformist Welshmen buried there. In the church lies "CHARLES Y BALA," of whom some years ago a statue was erected in front of the Calvinistic Methodist Chapel in that town. It is noteworthy that the Rev. Dr. EDWARDS, President of Bala College, was a member of the Restoration Committee. Sir WATKIN WILLIAMS WYNN, who was chairman of the Committee, contributed with his accustomed liberality towards the work, and presided at a public luncheon held after the morning service. Mr. W. H. SPAULL of Oswestry was the architect of the restoration.

Much interest is attached to St. Beuno, the parish church of Llanycil, owing to the great antiquity of its associations. The history of the church is traceable to the ninth century. In the course of its history the church and churchyard have become endeared to thousands as the depository of the mortal remains of renowned and pious Welshmen. A most interesting article which appeared in Y Traethodydd, 1849, from the pens of the Revs. Roger Edwards, Mold, and the late Lewis Jones, Bala, terminates thus. "The Churchyard of Llanycil is the cave of the field of Machpelah or *Bunhill-fields* of the North Wales Methodists." The memorial of the far-famed Charles of Bala, one of the founders of the British and Foreign Bible Society, whose place of burial is situated near the east window, has, and will be, visited by thousands of his countrymen and others from all parts who take an interest in the world-wide distribution of the Holy Scripture. The works of this eminent man, next to the Bible most widely known and appreciated in the Principality, are the *Geiriadur Ysgrythyrol* and *Yr Hyfforddwr*. The following inscription is upon his tombstone :—"Underneath lie the remains of the Rev. Thomas Charles, B.A., of Bala, who died October 5, 1814, aged 59. By his indefatigable endeavours when in London (A.D. 1804) to procure a supply of the Holy Scriptures for the use of his native countrymen, he became the means of establishing the British and Foreign Bible Society. He was the reviver of the Welsh circulating charity schools, and the most active promoter of Sunday schools, both for children and adults; and North Wales, the more immediate field of his missionary labours for thirty years, will probably retain traces of his various strenuous exertions to promote the Kingdom of Christ till time shall be no more." In this church also lie the remains of his friends and fellow workers, the Rev. Simon Lloyd, B.A., of Plasyndre, author of *Amseryddiaeth Ysgrythyrol* and *Esboniad ar Lyfr y Dadguddiad,* and the upright and faithful minister of the gospel, John Evans of Bala, who, with Mr. Charles, contributed to the stirring dialogue recounting the deplorable moral aspect of the town of Bala and the Principality in olden times, under the signatures of Scrutator and Senex. The former represented Mr. Charles, the latter the Rev. John Evans. The dialogue related to the commencement and progress of religious revival in that period in some districts of North Wales. It appeared in the first numbers issued of *Trysorfa Ysprydol,* edited by the Revs. T. Charles, Bala, and T. Jones, Denbigh, printed in Chester, in St. Peter's churchyard, by W. C. Jones, and published at Bala by R. Saunderson. Book 1, part 1. April 16, 1799. Part 2 appeared in June, part 3 October, all in 1799, part 4 and 5 in January and October, 1800, part 6 in Dec., 1801, completed Book 1, which is now very rare. Also within the precincts of this building are the remains of the once celebrated poet and satirist, Evan Lloyd, of Fron, "a friend," says the *Gossiping Guide to Wales,* of Garrick and Jack Wilkes, the latter of whom made his acquaintance in the King's Bench Prison, and

wrote his epitaph. Amongst others buried here were Dr. Anwyl and Dr. E. Williams who were much beloved and respected. We must also add to the list the name of Dr. John Parry, whose memory is held in veneration in the town and vicinity, and throughout the Principality, as editor and principal contributor for many years to the "Encyclopædia Cambrensis," published by Mr. Gee, of Denbigh, and of the unassuming worker, poet, and patriot, Ioan Pedr.

Tradition says that this Church was built by St. Beuno whilst he was on his way from Montgomeryshire to the banks of the Dee in the sixth century. In the "Black Book of Carmarthen" there is an account of some of the Rhiwaedog family being buried in this Church in the ninth century. The "Taxatio," A.D. 1291, speaks of Llanycil as being both a rectory and a Vicarage, the income of the rector being at that time £4 6s. 8d., and that of the vicar, £1 13s. 4d. Edward Llwyd, 1670, says that opposite the Cross in Bala there was a place called "Monwent yr Eglwys" (we believe in some old documents and conveyances this is called "Monwent y Cappel "), where a Church once existed; probably this was the charge of the vicar mentioned in the "Taxatio," 1291, and to this Church probably belonged the famous "Cloch y Bala."

In the sixteenth century extensive alterations inside of Llanycil Church were made ; it was also re-roofed at this time. The oldest register now extant begins with 1615, which contains a copy of an order made by Commissioners from the Archbishop of Canterbury in 1636, which says "that for the future no one should claim a sitting place in the Church, and particularly that none should be allowed to claim by custom seats on either side of the chancel ;" and upon inquiry made at St. Asaph we are informed that there is no account of a faculty being granted for anyone to hold a pew in this Parish Church, so that practically before the Free and Open Church Movement was instituted, the principle was recognised in the parish of Llanycil.

At the time of the Reformation (Cromwell's) in 1649 and 1657, John Vaughan, of Cefnybodig, removed the old rooding or screen of the chancel, the old benches, and reading desk. The old bell was also taken away about this time.

In the year 1714 the Church is described as being filled with cushions and rushes, for the convenience of the congregation to kneel and sit upon. The Rector of the parish was desirous of removing these, when the parishioners made a bold stand, stating that they could not remain comfortable and quiet without them. However, the Rector removed a portion of them, probably those placed in the chancel, over which he had more direct control, when he discovered a large number of snakes had sheltered there from the inclemency of the winter, which fact being made known to the parishioners, they willingly consented to their removal.

In 1722, Robert Jones, the rector, presented the Church with a very handsome paten and chalice, and at this time a vestry was held, when the parishioners resolved to present the Church with a new bell, which was to be supplied by Williamson of Wigan. This same bell, bearing the maker's name, has been replaced from the old structure in the new cote. We append a list of the rectors of the parish from 1537 to the present time :— 1537, John ap David ; 1561, Robert Hughes ; 1583, Ellis Morrys ; 1598, Robert Morice ; 1615, John Piers, who built a school close by the Church, of which there is no trace at present ; 1626, Thomas Piers ; 1640, Andrew Maurice, M.A. ; 1641, J. Morgan, M.A. ; 1644, Thomas Edwards ; 1657, Edward Myers, M.A. ; 1658, John Jones, B.A. ; 1686, John Mostyn, M.A. ; 1688, Athelstane

5

15>

Savage, M.A.; 1705, Edward Humphreys; 1725, Peter Powell, M.A.; 1735, Robert Jones; 1753, David Lloyd, B.A.; 1760, Griffith Lloyd, B.A.; 1780, Thomas Mostyn, M.A.; 1782, Rice Anwyl; 1819, Robert Phillips; 1826, John Lloyd; 1841, Peter Price, M.A.; 1852, Richd. Pughe, M.A.; 1860, D. M. Thomas, M.A.; 1866, David Evans; 1876, Robert Jones, M.A.

SEPTEMBER. 1, 1880.

PURE ENGLISH.—It was incidentally mentioned on page 235 of *Bye-gones* for 1879 that purer English was spoken in Wales than in the English counties, where the uneducated classes speak a provincial dialect. We are informed by M. GAIDOZ, the editor of the *Revue Celtique*, that "the same has been observed with regard to French in Celtic Britanny."

NOTES.

THE QUEEN AT WELSHPOOL.—It was incidentally mentioned in one of the local papers of May, 1838 (in connection with the approaching coronation of the Queen,) that the Princess Victoria when on a visit to Powis Castle in 1832, had, "in the most gratifying and condescending manner visited the town, and National Schools, to which she generously gave £100."
BLACKPOOL.

SALOPIAN PICTURES.—The *Salopian Journal* for May 30, 1838, contains announcements of the publication of a "Print of Rice Wynne, Esq., on his favourite horse;" also a "Print of Mr. Stephen Denston, yeoman." The former was published by Ackermann of London, and the latter by Mr. J. B. Minor of Astley House. At the end of Nov. 1838, six views in Shrewsbury, "drawn from nature and on zinc," by Henry Blunt, were published, "tinted after the manner of Harding." After a few copies were printed the plates were effaced. About the same time Mr. Price, bookseller, of Oswestry, announced, by subscription, a highly-finished view of Brynkinalt, drawn by J. Ross, and lithographed by Day and Haighe. In Aug. 1839, Mr. Price also published a print, by Mr. Henshaw, of a view of Oswestry taken from a point above the Grammar School. In Nov. 1839, Mr. Pardon, dating from Pride Hill, Shrewsbury, announced his intention to publish "a Print from a Portrait he is now painting of the Hon. Thomas Kenyon." He further says, "The Engraving will be the size, and in the style of Dr. Darwin." The likeness of the doctor was advertised in Feb. 1839, at a guinea, prints; and £1 11s. 6d. and Two Guineas proofs.
SALOPIAN.

OSWESTRY HEIGHTS.—I once transcribed from an annotated copy of Price's *History of Oswestry* the following:—"Oswestry is 450 feet above the level of the sea, and 254 feet higher than the Shrewsbury meadows." In the *Oswestry Advertizer* some time back the following heights of places in and near Oswestry over the main level of the sea at Liverpool were given :—

Cambrian Station	402 feet
Castle Bank	487 ,,
Guildhall	442 ,,
Cross Fountain	420 ,,
St. Oswald's Church	430 ,,
House of Industry	410 ,,
The Hayes	530 ,,
Reservoirs	714 ,,
Rhydycroesau	786 ,,
Cernybwch	1019 ,,

I should have thought that the House of Industry stood on higher ground than the Guildhall, and certainly higher than the Cross.
L.C.

THE COTTONS OF COMBERMERE.—It-is very well known that the Cottons had been connected with Shropshire long before their settlement at Combermere in Cheshire; but their connection with Denbighshire is not so well understood, it being generally supposed they had become identified with that county through the marriage of Sir Robert Cotton to Hester Salusbury of Lleweni, and thereby acquiring that beautiful estate, and the one of Berain, which had vested in the Salusburies upon the marriage of a son of Lleweni to the celebrated "Katrin o'r Berain." I find however from Williams's *Records of Denbigh* that Charles Cotton of Combermere had been made a burgess of that borough so early as the year 1660, and I should be glad to know if he erected "Cotton Hall," a well-known house, not very far from the site of Old Lleweni. I can very well understand, how after acquiring Lleweni the Cottons were more intimately connected with Denbigh; but it is not clear how they came there at first; by way of guide to any of your readers who may look into the fact, first mentioned, I had better add the following entries, out of the same work :—

1665 Sir Robert Cotton of Combermere, Knt., sworn a burgess of Denbigh.
1700 Sir Robert Cotton, Knt. and Bart., elected an alderman.
1713 Sir Robert Cotton, Knt. and Bart., died.
1713 Sir Thomas Cotton, Bart., succeeded his father.
1717 Sir Thomas Cotton, Bart., died.
1717 Sir Robert Salusbury Cotton, Bart., succeeded him.
1729 Lynch Salusbury Cotton sworn a burgess of Denbigh.
1748 Sir Robert Salusbury Cotton, Bart., died.
1776 Sir Lynch Salusbury Cotton, Bart., died.
I do not quite know the succession of the above in title, but unless I am mistaken the first Lord Combermere was the very last of his family, born at Lleweni, and then the estates of Lleweni and Berain were sold to Lord Kirkwall, who afterwards sat in Parliament for Denbighshire, and, I think, became a member of the Denbigh Corporation. I conclude—subject to correction—that the connection of the Cottons with Denbigh commenced with Charles Cotton, and ended with the first Lord Combermere, and that they have not at this moment any property in that county.
GLADWYN.

QUERIES.

LLANDEN.—Does the opinion of Selden, that the name *London* is derived from two Welsh words, "Llan den"=Church of Diana, find favour with any scholars of the present day?
AP MEREDYTH.

CAPTAIN BRAMWELL OF OSWESTRY.—Can any of your readers state the circumstances that caused the following paragraph to appear in the *Shrewsbury Chronicle* of Apr. 6, 1838?

Captain Bramwell of Oswestry, of whom so much has been said, relating to the death of his wife, returned to that town on Saturday, and was immediately placed in the custody of Mr. Jones, in the Borough Gaol, where he remains for want of sureties to keep the peace; or until his person shall be placed under proper restraint by Trustees.

Who was Captain Bramwell, and under what circumstances did his wife die?
TELL.

THEOPHILUS JONES'S HISTORY OF BRECKNOCKSHIRE.—I shall be obliged if any reader of *Bye-gones* can give me, through that source, the following information regarding this model county history, published in two folio vols. in 1805 and 1809 :—(1) What was the original subscription price to this history? (2) Is there a good biography of the author in existence, and by whom published? (3) Does any person hold any copyright or other pecuniary interest in the history? (4) What has become of the original exquisite steel plates with which the vols. are illustrated? (5) What is the present market value (not fancy value) of a complete and perfect copy of the history?—Answers to these queries will greatly oblige

HISTORICUS.

REPLIES.

REMARKABLE STORM AT OSWESTRY (Aug. 18, 1880).—In reply to the question of JARCO, I remember perfectly well the storm in question in this neighbourhood (Welshpool). I was a boy at the time, and well remember my father taking me to the window, and telling me and my sisters to put our tongues to it, when the incrustation on the window had a saline taste. We have often since talked of it as a matter of recollection. EJ.

THE WELSH COAST (Aug. 4, 1880).—The verses quoted by TAFFY are from a poem of Dr. Johnson's entitled *London*, in which he imitates the Third Satire of Juvenal, commending the resolve of an imaginary friend, Thales, to withdraw from the whirl of city life to the sylvan solitudes of Wales. The poem commences:—

Tho' grief and fondness in my breast rebel,
When injur'd Thales bids the town farewel,
Yet still my calmer thoughts his choice commend
(I praise the hermit, but regret the friend.)

Then follow the lines alluded to—

Resolved at length, from vice and London far,
To breathe in distant fields a purer air,
And, fix'd on Cambria's solitary shore,
Give to St. David one true Briton more.

It will be perceived that since the subject of the piece is purely imaginary, no definite spot can be assigned as the retreat of "injured Thales." Verses 45 to 48 would seem to imply that it was inland, or at least not the lonely rockbound coast one would gather from the introductory lines. They run—

Some pleasing bank where verdant osiers play,
Some peaceful vale with nature's paintings gay,
Where once the harass'd Briton found repose,
And, safe in poverty, defy'd his foes.

The mention of the Cambrian national saint can scarcely be strained so far as to imply a retirement to the episcopal village which bears his name; the neighbourhood of St. David's, moreover, would have few attractions for the blasé citizen. We must therefore leave TAFFY's second question in abeyance. I may remark that the miserable poet Savage did actually visit the Principality under such circumstances as these in 1739. (Hales's *Longer English Poems*, p. 307.) LLWYD O'R BRYNLLWYD.

SHROPSHIRE SCHOOLS (June 23, 1880).— "Oxford, May 5, 1838. The Denyer Theological prize 'On the Divinity of the Holy Ghost,' has been adjudged to the Rev. Robert Scott, A.M., Fellow of Balliol College, and formerly of Shrewsbury School."

"Mr. Henry Marsh of Trinity College, Cambridge, has been elected a Scholar of that Society. He was educated at Shrewsbury School."—*Shrewsbury Journal*, May 9, 1838. SCROBBES BYRIG.

A correspondent has asked for the names of Scholars in our Shropshire Schools who have in any way distinguished themselves. My "reply" will be no answer, for it relates only to an event in the history of one of the Schools, and is copied from a newspaper of June 1838, as follows —"Her Majesty has been graciously pleased

to signify, through the medium of Lord John Russell, to the Rev. Thomas Rowley, M.A., Head Master of the Free Grammar School, Bridgnorth, her royal pleasure that a week be added to the usual term of the ensuing Midsummer holidays." R.

OSWESTRY INSTITUTIONS (Aug. 4, 1880).— It so happens that I possess the Rev. George Lloyd's private copy of the Reports of the "Oswestry Society for Bettering the Condition of the Poor," in which he has affixed his initials to all the reports he wrote, and which include the 2nd, 3rd, 4th, 5th, 7th, 9th, and 10th. The first and sixth have the initials "P.R." attached to them. The writer of these, the Rev. Peter Roberts, resided a good deal of his time in Oswestry, and was a very active man in public matters affecting the well-being of his fellows. Canon Williams, in his *Eminent Welshmen*, says Mr. Roberts supplied the MS. for the *History of Oswestry* published by Price in 1815-6. In some respects he may be looked upon as the founder of the Society for Bettering the Condition of the Poor, and his fellow-committeemen so far honoured his memory as to publish his likeness under the auspices of the Society, in 1821, soon after his death. Miss Parker of Sweeney Hall (afterwards Lady Leighton) had not long before "executed a very spirited and striking likeness of him," and Mr. W. Ormsby Gore undertook the engraving of it. He put the work into the hands of Mr. Scriven, who executed the task at a cost of £32 9s., which, I believe, included the printing of two-hundred copies for the subscribers. The Society netted £3 16s. by the transaction. But to return to the "Seventh Report" reprinted by Earl Hardwicke and the London Society. In Mr. Lloyd's copy of the Reports one of Lord Hardwicke's appeals is interleaved, which had been addressed to the Shropshire Court of Quarter Sessions, and reprinted by order of that Court, and circulated by the Clerk of the Peace, Mr. Joseph Loxdale. It has been stated that there are several "Associations for the Prevention of Crime" established on the Oswestry model of 1771; but how many places adopted the report of the Oswestry Society for Bettering the Condition of the Poor, in 1819, I cannot say. JARCO.

CURRENT NOTES.

THE BRITISH ASSOCIATION.

The British Association began its sittings at Swansea on Thursday, August 26. There was a large gathering at the Music Hall in the evening.

The MAYOR OF SWANSEA first addressed the meeting:— He welcomed the British Association for the Advancement of Science to Swansea with unalloyed pleasure. Thirty-two years, he said, had elapsed since that august body had visited the metropolis of Wales, and every year of that period had added to the celebrity, the usefulness, and the marvellous range of the labours of the Association. When they last favoured them with a visit Swansea was notable chiefly as a marine resort, the beauties of which Walter Savage Landor, the poet, had celebrated. Now it was a centre of industrial life, where science was applied with such grim reality as to shock the nervous system of men of the school of Ruskin. (A laugh.) He could assure them that the previous visit of the British Association had done much to turn the mind of his countrymen to the scientific capabilities of the district, which he hoped was not without scientific interest. Ingenious Bible critics had lately been telling them that Wales must have been part of Ancient Tarshish, the tin country of the Roman period. One thing at least was certain—they were at the present moment essentially the tin manufacturing country of the world, and it would not be their fault if the wise men of the East, our cousins in the country of the setting sun, and mankind in general, did not continue to get their manufactured tin from Wales. (Cheers.) They did not pretend to show the members of the British Association anything new, but rather hoped to receive many practical hints from them that might fructify in the future. His countrymen, speaking for the most part, even in the present century, the very language current when the legions of Cæsar did battle for Imperial Rome, had not had the benefit of 18th and 19th century research, for the simple reason that they did not understand the language in which science was expressed. They were now making up for the past, and had no doubt much to learn. It was colloquially said by his countryme n, in a tone of banter which he was sure would not be misunderstood by the assembly,—

> "Whatever men do, Welshmen dare,
> "For we the ancient Britons are."

(Cheers.) And he, in their name, dared hope that the British Association, which had shortly to celebrate a half-century of useful existence, would have no more teachable, willing, or humble followers in the three kingdoms than those in Wales. (Cheers.)

In the Anthropological department Professor F. W. Rudler, F.G.S., the vice-president, read an address of great interest to those who make the origin of race and language a particular study. The question which Mr. Rudler set himself to solve was what are the ethnical relations of the typical man of South Wales? He said it would be necessary to pass over the centres of population where the race is necessarily mixed. Glamorganshire probably contained at the present time more than one-third of the entire population of Wales. The temptation of high wages offered in seasons of prosperity had attracted hither a large number of settlers from different parts of the United Kingdom. Occasionally too (continued the lecturer), recourse has been had to the technical skill of foreigners; and thus ethnical elements have been introduced to a limited extent from outside the British Isles. It is worth while noting that the movement of population towards South Wales has been mainly determined by the geological structure of the district. It was the occurrence of coal that originally tempted Ulricke Frosse to bring his cargo of copper ore across from Cornwall to be smelted in the Vale of Neath; and it is still the working of coal which maintains the local industries and supports the vast population of Glamorganshire. The connexion between the geological structure of a district and the social and ethnic characteristics of its inhabitants has been recognized by no one more clearly than by the distinguished biologist who is presiding over the present meeting of this Association. Apart, however, from all foreign admixture, there is still in Glamorganshire, especially in the outlying districts, a very large proportion of the population who may be fairly regarded as typically Welsh, but when it is said that the true Welsh are Celts there arises a difficulty not disclosed by the language of the people—namely, the differences in their physical structure and complexion. Tacitus, in his "Agricola" described the Welsh as short, of swarthy complexion, with curly hair, probably related to the Iberians, but side by side with these are the tall fair natives, and of course individuals of intermediate character. If we can strip off all extraneous elements which have been introduced by the modern settler and the mediæval Fleming, possibly also by the Norman baron, and even the Roman soldier, we may eventually lay bare for anthropological study the deep lying stratum of the population—the original Welsh element. The researches

of archæological anatomists tend to prove that this country was tenanted in ante-historic or pre-Roman times by two peoples who were ethnically distinct from each other. It is difficult to resist the temptation of applying this to the ethnogeny of Wales. According to the view advocated by Thurnam, we have a right to anticipate that the oldest skulls found in this country would be of dolichocephalous type, and such I believe to be actually the case. Setting aside any archæological evidence derived from the bone-caves, barrows, or other sepulchres in Wales, we may finally look at the outcome of our inquiry into Welsh ethnogeny. If we admit, as it seems to me we are bound to admit, the existence of two distinct ethnical elements in the Welsh population, one of which is short, dark and dolichocephalic—call it Silurian, Atlantean, Iberian, Basque, or what you will; and the other of which is tall, fair, and brachycephalic, such as some term Cymric, and others Ligurian, then it follows that by the crossing of these two races we may obtain not only individuals of intermediate character, but occasionally more complex combinations; for example, an individual may have the short stature and long head of the one race associated with the lighter hair of the other; or, again, the tall stature of one may be found in association with the melanism and dolichocephalism of the other race. It is, therefore, no objection to the views herein expressed if we can point to a living Welshman who happens to be at once tall and dark, or to another who is short and fair. At the same time, I am by no means disposed to admit that when we have recognized the union of the xanthous and melanic elements in Wales with a predominance of the latter in the south, we have approached to anything like the exhausting limit of the subject. Still earlier races may have dwelt in the land, and have contributed something to the composition of the Welsh. In fact, the anthropologist may say of a Welshman, as a character in "Cymbeline" says of Posthumus when doubtful about his pedigree—

> I cannot delve him to the root.

It is possible that the roots of the Welsh may reach far down into some hidden primitive stock, older mayhap than the Neolithic ancestors of the Silurians; but of such pristine people we have no direct evidence. So far, however, as positive investigation has gone, we may safely conclude that the Welsh are the representatives, in large proportion, of a very ancient race or races; and that they are a composite people, who may perhaps be best defined as Siluro-Cymric.

CAMBRIAN ARCHÆOLOGICAL ASSOCIATION.

MEETING AT PEMBROKE.

The thirty-fifth annual meeting of this society was held last week at Pembroke. Mr. C. E. G. Philipps of Picton Castle, the new president, delivered his inaugural address, and the Rev. R. Trevor Owen, the secretary and editor, read the annual report. In the course of it the following reference was made to members who have died since the last meeting : "The society has lately lost by death several of its members, among whom are—M. Aymar de Blois, of the Chateau de Poulquinan, near Quimper, Finistére; the Rev. T. James, F.S.A., of Netherthong, near Huddersfield, one of the original members of the society, and whose extensive collection of Welsh books was lately dispersed at Sotheby's; Augustus Reed, Esq., of Acton, Wrexham; Rev. Canon Harries, late of Gelligaer Rectory, near Cardiff; Mrs. Laws, a member of long standing, and sister-in-law to the late James Deardon, the first treasurer of the society. But the latest and most serious loss of the society is by the death of William Watkin Edward Wynne, Esq., of Peniarth, near Towyn, in Merioneth, who died last July, in the seventy-ninth year of his age. Few men were better qualified and more willing to assist the Association in its earlier days, as the volumes of the *Archæologia Cambrensis* show. He acted as President at the Dolgelley meeting in 1850, and frequently attended subsequent ones. The restoration of the most interesting church in North Wales, namely, that of Llanaber, near Barmouth, was entirely his work, the rector wisely preferring his services to those of a professional architect, and the result has proved the wisdom of his selection and the judgment of Mr. Wynne. The last Sir Robert Vaughan of Nannau bequeathed to Mr. Wynne the celebrated Hengwrt collection, of which an exhaustive catalogue was inserted in Volume 15 of the third series of the journal. He was subsequently appointed constable of Harlech Castle, of which, in conjunction with Mr. G. T. Clark of Dowlais he published an account, at present the standard guide-book to the ruins. He also published a history of his parish of Llanegryn, and had promised one of Towyn. He rendered valuable assistance to Mr. E. Breese in his work of the 'Kalendars of Gwynedd,' and to Mr. Askew Roberts in his new edition of the 'History of the Gwydir Family.' He was at all times most ready to render assistance and advice to all who sought it. A full notice of him, by Mr. E. Breese, his intimate friend, may be found in the July number of this year." In enumerating the advantages conferred by the Association, the report says—"Another advantage arising from the existence of the Society is the formation of local societies, such as that of the Powys-Land Club. The first volume of its Transactions appeared in 1868, and has been annually followed by others of the same value and interest. In the introductory notice to the work it is stated that the idea broached in the first part of the *Archæologia Cambrensis* in 1846, 'on the study and preservation of the national antiquities of Wales,' led to the attempt of carrying out the idea for the county of Montgomery. The members of that Society know how successfully the work has been and is still being carried on. And it is to this success must be fairly assigned the establishment of the museum in Welshpool, not only the most valuable in Wales, but in some respects the only one, and it is a striking example of what the persevering energy and munificent liberality of one individual can effect. Important additions have been lately made to the building, rendered necessary by the additions constantly made to its collections. Wales at present has no museum of antiquities, although there are several local ones which contain a few objects of interest to archæologists, often passed over among cases of stuffed birds and geological specimens. A museum formerly existed at Carnarvon, some remains of the contents of which are in the Castle, and not very accessible to the public. The Royal Institution of Swansea possesses a few, and in time the newly-established museum at Tenby may be presented with some curiosities of the kind. There is a museum in Lampeter College, but it is a private one. None of these can supply what is wanted, viz., a general and central musuum for Welsh antiquities. The nearest approach to one is ready at hand in Welshpool, and could be made to answer the purpose at a small cost." The Report also contains the following reference to the work of some of its more literary members :—"The *Revue Celtique* started by one of our members and the corresponding secretary for France has nearly completed its fourth volume, and promises to become a work of great importance to Celtic scholars. No. 14, the last issued, con-

tains, among other articles, 'Supplement to Breton and French Dictionaries.' Some members of this society are supporters of this review, both as contributors and subscribers; but your committee think that were the work better known more would contribute to its support. The late Mr. R. Brash, for many years an active member of the Association, left a work on the 'Ogham inscribed Monuments of the Gaedhil in the British Islands,' which, by the assistance of Mr. G. M. Atkinson, his widow published last year. It is a work of considerable value, even if one or two of its statements are not admitted. Wales has so many Ogham monuments—some of them of considerable importance as having bilingual inscriptions— that the work must be one of special interest to Welsh scholars. It is very satisfactory to learn that it is the intention of the Rev. D. R. Thomas, late general secretary of the Association, to bring out a new and enlarged edition of his 'History of the Diocese of St. Asaph,' one of the most, if not the most important work of the kind that has yet been published in Wales. Such a work forms in itself a valuable contribution to a history of a part of Wales that at present has no recorded history. If other clergymen could be found as willing and competent as Mr. Thomas to do the same for their dioceses, a considerable step might be made towards supplying the want of county histories in Wales. Other members are not less active in adding to our stores of Celtic knowledge. Professor Rhys, in addition to the second edition of his 'Lectures,' is now engaged on a history of the Breton Celts, while the Rev. D. Silvan Evans, for some years editor of the *Archæologia Cambrensis*, is preparing a Welsh dictionary. Since the last report issued, part 5 of the Rev. Canon Williams's 'Selections from the Hengwrt MSS.' has been issued."

SEPTEMBER 8, 1880.

NOTES.

MISTRESS AND MAID IN 1714.—Looking upon *Bye-gones* as a receptacle for all kinds of information pertaining to a limited district, and of interest to any of the readers of the district, I have no hesitation in sending the following extract from the MS. Diary kept by Mrs. Savage, the daughter of Philip Henry. The lady in question resided at Wrenbury Wood, where her husband was a farmer and land agent :—

"Apr. 22, 1714. Too much disturb'd by the frow'dn'ss of a sev't, M. Ball, whom I have in many th'gs been as tender of as if a child ; yet because in a small thing I crost her will, presently runs away from me—like Hagar f'm her mistress, tho' I th'k I did not deal hardly with her—gave her no hard word, but only told her she must not th'k to trample on us all.——Afterward she came back, but seems uneasy. L'd make our way plain, for thou knowest my heart toward thee to be upright in this matter, & that it was the respect I had to her profession, least that should suffer, that made me send daut'r M. after her to speak peaceable to her.—Next morning she a little to relent, desired me to pray with her, w'h I did, as also she with me ; both of us beg'd of G. to mortify our corruptions and pardon us.——I find the difficulty of carrying it on in my p'ticular relations.—O for grace suitable."

By "her profession" of course Mrs. Savage refers to her avowed connection with a Christian Church. Mrs. S. was an excellent woman, and we have many excellent mistresses now-a-days, but such a method of dealing with a refractory servant is not the style of the present day !
PURITAN.

INTRICATE MARRIAGES. — The following scheme exhibits a most curious and unusual crosswise matrimonial alliance between the houses of Bodowyr and Myfyrion.
                                                                            T.W.H.

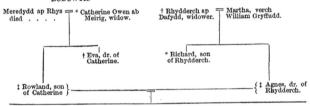

* Catherine Owen ab Meurig, widow, of the house of Bodowyr, was joined by a second marriage to Richard, son of Rhydderch ab Dafydd of Myfyrion.

† Rhydderch ap Dafydd, widower, of the house of Myfyrion, was joined by a second marriage to Eva, daughter of Catherine Owen ab Meurig of Bodowyr.

‡ Rowland, son of Catherine Owen of Bodowyr, also married Agnes, daughter of Rhydderch ap Dafydd, of Myfyrion.

Concerning this relationship, Sir Edward Trevor, of Brynkinallt [whose mother was the daughter of Richard in the above scheme, son of Catherine his mother], wrote an epitaph for the tomb of Eve, who was his grandfather's wife, thus :—

" Here lyes by name, the world's mother,
By nature my aunt, sister to my mother,
By law my grandmother, mother to my mother,
My great grandmother, mother to my grandmother,
All this may be without breach of consanguinity."

This Eve was Sir Edward Trevor's aunt, inasmuch as she was his mother's own sister ; by affinity she was his grandmother, because by a second marriage she became the wife of his grandfather, his father's father ; and she was his great grandmother, because she first married his great grandfather, Rhydderch ap Davydd. Catherine was her daughter by her first husband (Meredydd ap Rhys) ; by affinity she was his mother-in-law, since she was married to Richard Prytherch, the son in the pedigree, who was the father of the second husband. [Rhydderch ap Davydd was the father of Richard ap Rhydderch]. And thus was his step-mother and daughter-in-law, being sister by nature, and mother-in-law by affinity to Rowland Meredydd.

THE SUBJUGATION OF WALES.—The North Walians (and I confine my remarks to them) were probably not subjugated to the English even in theory, until Edward the Second was born at Carnarvon in the year 1284. It has been suggested that in April, 1884, the Prince of Wales should be invited to visit the Castle of Carnarvon, and that representatives from each county in North Wales should meet him there to celebrate the six hundredth anniversary of the birth of Edward of Carnarvon. I know not if there be at the present time constables of the border castles, which in English hands, helped to keep our ardent forefathers down, at the time when the Great Edward took possession of our country ; if not, then 1884 might be a fitting time to do honour to some of our brave men by giving them the titular lordships of those castles in a formal manner. Holt, Caergwrle, Hawarden, Ewloe, Flint, Rhuddlan, Denbigh, Ruthin, and Chirk, forming one chain in the Golden Union which · brought English and Welsh under one Royal head ; Conway, Beaumaris, Carnarvon, Criccieth, and Harlech being the other chain of fortresses Edward turned to good account ; more than a baker's dozen of them, each with a history of its own ; some erected by him, and others repaired, but all usefully employed in teaching the " wild Welshmen " how mighty and powerful a master they had in this first of their Saxon kings. Whether the noblemen and gentlemen of North Wales will take up the challenge, and prepare for the honourable reception of the Prince of Wales at Carnarvon in 1884, remains to be seen, but if some of your correspondents could be induced meanwhile to put upon record, shortly, when these castles were built; when first occupied by the English; and when they (or some of them) passed to private hands, and to whom, we might work out of the story a memorial to the Prince, which should suffice to secure the national visit suggested.
                                                    A WELSHMAN.

QUERIES.

OSWESTRY TOLL CAUSE.—I copy the following paragraph from the Oswestry Herald of Dec. 5., 1820 :—

OSWESTRY TOLL CAUSE.—We are authorized to state that the account of Mr. David Jameson, as to his receipts and disbursements in defence of this cause, has been examined and allowed by several of the principal Subscribers, an attested copy of which is left at the Town Clerk's Office, for the inspection of the public ; and that the balance is paid into the Oswestry Savings' Bank to wait the direction of the subscribers. What " Cause " was this ? With whom was the dispute and where and when was the action tried ?   TELL.

HAIL STORM AT LLANRHAIADR, 1556.— I once copied from a newspaper (which omitted to quote its authority) the following :—" Anno. 1556, 26th July, was such a tempest of rain and hail-stones in the parish of Llanrhaiadr, that the like was never seen before, bigger than tennis balls, and broke down the corn and broke the straw all to pieces, that they had no good of the corn in that year." Which Llanrhaiadr was this ? It is a likely event to be recorded in the parish registers.   TELL.

MONWENT YR EGLWYS, OR MONWENT Y CAPPEL?—In the account of the re-opening of the Llanycil Parish Church, both these terms are applied to some place situate in the town of Bala, of which it would be very desirable to have further information. In the conveyance of the property on which the old Calvinistic Methodist Chapel was built, dated 19 June, 1778, from the Rev. Simon Lloyd, Plasyndre, to Revs. Daniel Rowlands, Llangeitho; Peter Williams, Carmarthen; David Jones, Llangan; Messrs. Thomas Foulkes of Bala, mercer; John Evans of Bala, weaver,; and Humphrey Edwards of Bala, glazier, it is stated "that the said chapel was erected *on* or *nearly adjoining* the N.W. side of a certain place situate and lying in the town of Bala, commonly called Monwent y Cappel, and was certified to the Bishop of St. Asaph, and in the Ecclesiastical Court there registered as a place of worship." The present square known as Tegid Place or Square in front of the chapel, where Mr. Charles's monument is erected, must therefore have been Monwent y Cappel in olden time.

B.

REPLIES.

PHILLIPS'S *HISTORY OF SHREWSBURY*. (Feb. 18, 1880).—"W.H.SP." at the above date stated that Mr. James Bowen, Herald Painter, of Shrewsbury, was the real author of this history—or rather, we should say, compiler, for all he did was to make use of MSS Mr. William Mytton of Halston employed him to copy. "Phillips's History" was issued in 1779. It would appear that more than one member of the Bowen family was famed as a Heraldic painter, and decipherer of manuscripts, for amongst the deaths in the papers of June 1832, I read the following announcement:—"On June 19, aged 76, Mr. John Bowen, of St. Mary's Place, Shrewsbury, whose talent as a Herald painter, antiquarian, and reader of ancient MSS has been many years appreciated." This, I presume, was the son of the historian.   W.E.M.

PEARLS IN THE CONWAY (Aug. 25, 1880).—In the same book quoted by NORTH (viz., *Chambers's Miscellany*, No. 167, art. "Pearls and Pearl-Fisheries") which was published thirty years ago; there is an extract from Loudon's *Magazine of Natural History*, in which the writer says he has been informed "that a lady on the Conway nets nearly £1,000 a year by the pearls of that river, under a charter." Some of your readers may remember the law suit two years ago (see Reprint of *Bye-gones*, Apr. 3, 1878), in which Lady Willoughby d'Eresby (the owner of the Gwydir Estate, and descendant of the Wynns) claimed the exclusive right of fishing in the Conwy river. In the claim nothing was said about the Pearl Fishery. Is that a matter of the past, so that its "rights" are not worth protecting? From the tone of the article in *Chambers's Miscellany* one would be led to suppose "many of the inhabitants of that part of the country" still "obtain their livelihood entirely by their industry in procuring the pearls," or, at least, did so when the book was published. The writer in the *Miscellany* goes on thus to quote Loudon:—"When the tide is out, they go in several boats to the bar at the mouth of the river, with their sacks, and gather as many shells as they can before the return of the tide. The mussels are then put in a large kettle over a fire, to be opened, and the fish taken out singly from the shells with the fingers, and put into a tub, into which one of the fishers goes bare-footed, and stamps upon them until they are reduced into a sort of pulp. They next pour in water, to separate the fishy substance, which they call *solach*, from the more heavy

parts, consisting of sand, small pebbles, and the pearls, which settle in the bottom. After numerous washings, until the fishy part is entirely removed, the sediment, if I may so term it, is put out to dry, and each pearl separated on a large wooden platter, one at a time, with a feather; and when a sufficient quantity is obtained, they are taken to the overseer, who pays the fisher so much per ounce for them."   UNCLE.

CURRENT NOTES.

NATIONAL EISTEDDFOD OF WALES.

TRANSLATION OF THE POEMS OF GWALCHMAI (ADJUDICATION BY THE REV. D. SILVAN EVANS, B.D.)

Two competitive translations of the poems of Gwalchmai have been received, signed respectively "Meilyr" and "Ieuan Brydydd Hir." Both are productions of merit; but I consider that of Meilyr to be the best, and to him therefore is the prize awarded. If "Ieuan Brydydd Hir" were alone in the field, he might justly claim the prize.

In the earlier years of the modern Eisteddfod there frequently used to be a prize for the composition which ranked second in point of merit as well as a higher prize for the best. There is much to be said in favour of that mode of distributing literary rewards, for, among other advantages, it encouraged a greater number of competitors to enter the lists, and enabled adjudicators to acknowledge merit, though it might not be of the (comparatively) highest order. The division of prizes indicates, or ought to indicate, equality of merit, which is but seldom the case, and it often fails to satisfy either party. I think therefore that the former custom of offering second prizes, might, in many cases, well be revived.

The poems of Gwalchmai, of which twelve have come down to us, are confessedly difficult; and until we have a more trustworthy text than we have to work upon, no translation of many passages can be much more than tentative. These poems, as is well known, were printed for the first time in the "Myvyrian Archaiology of Wales" in the beginning of the present century. Like the other poems contained in the first volume of that collection, they were not printed from the best and oldest manuscripts; no classification of codices seems to have been attempted; and the variants are apparently given according to no system. The so-called second edition, which appeared a few years ago, and is the only one accessible to most students of the present day, is much less trustworthy than the first, being anything but a faithful reprint of it. Such being the case, the difficulties that meet a translator of these and similar mediæval poems cannot easily be overrated; and what makes these difficulties still greater is the fact that the language of these poets is very intricate, and highly artificial, and many of the rules of prose construction are not unfrequently set at nought.

I hail it as a promising sign that the Eisteddfod has made a literal prose translation of the Poems of Gwalchmai the subject of a prize. This is undoubtedly a step in the right direction; and I cannot but express a hope that the poems now clothed in an English dress may be the beginning of a long series of bardic translations produced under the influence of our National Institution. We can now conveniently dispense with particular ebullitions of self-laudation, and apply ourselves in sober earnestness to the cause which we profess to have at heart. It is greatly to be desired that the Eisteddfod should year after year offer a prize, and that of some value, for the best translation into English of one or another of our middle-age poets, so that ultimately we may possess a version of the whole corpus poeticum of the period to which they belong. The Eisteddfod should have a higher mission than being simply a holiday amusement; and these gatherings need not be in the least less attractive to the thousands that attend them because they produce solid and lasting work. The useful and the sweet may in this as well as in hundreds of other instances, be successfully combined.

If Meilyr will look over his translation, supply additional notes, where such notes are required, and append a Glossary of Uncommon Words, which he appears to have prepared, as well as the Index of Proper Names which he has subjoined, the work might advantageously be sent to press.

(Signed) D. Silvan Evans.

[A prize of £10 and silver medal had been offered by the Eisteddfod Committee for the best translation. "Meilyr" appeared in the person of Mr. Llywarch O. Reynolds, Merthyr Tydfil, son of the well-known Welsh bard, Nathan Dyfed.—Ed. O. A.]

RE-OPENING OF HORDLEY CHURCH.

This old church, which has been closed for over twelve months, was re-opened on September 2, after a complete restoration. Some time ago it was apparent that the fabric was far from safe, and would before long fall if something was not done to it. The restoration is a very complete one, carried out from plans by Mr. W. McCarthy (the architect who was employed at Criftins), and comprises a new roof and bell turret, the munificent gift of Lord Brownlow (the timber of the roof is particularly fine), a new porch, a new window pierced through the west end, which makes the church considerably lighter; and the whole of the east end has been re-built, with a new window placed in it. A nice vestry, also new, completes the external restoration, except two buttresses to strengthen the north wall. Inside the improvement is great, and those who knew the old church well, with its curious arrangements and fittings, will be most agreeably surprised at the alterations for the better. The removal of the ceiling, the new windows east and west, the handsome alabaster reredos, thrown out by dark hangings on each side, the lowering of the pulpit, the new tiling of the sanctuary, all combine to give an air of worship and reverence to the church. There was an afternoon service at three, at which most of the ladies and gentlemen of the neighbourhood were present. The Rector, the Rev. J. W. Moore, read prayers, the Rev. R. K. Haslehurst, Rural Dean, read the first lesson, and the Rev. Loftus Owen the second. The sermon was preached by the Rev. W. C. E. Kynaston of Hardwick. The following clergy were also present in their surplices: Rev. W. E. Belson, Rev. F. P. Wilkinson, Rev. O. M. Feilden, and Rev. G. G. Monck, and others were in the body of the church. The collection at the close of the service amounted to £38 11s. 10d. After service tea was provided for all at the Rectory in a large tent; about 150 sat down. The second evensong was at 6 p.m.; the church was not so crowded as at the first, for, owing to the beautiful weather, everyone was busy in the harvest field. The sermon was preached by the Rev. G. G. Monck, Vicar of Welshampton, and the collection amounted to £2 12s. 3d., making a total of over £40, which will go a long way to clear off the debt of about £50 that was still owing for the restoration. The music of the services was entirely done by local voices, and very creditably done too, Mrs. Kynaston presiding at the harmonium. The decorations, which showed a good deal of taste and skill, were done by Miss Dodd, Miss Cureton, and Mr. Williams, gardener at Hardwick.

WHITCHURCH ART EXHIBITION.

The Whitchurch Art Exhibition was opened Sept. 7th by the Countess Brownlow. The high quality and interesting character of the exhibition bear testimony to the admirable skill and taste, as well as industry, with which the promoters of it have performed their arduous enterprise, and it only remains for the public to do their part, in order to ensure its being brought to a successful issue. The idea of organizing an exhibition of this kind originated with the Committee of the Whitchurch Young Men's Institute, and the idea was no sooner conceived than a plan was sketched out for its execution. The objects sought to be attained were two-fold, first, to promote the love of art in the town and district, and secondly, to benefit the funds of the Institute. The owners of the principal private collections of pictures and other art treasures in the district were communicated with, for the purpose of ascertaining whether they would be willing to lend them for exhibition, and the consent of several of them having been obtained, it was resolved to carry out the project. A general committee was accordingly formed, consisting of the members of the Institute Committee, together with a number of active and influential men who were likely to give effective help in carrying out the details of the scheme. The Rector of Whitchurch, the Rev. W. H. Egerton, was appointed Chairman of the Committee, and the following gentlemen consented to act as honorary secretaries—Major Lee, and Messrs. R. Pearson, H. H. Etches, and T. T. Chubb. Several Visits of inspection were paid to the treasure-houses of art in the neighbourhood, and a basis of operations having thus been established, various sub-divisions of the committee were formed, and special duties were assigned to each. Amongst these duties was that of selecting pictures for exhibition. Upon what was called the Arrangement Committee devolved the important function of setting out all the articles sent for exhibition (except the pictures), and making various arrangements, including those of the refreshment department. The duty assigned to the Receiving Committee was that of attending to the receipt and delivery of all the things sent for exhibition, and of giving receipts to the owners. This, of course, entailed a large amount of correspondence and other work. The task of hanging the pictures was entirely performed by the Hanging Committee, and although their function was not quite so invidious as that of the Hanging Committee at Burlington House, it was sufficiently delicate and difficult. The General Committee very wisely resolved from the first to adopt a strict policy of prudence and economy. They were extremely anxious that the Exhibition should succeed financially, in order to be able to give practical proof that it is possible to organize art exhibitions in country towns without losing money by them, and because they felt that a balance on the wrong side would have the effect of discouraging similar efforts in other places. They therefore courageously determined to do all the work themselves without calling in any professional aid. The Committee decided at the outset not to give any special guarantee to the owners of articles contributed, and they also succeeded in obtaining the consent of the owners to send them at their own cost of carriage, to and from the Exhibition. The generous terms upon which the contributions have been made deserve, therefore, the heartiest acknowledgment. We may add that a guarantee fund was formed in order to meet a possible deficiency; but all chance of any call being made upon the guaranrs has been precluded by the large sale which has taken place of 'untransferable' season tickets, issued at a large of five shillings each for the whole period of the exhibition. In order to afford the most ample facilities or people of every class to visit the Exhibition, the Committee decided to keep it open from ten o'clock in the morning till ten at night, except upon the first day, when it was opened at half past twelve and closed at seven o'clock.

The Committee were fortunate in having placed at their disposal a building so suitable for a purpose of this kind, as the New Town Hall, of Whitchurch. The Assembly Room, in which the greater part of the collection was arranged, is an apartment of handsome and convenient proportions, and, what is of the first importance in an exhibition of pictures, is well lighted. The Hanging Committee have done their work so well that but very few of the pictures suffer from being seen in a bad light, and upon entering the room the visitor is at once struck with the effective manner in which the whole collection is arranged. Besides the many noble and beautiful pictures which adorn the walls, the room contains a display of art treasures, antiquities, and curiosities of an exceedingly varied and interesting character. Conspicuous among them are the contributions which have been made upon very liberal terms by the authorities of the South Kensington Museum, and which add a good deal to the attractions of the Exhibition.

Of oil paintings there are 184 entries in the catalogue. Of these, as might be expected, by far the greater number (138) are productions of the English School of painters. The rest are divided into two sections, one Italian, Spanish, and French, and the other German, Flemish, and Dutch.

In a brief reference to the principal pictures we will take the works of the English school first. Of Sir Joshua Reynolds, whom Mr. Ruskin declares to be not only the greatest of English painters, but "than whom there is, indeed, no greater among those of any nation or any time," there are several examples. A portrait of Mrs. Massey of Rosthern, contributed by Mr. C. H. Poole, is ascribed to Sir Joshua apparently upon uncertain grounds. The other pictures by Reynolds are a portrait of Dr. Myddleton Massey, belonging to Mr. T. H. Sandford, a portrait of Joseph Baretti (seated, reading a book, which he holds close to his face), the painter's well known portrait of himself from Sir Watkin's collection, "A Child and Lamb," also from Wynnstay, and a portrait of Sir John Larpent, contributed by the Rev. W. E. Belson. Sir Peter Lely is represented by three portraits, one of William Farmor, Baron Lempster, sent by Admiral Cotton, another a graceful "Portrait of a Lady," sent by Mr. J. F. Lowe, and the third, a large portrait, with a face and figure expressive of calm dignity, of Admiral Sheffield, who commanded the fleet sent out against the Spanish Armada, and was raised by Queen Elizabeth to the peerage under the title of Earl Mulgrave. Two portraits by Sir Godfrey Kneller are exhibited by Lord Combermere, a third by Mr. T. H. Sandford, and a fourth by Dr. Groom. A small portrait of Dr. Johnson in his old age by John Opie has been sent by the Hon. and Rev. W. T. Kenyon, one of the rectors of Malpas. A portrait of Admiral Byng, ascribed to Gainsborough, is contributed by Mrs. Atkinson. Of the works of another great English portrait painter, George Romney, there are several noteworthy examples. A portrait of Lady Hamilton, which seems to do but scant justice to the charms of that famous beauty, is ascribed to Romney, but is probably not by that painter. The picture belongs to Sir E. A. Hamilton. A pair of Romneys sent by Admiral Cotton are portraits of Mr. and Mrs. Henry Calveley Cotton;

there are also portraits by Romney of Lady Margaret Hanmer, and Mary, Lady Kenyon, and a very fine portrait of Lord Chief Justice Kenyon in his judicial robes, exhibited by Lord Kenyon's trustees, who have also sent a painting by Sir Thomas Lawrence of this distinguished lawyer and his wife, and another portrait by Hoppner of Lady Kenyon. The only other portraits in the collection by Hoppner (who, in his day, was one of a trio of fashionable portrait painters, Lawrence and Opie being the other two) are from Wynnstay. One is a portrait of Lady Williams Wynn, daughter of the Right Honourable Sir George Grenville, and second wife of Sir Watkin Williams Wynn, fourth Baronet. This lady, who was a sister of the Marquess of Buckingham, died in 1832. She was described as a "beautiful and accomplished woman, twice painted by Sir Joshua." The other is a striking portrait of the Right Honourable Charles Williams Wynn, the distinguished father of the late member for Montgomeryshire and present Recorder of Oswestry. Mr. R. Gill exhibits a portrait by Lawrence of Lady Elizabeth Whitbread. There is but one Hogarth in the exhibition, and that is from Wynnstay, "A Musical Party." Mr. P. W. Godsal contributes three pictures by Francis Wheatley, Mr. J. J. Beckett fourteen pictures by modern English artists, Mr. T. Betton Gwynn, nine pictures (three of Highland scenery) by McInnis, and Mr. James Joyce, five pictures by different painters. Viscount Hill sends a picture by the late President of the Royal Academy, Sir Francis Grant, and a hunting group, of which the late Lord Hill is the most conspicuous figure ; and Sir E. A. Hamilton a portrait by a former president, Benjamin West, of Mrs. Macnamara. Among Sir W. M. Honyman's contributions are a portrait of Lord Braefield by Sir H. Raeburn (1786—1823), and a portrait of an ancestor, Andrew Honyman, Bishop of Orkney, and of Archbishop Sharpe, by unknown artists. The Rev. H. B. Finch exhibits amongst other pictures, Mr. J. Bridge's portrait of the late Dr. Selwyn. In the collection are to be found five animal pictures by a local artist, Mr. E. Lloyd, of Ellesmere. Two of these, "Terriers and Rabbit," and "Pony and Spaniel," are exhibited by Mr. J. Bateman, and the other three, "Welsh ponies and Scotch terrier," "Cat and rabbit," and "Brood mare and foals" by Lord Hanmer. The works of a well-known artist, Mr. R. Caldecott, whose "John Gilpin," "The House that Jack Built," Goldsmith's "Mad Dog," and other picture books have afforded so much delight to children of all ages, and who, until recently, lived at Whitchurch, are also represented. The humorous picture of "Three Ravens on a Tree,"— three ancient birds seated in solemn deliberation upon some affair of State, which was exhibited at the Royal Academy in 1876, is contributed by Mr. Pope, Q.C. An engraving of this picture has been chosen to adorn the cover of the catalogue. Three works of the same artist are exhibited by Mr. H. Beck, another by Mr. C. H. Mitchell, and another by Mr. H. H. Etches. A beautiful picture by Clarkson Stanfield, of "The Church of Santa Maria at Venice," with the Dogana in the foreground, is contributed by Mr. S. H. Sandbach. Mr. A. P. Heywood Lonsdale sends portraits in chalks of two of his children by Mr. J. Sant, R.A. It would have been rather strange if Sir Edwin Landseer had been left out of such a collection of pictures by English artists, and he is represented by three pictures. One of these, "A Terrier and Cat," sent by Sir P. de M. G. Egerton, derives its chief interest from the fact that it was painted when the artist was only sixteen years of age. The other two are among the fruits of his fully matured genius. One of them is the charming "Titania," from the "Midsummer's Night Dream," and is from Earl Brownlow's

5

16

Ashridge collection. The picture will be, no doubt, familiar to many of our readers from the engraving in which it is so admirably reproduced. The scene is that in which the gentle Queen of the Fairies, with amorous glances, invites the "translated" weaver to

Come sit thee down upon this flowery bed,
While I thy amiable cheeks do coy,
And stick musk roses in thy sleek smooth head,
And kiss thy fair large ears, my gentle joy.

The exquisite painting of the white rabbit is one of the most charming features of the work. The other picture by Landseer will, no doubt, be the most popular work in the Exhibition. It is the great picture called "Saved," which was dedicated by the artist to the Royal Humane Society, and belongs to Mr. John Naylor, Leighton. The subject is a half-drowned child brought to shore by a magnificent Newfoundland dog. Never was a grander dog painted even by "the Shakespeare of the world of dogs," and the expression of his upturned face is almost more rather than less than human. Among the contributors of pictures of the English school, whose names we have not already given, are the Rev. W. H. Egerton, Mr. James Joyce, Rev. J. Morrall, Mrs. Churton, Mr. J. Brown, Mr. J. Beckett, Mr. W. L. Brookes (a portrait of Matthew Henry, by an unknown artist), Mr. W. B. Etches, Mrs. J. Lee, Rev. J. Peake, Major Cust, Mr. P. W. Godsal, and Mr. T. H. Briscoe. There are about thirty paintings by masters of the Italian, Spanish, and French schools. Four Canalettos are exhibited by the Rev. W. H. Egerton, Viscount Combermere, and (two by) Mrs. Heywood, respectively. There are two Claudes, one "An Italian Port," from Wynnstay, and another, a landscape, by Lord Kenyon's trustees. Mr. P. W. Godsal exhibits a fine Zuccarelli and a "Madonna and child" by Sasso Ferrato. This last-named picture is remarkable not only for the beautiful faces of the mother and the sleeping infant, but also for the perfect manner in which the rich colouring is preserved, although the picture was in all probability painted more than two centuries ago. Two works of Gaspar Poussin's—1613—1675—"Boys plaiting Rushes" and a landscape are contributed by the Rev. W. H. Egerton, and the Rev. John Morrall; one of Nicholas Poussin's, 1594—1665, by Sir Watkin. The two Poussins were Italian painters of French extraction. They were only related by marriage. Mrs. Heywood sends a Salvator Rosa, "Italian Peasants"; and Sir Philip Egerton a pair of heads of old men by Guido, one of which is called a "Head of St. Paul" and the other a "Head of St. Peter." Among the other exhibitors in this department are Mrs. Atkinson (who sends seven pictures) Mr. T. H. Sandford and Mr. James Joyce. Seven sketches by Old Masters, formerly belonging to the Wynn collection, exhibited by Mr. Stanley Leighton, M.P., are included in this part of the catalogue, although they are exhibited in one of the lower rooms. Of the fifteen pictures by German, Flemish, and Dutch artists, there are two Teniers, sent by Mr. P. W. Godsal, and but one Rubens—and that not a very characteristic work—"Stag Hunt in a Wood," from the Wynnstay Collection. There is but one Cuyp, a "Child and Lamb," by Mrs. Heywood. Sir Watkin sends a beautiful Dutch River Scene by Van Goyen; Major Cust contributes a Cathedral Interior in Holland, by Berkhuyden, and other pictures are contributed by Mr. E. Tudman, Mr. T. Powell, Mr. Joseph Beckett, Sir Edward Hamilton, and the Rev. W. H. Egerton.

We have dwelt so long on the paintings, that we have left but little space to describe the other varied objects of interest in which the Exhibition abounds. Among the statuary and carvings is the ivory figure of an Highlander, given by Charles Edward Stuart to Mrs. Legh of Addington, and exhibited by Sir W. M. Honyman. In the department of Oriental and other curiosities a number of Indian, Japanese, and Chinese articles are exhibited; among them an Indian fan in gold and enamel, which belonged to Tippoo Sahib, and a carved tortoiseshell fan given to the wife of Sir C. Hamilton in 1820, and exhibited by Sir E. Hamilton. In the collection of old deeds, manuscripts, &c., are some interesting relics of Philip and Matthew Henry whose names are so intimately associated with the neighbourhood of Whitchurch. Mr. B. L. Vawdrey exhibits a day book kept successively by Philip and Matthew Henry; original letters of Philip Henry, his wife Katharine, his son, Matthew Henry, and his daughters. Matthew Henry's preaching bands, and a diary of Matthew Henry's for 1705, of nine belonging to Miss Parsons of Redbrook. The writing in these documents is remarkable for its extreme regularity and clearness. Diaries kept by Philip Henry are also contributed by Mrs. Lee, senior. A deed with the Mayoralty Seal of the City of London, dated 1464, and a Bull of Pope Innocent II., are exhibited by Mr. Vawdrey. Viscount Combermere sends the remains of an original deed of grant of Combermere Abbey by Henry VIII. to Sir G. Cotton, and Mr. R. T. Smith a curious map of Whitchurch, dated 1761. In the collection of armour, &c., Sir E. Hamilton exhibits a sword of honour presented to the late Sir E. Hamilton, to commemorate the capture of the Hermione, 1779. Mr. Vawdrey sends a dress sword of the Baron of Kinderton's of the date of about the end of the 16th century, and Sir W. M. Honyman, Mameluke's sword, taken in action in Egypt by Colonel Robert Honyman, aide-de-camp to Sir R. Abercrombie, whose life he saved in 1701. In the collection of embroidery, the Rector of Steeple Aston, the Rev. J. S. Brookes, exhibits an altar cloth and part of a cope of the 14th century. There is a very interesting collection under the head of plate and miscellaneous articles. An old brass alms dish, with a quaint treatment of the subject of Eve's Temptation, is contributed by Mr. T. L. M. Vernon. Mr. Vawdrey has a number of specimens of Samian ware and other Roman pottery, found chiefly at Kinderton, near Middlewich (believed by many to be the Roman station of Condate). Collections of Roman and English coins and tokens are exhibited by Mr. Vawdrey, Major Cust, Mr. T. R. Jones, Mr. R. T. Smith, and others. Lord Combermere exhibits the tusk of an elephant, weighing 113 lbs., killed at Rampore, and brought to England by the late Viscount Combermere in 1836. Lord A. Paget exhibits the uniform worn by the Marquis of Anglesey at Waterloo, and a gold cup, knife, spoon, and fork, presented to his lordship by Her Majesty the Queen. The cup bears the following inscription:—"To Alexander Victor Paget, from his godmother, Queen Victoria, 5th Oct., 1839." Mr. J. M. Wood shows an enamelled gold watch which belonged to Edmund Burke, and pendant heart-shaped ornaments set with six miniatures of the Stuart family. Dr. W. Copeman, a snuff box in gold and enamel, presented by the Empress Catherine of Russia to Mr. A. Young, the agriculturist. The Rev. J. H. Brookes, a ring with portrait of Napoleon I., given by him to his Minister, Fouché, and by Fouché to Captain Christie, grandfather of Mrs. J. H. Brookes, the present owner of the ring, and bracelets found on a skeleton at Steeple Aston. Mr. T. H. Sandford has a beautiful collection of miniature portraits, and Col. R. F. Hill exhibits a number of Chinese and Japanese curiosities. The collection of objects lent by the South Kensington Museum include the following :—

Pottery.—Italian, French, German, Russian, and English. 16th to 19th Century.

Glass and Enamels. — French, Spanish, Austrian, Venetian, Bohemian, and English. 17th to 19th Century.

Textile Fabrics.—Greek, Turkish, Persian, French, and English. 17th to 19th Century.

Electrotype re-productions.—From various private and public collections.

FRAMED EXAMPLES.

Lace.—Specimens of Spanish, French, Belgian, and Flemish. 17th and 18th Centuries. (Six frames.)

Coloured Photographs.—Enamels, Crystals, Pottery, &c., from various collections. (Twenty frames.)

Coloured Photographs of Fans.—From the Fan Exhibition, S. K. Museum. (Six frames.)

Illustrations of Works produced by Students in connection with the Science and Art Department. (Twenty-five frames.)

In the collection of china and other ware, amongst the articles deserving especial notice is a very handsome large china bowl lent by Mrs. Soper ; a cabinet of Sèvres china, consisting of two large vases and covers, two smaller ones, a centre vase and plates, which once belonged to the Empress Josephine, the set being lent by the Viscount Combermere. Some old Derby china pieces, lent by Major Starkey, should not be passed unnoticed ; two Belleville china jars, lent by Mr. R. P. Ethelstone, are of peculiar value and note ; a blue jug of the time of George I., lent by Mr. T. M. L. Vernon. An ornamented china howl, exhibited by the Hon. E. Kenyon, is one of the best pieces of china in the exhibition. A Dresden cup, cover, and saucer, of the Marsoline period (1796) is very good, and is also contributed by Mr. Kenyon. A prettily-flowered plate—"girls shrimping," lent by the Hon. and Rev. W. T. Kenyon. Among the contributions of Sir E. Hamilton are a Berlin china box, with groups of figures. A Sevres jug and dish for rosewater ; an old Delft octagon bowl, a flower bowl and cover (No. 73), Minton, Dresden style, some oriental china dishes, with raised surface, and a Chinese round dish with open border. Mr. B. L. Vawdrey lent a considerable number of articles in this collection, including an old blue-and-white Delft cup, dated 1650, and bearing the legend, "Be merry and wise," an old blue-and-white Delft puzzle jug of about the same period, an old blue-and-white Nankin dish, a genuine Indian Porcelain dish, a vase of Derby china, with blue-and-gold ornaments, an old stoneware grey jug, with ornaments and inscription of about 1691, another jug with figure of William III. ; a bottle jug, blue ground and raised grey rosettes, of about the same period ; and a quart cup, blue and grey, with scroll work and ornaments in relief of the same period. The same gentleman lent a finger glass and three wine glasses, which formed part of a set made for the Corporation of Liverpool, when they entertained the then Prince of Wales, afterwards George III. Mr. J. M. Wood lent a quantity of Ratisbon China, consisting of jars with covers and "beakers." The central ornament of the room consisted of a large vase and stand belonging to Mr. Kent. It is surrounded by Parian figures belonging to the Rev. W. H. Egerton and Mr. W. W. Brookes. The stand also bears two very choice pieces of old Chelsea pottery. Dr. W. Copeman's cups and saucers (104) with blue dragon-looking ornaments, clouded on white ground, are considered very good specimens. The same gentleman also lent an old China scollop-shell dish, a raised open-work cup in the centre, with flowers and figures ; and a delft two-handled quart cup with blue and red ornaments on a white ground. Mr.

Wilding Jones contributed a considerable number of articles, including two beautiful old Majolica jars, with snake handles (124), and two large Japanese dishes, with blue and white ground (128). A pair of hand-painted plates by Regnier are deserving of attention ; the subjects are crab and pear blossoms. The same gentleman lent a flower pot with birds and flowers ; a very handsome pair of large scent jars and covers, with butterflies and baskets of flowers on a white ground ; and a pair of very scarce old blue and white willow pattern plates. Mr. C. W. Dod lent two very curious delft bottles with the Dod arms upon blue and white ground. A set of Wedgwood, belonging to the Hon. E. Kenyon, deserve notice. Mr. Joyce lent a remarkable oriental bowl.

In the corridors and lower rooms of the building are exhibited an exceedingly good collection of water colours, engravings, and photographs. The largest contributors of water colour drawings are Mr. James Joyce, Mr. Wilding Jones, and the Rev. J. Lee, who exhibits four admirable pictures by Mrs. Lee ; a drawing of the Welsh bridge at Shrewsbury by P. Sandby, and a view of Aberystwyth by E. Bolton. A picture of the Madonna enthroned, a copy we presume of some old master, was painted by Lady Marian Alford. In the collection of engravings in the Local Board room are some fine old engravings, contributed by the rector of Whitchurch ; original drawings for the *Graphic* by R. Caldecott, and original pen and ink sketches for *Punch* by Du Maurier.

SEPTEMBER 15, 1880.

NOTES.

LOCAL "NOTES AND QUERIES."—Newspapers all over the country during the past few years have been publishing local columns of notes of Antiquarian and Historical interest. In Wales and the Border Counties we have had the following :—

1—"Bye-Gones," *Oswestry Advertizer*—1871
2—"Past Days," *Wrexham Guardian*—1873
3—"Shreds and Patches," *Shrewsbury Journal*—1874
4—"Montgomeryshire Mems," *Newtown Express*—1874
5—"Cambrian Remembrancer," *Carnarvon Herald*—1877
6—"Cheshire Sheaf," *Chester Courant*—1878
7—"Local Gleanings," *Shrewsbury Chronicle*—1879
8—"Welsh Antiquities," *Cambrian News*—1880.

Of these nos. 1, 3, and 6, are reprinted in quarterly parts ; and nos. 2, 4, 5, and 7, are either suspended or given up. Those that are reprinted bear on their title pages suitable mottoes ; thus on—

BYE-GONES.

"MRS HARDCASTLE.—Ay, *your* times were fine times, indeed. . . . I hate such old-fashioned trumpery.

"MR. HARDCASTLE.—And I love it. I love everything that's old: old friends, old times, old manners, old books, old wine. . . ." *She Stoops to Conquer*, Act 1, Sc. 1.

SALOPIAN SHREDS AND PATCHES.

"A snapper-up of unconsidered trifles."
Winter's Tale, Act 4, Sc. 2.

CHESHIRE SHEAF.

"O, let me teach you how to knit again
This scatter'd corn into one mutual sheaf !"
Titus Andronicus, Act 5, Sc. 3, 1. 70.

It is to be hoped that where these columns are not reprinted there may be found amongst their readers those who cut them out and mount them in Scrap Books. Such collections will one day be valuable. JARCO.

A YANKEE AUTHOR IN WALES.—Nathaniel Hawthorne the American writer, who became American Consul at Liverpool in 1853, has several references to the Principality in his *Note Book*. Like other Yankees when in the Old Country he seems to have found everything on.

a scale so small as to be almost contemptible. He does not appear to have been so inquisitive as many of his countrymen, and was almost as superficial in his observations as the distinguished foreigner at Mrs. Leo Hunter's *fête champêtre*. In July, 1854, he took a little tour in North Wales with Mr. Bright. He says :—

At Bangor we went to a handsome hotel, and hired a carriage and two horses for some Welsh place, the name of which I forget ; neither can I remember a single name of the places through which we posted that day, nor could I spell them if I heard them pronounced, nor pronounce them if I saw them spelt. It was a circuit of about forty miles, bringing us to Conway at last. I remember a great Slate-quarry ; and also that many of the cottages, in the first part of our drive, were built of blocks of slate. The mountains were very bold, thrusting themselves up abruptly in peaks,—not of the dumpling formation, which is somewhat too prevalent among the New England mountains. At one point we saw Snowdon with its bifold summit. We also visited the smaller [sic] waterfall (this is a translation of an unpronounceable Welsh name), which is the largest in Wales. It was a very beautiful rapid, and the guide book considers it equal in sublimity to Niagara. Likewise there were one or two lakes which the guide book greatly admired, but which to me, who remembered a hundred sheets of blue water in New England, seemed nothing more than sullen and dreary puddles, with bare banks, and wholly destitute of beauty. I think they were nowhere more than a hundred yards across.

The translation of "Rhaiadr y Wenol" into the "smaller waterfall" is amusing, but what will the thousands of tourists who every year admire Llyn Ogwen and Llyn Gwynant say to the New England notion of them? Further on Mr. Hawthorne says :—

At some unutterable village we went into a little church, where we saw an old stone image of a warrior, lying on his back, with his hands clasped. It was the natural son (if I remember rightly) of David, Prince of Wales, and was doubtless the better part of a thousand years old. There was likewise a stone coffin of still greater age ; some person of rank and renown had mouldered to dust within it, but it was now open and empty. Also, there were monumental brasses on the walls, engraved with portraits of a gentleman and lady in the costumes of Elizabeth's time. Also, on one of the pews, a brass record of some persons who slept in the vault beneath ; so that, every Sunday, the survivors and descendants kneel and worship directly over their dead ancestors. In the churchyard, on a flat tombstone, there was the representation of a harp. I supposed that it must be the resting-place of a bard ; but the inscription was in memory of a merchant, and a skilful manufacturer of harps.

By "some unutterable village" Mr. Hawthorne means Llanrwst, and before he leaves it he calls the place "a very delightful town," though he does not tell us in what he delighted. On another occasion he visits Rhyl, which he finds entirely "destitute of attraction," and where "life seems to pass away heavily." The English, he thinks, "do not have a turn for amusing themselves ;" and on Sunday he sets out for a walk "not well knowing whither." He reaches Rhuddlan :—

I plodded on, and by-and-by entered an antiquated village, on one side of which the Castle stood. This Welsh village is much like the English villages, with narrow streets and mean houses or cottages, built in blocks, and here and there a larger house standing alone ; everything far more compact than in our rural villages, and with no grassy street-margin nor trees ; aged and dirty also, with dirty children staring at the passenger, and an undue supply of mean inns ; most, or many of the men in breeches, and some of the women, especially the older ones, in black beaver hats. The streets were paved with round pebbles, and looked squallid and dirty. . . . . On the bridge stood a good many idle Welshmen, leaning over the parapet, and looking at some small vessels that had come up the river from the sea. The author evidently forgot when he spotted the lazy Welshmen that it was Sunday, but one would have thought the children would have been polished up on the day when all go to "Hermon," "Zoar," and "Bethesda," as the women evidently had done if they sported their tall hats. G.G.

LONDON MISSIONARY SOCIETY. — The *Salopian Journal* of Dec. 2, 1795, contained the following announcement :—

We are requested to inform the publick, that a Missionary Society, consisting of various denominations of Christians, is established in London, for the important purpose of spreading the Christian Religion in Heathen and other unenlightened nations.—A handsome collection was made yesterday at Mr. Lucas's chapel, on Swan Hill, for the benefit of this institution. —Those who are disposed to encourage the design, are requested to deposit their contributions with the printers of this paper, the printer of the *Shrewsbury Chronicle*, the Rev. Mr. Whitridge, Oswestry ; the Rev. Mr. Wilson, Drayton ; or the Rev. Mr. Edwards, Wem ; at which places collections have already been made.

Mr. Whitridge, referred to in the foregoing, was one of the originators of the Society, riding up to London on horseback to attend its first meeting. And he seems to have acted as general secretary for the Society in Shropshire. I have before me a memorandum book he kept at this date, and in it I find the sums subscribed in the county during the early years of the Society's existence. The following is an extract :—

			£	s.	d.
1795.	Dec. 1.	Received at Mr. Lucas's Chapel	18	7	7¾
		Corrie and Craig	8	8	0
		Mr. John Mitchell	2	2	0
		„ Joseph Gittins	2	2	0
		„ Joseph Parry	5	5	0
	1796. Feb. 2.	Of Mr. Lucas, by the hands of Miss Edwards	2	8	6
		Drayton and Wollerton Collection	19	5	6
		A Friend, by Mrs. Corbett	1	1	0
		Ellesmere : Mr. Langford	2	2	0
		Whitchurch : Presbyterian Congregation ; Rev. Mr. Jenkins	1	19	6
		Wem : Collection, sent by Mr. Edwards	„	„	„
		John Henshaw, Esq.	20	0	0
		Oswestry Collection	13	17	6½
		Llanfyllin Collection	1	4	6
	Apr. 11.	Sarney, Montgomeryshire, Rev. Mr. Richards' Congregation	10	6	
		Welsh Pool, Rev. Mr. Francis's	4	11	0
		Mrs. Corbett, Shawbury Park	2	2	0
		Rev. Mr. Wilson, Drayton	1	1	0

In all Mr. Whitridge acknowledges £125 1s. 2¼d. as the subscriptions of 1795-6. His expenses to London, and amount paid in postages (an important item in those days) amounted to £5 18s. 3d.   J.?.R.

QUERIES.

THE GOAT OF THE 23RD.—How did the custom of having a goat to march at the head of this regiment originate? I see by a note in the *Cambrian Journal* for 1855 (page 252), that the regiment was formed in 1688. Was it previously one of local militia, who had already adopted the custom of having a goat to accompany them? Paris.   H. GAIDOZ.

QUEEN'S HEAD CLUB.—Can any old Oswestry reader tell us anything about a club so called that once existed in the town ? I have recently accidentally seen a printed label connected with it, worded as follows :—

QUEEN'S HEAD CLUB.
BRING in your hand a social Friend,
And then with wit and mirth we'll spend
This joyous night, and drown all care ;
No churlish sot admitted here.
Mr. —— Master.

The label is 3 in. by 2 in. and has a blank left for the name of the "Master," who, I presume, was an elected chief. In the label (or card) I have seen the name "Owen" is written in. It is evidently of considerable age.   JARCO.

GOLDEN CUP AT MOSTYN HALL.—"E.M." writing to the *Bath Chronicle* in May 1828, says that when visiting Mrs. Piozzi in 1816, she told him "that in the family of Mostyn, in Denbighshire, with whom she was connected, she had frequently seen a Golden Cup, the history of which was then repeated to her by the present possessor. King Henry the Seventh, when Duke of Richmond, and on his way to fight Richard the Third at Bosworth, stopped for a day at Mostyn Hall, and at leaving told Lady Mostyn that should he be victorious, as he hoped to be, he would, when the battle was over, send her his sword by a special messenger, whom he should despatch from the field. He won the day, and sent the sword, as promised ; and for ages it hung in the armoury at Mostyn, but a good old lady of the family at length observing that the hilt was of pure gold, and that it was a pity metal of such value should be neglected, had the handle melted down, and converted into a caudle cup : the blade was lost !" Does this story appear anywhere else ? I don't think Mr. Heyward refers to it any where in his *Autobiography, Letters and Literary Remains of* Mrs. Thrale.　　　　　　　　　　　　　　　G.G.

REPLIES.

CHURCH BELLS (Dec. 24, 1879).—On one of the bells at Baschurch is the following inscription, in old black-letter form :—"+Maria . iaer . ous . veren . mcccc . ende. xlvii . ian . van . ven . ioe," which, being an ancient Welsh inscription, would, in more modern language, read thus :—"Maria iar oes merin [1400] ende [47] iaw van ven ioe." In English :—"When cut off from life, we become dead earth ; the soul departs, and proceeds through the air to eternal glory." It is probable this bell once belonged to Valle Crucis Abbey, or some other Welsh monastic establishment. *(Joseph Morris's MSS.)*　　　　W.A.L. (In *Shreds and Patches.*)

CAPTAIN BRAMWELL OF OSWESTRY (Sep. 1, 1880).—I remember this singular character very well. He lived in a house at the top of the passage in Beatrice. street leading to Vaughan's Timber Yard. The late Mr. James Vaughan had not long built Claremont House now occupied by Mr. Cottam. One day Mr. Vaughan and his family were startled by the report of firearms, and break. age of glass, and on going up stairs found that a window had been smashed by a ball, which had then pierced a door between two rooms, and lodged above a bed in which lay one of their children ! It transpired that Mrs. Bramwell having died that day, her husband fired over her dead body as a mark of honour to her memory ! The bullet passed through an open window in his house overlooking the tim. ber yard. He was eventually taken to an Asylum, from which a few years ago it was rumoured, he had escaped. Who he was I never heard. He had two or three children of whom he was very fond ; and I have often, when a boy, met him going along the street with them, loaded with toys. The bullet mark in the door remains to this day for all I know.　　　　　　　　　　　　　　　N.W.S.

CURRENT NOTES.

APPARITIONS AT LLANTHONY.

Father Ignatius has written to a Hereford paper respect-ing certain alleged apparitions at Llanthony. He says this monastery was founded ten years ago in order to afford the Church of England a house where men might conse-crate their lives altogether to God in prayer, praise, and labour. Two very important ideas and intentions have attached themselves to this monastery—one being to offer reparation to our Lord Jesus Christ for the insults he has received in our Church and country since the Reformation, in the holy sacrament, from the men who declare that it is not his body, whereas He himself declares "This is my body." The letter proceeds :—The events to be recorded took place during the time of adoration before the blessed sacrament. One person kneels in silent devotion for an hour before the shrine, after which another person takes his place. On August 30, while the senior brother was before the shrine, all at once on looking up he saw distinctly the silver monstrance appear out-side the thick doors of the tabernacle. [The mon-strance is the vessel in which the host is held at Benediction.] A schoolmistress from Hay saw the same apparition, neither person being of an imaginative turn of mind. The same evening four boys were playing in the recreation grounds after vespers when one came running up to Father Ignatius, saying, "Dear father, we have just seen such a beautiful spirit in Abbot's meadow." He replied, "Oh, nonsense," and resumed what he was about, when other boys came and confirmed the statement, saying they had seen the figure of a woman dressed in white alb, hands both raised, and from head to foot was a dazzling white light, oval shaped, shining round the body. The apparition moved through the meadow. A boy named Foord, frightened, caught up a stick and said he would strike it if it came near him. The figure and light, how-ever, entered the hedge and remained standing in it. The boys afterwards on strict cross-examination stuck to the same details, one saying he believed he saw the blessed Virgin Mary. Father Ignatius adds, "These are extra-ordinary but absolute facts. That the two apparitions occurred the same day seems most marvellous, as though God intended us to corroborate the other." Letters cor-roborative of this statement are also published in the same paper, containing extracts from the letters of the senior and another brother, and extracts from a boy's letter.

𝔏amentable 𝔇eath of the 𝔥eir to 𝔚ynnstay.

News of the death by drowning of Mr. EDWARD WATKIN WILLIAMS WYNN of Cefn, St. Asaph, heir to the baronetcy and estates of Wynnstay, has excited wide-spread regret. Mr. WILLIAMS WYNN, who was a lieutenant in the Scots Guards, was shooting a weir, in a canoe, on the Thames near Windsor, last Wednesday, Sept. 8th, when his frail craft was upset, and he almost immediately lost his life. He had performed the feat once, and was attempting to repeat it, against the advice of another officer, who had been upset but struggled safely to land, when the accident occurred. Assistance was out of the question, and half-an-hour afterwards his dead body was recovered from the river. On Saturday it was removed, with every demonstra-tion of respect from his com rades, who liked him well, to the residence of his bereaved mother, with whom the deepest sympathy will be felt ; and on Monday the re-mains were interred with those of his father in the family vault at Cefn. The heir to Wynnstay is now Mr. HERBERT LLOYD WATKIN, Mrs. WILLIAMS WYNN's second son. This is the second great sorrow which has suddenly befallen that lady, for her husband, Col. WILLIAMS WYNN, was killed in June, 1862, only seven years after his marriage, by falling from his horse close to his own resi-dence. A similar accident befell his great grandfather, the first Sir WATKIN, in 1749.

SEPTEMBER 22, 1880.

NOTES.

JOHN WILLIAMS, HARPER.—"Died, Sep. 20, 1832, after a short illness, brought on by a severe cold and over anxiety at the Eisteddfod, Mr. John Williams, Harper at the Cross Keys Inn, Oswestry; the successful candidate for the Silver Harp at Beaumaris Eisteddfod; which was presented to him by their Royal Highnesses the Duchess of Kent and Princess Victoria.—*Salopian Journal.*" As far back as Nov. 22, 1871, I put a query in *Bye-gones* relative to this Oswestry Harper, and

in reply was informed that at the time of the Beaumaris Eisteddfod he resided at the Ball, near Oswestry, but that he afterwards for many years resided at the Golden Lion, in Oswestry. The foregoing extract from the newspaper of 1832 will show that the "reply" of ten years ago was an error; the writer being evidently mistaken in the man. JARCO.

THE PEDIGREE OF SIR EDWARD TREVOR. The following table of the Pedigree of Sir Edward Trevor is taken from the Add. MSS. 14,909, in the British Museum. It differs in form and extent, &c., from the one given in the scheme headed "Intricate Marriages," on Sep. 8.   T.W.H.

THE PEDIGREE OF SR. EDWARD TREVOR, KNIGHT.

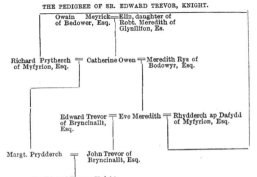

The above said Eve Meredith's Epitaph, by Sir Edward Trevor :—

Here lies by name the world's Mother,
By nature my Aunt, sister to my Mother;
My Grandmother, mother to my Father;
My great Grandmother, mother to my Grandfather;
My Grandfather's daughter, and his Mother,
All which by the antient Laws might be
Without ye breach of consanguinity.

TOMEN-Y-MUR.—Being at Festiniog last week I could do no less than walk over to Tomen-y-Mûr. I found the resident farmer there to possess but very little English, and our communications were therefore Very short and imperfect. I went with him round the camp and up the mound, and was very much interested. At the N. W. corner of the mound or tumulus (is *tomen* a corruption of the word tumulus?) he showed me on the top of the wall a stone about two feet long and about eight inches thick having three sides not very irregular, yet not sufficiently regular to be regarded as artificially wrought, on two sides of which were transverse marks or scratchings, the cause of which I could not determine exactly. They were either (1) striæ, i.e. glacier marks, (2) runic letters, or (3) incised marks made by a very careless mason intending to record something. The stone was granite, and had been dug up, I apprehend lately, in the adjoining ground, and placed on the top of the wall by the tenant. The conclusion I have come to is, that the stone needs examination by a more competent person than

myself, and if the first hypothesis be correct it is still of some interest; if either of the two others, we have there a national monument. If the Roman roads in Wales were carefully traced, I believe we should arrive at very important conclusions. I cannot think that the present race of Cambro-Britons inhabited the country at that time. There seems to have been a chain of fortresses and communications made, not so much to dominate a conquered people as to guard against invasion from the sea. I may be wrong, but I like to support strange theories because controversy elicits light.   BOILEAU.

QUERIES.

THE PORCUPINE YOUTH. — An Oswestry paragraph in the *Salopian Journal* of Feb. 24, 1841, was as follows :—"That living curiosity, described in the bills as 'the Welsh Porcupine Youth,' is at present being exhibited at Oswestry. His lively conversation and interesting features contrast strongly with the horny excrescences with which his limbs and other parts of his body are covered, and render him at once an object of great attraction and sympathy." Do any of your readers remember this youth? Some account of his history would be interesting.   TAFFY.

CHIRK CASTLE.—In the year 1781 there was published in London a small duodecimo volume entitled *A Gentleman's Tour through Monmouthshire and Wales*, and upon page 179 it is thus written : "We now ascended the long narrow ridge of a mountain, which soon

rought us within sight of Chirk Castle. The ancient
utward walls and towers of this Castle still remain, but the
ourt or quadrangle has at different times been made habit-
ble ; the apartments range all around it, and the principal
uite of rooms are grand, and handsomely fitted up in the
modern fashion." On page 246 of the same volume Lord
Lyttleton says : "Our last visit in Wales was to Chirk
Castle ; it was destroyed in the Civil Wars, and hath been
ebuilt ; it is a bad imitation of an old castle, the most
isagreeable dwelling-house I ever saw ; nor is there any
magnificence to make amends for the want of convenience ;
he rooms are large indeed in one part, but much too low ;
nd the ceilings are so heavy with clumsy fretwork that
hey seem ready to fall upon one's head." Which of these
ecounts is the true one? In some respects the castle un-
oubtedly is "a bad imitation of an old castle ;" that is
o say, outwardly, but is it a mere imitation? I have
eard it said by those who pretended at least to under-
tand such matters, that it is a restoration of that which
ad preceded it. Roger Mortimer has the credit of being
ts first builder in the thirteenth century, and looking at
he Castle from the Glyn Valley, I myself was struck with
ts grandeur, for the situation did for it naturally far more
han art could do for Carnarvon Castle for instance, and
pon a closer examination of it, I rather incline to the
estoration doctrine than I do to Lord Lyttleton's dictum
n relation to it. What say the learned pundits who make
hese questions a study? The spot upon which the Castle
tands, the Castle itself, the great people who have occu-
ied it, are each and all historical, and I may venture
herefore to hope that some of your learned readers, who
an do so, will try and resolve the doubts above mentioned.
                                                     KEVAN.

ST. MARTIN'S BIRD,—What bird is the Bird of
St. Martin, and why is it called by the saint's name? Is
here any mediæval legend on the subject? MINAFON.

WELSHMEN IN DORSETSHIRE.—I have read
omewhere of a colony of Welshmen settling in Dorsetshire
,bout the middle of the seventeenth century. Will some
ne kindly tell me the county in Wales whence they came,
,nd why they migrated thither; also, if any list of the
names of the families exists.   TINY TIM.
[In Notes and Queries.]

REPLIES.

JONES'S HISTORY OF BRECKNOCKSHIRE
Sep. 1, 1880).—This history was published at £7 19s. 6d.
The author gave up his practice (that of a solicitor) to
vrite, devoted much time to it, but lost £400 in cash in
ringing it out. There is a short biography of the author
n Beauties of England and Wales (South Wales Division)
y Rev. Thomas Ross. I am not aware of anyone claim-
ng the copyright. Some twenty years ago a dealer in
Brecon purchased the surplus copies of Vol. II., and the
opperplates from I. Booth,—the London publisher, the
ormer at 5s. per vol., and the latter for their value as old
netal. The writer secured some of the plates. A copy
f the work in good library condition is seldom to be met
vith under £8, which is a fair price for it.   F.S.A.
  Brecon.

OWAIN GLYNDWR AT MACHYNLLETH
May 5, 1880).—In June, 1838 (I believe the month to be
:orrect), workmen were employed in improving and en-
arging the "Eagles" Hotel in the town. The contractor
vas Mr. John Peters of Rhiwgreuddyn. When digging
'or a foundation for the extension of the house, garden-
vards, or for a new cellar, the earth suddenly gave way
ind John Peters, who was with his men, and another man,
suddenly fell into a hole with a quantity of earth running

upon them, entombing them. The workmen, after extri-
cating the two men, found out that the place was a well-
formed underground room, or cellar of considerable size,
previously unknown to anyone, and which contained much
ashes, the remains of a fire apparently. It was at once
decided to be the remains of Owain Glyndwr's occupation
of the town, and a dungeon used by him as a prison.
There was no tradition existing that I could learn about
Glyndwr's connection with the town beyond holding a
parliament there, the old parliament house being near the
top of Maengwyn-street. This room would scarcely
partake of the nature of a "dungeon" where the old
chieftains were said to be wont to imprison malcontents.
It would be more in accordance with presumable facts
to say that the place in question was the remains of the
Roman station, or town of Maglona. The site also abuts
on the part of the town called "The Garsiwn," which
evidently has a fraction of Roman in the word. When
the occurrence here referred to took place I was myself at
the time within thirty or forty yards of the spot, and being
acquainted with John Peters, I often spoke to him of his
escape from being killed. I am unable to account for the
circumstance of the report your correspondent quoted
stating that the discovery was made at Col. Edwards's of
Greenfields. There were no alterations going on there at
the time, so far as I remember.   T. W. H.

WELL AT WOOLSTON. (Aug. 11, 1880.)—In
the Liber Ecclesiasticus (London, 1835) are given, besides
the place of this name in Alberbury, Salop, Wollaston in
Northamptonshire, Wollastone and Woolstone in Gloucestershire, Woolstone in Bucks, Wolstan in Warwickshire,
and Wolstanton in Staffordshire. There are also Much
Woolton in Lancashire, Wollaton in Notts, Wolterton in
Norfolk, and Wolley in Somersetshire, Woolley in Hunts,
and Yorkshire, besides Wool and Woolland in Dorset,
Woolavington in Somerset, Woolavington and Woolbeding
in Sussex, Wooler in Northumberland, Woolborough, and
Woolfardisworthy (2) in Devon, Woolhampton in Berks,
Woolhope in Hereford, Woolpit in Suffolk, Woolstaston
in Salop, and Woolsthorpe in Lincolnshire. The close
resemblance of these names would seem to point to one
common original for them all, and, unless there be good
conceivable grounds for ascribing them to a Saxon
derivative, of the existence of which I am unaware,
unless it be in the name of St. Wulstan, then,
if a Celtic one can be proved for any one of the number,
that they all originated in the same will be no unreasonable
hypothesis. Now, there is no doubt that the parish
Church of St. Woollos at Newport, Monmouthshire, is so
named from St. Gundleus, in Welsh Gwynllyw, of which
Woollos is a corruption, although the fact of its origin is
lost to the inhabitants themselves. Gwynllyw Filwr is
given by Rees in Appendix III to the Essay on the
Welsh Saints, p. 344, as the Patron Saint of "Newport,
alias St. Woolos." He was a chieftain, or petty regulus
of the territory called after him Gwynllywawg, and Gwyn-
llwg, in English corruptly written Wentloog, which he
inherited from his father Glywys ab Tegid ab Cadell,
from whom the district, of which Newport became the
principal town, has been also termed Glywyseg. According to the Genealogies of Gwladus, a daughter of King
Brychan, of Brycheiniog, and the father of 7 sons, all of
them Saints, among them St. Catwg (Cadoc) the Wise,
some of whose writings are extant, and Hywgu, the father
of St. Beuno, the celebrated spiritual director of St.
Winifrede. In the Lives of the Cambro-British Saints,
published by the Welsh MSS. Society in 1853, there is one
of this Saint, and another of his son St. Cadoc. The
former is there described as having commenced life as a
lawless warrior ; but being

reformed by the exhortations of his son, he committed the government to S. Cadoc, and retired to a desolate spot, considered by the late eminent antiquary, Mr. Wakeman, to have been "certainly St. Woollos," where he passed the rest of his days in retirement as a hermit, an example which was imitated by his queen in a place at some little distance from her husband. It is sufficiently probable that churches should have been dedicated to him elsewhere, as well as at Newport, some of which, under Saxon rule, would have changed their patron Saints, together with their names; while others, falling into decay, would, in process of time, leave nothing behind them but the name attached now to the locality, and often incorporated with another.   H.W.L.

CURRENT NOTES.

The Art Exhibition at Whitchurch, we are glad to say, was successful. It is estimated that over 7,000 visits were paid to it, and that something like £100 will be handed over to the Young Men's Institute.

Since the visit of the Archæological Society to Pembroke, two tumuli, in the neighbourhood of Brownslade have been opened. In the centre of the first a cistvaen was discovered containing the remains of a body, an almost round hard stone, with a small cavity in its side, and a flat stone, which was unfortunately broken by a pick, and which is said to represent a rude cross in a rough circle. Two bronze rings were also discovered in this tumulus. The second one, near the sea, contained the remains of a body in a sitting posture, under a heavy slab, above which were found the remains of a jar of rude pottery, and a quantity of burnt human and animal bones.

The LORD CHIEF BARON whose death is recorded, was engaged as counsel in several famous peerage cases. In 1853 he obtained a decision in the House of Lords to set aside a clause of forfeiture and let in Lord ALFORD (in whose right Earl BROWNLOW succeeded) to the Bridgewater estates. The decision regulated the right to £60,000 or £70,000 a year, and in obtaining it Sir FITZROY KELLY induced Lord LYNDHURST, Lord BROUGHAM, Lord TRURO, and Lord ST. LEONARD'S to reverse the decision of the Vice Chancellor (Lord CRANWORTH) and to disregard the opinions of a large number of the Common Law Judges. The great law-suit which decided claims to the earldom of SHREWSBURY and TALBOT, and estates of the value of £40,000 or £50,000 a year, was also won, it is believed, mainly through Sir FITZROY'S assiduity and ability, for the Protestant claimant.

DAVID COX'S SIGNBOARD AT BETTWS-Y-COED.

At Bangor district Court of Bankruptcy on Wednesday, the Judge (Mr. Horatio Lloyd), gave judgment in a case of considerable interest, viz., the ownership of the celebrated signboard painted by the late David Cox for the Royal Oak Hotel, Bettws-y-Coed. His Honour said— "This is an application by Lady Willoughby d'Eresby, the owner of the Royal Oak Hotel at Bettws-y-coed, for an order upon the trustees of the debtor's estate to deliver up to her a picture called 'The Signboard of the Royal Oak Hotel,' which was painted by the late David Cox, R.A. The trustees claim this signboard as having been in the possession, order, and disposition of the debtor within the meaning of the 15th section of the Bankruptcy Act, 1869. Lady Willoughby, on the other hand, claims it on the several grounds that it was originally painted for the inheritance; that it was a 'fixture' at the time of the bankruptcy, and that by reason of its history any infer-

ence as to reputed ownership is rebutted. Very voluminous affidavits have been filed, and the facts to be gathered from them and from the oral evidence are shortly these. In 1847, David Cox, who had been for many years a visitor at the Royal Oak, painted the sign in question upon a board, which had been to that time the signboard of the house, and which was fixed to the outside wall by means of iron holdfasts driven into the brickwork. At the time the sign was painted, in 1847, a Mr. Edward Roberts was the tenant of the house, his tenancy being from year to year. He was succeeded in the tenancy by his son, Robert Roberts, and in 1861 a lease for twenty-one years was granted to him. He died in 1863; his widow remained in the house, married a Mr. Rae, and subsequently Mr. Richards, and the latter in 1871 surrendered the lease then existing, and received a new lease for 58 years. He shortly afterwards died, and his widow, Mrs. Richards, held the house until she assigned her interest in it to the debtor, Miss Thomas, in 1876. Miss Thomas filed her petition in 1879. During all this period the signboard remained on the premises. It was fastened to the outside wall of the house from the time it was painted, in 1847, until the year 1866, having been retouched in 1849 by David Cox, who mounted a ladder for the purpose. In the year 1866, at the suggestion of some eminent artists then staying at the hotel, the signboard was brought inside the house for protection from the weather, and it remained for a short time in one of the sitting rooms. It was then placed in the hall of the hotel, having been framed by the tenant, and was then screwed to a wooden plug let into the wall, and in that position it has remained for the last 14 years. I entertain no doubt that David Cox painted the signboard for the house, and that his intention was that it should remain as the signboard of the hotel. I incline to think that, as it was placed, and having regard to all the circumstances, it was a 'fixture,' and as such not a 'chattel' within the meaning of the order and disposition clause. But I rest my judgment mainly on the ground that the notoriety of the article, and the general knowledge of its history as the signboard of the hotel, absolutely exclude all legitimate ground for supposing that there could be any reputation of ownership in Miss Thomas as the person having the actual possession." After referring to legal authorities upon the question, His Honour continued: "I am of opinion that the circumstances of the history of this signboard, known to all interested parties, were such as to lead to the conclusion that it belonged to the house, and not to the debtor or to any tenant for the time being of the house. It is idle to suppose that any credit was given to the debtor upon the faith of this particular article being her property. She was possessed of a large and valuable stock and furniture, and this was doubtless the security upon which her creditors relied. I confess that it is difficult for me to imagine that any tradesman dealing with her, and having any knowledge of the house, could be ignorant of the fact that this picture was notoriously the signboard of the house, the history of which was well known to every frequenter of the district. I find the circumstances to be such as to exclude the possibility of any reputation of ownership in the tenant, and I must therefore hold that the order and disposition clause does not apply. It is on this ground only that the trustees rest their claim, and as Mrs. Richards in her evidence says that she relinquished any claim she might have to Lady Willoughby, I make the order as prayed, that the trustees do deliver the sign to the present applicant."—In allowing the costs of the application to be paid out of the estate, His Honour stated that he should only allow two-thirds of the costs of the voluminous affidavits which had been filed.

EISTEDDFOD REFORM.—FORMATION OF A
NATIONAL EISTEDDFOD SOCIETY.

At a meeting of the Cymmrodorion Section of the National Eisteddfod held at Carnarvon last month, papers were read on "Eisteddfod Reform" by Mr. Hugh Owen and Mrs. Thomas, St. Ann's Vicarage, Llandegai, and after a long discussion, in which some of the leading supporters of the Eisteddfod took part, the following resolutions were unanimously adopted :—

1. That a "National Eisteddfod Association" be forthwith established.

2. That the following gentlemen (with power to add to their number) be invited to act, in conjunction with the Cymmrodorion Society, as a Provisional Committee, which shall consider and define the scope and functions of the Association :—Clwydfardd, Dewi Wyn o Essyllt, Hwfa'Môn, Ceiriog, Gwalchmai, Ioan Arfon, Llew Llwyfo, Dafydd Morganwg, Gianmor, Iolo Trefaldwyn, Gwilym Alltwen, Nathan Dyfed, Owain Alaw, Myfyr, Cynfaen, Alaw Ddu, Mr. D. Jenkins, Mr. Emlyn Evans, Eos Morlais, Idris Vychan, Glan Menai, Mr. B. G. Evans, Mr. C. W''kins, Rev. E. T. Davies, Mr. Owen Parry, Mr. W. R. Frimston, Mr. D. C. Davies.

3. That the Committee shall meet at the Raven Hotel, Shrewsbury, at 10 a.m. on Friday, the 17th Sept.

4. That Mr. T. Marchant Williams be requested to act as Secretary (pro tem.) of the Committee.

A meeting of the Committee was accordingly held at the Raven Hotel, Shrewsbury, on Friday. Mr. J. H. Puleston, M.P., presided, and amongst those present were Professor Rhys, Mr. Lewis Morris, Mr. Hugh Owen, the Rev. J. Eiddon Jones, Iolo Trefaledwyn, Clwydfardd, Mr. Stephen Evans, Mr. Askew Roberts, Mr. T. Marchant Williams, honorary secretary (pro tem.), Mr. Howel Thomas, Mr. W. E. Davies, Mr. W. St. John H. Hancock, Mr. Owen Morgan, Mr. J. Ceiriog Hughes, the Rev. Evan Jones, Rev. J. Williams (Glanmor), &c.

The CHAIRMAN, in opening the proceedings, said he was present for two reasons, first, because he was in sympathy with the object which that meeting had been convened to promote; and secondly because several gentlemen had represented to him that his humble presence there might contribute in some degree to the usefulness of that gathering. (Hear, hear.) He would now call upon the Secretary to read the minutes of the meeting held at Carnarvon.

The SECRETARY then read the minutes, and also a number of letters of apology for non-attendance, and nearly all expressing sympathy with the movement. Mr. W. Cornwallis West wrote to say he regretted very much that he should be in Scotland on the 17th, or he would gladly have attended the preliminary meeting of what he soon hoped to learn had become a "National Eisteddfod Association." The proposal to publish in a volume the poems and prize essays was an excellent one, and would enable the public to judge of the literary talent of Welshmen. He would also suggest that any musical compositions deemed worthy of a prize at one eisteddfod should be played at the next. Would it be impossible to get up an Eisteddfod orchestra? Surely in all Wales forty or fifty excellent instrumentalists could be got together to interpret those original compositions; and this would give a variety to the evening concerts which they now lacked. He would also suggest that the evening concerts should be simply musical performances and nothing else; no president, no conductor (except the leader of the orchestra), and no speeches. As to the fine arts, unless they could attract first-rate Welsh artists, like Lewin Thomas and others, it was useless offering a prize for an historical picture in oils. No one could paint such a picture who was not in the foremost rank of artists. The prizes should be limited to drawings in pencil, chalk, and water colour, and he would limit the

competition to natives of Wales under 20. In conclusion, Mr. Cornwallis West said he wished them every success in their efforts to raise these national meetings into something worthy of the age.—Mr. D. C. Davies's son wrote to say that his father was in Norway, on mining business, and deeply regretted that he was unable to be present.—Letters were also read from Mr. Brinley Richards, Mr. John Thomas, Hwfa Môn, London, Dafydd Morganwg, Hirwaun, Y Thesbiad, Beriah Gwynfe Evans (Welsh novelist), Llangadock, Idris Vychan, Joseph Edwards, sculptor, London, Owain Alaw, Chester, Eos Morlais, Gwilym Alltwen, and Alaw Ddu.

A discussion then took place as to the name by which the new association should be called, and the functions it should perform. The title of "The Society of the National Eisteddfod"="Cymdeithas yr Eisteddfod Genedlaethol," was agreed upon, and its functions were defined to be such as would aid, counsel, and advise the promoters of Eisteddfodau, and, in course of time to strive to be the Eisteddfod itself. The subscription of membership was fixed at half-a-guinea per annum.

The CHAIRMAN then read the following extract from a speech made by Mr. Hugh Owen at a meeting of the Cymmrodorion Society in March last, in which he gave the outline of a scheme for forming a permanent Council in connection with the Eisteddfod :—

The following are some of the matters which will engage the attention of the Council :—(a) Raising by means of annual subscriptions and donations an eisteddfod fund that shall enable the Council to offer prizes for competition, and in other ways to promote the usefulness of the eisteddfod. It is believed that contributions to the extent of at least £1,000 a year may be obtained towards this fund. (b) Securing the holding of only one National Eisteddfod in each year, in North and South Wales alternately, and selecting the place at which it shall be held, as well as stipulating the conditions to be attached to the selection. It is hoped that in deference to the desire of the general public (llais y wlad) upon the subject, the local eisteddfodau will cease to assume the title of "national," when the proposed association is formed and in active operation. (c) Assist in providing a suitable pavilion in which to hold the eisteddfod in places where the accommodation does not exist. It may be found practicable to provide a movable pavilion for the purpose, and thereby reduce the expense which has usually attended the erection of the eisteddfod pavilion. (d) Assist in selecting appropriate subjects for competition, and in determining the sum to be awarded in each case. The council will recommend the reduction, to some extent, of the number of prizes, and the increase of their value; whereby the quality of the competitors will be raised, and the importance of the competition enhanced. They will endeavour to widen the range of subjects for competition, by embracing to a greater extent than has yet been attempted works of art, the productions of the manufacturer and the handicraftsman. (e) The council will discourage the acceptance of prizes offered by individuals, where the subjects in respect of which they are offered are unsuitable for the National Eisteddfod, or where the conditions attached to them are objectionable. (f) They will assist in securing men of eminence to preside at the eisteddfod meetings, and in selecting well-qualified persons to act as adjudicators. (g) They will assist in preparing the eisteddfod programme. The experience which they will acquire will enable them so to arrange the programme as to economise time and obviate the inconvenient length of the morning sittings. These might with great advantage be limited to three hours instead of four hours and a half. (h) They will uphold the gorsedd, with its mystic rites and high claims to veneration, and will gladly encourage any efforts that may be made to secure for the gorsedd degrees the weight and value which a proper examination of the candidates alone can give them. A proposal having this object in view has lately been prepared by Mr. Dan Rhys, the very able secretary of the forthcoming Carnarvon National Eisteddfod, and is now under the consideration of some of our chief bards. (i) The curtailment of the morning sittings, as suggested, will render it practicable to devote some time at an earlier hour for the reading and discussion of papers bearing on the condition of the people as regards health, food, dwellings, occupations, earnings, thrift, morals, and education, as well as on other questions of public interest. The attempt to do this was made by the Cymmrodorion section of the eisteddfod at the Birkenhead National Eisteddfod, but failed from the want of a suitable opportunity to carry out the object. *(j)* The council will publish a volume of the eisteddfod transactions annually, which will contain, among other matters, the chief prize essays, poems, and musical compositions of the year. A copy of the volume will be presented to every subscriber or donor of the requisite amount. *(k)* It will be the endeavour of the council to assist in making the eisteddfod the upholder of public virtue, as well as the promoter of excellency in literature, poetry, music, art, manufacture and handicraft. It will be their endeavour also to assist in excluding from the eisteddfod proceedings whatever may be deemed low, vulgar, or in bad taste ; as this highest court of the nation ought to be characterised in all its aspects by propriety, decorum, and even dignity, while its decisions ought to be marked by soundness of judgment and the strictest impartiality.

Mr. HUGH OWEN proposed that Sir Watkin Williams Wynn, Bart., be elected President of the Society. Mr. Owen said that Sir Watkin, the Prince in Wales, was held in the highest possible respect by all classes in the Principality, and he did not know anyone whom it would be more fitting to elect as their President. (Cheers.)

The motion was carried unanimously, amidst cheers.

The CHAIRMAN said he had no doubt the worthy baronet would be very much gratified with the deservedly kind way in which his name had been mentioned, and the hearty unanimity with which he had been elected President of the Society.

Mr. LEWIS MORRIS proposed, and Mr. ASKEW ROBERTS seconded, that the Vice-Presidents be nominated by the Council at their next meeting.

This was carried, and it was also agreed, on the motion of Mr. HUGH OWEN, that Mr. J. H. Puleston, M.P., and Mr. Cornwallis West, and all the Welsh peers, bishops, and members of Welsh constituencies, be invited to become Vice-Presidents of the Society.

On the motion of Mr. HUGH OWEN it was also agreed that the members of the Council should not exceed fifty in number, due regard being had to the proportionate representation of North and South Wales.

Mr. STEPHEN EVANS proposed that every chaired bard in Wales should be an ex officio member of the Council.

Mr. LEWIS MORRIS seconded the motion.

The CHAIRMAN said he thought that suggestion an extremely good one.

Mr. HUGH OWEN said that they had distinguished bards, men of great literary ability, who might render them very great assistance, but who were not chaired bards.

Mr. STEPHEN EVANS pointed out that such bards might be elected members of the Council.

Mr. HUGH OWEN proposed that Mr. Stephen Evans be appointed treasurer of the Society.

Mr. STEPHEN EVANS declined the honour. He said that as their worthy chairman was a banker, he begged to propose that Mr. J. H. Puleston, M.P., be appointed treasurer.

GLANMOR seconded the motion which was carried unanimously.

It was agreed that the gentlemen nominated at Carnarvon, with others, be appointed members of the Council.

Mr. HUGH OWEN then proposed that Mr. Lewis Morris be elected chairman of the Council. He said that the high place Mr. Morris held as a poet in the estimation of the English and Welsh public, and the fact of his being a Welshman, and thoroughly in sympathy with the Welsh national feeling and all the interests of the Principality, rendered it peculiarly fitting that he should occupy that position. (Cheers.)

The CHAIRMAN said he did not think there could be two opinions about that.

Mr. LEWIS MORRIS—I am sure there will be two opinions.

The CHAIRMAN having declared the motion carried unanimously,

Mr. LEWIS MORRIS said he appreciated highly and deeply the great honour done him, but when his friend Mr. Hugh Owen mentioned the fact that he was going to propose him, he at once said that he must positively and absolutely decline the honour. He was the more moved to that by the definition of the object of the Society, as not that of assisting in developing, but as the development and carrying out the purposes of the National Eisteddfod. He thought it was essential that anyone who accepted the chairmanship of a council of an association like that, should not be merely Welsh by birth, Welsh in sympathies, and Welsh in heart, but that he should also be a Welshman in language. He could not imagine a more ridiculous, he might say a more scandalous position, for a man who did not speak Welsh to occupy.

Mr. HUGH OWEN said he was very anxious to press the appointment of Mr. Lewis Morris as chairman of their Council. He was quite sure it would meet with universal approval, and that there was not a bard in Wales who would not recognize the appointment to that post of the author of the "Epic of Hades" as the most appropriate that could be made. In order to remove any difficulty Mr. Morris might feel in reference to the Welsh language, he would suggest that they should appoint a practical man who spoke that language as vice-chairman.

The CHAIRMAN—Professor Rhys suggests that we should appoint as vice-chairman a man who cannot speak English. (Laughter.)

Mr. CEIRIOG HUGHES also expressed his hope that Mr. Lewis Morris would re-consider his refusal to accept the post. He thought the appointment would do something to modify the feeling of clannishness which was supposed by English people to characterise the Eisteddfod.

Mr. Lewis Morris ultimately consented, amidst cheers, to accept the office for twelvemonths.

On the motion of Professor RHYS, seconded by Mr. HOWEL THOMAS, the following gentlemen were appointed to act as an Executive Committee until the next general meeting:—Messrs. Hugh Owen, Lewis Morris, Ceiriog Hughes, Askew Roberts, the Rev. Eiddon Jones, Clwydfardd, Dewi Wyn o Essyllt, Alltwen, with Mr. T. Marchant Williams as secretary pro. tem. It was agreed that this Committee should select names for the Council.

CURRENT NOTES.

Sir Watkin Williams Wynn has sent to the Ecclesiastical Art Exhibition in connection with the Leicester Conference two Missals printed in Paris in 1501 and 1503.

We hear that Professor John Rhys of Jesus College, Oxford, will bring out for the delegates of the Clarendon Press a revised edition of the "Mabinogion," with an English translation, a glossary, and a literary introduction.

The Menai Society of Natural Science recently paid a visit to Gloddaeth and Llandudno. At Gloddaeth they were sumptuously entertained by Lady Augusta and Mr. Ll. Mostyn, and after going over the house they descended the subterranean caverns, some of which they believed were excavated for mines, while others were of natural formation. They afterwards proceeded to a cave in the Orme's Head, where prehistoric remains have been discovered. The Rev. R. Parry (Gwalchmai) rendered the party valuable assistance by his local and antiquarian knowledge.

NOTES.

A WELSH EPIGRAM.—Six Things that dry rapidly :—

Chwech peth sy'n sychu chwippyn :
Carreg noeth a genau meddwyn,
Cawod Ebrill, tap heb gwrw,
Pwll yr hâf, a dagrau'r widw.

The following is a literal translation :—

Six things soon lapse to drowth :
A naked stone, a drunkard's mouth,
An April shower, tap without beer,
A summer pool, a widow's tear.

CWM CYNON.

OLIVER THOMAS.—The following extract from Wood's *Athenæ Oxonienses*, vol. 1, p. 860, may be of interest, as it relates to a person who did much for Wales, and of whom little is known :—

July 8. OLIVER THOMAS of Hart Hall.—The time when he took the degree of Bach. of Arts appears not, nor when or of what House he was matriculated. And therefore all I can say of him is, that he was afterwards, perhaps now, beneficed in Shropshire ; that he wrote and published a book in Welsh entitled *Carwr y Cymru* &c. Printed 1630 or thereabouts ; and that dying at Felton in that county* was there buried. In the year 1647, one Oliver Thomas of Oswestry did subscribe among other ministers of Shropshire to the lawfulness of the Covenant ; who, I suppose, is the same with the former.

There is no mention of Oliver Thomas in Browne Willis's *Survey of St. Asaph*, amongst the clergy of Oswestry, or its neighbouring parishes lying in that diocese. His name does appear amongst the twenty-five ministers named as "approvers of public preachers" in the Act for the Better Propagation of the Gospel in Wales, &c. 1649-50, "Thomas Baker, Esq., of Swiny" being, I believe, one of the Commissioners for putting in execution the powers of the Act. Oliver Thomas in his book *Carwr y Cymru* tells a pitiful tale of the character, fitness, and ability for their high calling, he having gained his knowledge of the Welsh Clergy when acting as "Approver."

CYFFIN.

* The following note is added after this passage :—" So I have been informed by Dr. Mich. Roberts, some time Principal of Jesus Coll : his contemporary."

[In the list of Shropshire Ministers signing the Testimony to the Solemn League and Covenant in 1647, the name of Oliver Thomas does not appear. See *Bye-gones* p. 185, Series 1876-7.—ED.]

QUERIES.

THE HARLECH EXHALATIONS.—Most of the Guide Books mention the mysterious fires on the Coast at Harlech in 1693-4, and some of them attribute the phenomenon to the exhalations caused by the dead bodies of locusts. I have just met with the following account, which I never saw before :—

LOCUSTS.—In the year 1747-8, England, with France, and many other countries of Europe, were visited by these insects ; but here they did little mischief, as the natural coldness of the climate soon put a period to their existence. But in the year 1693, two vast flights of locusts were observed in the counties of Merioneth and Pembroke, in Wales, where they made considerable depredation among the young wheat.—*Encycl. Edin.*

Perhaps some reader may be able to say how far the swarm of locusts affected Wales in 1747-8, and what form the visitation of them took in Pembroke in 1693 ?

G. G.

DANIEL JONES OF RHUABON.—The following is a copy of the title page of a book printed in Oswestry in 1790 :—

Cynnulliad Barddorion, i Gantorion : Sef Carolau, Cerddi ac Englynion. Gan DANIEL JONES.

Cynnulliad synniad y senedd—y Beirdd
S' au bwrdd ym mrô Gwynedd :
Canwyd, lluniwyd y llynedd,
'N odiaethol gan wyr doethedd.

SALM CXXXIX. 4. "Nid oes air ar fy nhafod, ond wele ARGLWYDD, ti a'i gwyddost oll."

CROESOSWALLT : Argraphwyd ac ar Werth gan J. SALTER. M,DCC,XC. Pris Swllt yn rhydd, neu Ddeunaw yn rhwym.

In the Introduction, which is signed "Daniel Jones, o blwyf Rhuabon," the author, or rather compiler, explains his reasons for publishing, and he asks those who would sing the songs and carols in the book, not to do so in the company of drunkards, or those who curse and swear. He pleads the want of an early education as an excuse for any imperfections of language, but hopes his more scholarly readers may find something to admire in his book. He acknowledges the services of those who kindly assisted him, and grieves that the book was not issued earlier, and explains that the delay had been caused by a dispute with the printer in the middle of the work, otherwise it would have been published at the time promised.

The book extends to 156 small octavo pages. How far Mr. Daniel Jones was an author as well as compiler cannot be inferred. Several of the pieces have no name attached to them : others have names at the end. These include Jonathan Hughes, Thomas Edwards, Dafydd Tomas, William Jones, and Phillip Humphrey. One by Jonathan Hughes is thus headed :—

Ystyriaeth ynghylch yr arwyddion a'r damweiniau hynod a ddigwyddodd yn yr Oes bresennol ; y Tymhorau anhwylus, a'r diweddar Gynhauaf yn y flwyddyn 1782 ; i'w chanu ar y mesur a elwir "Susannah."

There is also another by Jonathan Hughes, bearing the following title :—

Cerdd ar fesur a elwir "Gorweddwch eich hun." Darfoddigaeth goffadwriaeth am *Mr. Edward Lloyd*, gwr o Ial, a fu farw yn *Nwyrain India*.

One to which no signature is attached, is entitled

Cerdd berthynnasawl i *Richard Middleton*, Esq., Castell y Waun, yn swydd Dinbych, i'w chanu ar fesur a elwir "Breuddwyd y Frenhines."

The only piece with which the compiler's name is connected is one headed :—

Cerdd o ddiolchgarwch tros *Daniel Jones* i *Trevor Lloyd*, Esq., Trevor, am ei aml groeso mae ef yn ei gael ganddo, i'w chanu a'r y mesur a elwir "Belisle March."

This, it will be observed, is not claimed as Jones's own composition. Another "Cerdd" has, at the end of it, "*Jonathan Hughes* a'i gwnaeth, dros *Richard Barkley*, Gôf, o Landdoged."

There are thirty-one pieces (mostly carols) in the book, of which only eleven are signed. Were the rest by Daniel Jones? Is anything known of the men whose compositions are quoted?

JARCO.

REPLIES.

YSTWYLL, YNYD, GARAWYS, (Apr. 2, 1879.)—A correspondent asked for the derivation and meaning of these Welsh names of the feasts. *Ystwyll* is from the Latin *stella*=star ; *ynyd* from *initium*=beginning (i.e. of Lent) and *garawys* from *quadragesima*=the fortieth day (i.e. before Easter). Christianity having been brought to the Celts in a Latin form, the Latin name of

the Feasts were generally kept. On the first two of these names consult Prof. Rhys' valuable list of Welsh words borrowed from Latin, Greek and Hebrew, in *Arch : Camb :* for 1873-4-5. "Garawys" has been omitted by an over-sight of the learned author. H. GAIDOZ.
Paris.

THE BEDDGELERT PINT (July 14, 1880).— This old pewter tankard (out of which I have drunk) was at the Goat Hotel, Beddgelert, up to the dispersal of the effects of the late Mr. Prichard, some few years ago. It used to be always kept on the table in the hall of the hotel, and frequently have visitors tried to perform the feat of emptying it, when filled with ale, at one draught, without drawing breath. This was rather a formidable feat, and rarely achieved, because the vessel contained nearly two quarts of liquid, though called a pint. If any-one attempting the feat succeeded, he was entitled to the ale gratis. But if he failed, he had to pay double its price. This was the historical pint referred to by your correspondent as mentioned by Williams in his *Observa-tions on the Snowdon Mountains*, and came into the possession of Mr. John Prichard (the father of the late Mr. Robert Prichard) probably fifty or sixty years ago. With it on the table lay a sword given to Mr. Prichard by the late Mr. Searell of Sygun, and which was, locally, believed to be the weapon with which Llewelyn ap Iorwerth killed the famous hound Gelert! Above the table on the wall, and framed, was a notice to visitors in the handwriting of the late Professor Buckland, and signed by him, drawing their attention to the glacial marks and flutings on the rocks below Aberglaslyn Bridge. All these relics were removed by the agent of the owner of the hotel before the sale of the late Mr. Prichard's effects, and are I hope safe in the custody of Mr. Frank Walker Jones, to whom the hotel then be-longed. I trust that courteous gentleman will some day see his way to allow them to be placed for permanent exhibition in their old home, where the Pint and Sword excited the merry scoff or profound veneration of the pleasure-pilgrims, according to their several capacities for legendary belief, and where Buckland's geological "finger post" was of practical use. Of course, such an exhibition would not affect the ownership of the articles.
(In *Arch : Camb :* July.) E. BREESE.

STRAY NOTES.

MILTON A WELSHMAN.—The silly season, being de-layed this year by the press of parliamentary business, has set in with more than its usual severity. The first crop of the *Western Mail* is a "Remarkable Genealogical Discovery," from which we extract the following :—In the year 1605 there lived in the parish of Glan-pwll-y-domen, Montgomeryshire, a blacksmith, Shon ap Shenkin by name, who was as celebrated for the quality of his voice as for his skilled workmanship. His fame penetrated to the remotest corners of Wales, whence farmers brought their ploughshares and reaping hooks to be repaired and sharpened, while their wives and daughters accompanied them, attracted by the hope of hearing the harmonious blacksmith warble out some of his melodious notes. I pass over sundry incidents of a romantic nature which are not essential to this narrative, and come to the year 1607, when our hero was induced to compete for admission to the sacred circle of the Bards of Britain, in which he was not only completely successful, but the assembled bards were so struck with the number and variety of his songs that they unanimously dubbed him Mil Tôn, and he was thereafter known to his contemporaries as Shon Mil Tôn, or John of the Thousand Songs. Soon after this Shon got

married to a lassie from Cardiganshire, and settled down in his native village, where, in the ye..r following, his eldest son, afterwards the great poet, was born. A few years after this event, troublous times befel the country, when men began turning their ploughshares into swords, and, seeing a chance of bettering himself at this, Shon migrated to London, where he eventually set up at the sign of the Spread Eagle in Bread-street. His name Shon Mil Tôn was Anglicized to John Milton, which name his son was destined to immortalize.

DR. ROBERT DARWIN, FATHER OF CHARLES DARWIN.— In Dr. Robert Darwin (whom some of our older readers remember at Shrewsbury) the love of children was a striking feature. He would address them in his small, high-pitched voice, and occasionally lifting them on to a chair or table he would measure their head with his broad hand, as though reading character and mentally prognos-ticating their future fate. The writer of this sketch remembers well being taken by his father when a delicate child to Dr. Darwin's house to ask his advice. The kind doctor's prescription was, "You may have as many pies and puddings, apples and pears, as you can eat, and an egg every morning for your breakfast, but," he added, "you must eat the shell of it." This last proviso was not so palatable, still the prescription was for a long time obeyed to the letter, and the shell of every egg eaten up when the contents were finished. It was a quaint way of giving lime to make bone, and in keeping with the doctor's family motto, *Econchis omnia.* After this advice, when the child's father handed the usual guinea fee, Dr. Robert received it out of his right hand and put it back into his left with a pleasant laugh, saying, "Thank you, my friend." He was often purchasing beautiful ware for his table from the works of his father-in-law Wedgwood ; and so greatly did he feel the importance of making the mouth do its work before sending the food to the stomach, that he had a dinner-service made with the words printed round the border of each plate, "Masticate, denticate, chump, chew, and swallow." He also made a design for a nursery lamp for use in feeding children, which was manufactured in Etruria and had a large sale.—*Leisure Hour.*

CYMRU FU. ·

When Prince Owen Gwynedd was carrying on his war-like excursions with vigour and success against Henry II., the two armies met on the summit of the Berwyn Mountain, not far from Corwen. After Owen had gained the enemy's camp on the hill by Llangar, which was after-wards named "Bryn bu Gelyn," and whilst he was en-camping there, a white stag ran suddenly into the midst of the camp, and was chased by Owen's soldiers into the very spot where the chancel of Llangar church is situated at present. It was chased the following morning over the river Dee to Cymer, and was lost sight of in a place named afterwards "Fron Guddio." The stag was pur-sued the second time and crossed the river back, and was at last captured and slaughtered on the border of Berwyn, in a place called "Moel y Lladdfa." The incident was considered by Owen and his followers as a favourable omen, and soon afterwards came the overthrow of the English in the great battle of Crogen, on the banks of the Ceiriog, not far from Chirk Castle. In commemoration of this victory the Church of Llangar was erected, and endowed with tithes from the lands, the boundaries of which were the paths which the stag ran along when pur-sued by Owen Gwynedd's followers.

When Robin Ddu, the wizard, was crossing Garnedd-wen from Dolgelley to Bala, he said to his companion " that a ship in full sail would some time or other go betwixt those two mountains." The man, being a native of Dolgelley, was in great distress, because he thought that the ancient town would then be submerged and lost in the ocean if the water would ever be as high as the Garnedd-wen. Because Robin had foretold, so the event must come to pass, and from hence derived the following lines:—

Dolgelleu Dol a gollir,
Daear a'i llwnc a dwfr yn el lle.

The old saying was verified. Sir W. W. Wynn, Bart., bought a small vessel at Barmouth for his use on Bala lake, and as they were bringing it up Rhydymain, the horses could not draw the waggon and its contents. The wind happened to blow behind them, the sails were soon hoisted, and they went up the hill afterwards without the least difficulty.

Many years ago there resided at Hafotty yn Nhwrch a notorious thief named Shôn Bennion, who was living by plundering his neighbours. One night in the beginning of winter he went over Bwlchygroes to Llanuwchllyn, and stole a fat goose from one Thomas Lewis, Coedladur. Lewis in an instant suspected where the goose had gone, and followed the heels of Bennion to the Hafotty, where a fierce struggle took place. Bennion tried to kill his antagonist with a thick bludgeon. However, Shôn was overpowered, and was put in prison. During the following Christmas Bennion's wife took a fat goose to her husband to the county gaol, and instead of the usual stuffing, she managed to put a hammer and a small wedge inside the bird. Bennion soon made use of these tools by wrenching the iron bars of the prison, and in a short time gained his liberty. He was recaptured, and when before the Magistrates was asked how he escaped from the gaol. He answered indifferently amidst much laughter before a crowded Court that he made his escape with the remains of the goose—"the bones you know"—he uttered very coldly.

Alwen lake is situated on the Hiræethog mountain in Denbighshire. There was a man and wife living at Tanyllyn, near the place, possessed of an only daughter, who was considered very handsome and tall, and her name was Alwen. One day during the summer months one of the ancient Princes of Wales came by the lake, accompanied by his son and heir. Before they left the spot the young man was deep in love with Alwen. Both vowed to get married ; but before they could accomplish their object the young man was called to join the army in fighting against the English. Before parting they went according to their usual custom in a boat for pleasure on the lake. In the middle of the lake they yowed again to be faithful to each other until death. The young Prince went away, and was unfortunately taken prisoner during the war by the Constable of Chester ; but, being a Prince, he was soon released, on the condition that he would marry the Constable's daughter, and so he did. When Alwen heard the sad news she went to the boat, and rowed to the very spot where the young Prince and herself had made a solemn oath to each other, and threw herself into the lake. From that event the lake has been called ever since "Llyn Alwen."

Llywarch Hen.

OCTOBER 6, 1880.

NOTES.

MONTGOMERY BOROUGH ELECTION, 1802.—At the general election of July, 1802, Lieut.-Col. Cockburne, son-in-law of Lord Hereford, opposed the sitting member, Whitshed Keene, Esq., who had represented the Borough for 28 years. The contest, such as it was, came off on the 6th of July, with the following result :—Keene 62, Cockburne, 21 ; majority for Keene 41.

Blackpool.

LLANYBLODWELL.—In the Escheat Roll 56, H. 3, the place now called *Blodwell* is written *Bodowanhan. Wennen* (i.e. Gwên) was one of the sons of Meiric de Powys, a descendant of Tudor Trevor. This Gwên with his brother Greno, written in the grant—*Wrenoe* (Greno) and *Wennen* (Gwen), had a grant from King John in 2 year of his reign, of the Lordship of Whittington, of which Fulk Fitzwarine had been temporarily deprived. Whether by *Bod-o-wanhan* was meant *Bôd-o-Wennen* (i.e., the *Residence of Wennen*) I do not know, but the etymology of *Blodwell* has hitherto puzzled all our antiquaries (*Joseph Morris's MSS.*)
W.A.L.
(In *Shreds and Patches.*)

EDWARD JONES, *BARDD Y BRENIN.*—I have some of his writings in my possession, and out of one of his books, called "Piser Byr Edward Jones" I copy the following :—

"*Huw Machno,* or Hugh Owen of Penmachno in Carnarvonshire, flourished about 1600, and lieth buried in the Churchyard of the said place, as appears by his tomb on which the following inscription is still legible, 'H.O. obiit 1600.' Edmund Prys (the celebrated Archdeacon) sent him the following—

Rhyfeddod bennod drwy bant—a brynniau
Heb ronyn lliveiriant ;
Ddyfod afon (eigion nant)
Machno i Raiadr Mochnant."

"As to Edmund Prys's"—(he says)—"uncouthness of his version of the Psalms into Welsh metres, it must be attributed to the novelty of that kind of verse in our language, he being the first as far as I can find that introduced it ; for which he gave his reasons in a short preface to it."

I am very strongly of opinion myself, that Edmund Prys had latterly got into a more smooth and harmonious method of constructing his wondrous verses, and upon an old scrap dated 1654 I find John Salsbri of Llanrwst expressing a like opinion, adding " Yr oedd fy nghar Ffoulk Prys, mab Edmund, in fwy hyddysg nai Dad yn hyn," which means I suppose, the son had improved upon the father in smoothness and harmony, as indeed is the case generally ; for Mr. Jones remarks with some truth "the same is still more observable in the English metre of those times, when compared with the present." Edmund Prys died in 1624 according to Mr. Williams, and when we compare the Welsh poetry of that period, with the productions of the Bards of our own day we at once see how greatly the latter excel the former in smoothness and harmony.

Alluding to *Tudur Penllyn,* Mr. Jones says "he was a gentleman of fortune who lived at Glanllyn, near Bala, and was a great sheep farmer," and he seems to arrive at the latter conclusion from the *last words* in the following couplet, which begins—

Beth sy' ar ben Tudur Penllyn,
Ai Salad ai *Biswelyn ?*

And then follows the well known couplet,

Beth sy' ar ben Tudur Aled,
Ai Biswelyn ai Salad ?

I have seen it stated that Ieuan ap Tudur Penllyn, who flourished about 1480, was a far better poet than his father ; but Edward Jones does not seem to think so, and we must admit, he was no mean judge of poetical merit.
Goronwy Ddu.

OSWESTRY OBSTRUCTIVES.—On Oswestry fair day, June 21, 1820, Margaret Owen, widow, put up a stall or table, near the Cross, opposite the premises of Mr. Lewis Gwynne. The stall was not on the footpath, but between the gutter and the middle of the street. Mr.

Gwynne deemed this a nuisance to his shop, and proceeded forcibly to remove it. Mrs. Owen defended what she deemed her rights, and a struggle ensued, in which the widow incurred a slight bruise; whereupon she preferred an indictment against the shopkeeper for a common assault, and the case was heard at the Oswestry Quarter Sessions on July 14, before "Richard Salisbury, Esq., deputy-mayor; and Thomas Netherton Parker, Esq., coroner."[*] Mrs. Owen pleaded that she had been used to put up a stall, nearly on the same spot, for about 23 years, without interruption, and that her late husband having been a burgess, no toll had ever been demanded of her for so doing. The jury returned a verdict for the defendant.
                                                    JARCO.

[*] Mr. Parker was Coroner in consequence of his having been Mayor during the year preceding. There does not seem to have been a Recorder or Steward present; but under the provisions of the Charter of Charles II., two magistrates of the four Oswestry possessed, could act at Quarter Sessions, provided the Mayor (or his deputy) was one.

QUERIES.

THE CYMMRODORION.—Why is the Society of Cymmrodorion, past and present, styled *Honourable?* I am not aware that any of the other Societies are so denominated. What is the origin of the epithet as applied to this Association?   GLAN TRYWI.

HENRY JONES.—*Shrewsbury Quarry, &c.* Who was Henry Jones, who wrote, in 1770, a Poem entitled *Shrewsbury Quarry, &c.?* He is described on the title page as also author of "the *Earl of Essex, Kew Gardens, Isle of Wight,* the *Arcana, &c."* His printer was J. Eddowes of Shrewsbury, and he had no less than five London publishers! The work was dedicated as follows:—

To the Right Honourable ROBERT Lord CLIVE.

MY LORD,
A POEM upon SHREWSBURY will naturally make its approaches to your Protection; the Author's Judgment, and Inclination, directed by the Advice and Desire of the most discerning and respectable Persons of that Town soon determined him to lay this little Performance at your *Lordship's* Feet; he hopes it has some Claim to your Patronage derived from the Subject itself, and the Affinity you bear it. The Author means not in this Address, to interfere with the public Encomium so justly paid to your *Lordship's* merit, or interrupt the Voice of your Country. He also humbly intreats your Pardon for the Liberty he has taken in this Step; a Liberty, which the above incitements only, and your *Lordship's* humanity can excuse. Under this Hope of your Clemency, he ventures with the greatest Respect and Esteem, to subscribe himself
                    My LORD, *your* LORDSHIP's
                    Obedient Servant to Command,
                                        THE AUTHOR.

If the good man had been a malefactor seeking pardon from the Home Secretary he could not well have addressed a more abject petition,—but it was the fashion of the times; and books did not always so much succeed on their merits as on the merits of the "Patrons" of the Authors. Was Jones connected with Shrewsbury in any way? and how was he interested in the "Isle of Wight" and "Kew Gardens"?   AN UNPATRONIZED SCRIBBLER.

REPLIES.

SAINT MARTIN'S BIRD. (Sep. 22, 1880.)—In reply to MINAFON's query in *Bye-gones,* I have taken the following from Brewer's *Dictionary of Phrase and Fable:*—

St. Martin's Bird. A cock, whose blood is shed "sacrificially" on the 11th of November, in honour of that saint.

St. Martin's Goose. The 11th of November, St. Martin's day, was at one time the great goose-feast of France.

The legend is that St. Martin was annoyed by a goose, which he ordered to be killed and served up for dinner. As he died from the repast, the goose has been ever since "sacrificed" to him on the anniversary. The goose is sometimes called by the French "St. Maitin's Bird."
                                                    LANDWOR.

JOHN WILLIAMS THE HARPER. (Sep. 22, 1880.)—He was the son of Robert Williams, for many years parish clerk of Llangadwaladr, where he was born in a cottage, belonging to the Rev. John Phillips, now in ruin. Catherine, John's sister, was my sexton at Llangadwaladr for nearly forty years, until her death about five years ago, above eighty years old.
                                        ROBERT WILLIAMS.
Culmington Rectory, Bromfield, Salop.

TREES ON THE ASTON ESTATE. (July 21, 1880.)—It is stated in a note on page 276 of the Journal of the Shropshire Archæological Society, vol. 1, that the Rev. J. R. Lloyd of Aston, near Oswestry, "in 1796 received the gold medal of the Society for the encouragement of Arts, &c., for having planted 60,000 oaks." I have before me a leaf, which forms pages 244-5 of a Diary kept at the time by J. Fayel, who was farm-bailiff at Aston, of which the following is a copy:—

Planting att Aston by J. Fayel.

Oakes planted at Decoy New Plantation	3800
Elms planted at the same time along the Ditch	128
The Slip upon the Lay from Lawn gates to Smith Shop	1220
Hisland Common, now called the Square Field	284
The Scotch firs upon Decoy Meadows (the number omitted)	
Hentley, upon Mr. Munslow's farm	1870
At the same time lumbardy poplar cuttings	300
Beech upon John Manford's farm	93
Plantation on Stoney Field	860
1796. Making holes upon Aston Moor in 4 different Plantations. Larch 750, Oakes 3190, Spruce 2920	6860
1798. Trees planted in Townsend	1700
In little field at top of Aston lane	530
1799. Planted Beech in Bell and qiuking plantation where firs were thinned out	1860
1800. Planted in the hedges on Babin's Wood, Oakes	1150
Sycamore trees planted in Hedgerows, Babin's Wood	192
1801. Planted 60 Oaks between plantations, Babin's Wood	60
1802. Sycamores planted in Rithvin Clump	32
Planted Beeches in Hedgerows round Farm	116
Plantation on Aston Moor next Park grounds Ashes	400
Oakes	1400
Beech	850
Sycamore	50
Poplar Pitchers	550
Huntington Willow do.	950
Plantation by Aston lane field below the pool Spruce	100
Sycamores	190
Larch	40
Beech	75
Oakes	332
Poplar Pitchers	80
The oak plantation upon Babins Wood where My Master had the Medal from the Society of Arts and Sciences. Oakes 60020, Scotch fir 9300, all these planted and rose from seeds by J. Fayel	69320
	99992

It would seem from this that Mr. Lloyd caused something like 34,000 more trees to be planted than he got commended for by the Society.   BEN STARCH.
[We presume the leaf from which the foregoing list is copied belongs to the Diary from which extracts were given, in 1877, in the *Oswestry Advertizer?*—ED.]

LOCAL "NOTES AND QUERIES" (Sept. 15, 1880.)—The "Cambrian Remembrancer," which originally appeared in the *Carnarvon Herald,* was re-issued in January, 1880, in a quarto volume of 141 pages, a copy of which is now before me. I see it extends over from the

5th of Sept., 1877, to the 27th of December, 1879, when
it was discontinued. I have heard it stated that Mr.
'alisbury of Glan-Aber, Chester, had supplied nearly the
whole of the material comprising this volume, and that it
was discontinued because he was unable to spare time to
proceed with it further. I have often wished that some
friend had collected into a similar volume, "Past Days,"
"Montgomeryshire Mems.," and "Local Gleanings,"
to the end of 1879, for such a work would have been useful
to all who take an interest in Welsh and border county
literature, and I hope that it may be done. In like manner
I trust the Editors of the *Shrewsbury Chronicle* and of the
Cambrian News will arrange to collect their respective
"Notes" into convenient volumes, as from the 1st of
January, 1880.   ANTIQUARY.

HOPS IN WALES (Aug. 18, 1880).—Some one
connected with the Welshpool district must reply to the
more immediate question connected with the hop-growing
experiment mentioned by your correspondent at this date,
but on the question generally I may say that Walter
Davies, in his *Agriculture in South Wales*, vol. 1, p. 536,
says :—" Hops are growing wild in many places, but generally near dwelling ruins, &c., which, though now neglected,
prove their former culture, upon a small scale, for home
use. About ten years back [1804] a few small hop-
yards were planted in the valley of the Aeron, in Cardiganshire." The same author says that several extensive
hop-yards were in cultivation in the vale of the Wye in
1814.   CYFFIN.

CURRENT NOTES.

THE RE-OPENING OF BETTWS CHURCH, NEAR CORWEN.

(From a Correspondent.)

Bettws is a very common name of places in Wales.
There are three parishes of that name in the diocese of St.
Asaph :—Bettws-yn-Rhos, Bettws-Caedewen, and Bettws-
Gwerfil-Goch. The derivation of the word is uncertain.
Rees, in his "Welsh Saints," says the word is de-
rived from "Bead-house," a place to which, in Roman
Catholic times, people came to say their prayers for the
dead. Others derive the word from *Abatty*—"*Abbots'
House*;" and others again derive it from *Bedw*—"Birch."
It is supposed that in olden times these places were noted
for birch trees.
The parish of Bettws-Gwerfil-Goch is, upon the whole,
rather mountainous, but the church and village are very
prettily situated, resting on the brow of a hill at the junction of two beautifully wooded valleys on the banks of the
river Alwen, the largest of the tributaries of the Dee, and
on the Ruthin and Bala turnpike road. In days gone by
the village was noted for its fairs, and even now one of the
largest lamb fairs in North Wales is held here every
August. The church is very peculiarly situated. There is an
old saying that the Rev. John Lloyd (grandfather of Mr.
Townshend Mainwaring), who was rector of Bettws about
ninety years ago, could throw a stone from the churchyard
into three other parishes : Corwen, Gwyddelwern, and
Llanfihangel-Glyn-Myfyr. The parish of Llangwm is
also within a few minutes' walk of the churchyard.
Bettws, though one of the smallest parishes in North
Wales, contains parts of two counties—Denbigh and
Merioneth. At Bottegir, in this parish, lived Colonel
Salisbury, who during the civil wars defended Denbigh
Castle.
The old parish church, which is dedicated to St. Mary,
had for many years been in such a dilapidated state as to
be altogether unfit for a congregation to assemble in.
About twelve months ago its restoration was commenced

under the direction of Mr. John Douglas of Chester, who has
carried it out in the most careful and conservative manner.
The old church was built of local slatestone, with no
architectural features of interest. The windows were of
wood, circular-headed in shape—except the one in the
east gable, which was of the perpendicular period—but
poor in detail. Inside, the church was more interesting,
there being an old oak roof of good design, and similar in
character to those found in many of the small old Welsh
churches. In the restoration great care has been taken by
the architect to preserve everything of the smallest interest
or value. The old walls have been left, and new stone
windows inserted, of a late Gothic character ; the one in
the east gable being a three light, with traceried head,
and carved label terminations. The east gable is finished
at the apex by a stone cross. At the west end a bell
gable has been added in place of the old small gable. It
is carried up in the form of a spirelet and surmounted by
a gilt cross. The porch on the south side has been rebuilt,
with the insertion of a small window on each side. On
the north-east side a vestry and organ-chamber have been
added, the walls being built the same as the old ones of
local slatestone. The interior walls of the old church
having been pl astered, this has all been taken off, and the
old stone carefully pointed, as it had been originally. The
gallery at the west end has been removed, and the old
materials are used in the new seating, &c. The old roof
principals have been cleaned (having been whitewashed),
and the joints bolted up with wrought iron tie rods. The
spars are of new oak, exposed to view and pointed between. All the roofs are covered with the best green Port
Dinorwic slates of a small size, and have a very nice effect.
The windows are filled with cathedral glass in small square
quarries, each window having a metal casement. The
seats are of good design, in oak, framed and pinned together, the uprights having beautifully turned finals to
match the old ones, and pierced cut panels in elbows. The
chancel seats are also of oak, of a good substantial design,
having solid and framed elbow, moulded and cut fronts,
&c. The front prayer desk is from the old church, carefully cleaned and framed into new elbows. There is a very
handsome oak screen dividing the nave from the chancel,
in the position occupied by the old screen, of which there
were a few remains. The new screen has moulded uprights, filled in at the top by tracery panels, with moulded
cornice and carved cresting. The floors of the nave (under
the seats) and vestry are laid with Gregory's patent wood
blocks, the aisle and porch with 4in. red tiles, the chancel
with red and encaustic tiles. The pulpit is the old one
re-adapted and cleaned, and the altar rails are also old.
The font is of Cefn stone, of simple design, with steps of
local slate. An oak lectern has been given by Mr. Humphreys Roberts. The east window has been filled with
beautiful stained glass, representing the Ascension, given
by the late Mr. Roberts of Bottegir, in memory of his
parents, and executed by Messrs. Heaton, Butler, and
Bayne, of London. The south side window of the chancel
has also been filled with stained glass, in memory of the
late Rector ; it was given by his executors, and executed
by Mr. Swaine Bourne of Birmingham. The lighting has been done by Messrs. Hark, Son, Peard,
and Co., of London, and consists of neatly wrought iron
lamps and brackets, &c. The whole of the mason and
joiner's work has been carried out by Mr. George Aidney
of Gresford, the dressed stone being supplied by Messrs.
Chatham and Jones, Cefn. The plumbing has been executed by Mr. Isaac Williams of Chester.
The sum expended on the work is over £1,100. The
parish being so very small and poor, it was not possible to
raise so large a sum without appealing for help to the
friends of the Church generally. Under these circum-

stances the Rector was obliged to send out over 25,000 circulars soliciting a subscription of one shilling, to which about 10,000 persons responded. By this means about £650 was added to the funds, and we are glad to be able to state that the church was re-opened free of debt. Mr. Townshend Mainwaring gave £100, and other large sums were received. In addition, we may mention the following gifts :—A silver paten from Mrs. Sobieski Lynes of Chester, to match an old chalice given by her great grandfather, Mr. Robert Wynne, Garthmeilio, in the year 1761; altar cloth, the gift of Miss Brittain of Liverpool; cushions for altar steps from Miss Bertie, Weston Manor, Oxfordshire ; a beautifully carved oak chair for sacrarium from Mr. Hugh S. Roberts of Mold; hangings and tiles for east end, and windows in porch, from Mr. John Douglas ; communion linen from Miss Brittain of Malpas; a small oak chest for keeping Communion plate from Miss Lynes, Chester ; book-marks from Miss Brittain, Birkenhead, and alms bags from Mrs. Jones, Bettws Rectory. The re-opening services were held on Tuesday, Sept. 21. In the afternoon an eloquent sermon was preached by Archdeacon Smart from 1st Samuel xii., 24. In the evening the Bishop of the Diocese preached in his usual impressive manner to an overflowing congregation from Isaiah lii., 1. Amongst the clergy present we noticed Canon Wynne Edwards, rector of Llanrhaiadr, Canon Richardson, rector of Corwen, the Revs. Thomas Morgan, Rural Dean ; Owen Jones, Pentrevoelas ; John Jones, rector of Cerrigydrudion ; Ellis Roberts, rector of Llangwm ; T. E. Jones, vicar of Trofarth ; Richard Owen, vicar of Glyndyfrdwy ; Evan Evans, rector of Llanarmon ; W. Jones, rector of Clocaenog ; Joseph Williams, rector of Llanfihangel-Glyn-Myfyr ; T. Vaughan, rector of Gwyddelwern ; Morgan Rees, vicar of Llangwyfan ; John Williams, Holy Trinity, Bala ; J. Morris Jones, Corwen ; D. Davies, St. Cathrine's, Dinmael ; D. Evans, rector of Llansantffraid ; and T. M. Edwards, Yspytty Ifan.

OLD WELSH ALMANACKS.

You have from time to time published in the *Advertiser* some very interesting accounts of Welsh Almanacks ; and inasmuch as these old things are becoming more and more scarce every day, I have thought it would be both interesting and instructive to place on record a continuous account of the so-called "poetical effusions" which constituted the title pages of the early issues of these publications. I have a fairly perfect set of them between 1800 and 1835 as printed at Dublin*. I venture, therefore, to send you a first instalment of the Almanack story. Robert Roberts of Holyhead has always had the credit of preparing this particular set of Almanacks for the press, but as he died on the second of August, 1836, at the age of fifty-eight, it is difficult to believe that the *earliest* of them were wholly due to him ; that, however, is not of much moment in its relation to our present purpose, except when remarking upon the odd mixture of science and divinity which pre-distinguished the verses upon the title pages of the Dublin Almanacks. *Poetry* we cannot call these productions, they are not worthy of that designation ; " rhigwm " (as the Welsh call it) being the better term to use in relation to them ; but they contain much good sense, a store of useful information also, and are at times amusing. I can remember how, in my boyhood, the Welsh valued these Almanacks, and I have myself spent many pleasant evenings among the cobblers and nailmakers, listening to them singing "Caneuon yr hen Robert Roberts" (as they called them) in their workshops.

Glan-Aber, Chester.   E.G.S.

The one for 1800 is printed at Dublin, and is called " Cyfaill Cyfeillion ;" the price being three pence half penny, and on the title page are the following verses —:

1. Fy hên GYFEILLION cywyr,
O *Wynedd* i'r *Deheudir*,
Adwaenwch fi 'mhob *Tre* a *Llan*,
Mewn goleu pan y'm gwelir.

2. Pe byddai'r *Haul* mewn *Cylchau*,
Mor bell a rhai *Planedau*,
Ni wuai ei *oleu* mawr a'i *wres*,
I ni fwy lles na hwythau.

3. Yr *Esop* gall ddysgedig,
Roes anair i *Gi* diddig ;
Ei holl gyfeillion uchel radd
Ymroes i'w ladd a *cherrig*.

4. 'Does ond cymdeithas oeredd,
Er rhedeg mewn anrhydedd ;
Os na bydd Mab *Tangnefedd* cu ;
Yn cadw'r *Ty*'n gyfanedd.

5. Er maint y llid a chynnen,
Sy'n magu gau gynfigen ;
Mwynhâu yr y'm drugaredd *rad*,
Fel Israel yng Ngwlad *Gosen*.

6. Where God send forth a *Preacher*
His *people* believe together ;
Strangers to the light above,
They never love to hear.

The one for 1801, called " Cyfaill Tawel," is printed at Dublin ; price four pence, and the following lines are on the title page :—

1. Fy hên GYFEILLION hybarch,
Sy'n llon yn llawer Llanerch ;
A rhyw *newyddion* tra b'o chwyth.
Rwy'n chwenych byth eich annerch.

2. Tra byddo'r *Lleuad* newydd,
Yn myned ar ei chynnydd ;
Ein *Dacar* ni i'r *Lleuad* fydd,
Yn llai o ddydd i gilydd.

3. Er gwrando *Gwirioneddau*,
Odiaethol mewn *Pregethau* ;
Mae'n rhaid i'r sylwydd roddi *ffydd*,
Cyn derbyn *budd* o'r geiriau.

4. Gwyn fyd y rhai a *gredant*,
Hwy ganant hyd *Ogoniant* ;
Fe roddir iddynt, yn ddifeth,
Byth byth, bob peth a geisiant.

5. Oh ! *Gwmmwl* amryw liwiau
Sydd bαunydd uwch ein pennau ;
Yn darth, a niwl, yn dân, a mwg,
Oddi wrth ein *drwg* fucheddau.

6. If *Death* and *War* come nearer,
Again than former *ycar* ;
We ought agree with *God* above,
Where's plenty and love for *ever*.

I have so far confined myself to the *out side covers* of the Almanacks noticed ; but there are some verses upon the inner pages of some of them which should be preserved. The one for 1801 has the following :—

Ple'r acth yr *Effeithiau*, fu'n dilyn *Pregethau* ;
Mewn *Llannau* a *Theiau*, bu *Odleu*'n parhau ;

* All, in fact, except the years 1809 and 1812, and I should feel much indebted to any one who could, and would kindly supply me with copies of the two years in question.

Rhai'n caru'r *Cyfammod*, rhai'n cwyno gan *bechod*,
Hyfrydwch oedd '*nabod* wynebau?

Cynfigen a *balchder*, du gilwg ysgeler,
A fagodd wag *hyder*, rhy dynner bob dydd ;
Prin iawn ydyw *Crefydd*, o wythnos i gilydd,
Ond *Llanau Capelydd* cip hylwydd.

Yr *Arglwydd* sy'n dysgu, Athrawon *bregethu*,
Lle byddo'n eu *gyrru*, i *dreuthu* bob tro ;
Bydd Ef yn cyd *weithio*, iw *calyn* heb gisio :
Fe beru nes *llwyddo*, ei holl eiddo.

Mae *Gwyntill* Duw'n dyfod, i buro *rhai'n* barod
Oddiwrth eu holl *sorod*, trwy *ammod* rhad ras :
Caiff *us* ei wasgaru, Drwy rinwedd *Pregethu*
Bydd *nithio'n* ol *Dyrnu*, trwy'r *Deyrnas*.

n the one for 1802 I find the following :—
*Pry' *Rhwd* a fu brysur, i'n gwneuthur yn gaeth ;
†*A Cheiliog y Rhedyn*, yn ddygyn a ddaeth ;
Mae *Duw* yn darparu, pob teulu, Bwyttewch,
Os cerwch *wirionedd* digonedd a gewch.

*Yr hwn a gasglodd yd i ddifetha cyn ei werthu,
†Yr Anghenus, gwan ac ofnus, oedd yn faieh.

The Álmanack for 1802 is called "Cyfaill Cymmeredig."
t was printed at Dublin, price fourpence, and has the
following verses on the title page :—

1. GYFEILLION mwynion *Cymru*,
　Mae mwriad eich difyrru ;
　Er bod ynof fynnych *Fai ;*
　Ni fedrwch lai na'm *Prynu*.

2. Chwe mis o Hâf cyfannedd,
　Goleua'r *haul y Gogledd ;*
　A chwe mis eraill ceidw ei le,
　Ym mharthau'r *De* mae'n rhyfedd.

3. Mae rhai'n ymyrru'n fawrion,
　Mewn *Crefydd* yn dra chryfion ;
　Heb brofi dychryn *Sinai* serth,
　Na thawel nerth o *Seion*.

4. Mae amryw yn rhyfeddu,
　Awdurdod rhai'n *Pregethu ;*
　A chael gwrandawyr wrth eu trin
　Mor wan a *llin* ym mygu.

5. Gan fod cynhaiaf SEION,
　Yn fawr, a llafur ffrwythlon ;
　Duw, anfon *weithwyr* iddo'n rhodd.
　Fwy fwy, wrth fodd dy galon.

Some times we are like *Christians*,
But parted as *Samarians*,
Appear at other times, by *works*,
As bad as *Turks* or *Pagans*.

The one for the year 1803 was printed at Dublin, and is
called "Cyfaill Enwog," price fourpence, with the following verses on the title page :—

1. GYFEILLION mwyn di absen,
　Sy' heb fagu hen *gynfigen ;*
　Masnachwyr *Trefryw* rydd i'm sen ;
　Wrth grafu ar *Bren*, fy serifen.

2. Yr *Haul* mawr sy'n amgylchu,
　Y *Ddaear* i'w chynhesu ;
　Fel yr â ym mlaen goleua'r dydd ;
　O'i ol y bydd yn t'wyllu.

3. Ni all dysgeidiaeth *dynol*,
　Er seinio'n *ddefasionol ;*
　Heb Ysbryd Duw'n cydweithio'n rhydd,
　Briodi *Budd* ysprydol.

4 Er bod yr enw *Crefydd*,
　Mewn *clod* ar hyd y Gwledydd ;
　Mae'n dra chyffredin *bechod* drwg
　Mewn golwg yn ddig'*wylydd*.

5. Rhaid i bob Dyn *ymdrechu*
　Am fendith i gynyddu ;
　Ni welir fyth ddim llwyddiant dâ
　Heb *gredu* a *gweithreda*.

6. God is sufficient *Ransome*
　All sinners come and *welcome ;*
　Believe in *Him*, you never *fall*,
　But shall to *all* is freedom.

I shall proceed in my next communication to the poetic
title pages for the next four years, viz., 1804—1807, both
inclusive.

OCTOBER 13, 1880.

NOTES.

THE MOATED MOUNDS OF THE UPPER
SEVERN.—In reading an interesting paper on the above,
reprinted from the *Montgomeryshire Collections*, in the
July number of the Journal of the Cambrian Archæological Association, I observed that the learned compiler describes what we locally have known as the "Gro Lumps"
=*Rhôs Ddiarbed Earthwork*. I should take it as a favour
if some of your correspondents would indicate the source
whence this name for the works has been obtained. It
has occurred to me that possibly the name has been con-
founded with the earth works at the Moat Farm, near
Moat Lane Station, as there is a moor adjacent to the latter known as
Rhôs Ddiarbed. I have good grounds for saying that a
hundred years ago the field of which the Moat forms the
eastern corner was known as *Cae Moat*, and the triangular
field lying to the south of the Moat between and the
Welshpool turnpike road was called *Cae Henry*, as also
was a field on the opposite side of the Welshpool road.
At this period, starting from the present turnpike gate,
there was a wide road which led down to
the Moat. The bottom part of this is what Mr. Clark
describes as "the natural bed of the brook on the south
side." The short township road leading from the Moat
to the Welshpool road, and the Welshpool road itself
back to the turnpike gate, encloses the small field called
then "Cae Henry," as it were within three roads. It is
worth noticing that this old road, now obliterated, may have been a branch from the Roman
Road, which is known to go down the valley
between the Cambrian Railway and the Welshpool Turnpike Road, and opposite the Moat on the south side, is
not more than 200 paces from it. The large field west of
the Moat field, occupied by Mr. Miller, The Court, was
then called *Cae Draênog*, and the old race course, still
nearer the town, on part of which the new Cemetery will
be laid out, was then described as *Maes Castell*, and the
field between this and the Severn river, around to the
Moat, was called *Dol Iago*. Is it possible there could have
been a castle at some former period on the Race Course?
Some of your correspondents may, after this hint as to the
ancient name of the field, pursue the enquiry. In
describing the earthwork at Brynderwen, I notice a very
pardonable error of Mr. Clark's. He thought he was correcting an error of the Ordnance Map when he said the
work is on the *north*, not the *south* side of the bridge. The
fact is the old wooden bridge which was in existence when
the Ordnance Survey was made was *north* considerably of
the earthwork, but the memorable flood of Feb. 5, 1852,
swept that and many other bridges on the Severn away,.

and the new iron bridge which Mr. Clark saw was erected after this flood, south of and close to the earthwork. This note is only made with the object of securing accuracy, and thus making a most interesting paper more valuable.

EDROMO.

DIARY OF MRS. SARAH SAVAGE.—The following extracts are taken from the "Memoirs of the Life of Mrs. Sarah Savage, eldest daughter of the Rev. Philip Henry." The copy from which I made my extracts is in MS., and is evidently an early copy of the original. It comprises two thick 8vo volumes, neatly written, and extends from March 28, 1687, to Oct. 7, 1750. PURITAN.

Aug. 2, 1709. A sudden disaster at Bro. Henry's * by the falling-in of the Brewho: floor into the cellar with the furnace fire & maid-serv't, washerwo' &c. the poor wo'm much scalded. One died. God fit us for all events.

Mar. 28, 1711. To us a Thanksgiving day, now 24 years since the good providence of God bro't us together in the married state. Yet this being appoint'd by Authority for a National Fast, we join with them to implore the Divine bless'g on our sinful land, especially in respect to this tedious War. My husband and three of our children went to Namptwich ; it was my lot (as often) to stay at home & had my hands busy employ'd in one of the duties of a Fasting-day (this one of the least) Dealing my bread to the hungry. So great a numb'r of poor com'g now before East'r. Lord give me a charitable heart.

Sep. 21, 1713. We hear y't I'd. Newport was chose parliam't man at Salop after a hot dispute for several days. O Lord give to our senators y't wisdom needful to discern those things which make for peace.

July 18-25, 1714. This week I hear from Borreaton, they take their turn in sorrows, a bitter cup,—they who were deservedly dear to us snatch'd from us, her dear & worthy Father—L'd Chief Baron Ward is lately dead ;—great, wise and good men their breath is in their nostrils—therefore put not your trust in princes.

This week S'r Thos. Manwaring comes to Namptwich where my husband is daily attending him.—I should be diligent to get ready to attend my dear Lord on Sab : day ; who uses to meet his people in his own ordinances.

Aug. 1.—8, 1714. By the events of this week I may become fully convinced of our darkness & unaquaintedness of things at a distance : this morn, we heard of the death of Queen Ann on Aug. 1, of an apploplexy. We well know y't riches profit not in the day of wrath. As one once said "all the world for one inch of time." Who w'd desire to live such a life as she who liveth in pleasure & is dead while she liveth.

Aug. 4, 1714. Wed. Was proclaimed our new King Geo. I. at Namptw'h by L'd Cholmondeley the High Sheriff & their attendants. Lord if it be thy will make him a blessing to us & quiet the minds of unreasonable men such as bear illwill to the peace & prosperity of thy people ; let them be as grass on the house top. Some cannot but observe that the Queen should die the very day, Aug. 1., y't y'e Malicious Act was to take place.

Aug. 10, 1714. My son came home from Newmarket—the new Act† not permitting his master go on in the School as formerly. Blessed be God who has been with him there & kept him going out & coming in & will I trust make our way plain concerning him.

(To be continued.)

* Rev. Matthew Henry.
† The "Schism Bill" introduced by Bolingbroke, which enacted that no person in Great Britain should keep a School or act as Tutor who had not subscribed to the declaration of Conformity to the Church of England, and received a licence from the Diocesan, and in default might be committed to prison without bail.

QUERIES.

CADER IDRIS.—There is a paper on a visit to Barmouth in the Oct. no. of the Ellesmere Ruridecanal Magazine, which contains the following passage :—" Beginning the ascent of Cader Idris, two springs are met with on the west side, protected from loose stones by a kind of palisade of enormous plinths stuck into the ground. This work, as well as the Cyclopean building at the top, gives the impression of some person or persons having lived on the mountain for a length of time. The Cyclopean hut is upon the same plan as that of the Dwarfie Stone in Hoy, namely, a chamber on each side and an intervening passage." Has this theory ever been advanced before? I never met with it. G.G.

WELSHPOOL AND OSWESTRY.—In May, 1820, as you have stated in Bye-gones, a meeting was held in Welshpool, to petition the Post-master General to establish a daily mail between that town and Oswestry "in order to facilitate the intercourse between Montgomeryshire and the Northern counties of England." In Dec. of the same year Thomas Rogers of Cross-street, Oswestry, announced his car as running between the towns every Monday and Thursday, but as he left Oswestry for Pool until night, his object could not have been the same as that of the promoters of the May meeting. What was the local trade that warranted the proprietor of the car in thus doing? OSWALD.

THE DUKE OF NORFOLK, 1571.—Our county histories tell us of a bag of gold, for the use of Mary, Queen of Scots, being sent in a roundabout way, by the Duke of Norfolk, to Shropshire, to Banister his lordship's agent. Mr. Froude (Hist. Vol. 10, p. 290) alluding to this says that "A Shrewsbury merchant, who had been in London making purchases" was entrusted with the bag, and when he neared Shrewsbury, the weight of its contents aroused his suspicions. He opened it and handed over the money and a letter in cypher to the authorities ; going back to London for the purpose. His name was Brown. Were "Merchants" employed as "Carriers" in those days? I observe that Mr. Hulbert speaks of Brown by the latter designation. SALOPIAN.

A WELSH HUNT IN 1797.—An action was tried at the Hereford Assizes in April, 1797, to recover the sum of twenty-four guineas, for a pack of hounds. The plaintiff was Mr. Thomas Evans, who sold the hounds to the members of the Red Coat Hunt, Carmarthen, through the defendant A. L. Davids, Esq., one of the members, and delivered them to his servant in the kennel. "They were hunted a fortnight when it was discovered that the funds of the club were too scanty to pay for them. A meeting was called, when it was resolved that the hounds should be returned, and the defendant was requested by the secretary of the hunt to write to the plaintiff to inform him that they had no cash. Defendant refused to write, as he was ashamed of the transaction, however the animals were returned, and plaintiff refused to receive them, so they have been wandering about ever since. Judgment went for plaintiff, so the defendant will be compelled to bring actions against all the members, twenty-four in number, unless the matter can be amicably arranged." Does any reader know how the matter ended? TALLY-HO.

REPLIES.

EDWARD JONES, BARDD Y BRENIN (Oct. 6, 1880).—Here's another very interesting bit out of Y Piser Byr. "John Jones of Gelly-lyfdy, in the parish of Ysceifiog, was confined in Flint castle nearly twenty years, for enclosing a common. During his confinement he amused himself in transcribing the most ancient and curious Welsh MSS., and he was esteemed one of the most judicious antiquaries of his time; many of the oldest and valuable Welsh manuscripts would inevitably have been lost or decayed had it not been for his great industry. I have seen about a dozen different MSS. of his hand writing which were transcribed in a plain old hand with infinite labour, with an index, and greatly ornamented." What has become of these treasures? Are they at Peniarth? Mr. Canon Williams has a notice of John Jones, but he says not a word of this Flint incident. He (Edward Jones) gives us the following note, which John Jones had written in a manuscript copy of the Triads :—" Y triodd uchod a gefais i yn ysgrifennedig mewn llaw ewingron a ysgrifennesid uwchlaw chwechan mlynedd cyn hyn, ac a gollasir eu dechreuad hwynt, ond cymmaint ac a gefais mi au hysgrifennais yn y modd i cefais." This is dated 1640. In another place it is added—

"Llyma enwau arfau Arthur :
　Bongogoniant, ei Wayw ;
　Caledfwlch, ei Gleddyf ;
　Carwennan, ei Ddager.

Ac fal hyn a ascrifennais i o law Simwnt Fychan y terfyna y=2=dydd o fis Chwefror 1640. Jo. Jo."

Edward Jones in another part of the same book gives the names of the maids of honour at Arthur's Court thus:—

"1. ESYLLT, ferch Garymanwyd post prydain ; ei chariad oedd Trystan ab Sallwch.

"2. MORFUDD, merch Urien Reged ; ei chariad oedd Clydno Eiddyn.

"3. TEGAN EURFRON, ferch Nadd law hael, Frenhin y Gogledd ; ei chariad oedd Caradog Freichfras."

Doubtless many of your English readers will smile at the simplicity of a man who could thus keep on record the names of these three maids of honour and of their "sweethearts ;" but I am of the Welsh Welshy, and see in all this, the one pre-eminent characteristic of the nation's antiquity, for like the Jews of old, they esteem the remembrance of their sires as sacred.

Robyn Ragad when assailed at Warrington once upon a time "turned short upon his antagonists, and spoke the following extempore reply—

'Despise the Welshman if you dare,
For we the Ancient Britons are ;
We kept this nation safe and sound,
Before you Saxons trod the ground.'"

　　　　　　　　　　　　　GORONWY DDU.

CURRENT NOTES.

THE POWYS-LAND CLUB.

The thirteenth annual meeting of the Powys-land Club was held at the Powys-land Museum and Library, Welshpool, on Friday October 8. The chair was taken by the President, the Earl of Powis, and amongst those present were :—The Bishop of St. Asaph, Lady Charlotte Montgomery, Mr. Hugh Montgomery, Miss Montgomery, Mrs. Willes Johnson, Llanerchydol, Mrs. Lovell, Miss Harrison, Mrs. Howell, Rhiewport, Mrs. Edward Jones, Welshpool, Mrs. and Miss Morris Jones, Gungrog, the Revs. Canon Wynne-Edwards, D. P. Lewis, Rural Dean, J. McIntosh, Rector of Llanerfyl, J. E. Hill, Vicar of Welshpool, John Williams, Rector of Newtown, Jos. Matthews, Rector of Llandysilio, D. R. Thomas, Vicar of Meifod, T. Jeffrey Jones, Vicar of Llanfair, E. Price, Rector of Llanymynech, Ang, Field, Vicar of Pool Quay, Griffith Edwards, Rector of Llangadfan, D. L. Boyes, Welshpool, J. David Jones, Welshpool, and H. Williams, Llanfair, Messrs. A. Howell,

Rhiewport, G. D. Harrison (Mayor of Welshpool), P. A. Beck, Trelydan Hall, W. Withy, Golfa, D. Pryce Owen, Welshpool, C. S. Burton, Hanwell, T. Morgan Owen, Rhyl, Lieut.-Col. Walker, Messrs. Elijah Pryce, Trederwen, Thomas Savin. Oswestry, Edward Jones, Town Clerk, Welshpool, Charles Jones, Welshpool, Richard Williams, Newtown, William Wilding, Town Clerk, Montgomery, R. Hurst, Borough Surveyor, Welshpool, L. Hutching, Welshpool, T. Hoblyn, Welshpool, M. Paterson Jones, Liverpool, T. Simpson Jones, Lincoln's Inn, T. Rutter, Welshpool, and Morris C. Jones, F.S.A., Hon. Secretary.

The CHAIRMAN called upon the Secretary to read the annual report, which was as follows :—

The Committee have the pleasing duty of reporting that, in pursuance of the resolution of the last annual meeting, £200 four per cent. Debenture Stock of the London and North-Western Railway Company was, on the 13th November, 1879, purchased out of the funds of the Club, at a cost of £216, in the names of the Trustees of the Museum, to be held by them as part of the repair fund, as provided by the Constitution deed.

In addition to this necessary measure of precaution, the Committee have the pleasure to report that the proposed new room has been built on the eastern side of the Museum, which will afford as much further accommodation as will, under ordinary circumstances, be required for some years. The scheme for the addition met with general approval, and the amount required for erecting the building has been fully subscribed, so that no debt remains upon it. Some glass cases and internal fittings are required, the expense of which the dividend from the repair fund will in part provide, and the sanction of the meeting is requested to the residue being paid out of the funds of the Club to the extent of £20 or £30.

In consequence of members of the Cambrian Archæological Association liberally supporting the extension by their subscriptions and influence, it is proposed to place an inscription in the new room that it was erected in commemoration of the successful meeting of the Cambrian Archæological Association in Welshpool in 1879.

It will not be necessary in this report more than to allude to the terms in which the Powys-land Club and Museum are referred to by the Council of the Cambrian Archæological Association in their recent report, inasmuch as the effect of such report has been already printed on the cover of the last issue of the _Montgomeryshire Collections._

The finances of the Club are in a satisfactory condition, and, notwithstanding the outlay in the repair fund, there is a substantial balance in hand, although an unusual number of subscriptions are in arrear.

A considerable number of donations to the Museum has been received. The Museum has been kept in confusion owing to the building operations, and it will take some time to procure the necessary fittings, and to effect the re-arrangement of the objects. When these are done, all objects contributed can be properly arranged and displayed.

Mr. Charles Thomas has removed his Peruvian collection, and the thanks of the Club are due to him for exhibiting them for a period of six years, during the infancy of the Museum, when they were useful to the institution.

Mr. James Williams has offered his assistance to arrange the geological specimens, and has kindly presented from his own collection many typical specimens that were lacking. The collection is small, but it is hoped it will soon assume an educational value, and in time increase, and become important in that respect.

The Committee trust also that the Club will soon obtain similar amateur help for the arrangement of the Caine collection of shells, when its extent, completeness, and value will more fully appear.

The literary work of the Club has proceeded satisfactorily, and although a large amount of material has been already printed in the Transactions, the sources of information are not yet by any means exhausted. The Club would nevertheless welcome more and fresh literary contributors.

The Club has lost five members by death, viz., W. W. E. Wynne, Esq., of Peniarth (a vice-president of the Club), the Rev. F. Tompson, Rev. J. J. Turner, Rev. D. P. Pritchard, and Miss Hinde-Lloyd. Four members have also resigned.

On the other hand, four new members have joined the Club. The rule which has obtained in the Club, of sons succeeding their fathers in their membership, has been illustrated in the case of Mr. Wynne of Peniarth.

The TREASURER, Mr. Peter Beck, then read the financial report.

The CHAIRMAN then said—Ladies and gentlemen,—Through the never tiring energy of our excellent Secretary, Mr. Morris Jones, we are met to-day under favourable auspices, and with enlarged premises, which are already beginning to look as though they were fairly occupied, and which show that as fast as we are able to give room to the various objects of interest and curiosity connected with Wales, donors are found to provide specimens which save our rooms from looking bare and empty. In these days of universal depression it is cheering to find any interest, however small, and any institution, however modest, that is able to expand and extend itself. The report states that some fittings are wanted for the new apartments, but that is a deficiency which we trust will shortly be supplied, and in which we are countenanced by two great institutions, the British Museum and the South Kensington Museum; because, although a magnificent building has been erected at South Kensington to which they might remove the Natural History collections from the British Museum in order to make the valuable space at the British Museum available for other and more important objects, the birds and beasts still remain in statu quo, and the British Museum still continues to keep magnificent antiquities, brought at great expense from Greece and Egypt in its basement stories because no Chancellor of the Exchequer has been found sufficiently liberal to give a grant for the fittings of this new apartment. (Laughter.) I hope we shall have completed our fittings before the British Museum. (Cheers and laughter.) Among the members whom we have lost in the course of the last year, the death of our Vice-President, the late Mr. Wynne of Peniarth, is much to be regretted. He had a very valuable collection of ancient Welsh MSS., records, and writings, in his possession, and there was no one who was more heartily interested in the antiquities of the Principality, or who personally possessed a more thorough and scholarlike acquaintance with its ancient lore. (Hear, hear.) Through the kindness of Mr. Caine, a friend of Mr. Morris Jones's, a very handsome collection of shells has been given us. They have been placed in the other room, where they form an attraction, and give new interest to the Museum, in place of the very curious things we have lost —I mean those Peruvian antiquities which Mr. Thomas was good enough to lend us for six years. You will not have forgotten that curious bottle which was so harmonious and almost articulate in its utterances, as though it had stolen from the human race that power of utterance of which it sometimes in Wales deprives them. (Laughter.) I may invite your attention to the other apartment in which some of our new things are exhibited. I will now move "That the report now read be confirmed, printed, and circulated amongst the members, and that the financial recommendations therein made be carried out." In connection with the report we may congratulate ourselves, that we have laid the foundation of a repair fund, which is a thing most necessary for the permanent welfare of an institution like the present, because, being voluntary, we cannot depend upon rates, and we know that with buildings age soon begins to tell, and that if they do not receive early attention they may soon become as dilapidated as some of the old worm-eaten remains to which they now give shelter. (Cheers.)

The Bishop of ST. ASAPH said he had been requested to second the motion before the meeting, and he rose to do so with great pleasure. He had heard much, and had read a little of what had been going on in connection with that institution. It could not but be a very great advantage to the locality to have connected with it such a building for the purposes intended. If they cared to study natural history it gave them an opportunity of cultivating their taste for that pursuit. He thought that that institution was a very important gain, if they regarded it as affording opportunities for social gatherings of those who were drawn together by similar tastes, and who might thus possibly be encouraged to pursue with greater assiduity those studies to which the objects collected there directed their attention. Again, a great deal of historical research would, he was sure, be originated there, which would be of very great advantage to them, not only in that county, but throughout the whole Principality. There were many facts in past history which they would be very sorry to lose sight of, but which were often regarded as mere myths. That Society, he had no doubt whatever, would prove that they were not myths. Historical facts were important; but principles were still more important, and he, for one, regarded the labours of that institution with peculiar interest on account of the principles which it would enable them to lay hold of and to appreciate. Montgomeryshire had been highly distinguished in distant ages. It was distinguished for having had connected with it the great name of Brochwel Ysgythrog, who, he believed, was one of the Princes of Powys-land. He did not at all refer to him in order to give them the slightest desire to revive the state of things which existed in his day; but there was one very important fact in his history. Brochwel was instrumental in turning back the tide of war which was then advancing in the Principality; and not only the inroad made upon our civil institutions but upon our religious institutions. Upon the occasion of that successful struggle a terrible slaughter took place on the borders, near the great Abbey and College of Bangor Iscoed. As to the question whether the Romish missionaries had anything to do with it, historians agreed among themselves as a rule to say " No ;" but let that be as it might, they knew that an attack was made upon the institutions and liberties of this country, but Brochwel came forward, stood boldly out against the aggression, turned the tide of war, and saved us for a long period, our freedom, our institutions, and our learning. They must not suppose that the learning was a myth, even at that remote period ; for there were, he believed, at that time in that institution, about two thousand inmates, just the number the great University of Oxford could boast of at the present day. A distinguished individual, wrong-headed as he was, Pelagius, was educated there, and the famous Abbot Dunawd, or Dinoth, was the head of the institution, when Augustine first came to England, and acted as the leader of the British Bishops in resisting his pretensions. The men of Montgomeryshire, joining heartily with Brochwel, were instrumental under Divine Providence, in turning back the tide, and not only in securing to their countrymen a certain amount of liberty, but also in maintaining in its integrity the religion they had received from apostolic times. He believed that the candle of God's truth was lighted in this land at a very early period. He could not bring his mind to suppose that the apostolic age had passed away before the gospel was preached to our forefathers. There was one singular circumstance which the language of their country, whether they valued it or not, had preserved to them, in the use of one expression — the name given to Confirmation, " Bedydd Esgob"—("Bishop's Baptism.") The question of the realization of the baptismal covenant, by the ministration of the Bishop at Confirmation happened to be one of the points in dispute between the British Bishops, seven of them in all, and Augustine and his companions. It might appear strange that they should attach so much importance to it, but it was in reality of infinite importance. It was the Protestant religion showing itself long before its day. Rome then held that Confirmation was to be administered immediately after baptism, as something opus operatum or ex opere operato. This was resisted by the representatives of the British Church, who contended that a sufficient interval should elapse to give an opportunity of seeing whether the conditions of the baptismal covenant were realized and fulfilled, and that not till then should the rite of Confirmation be administered. That one circumstance was of the greatest possible advantage to us, because it showed that in those early days our forefathers appreciated the truth that religion was a matter of personal faith, and not a mere empty profession. But he must not detain them any longer. He could only say it gave him the greatest possible pleasure to be present at that gathering. He trusted that before very long they would fill their new room, and not only so, but require in course of time other rooms to be added to it. Lord Powis had referred to the British and South Kensington Museums. He (the Bishop) believed those Museums were full to overflowing, and if they in Montgomeryshire were prepared to take charge of them they might possibly become the recipients of some of those superfluous treasures, and possess a collection such as no other county in Wales possessed. He hoped great success would attend their efforts. He thoroughly agreed with his Lordship that the greatest credit was due to their Secretary, Mr. Morris Jones. But for that gentleman he (the Bishop) should not have known much about their institution, and he was very much obliged to him for writing to him from time to time about it. (Cheers).

The motion was then put and carried unanimously.

Mr. HOWELL said that Lord Powis had referred to the want of accommodation at the British Museum. They did not propose to supply that want, but they proposed to extend the operations of the Powys-land Museum, and to make it more or less a Museum for the whole of Wales. The resolution he had to propose was the following :—

Having considered the report of the Council of the Cambrian Archæological Association to their last annual meeting, wherein it is stated—
"That the Powys-land Museum is not only the most valuable in Wales, but in some respects the only one :
"That Wales at present has no Museum of Antiquities :
"That the Museums at Carnarvon, Swansea, Tenby, and Lampeter College cannot supply what is wanted, viz., a general and central Museum for Welsh Antiquities ;
"That the nearest approach to one is at hand in Welshpool (viz., the Powys-land Museum), and could be made to answer the purpose at a small cost" ;
Resolved, that the Powys-land Club is prepared to make arrangements with the Cambrian Archæological Association, whereby the Powys-land Museum may become a general and central Museum for Welsh Antiquities, and that an intimation to that effect be conveyed to the Council of the Cambrian Archæological Association, and that the Council of the Powys-land Club be a Committee to negociate with them, three to be a quorum, and to report to a general meeting of the Club.

They would bear in mind that the proposal emanated from the Cambrian Archæological Association. The first mention of it was contained in the report of the meeting of the Association held at Welshpool in August, 1879. At that meeting the following remarks were made by the Rev. E. L. Barnwell, the treasurer, respecting the Museum :—

With regard to the Museum, there was nothing of the kind, so far as he knew, in any other part of Wales ; and, from his knowledge of the Principality, which extended over thirty years, he did not see much probability of the example being followed in the other counties. The Museum was not only for the benefit of the town, but also for the whole community. They had articles in their Museum which were perfectly unique, rare, and of inestimable value.

In the report of the Powys-land Museum and Library Committee, presented to the annual meeting last year, the proposal was referred to in the following terms :—

A suggestion has been made that the Powys-land Museum—secured, as it is, by deed upon public trusts—rendered stable by a repair fund—endowed with a cottage residence for a care-keeper—prohibited by its trust deed from being used for political or polemical purposes—affording, with the proposed addition, ample present accommodation, and having vacant land sufficient, when required, to double the present ground-floor accommodation—that this Museum, thus advantageously placed, and centrally situated in Wales, could form a fit, indeed, the most suitable receptacle, which the Cambrian Archæological Association could adopt as a "Museum of Antiquities" for North and Central Wales. The Committee concur in the wisdom and expediency of this suggestion ; and, on their part, are ready to adopt and carry it out, when the proper time for so doing has arrived ; and, in the meantime, express their willingness to take charge of such objects as may be entrusted to them.

At the recent meeting of the Cambrian Archæological Association at Pembroke the matter was again referred to in the report of the Council of the Association. Having read an extract from the report, which was to the effect stated in the preamble of the resolution, Mr. Howell said he thought that all those who had been associated with that institution from its commencement might well concur in the sentiments there expressed. He did not wish to make personal references to their friend the Secretary, but it was difficult to avoid it, as they were so much indebted to him in every way for what had been done. There had been a continuous and steady advance, with no chance of retrogression. Every inch of fresh ground which had been gained had been permanently secured. He could see, therefore, no objection to the proposed extension, and he believed they would agree with him that it was likely to be of great benefit both to themselves and to the Principality at large. He therefore begged to move the resolution he had read. (Cheers.)

The Rev. D. R. THOMAS said so much had been said about the sentiments of the Cambrian Archæological Association upon this matter that it became a very easy and pleasant office to second the proposal brought forward by Mr. Howell. It had been the object of the Association from the very commencement to try and stir up different parts of the country to form museums in which local antiquities might be brought together, so that there might be in every county, if possible, a nucleus of information and instruction upon the antiquity and history of that county. To a certain extent that object had been attained, in so far as in several places, Carnarvon, Swansea, Tenby, and Lampeter, museums had already been formed. At Carnarvon, which had ample opportunities and means of acquiring objects of interest in the neighbourhood, the museum itself was, he believed, much inferior now to what it was twenty or thirty years ago. At their recent meeting there they were unable to find some objects of interest which had been there when the Society met at Carnarvon about the year 1848. At Swansea there was a museum of considerable value. When the Cambrian Archæological Association was started, it was intended to make it the focus and centre of its own antiquities; and many of their books were placed in charge of the Swansea Royal Institution ; but for some reason or other, probably on account of the inconvenience of the situation, the scheme was not carried out. At Tenby an admirable museum was being vigorously worked, and the time would perhaps come when it would run the Powys-land Club very hard, and the harder it ran them the better. There was also at Lampeter an admirable museum of its kind. There was one antiquity in that museum they could never hope to match—an ancient copy of the Scriptures, dating, he believed, from about the eleventh or twelfth century, and marked with the blood of some of the martyrs at Bangor Iscoed. At Aberystwyth a museum had been started which was likely to be of very great value. The more museums there were the better pleased they would be, because every one who wanted to study the antiquities of his country and his district would learn a great deal more from looking at objects which illustrated them than he could possibly learn by mere reading. (Cheers.) He would say everything he possibly could in favour of other museums, and if any one present had any objects of special local interest or value, he (Mr. Thomas) would not be jealous, and he was sure Mr. Morris Jones would not be jealous, if either of those museums was chosen as the depository of those treasures, but there was really more to be said in favour of the Powys-land museum than of any of the others. It formed a better nucleus and was situated more centrally and more conveniently for access by railway from different parts of the Principality. Aberystwyth had one leg in the sea, but their museum was situated very centrally for North and South Western Wales, and also for the Marches. He therefore had great pleasure in seconding the resolution proposed by Mr. Howell, and he thought the Council of the Cambrian Archæological Association would be the more ready to accede to the proposal when they were told in what a winning, wily way the new room had been dedicated in their honour. (Cheers and laughter.)

The CHAIRMAN then put the resolution to the meeting and it was carried unanimously.

The MAYOR OF WELSHPOOL said that the Secretary had done him the honour of placing the next resolution in his hands, and he was quite sure it would be as acceptable to the meeting as it was gratifying to him to propose it to them. The Earl of Powis had held the office of President of the Club ever since its formation thirteen years ago, and he hoped that his lordship would continue for many years to come to preside over its meetings, and to give it the benefit of his kind and active support. (Cheers.) He was sure it must be gratifying to his lordship as President of the Club to see the success which had attended the efforts of their untiring and energetic Secretary, Mr. Morris Jones. (Cheers.) He begged to move that the thanks of the meeting be given to Lord Powis for presiding over it. (Cheers.)

The Rev. D. P. LEWIS seconded the motion, which was carried amid cheers.

His LORDSHIP said he was much obliged for the compliment they had been good enough to pay him, and on behalf of the Committee of the Club he begged to thank the visitors who had attended the meeting. (Cheers.)

The proceedings then terminated.

GOD BLESS THE PRINCE OF WALES.—Some songs for soldiers and for the volunteer forces have appeared at intervals, but since Dr. John Bull, the professor at Gresham College, produced "God save the King," which was composed and performed on the occasion of King James's visit to Merchant Taylors' Hall in 1607, in commemoration of his Majesty's escape from the Powder Plot, there has appeared but one truly national anthem, which has been loyally and emphatically accepted as one of the patriotic songs of the people. We mean "God Bless the Prince of Wales," by Mr. Brinley Richards, and by a curious co-incidence this air emanated from a Welshman. The origin of Mr. Brinley Richards's "accepted National Anthem," so called by the Daily News, was due to the Eisteddfod held in the ruins of Carnarvon Castle. It was at the request, in 1862, of one of the judges, Mr. Ceiriog Hughes, that Mr. Brinley Richards set the Welsh words by the former, an English translation of which was made by the late George Linley, under the title of "The Prince of our Brave Land," till the composer re-wrote the first four lines, and entitled the air, "God Bless the Prince of Wales." It was Mr. Sims Reeves who first sang it at St. James's Hall on Feb. 14, 1863. Its success was immediate and immense. The new lease for its popularity naturally was signed by the general public, not only of this country, but also by that of the most distant colonies—indeed wherever the sun shines on Britishers the anthem was sung during and after the dangerous illness of the heir to the Crown—a revival for royalty and loyalty after some sinister democratic signs which was unparalleled in history. . . . At all the festivals in Wales, Mr. Brinley Richards's choral compositions, both sacred and secular, are sung. As a native of Carmarthen, where he was born in 1819, this was natural enough, but his works have stood by the side of those of the greatest composers, so that there is something more than nationality in this appreciation. A Welshman has achieved for his country what Rouget de l' Isle has done for France in the "Marseillaise," which, by the way, by the turn of the political wheel of fortune in that country, is now recognized as the "national song." . . . The Russians have recognized "God Bless the Prince of Wales," for the military band of St. Petersburg played the anthem on the occasion of the marriage of the Duke of Edinburgh, whilst her most gracious Majesty commanded a performance of the air at a banquet at Balmoral Castle, after the toast of the Prince of Wales. Mr. Brinley Richards has added to the songs of the people, and what he has written will be enduring like our ancient ballads.—Temple Bar Magazine, May, 1879.

The following appears in the October number of The Antiquary :—"In the latest volume of his 'Collectanea Antiqua' Mr. Roach Smith has published some interesting anecdotes of his late friend and colleague, Mr. Thomas Wright, F.S.A. Our readers will regret to learn that Mrs. Wright is in severe suffering, and almost in a state of destitution. It has been suggested that a portion, at least, of the literary pension which was awarded to Mr. Wright should be continued to her; and it is to be hoped that Mr. Gladstone will recommend the proposal."

A new church, dedicated to St. John, which has been erected in Waenfawr, a chapelry of Carnarvon, and the centre of a large mining population, was opened on September 29. The services were in Welsh, and the preachers were the Bishop of Bangor and the Rev. Griffith Roberts, vicar of Llanegryn and rector-designate of Dowlais. The site is the gift of the late Mr. Holman, and a stained glass window to his memory is placed in the new church by his widow. The cost of the building is about £1,200. Mr. Kennedy of Bangor was the architect.

The Builder mentions "some grotesque modern carvings which a friend of ours lighted upon lately at Chester Cathedral. These corbels will be found on the north-east corner of the north transept of the Cathedral, and seem to be known locally as Political Contention and Religious Contention. In the first, Lord Beaconsfield and the late Dr. Kenealy are readily recognizable engaged in a struggle in which a crown and a cap of liberty are concerned; and in the second Mr. Gladstone is using his learning as a fulcrum for the upsetting of the Romish Church."

NONCONFORMITY IN OSWESTRY.

Statement of Accounts connected with the Building of the Old Chapel and Repairing the Vestry and the Houses. 1830.

	£	s.	d.		£	s.	d.
To Bills paid...	1047	9	8	By subscriptions			
„ to pay	65	17	9	received	461	5	2½
				„ to receive	48	10	0
	1113	7	5				
					509	15	2½
To Balance ...	603	12	2½	Balance	603	12	2½
					1113	7	5

Examined, John Francis, Aug. 6, 1830.

November, 1833. Average number of the congregations in the respective places of worship in Oswestry, as stated to the Commissioners for enquiring into the state of Municipal Corporations, in the Town Hall; with the number of scholars in the Sunday Schools :—

Church Congregation, about 700, and has an adult Sunday School.

Independents,	congregation,	600,	school,	180
Baptists,	do.	260,	do.	60
Wesleyans,	do.	300,	do.	60
WelshCalvinisticMethodists,260,			do.	100
Primitive Methodists		100		

OCTOBER 20, 1880.

NOTES.

SHROPSHIRE AND SLAVERY. — In the Division on Mr. Wilberforce's Slavery Abolition Bill, Mar. 26, 1796, one Shropshire member voted against it, but my authority (a newspaper of the name) omits the name. Sir Richard Hill was absent, but he paired in favour. It was the opinion of the opponents of the Bill, that "it destroyed private property, and violated the dearest part of the British Constitution." The Hon. R. Clive, member for Ludlow, voted for the Bill, and W. Clive, Esq., member for Bishop's Castle, was prevented by accident from voting.   N.W.S.

THE WELSH ALMANACKS (Oct. 6, 1880).—In resuming the account of the old Welsh Almanacks, I would remark that some writers made fun of them, whereupon the compiler (Robert Roberts), as we have seen, in his issue for 1803 sets this down to *spite*. Be that as it may, it is no part of our business to discuss the question at issue, and we therefore proceed to give the title pages of those for 1804—1807.   E.G.S.

The one for 1804 is printed at Dublin, and is called "*Cyfaill Glandeg.*" The price is fourpence halfpenny, and the following verses are on the title page :—

1. Fy hen GYFEILLION Gwisgi,
   Sydd *etto* yn fy hoffi ;
   Mae *Llyfrau'r* Byd, gan *gall* a *ffol*,
   Mewn *parch* yn ol eu *ffansi*.

2. *Haul, Lloer*, a sêr hâf dirion,
   Ymladdodd â *Gelynnion ;*
   Ymladdant etto, os bydd raid,
   Mor gryf o blaid *Duwiolion.*

3. Mae rbai yn synnu'n erwin,
   Fod *Sectiau'n* coethi'n gethin ;
   Er bod hynny yn ddi ball,
   Cyn *Calfin* gall, nac *Armin.*

4. Rhoed i ni siamplau cyson,
   Gan *Grist* a'i *Apostolion !*
   Mae yma fywyd i barhau,
   Rhag byw ar ddoniau *dynion.*

5. 'R un modd â *gwlaw* ac *Eira*,
   I'r *Ddaear* pan fo sycha ;
   Mae *Duw'n* cynnyddu gwaith ei law,
   A'r *Gair* a ddaw o'i *Ena.*

6. There's many *roads* to a *City*,
   Says *People* of different *Party* ;
   No ways to *Heaven*, they bear accord ;
   But *Christ* our *Lord* Almighty.

The one for 1805 is printed at Dublin ; is called "Cyfaill Taeredd." The price fourpence halfpenny, with the following verses on title page :—

1. GYFEILLION sydd mewn 'wyllys,
   I gael ymgomio'n gymmwys ;
   Am gwrs y Byd a threfn y *Rhod ;*
   Er mwyn cael bod yn hysbys.

2. Mae'r *Ser* yn rhedeg beunydd,
   I linell y *canol ddydd ;*
   'Bron pedwar *munud* ar eu hyut,   3′55″
   Bob nos yn gynt na'u gilydd.

3. Fel *Lleuad* ar ei chynnydd,
   Y mae'r *Creadur* newydd ;
   Mwy fwy ei Gariad, Ffydd, a Dawn,
   Nes myn'd i'w lawn *lawenydd.*

4. *Rhagrithwyr* cynfigenllyd,
   Ar ol *professu* ennyd ;
   Ant yn llai lai, gan gnawd a byd,
   Fel *Lleuad* hyd y newid.

5. Un peth sydd *angenrheidiol*,
   Goruwch holl *Ddoniau* dynol ;
   Adnabod *Iesu Grist* yn *Rhann*
   I'r *Enaid* gwan anfarwol.

6. Our Enemies are many ;
   In force of *Pride* and *Envy ;*
   We beg of GOD both Night and Day,
   To keep away their *Army.*

The one for 1806, printed at Dublin, price fourpence halfpenny, has these verses on the title page :—[Called "Cyfaill Cymmeredig."]

1. GYFEILLION pur eu bwriad,
   Sydd ystwyth iawn yn wastad ;
   I wrthod *Enllib* o bob rhyw,
   Er mwyn cael byw mewn *Cariad.*

2. Mae'r *Byd* yn troi rwy'n teuru,
   I *Haul* mawr ei lewyrchu ;
   O'i flaen o hyd mae'n torri dydd ;
   O'i ol y bydd yn t'wyllu.

3. Cyn Angeu mae *Duw'n* golchi,
   Ei Blant oddi wrth ddrygioni ;
   A'r Annuwiolion (ond y chwith)
   Oddi wrth eu *rhith* ddaioni.

4. Mae *Crist* a'i Ras yn puro,
   Pawb ynddo sydd yn ffrwytho ;
   Y rhai na arhoso dan ei law,
   A deflir draw i wywo.

5. Os oes *Pregethwyr* ffyrfiol,
   Am gasglu Tyrfa ddynol ;
   Mae rbai am *Filwyr* teg eu gwawr ;
   I'r *Brenin* mawr Tragwyddol.

6. This *Morning* we appear ;
   Our *Night* is coming near ;
   All *Friends* and *Goods* we leave behind,
   And cannot find them ever.

The one for the year 1807; printed at Dublin, price fourpence halfpenny, is called "Cyfaill Distaw," and has the following verses on the title page :—

1. Hyd attoch unwaith etto,
   Y daethym wrth ymlusgo ;
   Ac er nad wyf ond burgyn gwael,
   Chwenychaf gael fy nghroeso.

2. Y ser sefydlog golau,
   I'w dolbyrth sydd yn hauliau ;
   A'r rbai tramwyol'n ol eu rhyw,
   Sydd dywyll clyw, yn ddiau.

3. Rhyw lyfyr mawr yw'r awyr,
   Y ser llyth'rennau eglur ;
   Hwy a argraphwyd oll gan Dduw,
   A dynion yw'r darllenwyr.

4. Yr Haul a'r Lloer wrth enw,
   Sy'n llywio trai a llanw ;
   Cyd lithant hwy y gorllif can,
   Gwrth dynnant pan fo'n marw.

5. Ein dosparth fer sy'n darfod,
   Pob munud awr a diwrnod,
   Boed i'n ei nabod Ef yn well,
   Cyn myn'd i briddell beddrod.

6. May God the source of mercy,
   Protect our King and country,
   May he (to Britain's joys) increase
   The bliss of peace and plenty.

QUERIES.

SHREWSBURY ASSIZE OF BREAD.—From a Shrewsbury paper of Oct. 15, 1795, I take the following:—
Shrewsbury Assize of Bread. By order of the Mayor :—

		lb.	oz.	dr.
The Penny Loaf or two	White	0	4	4
Half-penny loaves	Wheaten	0	5	11
	Household	0	7	9
	White	0	8	8
The Two-penny Loaf	Wheaten	0	11	6
	Household	0	15	2
Three-penny Loaf	Wheaten	1	1	1
	Household	1	6	11
Four-penny Loaf	Wheaten	1	6	12
	Household	1	14	4
Six-penny Loaf	Wheaten	2	2	2
	Household	2	13	6
Twelve-penny Loaf	Wheaten	4	4	4
	Household	5	10	12

Can any of your readers explain what this means?
TELL.

OLD OSWESTRY BALLAD.—Has anyone preserved a copy of a ballad once written and published by "Minshull the Printer" entitled *The Twelve Tribes*, or *The Town in Danger of a Siege*? I only remember three of the verses, which ran as follows :—

The Owenites will Pave the way
To share the glories of the day,
Can use the Pickaxe and the Spade
If deepened trenches must be made.

The Robleyites will never halt
Till they have Ground their foes like Malt,
And turned them bravely o'er and o'er
Like Barley on a Malthouse floor.

The Minshullites, a noble train,
Will strip the bodies of the slain,
And Sell their Clothes (now don't turn pale)
Or Serve the Camp with famous Ale.

To explain the last verse it must be stated that Minshull kept a beerhouse, and dealt in old clothes, as well as following his trade of printer. Owen was the town pavior, in the days when Oswestry was laid with "petrified kidneys." Mr. Robley was a maltster living in Salop Road. I should feel greatly obliged to any one who would lend me copies of Minshull's ballads and squibs. They should be promptly copied and carefully returned.
JARCO.

THE YEOMANRY CAVALRY.—At the beginning of the year 1820 several of the regiments of Yeomanry Cavalry were increased in number ; thus Montgomeryshire had the addition of two troops ; and Flintshire, through the exertions of Lord Kenyon, the same. In Denbighshire, it was stated, the subscriptions for increasing the force amounted to £1,300. What was all this money wanted for, and why were the troops augmented at that particular period? VOLUNTEER.

REPLIES.

SHREWSBURY SCHOOLS (Sep. 1, 1880).—The *Shrewsbury Chronicle* of June 15, 1838, says—The Porson prize "for the best translation of a passage from Shakespeare into Greek verse" was adjudged to Mr. Thomas Evans, of St. John's College, Cambridge, formerly of the Shrewsbury Royal School. Mr. France, also of Shrewsbury School, carried the Declamation prize. And the prize for the best Classical Scholar among the Freshmen was adjudged to Mr. Thring. (For "Porson prize" of 1880 see Reprint of *Bye-gones*, p. 66.)

The Rev. James Wilding, M.A., who has recently been presented to the Vicarage of Chirbury, in this his native county, by the trustees of Shrewsbury School, has had presented to him a service of plate from the inhabitants of Cheam, Surrey, as a memorial of his 32 years ministerial labours. Some time previously Mr. Wilding was presented with a Silver Tea Service by the pupils on his retirement from the mastership of the school at Cheam.—*Shrewsbury papers*, Oct. 1838.

The *Salopian Journal* of July 11, 1838, says, "We are authorized to state that the Viscount Dungannon has intimated to the Rev. Stephen Donne his intention of presenting two prizes annually to the boys of *Oswestry* School." What were these prizes, and how long did his lordship continue the practice? In Mar. 1839 his lordship intimated to Dr. Kennedy his intention of presenting Fifteen guineas annually for the encouragement of classical literature in *Shrewsbury* School.

The same paper of Sep. 26, 1838, says that the day-scholars of *Shrewsbury* School, desirous of showing respect to the Rev. Arthur Willis, one of their masters, on his becoming head-master of *Ludlow* Grammar School, presented him with a silver tea-service. The presentation took place at the house of Mrs. Scoltock of Princess Street, and Mr. James Tomlins, the head day pupil, was the spokesman for his fellows. SCROBBES BYRIG.

CURRENT NOTES.

TRANSACTIONS OF THE SHROPSHIRE ARCH. ÆOLOGICAL SOCIETY. Shrewsbury : Adnitt and Naunton. Oswestry : Woodall and Venables.
PART 3, completing Vol. 3, has just been issued to subscribers, and contains the completion of "Taylor's MS." transcribed by the Rev. W. A. Leighton ; also a valuable genealogical paper, under the somewhat misleading title of "Lord Herbert of Cherbury's MSS.," by Mr. H. F. J. Vaughan. Mr. Phillips contributes a paper on "The Hymenomycetes of Shropshire," and Mr. Calloway one on "Further Geological Discoveries in Shropshire." Again

we would urge on such of the more intelligent of our readers who have not yet become members of the Shropshire Archæological Society, that they should by all means do so without delay; before the number is filled up, and the copies of the Journal of the Society are exhansted. To Oswestry men, especially, would we urge this, for in no other form can they ever secure the interesting Corporation documents Mr. Stanley Leighton has at so much expense and labour, placed in so attractive a form before the public. In the three volumes that have, so far, been issued, there has been much of interest to our locality, and other papers are in progress. Application for membership must be made to Mr. Adnitt, hon. sec., Lystonville, Shrewsbury, or we shall be only too happy to receive names at our office.

ATHRAVAETH GRISTNOGAVL. 1568. Printed for the Honourable Society of Cymmrodorion. London 1880.

WE cannot quite see who will be interested in this reprint, which professes to be "Reproduced in fac-simile from the unique copy in the possession of H.I.H. Prince Louis-Lucien Bonaparte," but which, after all, is *not* a fac-simile—such as would have been secured had the pages been photographed—but a reprint, as nearly as possible copying the original. The Prince has taken great pains to secure correctness, and where he has overlooked errors has noted them at the end of the book. But these "errata" are curiously jumbled by the printers, who have so arranged some of the lines that you have to look twice before you can see what is really meant. Something about the book itself will be found on page 81 of the Reprint of *Bye-gones* 1880' under date of July 7th. The *Athenæum* says: Among the many languages which Prince Louis-Lucien Bonaparte has studied are those of the Celtic nations, and among them that of the Welsh. A short while ago he called attention to the fact that he had in his possession a unique Welsh book, called *Athravaeth Gristnogavl*, published by Griffith Roberts at Milan in 1568, where he also printed the only portion published of his Welsh Grammar, the first book of the kind ever printed in the language. The small quarto before us is a kind of Roman Catholic catechism, the language and orthography of which are highly interesting. The editor tells us that the illustrious owner of this treasure spared no trouble in directing the work, and on inspecting it we are at once convinced of the truth of a remark in the preface, that the printing has been done line for line and word for word, even the obvious typographical errors, in which the text abounds, being scrupulously reproduced. Among other things the Prince points out several arguments supplied by the typography in confirmation of the opinion that "Mylen," whence Griffith Roberts dates, is Milan, and not the hypothetical town in Wales suggested by Panizzi some years ago. Prince L. L. Bonaparte deserves the heartiest thanks of the Cymmrodorion for his painstaking generosity, and that Society in its turn deserves the thanks of the Welsh for the highly creditable fashion in which the work has been executed.

MONTGOMERYSHIRE COLLECTIONS, issued by the Powys-land Club. London, printed by T. Richards. THE present number completes the thirteenth volume, and is in no way inferior to its predecessors. The part opens with a continuation of Mr. Morris Charles Jones's history of Welshpool, in which the troublous times of Charles the First are rapidly sketched, and many valuable and trustworthy authorities quoted. A graphic incident in the history of the town, at an earlier period, 1615, is also noted, viz., the murder of Mr. Thomas Jones of Llanerch-brochwell in the streets by Mr. John Lloyd, who ran him

through with a rapier, in consequence of a quarrel at an ale-house. The Welshpool paper is illustrated by a curious old map of "The Welsh Poole in 1629," and a drawing by Mr. David Pryce Owen (from an old engraving,) of the Old Church, in 1587. The Rev. Elias Owen continues his interesting paper on "Weather Signs," and Mr. Askew Roberts supplements Mr. Charles Williams Wynn's article on the Montgomeryshire Volunteers of 1803, by some additional details. Other papers are advanced a stage, and some are completed. Of the latter we may mention Mr. T. G. Jones's "Welsh Proverbs," and of the former, Mr. Fewtrell's (shall we say too exhaustive ?) history of the parish of Llanymynech. In "Montgomeryshire Worthies" Mr. R. Williams gives an outline of the Rev. R. Ellis (Cynddelw) one of the early contributors to *Bye-gones*, and the Rev. Wolseley Lewis gives a list of the recipients of the Powis Exhibition at Oxford, amongst whom we find the name of one since deceased (Mr. Nicholas) who was a constant contributor to the columns of the *Oswestry Advertizer*. Another of our valued contributors to *Bye-gones*, Mr. Howel W. Lloyd, furnishes an excellent paper on "Reliques of Valle Crucis &c.," and the Rev. J. Davies, M.A., one on a "Welsh Marriage Deed." Lastly the Rev. G. Sandford has presented a most readable account of the Lordship of Leighton, and its strange vicissitudes. In the "Miscellanea" there are some papers on Nonconformity in Montgomeryshire, which point to the fact that the Rev. Dr. Edward Williams of Oswestry, was something like a 'Bishop' of the order in this district, at the end of the last century.

Amongst the notices of deceased ministers mentioned in the Wesleyan "Minutes of Conference" for 1880, is one of the Rev. Evan Pugh, who was born at Bryncrug, Merionethshire, and who "for forty-three years exercised His sermons were carefully prepared and delivered with earnestness and pathos. He loved his work, continued his hallowed toil so long as his strength lasted, and literally went from the pulpit to his bed to die."

A new church, dedicated to the Holy Trinity, has been built at Rhosygwalia, Bala. The late Mr. H. T. Richardson of Pwllheli, formerly of Aberhirnant, near Bala, left by will a sum of £2,000, to be expended in the restoration of the church, and the interest on £1,000 towards keeping the church and Vicarage in repair; but although the church was erected only forty years ago, it was so dilapidated that it was decided to re-build it entirely. Mr. E. B. Ferrey of London was the architect.

OCTOBER 27, 1880.

NOTES.

OSWESTRY SCHOOL.—Several references have been made in *Bye-gones* to David Holbach, the founder of our Schools, and it has been stated that diligent search has been made for his will, without effect. But it is by no means certain that his will would throw any light on the question, because we are no where told that he bequeathed the property, only that he founded and endowed the School. In Price's *History of Oswestry* the date of his doing this is vaguely fixed as in the reign of Henry IV., and Cathrall (with what authority I know not) says "the munificent founder granted, for the maintenance of a schoolmaster, and the reparation of the school-house, certain lands in Sweeney, Treflach, Maesbury, and Crickheath, in addition to a house on the south-west side of the parish church." The Rev. D. R. Thomas

5
19

(Hist. Dio. St. Asaph) is of opinion that some fields still known as "The Holbeches" at Sweeney, were the only lands originally given by the founder, and that the rest has been acquired at various times since. I have been for some time trying to get all the information I can on the subject, for a paper to be published in the *Transactions of the Shropshire Archæological Society*, and although I have not found anything about Holbach's gift, I have found, in an attested copy of an original document, the following :—

"Presens Indentura facta inter Thomam Lestrange, Jo-h'em Hanmer, Will'm Burley, armiger, Edr'um Trevor, Joh'em Wyckle, David ap Thomas, Ric'um Hova, clericos, Will'm Hord de Salop, Cadwalladrw ap Owen, Evan ap Arthur ap Evan, Ric'um Ireland, Edr'um ap David, Job'em Eton, Thoma' Lloyd, Madocum ap David Gethin, Ric'um ap Thomas, Griffith ap Thomas, Griffith ap David Gethin, et Edr'um ap Goch in ex p'te una, et Gwenhwyvar que fuit uxor David Holbadge p'te ex alt'a testatur quod p'd Gwenhwyvar dederit, concesserit, et p' carta sua feofament' confirmaverit p'dicis Thome & co'feoffats suis supd'cis molendinum granaticum de Maesbury, ac omnia terr' tant' prata, boscos, et subosc' cu' eoz p'ti'n que p'dca Gwenhwyfar h'uit infra Domn' duaz p'tin hundred' de Oswest' *Habend'* & tenend' eis hered' et assign' suis imipp'm pro ut in carta feod' sim'plis inde confecta plenius continetur. Idem tamen voluntate concediunt pro eis hered' & assign' eoz ut intencio David Holbach nuper mariti d'ce Gwenhwyvar in omnibus et pro omnia in hac p'te debeat observari, viz., quod redditu' exitus et pro-ficicu'm annualia duoz terraz, tenementorz, pratorz cu' p'tin ad annualia et sustentac'oe unius M.ri Scolaria apud Villa de Oswest' ordinari et applicati debent de anno in annu' impp'm. *In cujus rei,* & . . . "

"This is the Substance and Effect of the deed made by the within named Gwenhwyvar to the said Feoffees, the which deed beareth date about the 9th of Hen. 4th, the true and authenticall copy thereof is to be seene. Besides it is to be proved that the first purchase was made from Lhew Llewku Haston of Trevelech, the daughter of Gwillim ap Einion Goch, &c. . . . "

The names of the Feoffees that were put in trust by David Holbadge for the S^{ch}ool lands.

Thomas Lestrange	} Esqrs.	Richard Ireland
John Hanmer		Edward ap David
William Burley		John Eyton
Edward Trevor		Thomas Lloyd
John Wilke		Madock ap David Gethin
David ap Thomas, clerk		Richard ap Thomas
Richard Hova		Griffith ap Thomas
William Hord of Salop		Griffith ap David Gethin
Cadwallader ap Owen		Edward ap Gochin
Evan ap Arthur ap Evan		6 Hen. 4.

The foregoing points to two things ; 1, that Holbach had a wife who was interested in Oswestry and, who, really, was the donor of, at least, part of the property, viz :—a mill, granaries, &c., at Maesbury ; and 2, that the original grant comprised property not included in the Holbaches. It also gives definite dates, 6 and 9 Hen. 4.

We have no evidence that Holbach was a native of these parts. He was Steward of Oswestry at the beginning of the fifteenth century ; but had not then held the office long, for in 1393 it was held by John Boerley (see *Bye-gones* July 21, 1880). There was a John Boerley member for the county as early as 1399, and in 1409 Holbach was his fellow-member. Two years later, John Boerley drops out of the scene, but we have Holbach as member either for the county or county town, as late as

1417. Two other names in the list of Feoffees also appear in the Parliamentary lists; viz. : William Boerley, as member for Shropshire in 1417, and subsequently ; and William Hord, as member for Shrewsbury in 1414, &c. He was fellow member with Holbach in 1417.

If any of my London readers could trace the documents quoted above, I should be truly glad to hear from them ! It will be observed that Richard Hova is styled clergyman in the deed executed by Gwenhwyvar, the wife of David Holbach ; but in the list of Feoffees put in trust by the founder, David ap Thomas is described as the clerk. It will be noticed that two names, viz., Thomas Lestrange and John Hanmer, are bracketed. They were probably the Bailiffs, or rather the "Two Burgesses elected to hold pleas of the Crown" which were appointed under the provisions of the Charter of Rich. II, granted 1398 (see *Sh : Arch : Trans.* Vol. 2). Our town did not possess Bailiffs, so called, until 8 Hen. 4. It may be that Hova or David ap Thomas (as the case may be) was the vicar.
                                                          JARCO.

THE LLANDUDNO STONE.—The *North Wales Chronicle* in a report of the visit of "The Menai Society of Natural Science" to Llandudno in September, says : On the road side leading from Gloddaeth to Llandudno, in front of a cottage called Tyddyn Holland, between Bodafon and Rhiw, there is a grit stone, about a yard long, from which the following inscription is copied :—

SANCT
ANVS
SACRI
ISIS

This happens to be the reading given nearly half-a-century ago in Mr. Williams's *History of Aberconwy* ; and a reading he will no doubt amend when he issues (as I trust he may) a new and enlarged edition, which I have reason to know he has ready for the press. As far back as 1877 Professor Rhys, in *Arch : Camb :* (p. 135), called attention to this stone, and said, "I guess what remains of the three first lines to have been

SANCT
FILIXS
SACER

the fourth line I can make nothing of ; it looks as if it had been

1618

with the enclosed spaces frayed off ;" adding that he thought the first lines might be completed thus :—

SANCT ANVS (or SANCTAGNUS FILIUS) SACERDOTIS.

"The son's name may have been Sanctus, but 'Sanct-agnus' or 'Sanctánus' would have in its favour a passage in the preface to Sanctan's Irish hymn in the *Liber Hymnorum*, thus rendered by Mr. Whitley Stokes, 'Bishop Sanctum made this hymn,' &c. St. David's father is also said to have borne the name of 'Sant.'" In a further page Mr. Rhys pursues the subject *(Arch. Camb.* 1877, p. 239), where he suggests that "we have the name Sancagnus accurately contained in Sannan in the name of the church of Llansannan in the same district. This would put Sanctánus out of the question, and the suggestion that Sannan is identical with the Irish saint's name Senanus *(Lect. Welsh Philol.,* p. 25) is to be cancelled, and those on 388 to be modified." The conclusion Prof. Rhys comes to is that the Llandudno stone "probably commemorates the very Briton who is mentioned as Sanctan in Irish hagiology." Professor Westwood, in his *Lapidarium Walliæ,* gives an engraving of this stone, and states (p. 182) that in the narrow lane in which it is situated, "it is liable to be run against by the wheels of passing carts."
                                                          J.?.R.

QUERIES.

QUOITING IN SALOP.—It is announced in the *Salopian Journal* for June 27, 1838, that "The Great Quoit Match at Uffington, between the Gentlemen of North and South Shropshire" would be played on the Bowling Green of that place on the following Friday. Was the game of quoits ever a general one in Shropshire and the Borders, and is it ever played now-a-days? TELL.

DR. LINDEN.—In a poem called *Gayton Wake*, by Richard Llwyd, published at Chester in 1804, two lines run as follows :—

> Dr. Linden also crossed the Dee,
> And brought his magic rods.

To this the following note is added :—"A foreign adventurer, who a few years ago resided for a long time in different parts of Flintshire, and imposed upon many by a pretence of discovering minerals by the *Virgula Divinatoria.*" What does this refer to? I presume Dr. Linden, who wrote so much about the mineral waters of Wales about the middle of last century, is meant? Was he a quack? He is often quoted as an authority. G. G.

REPLIES.

CHURCH BELLS (Sep. 15, 1880.)—In the tower of the noble church of St. Lawrence at Ludlow is a melodious peal of eight bells, the inscriptions on which are thus given in Wright's *History of Ludlow*, 1852, page 469 :—

First.—Richard Perks, Town Clerk, A.R. 1732.
Second.—Abraham Rudhall, of Gloucester, cast us, 1732.
Third.—Rogers Phillips and William Bright, Churchwardens, 1732.
Fourth.—Prosperity to the town and our benefactors.
Fifth.—Prosperity to the town and parish.
Sixth.—Prosperity to the Church of England, A.R. 1732.
Seventh.—Somerset Jones, Esq. and Cæsar Hawkins, Gent. Bailiffs.
Eighth.—Tenor. The Rev. Richard Baugh, Rector, Mr. John Smith and Mr. John Smith, Churchwardens, 1823.

> May all whom I shall summon to the grave
> The blessings of a well spent life receive.

Shrewsbury. R.E.D.

WELL AT WOOLSTON (Sep. 22, 1880.)—The name connected with this well has been variously suggested as St. Wulston, St. Goustan, and St. Woollos. Mr. Anderson, in his *Shropshire Antiquities*, does not mention the Well, but he refers to the place as belonging to Mereseté (now Oswestry) Hundred. "When the Conqueror's record was compiled, Rainald the Sheriff held all these different manors of the Norman earl." Woolston was one of them, and the following quotation is given by Mr. Anderson : "'The same Rainald holds *Osulvestune* and a knight [holds the manor] of him. Uluric held it in King Edward's time with one berewick. Here i hide and a half. The land is for iii ox-teams. Here iiii Welsh have i team. It is worth 6s.' *Domesday*, fo. 255, a 1." NEMO.

LOCAL "NOTES AND QUERIES" (Oct. 6, 1880). On Sep. 15 I stated that the "Local Gleanings" in the *Shrewsbury Chronicle*, had either been given up or suspended. I am glad to see in the issue of that paper for Oct. 8, that the column in question has only been suspended, and after an interval of some months has been revived. I wish the editor could see his way to half a column every week, instead of nearly three columns once in as many months. The interest would be kept up and many of us would be on the look out. He has a splendid supply of material within his own doors ; and by throwing overboard one writer—who so far has filled the bulk of each instalment with somewhat stale matter—the Editor could profitably work his own mine, as he has done very partially in the last issue, for instance. I need scarcely say that by his "own mine" I mean the file of *Shrewsbury Chronicles*, beginning more than a century ago. A systematic search into the columns would bring to light many quaint events, and customs that interested the grandfathers of this generation, and would be none the less interesting to us. JARCO.

NOVEMBER 3, 1880.

NOTES.

THE LATE W. W. E. WYNNE OF PENIARTH. Having occasion to examine some old letters in my possession, I came across the following one from my lamented friend Mr. Wynne, addressed to Richard Llwyd the Bard of Snowdon. The column which he so often graced with his pen when alive, is the most suitable tablet upon which to inscribe this memorial of him, now that he is dead ; and I send it to you accordingly.

I have to return my thanks for your letter, and for the valuable information that it contains as to the History and Armorial bearings of Osburn Wyddell.

My Pedigree of the Drenewydd family compiled from the Harl. MSS. and the authority of my friend Miss Angharad Llwyd differs in some respects from yours, as will be seen by the following extract :—

Edward Lloyd of Llwynymaen ══ Elizabeth daughter and heiress of Richard Stanney of Oswestry.
|
John Lloyd second son of Whittington ══ Ellen daughter of John Rees.
|
Edward Lloyd ══ Catharine daughter of John Trevor Vychan diweddar o Groes Oswallt.
|
Marmaduke Lloyd Ob. 1670 ══ Penelope daughter of Charles Goodman of Glanharfin.
|

1	2	3	4
Edward, Ob. 1715	Charles	John	Catharine

All living 1676. So far from my Pedigree.

From an extract of the Whittington Register I find a Catharine Lloyd of Trenewith was buried on the 9th of September, 1740. I suppose her to have been the wife of Edward Lloyd, who died without issue, but whose daughter she was I know not. Certainly Catharine, the mother of Marmaduke Lloyd, could not have been alive at this period. If I may trouble you, I should feel obliged for some further particulars as to the matches of this family. I have little doubt that Charles Lloyd, who married Annabella Kingston, was the father of Annabella, heiress of Trenewydd, who was born in 1722, and who married in 1744 Richard Williams of Penbedw, my great-grandfather. I have every match from the third descendant from Hedd Molwynog down to Edward Lloyd of Llwynymaen, who married Elizabeth Stanney.

Did you ever observe a paragraph in Mr. Pennant's Tour, as follows?—"After leaving the village (Whittington) on the road towards Oswestry, I observed on the left Tre-Newydd, a seat of Watkin Williams, Esq., in right of his mother, heiress of the place. Her grandfather, Edward Lloyd, Esq., who died in 1715, was eminent for his learning, and had prepared materials for the History of his native county." Edward Lloyd of Trenewydd, son of Marmaduke, certainly did die in 1715, but I think that Mr. Pennant, who is not always the best authority, has mistaken him for the well-known Edward Lloyd, a natural son of Llanforda, who died in 1707.

I lament to say that my knowledge of my native tongue is not what it should be, and I must plead guilty of great ignorance in my orthography of Tre-Newydd. I believe that I am possessed of a copy of the book you mention, though not very perfect. If I should hear of any person in want of this work, or any one likely to purchase it, I will let you know. Mr. Williams Wynn's frank will bear a vol. such as you mention. It should however be packed up in *white paper* and as much as possible in a convenient shape for the post.

There is no date on the letter, but Mr. Wynne, looking at it one day with me, believed he had written it in the year 1830, so that he lived for another half century beyond that year to work up the heraldic history of families, and to enrich his own and other people's papers with those "notes" in which he so much delighted and excelled. It is probable that after Richard Llwyd he was the greatest master of genealogical and historic facts that we have had in North Wales in modern times, and latterly he stood alone, the one authority to whom all bowed ; nor do I derogate from Richard Llwyd's fame when I say that Mr. Wynne was in many respects superior to him, partly because he had better means of good information' at his command, a wider knowledge of history, and a more exact acquaintance with the cramped language in which old masters in these arts had conveyed their thoughts in MS. Ah, me ! we shall never look upon his like again, nor will the void his death has left in the ranks be ever filled up by scholars and antiquaries. The genial, kind, unselfish manner in which he did the duty of friend and adviser to all who stood in need of his help and assistance, will never be forgotten by those who had the pleasure of his acquaintance. Peace to his ashes ! E.G.S.

DIARY OF MRS. SARAH SAVAGE.
(Oct. 13, 1880.)

Feb. 16, 1715. My husband went to Chester. A public Election for parliam't men for the county. A hot poll—lasted three days. Sir Geo. Warburton & Mr. Booth were chosen by a majority of 500 votes. Lord wilt thou meet the great assembly when these meet ; let good laws be enacted & good men intrusted with the execution of them.

June 1, 1715. Tydings of much disturbance by the Jacobite mob ; great outrages in London, Oxford, York, Manchester & Shrewsbury. Fire kindled in some meeting-houses. God in mercy I trust will set bounds to their rage, as he does to the seas proud waves—hitherto shall ye come but no farther.

June 3, 1715. Mr. Thos. Hunt from Boreaton & his sister Jenny came to make us a visit.

June 14, 1715. We had the tidings of the death of S'r J. Cotton at London, June 12, being seiz'd with a palsy stroke in his coach last Thursd'. A great man fall'n. I suppose not 40. He is gone to his place. His fine houses, gardens, furniture, &c., shall know him no more. Lord let me be enrich'd with someth'g w'h death cannot strip me of.

July 11, 1715. We sent son Phil. to Wem & Moathouse to enquire of their state. Tuesd, he return'd, found it true y't Shrewsbury meeting ho : is destroy'd by violent hands—y't at Wem has no harm as yet, nor Whitechurch. O Lord be pleas'd to quiet the minds of unreasonable men.

This week it pleas'd the Almighty to permit it y't on Tuesd. Wem chapel & on Friday Whitch. was pulled down. Of the latter I was an ear witness (July 15) in the afternoon, (we going to Wh'ch y't day) at 5 or 6 o'clock. The rabble crowded to the chap. & with g't heat & violence broke all to pieces. They triumph & rejoice but the city Shushan was perplex'd. I co'd not but be affected to see so many good p.p. with their eyes & their hearts failing, while others are making the town ring with their acclamations, bringing some parts of the building to burn in

different places. Sais a good man—it's sad work, but blessed be God we have a Tabernacle above not made with hands, out of their reach. I staid with my daugh'r Keay fryday & Satt'y night. On Sab : day no solemn assembly, yet two or three in an upper chamber met to repeat a pray'r and sing, & found it good to be there.

July 17, 1715. Mr. King of Stone preach'd to-day at Nampt'h (his own meeting being in ruins).

The beginning of this week my husband had some trouble with one of the villians, y't help'd to pull down Wt'chyrch Meeting, who came y't night to Wrenbury, & behav'd insolently & being drunk spoke treas'able words ag't the King, w'h being proved against him he was on Wed : committed to Chester Castle, the Justices meeting at Chomley ; w'h act of necessary justice we hope may help to suppress the rioters. Mr. S. Lawrence was here all night on Tues : we had fears of a mob coming upon us in the night, who were gathered at Wrenbury, but our good God who is a witness to the innocenc'y and integrity of his poor serv's did watch about and protect us from all evil, to his name be all the praise.

July 26, 1715. P. and M. went to Motehouse and Boreaton near Wem, to see how they fare in this day of rebuke.

Aug. 8, 1715. A buisy day at Whit'ch ; the high sheriff & Justices came to examine ab't y'e riots lately committed in pulling down ye chappel—the mob insolent & justices not zealous, so little done ; but they were found guilty of a riot.

Sep. 27, 1715. This week my husband has been employ'd in the prosecution of one of the Rioters taken in July last at Nampt'h & now found guilty of treas'able-words. He is fined and sentenced to stand in the pillory in Chester, Namptw'h & Middle-Wich, &c.

Sep. 24, 1715. Early this morn our house was broke open at my husband's closet window, whence they took about thirty pound in money, whilst we securely slept. We found 2 ladders on the outside. Let us do good by this calamity. Set our affections higher on things above, where only they can be safe.—there theeves break not thro'.

Sep. 6, 1720. We attended the funeral of sister Eddowes at Nampt'h—her husband died there last March. . . She was a pious useful woman, daut'r of a worthy Nonconformist Mr. Rowl'd Nevett of Oswestry, a g't frien'd and lover of my d'r father. She lived to a good old age, 68.—was very desirous to have gone back to her old frn'ds at Whch. but God said No.   PURITAN.

QUERIES.

LLYN IRDDYN.—This lake, which is situated under the shadow of Diphwys mountain in Merionethshire, is called in the *Gossiping Guide to Wales* " The Priest's-Lake." Can any one tell me why it is so called ? Is it from the name Irddyn, or Urddyn, or from some known tradition ?   H.P.

OSWESTRY BOROUGH GAOL. — I have just come across the following paragraph in a Shropshire Tory paper for Sep. 12, 1838 :—

OSWESTRY BOROUGH GAOL.—*Effects of " The Bill."*—This building, rendered useless to any purposes of the town, is about to be disposed of.

Oswestry must have been better in its manners forty years ago than it is now-a-days, if its gaol was useless ! What gaol is referred to, and was it sold ?   OSWALD.

WELSHPOOL STREET NAMES. — In the thirteenth volume of *Mont: Coll:* p. 242 we have a singular example of how the names of minor streets change without the action of public authorities. What is now known as Powell's Lane, in Welshpool, was, not so very long ago, called Bowling Green Lane ; and now we are told, on the authority of legal documents in the possession of Mr. E. Maurice Jones, solicitor, that in 1741 and 1755 the same street was called Yocking Hen's Lane ; in 1778 Yorking Hene Lane, and in 1801 Yoking Hen's Lane. What do these names mean ? The alteration in spelling of course means nothing ; that is always to be found. Earlier still, according to a curious old map by Humphrey Bleaze, dated 1629, and preserved in Powis Castle office, there is another variation in the spelling, viz., Cocken Hesne Lane. Has the origin anything to do with poultry ? BLACKPOOL.

A WEM PROFESSIONAL.—The following advertisement appeared in the *Salopian Journal* for Dec. 21, 1803 :—

A. BEETENSON,
(Younger Brother of SAMUEL BEETENSON, late
of WEM)
MOST respectfully informs the Inhabitants of WEM, and the neighbouring Country, that he has taken the late Mr. HIGGINS's House, and solicits a Continuance of their Favours in all the different Branches of the Profession, which the late Mr. Higgins practised with such general Satisfaction.
A. BEETENSON flatters himself, from an experience in full Practice for more than 20 Years, he will be found in every respect perfectly qualified for such Engagement, and assures them the most unremitting Attention will be paid to those Friends who may honour him with their Calls.
The question is, 'what was Mr. Beetonson's ' profession' ? He omits to state it ! SCROBBES BYRIG.

REPLIES.

THE YEOMANRY CAVALRY (Oct. 20, 1880).—I cannot answer the query of VOLUNTEER as to why the Yeomanry Cavalry force was augmented in 1820, but from *Mont : Coll :* Apr. 1880 (in a paper by Mr. Charles Williams Wynn, Recorder of Oswestry), I glean the following details as regards Montgomeryshire :—"Dec. 10, 1819 : A further augmentation of the establishment to the extent of two troops (making in all six troops of forty-four men each) sanctioned by Government. Dec. 23 : Capt. John Buckley Williames to be major; Wythen Jones, Esq., to be captain ; David Pugh, Esq., to be captain; Thomas Jones, Esq., to be captain ; Edward Williames, Esq., to be lieutenant ; Joseph Jones, Esq., to be lieutenant. Feb. 22, 1820 : Gilbert Ross, gent., to be cornet ; John Beck, gent., to be cornet ; Richard Weaver, gent., to be veterinary surgeon." EX-VOLUNTEER.

CURRENT NOTES.

We are glad to understand that Sir WATKIN WILLIAMS WYNN has accepted the office of President of the National Eisteddfod Association, to which he was elected at the meeting at Shrewsbury on the 17th of September.

Mr. Lewis Morris delivered on Thursday evening the inaugural address at the opening of the second Session of the Menai Society of Natural Science and Literature. The author of the "Epic of Hades" is clearly not a disciple of the Apostle of Modern Culture. He has indeed a "perfect horror" of the very word "culture" for to him "it is connected with some of the most devastating intellectual pests of modern times, with 'sweetness and light,' with 'the general stream of tendency,' with every insincerity and affectation." After this rather decided language, one is a little surprised to find that the obnoxious and even "impossible" word recurs more than once in the course of the address. Mr. Lewis Morris is a great believer in modern progress, and his eloquent address calls to mind the words of The Preacher—"Say not thou what

is the cause that the former days were better than these? for thou dost not enquire wisely concerning this." He has no sympathy with those who magnify the past at the expense of the present, and who would assert that " no great poem for instance can be written now or in future to compare with those of ancient days." He thinks it cannot be doubted "that the general level of literature is immensely higher now than it has ever been before," and he believes that " a wider knowledge and a more reasonable faith, as they have led already to an immensely higher standard of general excellence, must infallibly lead before long to higher and supreme efforts of genius in literature than the world has known thus far. I think it likely that we are on the threshold of great discoveries in science and great achievements in literature, and I believe that the young people who get themselves born about the year 1900 will know before they go hence a good deal more, and live fuller and more satisfying lives than we have any idea of now."

An attempt to revive the old Welsh form of lynching called "Cludo ar ysgol " (" to carry on a ladder"), in which the victim is seized, strapped lengthways to a ladder, and carried or jolted through the place, was made last week at Talysarn, a village near Carnarvon. It appears that an Englishman named Joseph Preston had taken legal proceedings against a Welshman in his employ, but the verdict was in favour of the latter. When Preston arrived at Talysarn he was met at the railway station by a large crowd. A ladder could not be found, so a wheelbarrow and ropes were in readiness to lynch the Englishman. Preston, fortunately, managed to escape, but not without being roughly treated. At Carnarvon, on Saturday, nine persons were charged before the county magistrates with rioting and committing an assault upon Preston, and were remanded.

Mr. T. J. Hughes, the well-known vocalist, died on Wednesday, at Liverpool, aged 49. The *Liverpool Mercury*, in a notice of his death, says—"He was born at Llanfyllin, Montgomeryshire. His father was Lot Hughes, one of the pioneers of Wesleyan Methodism in Wales, who died a short time ago at Chester, having reached fourscore years. Mr. Hughes was for many years one of the most popular baritones in this part of the country. He was a great favourite at the principal eisteddfodau held during the last fifteen years, and had a marvellous capacity for rendering the old Welsh airs in all the charm of their simplicity. Many who heard him at these festivals will not soon forget the delight with which they listened to ' T. Jai,' as Mynyddog used fondly to call him. From the first he was one of the principals at Lea's Saturday Evening Concerts, and continued so this season until illness intervened. For many years he acted as precentor at St. Nicholas's Church, and contributed greatly to the well-known efficiency of the singing at that place of worship. Mr. Hughes has left a numerous family and a large circle of friends to mourn his loss."

THE BISHOP OF ST. ASAPH AT THE
POWYSLAND CLUB.

SIR,—In your report of the annual meeting of the Powys-land Club, in your number of the 13th October, among the remarks made by Dr. Jonathan Hughes appears the following :—"It (Montgomeryshire) was distinguished for having had connected with it the great name of Brochwel Ysgythrog, who, he believed, was one of the Princes of Powysland. . . . There was one very important fact in his history. Brochwel was instrumental in turning back the tide of war which was then advancing in the Principality ; and not only the inroad made upon our civil institutions but upon our religious institutions.

Upon the occasion of that successful struggle a terrible slaughter took place on the borders, near the great Abbey and College of Bangor Iscoed. As to the question whether the Romish missionaries had anything to do with it, historians agreed among themselves to say ' No,' but let that be as it might they knew that an attack was made upon the institutions and liberties of this country, but Brochwel came forward, stood boldly out against the aggression, turned the tide of war, and saved us for a long period our freedom, our institutions, and our learning." Now with regard to the " Romish missionaries," the Bishop's sneer, " be that as it might," after the acknowledgment that it was agreed by historians that they had no part in the massacre, strikes me as alike uncharitable and disingenuous ; but this by the way. Let us pass on to Brochwel Ysgythrog, who, we learn for the first time from this Anglican prelate, " turned the tide of war, and saved us" when " the inroad was made not only upon our civil but our religious institutions." Now all we know that is historical of Brochwel Ysgythrog's conduct at the battle of Bangor Iscoed is contained in the Ecclesiastical History of the Venerable Bede (a), who lived within a century of the battle, and is to the effect that while the monks were praying on the hill, he was set, with the force which he commanded, to guard them from harm. Instead of fulfilling this duty, or even attempting it, at the first advance of the enemy upon the monks he fled precipitately with his horsemen and left them to their fate (b). Is this the sense intended by the Bishop when he said that Brochwel Ysgythrog "turned the tide of war"? We know that the coat of arms borne by the descendants of this Prince is sable, three nags' heads erased, argent. Can it be that the sable tincture was intended to signify the sad disgrace of his cowardice, and the nags' heads the pleasant safety to their skins acquired by him and his runaway horsemen through the swiftness of their steeds?

It needs not, however, to be supposed that because the Bishop has been romancing, the web of his romance has been wrought in his own imagination alone. It did not proceed from Bede, the nearly contemporaneous and only genuine authority. Whence, then, did he derive it? And whence his misplaced confidence in its accuracy? The reply is not far to seek. Turn to "Williams's Dictionary of Eminent Welshmen," and you find it substantially epitomised, with a reference to a page in vol. ii. of the Myvyrian Archæology. Turn again to the " Hanes Cymru " of the late Mr. Price of Cwm Du, and you find it again in fuller and more circumstantial detail, but without reference to any authority at all. Bede, indeed, is quoted, but only for the number of the monks. In default, then, of other evidence, turn once more to the Myvyrian Archæology, and the writer referred to by Williams ; and there, to your amazement, you discover it, in the Welsh version of the romance of Geoffry of Monmouth, entitled " Brut Gruffydd ab Arthur," thus, by these Protestant, Anglican, and clerical writers made to do duty for history ; Dr. Hughes took his story, doubtless, at second hand, from one or both of these authors, the one of whom gives us mythology and history in his Dictionary, as he finds it, without professing to be critical, or to separate the chaff from the wheat ; the other often hypercritical to a fault, but more than ever so when the facts seem to bear in favour of Catholicism. To the eye of the Establishmentarian theorist, they present too precious a windfall to need to be sifted thoroughly.

(a) Born 672, died 762.
(b) The words of Bede are these : —"Brocmalius ad primum hostium adventum cum suis terga verteus, eos quos defendere debuerat, inermes ac nudos ferientibus gladus reliquit."

Like Bob Acres, he would reason, "The quarrel is excellent as it stands 'twere a pity to spoil it." So the charge is held in reserve for the first happy opportunity ; and what more convenient for its explosion than the meeting of the Powys-land Club ?

I have yet some remarks to offer on some other points raised by his Lordship, but, fearing to trespass on your space, I propose, with your permission, to defer them to your next issue.—I am, &c.,   H. W. LLOYD, M.A.
26th October, 1880.

AGRICULTURAL DISTRESS IN 1816.

The following are the reports that were received from North and South Wales in reply to the inquiries of the Board of Agriculture in 1816 :—

NORTH WALES.

S. Lloyd, Bala—Three or four considerable farms unoccupied ; twenty notices to quit ; 20 to 33 per cent. abatement of rent ; hundreds of the labouring poor in some of the counties out of employ and starving ; poor-rates lowered ; remedies, lower rents and taxes.

H. W. Jones, Treiorwerth, Anglesey—Seven farms, containing 1,300 acres, unoccupied ; many intend giving notice to quit ; 20 to 30 per cent. abatement of rent ; labouring poor seldom worse for want of employ ; poor-rates stationary ; remedies, malt, salt, and other taxes.

W. Davies, Welshpool, Montgomery—Many farms unoccupied, among them ten averaging 150 acres each ; many notices to quit ; 25 to 50 per cent. abatement of rent ; great want of employment among the labouring poor—some work for food only ; poor-rates increased one-fifth ; remedies, increase circulation, reduce taxes, rent, and tithe, regulate poor rates.

WALTER DAVIES.

The circumstances denoting the distress of the farmers are very evident, for at the present price of grain and stock they can scarcely find money enough to pay tithes, rates, and taxes. The most striking feature of distress of tenants is the unparalleled frequency of sales by auction of live stock and properties of farmers, under execution for rent, debts, &c., insomuch that sheriffs' officers are the only class of men who in these days are fully employed and make their fortunes. Country banks stopping payment have of late been too frequent. The notes of such banks in circulation are for a considerable period of time useless ; and seldom, if ever, of prime cost value at last. The remaining banks, apprehensive of a reflux of their notes, commonly termed a run, are become very cautious in issuing out notes, or of giving the customary credit to farmers. The consequence is a general scarcity of circulating paper, as well as of real money. Bank of England notes are extremely scarce, and many of the few in circulation are apparently forgeries, especially of the one and two pound notes. This scarcity of a circulating medium is one co-operating cause of the depression of live stock. At market there may be buyers enough, but they have not the where-withal. Rent days are fixed as usual, but the payments made are very few. In a comparatively wealthy part of the county I am credibly informed of an instance where only £70 was paid out of a rental of £1,600. Defaulters in the last payment of the property tax are four times the number they were last year.

Handicraftsmen are worse off than when they paid double the price they now do for bread corn. They may have corn cheap, but they find it difficult to procure money to pay for it, low as it is. Labourers in husbandry are much out of employ. Some even without children have in consequence applied for parochial relief. Others offer their labour for food only ; some at half the last year's wages, and most at a diminution. The indispensable work only is attended to. Other works are deferred for the time, owing to the inability of the farmers to find weekly payments for their labourers. As to poor-rates, the weekly pay of invalids may have been lowered, owing to cheapness of provisions, but new paupers crowding upon the lists, owing to want of usual employment, more than counterbalance the former reduction ; so that the present rates compared with those of 1811 and 1812 may be as five to four.

Remedies.—Every means of increasing the circulating medium. Country banks under the sanction and control of Government ; one, two, three, or more, in each county, according to its extent, commerce, and population, and upon a kind of Tontine principle, so as to restore universal confidence.

Rent should be reduced, or rather restored to its proper level, universally and immediately, whilst the remaining farmers have any capital left. The charging of the present rent on lands, owing to a rise, which, in the nature of things, could not but have been temporary, was an avaricious absurdity; and the sooner a recurrence to former principles takes place the better: it is a question whether anything short of this can possibly save the country.

H. JONES.

A general inability to pay rents, and a total cessation from any agricultural improvements. Instances are frequent where no more than about 30 per cent. of rents due at All Saints last (Nov. 12) have yet been paid, and many where nothing has yet been received by the landlord.

There are few grass farms in this county where a mixed or convertible system of husbandry is general. The distress on these farms must be considerable, when oats are sold at 9s. per quarter of eight bushels, which must weigh 315lbs., and barley unsaleable in any quantity at 20s. per quarter, weighing 420lbs. Beef from 2d. to 4d. per lb., and fat pigs 2½d. per lb. live weight.

There is hardly any circulation whatever except silver. The difficulties under which the agricultural part of the community labour having, as I conceive, arisen from the importation of corn, added to the produce of two very abundant harvests, I apprehend that no immediate relief can be expected.

The duty on culm and coal carried coastways is also severely felt in this country. The former materially affects the price of lime, and the latter puts coal out of the reach of the cottager in a country where fuel is extremely scarce. A ton of coal cannot be had in Anglesey under 38s. or 40s. (measuring 8 barrels).

S. LLOYD.

The circumstances that denote the distress of the farmers are many, and very sensibly felt, not only by them, but by the whole community at large. Horses and pigs are lowered in price one half, milch cows one-third, and other horned cattle more than one half, comparing the present year with 1814. Farmers are in debt to each other without the means of paying, in some instances the smallest portion. They are generally in arrears of rent and taxes, both parliamentary and parochial. In debt to shopkeepers and all sorts of tradesmen, and for lime, which prevents their carrying that necessary manure for their lands. In short, all agricultural improvements are in a great measure suspended, the ill effects of which must be felt in this and succeeding years, besides sales by auction take place almost every week, and in every direction. And this, I hear, is the case generally in most districts throughout the Principality, from which an alarming increase of paupers is to be apprehended.

Oats and barley have lowered more than one-half even of last year's prices; wheat about one-third. The depreciation may be attributed to the abundant harvest of last year—the immense quantities, especially of oats, raised at a great expense on several large tracts of enclosed commons. But the price of corn is very unequal in different counties of the Principality. In this neighbourhood (Bala) the prices at present are :— Oats 15s., barley 22s. 6d., wheat 60s. per London quarter, that is, by reducing the customary measure to the London quarter.

The diminished circulation of paper may be justly reckoned as the principal distress under which this part of the country now labours. It may be safely attributed to the immense drain of taxation, which, at present, exceeds the influx of bank and provincial paper from the sale of stock and produce sold in English counties, chiefly horses, pigs, sheep, cattle, butter, and cheese. These, except sheep, being sold at half the price they formerly fetched, the paper circulation must be diminished nearly one-half. Besides, sales are with difficulty effected at the present reduced prices. Another cause of the diminution of the paper currency is the reduced state of the manufactures of this county, which are stockings in this part, and webs in the maritime part. The wool has of late years been sold to the Yorkshire clothiers at high prices, so that the manufacture of those articles has been considerably diminished at home.

The state of the labouring poor is in general better than that of the farmers who employ them, as there has been yet no general diminution in their wages. But it is in contemplation, and some agreed to a reduction of one-fourth, taking the year through, that is from £16 to £12, the farmer finding victuals. Hundreds of labourers are out of employ in some counties, as I am informed, and nearly starving in the midst of plenty.

They are mostly employed in this neighbourhood. In the year 1812, 20½ rates were collected for the poor of this parish at 6d. in the pound, according to the valuation of farms made in King William's reign. In 1812, 23 similar rates were collected. In the present year it is expected that 22 rates will be sufficient. Though the poor have increased, the relief that was usually given was this year diminished nearly one-half, owing to the lowering of almost every article of provision. Besides the relief paid in money, begging from door to door is not only permitted, but even encouraged at vestries. What is thus given, if valued, would increase the poor-rates at least one-third.

I know a respectable farmer, an honest and industrious man, who pays nearly £40 per annum as a tax upon occupation, no doubt intended as a tax upon profits; but this person declares, and is willing to verify on oath, that he is a loser by £200 a year by his farm, and that he has no remedy, being tied down by lease. I am persuaded that there are thousands in the same predicament, who will undoubtedly be ruined unless seasonable relief be administered.

SOUTH WALES.

A. Murray, Cardigan—Near 60 farms, from 50 to 250 acres, unoccupied.

T. P. Lewis, M.P., Radnor—Very many farms unoccupied, from £40 to £250 per year; many notices to quit; more than half the farmers have reductions of rent; poor rates increased; remedies, taxes, regulate poor rates, increase circulation.

J. Franklen, near Cowbridge—Several farms unoccupied; some notices to quit; 33 per cent. abatement of rent; labouring poor better than for many years past; poor rates stationary.

P. Williams, Penpont, near Brecknock—Three or four farms unoccupied, from 100 to 300 acres each; many notices to quit; 20 to 30 per cent. abatement of rent; labouring poor in greater distress than ever; poor rates increasing rapidly; remedies, reduce taxes, and regulate poor rates.

Rev. J. Jones, Pembroke—No farms unoccupied; no notices to quit; no abatement of rent; few labouring poor out of employ; poor rates increasing.

T. Gough, Swansea—Farms rent free, better than occupation by landlords; poor rates doubled; remedies, Government to manage the poor.

Rev. D. Williams, Lampeter, Cardigan—Twelve of the largest farms unoccupied; all not under lease have notice to quit; 25 to 30 per cent. abatement of rent; great want of employment among the labouring poor; poor rates stationary; remedies, taxes, lower rent.

E. L. Loveden—Seventeen on his estate have notice to quit.

T. GOUGH.

Nothing within the experience of fifty years would have led me to believe that the agricultural classes of society could have been so wretchedly and hopelessly depressed as I have lived to see them. It is futile to talk here of lands being given up to landlords: they had rather tenants should occupy them rent free than accept their resignation. In the first case they know what they have to lose, the other is *incalculable*. The distresses of arable and grass farmers arise from many causes : wheat for one-third; barley for less; oats one-fourth the former prices; cattle for one-third; pigs for one-third; sheep half price. The Government taxes as high as ever. The poor-rates from double to quadruple to what they were. Paper circulation plentiful in this district, where mineral and coal-works abound, and there is a water communication. These subterraneans are well off. Such labouring poor as have employment are better off at 8s. per week wages, than our *small farmers*, whose lands present the melancholy picture of neglect and abandonment. The only remedies for these mental pangs of expiring agriculture appear to me to be such rigid economy in all departments of Government, as may enable them to relieve landed proprietors and occupiers from their most oppressive taxes, Taking the management of the poor, at *moderate rates*, into their own hands, and building appropriate houses, and appointing steady and impartial overseers to manage them, which in a few years would reduce that ruinous burthen, now augmented by fear and favour, to one-fourth the present weight; and meliorate the morals of the indigent classes. Above all, devoting to the relief of the immediate distress of despairing agriculture, a due proportion of that fund, appropriated now to relieve posterity from an enormous, but, perhaps, unavoidable debt; when all those, who have borne the burthen of a war of unprecedented continuation and expense, shall have paid the debt of nature.

JOHN JONES.

We have few of the labouring poor out of employ at present, for many that were lately employed in agriculture, are now employed in the new dockyard at Pater.

T. F. LEWIS, M.P.

General inability in the farmers to make good their payments; poor-rates paid in kind, not in money; executions, sales, &c., &c.

Limiting the poor-rates, and defining who are really the proper objects of relief.

JOHN FRANKLEN.

I have been a land steward above fifty-five years, and a farmer nearly fifty. I have not heard of the failure of so many tenants, and their stock distrained upon as in the last six months, within many years, owing to the very sudden and great fall of the price of all farming produce, except wool, which is not a considerable article but in the north and hilly and mountainous parts of the country.

It is difficult to lower the price of wages much, though corn and other necessaries are cheaper, because the workmen have altered their habits of life, both as to food and clothing.

I think that trade and commerce in general, is distressed by a diminished circulation of paper, owing (I believe) to the failure of many country banks, and the consequent decrease of credit and mutual confidence.

I think that the state of the labouring poor in the last two years is better than it has been for many years before, because most of the necessaries they use are lately much reduced in price, and their wages not: therefore the poor-rates in this small inclosed parish (where I have farmed for many years) have been very little advanced, owing, I think, to taking to find them constant employment, the want of which encourages idleness, and is a chief cause of high rates.

P. WILLIAMS.

Considerable difficulty in procuring any portion of rent or taxes; and, in some instances, the overseers have been obliged to collect the poor rates in corn, butter, and cheese.

Some regulation as to the maintenance of the poor seems requisite; for, as the law now stands, men of funded property, as well as the mercantile interest, contribute little or nothing towards the poor rates.

REV. D. WILLIAMS.

The heavy burthen of parish rates, on account of the labouring class finding little or no employment, and the hitherto undiminished continuation of Parliamentary taxes contrasted with the present low prices of stock and corn, have contributed to impoverish the farmers here so, as to make them liable to law processes, and thereby ruined.

This country is in great distress from a diminished circulation of paper, and has considerably suffered from banks who have stopped payment.

NOVEMBER 10, 1880.

NOTES.

WELSH HERALDRY.—The new Peerage and Baronetage, by Joseph Foster, affects a higher degree of accuracy than Burke, Debrett, or Walford, and abounds in new views. In the Baronetage, under "Williams-Wynn," Bart., of Wynnstay, the Arms are thus given :—

"Arms (not exemplified, but the following are used)—Quarterly, 1st and 4th, Vert, three eagles displayed in fesse, Or, WYNN; 2nd and 3rd, Arg., two foxes counter salient in saltire, Gu., the dexter surmounted of the sinister, WILLIAMS."

Under "Williams," Bart., of Bodelwyddan, the Arms for "WILLIAMS" are given as above. The "non-exemplification," whatever that may mean, must be intended to apply to the "WYNN" quartering only. Foster also gives the crest merely as "An eagle displayed, Or," and does not place the shield on the breast of the eagle in the way which is so familiar to all Welshmen. These innovations will offend the Welsh taste.   A CAMBRO-BRITON.

EARLY PRINTING IN SHROPSHIRE.—In January 1867, the late Mr. Thomas Wright, F.S.A., gave a lecture on Printing, at Ludlow. In the course of his remarks he observed that the earliest known book published in Ludlow bears date 1616, and is in the Oakley Park library, and is a curious account of the political loyalty of Wales. The book was printed by Nicholas Oaks. The author, Daniel Powell, on its publication, formed a grand procession of the school-boys and marched to the Castle. The next publication was in 167 6, a sermon by Richard Herbert, the parson of Bromfield. Shortly afterwards appeared another publication of a somewhat notorious but not very creditable occurrence. Robert Foulkes, vicar of Stanton Lacy, was executed for the murder of a young woman whom he had seduced; from this account it appears he was carried to London, and, after making a confession, was there hung. In 1685 a sermon, indicating the political character of Ludlow, by the Vicar of Munslow, was published. This was followed by the publication of a pamphlet in 1710, entitled "Zeal for Religion," by — Cornewall, and dedicated to Charles Walcot. In this publication mention is made of the principal Shropshire families of that date. The next publication appears to have been a sermon preached in Ludlow Castle, on the 13th Feb., 1720. At that time there was a newspaper printed in Ludlow, the first and only newspaper then printed in Shropshire. Seven numbers of this unique Shropshire newspaper, *The Ludlow Postman*, are preserved in the British Museum. The first of these, No. 14, is dated October, 1719. This curious newspaper appears to principally contain, in its local interest, recitals of love-making by the young maidens of Ludlow, several humorous extracts of which were read by the lecturer. There is but one solitary advertisement in the seven numbers, and that relates to the loss of a horse which had been stolen or strayed from Shobdon, near Leominster, and for which John Taylor offers one guinea reward. Coeval with the period of this newspaper was published an engraving of the town of Ludlow, published by W. Parks, a copy of which the lecturer exhibited, and which he believed until recently was the only one extant, but it appears there is another in the possession of Mrs. Stackhouse Acton, at Acton Scott, in this county. In the year 1794 three printing and bookselling establishments were severally commenced by Henry Procter, Thomas Griffiths, and William Felton. In the establishment of Procter, who was a son of the incumbent of Orleton, the late Mr. Thomas Wright, father of the lecturer, was apprenticed. Amongst the earliest publications which were issued from the press of Procter was a "Treatise on the Culture of the Apple and Pear," by the late T. A. Knight, Esq., of Downton Castle, which was succeeded by "Bowker's Art of Angling," which has since passed through several editions. The earliest history published of Ludlow Castle was printed by Felton; who afterwards published "Political remarks on the Game Laws," and the "Beauties of Ludlow," by John Bullock.   TYPO.

QUERIES.

HYWAL AB IEUAF AB YWAIN, Lord of *Cedewain* and *Dolfor* bore, argent a lion rampant, sable armed and langued gules crowned or *(Jos: Morris MSS.)* Where did Joseph Morris obtain the information that the above was Lord of Cedewain and Dolfor? When was he Lord?   DWN.

CASTLE CILRHON.—In the western part of Clun Forest, near the Anchor Public House (a wayside Inn on the road leading from Newtown to Newcastle, near Clun) is the remains of an old Castle, marked on the Ordnance Map as Castle "Cefn Fron," but locally called Castle "Cilrhon." Can any of your readers give me any reference to this ruin in any work—little seems to be known about it.   Q.

REPLIES.

SHROPSHIRE WORDS (Aug. 11, 1880).—A writer in *Notes and Queries* has recently spotted "Fairation" as positively a new word. Numerous readers of *Bye-gones* will recognize it as a very old friend in the Oswestry district, and perhaps elsewhere; although strange to say it has been overlooked by Hartshorne and Miss Jackson. More than thirty years ago I remember an old man who used the word oddly, as, for instance, in "Let's have *fairation doos*," when those with whom he came in contact were not inclined to deal above-board.

JARCO.

CAMBRIAN INSTITUTIONS (Aug. 4, 1880).— The *Chester Chronicle* of July 5, 1833, contained the following relative to the

CYMMRODORION SOCIETY.

We have received the Address of this Society, from which we extract the following, which, as an exposition of the operations of the Society from its commencement, will prove interesting to our readers:—

The Cymmrodorion Society was established in 1820, on the basis of an institution founded about the year 1750, which, through various causes, had been suffered to sink into inaction. Its principal objects are the preservation of records illustrative of Ancient British History; the discovery of Cambrian literary relics; the elucidation of the works of the old Bards; the cultivation of the National Muse and the language of the Principality; and the general encouragement of Native genius. In furtherance of these views, several books and documents, both in print and manuscript, have been diligently sought for and purchased by the Society, and now form a valuable collection. The Premiums, which have been annually offered for Essays illustrative of certain periods of early history, have awakened a spirit of enquiry and of deep research, that must eventually clear up many doubts and historical inaccuracies, and have already produced papers of extraordinary interest both to the historian and the Antiquary. The following is a list of the subjects which have been proposed by the Society, and the prizes awarded to successful candidates:—

1821. The Revival of the Cymmrodorion, an Ode in the Welsh language. (The late Thomas Jones, Esq., Bardd Clôff.)

1822. Hu Gadarn, or Hugh the Mighty, a Poem in the Welsh language. (The Rev. Edward Hughes, rector of Bodfarry.) On the Cultivation of the Welsh Language, an Essay in English. (The late John Humphreys Parry, Esq.) The same subject in a Welsh essay, written by students at the Grammar Schools of Wales. (Mr. Evan Williams, and Mr. David Jones.)

1823. Caswallon, and his resistance of the Romans, as Pendragon of the Britons, a Welsh Ode. (The Rev. Walter Davies, rector of Manafon, Montgomeryshire.) Ancient Genealogies, as illustrative of the laws and customs of the Britons, an English essay. (The Rev. William Probert of Walmsley, near Bolton, Lancashire.) O Dduw y mae pob peth, from God proceedeth all things, a Welsh essay.—Grammar Schools.—(Samuel Roberts of Llanbrynmair, and Griffith Griffiths.)

1824. The Royal Medal was presented to Dr. William Owen Pughe of Dolydd y Cau, Merionethshire, as a token of the esteem in which his eminent talents were held by the Institution, and as an acknowledgment of the invaluable services rendered by him to the literature of his country. The Royal Medal was also presented to J. Flaxman, Esq., R.A., for his classical design on the medal.

5

1825. An Enquiry as to the Several Tribes comprehended under the general appellation of Ancient Britons. (The Rev. William Probert.) On the Life and Character of Hywel Dda; Howel the Good; a Welsh essay.—Grammar Schools. (Mr. William Davies.) The Royal Medal was presented to Mr. John Parry, Bardd Alaw, as a tribute to his eminent services in preserving the National Music of Wales, and rendering it attractive to the world.

1826. The several Invasions of Britain, and their Effects on the Character and Language of the Inhabitants. (The Rev. William Probert.) Owain Glyndwr, a poem in English. (The Rev. John Vaughan Lloyd.) Owain Glyndwr, a poem in Welsh. (Robert Davies, Bardd Nantglyn.) Calondid, courage, a Welsh essay, written by the students at the Grammar Schools in Wales. Three compilations were deemed worthy of medals. (Samuel Roberts, John Jones, and Joseph Hughes.) The Royal Medal was presented to Miss Angharad Llwyd of Caerwys, for her great zeal in promoting Welsh literature in general. Medals were awarded to two Pennillion Singers with the Welsh Harp.

1827. On the Mythological Traditions of the Britons, an English essay. (David Lewis, Esq.)

1828. Cantre'r Gwaelod, the Lowland Hundred, an ode in Welsh, awarded at the Royal Eisteddfod held at Denbigh. (The Rev. William Rees; Gwilym Hiraethog; of Llansannan.)

1829. The Normans in Wales, an English essay. (Henry Davies, Esq., and Thomas Richards, Esq.)

1831. An Enquiry into the Coinage of the Ancient Britons. (None received, vide *Cam. Quar. Mag.* Vol. 5, p. 244, for article on the subject by Sir Samuel Meyrick.) A Biographical Sketch of the most eminent individuals Wales has produced since the Reformation. (Robert Williams, Esq.) The Causes which in Wales have produced Dissent from the Established Church. (Arthur James Johnes Esq.) An English Poem, by a Native of the Principality, on any subject connected with Wales. (Robert Folkestone Williams, Esq.,—the subject chosen was The Revolt in Wales under Owen Glyndwr). An argumentative essay, in Welsh, on the Advantages and Disadvantages of cultivating the Welsh Language as a Living Tongue. (The Rev. William Williams—Gwilym Caledfryn—late of Denbigh). A Welsh Englyn on Woman. There were upwards of fifty candidates. (Mr. William Edwards—Gwilym Gallestr—of Ysgeifiog, Flintshire).

1832, A Welsh essay on the Syntax of the Language. Two medals were awarded at the Royal Eisteddfod held at Beaumaris. (The Rev. J. H. Williams, and Mr. Hugh Jones—Huw Erfyl—of Chester).

1833. A Historical account of the Monasteries and Abbeys in Wales. (The Rev. Peter Bayley Williams, rector of Llanrug, Carnarvonshire). An essay on the General Character of Welsh Literature, commencing with the Nineteenth Century. (Robert Williams, Esq., B.A. of Conway).

1834. The subjects proposed for next year are: A Historical Account of the Castles in Ancient Dimetia, namely, Pembrokeshire, Carmarthenshire, and Cardiganshire. The Royal Medal and Ten Guineas. (It is proposed to continue this interesting subject annually until a complete account of all the castles in the Principality be obtained.) An essay in Welsh on Welsh Poetry, stating whether the four-and-twenty metres have been of benefit to the language or otherwise. An essay in English on the same subject, giving specimens of Welsh poetry, with translations, &c. The Royal Medal for each.

20

The Society has had Mr. R. Williams's Biographical Sketch of Eminent Welshmen, translated into Welsh, and printed for general circulation in the Principality. The English Biographical account will be inserted in the fourth number of the Society's Transactions, which will be forthwith printed, and copies presented to the members. The Poems of Lewis Glyn Cothi, a celebrated bard of the fifteenth century, will be also published by the society, prepared for the press, with an English translation, &c., by the Rev. John Jones; Ioan Tegid; of Christ Church, Oxford.   NEMO.

CURRENT NOTES.

A new church at Aberganolwyn was consecrated a few days ago by the Bishop of Bangor. Amongst the principal contributors to the building fund were the Marquess and Marchioness of Londonderry and Sarah, Lady Harlech. Last week the Bishop of St. David's consecrated a new church at Llangwyryfon. A new church tower was opened at Aberaeron on Thursday.

Among the wills recently proved is that of the Right Hon. Margaret, Dowager Baroness Willoughby de Broke, late of Plasnewydd, Anglesey, of which Mr. S. K. Mainwaring is one of the executors. The personalty was sworn under £120,000. The testatrix bequeaths £1,666 13s. 4d. reduced three per cent. annuities upon trust to apply the dividends towards the support of the Bodelwyddan National Schools so long as they are conducted according to the Protestant principles of the Church of England as now by law established, and if the said schools should hereafter become vested in a School Board under the Elementary Education Act the trust is to cease, and the money is to go over to other purposes. There are also a number of family bequests. The deceased was the widow of Henry, eighth Lord Willoughby de Broke.

MR. JUSTICE WILLIAMS.—Mr. Watkin Williams was sworn in as a judge of the High Court of Justice on Friday morning before the Lord Chancellor in his private room in the House of Lords, and afterwards proceeded to hear summonses at Judges' Chambers. Mr. Justice Lush was also sworn in as a Lord Justice of Appeal. On Monday Mr. Justice Williams took his seat as a puisne judge of the Queen's Bench Division. Mr. Williams is the eldest son of the late Rev. P. Williams, rector of Llansannan, and represented the Denbighshire Boroughs from 1868 to 1880, when he came forward for Carnarvonshire, and was returned by a large majority. He is a Liberal in politics, and married a daughter of Lord Justice Lush.

THE CULTIVATION OF LAND IN SHROPSHIRE.—It appears from the official return that there are now in Shropshire 3,248 acres of orchards, and the like; 44 acres are under cultivation by market gardeners, 95 are in the hands of nurserymen, and 45,795 are in coppices or plantations, not including gorse land and garden shrubberies. In June last there were in Shropshire 8,528 holdings of 50 acres and under, an increase of 247 compared with 1875; from 50 to 100 acres, 918, an increase of 15; from 100 to 300 acres, 1,934, an increase of 9; from 300 to 500 acres, a decrease of 13; holdings from 500 to 1,000 acres number 47, and remain stationary, whilst one holding has grown into above 1,000 acres—the total number of holdings being 11,872, an increase of 259 upon 1875, when the number was 11,613. It appears from the same return from which the above figures are taken that the acreage of arable land in this county has since 1875 increased to the extent of 10,086 acres. In June last, in farms under 50 acres, there were 85,876 acres, against 85,619 in 1875; in farms from 50 to 100 acres, 63,196 acres, against 66,611 in 1875; farms from 100 to 300 acres, 359,113, against

349,284; farms from 300 to 500 acres, 163,796, against 166,811; farms from 500 to 1,000 acres, 28,654, against 28,304; one farm above 1,000 acres, 1,080. From these figures it will be seen that the acreage of holdings of 50 acres and under has increased 257 acres; holdings from 50 to 100 acres, 1,585; holdings from 100 to 300 acres, 9,829; holdings from 300 to 500, a decrease of 3,015; and in holdings from 500 to 1,000 acres, the increase has been 350 acres.

NATIONAL EISTEDDFOD ASSOCIATION.
MEETING IN LONDON.

The Executive Committee of the National Eisteddfod, Association met on Tuesday evening, Nov. 9, at 18, St. James-square, London, the residence of the president of the Association, Sir Watkin Williams Wynn, Bart, M.P. The chair was occupied by Sir Watkin, the other members present were Mr. Puleston, M.P., Messrs. Hugh Owen, Stephen Evans, Brinley Richards, John Thomas, Ceiriog Hughes, W. E. Davies, and T. Marchant Williams, hon. sec. Letters were read from Mr. Cornwallis West, Mr. Justice Watkin Williams, Mr. John Roberts, M.P., and the Ven. Archdeacon Griffiths, each of whom has consented to become a vice-president of the Society and a subscriber to its funds. The Secretary also read letters from the following absent members of the Committee—Mr. Askew Roberts and the Rev. J. Eiddon Jones. After considerable discussion the following resolutions were passed:—(1) That the Committee, after duly considering the application received from Bangor relative to the National Eisteddfod which it is intended to hold there in 1882, have resolved to give the movement their countenance and support, provided that the Eisteddfod be conducted on principles which are consistent with the true interests of the institution. (2.) That the following gentlemen be elected members of the Council: Yr Estyn, Dr. Evans, Mr. Isaac Foulkes, Mr. Cadwaladr Davies, and Andreas o Fôn. (3.) That an advertisement be forthwith issued for a paid secretary. 4. That the meeting be adjourned to the second Tuesday in December.

The next meeting will be held at Sir Watkin's residence. A most cordial vote of thanks to the president, who evidently takes the greatest interest in the Association, terminated the proceedings.

The little village of Hawarden, though now principally known through Mr. Gladstone's residence there, has (says One and All) a very ancient history of its own. Here is a curious story of the place—taken, according to Willett, the learned historian of the county, from old MSS.—which has a droll quaintness of its own. In it is explained, with more or less of historical accuracy, the origin of the name of a large open space on the banks of the river Dee at Chester, called the Roodee, which all who have visited or passed through the town must have noticed, and where all the annual races, reviews, and public sports are held. In the reign of King Conan, one of the Welsh Kings, it is said that the Hawarden Church contained a very large image of the Virgin Mary. One summer, during a great drought, the country people flocked to the church to pray for rain, and amongst them came the sheriff's wife. While the lady was praying, the great rood or cross in the church fell upon and killed her. Thereupon an inquest was called, and the people, with less reverence for sacred things than might have been expected, brought in a verdict of murder against the Virgin as the patron saint of the church. A member of the community then suggested that, as she did not belong to their country, some variation in the ordinary mode of execution should be made, and, after discussion, it was agreed that the image should be thrown into the river, so that if it really possessed miraculous power it might have a chance of saving itself. This was done. The story goes on to tell that the image straightway floated down to Chester, was taken by the inhabitants out of the river, and was there buried by them in a large field on its banks, where a cross with this rude inscription was erected—

> The Jews their Lord did crucify,
> The Hardeners their's did drown;
> For she did not to their wants agree,
> So she lies under this stone.

Hence, according to this quaint old legend, arose the name of Roodee, by which for several hundred years this large open ground has been known. [A translation of the old Saxon MS. referred to here was given in *Bye-gones*, Nov. 19, 1873.]

WELSH BEEF IN 1801.—Three fine oxen the largest of their kind in this part of the kingdom, were bred by Sir John Williams, Bart., of Bodelwyddan, in Flintshire, and sold at Chester in 1801, at £75 each.

"THE COCK INN."—It seems fitting to record the departure of old friends. This ancient hostelry came to an untimely end on Saturday, the 30th October. It was a remnant of old Welshpool, being a timber-house with an antique gable and dormers, with a thatched roof. It has long been in a dilapidated state, but it did not actually tumble down of its own accord. Being observed to be in an unsafe condition, the corporate authorities, through the borough surveyor, interfered, and at his instance the owner took measures for its demolition. It did not require much to bring it down; the removal of some of its under portions, and a few tugs at ropes fastened to its roof, soon rendered it a heap of ruins. Although so dilapidated, it was a picturesque and interesting object, and has formed the subject of many a sketch, some of which happily still survive. Tradition gives it a very early date. One authority, the late Robert Jones, well known as "the Prothonotary's Clerk," used to say there was ground for thinking it was a licensed hostelry as far back as Edward the Second's reign. However that may be, its massive old beams, some of them still undecayed, and the old wattled partitions now piled up in the heap of ruins, testify to a very early date. Very lately it had a quaint sign-board which attracted attention and yielded amusement, "The Cock Inn, by Luke Peacock." Although its picturesque outline is missed, yet the removal of the old building has revealed, as a compensation to its opposite neighbours, a pretty view of Leighton Church and its surroundings.

NOVEMBER 17, 1880.

NOTES.

WILLIAM MORGAN, F.R.S.—Died, in 1833, at his residence, Stamford Hill, near London, aged 83, William Morgan, Esq., F.R.S., the Eminent Mathematician and Calculator—upwards of sixty years Actuary to the Equitable Assurance Office. Mr. Morgan was a native of Bridgend, in Glamorganshire, and nephew to the celebrated Dr. Price, who with his nephew may be styled the Fathers of Benefit Societies; for it was they who placed them on a rational basis. Few men have passed through life more beloved and esteemed than Mr. Morgan: his distinguished talents made him early known to, and his friendship sought by, persons of all ranks; and his advice on subjects of Finance was eagerly solicited by the Government of all nations.—*Chester Courant.* For notice of Dr. Price see Williams's *Eminent Welshmen*, p.p. 417—20.   TAFFY.

POVERTY AND PIETY.—Under this heading some of the newspapers of Feb. 1821 introduced the following petition from "the Poor Parish of Cilcennin, in the County of Cardigan, and diocese of St. David's:"—This petition sheweth "That the parish church of Cilcennin having fallen down, a new church is become indispensably necessary; that owing to the scarcity which has prevailed of late years, and the badness of the times, there is a total inability to build a new church. The parish is barren and hilly, having that well-known barren mountain, Tri Chrug, within its boundaries; and no less than 15 farms have failed in the course of a year, and not 40 farms are assessed to the poor rates. The population is great in proportion to the extent of cultivated land, having above 700 inhabitants; the cottagers, who are numerous, are generally maintained by parochial aid; whilst the parish is reckoned the poorest in the neighbourhood, and perhaps in the country. They are therefore constrained to adopt this humble method of petitioning for the assistance of their opulent and charitable neighbours, and all other their fellow-Christians, to enable them to erect a decent House for the worship of their common Redeemer. That the parishioners are well-attached to the Church of England, their constant attendance at Church affording the best proof, having had to boast of a regularly crowded congregation; consequently they are highly distressed to see their place of worship fallen into ruin, without the means to rebuild it."   NEMO.

SIR WILLIAM MAURICE OF CLENENNEY.
(Aug. 4, 1880).

From John Lloyd at Ludlow, to Sir William Maurice, 1618. From the original at Brogyntyn :—

Right Wor: After respect of my humble duty, yo'u shall vnderstand that my lord pr'sydent was at the assizes in Chester, fflynt shire, and Denbighe shire, last holden in aprell last and Contynued in fflynt shire & Denbighe shire all the whole assizes, and from thence came to the app'ance [appearance] and the ffyrst night of his retorne he laye att the howse of S'r Edward broughton by wrexham; the second and third nights he laye at the howse of S'r Edward Kynaston, the iiij night beinge vpon monday my lord and the Chief Justyce laye at S'r henry Towneshend his howse.

Nowe my lord pr'sydent vpon monday the xj*th* of this maye is gone towards london : beinge as I am Credibly enformed, sent for by his Ma'tie and whether he will retorne the next terme or not y't is not yet knowne.

Mr. Justice doth vpon friday the xvth of this moneth, travill towardes london also : what his occasions are I knowe not.

my lord pr'sydent tooke the vieu and sight of all the trayned souldiers of fflynt shire and denbigh shire, and dyd see them trayned : and intendeth at the assizes tyme to goe through all wales to that end.

Mr. Samuel Parker, a man of this towne, worth xx*ty* thowsand pounds at his death, dyed this last weeke, having but one daughter : and I am at this tyme sore greved w'th an ague.

I meane godwillinge, to be at london the next t'me, [term] if it pleaseth Almighty god to restore my health : and if yo'r wor' or any of yo'r servants be then there, I shall, w'th them, not be forgetfull of my duty in gyving the best dyrec'cons in yo'r cause that I can, as occasion shall require.

It is credibly reported here, in secret man' [manner], that there cam' al're [a letter] to my lord pr'sydent very lately, menc'oning grete musters to be very shortly, the tyme certen I cannot learne, and many to goe furth out of all cuntreyes, in armo'r. I have noe newes, other then the newes before menc'oed, to adu'tize yo'u of at this tyme: But I hartily pray to almighty god to blesse yo'u with health and p'speritie, and to defend yo'u from the wicked wills of yo'r adu'saries whosoever ; and soe I comitt yo'u to gods blessed tui'con, and rest ever

Yo'r wor' faithfull
solicitor to comannd

ludlow, xij° maij   duringe lief,
1618   John lloyd.

Addressed : "To the right wor' and his much respected wor' ffrend S'r Wm Maurice, Knight, d'd."   A.R.P.

ELECTING BAILIFFS AT WELSHPOOL.— The following curious way of electing Bailiffs at Welshpool before the passing of the Municipal Corporations Act, is incorporated in the report of the Commissioners who sat in 1833 to enquire into the Municipal affairs of that borough. I extract it from No. 2, Vol. 13, of the *Montgomeryshire Collections* of the Powys-land Club, published last month.   ANON.

" The bailiffs are chosen annually on Michaelmas day by a jury composed of such of the burgesses as happen to be in court ; the jury always consists of fifteen persons. Balls of wax are made of equal weight, as many as there may chance to be aldermen present ; the name of each alderman is written by the town clerk on a slip of parchment, and one name is introduced into every ball ; the balls are put into a bag, and shaken, and the bag is presented to the outgoing chief bailiff, who takes out a ball, opens it and reads the name aloud. The alderman so named nominates eight of the jury. The bag is next handed to the out-going associate bailiff, who draws out another ball, and proceeds in a similar manner ; the alderman thus drawn names seven of the jury. The proceeding is conducted in this fashion : moreover, the bailiffs tuck up their sleeves to the elbow before they put their hands into the bag. They do not see the balls ; the names written on parchment and introduced into the wax are completely concealed. All except the jury retire after the jury are impannelled and sworn. The jury then consider of their verdict, and nominate the next chief bailiff and the next associate ; unanimity is not required, but nine must agree. The bailiffs are selected from the burgesses at large; the party chosen must be a burgess, he has occasionally been elected a burgess the moment before he was made bailiff. They cannot nominate a person who is not a burgess, but they may nominate one who has been previously admitted at the same meeting.

" The sage who devised this singular mode of procedure was probably very proud of his invention ; but it may perhaps be doubted whether he conceived, like the modern philosophers, who so warmly enforce the ballot, that he had discovered a radical cure for every disease incident to the body politic.

" It having been asked if it were ever possible, notwithstanding the balls and the bag, and the tucked-up sleeves, to learn before the election who would be the bailiffs, all present laughed assent. Alderman Thomas Lloyd Dickin deposed thus : ' I reside within the borough ; I have always resided there ; my age is fifty-six years. I was brought up to the law ; I practised about a year, but I gave up the profession through ill health. I was the chief bailiff in 1804. I knew I was to be the chief bailiff, for I was applied for I was a burgess to take the office ; so I became a burgess, and was immediately elected the chief bailiff.' It appeared, indeed, that the names of the future bailiffs are only all the better known on account of the secrecy that shrouds their election ; but the manner of acquiring this knowledge is a State secret, and possibly a very valuable one. Previous arrangements are commonly the more perfect in proportion to the efforts that are made to prevent and disconcert them."

WHITSHED KEENE, ESQ. — Who was the above ? He represented the Borough of Montgomery for many years in Parliament. How came he connected with the county ?   QUERIST.

OSWESTRY MARKET DAY.—The following is an extract from Heylyn's "Microcosm," Edition 1627, pp. 490, 491. Speaking of Wales, he said, "The country is very mountainous and barren. There chief commodities are woollen cloathes, as cottons, bags, &c. These merchandizes are from all parts of *Wales* brought up into *Oswestre* (which is the furthest towne in all *Shropshire*) as unto a common emporie. For hither on *Mundaies* (which are the market dayes) come from *Shrewsburie* the cloath-merchants, and drapers there dwelling, buy these commodities, carry them home, and from thence disperse them into all places and parts of the kingdom." When was Oswestry Market changed from Monday to Wednesday ?   MARCHER.

[The Oswestry market day was changed from Monday to Wednesday under the Charter of Charles II. granted in 1674.—ED.]

PEARLS IN THE CONWAY.—(Sep. 8, 1880.)— It is stated in a Guide to Llandudno, published by William Bridge of Conway nearly thirty years ago, that about seventy years earlier "Sir Robert Vaughan went to Court with a button and a loop in his hat, set with pearls from the Conway."   NORTH.

[Probably it was one of these pearls that Sir Robert Williames Vaughan gave to Mr. W. W. E. Wynne. See "Memorials" in *History of the Gwydir Family*, published by Woodall and Venables, 1878.—ED.]

SHREWSBURY ASSIZE OF BREAD.—(Oct. 20, 1880.)—Each item in the table quoted by TELL is to be read in the same way as the following—

		lb.	oz.	dr.
	White must not weigh less than	0	8	8
Two-penny Loaf	Wheaten ,, ,, ,,	0	11	6
	Household ,, ,, ,,	0	15	2

The table was, of course, issued by the Mayor of Shrewsbury to regulate the weight of bread sold at *certain prices* within the borough.   C. J. D.

LLANRWST CHURCH.—Visitors to this church are shown a card in the Gwydir Chapel which professes to be a description and copy of the monuments. But this is very scanty and imperfect. Something more complete and trustworthy seems to me desirable. The other day I copied the inscription on the centre one of three small brasses at the back of a square pew at the head of the nave, as follows :—

Prope Iacet Corpus Griffini Lloydd
Brynniog Olim Ludimagistre
Indigni Llanrustiensis Nuper
Lecturarij Indignioris et Rectoris
Indignissimi Doegensis Sepult
Decimo Quinto die Martii
Anno domini
1719
Nil de Defencto dic Scribe
Puta ve Maligne

Beneath this there was the skull and cross bones engraved. The card I have referred to contains a translation of this, but does not give the original text.   R.D.

[The *Gossiping Guide to Llandudno*, announced for issue next season, will give correct copies of all these monuments, as well as other information about Llanrwst, under the heading of "Day Trips from Llandudno."—ED.]

THE CYMMRODORION SOCIETY.

The Honourable Society of Cymmrodorion (or, as the late Gwallter Mechain would prefer to call it, Cymmrydorion) held its usual annual meetings on Wednesday, Nov. 10, at the Freemasons' Tavern, Great Queen-street, London. The Council met at five o'clock, under the presidency of Mr. Stephen Evans. The annual meeting of members was held at six o'clock, under the presidency of Sir Watkin Williams Wynn, Bart., M.P. (the Society's president). At the general meeting there was a good attendance of members. The President on his appearance was most warmly greeted, and after taking the chair, proceeded to call upon the Secretary to read the report of the Council for the year ending November 9.

The SECRETARY (Mr. C. W. Jones) then read his report, which congratulated the Society on the great success that had attended it during the past year. 110 new members had joined, and the Council had the pleasure of adding the distinguished names of Prince Louis-Lucien Bonaparte and Professor Cowell of Cambridge as honorary members. The death of Mr. Sergeant Parry was a loss to them, and to supply his place the Very Rev. Dr. Vaughan, Dean of Llandaff, and Master of the Temple, was elected. The Rev. E. T. Davies, B.A., and the Rev. Owen Jones, B.A., had been appointed corresponding members for Liverpool, and Owain Alaw an additional corresponding member for North Wales. The publications which the Society had issued included the Report of the Council, and the third volume of "Y Cymmrodor," and a re-publication of that extremely rare and unique work—the "Athravaeth Gristnogavl," originally published at Milan in 1568. The meetings held during the past year were well supported, and important papers on Literature, Art, &c., had been read, including the following :—A Lecture on "Prehistoric Wales," by Professor Rudler; another on "Celtic Art," by Mr. St. John Hancock; one on "Eisteddfodic Reform," by Mr. Hugh Owen, and another "On Welsh Books printed on the Continent in the 14th and 15th centuries," by Mr. Howel W. Lloyd. There was also held in London a very successful conversazioné, and at Carnarvon the Society was well represented, important papers having been read in connection with the Eisteddfod. Meetings of the sub-committee, elected to work in harmony with Eisteddfod promoters, had also been held, and had proved very successful. The work of editing their publication "Y Cymmrodor" was in the hands of Mr. Thomas Powell, M.A. (Oxon), ably assisted by Dr. Isambard Owen, M.A., in London. The publication of the poems of Iolo Goch, commenced by the late editor, was being continued by the present editor, assisted by Professor Silvan Evans. The transcription and collation of the numerous MSS., of his poems, &c., contained in the British Museum, had been completed by Mr. Thomas W. Hancock. The Council were forwarding the issue of the medal, designed by Mr. Joseph Edwards, and members were urgently invited to subscribe to get the die speedily struck. A committee, consisting of Dr. Owen, Mr. Howel W. Lloyd, Mr. St. John Hancock, the Rev. J. Davies, and others, had been elected to consider the possibility and necessity of collecting materials for a new and complete Welsh Bibliography, and their prospectus would be issued very shortly. Such are a few of the points touched upon in the report. The accounts were audited by Mr. Howel Thomas, and Mr. St. John Hancock, and showed a cash balance to the Society's credit of £70 12s. 4d., and to the Medal Fund of £16 14s.—The adoption of the report was moved by Mr. W. Jeremy, barrister, and seconded by Dr. Isambard Owen, who wished to impress upon the meeting that the report was now submitted for free discussion. The work done in the

past, he viewed, as real and substantial work, and the future also, he trusted, would be equally satisfactory, if not more satisfactory than the past. The report alluded to the publication of the poems of Iolo Goch, which he believed would be found interesting ; and again there was the important Bibliographical work, which he considered would be of very great service to Welsh literature. He hoped all literary Welshmen and Englishmen, and our distinguished neighbours over the channel, would give every assistance to get a complete work.—The report having been unanimously adopted, the Secretary next submitted the names of the following gentlemen as members of the Council, in lieu of others who were retiring :— Mr. W. Evans, Mr. Thomas W. Hancock, and Mr. Howel W. Lloyd. These names were proposed by the Rev. John Morgan, and seconded by Mr. Stephen Evans, and adopted.—On the proposition of Dr. Owen, votes of thanks were moved to the gentlemen mentioned before, for their papers delivered before the Society.—This was seconded by Mr. D. Lewis, barrister, who, in so doing, called also special attention to the importance of the work proposed by Mr. Hugh Owen, in his paper on Eisteddfodic Reform, which was already bearing good fruit. Thanks were moved and seconded to Mr. Stephen Evans, the chairman of the Council, whose attendance and business tact had been of the greatest assistance, to the Editor, Assistant Editor, the Secretary, and the Auditors, and there was also a special vote of thanks to Mr. Hugh Owen for the use of his offices for the Council. Mr. Howel Thomas and Mr. E. W. Davies of the Exchequer and Audit Offices were appointed auditors for the present year. Mr. Ignatius Wilhams of the North Wales Circuit proposed a vote of thanks to Sir Watkin for his kindness in presiding that evening, which was carried with acclamation. Sir Watkin replied in a patriotic speech, and remarked that he was sensible of the kindness of his friends, both in Wales and in London. It gave him great pleasure to preside over them and over the Executive Committee of the National Eisteddfod Association, which had met the previous evening at his residence in London. He hoped to see the gentlemen who were at that meeting also at dinner, when they would be as agreeably engaged as they were in discussing the best means of promoting Welsh literature, and more agreeably, he was sure, than in listening to his remarks. (Laughter.) Sir Watkin resumed his seat amidst great cheering.

At the close of the meeting the members and other gentlemen connected with the Principality, and otherwise interested in promoting the interests of Wales and Welsh literature, assembled in another room to a most sumptuous dinner. On the list were the following names of those who attended both the annual meeting and the dinner : Sir Watkin Williams Wynn, Bart. M.P., Mr. Charles W. Wynn, Recorder of Oswestry, The Dean of Bangor Mr. Hugh Owen, Mr. Stephen Evans, Mr. W. D. Jeremy, Mr. Ignatius Williams, Mr. D. Lewis, Rev. John Morgan, Mr. L. P. Pugh, M.P., Mr. John Thomas, Mr. Brinley Richards, Dr. Isambard Owen, M.A., Mr. John Davies, of the Treasury, Mr. Marchant Williams, Mr. Howel Thomas, Mr. St. John Hancock, Mr. C. W. Jones, the Secretary, Mr. Howel W. Lloyd, Mr. Joseph Edwards, Mr. John Davies (Mynorydd), Revs. J. Ricketts, Evan Jones, John Evans, Mr. Bernard Quaritch, Mr. Wyman, Mr. Christopher Thomas, Bristol, Mr. Lloyd Roberts, Mr. Dix Lewis, Mr. Hilton, Dr. J. T. Jones, Mr. Nichol, Mr. Morgan, Mr. Ellis Jones, Mr. T. J. Thomas, and Mr. Lewis Wingfield. Amongst the speakers after dinner were Sir Watkin W. Wynn, Mr. C. W. Wynn, Mr. Hugh Owen, Dr. Isambard Owen, the Dean of Bangor, Mr. Ignatius Williams, &c.

AGRICULTURAL RETURNS.

We have compiled the following figures from the Official Return for 1880 :—

COMPARATIVE STATEMENT, 1880 AND 1879.

	Salop.		Montgomery.		England.		Wales.	
	1880.	1879.	1880.	1879.	1880.	1879.	1880.	1879.
	Acres.	Acres.	Acres.	Acres.	Acres.	Acres.	Acres.	Acres.
Total Area	841,167..	841,167..	485,351..	485,351..	32,597,398..	32,597,398..	4,721,823..	4,721,833
Total Acreage under Crops, Bare Fallow, and Grass....	706,613..	704,980..	252,961..	252,039..	24,596,266..	24,503,882..	2,767,516..	2,758,743
Wheat	69,166..	67,114..	16,474..	17,879..	2,745,733..	2,718,992..	89,729..	94,639
Barley or Bere	53,171..	58,606..	10,793..	11,619..	2,060,807..	2,236,101..	142,514..	152,491
Oats	29,367..	24,468..	22,692..	21,483..	1,520,125..	1,425,126..	239,526..	226,967
Rye..........................	842..	995..	65..	71..	31,683..	39,808..	1,765..	1,464
Beans........................	3,577..	4,186..	142..	448..	404,071..	419,504..	2,619..	3,081
Peas	2,999..	4,268..	577..	959..	231,280..	273,591..	1,963..	2,985
Total of Corn Crops....	159,122..	159,637..	50,743..	52,464..	6,993,699..	7,113,122..	478,116..	481,577
Potatoes	5,747..	5,088..	2,519..	2,732..	324,931..	323,992..	38,940..	42,600
Turnips and Swedes	45,040..	46,293..	7,534..	7,672..	1,473,030..	1,457,762..	65,190..	67,349
Mangold	5,18L..	5,744..	449..	274..	333,609..	352,671..	7,685..	8,410
Carrots	252..	234..	16..	14..	15,186..	13,992..	503..	469
Cabbage, Kohl-Rabi, & Rape	164..	141..	34..	64..	155,001..	162,296..	1,096..	1,237
Vetches and other Green Crops, except clover or grass	1,657..	2,269..	509..	576..	357,377..	425,775..	6,659..	6,877
Total of Green Crops ..	58,042..	59,769..	11,061..	11,332..	2,659,134..	2,736,488..	120,073..	126,951
Clover, Sanfoin, and Grasses under rotation	67,854..	73,202..	24,966..	28,213..	2,646,241..	2,674,949..	332,353..	347,473
Permanent Pasture (exclusive of heath or mountain)	407,010..	398,158..	161,866..	156,303..	11,461,856..	11,233,526..	1,805,750..	1,773,811
Bare Fallow or Uncropped Arable	14,488..	14,124..	4,322..	3,726..	759,845..	671,156..	81,207..	28,919
Horses used solely for agricultural purposes	19,097..	19,218..	6,782..	7,047..	766,527..	769,590..	72,605..	73,130
Unbroken Horses and Breeding Mares...................	11,000..	10,967..	7,053..	7,368..	325,745..	331,117..	62,290..	63,261
Cattle	138,036..	137,876..	62,906..	63,128..	4,158,046..	4,128,940..	654,714..	643,815
Sheep	408,240..	488,406..	325,980..	354,465..	16,823,646..	18,445,522..	2,718,316..	2,873,460
Pigs	50,783..	52,598..	19,417..	20,949..	1,697,914..	1,771,081..	182,003..	192,757
Orchards (arable or grass land also used for fruit)	3,243..	— ..	378..	— ..	175,200..	— ..	2,834..	
Market Gardens (for vegetables, &c.)..............	44..	— ..	3..	— ..	40,289..	— ..	596..	
Nursery Grounds	95..	— ..	27..	— ..	9,891..	— ..	316..	
Woods	45,795..	— ..	22,630..	— ..	1,435,434..	— ..	162,135..	

Note.—There are four acres of flax in Salop in 1880 as against none returned in 1879, and 93 of hops against 90. In Montgomery 3 of flax against 1 ; no hops. In England, 8,788 of flax against 6,970, and 66,703 of hops against 67,671. In Wales, 15 of flax against 12 ; 2 of hops against none. The greater part of the acreage of Orchards and some part of the acreage of Market Gardens are included in the general Returns under separate Crops or Grass.

SIZE OF HOLDINGS AND NUMBER OF LIVE STOCK, 1880 AND 1875.

	Salop.		Montgomeryshire.		England.		Wales.	
	1880.	1875.	1880.	1875.	1880.	1875.	1880.	1875.
50 Acres and under..........	8,528..	8,281..	3,572..	3,731..	295,313..	293,400..	40,836..	40,161
Number of Agricultural horses on 50 acre holdings	2,882..		1,738..		141,252..	—	19,445..	
Number of Cattle............	24,833..	25,620..	17,322..	20,049..	924,407..	963,651..	192,355..	196,192
Number of Sheep and Lambs	28,002..	37,958..	85,552..	110,484..	1,497,760..	1,808,413..	705,959..	831,618
50 to 100 acres	918..	903..	958..	910..	44,602..	44,842..	9,767..	9,656
Agricultural horses	2,249..		2,057..		113,433..	—	20,861..	
Cattle	14,130..	14,830..	17,395..	18,157..	659,165..	699,548..	172,945..	175,915
Sheep and Lambs............	28,602..	38,003..	92,014..	100,470..	1,754,255..	2,126,590..	749,807..	807,332
100 to 300 acres..............	1,934..	1,925..	692..	663..	58,677..	58,450..	7,690..	7,316
Agricultural Horses	9,622..		2,654..		314,252..	—	23,746..	
Cattle	66,546..	68,981..	24,398..	24,427..	1,677,622..	1,695,295..	254,406..	244,140
Sheep and Lambs	198,779..	244,516..	117,971..	119,968..	6,432,090..	7,592,104..	1,027,076..	1,007,426
300 to 500 acres..............	444..	457..	38..	44..	11,617..	11,245..	454..	433
Agricultural horses	3,774..		265..		119,655..	—	2,915..	
Cattle......................	27,346..	29,411..	2,889..	3,619..	673,135..	562,836..	27,927..	27,581
Sheep and Lambs	127,423..	150,463..	14,905..	21,442..	3,694,344..	4,038,957..	139,790..	67,150
500 to 1,000 acres..........	47..	47..	5..	4..	4,005..	3,871..	75..	84
Agricultural horses	570..		43..		65,651..	—	585..	
Cattle	4,943..	4,358..	523..	510..	259,609..	244,023..	6,077..	6,419
Sheep and Lambs	24,976..	25,478..	2,504..	2,529..	2,735,584..	2,865,219..	57,246..	63,419

Over 1,000 acres	1.. —	2..	2..	500..	463..	6..	10
Agricultural horses		24..		12,243..		47..	
Cattle........................	220.. —	325..	450..	46,957..	40,050..	562..	757
Sheep and Lambs..	300.. —	3,065..	2,436..	704,752..	656,504..	7,596..	13,691
Totals :—							
Holdings	11,872.. 11,613..	5,267..	5,354..	414,804..	412,340..	58,834 ..	57,660
Horses	19,097.. —	6,781..		766,486..		72,599..	
Cattle...................	138,023..143,200..	62,857..	67,212..	4,140,955..	4,205,403..654,272..		651,004
Sheep and lambs	408,172..496,418..316,011..357,387..16,818,785..19,087,787..2,087,474..2,950,686						

CROPS, PASTURE, AND LIVE STOCK IN 1871 AND 1880.

	Salop.		Montgomery.		England.		Wales.	
	1871.	1880.	1871.	1880.	1871.	1880.	1871.	1880.
	Acres.	Acres.	Acres.	Acres.	Acres.	Acres.	Acres.	Acres.
Corn Crops	183,830..159,122..		59,973..	50,743..	7,683,692..	6,993,699..	560,700..	478,116
Green Crops................	69,441.. 58,042..		13,379..	11,061..	2,897,545..	2,659,134..	136,541..	120,073
Clover	79,567.. 67,854..		34,615..	24,966..	2,694,870..	2,646,241..	375,086..	332,353
Permanent Pasture	342,646..407,010..131,512..161,866..				9,881,833..11,461,856..1,494,465..1,805,750			
Horses	26,274.. 30,097..		11,968..	13,885..	962,840..	1,092,272..	117,176..	134,895
Cattle.......................	120,548..138,086..		61,657..	62,906..	3,671,064..	4,158,046..	596,588..	654,714
Sheep.......................	438,240..408,240..330,277..325,980..17,530,407..16,823,646..2,706,415..2,718,316							
Pigs	64,303.. 50,783..		25,040..	19,417..	2,073,504..	1,697,914..	225,456..	182,003

The tenants of the Peniarth estate have resolved to erect a window in Llanegryn Church in memory of the late Mr. W. W. E. Wynne, who was held in the highest respect amongst them. To the present owner of the estates, Mr. W. R. M. Wynne, they have presented an address of condolence and cordial regard.

The death is announced of the Rev. J. L. Hulbert, B.A., English Chaplain at Christ Church, Carabacel, Nice, second son of the Rev. Canon Hulbert, vicar of Almondbury, near Huddersfield, and a grandson of the late Mr. Hulbert, the author of "The History and Description of the County of Salop."

The Anglesey Hunt is said to have a known existence of 123 years. A writer in the *Carnarvon Herald* says— "In one year during the last century a receipt is given for 'all the expenses and demands of the hunt ; likewise for providing a French horn, or trumpet, as a call in the morning and notice for dinner.' In 1775 two French horns (or rather the horn blowers) cost the hunt £10 10s.; fiddles and harp £5 5s. ; and in 1786 the tambarine man cost £1 10s."

THE RECORDER OF LUDLOW.—Several false rumours are set at rest by the announcement that Mr. Smythies, Q.C., has been appointed Recorder of Ludlow.

Mr. JUSTICE WATKIN WILLIAMS.—The *Lancet* says :— "It may interest our readers to be told that Mr. Watkin Williams many years ago diligently studied medicine and completed his curriculum at University College. He acted as house-surgeon under Mr. Erichsen, the present distinguished president of the Royal College of Surgeons."

THE REV. D. R. THOMAS.—The newly elected proctor for the diocese of St. Asaph, the Rev. D. R. Thomas, M.A., vicar of Meifod, was educated at Ruthin school, from whence he passed to Jesus College, Oxford, graduating with honours in the final classical school. He is the author of several works both in the English and Welsh languages, but is best known for his "History of the Diocese of St. Asaph." He was for some years editor of the *Archæologia Cambrensis*. His proposer and seconder, the Rev. H. Humphreys, vicar of Henllan, and the Rev. B. M. Jones, vicar of Llanfair, were also educated at Ruthin school and were both scholars of Jesus College, Oxford.

CYMRU FU.

Tradition relates that one of the owners of Ystumcolwyn, an ancient seat situated in the beautiful vale of Myfod, while he was one evening enjoying himself in the adjacent fields, perceived smoke coming through one of the chimneys, and knowing that it was not requisite to have a fire in that part of the hall, grew suspicious, thinking that something must have been going wrong in the house. He hastened to the spot, armed with a sharp dagger or sword, and whilst searching the rooms upstairs he soon perceived secreted in a small apartment one of his wife's old admirers. His jealousy was inflamed, and a fierce struggle took place, which ended in the death of the intruder. A ghost afterwards haunted the place occasionally during many generations, and blood stains were left on the stairs. If one of the servants had to wash the stains away the hall would be troubled with dismal sounds during the night for weeks continually.

Whilst one of the servants at Cynon, Llanwddyn, was staying up very late one bright moonlight night waiting for her master and mistress home from Llanfyllin fair, a distance of about eleven miles, sometime in the middle of the night, when looking through the kitchen window, she could perceive two persons bringing, as she then thought, a naked dead child in their arms, smeared all over with blood, and placing it opposite the front door. They afterwards went away towards the road. In about an hour or so, the inmates made their appearance, and the girl related her story, but nothing could be seen outside of the child. Moreover, the house was soon afterwards troubled by such a savage spirit that people scarcely dared live there. Stones and slates from the top of the buildings were hurled at the inmates in all directions until they were obliged to get some one to lay the ghost. The old people in the neighbourhood used to relate often in the winter nights before a turf fire about the trouble and labour they had had with the ghost, especially in placing him in a bottle under a large stone under Cynon bridge. It is to be hoped that the navvies of the Llanwddyn Water Works will not apply their pickaxe so heavily as to break the bottle, or it is to be feared the Liverpool Corporation will suffer much from damage committed by the ghost, for he must have gained a vast deal of strength after resting so many years.

LLYWARCH HÊN.

NOVEMBER 24, 1880.

NOTES.

A HAPPY BOROUGH.—The *Shrewsbury Chronicle* for Nov. 3, 1837, contains the following paragraph :—"The election of Councillors for Oswestry went off in quietness ; only one new one was introduced, viz., Mr. Davies, saddler ; so that the town has the *happiness* to say they have a Corporation 'all on one side like Bridgnorth election,' except one Whig, Mr. Sabine." This would be the third election after the passing of the Municipal Corporations Act. Mr. Sabine was returned in 1835, and was the only Liberal who was successful.
OLD OSWESTRY.

CARDIGANSHIRE TRADITION.—A writer in *Arch : Cam:* 1850, p 73, the first vol. of the New Series, says :—" In the churchyard of Llanarth, near Aberaeron, on the south side of the church, is an inscribed stone (not hitherto published) of the twelfth century. It bears a cross, covering the stone, with four circular holes at the junctions of the arms. The inscription is on the lower limb of the cross ; but, as it is made of a micaceous sandstone, part has been split off, and the inscription is much mutilated. . . The current tradition of the place concerning it is, that one stormy night, some centuries ago, there was such a tremendous shindy going on up in the belfry that the whole village was put in commotion. It was at last conjectured that nobody but a certain ancient personage could be the cause of this, and, therefore, they fetched up his reverence from the Vicarage to go and request the intruder to be off. Up went the vicar with bell, book, and candle, along the narrow, winding staircase, and, sure enough, right up aloft among the bells, there was his majesty in person ! No sooner, however, had the worthy priest began the usual ' Conjurate in nomine, &c.,' than away went the enemy up the remaining part of the staircase on to the leads of the tower. The vicar, nothing daunted, followed, and pressed the intruder so briskly that the latter had nothing else to do than to leap over the battlements. He came down plump among the gravestones below ; and, falling upon one, made with his hands and knees the four holes now visible on the stone in question, which, among the country people, still retains his name." This was written more than a quarter of a century ago, perhaps the parishioners of the present day are scarcely aware of the former presence of the devil amongst them.
M.C.A.S.

MR. T. N. PARKER OF SWEENEY.—The older Oswestrians will remember, personally, and others will often have heard of the late genial and respected Thomas Netherton Parker, Esq., of Sweeney Hall, who seldom, when at home, omitted a daily visit to our town. Several references have been made to him in *Bye-gones*, especially in respect to his mechanical powers ; but nothing has hitherto been said of his powers of humour, and the life that he sometimes threw into " Mayor's Feasts " by the original and racy songs he composed and sang. On Nov. 25, 1836, we are told by a newspaper of the time, " at a dinner which took place at the Wynnstay Arms, to commemorate the election of Mr. F. Campbell as Mayor of Oswestry, Mr. Parker made a good deal of merriment by a song upon Temperance Societies, and the introduction he made to it." The following sample-verse is given :—

The folks that would take from us good wine and beer,
Would also deprive us of one Mr. Shakspeare,
And when they came to me, they'd take no denial,
And so I thought to go a month upon trial ;
But before I embark, I think it but fair,
That I should be allowed for to dine with the Mayor.

The Municipal Corporations Act not coming into operation until the month of January, 1836, Mr. James Edwards, who had been appointed mayor in the autumn of 1834—and who should have retired in ordinary course at the end of twelve months—retained office to the end of 1835 ; and on the 1st of Jan., 1836, the late Mr. John Croxon of Llanvorda-issa was elected first mayor under the new regime. The commemoration dinner came off on Jan. 22, 1836, and I have before me the original MS. of a song prepared for the occasion by Mr. Parker, but which he was prevented from singing by a death in his household. The MS. is accentuated for the guidance of the gentleman deputed by Mr. Parker to sing it ; for, as I need scarcely observe, the author's verse was not of that flowing quality Bond-street music publishers like to set to equally flowing music. The lines are headed " Air, 'Golden Days of Good Queen Bess,'" and are as follows :—

The watchwords of the present day
　Are Reform and Innovation ;
Old fashions have no more fair play
　Than our ancient Corporation.
To changes and to chances we
Submit, with some objections,
But those befalling Oswestry,
We trust will prove exceptions.
　CHORUS :—
'Twas different in the glorious times of Good
　Queen Bess,
Blessed be the memory of Good Queen Bess !

Our High Steward, and our Right Honourables,
　And Doctors in Divinity,
Privy-Councillors and Baronets,
　No longer Aldermen shall be :
While in the midst of change arise
　Political commotions,
All canvassing to gain a prize
　In Municipal promotions.
　　'Twas not so in the happy times, &c.

Although our Corporation's formed,
　For the greater part of new-men ;
Long may it boast of being adorned
　By a loyal host of true-men !
With patriotic zeal to shew
　How worthily selected,
Were those for civic honors who
　Have lately been elected.
　　To remind us of the golden days, &c.

The *agitation*, that we dread,
　Like a Comet with a *tail* is :—
As moon-shine, or suppose we said,
　The Aurora *Bore*-ealis.
New fangled orders of the day,
　Occasion much confusion ;
Which threaten soon to sweep away
　Our glorious constitution.
　　'Twas not so in the happy days, &c.

New lights are shining brilliantly,
　From Pluto's territories ;
Surprising us infernally,
　Till they scorch both Whigs and Tories.
While our intellects are on the march,
　As we fully are persuaded ;
But I fear they'll leave us in the lurch,
　By movements retrograded.
　　'Twas not so in the glorious days, &c.

The improving of our good old Town,
　Is greater than expected :
The redemption of our Market-Tolls,
　Has lately been effected.—
It now remains for you to try,
　And meet the bonny lasses' call,
To keep their eggs and butter dry,
　By building a new Market-Hall.
　　In honor of the golden days, &c.

Another very great event,
　Did equally concern you ;
The erection of a noble Bridge,
　Across the River Viernew :
Instead of splashing through the fords,
　All travellers confounding :
Which often was accompanied
　With narrow escapes from drownding.
　　Before and since the golden days, &c.

Some other boons, I'll just record,
　Not wanting much description ;
A new clock on the old Church tower,
　Is provided by subscription.
A chapel at Trefonen raised,
　For our Cambrian population ;
And another built on the Salop Road,
　For an English congregation.
　　All worthy of the golden days, &c.

But our present body corporate,
　Have incurred no little danger ;
(May this warning voice not come too late)
　About their Council Chamber.
For many have expressed their fears,
　And venture upon prophecies ;
That they'll pull an old house 'bout their ears,
　And swamp the Town Clerk's Offices.
　　'Twas not so in the golden days, &c.

Most of the allusions in the foregoing are palpable
enough. Under the old regulation our High Steward and
Recorder were the one an alderman and the other a councillor. The redemption of the Market Tolls refers to the
time when they were the property of the Earl of Powis,
and all produce that came into the town was taxed at the
gates. The new clock on the Church has long been worn
out, and replaced. The Chapel at Trefonen—built for
the Welsh—is now an English place of worship. The
"Chapel" referred to in Salop-road, and which was called
"Trinity Chapel," when it was consecrated, is now "Holy
Trinity Church." The only allusion I cannot quite understand is the last of all, touching the Town Clerk's Office,
unless the author spoke figuratively.　　　　JARCO.

QUERIES.

CYDEWAIN.—This place name, if it be a place
name, I have seen written in several forms—Kedewen,
Kiddewy, Kidowen, Caedewen, &c. Can any correspondent give the meaning of the word ? and name the earliest
instance of its application as the name of a district, so far
as is known.　　　　DRENEWYDD.

NOVELS RELATING TO WALES.—Dutton
Cook's *Trials of the Tredgolds* lays some of its scenes in
Llanidloes ; Miss Braddon portrays Llandrindod Wells in
her *Hostages to Fortune.* Miss Hesba Stretton has much
to do with Barmouth in *David Lloyd's Last Will,* and Miss
Beale's story of *The Pennant Family* wholly relates, I
think, to Merionethshire. Mr. Black's *Strange Adventures
of a Phaeton,* reveals an interesting scene in the Fairy
Glen at Bettws-y-Coed. What other novels refer to
Wales ? And can any reader give the name of a novel
about a "Welsh Heiress" that was issued a few years ago,
and said to contain some striking descriptions of Welsh
Scenery ?　　　　G.G.

ST. OSWALD'S PILGRIM SIGNS.—In an
Article on "Pilgrim Signs" by Cecil Brent, F.S.A., in
the *Archæologia Cantiana* Vol. xiii., p. iii., there is a
plate entitled "29 Medieval Broaches and Pins worn by
Pilgrims after visiting Shrines at Canterbury." They are
mostly relating to St. Thomas à Becket, being purchased
by Pilgrims to shew that they had visited the Shrine of
the Martyr at Canterbury. The four last signs, however, are stated to relate to "St. Oswald, King of

Northumbria, who reigned 9 years, and was killed by
King Penda. He was first buried at Barching, in
Lincolnshire, his body was removed to Gloucester in
A.D. 909. To him is dedicated the church of Paddles-
worth, near Folkestone." Nothing further is said about
the St. Oswald pilgrim signs, and the plate is on too small
a scale (2-5ths of the actual size) to enable one to distinguish what the figures upon them represent. Was the
Shrine of St. Oswald at Gloucester, or Canterbury, or
where ?　　　　F.S.A.

REPLIES.

SHROPSHIRE WORDS (Nov. 10, 1880).—The
other day, walking down Oswald Road, Oswestry, as our
country neighbours were coming from the Llanymynech
train to our market, I just heard in passing one woman
say to another :—"And there she wun as big as Ess."
Now, I have heard this description "big as ess" often,
and have as often puzzled over its origin. What does it
mean ?　　　　N. W. S.

EDWARD JONES, *BARDD Y BRENIN* (Oct.
13, 1880).—A few weeks ago, in Market Street, Manchester, the identical harp which Jones played, and which
he pourtrayed in his *Bardic Relicks,* was discovered by the
well-known penillion singer, "Idris Vychan." On an
old corroded brass plate the name

Edward Jones, Henblas,

Llandderfel,

-----

is quite distinct. Certain carvings and fluting correspond
exactly with the harp engraved in the *Bardic Relicks.* The
instrument is smaller than harps now in use, and is in
excellent condition. It ought to be purchased for some of
our public museums.　　　　J.C.H.

THE HARLECH EXHALATIONS (Sept. 29,
1880).—Our learned countryman, Edward Llwyd, wrote
an account of these somewhat mysterious exhalations in
the *Philosophical Transactions.* It would be interesting
to know what that eminent man had to say respecting
them, and any reader of these columns having access to
the *Transactions* of the period would confer a favour upon
many besides myself by supplying a copy of the paper
referred to for re-publication in *Bye-gones.* Llwyd was
not only the first philologist of his age, but also a naturalist of no mean order. The *Cambrian Plutarch,* p. 338,
refers to no less than fourteen papers in the *Phil. Trans.* as
the work of Llwyd. Most of these are stated to relate to
natural history, but some of them are on antiquarian and
philological subjects.　　　　DYVNIG.

A writer in *Notes and Queries* points out the fact that the
Heralds' Visitations of Salop, Stafford, and Worcester counties
have not "received attention at the hands of any of the Societies
which have done such valuable work in printing the genealogical
accounts of other districts."

TRANSACTIONS OF THE SHROPSHIRE ARCHÆOLO-
GICAL SOCIETY. Shrewsbury : Adnitt and Naunton.
Oswestry : Woodall and Venables.
ANOTHER instalment—forming Pt. I. of Vol. 4, has just been
issued, and contains a further chapter of Oswestry Corporation
history compiled by Mr. Stanley Leighton, M.P. This is chiefly
devoted to the Charter of Charles II. by which Oswestry was
governed from 1674 to 1836. The Charter has never been hitherto
published entire, and Mr. Leighton adds a clear and concise abstract of it. Another document relates to the Tolls in 1673, and is
signed by Richard Jones and John Glover, bailiffs, and *Morgan
Wynne,* recorder ; which answers a question put in our columns
July 7, as to whether this gentleman served under James's Charter.
The remainder of the part includes papers on Moreton Corbet,
Rossalls of Rossall, Shrewsbury of Past Ages, Manor of Condover, and Leland's Itinerary. There are several illustrations.

MONTGOMERYSHIRE COLLECTIONS of the Powys-Land Club. London : Richards.

THE supplementary part of the *Montgomeryshire Collections* of the Powys-land Club—completing the thirteenth volume—has just been issued. It contains notices of the late Rev. Robert Jones of Rotherhithe, and W. W. E. Wynne, Esq., of Peniarth ; with lists of their contributions to the papers of the Society, The fine portrait of Mr. Wynne, subscribed for by members of the Powys-land Club and the Cambrian Archæological Society, is added as a frontispiece to the volume. A letter from Canon Williams, rector of Culmington, is also published, urging that the Museum at Welshpool should be made the grand library for the reception of Welsh-printed books ; and calling attention to the fact that even the most unimportant works may sometimes be useful to scholars ; instancing as a proof of this the extracts from old Welsh almanacks recently given in *Bye-gones* by Mr Salisbury of Glan Abei, Chester.

CURRENT NOTES.

Grinshill Church, which is dedicated to All Saints, was re-opened on Thursday after reparation, re-seating, and other improvements, which have been carried out at a cost of £300. The sermon was preached by the Bishop of Lichfield. Amongst the special gifts to the church was an alms dish presented by Miss Bettenson of Wem.

On Friday, the Shirehall at Shrewsbury was partially destroyed by fire. Fortunately the fire occurred in the morning, and was soon discovered, or the whole of the building, and many of the adjoining houses, would very likely have fallen before the flames. The fire is said to have been caused in some way by the action of workmen who were repairing the roof.

DEATH OF MR. R. L. BURTON.—The death is announced of Mr. Robert Lingen Burton, of Longner Hall, near Shrewsbury. Mr. R. L. Burton, who was forty-four years of age, was the son of the late Mr. Robert Burton, of Longner, who served the office of sheriff in 1852, and was twice Mayor of Shrewsbury. Mr. Robert Burton married first, in 1821, Catherine, daughter of William Walcot, Esq., of Moor Park, and, secondly, in 1835, Catherine, eldest daughter of the Rev. Herbert Oakeley, D.D., Oakeley House, Bishop's Castle, and the gentleman now deceased was their eldest son. Mr. Burton, we believe, was a member of the county Bench of magistrates, but seldom took part in public business. As a sportsman he was very popular. He did much to keep together the Shrewsbury Hounds, of which he was twice master, and his tact, pluck, and genial manner in the field won for him friends among all who frequented the meets and indulged in the many fine runs he gave them cross-country. As a breeder of stock his name was also well known. The family of Burton dates as far back as the fourteenth century.

THE BISHOP OF ST. ASAPH AT THE POWYS-LAND CLUB.
(Nov. 3, 1880.)

SIR,—Mr. H. W. Lloyd has tilted in such violent fashion, and in language which it is a pity he should have been tempted to use, that it is amusing to read his warning to the Bishop about what was due to a Historical Society, and his suggestion that perhaps the Bishop's statements were attributable to "ignorance and prejudice" rather than "deliberate slander and malevolence."

But is Mr. Lloyd's self-confidence justified? and are his own statements so incontrovertible?

First of all, he rates the Bishop for his statement about Brochwel Ysgythrog : and it is not easy to say which of the two he is most virulent against. He traces the statement back to what he calls the "romance of Geoffrey of Monmouth by these Protestant, Anglican, and Clerical writers made to do duty for history." But why did Mr. Lloyd stop short here? Does he not know that however

Geoffrey may have romanced about some things, he had an earlier "Brut" or Chronicle for his historical matter : and this original Chronicle we have still under the name of "Brut Tyssilio." Now this Tyssilio lived nearer to the time in question than even the Venerable Bede : in fact he was the son of Brochwel, and therefore may be supposed to have known as much about the facts, as one who lived nearly a hundred years later. At all events the two versions are entirely distinct and independent. And if it be objected that the version of Brochwel's son would naturally be partial : it may be equally replied that the version of his enemy would not necessarily be impartial. Indeed, no one I think, can read Bede's account of the whole matter without seeing what a strong partisan he shows himself against the Britons. And whether the Bishop conceded too much, or too little, as to what "historians are agreed to" as to the incentive to the slaughter of the Monks, Bede himself, Mr. Lloyd's great authority, rejoiced in it as a just judgment on "that perfidious people," and believed it to be the fulfilment of the prediction "which the man of God, Augustine, was said in a *threatening manner* to have foretold."

Now, Bede's version is that "Brochwel was set to guard the monks while praying, but that at the first advance of the enemy he fled precipitately with his horsemen, and left them to their fate."

The "Brut Tyssilio," on the other hand—to quote the account a little more fully, relates—that "when the Saxons came to punish Dunawd and his Abbey for their disobedience, Brochwel commanded the Cymry at Caerllion, and there came to him religious men from all the Abbeys, and chiefly from Bangor Vawr, and they fought the Saxons, and Brochwel fled as far as Bangor, and drew to him all the Britons. Then Ethelfled seeing so many religious men, slew twelve hundred of them. After this the other British chieftains from Cornwall, Dyfed, and Gwynedd, came to the aid of Brochwel. Whereupon a bloody battle ensued between the Britons and the Saxons, the result of which was that the Britons gained the victory, and that Ethelfled was wounded, and fled."

This is evidently the version that the Bishop of St. Asaph followed in his Eulogy on Brochwel. Whether it is less reliable than that of Bede let scholars judge. The action of Brochwel, at all events, stands in quite a different light from what Bede would place it in. And when the "Brut Tyssilio" goes on to state that the combined Britons under Cadvan "pursued the Saxons across the Humber," it was no particular mark of "ignorance" or even "prejudice" to state that "Brochwel was instrumental in turning back the tide of war."

One or two other points raised shall be touched upon another time.   D.R.T.

HIGHER EDUCATION IN WALES.
THE DEPARTMENTAL COMMITTEE.

WELSHPOOL.

The Committee appointed to enquire into the subject of Intermediate and Higher Education in Wales sat at the Town Hall, Welshpool, Nov. 30. Lord Aberdare presided, and the other members of the Committee present were Viscount Emlyn, M.P., Mr. Henry Richard, M.P., Professor John Rhys, Canon Robinson, and Mr. Lewis Morris.

The Earl of POWIS was the first witness examined, and he was followed by Mr. M. S. FORSTER, Head Master of Oswestry Grammar School. Mr. Forster explained the constitution of the Governing Body, and the nature of the education given in the School. Upon being questioned as to the number of Welsh boys he had, he said he had

twelve boys who were born in Wales, eight who were
resident in Wales, and three who spoke the Welsh language. The School was a first grade school, and he sent
boys to the University. He recommended that exhibitions for Welsh boys should not be limited to any
particular school or college, but should be tenable at any
place of higher education of which the trustees of the fund
might approve. In answer to the question whether the
charges at the Grammar School were not too high for the
class of boys with which the enquiry was most concerned,
the witness replied that it might possibly be so. Some
stress was laid upon the question whether it would not be
better for boys to leave such a school as Oswestry at an
earlier age than eighteen or nineteen, in order to go to
some such College as Aberystwyth before proceeding to
Oxford or Cambridge. Mr. Forster's reply to that question was, although it might make the working of the
school less heavy, he still thought it would be undesirable
for boys to change their school at that late period of their
education. In answer to a question whether Oswestry
might not be included in the Welsh Marches, the witness
said he thought it might be included in the district with
which the Committee had to deal, because Oswestry School was not included amongst the Shropshire Grammar Schools, which enjoyed the
benefits of the Careswell Exhibitions, nor yet
amongst those which enjoyed the benefits of exclusively
Welsh exhibitions. The extent of the Welsh element in
Oswestry was shown by the fact that there was a Welsh
Church in connection with the parish church, as well as
several Welsh chapels.—In answer to Mr. Richard, Mr.
Forster said that he himself and the other masters were
members of the Church of England, and there was a
chapel in connection with the School. There was a Conscience Clause in operation. Oswestry was convenient for
access from different parts of Wales.—The next witness
was the Rev. W. HOLT BEEVER, incumbent of Llandyssil,
formerly master of Cowbridge School, who deprecated the
proposal to found a Welsh University, and was opposed
to close scholarships for Welsh boys. Welshmen suffered
from their isolation. It was most desirable that natives
of the Principality should be educated as far as possible
at school and college with English boys and young men,
for they had plenty of ability to cope with them if they
were efficiently taught. One great need of Wales was to
provide efficient masters for the existing Grammar
Schools. In his opinion close scholarships afforded little
real stimulus to competition, and were injurious because
the boys knew almost exactly what was necessary to win
them, and would not stretch an inch beyond what was
actually required.

A deputation from the County Conference, recently
held at Newtown, attended the enquiry, and was com-
posed of the following gentlemen:—Hon. F. S. A.
Hanbury-Tracy, M.P.; Mr. Stuart Rendel, M.P.;
Captain R. D. Pryce; Mr. C. R. Jones; Mr. John
Jones, Llanfyllin; Mr. Richard Williams; Mr. W. T.
Parker; Mr. J. Smout; Mr. T. G. Jones; Mr. E. S. R.
Trevor; Mr. J. Jones, Varchoel; Mr. Maurice Evans;
Mr. James Hall, and Mr. Samuel Davies, Welshpool.

Mr. STUART RENDEL, M.P., said he had the honour to
head a deputation in pursuance of a resolution passed at
a Conference held at Newtown, on the 1st Nov., at which
Lord Sudeley presided, and at which the County and
Borough members were present, together with gentlemen
from all parts of the County, especially representing
the class interested in intermediate and higher
education in Wales. The hon. gentleman then
submitted the names of the members of the deputation, and copies of the resolutions come to by

the Conference, which he said he would not take up the
time of the Committee by reading. In reference to the
first resolution stating that the main provision for education other than elementary in the county was given by a
few private adventure schools, the witness submitted a
tabular statement conveying information respecting those
schools, from which it appeared there were only six for
boys, and eight for girls of any sort of importance; that
the approximate number of children for whom those schools
provided education was 350, and that the education was to
a large extent of a very elementary character. Only one
of them had any endowment, namely, that at Deytheur,
which had £109 a year. Such funds as might have been
devoted to Grammar Schools had been gradually absorbed
by elementary schools, in which, however, in many cases,
intermediate education was provided for the more promising
pupils, and for that reason the Conference had not
sought to express any opinion as to disturbing the present
uses to which those funds were applied, although members
of the deputation would in their individual capacity
like to make statements on the subject. With regard
to the second finding, the Conference wished to point out
that, of the sum of £1,640 per annum, summarized from
Lord Robert Montagu's return as the total charitable endowment of the county for all purposes, only £752 was devoted to education. As he had already shown, only a
small portion of that sum, namely, that which went to
Deytheur, was applied, strictly speaking, to schools for
secondary education. As to the third finding, that large
sums of money arising from property within the county
were annually paid for purposes of education elsewhere,
Mr. Stuart Rendel handed in a statement showing that
£4,011 a year went out of the county for the benefit of
two Oxford Colleges, namely, Christ Church and University College, from which no sort of special benefit was
derived either by Montgomeryshire or the Principality,
though they did not allege this as a grievance, inasmuch
as nobody's pocket was the worse for it, but it was a contribution from the soil of the county. In reference to
a further finding of the Conference, and also in answer to
a question by the Chairman, the hon. gentleman said that
large sums of money had been spent by the middle classes
in circumstances which the Conference deemed worthy of
notice. Prior to the recent educational legislation the
county, in order to make provision for unsectarian
elementary education, had provided by voluntary effort
accommodation for fully two thousand children, and it
would be seen from the statement he handed in how this
accommodation was distributed. In addition to grants of
£1,311, at least £5,000 must have been raised by the people
themselves, which would still represent a much smaller
total sum than would be sufficient to provide accommodation
according to the lowest rate at which such schools were
being built. The cost per head at a modern Board School
varied from £5 to £10 per head. They did not forget that
the present generation had the benefit of those British
Schools, in the shape of a reduction of School Board rates.
Their existence nevertheless constituted an evidence of
the zeal of the people, and a claim for present consideration. In view of the admission by the legislature of the
principle of unsectarian elementary education, the Conference also thought it not unreasonable to submit for the
consideration of the Committee the fact that circumstances had compelled Montgomeryshire to make a
great effort to provide for the spiritual necessities
of the people. Mr. Rendel then handed in a paper
showing, upon the authority of Mr. Richard Williams
of Newtown, that in round numbers £175,000 had been
spent in the erection of over 300 chapels, and of that sum
£10,000 a year was raised for the support of the ministry.

In common with the rest of Wales, but in a degree which the foregoing facts shewed to be peculiar, it might be said that, while the labouring classes in the county received education at the public cost, and the wealthier classes enjoyed the enormous advantages arising from the ancient educational endowments of the county, the great bulk of the middle classes was without corresponding assistance. The Conference considered that the best educational aid that could be given to the county was by annual grants to an intermediate school for girls as well as boys, established in some convenient part of the county. The Conference were in favour of a technical and commercial education being given in such school, and especially in subjects connected with agriculture and mining pursuits, but conjoined with their scheme they desired to see bursaries, scholarships, or exhibitions established at the University, as prizes for superior talents and industry in connection with the school, so as to graft the advantages of a higher education upon the main object they had in view—a system of intermediate education. The Conference would be glad to see a college in North as well as in South Wales; and they were in favour of granting substantial support to the College at Aberystwyth, which they considered ought to be affiliated to a University or other degree-giving body in Wales, which should be of a distinctly national and Welsh character.

Mr. T. G. JONES of Llansantffraid next gave evidence. He said that the endowment of Deytheur, which amounted to £109 a year, was not sufficient to fulfil the intentions of the donor, the Hon. Andrew Newport, namely, that girls as well as boys should receive the benefits arising from it. He (Mr. Jones) suggested that the Deytheur endowment should be so far supplemented by the county educational endowments, as to enable the master to engage a sufficient staff of teachers for girls as well as boys.

Mr. C. R. JONES, of Llanfyllin, the convener of the Conference, said that the endowments, which according to the returns moved for by Lord Robert Montagu amounted to £1,640 10s., were in the hands of a small section of the community, and afforded opportunities for waste and extravagance, not in accordance with the wishes of the donors. Out of that sum only £750, according to the return (but the actual amount was nearer £850) was devoted to educational purposes. The witness contended that these endowments were not required now, and that provision had been made by the Education Acts of 1870 and 1876 for elementary education throughout the country. For example, in the Llanfyllin National School, at which the average attendance was 117, the grants gained last year amounted to £116 10s. 3d.; and the endowments for Llanfyllin and Llanfihangel Schools were £132 10s. At the Llanfyllin British School the average attendance was 113, and the capitation grant, £99 7s. 11d.—seventeen shillings per head on the average attendance. This school had received special praise from the Rev. R. Temple, the Inspector, as being one of the best schools in his district. In Kerry National School the average attendance was 156; the Government grant, £116 9s.; and the endowments, £153—total, £269 9s., or £1 14s. 6d. per head. At Berriew National School the average attendance was 120; £104 13s. was raised by the capitation grant, and the endowment was £90—total, £194 13s., or £1 12s. 5½d. per head. At Newtown National School the average attendance was 186; the grant, £161 17s. 6d.; and the endowment, £55 11s. The British Schools only obtained on an average 17s. 6d. per head. The witness suggested that the endowments for educational purposes should be applied to giving exhibitions in grammar schools, for both sexes, or as an alternative, that they should be applied in liquidation of the rates in their

respective parishes. Mr. Jones also gave evidence in respect to doles, which he said were worse than useless, and to money for apprenticing, and he suggested that such endowments should be applied to educational purposes in connection with middle class schools. He was in favour of establishing a boarding school in the county for boys and girls separately. In answer to a question by Mr. Richard, as to the difficulty in regard to religious teaching, Mr. Jones said he would have the school perfectly unsectarian, but at the same time Protestant. He thought the Bible should be read, and prayers said.

Mr. JOHN JONES of Guilsfield, another member of the deputation, gave further evidence.

The CHAIRMAN, in thanking the deputation for their attendance, said he only wished other counties had taken as much pains in preparing evidence for the enquiry as the County of Montgomery had done.

Mr. C. W. W. WYNN then gave evidence in respect to the Welsh Charity Schools at Ashford, Middlesex, of which he was for ten years the treasurer. He said that whereas by the original constitution no children were eligible unless they had been born in London or within ten miles of the Royal Exchange, now one-fourth of them might be sent from the Principality, but one of the parents must have been born in Wales, or in the Welsh parishes of Shropshire or Monmouthshire. Owing to reduced subscriptions the number of children upon the foundation had fallen from 200 to 77. The amount of funded capital was £49,000.

Mr. STANLEY LEIGHTON, M.P., the present treasurer, then gave evidence on the state of the Welsh Charity School at Ashford, founded in connection with the Society of Ancient Britons. The income of the school consisted of £1,468, being the interest of £49,500 consols, which had arisen from donations and legacies. The rent of land was £42 a year, and the annual subscriptions £800. The pay of scholars amounted to £1,500. The numbers of scholars on the foundation were 49 boys and 34 girls. These were children of Welsh extraction, chiefly from London. The pay scholars were 37 boys and 20 girls, making a total of 57 pay scholars. The pay scholars were chiefly the children of English farmers. They paid £24 a year. The foundationers were children of the really indigent, and their parents were sometimes actually paupers. The children wore uniform, and they usually went into domestic service. The school was a Church of England School, and the instruction consisted of the ordinary elementary education. The demand for admission had lately fallen off. Since 1876, there had been no competitions for elections. The subscriptions also showed a great diminution. As to the history of the foundation, the first record of the founders' intentions was contained in a resolution, that all the charity money of the Society should be disposed of for the benefit of the Welsh nation in general. That was passed in 1714. Shortly afterwards the charity money was applied to the apprenticeship of boys. In the year 1718, schooling and clothing were added to the apprenticeship, as follows, "for children descended from Welsh parents, having no parochial settlement, and living within ten miles of the Royal Exchange, London." In the year 1771, a new School was built in Gray's Inn Road, where the School House remained until 1854, when it was removed to Ashford, Middlesex. In the year 1841, there were 200 children on the foundation, and at the present time there were only 83. In the year 1874, the children of English parents were first taken on payment. This year, at a meeting of the House Committee that had the management of the School, it was proposed to consider a scheme for converting the School into a Middle class school, of exclusively Welsh character. Sir Watkin

Williams Wynn, and General Brownrigg, C.B., proposed, and it was carried *nem. con.*, "That a committee should be appointed to prepare a draft scheme." That scheme was still under the consideration of the governors, and, under it, it was proposed to establish a school for girls of the higher middle-class, somewhat after the pattern of the Howell's Schools at Denbigh and Llandaff.

The Rev. E. ROBINSON of Deytheur gave evidence in regard to Deytheur Grammar School, of which he had been master for twenty-four years. The education provided there embraced classics, mathematics, French, and the general course of an English education, qualifying the pupils for the Cambridge Local Examinations which some of the boys had passed for the last fifteen years. There were two classes of day pupils, those living in the Hundred of Deytheur being free, and those living outside the Hundred paying £2 per annum. The Head Master took boarders who received their instruction along with the day pupils. The day boys were generally the sons of farmers, tradesmen, and cottagers, in the neighbourhood and adjacent districts. The pupils on the foundation paid a small entrance fee, and found their own books and other requisites. The average attendance of boys had been about fifty. The elementary schools lately established in the neighbourhood by Capt. Mytton had reduced the number of the poorer children attending the school, and the day scholars now attending were mainly the sons of farmers and tradesmen. The fact that they generally ceased their attendance at school about the age of fifteen showed that there was no great desire among that class to continue their boys at school sufficiently long to receive more than a sound education within limits, and that they did not aspire to that higher education which the school was perfectly capable of giving to fit youths for matriculation at a University or the various Civil Service examinations. The boarders, who varied in numbers reaching to thirty-two, had belonged to various classes in various towns in Montgomeryshire, Shropshire, Cheshire, &c. The extreme healthiness of the School was shown by the fact that not one serious case of illness had occurred during the last twenty-four years. While the School was sufficiently removed from any town, it was yet in easy communication with all parts of Montgomeryshire. He did not think, from his own experience, that there was at present any very great desire for higher education among the humbler classes in Wales, nor was there very much willingness, on their part generally, to make any great sacrifices in order to obtain it. He strongly thought that several existing endowed schools at suitable places, and at proper distances from each other, should be improved both as to buildings, endowments, and scholarships, and made as efficient as possible with a View of providing good intermediate education in certain centres for the surrounding districts. This would be very much better and very much more economical than any attempt at building any large and necessarily expensive buildings in any one place. Building upon the present lines, and improving present means, was, he apprehended, the best plan. The present Grammar Schools in certain places, and at their efficiency largely increased by improving the buildings where required, by enlarging somewhat their endowments, by providing scholarships to and from them, and by excluding junior pupils, who, upon examination for candidates for admission, did not reach a certain minimum standard. There might be a great improvement in applying endowments of small or questionable utility. He did not think it desirable, in the interests of higher education in Wales, to have a University for Wales with power to confer degrees in Arts; but that it would be infinitely better that those proceeding to a degree should do so at one of the existing Universities.

Mr. R. E. JONES of Bryntalch said he wished to correct a statement which had been made to the effect that the endowments of the Kerry School amounted to £153 a year, and that they were given for the purposes of secondary education. That was not so. The school was fulfilling in the most satisfactory manner the purpose for which it was intended; and the trustees hoped that when a portion of the endowment which was now suspended fell in they would be able to give an elementary education of a very high class, so as to meet the wants of many of the middle classes. He agreed with the suggestion made by the Deputation that there should be two schools in Montgomeryshire, one for boys and the other for girls. He thought, however, that it would be best to proceed by developing existing schools instead of setting up new ones. He was of opinion that Deytheur School, if enlarged, might be made the nucleus of a very excellent school; but he thought that in its present situation that would be impracticable, and that it should be removed to some more populous place. By so doing the accommodation would be very much greater in proportion to the cost than if given in a remote country district, as in the one case provision would have to be made for boarding all the pupils, while in the other a very large number of the pupils would be day scholars. It appeared that the education could not be given in a small school remuneratively at the price now charged, while in large schools, such as those established on Canon Woodard's principles, it had been found practicable to give board and education for from £25 to £30 a year.

Mr. A. HOWELL, Rhiewport, referring to Mr. C. R. Jones's remarks, said that he did not quite know in what sense Mr. C. R. Jones had called Berriew School a Church School. The fact was that all the children of the parish, whatever their religious profession might be, were educated in a similar manner.

Mr. OWEN OWEN, B.A., of Willow-street Academy, Oswestry, said that he was inclined to believe that no educational scheme could meet the wants of the Principality which did not bring schools of all grades to work together in perfect harmony, and which did not remove the last obstacle or difficulty from the path of a poor boy from the village school to the university. One way to remove these difficulties would be to connect three distinct grades of schools by means of exhibitions created out of result fees. In an elementary school of 100 boys, 20 ought to be able to pass an examination in arithmetic, English grammar, orthography, English history, geography, and writing; if the Government allowed 5s. for each pass in those six subjects, that school would receive £30 annually towards sending the best boy to a higher grade school. The school might receive more than £30 one year, so that the surplus of that year might cover the possible deficit of another year, or they might by means of three or four years' surplus be able to offer an additional exhibition occasionally. He would call elementary schools fourth grade schools; all endowed, proprietary, and private schools he would call third grade schools. A third grade school, if at all efficient, could train 60 boys out of a 100 to pass a good examination in the above-mentioned subjects. If the Government allowed 7s. 6d. for each pass, that school would receive £135 towards maintaining worthy boys of limited means. Such a school ought also, in addition to this, to secure twenty passes in each of the following subjects—Euclid, algebra, Latin, Greek, French, German, and music; if 10s. was allowed for each pass it would be possible to offer two exhibitions of £40 annually for competition to such as wished to enter one of the second grade colleges. To secure thoroughness in elementary subjects, it would be well if no result fees were allowed except in the case of those who had satisfied in arithmetic, English grammar, orthography, and writing. He advocated three second grade colleges for Wales ; one to be at Swansea, one at Aberystwyth, and one in Carnarvon. If each of these colleges could secure 100 passes in each of the above mentioned subjects, and the Government allowed 10s. for each pass, they could offer 10 Scholarships of £70 a year to their best men, tenable at Oxford or Cambridge. The control of the Examinations, and result fees should be left to a central council elected by head-masters. He felt very strongly in favour of a system of result fees ; there ought to be no obstacle in the way of schools, any more than in the case of individuals, to reach the status which they were capable of reaching. He thought it would be much better if the Government, instead of fortifying certain schools against the inevitable consequences of bad management and bad teaching, were to assist all schools alike on the principle of payment by results. He referred to the enormous wealth of Jesus College, the "National College" of Wales, as compared with the comparative poverty of the Principality. He thought that if Keble College, without a farthing of external income could educate 130 undergraduates at a cost of £81 a year, Jesus College, with a corporate income exceeding £8,000 a year, ought certainly to be able to educate 200 Welsh youths at a cost not exceeding £60, and so be more accessible to students of limited means. All were ready to admit that Welsh endowments were far too meagre to meet the educational wants of the Principality. He advocated that all such endowments as might be available for educational purposes should be brought together into one fund, subsidized by Government aid ; and that schools should receive from this general fund precisely according to their merit.

The Rev. D. R. THOMAS, Vicar of Meifod, was also examined, and said he assumed that "higher education" meant higher than elementary ; that they were asked to fill up the stages to the highest or final form ; that the special object of that meeting was to promote "local effort" in its connection with Montgomeryshire. He had therefore confined himself to that aspect, and he had come to the conclusion that the best way of attaining that object would be to make such a wise and just use of existing resources, as to elicit further support for the supply of existing deficiencies. For that purpose it appeared to him that the best plan would be to have a number of intermediate schools so placed as to be convenient for the middle classes in different parts of the county, and a higher school, into which they might be drafted by examination from the intermediate ones. Such intermediate schools already existed at Deytheur and in Welshpool, and he would establish others at Berriew, Kerry, Llanfyllin, Llanerfyl, Llanidloes, Newtown, Llanbrynmair, and Machynlleth. He would not interfere with the trusts, otherwise than by the insertion of a conscience clause, but he would utilize the endowments for the higher education of the children of the parishes to whom those endowments belonged. The Elementary Education Acts had so affected the pre-existing conditions that many of these educational endowments might fairly be applied now to at least the intermediate stage of higher education, and he would propose to apply them in full or part payment of the fees of clever boys in or from the respective parishes. The schools themselves should be subject to examination, and upon examination earn a Government grant upon the same principle as was already acted upon in elementary schools. From these intermediate schools to the higher

schools there should be further exhibitions. For those who wished for a technical education, in such a school as was indicated by the deputation from Newtown, the Government should provide an ample endowment, and for those wishing to proceed to classical schools, either at Oswestry, Shrewsbury, or elsewhere in Wales or the borders, the capitalized portion of the Meyrick fund at Jesus College might be available in the form of entrance exhibitions to be competed for under the direction of the Fellows of that College. Until lately educational endowments had been provided all but solely by Church people, and these should not be alienated. Now that the Government was awaking to its obligations, let it supply the requirements of Nonconformists with a liberal grant ; but it should be remembered that among those requiring Higher Education, Churchmen were hardly to be put down as a minority. A Higher School for girls was most desirable, and he thought Welshpool was the most convenient place for such an institution for Montgomeryshire, and that Christ Church, Oxford, which received so much from this and adjoining parishes should contribute towards the funds of such a school. Besides educational endowments, there were also some others of such a character that they might probably be better applied to the purposes of intermediate education than continue to be devoted to their present uses, but each case would require to be dealt with separately upon its merits. Such for instance would be some of the doles. Apprentice funds also in some cases might be available to help boys on to technical schools whether at Newtown, Birmingham, or Manchester. And he would suggest that the fines inflicted in the different unions for infraction of the new by-laws, should be employed as a fund for exhibitions to be competed for by the scholars in the elementary schools of the district. Such a system of intermediate schools would form a network through the County, and would supply better material for, and produce better results in, the higher schools. Mr. Thomas would not disconnect the Meyrick Funds, other than as already suggested, from Jesus College, Oxford, nor would he diminish the exhibitions and scholarships belonging to that College, for he believed it had yet a great future before it as the Welsh College, and would produce as good fruit as it had done in times past. Better prepared material and a better staff of tutors must produce corresponding results, and he thought that Dr. Harper's plan to connect the Higher class schools with the College by enabling the masters to hold fellowships concurrently with their masterships, would promote very efficiently higher class education, and it would place the College as it should be placed, at the head of an active, intelligent, and connected scheme for the promotion of the highest educational interests of Wales. In answer to a member of the committee, Mr. Thomas said that he would by all means limit endowments in favour of any particular denomination when the donor wished it, as being the principle to which all existing ones were due, and the only one at all likely to enlist more in the future.

ABERYSTWYTH.

The Departmental Committee appointed to inquire into the state of education in Wales met at Aberystwyth on Dec. 2, under the presidency of Lord Aberdare.

The Bishop of BANGOR was examined as to the state of Beaumaris, Bangor, and Bottwnog schools. Respecting Beaumaris, he said that though the governing body consisted of twelve Churchmen and only two Nonconformists, he did not consider the school improperly managed. It was true the population of Anglesey was mostly Nonconformist, but the moral influence of two Nonconformists on the governing body, backed by public opinion, would not be without weight. He did not think the benefit to be derived from the suggested change of situation would compensate for the expense of new buildings. If, however, the cost of new buildings could be obtained from an independent source he might see fit to change his opinions. His lordship's connection with Bangor only dated from the time when the new scheme came into operation, the school was well conducted, and produced good results. It had been proposed to transfer the Bottwnog School elsewhere —Pwllheli, for instance ; and it was a fair subject for consideration whether that could not be effected, if adequate compensation were given to the district from which the school was taken. Speaking on the general question of higher education, his lordship deprecated a narrow and mistaken patriotism in this respect. He contended that what was calculated to confer the greatest and most lasting good to the nation ought to receive attention, so far as Welsh education was concerned. If an institution existed in the Principality, or was henceforth founded, which had the power of conferring degrees, it was a question what the value of those degrees would be.

Lord ABERDARE pointed out that the Scotch system had been successful and beneficial to the natives of that part of the kingdom. Would not a similar system meet the needs of Wales?

The BISHOP replied that he was by no means adverse to a sort of intermediate university for Wales, which would be a kind of connecting link between higher class schools and the older universities. As long as Jesus College endowments were administered by Jesus College in such a way as to answer the purpose for which they were devised, he would not advocate any innovations in existing arrangements.

The PRINCIPAL of Aberystwyth College explained the present position of the College, and said there were fifty-seven students. The decrease which had occurred in the number was partly due to depression in trade, which had caused a decrease at Owen's College, Manchester, and other educational institutions ; and partly to the fact that people were beginning to understand what the College meant, and did not send so many unprepared youths, who ought to go to Grammar Schools. He was in favour of establishing a Science College in Glamorganshire, with sufficient classics as would be requisite for a pass degree ; and a Classical College at Aberystwyth, with sufficient science for a degree. He thought that arrangement would suit North Wales. The establishment of three colleges, as was proposed at the Aberystwyth Conference—one in Carnarvon, another at Aberystwyth, and a third at Cardiff—all three to be equally classical and all three to be equally scientific, would, in his opinion, swamp one, if not two, of the three. Religious training should be left entirely in the hands of parents and ministers of religion. He was strongly in favour of a University for Wales, established neither on the plan of London University, to which no college need be affiliated in order that students might be examined for degrees ; nor on the plan of the other Universities, in which the University itself taught through its professors ; but on the plan of Victoria University, which had its headquarters at Owen's College, but which was distinct from the College, the University to be composed of affiliated colleges. His arguments in favour of a University for Wales were that a degree was the natural culminating point of education, and that it bestowed upon that education the stamp of unity, without which it became scattered and aimless ; and in the second place, because there was already in Wales a quasi-university possessing power to grant degrees. Referring to Lampeter College, which has the power of conferring B.A. and B.D. degrees, he thought it would be an injustice to other sections of the population if an institution,

which was virtually a Church of England college, should be the University for Wales. Principal Edwards concluded by explaining the undenominational character of Aberystwyth College, and by reciting the number of students who had taken degrees since the College was opened in 1872.

Chancellor PHILLIPS, who represented the Church party, strongly urged the improvement of the means of intermediate education, believing that a greater necessity existed for that class than for elementary or higher education.

Mr. THOMAS BURY, town clerk of Wrexham, clerk to the Trustees of the Grammar School and Wrexham Charities, gave evidence as to the state of the Grammar School and educational endowments in that town. He informed the Committee that there was a general desire on the part of the inhabitants to have a first-class grammar school where classical education, as well as scientific and general attainments, might be imparted. The endowments being only some £30 or £40 per annum, rendered it desirable that there should be some extraneous aid for higher class education in that place. He also gave information as to the application of other charities in the town, which he said were devoted to purposes of elementary education.

Professor ANGUS (University College of Wales) was examined chiefly with reference to the question whether the ignorance of English occasionally displayed by the students was a drawback to the study of Latin. He replied that such was the case. Examined respecting the preparation of students on entering the College, he said that the standard was now superior to what it was when he first became connected with the institution.

Dr. HUMPIDGE, professor of science at the University College of Wales, gave his experience of educational institutions in Germany and Switzerland, and his information was fraught with much interest. He contended that the mechanism of the University College of Wales, and the nature of the teaching thereat, proved it to be entirely different in character from the grammar schools of the Principality, or those in other parts of the kingdom. The chemistry courses at the University College of Wales, he said, were the same as at Bristol College, and Owen's College, Manchester, except that those experiments requiring more expensive apparatus were not shown, and the course of training qualified the students to take the B.A. degree at the University of London.

The Rev. DICKENS LEWIS, Shrewsbury, advocated the desirableness of establishing an Undenominational University for Wales, and he was followed by

Mr. JOHN GIBSON, who thought that private adventure schools should be placed under trust, in order to secure the permanence of the schools and excellence in teaching. He spoke in favour of widening the charter of St. David's College, and the appointment of an examining body in which all denominations would have confidence, and expressed the great need that existed for girls' schools in the Principality.

LAMPETER.

The Committee met at Lampeter on Friday, Dec. 3. The Bishop of St. David's and the Rev. F. J. Jayne (principal of the College), gave evidence, which occupied the attention of the Committee from eleven till four.

The BISHOP explained that prior to the establishment of Lampeter College, certain schools were licensed for the training of young men for the ministry in the Welsh Church, and among those schools was that of Ystrad Meurig, between Aberystwyth and Lampeter. He was not satisfied with the way the school had been conducted, and a scheme had recently been formulated for its better management, and that scheme had his approval. He advised the removal of the school either to Llanbadarn, near Aberystwyth, or to Lampeter. His lordship then explained how that Lampeter College had been founded about fifty years ago by Bishop Burgess, mainly for the purpose of providing ministers for the Church of England. Subsequently the College was granted charters, empowering it to grant B.D. degrees and afterwards B.A. degrees. Though the students at the present time were nearly all intended for the Church of England ministry, there was nothing in the constitution of the College to prevent Nonconformists becoming students. He considered that the present means of intermediate education should be improved, and higher education provided for girls, something similar to that which had been provided at Carmarthen; and he was not adverse to the extension of the Lampeter charter, so as to give degrees to students from other colleges examined by an extraneous Board, if due provision were made for the examination of theological students as at Cambridge. He considered the existence of Lampeter necessary for the welfare of the Church, because it was in a position where students could be drawn from Welsh speaking counties. The difficulty was in getting candidates for holy orders with a thorough Welsh education; and for that reason he deprecated young Welshmen intended for the ministry going to St. Bees.

Principal JAYNE explained that at present there were 80 students on the books of the College, a very considerable proportion of whom were destined for the ministry in the Church of England, though it was not a denominational college so far as its constitution was concerned. He had been connected with Jesus College for eleven years, and was appointed principal of Lampeter College in 1879. He was agreeably surprised at the standard of preparedness shown by students at the entrance examination, which, he thought, was equal to that of the rank and file of Jesus College. The want of preparation had been a common complaint, and he admitted that the preliminary education could be improved. The present deficiency in this respect, he thought, was due to the want of organisation in intermediate schools. There seemed to be no adequate endowment to meet the linguistic difficulties, and the comparative poverty of the class from which students were drawn. The grammar schools of Wales seemed all to have been attempting to do the same kind of work, whereas, he thought, there should be schools of different grades. Speaking of the general question of higher education, he admitted that local universities were feeders to the older universities, and that the power to grant the B.A. degree had been beneficial to Lampeter. He, however, expressed his feeling that the Welsh as a nation were not noted for accuracy; and he thought that accurate knowledge could be better obtained under a tutorial system of instruction than under a professorial system. As a rule, students in Colleges between nineteen and twenty-three years of age, intended for the ministry, and he did not think it would benefit young men of sixteen, intended for the professions, to leave good intermediate schools for colleges where general instruction was given, though he thought it would be beneficial if they could leave for schools established for the teaching of special sciences. He had been told by Oxford examiners that the Lampeter degree was equal to an ordinary Oxford or Cambridge B.A. degree, and he believed it was a fact. If an M.A. degree were established in connection with a Welsh University, he thought it should represent advanced merit, like that of London. Principal Jayne concluded by expressing his belief that the establishment of a school of science would be beneficial to South Wales, and he thought that a knowledge of agricultural chemistry, as well as of general chemistry, would be eminently useful to the theological students of St. David's College.

NOTES.

SIR WILLIAM MAURICE OF CLENENNEY.
(Nov. 17, 1880).

John Lloyd to Sir William Maurice. From the original at Brogyntyn.

Right Wor'—After respect of my humble dutie, yo'u shall vnderstand that I'res came hither, ijo dayes past, by a post w'ch menc'oed that my lord pr'sydent would be heare at ludlowe vpon the xviijth of this moneth : and y't is credibly thought that his l'p will travell w'th S'r ffraunc' Eure (1) throughe all his Circuitt : but whether he will soe doe or not is not certenly knowne till his l'ps coming hither—here attendeth of the Councell, Mr. Justice, S'r henrie Towneshend, S'r ffrauncis Eure, and Mr. Justyce overburye—this terme is a reasonable terme : but I haue knowne many a better ; but for my part I haue for fyve weeks past byn trobled w'th an Ague, w'ch as yet hangeth vpon me and sore vexeth me, to my litle p'ffytt this term tyme. S'r Walter Rawleighe his voyage is quite ou'throwne, to the grete hindrance of many ap'son [a person.]

And y't is Credibly reported, That S'r Thomas Bromley, a Knight borne in the coun' of Salopp sonne & heyre to S'r henry Bromley K'ght decessed, who was lycenzed by his Ma'tie to travell, hath Robbed the Kinge of Spayne his Tresurie howse, and hath taken millions (yee vnknowne riches and tresures from thence) and now he lyeth vpon the Narrow Seas, expectinge his Ma'ties gracious pardon ; And y't is also reported that the Kinge of Spayne sent to his Ma'tie, signifyeinge the pr'miss's [premises], and request'g restituc'on of the goods & riches by him taken, but I doe not heare of any assent of restituc'on yelded vnto. I haue noe newes other then before to adu'tize yo'r wor' of, And therefore I for this tyme leave to troble yo'u any further, but betake my self to ffeede my quakeinge and burninge Ague, that forgetteth not to visit me, and thus with my daily pr'yers to Almighty god for to blesse yo'u and all yo'rs, and to Contynue his grace & favor towards yo'u, and for the contynuance of yo'r health & p'speritie, I comitt yo'r Wor' to the blessed tuic'on of Almightie god, And rest ever

Most redy at yo'r Wor'
Comaundement till
deathe,
ludlow 7o Junii 1618   John lloyd

Addressed :—" To the right Wor' his verie lovinge and muche respected Wor' frend S'r Wm. Maurice, Knight, d'd theis."   A.R.P.

(1) " Sir Francis Eure was, I think, at this time Chief Justice of the North Wales Circuit. He married a grand-daughter of Sir Wm. Maurice and his heiress."—Note by the late W. W. E. WYNNE, Esq., of Peniarth.

PARISH RECORDS OF TOWYN-MERION-ETH.—A correspondent of the *Carnarvon Herald* (who unfortunately is not able to decipher the Court-hand) has recently inspected some old parish records of Towyn, and has given several extracts in the paper. Shorn of his notes and comments, which readers of *Bye-gones* will scarcely care for, the following are amongst the most interesting entries. I may premise I have only the printed "copy" to follow, my extracts not having been compared with the original.

The Vicar of Towyn's share of tyth by.........was not taxed at all to the land tax till a heir of Caethley, upon a vacancy with one Mr. Hughes, Vicar, taxed the tithe corn in Ddauddwffryn at 20th, and the vicar contrived to be taxed at the same rate untill Mr. Ll : Edwaryds' of

Talgarth, Mr. Wm. T. Anwyl o Botalog, and Mr. Oliver Morrice of Penal coming gioned were pleased in 1742 to tax Edd : Morgan, vicar, at 8th more for his share of lambswool for no other alleged reason than that the farmer (who then was Mr. Edwards) used to be taxed in Vaenol at ye rate of 40th for lambswool.

We whose names hereunto subscribed, at a vestry meeting held ye 27th day of Maye, 1729, have agreed if ye above poor [names mentioned] shall [not] wear badges on ye right shoulder, upon their upper garment, visibley, they forfeit their allowances.

1731.　Paid to Griffith Owen for killing four ravens, 00. 02. 00.

Memorandum : I was informed Aug : 27, 1733, that one or other of ye owners of Towyn boat took ye long pole, bought for a crossing pole for ye use of ye Church, and converted it into a hook pole for their last fishing season at Dovey, without leave, and ye pole is missing ever since. Enquire about it next vestry as an uncommon pitch of impudence.

At a vestry held and lawfully called and registered by Mr. Lewis Vaughan, ye first day of November, 1733, we, the persons undernamed, have agreed to advance the tax sixpence in the pound towards the rebuilding of the steeple of ye Church of Towyn ; ye said sixpence in the pound to be paid over and above the yearly tax of ye Church and poor, as witness our hands this day and year above written.

1734.　At a vestry then held, we whose names are hereunto subscribed have agreed to.........that four pounds twelve shillings, money received from Evan Meredithe, ye old warden, should be layd out towards making a new tower to ye Church, and towards other necessary repairs of the Church, as witness our hands.

The four pounds twelve shilling payd by Evan Meredith is lodged at present with me, and I acknowledge the receipt of the sam, and will be accountable w'n called upon. As witness my hand Edd. Morgan.　　　　　G.G.

(To be continued.)

QUERIES.

J. DUNCOMBE, ENGINEER AND "POET."— In the *Salopian Journal* for Oct. 28, 1795, there is a notice of the election of the Rev. J. R. Lloyd of Aston, to the office of Mayor of Oswestry ; "on which occasion a very elegant entertainment was provided at the Cross Keys Inn, and a most numerous and respectable company assembled. A new song, written by Mr. Duncombe, engineer, was received with great eclat." Two verses are given as a specimen :—

> Blest may'st thou Oswestry
> And Corporation be
> 　With every store;
> Benevolent and Great,
> In honours quite replete,
> Thy Praise shall Time relate
> 　Till Time's no more.
>
> Let Friendship quite sincere
> Attend our worthy May'r,
> 　Long may he live,
> Blessed with Plenty's Store,
> Joy, Health, and whate'er more
> Heaven's all-bounteous Pow'r
> 　To him can give!

The same " poet " has previously figured in *Bye-gones*, in a song sung at an Oswestry banquet in Nov. 1799, on the occasion of Mr. Owen Ormsby of Porkington joining the Oswestry Rangers as Major. "J.D., Whittington," for thus he modestly signed his effusion, was, like every body else in those days, a very pronounced Jingo indeed, only it was France then and not Russia that was the bete noir of

5

our countrymen. One verse of the song that heralded the advent of the new major ran as follows :—

> The atheists of France, who their God have forsaken,
> Who live by the ill-gotten spoils they have taken ;
> Who are bound by no law, either sacred or civil,
> On Liberty's tree may they swing to the devil.

In 1801, when Richard Croxon, Esq., was chosen mayor of Oswestry, the poet again came to the front; and sent the following song to his Worship :—

A Song composed for the Feast of Richd. Croxon, Esq., Mayor of Oswestry, Oct. 29, 1801, by his very humble servt.
　　　　　　　　　　　　　　　　　　　J. DUNCOMBE.

Tune, *God Save the King.*

> Fill, fill the friendly Bowl,
> Let naught our Mirth controul,
> 　The Music bring,
> Now strike the Lyre again,
> A loud yet louder strain,
> While we in Chorus join,
> 　God save the King.
>
> Peace from long absence turns,
> Industry's ardour burns,
> 　Wealth to increase:
> Commerce resumes the Main,
> Plenty bedecks our Plain,
> May it with Time remain,
> 　Never to cease.
>
> Britons with Conquest crown'd,
> Your Praise does Fame resound,
> 　From Pole to Pole ;
> Renown'd your Virtues be,
> But while thus nobly Free,
> Licencious Liberty
> 　Do you Controul.
>
> Let us the Laws revere,
> And aid our worthy May'r,—
> 　Long may he live.
> A friend to Church and State,
> May he with Honour great,
> In his exalted seat,
> 　Strict justice give.

From these effusions it would appear that "J. Duncombe, engineer," resided at least six years in the district. Who was he, and what engineering was there to occupy him?
　　　　　　　　　　　　　　　　　　　JARCO.

GAS IN OSWESTRY.—The first public building lighted with gas in Oswestry was the Theatre in Willow street : indeed it was the first experiment made in the town. Progress is thus reported in the *Oswestry Herald* for Oct. 3, 1820 :—" The beautiful effect of this light is exemplified with great advantage at our Theatre, and every additional night's experience renders it more and more complete. The means of purifying the gas have now undergone so much improvement, that *scarcely any perceptible smell exists, while the gas is ignited* ; but invention has hitherto failed in preventing an unpleasant effluvia, whenever the gas is allowed to escape without being instantly lighted. The spirited and successful attempt of an ingenious individual of this town, at the introduction of this light, deserves the encouragement, as well as the praise of the inhabitants ; and every one must reprobate the juvenile trick, which was played off on Friday night, by putting out one of the back lights in the boxes. The stop cocks have been so contrived, that the gas cannot be turned on or off without a key ; and therefore the trick which occasioned the offensive smell of the gas is not likely to happen again. Besides, it might throw an obstacle in the way of the manager of the gas, in the pursuit of a fair and just remuneration for his ingenious and expensive apparatus, which is calculated to extend the use of this beautiful and economical light beyond the precincts of the Theatre."
　　　　　　　　　　　　　　　　　　　OSWALD.

REPLIES.

CASTLE CILRHON (Nov. 10, 1880).—This is a rare and curious word and serves as a key to another curious word. There are several *Rhongils*. A house named Pant-y-Rhongil near Llanidloes—Bwlch yr Hongil near Llansilin, and on the Mawddwy line Aber Rhongil, spelt now Aberangel. The roots Cil and Rhon are reversed as in Gwenfron, Gwelltglas, Bronwen, and Glaswellt. Cil Rhon and Rhongil probably mean Dingle of the Bottom, and Bottom of the Dingle. *Gwlan Rhoniau*, wool of the tails. Or does Rhongmean a river, as the Rhone in Celtic France and Aber Rhonddu in Wales. Will your correspondent say if Cilrhon Castle is at the top or bottom of a dingle, and if in a dingle at all.
Caersws.   J.C.H.

HOPS IN MONTGOMERYSHIRE (Oct. 6, 1880). Anyone travelling in the old Coaching days when the Mail from Welch Pool to Aberystwyth went through Llanfair and Cann Office, might have often seen Hops growing in a large Orchard adjoining the Llanfair-road, belonging to Spring Bank, then occupied by Mr. Thomas Newill, now of Powis Castle Park, during the year 1842 &c. Mr. Newill being a practical farmer, used to try, I believe, various experiments in order to endeavour to introduce fresh material as it were for the benefit of the various farmers on Lord Powis's Estate, and for about four years grew very good Hops, which he used for his own purposes, but gave up the growing because of the nuisance connected with the Excise returns. As it was only experimental, there was only about ¼ of an acre grown. This is believed to be the only attempt in introducing the "Hop" into Montgomeryshire.   SESQUIPEDALIUM.

SHROPSHIRE SCHOOLS (Oct. 20, 1880).— On Thursday the Town Council of Bridgnorth, who are the Governors of the Bridgnorth Grammar School, elected the Rev. R. Lucas, M.A. LL.D. (London University), headmaster of Moulton Grammar School, Spalding, to succeed Mr. F. Ellaby, M.A., who has taken a high preparatory school at Bath.
The Rev. Dr. Bateson, master of St. John's College, Cambridge, and one of the Governing Body of Shrewsbury Grammar School, has been appointed a member of the Cambridge University Commission, to supply the vacancy caused by the death of Lord Chief Justice Cockburn.

CURRENT NOTES.

FREEMASONRY IN OSWESTRY.

The Lodge of St. Oswald, whose annual festival was celebrated on Monday evening, was the first lodge ever established in Oswestry. There were previous to its consecration several Masons in the town, and during the month of September, 1866, a few of these met for the purpose of memorializing the Grand Master for a Warrant, under which they could form a lodge at home, and so not have to visit distant towns when they wished to enjoy the sociality and good fellowship of Brethren. On Oct. 1, 1866, the new lodge met for the first time, when there were present—Brothers W. H. Hill, George Owen, B. H. Bulkeley Owen, Askew Roberts, J. Hamer, W. H. Spaull, Henry Davies, and E. Elias; J. Duncan, Tyler. At the same lodge Mr. J. R. Ormsby Gore, M.P., was proposed as a candidate for initiation, and at a future meeting he was duly initiated, and in due course passed the chairs, and became W.M. On Monday evening Mr. Stanley Leighton, the successor of the late lamented member for the county, was installed in the seat he once

held in Masonry. He, too, is an initiate of the St. Oswald Lodge, and has filled all the offices necessary for promotion ; and that his election to the post of Worshipful Master by the Brethren was popular is amply evinced by the very numerous attendance at the Installation.

EDUCATION IN WALES.

The following statistics were submitted to the Departmental Committee at their sitting at Welshpool plast week, by Mr. Richard Williams of Newtown :—

MONTGOMERYSHIRE.
Endowments belonging to Colleges and Schools out of the County.

Parish.	College or School endowed.	Name or Situation of Property.	Extent.	Gross estimated Rental.
			a. r. p.	£ s. d.
Berriew....	Shrewsbury School ..	Llandinier	332 3 38	260 0 0
		Do., Woods	—	10 16 0
Kerry	BitterleySc. (Ludlow)	Little Perthybeel	40 2 3	40 0 0
Buttington	Christ Ch., Oxford ..	Rectorial Tithes..	—	276 10 0
Guilsfield ..	Do.	Do.	—	1129 10 0
Meifod	Do.	Do.	—	488 2 6
		Glebe Land	4 3 37	
Welshpool..	Do.	Rectorial Tithes..	—	476 0 0
Llandinam..	University Col. Oxford	Park	333 2 22	114 0 0
		Do., Woods	—	0 10 0
		Garthfawr	357 2 11	123 0 0
		Do.. Woods	—	0 12 0
		Garthfach......	182 1 1	55 0 0
		Do., Woods	—	0 9 0
		Brynhafod	241 3 30	65 0 0
		Lodge .... }	184 0 24	55 0 0
		Cold Harbour .. }		
		Troedrhiwfelen.		
		Glanyrafon	112 0 8	30 0 6
		Do., Woods	—	2 2 0
		Total	1411 2 16	445 13 0
Llanidloes..	Do.	Ffridd	225 0 16	20 0 0
Llanwnog ..	Do.	Park .... }		
		Do., Woods }	625 0 4	515 2 4
		Colwyn .... }		
		Belan .... }		
		Ffridd	80 1 28	60 0 0
		Llechwedd-dyrees	50 3 26	
		Do., Woods	—	55 5 0
		Bron-nant	26 1 18	
		Moor Cottages ..	—	10 0 0
		Total	782 2 36	640 7 4
Penstrowed	Do.	Ffridd	99 1 33	35 4 0
		Do.. Woods	—	18 6 0
		College	12 3 37	8 0 0
		New House	0 0 20	3 0 0
		Total	112 2 10	64 10 0
Trefeglwys.	Do.	Borfanewydd	62 2 29	20 0 0
		Esgarnain	73 0 29	20 0 0
		Fairdrefawr......	144 1 12	42 12 0
		Penrhyn	60 0 7	20 0 0
		Part of Tithes of }		
		Esceirieth and }	—	37 0 0
		D o l g w d e n }		
		Townships .... }		
		Total	340 0 37	130 12 0
Forden	Chirbury Sc.	Hem	—	20 0 0

SUMMARY.

		£ s. d.	£ s. d.
Shrewsbury School	Berriew	270 16 0	270 16 0
Bitterley School	Kerry	40 0 0	40 0 0
Christ Church, Oxford ..	Buttington	276 10 0	
	Guilsfield	1129 10 0	
	Meifod	488 2 6	
	Welshpool......	476 0 0	2370 2 6
University College, Oxford	Llandinam	445 13 0	
	Llanidloes......	20 0 0	
	Llanwnog	640 7 4	
	Penstrowed	64 10 0	
	Trefeglwys	139 12 0	1310 2 4
Chirbury School	Forden	20 0 0	20 0 0
		Total	4011 0 10

MONTGOMERYSHIRE.
Nonconformist Chapels and Ministers.

	Chapels.	Ministers not including Local Preachers.
Calvinistic Methodists	94	34
Congregationalists	72	25
Wesleyan Methodists	59	16
Baptists	23	8
Primitive Methodists	5	2
Total	253	85

Estimated original cost of Chapels	£125,000 0 0	
Do. expenditure during last 20 years in enlargement and rebuilding	£50,000 0 0	
	£175,000 0 0	
Estimated annual cost of Ministry	£10,000 0 0	

In an interesting pamphlet upon the subject of Higher Education in Wales, the Rev. D. J. Davies, Fellow of Emmanuel College, Cambridge, has set forth some remarkable facts concerning the ability of Welsh children. Taking the statistics given in the two last reports of the Committee of Council on Education, he finds that the chief sources of income of Board Schools are the rates and the Government grant which varies with the proficiency of the children. Now the average English child earned, in 1875, 15·4 per cent. of the total maintenance at school, while the average Welsh child earned 22·6 per cent. of the cost of its maintenance. In the following year the percentages were 16·0 for England, and 24·4 for Wales; in 1877, 18·3 for England, and 29·0 for Wales; in 1878, 19·6 for England, and 31·1 for Wales. Or, as Mr. Davies forcibly puts it, " an English ratepayer who pays £5 towards his school would have to pay only £4 17s. 6d. if all his geese were swans—if all his children were Welsh children."

DECEMBER 8, 1880.

NOTES.

MARRIAGE ANNOUNCEMENTS LAST CENTURY.—A modern newspaper editor would wonder if asked thus to announce marriages :—" Sep. 2, 1735. Married, Morgan Williams, Esq., of Denbighshire, to the sole daughter of John Craddock, Esq., of Chester: a fortune of £8,000." "April 8, 1736. Tho. Whitmore, Esq., M.P. for Bridgnorth, to Miss Cope, of Oxfordshire, worth £20,000." "May 27, 1738. Sir Bryan Broughton, Bt., to Miss Forester, daughter of William Forester, mem-

ber for Great Wenlock, Salop, with upwards of £10,000." "Oct. 10, 1741. Edward Lloyd, near Oswestry, Esq., to Miss Devenport of Cloveley, in Cheshire ; a fortune of £8,000." "Ap. 20, 1755. Frederick Herbert of Shrewsbury to Miss Owens of Ludlow, with a fortune of £700 per annum." NEMO.

MEETING HOUSES.—Time was when our sturdy Nonconformist fathers rejoiced in calling their places of worship "Meeting Houses," and this term they often abbreviated ; as, for instance,—" On Sunday next (June 30, 1805), in the afternoon, a sermon will be preached at Swan Hill Meeting, Shrewsbury, for the benefit of the Sunday School at that place, by the Rev. Thomas Grove of Walsall." The buildings were plain and substantial, without pretence ; and if often ugly, at least did not cause men of cultivated taste to sneer at the attempts to ape and mar a style of architecture unfitted for the simplicity of Nonconformist worship. NONCON.

A KERRY DIARY, 1771.—The following extracts from a Diary kept by some person in the Parish of Kerry, Montgomeryshire, for the year 1771, may be worth printing in Bye-gones, as showing the price of corn, wool, &c., and other information at that period :—
1771.
Jan 5 John Jones of ye New Inn had 2 lb of Butter, at 7d. pr lb. unpaid.
Jann 6 Paid for one lb of sugar. 6d
Jan 14 Sold 1 Strike of Corn for 6.6
  „ „ ,, 5 Bushels of Oats at 7/- 1.15.0
  „ 17 Sold 1 Strike of Wheat for 7.6
[" Corn " doubtless was a mixture of Rye and Wheat : it was grown at a much later date than 1771 in Kerry parish.]
Jan 21 Father went to Pool for Solt
  24 Sarah Jennings had 1 lb of wool. 5.6
  29 Sarah Jennings had a little Hop of corn 1 - 10½
[" Hop " is a measure unknown in the district now. it seems to be the fourth of a strike, judging by the money it came to. Has the measure any connection with the Welsh " Hobbet "?]
Feb 20 (Thursday) I was at Carecose Market.
[When was Caersws Market discontinued ?]
March 11 Phillip Swaincot had for wife 1 lb of wool 6/-
  19 I was at Nancy Stoake's Burrying
  29 Mrs. Barrington had by the hand of James Gildon a Couple of fowls.
April 20 Patty went to Montg : with the Bacon and did put her measure for a Stays.
April 27 Paid Graty pr. wife 10/ for mending ye Church Windowe at same time rec : in full 4.8
[This 4/8 was for barley supplied on January 16th preceding.]
May 1 Mr. Edward Pryce had 17 lbs of Cheese at 3¼ pr lb, at 4. 7¼ at ye same time he had a bushel of oats in all 12. 7¼
May 7 I was at Montg : fair
  8 I tooke a voment.
[A frank, but rather suggestive entry.]
May 13 (Wednesday) there was a sheep roasted upon Kerry Street.
  14 Mr. Edward Pryce had 1 Strike of Muncorn—7/-
  16 I was at the Little Mill.
  27 Phillip Swanket had 1 lb. of Wool 6/- due 8.10. I was at the Sale at Newtowne. We had of Mr. Williams 1 lb. of soap.
  28 Mrs. Jones of the Little Mill and her sister was hear drinking tea.
  30 Mr. Edward Pryce had 1 strike of Muncorn. Mr. J. Matthews & Edward Phillips was at dinner.

June 11 Sent for a blistering plaster; paid 6d. for it.
    24 I went to the Row from ye fair.
       [Meaning the Gro, near Newtown.]
July 10 I went to Town about some beef, and I went to
      the Row and staid there all day.
    20 I was at Vincent Owen's Burrying.
Aug. 2 (Sunday) Patty & me was at the Red House
      drinking tea.
     9 (Sunday) Mr. Gwdden and his wife was drinking
      tea at Dolforgan.
  [Query, did the writer of the Diary reside at Dolforgan?]
    16 Bety and me was at Llandiesil. Mother was at
      the Red House.
    23 Patty and me was at Mr. J. Stoakes drinking
      tea.
    27 I was at Gwernygo.
    31 (Monday) we did reap the wheat.
  [The entries all through September have been cut out.]
Oct. 1 Miss Molly Stephens was hear for tea and Mr.
      Lewis came for her home.
  [From this to end of year the entries have been cut out.]
  The following list of Country Dances are given as the
Dances for the year 1772 :—" The Rattle," "The Round-
about," " Aldridge's Rant," "The London Assembly,"
"Brighthelmstone," " Hot Bath," "Charles Street Walk,"
"Windsor Terrace," "Knights of the Garter," " La
Tonva," "Portsmouth Harbour," "The Installation,"
"The Bells of Osley," "The Favorite," "The Whim,"
"Paddy Wack," "The Hamburgh Dance," "Vicar and
Moses," "The Maid of Bath," "Lord Clive" [The
figures of this dance were, Hands all four across and
foot it, hands all four across back again and foot it;
cross over two couple, and half figure; right hands and
left.] "The Slipper," "The Teapot," "Hob and his
Nob," "The Brill," "The Petticoat White." This was
by no means a scant list to select from, and the figures
of each are given.   BOOKWORM.

QUERIES.

CLUN FOREST.—Some years ago I think Mr.
Salt of Shrewsbury printed for private circulation a pamphlet containing an account of Clun Forest. Can a copy
of this be obtained? If not, could it not be reprinted in
this column? It was, so far as I remember, a very interesting sketch.   Q.

MACHYNLLETH—FAZAKERLY.—At the be-
ginning of the eighteenth century there resided in Machynlleth a tradesman named Owen Fazakerly. His children, it is said, abandoned the name Fazakerly as strange
to Welsh ears, and, in accordance with Welsh custom at
that period, took their father's Christian name Owen as
their surname. Can any one inform me as to the correctness of this tradition? Is the name Fazakerly still known
in Machynlleth? Are any analagous cases of abandonment of English surnames for Welsh known in Wales in
comparatively recent times?   LLWYD.

LLOYD'S HISTORY OF SHROPSHIRE.—
Allow me to call attention to the following paragraph in
a MS. account of Halston, written in 1821, by the late
Rev. C. A. A. Lloyd, rector of Whittington :—
  Mr. W. Mytton [grandfather of the sporting John Mytton]
was engaged for many years in collecting materials for a History
of the County [of Salop] but unfortunately died before he ar-
ranged them. Among the collection is a manuscript copy of the
History of the County by Mr. E. Lloyd of Trenewydd, which
Mr. Pennant, by some blunder, mistook for Mr. Mytton's.
Where is the MS. alluded to by the Rev. Charles Lloyd
now, and what has become of his own MS. account of
Halston?   SALOPIAN.

ROBERT KNIGHT, EARL OF CATHER-
LOUGH.—If any correspondent to Bye-gones is in possession of a peerage (1750 to 1770) and would give a short
sketch of the above gentleman's pedigree, he would confer
a favour, particularly if he could indicate how the Gwern-
y-goe and other estates in Montgomeryshire devolved
upon the above Earl of Catherlough?   MEHELI.

CEUBREN YR ELLYLL.—We are told in the
Cambro-Briton, vol. 1, p. 227 (published in 1820) that
about seven or eight years earlier a violent storm blew
down the Nannau Oak, near Dolgelley, and that "the
worthy baronet, in whose domains it was situated, caused
its wood to be manufactured into a variety of utensils,
the same to be distributed among his friends." We are
further told that " a short time before it was blown down
an eminent amateur artist made a sketch of it, from which
engravings have since been taken, and there is scarcely a
house in Dolgelley, but what contains one at least of these
engravings, framed in the very wood (which is of a
beautifully dark colour approaching to ebony) of the
Ceubren yr Ellyll." Sir Richard Colt Hoare, writing in
Aug. 1820, states that the tree was not destroyed by a
storm. He says that during a visit to Sir Robert Vaughan
in the summer of 1813, the tree attracted his notice, and he
made a sketch of it on the 13th July. The day was intensely hot, and during the night succeeding the tree fell
down. Sir Richard's drawing was etched by Mr. George
Cuitt of Chester, and published by Mr. Colnaghi of London. He had the original framed in the wood of the tree.
Has this old picture ever been copied into any modern
book or serial? And is it still to be commonly met with
at Dolgelley?   TAFFY.

REPLIES.

DICK OF ABERDARON (July 21, 1880).—
Mention was made at this date of Mrs. Dawson Turner's
etching of Jones which is prefixed to Roscoe's life of the
linguist. Mr. JOSEPH MEYER, F.S.A., writes to the
Cheshire Sheaf of another likeness—a full length one—
engraved by Burt of Chester. There are two full-length
portraits in a sixpenny pamphlet life published by
Humphreys of Carnarvon. Is it one of these Mr. Meyer
refers to? The frontispiece to Roscoe's life is a half-length
as described in the Bye-gones extract June 23. N.W.S.

SHROPSHIRE WORDS (Nov. 24, 1880).—A correspondent of the Carnarvon Herald has copied several
entries from the parish records of Towyn, and one of his
transcripts is as follows :—"1678, fines levied for byrying
in flannen 2li 10s." The transcriber adds a query as to
whether the word should not have been flannel; oblivious,
I presume, of the fact, that burials in woollen were at
one time common, and that " flannen" is a word in use in
some parts even to the present day. On the borders I
don't wonder to find it, because we have several words in
use adapted from the Welsh; and such the word in question is—gwlanen being the word corrupted—but I am
rather surprised that two centuries ago such a word should
have been in use in a town in the heart of Wales.
                                          OLD OSWESTRY.

WHITSHED KEENE (Nov. 17, 1880).—From Parliamentary Return, just published, " Members of Parliament, p. 2," it appears that " Whitshed Keene " was first
elected for the Montgomery Boroughs, which then consisted only of Montgomery, Llanidloes, Llanfyllin, and
Pool, October 10th, 1774, re-elected after accepting Chiltern
Hundreds July 4th, 1777, re-elected Jany. 1, 1779, on
appointment as Surveyor General of Works. Again at
general election 13th September, 1780, and re-elected 16th

April, 1783, after appointment as one of the Lords Commissioners of Admiralty. Re-elected general elections 5th April, 1784, June 19th, 1790, June 2nd, 1796, July 6th, 1802, October 31st, 1806, May 6th, 1807, October 7th, 1812, and was succeeded by Henry Clive June 17th, 1818, who represented the boroughs until December 10th, 1832, when he also was succeeded by the late David Pugh of Llanerchydol, whose election was declared void, and the seat occupied by Sir John Edwards on April 8th, 1833.

D. P. OWEN.

CURRENT NOTES.

The *Antiquary* has just completed its second volume. In its programme of the future a paper is promised by Capt. P. H. Salusbury on the Welsh and Border Counties Collection in his father's Library at Glan Aber, Chester.

THE BISHOP OF ST. ASAPH AT THE POWYS-LAND CLUB.
(Nov. 3, 1880.)

From the familiar initials appended to the second letter I trust I am justified in presuming it to emanate from the Rev. D. R. Thomas, vicar of Meifod, author of the History of the Diocese of S. Asaph, &c., and recently elected proctor of Convocation for the Diocese of St. Asaph. I am almost at a loss for an answer when he says I have "tilted in violent fashion, and in language which it is a pity I should have been tempted to use" in suggesting that perhaps the Bishop's statements were attributable rather to ignorance and prejudice than deliberate slander and malevolence. I certainly preferred to attribute them to his either not knowing the full import of what he said, or not having deliberately weighed it before he uttered it. For one Christian Bishop, as Dr. Hughes professes to be, to attribute to another Christian Bishop, no matter when he lived, the deliberate formation and execution of a design to set on a number of Saxon savages, whom he had come to England to convert, to murder a number of Christians because they would not join him in preaching the Christian Faith to those savages, would, I still think, have been deserving of whatever strong language I may have bestowed upon it, and the more so, when, as he admitted, it was opposed to the concurrent testimony of historians. The gravity of the charge is greatly enhanced when the dignity of St. Augustine's character and position are considered, as the first apostolic preacher of Christianity to the English, and the first Archbishop of Canterbury, venerated by his contemporaries not only for the holiness of his life, but also for his miraculous powers. The charge extends itself also from the person of St. Augustine to all Catholics from his day to ours, who venerate him as a canonized Saint who is reigning with Christ in heaven. In the feelings inherent in us from this fact, neither the Bishop nor Mr. Thomas will naturally participate as Protestants, but inasmuch as such a charge conveys by implication one against the Church which, by the hypothesis, canonizes persons guilty of such crimes, those who make them should be careful to do so only on solid grounds, and to choose, moreover, an appropriate time and place for the purpose. Amusing as it may be to Mr. Thomas, while I am free to admit, and have never controverted that the conduct of the Prince of Powys was a fair topic for remark in a Historical Society, he has neither proved, nor attempted to prove that the Bishop was justified in airing his Protestant opinions on religion at the expense of Catholics at an annual meeting of the Powys-land Club.

Mr. Thomas proceeds to ask whether I "do not know that, however Geoffry may have romanced about some things, he had an earlier 'Brut' or Chronicle for his historical matter; and this original chronicle we have still under the name of 'Brut Tyssilio.'" I know that Geoffry states that his history was founded on a chronicle brought out of Brittany by or to Walter de Mapes. But I do *not* know that this chronicle was the "Brut Tysilio." On the contrary, I have very certain evidence to the contrary; a statement, namely, to that effect at the end of the Brut Tysilio itself—"I, Walter, Archdeacon of Oxford, turned this book from Welsh into Latin, and in my old age I turned it again from Latin into Welsh," a statement repeated, with some additions, at the end of the other version of Geoffry's History, called that of G. ap Arthur. There is abundant internal evidence in both of these that, whatever foundation of history they may have possessed in an earlier chronicle, every fact propounded in them as historical is not to be accepted for history. On the contrary, I know not what historian, critic, or archæologist would venture to put them forward as reliable without corroborative testimony from elsewhere. As far as the narrative in question is concerned, my perusal of it in these two versions of Geoffry has led me to the inference that they consist merely of the narrative of Bede, enlarged, altered, and embellished, with variations, according to the object or the fancy of the writer; and I believe that no competent person who studied them otherwise than superficially could come to a different conclusion. In 1875-6 I addressed some letters to the *Oswestry Advertizer*, in reply to Mr. Morgan Owen, in *Mont. Coll.*, in which I endeavoured to show that it was chronologically impossible that S. Augustine could have suggested the massacre; nor am I aware that the reasons then adduced by me have ever been seriously answered. As to Ven. Bede, he is still the only authority on the subject, admitted by all, I believe, Mr. Thomas excepted, to be genuine and honest; and if his authority is accepted for some parts of his narrative, there is no reason that has yet been shown why it should not be equally admissible for the others.(a)

H. W. LLOYD, M.A.

Feast of St. Francis Xavier,
　Apostle of the Indies, 1880.

CARNARVONSHIRE ELECTION.

The poll for the election of a member of Parliament for Carnarvonshire, in the room of Mr. Justice Watkin Williams, took place on Tuesday, Nov. 30. The counting took place the following morning, and the result was declared soon after noon, as follows :—

Rathbone (Liberal)	3,180
Ellis Nanney (Conservative)	2,151
Liberal Majority	1,029

The numbers in April last were—

Williams (L)	3,303
Pennant (C)	2,206
Majority	1,097

Mr. William Rathbone of Green-bank, Liverpool, is the eldest son of the late Mr. William Rathbone of Green-bank, by his marriage with Elizabeth, daughter of the late Mr. Samuel Greg of Quorn-bank, Cheshire. He was born in the year 1819, and is well known as one of the leading

(a) This "Brut" alone contains the forged statement of the British Bishops relative to their subjection to the Archbishop of Caerlleon, now proved to be an anachronism. For other falsifications of fact see "Where did St. Oswald die?" p. 38. (Woodall and Venables.) The very title of the Brut is manifestly a forgery. The other versions of the Brut are silent as to Brochwel's part in the battle under Cadvan.

merchants at Liverpool. He is a magistrate and deputy-lieutenant for Lancashire, and sat as one of the members for Liverpool from 1868 down to the last general election, when he retired. Mr. Rathbone has been twice married; firstly, in 1847, to Lucretia, daughter of Mr. S. S. Gair; and, secondly, in 1862, to Emily Acheson, daughter of the late Mr. Acheson Lyle of the Oaks, county Londonderry. Mr. Rathbone is the 29th new member returned to St. Stephen's since the general election.

DECEMBER 15, 1880.

NOTES.

TOWYN-MERIONETH PARISH RECORDS

(Dec. 1, 1880).—Your readers must take my transcripts with all their faults. I have no doubt the newspaper I copy has not been painfully particular to secure accuracy: and the copyist has in most cases omitted names of persons signing the parish books.

1 June 1740. At the same vestry ye Churchwardens were ordered to return the names of all the parties in arrears to the Court of Bangor, and there be prosecuted according to law, as witness our hands.

Memorandum: That Mr. Henry Edwards of Talgarth; Mr. Anwyl of Botalog; and Mr. Oliver Morrice, being acting commissioners of the land tax, were pleased to tax the vicar in 174?, after ye rate of 8th for wool in Vaenol, because the tyth farmer was rated allways at 40th for ye same in ye said township. He desired Mr. Corbet Owen to act that he might appeal, but he refusing, he had nothing to doe but to acquiess till some more favourable opportunity—in whose time that may happen God only knows.

1737. Memorandum: that I yearly pay on ye 7th day of January fifteen shill: 00 15 00 to the poor of Towyn parish, viz:—five shillings for my father's legacy, five shillings for my mother's legacy, and five shillings for Mrs. An: Lewis, added to the late vicar of Towyn's legacy, which legacys I shall leave paiable on my son and heir Corbet Owen, and his heirs, except they can be better laid out for the use of the poor. Witness my hand, An: Owen.

Memorandum: the sum of five pounds is now at interest with W. Rowlands of Crychnant, February 24th 1775. Jer: Griffith, vicar.

Memorandum: that I yearly pay to from the date hereof, January 5th 1740, five shillings on Good Friday, to the poor of Towyn parish, being interest of five pounds given to the said parish by Mrs. Elizabeth Hall of Bridgenorth, which interest I shall leave payable on my executor, except I find a place in my lifetime to lay out all the poor's money in the hands of me An: Owen.

[My authority says that these legacies of the Corbet family, according to the report of the Commissioners issued some years back, had not been paid since 1782, in which year Mr. Henry Arthur Corbet died insolvent].

Memorandum: that the overseers of the poor received from me £13, being Gwen Owen's legacy to the poor of this parish, November 12th 1768. Witness my hand Jer: Griffith, vicar.

[No mention of this legacy, we are informed, is made in the Charity Commissioners' report previously alluded to.]
G.G.

(To be continued.)

PEDIGREES OF BORDER FAMILIES.—The

writer has in his hands a very interesting manuscript, written between 1650 and 1680 by William Maurice of Cefn Braich, Tregeiriog, in the parish of Llansilin. The Rev. Robt. Williams, M.A., late of Rhydycroesau, states he was a gentleman of landed property and good family,

was a learned antiquary, and an industrious collector and transcriber of Welsh manuscripts. Adjoining his house he built a library three storeys high, in which he spent most of his time. The book before me contains a great number of poems or Cowyddau, by Gutto'r Glyn and about twenty other poets of the 15th and 16th centuries, also pedigrees of the following families :—

Edward Owen of Crogen Ithon, near Chirk.
The Middletons of Chirk Castle from Lord Penllyn down to Sir Thomas (altered by pen into Richard in MS.) Middleton, Baronet, 1672.
The Eytons of Coed y Llai (Leeswood) Flintshire.
The Vaughans of Glan-y-Llyn and Llwydiarth (1673 and previous).
The John Edwardses of Chirk.
The Wynns of Plas Uchaf, Llangedwyn.
The Wynns of Maes Mochnant in the parish of Llanrhaiadr.
The Morrises of Lloran Uchaf a'r Plas yn Glan Tanat.
The Lloyds of Llwyn-y-Maen (seat of C. H. Wynn, Esq.)
The Rhyses and Thomas Tanads of Abertanad.
The Rogerses and Kynastons of Hordley.
The Richardses and Morrises of Bryn y Gwaliau, Llangedwyn.
The Lloyds and Morrises of Lloran Isaf yn mhlwyf Llansilin.
The Salisburys of Lewenny, Denbighshire.
Ditto of Rhug, near Corwen.
The Hugheses of Pen y Bryn, Llanarmon Dyffryn Ceiriog.
The Hughes of Gwernlâs.
The ? (? Owens) of Clenaney.
The Roger Evanses of Dryll y Pobydd and Croesoswallt. (Is this Drill?)
The Lloyds, Tudors, and Llewelyns and Thelwalls of Iâl.
The Thomases, Edwardses, and Lloyds of Lledrod, Llansilin.
The Hamners of Pentre-pant, Llanarmon. (This family still holds the estate.)
The Foulkes of Rhiwlas, near Oswestry.
The Mostyns, Goodmans, Wynns, and Salisburys, of Pengwern.
The Lloyds of Estyn yn swydd y Drewen (id est. Hope, in the county of Whittington or Whitchurch?)
The Kyffins, Lloyds, and Vaughans and Eytons of Bodfach and Llanerch-yr-aur.
The Lloyds of Llanvorda.
The Morrises, Merediths, and Vaughans of Pen-y-Bont.
The Morrises and Hollands of Cefn Braich. (W. Maurice's own Family.)
The Lloyds of Lanhawon Mochnant uwch Rhaiadr.
The Middletons, Lloyds, and Foulkes of Plasnewydd and Bodlith, Llansilin.
The Sion ap Arthur ap Edward ap Morris of Rhiwlas.
The Lloyds, Kyffins, Meredydds, Holts, Blodwells, Tudors, and Hugheses of Sarphle.
The Hugheses and Erddigs of Adwy'r clawdd and Wrexham.
The Powells and Holts of Parc y Drewen (id est, Whittington Park?)
The Thomases, Edwardses, and Hughes of Pant-Glas-uchaf, Llangadwaladr.
The Trevors and Wynns of Trevor yn mhlwyf Llangollen.
The Lloyds and Trevors and Wards (Oswestry) of Carrog in Edeyrnion.
The Morrises, Trevors, and Rogerses of Pentre Cynwrig (sic) Oswestry.
The Lloyds of Ednal or Sarn yn Swydd y Drewen.
JESSIE H.

PARLIAMENT OF ENGLAND (June 23, 1880)

Our last instalment of Shropshire members appeared on June 23, 1880. Since that time the Blue Book containing lists from 1702 has been issued, so we shall be able, from week to week, to complete our records of Shropshire and the Welsh counties.

COUNTY OF SALOP.
1705 Sir Robert Corbett, bart.; Robert Lloyd, esq.
1708 Henry Newport, esq.; Sir Robert Corbet, bart., of Adderley.
1710 John Kynaston, esq.; Robert Lloyd, esq.
1713 Henry Newport, esq., commonly called Viscount Newport; John Kynaston, esq.
1714 Henry Lord Newport; Sir Robert Corbet, bart.

1722	John Kynaston, esq., of Hardwick ; Robert Lloyd, esq., of Aston.
1727	John Walcott, esq., of Walcott ; William Lacon Childe, esq., of Kynlett.
1734	Sir John Astley, bart.; Corbet Kynaston, esq.
1741	Ditto ; Richard Lyster, esq.
1747	Ditto ; Ditto.
1754	Ditto ; Ditto.
1761	Ditto ; Ditto.
1768	Ditto ; (1) Charles Baldwyn, esq.
1774	Charles Baldwyn, esq.; Noel Hill, esq.
1780	Noel Hill, esq.; Richard Hill, esq., of Hawkestone.
1784	Sir Richard Hill, bart.; John Kynaston, esq.
1790	Ditto ; Ditto.

(1) Sir Watkin Williams Wynn of Llanvorda, co. Salop, elected *vice* Sir John Astley, deceased, 5 Mar. 1772.

BOROUGH OF SHREWSBURY.

1705	John Kynaston, esq., of Hordley ; Richard Mytton, esq., of Hallston.
1708	Sir Edward Leighton, bart. ; (1) Thomas Jones, esq. (2)
1710	Edward Cressett, esq., of Cund ; Richard Mytton, esq.
1713	Corbet Kynaston, esq. ; (3) Edward Cressett, esq.
1714	Ditto. ; Thomas Jones, esq.
1722	Orlando Bridgman, esq. ; Sir Richard Corbett, bart. (4)
1727	Richard Lyster, esq. ; Sir John Astley, bart.
1734	Sir Richard Corbett, bart. ; William Kinaston, esq.
1741	Ditto. Ditto.
1747	Ditto. Ditto.
1754	Thomas Hill, esq., of Tern ; Robert More, esq.
1761	Ditto ; Robert Clive, esq., of Berkeley Square.
1768	Noel Hill, esq., of Tern ; Robert Lord Clive.
1774	Robert Lord Clive, Baron Clive of Plassey in the kingdom of Ireland ; (5) William Pulteney, esq. (6)
1780	Sir Charlton Leighton, bart. ; Ditto.
1784	Ditto. (7) Ditto.
1790	William Pulteney, esq. ; John Hill, esq.

(1) Return amended of the House dated 20 Dec. 1709, by erasing the names of John Kynaston, esq., and Richard Mytton, esq., and substituting that of Sir Edward Leighton, bart.
(2) Vice John Kynaston, esq., and Richard Mytton, esq., whose election was declared void.
(3) Return amended by Order of the House, dated 27 May, 1714, by erasing the name of Thomas Jones, esq., and substituting that of Corbet Kynaston, esq.
(4) Return amended by Order of the House, dated 9 Apr. 1723, by erasing the names of Corbett Kynaston, esq., and Richard Lyster, esq., and substituting Bridgman and Corbett.
(5) John Corbet, esq., of Sundorne, elected *vice* Robert Lord Clive, deceased, 17 Mar. 1775.
(6) Return amended by Order of the House, dated 16 Mar. 1775, by erasing the name of Charlton Leighton, esq., and substituting Pulteney.
(7) John Hill, esq., elected *vice* Leighton, deceased, 29 Oct. 1784.

QUERIES.

BRYNBEDWIN—This is the name of two farms between Newtown and Dolfor—one called "Little" Brynbedwin. Near the road side, just beyond Brynbedwin proper, are two very ancient looking *Yew* Trees. What is the English equivalent of the word Brynbedwin ? Is there any local tradition connected with the place ? In a very secluded spot, about three quarters of a mile south west of and in a line almost between *Brynbedwin* and *Cincoed* is a very fine Mound marked on the ordnance survey, "Tump." Is there any local name to this, or is any tradition current about it ? DOLFOR.

ROBBER'S CAVE AT THE DEVIL'S BRIDGE. A writer in *Blackwood's Magazine* in 1839, speaks of a Robber's Cave above one of the falls at the Devil's Bridge. He says it is " a cavern of no great depth, and where, it is said, a robber once lived, with, we believe, two companions, a sister and another female. The habitation must have been very small for three persons, but certainly very safe from surprise. It is said that, one having betrayed the watchword, the robber was taken ; he had committed a murder." Is more known, locally, of this tradition, or has any topographer mentioned it ? G. G.

HISTORICAL NOTICE OF WHITTINGTON.— In Aug. 1855 Shrewsbury was made the head-quarters for a week of the Archæological Institute, and one of the days' excursions included a visit to Whittington. In looking over a file of the *Oswestry Advertizer* the other day to find something else, I came across the report of this meeting, in the course of which I find the following paragraph :—" A curious book was shewn, containing in manuscript a history of the parish and castle of Whittingtou, with miniature portraits of some half-dozen incumbents of the church." Where is this MS. Volume now ? It is only a quarter of a century since it was exhibited. The possessor of it would confer a boon on the county if he would permit its publication by the Shropshire Archæological Society. JARCO.

REPLIES.

SHROPSHIRE WORDS (Nov. 24, 1880).—I have more than once heard an expression since I came to live at Oswestry that strikes a stranger as singular. "He called him all to pieces" said a poor woman to me the other day, complaining how a neighbour had by tongue abused her husband. Is this a Shropshireism ? Another familiar expression in the Oswestry district is, "Don't drown the miller ;" used when too much water is put in the tea pot. Is this local ? SOJOURNER.

OLD FOLKS (July 16, 1880).—I have copied from a MS. collection of epitaphs, made in 1833, the following, which was on a brass plate on a pew door in *Mold* Church :—" Underneath lyeth the body of Thomas Wynne, of Llwynegryn, son of John Wynne, late of Argoed, Esq., and grandson to Peter Wynne, late of Tyddyn, Esq, who dyed Dec. 13, 1753, aged 106." J.B.

CURRENT NOTES.

HIGHER EDUCATION IN WALES.—THE DEPARTMENTAL COMMITTEE.
(Dec. 1, 1880.)

The Committee took evidence at Carmarthen on Monday and Tuesday, December 6 and 7, Lord Aberdare presiding. —The Rev. Alfred Edwards, Warden of Llandovery College, disapproved of the boarding-out system. It was cheaper, and sometimes the boys accomplished more work in private houses than in a large boarding-house, but they lost, through lack of supervision and the advantage of contact with their fellows. He had found boarders-out wanting in platform sharpness and public spirit. Welshspeaking boys had great difficulty in classics ; they were heavily handicapped in this respect, and he would therefore like twelve close scholarships in Jesus College to be reserved exclusively for Welshmen. Boys whose home language was Welsh were astonishingly little acquainted with English literature ; the works of the great English authors were sealed books to them. There was, further, among Welsh people a tendency to discourage novelreading, this probably being a portion of the old heritage of Puritan gloom. A deputation from Llanelly stated the need there of intermediate general and technical schools ; a University for Wales was urged, and Swansea stated as a more central place for it than Cardiff.—Mr. J. Bancroft, her Majesty's inspector of schools, Tenby, said the grammar schools of Wales were insufficient, principally because they were not sufficiently endowed to pay good and capable masters. Private-adventure schools were numerous, and they were the bane of the country. There should be a high-grade school in every county, with one or more small second-grade schools to feed the former ; the money now spent in doles should be utilised for scholarships. If a Welsh University were established, its senate should be given the general oversight of the education in the Principality, including grammar schools. In any case, such a Board of Education was desirable, its members to be appointed by Government, the Universities, the Education Department, and learned societies ; fellowships at Jesus College, Oxford, should be open, to strengthen the tutorial staff.—The Chairman of the Carmarthen School Board said that, as a Calvinistic Methodist minister, acquainted with almost every town in Wales, he had no hesitation in saying that the Welsh nation earnestly desired a University. They were not fairly treated compared with England, Ireland, and Scotland. What St. David's College had done for the Church of England section of the community a University would do for the nation. The great need of the Principality, however, was intermediate schools.—Dr. Vance Smith, principal of the Presbyterian College, Carmarthen, said he failed to see the advantage of a degree granting authority in Wales over that of the London University.

On Wednesday, the Committee took evidence at Haverfordwest. The balance of a large mass of testimony was favourable to the foundation of a Welsh University, though some witnesses thought such an institution now would be 100 years too late, seeing the facilities that existed for taking London degrees. Witnesses representing Church interests pleaded for the retention intact of the degree-granting charter held by Lampeter College, but offered no objection to the granting of a similar charter to an undenominational institution which would meet the wants of Nonconformists. High-class colleges were generally approved of.

At the sitting of the Committee at Swansea on Thursday, it was stated that the income of the grammar school (£650) might be quadrupled if the mines and farms were properly let. The Mayor advocated a college for higher and technical education, saying that the town would do its part if the Government would assist.

Mr. C. W. W. Wynn, in giving evidence before the Committee at Welshpool with regard to the Welsh School at Ashford, Middlesex, said that its first, and, for some years, its only object, was convivial dinners, which were given on St. David's Day. On the 9th of May, 1717, it was instituted that two children should be apprenticed, with a premium of £10 each. In 1718 subscriptions for a school were set on foot for Welsh children, born in or near London, and having no parochial settlement within 10 miles of the Royal Exchange. A room in Hatton Garden was provided for 12 children, and the accommodation was subsequently increased to 40. Building of premises was begun in 1737 at Clerkenwell Green. In 1762 there had been 250 children apprenticed, 114 sent to sea, 93 put out in service, and 42 children were in the school. Until 1768 the children were neither fed nor lodged. In 1771 premises in Gray's Inn-road were erected. In 1816 the premises were enlarged and a dormitory built, and in 1818 further enlarged again, and 50 more children admitted. At that time there were

150 children in the school. In 1837 the number was increased to 160 children, and further enlargement. In 1839-40 the premises were again enlarged, and the number had increased to 200. The Society was incorporated in 1846, new schools were erected in 1857, the whole cost being £20,000. £14,000 was received for the premises in Gray's Inn-lane. Another subscription was set on foot to procure the odd £6,000, but only £1,500 had been received. In consequence of decreased subscriptions, the original number of 200 children was now reduced to 77, namely, 44 boys and 33 girls, besides 46 boys and 22 girls, whose cost is otherwise defrayed, being taken in on payment of £26 each per annum. The dividends on capital amounted to £1,468. The donations and subscriptions now amounted to £710; income from pay scholars, £1,555. In 1878 one vacancy in every four was decided to be filled up by children born in Wales (the father being dead) within the limits of the Act. This had not resulted in any fresh subscriptions.

SHROPSHIRE ARCHÆOLOGICAL SOCIETY.

ANNUAL MEETING.

The annual meeting of the Shropshire Archæological and Natural History Society was held in the Museum, at Shrewsbury, on Tuesday, Dec. 7, at half-past eleven, Mr. Stanley Leighton, M.P., one of the vice-presidents, in the chair. The attendance was unusually large, owing, no doubt, to the fact that Mr. Leighton had been announced as chairman, and the natural wish of the members to support him on the occasion. Before we report proceedings we may perhaps be allowed to say that the Council of the Association would be acting for the best interests of the Institution, we think, if they arranged each year beforehand for a president at the annual meeting, so as to secure, as on the present occasion, an Inaugural Address worthy a place in the Transactions of the Society.

Amongst those present were, the Revs. Canon Butler, W. A. Leighton of Shrewsbury, J. Evans, Whixall, J. Mitchell, Alberbury, Messrs. W. Wilding, Church Stretton, J. Bodenham, Newport, Askew Roberts, Oswestry, Dr. Cranage, Wellington, Revs. C. H. Drinkwater, T. Auden, S. W. Allen, Messrs. J. Morris, J. Sharpe, T. Onions, Oldroyd, T. Southam, S. C. Southam, J. P. White, W. Beacall, C. Cortissos, J. Calcott, W. Phillips, R. Taylor, J. P. Smith, E. J. Parry, A. B. Deakin, H. W. Adnitt of Shrewsbury, &c., &c.

The HON. SECRETARY (Mr. Adnitt) read the annual report, which was as follows :—

The Council of the Shropshire Archæological and Natural History Society again have pleasure in presenting their report and statement of Accounts to the members. The accounts show that the number of members has but slightly decreased, and this has been occasioned by deaths and removals ; the Council venture to hope that the number may be made up by the exertion of the present members, and believe that if a special effort was made by those interested, the list might easily be increased to 350, which is the number of the copies of the transactions printed.

The accounts show a balance in hand of £63 5s. 4d., which is less than the balance in hand at the commencement of the year by £5 14s. 9d., but it must be remembered that the Council have purchased during the year a fine copy of Eyton's Antiquities at a cost of £22, and made also other purchases of interest to the Museum.

During the year the Transactions have been issued to the members, and the Council beg to thank all the contributors for their valued papers, and especially Stanley Leighton, Esq., M.P., for a further instalment of the Corporation Records of Oswestry, and the Rev. W. A. Leighton for his transcript of Taylor's MS., so far as it relates to Shropshire.

The Council in doing this cannot but refer to the late disastrous fire at the Shirehall, and venture strongly to suggest that the records of the county and borough may be at once carefully gone over, and, as far as possible, copies made. They feel thankful that those valuable documents, which were in the Strong Rooms, and the paintings were entirely preserved.

At the Museum a considerable amount of work has been done by the curators in arranging the different sections, but they find that, as referred to in the last report, they are sadly hindered for want of room, and the Council feel strongly that the time must shortly arrive when it will be imperative to take steps to erect or acquire a building worthy of the county and borough.

During the year valuable donations to the Museum have been received, and which are acknowledged in the *Transactions*. The Council, in presenting their thanks to the donors, would especially mention a most interesting collection presented by Mr. T. C. Walker, formerly of, Shrewsbury, and also W. Muckleston, Esq., of Meole Brace, for his donation of the Records and Charters, &c., of the Guild of Mercers and Goldsmiths, he being the last surviving member. Since the year has closed, a very large and valuable donation has been received at the Museum from T. Slaney Eyton, Esq., and the Misses Eyton, consisting of the late T. C. Eyton Esq.'s, choice collection of shells, fossils, &c., which will be more fully recorded in the next year's report.

The Committee feel they cannot conclude without referring to the death of the late T. C. Eyton, Esq., who, from the foundation of the Museum, was a most earnest worker in the Zoological Section, and also the donor of many of its contents.

The number of visitors to the Museum have been by payment of 6d., 411, £10 15s. 6d.; 3d, 156, £1 19s. 0d.; total, £12 4s. 6d. members' orders, 605; total, 1,172. Several societies have also been admitted free.

The Council have only to add that their thanks and those of the members are due to the Editorial Committee, especially to the Rev. W. A. Leighton, and also to the hon. sec., Mr. Adnitt, for his willing exertions for the welfare of the Society.

The Council again solicit donations of objects of interest relating to the county, especially books, prints, drawings, coins, and specimens illustrating the archæology, botany, zoology, and geology of the county.

Mr. STANLEY LEIGHTON, M.P., said—Gentlemen, as your chairman it is my duty to move the adoption of the report. The development of this and kindred societies is a most undeniable evidence of the attractiveness of archæology, and of the natural and becoming pride which intelligent men feel more and more, in what remains to them from generations past. I think I may congratulate the Society on the character of its supporters. The list, I hope, may become even larger, but nevertheless at present I think it contains the names of almost every peer connected with the county, and most of the principal landowners. It contains moreover a number of professional men, and men whose occupation lies chiefly in trade and agriculture; and I think it contains, without exception, all the men and women in Shropshire who are professed antiquaries. Gentlemen, as a member myself of several antiquarian societies, and also of what I suppose may be called the parent society, namely, the Chartered Society of Antiquaries in London, I have often wished that a more direct intercommunication between antiquarian societies could be brought about. The affiliation of local societies to the London Society would add strength to the one and dignity to the others, and give great encouragement to antiquarian pursuits throughout the whole country. I understand that we may have an opportunity ourselves this year of showing hospitality and attention to the Cambrian Archæological Society, which proposes shortly to meet in Shropshire. I hope it will be found acceptable to our Council to give them an appropriate welcome. Gentlemen, the historical monuments of England will never be safe until they are regarded as precious in the eyes of all Englishmen. Not the Government or a committee of the British Museum but the people themselves must guard the evidences of their history. The antiquarian societies are fitting custodians of such treasures, and upon us is voluntarily imposed the obliga-

tion to set the example. More often than some persons think an ancient monument has an absolute commercial value, and people will pay money for the privilege of seeing. As an example I will mention Shakespeare's house at Stratford, and the famous stones on the Salisbury Downs. But in cases where money is out of the question, sentiment is usually found to be strong enough to induce the educated to subscribe for the sake of preserving an old landmark, even though the mark can be only recognised by the eye of an antiquary. Let me mention some instances in our own immediate neighbourhood. The mound of Oswestry Castle, the ruins of Ruyton Castle, the remnants of Wroxeter, the very hall in which our own museum is collected, "Vaughan's Palace," as it was called in the old days, one of the rare specimens of the Domestic architecture of the 14th century, still extant in Shrewsbury, all these are examples of places saved from neglect by the associated action of private individuals. Perhaps, gentlemen, I shall not be overstepping the scope of a chairman's address, if I venture to throw out a suggestion. There is in Shrewsbury, as we all know, a precious and almost unique example of mediæval architecture and monastic manners, in the stone pulpit of the Abbey. Its conventual surroundings have now for a long time been removed from its neighbourhood. It stands like an unwelcome monitor in the centre of a railway station. There is difficulty in approaching it, to examine it is almost impossible. Danger threatens it on every side. Could not the Council of our Shropshire Archæological Society, or might not individual antiquaries, enquire how far it would be practicable to move the pulpit to some more congenial site—and how far those most interested in the Abbey to which it belongs would be willing to afford to it a safe and dignified resting place, where it might be seen and appreciated? The removal of Temple Bar and the erection of it afresh elsewhere, stone for stone the same as it was, is a precedent in point. The figures in the front of the Town Hall, the one of Richard Duke of York, removed from the Tower of the Welsh Bridge, the other of an angel bearing the arms of France and England, removed from the Castle Gate Tower, are precedents of our own. Gentlemen, it is an agreeable subject of congratulation that we are growing too big for our present premises, which we have occupied for 45 years. No more appropriate hall than the one we now rent could we possibly obtain, and we should certainly make the most of it. I should be very sorry for it to be given up, but it is crowded to excess; we have been obliged to decline some valuable collections of natural history for want of room. We have lately received from the family of Mr. Eyton a most rich gift of shells and fossils. Our library is increasing; our maps and pictures require wall room which we cannot give them; so the time seems to have come when the antiquaries and naturalists of Shropshire might endeavour to provide themselves with two houses, one wholly devoted to natural history, and the other wholly devoted to archæology. For my part, I should be sorry to see a new building erected. I should like an old building better. One of the many ancient houses of Shrewsbury would afford a characteristic habitation for the Archæological Society of Shropshire. Gentlemen, if I am not improperly detaining you, I would say a word on the literary work and objects of our Society. The tendency of modern thought, which affects archæology as well as every other branch of knowledge, demands the production of proofs rather than the repetition of tradition. Therefore, we are more and more desirous of publishing original documents, noted and explained, of course, but yet depending

5

23

for their main value on the fact that they are original. The number of original documents in Shropshire is enormous. Some of them have lately had a narrow escape. The contents of no manuscripts are safe unless they are printed. I will only refer to one class of them now—namely the parish registers. They form one of the principal sources from which parochial histories are written. We are particularly desirous of encouraging that branch of our work. The church register is usually the oldest book in the parish, and the parish books often contain a fund of information beyond mere entries of account. The more of these original facts and figures which we can publish the better. The parochial registers are the annals of the people. They are the only authority to which we can refer, previously to the present century, for an approximate census of the people. They mark the migration of the population from one locality to another. In the prevalence of certain names they indicate varieties of race. They are our guides in testing the average duration of human life in the past three centuries. They are the highest evidences for proving family descent and pedigree. But, gentlemen, not one of these invaluable records of the English nation is perfect. They have perished, and they are perishing. 15,000 unindexed volumes in 15,000 places are from necessity a sealed book both to the student and to the nation. By those who have thought of these things, frequent proposals have been made to provide a remedy. Sir Thomas Phillips in 1832, Lord Romilly in 1837, Horace Mann in 1857, Lord Lyndhurst in 1860, Southerden Burn in 1868, have all endeavoured to draw attention to this subject, and have all failed to bring about a practical remedy because the popular mind remains still uninstructed and only partially interested, If the clergy, who are the custodians of these priceless records, and the antiquaries, whose business it is to teach the people the value of such things, were to combine in urging upon the Government the paramount importance of saving the Registers from further decay, I doubt not but that a plan might be devised, at comparatively small cost, for printing and indexing every Register in England, and making up the volumes according to counties, and indexing again the larger collections, and thus making reference easy and destruction impossible, and removing from amongst us a national discredit. Gentlemen, I regard this Association as the highest and indeed the only collective authority in Shropshire which has a claim to speak to the public on archæological matters. The occasion of our annual meeting appears an appropriate one for making known our opinions and endeavouring to give effect to them, and for enlarging our influence. I beg leave to move the adoption of the report.

The adoption of the report thus moved by the Chairman was seconded by Dr. Cranage and carried.

The Rev. J. Mitchell then proposed and Mr. Oldroyd seconded the re-election of the Council, with the addition of the names of Dr. Calvart and Mr. Calcott. The Rev. S. W. Allen proposed and the Rev. J. Evans seconded the re-appointment of the office-bearers of the Society. Mr. R. Taylor proposed and Mr. Askew Roberts seconded Mr. Onions and Mr. Oldroyd as auditors. Mr. Beacall proposed and the Rev. C. H. Drinkwater seconded a vote of thanks to the Donors to the Museum. Mr. Phillips proposed and Mr. Calcott seconded a vote of thanks to the editors of the Society's *Transactions* and to the Hon. Sec., to which the Rev. W. Allport Leighton and Mr. Adnitt responded.

This was all the routine business. Canon Butler proposed the vote of a further sum of £10 to increase their collection of specimens of Birds, and suggested the destruction of some of the worm-eaten animals that now took up too much space in their rooms. Dr. Cranage, in seconding the motion, urged that they should not attempt to make a little British Museum of their building, but confine themselves to Shropshire specimens. Mr. Parry and the Rev. C. H. Drinkwater urged that the Council should keep an eye on the Schools with a view to its being a probable museum of the future.

THE RUINS AT WROXETER.

The Rev. T. Auden said he and Mr. Phillips had been appointed by the Council to report on the condition of the excavations at Wroxeter, and they had done so. The man in charge did his work on the whole satisfactorily, but new fencing was wanted. Mr. Phillips supplemented what Mr. Auden had said, and it was agreed that they, with the addition of Mr. Beacall and Mr. White, should form a committee to execute the necessary repairs. It was also resolved that the question of rent should be laid before the Duke of Cleveland, who owned the property.

THE ABBEY PULPIT.

In reference to the remarks of the Chairman as to the removal of the Abbey Pulpit an interesting discussion arose, in which Mr. J. P. White, Mr. Taylor, and others took part. The general feeling was that no removal should be made unless the safety of the structure required it, although some held strongly to the opinion that as it now stood, a desolate looking object shorn of its surroundings, it would be better at once to take measures for its removal to a public spot near the Abbey.

CAMBRIAN ARCHÆOLOGICAL SOCIETY.

The Hon. Sec. said he had received a letter from the Rev. Trevor Owen, secretary of the Cambrian Archæological Society, saying that they purposed meeting at Church Stretton in August.—The Chairman thought that arrangements should be made to co-operate with the Society when it made its visit, and give it a welcome.

Mr. STANLEY LEIGHTON's interesting speech at the annual meeting of the Shropshire Archæological Society is reported in our columns to-day. Mr. LEIGHTON's suggestions, we hope, will not be allowed to pass unheeded by what he called "the only collective authority in Shropshire which has a claim to speak to the public on archæological matters." We may mention more particularly a proposal which has more than once claimed attention in these columns—the printing of parish registers. Several thousand volumes exist in the country, but they are gradually perishing, and unless steps are taken to preserve them we shall lose some priceless memorials of the past. Mr. LEIGHTON seems to think the Government might be induced to take the work in hand; but meanwhile it lies with the antiquaries and archæological societies of the country to do what they can in the way of printing the registers, which, as Mr. LEIGHTON justly says, is the only method of making them secure. A direct appeal to the clergy of Shropshire would certainly meet with a response. Some of the custodians of the parish registers, perhaps, are scarcely aware of their value; others would respond to a direct appeal who would not unasked undertake the work; and others, again, who would shrink from the task themselves, would allow some zealous archæologist to carry it out. In one way or another, we believe all the parish registers of Shropshire might be collected; but something more is wanted. Authentic parish histories would be more interesting than the registers, though often not so valuable. Parish histories, not overloaded with petty details, yet taking in those minute touches of conduct and character which are to be recovered from existing manuscripts and floating traditions, would be a most useful and attractive feature of the Archæological Society's Transactions.

DECEMBER 22, 1880.

NOTES.

THE OLD WELSH ALMANACKS (Oct. 20
1880).—The internal verses in the issue for the year 1804 are
as under :—

Y mae Arwyddion daw i'n *Gwlad* :
Newyddion *Hedd*, a Chariad rhad :
Dadseiniad Byd, a *Seion* fro,
Amen, Amen, fel hynny bo.

Hen *bechod* câs ysgeler, a roist i *Loegr* glwy :
Ofn colli hen drigfannau, a *Breintiau* fwy na mwy ;
Ac hefyd rhoddi'n bywyd, i *Dân* a blin-fyd croes,
Meu fyw dan ryfyg *Rhufain*, i ochain hyd ein hoes.

Mae *Awdwyr*, wedi addo, os wyf yn cofio'n glir,
Y bydd raid i *Babyddion*, rai taerion ddod i'n tir ;
Gobeithio na chant odfa, i wneud *Sefyllfa* lân :
Ddim mwy na ch'lomen *Noa* ymhlith y tonnau mân.

Yr Arglwydd yw *Rhyfelwr*, Efe yw rhoddwr hedd ;
Efe a ddichon gadw, a bwrw i lawr y *Bedd :*
Fe fathrodd Fyrdd o '*Lynion* yn feirwon dan ei *draed*,
Maddeuodd Feiau *Anfawr*, er mwyn ei werthfawr *waed !*
Duw cynnal *George* ein Brenin yn ddiflin yn ei daith,
Ynghyd a'i holl swyddogion, sydd union yn dy waith
Bydd gyda ei *weision Rhyfel* ymafel yn eu llaw,
I ymlid y *Gelynion*, sy hyllion drawsion draw.

NATTURIAETH Y SAITH BLANED AR DDYNION WRTH
NATUR.

1. Pob mab a merch gwrandawed, yn dirion ac ystyried ;
　Yn ol y rheol treiaf drin natturiaeth ffin eich *blaened.*

2. Y *Sadwrn* yw'r uchelaf, natturiaeth hon sydd waethaf ;
　Gosodwyd hi gan faint ei thwyll, gan dduwiol bwyll yn bellaf.

3. Ei phlant i gyd fy 'greulon yn sadaf am ymryson ;
　Ac ni phlygant ddim yn hir, er clywed gwir yn gyson.

4. Chwenychen' ladd neu losgi, rhai mwd a hwy Gamwri ;
　Y Dydd a'r Nos yn hanner cla' o falais a drygloni.

5. Danghosant ragrith ofer, cyhyddnod twyll a ffalster,
　Ac yn llawn o ofnau caeth, gael byd yn waeth ar fryder.

6. Rhai pryddion wyneb galed, yn edrych ar ei wared,
　A golwg hen cyn deugain llawn, ofnadwy iawn eu tynged.

7. Mae Plaenad *Iau* a'i meiblon, yn Gelfydd, call ac union,
　Mwyn a theg a llariaidd yw, a'i bryd ar fyw'n heddychlon.

8. Ymdeithiant gyd a doethion, myfyriant bethau mawrion ;
　Mewn achos caled byddant ffel, ymddygant fel bon'ddigion.

9. Yn fynnych rhai cyfoethog, yn casglu'r byd yn enwog,
　Mewn amser caled rhoddant gais, i wrando llais anghenog.

0. Gwrid goch a danedd hirion a llygaid teg a gleision ;
　Gwrol gyrph cryf syth a llon, ond yw plant hon yn dirion.

1. Plant *Mars* sydd wrthryfelgar, hyf, gwaedwyllt, ac ysgeler :
　Am fatter bychan digio wnant er tegwch nid ant hawddgar.

2. Rhai hywiog mewn rhyw gweryl a drawant cyn b'o disgwyl,
　Am swyddau creulon maent i fyw, ond erchyll yw y gorchwyl.

3. Tyngwyr cas ac efrydd, na wridant, er cael gwradwydd
　Yn dra mynych bydd eu bryd, i lanw'r byd a ynfydrwydd.

4. Lliw coch ac wyneb ffyrnig, brych wedd gwallt du cyrledig ;
　Melyn groen a llygaid llym, corph byrr o rym canolig.

5. Mae plant fy dan *So*! dirion, yn uchel iawn a beilchion
　Myfyriant Gelfyddydau maith, i gaffel gwaith i'r doethion.

6. Ymgomiant am gael cymmod, a dwrdiant drwy awdurdod
　Lle byddo ymryson gwael hwy dreiant gael eu datod.

7. Bodlonant hwy yn helaeth pan ddelo croes Ragluniaeth
　Uwch law disgwyliad yma cair hwy'n cadw eu gair yn odiaeth.

8. Gwallt melyn wyneb crynno, a gwawrled felyn aruo ;
　Chwimyth rai ac ysgrifn droed, yn ol yr oed yn rhodio.

9. Plant *Venus* sy'n fwynhynod, ar eiriau peraidd parod ;
　Etto ant er chwaer na brawd, ar ol y cnawd yn ormod.

20. Cellwerus di ymdeuru yn hoffi dawns a chanu ;
　'N segur fyw mewn lloches glyd, neu rodio'r byd o bob tu.

21. Rhai hael a hylaw ddigon, rhag digio cymmydogion ;
　Gwell ganddynt hwy gymmeryd senn, na myn'd ymhen cy-
　feillion.

22. Crwn wyneb, aeliau goleu eu gwallt yn dew a gwineu ;
　Hardd ac uchel eu dwy fron a llygaid llon yn chwareu.

23. *Mercury* fy'n ymgyredd am wegi ffol a gwagedd ;
　Yn fawr ei phoen o bryd i bryd am bethau'r byd i'r annedd.

24. Rhai hylaw y'nt am holi pan ddelont i gwmpeini ;
　Am amryw bethau heb ymdroi cynhygiant roi peth cyfri.

25. Ymryson ac ynddadleu a wnant am groes gwestiwnau
　Os cynnyger iddynt gam hwy redent am gyfreithiau.

26. Y rhain sy ddynnion cryflon aelodau grymus hirion,
　Gwallt nod ddu a thalcen mawr yn rhodio'r llawr yn sythion.

27. Plant *Luna* lawn ffolineb dull hynod a dallineb ;
　Garant heddyw hyd brydnawn y foru'n llawn casineb.

28. Eu *Blaenad* sy'n eu blino, cas gan eu gwithi weithio ;
　Cas ganddynt glywed ar un pryd, fod neb o'r byd yn llwyddo

29. Mae rhai e'r dynion yma yn erwin am chwilena,
　Neu siglo'r byd yn wael eu llun au gado eu hun a geisiau.

30. Lliw gwan a llygaid duon trwyn mawr talceni hirion,
　Eu gwallt yn grych a du ei wawr yn ddynion mawra thewion.

31. Wel dyma'r saith natturiaeth, a hidlwyd i'n cenhedlaeth,
　Os wyt ti well yn byw a bod, Duw biau'r clod yn helaeth.

32. Nid oes ar y *Duwolion* ddim ofn *Planedau* croesion
　Mae eu serchiadau gyd a *Duw*, ac felly 'n byw yn foddlon.

33. Maent hwy yn ddigon hysbys caiff cyfyngderau dyrus
　Gyd weithio er eu lles o hyd, tra b'o eu byd helbulus.

34. Y pechaduriaid mwyaf a gaiff y poenau pennaf ;
　Ond o's edifarhant trwy ffydd hwynt hwy a fyd y blaenaf.

35. Os bydd yn Uffern boeni pob pechod a dryglonl,
　Mil mwy am wrthod un Mab Duw, caiff dynol ryw eu cospi.

36. Rhad gariad Duw raid alw, pechadur wrth ei enw,
　Gan ddwedyd co'd gysgadur swrth, ar frys oddiwrth y meirw.

37. Rhai gafodd y Dystiolaeth eu bod yn blant yr *Arfaeth*
　Fe fydd eu hamcan ymhob lle am dirion *Iechydwriaeth.*

38. Y maent fel dan boen bywyd, yn cosbi'r cyrph yn ddiwyd ;
　Gan ofni hyd eu taith rhag diffodd gwaith yr *Yspryd.*

39. Rhai sydd a hanes hynod, am *Arfaeth* ar flaen tafod ;
　Bydd y rhai'n a geiriau ffraeth yn llarpio'n waeth na *llewod.*

40. Er *Ysgythyrau* cywir mewn *Llanau* a ddarllenir
　Y mae rhai yn byw gwel'd yn glir, fod ynddynt *wir* ni cherir !

41. Mae tirion blant y *Daran* y llwyr gyhoeddi allan ;
　Am edifeirwch, a gwir *ffydd* dwy *efaill* tydd un oedran.

42. Lle byddo bur *bregethu*, mae'r ddwy yn cyd gynyddu,
　Fe fydd *Gobaith* yn eu plith ond *Chariad* byth a beru.

43. Holl *eiriau'r* Arglwydd Iesu fy o *les* heb ddim i lysu,
　Na dim iw arfer megis Sarn i gynnal *Barn* i fynu.

44. *Duwiolion* sydd yn bwytta y *gair* fel peraidd *fara*,
　Ac yn parchu pawb mewn *head* fu'n caru *gwledd* Jehofa.

45. Bydd llawer yn wyllylio myn'd tros fy *Nghaniad* etto,
　Eraill gan y *Gwahanglwy*, ni fynant mwy ei gwrando.

Ffarwel gyfeillion *mwynlan*, yn gyfan oll i gyd,
Eich annerch mwy ni allaf, tra byddaf yn y *byd ;*
Mae fy synhwyrau'n *darfod*, hawdd i mi wybod hyn,
A bod y *Dydd* yn nesu i'm *claddu* yn y Glynn.

　　　　　　　　　　　　　　　　　　　E.G.S.

QUERIES.

OSWESTRY FORTY YEARS AGO.—"Two
ruffians fought a battle of nearly 39 rounds, on *Sunday*
evening last. within 300 yards of Oswestry church, and during
Divine Service ! This, in a Christian country, and on
Christmas Day too ! Shame ! Where were those authorities who often, on trivial occasions, are conspicuously
officious ? We hope the Mayor will institute some en-

quiries as to this disgraceful exhibition."—(*Salopian Journal* Dec. 28, 1836.) Did the Mayor do as the writer hoped he would? Mr. Campbell, the watchmaker, was in office, being the second Mayor elected after the passing of the Municipal Reform Act. OSWALD.

REPLIES.

CASTLE CILRHON (Dec. 1, 1880).—Will "J.C.H." be so good as to inform us on what authority is the statement made that *Aberangell*, between Cemmaes and Dinas Mawddwy, is a corruption of *Aber Rhongil?* I have some slight acquaintance with that locality, and I have never heard the name pronounced in any other way than *Aberangell* (that is, with the final Welsh *ll* as in asgell, castell, padell, and the like, and not *Aberangel* as given by "J.C.H.") Can the writer of the note refer me to any old, or comparatively old, document, in which the name is given as *Aber Rhongil?* I know of none; but it is just possible that some English scribes may have corrupted Aber *Angell* into Aber *Rhongil.* Such blunders are not uncommon. I may mention also that Aber *Hodni*, not Aber *Rhonddu*, is the older form of the name now generally spelt Aber Honddu or Aberhonddu. The Honddu which falls into the Usk at Brecon is not the only river of that name in the Principality.
COCHWILLIAD.

In reply to the enquiry of "J.C.H." as to how the above Castle is situated, I may say it is not in a dingle, though it stands on a slope at foot of which a rivulet flows. It stands on high ground in the western corner of Clun Forest, and not above half a mile, if so much, from the point where the counties of Radnor, Salop, and Montgomery meet, where also England and Wales and North and South Wales meet. One of the names (marked on the Ordnance Survey) by which the Castle is known, is "Castell Bryn Amlwg," which, I suppose, may be *anglicised* as the "Castle on a conspicuous hill." Could this be "Withybrook" Castle, referred to by Eyton in his work, and which he failed to identify? Geographically it would answer. RHYDDWR,

OLD FOLKS. (Dec. 8, 1880.)—In an old MS. book of matters interesting chiefly to Wales, I find the following record of deaths :—William Edwards died at Caeren, near Cardiff, in Glamorganshire, in 1668, aged 163. Gaynor Fechan died Sep. 16, 1686, at Abercowarch, near Dinas Mawddwy, in Merionethshire, aged 140. I don't ask anybody to believe these statements, but I should like to know the ground they rest upon. A.

The following records of the deaths of old people are taken from various volumes of the *Annual Register* :—Oct. 1761, Widow Rogers at Wrexham, 107 ; Dec. 1761, Francis Watkins of Trevethin, Monmouthshire, 102 ; Dec. 1862, Evan Owens at Denbigh, 100 ; July 1763, John Bates, near Wem, Salop, 103 ; Oct. 1763, Jane Grey, at Wem, 100 ; her husband, a shepherd still living, is 98 ; Apr. 1767, Mrs. Elizabeth Mason, at Hales Owen, 104 ; Oct. do., Elizabeth Harwood, at Whitchurch, Shropshire, 102 ; her husband, a shepherd, living, aged 98 ; Dec. do., Margaret Edwards of Bestieth (sic) in Montgomeryshire, 118 ; Jan. 1770, Ralph Nied, near Chester, 107, he had buried six wives : Aug. do., Jane Hammond, Whitchurch, Shropshire, 107 ; Aug. 1771, one Ap-Jones, a shepherd in the Isle of Anglesey, 107 ; his fourth wife he married when he was 90, and he had children by her ; Sep. 1772, Mrs. Redrick, at Shrewsbury, 105 ; Nov. do., John Jones, of Horton Lane, near Shrewsbury, 102 ; do. Mary Butler, of Shrewsbury, 102 ; Apr. 1773, Mary Jones, Wem, 100 ; she was only 2ft. 8in. high ; Aug. 1776, Mrs. Mary Yates, of Shifnal,

128 ; she walked to London after the fire in 1666, married a third husband in her 92nd year, and was hearty and strong at 120 ; Dec. 1778, Mr. Rice Morgan, Llanerwisse, South Wales, 103 ; Dec. 1780, Mrs. Elizabeth Dallass, near Ellesmere, 103 ; May 1785, a man named Froome, at Holmes Chapel, Cheshire, 125 ; "he was guardian to the late John Smith Barry, Esq., who left him an annuity of £50 a year." Feb. 1787, Catharine Jeffreys, Alberbury, Shropshire, 104 ; "The noted old Par was a native of the same parish ;" 1792, Mr. Hammond, Senern (sic) Hall, Shropshire, 107 ; July 1801, Elizabeth Rogers, Cynllwyd, near Llanrwst, 105 ; "leaving children, grandchildren, and great-grand-children to the number of 140." S.

SHROPSHIRE SCHOOLS (Dec. 8, 1880.)—Dr. Kennedy, the Head Master of *Shrewsbury* School, published, on Apr. 10, 1839, the qualification of candidates for the prize offered by Sir Richard Jenkins "of a Writership to be competed for by Shrewsbury boys." Sir Richard was deputy-chairman of the East India Company.

Mr. F. S. Bolton, who was educated by the Rev. Dr. Rowley, Head Master of *Bridgnorth* Grammar School, has lately very highly distinguished himself at the University of Cambridge, by taking a first class in the Classical Tripos, being previous to this a Senior Optime at the last general examination for degrees.—*Salopian Journal*, Nov. 20, 1839.

The same paper of Apr. 3, 1839, states that Mr. R. Lingen, who had previously distinguished himself, obtained the Hertford Scholarship at Oxford, for which there were twenty-four competitors ; and Mr. Webster obtained a scholarship at Lincoln College against twenty-eight com petitors. They were both educated at *Bridgnorth* school.
SCROBBES BYRIG.

CURRENT NOTES.

It is stated that Mr. Darwin is confined to his bed from physical debility, but is happily not prostrated to the degree of being unable to read and converse. He is now 72 years of age.

DEATH OF MR. WM. LACON CHILDE.—We have to record the death of one of the oldest ex-M.P.'s, Mr. Wm. Lacon Childe, of Kinlet-hall, Shropshire, and of Kyre, Worcestershire, who in three weeks would have attained the age of 95. The deceased was the only son of the late Mr. William Baldwyn (who assumed the surname and arms of Childe only), by his marriage with Annabella, second daughter of Sir Charlton Leighton, of Lotou-park, Shropshire (great great grandfather of Mr. Stanley Leighton, M.P.), and was born on the 3rd of January, 1786. He was educated at Harrow, where he was school fellow of the late Lord Palmerston, Sir Robert Peel, Lord Byron, and the late Duke of Sutherland. He afterwards entered Christ Church, Oxford. He sat in the House of Commons, in the Conservative interest, as member for Wenlock, in the first Parliament of George IV. He moved the address in reply to the King's Speech in February, 1823. Mr. Childe was a magistrate and deputy-lieutenant for the counties of Worcester and Salop, and served as High Sheriff of the latter county in 1859 ; he was also a magistrate for the county of Hereford. He married in 1807 Harriet, second daughter of the late Mr. William Cludde, of Orleton, Shropshire, by whom he has left a family. He is succeeded in his estates by his eldest son and heir, Mr. William Lacon Childe, who was born in 1810, and married in 1839 Barbara, daughter of the late Mr. Thomas Giffard, of Chillington, Staffordshire. Mr. Childe's grandfather, Sir Charlton Leighton, was born in the reign of Queen Anne, and Sir Charlton's father (Mr. Childe's great grandfather) in the reign of Charles II.

EDUCATION IN WALES.
(Dec. 15, 1880).

The departmental Committee sat at Brecon on Wednesday, Dec. 15, when the Rev. Lewis Lloyd of Christ's College suggested the establishment of colleges in North and South Wales, with a third for science teaching. He was not in favour of creating a Welsh university with degree-conferring power; the population of the Principality was too small to supply such a number of students as would give life and character to degrees bestowed by the university.

At Cardiff on Saturday, Dec. 18, the Bishop of Llandaff was examined.

At Newport on Monday, Dec. 20, the following suggestions were submitted to the Committee by a deputation :— 1. That intermediate schools, both for boys and girls, assisted by grants from Government for their erection and maintenance, and with admission fees not exceeding five guineas per annum, are urgently required for Wales, the number and position of such schools in various districts of the country to be determined by a Government commissioner. 2. That all public intermediate and elementary schools, if unsectarian in teaching and management, be encouraged by exhibitions and scholarships, and by payment for results. 3. That existing educational endowments of their surplus funds be utilized for the purposes contemplated in the two previous resolutions. 4. That intermediate schools thus assisted should be managed by a County Board popularly elected, such Boards in the meantime to be elected by the various School Boards in each county. 5. That there be two colleges established in Wales, one in the north and the other in the south, for which grants shall be given by the Government towards their erection and maintenance, and that the southern college be erected in Cardiff. 6. That it is desirable that there should be an examining body, to be called "The Cambrian University," empowered by Royal charter to confer degrees in arts and science. 7. That all educational institutions so assisted should be entirely unsectarian in constitution, teaching, and management.

The Committee concluded their sittings at Newport on Tuesday. Amongst the principal witnesses who have given evidence is Professor Marshall, Bristol University College. The Professor gave the Committee some interesting particulars with regard to the institution with which he is connected, and showed that before that can be placed on a proper footing it will require a considerable sustentation fund. Though he would like to see the day when colleges would be established in large towns, he did not think the time for it had yet arrived ; and he candidly confessed he would not like to see a college in Cardiff very soon, as it might, and probably would, affect the number of students at Bristol. A University for Wales would be decidedly objected to on the ground that the only way of keeping up the standard of a degree was to centralise the examinations for it as much as possible ; but he would abolish probationary residence, and let any student of a college like his own stand the examination for a degree.

There was a general concurrence as to the pressing necessity of better intermediate education facilities. The Newport inquiry concludes the sittings of the Committee.

The Welsh Education Committee concluded their enquiries last week, when they sat at Newport in Monmouthshire. Notwithstanding the exclusion of reporters, the evidence has been placed before the public at considerable length. In these days, when the London dailies profess to be regularly supplied with the secrets of Cabinet Councils, it was scarcely likely that the proceedings of an enquiry which excited lively interest from one end of the Principality to the other could be conducted in privacy. The net result of the evidence seems to be this : that there is a unanimous opinion in favour of improving the means of intermediate education in Wales ; a very strong opinion, amounting in effect almost to unanimity, in favour of a Government endowment for one or more colleges ; and a wide-spread desire for a national university. The third proposal has a large number of determined opponents, and though they are chiefly old University men, who have an excessive veneration, perhaps, for Oxford and Cambridge, the opposition is not confined to that class. Men of various shades of sentiment have expressed their belief that a Welsh University would not secure a sufficient reputation to make its degrees of any value. On the other hand, it is urged that a University will crown the edifice of Welsh education, and that the strong national feeling in favour of it ought to be satisfied. Fortunately the present Government can be trusted to consider the question with an open mind, and with a single desire to promote the interests of the Welsh people, and to give them the greatest facilities for acquiring the knowledge which they have shown they love, and the culture which they have not yet perhaps learnt to appreciate as it will be appreciated when the educational defects of the present day are re moved.

There were great floods at Aberystwyth last week. The railway station was flooded, and looked more like a dock than anything else. Part of the Manchester and Milford Railway was washed away.

The ancient Church of St. Michael, Abergele, has lately been thoroughly restored internally at a cost a little exceeding £2,000, which, with the purchase of an organ and other incidental expenses, brought up the total outlay to £2,900. It is believed that the debt will be wholly cleared off by the end of the year.

The death is announced of Miss Evans of Darley House, Derby, at the venerable age of 94. Deceased was noted for her charities. She was the owner of Boscobel, and the farms of Blackladies and Whiteladies, near Shifnal, celebrated in English history as the place where the Penderels temporarily sheltered King Charles.

DEATH OF THE REV. MACKENZIE WALCOTT.—The death is announced of the Rev. Mackenzie Edward Charles Walcott, B.D., Precentor of Chichester Cathedral, who was well known in the antiquarian world. He was the only son of the late Admiral John Edward Walcott, formerly M.P. for Christchurch, was born in 1822 and was educated at Winchester, and at Exeter College, Oxford. He was for some years curate of St. Margaret's, and evening lecturer at St. James's, Westminster ; was appointed Precentor and Prebendary of Chichester Cathedral in 1863, and was minister of Berkeley Chapel, Mayfair, from 1867 to 1870. Mr. Walcott was the author of a large number of antiquarian and ecclesiological works, including "Four Minsters Round the Wrekin," and was a member of several learned societies both at home and abroad. He wrote the first paper in the first volume of the Shropshire Archæological Society's *Transactions*, and was an occasional contributor to our own *Bye-Gones* column. Mr. Walcott died in London, Dec. 21, at the age of 59. The deceased was descended from a common ancestor with the Walcotts of Bitterley, Salop, who flourished in the sixteenth century, and on that ground, however remote, he might be claimed as a Salopian.

MARKET IMPROVEMENTS AT OSWESTRY.

OPENING OF THE CROSS MARKET EXTENSION.

(From the *Oswestry Advertizer*, Dec. 22, 1880.)

A new wing to the Cross Market Hall, Oswestry, was opened with civic ceremonies, by the Mayor (Mr. Alderman Minshall) and Town Council, on Tuesday, Dec. 21, 1880. The Lord of the Manor (the Earl of Powis), Mr. Stanley Leighton, M.P., and others, took part in the demonstration, which culminated in a lunch at the Queen's Hotel.

The history of the Oswestry Markets has yet to be written, and there is plenty of material available to any one who has time and patience at command who will undertake the task. In olden times the feudal lord was paramount, and all the tolls belonged to him, and were paid without a murmur; but, as people became more energetic and independent, the laws were relaxed and, eventually, ratepayers taxed themselves, and saw that they had a return for their money.

We have said people in times gone by paid without a murmur, but this was not always so, for as far back as 1751 we find grumblers who took their grievances into a court of justice; and a Mr. Griffiths, attorney, was sent to London by the Mayor and Corporation to assist in the defence of some causes in the Court of King's Bench, touching the payment of "An Ancient Duty called Tensery."

At the period "the Right Hon. George Edward Henry Arthur Earl of Powis" was Lord of the Manor, that is to say in 1782, the old gateways that arched Church-street and Beatrice-street had become in such a tumble-down condition that the Corporation asked his lordship to take them down. The walls of the town, with which they had been connected, had been demolished a century earlier. That the Lord of Powis had full power over these gateways (as he had over other matters) was shown in the fact that they were always repaired at his expense. Thus, in 1752, one of the gates tumbled down, and "Thomas Jones, for removing the rubbish," and taking down the rest, was paid £1 18s. 7d. In 1763 the Willow Gate was "presented" (i.e., reported to the authorities as defective) and "William Griffiths" had "2d. a yard for paving 31½ yards, with stone and gravel under it." In 1776 a new pillory (probably near the New Gate, over which was the prison) was put up at a cost of £2 7s. 0d. In 1791 a Table of Tolls, for the use of the "Toll Gatherer" was painted, at a cost of 7s. 6d. In 1803 repairs to the clock on the Town Hall (now the "Powis Hall"), amounted to £5 15s. 6d., and a new dial to £12 14s. 3d. All these and other payments were made by the Lord of the Manor, so there could be no question as to his right. Still, as time wore on there were grumblings, and before the end of the first quarter of this century there were law suits pending which ended in an amicable settlement of the question, and a redemption of the Tolls.

It will be seen from the foregoing that our lord had the command not only of our markets, but of our time and our punishments! This power became centred in the Herbert family in 1697, on the death, without issue, of the Earl of Craven, from whom William Herbert, second Marquess of Powis, inherited. It was not until 1801 that the lordship was carried into the family of Clive. Those who have examined the very well executed coat of arms, on a pillar let into a wall in Church-street (which marks the spot where the New Gate once stood) will have observed that it is the Herbert Arms that are there depicted. This was erected in 1782. At what precise date

the Tolls were redeemed we cannot say,—further than it was when the grandfather of the present lord was Earl of Powis—but it was not until the period when the new markets were inaugurated that the old premises on the Bailey Head became "The Powis Hall," a name adopted in commemoration of the gift of the present noble Lord's father.

Some of the customs in connection with the "Toll gathering" were curious. Another week we may recount some of these. Our older readers will remember the time when sacks of grain were "pitched" on the Bailey Head, and toll taken out of each with a dish! In those days the paving-stones on "The Biley" were so arranged in lines as to show where these bags were to be placed, and the Town Hall bell was rung at half-past one o'clock on market days to call the farmers and millers from the neighbouring public houses, in order that they may all commence business at once. Bargains were struck, and the parties speedily returned to their respective houses, and paid or received their cash—as the case might be—over a friendly glass.

In those days a public house was a necessity in a borough like Oswestry, and the first question asked by the magistrates of a would-be publican was, "What stable accommodation have you?" and, "Have you a good Market-room?" We had no railways; and "farmer's traps," especially on Fair days, were ranged in order along the back streets, with scarcely room for vehicles to pass. We have seen those in Upper Brook-street reach from the Coach and Dogs corner up to a point near the Grammar School. From the Welsh country many rode on horse back to market, and "horse-blocks" stood outside some of the inns for the convenience of ladies (who rode on pillions behind their husbands) mounting the steeds. This manner of locomotion was called "Peggy behind Marget!" In these railway days, it may be observed in passing, the stables are many of them abolished, and the "Market Rooms" of the public-houses turned into a "Spirit-vaults."

In the days of which we speak the fair sex were treated in a most unfair manner. In all weathers they had to squat themselves down on the curb-stones with their baskets of butter, apples, potatoes, and other commodities, in the channel before them; and it was no unusual sight to see rows line each side the Cross and Church-street as far up as Cae Glas. Naughty boys on the causeways became expert in the way in which (by means of a stout pin at the end of a long stick) they extracted fruit from the basket of an unwary owner; and there were no "Bobbies" to circumvent them, and but few "Beaks" to punish the evil doers.

The Market for horses was ostensibly "Under the Welsh Walls, but really — everywhere! — and you had to look out as you paced the streets. Cattle had full possession of the Bailey Head, and Sheep and Pigs of Brook-street; and, generally speaking, Oswestry was about as uncomfortable a place on a Fair Day as you would find anywhere.

Interesting remarks have fallen from official lips as to how and when our Cattle Market, and Corn Market, and Horse Market, and [very] Cross Market were achieved. On the 26th Dec., 1850, a presentation was made to Mr Alderman Peploe Cartwright, of a silver salver, &c., in recognition of the energy and ability he had displayed in prosecuting the good works. The town has grown rapidly since then, and is growing so fast, that probably in a shorter time than some think for, the Three Tuns and Grapes Public-houses will have to be swept away still further to enlarge the Domestic Market, an important addition to which was opened yesterday.

An important extension of the Cross Market, at Oswestry, was formally opened yesterday. The town of Oswestry, as the convenient centre of a large agricultural district, owes its prosperity chiefly to its markets and fairs. The Town Council have not only been careful not to kill the goose that lays the golden eggs, but with wise forethought they have done their best to stimulate the growth and development of the markets by making them as free as possible and by enlarging and improving the market accommodation whenever it seemed desirable to do so. The Cross Market was erected in 1842 for the sale of agricultural produce upon a site which cost £2,700, and the expenditure was defrayed in part by public subscription and in part by a loan raised upon the security of the rates. About £3,200 was raised by the former means, and, with a sum of £5,000 borrowed for market improvements, the Council added a large building to the old Guildhall, and converted it into the Powis Market, which was so named after the late Earl of Powis, who gave the Guildhall and the site; one room is used as the Corn Exchange, and another as the butter and cheese market. The Powis and Cross Markets were both opened on the 6th of June, 1849. (?) About a month later the Smithfield (the site of which cost upwards of £1,000) and the Horse Market were opened. In 1876 the Powis Hall was enlarged, at a cost of £814, so as to accommodate nearly two thousand persons. The Powis Market is free for the sale of grain, though an annual charge is made for a standing; and one basket of agricultural produce is admitted free to the Cross Market, with a charge of one penny for each extra basket. The Markets and Smithfield tolls generally are extremely moderate, and in this respect Oswestry may, we believe, challenge comparison with any other town in the kingdom. Monthly fairs were begun in September, 1845; fortnightly cattle fairs in 1863; and weekly fairs in October, 1872. The following statistics as to the letting of tolls shows that the enterprising policy of the Town Council has been amply justified by results :—

HORSE MARKET AND SMITHFIELD TOLLS.

1860 (monthly fairs)	..	..	£185
1863 (fortnightly fairs began)	..	..	£200
1870	..	..	£351
1872 (weekly fairs began) ..	..	..	£450
1879	..	..	£785
1880	..	..	£700

POWIS AND CROSS MARKETS.

1860	..	..	£265
1870	..	..	£340
1880	..	..	£525

The falling off this year in the Horse Market and Smithfield tolls is known to have arisen from artificial causes, as well as, in part, from the depressed condition of agriculture.

The accommodation in the Cross Market having become wholly inadequate to the purposes of the market, the Town Council resolved to improve and extend it, and to this end they purchased adjoining property which happened to be in the market, the Grapes Inn and premises in Willow-street, and the Three Tuns Inn and premises in Bailey-street. In order to carry out the present extension it was not found necessary to demolish either of these inns, and the Corporation retain them in their possession, together with a shop in Willow-street, and the premises now known as the "Oswestry Castle" (temperance) public house, in order to facilitate a further enlargement of the market at any future time. We may here mention that the total amount borrowed by the Corporation for market improvements up to November last was £20,530, of which £7,750 has been repaid.

The new portion of the Cross Market is a rectangular building at the north of the existing market, 83ft. 0in. by 77ft. 0in., with an area of 6,391 superficial feet, exclusive of offices, &c., and is entered either from the existing market or from Willow-street, by a cartway through the "Grapes Inn" Yard or from Bailey-street, by a similar cartway through the "Three Tuns" Inn property, all of which belongs to the Corporation.

In the *Salopian Journal* for April 27, 1842, appeared the following paragraph :—

OSWESTRY NEW MARKETS.

One portion of these buildings (that intended for the sale of provisions) is nearly completed, and will be ready for the accommodation of the public in about a fortnight. The principal entrance, now finished, presents to the eye a remarkably chaste and well-executed design; it is also a great ornament to the town, and reflects much credit on the skill and perseverance of those highly-respected gentlemen under whose superintendence it has been erected.

The front (facing the Cross) remains to this day, and it may be compared to one of those wonderfully useless knives boys affect, which contains corkscrew, bradawl, hammer, and so on; for in the market front we have, or had, pump, weighing machine, clock, volunteer notice board, and policeman's box. Useful, no doubt, but not "chaste," certainly.

Mr. Hulbert in his *History and Description of the County of Salop* says, p. 217, "Recovering from every disaster, Oswestry soon after [the civil wars] became one of the principal towns on the Welsh borders, and is now perhaps the most flourishing and prosperous of any in the county. I have been credibly informed that one Mercery and Drapery establishment receives and pays at least £30,000 per annum." To what establishment did the author refer? Then at page 359 it is stated that "grazing land was recently sold at £200 per acre, and building land on the outskirts of the town at the rate of ten times that sum." The book was published in 1837. What, I wonder, was land in Leg-street worth then? As the recent sale of land in the street has shewn us, it is now worth £60,000 an acre!

In 1854 the clock, which was placed over the Cross Market Hall, in Oswestry, was put up chiefly through the exertions of the late Mr. Sabine, sen. On the stone work each side of the face, he caused to be placed the motto, "Nummi, Ponderis, Mensuræ et Temporis, norma sit una." The clock was paid for by subscription, most of the tradesmen and professionals of the town giving sums varying from half-a-crown to ten-shillings. The motto notwithstanding, butter inside has often been 18 oz. to the lb. on one stall, and only 16 oz. on another; and the clock itself has not always agreed with its neighbours on the Church Tower and Powis Hall.

A vault in the Oswestry churchyard was opened last week (to admit the body of the last of a respected family of the district) over which there has long existed a stone, bearing an inscription the late Mr. Shirley Brooks described as being the most depressing bit of churchyard literature he ever met with. Here it is :—

"Never more shall midnight damps
Darken round these mortal lamps
Never more shall noonday glance
Search these mortals' countenance.
Damp the pit and cold the bed
Where the spoils of death are laid,
Stiff the curtains, chill the gloom,
Of man's melancholy tomb."

Q.

Sir James Bacon, in the London Bankruptcy Court, has reversed the decision of the County Court Judge, and decided that the sign of the Oak, painted by David Cox for the Oak Hotel, Bettwsycoed, must go to the trustees of Mrs. Thomas, the former landlady, whose affairs are in liquidation.

The disputed ownership of the signboard painted by David Cox for an hotel at Bettws-y-Coed has more than a merely artistic interest. The County Court judge of Chester, in awarding it to Lady Willoughby d'Eresby, carried the legal presumption in favour of the freeholder to an extreme point. The signboard was painted by Cox for a former innkeeper, and after a time was taken indoors, framed as a picture, and attached by loose fastenings to the wall. How a picture in this condition could be called a landlord's fixture, or a fixture of any kind, is rather difficult to understand; and the County Court judge appears to have fallen back on the presumed but most improbable intention of Cox that the picture should go with the inheritance. Sir James Bacon has decided that the picture belonged to the innkeeper "as much as the coat on his back," and he added that the judicial treatment of fixtures has lately been greatly modified in favour of the tenant. If the decision of the County Court judge had been sustained, this beneficial development of the law would have been arrested, and some of the harshest privileges of "landlordism" revived.—*Pall Mall Gazette.*

General Garfield, the President Elect of the United States, is a Freemason, and is said to have claimed to have Welsh blood in his veins. In this respect, however, he was beaten hollow by General Hancock. The Democratic candidate held quite a levée of Welshmen, who waxed quite enthusiastic on his behalf after he had assured them that his great grandmother on his mother's side was descended from Jenken Jenken, an emigrant from North Wales who settled in Pennsylvania before 1728. General Hancock, however, was of very composite nationality, claiming during the election to be by turns American, Welsh, Scotch, and English. His fourfold nationality, however, did not save him from defeat, and in March next his successful rival will exchange the homely country residence near Mentor for the White House at Washington.

An old handbill, dated June, 1808, of which the following is a copy, throws some light upon the Cheshire wakes in the olden times—

Wanted a person to conduct the performances at BUNBURY WAKE, which will be celebrated on Monday, Tuesday, and Wednesday, the 20th, 21st, and 22nd inst. It is necessary that he sh'd have a complete knowledge of pony and donkey racing; wheelbarrow, bag, cock, and peg racing; archery, singlestick, quoits, cricket, football, cocking, wrestling, bull and badger-baiting, dog-fighting, goose-riding, bumble-puppy, &c.
In addition to the above qualifications, he must also be competent to decide in dipping, mumbling, jawing, grinning, whistling, jumping, jingling, skenning, smoking, scaling, knitting, bobbing, bowling, throwing, dancing, snuff taking, singing, pudding eating, &c. For further particulars apply to Mr. Farral of Bunbury; Mr. Vickers of Spurstow, or Mr. S. Mintcake of Nantwich.—June, 1808.

Bear-baiting, which, rather oddly, is not mentioned in this list of sports, was, it is said, the great attraction of Wake Monday at Bunbury till about fifty years ago.

The new scheme of the Charity Commission in regard to the Ludlow Municipal Charities has been made public. It deals with "Hoseyers' Almshouses," "the preacher of the town of Ludlow," and the "Assistant to the Rector of Ludlow." It is proposed by the new scheme to empower the trustees of the several charities, subject to the order or direction of the Board, to select the future inmates of the almshouses from poor men and women of good repute, who shall have resided within the parliamentary boundary of the borough of Ludlow for not less than ten years next preceding their election, and to utilize the surplus annual income of the several charities, as to two-third parts thereof, in the grant of out pensions of suitable amounts to be assigned to the same class of persons as will in future be eligible for election as inmates of the almshouses, and, as to the remaining one-third part thereof, in the payment of the salary of a stipendiary curate, who shall be appointed by the rector of Ludlow, and shall be licensed by the Bishop of the diocese, and who shall be removable from his office in the same manner as other stipendiary curates.

THE LATE ARCHDEACON WICKHAM. — Old Wykehamists generally, and many friends in this district, will have learned with regret of the decease of the Venerable Robert Wickham, late Archdeacon of St. Asaph, which occurred on Tuesday, Dec. 21, at Gresford Vicarage. The venerable archdeacon was for many years the master of one of the largest and most flourishing private schools at Twyford, near Winchester, where his name was a "household word;" when the foundations of Eton and the other public schools were thrown open to competition, many of his old pupils were among the first so elected. He was educated at Christ Church, Oxford, where he took his Bachelor's degree in 1823-4, obtaining a second class in the School of Literæ Humaniores. Mr. Wickham was a brother-in-law of the late Dr. T. Vowler Short, Bishop of St. Asaph, who conferred on him in 1847 the Vicarage of Gresford, Denbighshire, and appointed him his chaplain and archdeacon of St. Asaph. This latter post he resigned about three years ago. Archdeacon Wickham was the author of "Sermons on the Lord's Prayer," and of one or two small works on "The Sacraments of the Church of England," on "The Offertory," and on "The Rubrics of the Communion Service." The funeral took place on Dec. 28, in Gresford Churchyard. The procession left the house in the following order :—The Revs. R. E. Jones and — Lewis, Rowland Ellis, A. M. Colley, E. B. Smith, J. Dobell, and J. Rowland. The body. Pallbearers, Mr. T. H. Ffoulkes, Mr. Trevor Parkins, Mr. J. Sykes, and Mr. Ed. Roberts. Mourners, the Rev. L. Wickham, Rossett, Miss Wickham, the Rev. Canon Wynne-Edwards, Mrs. Wynne-Edwards, the Rev. T. V. Wickham, Mrs. T. V. Wickham, Mr. Chas. Townshend, Mr. J. Boydell, the Rev. A. Short, the Rev. H. J. Williams, Mr. W. H. Williams, the Rev. J. R. Williams. There was a large concourse of people in the church. The remains of Mr. Wickham were laid by those of his wife, who died in 1875. The curates of Gresford officiated at the grave.

DECEMBER 29, 1880.

OLD OSWESTRY BALLAD (Oct. 20,1880).—At this date JARCO asked for the completion of an old Oswestry Ballad, "The Twelve Tribes," of which he gave three verses. The following contribution towards the whole has been sent by "E. O., Treflach":—

1. Thy vassals O Most Noble Clive,
   Are sworn the Manor foes to drive;
   And while such Tribes are in the train
   Thy chieftains shall not fight in vain.

2. The MORRISITES on Oak or Ash,
   Will soon across the Ceiriog dash;
   And lead the valliant heroes on
   If by the toe the bridge is gone.

NOTES.

SIR WILLIAM MAURICE OF CLENENNEY.
(Dec. 1, 1880.)

Extract from a letter of John Lloyd to Sir Wm. Maurice. From the original at Brogyntyn :—

—heare attendeth this app'ans [appearance], my lord Presydent, Mr Justyce Chamberlen, S'r henry Towneshend, S'r ffraunce' Eure, S'r Vincent Corbett, and S'r ffraunce' lacōn, and S'r Edward ffoxe, but these 3 last named I take it came of purpose to see my lord. S'r James Skudamore of heref' shire decessed late deputie livetenant to my lord pr'sydent his sonne & heire, aged about eighteene yeres of age, hath bin here to visit my lord pr'sydent, Who is by his honor highely esteemed, and made deputie livetenant as his father was, & meaneth w'th all favor to raise him &c

S'r Wm. herbert of the red castle cometh into the cuntrey against the Sessions of Mountgom'y shire, w'ch beginneth vpon Munday next. I doubt not but you have hard how mr Robt vaughan of lloydiarth, now being S'r Robt vaughan, hath m'yed [married] his daughter.

I must assure yov there came about vje weeks past, such a svdden flud in the p'ishes of garthbibio, llangadvan, llanvaire in kerrynion, & p'te of llanothin, being in the Coun' of Mountgom'y, w'th such horrible & Cruell thunderinge, lightning, and tempest, as the like in the memory of man hath neu' [never] bin seene, and the hurt therby donne hath bin grete both to man & beast : for the pr'venc'on of all w'ch like & all other accidents of ill nature happininge, the lord by his infynite m'cies sake give vs all grace to retorne from synne, & to obteyne m'cie & favor at his hands, & to live & dye in his feare—hayle stones also fell in the coun' of heref' abouts that that tyme, the like neu' [never] seene in the memorye of man, w'ch have don grete hurt.

My lord pr'sydent goeth to bewdley the beginninge of the next weeke, and there styeth for a while, & then into his owne cuntrey

S'r henrie Towneshend comends him very hartilie vuto yo'r Worshippe, and to yo'r vertious good lady, and hopeth to meete yo'u at london in mychaelmas t'me [term] next, that he and yo'u m.ye dyne and be mery at the nagge head in Cheape syde, and he charged me to write this to you.

If I had greter newes of moment yo'u shuld be p'taker thereof, but havinge non' I crave p'don for my ou' [over] bouldnes in beinge so tidious ; and w'th my daily prayers to Almighty god to pr'serve yo'u and yo'r vertious good ladye & all yo'rs from the evill will & desires of yo'r adu'saries, and to contynue his love ond favo'r toward' yo'u and yo'rs w'th heath & p'speritie ; Remembringe my true love & service to yo'r wor' sister m'res Anne Wynn Brynkir, I humbly take leave & rest

Yo'r Wor' faithfull solicitor

ludlow, vijo septembris   John lloyd
1619

Addressed.—To the Right Worshipfull, S'r William Maurice, Knighte, d'd these

· (Impression on the seal a stag tupping).

THE FIRST OSWESTRY NEWSPAPER.—The
first that was started was called the *Oswestry Herald*. The first number made its appearance on Tuesday, March 21, 1820, and the following extracts from its original flourish of trumpets will show what it was intended to do. We are told that the Managers intended to—

oppose themselves ,to that class of dangerous characters who under the specious pretext of effecting a Reform of our present unparalleled Constitution, have long been endeavouring to destroy that fair fabric, and to raise upon its ruins, the Temple of Democracy.

So much for its politics, at which we in the present very advanced age can afford to smile as perhaps those who live another sixty years hence will smile at us! The programme then becomes practical, and says—

A faithful record of every public event worthy of notice in this district, will be given in our columns, and a copious and interesting selection of matter, emanating from occurrences in various parts of the Kingdom, without the limits of this neighbourhood, will be weekly presented.

"Mar^{k}et Reports" were to be made much of, and advertisements were, of course, eagerly solicited. And the editor proceeds—

We are aware, that in the precincts of "fair Oswestry," there are a few " choice spirits," of whose competency to infuse a vigour into our columns, " confirmation strong" has already been given. The literary aid of these, we would respectfully intreat ; and humbly trust, our solicitation will not be made in vain.

It is to be presumed that the "confirmation strong" already given would readily be discovered in the first number, but I fail to discover any evidences of the talent of " fair Oswestry."

The preliminary address concludes with the inevitable bounce as to circulation, mention being made of "the extensive circulation we already possess" before even a number was issued ! The paper existed until the end of 1822, a period of nearly three years, and (Mr. Cathrall says in his *History of Oswestry*, published in 1855) " was swamped by excessive taxation."   JARCO.

TOWYN-MERIONETH PARISH RECORDS
(Dec. 15, 1880).—Herewith I offer another instalment of the old Towyn parish registers :—

At a vestry meeting holden on the fifth day of February, 1773, it was then agreed by us, the freeholders and other the parishioners of the parish of Towyn, in the county of Merioneth, that the north and south ayles from the pillars to the side walls in the body of the lower part of the said church and the alley leading from the great door to the opposite wall of the said church shall be flagged with stones at the parish expense, and the said work to be Sott to and done by Rowland Jones mason, at 1s. 6d. per yard. Signed, John Garnon, for William Jones, Esquire ; John Edwards, for William Wynne, Esquire ; William Martin, for Henry Corbet, Esquire ; Serwan Hughes, John Pritchard, David Jones, David Pughe, Owen Williams, John Davies, Hugh Richard.

Wheareas at a vestry summoned on the 19th day of September, 1773, and held on the 24th of the said month, in the parish church of Towyn, it was ordered that part of the south ayle of the said church should be roof'd, and that the same, together with part of the gable end of the north ayle, should be plaistored within.

It is further ordered at a vestry summoned on the 3rd October, and held the 8th day of the same month, by the major part of the inhabitants then present, that a new Communion table, and a new gate leading eastward to the churchyard be immediately made at the expence of the said parish. And whereas the main timber work in the roof of the body of the said church is, to all appearance, in a ruinous and tottering condition, it is hereby further ordered that the said timber-work be secured at as small an expence as possible. Given under our hands, Jer : Griffith, vicar ; L. Edwards, Griffith Owen, William Morton, Edward Daniel, Serwan Hughes, Hugh Pugh, Griffith Evan, Owen Williams, David Jones, William Evan, David Owen. Signed, David × Pross, October 8th, 1773. Received then of J. Griffith the sum of five pounds in part of the legacy bequeathed by Richard Jones, late of Perfeddnant, to the poor of the parissh of Towyn by us Ll. Edwards, Edward Daniel.

To drink at five several vestries, 2s. 6d.; to mending the Church Common Prayer Books, 8s. 6d.; to washing the church linen and mending a surplice, 4s.; to Peter Roberts in part of flagging the Church, £1 14s. 8d.; to ditto for the same work, 3s. 4d.; to Morgan David for carrying earth to put under the flags, 8s.; to Christmas candles, 11d.; paidpfor killing a fox, 5s.; paid for killing a pole catt, 2s. 6d.; paid for killing four ravens, 2s.; paid for bell ropes, 8s. 9d.; to my journey to Machynlleth, for the said ropes, 1s.

[This was the account of David Evans, one of the wardens, in the year 1773.] G.G.

PARLIAMENT OF ENGLAND (Dec. 15, 1880). From the date at which our list of this week commences, The House is styled "The Parliament of the United Kingdom," instead of "Parliament of Great Britain."

COUNTY OF SALOP.

1801 Sir Richard Hill (1); John Kynaston, esq. (1)
1802 Ditto; John Kynaston Powell, esq
1806 John Kynaston Powell, esq.; John Cotes, esq.
1807 Ditto; Ditto.
1812 Ditto; Ditto.
1818 Ditto; Ditto.
1820 Sir John Kynaston Powell (6) Ditto (7)
1826 Sir Rowland Hill, bart.; John Cressett Pelham, esq
1830 Ditto; Ditto.
1831 Ditto; Ditto.

BOROUGH OF SHREWSBURY.

1801 Sir William Pulteney, bart. (2); William Hill, esq (2)
1802 Ditto; Ditto.
1806 William Hill, esq.; Henry Grey Bennett, esq
1807 Ditto; Thomas Jones, esq (3)
1812 Henry Grey Bennett, esq.; Lient.-Gen. Sir Rowland Hill, Knight of the Bath (4)
1818 Ditto; Richard Lyster, esq. (5)
1820 Ditto; Panton Corbett, esq
1826 Panton Corbett, esq.; Robert Aglionby Slaney, esq.
1830 Richard Jenkins, esq.; Ditto.
1831 Robert Aglionby Slaney, esq.; Richard Jenkins, esq

This was the last Parliament before the passing of the Reform Bill. The list from that period to the present time will be found in the Reprint of Bye-gones for April, 1880. ED.

(1) Returned June 6, 1796.
(2) Returned June 8, 1796.
(3) Henry Grey Bennett, esq., elected 23 Dec. 1811, vice Sir Thomas Tyrwhitt Jones, bart. deceased.
(4) Richard Lyster, esq., elected 27 May, 1814, vice Sir Rowland Hill, called to the Upper House as Baron Hill.
(5) John Mytton, esq., elected 25 May 1819, vice Richard Lyster, esq., deceased.
(6) John Cressett Pelham, esq., of Cound Hall, and of the Castle at Shrewsbury, elected 2 Dec. 1822, vice Sir John Kynaston Powell, bart., deceased.
(7) Rowland Hill, esq., of Hawkstone, elected 18 Oct. 1821, vice John Cotes, Esq., deceased.

QUERIES.

LORIN.—In Davies Leathart's *Origin and Progress of the Gwyneddigion Society* (1831), p. 61, mention is made of "Jones, the author of *Lorin.*" Who was this Jones, and what is the subject and date of *Lorin*? UST.

WALTER THE STEWARD.—In Aug. 1853 a letter appeared in the *Oswestry Advertizer*, in the course of which the writer said, "It may interest many of your readers, all of them in fact who are interested in matters of local interest, to hear that in the transitive state through which the Castle Hill is gradually passing, from neglect to culture, that a coin was found there a few weeks ago which strongly corroborates the statement in *Oswald's Well*, a statement made on the authority of Chambers and Pinkerton, though questioned by some Scottish authors who are naturally jealous of parting with such an honour as that claimed for Oswestry and its venerable Castle Hill, from whence Walter [Fitz] allan sailed out with his military retainers. The coin is a David the First, Rex Scottorum, into whose service Walter is said to have entered. True, it does not amount to proof of the Oswestry claim, but it is a strong link in the chain of evidence. At all events it proves that centuries ago there was a connection between Scotland and the spot where the great and good King Oswald fell. Those who question the claim may say it proves nothing: those who maintain it, that it goes to strengthen if not confirm the statement." On the strength of this "find," and the previous statements in *Chambers's Journal*, &c., Mr. Sabine caused a stone to be placed on the Castle Bank, inscribed "A.D. 1538: Walter son of Allan the progenitor of the Royal House of Stuart, left this his ancestral Castle, in the reign of Stephen, King of England, and of David I., King of Scots." What has become of the stone?
OLD OSWESTRIAN.

REPLIES.

CEUBREN YR ELLYLL (Dec. 8, 1880.)—The Etching of this tree by Mr. George Cuitt of Chester, alluded to by TAFFY, was issued in a series of six views in Wales by that artist, and sold in a loose wrapper for £1 5s. I am not aware that it was ever published separately, or issued in any work in a reduced form. Cuitt's etchings are all scarce now. W.P. Wrexham.

LLOYD'S HISTORY OF SHROPSHIRE (Dec. 8, 1880).—The Halston MSS. were given by the Hon. Thomas Kenyon, the executor, to Lord Hill when the place was sold. L.

DICK OF ABERDARON (Dec. 8, 1880).—Mr. H. R. Hughes of Kinmel, writing to the *Cheshire Sheaf* of Dec. 8, 1880, says, "The [qv. 'an'] original portrait of the above, painted in oils by Roose, is at Kinmel." There is no mention, either in the *Sheaf* or in *Bye-gones*, of any engraving of this. N.W.S.

PEDIGREES OF BORDER FAMILIES (Dec. 15, 1880).—There are more than one error of description in this list, such as "The Lloyds of Llwynymaen (seat of C. H. Wynn, Esq.)" Mr. Wynn's seat is "Coed-y-Maen, Meivod." "The Lloyds of Estyn yn swydd y Drewen (id est. Hope, in the county of Whittington or Whitchurch?)" This should be "Lloyds of Aston, in the lordship or manor of Whittington." William Maurice the Antiquary lived at Cevnybraich, in the township of Ystum Allan, near Llansilin. Cevnybraich in the township of Rhiwlas, opposite to Tregeiriog, is quite a different farm. R. WILLIAMS.

BRYNBEDWIN (Dec. 15, 1880).—The exact English equivalent of Brynbedwin (more correctly Bryn Bedwin) would be "Birchen Hill," bedwin being formed from bedw = birch, just as birchen is a derivative of birch. But Bedwin in this case *may* be a proper name (compare Bedwini Esgob), and if so, Bryn Bedwin would signify Bedwin's Hill, with which we may compare such placenames as Bryn Llywelyn, Bryn Gronwy, Bryn Sion, Bryn Dewi, Bryn Meirig, &c. The other queries in DOLFOR's communication I must leave to others acquainted with the locality to answer. GWYDDAN.

CURRENT NOTES.

We have been favoured with the sight of some sketches by a townsman—Mr. W. Charles Evans, son of Mr. John Evans of Upper Brook-street—of objects of local interest. Mr. W. C. Evans, who has recently commenced business as an architect in the Old Palace Yard, Westminster, does the illustrations for the *Building World*; and one of the most recent of his productions is a beautifully executed representation of Mr. Fletcher Rogers's house, Haye Lea, Oswestry. We should like to see some of Mr. Evans's sketches illustrating the Oswestry papers in the *Transactions* of the Shropshire Archæological Society, and would suggest to the editors the new Reredos in the Old Church as a subject to begin with.

The Rev. T. Williams, Rector of St. George, St. Asaph, died on Monday, Dec. 27, at an advanced age. He was a well-known and much-respected clergyman in the diocese. Mr. Williams was rector of the same parish for twenty-five years, and was recently appointed by the Bishop as Rural Dean of Denbigh Deanery. He was a musician and musical composer of considerable ability. The deceased clergyman was a magistrate of the county of Flint, and regularly attended the meetings of the St. Asaph Board of Guardians.

"M. M." writes from Llanfairfechan, North Wales, December 29 :—"Noticing in *The Times* of the 27th inst. a paragraph as to flowers in bloom at Ventnor, you may perhaps think it worth while to publish the subjoined list of flowers and shrubs which were found in good bloom in a small garden here on Christmas morning. I send it with no view of making comparisons, but merely as information. The garden is some 200ft. above the level of the sea, and about half a mile from the shore :—Roses, scarlet, white, and pink geraniums, violets, veronicas (three varities), escallonia, hydrangea, single and double stocks, wallflower, chrysanthemums, pansy, mignonette, Christmas rose, French Marguerite, white alysam, Daphne, polyanthus, yellow jessamine, fuchsias, campanula, heath, lavender, buttercups, daises, laurustinus, and arbutus."

Some days ago the Rev. T. K. Davies, J.P., of Croft Castle, about six miles from Ludlow, was served with a notice from a man named Timothy Payne, of Yatton, and other parishioners, to the effect that on the 27th of December they should proceed to Yatton-hill Wood, and take possession of the wood by cutting part of it as their legal right. Accordingly, at twelve o'clock on the 27th, about forty persons assembled at Yatton Wood, near Croft Castle ; they entered the wood, and some of them cut part of it and carried it away. There was a detachment of the district police in attendance, but no disturbance took place, the parties confining themselves to carrying out the intentions of the notice. There is a tradition that the wood is allowed to grow twenty-one years, and is then to be cut down and sold. It is asserted that parishioners have the right of grazing their cattle in the wood for sixteen years, and that the Rev. T. K. Davies then is entitled to close it the next five years, previously to cutting it down. The matter will shortly come before the law courts.

The poem of "The Northern Cobbler" in Mr. Tennyson's new volume is taken from a story, whether fact or fiction nobody knows, published in the *Chester Gazette* forty years ago, and revived in the Rev. E. Paxton Hood's "World of Religious and Moral Anecdote." The cobbler's name was Henry Parker, and the bottle scene is thus described —" 'Betsy,' said he to his wife, as he rose from his work, 'give me that bottle.' These words pierced her very heart, and seemed to sound the knell of all her cherished hopes ;

but she could not disobey him. He went out with his bottle, had it filled at the alehouse, and, on returning home, placed it in the window immediately before him. 'Now,' said he, 'I can face an enemy.' With a resolution fixed upon overcoming his pernicious habits, he went earnestly to work, always having the bottle before him, but never again touched it. Again he began to thrive, and in a few years he was once more the owner of his former delightful residence ; his children grew up, and are now respectable members of society. Old age came upon Henry, and he always kept the bottle in the window where he had first put it ; and often, when his head was silvered over with age, he would refer to his bottle, and thank God that he had been able to overcome the vice of drunkenness. He never permitted it to be removed from that window while he lived, and there it remained until after he had been consigned to his narrow home."

Mr. W. C. Owen of Burton-on-Trent, writing in the *Daily News*, says—Last summer the Burton Natural History and Archæological Society had an excursion to Wirksworth, and some very pleasant discoveries were made relating to "Adam Bede" and its gifted authoress. In Coldwell-street there lives a Mrs. Walker, cousin of "George Eliot," and daughter of the veritable Dinah Morris. Mrs. Walker has in her possession an oil portrait of Dinah, also a rich brown satin Quaker bonnet worn by Dinah in her later life. In the Wesleyan Chapel at Wirksworth, there is a tablet with the following incription :—"Erected by numerous friends to the memory of Elizabeth Evans, known to the world as Dinah Bede, who during many years proclaimed alike in the open air, the sanctuary, and from house to house the love of Christ. She died in the Lord, November 9, 1849, aged 74 years. And of Samuel Evans, her husband, who was also a faithful local preacher and class-leader in the Methodist Society. He finished his earthly course December 8, 1858, aged 81 years." It will be seen, therefore, that the principal characters in "Adam Bede" were no mere creations, but living men and women, though disguised and somewhat transposed, as proved by the tablet. Mrs. Walker stated that the tragic story of Hetty Sorrel was suggested by that of a Mary Boce, who for poisoning her child was executed on Nottingham Forest, and who had previously been visited in prison by Dinah, that good woman also accompanying her in a cart to the scaffold as in the case of Hetty in the tale.

A LLANYMYNECH SUPERSTITION.—Some years ago there was a general belief among the inhabitants of Llanymynech that a field called the "Pigeon House Field," a part of the glebe attached to the Rectory, was bewitched. It was always supposed that at the time of hay harvest a shower of rain would fall when the mowing of this field had been commenced. So general was the belief in this not supernatural occurrence that many persons were accustomed to put off the commencement of cutting their hay until after the crop on this field had been cut.—*Salopian Shreds and Patches.*

THE OSWESTRY MARKETS.
(Dec. 22, 1880.)

The question of market accommodation was first seriously entertained in Oswestry early in the year 1838. Mr. Peploe Cartwright introduced the subject at more than one meeting of the Town Council, and so far had the idea taken hold of the public that in April of that year, at a Corporation dinner, presided over by the Mayor, C. T. Jones, Esq., "the best affair of the meeting was the offer of a subscription of upwards of £600 towards erecting a market hall." Among the guests at this dinner were

"W. Ormsby Gore, Esq., M.P., Messrs. Parker, Sweeney; Lloyd, Aston; Aubrey, Broomhall; Lovett, Belmont; Lovett, Fernhill; &c., &c." Mr. F. Campbell was vice-chairman.

Early in May, 1838, the papers were able to announce that "the subscription set on foot some time ago, for the purpose of raising a fund to be applied to the purchase of a site whereon to erect a Market Hall and Public Rooms in a central part of the town of Oswestry" was progressing well, and one (the *Salopian Journal*) of May 23, 1838, gave circulation to a rumour that Viscount Clive had, in the most liberal manner, "made an offer to the Council of the present Town Hall, and other old buildings in the rear." The "Viscount Clive" here referred to was the father of the present Earl of Powis. His father dying the next year, he became Earl of Powis in May, 1839.

On the 24th of May, 1838, the Oswestry Town Council met to talk over the question of Market Arrangements. In the absence of the Mayor, Mr. Cartwright presided. This gentleman had at a former meeting submitted certain resolutions to the Council, and on the basis of these, he said, he should now offer certain propositions for their consideration. Mr. Cartwright proceeded to explain very fully his scheme, and from it we gather the following leading propositions:—

First as to the Cattle Market. According to the previous resolution of the Council he proposed that they should enclose the ground at the back of the Town Hall, and purchase about an acre and a half of the Castle Field to add to it, therewith to form a square in which all the Cattle Fairs may be held, instead of being, as they then were, a dangerous obstruction to the central thoroughfares of the town. It should be observed in passing that the "Town Hall" alluded to was the building the present generation knows as the Powis Hall. The Guildhall of the present day was formerly used for school purposes. Mr. Cartwright, in support of his scheme, suggested that roads should be made from it, one to Beatrice-street, and the other to the top of Lower Willow-street; a plan, he thought, more than usually feasible then as the property was for sale.

His next point was a Corn Market. The Council had, at a previous meeting, agreed to send a respectful application to Lord Clive to dispose of the Town Hall. Knowing, as they did, the generosity of his lordship, as evinced on previous occasions, it was evident the Council felt his lordship would comply with their request, and on liberal terms. Mr. Cartwright alluded to some former acts of liberality on the part of his lordship, including "the more recent instance of the purchase of the tolls." Mr. Cartwright's plan was to convert "the ground floor, with a colonnade in front, into a Corn Exchange, suitable to all the wants of the farmers."

Lastly the attention of the meeting was called to the necessity of a Mart for Butter, Poultry, Butcher's Meat, &c. The stumbling-block in their way was the high value of property in The Cross, where the markets had hitherto been held. Mr. Cartwright said one or two sites had been thought of. "The first was to take the range of buildings between Mr. Dorset Owen's Wine-Vaults and the Cross Keys, and form a new street from the Cross into Salop-road, providing market accommodation on either side." Another site was "the Three Tuns property, on which a price could be had, and which being a locality central to the three main central streets of the town, was admirably adapted to their purpose." Mr. Cartwright proposed, if this site was adopted, to "have a main opening into the centre of the Cross (from which it was not distant thirty yards) and one into Willow-street, as well as retaining the one which now existed into Bailey-street." Mr.

Cartwright ended by moving that the sites should be surveyed and reported upon.

Mr. Penson in seconding Mr. Cartwright's proposition, strongly urged the demolition of some old houses in the Clawdd-du, not only for the purposes of a market, but "as a great public improvement in the clearance of a small confined street that was now a nuisance." The resolution was carried unanimously.

In speaking of the services rendered to Oswestry by the family of Powis, Mr. Cartwright mentions as one of the more recent the settlement of the Market Tolls. The precise date of this he does not give, but we have other reports that show these dues were relinquished a few years earlier than the date of Mr. Cartwright's speech. As early as 1814, when Price printed his *History of Oswestry*, it was in contemplation to get rid of these tolls, and "a case was prepared for a Committee appointed to manage the affair." They do not seem, however, to have "managed" it very soon, for in 1820 there were threatenings of actions, if not actions themselves, against non-payers of Toll. In 1836 a writer in the *Salopian Journal* speaks of "the praiseworthy exertions of a highly-talented gentleman" as instrumental in removing the "obnoxious tax," the good work being effected by "Voluntary subscriptions of the town and neighbourhood." During the same year as the letter quoted was written, Mr. Parker of Sweeney's song, given in *Bye-gones* a week or two back, was sung, and it points to the settlement of the Toll question as being recent, and that of a New Market Hall as a project talked of.

The "Viscount Clive" referred to by Mr. Cartwright, was the father of the present Earl of Powis, and his father dying as we have stated in 1839 (the year after the meeting was held) he became Earl, and, in Nov. of the same year, came to Oswestry on the occasion of the celebration of the coming-of-age of his son—then Viscount Clive, now Earl of Powis. It was on that day (Nov. 11, 1839) the "Earl and his son presented us with the old hall on the Bailey Head." Two years later, viz., Sep. 1841, the late Earl of Powis again visited Oswestry; and it was to commemorate the coming-of-age of Sir Watkin Williams Wynn, and to lay the foundation-stone of the Cross Market.

It will be needless to go through all the various discussions that led to the adoption of the site in question. Doubtless there were obstacles in the way, or such an inconvenient wind-trap as the Cross Market was when first opened would never have been erected. The chief stone was laid amidst loud popular applause, none the less hearty because the public had not been rated to build it. The works rapidly proceeded, and by April, 1842, it was considered on the eve of completion. That is to say, the first portion of it, the area opening to The Cross. We are told in the *Salopian Journal* for May 18, 1842, that the building was then "ready for the purposes intended," and on June 15, 1842, the same paper states that at a meeting of the Market Committee a further contract was let to Messrs. G. and W. Morris "for an extension into Willow-street, with approaches and entrance from the latter; the whole to be completed within three months."

So much for the Cross Market, which formed the first portion of the grand scheme for Market accommodation at Oswestry. Another week we may, perhaps, give some particulars connected with the Corn, Cheese, and Cattle Markets, which were not accomplished until eight years later. Speaking under correction we assume that there was no public dedication of any of these market places, but that all were quietly taken possession of on market days.

BYE-GONES FOR 1881.

NOTES, QUERIES, and REPLIES, on subjects interesting to Wales and the Borders, must be addressed to "ASKEW ROBERTS, Croeswylan, Oswestry." Real names and addresses must be given, in confidence, and MSS. must be written legibly, on one side of the paper only.

JANUARY 5, 1881.

NOTES.

FULK FITZ WARREN OF WHITTINGTON.

The following interesting document is from "a true translation" made by "John Caley, Grays Inn, 12 March, 1817." Why it was made, or for whom, I cannot say.

JARCO.

Among the Records of ye Court of Chancery in the Tower of London, that is to say, the *Inquisitiones post Mortem* of the 23 Edw. 3d. Part 1, No. 39, is thus contained. Ao. 1349.

EDWARD by the Grace of God, King of England and France and Lord of Ireland, To his beloved John de Swinnerton his Escheator in ye county of Salop Greeting *Inasmuch* as Fulk fitz Warren held of Us in Capite on the day of his death as we are informed, We command you that without fail you take into our hands all the lands & tenements of which the said Fulk was seised in his demesne of as of fee of your Baliwick on the day on which he died and cause the same to be safely kept untill We shall thereupon otherwise command And by the oath of good & lawfull men of your Baliwick by whom the truth of the matter may be better known you diligently enquire how much lands the said Fulk held of Us in Capite as well as in demesne as in Service in your Baliwick on the day on which he died and how much of others and by what Service & how much those lands are worth yearly in all issues, and on what day the said Fulk died and who is next heir and of what age *And* the Inquisition thereupon distinctly and openly made, without Delay you send to Us under your Seal and the Seals of those by whom the same shall be made and this Writ. *Witness* myself at Westminster the 20th day of August in the year of our reign of England the 23. and of our Reign of France the tenth.

The Marches of Wales.

AN INQUISITION taken before John Swynnerton Escheator of the Lord the King in the County of Salop and the marches of Wales adjacent at Shrewsbury on Friday next after the Feast of S't. Michael in the 23d year of the reign of King Edward the third after the Conquest that is to say according to the tenor of the Writ of the said Lord the King to this Inquisition served, by the oath of Madoc ap Zerward David ap Kenewrick, Howell ap David, Madoc ap David ap Howell Payn ap Ithel Ievan ap Ada, Ierwerth

Vauchan, Ievan ap Ithell Ievan Meiller, Madoc ap David Payn ap Ierworth & Howell ap Heillez. *Who* say upon their Oath that Fulk fitz Warryn held in his demesne as of Fee on the day on which he died the Manor of Whytynton with the Appurt's in the Marches of Wales aforesaid of the Lord the King in Capite by service of one Knights fee, In which Manor there is a certain Castle which is worth nothing yearly beyond Reprises, because it wants every year for repairing of the Houses and Walls there 40s. And there is a certain Garden which is worth yearly 6d. And there is a certain Dovehouse which is worth yearly 12d. And there is there two Water Mills which used to be worth yearly 40s. and now are worth only 20s. by reason of the Pestilence, because the tenan's are dead in the present pestilence And there is two Ponds, the fishery thereof is worth yearly 2s. And there is a certain Wood, the underwood whereof is worth yearly 2s. and the Past're thereof is common. And there is a certain Park in which there is no underwood and the Pasture thereof is worth nothing yearly beyond the sustentation of the wild beast there. And there is a certain Chase which the Jurors know not how to extend because there is no wood and Pasture there but in Common. And there is there two Carucates of land which used to be worth yearly 20s. and not more because the land could not be ploughed by reason of the Stones and now is worth only 10s. because no one would lease the same. And there is fiue Acr.s of Meadow which are worth yearly 20s. and they were mowed and taken away In the life of the said Fulk, there used to be rent of Assise of free (tenants) there 60s. and it was paid at the terms at the Birth of our Lord and the nativity of S't John the Baptist in equal Portions, and now there is only 20s. at the terms aforesaid and this by reason of the Pestilence The Pleas and Perquisites of Courts there used to be worth nearly 40s. and now they are worth only 13s. 4d. Also they say that the said Fulk died on Wednesday before the feast of the Nativity of the blessed Virgin Mary last past. And they say that Fulk son of y'e said Fulk is the next Heir of the said Fulk and was of the age of 9 years at the feast of S't James the Apostle last Past. *In Testimony* whereof the said Jurors to this Inquisition have put their Hands and Seals.

AN OSWESTRY WILL, 1559.—(30 Chaynay). *Gwen verch Meredeth* of Oswestrye "unto my sonne John the house wherein he dwillith, . . . and the greate house wt the garden wherein I dwellid wt the horse myll and the bygger barne wt theire appurtenaunces so that he do paie or cause to be payde unto Katheryne verch John his base doughter the somme of five poundes . . . out of the aforesaide Horse Myll at his furst entrye with the fourthe part of the profettes growing upon Maefthyn Boola or that shall hereaftre growe thereupon untill yt be

Redemed and then to have twentie nobles of the money
. . . . . unto my sonne Thomas the howse wherein
Richarde the hewster dwellith . . . . with the
fourthe part of the proufett growing upon Maeffethy boola
. . . . unto my sonne Richarde the howse wherein
he dwellith . . . . and the lasse barne . . . .
with the fourthe parte of the proufettes growing . . .
upon Maesfithy boola . . . . unto my sonne Roger
the house wherein lewes Bocher dwellith . . . . my
sonne John . . . Alice my doughter and David ap ll'enn
my sonne in lawe . . . . . I do make . . . .
executours of this my Will and testament my sonne John
Thomas and Richard and David ap ll'enn my sonne in law .
. . Aud oversears . . Nicholas Pursell and Richarde
lloydde ap Edwarde gent. Witnesses present Mr. Rolande
Buckley Hughe Buckley Thomas Elys and others." S.

[In a list of Burgesses of Oswestry dated 1553-4 (in *Bye-gones*
Mar. 20, 1877) there is the name of "nycholas pursell of Salop."
And in the Muringer's Account for 1560 (see Mr. Stanley
Leighton's account of the Oswestry Corporation Records, in
Transactions of Shropshire Archæological Society) there is mention made of two of the name of "Lewys bucher," one of whom
fled during the Plague that visited the town in 1559, and the
other who fell a victim to the epidemic. Was the property in
question that we now know as "Maes y bwlyn"?—ED.]

QUERIES.

THE ELLESMERE GHOST.—Who was Miss
Sadler of Shrewsbury, afterwards Mrs. Worth,
who wrote a poem on the "Ellesmere Ghost" which was
published in the first number of Hulbert's *Salopian
Magazine*, issued in Jan. 1815? She is there described as
"the late Mrs. Worth." I have been told that after her
death her husband published a volume of her poetry, with
memoir. Who and what was he, and where was the book
printed?   TELL.

EVELINA'S SARCOPHAGUS.—Where shall I
find an account of the discovery of a rude Sarcophagus at
the foot of Snowdon, with "Evelina" carved on it? A
poem on the subject was published in 1774, written by J.
H. Wynne, and dedicated to Sir Thomas Wynn, Bart.,
Lord Lieutenant of the County of Carnarvon. Who was
the author? Was he in any way connected with the
Wynn families?   R. ROSSE TEWK, B.A.

WREXHAM AMICABLE SOCIETY.—The mem-
bers of this society assembed at the Wynnstay Arms Hotel,
Wrexham, on Aug. 1, 1820, and marched to Church, for
service, after which they returned to the hotel for dinner.
What was the object of this society? The report I quote
states that "this truly respectable society has been established upwards of sixty years, and on its list of members may be found the names of the most respectable inhabitants of the town and neighbourhood of Wrexham."
                                              WREXHAMITE.

AN OSWESTRY LOTTERY.—In July, 1833,
Mr. Robert Roberts, gas proprietor of Oswestry, advertised "An Ornamental Conservatory" to be disposed of
"in Five Prizes, by way of Ticket at one Guinea each:
800 subscribers." The draw was to take place on Sep. 30,
and tickets were to be had at booksellers'shops in Oswestry,
Shrewsbury, Chester, Ellesmere, Welshpool, Wrexham,
and Liverpool. Mr. Roberts stated that his conservatory
had cost him £1,500. Did the raffle ever come off, and
what was the fate of the Greenhouse? Mr. Roberts was
the man who introduced gas into Oswestry some 14 years
earlier. (See *Bye-gones*, Nov. 17, 1880). He was in some
respects a singular character, and for many years his portrait hung over the fireplace in the smoking-room of
Osburn's Hotel.   JARCO.

EARL OF CATHERLOUGH (Dec. 8, 1880).—
Mr. Robert Knight was of Barrells, Co. Worcester. He
married a daughter of Lord St. John. She was sister to
the first Lord Bolingbroke. (? There was no issue). There
had been a Lord Catherlough before. The seventh Earl
of Westmorland received the title for services under Marlborough.   L.

WHITSHED KEENE (Dec. 8, 1880).—Whilst
thanking your correspondent, D. P. OWEN, for his reply,
he will perhaps permit me to say that what I wanted to
know was who was Whitshed Keene, and how he was
connected with the county. If he or any contributor to
Bye-gones can answer he will oblige.   QUERIST.

JANUARY 12, 1881.

NOTES.

PORTRAIT OF SIR ROWLAND HILL.—In
1839 Messrs. Eddowes of Shrewsbury, and Ackermann of
London, published a portrait of Sir Rowland Hill, Bart.,
M.P. forth North Shropshire. The work was described
as "lithographed in fine style." The price was 10s. plain,
15s. coloured. It was taken "from a picture by
Richmond."   SCROBBES BYRIG.

TOWYN-MERIONETH PARISH RECORDS
(Dec. 29, 1880).—Your readers will have noticed
that no regularity is preserved in the dates of the
entries. I give them in the same order as I find them in
the newspaper I copy:—
    At a vestry summoned on the 7th and held on the 12th
day of April, 1776, in the Parish Church of Towyn, it was
agreed upon by a majority of the parishioners then and
there present that the bell loft in the steeple of the said
church shall be raised up by means of screws and wedges,
or otherwise, to a sufficient height above the clock that is
already subscribed for by the gentlemen freeholders and
others in the said parish and the neighbourhood thereof,
and that the loft where the clock is to be set up be made
convenient and fit for the said purpose, together with the
frame, case, and weights, at the expense of the parish.
    At a vestry meeting summoned on the 20th July, 1777,
to be held on the 26th and adjourned to the 27th day of
the same month, it is agreed upon by a majority of the
inhabitants present that a rate not exceeding one shilling
in the pound be assessed and levy'd of and from the
several occupiers of lands in this parish towards the relief
of the poor for the year eading at Easter, 1778. And it
is further ordered that no person whatsoever shall have
the benefit of the said rate but such as shall wear badges
constantly on their outer garments. Witness our hands,
Jer. Griffith, vicar; Wm. Hughes, Owen Rees, Hugh
Richard. Humphrey Daniel, John Pugh, John Lewis,
David Pugh, Hugh Owen, the mark of Thomas + Owen.
    At a vestry suumoned November 23rd, 1777, and held
on the 28th in the parish church of Towyn, the inhabitants
then and there present have agreed and assented that a
rate of four pence in the pound be assessed and raised by
the Churchwardens towards defraying the expenses of an
appeal for settling the county rates of Tow : P'sh : equally
with the rest of the county of Merioneth. And at the
same time it is agreed that the Church rate shall be two
pence in the pound for this present year.
    Whereas at a vestry held in the parish church of Towyn
on the 27th day of July, 1777, it was agreed that the
poor's rate should not exceed one shilling per (per mark)
pound; and whereas the said rate is found to be, or at
least pretended to be, insufficient for the purposes in-

tended, either thro : the neglect or partiality of the overseers is not insisting upon the poors wearing of badges :
it is the 20th day of March, 1778, agreed upon by majority
of the inhabitants present that an additional rate not exceeding four pence in the pound be assessed, levied, and
collected of and from the several occupiers of lands and
tithes within the said parish of Towyn.　Given under our
hands this 20th day of March, 1778.　William Morton,
the mark+of Evan Edwar : Churchwardens ; Richard
Edwards, the+of Hugh Owen, the mark I. H. of John
Humphrey.　　　　　　　　　　　　　　　　　　G.G.

THE OLD WELSH ALMANACKS (Dec. 22,
1880).—In the inner sheets of the one for 1805 are the following verses :—

　　1.　Nid yw yr *Athrawon*, ond brau lestri priddion,
　　　　A lenwir yn llawnion, a digon i'w Dydd ;　2 Cor. 4., 7
　　　　Os cyrant a geiriau, fe gyll eu *Trysorau*,
　　　　Heb adwyn mewn *goleu* mo'u gilydd.　　　Cor. 9., 27

　　2.　Bu *Luther* a *Chalfin*, yn lân yr un llinyn ;
　　　　Y yn cid borthi'r weren yn un fin am fod,
　　　　Ond Meistress *Partiaeth*, mewn bwrlad a bariaeth,
　　　　A wnaeth eu gwahaniaeth yn hynod !

　　3.　Mae hon yn ymochu, yn *Lloegr* a *Chymru*
　　　　Gan daeredd ymdeyru, i *fraenu* pob *Bro;*
　　　　Gobeithio nad *Boni*, yrr luoedd i'n cosbi,
　　　　O herwydd drygioni'n drwg *uno*.　　　　　Calvin

　　4.　Ffordd gul yr Ysgrythyr, aroglaidd sy' eglur　　Armin
　　　　Ffynnonau llawn cysur, i *Frodyr* bob pryd :
　　　　Maent byth i'w *pregethu* 'n gariadus a'i *credu*,
　　　　Heb *gnaud air* i'w helpu mewn *Pwlpud*.

　　　Duw cynnel ein Brenin i faeddu'r hyll *Fyddin*,
　　　Sydd megis *cun drycin*, yn dychryn bob Dydd ;
　　　A boed ei *swyddogion*, yn dirion *Frodorion*
　　　A'r *Milwyr* un galon a'u *gilydd*.

In the one for 1806 are these :—

　　　Duw cynnil *George* ein Brenin, yn ddiffin yn ei daith,
　　　Ynghyd a'i hoil *Swyddogion* sudd unien yn ei waith ;
　　　Bydd gyda ei *weision Rhyfel*, ymafael yn eu llaw
　　　I ymlid y *gelynion* sy' hyllion drawsion draw.*

　　1.　Mae pedwar ugain mlynedd, a saith gyfanedd glir,
　　　　Er pan ddaeth goleu rhyfedd, i barthau'r gogledd dir ;
　　　　Rhai gwael oedd yn Pregethu a Duw'n cynnyddu'r Ddawn,
　　　　Rhoi goleu'r boreu beunydd, a,newydd beth brydnawn.

　　2.　'Doedd neb yn rhoddi galwad, ond cariad yn ei rym ;
　　　　Oedd yn eu cadw'n gefnog ym mhlith rhai llidiog llym :
　　　　Pan welant rai yn edrych mewn tre' neu bentre' plwy ;
　　　　Cyhoeddant Air y Deyrnas yn addas iddynt hwy.

　　3.　Ar ol diweddu'r Bregeth, Rhai oedd a hiraeth dwys,
　　　　Am ysgafnhâu meddyliau, am bethau mawr eu pwys ;
　　　　Wrth ail ymddiddan weithiau, fe chwythai Deheu wynt ;
　　　　Cânt *fyned adre'n foddlon*, fel y Disgyblion gynt.

　　4.　Bywiogodd rhai Eglwyswyr, ac Ymneillduwyr maith,
　　　　Rhoddasant eu Deheulaw; yn hylaw at y gwaith,
　　　　'Doedd dim yn maddeu pechod, yr amser hynod hyn,
　　　　Ond Crist y gwir Fessiah, fu mhen Calfaria fryn.

　　5.　Oes neb yn coflo darllain, yn Llyrfau Prydain fawr,
　　　　Am amser cyd mor lonydd, i grefydd ac yn awr ;
　　　　Camrau Duw sy' ysgafnau, a'i Ddyrnau megis Plwm,
　　　　Pan ddelo yn ei ddialedd, fe deru'n chwerwedd drwm.

　　6.　Pa le yn awr mae cariad, fu'n wastad yn ei nyth ;
　　　　Er iddo oeri'n'arw, ni ddichon farw fyth :
　　　　Er maint y llid a rhagfarn, fy' gadarn ar bob llaw :
　　　　Bydd ef yn bur a hyfryd, yn nheulu'r bywyd draw.

In the one for 1807 there is but this one verse :—

　　　Myn'd heibio mae'n Blynyddoedd, 'run modd a'n misoedd maith
　　　Cyd nesu mae Wythnosau, a Dyddiau pen ein taith ;
　　　Mae'r awr ddiwedda'n dyfod ; gwyn fyd y parod rai,
　　　Sy' au pwys ar Iesu brydferth, heb geisio Aberth llai.

　　　　.* This verse had appeared in 1804 also.
　　　　　　　　　　　　　　　　　　　　　　　　　E.G.S.

QUERIES.

A JUDGE'S ESCORT AT WELSHPOOL.—I read
in the papers of July 1839, that on the 13th of that month
Mr. Justice Pattison was escorted into Welshpool for the
assizes, not only by the High Sheriff and his retainers, but
by the Mayor and Corporation.　When they reached the
Judge's lodgings the Mayor congratulated his lordship on
his safe arrival into Wales.　Was all this a usual . ceremony in past days, or was it exceptional? I note that
the town was much excited on the occasion, and thronged
with people interested in the trials of the Chartist rioters,
which were to come off at the assizes.　　　　　　TELL.

BANGOR ISYCOED, FLINTSHIRE.—Can any-
one give me a more complete history of this ancient and
very interesting little place, than the following, which is
an extract from Mr. W. Garratt-Jones's *Geography and
History of North Wales?*—Bangor stands in an open fertile
valley, and is famed for the monastery it contained, but
of which there are now no traces.　It was founded about
the year 180, and contained in the year 596 no less than
2,400 monks.　In 613 the King of Northumberland having
besieged Chester, fell upon 1,200 and slew them ; the rest
escaped to Bardsey Island.　Sir Walter Scott has written
a beautiful poem on the solemn event.　　　　RALPH.

OSWESTRY GRAMMAR SCHOOL (Oct. 27,
1880).—In the third volume of the *Transactions* of the
Shropshire Archæological Society, p. 21, Mr. Stanley
Leighton, M.A., refers to the postponement of the hearing
of a case before the Court of the Marches at Bewdley
(38 Eliz.), in which "Henry Jonse, M.A.," was plaintiff,
and "Edward Hanmer" defendant.　The matter was
adjourned because the defendant was "high collector of
H.M. subsidies, and having to repair to London."　Who
was "Mr. Jonse?"　In an attested copy of an original
document before me, I find that this case related to some
of the Grammar School property, and a Commission was
issued for the hearing to take place in the Oswestry
Parish Church.　The document will appear in a paper on
the "Grammar School" which will be published in the first
part of Vol. 5 of the *Trans.* of the S.A.S., to be issued
next October.　In the MS. referred to the plaintiff's name
is spelt "Jones," but the familiar name is often to be met
with "spelt as spoken" by the common people on the
borders !　In an Old Chapel document of a century and a
half ago, there is the name "Nathaniel Jonse" attached.
　　　　　　　　　　　　　　　　　　　　　　　　JARCO.

　　On page 143, Part I., Vol. 4, of the *Transactions* of
the Shropshire Archæological Society, Mr. ADNITT extracts from Leland's *Itinerary* the reference to "Davy
Holbeche" and the "Fre Schole" he founded.　In this
the following passage occurs :—"Sum say that this *David*
made David Yn yn *London*."　What does this mean ?
　　　　　　　　　　　　　　　　　　　　YOUNG OSWESTRY.

REPLIES.

MONTGOMERYSHIRE YEOMANRY (Nov. 3,
1880).—At this date Ex-VOLUNTEER quoted the *Mont :
Coll :* for the fact that the Moutgomeryshire Yeomanry
Cavalry were augmented in 1820.　I have accidentally
seen in the *Salopian Journal* of 31 July 1839, a letter referring to a statement in a previous paper to the effect
that there was an intention of still further augmenting
the force then, in consequence of the Chartist riots that
had been prevalent.　This was not done, I presume, or we
should have been told of it either in the papers by Mr. C.
W. Williams Wynn, or by Mr. Askew Roberts, in Vol. 13
of the *Mont : Coll.*　　　　　　　　　　　　BLACKPOOL.

SHROPSHIRE WORDS (Dec. 8, 1880).—Referring to the extract from Towyn Parochial Records—" 1678, fines levied for byrying in *flannen*," whilst concurring with OLD OSWESTRY that the word " flannen" is in use now (I hear it almost daily) it is worth noting that there may have been a meaning to the word at that period other than the one we give to it now, namely, a flannel, made of *wool*, for by an Act passed in 30 Charles II, c. 3 (1678—9) the very year in which the Towyn entry was made, it was enacted " that some one or more of the relations of the party deceased, or other credible person, shall within eight days next after interment bring an *affidavit* in writing under the hands and seals of two or more credible witnesses (and under the hand of the Magistrate or Officer before whom the same was sworn, for which nothing shall be paid) to the Minister or Parson—That the said person was not put in, wrapt or wound up, or buried in any shirt, shift, sheet, or shroud, made or mingled with flax, hemp, silk, hair, gold or silver, or other than what is made of sheep's wool only, or in any Coffin lined or faced with any Cloth, Stuff, or any other thing whatsoever, made or mingled with Flax, Hemp, Silk, Hair, Gold, or Silver, or any other material but sheeps wool only." And by the same statute, and also by 32, Ch. II., cap. 1, it was enacted "that the Curate of every parish is to keep a Register, to be provided at the charge of the parish, wherein to enter all Burials, and affidavits of persons being Buried in Woollen, and if no affidavit be brought in eight days (which are to be reckoned from the hour in which the Corpse was Buried) he must enter a memorial of this default, over against the name of the party interr'd, and of the time when he gave notice of this default to the parish officers, which notice must be given in writing under the Curate's hand." "The Curate making default in any particular forfeits £5." It would have added to the interest of the Towyn extract if the day of the month had been copied—for it would have been then seen whether the Act had become operative, and, if so, it would permit a suggestion, (a) that the word " *not*" was omitted in making or copying the entry, or (b) that " flannen" at the period meant a mixture of something other than pure wool. EDBOMO.

CURRENT NOTES.

ENGLISH LAND AND ENGLISH LANDLORDS.

A volume bearing this title, by the Hon. George C. Brodrick, has just been published by the Cobden Club. It is of great interest and value, especially at the present time, when we are on the eve of a general reform of the land laws, for there is no doubt that legislation in Ireland must be followed by legislation for the rest of the kingdom. Mr Brodrick, with singular perspicuity and impartiality, gives a sketch of the history of the laws which govern the possession of land, describes the distinctive features of the English land system at the present day, and concludes with a discussion of the proposed reforms. Amongst the appendices to the volume are two by Mr A. C. Humphreys Owen : one on the Land Tax and the abolition of Feudal Tenures, exposing a fallacious statement in the *Financial Reform Almanack*; and another on the liability of personalty to Poor Rate, which is calculated to correct certain erroneous impressions in the public mind. We extract from the book the following statistics compiled by Mr Bateman :—

SALOP.

No. of Owners.		Class.				Acres.
8	..	Peers	..	..	..	195,276
44	..	Great Landowners	..	..	..	223,429
65	..	Squires	..	..	..	116,500
222	..	Greater Yeomen	..	..	..	111,000
447	..	Lesser Yeomen ..		..	..	75,990
3,841	..	Small Proprietors		..	..	57,738
7,281	..	Cottagers	..	..	..	4,544
211	..	Public Bodies ..		..	..	13,464
		Waste ..	..	..	..	19,674
12,119	..	Total	..	..	..	811,615

ANGLESEA.

3	..	Peers..	..	..	..	31,339
8	..	Great Landowners		..	..	66,175
6	..	Squires	..	..	..	10,200
31	..	Greater Yeomen		..	..	15,500
86	..	Lesser Yeomen		..	..	14,620
955	..	Small Proprietors		..	..	20,421
3,015	..	Cottagers	..	..	..	234
37	..	Public Bodies	..	..	..	3,447
		Waste ..	..	..	..	5,678
4,141	..	Total	..	..	..	167,614

CARNARVON.

4	..	Peers	..	..	..	102,470
10	..	Great Landowners		..	..	100,861
19	..	Squires	..	..	..	32,300
42	..	Greater Yeomen		..	..	21,000
96	..	Lesser Yeomen..		..	..	16,320
1,407	..	Small Proprietors		..	..	23,527
4,610	..	Cottagers	..	..	..	373
52	..	Public Bodies	..	..	..	4,382
		Waste ..	..	..	..	14,563
6,240	..	Total	..	..	..	315,796

DENBIGH.

0	..	Peers..	..	..	:	20,812
16	..	Great Landowners		..	..	130,165
38	..	Squires	..	..	..	64,600
106	..	Greater Yeomen		..	..	53,000
254	..	Lesser Yeomen..		..	..	43,180
1,773	..	Small Proprietors		..	..	31,436
3,486	..	Cottagers	..	..	..	721
85	..	Public Bodies	..	..	..	4,503
		Waste ..	..	..	..	18,812
5,708	..	Total	..	..	..	367,229

FLINT.

3	..	Peers	..	..	..	25,416
5	..	Great Landowners		..	..	30,113
9	..	Squires	..	..	..	15,300
44	..	Greater Yeomen		..	..	22,000
111	..	Lesser Yeomen..		..	..	18,870
1,225	..	Small Proprietors		..	..	15,179
2,043	..	Cottagers	..	:	..	562
65	..	Public Bodies	..	..	..	5,847
		Waste ..	..	..	..	4,312
3,510	..	Total	..	..	..	146,599

MERIONETH.

		Peers..	..	..	..	16,084
12	..	Great Landowners	:	..	..	128,593
37	..	Squires	..	..	..	68,800
96	..	Greater Yeomen		..	..	43,000
135	..	Lesser Yeomen..		..	..	22,950
346	..	Small Proprietors		..	..	14,244
1,044	..	Cottagers	..	..	..	212
25	..	Public Bodies	..	..	..	3,174
		Waste ..	..	..	.:	416
1,095	..	Total	..	..	..	303,073

MONTGOMERY.

2	..	Peers	..	..	..	61,070
9	..	Great Landowners		..	..	86,587
42	..	Squires	..	..	..	71,400
123	..	Greater Yeomen		..	..	64,000
280	..	Lesser Yeomen..		..	..	47,600
1,418	..	Small Proprietors		..	..	43,956
1,314	..	Cottagers	..	..	..	262
48	..	Public Bodies	...	..	..	5,510
		Waste ..	..	..	..	6,956
3,241	..	Total	..	..	..	387,341

SUMMARY TABLE OF ENGLAND AND WALES.

No. of Owners.		Class.			Extent in Acres.
400	..	Peers and Peeresses	..	..	5,728,979
1,288	..	Great Landowners	..	..	8,497,699
2,529	..	Squires	..	..	4,319,271
9,585	..	Greater Yeomen	..	..	4,782,627
24,412	..	Lesser Yeomen	..	..	4,144,272
217,049	..	Small Proprietors	..	..	3,931,806
703,289	..	Cottagers	..	..	151,148
14,459		The Crown, Barracks, Convict Prisons, Lighthouses &c.			165,427
		Religious, Educational, Philanthropic, &c.			947,655
		Commercial and Miscellaneous			330,466
		Waste	..	..	1,524,024
973,011	..	Total	..	..	34,523,974

"Peers" include Peeresses and Peers' eldest sons.

"Great Landowners" include all estates held by commoners owning at least 3,000 acres, if the rental reaches £3,000 per annum.

"Squires" include estates of between 1,000 acres and 8,000, and such estates as would be included in the previous class if their rental reached £3,000, averaged at 1,700 acres.

"Greater Yeomen" include estates of between 300 acres and 1,000, averaged at 500 acres.

"Lesser Yeomen" include estates of between 100 acres and 300, averaged at 170 acres.

"Small Proprietors" include lands of over 1 acre and under 100 acres.

"Cottagers" include all holdings of under 1 acre.

"Public Bodies" include all holdings printed in italics in the "Government Return of Landowners, 1876," and a few more that should have been so printed, being obviously public properties.

"Peers" and "Great Landowners" are assigned to those counties in which their principal estates are situated, and are never entered in more than one county. The column recording their numbers in each county must be taken with this qualification, but the acreage of all the "Peers" or "Great Landowners" in each county is correctly given, and their aggregate number, as well as their aggregate acreage, may be learned from the summary.

In Merioneth, for special reasons, the classification mentioned above in the 3rd, 4th and 5th classes is not exactly followed. The division into classes is, of course, to a large extent an arbitrary one; "Yeomen," for example, would include an ambassador, an ex-Cabinet Minister, a well-known Dean, a Master of Fox Hounds, and the Poet Laureate. But the table shows, with such an approach to exactitude as can yet be made, the number of holders of land classified according to the size of the holding.

JANUARY 19, 1881.

NOTES.

SIR WILLIAM MAURICE OF CLENENNEY
(Dec. 29, 1880).

From the original (at Brogyntyn) addressed "To the woorshipfull Willia' Moris esq'r as his house in Clennene d'd this."

Woor: good Coozen sence yo'r dep'ture I receved two l'res fro' yo'u the one dated the ,9. of Janur : the other 12 of the same, both to the same effect, full of love and Curtesie farre above my diserts : A man of yo'r Callinge and credyt to make me a poore gentl : borne to nothinge, head and hono'r of so anncient a house, so woor : a lyvinge, so fayre and vertious a gentlwoma', what demiretts of myne may ever come neere, to Countervayle these Curtesies. All I can doe is to beare a thankfull mynd, expecting oportunitie to show the same. Protestinge w'th all that yf I might match w'th yo'w, w'thout to much p'indiciuge myestate : her person, and yo'r frindshippe, should blyndfield me, for any other respect of wealthe or worldlie posibiltie. But syth yt is not so, geve mee leave bothe for yo'rs, bers, and my owne good, to take dew advice and consideration in this case. Now yf yo'w be remembered at ou'r fyrst conference matters being debated w'th yo'w by my frinds wher no offer that they could make thoughe never so large (and farre out of my likinge) would be accepted. Then wee brake of, w'th these condic'ons, (eftsons repeted) that at cominge to the countrie at mydsomer, yf wee should fall to a second conference, vpon my coozens and yo'r likinge that no mentio' or hould should be taken of any former p'fers. But to debate of matters a new (by mediation of frinds) as opportunitie should then serve. And hearin I take my selfe sumwhat iniured in the last l're, wher yo'w reguyre in me Constancie, and w'thall yo'w urge my constant liking of the gentlwoma', yt is the same, yf to former profer, yo'w refused them. And for that yo'w vrge me w'th p'mise I know not vpo' what ground yo'w should gather yt, yf yo'w meane some former p'mise, yf yo'w meane that p'mise yt I past afor m'r henry lloyd m'r david Roberts & others to be ther about Mydsomer, to fynish it one way or other, God willing I will performe yt yf yo'w be also of the same mynd. In the meane tyme I will wade no further in this mattr : but wholie reserve yt vntill all those good frinds and wee meet together, by whom both yo'w and I may be resolved of our conclusio' then. In the meane tyme I leaue all to yo'r dispositio', to deale therin as yo'w see cause.

The cause that I dyd not then p'sentlie answeare both yo'r l'res and my Coozens, yt I had an intent to send Henry Hughes (w'ch brought yo'r l'res to me) of purpose aswell to conferre in some things w'th yo'w, as other negociations of myne in Wales, for ye sayd Hughes had signifyed to me in a l're he left behind, that he would returne w'thin les then a monnthe, and offered hymselfe to be imployd in any service that I would put hym to. And still expecting his retorne, I have disappointed my selfe and (I fayre mee) offended yo'w. And now I am fayne to send other wise, as I might have done at fyrst. Thus having tould yo'w the truth in all respects I hope yo'w will conceave no vnkyndness thereat.

You see how I wrytte to my Coozen Ellin, And yt may be yo'w will conceave hardlie thereof. But p'don mee, yt is my mane'r, and vse of dealing in all things to make show of the worst side, and to lay open all inconvenienc'e's. Yf bettr be found I shall not afterwards be accused of sinister badd dealings. And therefore I will not spare my self in my most deerest and nerest mattr of mariage.

Thus hoping that I have writte nothinge that yo'w will take any discontentment or exceptions agaynst, w'th my humble dutie to yo'r selfe, Coozen Sheryffe (1) and my goode Coozen his bedfellow and Mr. Jo : Roberts and Mr. R : Elza [Ellis] the rest as yo'w se cause. I comytt yo'w to god's p'testio' at Lords' the xxth of March 1594.

Yo'r assured most lovinge
poor Coozen & frinde allways
Tho : Owen.

[Seal—Idnerth Benfras, first and fourth ; quartering, 2d and 3d. Ireland, I think (six fleurs de lys 3, 2, and 1 a crescent for difference.)]

TYDDYN INCO.—In the year 1872 a writer in Notes and Queries, in a query suggested by a passage in the Gossiping Guide to Wales, asked the meaning of Tyddyn Inco, the name of a farm house at Llandderfel. One reply was given to the effect that Inco was a corruption of Inigo, and that the farm was called after the cele-

---

(1) Robert Wynn Brynkir, Esq., of Brynkir, sheriff for Carnarvonshire that year.

brated architect who designed the house. Another correspondent thought the words meant "Memorial farm." He remarked that " *Tyddyn* is a farm, *co* a part or the verb *cofio* = to remember ; and *in* the same as our preposition *in*." Pennant, in his *History of Whiteford and Holywell*, p. 3, speaking of the ancient custom of sending children out to nurse in Wales, says—

Of the affection between the foster-father, foster-mother, and foster-brother, the instances were frequent. The fidelity of *Robin ap Inko*, foster-brother to Jevan ap Vychan, of the house of Gwedir, in the reign of Edw. IV. was a most neted one. In a fatal feud between Jevan and his brother-in-law, Rys ap Howel, the latter, expecting a fray, provided a butcher to murder Jevan in the confusion of the battle, and to him he gave orders in these terms. The butcher, not being acquainted with Jevan, Ap Rys said, "Thou shalt soone discerne him from the rest by his stature, and he will make way before him. There is a foster-brother of his, one *Robin ap Inko*, a little fellow, that useth to watch him behind ; take heed of him, for be the encountre never soe hot, his eye is ever on his foster-brother ;"— and so it happened. Robin suspected the treachery, and seeing the butcher watching his opportunity, came behind him and knocked him on the head in the moment in which he had come behind Jevan, and had aimed one at his beloved foster-brother. The patrimony of his faithful follower was in the parish of Llanderfel ; and to this day retains the name of *Tyddin Inko*.

This " knocks on the head " the other theories of meaning of name, as completely as Robin's staff did the head of the butcher !   N.W.S.

QUERIES.

HATRED OF JEWS.—I well remember as a boy, 30 years ago, hearing a farmer's wife in Montgomeryshire using as a term of opprobrium to provoking and intractable animals, especially to pigs, the words " Hen Ddewon." Was this " Iddewon," Jews, or a softened form of a still more formidable, though more familiar, epithet ? If the first, it was an instance of the " survival " of the intense mediæval hatred of the Jewish race.   CYNWYL.

A SHROPSHIRE MARTYR.—In the " Early Chronicles of Shrewsbury" printed in the *Transactions* of the Shropshire Archæological Society, vol. iii., August, 1880, this paragraph occurs :—" The next daye followinge, being the xijth day [July, 1598] there was one Joanes a Shropshyrma' executyd at at Sainct Mary Watterings who studd stowtely against the Queene's *Mts* proceedings, being a seminary " (i.e. Priest). Having failed to identify this martyr with any of those of the same surname in the Douay Records, I should be much obliged to any one who would communicate to *Bye-gones* his Christian name, or any further particulars respecting him ?   H.W.L.

A WELSH CANNIBAL. — Where, in Welsh history, are we told of the following cannibal prince ? " It is recorded that a certain prince of Britain, named Gwrgi Garwlwyd, was a cannibal, and that he acquired a taste for man's flesh at the court of Edelfled, King of the Saxons, whose sister he married. He had a particular passion for making his meal of little Cymri boys ever after : his name signifies the ' rough brown dog-man.' Edelfled was in the habit of eating two noble maidens of the Cymri every morning for breakfast, and Gwrgi, on his return from the fashionable court of the Saxon king, found it impossible to exist without his table was supplied every day with a male and female of the Welsh nation : he was, however, considerate in his cruelty, for on a Saturday he killed two of each, that he might not be compelled to kill on Sunday." This extract I take from a foot note on pp. 208-9 of Miss Costello's *Falls, Lakes, and Mountains of North Wales*, Longman, 1845.   ANON.

THE ELLESMERE GHOST.—(Jan. 5, 1881.)— I have before me a small octavo book, the bastard title page of which is worded " Poems, Moral and Sacred." The title page itself is missing, but the imprint on the last page bears the name " J. Wilson, Macclesfield." Seventeen pages are occupied with the "Experience of Mrs. Worth," by her husband, and the rest (forty pages) is devoted to her poetry, which includes an ode "on the Death of the late Rev. Mr. De Courcy, Vicar of St. Alkmond's, Shrewsbury," one " on the Death of Miss Menlove of Bradenheath, 1804," another, written in 1806, referring to the death of the mother of the authoress. In addition to these there is a hymn " written for the Sunday School at Shrewsbury, 1812," and one " To my Husband on his Birthday, 1812." " The Ellesmere Ghost " is included in the book. I fancy Mr. Worth must have been a " Travelling Preacher " connected with the Wesleyan Methodist body, and therefore they would move from place to place. Another week I will give an abstract of the memoir.   R.D.

It is stated on the title page that Mrs. Worth's poems were " Printed for the Editor by F. Wilson, Macclesfield, and sold by Baynes, Paternoster Row, London, 1813."   F.

I have an imperfect copy of a volume of Poems by Miss Sadler, afterwards Mrs. Worth. She was Teacher at Miss Dorset's School in Oswestry. Mr. Worth was Wesleyan Minister at Oswestry. One of the pieces in the book was " Written for the Sunday School at Oswestry," the Old Chapel School being the one in question. There is also a hymn " to be sung by the Children," dated 1810. There are also some lines " On the death of Miss Hilditch of Oswestry," written in 1811. This was Mary, eldest daughter of Mr. Hilditch of The Cross, who was Mayor of the town in 1810-11.   E.C.

[The *Salopian Journal* of Apr. 3, 1798, contained the following advertisement :—" Ladies Boarding School, Oswestry. Mrs. Holbrook and Miss Dorset return thanks for the very liberal encouragement they have experienced, and beg leave respectfully to inform the Public, that they have entered upon a commodious House, in a fine airy Situation, (formerly occupied by the late Mr. Trevor), which they have fitted up for the Reception of Young Ladies."—ED.]

THE RECORDS OF OSWESTRY (July 7, 1880). A correspondent asked if " Morgan Wynne " the Recorder named for Oswestry under the charter of Charles II., granted in 1673, acted under the previous charter of James I. By reference to the Corporation documents, quoted by Mr. Stanley Leighton, I find that he did. The last Bailiffs were " Richard Jones and John Glover," and their names, with that of Morgan Wynne as Recorder, are attached (as was stated in *O.A.* Dec. 1) to documents still in existence. Mr. Wynne was re-appointed Recorder under the new charter, and the ex-bailiffs were made aldermen. The latter were among "the new elected Burgesses in 1674" sworn before Richard Pope, Esq., the first mayor. For this privilege " Mr. Bayliffe Jones " only paid 15s., whereas Glover had to pay £3 15s. 0d. Mr. Stanley Leighton, in his last instalment of Records in *Trans.* of S.A.S. names ten defaulting aldermen and councillors, under the charter of Charles II. (see also *Bye-gones*, Oct. 29, 1873), and gives the names of twelve chosen to fill their places. The extra two were required as councillors, because two of the defaulters were aldermen, and two of the original council were nominated to take their places ; which necessitated two fresh names to supply their places as common councilmen, as well as eight new ones. The question naturally arises why there were so many defaulters? Perhaps one reason is revealed in the documents Mr. Stanley Leighton has unearthed. The town was, financially, at a very low ebb : the late wars and "usurping powers" had wasted it sorely ; "a *quo warranto* issued out against them" had put the inhabitants "to great charges." At such a time a new charter was a costly piece of business, and we can understand some of the ratepayers rather shirking the responsibility of it. The Mayor himself would have declined office if he could have done so. The Earl of Craven, the Lord of the Borough, obtained the charter, and was to pay half the expense. The town half came to £93 13s. 8d. The money not being forthcoming, the Earl commenced an action against the Mayor, but the latter (Mr. Pope) and Mr. Ralph Devenport made such a representation "of the low estate of the Borough" that his Lordship relented, and "was content to receive" a sum of £50 "in full satisfaction." These documents are highly interesting to Oswestrians ; the wonder is there are not more members of the Society in our Borough. JARCO.

JANUARY 26, 1881.

NOTES.

A ROYAL VISIT TO OSWESTRY.—King John was at Oswestry from the 6th to the 10th August, 1216. He burnt the Town, if not the Castle to the ground,—*Eyton*, vol. IV. p. 250. JUNIOR.

EXPERIENCE OF MRS. WORTH.—The memoir of the authoress of the poem entitled "The Ellesmere Ghost" (referred to Jan. 5, 1881), is worded in the peculiar phraseology of the old Methodist records. All I propose doing is to weed out what is strictly biographical, as the rest is scarcely fitted for *Bye-gones*. The notice of her life and death is penned by her husband, whom I presume to have been a Wesleyan Minister. "Mrs. Anne Worth was born in Shrewsbury, Feb. 4, 1776: she was the youngest daughter of Mr. Joseph Sadler of that town." Her father died when she was a child, and her mother had her carefully educated. They were attendants at St. Alkmond's Church, during the time that the Rev. Mr. De Courcey was Vicar. In 1801, just as Miss Sadler was "first entering into life, she was much given to gaiety and fashion," but under Mr. De Courcey's "ministry she was convinced of the impropriety of her conduct." Soon after this she became a "teacher in boarding schools," and in 1806 was engaged as governess in the family of Sir Andrew Corbet, bart. During the same year her mother and Mr. De Courcey both died, and Miss Sadler "became a member of the Methodist Society of Shrewsbury." We are not told how long she remained in the family of Sir Andrew; the memoir rather abruptly goes on to speak of "her subsequent residence in Oswestry, which was then attended by Welsh Preachers, whose language she did not understand." In consequence of this she, whilst resident in Oswestry, although deprived of "many advantages she had enjoyed in Shrewsbury," was "often blest in attending the ministry of a pious Calvinist in that town." As a passing picture of the Methodism of those days I will add one passage in her life at Oswestry. "During this period she was solicited to attend the Theatre ; she repeatedly resisted, and overcame the temptation; but at length was vanquished. Even while there the horrors of her mind were inexpressible ; she trembled to think what a deplorable state her mind must have been reduced to, before she could have consented to attend such a place !" In March 1811, whilst still at Oswestry, Miss Sadler had a dangerous fever, and, says

Mr. Worth, "whilst she was recovering from this affliction, I was providentially led, at the request of a friend at Wrexham, to preach at Oswestry." He had an interview with the lady, and on the 30th of the following July was married to her at Shrewsbury. Mr. Worth was "re-appointed to the Wrexham circuit," and his wife became very active in good works, especially as a visitor of the sick connected with "a society then formed in Wrexham for that benevolent purpose." From Wrexham the Worths went to reside at Burslem, and here Mrs. Worth caught cold, after the birth of a son, and she died on Sunday, Apr. 4, 1813. R.D.

TOWYN-MERIONETH PARISH RECORDS. (Jan. 12, 1881).—The entries I have placed before your readers have been extracted from two books, the first of which is entitled "Lyfr Cyfrif Eglwys—Dowyn a Brynwydd—am 2s. yn y flwyddin 1728—Edward Morgan, vicar—John Hughes, O'r Dyffryngwyn—ag—Humphrey David o Benowern—wardeiniaid—writ by Edward Hughes of Towyn—Pa bethau bynnog oll a ewyllygioch eu gweuthier o Ddynion i chwi selly gwnerwch chwithau iddynt hwy canys hyn yw's gyfraith a'r—Trophwyd Mathew 7. 12." From this book the transcriber has summarized several entries "taken out of an old booke," as follows :—"For a winding sheet in 1666, 6s. ; for ditto in 1664, 5s. 7d. ; for ditto, ditto, 1s. 4d. ; for ditto in 1666, 3s. 6d. A warden for uch byga and Vaenol in 1666 made use of lime belonging to Vaenol which was to be defrayed by uch byga. For writing a wardens account in 1666, 8d. ; one wardens charge in ye .... or 1664, 2s. The part of ye chch repaird by uwch byga in 1666 with the steeple. In 1662 there was a warden for uwch byga and Vaenol, another for Dauddyffryn and Cefnrhos, and another for Ysyrafon. Ysyrafon pd them for their part of the chch fair, 10s. ; Cefnrhos, 3s. ; Vaenol, 3s. Uwchbysga towards repairing the steeple, £1. In 1668 proportion towards repairs in Ysyrafon, 10s. ; in Kefu-rhos, 10s. ; in Dauddyffryn, 5s. In 1667 ditto as under:—In Dauddyffryn, 1*li* 12s. ; in Cefnrhos, 2*li* ; in Ysyrafon 1*li* 15s. In 1677 a chch bible cost 4*li* 4s. In 1678 fines levied for byrying in flannen came to 2*li* 10s. In 1678 a crown was paid for writing the Register Roll. In 1681 6s. was paid for ditto; for ditto in 1683, 6s. ; 1784, 6s. ; ditto in 1691 and 1692. In 1603 a quart of wine against Whitsontide cost 9*l*. In 1690 writing ye Register Roll Pejent and parchment cost 15s. In 1693 Register Roll cost 6s." These are the last entries up to "Aprill ye 13th 1724." G.G.

SCARCITY OF GRAIN IN 1783 & 1800.—The *Salopian Journal* for Sep. 10, 1800, in calling attention to the formation of Associations in various parts of the country, for the purpose of resisting the increase in the price of grain, &c., in times of scarcity, and breaking up the "abominable combinations for keeping up unreasonable prices," said that "In the year 1783, upwards of £2,000 was subscribed in *Shrewsbury* for the like laudable purpose, and very large quantities of wheat were purchased in the ports ; which had the happy effect of very considerably lowering the markets ; and after the sale had been continued for near six months 18s 6d. in the pound was returned to the contributors." In Dec. 1800 the same paper gave a list of *Oswestry* subscribers "of money and grain," with the following explanation :—"Oswestry 13 Nov. 1800. A subscription in money, and engagements to deliver corn at sixteen shillings, wheat, and ten shillings, barley ; from the undermentioned persons, towards supplying poor families in the town and parish of Oswestry with provisions, at a reduced price." Here follows the list of subscribers, and then we read :—"The Committee hope and expect that other owners of estates, and inhabitants of the town and parish, will follow the above good examples; and they are informed the list is left open at Mr. Lewis Jones's, in Oswestry, where they who intend to contribute in cash or grain will enter their names, which will be published hereafter." I have only found one further list, viz : on 14 Jan. 1801, and this is confined to four names, with the information that "the subscriptions, in cash, amounted to £487 4s. 0d. and engagements, wheat 670 and barley 680 [measures]." Through the courtesy of an old inhabitant of Oswestry I have before me a complete list of subscribers issued by "Salter, printer" on Dec. 16, 1800, with a statement of accounts, &c. This I will give another week. JARCO.

QUERIES.

AUGUSTINE'S OAK ON THE SEVERN.— Dean Howson, in his book on the Dee, says there are only two places connected with the meeting of Augustine and the British Bishops; viz.: "Augustine's Oak on the Severn and Bangor on the Dee." Can any of your readers tell me the exact locality of "Augustine's Oak on the Severn"? W. A. L.

ARWYSTLEY—SEAL.—A large seal has been found with the following arms upon it :—1 & 4, Three fleurs-de-lis. 2 & 3, Three lions passant guard. Supporters: Dexter, A lion rampant. Sinister, A Dragon; with the legend, "Sigillu. Regiae Majestatis ad causas Ecclesiasticas pro comissario Arwystley." Can any of your readers tell whose seal it would be? Was there any Ecclesiastical jurisdiction peculiar to Arwystley? A.

DAVID COX'S SIGNBOARD.—Can anyone say, for certain, when and under what conditions the signboard at Bettwsycoed (which has recently been the subject of litigation) was painted? Some affix the date at 1847; others a year or two later. Some say Cox painted it to clear off his score at the house, others that he did it out of pure good nature. Some say the board was affixed to the wall of the little public house when he painted it—he standing on a ladder; others that he painted it in the house, but retouched it from a ladder on future occasions. Some say the signboard was never affixed to the wall, but swung in the wind. Will some one who can speak with authority tell us all about it? N.W.S.

OUR MONTGOMERYSHIRE NEIGHBOURS.— The following letter from the late Hon. Thomas Kenyon has been preserved. Can any reader supply the date, and the occasion, when the Oswestry Yeomanry were paraded to "shew respect to our Montgomeryshire neighbours?"

DEAR CROXON. I have just received the enclosed from Chas. Wynn & am sure there will but be one wish, if the short notice enables us to do so, to comply with his wishes & shew respect to our Montgomeryshire neighbours. I would certainly go myself but am obliged to go to Salop for the Sessions. I must therefore, and indeed cannot do better, leave the matter in your hands. Gardner also I find is out.

If you could muster to the number of one troop it would be very handsome, or half a troop I should think would do; but let them be men and horses that will do us credit.

Have the goodness also to send the enclosed to Chas. Wynn.

Yours very truly,
Pradoe, Sunday. THOS. KENYON.
Of course you will get the men from the Oswestry neighbourhood.

Mr. John Croxon of Llanvorda Issa was a Captain in the North Shropshire Yeomanry, and Gardner was Drill Sergeant residing in Oswestry. These, I presume, are the parties mentioned. Gardner was an old Waterloo man, and his son, Douglas, lost a leg in the Balaclava charge. JARCO.

SALOPIAN LITERATURE (Aug. 18, 1880).— The attention of your readers is called to the following queries :—

ALMIRA.—A writer, who, under this name, published a small volume of "Poems on Several Occasions : Never before Printed," is said to have been born at Roden near Shrewsbury; and I am anxious to get some information about him. The volume was printed at Shrewsbury in 1727 "by Thomas Durston for the Author," and contains eighty-eight pages duo.

THOMAS RODENHURST. — Can anyone give a short account of this Salopian writer, who published "A Description of Hawkstone?" The sixth edition "with a second part, and several alterations and additions" was printed in 1799; and I should also like to know the dates of the five preceding editions, and of any later ones published.

ROWLAND HILL'S HYMNS.—"Good old Rowley" published a small volume of "Psalms and Hymns, Chiefly Intended For Public Worship," in the year 1783; and I believe that to be the first edition. In the year 1794 a third edition appeared. Can any one tell me when the second edition was published? The first edition is very scarce, and is priced at a very high figure in the London catalogues. G.R.

REPLIES.

WREXHAM AMICABLE SOCIETY (Jan. 5, 1881).—This society was an ordinary benefit society, better known in Wrexham as "The Gentlemen's Club." It originally held its meetings at the Wynnstay Arms, whence it was removed to the Sun Inn in Abbot-street, and thence to the Blossoms Inn in Charles-street, where it ultimately expired—in its latter days it was known as the "Greasy Hat Club." An offshoot of this society consisting of twenty-nine members, upon the 22nd of June, 1807, formed the nucleus of the Friendly Union Society, which held their meetings at the Fleece Inn, in Hope-street, which was remarkably successful, its funds amounted in 1848 to about six thousand pounds, of which amount the members were robbed by the Insolvency of their Treasurer, the notorious R. M. Lloyd, the Banker. Wrexham. LANDWOR.

ROBBER'S CAVE AT THE DEVIL'S BRIDGE (Dec. 15, 1880).—In reply to "G.G." respecting the above, I forward the following account from Nicholson's Cambrian Travellers' Guide, 8vo. edition, 1840, page 507, under the heading of Pont-y-Mynach. "After repassing the Bridge, a fourth descent may be made at the side of the Mynach Falls, to the Robber's Cave, at the part of the lowest fall. Nothing extraordinary attaches to it except an uncommon tradition. About the middle of the 15th century, it was inhabited by two men and a woman known by the epithet 'Plant Matt,' or Matthew's children. The father kept a public-house at Tregaron. These persons were notorious robbers. The entrance to the cave admitting but one at a time, they were able to defend it against hundreds. Here they lived several years, but at length being found guilty of committing murder, they were taken and executed. A descent to the falls of the Mynach may be made by winding behind the house almost as far as the spot called Llyn Fate's Cave, a traditional personage said to have followed the vocation of Plant Matt, and to have made this a retreat from the pursuit of justice." Mr. Nicholson's Guide gleans a great deal from other authors, and it does not appear clear whether he quotes these legends from Newell's Scenery of Wales, or from Mr. Barber's Tour, as both names are mentioned in the course of his descriptions of the Devil's Bridge and Falls. W.P. Wrexham.

CURRENT NOTES.

An addition has been made to the beautiful memorials in Chester Cathedral of the late Mr. Thomas Brassey, the great civil engineer (who was born at Aldford, near Chester, in 1805, and was educated at Chester), and of his wife. An admirable bust in marble of Mr. Brassey, by M. Wagmüller, has been placed on a pedestal of red sandstone, erected and partially incorporated with the northern wall of the apse, at the south-eastern angle of the Cathedral, called St. Mary Magdalen's Chapel, which was restored by his sons in memory of their father during the general restoration of the edifice a few years ago. It is proposed to extend the series of very fine mosaics already placed in the space beneath the windows of the apse by others on each side of the bust, and also on the opposite wall, in memory of one of Mr. Brassey's children.

SUNDAYS IN THE OLDEN TIME.

At a meeting of the Historic Society of Lancashire and Cheshire held at Liverpool on Thursday an interesting paper was read by Mr. W. E. A. Axon, upon "Sunday in Lancashire and Cheshire." In the course of his paper he said :—In 1512 the Mayor of Chester enjoined that all children over six shall be taken to church in the morning, and in the afternoon the males shall be exercised in shooting with bows and arrows for pins and points only. In Elizabeth's reign, the aldermen, justices, sheriffs, and leavemen of Chester met in the Inner Pentice every Sunday for a shot or a drinking. As late as 1657 the Mayor sat for the administration of justice. In this he followed the example of the higher courts, which before the time of Edward IV. sat on Sundays. Legal documents are frequently found dated on that day. The Chester plays were acted not by clerics, but by members of the trading guilds. There are many indications of coarse manners, the comic element being either rude pictures of domestic strife or grotesque diablerie. In one play, the shepherds make a homely supper, in which Halton ale and a jannock of Lancashire figure, and have a stiff wrestling bout. This, one of the earliest attempts at a realistic presentation of common life, must have been very popular. Amongst other Chester plays were "Robert of Sicily," "King Ebrauke" (an ancient British king, who had twenty wives, twenty sons, and thirty daughters), and "Æneas and Dido." The last-named was produced with great spectacular display in 1564, on the Roodeye, on the Sunday after Midsummer. There were made about this time four giants, one unicorn, one dromedary, one camel, one dragon, six hobbyhorses, &c., to be borne in procession on St. John's Eve. The giants were enormous figures, made of hoops, deal boards, and paper, held together partly by nails and partly by paste, in which it was found requisite to mix arsenic to prevent them being eaten by the rats. In 1542 Bishop Bonner prohibited these amusements, and in 1599 the Mayor of Chester broke the civic monsters so that they could not go. They were set out again in 1601, and not finally abolished until 1678. The stage was now taking up an independent existence. Sunday was the chief day for social ceremonials. It was decreed in 1566 that the Manchester wedding-feasts and bride-ales should not cost more that fourpence a head, and were not to have any music except that supplied by the town waits. In 1574 it was ordered that any person "found drunken in any alehouse" should pass a night in the dungeon, and pay a fine of sixpence, and if he could not, the "goodwife" of the alehouse had to pay for him. In 1634 we are gravely told of a woman gathering plums upon the walls of Chester who fell down and broke her neck as a "judgment" for Sabbath breaking. Under the Parliament the

theatres were closed, the fairs reduced to markets, and the maypoles prohibited. Yet those who were supposed to be Puritanically inclined were not always strict in carrying out their principles. Roger Lowe records in his diary being measured for clothes, many visits to friends and to the alehouse, where he was sometimes "merry," much sweethearting, and much chapel-going. The Lancashire folk were fond of amusement. The proprietor of a travelling dromedary, in 1662, testified that he derived more profit in that than in any other county. In conclusion, Mr. Axon referred to the decline within recent years of the Sabbatarian spirit, and the rapid growth of sympathy with the proposals of the Sunday Society. This had been conspicuously proved by the action of Manchester and Wigan in opening their libraries and picture galleries on the Sunday, and by the refusal of the Corporation of Oldham to accept the gift of a library that was clogged with the condition that it should not be opened on that day. The licence of the middle ages had fortunately passed away, and the Sabbatarianism of the seventeenth century was fast following it. The future, they might hope, Mr. Axon said, would bring us a Sunday equally removed from extravagance and from bitterness— a day sacred to worship, to education, and to recreation ; a day whose high thought and inspiration should permeate the entire week.

WELSH SHEEP DOGS' "TRIALS."

The *Manchester City News* of Jan. 15, 1881, contains a report of a meeting of the "Literary Club" on the previous Monday evening. We are told that—

"Mr. Joseph C. Lockhart read a short communication on the treatment of their sheep dogs by the Welsh farmers and shepherds. He first described the operations of two collie dogs when dividing a flock of sheep on the steep bluff that rises above the hostelry at Tal-y-Llyn, as seen from a boat on the lake. The shepherd who was with the dogs would sing out some very dreadful language about the length of one's arm, and off one of the dogs would go almost to the top of the bluff, whilst something still more awful would despatch the other in an entirely different direction. It was marvellous to see these two creatures at work separating two sheep from one point of the mountain, and three from another, and carefully bringing them down or up to the shepherd for examination. And he (Mr. Lockhart) could not help wondering how long it would take a dog of ordinary ability to master the niceties of the Welsh language. (Laughter.) During the same holiday he happened to be near Penmaen Pool, midway between Barmouth and Dolgelley, when he was overtaken by a young Welsh shepherd driving a flock of fat mountain sheep. He had with him a handsome collie bitch. He said that he was a tenant of Sir Edmund Buckley, and his farm was on the Aran mountain ; the sheep in front of them had been fattening in the richer pastures of the Mawddach valley. They had four other dogs besides that one. 'And what do you do with them in the winter?' 'We always turn them out in winter time.' 'That is, of course, after they have served you during the spring, summer, and autumn. What do they feed on, then, during the winter?' 'Oh! sometimes there are dead sheep—sheep that have fallen down the rocks or been starved to death.' 'But if it doesn't suit the sheep to die either by accident or starvation, how are the poor brutes to be fed?' 'They sometimes take bad ways, and they kill a sheep or a lamb for themselves. The brother of that little bitch took such ways, and he was very cunning with it. We lost lamb after lamb, but we never suspected him till one day I was out with him on the mountain, and with my own eyes I saw him seize a lamb, worry it, make his meal out of it, and then go and wash himself in a pool ; then rub himself dry on the heather, repeating this until not a trace of the blood could be seen on him.' 'What did you do with him ?' 'Oh ! I took him by the hind legs and banged his brains out on a rock.' 'Is the custom common in your neighbourhood to turn out the dogs in winter ?' 'Yes, we all do it.' 'Then you are all a set of infernal wastrels !' 'Yes, indeed, sir, we wass.' 'How you could possibly go about with a faithful, beautiful creature like that little bitch, and have her staring into your eyes for nine months out of the twelve, no hours too long for her, no labour too hard, and then, in the hardest weather, turn her adrift, and beat her from your door with staves, I cannot possibly imagine. You richly deserve to have all your sheep worried.' And with this parting benediction the talk ended."

The distinguished foreigner in *Pickwick* took a whole fortnight to compile a " book full of notes" on England, " music, picture, science, potry, poltic ; all tings ;" but Mr. Lockhart would scarcely need such an expenditure of time to do one on Wales. A single glance, and a solitary conversation makes him master of a very important element of Welsh farming,—the ways of farmers with their dogs, and dogs with the sheep. And yet it might be hinted that—sinking "humanity" altogether — Welsh farmers are not such fools as to turn their best shepherds into wild animals at a period of the year when they may any day require their services ; and beat from their doors with staves animals worth their weight in gold. That "the dogs sometimes take to bad ways" is true, but the "brother to the little bitch " who came to so untimely an end, evidently, did not do so from hunger ; but (as is invariably the case) from mischief. However we need not argue on a matter like this. The simplest thing to do is to give the charge a flat denial. Whether the 'gentle shepherd' the tourist met was having his joke with the Saxon, or not, we cannot say ; but we can say to the gentleman making the charge—" Indeed, truth, he wass tell you a lie, whatever, Mr. Lockhart !"—*Oswestry Advertizer.*

FEBRUARY 2, 1881.

NOTES.

MR. MADOCKS AND JOHN GIBSON.—I have recently been fortunate enough to come across a very interesting correspondence between two eminent Welshmen of the present century, of which I send you a copy. Mr. W. A. Madocks, who was a great patron of Art, and especially of Welsh Art and Artists, did not live to see his great commission executed by John Gibson the sculptor, for he died in Paris in the year 1828, soon after the date of the subjoined correspondence, and Gibson presumably never went on with the work. Gibson survived Mr. Madocks nearly forty years, and died at Rome 27 January, 1866.   E.B. Portmadoc.

" Rome, 15th Novr., 1827.

"Dear Sir,—I have returned to Rome, and it is with feelings of gratitude and pleasure I acknowledge the honor of receiving your kind enthusiastic letter, you do inflame my soul with feelings of patriotism and with high ambition to produce some grand work for my native country, for my generous countryman and for posterity.

"Your idea of building a little Greek temple over the sea in our land of original poetry and musick of the island is a very noble thought, and what a classical beautiful object it would be viewing it from the sea.—I do assure you the honor of placing a work of mine within would rouse up all the enthusiasm and ambition I am capable of, and would give up all my time, all my soul, to produce a work for you and for posterity.

"The subjects you are so good to suggest are very beautiful, but the one I feel the most partial to is Neptune as a subject which gives scope to genius and grandeur of conception.

"The God might be represented turning his face towards the sea as if commanding the waves, and to give to his whole figure some energetic attitude with a terrific majesty to his look and air, his uplifted trydent would also be an ornament of beauty.

"There might be sculptured on the pedestal 3 basso re-lievi subjects from the Greek Mythology that would have some relation to the circumstance of your having founded Tre Madoc, for instance, this fable might be one—In the time of Inachus Neptune and Juno disputed for the sovereignty of Argos, Inachus was appointed Umpire, and he decided for Juno. Neptune, in revenge, deluged the country, but at last, overcome by the sacrifice of Inachus and the authority of Juno, he ordered the waters to retire by a subterraneous channel ; and on this spot the gratitude of Inachus and the Argives erected a temple to Neptune Proclystius (who causes to flow off). The contest between the air and the sea for the possession of the earth in allusion to Inachus having driven back the sea, and built Argos, is the subject of this fable.

"The other might be Neptune and Minerva contending for the right of giving a name to Athens—another might be Cybele, goddes of the earth, repelling Neptune from her teritories.

"There is another subject which I shall take the liberty of mentioning fine for the display of art, and repre-sents a mortal contending with the waters, it is Achilles contending with the river Scamander.

"For a light elegant work Venus rising out of the sea is a very beautiful subject. By the time you return to Rome I will make some small models for you to see. "At present I am finishing a group in marble of Venus and Cupid, and the marble is unusually beautiful. This work is not yet ordered, but you will see it when you re-turn to Rome.

" I have the honor, dear sir, to be " Your very obedient Humble Servt., JOHN GIBSON.

" To W. A. Madocks, Esqre., Naples.'

" Rome.

" I have the pleasure of acknowledging the honor of receiving your second letter. At this very time I am making a small model of Neptune, upright, majestic, ' with energy divine,' commanding the waves to retire. Let the statue be facing the sea, and we may imagine that he is commanding the waves to retire from the land, and there might be put in gold letters on the front of the pedestal Neptune Proclystius, and on each side, and back, basso relievi from the Greek Mythology, such as the fable of Inachus and Argos, and Athens, &c., all bearing some relation to your foundation of Tre Madoc.

" An upright posture for the Neptune would be more in conformity with the system of the refined Greeks, who always represented their Gods in the most dignified, majestic attitudes. The lesser Gods, who presided over rivers, &c., were represented laying on the ground like the sketch you have made.

"I shall feel very thankful to you for all the hints you can give to throw light and interest on the subject, and I should wish very much to know the sentiments of Sir William Gell on such a subject being a man of high clas-sical taste.

" The Venus and Cupid which I mentioned to you will be in a forward state by your return to Rome, and if the price, which is 400 pounds, as well as the work itself should meet your approbation, I should feel very proud to have it in your possession. Neptune commanding the waves to retire (turning his front to the sea) is not inconsistent with the lines you have sent me, 'The sea is His, and He made it, and His hands prepared the dry land.'

"May I beg you to do me the favour to return my best thanks and respects to the ladies for their kind mention of me, and believe me,

"dear sir, to be always most respectfully,
"Your humble servt,
"W. A. Madocks, Esq.,   "JOHN GIBSON.
Messrs. Falconets & Co., Napoli."

"I copy your letter which I admire so much.
"Naples, 13th Novr., 1827.
"My dear Sir,—I hope you are returned from Carrara quite safe and well. I long to be returning to Rome, which I hope we shall do before Christmas. Whenever we reach Rome we shall stay till the holy week. I write this principally to invite your attention to a figure of Neptune, Ocean or Thetis, or Venus springing out of the sea. My place in *Carnarvonshire* is close to the sea, and I am very ambitious of having some marine subject from the chisel of a Welsh sculptor, and one so eminent as you. I consider you are a great honour to our country, the land of the original Poetry and Musick of the Island, and I trust you will bring sculpture in to add to and complete the reputation of Cambria for her love of the arts. Whatever you design to meet my views of a marine subject, I shall be happy to give an order for. Indeed I should like *two*, one on a small scale, to be executed out of hand directly, and the other to be subject to your other occupations in point of *time*. I long much to take something *home with me* from your studio. Pray have the goodness to give me a few lines to *feed my hopes* on this subject, and direct your letter to me at Mr., &c.

"Believe me," &c,
"I have rescued from the sea several thousand acres of land in Carnarvonshire; founded a town, Tre Madoc, nine feet under high water mark, with a church; established weekly markets and made a harbour called Port Madoc, where vessels of 200 tons come up and load, for which I obtained two Acts of Parliament and a gold medal from the Agricultural Society, which I will show you at Rome. There is a considerable trade in slates and copper from Port Madoc, and last year 12,000 tons of shipping came in and out with various cargoes. I am anxious for some marine figure to put on a pedestal in a Temple over the sea. How apropos from a Welsh sculptor at Rome a pupil of Canova. Let me inflame your patriotism, and do something for Wales and a Welsh Improver!!—W.A.M."

PARLIAMENT OF ENGLAND (Dec. 29, 1880).
Denbighshire, County and Borough. The first name under each date relates to the County, and the other to the Borough:—

1541-2	Johannes Salisbury, senior, armiger.	Richard Middilton, gent.
1547	Omitted (1)	
1552-3	Robertus Puleston.	Simon Thelwall, generosus.
1553	Johannes Salisbury, miles,	Ditto.
1554	Ditto.	Johannes Salisbury, armiger.
1554	Johannes Salusbury, miles.	Omitted (2).
1555	Edwardus Almer, armiger.	Johannes Evans, generosus.
1557-8	Omitted (3).	Johannes Salesbury, armiger (4).
1558-9	No Returns found (5).	
1562-3	Simon Thelwall, Esq.	Humphrey Lloyde, Esq. (6)

1572	William Allmer, Esq.	Richard Candishe, gent.
1584	Evan Lloyd (de yod?) (7).	Ditto.
1586	Robert Salesbury, Esq. (8), of Ruge.	Robert (Wrote, Esq).
1588-9	John Edwardes, Esq., of Chirke.	John Turbridge.
1592-3	Roger Puleston, Esq.	Simon Thelwall, gent.
1597	No Return found (9).	John Panton, gent.
1601	Sir John Salusburye, Knt.	Ditto.
1603-4	No Returns found (10).	
1614	No Returns found (11).	
1620-1	Sir John Trevor, junior, Knt.	Hugh Myddleton, Esq.
1623-4	Sir Eubule (Thelwall) Knt., a (Master in Chancery) (12).	Sir Hugh Middleton, bart.
1625	Sir Thomas Middleton, jun., Knt. (13).	Sir Hugh Middleton, Knt. and bart.
1625-6	Sir Eubule Thelwall, Knt.	Ditto.
1627-8	Ditto.	Ditto.
1640	Sir Thomas Salusbury, bart.	Omitted (14).
1640	Sir Thomas Middleton, Knt. jun., Esq., of Plasward.	Simon Thelwall,
1654	No Return found (15).	
1656	Col. John Jones (16).	Omitted (17).
1658-9	No Returns found (18).	
1660	No Returns found. Sir . . . . . ., Knt. (19).	
1661	Sir Thomas Middleton (20).	Sir John Salusbury, Bart.
1678-9	Sir Thomas Myddeton, bart.	Sir John Salusbury, Bart.
1679	Ditto.	Ditto.
1680-1	Sir John Trevor, Knt.	Ditto.
1685	Sir Richard Myddleton, bart.	Sir John Trevor, Knt. (21).
1688-9	Ditto.	Edward Brereton, Esq. (22)
1689-90	Ditto.	Ditto.
1695	Ditto.	Ditto.
1698	Ditto.	Ditto.
1700-1	Ditto.	Ditto.
1701	Ditto.	Ditto.
1702	Ditto.	Ditto.

(To be continued.)

(1) Denbighshire is omitted from the Official Return of this year; but in Williams's *Records of Denbigh* the following names are given:—John Salusbury and Simon Thelwall of Plas-y-Ward.
(2) John Salusbury, re-elected—*Ibid*.
(3) Williams gives "Return lost" for County, (4) but puts "Evans re-elected" for Borough.
(5) Robert ap Hugh (of Creuddyn, Esq.) and John Evans, gent.—*Williams*.
(6) Alias Cavendish—*Ibid.*
(7) Evan Lloyd de Yale—*Ibid.*
(8) Richard Salesbury de Rug—*Ibid.*
(9) John Salesbury, Knt.—*Ibid.*
(10) Peter Mutton (afterwards Sir Peter Mutton, Knt., Chief Justice of North Wales), and Hugh Myddleton, Esq.—*Ibid.*
(11) John Trevor, Knt., and Hugh Myddleton, who this year brought the New River to London—*Ibid*
(12) Eubulus Thelwall (Esq.)—*Ibid.*
(13) Williams gives Thelwall again.
(14) John Salusbury, Esq., junior—*Ibid.*
(15) Col. Simen Thelwall: Col. John Carter: County.
(16) The Official List gives Col. Lumley Thelwall, vice Col. Jones, who elected to serve for Merioneth, chosen 31 Dec., 1656. Williams gives Col. John Carter as succeeding Col. Jones.
(17) Williams also omits the Borough in his return.
(18) John Carter of Kinmel, Knight. John Manley, Esq.—*Ibid.*
(19) Sir Thomas Myddelton. Sir John Carter—*Ibid.*
(20) The Official List also gives John Wynne, Esq., of Melay, elected to the County on the decease of Sir T. Midleton, 4 May, 1661.
(21) From this time forward the Official Return describes the Borough" as "Leon (*alias* Holt) and Ruthin Borough."
(22) Williams gives Sir John Trevor.

QUERIES.

A SHROPSHIRE GIANT.—I one day read in a newspaper the following :—"Died at Tetchill, near Ellesmere, in 1792, aged 77, William Framston formerly known by the name of 'The Moreland Boy,' a Shropshire Giant. He was remarkably active for his age, and a surprising height, his coffin measuring 8 ft. 2 in. inside." Can any of your readers give further information respecting this man—who he was and why called "The Moreland Boy"?   E.O.

BURIAL TAX.—In a letter to the Independent Church at Sarney, Montgomeryshire, from a former minister, dated 1787, I find reference to an attempt made by a Parish Clerk to levy a fee upon burials in the Chapel burying ground. The letter, after pointing out the illegality of this attempt, proceeds "One thing you must be mindful of, namely, the tax levied by Parliament upon all the dead in the kingdom ; For it is enacted that 3d. are to be paid to the public revenue for each Burial ; and if you do not pay the 3d. you are liable to a fine of £5. The Ministers that bury your dead are to receive the tax, and in order to that they must be qualified ; That is, they must have a License or a Stamp'd Book ; or else any Minister that will receive the Tax for Births or Burials may be fined £5. I would advise you to have a Stamp'd Book fr yourselves as a Church that the Births & Burials may be properly registered on the spot. You must get Mr. Williams of Oswestry to put you in the way of having one." I presume "Mr. Williams" was the Minister of the Old Chapel, Oswestry. Can any correspondent give any information as to the history of this tax on burials, and when it ceased to be paid?   W.H.
[The letter quoted by our correspondent was published in *Mont : Coll :* Vol. 13, and was signed "John Griffiths," and addressed :—"Mr. Edward Astley, near New Chapel, to be left at Mr. Thomas Evans's, mercer, Welshpool."—ED.]

REPLIES.

JUDGE'S ESCORT AT WELSHPOOL (Jan. 12, 1881).—It was a usual custom not very long ago for the Mayor and Corporation of Welshpool to meet the Judge of Assize and wait upon him.
A FORMER MAYOR OF WELSHPOOL.

NOVELS RELATING TO WALES.—(Nov. 24, 1880.)—In a novel published by Macmillan in 1875, entitled *Janet's Home*, by Annie Keary, there is much about Wales. Amongst the names of persons introduced are Llewelyn Wynne, and Nesta; and amongst the places mentioned Morfa and Bangor.   K.A.R.

CURRENT NOTES.

The Rev. John Brooke of Haughton Hall, near Shifnal, died on Thursday. Mr. Brooke was formerly vicar of Shifnal and was patron of the living. He was also for many years chairman of the Shifnal Board of Guardians. The rev. gentleman was much beloved and esteemed by all his friends and neighbours. Mr. Brooke was one of the contributors to the *Shropshire Archæological Transactions*.

In a return made to the House of Commons by the Commissioners of Woods and Forests, it is stated the acreage of all Commons, and Waste Lands, belonging to Crown Manors in Wales, is given at 85,150 acres. The return gives the acreage of all the commons and waste lands of which surveys and measurements exist, but it must not be regarded as comprising everything to which the Crown is entitled. The acreage is also subject to revision de-

pending on the issue of adverse claims to portions of land claimed as belonging to the Crown. No profits are received by Her Majesty's Commissioners of Woods and Forests from the tenants of Crown manors for the exercise of commonable rights. It is not the enjoyment of a privilege subject to the will of the Lord, but of an ancient prescriptive right for which no payment is due. But although no profits are received from this source, the annual profits from other sources are considerable, including profits of mines, rents of sporting, acknowledgments for encroachments, estrays, &c.

It is probably forgotten by many that Davitt was connected with the Fenian attack upon Chester Castle in February, 1867. At the trial of Davitt one of the witnesses, John Joseph Carydon, who had been an officer of the Federal Army and a member of the Fenian organization, described the projected attack. The Holyhead Mail was to be seized as it passed Chester, and the telegraph wires were to be torn, and some of the rails taken up. The arms captured at the Castle were then to be placed in the train, and taken to Holyhead, where the mail boat was to be seized, to convey the arms to Ireland. The witness saw as many as 600 Fenians starting from Liverpool for the attack, and it was arranged that 1,200 or 1,400 were to take part in it. After the enterprise had failed, meetings were held to discuss the matter, and to arrange for a rising in Ireland, and Davitt was present at all of them. It was the witness Carydon who gave information of the projected attack on the Castle.

SHREWSBURY IN 1601.—"This yeare and upon Christmas Daye in the morninge throughe grete tempests of weather and rayne that Severn water did rise in the suburbs of Shreusberie into the inhabitants howses there wch contynewed 5 dayes together yt the people there keapt a loft in theire chambers withe sutche p'vision the had or coulld be brought to them by water and at the 5th dayes ennd began to fall that the inhabitants might goe downe to their bowses, but w'thin two days followinge it did rise agayne within a foote of the same height wch contynewid two dayes beinge a very hevye Christmas & discomfortable to the sayd inhabytaunts for it troublyd them sore in washinge downe their walles ovens & furnases to their greate hinderance & losses besides."—*Taylor's MS.*

THE LATE MRS. STACKHOUSE ACTON.—We regret to record the death of this lady, which occurred on Sunday evening, Jan. 23. Mrs. Acton had reached her eighty-seventh year, and although she was considered exceedingly robust for her advanced age, there is no doubt that the late extraordinary severity of the weather hastened her decease. The actual malady to which she succumbed was bronchitis. The deceased lady was the eldest daughter of the late Mr. Thomas Andrew Knight of Downton Castle, the first president of the Royal Horticultural Society, and a distinguished pomologist, and her uncle was the late Richard Payne Knight, the famous critic and virtuoso. She was married in 1812 to the late Thos. Pendarves Stackhouse Acton of Acton Scott, their olny child being a daughter, who died in early life. From the period of her marriage to the present time Mrs. Stackhouse Acton has been a constant resident at Acton Scott, and endeared herself to a verly large circle of friends by her many unceasing kindnesses, and more particularly to her poorer neighbours by the ready help which every case of distress never failed to receive. Those who had the privilege of her acquaintance will not readily forget (says the *Shrewsbury Chronicle*) the delight they experienced from her conversational powers, for she was both an artist and an authoress, and those gifts were increased by extensive reading and intercourse in early life with many of the scientific men of the day, the friends of her father, whose favourite daughter and constant companion she was in all those experiments by which he gave an impetus to scientific horticulture, all of which her retentive memory enabled her to describe as though they had been passing events of the hour. It was something more than the smattering that the present generation in our busier world usually contents itself with that she possessed of geology, horticulture, botany, architecture, and all branches of antiquarian research, and many a county drawing-room has, in "The Old Houses of Shropshire" and other publications, proofs of how her ready pen and pencil delighted to rescue from oblivion many relics of the past. The profits derived from her works were given to the Infirmary and the Eye and Ear Hospital, both of which institutions always had her warmest sympathy. Her funeral took place on Friday at Acton Scott.

Death of the Chairman of Denbighshire Quarter Sessions.

We regret to record the death of Mr. Thomas Hughes of Ystrad, the venerable Chairman of the Denbighshire Quarter Sessions. It will be remembered that Mr. Hughes was prevented by illness from attending the January Sessions, and it was then remarked that he had never been absent before since his appointment, almost a quarter of a century ago. The deceased gentleman, the son of John Hughes, Esq., of Llainwen, Denbighshire, was born at Denbigh, December 7th, 1799. He was educated at the Grammar School, Manchester, and married in 1827, Margaret, only daughter of Robert Williams, Esq., of Pentremawr, Denbighshire, by whom he had a son and three daughters. He succeeded to the estates in 1830. Mr. Hughes was appointed Steward of the Crown for the Lordship of Denbigh in 1851, and was a magistrate for Flintshire as well as Denbighshire; and he had just been elected for the 25th time Chairman of the Committee of Visitors of the North Wales Asylum. He died at his residence, Ystrad, near Denbigh, yesterday, at the age of 81, and is succeeded by his son, Major Hughes.

During Mr. Hughes's tenure of the Chairmanship of Quarter Sessions we believe there was only one appeal against his decision, and that resulted in his favour. He was an excellent man of business; and highly respected by all who came in contact with him, and his memory will be held in honour and affection by a large circle of friends. His only son and daughter-in-law, and a large family of grandchildren, to whom the old gentleman was devotedly attached, shared his home at Ystrad.

THE WEATHER.—Lowest Readings of the thermometer (Far.) at Oswestry from January 12 to 31.

Jan.			Jan.		
„	12	15	„	22	5
„	13	16	„	23	25
„	14	5	„	24	20
„	15	4	„	25	7
„	16	3	„	26	4
„	17	5	„	27	18
„	18	18	„	28	31
„	19	22	„	29	31
„	20	10	„	30	32
„	21	7	„	31	31

The cost of removing the ice, which was estimated to weigh from 190,000 to 200,000, tons from the public streets and high road in the borough of Carnarvon, will, it is said, be equal to a penny rate; and the parish of Llanddeiniolen will have to pay an ice rate of threepence in the pound.

The antedeluvian joke about the Spanish grandee last week reminds us of the various ways in which writers have got a rise out of the Welshmen in the same way. Thus, in Sir Walter Scott's *Ivanhoe*, in Wamba's song, "The Widow of Wycombe," we have :—

The next that came forth swore by blood and by nails,
  Merrily sing the roundelay;
Hur's a gentleman, God wot, and hur's lineage was of Wales
  And where was the widow might say him nay?

Sir David ap Morgan ap Griffith ap Hugh
  Ap Tudor ap Rhice quoth his roundelay,
She said that one widow for so many was too few,
  And she bade the Welshman wend his way.

Shakespear, too, that is if Shakespear wrote *Sir John Oldcastle*, as some suppose; has a similar joke. The scene opens with a quarrel in the streets of Hereford, between Lords Powis and Herbert, and their followers. The Mayor and Sheriff interfere, and, to save his master's arrest, a Welsh servant, Davy, offers to put in bail. The judge of assize puts in an appearance and asks "What sureties?" and Davy replies, "Hur cozen ap Rice ap Evan ap Morice ap Morgan ap Lluellyn ap Madoc ap Meredyth ap Griffin ap Davy, ap Owen ap Shinkin ap Shones." The Judge thinks "two of the most sufficient are enough," when the Sheriff interposes with "And please your worship these are all but one !" These illustrations appeared in *Bye-gones* some years ago, but they will bear repeating.

FEBRUARY 9, 1881.

NOTES.

MAEN PEN VOEL GWALT GWYN.—*The Stone of the bald top, O thou man of the white hair !* (Prof. Westwood's *Lapidarium Walliæ*). This portentous stone lies on a moated mound near the Sarn Helen, on the boundary of Cardigan and Carmarthen counties. As the writer, from his recent acquaintance with it, may have helped to mislead Prof. Westwood as to its proper name and signification, and thereby leave it open to the *Saturday Review* in its notice of *Lap: Wall:* to refer to him as a "wag," he feels he ought to try to make some amends to the stone and the learned Professor. The original form of the name is clearly given in the Talley Abbey charters (5 Edw. III.) as "Prenvol gwallwin." Prenvol means a wooden chest. Lewis Glyn Cothi refers to a coffin as being "Llun preavol," in the shape of a wooden chest. Gwallgwyn = white flaw. Maen Prenvol gwallwyn = The chestlike (or coffin) stone with the white flaw. C.C.

THE ANCIENT BRITONS IN 1815.—In a letter dated 3rd March, 1815, written by a gentleman who is still living, to a Montgomeryshire friend, the following passage occurs, which, perhaps, may not be without interest :—"I dined on Wednesday with the particularly ancient and honourable Society of Welshmen at Freemason's Hall. Six hundred worthy fellows dined tog'r in the same room and afts. diluted their meal with Twelve hundred Bottles of Wine. You may imagine our Ancient & honourable hearts were much gratified by the appearance of Sir Watkin amongst us who only arrived in England 3 days before. Towards ten & eleven the ancient boys became more and more noisy and riotous, and such a scene ensued as I am unable fairly to describe ; the truth is I was in no condition for making calm observations, but I desire you will give no countenance to the report that I danced a hornpipe on the table. Those who are in a certain condition, you are well aware, think every object before their eyes is dancing, but they are generally deceived."
Z.

SCARCITY OF GRAIN, &c., IN 1800. (Jan.

26, 1881.)—Amongst the other plans to meet the scarcity in 1800 was the following, which appeared in the *Salopian Journal* of March 19 that year :—" *Celery.* We understand that the seeds of this wholesome plant answer the purpose in making soup as well as the root itself ; and it may likewise be acceptable to readers to know that the green tops of celery hung up and dried like mint, make when pounded a good substitute for the root." An invention called "The Digestor" was also recommended, and it was said experiment had proved that a bone of beef, from which all the meat had been scraped away, weighed, when put into the Digestor, 25½ ounces, and when it came out only 10 ounces, "thereby gaining 15½ ounces of wholesome food." In Dec. 1800, turnips mixed with potatoes were recommended in Shrewsbury as a good substitute for butter ! To save milk—rice and onions with allspice and salt were boiled up in a large quantity of water ! All this may have done in 1800, but I fancy in 1881, "the working classes" when trade is slack and they cannot buy sausages, would prefer that their womankind should " go round with a book," and so provide more tasty food than stewed bones and turnip butter !

JARCO.

QUERIES.

THE GOAT OF THE 23RD REGIMENT.—Under this heading I put a query on Sep. 15, 1880, respecting the origin of the custom of having a goat to march at the head of this regiment. I observe in the *Oswestry Advertizer* of Jan. 19, 1881, that the same custom is followed with the Royal Carnarvonshire Militia. Is this the case with any other regiments of Militia ?
22 Rue Servandoni, Paris.   H. GAIDOZ.

BR—SL—Y TRIUMPHANT.—I have just had put into my hands a quarto pamphlet of 24 pages, published most likely in the spring of 1783, the title-page of which is as follows :—

BR—SL—Y TRIUMPHANT, over Tyrants and Pickpockets, a Pilfering Poet, and a Paltry P-rs-n. "Keep thy Hands from Picking and Stealing and thy Tongue from evil Speaking, Lying and Slandering."—*Ch. Catech.* The Fifteenth Edition, with several valuable and curious Additions, and Improvements by the Editors. Brecknock : Printed for Evan ap Griffith ap Rees ap Morgan ap Shone ap Walter. Sold by several Booksellers in Shropshire.

This pretended imprint gives a clue to the real name of the party attacked. As far as I can unravel the blanks and dashes, and hints and insinuations, the matter stands thus :—The Rev. Morgan Jones, rector of Willey and Barrow, Shropshire, (son of a blacksmith named John Walter residing at Brecon) made himself unpopular in the neighbourhood of Broseley. The first sentence of the preface of the pamphlet brings the charge against him thus :—

During the proceedings in the last Sessions of Parliament for an Act to establish a Court of Requests at B—sl—y, M—n J—es the R—ct-r of W—l-y, by every artifice in his power, endeavoured to raise an opposition to the Bill, and with great pains and trouble framed a ridiculous Petition, got it signed and sent to L—N—N, from whence it was returned with the contempt it deserved :—Yet, notwithstanding his disappointment, and the despicable Figure he had made, he came to the first Court at B—SL-Y ; and in the face of a large and respectable number of Gentlemen, assembled to qualify themselves for Commissioners, he privately stole one of the printed Acts of Parliament.

Mr. Jones, it is said, returned the Act on an officer of the Court being sent after him for it, and then wrote a poem, which he handed about, lampooning the Commissioners. It is in reply to this that the pamphlet before me is published. It is chiefly made up of bits of doggrel, most shockingly scurrilous ! In one of the pieces, "The Lamentation of M—g-n ap S—ne," several names connected with the Broseley Commission are given, such as B—ke—y, M-c-l-st-r, Dan. B-d-n, W-ke, B-n-ks, J-n-gs, J—m-s, P—ry. M-r-s, &c., and in the introduction to the pamphlet it is insinuated that the opposition of the parson is instigated by a Wenlock attorney. The book winds up with the following elegant advertisement :

TAKEN UP, on Sunday Night last, on the Turnpike-Road leading from B—gn—th to M—h W-nl—k, through N-l-y ; A BLACK HE GOAT, with a white Face, in very poor Condition, and from the appearance of his Coat, he had been worried by a set of *Sabbath Breakers :* (too notorious in that Country). Whoever is the Owner may hear of him, by applying to the Printer of the *Shrewsbury Chronicle.*——See the Paper of the 28th of September, 1782.

Perhaps some reader of this will be able to tell us something about the Broseley Court of Requests and the opposition of the Parson ?   J.?.R.

REPLIES.

TALHAIARN (Apr. 21, May 5, 1880.)—In looking over the reprint of *Bye-gones* for last year I observed two paragraphs on dates as above, referring to the assumption of the Bardic name *Talhaiarn* by the well-remembered John Jones, but I have been under the impression that he adopted it rather from the parish of his nativity (Llanfair *Talhaiarn*) than in imitation of his ancient predecessor. Our friend "Ceiriog" is a living instance of a similar selection, and not in imitation of another Welsh poet who flourished about 1580-1620.   TYRO.

THE ORIGINAL CADER IDRIS GUIDE (Aug. 26, 1880).—The writer in the *Gent.'s Magazine* which "N.W.S." quotes, has taken his description almost word for word from Pugh's *Cambria Depicta,* vide page 206-7, who gives a very characteristic portrait of the eccentric guide, and thus prefaces his description—

Here is an eccentric old man, not unknown to many of those who have visited this place : he fills the office of a guide to Cader Idris with as much credit to himself as pleasure to the strangers whom he conveys.

I have given a portrait of him from the life, seated upon his poney, conducting a party up the mountain. This I trust, with the following ludicrous description, will give a just and proper idea of the little fellow.

Then follows the description as quoted by "N.W.S."
LANDWOR.

METHODISM IN OSWESTRY (Apr. 21, 1880.)—At this date I stated that the Wesleyans had worshipped in Oswestry previously to the erection of a chapel in Salop Road, in what is now the Guildhall. From a little book just lent to me (and which has been mentioned in *Bye-gones*) I infer that these services were, originally, in Welsh. The chapel, as we know from our published histories, was erected in 1813. Between the years 1806 and 1811 a Miss Anne Sadler of Shrewsbury came to reside in Oswestry, and being a Methodist was naturally anxious to have the ministrations of her own community ; but "Oswestry was then attended by Welsh Preachers." Occasionally, however, it would seem they held English services, for in 1811, the Minister from Wrexham, Mr. Worth, came over to preach, and "she rejoiced at the opportunity to make known her state to a preacher in the Connexion to which she belonged." I need not say more about Miss Sadler (afterwards Mrs. Worth) as you have already given an outline of her life and work. In one of these communications I observe that "E.C." says that Mr. Worth was "Wesleyan Minister at Oswestry." This perhaps only means that he came over occasionally from Wrexham to preach. He had certainly left the district before there was any chapel built. Mr. Jones of Creaton, who was curate in Oswestry in 1782, refers to Wesleyan Methodists in his time, but does not say whether they were Welsh or English.   JARCO.

OLD PARR'S PORTRAITS (Apr. 14, 1880).—At this date Col. HEYWARD stated that the Likeness by Rubens was sold at Christie's for £189 in June, 1878. Will he kindly describe the picture? I ask for this reason: In Chambers's Book of Days, vol. 2, p. 583, we are told that "the portrait which is frequently attached to the puffing placard advertisements of Parr's Pills is derived from a likeness by the celebrated painter Rubens." Now it so happens that the proprietors of the quack medicine use more than one likeness. That on the pill boxes represents a man in the full possession of his sight, and with a flowing wig and beard; and one in a penny almanack, in the interest of the pills, has an older, but still wide awake, man with shorter and scantier hair, parted at the side. This has under it "by Rubens," and is stated to have been taken when Parr was 152 years of age. Amidst the mass of fable surrounding Parr's life, at least one fact is undeniable, which is that he was blind for more than 30 years before he died. The Arundel Society had copies of two likenesses of Old Parr in their collection of photographs; viz., the one in the possession of Mr. Reginald Cholmondeley (exhibited at Wrexham in 1876), which is described as 'Bust; conical cap and dress brown; white collar; canvass 23-in. × 18-in;" the other in possession of the Ashmolean Museum, Oxford, "half-length; looking to right; brown dress; stick in right hand; canvass 42-in. × 31-in." In both cases Parr is described as 152 years old; and in Mr. Cholmondeley's likeness (which I believe is by Dobson) he is represented as blind, or nearly so.   N.W.S.

THUNDER ON THE ORGAN (Feb. 4, 1880). The "Organ Thunderer," Mr. Joseph Weston, was a native or resident of Solihull, near Birmingham, of great musical abilities, good education, but very irritable and eccentric, and given to deep potations. He imported himself into Shropshire as a candidate for the organist's place at Whitchurch. Being unsuccessful, he stayed a while in Shrewsbury, where he astonished the people with his clever "Organ Recitals." He visited a good deal at Mr. David Parkes's, in Castle-street, but his habits became so obnoxious that the family was obliged to show him "the cold shoulder." He always went to his Organ Recitals in a state of great intoxication, and as Mr. Blakeway, the then Minister of St. Mary's, and his Churchwarden, Mr. D. Parkes, were both enthusiastically fond of music, and from their knowledge of the science could appreciate it, there can be little doubt but that the intoxication was the real cause of his performance being veto'd at St. Mary's. I suppose he received some hospitality from my father and mother also, as I have a letter dated June 26, 1805, in which "Mr. Weston begs Mrs. Leighton's acceptance of the enclosed lines on her dear little Cherub, as a trifling acknowledgment for the kind attentions which he has received during his residence at Shrewsbury." The lines enclosed are entitled "The Wish written on seeing a beautiful Babe, of about a month old." The "beautiful Babe" was my own sweet self, my birthday being May 17, 1805. Mr. Weston returned to Solihull, and soon after succumbed to his habits.   W.A.L.

CURRENT NOTES.

"An American Journalist" writing to the Nonconformist newspaper, relates the particulars of an interview he has recently had with the Rev. John Morris, who was for more than fifty years Congregational minister at Tattenhall, and who is now—in his 94th year—hale and well, at Chester, residing with his daughter, Mrs. Marsh. The "Journalist" says, Mr. Morris "distinctly remembers, and describes in a very interesting way, being taken to hear John Wesley preach at Oswestry, shortly before Wesley's death, and when Mr. Morris was three years old." Some of the readers of the Oswestry Advertizer will perhaps remember that this fact was once stated in "Byegones." Mr. Morris was a native of Oswestry, and has relatives still living in the town. The American writer we have been quoting goes on to say that on the occasion when John Wesley preached in Oswestry the hymns sung were "lined out by the Rev. Mr. Tompkinson, an ex-clergyman of the Church of England, who afterwards presented the little boy, Morris, with a Bible, which is still extant." Before the visitor left, Mr. Morris sang him a Welsh hymn, with which the American was very much delighted, and he says if "the reverend gentleman reaches his century" he thinks he shall cross the Atlantic to join in it! Meanwhile he wishes others to interview Mr. Morris.

THE LATE LORD WENLOCK'S WILL.—The will (dated January 23, 1877) with two codicils (dated January 23, 1879, and June 3, 1880) of the Right Hon. Beilby Richard, Baron Wenlock, late of Wenlock, Shropshire, and of Escrick Park, Yorkshire, who died on November 6 last, has been proved at the district registry, York, by the Dowager Baroness Wenlock, the widow, and John Coleman, two of the executors, the personal estate, including leaseholds, being sworn under £250,000. The testator bequeaths to his wife, Elizabeth, Lady Wenlock, £2,000, certain horses and carriages, and the jewels usually worn by her; she is to have the use for life of the family jewels and such plate as she may select; at her decease these are made heirlooms to go with the estates; he also leaves her £1,000 per annum for life, in addition to the jointure secured to her by her marriage settlement, and Monk Hopton House, Salop, with the furniture, or Escrick Villa, Yorkshire, for a residence, as she may elect. All his manors, messuages, lands, tenements, and hereditaments in the counties of York and Salop (except Weel, Yorkshire, and Monk Hopton and Priors Ditton, Salop) he devises to the use of his eldest son, Beilby Lawley, for life, with remainder to his first and other sons successively in tail male. His property at Monk Hopton and Priors Ditton, Salop, he devises to the use of his second son, Richard Thompson Lawley, for life, with remainder to his first and other sons successively in tail male. He gives to his eldest son absolutely all his live and dead farming and agricultural stock and implements of husbandry, and the use of all his furniture, plate, pictures, and household effects for life, after which they are to go with the estates; to each of his four younger sons £30,000, except Weel, each of his four daughters £15,000, and legacies to many of his servants, conditional on their being in his service at the time of his decease. The advowson and rectory of Marston, Yorkshire, is left to trustees, for the purpose of his son, Algernon George, if in holy orders, being presented to it at the next vacancy. The residue of his real estate is directed to be sold, and the proceeds, with the residuary personal estate, laid out in the purchase of land about Escrick, to be settled the same as the family estates.

FEBRUARY 16, 1881.

NOTES.

THE OLD WELSH ALMANACKS (Jan. 12, 1881).

—I am sorry that I can only send you the titles of *three* out of the four Almanacks for the years 1808—1811, the one for 1809 being missing ; and as only one of these has *internal* lines to mention, I at once proceed to quote the one verse met with, viz., in the issue for 1811 :—

O Frydain Fawr dy freintiau, na hir freuddwydia'n hwy;
Rhag i dy hedd ddiflanu, heb obaith t'wnnu mwy;
Gwel wledydd cymdogaethol, dan *farn*, aruthrol ief,
Ers blwyddau heb ymwared, a *ni* dan nodded nef.

The Almanack for 1808 is called "Cyfaill Llesawl." It was printed at Dublin, and sold at fourpence halfpenny. The verses on the cover are as under :—

1 Fy hen gyfeillion tyner,
　Rwy'n d'od yn ol fy arfer;
O wlad i wlad, o Dre' i Dre,
　I ymofyn lle dres amser.

2 Mae lle chwe mis heb amau,
　Na welir Haul ar fryniau :
A chwe mis arall mewn rhyw-
　　　　　　　　　　fan,
Heb fyned dan ei gaerau.

3 Y Ddae'r a'r Lloer yr hunwedd
　A'r holl blanedau hôywedd;
Sy'n cylchu'r Haul-wen yn
　　　　　　　　ddidawl
Ac yntau'n bawl cymher-
　　　fedd.

4 Pe byddai Haul y Nefoedd.
　Yn cylchu'r Byd a'i lueedd;
Fe â bob munud yn ei dro,
　Dri chan' mil o Filldiroedd.

5 Mae'r Ddaear hithau'n ymdro
　I'r dwyrain fel maen llife ;
Rhyfeddol Drefnwr　arfaeth
　　faith,　　　　　　[syrthio.
Sy'n　cadw 'i　waith　rhag

6 As darkness must be flying,
　When light is but ap-
　　proaching ;
So superstition loses ground,
　Where learning's found in-
　　creasing.

The one for 1810 is called "Cyfaill Gwaraidd ;" was printed at Dublin ; sold at fourpence halfpenny, and has these verses on the title page :—

1 Rwy etto'n dyfod attoch,
　I'm cannol fel y'm gweloch,
Os am iawn lê y gwyrif ddim,
　Boed hamdden,chwi'm had-
　　waenoch.

2 Mae'r *ongl* hynod hoywedd
　Rhwng Henlawd a Chyhyd-
　　　　　　　　　edd ;
Bob deuddeng mis yn cael ei
　ladd,　　　　　[fanedd.
Chwech ailiad grâdd gy-

3 Os felly, daw'r Tymhorau
　Yn un y'mhen blynyddau ;
Bydd *Rhagfyr* oer mor deg ei
　le
A *Mai* neu *Hefin* olau.

4 Mae sêr y *Nef-wen* dirion,
　Yn Fydoeddmedd y Doeth-
　　ion ;
Heurant hefyd drwy ryw
　ddawn,
Eu bod yn llawn *Trigolion*.

5 'Mofynwn am Wirionedd
　I'n cynnal uwchlaw gwag-
　　edd ;
A gwir adnabod Castell clyd,
　Yn gysgod hyd y diwedd.

6 Soon may the *Arms* of Envy,
　Abate their ardent Fury ;
Another JUBILEE shall sound,
　When *Peace* surround our
　country.

The one for 1811 is called "Cyfaill Mwynaidd," the price fourpence halfpenny. It was printed at Dublin, and has the following verses on its title page :—

1 GYFEILLION mwynion Cymru,
　Rwy'n chwennych eich di-
　　ddanu ;
Drwy ym'ch byd i roddi tro,
　I chwilio'r fro i fynu.

2 Ein Daear fawr sydd gyfrgron
　(Fel pêl) yn rhodio'r eigion;
O gylch yr haul rhydd gyflawn
　　daith,　　　　　　　　　　　　　　　　　　　　[gyson.
Mewn blwyddyn faith yn

3 Ac ar ei ffûg begynnau,
　Hi dry yr un amserau ;
I lunio boreu, hwyr a nawn,
　Dros *ugain* llawn o oriau.

4 Lliosog iawn yw'r teulu,
　Sydd arni yn byw o bobtu ;
Rhyfeddol DREFN sy'n cadw'n
　　　　　　　　　fyw,
Holl ddynolryw o'i deutu.

5 Mae difyr ddyddiau'n dyfod,
　Gwyn fyd a'i gwelai'n barod;
I'r *Llesgard*, *Llew*, a'u dan-
　　nedd câs
A'r *Nifail* brâs i gydfod.

6 May Britain's Sons be steady,
　In doing well their duty ;
At home, abroad in foreign
　land,
May they command in safety.

*23a, 56½m.

　　　　　　　　　　　E.G.S.

THE SCARCITY IN 1800. (Feb. 9, 1881.)—The following is the document referred to Jan. 26.

OCTOBER, 1800.

OSWESTRY SUBSCRIPTION FOR THE RELIEF OF THE POOR.

	£	s.		£	s.
Earl of Powis	50	0	John Probert, Esq.	5	5
Lord Bradford	10	0	Lazarus Venables, Esq.	20	0
Thos. Jones, Esq., M.P.	20	0	George Withers, Esq.	10	10
Mrs. Barrett	50	0	Mr. Thomas Whitehurst	10	0
Rev. William Roberts, and			Mr. Edward Rees	10	10
Mrs. Roberts	45	0	Mr. Richard Bickerton	5	5
Owen Ormsby, Esq.	20	0	Mr. John Croxon, Jun.	10	0
Mrs. Owen, Porkington*	15	0	Mr. William Lacon	5	0
Rev. J. R. Lloyd	10	0	Mrs.　Hopkins,　Park		
Rev. Joseph Venables ..	20	0	Promise	5	5
John Gibbons, Esq.	20	0	Mr. John Frank	10	0
Rev. Turner Edwards	20	0	Mr. John Stoakes	10	10
Lewis Jones, Esq.	15	15	Mr. Richard Bill	5	5
Mrs. Susanna Price	10	0	Rev. Mr. Whitridge	4	4
Rev. Owen Owen	15	15	Mr. Davies, Maesbury .	5	5
Mrs. Owen	5	5	Mr. Rice Roberts	5	0
Mrs. Humffreys	15	15	Mr. Richard Jones	3	3
Mrs. Hilditch	10	10	Mr. Pritchard, Moreton	1	1
Rev. James Donne	10	10	Collected at　Quarter		
Rev. Richard Maurice ..	5	5	Sessions	1	1
Mr. Thomas Longueville					
Jones	5	5		543	4
Mr. H. O. Gibbons	5	5	Mr. J. Downes, in lieu of		
Mr. Edmonds	5	5	63 strikes of grain	6	6
Mr. Cartwright	5	5	Mrs.　Evans,　Sweeney,		
Robt. Lloyd, Esq., Swan-			do. 30 do.	3	0
hill	10	10	Mr. A. Davies, do. 54 do.	5	8
Thomas Davies, Esq.	10	10			
Thomas N. Parker, Esq.	5	5		£557	18

OCCUPIERS OF LAND WHO DELIVERED WHEAT AT 16s. AND BARLEY AT 10s. A STRIKE.

	Strikes of Wt. B'y.			Strikes of Wt. B'y.	
Mr. J. Jones, Oswestry	50	50	Mr. Manford	20	40
Mr.T. Jones, Milehouse	50	50	Mr. Arthur Davies	46	—
Mr. T. Jones, Foxhall	60	60	Mr. Jebb, Maesbury	20	20
Mr. Croxon	50	50	Mr. Edward Roberts	20	20
Mr. Richard Croxon	—	100	Mr. Thos. Howell, Llys.	20	20
Mr. John Downes	37	—	Mrs. Evans, Crickheath	9	20
Mr. Richard Menlove	—	100	Mrs. Evans, Sweeney	30	—
Mr. Peploe	20	20	Mr. Thomas, Moreton	20	20
Mr. Richard Downes	40	—	Mr. Edwards, Maesbury	80	30
Mr. E. Davies, Waen-wen	20	20	Mr. John Davies, Nant	10	10
Mr. Clemson	20	20	Mr. Jarvis, Nant	—	40
Mr. Ellis Jones, Drill..	—	40			
				572	710

The foregoing, which was in the form of a foolscap folio circular, was probably issued at the time it is dated, viz., Oct., 1800.　Fourteen months later another statement was issued, printed on the back of it, as follows :—

December 16, 1801.

ABSTRACT OF THE ACCOUNT OF THE COMMITEE :—
The particulars of which may be seen at the Oswestry Bank.

THE Committee appointed to manage the Fund raised by voluntary contribution for the Relief of the Poor resident in the Town and Parish of OSWESTRY, during the late Season of Scarcity, trust that the Measures they adopted in conducting the Business, met the approbation of the Subscribers and Occupiers of Land who delivered their several Quantities of Corn according to Agreement, at reduced Prices, and tended effectually to relieve the Objects of their Charity,

By having the principal Part of the Grain ground for 6d. a Strike, a very considerable Saving was made for the Benefit of the Poor, (perhaps more than 125l.) and thereby, it is apprehended, much Waste was prevented in the Use of fine Flour, a Matter of no small importance during such a Season.

The average Number of Persons relieved weekly with Corn, Flour and Herrings, at reduced Prices, from the 20th of *October*, 1800, till the 3d of *August*, 1801, was about 1780.　The Articles were sold for about two-thirds of their Value, for a considerable Part of the Time, and never at a higher Rate than about three-fourths of their Value.

Committee for Supplying the Poor with Flour, &c.

DR.

	£ s. d.
Subscriptions amounting to	557 18 0
Received for—	
Blend-Corn 230¾ Strikes at 10s.	115 8 9
17,355 lb Flour, at 6 lb for 1s.	144 12 6
56,960¼ lb ditto, at 5½ lb for 1s. ..	517 16 6
65,360 lb ditto, at 5 lb for 1s.	653 12 0
42,756 lb ditto, at 4 lb for 1s.	534 9 0
One Barrel of Flour	2 4 6
Damaged Flour	1 4 6
Bran	26 6 3
Herrings	48 10 9
Casks	4 11 2
Bags, Weights, &c.	8 14 0
	£2615 7 11

Per Contra CR.

	£ s. d.
Paid for—	
Wheat, delivered by several Persons according to Agreement, 572 Strikes & 45 1b. at 16s. ..	458 1 8
Barley, ditto, 710 ditto, at 10s. ..	355 0 0
Wheat bought at Market Prices, 160 ditto ..	182 7 0
Barley, ditto, 1273¾ Strikes & 15 lb ..	967 0 9
Peas, ditto, 15 ditto, at 14s.	10 10 0
Herrings	51 1 8
155 Barrels of American Flour	312 18 2
Carriage of Flour and Herrings.. ..	33 14 0
Printing Notices of Meeting, inserting Notices in Salop Papers, Postage, &c. ..	5 5 4
Assistance to Edw. Jones, Rd. Llewellin, and others, in selling Corn, Flour, &c., and other petty expenses	24 15 6
Sacks, Weights, &c.	22 6 4
White-washing and repairing the Hall ..	0 18 4
Counterfeit Coin received	5 11 4
Grinding 2,497 Strikes of Grain.. ..	62 10 6
Toll ot Corn to the Mayor	28 7 0
	2520 7 7
By Balance in the Oswestry Bank ..	95 0 4
	£2615 7 11

N.B. A Meeting of Subscribers in Money and Grain, will be held on *Wednesday* the 23d Instant, in the *Town-Hall*, at Twelve o'Clock, to determine upon a proper Mode for the Application of the above Balance, for the Benefit of the Poor.

* "Mrs. Owen, Porkington," is described in the newspapers as " Mrs. Owen, St. James's Place."

QUERIES.

MAGIC AT MAIN, MEIFOD.—As a boy, living in this parish, I used to hear very minute and circumstantial accounts of certain supernatural occurrences which must have taken place, if at all, about the year 1807, at the above farm. Will some one take the trouble to collect what can be known of the phenomena, real or imaginary? It surely can hurt no one's feelings at this length of time, and the firm credence given them seems to me not without its value in considering the credibility of such testimony generally.　　　　C.G.T.

SHIPWRECKS AT LLANDUDNO.—In Nicholson's *Cambrian Traveller's Guide* ed. 1813, allusion is made to the wreck of the Hornby Castle, near Llandudno. What were the circumstances of this shipwreck? When at Llandudno many years ago I questioned some of the older inhabitants about it, but though they were very ready with stories of the wreck of the Rothsay Castle (which, as we know, took place in 1831) they knew nothing about the Hornby Castle. It must have been before 1813. What was the name of the author of a book called *The Wreck of the Rothsay Castle*, published some time between 1831 and 1835? It is on the title page, but I have forgotten it.　　　　C.

5

REPLIES.

A WELSH CANNIBAL (Jan. 19, 1881).—The passage quoted from Miss Costello's book is a nearly exact translation of the text of one of the so-called " Historical Triads" published in the *Myfyrian Archæology of Wales*; Gee's edit. p. 404.　　　　H. GAIDOZ.

I suspect that the quotation from Miss Costello's *Falls, Lakes, and Mountains of North Wales* comes originally from ."The Triads." It will be found duly set forth on page 405—*Triad* No. 45—Gee's Edition of the *Myfyrian Archaiology of Wales* where *Gwrgi Garwlwyd* is described as one of the three " *Carnvradwyr* " or Arrant Traitors of the Island of Britain—the other two were *Medrawd* and *Aeddan.*　　　　BOOKWORM.

A SHROPSHIRE GIANT (Jan. 26, 1881).—Mr. Hulbert, the gossiping chronicler of our boyish days, has recorded this giant on page 239 of his Salopian *History*. He says, "Ellesmere parish has not been without its giants any more than its patriarchs; in 1792 died at Tetchill, William Formston, aged 77, known by the name of the Moreland Boy, or Shropshire Giant, he was, it is said, remarkably active for his age and surprising height; his coffin measured eight feet two inches inside."
　　　　SCROBBES BYRIG.

CHURCH BELLS (Sep. 15, 1880.)—*The Ancient Bell at Baschurch.*—In examining Bells, and especially old Bells, copies of their inscriptions are always more or less unsatisfactory :—rubbings alone are thoroughly reliable. Mr. Morris was misled by an imperfect copy of that on the Baschurch "Lady bell." It is not Welsh but Dutch, and no doubt the bell itself originally came from the Low Countries. The inscription is as follows :—"+ maria : int. jaer. ons. heren. m.cccc. ende. xlvii. jan. van. venloe." (Mary—In the year of our Lord 1400 and 47—Jan van Venloe). The use of " ende" for *and* occurs frequently in the *Essen Muniments.* John of Venloe (Venloo) was in all probability the founder. A bell at Nicholaston, Glamorganshire, bears a similar Low Dutch inscription :— " Ic ben ghegoten int jaer ons heeren mccccxviii." (I am cast in the year of our Lord 1518.) Another at Bromeswell, Suffolk, quoted by the Rev. Dr. Raven in a paper read at Lampeter, August, 1878, reads :—"Ihesus : ben ic ghegoten van cornelis waghevens int jaer ons heeren mccccxxx." The Baschurch bell is a handsome well-shaped bell with a good musical tone. The initial cross is engraved by the Rev. H. T. Ellacombe in his *Bells of the Church* as occurring at Vowchurch, Herefordshire, on a bell since melted down. Besides the Cross there are two other stamps, a lion and an eagle, perhaps intended as two of the four evangelistic symbols. These stamps, popularly supposed to represent a goat and a harp respectively, are considered by the villagers to prove the Welsh origin of their Bell. It would be interesting to discover if any foundation exists for the tradition that this bell once belonged to Valle Crucis Abbey, and if so, how it came to Baschurch.　　　　W.H.J.
Malvern.

PHILLIPS'S *HISTORY OF SHREWSBURY* (Sep. 8, 1880).—Mr. James Bowen, a very skilful herald painter, and an expert in deciphering old deeds and MSS., was employed by Mr. W. Mytton of Halston to make MS. Collections from ancient Records and Registers for a projected *History of Shropshire.* Mr. James Bowen painted and engraved four views of Shrewsbury from different points, which are now very scarce. They are exceedingly interesting, being faithful representations, and shewing the aspects of the Town at that particular period, about 1700. He was 'no doubt the author

27

of Phillips's *History*, at least such was always asserted by his son. His son, Mr. John Bowen, succeeded him in his business, and followed in his steps as a herald painter and expert in old MSS. Those who have witnessed him when engaged in heraldic painting, were always astonished at the ease, rapidity, skill, and spirit with which he executed his work. He was continually employed by the nobles and gentry of Shropshire and adjoining counties to decipher and translate their family muniments, and he had splendid opportunities of amassing large local historical information, but he unfortunately was of such an indolent disposition that those opportunities were unimproved. He died in 1832, and was succeeded by his second son, the late Alderman Bowen, who inherited his father's talents, and was an artist of considerable excellence. W. A. L.

CURRENT NOTES.

The fallow-deer for which Eyton Park, near Wellington, has long been famous, left their old quarters on Thursday, having been purchased by the Earl of Derby for £125, to augment his splendid herd at Knowsley Park. Lord Derby had entrusted the arrangements for catching the deer and conveying them to Prescot, to Lord Eustace Cecil, and a large number of people assembled at Eyton on Thursday to watch the operation. The chief work was done by three muzzled deer hounds which Lord E. Cecil had brought with him for that purpose. Four of the deer were killed. The live deer were placed in two large caravans, which were taken to Wellington goods station.

A gentleman in Denbighshire lost a large silver cup of much value, which had been an heirloom in the family for many generations. After making diligent enquiry respecting the cup, without the least success, he at last determined to place the affair in the hands of Robin Ddu the Wizard. Robin without losing much time attended at the Hall, and after placing his red cap on his head, and a large wooden pair of spectacles on the bridge of his nose, he soon called all the inmates of the Hall before him, and declared that he would find the thief before midnight. All the servants firmly denied the theft; then, said Robin, "if you are guiltless you will have no objection to undergo a magic proof." He then ordered a cockerel to be placed under a pot in the pantry, and told all the servants to go one by one and rub the pot well with their hands. If any of them were guilty of the theft the cockerel would immediately crow whilst the guilty person was rubbing the vessel. After all the servants had gone through the ceremony the wizard ordered them to show their hands, when he perceived that the hands of the butler were clean. His conscience had stricken him, so that he could not touch the pot. Robin accused him of the theft, which he reluctantly admitted, and the cup was restored to its owner.

OSWESTRY SCHOOL.—The last number of *Land and Water* contains the result of a competition for prizes offered by the proprietors for English compositions by schoolboys in the United Kingdom, under nineteen years of age. The first prize of three guineas has been gained by H. P. Cuthbert, and the third prize of one guinea by C. J. Pugh, both of Oswestry School. The subject was "Lieut.-General Sir F. Roberts's Victory over Ayoub Khan at Baba-Wali on September 1st, 1880."

OSWESTRY PARISH RECORDS.

At the annual meeting of the Shropshire Archæological Society held in Shrewsbury last December, Mr. Stanley Leighton lamented that no Government had taken up the question of copying the Parish Registers of England and Wales. There are many of us who entirely agree with Mr. Leighton in this, but I fear it will be a long time to wait before so good a suggestion is adopted. In some parishes local subscriptions have been collected, in order to accomplish the work, and the local Parish Magazine has been the vehicle through which the result has been published. Not the Registers alone, but the Records, generally, should be transcribed and printed. There must be much that is deeply interesting and curious locked up in the parish chests of Oswestry—quite independent of the Registers. For instance, it was stated in *Bye-gones* on Jan. 12, that "a Commission for the hearing of a case connected with the Grammar School" was issued in the reign of Queen Elizabeth, "the hearing to take place in the Oswestry Parish Church." If records such as these should happen to be preserved, the money spent in unearthing them will not be thrown away. I, for one, would be very happy to contribute a guinea to a "Copying Fund," and I am sure the publishers of the *Oswestry Parish Magazine* would print a four page supplement every month for the bare cost of paper and working. Does the idea commend itself to any of your readers?

JARCO.

THE WELSH EDUCATION COMMITTEE.

The Welsh Education Committee held their final sittings for taking evidence on Thursday and Thursday week. Last Thursday Lord Aberdare presided, and all the members of the Committee were present. Archdeacon De Winton of Brecon, and Mr. Beck, clerk of the Ironmongers' Company, London, were examined. It is understood that the report will now be considered. Lord Aberdare and Canon Robinson have undertaken to draw up a digest of the evidence, a copy of which will be furnished to the members of the Committee, who will thereafter meet again with the object of considering their report; but this will not happen for some time. At the last sitting but one, Mr. Stephen Evans gave an account of the finances of the University College of Wales. The subscriptions and donations received between 1863 and the 30th of June, 1880, amounted to £51,131 18s. The college was established in 1872. The expenditure for the last two or three years had been £3,400 a year; the income from students' fees and investments about £1,000 per annum; leaving £2,400 to be raised by voluntary subscriptions. Up to the present the receipts had been sufficient to meet all the necessary expenses, but the future maintenance of the college by voluntary subscriptions was impossible. The difficulty of obtaining subscriptions was constantly increasing. Appeals had been made to the great landowners of Wales, but with very small success, except in a very few instances. The college had been supported chiefly by wealthy men engaged in commerce, and by the middle and industrial classes. A Government grant was indispensable; without it the college, in its present form, must collapse. As to the students at the college, their number was small, much smaller than was anticipated. This was partly owing to the deficiency of means for preparing youths for college education, and partly to the poverty of intending students; and also, and perhaps, chiefly, to the scattered nature of the population in that part of Wales, although that would apply to any other county in Wales, with the exception of Glamorganshire. Another reason might be found in the want of co-operation —not to say hostility—on the part of existing endowed grammar schools of the country. No scheme of education would meet the want of Wales unless it provided exhibitions from elementary schools to secondary schools, and, again, from secondary schools to the college or colleges. It was also very important that some efficient secondary schools should be established in each county, and the fees fixed on a very moderate scale. He hoped that it would be found practicable to establish an examining Board with power to grant degrees in arts. This would give a great impetus to education throughout Wales.

Mr. T. Marchant Williams, B.A., one of the inspectors of schools for the London School Board, suggested that all available Welsh educational endowments should be concentrated in one fund, to be vested in and administered by the Charity Commissioners, or by Commissioners specially appointed. The next step would be to establish county public schools for boys and girls, the number, size, and geographical position of such schools to be determined by the Commissioners after they shall have made a searching enquiry into the existing grammar schools and private adventure schools, which shall be placed on much the same footing as the new county public schools if they satisfy the Commissioners in respect of their discipline, the scope, character, and extent of their teaching, their geographical position, and their suitability in the way of premises, apparatus, &c. It should also be a condition that such schools should be open to the periodical visits and inspection of any person or persons authorised by the Commissioners. The grammar schools to be managed in precisely the same manner, and by the same persons, as the county public schools; the private schools to be managed by private individuals, who would fix the fees and superintend and control all the arrangements of their schools; all such arrangements, however, to be annually inquired into and approved by the Commissioners' representative. The building fund for these county public schools to be raised by private donations supplemented by a county rate; these schools to be managed by a Board elected triennially; every person within the county rated to poor rate at not less than £30 per annum to have a vote. The school buildings to resemble the Ecole Modele at Brussels, or the North London Collegiate School for girls. All the teachers to be adults, and to be appointed by the Board of managers.—Canon Robinson: Do you suggest that the schools should be unsectarian?—Mr. Marchant Williams: Decidedly.—Canon Robinson: Suppose parents should require their children to receive religious education?—Mr. Marchant Williams: That might be compassed by private arrangement. Religious instruction should not be imparted in the schools during school hours.—Proceeding with his evidence, Mr. Williams said: I would suggest that the syllabus of the subjects of instruction should be arranged by the Commissioners, and that it should comprise English, mathematics, Latin, Welsh, French, German, natural science, elementary, social, and political economy, laws of health, vocal and instrumental music, physical exercises, and also, in the girls' school, domestic economy, sewing, knitting, and cookery. The fees to be fixed by the managers, subject to the approval of the Commissioners. The schools to be inspected and reported upon, and also to be visited once a year, at least, by the representative of the Commissioners. Scholars not to be under ten or over sixteen years of age. The entrance examination to be fixed upon by the managers and the representatives of the Commissioners, but to be dispensed with in the case of boys and girls who have passed the Standard IV in the elementary schools, or any other examination specified by the Commissioners. Exhibitions—out of the Welsh Educational Endowment Fund—to be awarded at the beginning of each year, in accordance with the official inspectors' reports. Results fees to be awarded out of the same fund; the scale and other conditions to be arranged by the Commissioners. Graded public elementary schools are possible only in populous places, such as Swansea, Cardiff, and Merthyr Tydvil. They should be established by the School Boards, independently of the Commissioners. As provision for higher education in Wales, I would suggest two colleges, one at Swansea and the other at Bangor, to which place I would suggest that the University College of Wales, now at Aberystwyth, should be, so to speak, transferred. Lampeter College and the Theological Colleges at Bala, Trevecca, Carmarthen, Brecon, Haverfordwest, and Pontypool to remain as they are and where they are. As to the two colleges, I would suggest that a Government grant should be obtained in aid of the building of the new college at Swansea, and to defray the expenses incurred in transferring the college at Aberystwyth to Bangor; also that an annual grant should be obtained from Government to be administered by the Commissioners. The annual grant to be apportioned by the Commissioners to each college according to the report of the representatives of the Commissioners, dependent, not only upon the attainments of the students, but also upon the attendance. I think that the colleges would only in a measure be self-supporting. Scholarships and exhibitions to be provided out of the Welsh Educational Endowment Fund. Mr. Marchant Williams further said that he was opposed to clerical head teacherships, and in favour of a Welsh University, with the power of granting degrees. As to the Jesus College endowments, he advocated their being preserved for the Welsh, but that the scholarships should be tenable at any college in Oxford or Cambridge.

<hr>

FEBRUARY 23, 1881.

BARRINGTON.—Mr. W. Barrington of 19, Green-park, Bath, would be glad to know any particulars respecting his grandfather, who left Wales about the beginning of this century. His tombstone at Calcutta bears the following inscription:—"Wm. Barrington, Esq., born N. Wales, June 17, 1789, died in Calcutta, June 25, 1843." The grandson wishes to know whether any of the family are still living in Wales.

NOTES.

ANCIENT HILL CULTIVATION.—On several hills in North Carmarthenshire there are clear evidences of cultivation, which those best qualified to judge consider to be very ancient. The ridges or "butts" are quite distinct, never more than 6 or 8 feet wide, and sometimes curved according to the nature of the ground. From the ancient poem of the "Gododin," it would appear that the hill ground was then cultivated.

"Pan vuost di kynnivyn clot
En amwyn tywyssen gordiret."

"When thou, famous conqueror!
Wast protecting the ear of corn in the uplands."
                                                    CYNWYL.

MR. MADOCKS AND JOHN GIBSON (Feb. 2, 1881).—The following letter from Sir Wm. Gell, F.R.S., the eminent describer of classical ground, on the subject of Mr. Madocks' proposed Temple at Portmadoc, bears no date, but was probably written about the same time as Gibson's—in 1827.   E.B.

"My dear sir,—I received your letter late last night and though it has been in my mind's eye the whole day it is only just now I have a moment to write, as I have been bevisited till the present moment most terribly. Of course Mr. Gibson would be too happy to do any thing you might like for Tremadoc, but very difficult will it be to get a subject proper for the purpose. Neptune ought to be struggling with you for the possession of the soil. Thus Hercules fights with the river Achelous, that is, the river was dammed out or d——d out, and a great accession of land was the consequence, whereas Achilles gained nothing but wet boots by his battle with Scamander. As to a Cyclopean temple such a thing was never heard of except a fine tower with one window. Temples are of all things the most difficult to execute well, for it costs too much money to make and erect the columns and architraves. The only thing is a four column temple or 4 columns and two antae at most. Unless a temple has a certain size it does not make any great figure. This is about what is produced by 2 columns and 2 antae*. Here is the sort of thing to be made with 4 columns and may produce a fine effect*, but the truth is, it is pitch dark, and I have had another call in the middle of this, and it is now ¼ past 5, and I am to dine at your aunt's at half-past. It is therefore in vain to think of drawing or making temples to-day, and I must put it off.

"As to Lycophron, some cruel person to whom I lent it has stolen it, so it is without remedy, and not to be found in my book case any longer after a good hunt.

"So I must now stop, and will end by telling you I will consult on the temple and statue with you when you like, and that I am, ever yours most truly,   W. GELL.
"W. A. Madocks, Esq., M.P."

* Sir William here gives sketches, which, of course, we cannot well reproduce. Our correspondent informs us that an exact copy of Sir W. Gell's first sketch may be seen in the façade of the Calvinistic Methodist Chapel, near Tremadoc; though it is disfigured by a round window not in the sketch.—ED.

DRWSYNANT.—The little Inn between Bala and Dolgelley at which Mrs. Presland stopped (see Bye-gones, Jan. 7, 1880) must have been the "Howel Dda," at Drwsynant. In 1856, in my walk from Shrewsbury to Barmouth, I went into this inn, and found it in the same miserable state as described, but in 1871 I stayed there four days and found everything changed—all things clean and comfortable, provisions good and well cooked, charges moderate : altogether the nicest country inn in N. Wales. Drwsynant is the best station from which to ascend up the broad beautiful valley to Arran Mowddwy and Arran Benllyn, and in crossing the river Wnion, before entering the valley, one of the best views of Cader Idris is obtained.
W.A.L.

QUERIES.

A CHURCH-YARD SUPERSTITION.—Forty years ago I remember the people of Newtown had an objection to being buried on the North Side of the graveyard, saying, that only murderers, suicides, and unbaptized persons ought to be buried on that side. The superstition appears to have died out. Does it exist in any Welsh or Border parish at the present day? What was the supposed origin of it?   MAES-Y-DRE.

REPLIES.

ARWYSTLEY—SEAL (Jan. 26, 1881).—The arms on the seal described by "A." are those of Queen Elizabeth, precisely as sculptured on the west front of the old Market Hall in Shrewsbury with the date 1579.
W.A.L.

OUR MONTGOMERYSHIRE NEIGHBOURS (Jan. 26, 1881).—I don't remember any occasion when the Oswestry Yeomanry can be said to have done honour to their Montgomeryshire neighbours, except on Aug. 4, 1832. I remember it as well as if it were yesterday. Captain Croxon took his troop to Llanymynech to escort the Princess Victoria who came from Powis Castle, through Oswestry to Wynnstay. The troop attended the Princess and her mother

from the Montgomeryshire border at Llanymynech to the Denbighshire border at Chirk Bridge. Mr. Parker of Sweeney sent two barrels of ale and a hamper of sandwiches to Llanymynech for the refreshment of the Oswestry troop whilst they waited there. At Chirk Bridge they were met by the late Sir Watkin Williams Wynn. He introduced Capt. Croxon to the royal ladies, who thanked him for his escort.   T.W.
Oswestry.

When I read the query put by JARCO, I at once supposed that the period referred to was the occasion of the visit of the Princess Victoria to Wales in 1832 ; but there are two circumstances that made me doubt it : 1, that the Hon. T. Kenyon was not at that time connected with the Yeomanry ; and, 2, that he was present at Oswestry, and not at a sessions at Shrewsbury, as he said he must be on the occasion enquired about.   OSWALD.
[The Hon. T. Kenyon was present at Oswestry on this occasion as a civilian, and as High Steward of the Borough received the Royal guests in the absence of the Mayor.—ED.]

EARL OF CATHERLOUGH (Jan. 5, 1881).—The Annual Register of 1772 records the death on March 30th of Robert Knight Earl of Catherlough Viscount Barrels and Lord Luxborough of Shannon. He was M.P. for Milbourn-Port, Dorsetshire, and Recorder of Great Grimsby in Lincolnshire. John, 7th Earl of Westmoreland, received the title for services under Marlborough, patent dated 4th Oct., 1733, but he, dying without issue 26th August, 1762, the Irish Peerage expired. It is probable that Robert Knight was elevated after this date. In the 48 George III. (1808) a Private Act was passed "for vesting certain estates in the counties of Warwick, Middlesex, and Montgomery, late of the Right Honourable Robert Earl of Catherlough, deceased, in Trustees, in Trust, to be sold, and for investing the money arising from the sale thereof in the purchase of other estates to be settled to the subsisting uses of the will of the said Robert Earl of Catherlough and for other purposes therein mentioned."

In the preamble, the will of the said Robert Earl of Catherlough is recited, and which appeared to have been executed on the 11th February, 1772, by which he charged his estates in the counties of Warwick, Lincoln, Middlesex, Montgomery, Salop, Flint, and Chester, any or either of them, with an annuity of £400 per annum to Jane Davies for life, if she should continue unmarried, but in case she should marry, then from and after her marriage with an annuity of one hundred pounds for life. After charging his manor of Edstone, part of his said estates, with the payment of an annuity of £300 to Henry Ralegh Knight (therein called his the said testator's son or reputed son of his body on the body of the said Jane Davies begotten), he wills the whole of his estates to "certain Trustees to hold the same to the uses upon the trusts for the intents and purposes and subject to the powers and provisoes thereinafter limited declared and contained." At the time of his death he left Robert Knight, the said Henry Ralegh Knight, Jane Knight, and Henrietta Matilda Knight, his only children or reputed children by the said Jane Davies him surviving.

Robert Knight, the eldest son, married the Hon. Frances, daughter of Charles Dormer, 8th Lord Dormer, June 12, 1791, and by an Indenture Tripartite, dated the preceding day, he charges his estates in the county of Montgomery with an annuity of £600 to the said Frances Dormer and her assigns from and after his decease for her natural life.

After describing the marriages and children of the Testator's other children, the preamble recites that the Manors and other Hereditaments in the First Schedule to this Act "be detached from the family mansion, and it would be for the benefit of the parties interested that the same should be vested in Trustees to be sold."

And it was enacted that they should be sold—the Bill receiving the Royal Assent on the 18th June, 1808.

Among the properties Scheduled was "The Manor of Barrels" Co., Warick,—acreage, 840,—rental, £912 17s. 8d. per annum—also in the County of Montgomery—Parish of Kerry.

Lot. 1. Gwernygoe, and part of Mount Nebo, with Sundry Allotments, and liberty for 600 sheep to run on Kerry Hills. Tenant, John Jones. Number of acres, 617a. 0r. 0p. Annual rent, £588.

Lot 1. Other Part of Mount Nebo, Cefnyberin, and Gwenthrew Farms, with run for 400 sheep on Kerry Hills. Tenant, Edward Cleaton. No, of acres, 174. Rent, £203.

Lot 1. Cwmearl Farm, with run for 500 sheep on Kerry Hills. Tenant, Richard Arthur. No. of acres, 190. Rent, £256.

Lot 1. Bahithlon Farm, with run for 500 sheep on Kerry Hills. Tenant, Jane Davies. No. of acres, 225a. 3r. 0p. Rent, £250.

Lot 1. Lands allotted to the Estate of the late Lord Catherlough, and let as sheep-walks with the above farms, 830 acres.

Lot 2. The Birches Tenement. Tenant, John Bree. No. of acres, 4a. 2r. 33p. Rent, £6 0s. 0d.

Lot 3. Highlands. Tenant, John Lewis. No. of acres, 11. Rent, £615s. 0d.

Lot 4. Oak Tenement. Tenant, Richard Lewis. No. of acres, 22. Rent, £20.

Lot 5. Great Yatt Farm. Tenant, John Withers. No. of acres, 64. Rent, £52.

Lot 6. Keven Perfa. Tenant, Robert Howells. No. of acres 255a. 1r. 16p. Rent £100.

Lot 7. Gilfach. Tenant, Thomas Morgan. No. of acres, 209a. 2r. 33p. Rent £130.

Lot 8. Little Bryn Bedwin. Tenant, John Rowlands. No. of acres 30a. 0r. 19p. Rent £15.

Llandinam Parish.

Lot 9. Tyn y pwll and Penybank. Tenant, David Hamer. No. of acres, 119a. 1r. 16p. Rent, £50.

Lot 10. Gilfach. Tenant, John Cleaton. No. of acres, 30a. 3r. 10p. Rent £25.

Lot 11. The Cwm Farm. Tenant, Abraham Hamar. No. of acres, 76. Rent £30.

Lot 12. Cefn. Tenant, Thomas Kinsey. No. of acres, 82a. 1r. 16p. Rent £35.

Lot 13. Wigdoor. Tenant, Evan Davies. No. of acres, 48a. 2r. 13p. Rent £30.

The Kerry property was offered for sale by Auction at the Dragon Inn, Montgomery, on the 6th of May, 1809.— Messrs. London and Son, auctioneers—when Lot 1 was bought in by Mr. Mather at the reserve of £40,000. The Great Gate was sold (after the Sale) for £1,300 (Reserve £1,500) to Mr. W. D. Davies. The Gilfach was knocked down to Mr. Evan Stephens, Solicitor, of Newtown, at £5,240 (Reserve £5,000) for Mr. Herbert of Dolforgan. Cefnperfa was bought in at £4,000. Brynbedwin was bought in at £600. The Birches was not put up. The Highlands were bought by Mr. Thomas Morris of Cefnwenthrew at £245 0s. 0d. (reserve £200). The Oak was bought by Mr. Stephens for Mr. Thomas Morris, Great Gate, for £625. The Llandinam property was offered at Llandinam on the 8th of May, 1809 (Monday), when Tyn-y-pwll and Penybank were bought in at £1,986. The Gilfach (£1,090), The Cefn (£960), and Wigdoor (£1,780) were all sold to Mr. Thomas Jones of Pen Bryn; and the Cwm was bought in for £1,000. I have entered into these particulars, which I trust may interest some of the readers of *Bye-gones*, with the view of repeating my query, asking if any correspondent can say how Robert Knight, Earl of Catherlough, became possessed of the Gwernygoe Estate and the other lots in Kerry parish, Gwernygoe, and probably all lot I., at the Dissolution of the Monasteries in 1542, being known then to have been a Grange belonging to Cwmhir Abbey.

MEHELI.

CURRENT NOTES.

The EMPRESS OF AUSTRIA arrived at Combermere Abbey on Wednesday, and was in the hunting field the three following days. On Saturday, her Majesty hunted with Sir WATKIN's hounds.

Miss Rhoda Broughton, the well-known novelist, is one of the Broughtons of Broughton, in Cheshire, and lived at one time with her sister, Mrs. Newcombe, at Upper Eyarth, near Ruthin, where two or three of her books were written.

On Thursday, an old custom of that part of the country was carried out at Lea Farm, Cheshire. All the neighbours sent their ploughs and teams, about thirty in number, for a day's work, to help the new tenant of the farm in breaking up his land. At noon the tenant gave his visitors a substantial luncheon.

Mr. Parnell seems to have an ancestral right to rebel. On his mother's side he is descended from "Old Ironsides," one of the leaders in the American rebellion, and on his father's, it is said, from Tobias Parnell of Congleton, Cheshire. Tobias was brother of Richard Parnell, mayor of Congleton, and held some office himself, for it is stated that both of them were put out of office for refusing to take the oath of allegiance to Charles II. after the Restoration.

The Bishop of Liverpool, as we stated last week, has announced his intention of confirming two at a time, placing his right hand on the head of one candidate, and his left on the other. The practice, we believe, is not uncommon, and if a statement in the papers of 1805 is true, some such course must have been adopted at Shrewsbury on May 28 that year; for we are told "The Bishop of the Diocese confirmed 2,080 persons at St. Chad's Church." On the day previous he had confirmed 550 at Wellington.

A correspondent of the *Gardeners' Chronicle* says of the late Rev. John Brooke of Shifnal, "Mr. Brooke was a keen and accomplished botanist, and an enthusiastic horticulturist. For many years he and his sister, who predeceased him, kept up at Haughton one of the largest and most interesting collections of hardy herbaceous and greenhouse plants and bulbs in the Midland Counties. They were especially fond of those good old-fashioned things which the bedding mania well-nigh extirpated, and many a garden has been re-stocked with the grand old perennials of the past from the glorious clumps which grew in the gardens at Haughton. Mr. Brooke was an English gentleman of the good old type, now, alas! somewhat rare to find, and everyone who knew him deplores the loss of a friend whom it would be difficult, if not impossible, to replace."

Mr. R. Oliver Rees, chemist and bookseller, of Dolgelley, died on the 12th of the present month in the 62nd year of his age. Mr. Rees was well known as the author of several Welsh books. He was buried on Wednesday in St. Mary's church-yard. The Rev. Canon Lewis officiated, and the funeral, which was a public one, was very largely attended. All the shops in the town were closed as the funeral procession passed through the streets. Mr. Rees was at one time the possessor of "Mary Jones's Bible." Mary Jones was the subject of the well known incident which led to the formation of the British and Foreign Bible Society. The Rev. Thomas Charles of Bala having enquired of a little girl whether she could repeat the text from which he had preached on the preceding Sunday, "instead of giving a prompt reply as she had been accustomed to do, she remained silent, and then weeping told him that the weather had been so

bad that she could not get to read the Bible. She had
been accustomed to travel every week seven miles over
the hills to a place where she could obtain access to a
Welsh Bible." This Bible Mr. Rees gave to the Library of the
Bible Society; and about a month ago he was invited to London by the Committee of the Society, and was presented with
a magnificent Bible with annotations as an acknowledgment of his interesting gift.

On Friday evening Mr. Henry Sweet read a paper before the Philological Society, at the University College
on "The Grammar and Pronunciation of the Welsh non-
literary vocabulary, illustrated by dialogues and proverbs.'
Having touched on the points of likeness between Welsh
and old English, the two languages being shown to have
influenced each other to a very appreciable extent, the
speaker proceeded to dwell upon the forms and inflections
of the former. Early in the 9th century it lost the latter,
and its grammar was reconstituted. The power of the
Welsh language to form new compounds differs from the
English in using the modifying power after the
word. In development of particles, Welsh has
gone as far as the Greek language did in the
some direction. The mutation of letters and syllables
was shown to be a great difficulty in the way of acquiring
the various dialects, &c. This was illustrated by the use
of the dialect of Nant Gwynant, Carnarvonshire, where
Mr. Sweet studied for some time. Having traced the
use of various English words by the Welsh, the speaker
concluded with a strong appeal in favour of the formation of a Welsh Dialectic Society, whose aim it should
be to preserve the many scraps of an old language soon to
be blurred and corrupted by the wholesale introduction
of School Boards.—In the subsequent discussion, Mr.
Alexander J. Ellis, Mr. Furnivall, Dr. Richard Morris,
Mr. Spurrell, Mr. Jenner, and others took part.

TITHES AT WELSH-HAMPTON.

A hand-bill, "R. B. Jones, Typ.," has been preserved.
Can any of your Ellesmere readers remember its being
published, or the object sought to be attained by its publication? The following is a copy :—

REFORMING PARSON.

The following Letter is a copy of one sent by the
Reverend Wm. HOBSON, the Incumbent of *Welsh-
Hampton*, in the County of Salop, to one of his Parish-
ioners.

Mr. HOBSON boasts of having been the Tutor of the
notorious DANIEL O'CONNELL, and calls himself a "Reformer."

ELLESMERE, Dec. 27, 1830.

SIR,—According to your Choice and advice, I have had
your Tithes valued, having first sent to Mr. BOYDEL a correct accompt of the Cows, Calves, and Sows had by you in
the last Summer, and also of the quantity of Potatoes and
Turnips raised on your Farm in my Parish, having at the
same time left with him a terrier of my Rights in the
name of Tithes, received by me from the Bishop's
Registry Office at Lichfield, some Days before. The enclosed is his Estimate of your Tithes for the Articles
mentioned therein only, and also herein above and these
mitigated according to my advice and directions, if otherwise, or according to my legal Rights, they would have
been about twice as much, without any other tithable
Article included. But be well assured, that besides the above
mentioned Particulars, I have an unquestionable Right to
the tenth of every Article produced by your Orchard &
Garden, whether Apples, Pears, Plumbs or Cherries, at
the time of gathering them, as well as the tenth of every
feathered Creature, whether Goose, Turkey or Fowl, but

what is of much greater value, I have also an inalienable
Right to an Adjistment Tithe of 3d. or 4d. a week according to the age, for every Beast bought by you, and brought
from any other Parish or Place, while it continues to feed
on your Farm; and also to a 1-10th of the value of the feed of
every Beast of whatever sort it be that is bred on your
Farm, and sold by you at any future time, that is for the
three years it was growing; besides the 1-10th value of every
young Creature fed by its Mother's milk, at the time it is
weaned. The great difference between the Parish of
Hampton, and those adjoining it, in general consists in
this; that in Hampton no modus exists. Mr. COTTON, for
example, is tied down to 1½d. for every Cow and Calf,
whereas, if there was no modus in his Parish for them, he
would be entitled by law to 1-10th value of the Milk or Cheese
made in his Parish, as I am, the which alone, would far
exceed all his other Tithes together, in amount. They
would it seems exceed £1,000 annually; or the Substitute
for this Milk or Cheese, which in this Neighbourhood is
generally the Herbage consumed by the Cows, would far
exceed all the other Tithes. Because no modus of any
kind exists in my Parish, I am entitled to a full tenth of
the whole produce of the Land, Corn, Hay, Lambs, and Wool
excepted, according to the Terrier; I am quite persuaded that
Mr. REDDROP, in valuing the Tithes of Hampton, must
either have omitted the Cows altogether, or charged them
at 1½d. each as in Ellesmere, where there is a fixed modus
for them; as your Tithe of Potatoes and Turnips in the
current year at 10/ and 4/ an Acre respectively, far exceeded your Estimate of 50/ by him without anything else
included. But let it be well noticed that the Milk or
Cheese is our legal Right, and not the tenth part of the value
of the Herbage consumed by the Cows, which is usually taken
in this Neighbourhood : and as this Herbage does not exceed perhaps ⅓ of the value of the Milk or Cheese, which
the law gives so far, that is by ⅔ does this custom profit
the Farmers to our disadvantage ? If therefore you still
object to the enclosed valuation, I warn you that I shall
from Easter next, take the Milk or Cheese in kind, as
well as the tenth part of your Potatoes & Turnips in the
next year, in quantity, or measure, or weight, after
digging or severing from the Ground; and also 1-10th of the
value of every sucking Beast, whether Calf, Colt, or Pig,
to be rated at the time of its being weaned, (Lambs excepted;) that is, that every 10th day's Milk be kept for me,
or that the 10th part of your Cheese, without fraud, in the
quantity or quality, be weighed off for me. It is the
farthest from my wish to raise any question or cause of
dispute with you, but I have now the most justifiable
reasons, for objecting to take what I offered to take, in my
late memorandum given you in the beginning of Oct.
last. In the first place, your objections to that very
moderate offer, has put me to an expense exceeding the
difference between it and the enclosed estimate ; viz., for
the valuation, for the advice of counsel, for the terrier, &
for law books on the subject of Tithes ; but in that offer
I was guided also by your assertion, that you had only
120 Acres of Land in my Parish, whereas, I have now had
seemingly good advice; that you have 200 Acres in it,
these are good reasons why I expect you to abide by the
enclosed valuation, or in future to pay your Tithes in kind
as above directed, & according to law, I am ready to maintain, that all that is herein said of my Rights is strictly
& legally correct, and if you doubt this, I only wish you
to submit this to the opinion of your own Attorney,
and I am quite sure he can neither disprove nor refute
any thing herein asserted. I am quite persuaded that
if your Tithes were rated according to my legal
and just claims, they would be little short of £30 a
year. You will hence see why your Tithes cannot any

year be ascertained till towards the end of it, why Mr.
BOYDEL also has not made you any charge for the Adgistment of Cattle bought by you, & fed on your Farm for a
time, and also why the law directs, that a verbal composisitiou for Tithes can only be from year to year : Please
also to notice, that nothing is charged by Mr. B. for the
three Foals you had last Spring ; notwithstanding all these
considerations, I have no objections to compounding with
you, for the current and the next year, for the sum estimated by Mr. BOYDEL, to which, if you yet object, you
will find an alternative above, as our only regular and legal
means of settling the question.

I remain, Sir, your obedt. servt.,
WM. HOBSON.

P.S. As this was written before I received Mr.
BOYDEL'S valuation, which I requested in my Letter to
him might be on a separate piece of paper, which I meant
to enclose to you, this will account for the inaccuracies
herein contained, he only in a Letter which you shall see,
put your Tithes at £11 15s. and Mr. MENLOVE'S also accordingly, as the only Objectors to my offers of a composition, & therefore only necessary to be valued ; notice
also that his valuation is only for Cows, Calves, Sows,
Potatoes, & Turnips as above, which were the only
things I gave him an account of on your Farm, & to
which I consented to his Tithing at any rate of valuation,
high or low.

All this only occurred half a century ago ; there is
doubtless some one left in the district who " remembers
all about it."   P.

THE WEATHER IN 1795.—A newspaper published in
Jan. 1796, stated that on the longest day of the previous
year the thermometer stood at 33½ deg., in Shrewsbury,
and on the shortest day at 52 deg.   Scarcely what we
now-a-days call " old-fashioned weather "!

MERIONETHSHIRE WRECKERS.—Somewhere in the month
of Oct. 1804, the " Princess of Wales " West-Indiaman
was wrecked on Wicklow sand banks ; and fifty puncheons
of rum, and other goods, floated ashore on the Welsh
coast near Aberdovey.   An exciting scene was the result :
the whole was speedily seized, and carried away inland by
the country people.

TRAVELLING EIGHTY YEARS AGO.—On the 16th Sep.
1804, Mr. J. Price of Llanfyllin was attacked on the
Wrexham road near Belgrave, by two men on foot, who
plundered him of Two-hundred guineas in cash ; and bills
drawn at Shrewsbury, Oswestry and Dolgelley ; making
the amount altogether £690.   Not content with this
booty they also stripped him of his coat and waistcoat.

A SHREWSBURY SCHOOL BOY.—Lieut.-Colonel Arthur
Need of Fountain Dale, Blidworth, Notts, Lieutenant of
the Yeomen of the Guard, upon whom the honour of
knighthood has just been conferred, was educated at
Shrewsbury School. Col. Need, who was in the 14th
Hussars, saw considerable service in India, having been
present during the whole of the siege operations against,
and capture of, Mooltan, and also taking part in the action
of Soorjkoond. . He was present at the surrender of the
fort and garrison of Cheniote, and at the battle of Goojerat.   He served in the Persian expedition of 1857, and
also with the Central India Field Force under Sir Hugh
Rose in 1857-8. He was likewise present at the siege and
capture of Rahutghur, the relief of Saugor, and the capture
of Garrakota and the pursuit of the rebels across the Beas.
He took part in forcing the Muddenpore Pass, in the
battle of the Betwa, the siege and capture of the town and
fortress of Jhansi, the battle of Koonch, and many subsequent engagements.

NOTES.

PARLIAMENT OF ENGLAND (Feb. 2, 1881).—
List of Members for *Denbighshire*, continued. The first
name is the Member for the County, and the second that
for the Boroughs :—

1705 Sir Richard Myddelton, bart. William Robinson,
Esq.
1708 Ditto.   Sir William Williams, bart.
1710 Ditto.   John Roberts, Esq.
1713 Ditto.   John Wynne, Esq.
1714 Ditto. (1)   Ditto.
1722 Watkin Williams Wynne, Esq. Robert Myddelton,
Esq., of Chirk Castle. (2)
1727 Ditto.   Ditto. (3)
1734 Ditto. (4)   John Myddelton, Esq;
1741 Ditto. (5)   John Wynne, Esq., of Melay.
1747 Ditto. (6)   Richard Myddelton, Esq. (7)
1754 Sir Lynch Salusbury Cotton, bart. Ditto.
1761 Ditto.   Ditto.
1768 Ditto.   Ditto.
1774 Sir Watkin Williams Wynne, bart. Ditto.
1780 Ditto.   Ditto.
1784 Ditto. (8)   Ditto. (9)
1790 Robert Watkin Wynne, Esq. Richard Myddelton,
jun., Esq.
1801 Sir Watkin Williams Wynn, bart. [Thomas Jones,
Esq.] (10)
1802 Ditto. Frederick West, Esq., Chirk Castle. (11)
1806 Ditto. Robert Myddelton Biddulph, Esq., of Chirk
Castle.
1807 Ditto.   Ditto.
1812 Ditto. John Hamilton Fitzmaurice, commonly
called Lord Viscount Kirkwall.

(1) Watkin Williams, Esq., elected 30 June 1716, *vice* Sir R.
Myddelton deceased.
(2) Succeeded to the Chirk Castle estates on the death of his
cousin, Sir William Middelton, in 1717. He contested the county
against Watkin Williams Wynn, Esq., in 1722. — Williams'
Denbigh.
(3) John Myddelton, Esq., of Chirk Castle, elected, *vice*
Robert Myddelton deceased, 27 Apr. 1723.—*Blue Book.* Brother
and heir to the late member. Elected for the county in 1741
against Sir W. W. Wynn but unseated on petition — Williams'
Denbigh.
(4) Sir Watkin Williams Wynne, bart., re-elected 24 Dec. 1740,
after appointment as steward of the lordships and manors of
Bromfield and Yale, Co. Denbigh, (see Commons' Journals 25
Nov. 1740)—*Blue Book.* Re-elected (as Sir Watkin) having on
the death of his father accepted the Stewardship.—Williams'
Denbigh.
(5) Return amended by Order of the House, dated 23 Feb.
1741-2, by erasing the name of John Myddelton, Esq., of Chirk
Castle, and substituting that of Sir Watkin Williams Wynne,
bart.—*Blue Book.* This was the "Election Mawr," the great
contest which established the victory of the family of Wynnstay
over their rivals of Chirk Castle.
(6) Sir Lynch Salusbury Cotton, bart., of Lleweny, elected
5 Dec. 1749, *vice* Sir W. W. Wynn, deceased.
(7) Richard Myddelton, Esq., re-elected 27 Dec. 1749, after
accepting the office of steward of the Lordships and Manors of
Bromfield and Yale.—*Blue Book.* He was Recorder of Denbigh.
(8) Robert Watkin Wynne, Esq., of Plasnewydd, elected 28
Aug. 1789, *vice* Sir W. W. Wynn, bart., deceased.
(9) Richard Myddelton, jun., Esq., of Chirk Castle, elected
20 May 1788, *vice* Richard Myddelton, jun. (qy. sen.) Esq. who
accepted the Chiltern Hundreds.
(10) Thomas Jones, Esq., of Carreghova, elected 12 Jan. 1797,
vice Richard Myddelton, Esq., deceased. The members under
the date of 1801 in the *Blue Book* (the "First Parliament of the
United Kingdom") include those elected in "The Parliament
of Great Britain" 1796.
(11) Williams gives him as the Hon. F. West.

1818 Ditto. John Wynne Griffith, Esq., of Garn.
1820 Ditto.　　　　　　Ditto.
1826 Ditto. Frederick Richard West, Esq. (12)
1830 Ditto. Robert Myddelton Biddulph, Esq.
1831 Ditto.　　　　　　Ditto.
For Return of Members from the passing of the Reform Bill to 1880, see *Bye-gones*, Apr. 7, 1880.　　ED.

WOLVES IN ENGLAND.—Eyton, quoting Blakeway, says :—A curious document informs us that Peter Corbet (of Caus), like his ancestors, was a lover of the chase, and that wolves, so far from having been extirpated in England by King Edgar, as the story goes, were existent in the time of Edw. I. A Patent of the latter King, dated May 4, 1281, informs all Bailiffs and Officers of the Forest that the King has commissioned Peter Corbet to destroy these beasts wherever they could be found in the counties of Salop, Stafford, Gloucester, Worcester, and Hereford, using men, dogs, and other devices for that purpose ; and the said Bailiffs, etc., are desired to assist (*Ant : of Shrop.* vii. p. 33). 　BOOKWORM.

THE QUEEN AND THE ANCIENT BRITONS. On the 1st of March, 1838, the Hon. Robert Clive, M.P., who presided at the annual gathering of the Ancient Britons in London, was able to announce that Her Majesty, then newly come to the throne, had consented to become their Patroness, and had subscribed the usual hundred guineas to the charity. After dinner the children of the school paraded the hall, and were marshalled in front of the chair, when they sang the following verses to the air of " Jenny Jones ":—

The last time our lips breath'd our kind Patrons' praises,
　Among them was numbered our late gracious King ;
But now, while we mourn for a father departed,
　A *Star* has arisen, new blessings to bring !
VICTORIA, our Sovereign, who rules and reigns o'er us,
　And towards the distress'd wears Charity's mien ;
For Her our young hearts swell in one joyful chorus,
　And thousands will join us—Long life to the Queen.

She has dwelt in the land of the flood and the mountain ;
　That honour from Cambria will ne'er pass away ;
And many a year be her bounty recorded,
　In aiding your efforts on Saint David's Day !
While the great and the good stand like bulwarks before us,
　To shield us from want, and their succour to lend ;
A prayer from our hearts flows in one grateful chorus,
　For *them* and VICTORIA, our Patron and Friend.

These lines were the composition of Mrs. Cornwell Barry Wilson, and we are told they received a hearty encore.
　　　　　　　　　　　　　　　　　　　　　G.G.

AN OLD TOWYN RENT BOOK.—In the Towyn parish records recently given in *Bye-gones* the name " An : Owen " figures more than once (see Dec. 15, 1880). I have before me an old rent book in which this lady's handwriting appears, and some of the entries are curious enough to bear transcribing. Thus on the first pages there are the following :—
" January ye 5th 1740. Stated then on account with Evan Rees of Pant : y : noiodd and upon allowing his whole demand for cattle for harvesting Hay & Turff this year and of my tax for Caithley that was allow'd him for a poor child one pound four shill : 01 : 04 : by which account and what receipts I allow from Owen Griffith &c Evan Rees will be indebted to me May next three p'd fifteen shill : nine pence half peny — 03 : 15 : 9½. AN : OWEN."

(12) Return amended by Order of the House, dated 29 March 1827, by erasing the name of Joseph Ablett, Esq.—*Blue Book*. Williams describes Mr. West as of " Ruthin Castle," and the petitioner as " Joseph Abbett, Esq., of Llanbedr Hall."

" Sep't : 6th, 1742. Allow'd then to Evan Rees for making a Barn at Hendu three p'd : twelve shill : 03 : 12 : 00. Allow'd also for David John Owens barn one pound four shillings—01 : 04 : 00. For harvesting 209 Loads in 1741 and for harvesting Turff 1742, eighteen shill : 00 : 18 : 0. I say allow'd by AN : OWEN."
The next entry worth transcribing is in a different handwriting, and shows the Market price of Cattle in Merionethshire a hundred and thirty five years ago :—
" Sep't ye 7th 1745. Then Bought of Evan Rees one yearling heifer for one pound & three shillings — 01 : 03 : 00. I say bought & allow'd for ye use of Mad'm Owen. By me JOHN OWEN."
" November ye 15th 1758. Memorandum that I then agreed with Evan Rees to make my malt for one peny p'r measure.
　　　　　　　　　" AN OWEN
　　　　　　" The Mark of EVAN REES ∃ "
The last signature of An : Owen dates 1758, and we have then, dated Feb. 19, 1761, that of " Wm. Morton " for " the use of Pryce Maurice, Esq., executor of Madam Owen, deceased." In 1763 Mr. Morton signs as " to the use of Pryce Maurice, Esq. as Guardian and next friend, &c., to his son Mr. Henry Corbet." The last signature of Morton's is dated Dec., 1772, and is followed by " William Hughes," who signs receipt in Jan., 1773, on behalf of Pryce Maurice for H. Corbet ; and in Dec. 1773, " Henry Ar. Corbet " signs in his own behalf. This gentleman signs up to June, 1782, and the next year we have " Edw. Corbet " whose signature is attached to all the receipts up to 1799. From this date there is a break, and the remaining items in the book are too recent to be of interest.
　　　　　　　　　　　　　　　　　　　　　T. S.

QUERIES.

WALTER THE STEWARD (Dec. 29, 1880.)—Will OLD OSWESTRIAN say what was the statement made on the authority of Chambers and Pinkerton in *Oswald's Well* ? Is not the date, 1538, four lines from bottom of paragraph, a misprint ? 　　　　　　QUERIST.
[We are glad QUERIST has called attention to this subject, for it has enabled us to look into the matter. The letter quoted by OLD OSWESTRIAN from the *Oswestry Advertizer* of Aug, 1853, was written by the late Mr. Sabine, sen., solicitor ; and the previous statements he refers to were afterwards (1855) amplified into a " Paper " which he contributed to Cathrall's *History of Oswestry* (see pages 176-181). The passage from *Chambers's Journal* is as follows :—" During the troublous conflicts of Maud and Stephen, in their competition for the crown of England, Walter, the son of Alan, the son of David, fled from the family seat at Oswestry, and settled in Scotland. David I. made him his Steward, and gave him lands to support the dignity of his office, &c , &c." Mr. Sabine showed that " by the marriage of one of these Stewarts with Margery Bruce, Robert the Stewart was born, and became, 1370-1, King of Scots. On page 178 of Cathrall's *History* he gives the descent to Queen Victoria. The date on the stone, as given in *Bye-gones* Dec. 29, was a printers' error ; it should have been 1138.—ED.]

PEARLS IN SHROPSHIRE.—In Christopher Merrett's *Pinax rerum naturalium Britannicarum* 1667, p. 210, it is said :—" Margaritæ frequentes satis in quibusdam Ostreis præsertim Scoticis, majores dicuntur extrahi ex Mitylis grandioribus ad Kerby Lonsdale in Westmorlandia, Cornubia, Cumbria & agro Salop." In what part of the County were these Pearls found ? 　　W.A.L.

GWEDDI'R FORWYN. — One of H.M.'s Inspectors of Schools, who is a native of Merionethshire, informs me that, twenty or thirty years ago, if he had asked the school-children in the neighbourhood of Towyn which of them knew " Gweddi'r Forwyn," about half their number in the higher classes would probably have held up their hands in token of their acquaintance with it. A young man acknowledged to him that he used it nightly as a preservative against bad dreams. It commenced "O Forwyn wen "=O blessed virgin. Has it been published and is it still in use? In the *Myvyrian Archaiology* the Prayers to the Virgin are omitted.   CYNWYL.

REPLIES.

A SHROPSHIRE MARTYR (Jan. 19, 1881.)— Challoner's *Memoirs of Missionary Priests* contains an account of the execution of John Jones alias Buckley, a "*Carnarvonshire* man," at St. Thomas Waterings, on the 12th of July, 1598. He was the only priest executed at this place in 1598. There were four executed at York and one at Carlisle. I am inclined to think John *Jones* must be the one your correspondent "H.W.L." refers to.
Brecon.   F.S.A.

MR. EVANS'S CEDARS (May 12, 1880).— The great and noble Cedar of Lebanon planted at the Nursery, Westfelton, was blown down by the great storm which devastated the woods and parks of Shropshire in 1839.
        W.A.L.

EVANS OF LLWYNYGROES (Aug. 4, 1880).— Mr. John Evans lived on his estate at Llwynygroes, which he planted with rarer trees. He was a land surveyor, and made and published a large map of North Wales, which was considered very accurate and comprehensive. His son, Dr. John Evans was a physician, and an excellent and learned Botanist, and author of a Poem called *The Bees*. He resided at the Council House, Shrewsbury, then all in one large mansion. His son was the Ven. Archdn. Robt. Wilson Evans, rector of Tarvin, Cheshire, and afterwards of some living in the North, where he died.   W.A.L.

WELSH SHEEP DOGS' "TRIALS."
(Jan. 26, 1881).

The charge of cruelty to sheep dogs against Welsh Farmers by Mr. Lockhart has called forth so many replies, that the accuser has retracted, as will be seen by the letter appended, which has just been published in the *Manchester City News*. We observe by the last passage in his withdrawal of the charge he has adopted the *Oswestry Advertizer* explanation of the conduct of the shepherd, except that the remark as to "the traditional bad character" of Welshmen is not ours.

"No doubt both you and your readers will be glad to have the last word in reference to the subject of Welsh sheep dogs. It did not appear in the extracted portion of my paper that was published in the *City News* that the conversation took place ten years ago.

"I was then spending a holiday in the neighbourhood of Tal-y-llyn, and after our six o'clock dinner the subject turned up of sheep-worrying by stray dogs in this particular neighbourhood. One gentleman who was present, and who had then resided in the inn for several months, attributed the cause to the carelessness of the shepherds in the district. On the following morning I left the inn, Ty'n-y-Cornel, and crossed over the summit of Cader Idris by Llyn-y-Cae, and dropped down on the road that runs from Dolgelley to Barmouth Ferry, and it was there, whilst lazily enjoying a pipe on a green bank, that the young Welsh shepherd came up with his little flock. I called his handsome little bitch to me, and we became at once good friends, for I have been a lover of dogs from my very earliest recollection, and it was at this particular spot that the conversation commenced.

5

"In the dialogue published by you I gave the exact words used by each of us, and, after the post-prandial remarks of the day before, I had no cause to doubt the truth of the shepherd's statement, given as it was with much detail and circumstance. However, it is impossible for me to prove his assertions, and the inquiries I have recently made go to prove that, at present, the very contrary is the fact, that the shepherds, even in the wildest districts, do not treat their dogs in the way I described in my note. It would have been wiser, perhaps, if I had inquired before making the statement, but 'Wisdom is justified by her children,' and I have the greatest possible pleasure in now believing that these faithful creatures are not now treated in the way I thought they were, and that the shepherd I met, besides being a Welshman, with the traditional bad character, must at the same time have been a perverter of the truth, or, as one of the papers commenting on my note puts it, 'Indeed, truth, he wass tell you a lie, whatever, Mr. Lockhart.'

"J. C. LOCKHART."

THE LATE MR. CHRISTOPHER JAMES OF MERTHYR TYDVIL.

The South Walians have every reason to be proud of their eminent countryman, Lord Justice James; and the following account of his family is interesting—"In the course of Merthyr history there have been migrations from various shires and districts at certain times; Pembrokeshire migration in, in later times, Cardiganshire; and Caermarthenshire migrations; but the earliest of all were supposed to be migrations from Breconshire; but very early in the prosperous days of Merthyr, a migration from the neighbourhood of Cardiff may be noticed. Amongst these were Mr. Rowlands, late parish clerk; Mr. Davies, late of the Bush; and the brothers, Christopher, Job, and William James. Mr. Christopher was a general dealer and wine and spirit merchant in the shop afterwards occupied by Mr. S. Davies, next door to the Bush. Here he sold draperies, groceries, and wine; and, with Mr. William Milburn Davies, and their father-in-law, Mr. David Williams, and Mr. Davies, of the Pond-side, he may fairly be said to have monopolized the trade of Merthyr. The site of his hotel was then simply a yard in connection with his premises, but subsequently he built the Bush Hotel, one of his happiest and most successful speculations. As he rose in life he became connected with other undertakings. One of these, the leasing of the turnpikes, was a fortunate hit; and old people say that from this venture he gained a great accession of fortune. He built a mill at Treforest, and supplied Merthyr with most of the flour consumed there. In the canal he was largely interested, and in a variety of ways influenced the trade and prosperity of Merthyr; his very servants becoming gentlemen; one of them, Davies by name, dying not many years ago, at a country seat near Abergavenny. In the prime of life, with a competence he retired to Swansea; but it was not in his nature to waste, unemployed, the term of life allotted to him. He rose at once into the ranks of the leading men of Swansea, and figured in various positions of note. For some years he was acting director of the Taff Vale Railway; a long time member of the Town Council of Swansea, and at length Mayor of that important town. In addition, he was one of the members of the Swansea Harbour Trust, and he long acted with energy as a county magistrate. It is gratifying to find that he did not forget his old Merthyr friends, and to the last was cordially attached to the village, where he made

28

his first essay in life, and so long as Merthyr has a name in history, Christopher James will be mentioned as of it. He died in the sunny month of May, at his seat, Belle Vue House, having reached the venerable age of seventy-nine.

"The eldest of his sons, Mr. D. W. James, figured conspicuously in local politics, eventually opening coal works at Cwm Rhondda; but, after his father's death, he, too, retired from the active scenes of life. The second son, Mr. William Milburn James, attained considerable eminence at the Bar. After a sound legal training he became a barrister; practised on the South Wales Circuit; shone meritoriously for a long time as Q.C.; and then he held the high post of Vice Chancellor of the Duchy of Lancaster, and now he is everywhere known as Lord Justice James. He married a daughter of the Bishop of Chichester; and by the marriage of other of his lordship's daughters, he is connected with Lord Romily and Lord Belper.

"Mr. Job James has been represented by gentlemen who have attained leading positions in the town and elsewhere. Messrs. Frank J. William Rupert, Christopher, and a most able medical officer, Herbert, who fell a victim to typhoid in the energetic pursuit of his profession. Mr. William James is represented by two sons; Mr. Charles H. James, one of the ablest solicitors in the county; the Rev. William James, a rector in Devonshire; and the latter gentleman again by Mr. W. H. James, manager of the West of England Bank, and Mr. C. H. James, C.E., Cyfarthfa." That is the story as it reached me in MS., and it deserves to be printed. CAMBRIAN.

CURIOUS EPITAPHS.—In Carno churchyard were found some few years ago several remarkable verses on the tombs. There is one inscription engraved on the tomb of a man who, it says, died of "chronicle abscesses." If this is still legible, perhaps some resident will supply us with a copy.—Cockshutt churchyard is responsible for the following:—

> Our parents dear are gone to rest,
> And left us here behind:
> To raise this stone we thought it best,
> To keep them still in mind.

EPITAPH ON A TOMBSTONE IN FORDEN CHURCHYARD.

> Beneath this tree
> Lies singers three,
> One tenor and two basses;
> Now they are gone
> 'Tis ten to one
> Such three shall take their places.

Choosing a clergyman by ballot is not a very usual course, but we are told in the newspapers of 1795, that on October 2 of that year, "at Christ's Hospital, London, came on the election by ballot of a clergyman to the Vicarage of Albrighton, Salop, vacant by the death of the Rev. Henry Binfield, when, after casting up the votes there appeared—for the Rev. M. Lloyd, 93; Rev. M. Richards, 90; Rev. M. Trollope, 45. Rev. M. Whittaker resigned before the ballot commenced."

A WELSH RAILROAD IN 1803.—A newspaper of Nov., 1803, says, "The Carmarthenshire railroad from Llanelly to Castle Garreg was opened on Nov. 7 to the extensive collieries and iron-mines in the neighbourhood of Bron. dinog and Gynhidre, on which occasion the gentlemen of the company went up the road in carriages constructed for the purpose, where they were met by a vast concourse of spectators." Up to that time iron-stone and coal had been conveyed on horses' backs. By means of the rails fewer horses were required, and a vast saving was effected.

FLOGGING AT THE CART TAIL.—On July 13, 1804, a couple of petty thieves were flogged at the cart tail in Monmouth. After the first had received his punishment, and was released, he coolly put on his clothes, and followed the cart the whole way to witness the flogging of his companion in iniquity.

CURRENT NOTES.

A correspondent of a contemporary says a good deal of the land in Cheshire is going out of cultivation.

A return of the foreign trade of the port of Chester gives 64 vessels from foreign ports, with a tonnage of 12,002 in 1878, and 141 vessels with a tonnage of 36,136 in 1880.

The *Athenæum* says that Canon Williams is proceeding diligently with his selections from the Hengwrt MSS. in the Peniarth Library. He has now brought out part v., and part vi. will complete the second volume. The first volume contains the Welsh text of the 'Seint Greal,' with an English translation and glossary. We are sorry to find the Canon complaining of lack of proper support.

The parish church of Clunbury, which has been restored at a cost of about £1,400, was re-opened on Thursday by the Bishop of Hereford. Mr. J. P. St. Aubyn of the Temple, London, was the architect, and Mr. Birrell, builder, of Shrewsbury, was the contractor. The church was originally Norman, and the western doorway is of that period; but the greater part of it is of the Decorated period. The Earl of Powis contributed £500 towards the work of restoration.

DEATH OF MISS DAVIES, PENMAEN DYFI.—We regret to hear of the death of Miss Jane Davies, Penmaen Dyfi, only daughter of the late Rev. Walter Davies (Gwallter Mechain), which took place on Tuesday, Feb. 22, at her residence. The deceased lady was well known to many of our readers, especially amongst Welsh literati. She possessed a splendid library, including most of the books and manuscripts of her late father, and she was most courteous and obliging to all who wished to inspect its rare contents.

THE NEW RECTOR OF LLANDRINIO AND VICAR OF GUILSFIELD.—The Rev. D. Phillips Lewis, M.A., vicar of Guilsfield, and Rural Dean, has been appointed to the Rectory of Llandrinio, vacant by the appointment of the Rev. E. B. Smith to the Vicarage of Gresford. Mr. Lewis has been at Guilsfield since 1863, before which year he was Perpetual Curate of Buttington. From 1845 to 1847 he was curate of Oswestry, from 1847 to 1850 he was curate of Welshpool, and in the latter year he removed to But. tington. Mr. Lewis's residence at Guilsfield will be associated with the restoration of the church, in which he took a deep and active interest. The fabric, as the Rev. D. R. Thomas says in his valuable History of the Diocese of St. Asaph, is probably the finest in the county, and the work of restoration therefore excited an unusual amount of interest amongst antiquaries and students of ecclesiastical architecture. Mr. Lewis is a vice-president of the Powysland Club, and was one of the original members of the Oswestry and Welshpool Naturalists Field Club. The living of Guilsfield has been offered to the Rev. J. Lewis, now curate of Rhyl, and lately curate of Gresford, and it is probable that the rev. gentleman will accept it. Both Llandrinio and Guilsfield are in the gift of the Bishop. The former is put down as worth £556, together with a house and forty acres of glebe; the latter, £380, and there is a house with fifteen acres of glebe.

NOTES.

BRYCHAN.—Giraldus (*Itin.* Ch. 10) says the single bed-cover used by the Welsh in his day was so called no doubt from its variegated colour. Dr. Pughe (*Dict.* s. v.) quotes from C.C., "Y *brycan* a'r gobenydd =the rug and the bolster." I suspect that under both forms it has long passed out of use. The Scotch plaid was formerly called by the same name and applied to the same use.

> "He's turned him richt and round about,
> And rowed him in his *brechan*,
> And he has gone to tak' a sleep
> In the Lawlands o' Baleighan."
> (Ballad of "Sir James the Rose.")
> CYNWYL.

THE SCARCITY IN 1800. (Feb. 16, 1881.)— The year 1800 opened badly for the poor and the improvident, (too often synonymous terms). At the outset there was a severe frost, and "thousands of poor people being thrown out of work, public benevolence was largely taxed." On the first day of the year the thermometer stood at 20 below freezing in some parts of Shropshire at 8 o'clock in the morning. The complaints at *Shrewsbury* of the exorbitant price of coals, were loud, and on the second week of January it was agreed at a parish meeting at *Wroxeter* to purchase 500 bushels of wheat to sell to the poor at a reduced price. At the Shropshire Sessions the Magistrates agreed to issue orders for enforcing the Act prohibiting the making of any but Standard Wheaten Bread. Soup shops were opened at *Ludlow* and *Wellington.* At *Chester* soup was sold to the poor at a penny a quart, and at a town meeting held in *Shrewsbury* on Jan. 30 more than £100 was promised "towards establishing a soup-shop on the plan of the Government for the relief of the poor." In March several plans were adopted for the saving of wheat, and the use of potatoes, rice, &c., was urged. At *Machynlleth* the danger of a riot in consequence of the scarcity of grain became so imminent that on March 11, a detachment of the 21st Light Dragoons was sent there from Shrewsbury. In May the Shrewsbury soup house served out to each applicant "a pound of bread with four quarts of soup, and a proportionable quantity of rice" at half price. On May 6, Mr. Jeffreys of Sutton, Shropshire, a farmer, whose stacks had been fired on the 27th of the previous month, made oath before the Mayor of Shrewsbury that "he had never said he would keep his corn until it was at the price of a guinea-and-a-half per strike." During the same month of May "in some districts several respectable families agreed to eat no more lamb until after midsummer." Later on in the month "printed receipts for the preparation of potato-flour and rice, &c., as substitutes for wheat," were given away to the poor in Shrewsbury. The gentry and farmers everywhere sold of their stock of wheat in small quantities, and at reduced rates to the needy, so long as the high prices kept up ; and at the beginning of June, 1800, it was stated that on the previous week 3,390 quarts of soup had been sold at the Shrewsbury soup-house. JARCO.

QUERIES.

J. TOMKIES OF OSWESTRY, 1789.—Who was he? I have before me a pamphlet (published by J. Salter of Oswestry) which contains a letter dated "Oswestry, Aug. 20, 1789," that had been written by him to an Oswestrian waiting for execution in Shrewsbury gaol, and which seems so much to have excited the curiosity of the inhabitants that it was printed for the author, with an introduction, in which the public are very seriously warned that all are sinners alike "guilty before God, and in equal need of the same mercy as the late unhappy sufferer." The copy in my possession is the second edition, and the title page contains the names of Mr. Wood, Shrewsbury ; Mr. Poole, Chester ; Mr. Maddocks, Ellesmere ; Mr. Hughes, Wrexham ; Mr. O. Jones, Welshpool ; Mr. Swinney and Mr. Lucas, Birmingham, as vendors of the book. On the last page there is the following advertisement :—

> Lately published by the same Author, price 9d. and may be had of him ; and likewise of every bookseller in the Kingdom:—
> "*The Believer nothing to do with the Law of the Ten Commandments, proved on Scripture-Grounds,*" &c., &c.

The following lines were found annexed to one of the said books on reading it.

> "This little David, with a sling and stone,
> Hath the whole host of Philistines outdone ;
> Hath changed the massy staff, the weaver's beam,
> Into a spotless robe, without a seam,
> Hath on the head of their great champion trod,
> And taught true Israel the way of God :
> Hath taught, whence peace of conscience truly springs,
> And given the glory to the King of Kings."

The name of "Richd. Bickerton, Roden, 1792" is written on the title page ; so I presume my copy once belonged to that gentleman. He is one of the "Border Counties Worthies" mentioned by Mr. Salisbury.
H.W.A.

WELSH DWARFS.—In a recent number of the *Cheshire Sheaf,* mention is made of a couple of Welsh Dwarfs known as "Dick and Mary Bach," who lived in the last century. They are referred to as "walking under a dresser at Cwmmain." Did any of your readers ever hear of little Dick and Mary ? TELL.
[Pennant mentions these dwarfs in connection with Penmorva. —ED.]

PHILIP HENRY'S DIARIES extend from 1656-96, and are written with a crow quill in *Goldsmith's Almanacks* (interleav'd) which measure 4 in. by 2 in. Anyone who knows where these are will oblige by writing to
MATH. HENRY LEE,
Hanmer, Whitchurch, Salop.
[It may interest the Rev. M. H. Lee to know that several memoranda in the autograph of Philip Henry have recently been copied and sent to the editor of the *Cheshire Sheaf,* who intends to publish them.—ED.]

REPLIES.

OLD CANOE AT ELLESMERE (May 5, 1880).— The late Counsellor Dovaston of Westfelton told me that he recollected a similar vessel and great quantities of black oak trees of considerable size being dug up out of a drained peat moss near Westfelton called Twyford Vownog. W.A.L.

NOVELS RELATING TO WALES (Feb. 2, 1881).—The following is a portion of a paragraph which appeared in a Liverpool paper Nov. 23rd last year :— "The [Royal] Commissioners [on Higher Education in Wales] are now engaged in taking evidence in London. Amongst the testimony which has already been given one fact is worthy of notice. A witness who is a bookseller stated of thirty works of various kinds printed in the vernacular, not one novel is included in the list." Have no original Welsh novels been printed in Welsh ? If I remember rightly, more than one original novel written in

Welsh has appeared in the columns of Welsh newspapers. The number is not large, but a list of their titles would be interesting. At the risk of repeating titles which have already been mentioned, I may mention the following works as a contribution to the list of "Novels relating to Wales" :—*Hirell*, by J. Sanders ; *The Betrothed*, by Scott ; *Hidden Fire* treats of the Chartist outbreak in South Wales ; *Sir Cosmo Digby*, a tale of the Monmouthshire riots, by J. A. St. John ; *Trial of the Tredgolds*, by Dutton Cook ; two written by Henty, the war correspondent of the *Standard*, the titles of which I forget, but some of the scenes are laid in the neighbourhood of Llanidloes, Mr. Henty being once engaged on the construction of one of the railways near that town ; *Bronwen*, by a Carmarthenshire schoolmaster (Mr. B. Evans) an Eisteddfodic prize tale of the times of Owen Glyndwr ; the *Rebecca Rioter ; Fitzhammon*, by Mr. Wilkins of Merthyr ; *Nest*, by the same author, now appearing in the columns of the *Weekly Mail*. There also appeared a serial tale in *Chambers's Journal* a short time ago, in which North Wales scenery was depicted.   GOGLEDD.

[Of the foregoing list only *The Trials of the Tredgolds* has been previously mentioned. A brother of the author's (Mr. Cook) was engaged on the Mid-Wales railway works, we believe. Mr. Henty is supposed to have drawn from life at least one character he met with in his railway experiences.—ED.]

DR. JOHN DEE (March 10, 1880).—In the interesting extracts relating to the above, copied by your correspondent NEMO from *Local Gleanings*, he quotes "1595, June 29. Mr. John Blayney of Over Kingesham in Radnorshyre, and Mr. Richard Baldwyn of Duddlebury in Shropshire, visited me at Mortlake. The great grandfather of the sayd John and my great grandmother by the father side were brother and sister." The following skeleton pedigree will show the relationship :—

LLYNWENNY.	BLAYNEY OF EVESHAM.
(*L. Dwnn* I. p. 268).	(*Burke's Commoners*, IV. p. 632).
Davydd ddu ╤Eva v Ieuan Blayney (ap Hywel ap Cadwgan Vychan)	John Blayney Melyneth
Bedo du ╤Eva v Llewelyn Goch	Richd. Blayney of Kinsham ╤
Rowland Dee╤Jane Wylde Gentleman server to King Henry VIII.	Thomas Blayney╤ of Kinsham (living 1573)
Dr. John Dee╤Jane Fromage	John Blayney of Kinsham

These Blayneys of Kinsham, I imagine, were a branch of the Gregynog (Montgomeryshire) family, as in Meyrick's *Visitations of Wales*, among the Radnorshire pedigrees, several intermarriages of daughters of a grandson of Ieuan Blayney of Gregynog with Radnorshire families are seen, though there is no pedigree of the Radnorshire family of Blayney to be found in it. In a search made in Heralds' College a Herefordshire and Radnorshire Blayney family were found, but both emanated from Montgomeryshire.

Benjamin Blayne, D.D., the celebrated Hebrew Scholar, was of the Kinsham stock.

An account of the family of the Richard Baldwyn of Duddlebury, referred to in same paragraph, will be found in Blakeway's *Sheriffs*, p. 212, *et seq.* It is rather singular that

this family subsequently became connected with the Gregynog Blayneys by the marriage of Jane, 4th child of Henry Blayney, Esq., of Gregynog, to Mr. — Baldwyn of Salop. They had issue two sons and one daughter, who all died without issue. I have several books with a book plate in, probably that of the son of the above *Jane*, and which may be thus described, on a Banner Gules—per pale argent. a saltire sa : on Dextra and Sinistra sides. *Crest*, a Cockatrice resting on a mount, supported by the helmet of an Esquire ; supporters, two angels, naked ; over the crest, the motto, "Nunquam Non Paratus ;" on a label at foot of banner, "Per deum Meum Transiliom Murum."—Blayney Baldwyn, M.A. Blakeway has some interesting observations on the origin of the assumption of the latter motto by the Baldwyn family.

The Mr. Oliver Lloyd of Welshpool, styled by Dee "his cousin," was doubtless Oliver Lloyd of Leighton, who was "one of the aristocracy by whom I (Lewys Dwnn) was permitted to see old records and books from religious houses that had been written, and their materials collected by Abbots and Priors." This Oliver Lloyd represented the County of Montgomery in the Parliament of 29th Eliz. (1586-7). There was an Oliver Lloyd Vaughan —or *Vychan*, Junior, Bailiff of Welshpool in 38, Eliz. (1595-6) who might have been the donor of the MS. No. 847 in the Ashmolean, and who was in the judgment of the Rev. W. V. Lloyd (*Montg. Sheriffs*, p. 280, n 1.) the son of Oliver Lloyd of Leighton. Was he identical with Mr. Sergeant Oliver Lloyd, referred to in the preceding paragraph? If not, to what branch of the Lloyd family did Mr. Sergeant Oliver Lloyd belong? This family, like the Baldwyns, were a connection of the Blayneys by marriage, and hence perhaps "the cousinship."

There is a pedigree or rather pedigrees of the *Gwyn* family of Llanidloes in *L. Dwnn*. The one commencing on p. 309, vol. I. is headed LLANIDLOES THE GWYNN'S to ADAM, and on page 310 occurs "This pedigree was testified by John Wynn ap David ap Griffi—Written by his own hand 60 years before the original of this Book, which was written about the year 1610 or thereabouts"—and in a foot note by Sir S. Rush Meyrick, "This observation appears to have been written by John Rhydderch, *who does not however explain how John Wyn could certify this ascent to Adam !*"

Sir Sam. Rush Meyrick, *Visitations of Wales*, at p. 167, vol. I., n. 7, makes the following reference to Dr. "John Dee. He was the son of Rowland Dee, a vintner in London, in good circumstances, descended from an ancient family at *Nantygroes* in Radnorshire, and was born on the 15th of July 1527. In 1542 he was sent to St. John's, Cambridge, where he applied assiduously to study. He visited the principal universities abroad, and was distinguished for his knowledge of mathematics and alchemy. In 1553 he was presented by Edward VI. to the Rectory of Upton upon Severn. He merits the gratitude of posterity for the memorial he presented to Queen Mary for the preservation of Ancient MSS. and muniments. He recommended himself to Dudley, Earl of Leicester, and to Queen Elizabeth, as an astrologer ; and when ill at Lorrain in 1571 the Queen sent him two physicians. After his return to England he collected a noble library of books of Science and MSS., comprising 4,000 volumes, 1,000 of which were MSS., among them were large collections of original Irish and Welsh records, Welsh grants, donations, and pedigrees. The ignorant populace, who believed that he dealt with the Devil, broke into his house in 1583, during his absence abroad, took away and dispersed or destroyed what had cost him the labour of forty years and a great expenditure of money. He did, actually, after this, practise necromancy, and disgusted foreign Courts, to which he travelled, with his absurdities, so that the Queen sent for him to return. When he came to England, his friend Sir Thomas Jones offered him his Castle of Emlyn in Carmarthenshire to live in, with all necessary accommodations, but this he declined, still choosing to live in his house at Mortlake, Surrey. King James did not at all notice him, so that he died very poor, in the year 1608, at the age of 81."　BOOKWORM.

CURRENT NOTES.

The number of volumes taken out of the Chester Free Library in February was 3,450.

The frequent floods on the Dee have aggravated the losses of the farmers about Holt and Farndon and other parts to such an extent, that many of them are abandoning agriculture. Several large farms are without tenants.

Among the most recent additions to the list of vice-presidents of the National Eisteddfod Association are the Right Rev. the Lord Bishop of St. Asaph, Lord Tredegar, Lord Dynevor, and the Right Hon. G. Osborne Morgan, M.P., Judge Advocate General.

At a recent meeting of the Cymmrodorion Society, when Mr. Howel Lloyd presided, Dr. Isambard Owen stated that Mrs. Stephens of Merthyr had consented to hand over the manuscript of her late husband's edition of the "Gododin" for publication in the Society's Transactions. It was also stated that Mr. Stephens had written a historical introduction to the poem.

On Thursday John and Albert Roberts, the Welsh harpists, performed before the Empress of Austria at Combermere, and Charles Wood gave her Majesty some specimens of pennillion singing. Mr. Linger conveyed to Mr. Roberts and his son the expression of Her Majesty's pleasure with their performances on the Welsh national instrument.

Mr. Brinley Richards started on Tuesday on a tour of several weeks' duration, as official examiner on behalf of the Royal Academy of Music, an appointment that was recently unanimously conferred upon him. In addition to the large towns in the South and West of England, Mr. Richards will personally visit the principal towns of North and South Wales. The applicants for examination are so numerous that Messrs. Walter Macfarren, A. O. Leary, and W. Davenport have been appointed to assist Mr. Richards as assistant examiners.

THE REV. E. D. WILKS.—The Rev. E. D. Wilks, whose removal we announced last week, has accepted the charge of the Baptist Church at Kingsbridge, Devon. Mr. Wilks has laboured at Oswestry for not far short of a quarter of a century, having entered upon the pastorate of the Baptist Church in 1857, and his departure will be regretted by many friends.

DAVID COX'S SIGNBOARD.—The much-coveted sign which David Cox painted for the Royal Oak Hotel at Bettws-y-coed was again the subject of litigation last week, when the Baroness Willoughby D'Eresby appealed to the High Court from the order of the Chief Judge in Bankruptcy, who had reversed the decision of the judge of the Bangor County Court, and had decided against the claim of the Baroness. Their lordships were unanimous in allowing the appeal, holding that the picture belonged to her ladyship as part and parcel of the freehold of the house.

Some of the Welsh members wore the leek in the House of Commons on St. David's Day. Let us hope none of them will ever be compelled to eat it there.

The Society of Ancient Britons held their 166th anniversary on St. David's Day at the Freemasons' Tavern. The chair was taken by Lord Windsor, who was supported on the right by Lord Powis, Sir Watkin Williams Wynn, Bart., M.P., Captain Verney, R.N., Rhianva, and Mr. C. W. W. Wynn, and on the left by Lord Harlech, Sir Alexander Wood, the Mackintosh of Mackintosh, and Mr. Pryce Jones, Newtown. Among other gentlemen present were Sir J. R. Bailey, Bart., Mr. Stanley Leighton, M.P., Mr. Brinley Richards, Mr. R. L. Kenyon, Mr. Calvert, Q.C., &c., &c. The loyal toasts were proposed by the chairman and drunk with much enthusiasm, after which the Mackintosh of Mackintosh proposed the toast of "The Army, Navy, Militia, and Volunteer Forces." Touching on the annoyance felt by the Highland regiments at the threatened supercession of the tartan, the Mackintosh opined that a similar feeling would be engendered in Welsh regiments in the event of the Government threatening any of the national characteristics of those regiments, such as for instance the removal of the world-renowned goat of the Royal Welsh Fusiliers.—Sir Watkin, who received a remarkably warm welcome, spoke of his connection of nearly half a century's duration with the Denbighshire Militia and Volunteer forces, and expressed, as his opinion, that in view of wars and rumours of war, the auxiliary forces might be depended upon for the defence of their country. —The Chairman proposed "Prosperity to the Welsh Charity Schools, and perpetuity to the Honourable Society of Ancient Britons."—Mr. Stanley Leighton, M.P., acknowledged the toast, and regretted that at present the schools did not altogether satisfy his wishes on their behalf. The list of subscriptions was read by Mr. C. B. Shaw, and numbered among its names Her Majesty the Queen, 100 guineas, Lord Windsor, 100 guineas, Lord Powis and Sir Watkin Wynn, 50 guineas, Lord Tredegar, £50, Mr. Pryce Jones, 25 guineas, and other subscribers of smaller amounts, making in all over £800.—Lord Harlech proposed "The President of the day," and Lord Powis "The vice-presidents," to which Mr. Pryce Jones responded. — Other toasts followed.— Lady Llanover, with her usual liberality, sent her harper Gruffydd up to London for the occasion. He played several airs on the old Welsh triple-stringed harp. Gruffydd, by the way, was clad in the veritable costume of the Ancient Britons, a striped check, woven in Gwent, and known in the vernacular as "Gwlanen onglog a chymmwys." A highly successful concert, was given at St. James's Hall in the evening, under the patronage of Sir Watkin and Lady Williams Wynn, and in aid of the Penygraig Colliery Explosion Fund.

The death is announced, at the age of sixty, of the Rev. Moses Margoliouth, M.A., LL.D., vicar of Little Linford, Newport Pagnell, Bucks, one of the best Hebrew scholars of the present century, and a reviser of the English version of the Old Testament. The deceased gentleman, who was of foreign Jewish extraction, was born December, 1820, and became a convert to Christianity in his early manhood. At the Llangollen Congress of the British Archæological Association, in August, 1877, Dr. Margoliouth read an elaborate paper entitled "Whence the appellation of the term 'Kymry,' a problem for British Philological Archæologists." The object of the paper was to prove that the terms "Gael" and "Kymry" were of purely Hebrew origin. The learned Doctor's theory was, some of our readers may remember, rather mercilessly criticized by Professor Rhys.

The Late Mr. Edward Breese, F.S.A.,

(From the *Oswestry Advertizer*, March 16).

It is only some seven or eight months ago since we had the painful duty of recording the death of a gentleman whose contributions to the Literature of Wales, and whose services to the county of Merioneth, made his loss one which a generation could not well replace. And now the hand that penned the memoir we then published of Mr. Wynne is cold for ever.

Mr. Edward Breese of Morva Lodge, Portmadoc, whose death at the comparatively early age of 45 took place in London on the 10th of March, was the son of the late Rev. John Breese, by Margaret, second daughter of Mr. David Williams of Saethon, Carnarvonshire, He was born April 13, 1835, at Carmarthen, and was educated at Lewisham, Kent. On June 2, 1863, he married Margaret Jane, second daughter of Lewis Williams, Esq., of Vronwnion, Dolgelley, "the Old Banker," of whom we published an obituary notice in March 1879, and whose memory will be affectionately remembered in the district where he resided, as long as this generation lasts. Mr. Breese was Receiver for the Madocks estate — a property known far and near, comprising as it did some thousands of acres reclaimed from the sea by the enterprise of its owner—to which office he was appointed by the Court of Chancery on the resignation of his uncle, the late Mr. David Williams, M.P. He was also Clerk of the Peace for the County of Merioneth, Clerk to the Magistrates for the Portmadoc and Penrhyn divisions, and Clerk to the Lieutenancy of the County of Merioneth; and at the head of the well-known legal firm of Breese, Jones, and Casson, of Portmadoc.

Mr. Breese's sight was always defective, and at times he suffered severely from inflammation in the eyes. Probably had he lived he would eventually have become blind. In October last, when out shooting, by the explosion of a cap he completely lost the sight of one eye, and to save the other this had to be removed. But so fast did he recover —thanks to his cheerful temper and strong will—that in December he was able to write letters : letters, too, full of life and energy, as if he was a man of the most perfect and robust health. It may be that he attempted too much at that critical period ; we could not help thinking so when we heard of the correspondence the preliminary negotiations in connection with the Carnarvonshire election necessitated. However, he seems to have wonderfully recovered, and to those friends who resided at a distance the news of his death came with painful suddenness.

It is chiefly as a man of letters and as a genial and accomplished gentleman that we wish, in our present notice, to write of the deceased. He was one of the few Welshmen who have contributed to the literature of their native country with scholarly accuracy and painstaking research. Canon Williams (no mean authority), in a letter we have had from him since Mr. Breese's death, says "His views might be depended on, as he belonged to a superior school, where accuracy is the first requisite." The *Kalendars of Gwynedd* (published in 1873) is a good example of Mr. Breese's accuracy and painstaking care. To compile his lists of Lords-Lieutenant, Sheriffs, and Knights of the Shire, he laboriously searched through the musty files of the British Museum and Public Records Office, and the result is a book that is indispensable as a work of reference to students interested in the history of Venedotia as far as it relates to the counties of Anglesey, Carnarvon, and Merioneth.

To *Bye-gones* the deceased was a constant and regular friend ; his latest contributions being the interesting correspondence between Mr. Madocks, Sir W. Gell, and John Gibson, the sculptor, on the subject of a projected monument on the Portmadoc Embankment. Indeed as lately as Feb. 11, we heard from him on this subject ; and the reply was to be addressed to him at the Devonshire Club, London. He then intended to stay in London a fortnight, and he purposed, when he settled down again at home, to write some account of Tomen-y-Mûr, and a description of the Welsh MSS. in his library. But on Friday week he caught cold in London, rheumatic fever followed, and, weakened probably by the sufferings which he had previously undergone in connection with the injury to his eye, Mr. Breese passed away on Thursday. Mrs. Breese was summoned to London on the Saturday, and was with her husband during the last few days of his life.

Mr. Breese was the corresponding secretary for Merionethshire of the Cambrian Archæological Association, and a contributor to the pages of the *Archæologia Cambrensis*, the quarterly journal of that Society. In 1876, when there was a movement at Dolgelley to preserve the old building, "Cwrt Plas yn Dre" (so well known to tourists as "Owain Glyndwr's Old Parliament House") he wrote a paper that exploded the local theory as completely as the local theory of the Birth of the First Prince of Wales in Carnarvon Castle was exploded by the late Mr. Hartshorne. Mr. Breese's latest contribution to *Arch : Camb :*, we believe, was the memoir of Mr. W. W. E. Wynne of Peniarth, previously alluded to. This first appeared in *Bye-gones*, and was afterwards, at the suggestion of some of our prominent Welsh scholars, somewhat enlarged, and re-issued in that journal, accompanied by the beautiful portrait of Mr. Wynne, now so well known, copies of which were presented to the Cambrian Society by subscribers to a special fund for the purpose. Never was a biography penned where the writer entertained profounder regret at the loss of the object of his reminiscences. "I mourn for him as a friend," wrote Mr. Breese in sending his MS. to the editor of *Bye-gones* in June, 1880, " and feel his is a loss which can never be replaced. He was such a courtly, intelligent, and genial gentleman of the old school." Writing again a few days later, he said, "I attended the funeral of the late Mr. Wynne yesterday, at Llanegryn Church, and felt as the coffin was lowered to its last bedding in the vault under the chancel that the Silent Majority had gained a great acquisition indeed. He was a man whose like we shall not soon look on again."

Mr. Breese was also a member of the Powysland Club, and an occasional contributor to its *Montgomeryshire Collections.*

We need scarcely say that a man of Mr. Breese's culture would possess a good library ; and his collection was, as his attainments were, varied. Especially was it rich in rare books connected with the Principality. He possessed, what is all but unique, a perfect copy of Salesbury's Welsh Testament ; and he was always adding to his store. Especially valuable were the Welsh MSS. he possessed, and in 1877 he made some important additions to these by the purchase of the more valuable of those relating to Wales, from the famous "Mytton collection" sold in London in that year. He also preserved at his charming residence, Morva Lodge, several objects of antiquity interesting to Wales ; notably a Glas Hirlas of the 15th century, which had belonged to the Auwyl family. This he exhibited at Wrexham in 1876.

Amongst Mr. Breese's collection of Manuscripts was "The Diary of Peter Roberts," a work stated in the Report of the Camb : Arch : Society of 1878 to be "a MS. of great interest to the antiquaries and genealogists of Denbighshire and Flintshire," and it intimated that Mr. Breese was preparing it for the press : indeed in one of the issues of the *Arch : Camb :* a specimen page of the work was given. How far this work has progressed we are not informed.

He was a true friend, as many who now mourn his loss can testify. Socially he was beloved and respected, and at Portmadoc he will be especially missed. When the Madocks Fountain in that town was opened by Mrs. Breese (on behalf of the subscribers) in 1878, the late Rev. Robert Jones, rector of Rotherhithe, in *Y Cymmrodor*, said, "Towards the erection of this Fountain, and towards the carrying out of various improvements in the town and neighbourhood of Portmadoc, effectual help has been rendered by Mr. Breese, and we were glad to find how highly, in consequence, both he and Mrs. Breese were greeted by the inhabitants."

It is stated in a contemporary that in 1862, Mr. Breese obtained by purchase the Dolvriog estate. "This property in the 15th century formed part of the lands of the celebrated Welsh poet, Rhys Goch Eryri, the friend and patron of Davydd Nantmor. He lived at the adjoining Plasdy of Havodgarregog. It afterwards came into the possession of the Anwyls, a branch of the Anwyls of Park, one of whom, William Anwyl of Dolvriog, served the office of Sheriff for Merionethshire in the year 1694."

The news of Mr. Breese's death was received in Portmadoc with deep and general regret, a feeling which will be shared by numbers of his countrymen throughout North Wales. For many years Mr. Breese was chairman of Portmadoc Local Board, but he retired from that position some time ago. He was the first W.M. of the Madoc Lodge of Masons and a liberal contributor to its funds. He was initiated into the mysteries of the craft in the Provence of Herefordshire; we believe by the then Grand Master, the Rev. Dr. Bowles of Stanton Lacy ; and for some time he acted as Grand Registrar of that Provence. In politics he was a Liberal, and he was looked upon as the future member for Merionethshire. His services to the Liberal party, as a wise adviser, an able organizer, and an effective speaker, can scarcely be exaggerated, and there is no doubt that the triumphs of the Liberal party in Merionethshire and Carnarvonshire during the last twelve or fourteen years owed a great deal to Mr. Breese's help. But it will be as an accomplished Welshman, a man of singular kindness of heart, that he will be chiefly remembered by those who knew him best, his friends and neighbours at Portmadoc and elsewhere, and to these his loss is irreparable. Mr. Breese leaves six children, four boys and two girls, the eldest son being sixteen years of age.

The Late Lord Hanmer.

We regret to record the death of Lord Hanmer of Bettisfield Park near Whitchurch. Lord Hanmer was at Knotley Park in Kent at the time of his somewhat unexpected decease, which happened on Tuesday, March the 8th, in the 72nd year of his age. His ancient family seat, Bettisfield Park, though it is near Whitchurch, is in the county of Flint, in the detached portion of it which is surrounded by Shropshire, Cheshire, and Denbighshire, and the greater part of the late lord's public life was identified with the county in which his residence was situated, as well as the neighbouring village which bore his name.

The Right Hon. John Hanmer, Baron Hanmer of Hanmer and Flint, in the Peerage of the United Kingdom, and a baronet, was the eldest son of the late Lieutenant-Colonel Thomas Hanmer and Arabella Charlotte, eldest daughter and co-heiress of Mr. T. Skip Dyot Bucknall, M.P., of Hampton Court, and was born at Hardwicke Grange, Salop, Dec. 22, 1809. He was educated at Eton and at Christ Church, Oxford, graduating as B.A., in 1828. In 1833 he married Georgina, daughter of Sir George Chetwynd, the second baronet, and he was left a widower a twelve month ago. He was a deputy-lieutenant and J.P. for the county of Flint, of which county he was high sheriff in 1832 ; he was also a J.P. for Shropshire and a fellow of the Royal Geographical Society. He first entered Parliament at the General Election in 1832, as one of the members for Shrewsbury, directly after the passing of the Reform Act, being the colleague of Mr. Robert A. Slaney. On that occasion he headed the poll, the numbers being Hanmer 808, Slaney 797, John Cresset Pelham 634. At the election of 1835, he was again returned for that borough, the numbers being Hanmer 761, Pelham 629, Slaney 578. He did not contest the borough in 1837, but in 1841 he was returned for Hull, and he remained a representative of that borough until 1847, when he was returned for the Flint district boroughs. He continued to represent the latter constituency until his elevation to the peerage by Mr. Gladstone in 1872. In politics, he was a moderate Liberal, and he originated the Bill for the Commission to inquire into Corrupt Practices in 1848. During his Parliamentary career he displayed a perfect acquaintance with the constitutional laws of the country, but he took little part in the debates.

Lord Hanmer leaves no issue and the peerage becomes extinct. He is succeeded in the baronetage and the estates by Major Wyndham Edward Hanmer, his surviving brother, who was born on December 24th, 1810. The new baronet is a deputy-lieutenant and J.P. for Bucks, and a J.P. for Bedfordshire. He has been twice married, first, in 1842, to Victoria Mary Louisa (daughter of Sir John Conroy), who died in 1866 ; and secondly, in 1877, to Harriett Frances, daughter of the late Colonel the Hon. Hely Hutchinson, and niece of the second Earl of Donoughmore ; and he has a son and heir by this first marriage.

The deceased peer was descended from Sir John de Hanmere, governor of Carnarvon Castle, in the reign of Edward I., who, with a salary of 200 marks, is said to have maintained a force of fourscore men, a chaplain, surgeon, and smith. Sir John (says Burke) was possessed of Hanmer, and in 1258 married Hawys, daughter of Eynion ap Griffith ap Gwynwynwyn, Lord of Powis. His great granddaughter married Owain Glyndwr, whose brother-in-law, Sir John Hanmer, fell fighting against the king at the Battle of Shrewsbury. Several members of the family were distinguished men. One of them, Sir Thomas Hanmer, M.P. for Flintshire (which county each of his successors represented down to the last baronet of the first creation), a member of the Court of the Marches of Wales, attended the Earl of Derby with the Ensign of the Garter for Henry III., and married, first a daughter of Sir John Talbot, and second a daughter of Sir Thomas Mostyn. It is interesting to note that the grandfather of this Sir Thomas—another knight of the same name—married Katherine, daughter and heiress of Thomas Salter of Oswestry. Sir John Hanmer, Knight, was created a baronet in 1620, and his son, Sir Thomas, was cup-bearer to Charles I., in whose cause he raised two troops of horse during the Civil War. He was to have been one of the Knights of the Royal Oak had that order been actually instituted. His elder son, Sir John Hanmer, was colonel of a regiment under King William III. at the battle of the Boyne, and Sir John's nephew, Sir Thomas

Hanmer, was the most famous of all the line. He was returned to Parliament on the accession of Queen Anne, for the county of Flint, elected in 1707 for Suffolk, and in 1712 chosen Speaker of the House.

His Latin epitaph (at Hanmer) was admired by Dr. Johnson, who wrote an English paraphrase, in which occur the following lines :—

Resistless merit fixed the Senate's choice,
Who hailed him Speaker with united voice.
Illustrious age, how bright thy glories shone,
When Hanmer filled the Chair, and Anne the Throne.

Sir Thomas had an extensive correspondence, and letters addressed to him by Swift, Steele, Prior, Bolingbroke, Bishop Berkeley, Roger North, the Electress Sophia, the Duke and Duchess of Marlborough, and other famous persons, are given in " The Correspondence of Sir Thomas Hanmer, with a Memoir of His Life," edited by Sir Henry Burnaby, Bart., and published in 1838. A letter of Roger North's, in which he argues against the scientific explanation of the ascent of smoke, is extremely amusing. He says—"Ye smoak is really air, enely a little fowler," and " ye swift rising of ye smoak is but a consequence of ye air's swift motion, of which it is a part, or, at least passively contained in it." Sir Thomas is best known, however, for the edition of Shakespeare which bears his name, published by the University of Oxford, to which he presented the manuscript. With Sir Thomas, who left no issue, the baronetcy expired, but it was revived in 1774, in favour of Mr. Walden Hanmer, M.P. for Sudbury, great grandfather of the late lord.

Lord Hanmer was an accomplished man of letters, and a poet whose talent is recognized in a volume of " English Sonnets, collected by Samuel Waddington," and published by George Bell and Sons, in which some of his productions are included, side by side with those of Tennyson, Swinburne, &c. In 1838 he published " Fra Cipolla and other Poems," one of which, the " Friar and the Ass," tells the same story which is told by Longfellow, under the title of " The Monk of Casal-Maggiore," in " Tales of a Wayside Inn" in "Aftermath." His lordship was an occasional contributor to our column of Bye-gones; his first contribution was an old MS. from his library, containing a list of Flintshire Sheriffs from 1541 to 1764. We cannot conclude this notice better than by extracting from the volume already mentioned Lord Hanmer's lines

TO THE RIVER DEE.

By the Elbe and through the Rheinland, I've wandered far and wide,
And by the Save with silver tones, proud Danube's queenly bride ;
By Arno's vales, and Tiber's shore, but never did I see
A river I would match with thine, old Druid haunted Dee !

I've stood where Sorga gushes forth Valchiusa's marble cave
As bright as when to deathless verse its name Petrarca gave,
In fair Verona's palaces—the towers of Avignon,
But Adige was not like to thee, nor blue and sunny Rhone.

I've heard great Danube roaring far, and sailed upon his breast,
And seen beneath his sea-like wave the sun sink down to rest ;
And by the Po, which Virgil loved—and by his Mantuan stream,
And Iser hailed of poets now, bright with Art's favourite beam.

But though beside thy waters wild no Munich e'er will rise,
Far sweeter is their liquid voice, and it hath dearer ties,
And liv'st thou not in song my Dee, when of Milton thou canst claim
A portion of the awful love, and the everlasting name.

By the Moorish towers of Andernach, beneath a walnut's shade
Thus speed my faithful thoughts to thee, though a little Rhenish maid
Hast wine, da wreath of water-flowers, round a flask of Wurtzberg wine,
And bade me give of streams the palm to their old Fader Rhein.

MARCH 16, 1881.

NOTES.

THE SCARCITY IN 1800 (Mar. 9, 1881).—All provisions were dear in 1800, but "bread-corn" seems to have been especially scarce. On June 10, the richer and more provident inhabitants of *Shrewsbury* met to make a further subscription for their poorer and less provident neighbours ; and it was stated at the meeting that "upwards of 4,000 individuals had reaped the weekly benefit of the subscription entered into in February." Mr. Carless, the Mayor, accompanied by Sir W. Pulteney, the member, presented an address of congratulation to the King that month, on his escape from the shot of a madman, when his Majesty "anxiously enquired into the price of provisions and the state of growing crops in Shropshire." The second subscription at Shrewsbury (previously referred to) was chiefly for the supply of rice, "as the season of the year (June) was not so well adapted for the use of soup," but early in July the committee had temporarily to suspend operations "for want of a supply of that article." On July 5th, wheat in Shrewsbury market realized 22s. a bushel, and on the 26th of the same month fell 5s. a bushel "owing to the abundant promise of a good harvest." In *Ellesmere* market the same week wheat sold for 12s. a bushel. I find no further records until Sept. 10, 1800, when the *Salopian Journal* says :—" It is with great pleasure that we find gentlemen of landed property giving notice to their tenants to bring their corn to market for the supply of the country."
　　　　　　　　　　　　　　　　　　JARCO.

THE OLD WELSH ALMANACKS.
(Feb. 2, 1881.)

In this contribution one year—1812—is wanting, and I had better therefore preface the title pages of the other three by saying that within their covers, are the following verses :—

In that of 1813—

Ai pell ai pell yw'r dyddiau, hyfrydaf dan y nef,
I'r tion a'r cleddyf pybur, droi'n swch neu bladur gref :
A therfyn ar ryfeloedd yn nghylchoedd daear las :
Holl deulu'r byd mewn cydrod, yn erbyn pechod cas?

Pryd hyn bydd cyflawn derfyn ar waith y gelyn mawr,
Fu chwe-mil bron o flwyddau yn llywio graddau'r llawr :
Ni rwygir mwy deyrnasoedd, na dryllio lluoedd byd,
Ond senio mawl Hosanna, fydd gwaith y dyrfa i gyd.

In that for 1815—

O'r diwedd daeth y dyddiau, i sain cenhadau hedd
Orlenwi CRED yn unol, 'nlle brad anghaeol gledd :
Boed i ni bellach gwympo, wrth orsedd effro'r nef,
Rhag haeddu eto'n hoywedd, y farn mewn agwedd gref.

And now I proceed with the title pages of the Almanacks for 1813 to 1815.

The one for 1813 is called "Cyfaill Treiddgar." Printed at Dublin ; price fourpence half-penny, and has the following verses on title page :—

1 Fy hen Gyfeillion heini,
　Rwy' eto am eich lloni,
　A hanes deg am flwyddyn lawn
　Yn ol y ddawn sydd geni.

2 Mae *haulwen* oleu hyfryd
　Yn ganol bwynt i'r *holl-jyd ;*
　Sef i'r planedau mawr yn rhwydd
　O'i gylch bob blwydd ymsymud.

3 Ni syflodd ef (mae'n hynod)
　O'r man lle cadd ei osod :
　Ond ar ei begwm try yn gain
　Bob pump ar hugain niwrnod.

4 Y ddaear fawr yn unwedd,
　Sy'n troi ar *begwn* hoywedd ;
　I roddi i ddydd a nos eu bod :
　Mae *trefn* y rhod yn rhyfedd.

5 Boed *ini* megys teulu,
　Ymofyn nawdd o ddifri :
　Rhag bod rhyw *Seba* drwg ei wedd
　Yn rhwystro *hedd* reoli.

6 As malice, pride and envy,
　Causo war with all its fury,
　So *these* removed, we soon would trace
　The bliss of peace and plenty ;

The one for 1814, printed at Dublin, is called "Cyfaill Newydd," the price fivepence. The following verses being on the title page :—

1 Fy hen Gyfeillion hybarch,
Na roddes imi amharch,
Er dod i'ch plith yn waeth fy llw,
Na sothach *Trefriw* sybarch.

2 Ymrof yn lan eleni,
Mewn diwyg gwell eich lloni,
Am wg a gwên y sêr sy'n glaû,
O radd (medd rhai) 'n rheoli.

3 Y Lloer-wen oleu syber,
Sy rhwng yr haul a'r ddaear,
Pan fo'r goleuad mawr yn brudd,
O ddiffyg cudd ddisgleirder.

4 A'r ddaear ar ogwyddiad,
Ar oriau llawn y lfonad ;
Y sydd a'i chysgod tywyll byg,
Yn ddiffyg ar y lleuad.

5. Gan fod ein horiau'n dirwyn,
O ddydd i fis a blwyddyn,
Boed sail ar graig (nid eiddo yr ffol,)
I'n dal hyd farwol derfyn.

6 May God who reigns in mercy,
Protect in perfect safety,
Our King and constitution, free
From any foreign party.

The one for 1815 is called "Cyfaill Heddychol." It was printed at Dublin, price fourpence, and has the following verses :—

1 Fy hen Gyfeillion tawel,
Sy'n gyrch rhag brâd yn gochel :
Annerchaf chwi ar hyn o bryd,
Ar derfyn gwaedlyd ryfel.

2 Y fendith fwyaf hyfryd
O eiddo dynol fywyd ;
Yw meddu head (os ynddi loes)
Yn nghanol oes o ddrygfyd.

3 Ond fel trowd *Vulcan* hylla
O'r nef i ynys *Lemna :*
Rhaid eto fyrdd sy'n hedd ddihap
I fyw at *Nap* i *Elba.*

4 Nid rhaid ond cariad gola'
Ac undeb rhwng eneidiau,
Yn ddôr rhag twyll a rhagfarn hy'
I ddrygu unrhyw dyrfa.

5 Nis gall dim doniau dynol,
Er swnio yn ddefosionol,
Gyfnewid anian ffromllyd : clywch [lol.
Rhaid cael peth uwch natur-

6 The Bliss of peace and plenty,
In part has crown'd our country ;
Then may the Nation's *gait* impend
For God to extend his mercy.
E.G.S.

QUERIES.

OSWESTRY PRINTERS (Mar. 19, 1879).—In Hulbert's *Salopian Magazine* for July, 1815, the marriage is announced, at Oswestry, of "Mr. D. Oliver, printer, to Miss Griffiths." Was Mr. Oliver an Oswestry printer, and in business on his own account? TYPO.

COFFIN PLATES ON CHURCH WALLS.—Your occasional correspondent BOILEAU, writing in *Salopian Shreds and Patches* Jan. 19, says, "In the old church of Llandrillo I remember, forty years ago, seeing dozens of coffin-plates fixed to the walls." It is said that at Little Ness (Salop) there is one so placed. Can any reader say if the coffin-plates are still in so unusual a position at Llandrillo, and whether they are duplicate plates, or removed from the respective coffins they belonged to? Are other instances known where such strange monumental tablets are affixed? N.W.S.

[Since the above was published a further communication states that plates removed from old coffins used to be placed in like manner on the walls of Llanaber Church, Barmouth.—ED.]

TUMULI, OVAL AND ROUND.—On the Welsh hills are many barrows of earth and stone, but almost all with which I am acquainted are round—varying in diameter from 20 to 100 feet. There are a few oval ones. Would it not be well to collect a list of these latter, as in the opinion of antiquaries they belong to a different and earlier race—the dolicocephalous—which is supposed to have preceded the Celtic race in these islands? There are hundreds of barrows, earth and stone, on the mountains to the south of the river Teivy, but all I have seen, with some doubtful exceptions, are round. I have been present at the opening of some dozen of the smaller ones, and

those that have not been disturbed have generally a "cist" in the centre. This is formed by placing large slab stones in an upright position so as to enclose a space about 2 ft. in width and varying in length from 6 ft. to 3 ft. Generally it is covered by a cap-stone. The smaller ones were used for burial by cremation, as the burnt bones and ashes found in them still bear witness, and the larger ones for inhumation. The burial arrangements in the oval mounds are generally more elaborate than in the round ones, having frequently large chambers and walled passages leading to them from the outside. I believe that only one or two specimens of this class have yet been exposed in Wales. There is a very large oval cairn—some 150, ft by 80 ft.—within the ancient fortress of Carn Goch in Carmarthenshire, and another on the hills near Abergwessin in Breconshire. CYNWYL.

REPLIES.

DAVID COX'S SIGNBOARD (Jan. 26, 1881).—The history of this sign-board will be found in the life of the Artist published by his son. W.A.L.

The *Magazine of Art* for this month has the following :—Apropos of a paragraph in these columns concerning the signboard painted by David Cox, which has recently been the object of litigation, we have received some interesting communications from persons who were acquainted with the painter and with the circumstances of his strange gift to "mine hostess" of the "Royal Oak" at Bettws-y-Coed. "It was painted," writes a lady, "in August, 1847, for his kind friend Mary Roberts, as he always called her. I was staying at Bettws at the time, and it was our evening's amusement to go down to the 'Royal Oak' and watch David Cox mount a ladder to paint at the sign." The former sign, which he found there when he came, offended his taste, and no wonder. It consisted of a tree, out of the top of which appeared a crowned head, so large that had a body been added in scale it would have been far taller than the oak itself. "I want to paint out the horrid thing," said David Cox to another of our correspondents, who passed through Bettws one morning on a day's excursion, and who, returning by the same route at night, found Cox up the ladder, with a candle fastened to his palette, hard at work on the new sign, which has since been the subject of so much talk, and has been valued at a price which David Cox never dreamed of asking for the most careful and lovely productions of his brush. One of our correspondents, the daughter of an artist, makes a lament over the change that has come over Bettws-y-Coed since the good old days when David Cox stayed there, and not only painted the signboard at the inn, but also, she asserts, decorated the parlour with a fresco of "Margaret Douglas Barring the Door," and with another drawing, and made some sketches in the Visitors' Book. Even in 1847 it was, as it is now, a popular painters' haunt, and our correspondent well remembers "the low parlour at the inn, full of artists—and smoke. The village was then very different from the Bettws of to-day, which would have scared away gentle old David Cox. My father, who was a dear and intimate friend of his was last in Wales with him in 1853—at Capel Curig. Even then Bettws had become *too grand* for the simple, kindly old man." E.

AN OSWESTRY LOTTERY (Jan. 5, 1881).—The Lottery enquired about never came off. Mr. Roberts sold several guinea tickets, but there were found to be difficulties in the way and the money was returned. The Conservatory that was to be raffled for was at that time (1833) erected temporarily in a garden in Upper Brook-street. It was afterwards taken to pieces and sold to different parties. I believe a portion of it went to Brook Cottage, Woodhill, and another piece to Ashlands.   J.

TOMEN-Y-MUR (Sep. 22, 1880).—The only incised stones recorded at this locality and figured in Westwood's *Lapidarium Walliœ* are Roman sepulchral inscriptions. From BOILEAU's description I should conjecture the stone he speaks of to have on it an Ogham inscription, although no mention is made of one at Festiniog in Brash's valuable and exhaustive work on Ogham Inscriptions. If this be so, it would be well to have a cast and rubbing made of the Stone, or better still remove it to the Museum of the Welsh University College at Aberystwyth.   W.A.L.

BROSELEY TRIUMPHANT (Feb. 9, 1881).—In reference to this pamphlet, I may add that amongst the doggrel pieces there are one or two shewing that the parson was also chaplain to the squire of Willey. In one of these—"The Blessed Chaplain," there is this verse :—

My PATRON, God bless him, but why should I brag?
A SPORTSMAN has been—good as e'er cross'd a Nag;
But for Company's sake, it were Something divine
His old Friends to desert for the Pref'rence of mine.

In another one called "The Clerical Dupe" we have the following :—

This *meek-ey'd* Son of Charity,
This matchless Ancient Briton
To preach, and drink, as good you'll say,
As ever Bench did sit on:
The Squire's Sunday jovial Bowl
He deeply dips his Beak in,
And drinks as well becomes a Soul,
To all Friends round the Wrekin.

"The Court of Requests"—the cause of all this little tempest—was, I gather from Lewis's *Topographical Dictionary*, established under Act of Parliament passed 22 Geo. III., for the recovery of debts under forty shillings: though why Broseley should possess such an Act the author does not say.   J.?.R.

CURRENT NOTES.

Prince Lucien Bonaparte has consented to become a vice-president of the National Eisteddfod Association.

A volume of "Borth Lyrics," by the Rev. Edward Thring, M.A., Head Master of Uppingham School, has been published.

The Welsh are talking of erecting a statue to General Picton on the vacant pedestal in Trafalgar-square. He will be portrayed sitting on a cheese with a Welsh rabbit on his lap.—*The Cuckoo.*

The annual meeting of the Welsh Congregationalists worshiping at Fetter Lane Chapel, was held on Wednesday night, when the chair was taken by Mr. Puleston, M.P. After a hymn had been sung, the Chairman opened the proceedings in Welsh, and, in the course of his remarks, after passing into English, congratulated his hearers on their ability to understand both Welsh and English. Mr. Puleston said that when he was about eighteen years of age he was connected with a society for fostering the study of Cambrian literature. They had a dinner, and it was necessary to get a president for this dinner ; he (Mr. Puleston) went to ask that great Welshman, Sir George Cornewall Lewis, to take the chair. Sir George consented, and brought several friends with him, among whom was Sheridan Knowles, who, in the course of the evening, made the remark that "in proportion to the languages a man knew he was so many times a man." Let them then while cultivating English hold fast to their old Welsh tongue. The Chairman went on to say that he could not

sympathise with the idea which was now too popular a one, namely, that a knowledge of Welsh was a barrier to the progress of its possessor. Having had wide experience of the Welsh, not only in England, but in America, he begged with, he hoped, some authority, to contradict that statement. In the great Republic of the west no people occupied a higher position than the Welsh. In America it was a rare thing to see a Welshman in the police-court, and a Welshman was seldom found seeking relief.

An interesting story is (says a Manchester paper) told just now concerning Lord Sherbrooke. The noble viscount who, as is well known, suffers from defective sight, was staying some time ago at an hotel in North Wales, where he observed a little boy suffering from an affliction similar to his own. Lord Sherbrooke at once interested himself in the lad, and had him brought to London, where he is now under treatment by an eminent oculist, being in the meantime attentively watched by his distinguished patron.

The February number of the *University College of Wales Magazine* is not as interesting as usual. It is too serious. The number of readers who care for essays on "the Influence of Education," the "True Nobility of Life," "Natural Science and Religion," &c., is comparatively small, nor does a critical notice of Wieland appeal to a much wider circle, though it is appropriate enough to a College Magazine. What is wanted is more relief for the strained faculties, such relief as has been given with sound judgment in previous numbers, and will, we have little doubt, be given in future. We learn from the Oxford Letter that a Club of Aberystwyth College men, eighteen in number, has been formed there, and meets weekly for debate and social intercourse.

ST. DAVID'S COLLEGE, LAMPETER.—Professor Scott has been appointed an examiner in natural philosophy for 1881, under the Intermediate Education Board for Ireland. Professor Coolidge having been unexpectedly re-called to Oxford as law and modern history tutor of Magdalen College, of which he is a Fellow, the College Board of Lampeter, with the approval of the Visitor, has chosen Mr. T. F. Tout, B.A., of Balliol College, Oxford, to be professor of English and modern languages in his stead. Mr. Tout was a Brackenbury scholar of Balliol, and obtained in 1877 a first-class in the school of modern history, and in 1879 a second-class in the school of literæ humaniores.

MARCH 23, 1881.

NOTES.

PORTMADOC EMBANKMENT. — The recent publication of the Gibson—Madocks correspondence will make the following record additionally interesting.—"The embankment across the Traeth Mawr, near Tre-madoc," says the *Gent's: Mag:* for Sep. 1811, "has at length been closed, and this stupendous work is thus far executed. We say thus far executed, for as the embankment is composed of pieces of stone blasted from the rocks on either side, and then carried and promiscuously thrown together, the sea rushes through with almost as much facility as if there were no barrier to its tide. These tides however will, in process of time, fill up the interstices, and also deposit a sand bank on each side ; thus the enraged element will complete its own prison-wall. Along this stupendous barrier, which connects the two counties of Merioneth and Carnarvon, an excellent carriage road towards Tan-y-bwlch will be immediately made. The embankment is 1,500 yards in length, and eight or nine feet wide at the top. The extent of the land gained from the sea is not correctly ascertained, but it is supposed that it will be from 4,000 to 5,000 acres. This great work has been accomplished by W. A. Madocks, Esq., M.P. for Boston."—Early in Feb. 1812, the embankment was greatly injured by the high wind and tide. Four-hundred men with two-hundred horses and 67 carts were employed in repairing the breach.	G.G.

QUERIES.

SELION OF LAND.—"Madoc L'Estrange, Roger de Borghton, and Cecil his wife gave to John Loid of Oswestry seven *selions* of land together lying in the field of Weston between land of Richard de Haston on one side and land of Madoc L'Estrange on the other. To Have &c., for ever." This is an extract from an old deed (June 1341), printed in *Arch : Camb :* 1852. What is or was the quantity of land expressed by the term *Selion?*	QUERIST.

GRIFFITH JONES.—In Mr. Davenport Adams's *Dictionary of English Literature*, p. 318, mention is made of "Griffith Jones, author and publisher," who was born in 1722, and died in 1780. He is stated to have written "Great Events from Little Causes"; contributed to the "Literary Magazine" and the "British Magazine," and edited the "London Chronicle," the "Daily Advertiser," and the "Public Ledger;" and also to have published several translations from the French. Who was this Griffith Jones? He must have been a Welshman, for if there is such a thing as a real Welsh name, Griffith Jones must have a pre-eminent claim to that distinction. I do not think that the Griffith Jones in question is mentioned in any of our biographical Dictionaries; but perhaps when the Cymmrodorion will bring out their new Cambrian Bibliography we may learn something about him.	DEINIOL.

REPLIES.

A CHURCHYARD SUPERSTITION (Feb. 23, 1881).—I have never before heard of this as a superstition, but it is nevertheless a fact that in many churchyards, with which I am well acquainted, very few interments have taken place on the north side of the ground. It is also a fact that many persons who have suffered the extreme penalty of the law, and whose bodies were not claimed by their friends, have been buried in St. Mary's Churchyard, in this town, and, invariably, on the north side of the church, on which side not more than half a dozen other interments have taken place, whilst the south and west sides are crowded. The same remark applies to others ; St. Alkmond's, for instance, where on the north side the gravestones bear modern dates, as though it had not been used until the other side was full. At St. Giles's there are very few graves on the north as compared with the south side. At Condover the first person buried on the north side of the church, except in two or three family vaults near the east end, was alive less than fifty years ago, the south side being of course full.	W. H. Shrewsbury.

No doubt the practice of burying on the south side of the churchyard arose from the desire that relatives and others, as they passed into the church through the south door, would breathe a silent prayer for the repose of the soul. The north side was avoided as appropriated to the unbaptized and excommunicate. Change in religious tenets and increase of population have altered all this ; but in many sequestered villages it may be still discernable more or less.	W. A. L.

ANCIENT HILL CULTIVATION—(Feb. 23, 1881.)—I was accustomed some five and twenty years ago to go shooting over the hills in the neighbourhood of the "Anchor" a modern public house, located on Clun Fe rest, about midway between the village of Kerry in Montgomeryshire and Newcastle in Shropshire. The hills (then unenclosed) which form the water-shed on the South side of the Clun rivulet, lying between the road leading from the Anchor to the Bettws Church and the Hall of the Forest, were, on the slopes leading to the brook, in many places distinctly marked with ridges or Butts, and, similar to those observed in North Carmarthenshire, curved according to the formation of the ground, but the "Butts" were of various sizes, some narrow, some wide. It used to puzzle me why cultivation should have taken place up so high, leaving, as I then thought, better land lower down untouched, but since then I have considered that as Castell Bryn Amlwg (referred to previously in this column) lay closely adjacent—only a mile or so west—that it is probable this hill land was in some way connected with that establishment, and that it was cultivated to supply the requirements of the garrison, who, during the troublous days of the middle ages often were isolated, and cut off from their base of supplies. Since the period I referred to above, these hills have been allotted to the several freeholders and for the most part cultivated, so that all traces of the ancient culture are now obliterated.	RHYDDWR.

SEDAN CHAIRS (May 12, 1880).—I have clear remembrances of several Sedan Chairs being in use in Shrewsbury to carry ancient maiden ladies and invalids to church, or tea, and card parties, without disarrangement of dress or toilet. The last proprietor was an old servant of my father's, Thomas or Roger Yeomans, who lived on St. John's Hill, and on his death Sedans disappeared altogether. In 1827 my wife and her sister were conveyed in a Sedan from Castle-street to St. Mary's Church for the marriage ceremony. No doubt the *hired* Sedans were the cast-off furniture of the "quality," who in the seventeenth and eighteenth centuries used to winter in Shrewsbury in their town mansions, and each family had their own Sedan, as now their special carriages. It may be noticed that the mansions of the time of Queen Anne, and the early Georges have all wide doorways and spacious halls, into which the Sedans would be conveyed with their occupants. Figures of Sedans may be seen in Cassell's *Old and New London*, vol. 3, p. 336, and their use in Dickens's *Old Curiosity Shop* by Beau Charter. I have heard my father say that early in the present century some one attempted to introduce for hire "Flys" in Shrewsbury, but in a month or two ruined himself. The wants of society had not then progressed far enough.	W.A.L.

CURRENT NOTES.

The weekly attendance at Wrexham Free Library is about 1,000.

The list of vice-presidents of the National Eisteddfod Association is rapidly increasing. Among the later additions are Mr. Stuart Rendel, M.P., the Hon. F. S. Hanbury Tracy, M.P., and Mr. Hussey Vivian, M.P.

CURIOUS EPITAPHS.—A correspondent writes : As far as my memory serves me, the enclosed is the epitaph in Carno churchyard, asked for in your last :—

When on the stage of life my lot it fell to me,
Placed by my parents dear a carrier for to be,
In the exercise of my calling I travelled both far and near,
Till death by his last mortal stroke laid me silent here.

Died of a chronicle abcess in his right side.

The Rev. Wm. Houghton, M.A., Rector of Preston-on-the-Weald-Moors, has just been presented by the Trustees of the British Museum with a copy of their last published work on "The Cuneiform Inscriptions of Western Asia," in acknowledgment of his "researches in the languages of Assyria and Babylonia."

The Governors of the Welsh Charity Schools at Ashford met recently at the offices of the Society of Ancient Britons, St. James's Square. Mr. Pryce Jones of Newtown and the Mayor of Swansea were added to the Committee appointed to consider a scheme propounded by Mr. Stanley Leighton, M.P., treasurer of the Charity, for the reconstruction of the schools. Mr. T. Marchant Williams was appointed one of the House Committee for the ensuing year. It has been admitted that unfortunately the Welsh Charity Schools have not of late years been the success they might have been. In the absence of the requisite number of foundation scholars the doors have been opened for the admission of English pay children, much to the detriment of the original purpose of the founders. Mr. Leighton's scheme of reconstruction aimed at making the establishment a middle class school for Welsh girls. The consideration of this scheme has been postponed until the report of the Departmental Committee on Higher Education in Wales has been issued, these schools being among those enquired into by the Committee. I am given to understand that a strong feeling exists among the Governors that the schools should be thrown open for the education of Welsh orphan girls—upon lines similar to those upon which the Howell Schools at Denbigh and Llandaff have been established.

The Council of the Cymmrodorion Society, at a recent meeting, named Mr. Cadwaladr Davies of Bangor, and Mr. Wm. Davies (Mynorydd) as secretaries of the sectional meetings to be held under the auspices of the Society at the National Eisteddfod at Merthyr, and Mr. Hugh Owen, Dr. Isambard Owen, M.A., and others, will undertake committee duties. After some discussion as to the desirableness of forming a Welsh Folk Lore and Dialect Section in connection with the Cymmrodorion Society, a number of gentlemen, including the Rev. John Davies, M.A., Dr. Isambard Owen, M.A., Mr. Howel Lloyd, Mr. Ignatius Williams, barrister-at-law, Mr. D. Lewis, barrister-at-law, and Mr. T. W. Hancock, &c., were appointed to consider the practicability of forming such a section. The new number of the Cymmrodor will shortly be issued to subscribers, and will contain an article on Carnarvonshire Folk Lore by Professor Rhys. Papers on various subjects will be read before the Society during the season by Mr. Wirt Sikes, United States Consul at Cardiff, and author of "British Goblins," Mr. David Lewis (South Wales Circuit), the Rev. D. Jones Davies, M.A., and Professor Rhys, and a conversazione will be held on the 28th April.

MARCH 30, 1881.

NOTES.

THE SCARCITY IN 1800 (March 16, 1881).—The Landowners were not alone in their endeavours to bring down prices. In September 1800, at *Hereford*, a meeting was held of the Corn-factors, mealmen and bakers, who signed an agreement not to buy any wheat, or other grain, save such as was pitched in the public market-place; and the city authorities resolved to take no toll of wheat or other grain brought in and sold. At *Worcester* there was a meeting "to digest a plan for adopting such measures as would be most effectual in reducing the present exorbitant price of wheat, &c." The Millers of

Wellington district entered into a compact not to buy new wheat at a higher price than 12s. a bushel, with a view to "reduce the present unreasonable price of corn." Several of the gentry of Shropshire urged on their tenants the propriety of sending their wheat to market, and several farmers signified their intention of not asking more than 12s. a bushel. At *Ellesmere* a meeting was held to adopt measures to prevent Forestalling and Ingrossing, and a similar meeting was called in *Oswestry* by John Jones, Esq., Mayor. In Oct. Sir W. Pulteney's tenants in the Wellington district agreed to take to market grain mixed "one third barley and two thirds wheat, to be sold in single bushels." At *Market Drayton* on Sep. 27, 1800, it was the opinion of a public meeting that "notwithstanding the abundant harvest their market had not been sufficiently supplied with corn," and it was particularly urged that bags of grain should be sold to small tradesmen and labourers at not more than 12s. a bushel. A five-shilling subscription was entered into to defray the necessary expenses attending the business. On Nov. 1 there was another meeting at *Shrewsbury*, at which it was stated that there was less grain in the country than was usual at that season of the year, and that it would be advisable to import from abroad. Something like £3,000 was subscribed for the purchase of foreign flour. A meeting called for *Welshpool* on Nov. 28 was so thinly attended that it had to be adjourned. On Nov. 11 five rioters were lodged in Shrewsbury gaol by a party of the Oswestry Rangers; they had extorted money from several farmers in the neighbourhood of Oswestry.   JARCO.

QUERIES.

BISHOPS JOHN THOMAS.—During the latter half of the last century there appear to have been three bishops, nearly contemporary, bearing this same name.

1. Born at Dolgelley in 1681; Dean of Peterborough, 1740; nominated to See of St. Asaph in 1743, but before consecration transferred to Lincoln, and thence in 1761 to Salisbury, where he died in 1766.

2. Bishop of Salisbury 1757 to 1761; translated to Winchester 1761-81.

3. Bishop of Rochester 1774-93.

Can any readers of *Bye-gones* supply information as to the birthplace and antecedents of either of the two last named?   D.R.T.

MANORIAL CUSTOMS.—There were anciently many customs and customary payments peculiar to various Manors; reference is made to several in a deed of release dated 16th Oct., 4 Edwd. VI. (1550) from Sir James Baskerville, Lord of the Manor of Yrsley (Eardisley?), in the county of Hereford, to Johanni ap John, and as the names are in the Welsh Language perhaps some one of the readers of *Bye-gones* would favor the others by saying whether similar customs obtained elsewhere, and particularly in any Welsh Manor. The following are the services released:—Mochmeswrye Gwarthegan Claimai, Gwabr Merched, Arian Ythen (? Ychen) Gwasanethen, and Deiliad Moor.   QUERIST.

THE FIRST MAYOR OF OSWESTRY.—Such of your Oswestry readers as are members of the Shropshire Archæological Society will have seen in the most recent instalment of the Borough Corporation Records edited by Mr. Stanley Leighton, M.A., that "all that is known about Richard Pope, gentleman," who was first Mayor of Oswestry (1674) is that gravestones on the floor of one of the aisles in the Parish Church, previous to restoration, recorded his death, at the age of 83, in 1719, and that of his daughter, "Mrs. Mary Pope." In a list of

Burgesses of the probable date of 1553 or thereabouts, published in *Bye-gones*, Mar. 28, 1877, there is the name ' *Roger Pope of Shrewesbury, drap.*' By being sworn a burgess of the town he no doubt had some business connection with it. Can any Shrewsbury antiquary trace any connection between Roger Pope, the draper of Shrewsbury in 1553, and Richard Pope, the gentleman of Oswestry in 1674, and tell us something about the family ?
JARCO.

BLANCH PARRY WINDOWS AT ATCHAM.

Can any reader of *Bye-gones* inform me if these windows in Atcham Church, Salop, have been engraved or photographed, and, if so, state where copies can be obtained?
Kington. JAMES W. LLOYD.

[On 18 Mar., 1874, a correspondent asked in *Bye-gones* "whether Blanch Parry was ot Welsh extraction, and why Mrs. Burton" (who it was stated had done so) "was interested in getting the windows to Atcham?" The query was never answered. Perhaps the repetition of it will elicit a reply.—ED.]

REPLIES.

COFFIN PLATES ON CHURCH WALLS (Mar.

16, 1881.)—In the little, dilapidated church of Treflys, overlooking the sea, near Portmadoc, coffin plates are still to be seen nailed to the walls ; or were when I visited it last summer, rambling from Criccieth towards Moel-y-Gest. Anyone who visits this ancient church may like to know that in a field between the building and Moel-y-Gest the remains of a cromlech can be found. A.W.

OSWESTRY (June 16, 1880).—Variations in the way of spelling. I notice in *Arch : Cam :* Vol. III, 1852, the following, which may be added to the list supplied by " G.A." on above date :—

Oswoldustr
Osewastr
Oswald'tre

In the same volume we have also the following names of streets, &c., unknown in the present age :—

Midelstreet........................... 1341-2
Salter's way.......................... 1331
Wyhastreet........................... 1347
Widastrete........................... 1392
Maystade ways...................... 1397

Some of these have already been noted in *Bye-gones*, but not all. BOOKWORM.

EASTER CUSTOM AT CLUNGUNFORD (Mar.

31, 1880).—This reminds one of a similar custom which prevailed at Berrington, co : Salop, see *Trans. Shropsh. Archæol. Soc.,* vol. 3, p. 174.*

* " In the parish chest [at Berrington] is preserved a curious document under the hand and seal of Robert [Wright], Bishop of Coventry and Lichfield, dated Newport xxij day of August, 1639, reciting that 'As there hath beene tyme out of mynd an antient custome used w'thin the parish of Berrington, that the Parson of the said parish hath yearely upon Easter-Day feasted all the parishioners and landhoulders within that parish w'th a Lovefeast, the solemnization of w'ch feast was ever yet performed in the Church (a thing noe less profane than irreligious) ;' and reciting that the said parishioners for perfect establishment and confirmation of the said custom had petitioned Sir Richard Lea, Baronet, patron of the said Rectory, that they may yearly and without molestation of the incumbent, enjoy the liberty thereof. The Bishop, although he had prohibited the said feast—yet in accordance with the patron's permission he ' permits it to be held on Munday in the Easter week in any convenient place except the Church.'"
5

NOTES.

SEVENTEENTH CENTURY TOKENS.

THE recent publication in *Local Gleanings* of Mr. Nathan Heywood's valuable paper on the 17th Century tokens of Cheshire has suggested to me that if a list of all known tokens of this interesting series of Wales and the border counties were published in the columns of *Bye-gones*, with notes respecting the issuers, a subject which is of daily increasing interest would receive material assistance from your many readers by the publication of new tokens and information about the tradesmen who issued these pieces for the public convenience. With this view I send you as a first instalment a list of the Shropshire series as far as known to me. Boyne describes 80 specimens of this county in his valuable work on the 17th Century tokens, published in 1858, since which time many more have turned up and a few which he included are proved to belong to other counties. It is my intention to include Boyne's descriptions in the following list (omitting of course those which do not belong to the county), and these will be distinguished by the letter B. In compiling this list I have been greatly assisted by Mr. H. S. Gill of Tiverton, who has kindly furnished me with many new descriptions, and my thanks are due to him for his help so freely given. My own collection numbers nearly fifty of this county, and from some of these I am enabled to correct a few errors in Boyne's descriptions.
JAMES W. LLOYD.

Kington.

SHROPSHIRE.

The bulk of the tokens are farthings and half-pennies, but there are as many as 13 pennies, an unusual proportion, surpassed, however, by the adjoining border county of Chester, which boasts of 24 or more. Bridgnorth was the only town in the county that issued tokens in a Corporate capacity.

Bishop's Castle.

B. 1. Ob. RICHARD. AMBLER. APOTHC. HIS. HALF. PENNY 1670 (in six lines).
Re. IN . BISHOPS . CASTLE . SQVARE . DEALING . (in four lines). (A square token). ½

B. 2. Ob. WILLIAM . MALL—a lion rampant.
Re. OF . BISHOPS . CASTLE—W . L . M . ¼
Probably an Inn Keeper.

3. Ob. THOMAS . MASON . HIS HALFPENNY (in four lines).
Re. OF . BISHOPS CASTLE 1670 (in four lines). ½

4. Ob. EDWARD . WOLLASTON . IVNIOR—Arms of the Wollaston family, three pierced mullets of five points impaling——Ermine on a canton a fleur de lis
Re. IN . BISHOPS . CASLLE 1670—HIS HALF PENY. ½
Boyne gives an engraving of this token, but describes it wrongly.

B. 5. Ob. EDWARD . WOLLASTON—E . W .
Re. OF . BISHOPS . CASTELL—A castle. ¼

Bridgnorth.

B. 6. Ob. THE . CHAMBERLINS . OF . BRIDG—A castle
Re. NORTH . THEIR . HALFE . PENNY—1665 ½

B. 7. Ob. THE . CHAMBERLAYNES—A castle
Re. OF . BRIDGNORTH—A portcullis ¼
(There are two varieties of this token from different dies.)
30

B. 8. Ob. SIMON . BEAVCHAMP—The Drapers' Arms
Re. IN . BRIDGNORTH—S. B conjoined ¼

9. Ob. IOHN.HIGGINS OF—The Grocers' Arms
Re. BRIDGNORTH—I.C.H. ¼

B. 10. Ob. THO . WHEELER . OF—The Mercers' Arms
Re. BRIDGE-NORTH—T . M . W . ¼

Broseley.

B. 11. Ob. RICHARD . CROMPTON—HIS . HALF . PENY.
Re. IN. BROSLEY—1664. ½

12. Ob. WILLIAM . OKES . OF . 1669—Three Crowns on the Royal Oak
Re. BROSLEY . IN . SHROPSHIRE—HIS . HALFE . PENNY ½

Boyne gives an incorrect description of this token.

Church Stretton.

B. 13. Ob. IOHN . PHILLIPS . IN—I . A . P .
Re. CHVRCH . STRETTON—I . A . P . ¼

Drayton.

B. 14. Ob. DRAYTON . IN . HALES—The Merchant Tailors' Arms
Re. IN . SHROPSHIRE—1664. ¼

15. Ob. DRAYTON . IN . HALES—The Merchant Tailors' Arms
Re. IN . SHROPSHEERE—1664. ¼

B. 16. Ob. IOHN . COX . OF DRAYTON—HIS . HALF PENY
Re. IN . SHROPSHIRE . 1668—I . I . C . ½

B. 17. Ob. MATTHIAS . THVRSTON . RICHARD . CHAMBERLYN 1669 (in six lines).
Re. DRAYTON . IN . SHROPSHIRE—THEIR . HALFE PENNY. ½

Ellesmere.

B. 18. Ob. THOMAS . COOKE—HIS . HALF . PENY
Re. IN . ELSMEARE 1666—T . M . C ½

19. Ob. EDWARD . RENOLDS—HIS HALF . PENY
Re. IN . ELIZMERE—E . R . ½

Hodnet.

B. 20. Ob. THOMAS . ANNKER—The Mercers Arms.
Re. OF . HODNITT . 1665—HIS . HALF . PENY ½

Ludlow.

21. Ob. RICHARD . BEBB . IRON—A man smoking
Re. MONGER . IN . LVDLOW—R . B . ¼

B. 22. Ob. IOHN . BOWDLER . MERCER — The Mercers' Arms
Re. IN . LVDLOW 1664—HIS . HALF . PENY ½

John Bowdler was Bailiff of Ludlow in 1670 and 1684.

B. 23. Ob. IOHN . BRIGHT . MERCER . IN . LVDLOW—Three Cloves
Re. *His halfe . penny* 1669 (In four lines) (script) ½

Mayor in 1687, King James II., who visited Ludlow in that year, having granted a new Charter to the Bo ough, making it a Mayoral Corporation.

B. 24. Ob. EDWARD . DAVIES 1669 — The Apothecaries' Arms
Re. APOTHECARY . IN . LVDLOW . HIS . HALF . PENY. E . — . D . ½

B. 25. Ob. TAMBERLAINE . DAVIES—The Mercers' Arms T . D .
Re. MERCER . IN . LVDLOW 1669—HIS . HALFE . PENNY ½

26. Ob. TAMBERLAYN . DAVIES—The Mercers' Arms
Re. OF . LVDLOW—T . M . D . ¼

Boyne describes this token incorrectly. Tamberlayne Davies was Bailiff in 1668.

B. 27. Ob. BLANCH . HACKLVIT—A goat's head with an axe over it
Re. IN . LVDLOW 1669—HER . HALF . PENY ½

A Ralph Hackluit was Bailiff in 1636.

28. Ob. GEORGE . HAVGHTON . MERCER . HIS HALFE PENY
Re. IN . LVDLOV . 1669 . — An uncertain object ½

Bailiff in 1684. Boyne gives an engraving, but wrongly describes this token.

B. 29. Ob. WALTER . IONES—The Mercers' Arms without shield
Re. IN . LVDLOE—W . M . I . ¼

Bailiff in 1665.

30. Ob. EDWARD . MIELS . HIS HALFE . PENY ½
Re. IN . LVDLOW 1665—E . M . M .

B. 31. Ob. IOHN PEARCE—The Ironmonger's Arms.
Re. OF . LVDLOWE—1656 ¼

Bailiff 1666 & 1681.

32. Ob. WILL . RICHARDS—The Haberdashers' Arms.
Re. OF . LVDLOWE—1656 ¼

Described by Boyne as RICKARDS.

33. Ob. RALPH SHARETT—The Bakers' Arms.
Re. IN . LVDLOW—R.M.S. ¼

B. 34. Ob. CHARLES . VALLE—Three Crowns in the Royal Oak.
Re. IN . LVDLOW . HIS . HALF . PENNY . 1669—C.E.V. (in six lines) (*octagonal*). ½

Madeley Market.

B. 35. Ob. IOHN . HOLLAND . OF . MADELY—a pickaxe.
Re. IN . SHROPSHIRE 1667—HIS . HALFE PENY. ½

B. 36. Ob. EDWARD . LEWIS . OF . MADELY . IN . SHROPSHIRE—HIS . HALF PENY . 1669.
Re. (Badly preserved; the only part of the legend which is legible is SHROPSHIRE and in the field HIS . . . same as the obverse. It was apparently struck at a later time, from an old corroded die, on a large blank, the size of a modern halfpenny) ½

37. Ob. EDWARD . LEWIS . OF . MADELY . IN . SHROPSHER.—HIS . HALF PENY . 1669.
Re. MADELY . WOOD . & FILDS . COLE . THATS . GOOD—A collier's pick ½

Incorrectly described and engraved by Boyne.

B. 38. Ob. LAWRENCE . WELLINGTON . IN—The Ironmongers' Arms
Re. MADLY . IN . YE . COVNTY . OF . SALOP—HIS . HALF . PENY 1669 ½

Much Wenlock.

B. 39. Ob. THOMAS . OWSLEY . MERC—The Mercers' Arms
Re. IN . MVCH . WENLOCK—T.O. ¼

Newport.

B. 40. Ob. THOMAS . CHALONER—T.M.C.
R. IN . NEWPORT . 1664—HIS . HALF . PENY ½
41. Ob. SAMVELL . CLARKE—The Mercers' Arms.
Re. IN . NEWPORT. 1666—HIS .,HALF . PENY ½
42. Ob. SAMVELL , DOWNTON . OF .1669—HIS . HALFE.
PENY. S.D.
Re. NEWPORT . IN . SHROPSHIRE—The Mercers' Arms ½
Incorrectly described by Boyne.
B. 43. Ob. ROBERT . HVDDELL—A bird. R . M . H .
Re. IN . NEWPORT 1666—HIS HALF PENY ½
B. 44. Ob. ARTHVR . ROWE—A . E . R .
Re. IN . NEWPORT 1658—Arms of the Rowe family ; a beehive surounded by bees ¼

This token has been claimed for Newport, Cornwall, on the grounds that an old Cornish family of the name Rowe bear as their arms a beehive surrounded by bees, but as the adjoining county of Chester possesses a Rowe family whose connection with that county dates back as far as the fourteenth century with similar arms, I think we may justly maintain a Shropshire claim until dispossessed on better evidence. Probably an examination of the parish register will clear up the doubt, if some reader will take the trouble. The arms a beehive surrounded by bees appears on Charles Roe's Macclesfield token of the *last* century.

45. Ob. IOHN . THORNTON—A thorn tree
Re. IN . NEWPORT—I . E . T . ¼
46. Ob. THOMAS YOVNGE—The Mercers Arms.
Re. IVNIER . IN . NEWPORTE—HIS FARTHINGE ¼
Incorrectly described by Boyne.

Oldbury.

B. 47. Ob. OLIVER . ROVND—St. George and the Dragon
Re. IN . OLDBVRY 1663—HIS . HALF PENY ½

Oswestry.

B. 48. Ob. HVGH . EDWARDS . OF—A Shoe 1D
Re. OSWALSTREY . 1669—HIS PENY. 1D
Engraved in Boyne's Work.
B. 49. Ob. RICHARD . EDWARDS—A wool bag
Re. OF . OSWALSTREY . 1668—HIS . PENNY 1D
B. 50. Ob. PHILLIP . ELLICE—a roll of tobacco
Re. IN . OSWESTRY—P . E ¼
51. Ob. IOHN . IONES—a sword and pistol
Re. IN . CSWESTRE 1666—1D. between two cinqfoils 1D
B. 52. Ob. RICHARD . PAYNE . OF—R . M . P
Re. OSWALDSTRE . MERCER—HIS . HALF PENY ½
53. Ob. RICHARD . PAYNE 1667—A mortar and pestle
Re. IN . OSWALDSTRY—1D. 1D
B. 54. Ob. IN . OSWESTRY 1668—ARTHER . WARD
Re. IN . SHROPSHEIRE—A pheon 1D. 1D
55. Ob. IN . OSWESTRIE . 1668—ARTHEʳ . WARD
Re. IN . SHROPSHEIRE—A pheon 1D. 1D
54 and 55 probably the same token, Boyne's description being incorrect.

Prees.

B. 56. Ob. RICHARD . MADELEY—The Mercers' Arms
Re. IN . PREESE 1666—HIS . HALF . PENY ½

Shiffnal.

B. 57. Ob. ARTHVR . MANWARING—The Mercers' Arms
Re. IN . SHIPNALL 1664—HIS HALF PENY ½

Shrewsbury.

B. 58. Ob. THOMAS . ACHELLEY . 71. — A wheat sheaf.
T . A 1D.
Re. IN . SALOP 1670—A fleur de lys T . A . (Octagonal) 1D
59. Ob. THOMAS ACHELLEY . 71—A wheat sheaf between T.A. with 1D. over
Re. IN . SALLOP . 1671—A fleur de lys between T . A. 1D
B. 60. Ob. PETER . BAKER . DISTILLLER . AND . GROCER (In five lines)
Re. IN . SALOP . P . E . B . ½D. — A lion passant gardant (Heart Shape) ½
61. Ob. IOSEPH . BENYON . IN . — A wheat sheaf I . E . B .
Re. SALLOP . HIS . PENY 1669—A pair of scales. 1D. (Octagonal) 1D
Incorrectly described by Boyne.
B. 62. Ob. IOHN . BRIGDELL 1667—The Tallow Chandlers' Arms
Re. IN . SALLOP . CHANDLER—HIS . HALF . PENY ½
B. 63. Ob. EDMOND . CLARKE—Arms of Shrewsbury; three leopards' faces
Re. IN . SALOPP—E . C . ¼
B. 64. Ob. SAMVELL . CONEY . INKEEPER—A star with eight rays
Re. OF . SALOP 1669—HIS . PENNY 1D
65. Ob. ROBERT . DAVIES—The Mercers' Arms
Re. IN . SALOPP—R . D ¼
Incorrectly described by Boyne.
B. 66. Ob. WILLIAM HARRISON—HIS . HALF . PENY.
Re. OF SALOPE . 1666—The Stationers' Arms ½
67. Ob. BENIAMIN . HIND—The Arms of Shrewsbury
Re. IN . SALOP—B.H. ¼
Incorrectly given by Boyne.
B. 68. Ob. IOHN . HOLLIER 1668—The Mercers' Arms
Re. MERCER . IN . SALLOP—HIS . HALF PENY ½
B. 69. Ob. SAMVELL . MACHEN—A wheatsheaf S . H . M .
Re. BAKER . IN . SALOPP—HIS . HALF PENY ½
B. 70. Ob. PETAR . MACHEN . BAKER—A wheatsheaf
Re. IN . SALOP . 1669—HIS . PENY (Octagonal) 1D
71. Ob. THOMAS . MEYRICHE—The Vintners' Arms
Re. IN . SALOPP 1663—T . M . conjoined ¼
72. Ob. THO . MEYRICKE—The Vintners' Arms
Re. IN . SALOPP 1664—HIS HALF PENY ½
Both incorrectly described by Boyne.
B. 73. Ob. IOHN.MILLINGTON—The Bakers' Arms I . M . Mʳ
Re. OF . SHREWSBVRY 1664—HIS HALF . PENY. ½
B. 74. Ob. IOHN . MILWARD 1667—A still
Re. DISTILLER.IN.SALOP—HIS HALFE.PENNY ½
B. 75. Ob. CONSTANTINE . OVERTON—The Cordwainers' Arms
Re. IN . SALOPP . 1663—HIS . HALF PENY ½
B. 76. Ob. SAMVELL . RIDGEWAY—The Grocers' Arms
Re. IN . SALOP . 1671—HIS . HALF PENY ½
B. 77. Ob. OWEN . ROBERTS—A wheatsheaf O . R .
Re. IN . SALOPP . 1666—HIS . HALF . PENY ½

B. 78. Ob. IOB . SELBY . DISTILLER—HIS . HALF.PENY
Re. IN . SALLOP . 1667—I.S. ½
B. 79. Ob. THOMAS . STVDLEY—HIS . PENY
Re. OF . SHREWSBVRY—T . E . S . 1D
B. 80. Ob. IOHN . THOMAS . 1660—The Mercers' Arms
Re. OF . SALOP . MERCER—I . T . ¼
B. 81. Ob. WILLIAM . THOMAS . MERCER—The Mercers'
Arms.
Re. OF . SALOP 1666—HIS . HALF . PENY. ½
B. 82. Ob. MICHAELL . WILDING—The Mercers' Arms.
Re. IN . SALOF 1664—HIS HALF PENY. ½
B. 83. Ob. MICHAELL . WILDINGE—The Mercers' Arms.
Re. MERCER . IN . SALOP—M . I . W . ¼
B. 84. Ob. IOSHVA . WILLIS—The Arms of Shrewsbury.
Re. IN . SALLOP . MERCER—HIS HALF PENY. ½

Wellington.

Boyne includes all Wellington Tokens under Wellington, Somersetshire, with the following note: "It is doubtful whether these are correctly placed to Somersetshire, as Wellington in Shropshire is a larger town; the croppers, shears, and woolpack, emblems of the woollen manufacture, seem to belong to the Somersetshire Wellington, where the manufacture of druggets and serges was carried on to a considerable extent during the 17th century." In the following list I have therefore excluded the tokens which seem really to belong to the Somersetshire town, and hope some of the readers of *Bye-gones* will be able to verify the insertion of those retained for Shropshire.

B. 85. Ob. THOMAS . MARSH—A pair of Scales.
Re. IN . WELLINGTON—T . M . M . ¼
B. 86. Ob. CRISTOPHER . SAMFORD—The Grocers' Arms.
Re. IN . WELLINGTON—C . A . S . ¼
87. Ob. ANDREW . SOCKETT . 1666—The Mercers'
Arms.
Re. MERCER. IN . WELLINGTON—HIS . HALF PENY ½
B. 88. Ob. STEPHEN . WRIGHT . MERCER—A Greyhound
running.
Re. IN . WELLINGTON . 1668—HIS . HALF PENY ½

Wem.

B. 89. Ob. WILLIAM . ALANSON—Arms; a fesse between
three boars' heads.
Re. OF . WEM . 1666—HIS . HALF . PENY. ½
B. 90. Ob. THOMAS . IEBB—The Mercers' Arms.
Re. OF . WEM—I . T . (*sic*) ¼
B. 91. Ob. SAMVELL . ROYCROFT — The Ironmongers'
Arms.
Re. IN . WEM 1665—HIS . HALF . PENY. ½

Whitchurch.

B. 92. Ob. HVMPHREY . ROWLEY—A Ship.
Re. IN . WHITCHVRCH . 1669—HIS . PENNY . H . R.
conjoined (*Octagonal*). 1D

QUERIES.

EDWARDS OF MELIN-Y-GRUG.— Can anyone kindly give me any information regarding the descent, arms, crest, and connections of this Montgomeryshire family? Also, can anyone inform me whether William Edwards, who was in 1776 created Baron Kensington, in the Peerage of Ireland, was of the above family?
VIGILANTIA.

NEW WALES.—We are told in Chambers's *Book of Days* (vol. 2, p. 144), in a notice of William Penn, that "the name that Penn had fixed on for his provence was New Wales, but Secretary Blathwayte, a Welshman, objected to have the Quaker-country called after his land. He then proposed Sylvania, and to this the King added Penn, in honour of the Admiral." On what authority is this statement made, and from what district in Wales did Secretary Blathwayte hail? It is not a Welsh name.
TAFFY.

ALDERMEN OF OSWESTRY.—In the Charter of James I., dated 1617; the text of which is given by Mr. Stanley Leighton in vol. 3 of the *Trans.* of the S.A.S., no mention is made of Aldermen of Oswestry; and yet mention of Aldermen occurs in the same paper, under the heading of "The Welsh Cloth Trade." We have also the monument in the Old Church, to the memory of Alderman Hugh Yale, who was supposed to have died in 1616. The first mention of Aldermen in the Charters quoted by Mr. Leighton is in that of Charles II., which dates from 1674. Can any one explain this? MEMBER S.A.S.

REPLIES.

REMARKABLE TREES (Sep. 19, 1877; Aug. 4, 1880).—At these respective dates, and under this heading, correspondents of *Bye-gones* have noted a tree growing in the Glyn Valley. At the earlier date the writer, quoting the *Annual Register*, says:—"There was said to be growing in 1801, on the estate of Arthur Bush Baker, Esq., of Glyn Ceiriog, near Chirk Castle, Denbighshire, an oak tree that measured the following uncommon dimensions:
—length to the crown, 23 feet; circumference at bottom, two feet from the ground, 51 feet; ditto in the middle, 32 feet; making a total of no less than 1,472 cubical feet, which at 5s. the foot, the common trade price, amounts to £368." The account of the tree given on Aug. 4, 1880, gives the following dimensions:—"Girth, 41 ft. 3 in. at one yard from the ground; 44 ft. 8 in. at the ground." This measurement was taken several years ago, but since the other one. There must be some mistake in one of these measurements. The tree is still standing, and is situated within five minutes' walk of Pont Fadog on the Glyn Tramway. Perhaps some one will measure it. M.C.B.

EARLY PRINTING IN SHROPSHIRE (Nov. 10, 1880).—TYPO states that "Robert Foulkes, vicar of Stanton Lacy, was executed for the murder of a young woman whom he had seduced." This is not quite correct. The victim was their bastard babe. The unhappy man, during his reprieve, wrote "An Alarme for Sinners: containing the Confession, Prayers, Letters, and last Words of Robert Foulkes." I have a copy of this little work, which was published in small quarto, in 1679. The writer, who was evidently a person of learning and research, seems to have sincerely repented of his foul crimes, and he addressed words of warning and counsel to his family, his successor in the ministry, and his parishioners. There were two other publications relating to the affair. One was entitled, "The execution of Mr. Rob. Foulkes, late Minister of Stanton Lacy, in Shropshire, for Murder, with his penitent behaviour, &c., 1678-9," and the other, "True and Perfect Relation of the Tryal, Condemnation, Execution, and last Speech of that unfortunate Gentleman, Mr. Robert Foulks, late Minister of a Parish near Ludlow, 1679." Perhaps this last was the book which TYPO mentions as having been printed at Ludlow, but I have not seen either of them, and therefore cannot say certainly.
Shrewsbury. R.E.D.

CURRENT NOTES.

The Empress of AUSTRIA, who arrived at Comber-mere Abbey on Wednesday, February 16, left on Monday last, her Majesty's visit having extended over six weeks all but two days. It is estimated that during this time she has spent £40,000, but these popular estimates are worthy of very little credence.

The Earl of Powis, Lord Penrhyn, and the Bishop of Bangor have been added to the list of vice-presidents of the National Eisteddfod Association during the past week.

There is living at Taliesin, Cardiganshire, a woman named Margaret Morris, who was a convert of Daniel Rowlands's. Rowlands died in 1790, and Margaret Morris, who states that her age is 104, heard him preaching at Aberystwyth.

The Committee of the Hwfa Môn testimonial, which includes, among others, Mr. Morgan Lloyd, M.P., Mr. J. H. Puleston, M.P., Mr. Henry Richard, M.P., Mr. Lewis Morris, M.A., Mr. Hugh Owen, Mr. Stephen Evans, Mr. John Thomas (Pencerdd Gwalia), Mr. T. Marchant Williams, B.A., &c., recently issued its appeal for subscriptions. The Committee consider that the testimonial should take the form of raising a sum of money to be applied in the way that may be most agreeable to Hwfa Môn himself. It is pointed out that Hwfa Môn is well known in London as an earnest preacher and pastor, and ever ready to assist those needing his help without reference to religious or political sympathies. The subscriptions already promised amount to over £40.

A committee has been formed with the object of providing a fund for the erection of a suitable memorial over the grave of the late Dr. Nicholas, in Hammersmith cemetery. The efforts of Dr. Nicholas in the behalf of higher class education in Wales must be well known to our readers, but to the general public he is better known as the author of several works bearing on Welsh history, such as "Annals of the Counties and County Families of Wales," and "The Pedigree of the English People," &c., &c. Subscriptions towards the object mentioned will be limited to a guinea. A number of gentlemen have agreed to receive contributions, among them the Rev. J. Gwilym Roberts, The Grange Gardens, Shepherd's Bush.

The British Architect contains an effective sketch entitled "Suggestions for a Riverside Terra-Cotta Warehouse," for Mr. J. C. Edwards, of the Trefynant Works, Ruabon, adapted from an old design by Mr. T. Raffles Davison. The British Architect says:—The encouragement to terra-cotta design given by Mr. J. C. Edwards, of Ruabon, in the recent competition advertised and illustrated in the British Architect, and adjudicated on by Mr. Alfred Waterhouse, A.R.A., is likely to bear good fruit. Mr. J. C. Edwards, himself one of the most successful and extensive manfacturerers of terra-cotta (and now promising to compete in encaustic tile work with the very best "Minton"), will doubtless benefit by the juster appreciation of terra-cotta and the adaptation of designs in such manner as will do it justice in execution. We this week publish a design, the chief credit of which is due to an old building in the Netherlands, and adapted for Mr. Edwards, to show the sort of work which is suitable to terra-cotta manufacture, which offers much reproduction of similar features, and which would be likely in execution to produce good work, as it could be executed in small sizes with good result.

On Friday the Cambridge Classical Tripos list was published. Third on the list was the name of Mr. W. Rhys Roberts, son of the Rev. J. Gwilym Roberts, Nonconformist Minister, Shepherd's Bush, a native of Trawsfynydd, Merionethshire. Mr. W. R. Roberts received his education at the City of London School, under Dr. Abbott, and, while there, he gained the Fishmongers' Scholarship of £50 a year, tenable at the university for four years. On entering Cambridge he gained a Foundation Scholarship at King's of £80 a year with tuition free. tenable for seven years, and in 1879 gained the Carus Greek Testament prize for undergraduates. In this year's examination for the Chancellor's gold medal he was honourably mentioned by the examiners as having "highly distinguished himself." If we are not mistaken, the third place on the list of those who have passed in honours in the Classical Tripos is the highest place yet gained by a Nonconformist. The examination extends over nine days the subjects being translation, composition, philosophy, philology, history, &c. An early training being most essential to success in this Tripos, it speaks highly for the rapid advancement of Mr. W. Rhys Roberts that his knowledge of Latin and Greek only commenced when he was between fifteen and sixteen years of age.

THE MAINTENANCE OF PAUPERS IN SHROPSHIRE.—An official return has just been issued, showing the cost of pauperism in the half-year ending Michaelmas last. In the 15 unions of Salop in-maintenance cost £8,715, against £7,843 in the corresponding half-year of 1879 ; out-maintenance, £7,486, against £7,707—total, £16,205, an increase of £655, or 4·2 per cent. We subjoin the totals of the several Unions for the two half-years ending Michaelmas :—

	In-maintenance.		Out-relief.	
	1880.	1879.	1880.	1879.
	£	£	£	£
Ludlow	863	757	586	569
Clun	337	316	573	626
Church Stretton	308	270	194	204
Cleobury Mortimer	157	146	191	178
Bridgnorth	565	534	574	618
Shifnal	174	183	740	751
Madeley	877	792	454	589
Atcham	1,632	1,285	223	256
Oswestry	756	753	543	523
Ellesmere	530	489	359	338
Wem	284	260	420	390
Whitchurch	628	656	471	487
Drayton	332	320	207	188
Wellington	775	671	905	938
Newport	451	411	1,046	1,052

Further out-relief, in the shape of school fees, was given as follows :—Clun, £11 ; Church Stretton, £2 ; Cleobury Mortimer, £2 ; Bridgnorth, £1 ; Shifnal, £13 ; Madeley, £19 ; Oswestry, £15 ; Drayton, £8 ; Wellington, £21 ; and Newport, £21.

APRIL 13, 1881.

NOTES.

THE SCARCITY OF 1800 (March 30, 1881).—In Dec. 1800, potatoes became scarce and subscriptions were made in various places to purchase in large quantities, where available, and sell in small quantities and at reduced rates to the poor. It was stated in one paper that £10,000 was subscribed at Liverpool for the purpose. Farmers were compelled under a penalty of £10 to make known to the proper officers the prices at which they bought and sold corn in the market, and several informations were laid in Shrewsbury against those who had failed to do so. "In consequence of the King's Proclamation the servants at the Lion Inn, Shrewsbury, agreed not to eat bread but at their breakfasts." It was stated that "at the Royal Table pastry was discontinued," and (to save the consumption of animal food) soups were given up. The year closed with the announcement that at Shrewsbury £7,941 had been subscribed to import corn. His Majesty's Proclamation recommending "Oeconomy and Frugality in the use of every Species of Grain" was not issued until Dec. 4, 1800, although the scarcity had been felt all the year. Many of the gentry of Shropshire and elsewhere made arrangements for supplying the labourers on their estates with corn at very reduced prices. In Feb. 1801, it is stated in the papers that Sir Richard Hill sold to his workpeople as low as from 8s. to 10s. a measure, a course he had pursued in 1799. On Feb. 23, 1801, another public meeting was held in *Shrewsbury* "to consider the question of food for the poor." At this meeting a subscription was entered into "for the purchase of foreign and distant produce." On June 16 of the same year "The Shrewsbury Corn Committee" announced that they could supply the inhabitants with "superfine American Flour in barrels at Mr. Parsons's in Mardol, and in small quantities" at other places—which are enumerated. The announcement was signed by C. Wingfield, clerk to the Committee, and it was notified that there was to be cash on delivery. On July 11, 1801, it was stated that American flour had arrived in such considerable quantities at *Newtown* that wheat fell 4s. a bushel. In Nov. I presume matters were improving, or one of the papers would not have ventured on such a joke as the following :—" We have lately heard the best of all possible reasons alleged for the high price of butter ;—the grass was so high that the cows could not be found to be milked !" In Dec. 1801, says the same paper, "the Act, rendering it penal in bakers to sell bread that has not been baked twenty-four hours, is repealed."				JARCO.

THE OLD WELSH ALMANACKS.
(Mar. 16, 1881.)

I shall commence this letter by giving the verses within the covers of the Almanacks for the four years ending 1819. In the one for 1816 there is but this one verse :—

> Wel dyma ddyddiau tawel 'nol echrys ryfel hir,
> Fu'n farn am faith flynyddau' trwy holl *Europa* dir :
> Mae'n bryd in' weithian drydar, mewn hedd edifarhau,
> Rhag rhoi o'n du bechoda' ail rwysg i'r cledda clau.

In the one for 1817 are the following "Englynion i 4 ban Byd ar 12 Arwydd," by the celebrated DAFYDD NANMOR :—

Y Dwyrain twym sych, medd ymdaerydd,—llu,
Myharen, llew, saethydd,
Tân ei elment uwch nentydd,
Eira yw'r gwyntar wawr gwydd.

Oer sych yw'r Dehau, ni rusan' —y tir,
Tarw, Morwyn, Gafran :
Tir yw elment yr eilinan :
A gwla yw'r gwynt,gloyw hynt glân.

Gefell, Mantol, Dwfrwr, gefyn —twym wlyb,
Dyma wlad Gorllewyn :
Gwyntog, cawodog, ydynt,
Ac ael dew a gwegil dyn.

Sarph, Crange, Pysg ieuangc go oer,—a gwlyb,
Glybod elment dyfroer
Gogleddwynt, gwaglu addoer,
A roes les i'r rhewes loer.

There are two separate issues for 1818, in one these lines appear :—

> Er cael y byd yn dawel, heb ryfel maith na braw,
> Mae'r wialan heb ei symud, a'r drygfyd ymaith draw
> Os byw mewn gostyngeiddrwydd yn ufudd eto a wnawn
> Fe goña Duw drugaredd yn lle digllonedd llawn.

In the other copy, these :—

> O'r diwedd daeth y dyddiau, i barthau *Affrig* bell,
> A *China* fawr a *Ceylon*, i gael newyddion gwell,
> Efengyl a'i chref angor tros fôr yr India faith,
> Sy'n caffael hyfryd lwyddiant, gogoniant am y gwaith.

Ynysoedd y cenhedloedd rhai ydoedd dan hir wg,
Sy'n caru Iesu a'i weision, yn lle'r hen droion drwg,
Gwir gredu, meddu *moddion*, gwel'd Iesu a'i fron yn friw,
Sy'n golchi'r *Ethiop* aflan, a'r *Negro*'n lan ei liw.

Wel dwys ystyriwn ninau sy'n meddu breintiau heb ri,
Fod eisiau sail a *sylwedd* yn unwedd arnom ni ;
Rhag symud ein canhwyllbren a'n llusern aur o'i lle,
Ac i'r Gogoniant 'madal i dawel for y dê.

I now proceed with the title pages of the *five* issues for the four years 1816 to 1819.

The one for 1816, printed at Dublin, is called "Cyfaill Tangnefeddus ;" its price *fivepence*, and has the following verses :—

1 Gyfeillion mwynion medrus, Dysgedig, teg, a dawnus ; Boed i chwi 'leni flwyddyn dda, Helaethlawn a chysurus.	4 Yr Haul wrth union reol, I'r ddosbarth fawr sy'n ganol: Rhydd heb ymsymud, oleu clau, I'r holl blanedau siriol.
2 Nid all bro bell *Helena*, Ddim mwy nag ardal *Elba*, Byth gadw hedd yn *Europ*, os Yw'r drwg yn aros gartra.	5 Ein hamser byr sy'n treulio, Fel braidd cyn dechra'i rifo ; Mae troion dyrus byd diri A'u llais am i ni ddeffro.
3 Tra byddo eilun dduwia, O fewn y pyrth yn bena, Dychrynllyd farn, medd gair y Nef, Mewn gwlad a thref, reola.	6 The blissful days of plenty, With *Peace* have crown'd our country : *Brittania* wears the *Laurels* brave 'Twas God that gave the victory.

The one for the year 1817 is called "Cyfaill Ewyllysgar ;" it was printed at Dublin, sold for fivepence, and has the following lines on the title page :—

1 GYFEILLION union annedd, Da, Gonest, DE a GWYNEDD, Mae genyf 'wyllys i'ch bodd-hâu Hwyr a borau'n buredd.	4 Mae dau-le yma'n dilyn, Sef *Gogledd*, De gyferbyn : Mewn deuddeng mis un diwr-nod sydd, Un nos, un dydd yw'r flwy-ddyn.
2 Fe haerai'r dysgedigion, Trwy'u gilydd, fod trigolion Yn cyfanneddu ac ufuddhau Yn y planedau mawrion.	5 Mae moroedd a mynyddau, A mil o hên gymmalau, Yn dangos tywydd, nid o bell, Yn llawer gwell llyfrau.
3 Pa ryw ond rhyw dynoliaeth, Drwy degwch y gre'digaeth, Sydd i'r Creawdwr mawr ei fri Yn synio'n ddi wasanaeth.	6 Our time is getting shorter, By day, by month, by year ; Let us to ZOAR above the sun, For life all run together.
	E.G.S.

BOUNDARY STONES.

— From the Laws of Howel Dda it is clear that stones either cut or fitted together in the form of a cross were commonly used as boundary marks—" Croesvaen, sef yw hwnnw maen ffin," which it belonged to the "canghellor" (chancellor) to place in case of a suit at law. I have an extensive acquaintance with the hills of Powys and Dyfed, but have only found two stones which can be regarded as having served this purpose. They are near each other on Mallaen mountain, North Carmarthenshire. One has a groove across the face, upon which a cross may have formerly rested. They are about 4ft. above ground, and have always been considered as boundary marks, though now called *Meini hirion*. An old man affirms that in his youth this stone had a hole through it which is now filled up by the natural growth of the stone.				CYNWYL.

QUERIES.

ANCIENT CLUBS IN MONTGOMERYSHIRE.

In a paper on this subject in *Mont: Coll:* vol. 13, p. 184, mention is made of a secret society once held at Kerry, and of there being "some 45 years ago," at an inn there, "eight or ten chairs with crests or coats of arms painted upon each." It was the opinion of the late Capt. Jones

of Maesmawr that these chairs "belonged to a club of
gentlemen who met there for the ostensible purpose of
hunting only, but that their meetings in reality were connected with Jacobites' plots." There was published in
Bye-gones in Jan., 1878, a description of these chairs,
which are still existing at the Herbert Arms, Kerry.
The following were the initials and mottoes on some of
them : J.H.—Curo et rogo 1765. R.F.—Natale Solum.
J.C.P.—Quis. Ulla Aliena Sibi credat Mala. J.O.—
Better to hunt in fields for health unbought ; than fee the
doctor for a nauseaus draught. S.H.—May we see heaven
at last when we see no more hounds. W.H.—Ex Fumo
dare lucum. B.Ll.—Afiach pôb drom galon. W.M.—
Insanire Juvat. T.M.E.—Equis Canibusque. The
gentleman who contributed the list to *Bye-gones* asked for
translations of the mottoes and full names of the parties ;
but no reply, so far as I am aware, has appeared. I repeat
his query in the hope that some one who knows will throw
a little light on the doings of this club, and speculate on
any hidden meaning the mottoes may be expected to
convey ? I note by the passage from *Mont: Coll:* that
there used to be crests on the chairs. The writer in *Bye-
gones* says nothing about this in his description. TELL.

THOMAS MINSHULL OF SHREWSBURY.—
On the back of Price's *History of Oswestry*, which was
issued "in paper boards" about 1814-5, there appeared
the following advertisement :—

Posthumous Publication. To be published by subscription,
the Poetical Works of the late Thomas Minshull of Shrewsbury,
consisting of Monodies, Odes, Congratulatory Lines, Songs,
Satirical Pieces, &c., from MSS., &c., in possession of his son.

R.M. would gladly comply with the solicitation of several of
his friends to publish his father's Poems, if 100 subscribers at
5s. 6d. each could be promised ; otherwise, his circumstances
will not at present permit him to put the work in hand. The
booksellers at Shrewsbury will receive subscriptions, and also
Mr. PRICE of Oswestry, by whom it will be printed, and at
whose office specimens are ready for inspection.

"R.M." was, of course, Richard Minshull, the well-known
Oswestry lampooner. Canon Williams, in his *Eminent
Welshmen*, puts down the authorship of Price's *History of
Oswestry* to the Rev. Peter Roberts ; but Minshull had
much to do in completing it ; so much so that in Parry's
Royal Progresses he is styled the author. At the time
the advertisement appeared he worked (at least a portion
of each week) in Mr. Price's Printing-office.
Was the book ever published ? I presume " the father "
was the " M—nsh—ll " who figures in some of the Shrewsbury election squibs of 1795-6 ? He used to sign himself
" Q in the Corner ;" and, by all accounts, gave way to the
same bad habits that afterwards ruined the son. JARCO.

PEAT AND CLAY KILN AT SWEENEY.—In
the *Oswestry Herald* for July 11, 1820, there is a long
article, signed " P.," advocating burnt peat and clay as
manure. The writer (Mr. T. N. Parker of Sweeney Hall
of course) says, " I have ordered one or two clay kilns to
be set on fire in a field at Gwern-y-Bychan, in the township of Sweeney, adjoining the lane leading from the
turnpike road towards Weston Cotton ;" and he invites
those interested to watch the process. On the following
week the paper reported the experiment, but said nothing
of the probabilities of its success. How far was the plan
successful ? K. K.

REPLIES.

A SELION OF LAND (March 23, 1881.)—In
reply to QUERIST's query respecting the above, Nicholas
Bailey in his dictionary thus defines it, *Selion*—" a ltidge
of Land which lies between two furrows." LANDWOR.
Wrexham.

LLOYD'S HISTORY OF SHROPSHIRE (Dec.
29, 1880). — In 1844, T. F. Dukes, F.S.A., published *Antiquities of Shropshire*, and the ensuing
extracts from the preface to that work may be found of
interest in connection with this subject :—
The memorials detailed in the following pages were chiefly
compiled by Edward Lloyd, Esq., of Drenewydd, in the parish of
Whittington, near to Oswestry, in this county, a barrister-at-
law, during his residence in the Metropolis, who, in the early
part of his life, employed his leisure hours in transcribing from
the public records whatever might in any way relate to or
illustrate the history of this his native county ; and when he
retired to his patrimonial seat he digested a part of his extensive collections, which he entitled "Antiquities of Shropshire,"
and seems to have brought it to a conclusion about the close of
the reign of Queen Anne ; and to this manuscript reference is
made in Mr. Gough's edition of Camden.
The copy of Mr. Lloyd's manuscript, in the hands of the Editor,
is taken chiefly from a copy in the library at Halston, in this
county, the seat of the Mytton family, to which it is conjectured
some additions were made by Mr. William Mytton, who had
during a considerable part of his later years, and particularly
from 1730 to 1785, accumulated materials on an extensive scale
for a County History ; but, from illness, his labours were never
committed to the press.
The text has also been collated with the original manuscript
in the hand writing of Mr. Lloyd, formerly in the possession of
the late Rev. Francis Leighton, and now belonging to Mr. John
Eddowes, of Shrewsbury, as well as with other copies formerly
in the libraries of the late Rev. John Newling, B.D., Canon of
Lichfield, and of the late Rev. Richard Podmore, of Condover,
in this county.
Shrewsbury. R.E.D.

EPITAPHS IN BERRIEW CHURCHYARD.
In memory of Evan Edwards, who departed this life
Oct. ye 24th, 1777.

Whoso thou be that passest by
Where these corps interred lie,
Understand what I shall say,
As at this time speak I may :
Such as thou art one time was I,
Such as I am, such shalt thou be ;
I little thought on the hour of death
So long as I enjoyed breath.

In memory of John Rogers, who departed this life
December ye 16th, 1776, aged 60 years.

When God cuts off ye tender thread of life,
Then cruel Death he parts man and wife,
Then parted for a time they must remain,
We hope in heaven thair souls will meet again.

In silence here my son and I
Do take our long repose and lie
Till the last solemn trumpet shall rise
The dust of saints above the skies.—1804.

CURRENT NOTES.

There is now living at Bangor an old man named Griffith
Williams, who says he was born at Capel Curig in 1779,
and is therefore in his 102nd year. His birth is registered
in Llandegai parish. He has eighteen children, the
youngest of whom is aged forty-four. He married a few
years ago his second wife, who is eighty-five
years of age, and he is surrounded by children to
the fifth generation. The old man has never had
a day's illness in his life, it is said, and works a
few hours daily in his garden still. A correspondent of
a contemporary says that there are in the parish of Mold
an aged couple of the name of Bellis, who have had a family
of ten children, all of whom are alive, and whose united
ages (including the parents) amount to 692 years, the ages
of the father and mother being respectively eighty-three
and eighty-four years, and those of the children ranging
from sixty-one to forty-one.

Dr. Bateson, Master of St. John's College, Cambridge, whose death was recently announced, was the president of the Governing Body of Shrewsbury School.

Eddowes's Shrewsbury Journal states that Lady Willoughby D'Eresby intends to "refix David Cox's signboard on the Inn at Bettws-y-coed." So after all the costly litigation over a picture valued by some as high as a thousand pounds, it is to be placed at the mercy of the elements in a position from which, many years ago, it was removed, so that it should be saved from destruction! Surely our contemporary must be wrongly informed.

DAVID COX AT BETTWS-Y-COED.—A large double-bedded room was usually reserved for the artist, and on wet days Cox would have four of five drawings, in various stages of progress, spread out on the beds. The privilege of carrying his painting traps and easel was one for which there was keen competition among the village lads, for it was regarded by them as one of the highest of attainable honours. The artist was kind, and liberal even, to all with whom he was brought into contact, though his personal expenses were never very heavy. A clergyman, once curate of Harborne, testified to the fact that he had almost always found, when summoned to a cottager's sick bed, that David Cox had preceded him, and had fully cared for the temporal requirements of the family. A pleasing story is told of his kindness to a young artist whom he met at Bettws-y-Coed. Cox, noting his diligence, asked him to go out sketching with him. The young man's picture was progressing satisfactorily, when he stated that he must leave at the end of the week. Cox guessed the reason, and taking him quietly on one side, said that if it was on account of the state of his purse, he hoped that he would allow him to become his banker, and to defray the cost of his board and lodging at the Royal Oak for some little time to come. The parlour of the Royal Oak in those days was an artists' club, pur et simple, and Cox would always be seen there in the evening, seated on the sofa, with his cigar—he smoked no pipe—and his pint of ale, and one or two cronies by his side, willing to listen and willing to teach. "There was no racket, no shouting, no fastness nor slang," says Mr. Solly; "and I have heard French, German, Hungarian, English, and Welsh, flowing on, like a polyglot stream, at the same time in that same dingy parlour."—*Leisure Hour*.

THE LATE MR. ROCKE.—The death is announced of Mr. John Rocke, banker, of Clungunford, who traced his descent from the Rockes of Shrewsbury and Trefnanney, one of whom was Sheriff of Montgomeryshire in 1620. The deceased gentleman was a magistrate and deputy-lieutenant of the county of Salop, served the office of High Sheriff in 1869, and was for many years a lieutenant in the South Salopian Regiment of Yeomanry Cavalry. He was an ardent and indefatigable naturalist, and possessed one of the finest collections of British birds in the kingdom.

TEETOTAL MAYORS.—At Exeter Hall, on Thursday evening, a temperance meeting was convened by the National Temperance League to receive the testimony of various provincial Mayors in favour of total abstinence. The Lord Mayor of York presided, being supported by the respective Mayors of Leeds, Huddersfield, Gateshead, Reading, Wakefield, Scarborough, Poole, Oswestry, and Bootle, wearing their chains of office. Letters were read from sixteen other representatives of provincial towns. The Mayor of Leeds mentioned that twenty-seven Mayors were teetotallers.

THE LATE MR. BREESE OF PORTMADOC.—It is intended to place a window in Penrhyndeudraeth Church in memory of the late Mr. Breese. A large sum has already been subscribed, and it is proposed to devote the surplus to the foundation of a scholarship in the Portmadoc Board Schools. At the Merionethshire Quarter Sessions on Tuesday, April 5, the presiding Chairman (Mr. W. R. M. Wynne) said—Before we begin the ordinary business of the Court it becomes my painful duty to ask you to unite with me —and I am sure I shall not ask in vain—in passing a vote of condolence from this Court of Quarter Sessions to the family of one whose absence here to-day, I am sure, we all deeply and most sincerely lament. At our last meeting here our late lamented friend Mr. Breese had, to all appearance, recovered from the effects of a severe and serious accident. I think every one of us then congratulated him on his recovery, and hoped that he had before him a long career of usefulness and general activity, as we might reasonably have expected from his talent. Providence, however, has thought otherwise, and he has been taken from us, and I feel certain when we consider the number of years which he faithfully served this county—when I tell you that he was appointed Clerk of the Peace on the 22nd September, 1859, and took the oath of office at the following Quarter Sessions on the 18th October of the same year—when we think that for the long period of over one-and-twenty years he was Clerk of the Peace, I am sure it would be most ill becoming on my part were I not to ask you to join with me in a vote of deep and sincere condolence with his family. I am quite convinced that you will all agree with me in that, and I would ask you to let the present Clerk of the Peace send the expression of this Court to Mrs. Breese and Mrs. Breese's family. I am sure you will all unite with utmost sincerity in doing so. I cannot forget even six months ago I received at your hands that very kind vote on the occasion of my father's death; nor can I forget that it was Mr. Breese who wrote a most kind and touching memorial of my father. It is a matter of poignant regret to me to think that the hand who penned that memorial has ceased to act, and that my friend has passed from among us. Without saying more upon this sad and painful subject I ask you to join with me in a vote of deep and sincere condolence with the family of our late Clerk of the Peace, than whom it would be difficult to find one more worthy, or indeed for a time as worthy a successor. Looking back on these by-gone years, one and twenty, I believe I may say that not one ill word has passed between the magistrates of this county and our late Clerk, and I am sure I, for one, shall feel the greatest loss in finding anyone so ready and so kindly to turn to for that advice I often require during the time you allow me to sit here as your deputy-chairman. I much regret that the noble Marquess, our chairman, is not present, for he would have moved the vote in more touching and eloquent words, and would have supported it to the utmost of his language. I again ask you to join with me in a sincere vote of condolence with the family of our late lamented Clerk of the Peace.— Mr. Owen Slaney Wynne: I was asked particularly by Sir Watkin to say how sorry he was that he could not be here, to-day; and he most earnestly wished to be considered as joining in a vote of condolence with the family of our late Clerk of the Peace.—Mr. C. F. Thruston: I beg without saying more after the eloquent address of our Chairman, to second the motion. — The proposition was agreed to; and the Chairman said he should mention that Mr. R. Jones, the present Clerk of the Peace, produced his appointment that morning as Mr. Breese's successor.

APRIL 20, 1881.

NOTES.

BROGYNTYN.—As far as I can recollect I have never had any satisfactory etymology of "Brogyntyn," which is doubtless a Welsh compound, and I would suggest the following as by no means inapplicable :—*Bro cain din*= "The Fair Region of the Fort." Another, "Llynclys" : *Llynclws*= "The Beautiful Lake."

Bodvari Rectory.   T. B. LL. BROWNE.

[As far back as 1871, the name "Brogyntyn" came up for discussion, and its variety of spelling until the time it was corrupted into "Porkington," was given. "J.O.J." wrote (Dec. 27, 1871), "*Bro*—a region, or cultivated tract ; *cyn*—the preposition before ; *tyn*—a hill." The "*c*" he remarked was changed to "*g*" for the sake of euphony. We had a discussion over "Llynclys," in 1874-5. "J.C.H." said "Poor Llynclys, Llyny-clys, or the Lake of the Inclosure, is made into Llync-lys, or the Swallowed Hall, in spite of the unmistakable prefix Llyn, the existing lake, and the well-known words clys, clwys, and clois, used in Wales for any enclosed plantation, land, lake, or common."—ED.]

EDUCATION OF WELSHMEN.—Several witnesses examined recently before the Commission have spoken of the advantages to be gained by Welsh youths from association with Englishmen, especially in the final stage of the higher education. Something like this was recommended by Archbishop Peckham in the troubled time of Llewelyn and Edward I. The Archbishop travelled through the whole of Wales, and, notwithstanding the cruel interdicts he imposed upon it, appears to have taken a real interest in its welfare. Writing from Newport, Pemb., in 1284 to Edw. I., he says there is no other way to civilize the Welsh than to make them live together in towns, work, and *send their children to be taught in England.* In the same letter he deplores the condition of the young servant lads. (Wysshanbighan= Gweisionbychain). The letter is in Norman French, and a translation of it which I am unable to give, may interest some of your readers, as showing the condition of a class of people whom general historians are apt to overlook. It will be found in Haddan's "Councils" I. 570—1.

CYNWYL.

OSWESTRY.—*The Salter Family.*—In a collection of Welsh Deeds, translations of which from the originals (Latin) were supplied by a gentleman connected with the *Manchester Guardian*, and printed in *Arch : Cam :* Vol. III., 1852, the following names occur :—

Ficar le Salter	A.D. 1244
Thomas le Salter	No date.
Richard le Saltere	" "
Isolde de Saltere (mother of Richard)	" "
William the Saltere	A.D. 1341
Thomas le Saltere	" 1341-2
Richard son of William the Salter	" 1347
Richard son of Thomas the Salter	" 1352
Thomas le Salter	" 1392
Matilda (his wife)	" 1393
Richard son of Thomas Salter	" 1393

The family of Salter, whose names occur so frequently in the above, was, according to Mr. Jos. Morris of Shrewsbury, one of considerable importance at Oswestry for several centuries. This is supported by evidence in the document of 1393, where Thomas Salter and Matilda his wife at the Court for the Vill of Oswestry held at Oswestry on the 7th May, 1393, were granted for themselves and their heirs, male and female, all that land and tenement which Richard the son of Thomas Salter gave to him by his Charters in the Vills of Oswestry, Weston,

5

Swyney, Llanvorda, Llenclyde, Mersbury, Grucketh, Treforclauthe, and Coton*. The heiress of the principal line thereof, Katherine Salter, married Sir Thomas Hanmer of Hanmer, Knight, who died 5th April, 1530. John Salter, then the head of another branch of the family, was Sheriff of Shropshire in 1521.   BOOKWORM.

* See *Bye-gones* July 21, 1880.

PARLIAMENT OF ENGLAND (Mar. 2, 1881).—*Merionethshire.* County only : there is no Borough member.

1542	Edwardus Stanley, generosus.
1547	Lodowicus Owen, armiger. (1)
1552	Ditto.
1553	Johannes Salesbury, de Rydyok', generosus.
1554	Lodowicus Owen, armiger.
1555	Omitted. (2)
1558	Elizeus Pryce, armiger
1559	John Wyn' ap Cadwalader, esq.
1563	Elice Price, esq.
1572	John Lewis Owen, esq.
1584	Cadwallader Price, esq.
1586	Robert Lloid, esq.
1588	Robert Salesbury, esq., of Ruge, co. Merioneth.
1593	Griffith Nanney, esq.
1597	Thomas Mydleton, esq. (3)
1601	Robert Lloyd, esq.
1604	Sir Edward Herbert, Knight of the Bath. (4)
1614	No Returns found. (5)
1620	William Salisbury, esq., of Ruge, co. Merioneth. (6)
1624	Harry Wynn, esq., of Gwedyr, co. Carnarvon.
1625	Henry Wynne, esq.
1626	Edward Vaughan, esq.
1628	Richard Vaughan, esq. (7)
1640	Henry Wynn.
1640	William Price, esq., of Rulace, co. Merioneth. (8)
1654	No Returns found. (9)
1656	Ditto. (10)
1658	Lewis Owen, esq., of Penniarth, co. Merioneth.
1660	No Returns found (11)
1661	Henry Wynne. (12)

(1) Commonly known as "The Baron" from his having been Baron of the Exchequer of North Wales. Was murdered near Dinas Mawddwy in 1555.—Breese's *Kalendars of Gwynedd.*

(2) Elizeus (or Ellis) Price, esq.—*Ibid.*

(3) Afterwards Sir T. Myddelton of Chirk Castle.—*Ibid.*

(4) Afterwards the celebrated Lord Herbert of Chirbury.—*Ibid.*

(5) Robert Lloyd of Rhiwgoch, esq.—*Ibid.*

(6) Mr. Breese gives "Griffith Vaughan, esq.," and Mr. W. W. E. Wynne adds in a note, "of Corsygedol."

(7) Mr. Wynne adds the following note under the name of Richard Vaughan :—"Richard Vychan, the second of that name, of Corsygedol, and Plas Hên, represented the county of Merionedd, in Parliament, and was so fat and unwieldy that the folding doors of the House of Commons were opened to let him in, which is never done but when the Black Rod brings a message from the King, who being then in the House of Lords, the folding-doors opened, when the rumour in the House was ' The Black Rod, or the Welsh Knight is coming.' "—*Mostyn MSS.*

(8) This was the "Long Parliament" on 27 Apr. 1647, Roger Pope, esq., was elected, *vice* William Price, esq., disabled to sit. Afterwards John Jones, esq, was elected, probably *vice* Roger Pope, esq., deceased.—*Commons Journals,* 26, Aug. 1647. Price having adhered to the King, and gone with him to Oxford, was disabled, and John Jones (afterwards Colonel in the Parliamentary army), and one of the King's judges, was appointed by Parliament to fill the seat.—*Breese.* Col. John Jones, of Maesygarnedd, the Regicide, married a sister of Oliver Cromwell.—Note by Mr. *Wynne.*

(9) Mr. Breese gives John Vaughan, of Cefnbodig, esq.

(10) Col. John Jones was elected for Merioneth and Denbigh, but made choice to sit for the latter county.—*Breese.*

(11) Edmund Meyricke, Ucheldre, esq.—*Ibid.*

(12) William Price, esq, elected 25 Mar. 1673, *vice* Wynne deceased.

31

1679	Sir John Wynne, knt. and bart. of Rhiwgoch.
1679	Ditto. 1681 Ditto. 1689 Ditto. 1690 Ditto.
1695	Hugh Nanney, esq., of Nanney, co. Merioneth.
1698	Ditto. 1701 Ditto (13)
1701	Richard Vaughan, esq.
1702	Richard Vaughan, esq.
1705	Richard Vaughan, esq., of Corsygedol
1708	Ditto. 1710 Ditto. 1713 Ditto,
1715	Ditto. 1722 Ditto. 1727 Ditto.
1734	William Vaughan, esq., of Cors y Gedol.
1741	Ditto. 1747 Ditto. 1754 Ditto.
1761	Ditto.
1768	John Pugh Pryce, esq. (14)
1774	Evan Lloyd Vaughan, esq.
1780	Ditto. 1784 Ditto. 1790 Ditto. (15)
1796	Sir Robert Williames Vaughan of Nanney.
1802	Ditto. 1806 Ditto. 1807 Ditto.
1812	Ditto. 1818 Ditto. 1820 Ditto.
1826	Ditto. 1830 Ditto. 1831 Ditto.

For return of Members from the passing of the Reform Bill up to 1880, see *Bye-gones*, Apr. 7, 1880.

QUERIES.

THE SALOPIAN PULPIT.—Mr. Hulbert in his *Salopian Magazine*, vol. 1, p. 528, published in 1815, amongst a list of forthcoming books mentions the following:—"The Salopian Pulpit, containing Biographical Sketches of Living Clergymen, Dissenting Ministers and Methodist Preachers, within the County of Salop, with fair and candid Criticisms on the style and manner of their preaching, interspersed with many original Anecdotes of Eccentric Preachers, and curious specimens of Eccentric Sermons ; by a late Student of one of the Universities." Was the book ever published, and who was the "late Student"? TELL.

COST OF TRAVELLING IN WALES.—Mr. Philips on p. 29 of Vol. I. of his *Civil Wars in Wales*, speaking of travelling in Wales at the end of the sixteenth century, says, " A ten days' journey from Carnarvonshire to South Wales cost no more than fifteen shillings. Eighteenpence covered the outlay of a two days' journey from Tremadoc to Pwllheli, and half-a-crown was sufficient pocket-money for a man who had to travel from the former place to Oswestry and back." I infer from a note that these facts are gathered from a paper in *Arch : Camb :* (Orig. Doc. p. cix) contributed by the late Mr. W. W. E. Wynne. I do not possess the journal : will some one who does give your readers the benefit of a fuller abstract, and explain what was meant by "pocket money ?" TELL.

OSWESTRY CRITICIZED !—The circumstance I am going to refer to has already figured in *Bye-gones* (see Reprint for 1872, p. 73), but I allude to it now to mention a curious fact connected with it. It was stated in Hulbert's *Salopian Magazine* for 1815, at page 124, that Mr. Wood, the proprietor of the *Shrewsbury Chronicle*, soon after he established that paper in 1772, had to assume a "fictitious name and character, to protect himself from insult and injury " when he visited some friends near Oswestry, because he had published an unfavourable account of the town in the first number of his newspaper. On page 172 in the same volume of the magazine "G.P.,

(13) Richard Vaughan, esq, elected 29 Apr. 1701, *vice* Hugh Nanney, esq, deceased.
(14) Evan Lloyd Vaughan, esq, elected 24 Feb. 1774, *vice* John Pugh Pryce, esq, deceased.—*Blue Book*. Mr. Breese describes Mr. Pryce as of Rhug and Gogerddan.
(15) Robert Williames Vaughan, esq, elected 25 Jan. 1792, *vice* Evan Lloyd Vaughan, deceased.

Oswestry," gives the statements that offended our townsmen, the gist of which consisted in saying that the houses were " mean," the streets "dirty and ill paved ; " and that there was " not an inn in the place fit to accommodate a traveller." The magazine writer (and this is my reason for referring to the subject) gives one passage that does not occur in the *Chronicle* at all, which is as follows :— " There are many dissenters here, and they have a meeting, where they attend divine worship, according to their own form." The article in the newspaper was headed "A General History and Description of the County of Salop, wrote by a Gentleman who has lately made a Tour through the same." As the magazine writer introduces a passage not in the newspaper, it is evident he does not take his information from it. Probably he copies from the same source as the *Chronicle* editor. If so, in what form did the " Gentleman " making the Tour publish, and can any one, who has access to his work, give a complete transcript of his Salop experiences ? JARCO.

REPLIES.

COFFIN PLATES ON CHURCH WALLS (Mar. 30, 1881).—I visited Beddgelert in September, 1875, and was much struck upon entering the church to see coffin plates fixed to the walls and to the front of the gallery. The sexton informed me that they were removed from the respective coffins and placed there. ST. BEUNO.

THE SCARCITY OF 1800 (Apr. 13, 1881).—I have heard the late Mr. David Parkes frequently mention the great extravagance of the farmers in the years of scarcity. They held every Saturday a meeting to settle prices, and had an Ordinary at the Turf Tavern, Claremont Hill, Shrewsbury. Having occasion to see a farmer on business he called at the Turf, and was about to enter the Farmers' Room, when he was abruptly repulsed by the waiter. Being a resolute man, he insisted on entering, and there saw laid a table for twenty or thirty, and a bottle of wine beside every man's plate. W.A.L.

CURRENT NOTES.

THE CENSUS OF 1881.

REGISTRAR'S SUMMARY OF TOWN AND PARISH OF OSWESTRY.

TOWN OR BOROUGH OF OSWESTRY.						
	HOUSES.			PERSONS.		
MUNICIPAL DIVISIONS.	Inhabited.	Uninhabited	Building.	Males.	Females.	Total.
East Ward......................	570	41	9	1387	1509	2956
West ward......................	1020	51	10	2419	2476	4895
	1590	92	19	3806	4045	7851

ECCLESIASTICAL DIVISIONS.	HOUSES.			PERSONS.		
	Inhabited.	Uninhabited	Building.	Males.	Females.	Total.
St. Oswald's, or Parish Church....	945	52	16	2271	3384	4655
Holy Trinity	645	40	3	1535	1661	3196
	1590	92	19	3806	4045	7851

PARISH OF OSWESTRY.

CIVIL DIVISIONS, OR TOWNSHIPS.	HOUSES.			PERSONS.		
	Inhabited.	Uninhabited	Building.	Males.	Females.	Total.
Aston	13	..	..	41	53	94
Crickheath	90	3	..	201	199	400
Cynynion	22	2	..	53	50	103
Hisland	12	..	..	29	26	55
Llanforda	57	..	..	132	147	279
Maesbury	126	13	1	269	266	535
Middleton	16	..	..	38	42	80
Morton	32	2	..	68	73	141
Pentregaer	14	1	..	45	37	82
Sweeney	113	5	1	284	300	584
Trefarclawdd	76	10	..	160	155	315
Treflach	87	5	..	213	197	410
Trefonen	121	4	..	243	269	512
Weston Cotton	43	4	..	213	134	347
Wootton	28	1	..	71	66	137
	850	50	2	2060	2014	4074

TOTALS.	HOUSES.			PERSONS.		
	Inhabited.	Uninhabited	Building.	Males.	Females.	Total.
Town of Oswestry	1590	92	19	3806	4045	7851
Parish of Oswestry	850	50	2	2060	2014	4074
	2440	142	21	5866	6059	11925

ECCLESIASTICAL DISTRICTS IN TOWN AND PARISH OF OSWESTRY.

THE WHOLE OF ST. OSWALD'S OR PARISH CHURCH.	HOUSES.			PERSONS.		
	Inhabited.	Uninhabited	Building.	Males.	Females.	Total.
In Town of Oswestry	945	52	16	2271	2384	4655
In Parish of Oswestry, being Townships of Llanforda and Weston Cotton, with part of Sweeney	157	6	..	502	453	955
	1102	58	16	2773	2837	5610

THE WHOLE OF HOLY TRINITY CHURCH.	HOUSES.			PERSONS.		
	Inhabited.	Uninhabited	Building.	Males.	Females.	Total.
In Town of Oswestry	645	40	3	1535	1661	3196
In Parish of Oswestry, being Townships of Aston, Hisland, Maesbury, Middleton, and Wootton	195	14	1	448	453	901
	840	54	4	1983	2114	4097

THE WHOLE OF TREFONEN.	HOUSES.			PERSONS.		
	Inhabited.	Uninhabited	Building.	Males.	Females.	Total.
In Parish of Oswestry, being Townships of Trefarclawdd, Treflach, and Trefonen	284	19	..	616	621	1237

PART OF MORTON.	HOUSES.			PERSONS.		
	Inhabited.	Uninhabited	Building.	Males.	Females.	Total.
In parish of Oswestry, being Townships of Crickheath, and Morton, with part of Sweeney	178	8	1	396	400	796

PART OF RHYDCROESAU.	HOUSES.			PERSONS.		
	Inhabited.	Uninhabited	Building.	Males.	Females.	Total.
In Parish of Oswestry, being Townships of Cynynion and Pentregaer	36	3	..	98	87	185

SUMMARY.	HOUSES.			PERSONS.		
	Inhabited.	Uninhabited	Building.	Males.	Females.	Total.
St. Oswald's	1102	58	16	2773	2837	5610
Holy Trinity	840	54	4	1983	2114	4097
Trefonen	284	19	..	616	621	1237
Morton	178	8	1	396	400	796
Rhydcroesau	36	3	..	98	87	185
	2440	142	21	5866	6059	11925

IN THE WORKHOUSE, CENSUS 1871.

Males.   Females.   Total.
85   ..   98   ..   183

1881.
132   ..   80   212
Deduct Ellesmere children
not there in 1871   17

195 in 1881 against 183 in 1871.

The late Sir Philip de Malpas Grey Egerton, Bart., one of the two members of the House of Commons who were in that Assembly before the passing of the Reform Act of 1832, sat for Chester in the Tory interest in the Parliament of 1830, contested South Cheshire unsuccessfully in 1832, and was elected in 1835, and in 1868 for the Western Division of the county, which he has since continued to represent. The only other member of the unreformed Parliament now in the House of Commons is Mr. Christopher Talbot, who has sat for Glamorganshire without interruption since 1830. By the death of Sir Philip de Malpas Grey Egerton, Bart., the office of Antiquary to the Royal Academy, which the deceased gentleman had held since March, 1876, becomes vacant.

A serious accident, happily unaccompanied by any loss of life, occurred in Chester on Thursday night, when a portion of the lofty tower of St. John's Church, collapsed and fell with a great noise, injuring the beautiful and massive Early English porch, which is one of the chief beauties of the church. The church of St. John's is the most interesting ecclesiastical edifice in the ancient city from an antiquarian point of view, and was from the eleventh to the sixteenth century the cathedral church of the city. The church was first erected in Saxon times by Ethelred, husband of the Mercian princess Ethelfleda. Much of the nave and east end of the church are early Saxon work, said to be portions of the structure as rebuilt by Leofric, Earl of Mercia, in 1057. The steeple, which stood in the centre of the church, fell in 1468, and in its fall destroyed a great part of the choir and east end of the edifice.

This tower was soon after rebuilt, though another existed at the west end of the nave. The former again fell in 1572, and the parishioners then declined to rebuild it. The west steeple met with a similar fate in 1574, destroying the whole of the extremity of the fabric. The present tower must have been built after that time. In it was a peal of eight bells—the most melodious in the city. One half the tower is standing in a very precarious and dangerous state. On Sunday the Duke of Westminster (who is lay rector of St. John's), the dean, and some thousands of residents and excursionists visited the scene. In present circumstances the bishop's palace with some smaller buildings, are in danger should the remainder of the tower fall outwards.—Mr. Douglas, architect, of Chester, made a short time ago complete drawings and plans of the Norman porch and gateway destroyed on Friday. It is computed that at least a thousand tons of masonry have fallen, and competent authorities confess that the tower is completely ruined, and will have to be taken down. The precarious foundation on which it stands will make the work of demolition most dangerous. A strong wind would inevitably precipitate matters, and if the tower should fall across the old Norman church the damage would be irreparable. Some cottages bound it on the west, and these escaped the downfall on Friday morning. The residents describe the sensation when the tower fell as resembling an earthquake, while the sounds of clanging bells hit with boulders of stone was most weird. On the west portion of the tower, midway up, is a canopied niche in which stands the statue of the Abbot King Ethelred, caressing at his side "the white hind" of his vision. The founder of the abbey is said (according to the legend told of so many churches) to have had a vision from heaven that wherever he should kill a white hind he must build a church, and upon killing a white hind in the forest which then lay between the walls of Chester and the river Dee he founded a church upon the spot. This early Saxon structure was probably of wood, and it is questionable whether any traces of it are to be seen in the present edifice. Eminent antiquarian authority, however, supports the assertion that in the interior of the building there are considerable traces of very early Saxon work, probably contributed at the re-edifying of the building by Leofric, Earl of Mercia, in 1057. On closer examination it is found that the bells remain in the belfry almost concealed from view by the supporting beams.

THE LATE MR. BREESE BENNETT OWEN.—On Saturday the remains of Mr. Breese Bennett Owen were interred in the quiet little churchyard of Penegoes. Mr. Owen had many excellent qualities to which we will not refer, but we way say that seldom if ever higher proficiency in the art and history of Heraldry was attained by a student, as he was, of only twenty-six years of age. The golden lustre and multicoloured embellishments of his emblazonry, as well as the caligraphy which distinguished his artistic escutcheons, and the correctness of his shields and insignias, have not often been excelled. Mr. Deffet Francis, the well-known artist, after examining Mr. Breese Owen's armorial productions, wrote to a friend, "It would be difficult to express the thanks I owe you for the gratification caused me by so kindly obtaining for me a perusal of the fine MSS. work on the Heraldic Arms of the Welsh Princes, &c. It will remain, I hope, a lasting monument of the keen enthusiastic labour and literary acumen of Mr. N. Bennett, together with the tasteful caligraphic and exceptionally artistic skill of Breese Bennett Owen." His armorial collections were emblazoned from old manuscripts in the Glanyravon Library, and are as voluminous as they are beautiful.

CARNARVON CASTLE.—The renovation of this magnificent ruin is being effectively carried out under the personal supervision of Sir Llewelyn Turner, the deputy-constable, and the ancient fortress is being placed in a condition to withstand the ravages of time and weather. The outer walls have been divested of the vast quantity of self-sown roots which well nigh concealed them from view, and the joints have been carefully pointed and cemented. The stone staircase of the turret attached to the Queen's Tower has been completed to its full height of 80ft. ; the tower at the south-east end of the castle ditch and its ascending turret, which had been inaccessible for ages, have been thoroughly repaired, and the beautiful old chimney pieces entirely renewed. The work at present is chiefly confined to the turret and tower near the King's entrance, the entire staircase of which was destroyed through an explosion of gunpowder. The staircase is renewed to the top of the tower, and will in a few months be complete to the turret summit. The ramparts have been asphalted with the view of preserving the walls and corridors from wet ; the wall near the Queen's gate has been pinned and made secure, and the castle moat opened for a distance of 500 yards. There being no sand or gritstone quarry near Carnarvon, the materials for the mullions, staircases, and corbels, have been obtained from the Talacre quarries, Flintshire.

APRIL 27, 1881.

NOTES.

ENGRAVED PORTRAITS OF MONTGOMERY-SHIRE WORTHIES IN THE POWYS-LAND MUSEUM.

A Collection is being formed in the Powys-land Museum of engraved portraits of persons connected with Montgomeryshire by birth, property, marriage, office, or otherwise—the circumstance of any such person having had his portrait published qualifies him for the collection. The following is a list of those already obtained—arranged, so far as practicable, under families. They have all been presented. The list is printed in the hope of getting deficiencies supplied, and the collection rendered more complete. Inexpensive frames will suffice. Communications on the subject are invited by the Hon. Curator, Powys-land Museum, Welshpool.

Powis Castle.

1. Edward James, 3rd Earl of Powis, president of the Powys-land Club. Lithograph (Macguire, 1863).
2. His father, Edward Herbert, 2nd Earl of Powis. Copper plate, proof before letters.
3. His grandfather, Edward, 1st Earl of Powis (taken in Edinburgh in 1794, as Col. of the Shropshire Militia). The smaller figure is Major Skey.
4. His great grandfather, Robert, the great Lord Clive, ob. 1774, from the original in the Government House, Calcutta.
5. Cousin of his grandfather, and nephew of Robert, Lord Clive, Archdeacon Clive (formerly Vicar of Welshpool). Painted by S. Laurence and engraved by F. Holl.
6. His lineal ancestor in the 7th degree, Edward, 1st Lord Herbert of Chirbury. "From a drawing by Lady Lucy Clive, after the original painting."
7. George Herbert, "the Poet and Divine" (brother of the latter), from a scarce print by White prefaced to his poems. Nov. 1. 1822. Drawn by G. Clint, engraved by G. Smith.
8. Winifred (Herbert) "Countess of Nithisdale," daughter of the 1st Duke of Powis, who was lineal ancestor (through two successive heiresses) in the 6th degree

to the present Earl of Powis, from a drawing by C. Kirk-
patrick Sharpe, Esq., taken from the original picture by
Sir Godfrey Kneller at Terregles, engraved by Cook.

Gregynog.

9. Charles, 3rd Lord Sudeley (Vice-president) ; lithograph 1872.
10. His father, Sudeley, 2nd Lord Sudeley (also V.P.)
11. Arthur Blayney, Esq., of Gregynog. Painted by
Wm. Beechey, engraved by E. Hurley.

Wynnstay.

12. Sir Watkin Williams Wynn, Bart., M.P., Vice-
president, lithd. Published by Woodall and Venables,
Oswestry.
13. His father, Sir W. W. Wynn, Bart, M.P.
Drawn, engraved, and published by A. R. Burt., Miniature painter, Chester, Aug. 1, 1820.
14. His great-grandfather, Sir W. W. Wynn, Bart.
" Nich. Dahl,pinxit. George Vertue, sculpt. 1742. Printed
for T. Payne, Bookseller in Wrexham." A roll in his
hand, upon which is inscribed " An act for the more
effectual preventing Bribery & Corruption in the Election
of Members to serve in Parliament brought in . . ,"
15. His uncle, The Right Hon. Charles W. W. Wynn,
M.P. for Montgomeryshire from 1799 to 1850. Copper-
plate.
17. His cousin, Charles W. W. Wynn, Esq., Member of
the Council of P.L.C., M.P. for Montgomeryshire from
1862 to 1880 (Black, 1871).

Plas Machynlleth.

18. The Marquess of Londonderry and Earl Vane,
lithograph. Drawn by Walton.

Brogyntyn.

19. Ralph John, 1st Lord Harlech, lithograph (Walton).
20. His father, William Ormsby Gore, Esq., in his 80th
year (copper plate) ; painted by J. Lucas, engraved by G.
Zobel.

Glansevern.

21. Vice Admiral Sir Edward William Campbell Rich
Owen, G.C.B., G.C.H.; copper plate ; painted by
Pickersgill, engraved by G. T. Payne.
22. Edward Johnes, Esq., M.D. Copperplate.

Garth.

23. Devereux Herbert Mytton, Esq., of Garth. Lithograph (Walton).

Miscellaneous.

24. David Davies, Esq., M.P. Published by Woodall
and Venables, Oswestry.
25. Abraham Rees, D.D., F.R.S., the Cyclopedist ;
painted by Opie, engraved by W. Holl.
26. Peter Heylyn, S.T.P., engraved by Hopwood.
27. Sir Thomas Jones of Carreghova, Justice of King's
Bench, 1672, published in 1812 by Richardson.
28. Robert Owen of Lanark (born in Newtown),
painted in July, 1821, by Boys, engraved by Fry.
29. Edmund Edye, Attorney-at-law, œtat. 80, of Montgomery (from a portrait painted for his professional
brethren the Attornies of Montgomeryshire), 1836.
30. Thomas Drew, Attorney-at-law, Newtown, lithograph.
31. Rev. J. D. Jones, engraved by Greatbach.
32. Original sketch of Richard Jones, father of Henry
Jones of Welshpool.
33. Black and white Portrait of Mr. William Jones of
Welshpool.
34. Engraving of the Bards at the Powys Eisteddfod
Sept. 8, 1824, by [Lady] A. E. Delamere.

QUERIES.

PAWLS.—Lewis Glyn Cothy (fl. 1460) has this line
(Works I., 126) " Pawls y galwant plasau gloywon,"
Pawls they call the bright palaces. The " Brut y Tywysogion " says that before the advent of the Normans to
Wales even the castles were built of wood, and Giraldus
in A.D. 1200 describes the houses of the peasantry as very
ephemeral structures of branches, &c., " sufficient to last
a year," built on the edge of forests. In more settled
times, till this century, a favourite site for a mansion
would be a low-lying sheltered spot, where, owing to defective drainage, it was often necessary to build it on *piles.*
This use of timber may account for such houses being
called "Pawls" (from poles) and also for one perhaps
having given its name to " Bwlch-y-pawl." Are there
many examples of houses built on piles in our limits? I
believe Rhûg is so built.   CYNWYL.

, THE POOR CURATE OF FORD.—In connec-
tion with " the scarcity of 1800," recently referred to in
Bye-gones, I may remark that in the month of Oct. that
year, the Rev. James Matthews, M.A., who described
himself as " the Poor Curate of Ford," published a pamphlet on " Thoughts on Scarcity, and Remedies suggested,"
in which he suggested the reduction of large farms, increased culture and production of such articles as were
useful in themselves, least affected by accidents of weather,
and which would, consequently, render the return of
similar Visitations to that they had experienced impossible.
He advocated the increase of pigs for the victualling of
our fleets, and for the people on shore ; the preservation
of rivers, so as to increase the supply of fish ; an additional
tax on horses, so as to increase the use of oxen, and promote economy amongst farmers. He argued, too, that
corn ought only to be used for bread, and condemned the
" liquid fire " of the distilleries. Tithes, rents, and various
other matters are discussed, and the book, which was
issued by Messrs. Eddowes of Shrewsbury, was dedicated
to Sir Richard Hill, Bart., of Hawkstone. What moved
Mr. Matthews to publish ?   R.D.

REPLIES.

SHROPSHIRE SCHOOLS (Dec. 22, 1880).—A
copious list of scholars and eminent men educated at the
Shrewsbury Free School, will be found in Leighton's
" Guide through Shrewsbury."   W.A.L.

Mr. Arthur Moore, of the second year, and Mr. H.
B. Archer, of the first year, have gained classical Premiums at the recent November examination in Trinity
College, Dublin. These young gentlemen were educated
at *Oswestry* school.—*Salopian Journal,* Nov. 20, 1839.

[It is intended very shortly to publish a history of the Oswestry Grammar School in the Transactions of the Shropshire
Archæological Society ; and we shall be obliged if any of our
readers can give us the names of " old boys" who have in any
way distinguished themselves.—ED.]

WILLIAM OWEN PUGHE (Aug. 18, 1880).—
On July 28, 1880, a correspondent asked who was Mr.
Wynn to whom Southey wrote the opinion that " a more
muddier-minded man than William Owen Pughe " he
never met with. No doubt the correspondent was the Rt.
Hon. Charles Watkin Williams Wynn, an old friend and
benefactor of the poet, several letters to whom appear in
" Southey's Life and Correspondence " edited by his son,
and published in 1850. These do not contain all the letters
to Mr. Wynn, those written after 1820 not being received
in time by the editor. I hav'nt access to the Vol. of
Letters published by Southey's son-in-law in 1856, or
perhaps should find it there. The opinion of Southey, as
was shown by your correspondent, was more than shared in

by "Iolo Morganwg," but on Aug. 18, 1880, another writer pointed out how old Iolo was rather sweeping in his condemnation of those who did not agree with him. Southey had a high opinion of Iolo, and writes of him thus in a letter to Henry Taylor, Esq., Jan. 24, 1827 :—

My old acquaintance (those, I mean, who were elders when I was a young man) are dropping on all sides. One very remarkable one is just gone to his rest after a pilgrimage of fourscore years. Edward Williams, the Welsh Bard, whom, under his Welsh name of Iolo, some lines in "Madoc," were intended to describe and gratify. He was the most eccentric man I ever knew, in whose eccentricity there was no affectation, and in whose conduct there was nothing morally wrong. Poor fellow! with a wild head and a warm heart, he had the simplicity of a child and the tenderness of a woman, and more knowledge of the traditions and antiquities of his own country than it is to be feared will ever be procured by any one after him. I could tell you some odd anecdotes of him which ought not to be lost.

The lines mentioned in this letter refer to Madoc in Wales, and are as follows :—

"—— There went with me
Iolo, old Iolo, he who knows
The virtues of all herbs of mount or vale,
Or greenwood shade, or quiet brooklet's bed;
Whatever lore of science or of song
Sages and bards of old have handed down."

To return to William Owen Pughe. Mr. Southey did not always entertain so low an opinion of his powers, or he would scarcely have written thus—in a letter to Coleridge, June 11, 1804 :—

William Owen [Pughe] lent me three parts of the "Mabinogion," most delightfully translated into so Welsh an idiom and syntax, that such a translation is as instructive (except for etymology) as an original. I was, and am, still utterly at a loss to devise by what possible means, fictions so perfectly like the Arabian Tales in character, and yet so indisputably of Cimbric growth, should have grown up in Wales. Instead of throwing light upon the origin of romance, as had been surmised, they offer a new problem, of almost impossible solution. Bard Williams [Iolo] communicated to me some fine arcana of bardic mythology, quite new to me and to the world, which you will find in "Madoc."

Again; writing to Mr. Rickman, the same month, Southey says—"If William Owen will go on and publish them, I have hopes that the world will yet reward him for his labours." N.W.S.

THE WELSH CANNIBAL (Feb. 16, 1881).—The story of the Welsh cannibal, Gwrgi Garwlwyd by name, will be found in the Welsh Triads: *Myvyrian Archaiology* ii., pp. 9 (No. 37), 13 (No. 28), 65 (No. 46). The name signifies man-dog, and has been used by some Welsh writer as an appellative for "cannibal," and not as a proper name. DEINIOL.

NOVELS RELATING TO WALES (March 9, 1881).—I have a 3 vol. novel, written by the Rev. R. W. Morgan, formerly P.C. of Tregynon, and published by Rich. Bentley in 1853. The title of it is *Raymond de Monthault*. The Lord Marcher—a legend of the Welch borders. The plot is laid at Powis Castle, and many places in the neighbourhood are introduced into the tale. BOOKWORM.

Two or three of the novels by Thomas Love Peacock relate to, or have scenes laid in Wales. D.

COFFIN PLATES ON CHURCH WALLS (Mar. 30, 1881).—A great number of Coffin Plates were nailed to the front of the gallery in Llanwnws Church, near Ystradmeurig, Cardiganshire, up to the year 1872, but I don't know what was done with them when the church was restored. T.L.L.W.

MAY 4, 1881.

NOTES.

Y GOFITTY.—This is the name given to a farm house in the parish of Llandyssil, Cardiganshire. I have asked the derivation and meaning of many good Welsh scholars, but after several vain surmises all have given it up. Its history, which I have from a trustworthy source, is this :—About the beginning of this century the occupier found that a certain well near the house was possessed of marvellous health-giving properties, whose praise, at least, was frequent in his mouth. A quack doctor who lived near, being acquainted with Latin, naturally called the water *aqua vitæ*. The neighbours felt how appropriate the name was and applied it to the farm and all its belongings, calling it to this day, I believe, "Y Gofitty." I only give it from the pronunciation, being ignorant of the way in which it is usually spelt. Possibly if we could only get at the *history* of many a name it would confound the etymologists just as much as the above. CYNWYL.

SEVENTEENTH CENTURY TOKENS.
(Apr. 6, 1881).
MONMOUTHSHIRE.

The tokens of this county are few in number, and are all of late date; the earliest was issued in the year of the Restoration.

It is singular that no tokens exist of the now important town and port of *Newport*.

Abergavenny.

1. Ob. WALTER . DAVIDS . IN . 1661—OB in a diamond
   Re. ABERGENEYE—W. D. D. in a diamond ½

B. 2. Ob. *Edward . Lewis . his . Farthinge* (In three lines)
   Re. OF . ABERGAVENNY . 1667—Arms; a fleur-de-lys ¼

B. 3. Ob. PHILLIP . MORGAN—The Mercers' Arms
   Re. OF . ABERGAVENY . 1671—HIS . HALFPENY ½

4. Ob. PHILLIP . MORGAN—The Mercers' Arms
   Re. OF . ABERGAVENY—1667 ¼

Caerleon.

B. 5. Ob. WILLIAM . MEREDITH—1668.
   Re. OF . CARLINE . MERCER—W . M . ¼

6. Ob. WILLIAM . MEREDITH . 1669—Prince of Wales' Feathers
   Re. A . CAERLYON . FARTHING—A man holding a halberd. ¼

This token is as large as the usual halfpenny tokens. The Parish Register of Caerleon states that William Meredith was buried Oct. 19, 1715.

Chepstow.

7. Ob. THOMAS . DAVIS—HIS . HALFPENY
   Re. OF . CHEAPSTOL . 1671—I . D . (*sic*) ½

B. 8. Ob. WILL . DAVIS . OF . CHEPSTOW—The Mercers' Arms
   Re. MERCER . HIS . FARTHINGE—W . D . 1670 (*A large token*) ¼

9. Ob. RICHARD . MORGAN—HIS . HALFPENY
   Re. OF . CHEPSTOWE—1670 (*Octagonal*) ½
   Incorrectly described by Boyne.

B. 10. Ob. SAMVEL . MORGAN . 1670—S . M .
   Re. A . CHEPSTOWE . FARTHING—A portcullis ¼

B. 11. Ob. WALTER . MORGAN . 1670—W . M . conjoined
Re. A . CHEPSTOWE . FARTHING—A portcullis   ¼

Monmouth.

B. 12. Ob. GOD . SAVE . THE . KING—The King's Head
C . II . R .   ¼
Re. OF . MONMOVTH . 1661—R . A . B .

B. 13. Ob. RICHARD . BALLARD . OF . MONMOTH—HIS .
HALFEPENY . FOR . NECESARY . CHAING
Re. GOD . PRESERVE . OVR . GRACIOVS . KING —
Crowned bust of the King between . C . R
Crowned, and IID. below 1668   ½

B. 14. Ob. MICHAELL . BOHEWNE—The Mercers' Arms
Re. MERCER . IN . MONMOVTH—M . B .   ¼

15. Ob. MICHAELL . BOHEWNE—The Mercers' Arms
Re. MERCER . IN . MONMOTH—M . E . B .   ¼

16. Ob. EDWARD . BEVAN—A man making candles
Re. OF . MONMOVTH . HALFPENY—E . E . B .   ½
Incorrectly described by Boyne.

B. 17. Ob. THOMAS . EDWARDS . . . . — A portcullis
Re. MERCER . MONMOVTH—HIS . HALFE . PENY ½
FOR . NECESSARY . CHANGE

B. 18. Ob. THOMAS . MORGAN . 60—The Mercers' Arms.
Re. OF . MONMOVTH . MERCER—T . G . M .   ¼

Kington.   JAMES W. LLOYD.

QUERIES.

BELL LEGENDS.—In an article on this subject in Chambers's *Book of Days*, Vol. 2, p. 48, it is stated that "a certain Bishop of Bangor who sold the Bells of his Cathedral, was stricken with blindness when he went to see them shipped." When did this Bishop live, and is the legend recorded at any length elsewhere?   ANON.

"ENGINEER" COACH GUARD'S SONG.—When the above coach ceased to run between Oswestry and Aberystwyth on the completion of the Cambrian Railway, the well known guard, Goodwin, gave vent to his feelings in poetry on the morrow of his last start. I only remember two lines—

"A tear stands in Goodwin's eye,
He cannot blow his horn."

1 hope some one will give it complete.   CYNWYL.

HERBERT GOSSIP.—Is there any foundation of fact for the following extraordinary tale?—Henry Arthur Herbert, Earl of Powis, being single when about sixty years of age, bribed the Ladies' Maid of Lady Barbara Herbert (who was a wealthy heiress) to persuade her Ladyship, who was then very young, to marry him, with a reward of two hundred pounds per annum for the rest of her life. The Ladies' Maid fulfilled her part of the bargain, but after the Marriage his Lordship repudiated his promise ; the Ladies' Maid brought an action against his Lordship for the nonfulfilment of the bargain, which was tried in the Assize Court at Welsh Pool. His Lordship and her Ladyship attended the trial, his Lordship thinking to brave it out, but the Barrister for the plaintiff was very hard upon him, and the exposure was severe, his Lordship in a great passion called to her Ladyship to join him and leave the Court, but her Ladyship in a great passion also, replied, "*No*, I insist upon remaining to learn how I have been *bought* and *sold*," and his Lordship lost his case.   NEMO.

REPLIES.

THE ANCIENT BRITONS IN 1815 (Feb. 9, 1881).—Probably in the spring of 1815 Sir Watkin Williams Wynn—always popular—was the most talked of man in Wales. It was then, as we are told in *Wynnstay and the Wynns*, that he obtained the title of the Prince *in* Wales. The *Salopian Magazine* of April, 1815, in a note under the heading of "Provincial Intelligence," says, "Every mark of public respect continues to be paid to Sir Watkin Williams Wynne, Bart., by honest grateful Cambrians, and the public spirited inhabitants of Chester and Oswestry." Anyone who has access to the files of the Shrewsbury and Chester papers of March, 1815, could doubtless glean much valuable matter on the subject.
G.G.

THE FIRST MAYOR OF OSWESTRY (Mar. 30, 1881).—You will find ample particulars of the Pope Family of Shropshire in the Herald's Visitation of Shropshire, 1623 ; Blakeway's *Sheriffs of Shropshire* ; and Owen and Blakeway's History of Shrewsbury.   W.A.L.

About eighteen years ago I became possessed of a large number of old deeds consisting of feoffments, bonds, and leases, in which Roger Pope of Shrewsbury figured prominently. These documents related chiefly to the parish of Trefeglwys in Montgomeryshire. One of my deeds is a lease of the Vicarage and the Vicarial emoluments of Trefeglwys by him to a Lewys Gwynn of Llanidloes. I have not been able to trace how he became possessed of the right of dealing with this—but it is probable some one or other of the Shropshire Monastic Establishments had a connection with Trefeglwys and he obtained possession of its rights by purchase, the same as he did that of the three Friaries of Shrewsbury, shortly after the Dissolution of the Monasteries, temp. Hen. VIII. Blakeway in his *Sheriffs of Shropshire*, page 172, gives a sketch of the Pope family, which I tabulate for the purpose of assisting in discovering who Richard Pope, the first mayor of Oswestry, was. The information I give is not much, but it will limit the search required to clear the question up.

Walter Pope══? of Tripleton.

John Pope══? barker, admitted a burgess of Shrewsbury, 1504.   Richard Pope, draper, admitted a burgess of Shrewsbury, 1487.

Lewis Pope══?

Roger Lewis (*alias*) Pope══? who is written "Esq", he purchased from Richard Andrews in 1544 the scites of all the three friaries in Shrewsbury.

Roger Pope══? Alderman of Shrewsbury. He was admitted of Lincoln's Inn, 1574, lived in St. Austin's Friars, 1607, died 1628, (*a*)

Son══Lucia, daughter of Thomas Edwards.

Roger Pope══? of Wolstaston.
(*b*)

Roger Pope══? Equerry of Charles II., Bridgnorth.
(*c*)

Son══?

Bromwich Pope of Wolstaston, Sheriff 1722.
(*d*)

(a) Among the deeds in my possession is one dated 20th Sept. 1618, between Roger Pope of Shrewsbury and Hugh Wilson of Llanidloes. The subject was the lease for 21 years of a Tenement in the parish of Trefeglwys—one of the witnesses is a "Richard Pope," in whose handwriting the deed was endorsed—that a certain line was interlineated before the execution of the deed. The presumption thus is that he was in the legal profession —and was possibly a son of Roger Pope. He could not have been Richard Pope, 1st Mayor of Oswestry, for he was born, according to your query, in 1636.

(b) I have a deed executed by this Roger Pope, who is described as of Wolstaston, of which Manor he had livery as son and heir of Lucia daughter of Thomas Edwards in 1606. This document is dated 24 July 3. Ch. I. (1627), and is a demise for life to Henry Wharnebye of Trefeglwys of a farm called "Craigfryn" situated in that locality. It would almost appear from this that Blakeway had post dated the death of Alderman Pope, as the grand son is here dealing with the Alderman's property, who according to Blakeway was living in 1628. The father of this Roger Pope of Wolstaston apparently predeceased his own father.

(c) My next deed is dated 11 July 1686 and is between Roger Pope of Bridgnorth, and Edward Mitton of Halston, and was to secure the repayment of £500 to the said Edward Mitton which he had advanced to Roger Pope on his property in Montgomeryshire "of the yearly value of three score pounds." The witnesses to this deed were Thomas Lyster, John Ffowler, Edward Jones, Charles Chambre, and Thomas Davies.

(d) My last deed relating to this family is dated 21 June 1715, and is, Between Matthew Johnson and others, and Bromwich Pope of Wolstaston—it appears to be a surrender of the property of Roger Pope the elder and Roger Pope the younger to Bromwich Pope—under some antecedently created trust. This Bromwich Pope died, leaving an only daughter, Catherine. She dying (unmarried, in 1754) the Wolstaston estate passed to her cousin-german Sir Thomas Whitmore of Apley, K.B., son of her aunt, Elizabeth Pope.

As to who was the Richard Pope, first Mayor of Oswestry, I have not added much to the known facts, but I submit that he may be looked for either as descended from the Richard Pope witness to the deed of 1618, or he may be a son of Roger Pope of Wolstaston—who succeeded the alderman in 1627. An examination of Jos. Morris's extracts from Shropshire Registers, formerly, and doubtless now, in the Library of the Shropshire Museum at Shrewsbury, may afford evidence that would clear the matter up.

I have other, much older deeds, relating to Roger Pope.
BOOKWORM.

CURRENT NOTES.

The Council of the Cymmrodorion Society have resolved to establish a Dialect and Folklore Section, and appointed a Committee to superintend it.

The Literary Fund, over whose anniversary dinner Mr. Russell Lowell is to preside on the 4th of May, was founded in a humble way in 1790 by Mr. David Williams, a Welsh scholar and writer.

A large number of old Roman coins have been discovered in excavating for a new drive in course of construction at Baron-hill, the Anglesey seat of Sir R. Williams. Bulkeley.

Deadman-Dane's-Bottom, one of the deep valleys between two clay-covered chalk hills near Hughenden, is traditionally said to record a great battle between the Saxons and Danes, in which a company of Britons on the march gave their assistance to the Saxon churls and helped them to defeat the invaders. By prescriptive right, for which this legend was perhaps framed to account, the Welsh drovers, on their way with cattle from the Principality to the London markets, long claimed to depasture their herds freely on the heath or common land, Wycombe-heath or Pennwood, near the valley.

THE OSWESTRY SCHOOL OF MUSIC.

The following letter from Mr. Henry Leslie has appeared in The Times:—

Sir,—The interest you have shown in musical education emboldens me to crave permission for another letter on the subject, in order that I may narrate important practical events which have been obtained in this district during the past six months. In my letter of July last I bewailed the lack of efficient elementary teaching in the schools of this district, and protested against the enormous grant for music considering the unsatisfactory results of the instruction generally given, while the great question of high artistic training was left unrecognised and unsubsidised by the Government. But I was fully aware of the difficulties surrounding the subject, as one could hardly expect much from teachers who needed instruction almost as much as the children they taught.

You were so kind as to send a representative to the first Oswestry Musical Festival in the autumn of 1879, and the proceedings of that occasion were duly chronicled in The Times. The financial result of the festival was a balance of £130, and that sum was used to found the "Oswestry School of Music," of which I became president, backed by an influential committee. We offered class lessons in elementary choral singing at moderate terms to the well-to-do; to working men and their wives and families, for one penny a lesson; and to school children for one halfpenny a lesson. But next to no response was made. A "masterly inactivity" prevailed. The inhabitants of rural districts are slow to move.

When we commenced preparations for the Festival concerts of October, 1880, of which, owing to the unwillingness of the Festival Committee to undertake the responsibility, Lady Harlech most kindly assumed the financial liability, I determined to apply pressure in order to raise the standard of membership in the Festival Choral Society. No one was allowed to take part in the choral performance without undergoing a fresh trial of capacity, and they who could not pass the ordeal were obliged to go through a three months' training at the School of Music. Thus the Festival is made to help the school, and the school renders the members more competent for the required duties of the Festival.

But a solution of the problem did come, though in a manner entirely unexpected. Towards the end of last September a leading inhabitant of a neighbouring village asked me if I would do something to improve the singing in the Church services. Bad as the music in those services was, I declined acting on that basis, but said that if he could obtain the signatures of every representative man of every class in the village and its neighbourhood, irrespective of sect and politics, to the proposition "that it was expedient to establish a system of weekly choral practice in the village of Llansantffraid," I would act as chairman of the committee. In a few days every necessary signature was obtained, and in less than a fortnight the committee was formed and a conductor from a neighbouring town engaged. Work commenced on October 3, with elementary teaching from 6.15 to 7 p.m., and the advanced class, which consisted only of those who could read music and had some knowledge of it, practised from 7.15 to 8.30, membership being open to every one above five years of age, and no payment being required, as the expenses were to be covered by two concerts, which are given during the winter quarters.

Several important objects are thus gained at the same time—musical instruction is a free gift to every inhabitant of the parish; two entertainments are provided for those whose only chance of a change in the monotony of their lives is the public house ; the members of the choir have a pride in knowing that their exertions benefit the funds of the society ; the union of all classes increases cohesion and gives strength in local matters ; the services of Church and Chapel are certain to be greatly improved ; and a larger area of selection is gained for the future welfare of the Oswestry Musical Festival.

And now for the practical results. In this particular village one concert has already been given, and another, in which there is to be a selection from the "Messiah," will take place in a few days. The attendance for practice has averaged 100 each week. The movement spread with great rapidity, the initiative emanating entirely from the villagers themselves. At present fourteen parishes round Oswestry have choral societies, on the committees of which every class is represented, and at least 1,000 people are practising once a week. All these village societies are affiliated to the Oswestry School of Music, and thus we have under our direction elementary music, advanced music, and the annual festival, to the raising of the standard of performance of which all these varied organizations will be made subservient.

In the month of September a festival of fifteen village choirs will be held in Oswestry, and it is the intention of the committee to use every endeavour to make it the brightest of days to the many hundreds of children who will take part in the performance. I do not dare venture to enclose the programme intended for that performance, as I fear I have already transgressed in the way of length, but while it will be a most interesting one, and may even be a very brilliant one, the interests of art will predominate, for the festival must be specially considered as a step in musical education.

Now, all this has happened since 1879 in a district which was then called "unmusical Shropshire." But there is no magic in it. It is all the genuine outcome of a need that required a supply. The people desire rational amusement, and they eagerly grasp at the chance of a pursuit which cannot but tend to elevation and refinement. More especially do they wish it for their children, whose wits have become quickened by compulsory education and require more than they used in the way of intellectual work. Where it has once been carried out to success it can be repeated, and I trust to hear before long that in other districts centres are at work, and that the influence of music may make itself felt far and wide. Beyond the mere musical teaching this subject has a large social bearing, for, in the present strife of class interests, class antagonisms are arising, and everything that can bridge over the chasms in the body politic caused thereby merits the attention and consideration of those in power. It is as important to the Home Office as it is to the Education Department.

In *The Times* of November 2, 1880, there was a most important article on the subject of higher musical education. With one exception, it passed apparently unheeded, but it was so exhaustive that it closed the question. The exception was an important one, the offer of Mr. Sims Reeves to co-operate in the great work which would follow the establishment of a Conservatorium. The future of artistic musical education must before long receive the consideration of Government. Of course it is out of the question that aught can be done during the present Session, but if a Royal Commission could be appointed, it might collect valuable evidence which would materially shorten future discussion. If a few practical men well versed in the influence of music as an art and as a recreation were members of it, I am sure that evidence could be produced which would convince the most sceptical of the

good which would result from its receiving that assistance to which the musicians of Great Britain think it entitled.

I wish to add some observations on the doings of the People's Entertainment Society as having an important bearing on the social side of the subject, but dare not write another word.—I am, Sir, your obedient servant,

　　　　　　　　　　　　　　　　HENRY LESLIE.

Bryn Tanat, Llansaintffraid, April 16.

CONVERSAZIONE OF THE CYMMRODORION SOCIETY.

On Friday, Apr. 29, the Cymmrodorion Society held its second annual conversazione in the Crown Room of the Freemasons' Tavern, Great Queen-street. An exhibition of works of art, antiquities, books, and rare MSS., was opened at 7.30, The Rev. John Davies, M.A., exhibited a valuable collection of choice books, which, however, bore but little reference to matters of Welsh interest. Among them was " Parry's Welsh Bible, 1620," large folio, in black letter, containing Bishop Morgan's Preface, being the second edition published of the Welsh Bible. " Rastall's Collection of Statutes," 1585, containing laws relating to Wales from the time of Edward I.; a " Historia Atheismi," by Jenkin Thomas, printed at Altdorf ; the " Legend of Captain Jones," written 1671, by the Rev. D. Lloyd, dean of St. Asaph ; and books relating to the life and works of Pennant the antiquary. The next table bore the exhibits of Mr. Hancock. Among these were the " Oswestry Red Book "; the " History of the Gwydir Family;" " Bye-gones," " A memoir of the late Mr. W. W. E. Wynne," by the more recently deceased Mr. Breese ; Bede's Ecclesiastical History, in Latin, printed at " Lovanii, Anno, 1566," with two very curious vignettes, depicting, probably, a scene intended to illustrate the tradition of St. Melangell, of Pennant, and the Hare—the huntsman representing Prince Brochwel Ysgythrog, of Powys ; the First Welsh Concordance, printed at Philadelphia in 1730 ; Original Rent Roll, for 1719, of Lands in Denbighshire, Carnarvonshire, and Montgomeryshire, belonging to the Hon. Watkin Williams Wynn ; Fragment of a Welsh MS. on Agriculture, 16th century ; transcript of some early Parish Registers ; Drawings by T. W. Hancock, &c. The opposite table was occupied by the exhibits of Mr. Bernard Quaritch and Mr. Howel W. Lloyd, M.A. Among these may be noted Owain Myvyr's own copy of " The Myvyrian Archaiology of Wales, containing the collector's MSS. notes, a truly valuable copy of this excellent work ; a rare broadside relating to Owain Myvyr, printed at Chester about 1820 ; Caradoc of Llancarvan's " Historie of Cambria," translated by Humphrey Llwyd, continued by David Powel, first edition, 1584 ; Enderbie's (Percy) " Cambria Triumphans," 1661, an original edition and fine copy of a very rare book ; an original edition of Gambold's Welsh Grammar, published at Carmarthen, 1727. These formed part of the exhibits of Mr. Bernard Quaritch. Mr. Howel Lloyd displayed a number of rare and curious books, including " Llyfr y Resolusion," recently introduced to us by its possessor in an article on Old Welsh Books, which appeared in the last "Cymmrodor." At the next table Professor Rudler, F.G.S., exhibited specimens of pre-historic antiquities. Ranged round the room were various works of art, including paintings and drawings by Mr. W. Cave Thomas, Mr. B. S. Marks, and Mr. A. Howells. Sculpture was also well represented by Mr. Joseph Edwards, Mr. W. Davies (Mynorydd), Mr. D. Davies (who exhibits at this year's academy), Mr. Milo Griffith, and Mr. A. Plante. Most of the exhibitors made a few remarks on their respective exhibits, and Mr. B. T. Williams, M.P., gave a short address, in which he drew a somewhat gloomy picture of mining and agricultural prospects in Wales. The latter part of the evening was taken up by a concert, in which Madame Edith Wynne Agabeg, Miss M. J. Williams, Mr Hirwen Jones, Mr. John Thomas, and Mr. Brinley Richards, took part. Mr. John Thomas played on the harp, and Mr. Brinley Richards, though seriously indisposed, gave a pianoforte solo in which he introduced a " Welsh Hornpipe," a dance tune taken down by Herr Carl Engel on hearing it played many years ago by an old blind harper in Llangollen, and never before played out of Wales in any public meeting. In view of Mr. Richards's indisposition, Miss Mary Davies very kindly acted as accompanist. A vote of thanks, proposed by Dr. Isambard Owen, M.A., seconded by Mr. W. Jones, and carried by acclamation, brought the proceedings to a close.

The Late Canon Robert Williams.

(From the *Oswestry Advertizer*, May 11.)

We had last week the painful duty of recording the death of a well-known Welsh scholar, Canon Williams of Culmington, formerly of Rhydycroesau. who has soon followed his friends and fellow antiquaries, Mr. Wynne of Peniarth and Mr. Breese of Portmadoc, to the tomb. Canon Williams was for over forty years vicar of Llangadwaladr and rector of Rhyd-y-croesau, and was well known to a large number of our readers.   In 1879, having purchased the advowson of Culmington, near Craven Arms, Salop, he went there to reside, and there he died on Tuesday, April 26, 1881.

Mr. Williams was the son of the Rev. Robert Williams, perpetual curate of Llandudno, Carnarvonshire, and was born in Conway, on the 29th of June, 1810. He was educated at Christ Church, Oxford, where he took third class in classics, and M.A. in 1832.   The year following he became curate of Llangernyw, and in 1837 vicar of Llangadwaladr. In 1838 to this was also added the rectory of Rhydycroesau, near Oswestry, which, as we have said, he held up to 1879, when he removed to Culmington. And before we pass on from his clerical to his literary life, we may add that the present Bishop of St. Asaph conferred on Mr. Williams an honorary Canonry in St. Asaph Cathedral in consideration of his literary works, and (in 1871) offered him a living in Montgomeryshire, which he declined.

As a Welsh scholar and antiquary, Canon Williams took the foremost rank, and his death will be a severe loss to Celtic literature. Up to the last, his pen was active, and his literary services to the Principality covered more than half a century. His name to the general reader will be best known as the author of an admirable *Dictionary of Eminent Welshmen*, a goodly octavo volume of nearly 600 pages, which was published, in its present form, in 1852. This popular work first saw the light in 1831, as we gather from a minute in the Transactions of the Cymmrodorion Society of that year, which states that a prize was awarded to "Robert Williams, Esq.," for a "Biographical Sketch of the most Eminent Individuals Wales has produced since the Reformation." This was the same year, we may note in passing, that the Society awarded another prize to a "young Welshman"—Arthur James Johnes, Esq.—for an essay on the "Causes which in Wales have produced Dissent from the Established Church." The Society had Mr. Williams's Biographical Sketches translated into Welsh, and "printed for general circulation in the Principality," under the title of *Enwogion Cymru*, and the original English MS. was ordered to be printed in the fourth number of the Society's Transactions. In 1836, the author issued the first special edition of the book, "with addenda" containing notices of Dr. W. O. Pughe, R. Llwyd, and others. This was a thin duodecimo, of 115 pages, and was published by Hughes of 15, St. Martin's-Le-Grand, London.

Another of Mr. Williams's earlier works was his *History of Aberconwy*, which appeared, we believe, in its original form, as an "Historical Account of Conway Castle," and under the auspices of the Cymmrodorion Society. The book was published in its complete form in 1835, by Mr. Gee of Denbigh, and the author in a letter he wrote to us in September, 1880, stated that he had compiled sufficient matter to complete a new and revised edition of twice the size of the original. It is much to be desired that this labour should not prove in vain, for the book (now very scarce) is a valuable one, and an extended edition would be welcomed by a very large class of intelligent readers.

In 1865 Mr. Williams gave to the world his *Lexicon Cornu-Britannicum* ; a Dictionary of the ancient Celtic language of Cornwall. This was a quarto volume of which 500 copies were issued at a guinea and-a-half. The work is out of print, and so much is it esteemed that second-hand copies often realize as much as double the original price.   The Rev. D. Silvan Evans informs us that in a letter he had from Mr. Williams last year, it was stated that the author had a "new edition greatly enlarged ready for publication," which he hoped to have printed by the Oxford University Press. The mention of this laborious work reminds us of a note in relation to it that appeared in *Bye-gones* January 3, 1877. A well-known antiquary, under the signature of "S.," called attention to Professor Sullivan's article on "Celtic Literature" in the new vol. of the *Encycl : Brit :* where it was stated that, "the third relic of the Cornish language is a miracle play founded upon the life of St. Meriasek, son of a Duke of Britany, called in Breton St. Meriadoc.   This piece," says Mr. Sullivan, "which was written in 1504, was found a few years ago by Mr. Whitley Stokes among the Hengwrt MSS. at Peniarth." The correspondent of *Bye-gones* very properly claims for Canon Williams the discovery of the MS., and points out how much Mr. Stokes was indebted to the *Lexicon Cornu-Britannicum* for his knowledge of the Cornish language.

The most recent work of the deceased was the editing and translating of Selections from the famous "Hengwrt MSS." preserved at Peniarth. In 1876 Mr. Williams issued the first vol. of these, *Y Seint Greal*. In the preface he says :—"The Seint Greal is the most important of the prose works now remaining in manuscript, and it is written in such pure and idiomatic Welsh as to have all the value of an original work, and is well deserving of the study of the writers of the present day, few of whom can write a page without corrupting the language by the copious introduction of English idioms literally translated. Should I succeed in bringing out the Greal without incurring a heavy loss, I shall proceed with the publication of the Gests of Charlemagne ; Bown o Hamton ; Lucidar ; Ymborth yr Enaid ; Purdan Padrig ; Buchedh Mair Wyry ; Evengyl Nicodemus, &c., all of which have been carefully transcribed by me." The Greal, as we have said, appeared in 1876, in a complete volume, having been first issued in three parts. Two further parts—for the second volume—"Campeu Charlymaen," have since been issued, and in a letter we had from Mr. Williams in March last he says, "I am busy with part 6 of the Hengwrt MSS., which will complete the second volume;" and he adds jokingly, "I have astonished some people in asserting that I have done for Welsh Literature more than all the Esteddvods and Cymmrodorion put together !"

Mr. Williams's literary labours were by no means confined to his published books. He was one of the Editorial Committee of the Cambrian Archæological Association, and at various times contributed to the pages of *Arch : Camb :* the journal of that Society. He also wrote a few papers in the (now extinct) *Cambrian Journal*. To *Bye-gones* he also occasionally wrote, and his contributions were always valuable. The publishers of the *Gossiping Guide to Wales* were indebted to him for a thorough revision of the work, and the addition of a Glossary of Welsh words. In criticising this the late Rev. Robert Jones, rector of All Saints, Rotherhithe, in *Y Cymmrodor* for 1877, challenged one of the meanings as follows :— "'Dyfrdwy' is given as ' dwfr' and ' du,'=black water. But the beautiful Cymric name of the Dee comes from ' dwfr' and ' dwy'=divine or sacred water." In Jan., 1878, Mr. Williams, writing to *Bye-gones*, avowed the compilation of the Glossary as his work, and maintained

his position. To this Mr. Jones replied in the same pub-
lication, and the discussion was continued by other, and
minor critics, for some weeks in the Welsh newspapers.
In 1868 Mr. Williams translated, into English, the "Book
of Taliesin" for Mr. Skene's *Four Ancient Books of
Wales*, and in 1878 he revised several of the notes to
Mr. Askew Roberts's edition of the *History of the Gwydir
Family*.

In the spelling of Welsh words Mr. Williams was a
precisian. Nothing annoyed him more than the use of the
letter "f," which he held to be inaccurate. Instead of the
familiar modes of spelling we have been accustomed to in
newspapers and time-tables, he would write Llanvyllin,
Llanvair, &c., &c., and at his suggestion one of the editions
of the *Gossiping Guide to Wales* was issued with all the
names of places spelt after his theory; but it was soon
found that to teach philology was no part of a topographical
guide. In some cases, such as in the (to the Saxon) dreadful looking word "Dwygyvylchi," it was of small moment,
but in better known, and more easily pronounced localities,
a return to the modern form was imperative. Mr. Williams was no doubt right in his opinion, and we remember there was a discussion on the subject at one of the
National Eisteddvodau, where it was suggested to urge upon
the bards and literati of Wales, as well as editors and publishers of Welsh periodicals, the desirableness of thus returning to the original orthography of the Welsh language;
but, as was stated in the *Oswestry Advertiser* at the time,
"English critics who cannot enter into the arcana of Celtic
etymology may ask why we should return to the spelling
of former centuries on one side of the border and not on
the other."

Mr. Williams's literary labours speak for themselves
and need no panegyric. He was a hard-working student
to the last, and although over seventy years of age was
able to read the smallest type without glasses; and often
continued his studies until midnight without fatigue. As
a Welsh scholar he has been rivalled, but not surpassed,
and his library of Welsh books and books connected with
Wales is extensive and valuable. The *Montgomeryshire
Collections* of the Powysland Club published last year contain a letter from Mr. Williams to Mr. Morris C. Jones,
F.S.A., the Hon. Sec. of that Society, urging that the
Museum at Welshpool should be made the grand Library
for the reception of Welsh printed books; and calling
attention to the fact that even the most unimportant
works may sometimes be useful to scholars, instancing as
an illustration of this the extracts from old Welsh Almanacks published in *Bye-gones* by Mr. E. G. Salisbury
of Glan Aber, Chester. We wish we could express a
reasonable hope that the library of the deceased could be
secured to carry out this suggestion. The remains of the
deceased gentleman were interred at Culmington on Monday the 2nd of May, 1881.　　　　　　　　　A.R.

THE LATE MR. J. SIDES DAVIES.

It is with regret that we announce the death of Mr.
J. Sides Davies, surgeon, the Poplars, Oswestry, after a
lingering illness of two months' duration. He died on
Friday, Apr, 22, and the funeral took place on the following Monday at the Cemetery. Mr. Davies was a sur-
geon to the Cottage Hospital and Dispensary, as well as
Borough Coroner, to which office he was appointed in 1861.
He had previously contested the county coronership with
Mr. Blackburne unsuccessfully. He had a fine library,
particularly rich in topographical books connected with
Wales and the border counties, and our *Bye-gones* library
has often been enriched from its shelves. He was a member
of the Powys-land Club and the Shropshire Archæological
Society, in whose affairs he took a deep interest.

MAY 11, 1881.

NOTES.

"BYE-GONES."

The column of "Bye-gones" in the *Oswestry Advertiser*
has been continuously published for Five Hundred Weeks,
and during this period has contained Five Thousand
Notes, Queries, and Replies. During the whole period—
extending to nearly Ten years—no paragraph has been
repeated; and where (in rare instances) subjects have been
discussed twice, it has been for the purpose of shedding
additional light on an interesting question. The contents of the column are reprinted in volumes every two
years; and each volume forms a distinct work, without
being continued from its predecessors. Holders of the
earlier volumes are fortunate in possessing books that
have been "out of print" for a considerable period, and
are now much enhanced in money value. A copy was
recently sold at a book auction in London for 22s. that
had cost its owner 7s. 6d. And, as only a very limited
number are printed, the later volumes are fast becoming
scarce. Copies of the one for 1878-9 may still be had,
post free, for 10s. 6d., and the one for 1880-1 subscribed
for at the same price. These volumes will be found to be
perfect and distinct in themselves, and not numbered as
belonging to a series.

Every day adds to the list of contributors, and continually we have to lament the loss by death of those
who have been valued friends of the undertaking. Among
the latter we may name Mr. Alexander Andrews, author
of the "History of British Journalism," Mr. Breese,
F.S.A., Mr. Shirley Brooks, F.S.A., editor of "Punch,"
Rev. R. Ellis, "Cynddelw," Lord Hanmer, Rev. T. James,
F.S.A., Rev. R. Jones, rector of All Saints, Rother-
hithe, Mr. T. Jones, Cheetham Library, Mr. R. G. Jebb,
Rev. J. Peter, F.G.S., Mr. H. T. Richardson, Rev. T.
Salwey, Canon Williams, Mr. W. W. E. Wynne, Rev.
Mackenzie Walcott, &c., &c.

Our thanks are due, and are most cordially given, to the
friends who help us, by pen and by the loan of books,
MSS., and old newspapers; and we earnestly solicit a
continuance of public favour.　　　　　　　　　ED.

Croeswylan, Oswestry,
　　May 11, 1881.

THE OLD WELSH ALMANACKS.
(April 13, 1881.)

I now complete the years promised in my last. The
first one for 1818, printed at Dublin, is called "Cyfaill
Gobeithiol;" the price fivepence, and on the title page it
has these verses :—

1 Fy hen Gyfeillion cryno,
　Rwy'n dyfod attoch etto;
　Gan ddisgwyl, hefyd, er mor
　　　wael,
　Yn rhyw-sut, gael fynghroeso.

2 Os bu'r Hynafiaid hyfion,
　Cyn cyraedd plant ac wyrion,
　Yn heirdd eu drych, a gwych
　　　eu gwedd,
　Trwy degwch, hedd a digon.

3 Os rhodiad rhai 'dyw'r rhwyd-
　　　au
　A'u dyrys gyfyngderau,
　A ddylem rodio er mawrhâd,
　'Run m dd a'n tad a'n teid-
　　　iau? o

4 Er darllen Llyfr yr wybr,
　A'r Ser, llyth'renau eglur,
　Adwaenir tywydd, arwydd
　　　yw,
　Wrth rodiad rhyw Greadur.

5 I'w drin nid yw drudaniaeth,
　I'w bennu, na gwlybaniaeth,
　Gwres a sychder, gwynt a
　　　gwlaw,
　Ond g'leuni a llaw Rhaglun-
　　　iaeth.

6 Beware of false profession,
　Serving God and Mammon;
　We've reason to fear there i s
　　　but few
　Of lodgers true religion.

The *second* issue for 1818 is called "Cyfaill Hyfrydol;" it is printed in Dublin, price fivepence, and has these lines on the title page:—

1 Fy 'wyllys hen Gyfeillion,
  Eleni wrth reol union,
  Yw'ch annerch mewn amgen-
    ach gwawr,
  Na dirfawr sorod Arfon.

2 Pob casgliad wneis heb fethu,
  Diofer-waith i'ch difyru
  Gan eu cymhwyso i Ledred,
  A Hydred canol Cymru.

3 Byd mawr yw'r Haulwen ysol,
  Canol bwngc y cyrph nefol;
  A'r ddaear a'r planedau sy',
  'N ei gylchu yn ffynyddol.

4 Ein daear medd awduron

Yw lleuad y lloerolion;
Mae'n llawn a newid yn ei
  thro,
Yw eu goleuo 'n gyson.

5 Pan gaffo'r holl Ysgrythyr,
Ei llwyr gyflawni'n eglur,
Neshau wna'r amser (dyweda
  'n hy')
Bydd crynu'n neutu natur.

6 O! let no soul be silent,
But praise the omnipotent,
For HE alone's the only God,
That rules the rod of JUDG-
  MENT.

The one for 1819 is called "Cyfaill Gwasanaethgar"; it was printed in Dublin, the price fivepence, and has these verses on the title page:—

1 GYFEILLION, dynion dawnus,
  Drwy OGLEDD, DE, a PHOWYS,
  Yn eich plith, er bendith, bo,
  Wir ffwyddyn orfoleddus.

2 Yr awyr lâs ei hwyneb,
  Sydd megis trag'wyddoldeb,
  Heb ben na diwedd, mawredd
    maith,
  Yn llawn o waith cywreindeb.

3 Yn troi mae'r bydoedd beu-
    nydd,
  Fel gwelir, heibio'u gilydd,
  Yn nghanol yr ehangder
    maith,
  Gan ddangos gwaith yr AR-
    GLWYDD!

4 Ac anian rhai yn lleithion,
Rhai'n sych-gras, oer, a
  phoethion;
A barnu *Hin* yn ol eu hynt,
Am danynt y mae dynion.

5 Er *Orion, Mars* a *Ractus,*
Ceir tywydd yn fwy hyspys,
Gan lawer corphyn, briddyn
  brau,
A hen aeloddau clwyfus.

6 The Heavens, and all the
  Creation,
Remain in peace and union,
But EARTH is curs'd for man
  did fall;
He faceth all confusion.

                               E.G.S.

QUERIES.

SEVENTEENTH CENTURY TOKENS (Apr. 6, 1881).—Will someone explain what the middle letter stands for in the initials on so many of these Tokens? Take, for instance, No. 2, where William Mall is represented as W.L.M. In No. 10, Tho. Wheeler is initialed as T.M.W. In No. 13, John Phillips as I.A.P., &c., &c.,   TELL.

GWEDDI'R FORWYN (Mar. 2, 1881).—Is the prayer to the Virgin Mary alluded to a translation of the Catholic prayer, "Ave Maria," or a prayer of its own? A very quaint popular prayer to the Virgin Mary, in verse, and entitled "Breuddwyd Mair," or "Mary's Dream," has been published as obsolete—and nearly forgotten—in *Arch: Camb:* 3rd Series, Vol. xi., p. 397, and reprinted by me, with a French translation, in the *Revue Celtique,* Vol. iii., p. 447. It begins with:—

"Mam wen Mair, wyt ti yn huno?"
"Dear mother Mary, are you asleep?"

22, Rue Servandoni, Paris.   H. GAIDOZ.

CHURCH LEWN AT OSWESTRY.—In a squib bearing this heading, "Minshull the Printer," in January, 1834, opposed a Church Rate for lighting our old church. He complained that the parishioners' money was wasted, and said. "As a sample, take a few items from the parish books, from 1815 to 1829. Wine for the Church £337 6s. 4¾d. Thirteen dinners on the Wardens passing their accounts, £101 17s. 7d. (sic). Ropes, £29 4s. 9½d. Leather, £12 16s. 5d. Clerk's Salary and bills, £592 14s. 8d." Can any old Oswestrian tell me how many and who partook of these dinners, what the leather was for, and the meaning and derivation of the word "Lewu"? Eight

years later, by the way, we find objection to the account for lighting, and we are told that there was "a vestry held July 15, 1842, to assess a Church rate. Objections were raised against the Organist's salary, which upon vote was rejected by a majority of five. The following Sunday the organ was not played, nor was there any singing." It was fortunate the affair came off so near to Midsummer, or we may be led to suppose the evening service would be performed in darkness!   FITZOSWALD.

REPLIES.

J. TOMKIES OF OSWESTRY, 1789 (Mar. 16, 1881).—In 1768 there was a Benefit Club established at the Coach and Dogs Inn, Oswestry, and its annual sermon seems (from the minute book which is in my possession) to have been preached by the curate. In 1776 the preacher was "the Rev. Mr. Tomkies." If this was the party who wrote the letter to the culprit in Shrewsbury gaol, he must have been resident here, at least a dozen years.   JARCO.

REMARKABLE TREES (Apr. 6, 1881).—In reply to "M.C.B.," I made a visit to the above-mentioned tree Apr. 18, 1881. It is situate on Cilcochwyn Farm, near the roadside on the way to Llangollen, and close to Pont Fadoc in the Glyn Ceiriog Valley. The landlord of the Swan Inn accompanied me and we measured it together. Near to the ground it is 56 feet 6 inches in circumference, there is very little difference between the bottom part and the middle of the tree, it is in fact an enormous bulky tree, very solid, and the outside appearance not at all decayed, and during the summer has abundance of leaves. It is hollow on one side and open to the top. The opening into it is not large, the landlord and myself in going inside had to stoop in doing so, some five or six persons in addition could have stood with us. The tree is not high, its great curiosity is its enormous bulk; there is but one extending branch spreading to the right, and only small sprouts growing from the trunk towards the top, so that there is not much to draw life from it. It is certainly a Monster Tree, and well worth a visit.   W.P.

Wrexham.

BLANCHE PARRY WINDOWS AT ATCHAM. (Apr. 13, 1881).—In reply to the first part of your correspondent's inquiry repeated in your note in *Bye-gones* of above date, I beg to say Blanche Parry was undoubtedly of Welsh extraction, being descended from Moreiddig, second son of Idio Wyllt, lord of Llywel, who settled in the Golden Vale on his marriage with the widow of Thomas, Lord Lacy, or Lord of Ewyas Lacy. This Moreiddig, however, came originally from Ireland, being descended from Alured, King of Kyrian. His descendants settled at Old Court or Poston, in the Golden Valley; Griffith ap Harry a younger son of this branch, again settling at Bacton about the year 1400, building there a house which, in contradistinction to the name of his father's residence, he called New Court. His son, Harry ap Griffith ap Harry fought at Mortimer's Cross, and his grandson Miles ap Harry, who died in 1488, was commemorated by a beautiful stained glass window in the Parish Church. A similar memorial was erected to the memory of the grand-daughter of the said Miles, Blanche Parry, chief gentle-woman of the Privy Chamber to Queen Elizabeth.*

The above information I have obtained from Robinson's *Mansions and Manors of Herefordshire,* and Jones's *History of Breconshire,* which latter contains a pedigree of the family.

Blanche Parry was born in 1508, and died blind, February 12, 1589. She was an alchemist, astrologer, antiquary,

—————
* These are the windows which were removed to Atcham.

and herald, and a great friend of Dr. Dee, for whom she
obtained the mastership of St. Cross Hospital. Her body
was buried at Westminster, and her bowels at Bacton,
where a monument to her memory bears the following
curious inscription :—

I Parry hys daughter Blaenche of Newecourte borne,
  That trayned was in pryncys courts wyth gorgious
    white ;
Wheare fleetynge honour sounds wyth blaste of horne,
  Eache of accounte too place of worlds delyghts,
Am lodgyd heere wythein this stonye tombe ;
  My harpynger ys pacyde I owghte of due,
My fryends of speeche heerin doo fynde my doombe,
  The whyche in vaine they doo so greatly rue,
For so moche as hyt ys but the ende of all ;
  Thys worlde rowte of state what so they be,
The whyche unto the reste hereafter shall,
  Assemble thus eache wyght in hys degree ;
I lyvde allweys as handmaede to a Qreene,
  In chamber chieff my tyme did over passe,
Uncareful of my welthe there was I seen ;
  Whylste I abode the ronnyrge of my glasse,
Not doubtynge wante whilste that my mystresse liv'd,
  In womens state whose cradell sawe I rockte;
Her servante then as when shee her crowne attchiev'd,
  And so remaend tyll Death my doore had knockt ;
Preferrynge styll the causys of eache wyghte,
  As farr as I doorste move her graces care,
For to reward decerts by course of rygine ;
  As needs vrystle of sarvys doonne each wheare,
So that my time I thus did passe awaye,
  A maide in Courte and never no mans wife ;
Sworne of Queene Ellsbeth bedd Chamber allwaye,
  Wythe maiden Queene a meade did ende my lyfe.
Kington.   JAMES W. LLOYD.

CURRENT NOTES.

The Rev. T. F. Thistleton Dyer, in a paper on "Bees
and their Folk Lore," published this month in *Cassell's
Family Magazine*, says, " A Welsh belief informs us that
a short time previously to the death of the owner of bees,
the bees themselves will die without any apparent cause."
Mr. Dyer does not fix the locality in Wales where this
superstition prevails. In some parts of Shropshire, we
know, it is the proper thing to do to go and tell the bees
when any death takes place in the family.

DAVID COX AT BETTWS-Y-COED.—On Sunday morning,
as regular as Sunday came, there was Mr. Cox's car to
take him and any friend to Llanrwst Church ; at that
time there was no nearer English service. He was a sincerely religious man, with no show, but great earnestness ;
in fact this earnestness was a great feature in his character
in all that he did, and so great was his influence that the
most roystering son of the brush that ever ventured from
Cockayne never attempted to dispute his dictum. The
desecration of the Sabbath was the only way of raising
his indignation ; he banished his favourite colour-box and
brushes totally, and dressed distinctly different on that
day. Some time in the summer of 1849 or 1850 several
gay young artists had come down to Bettws, and had put
up at the Royal Oak. In the exuberance of their spirits
they had amused themselves with painting some coarse
caricatures on the walls under the Lych Gate of the church,
exhibiting the parson thundering from the pulpit in an
undignified attitude, the clerk fast asleep below, and so
forth. This much offended Mr. Cox's sense of propriety
and decorum ; so one evening, soon afterwards, just at the
close of the day, he called for a lantern, and said, "I'm

going off to Bettws Church to-night." A young man, a
friend, who was present, said, "Why, what for, Mr. Cox?"
"Oh," he replied, "I'm going to wash off all those unseemly drawings." The young man volunteered to accompany him, and shortly after they sallied forth in the dark,
one carrying the lamp and the other a large basin of water.
When they arrived at the porch, Cox worked away in his
usual energetic style until he had removed every trace of
the offending sketches. Many a worse subject for a picture might be chosen than this earnest and venerable old
man, with his youthful companion, under the porch and
the yew-tree shade, engaged in their pious errand.—*Leisure
Hour.*

CAMBRIDGE LOCAL EXAMINATIONS.—By a detailed report
just published by the University, it appears that high
distinctions were obtained by candidates examined at the
Oswestry Centre, including the first places in English and
French, and the second place in Latin among the junior
candidates. Junior candidates (under 16)—Religious
knowledge : C. S. Fearenside, Oswestry Grammar School,
23rd ; A. V. Williams, Oswestry Grammar School, and
Miss A. M. Galbraith, (the Misses Jebb, Ellesmere),
bracketed 69th, out of 4,878 candidates, of whom 170 were
distinguished. English (literature, history, and geography) : C. S. Fearenside, Oswestry Grammar School,
1st out of 4,878 candidates, of whom 103 were distinguished.
Latin : C. S. Fearenside, 2nd, and T. Frank, Oswestry
Grammar School, 119th out of 2,556 candidates, of whom
143 were distinguished. French : Miss A. M. Galbraith,
(the Misses Jebb, Ellesmere), 1st ; C. S. Fearenside, 28th ;
and D. E. Jones, Ruabon Grammar School, 128th out of
4,168 candidates, of whom 250 were distinguished. Senior
candidates—Music : Miss A. T. Attfield (the Misses
Harriman, Shrewsbury), 25th out of 475 candidates, of
whom 79 were distinguished.

AN INTERESTING ANTIQUARIAN DISCOVERY
AT TOWYN.

Mr. Humphrey Williams, of Plas Edwards, near
Towyn, while searching for stone to repair a wall, came
across what appeared to him to be the remains of an old
house, on land belonging to the Marquess of Londonderry,
within a short distance of the railway station. After removing some of the soil he, however, discovered that there
was something in the character of the structure different
from that of ordinary dwelling-houses. His conjectures
were further confirmed by the discovery of a rough slab
stone with hieroglyphic carved upon it. There were also
found many pieces of unglazed earthenware, iron pot, a
three-handled goblet, and other antique articles.

The house has a southern aspect, and is about forty-five
feet long from east to west by eighteen feet broad from
south to north. The walls are built of stone and clay
firmly bound together ; the floors made of burnt clay and
ashes, perfectly hard and as well set and smooth as concrete floors of the present time. There are two fire places,
one against the south wall and the other against the west
end, but there is no trace of a chimney or of a window.
To the north of the structure is a curiously shaped building, which is supposed to have been used for cattle and
horses. The stone containing the hieroglyphic was sent to
the Secretary of the Archæological Society, which resulted
in the arrival at Towyn of an experienced antiquarian,
who was able to decipher the characters on one side of the
stone, which turned out to be a plan of the house. It
is supposed by some that the house is of the early Roman
period, but, from remains of several relics found in it,
it appears that the place must have been used in a
much later period. Several stones were found which

bear indications of having been used as tools, such as hammers and stampers. The tables used by those who inhabited this rude dwelling consisted of a block of masonry, made as on the top and built against the wall. In excavating the ruins of the house, some of the men at work drove their picks into what appeared to them to be human bones, they at once stopped working, and nothing would induce them to go on. Some of them went home and declared it was not their mission on earth to disturb the repose of those gone to their last rest. Others less under the influence of duty to the dead, were persuaded to continue the excavation, and it was found that they were not human bones but ox horns which had possibly been used as utensils for domestic purposes. It was difficult, however, to convince the workmen that the old inhabitants of the house had not gone to sleep in their abode on the shore, and that it was an unpardonable sin to disturb their homes. A Roman road runs along the coast of Cardigan Bay. Some of its remains have been found on Morfa Gwyllt also by Glanydon and Penllyn. It is about twenty-four feet wide, and made upon the same principle as Macadam made his roads in modern times.

Mr. Park Harrison and Mr. Richard Williams, Newtown, have taken a good deal of trouble and have gone to some expense in making the excavations. Some of the objects found, such as stone implements, and in particular the slate, with some very remarkable figures or designs engraved on it, appear to be of very great antiquity; others, including bits of pottery and iron, of a later, probably mediæval, date, while some appear to be not more than 250 years old. The difference of dates assigned to the relics found in the house is very puzzling.

So far as any conclusion has been come to, it is that the house was originally put up by Irish marauders or settlers in the fifth or sixth century. Some of the objects found, however, are such as may have belonged to a period before the Christian era.—*Cambrian News.*

MAY 18, 1881.

NOTES.

AN ENTERTAINMENT AT LLANFYLLIN.—The following is a copy of a bill of an entertainment held at Llanfyllin in the year 1800. The original was lent me by Mrs. Bibby of Brynaber, to whom I am indebted for a variety of interesting "bye-gone" matters for my note book.

     T.W.H.

TOWN-HALL, LLANFYLLIN.

By Desire of several of his Friends, whom it is his pleasure to oblige,

Mr. DAVIS

Takes the liberty of laying before them the following Entertainment for SATURDAY evening, November 1st, 1800, called The

EVENING BRUSH,

For rubbing off the Rust of Care,

Selected from the Works of G. A. Stephens, Collins, Dibdin, &c., with

Transparent Paintings of the Characters;
And a variety of SONGS by Miss SMITH.

In the Course of the Entertainment the following

COMIC SONGS

Will be introduced by Mr. Davis;

The Brush	The Medley of Lovers
Captain Wattle and Miss Roe	The Whirligig
The Seven Ages	The golden Days we now possess
The Medley of Beggars	Nobody, &c.

Front Seats, 2/-; Back Seats, 1/-
To begin at Seven o'Clock.

[Salter, Printer.

VARIETIES OF WEATHER.—The following records of the weather in Wales and the Border Counties have been preserved in divers annals. In 1590 there was a severe winter and hard frost 'till the middle of April. In 1592 St. Mary's steeple and other buildings in Shrewsbury were blown down. "People played football on Severne" in 1607. Great flood in Shrewsbury on Christmas day 1628, when ten men and women were drowned in Frankwell. The great frost and snow in 1634 brought down Coleham wall, which had been repaired in 1629, also part of the stone bridge, and all the wears on the Severn. On June 23, the same year, "a great storm of hail as big as walnutts fell at Shradon (Salop) and destroyed all ye corne." On Feb. 1736, there was the deepest snow in Wales the oldest people could remember. "A great frost from Christmas to March, 1739. At Shrewsbury a tent was erected on the Severn—a sheep roasted and a printing press set to work on the ice." Violent wind in Shrewsbury Feb. 1750 did great damage. In Sep. 1752 upwards of 10,000 sheep were said to have perished in Wales in consequence of the heavy rains. The year 1757 was noted for a very high wind in March which blew down more than a hundred chimneys in Chester, and did much damage in the country adjacent. The snow lay so deep in Shrewsbury for some days in Feb. 1766 that the price of provisions rose, from scarcity; butter sold at 15d. a lb. Great storms and disastrous floods in Cheshire, July, 1768. Flood in the Severn at Shrewsbury Nov. 1770 which rose two inches higher than the one of 1672 when a plate was affixed to a house to mark the rise. There was a sudden and extraordinary storm in Montgomeryshire in June, 1781, which caused a flood. All the bridges in the neighbourhood of Abermule were carried away, and a blacksmith's shop was destroyed, all but the chimney, at the top of which a boy clung 'till he was rescued. In Dec. 1795, the nest of a robin was found in the neighbourhood of Chester, with four eggs in it. On the longest day of 1795 the thermometer stood at 33½ deg. in Shrewsbury, and on the shortest day at 52 deg.! In Jan. 1796 carnations were in flower in the open air. On Dec. 2, 1796, the Severn at Shrewsbury, opposite the Quarry, was, after an exceedingly short frost, frozen over. The thermometer stood at 14 deg. below freezing point; "an event so early, unparalleled." At 4 o'clock in the morning of Dec. 28, 1798, the cold in Shrewsbury was so intense, that the thermometer in the open air stood at 30 deg. below the freezing point, and during the day rose no higher than to 11 on the graduated scale. At Coalbrook Dale the same day the thermometer was "4 deg. below 0, or 36 deg. below the freezing point." In Feb. 1799, the poor everywhere were employed to clear away the snow: no stage coaches ran in or out of Shrewsbury from the first to the fourth of that month. During the winter several people perished in the snow. The roads in Shropshire were impassable early in Nov., 1799, in consequence of floods. Intense frost on Jan. 1, 1800. The year 1800 ended so mild that apples were gathered at Whittington the day before Christmas Day; a frost then set in. There was a tremendous hurricane in Shropshire on Jan. 21, 1801; upwards of 100 trees were blown down at Hardwicke, near Ellesmere. On Nov. 28, 1804, there were 50 rose buds ready to bloom in the garden of Mr. Jones, Chilton Grove, near Shrewsbury; roses were also to be seen growing in the open air in some parts of Wales, and some specimens grown "amidst the Cambrian mountains" were sent for exhibition to Shrewsbury. We talk, when we have a sharp Christmas, of "Old fashioned winters," but these records will show that our forefathers enjoyed, or deplored —as the case may be, "all sorts of weather" just as we do!   J.?.R.

VOLUNTEER ARMY OF 1803-4 (Aug. 25, 1880)—War Office List of Officers for *Carnarvonshire*, Oct. 1804.

CARNARVON, BANGOR AND CONWAY.

Lt.-Col. Comm. : Ashton Smith—24 Dec., 1803.

Bangor.

Captain : John Roberts—7 Oct., 1803.
Lieutenants : Thomas Roberts, James Price—7 Oct. 1803.
Ensign : David Price—7 Oct., 1803.

Conway (Loyal).

Capt. Comm. : George Thomas Smith—7 Oct., 1803.
Captain : Robert Hamilton—7 Oct., 1803.
Lieutenants : William Jones, Samuel Read—7 Oct., 1803.
Ensigns : Edward Woodcock, Owen Roberts—7 Oct., 1803.
Adjutant : John Haslam—24 Dec., 1803.

CARNARVON (Loyal Mercantile).

Lt.-Col. Comm. : Thomas Ashton Smith—7 Oct., 1803.
Major : David Ellis—7 Oct., 1803.
Captains : William Williams, Owen Anthony Poole, Robert Roberts, John Jones, Hugh Ellis—7 Oct., 1803 ; John Haslam—10 Apr., 1804 (Adjutant).
Lieuts. : Zaccheus Jones, William Roberts, Robert Humphreys, Owen Lloyd, Robert Williams, William Robyns, Samuel Lloyd, William Oakes, Edward Roberts, Robert Romsey Williams—7 Oct., 1803.
Adjutant : John Haslam—7 Oct., 1803.
Quarter-Master : John Sharp—7 Oct., 1803.
Surgeon : Thomas Jones—7 Oct., 1803.

EIVIONYDD (Loyal).

Captain : William Williams—7 Oct., 1803.
Lieuts : Griffith Thomas, John Evans—7 Oct., 1803.
Ensign : Morris Jones—7 Oct., 1803.

NEWBOROUGH (Loyal).

Lt.-Col. Comm. : Thomas Lord Newborough—7 Oct., 1803.
Lt.-Col.: Wm. Glynn Griffith—11 Feb., 1804.
Major : Robert Thomas Carey—11 Feb., 1804.
Captains : Robert Currie, Robert Rous, Robert Griffith, John Ellis, Griffith Williams, Griffith Roberts, Hugh Rowlands—11 Feb., 1804.
Lieuts : Robert Griffith, William Pritchard, Richard Griffith, Ellis Williams, David Jones, Richard Griffith, Evan Hughes, Hugh Jones—11 Feb., 1804.
Ensigns : Hugh Thomas, Robert Edwards, Humphrey Owen, Hugh Jones, John Pritchard, Robert Jones.

LOYAL SNOWDON RANGERS (Riflemen).

Captain : Robert Williams, bart.—7 Oct., 1803.
First Lieut. : Robert Morris—7 Oct., 1803.
Second Lieut. : William Price Poole.

In a return published in 1806, the following is put down as the numerical strength of *Carnarvonshire* : Loyal Eivionydd Infantry, Capt. W. Williams, 104. Snowdon Rangers, Capt. Sir R. Williams, 83. Carnarvonshire, &c., Infantry, Lt.-Col. Smith, 562. Loyal Newborough Infantry, Lt.-Col. Lord Newborough, 590.   ED.

QUERIES.

BERRIEW.—Will anyone possessing a copy of the *Gentleman's Magazine* for July, 1800, kindly give the readers of *Bye-gones* a brief epitome of the article on Berriew which then appeared, accompanied by prints from sketches from one of the Parslow family ? C.J.D.

DR. BELL'S AMANUENSIS. — Mr. Southey, writing from Keswick, May 20, 1833, to John May, Esq., says :—"Dr. Bell's amanuensis (Davies) has arrived with the poor doctor's papers : he is established in lodgings at the bottom of the garden, and I go to him every morning at seven, and remain with him till nine, inspecting a mass of correspondence it will take several months to go through." In a letter to the Rev. John Warter, Oct. 1, 1835, Southey says :—" The first fine day in next week, Bertha, Kate, Karl, and I are to accompany the Lord High Snab to his estate, and there each of us is to plant a yew tree, which planting I am to celebrate in a poem." It is explained that "Lord High Snab" is a "playful appellation given to Dr. Bell's late amanuensis, Mr. Davies, who had lately purchased a small mountain farm, near Keswick, called High Snab." A further letter, to Cuthbert Southey, incidentally mentions that "Davies is in Shropshire," and on Nov. 10, 1836, Southey writes thus to Grosvenor C. Bedford, Esq :—

We left home on Monday, the 24th, crossed the Mersey, and got to Chester the next evening, and the next day reached Lord Kenyon's to dinner. Gredington (his house) is in Flintshire, not far from old Bangor, where the monks were massacred, and one of the small meres which are not uncommon in Cheshire, touches upon his grounds. The view is very splendid : Welsh mountains in the distance, stretching far and wide, and the fore and middle ground undulated and richly wooded. There we remained till Friday morning, and then posted to Sweeny Hall, near Oswestry, where Mr. Parker had a party to meet me at dinner. I called there on Davies' mother and his two sisters, who are just such women as the mother and sisters of so thoroughly worthy a man ought to be. The former lives in a comfortable cottage which he purchased for his father some years ago, the two others are married ; and the pleasure of seeing these good people, and of seeing with what delight they heard me talk of Davies, would have overpaid me for my journey.

In a note, attached to a History of Oswestry Old Chapel (*Shrop. Arch : Trans :* Vol. 4, p. 187) it is stated that Joseph Lancaster, the educational reformer, married Miss Jones of Whitehall, near Aston, Oswestry ; so was in some measure connected with the district. By Mr. Southey's letters it would appear that there was a remote connection between Lancaster's rival Dr. Bell, and Oswestry, in the fact that his secretary hailed from the neighbourhood. Who and what were these Davieses?   JARCO.

REPLIES.

A SHROPSHIRE MARTYR (Mar. 2, 1881).— Your valued correspondent "H. W. L." on Jan. 19, referred to one "Joanes" a Shropshire martyr in Elizabeth's time (1598). The authority he quotes– *Taylor's MS*, published in Vol. 3, of the S. A. S. T.—contains also the record of another Shropshire martyr ; in the time of Henry VIII (1546). His name is there written "Nychilas Otterdon" (called by other authorities "Belenian.") Both Joanes and Otterdon are described as "preasts," and the latter suffered with Anne Askew.   SCROBBES BYRIG.

THOMAS MINSHULL OF SHREWSBURY (Apr. 13, 1881).—In a *Hand Book of Topography* the late Mr. Hotton once published is given the following title of a book :—

Salopian Guide and Directory, History and description of the Town, alphabetical list of the Inhabitants, &c. 12mo. Engravings of Abbey Church, &c., by Parkes. Shrewsbury, 1804.

The author or compiler was "T. Minshull of Shrewsbury." The book is not mentioned in the late Mr. Mackenzie Walcott's "Sources of Salopian Topography," that appeared in Vol. 2 of the *Trans.* of the Shrop. Arch. Socy.   R.

SOUTHEY AND HEBER AT LLANGEDWYN.

In a very interesting paper contributed to the *Montgomeryshire Collections* the Vicar of Meifod describes a "Visit of Southey and Heber to Powysland." The two poets were guests at Llangedwyn Hall, when it was occupied by the Member for Montgomeryshire, the Rt. Hon. C. W. Williams Wynn. Mr. Thomas says that at the time Mr. Wynn was in the Cabinet, and suggests that the visit, as far as Heber was concerned, was not unconnected with his nomination to the See of Calcutta. As we shall see further on, the facts are against this statement. Southey and Mr. Wynn were intimate and life-long friends. They were schoolfellows together at Westminster, and in the poet's earlier years it was Mr. Wynn's generous aid which enabled him to pursue his literary career. For some time he received from Mr. Wynn an annuity of £160, which he relinquished on receiving a pension from the Crown. Their long and honourable connection with one another is recorded by Southey in the lines—

My earliest friend, whom I
Have ever, through all changes, found the same,
From boyhood to grey hairs,
In goodness, and in worth, and warmth of heart.

At the delightful retreat at Llangedwyn Southey and Heber, Mr. Thomas says, made their first acquaintance with Powysland; but here again we see some reason to differ with Mr. Thomas, as we shall show. In "An Ode on Bishop Heber's Portrait" (again quoted from below three or four times), the laureate refers to the visit :—

Ten years have held their course
Since last I looked upon
That living countenance,
When on Llangedwyn's terraces we paced
Together to and fro ;
Partaking there its hospitality,
We with its honoured master spent,
Well pleased, the social hours.

Mr. Thomas mentions two interesting incidents which he learnt from " the honoured master's" son, the present Mr. Charles Williams-Wynn.

" It was during this visit that Heber, after hearing the old Welsh air of ' Ar hyd y nos ' played upon the harp, and while the tune was still ringing in his ears, composed to its music his well-known Evening Hymn.

God, that madest earth and heaven,
Darkness and light ;
Who the day for toil has given,
For rest the night,
May Thine angel guards defend us,
Slumber sweet Thy mercy send us,
Holy dreams and hopes attend us,
This livelong night.

Guard us waking, guard us sleeping,
And when we die,
May we in Thy mighty keeping,
All peaceful lie ;
When the last dread call shall wake us,
Do not Thou, our God, forsake us,
But to reign in glory take us
With Thee on high.

And it was when accompanying Mr. Wynn to Meifod, when the latter was about to purchase the Humphreys property in that parish, that Southey extended his expedition to the ruins of Mathraval, and there, after careful investigation into the stories and legends of the place, collected (says Mr. Thomas) the materials for one of the chief scenes, if not for the whole scheme of his poem, entitled ' Madoc in Wales :'—

He came
Where Warnway rolls its waters underneath
Ancient Mathraval's venerable walls,
Cyveilioc's princely and paternal seat.

Few are the vestiges that remain of this once famous palace of the Princes of Powys—nothing to betoken its royal splendour. The lofty mound, first raised to guard the river ford, and afterwards converted into a keep, when the castle was erected on its bank ; the broken ground which shows roughly where the foundations of the building ran ; an angle of the walling upon which it is probable that a wooden superstructure was raised, and the deep foss which enclosed the whole space : these are all that remain, perhaps all that ever survived the disastrous fire on the 2nd of August, 1212, when King John set it ablaze, in order to check the victorious rising of Llewelyn ap Iorwerth, and the chieftains of Powys. Decay and silence have been its after portion, a strange contrast to that life and splendour of its earlier days, which the poet has re-awakened in those vivid lines :—

From Cyveilioc's hall
The voice of harp and song commingled came ;
It was that day the feast of victory there ;
Around the Chieftain's board the warriors sate ;
The sword and shield and helmet, on the wall
And round the pillars, were in peace hung up ;
And, as the flashes of the central fire
At fits arose, a dance of wavy light
Played o'er the reddening steel. The Chiefs, who late
So well had wielded in the work of war
Those weapons, sate around the board, to quaff
The beverage of the brave, and hear their fame.
Mathraval's Lord, the Poet and the Prince,
Cyveilioc stood before them, in his pride ;
His hands were on the harp, his eyes were clos'd,
His head, as if in reverence to receive
The inspiration, bent ; anon, he raised
His glowing countenance and brighter eye,
And swept with passionate hand the ringing harp.
Fill high the Hirlas Horn."

Mr. Thomas, singularly enough, gives no date to this memorable visit to Llangedwyn, but it is fixed by a letter in Southey's own hand as having taken place early in 1820. The letter is written from Shrewsbury, on the 25th of April and Southey says Mr. Wynn had kept him at Llangedwyn until that day that they might visit Pennant Melangell. Now Madoc was published in 1805 ; so that Southey could not have collected his materials in 1820, and his first visit must have been paid many years earlier, if, as seems almost certain, he saw the scenes he describes. Indeed we know from his own pen that he had travelled in Wales more than once, and the evidence that he visited Powysland is almost overwhelming. In the Preface to the Fifth Volume of his poems he says, " It was my wish, before Madoc could be considered as completed, to see more of Wales than I had yet seen. This I had some opportunity of doing in the summer of 1801, with my old friends and schoolfellows, Charles Wynn and Peter Elmsley." Can any of our readers give us any account of this early visit to Wales and probably to Llangedwyn ? Turning now to Heber and the See of Calcutta, it must be remembered that Mr. Wynn did not enter the Cabinet until 1822, and it was in the following year that Heber accepted the bishopric. Indeed, in the life of Heber we read that the See fell vacant towards the end of 1822, and that Mr. Wynn, then at the head of the Board of Control for India, wrote to Heber, who, after some hesitation, accepted the appointment. To return to Mr. Thomas's paper. One of the excursions from Llangedwyn was to Sycharth, in the adjoining parish of Llansilin—

Together then we traced
The grass-grown site, where armed feet once trod
The threshold of Glendower's embattled hall.

Of the ancient palace no traces are left, but the site is marked out by the enclosing foss, the outer ward, and the inner keep, and Iolo Goch, Glyndwr's domestic bard, gives a minute description of it.

"The palace, he tells us, was surrounded by a well filled moat, and was entered through a spacious gate, standing on a bridge. It had a tower of Irish type, that reminded him of the Cloisters at Westminster, with their vaults and arches, and gilded chancel. The basement (apparently of stone) comprised eighteen compartments, and above were four stories, raised on four firm and richly-carved pillars, each story being subdivided into eight sleeping chambers. The whole was covered with a shingle roof, and there were chimney stacks to carry off the smoke. In the rooms were wardrobes, stored with apparel, not unlike the shops in London. It had a church, too, quadrangular in form, with chapels richly glazed. Around the palace he enumerates an orchard and a vineyard, a park with deer, a rabbit warren, meadows, and cornfields, a mill, a pigeon-house, and a fish-pond, stocked with pike and gwyniaid, and here, in the poet's trysting place,

　　　　Yn Sycharth, buarth y beirdd,

was abundance of Shropshire ale and malt liquor."
The nearest house is still called Parc Sycharth, probably the old deer park, and not far off is Pentref-y-Cwn, which tells of the pack of staghounds. The present Pandy was in earlier times a corn mill, and the Rev. Walter Davies has identified the site of the fish ponds. Here, fifty years after Southey, came George Borrow, who has given us a spirited translation of Iolo Goch's poem, which Mr. Thomas reproduces.

Another excursion, in which Southey and Heber joined, was to the secluded but wildly beautiful valley of Pennant (thus described in ' Madoc ') :—

　　　Melangel's lonely church—
　Amid a grove of evergreens it stood,
　A garden and a grove, where every grave
　Was deck'd with flowers, or with unfading plants
　O'ergrown, sad rue and funeral rosemary.

There they

　　Saw the dark yews, majestic in decay,
　Which in their flourishing strength
　　Cyveilioc might have seen—
　Letter by letter traced the lines
　　On Iorwerth's fabled tomb :
　And curiously observed what vestiges
　　　Mouldering and mutilate
　Of Monacella's legend there are left."

Mr. Thomas gathers from the epithet "fabled" that Southey was misled by the legendary tradition (as given in Pennant's Tours) that it was the tomb of Iorwerth Drwyndwn, with whom he connects it in his Madoc :—

　His glancing eye fell on a monument
　Around whose base the rosemary droop'd down
　As yet not rooted well. Sculptured above
　A warrior lay ; the shield was on his arm,
　Madoc approach'd and saw the blazonry....
　A sudden chill ran through him—as he read—
　"Here Yorworth lies"...it was his brother's grave.

Mr. Thomas says the legend on the effigy " Hic Jacet Edwart," and the local tradition that the neighbouring Bwlch Croes Iorwerth took its name from a memorial cross marking the scene of Iorwerth Drwyndwn's fall, harmonize well with this idea. The blazonry on the shield, however, connects the tomb with another Iorwerth, Edward ap Madoc ap Rhirid Flaidd, lord of Penllyn ; and it is probable that what is called " the rude image of St. Monacel," is that of Gladus, his wife. But we find the following note to ' Madoc' correcting Gough's ' Camden,' where the tradition of Bwlch Croes Iorwerth is given :—
"Mr. Gough has certainly been mistaken concerning one of these monuments, if not both. What he supposed to be the Image of St. Monacel is the monumental stone of some female of distinction, the figure being recumbent, with the hands joined, and the feet resting upon some ani-

mal. And the letters which he read for Etward are plainly Et Mado." Mr. Thomas remarks "that no notice is recorded of the giant rib " still preserved within the porch ; but in the letter we have already mentioned—a rhyming one the poet addressed to Edith Mary Southey, he says—" They show a mammoth rib (was there ever such a fib ?) as belonging to the Saint Melangel. It was no use to wrangle, and tell the simple people, that if this had been her bone she must certainly have grown, to be three times as tall as the steeple." The Paper concludes with a legend mentioned by Southey, and never met with before by Mr. Thomas :—

"The old house alluded to is evidently, from his account of it, ' Llechweddgarth,' an ancient mansion of the Thomases, from whom it passed by marriage to the late Mr. Griffiths of Caerhun :—

　We 'together visited the ancient house
　　Which from the hill-top takes
　Its Cymric name euphonious : there to view,
　Though drawn by some rude limner inexpert,
　　The faded portrait of that lady fair,
　Beside whose corpse her husband watched,
　　And with perverted faith,
　　　Preposterously placed,
　Thought, obstinate in hopeless hope, to see
　　The beautiful dead, by miracle, revive.'

The legend is not mentioned in Mr. Hancock's parochial account in the Montgomeryshire Collections, 1878-9 ; and though I have made inquiries, I can hear of no such tradition now surviving in the parish. It does not, indeed, follow that the lady was an actual resident here ; and a similar story exists relating to a former lady at Newtown Hall. Perhaps the inquiry may lead to further information relative to the Pennant legend and clear up the mystery."

LOCAL LITERATURE.

Mr. Alexander Ellis, President of the Philological Society, who was recently elected an honorary member of of the Cymmrodorion Council has sent the latter a copy of a curious old hymn, "To the Virgin," written in the sixteenth century, with Welsh phonetic notes.

If anyone has a right to speak with authority on matters connected with Archery, it is Mr. J. Sharp, of the Shrewsbury Journal. He was the man of all England selected by Professor Baynes to write on the subject in the new edition of the Encyclopœdia Britannica, and by the honorary secretaries of some thirty or forty Toxophilite Societies (from the " Royal" downwards) he is acknowledged as the authorized recorder of their proceedings. With such credentials to back our opinion, we have much confidence, as well as much pleasure, in recommending to the notice of our readers Mr. Sharp's Archer's Register for 1881, a "year book of facts" and fancies concueeted with the pastime. The book is full of archery news, and also contains much that is interesting in archery literature. Messrs. Adnitt and Naunton of Shrewsbury are the publishers.

Mr. Edwin Poole, of the Brecon County Times, has reprinted, from the columns of that paper, a "History of the Breconshire Charities," which he has compiled from official returns, and other sources. In his preface the compiler states his belief that he has given "all that is known " on the subject ; but he is evidently open to conviction, for he adds that he " will be glad to receive further communications ; " but these, he expects to 'partake of details in connection with the charities he has catalogued rather than the record of any he has omitted." There is

5

only one possible objection we can offer to the Reprint—it is too cheap. The work is valuable to a select rather than a numerous class, and the publisher might just as well have charged half-a-crown for it as eighteen pence. It will soon be quoted at the higher price in old book catalogues!

A bare enumeration of the contents of the last number [Pt. 1, Vol. 14] of the *Montgomeryshire Collections* of the Powysland Club will show how varied are the papers published. The Rev. D. R. Thomas contributes a pleasant article on the connection of Heber and Southey with Powysland, chiefly in their friendly relations with the Right Hon. Charles W. Williams-Wynn. We quote from the article in another column. Mr. A. Howell continues his history of the land and waterways of Montgomeryshire; and Mr. Fewtrell concludes his Parochial History of Llanymynech. The Rev. Elias Owen contributes further specimens of Archaic Words—chiefly words derived from the Welsh—in use on the border; and Mr Richard Williams continues his lives of Montgomeryshire Worthies. Mr. Askew Roberts sketches the life of Old Parr, and repudiates the old ge theory. He also compiles from the new "Blue Book" a list of Montgomeryshire M.P.'s, pointing out where it varies from lists previously published. More valuable papers to antiquaries will also be found in the part; such as an account of the family of Jones of Chilton, by Mr. H. F. J. Vaughan, some notes on the pedigree of Sir W. Humfreys by the Rev. W. V. Lloyd, and a further chapter of materials for a history of Welshpool, by the hon. sec., Mr. Morris C. Jones. Even now our table of contents is not complete, but we shall probably hear more about the papers from some of our *Bye-gones* contributors. It would be unpardonable to omit mentioning that the part contains a very beautiful autotype from a sketch by Mrs. A. Howell, the subject being the Old Packhorse, Welshpool. Altogether this part strikes us as a model of what a publication of this sort should be, and Mr. M. C. Jones is to be cordially congratulated on his judicious and successful editing.

The first part of the fourth volume of *Y Cymmrodor* has been in our hands for some time, and ought to have been noticed before. It opens with a paper by Prince Louis Lucien Bonaparte (translated from the Italian by Dr. Isambard Owen) on "The Pronunciation of the Sassarese Dialect of Sardinia, and on various points of Resemblance which it presents with the Celtic Languages." The second paper, by Mr. Howel Lloyd, on "Welsh Books printed abroad in the 16th and 17th Centuries," will have a wider interest for our readers. Mr. Lloyd answers the question how it came to pass that Welsh books were printed in Italy and France, by giving an extract from the preface (signed R.S.) to Griffith Roberts's *Drych Cristionogawl (Christian Mirror).* One copy of the book, it seems, was sent from France to Wales in manuscript, and "after being wetted by the salt water, it obtained (as I heard) a cover around it, and was dried, and lovingly and eagerly cared for," read and heard read with gladness, and copied for distribution. "Then there grew up in my mind a great hope that many souls in Wales might be saved from falling into Hell, if there were a way to point out to them their spiritual perils. In reflecting on this, I could see no convenient and fruitful way, unless the book could be put into and published in print. Within the kingdom I could see no hope of obtaining either money or workmen, nor a fit and suitable place. By long reflection, and seeing the energy of the English faithful in printing English books on this side of the sea in foreign lands, I conceived it within reason that printers of France might be able to print Welsh as well

as English, the two tongues being equally strange to them. And in view of the great number of English books that have been published since Faith and Religion were corrupted in the Island of Britain, through the toil and industry of the Catholic English : on pain of shame and loss to all Welshmen, I saw it expedient and honourable to set forth and publish one Welsh book, whereof there was so much need, and the Welsh so eager to get books, and God having provided printers on the sea-side, ready for hire to print Welsh as well as English." Further on, the writer says, "We have got English letters for the work, and instead of the doubled D. and L., we have put dh. and lh., according to the manner of the old Welshifiers, which is a more proper thing than to double the letters." Griffith Roberts, according to one account, was confessor to Cardinal Borromeo at Milan; and of him and other Welshmen and their works, Mr. Lloyd has a good deal that is interesting to tell us. In the course of his paper he quotes Mr. Richard Williams in *Mont: Coll:* for an opinion that a book was printed in Montgomery as early as 1648 ; and the suggestion of a writer in *Bye-gones* that the imprint may be fictitious. This suggestion was made in the issue of Jan. 17, 1877. A fortnight later, Mr. Williams wrote himself in the same column to express very strong doubt on the matter, and Mr. Allnutt of the Bodleian Library proved pretty conclusively that the imprint was fictitious. An article on "Welsh Anthropology" by Professor Rudler will be welcome to antiquaries ; while "The Present and Future of Wales," by Mr. Lewis Morris, the poet, brings us back to our own more prosaic times. Amongst the other contents is a Welsh description of the Day of Judgment, from a manuscript in the British Museum, with an English translation ; and the part concludes with miscellaneous Notes and Queries. From one of them we regret to learn that the Rev. Silvan Evans has not yet succeeded in finding a publisher for his long-expected Welsh Dictionary.

The Council of the Cymmrodorion Society met on Wednesday afternoon at Lonsdale Chambers, Chancery-lane, Mr. Howel W. Lloyd, M.A., in the chair. Three new members were elected, and the Rev. W. Watkins, M.A., vicar of Llanover, was appointed a corresponding member for South Wales. It was determined to present M. Gaidoz, the editor of the *Revue Celtique*, and a contributor to *Bye-gones*, with a set of back numbers of the Society's publications. With reference to the late Mr. Edward Breese, also a former contributor to *Bye-gones*, the following resolution was ordered to be placed on the minutes :—"That an expression of the tender sympathy and condolence of the Council be conveyed to the family of Mr. Breese on the sad bereavement which they have sustained. The Council feel that in the death of Mr. Breese the Society has lost a member distinguished by amiability of deportment and high character, and adorned with not a few rare accomplishments. They would specially note his extensive achievements in the department of archæological research as claiming special commemoration at the hands of a Society like that of the Cymmrodorion." In relation to the death of the late Rev. Canon Williams, Rhydycroesau, and the loss Welsh literature thereby sustains, a record was made of the Council's regret at the sad event. The date of Mr. David Lewis's (of the South Wales circuit) lecture on "The Welshman in English Literature" was fixed for May the 26th. The first portion of the *Gododin*, as edited by the late Mr. Thomas Stephens of Merthyr, is now in the press. Notwithstanding the considerable labour devolving on the present editor in completing references, &c., it is anticipated that the part will be ready for issue to subscribers, as announced, in June.

CYMRU FU.

AN EISTEDDFOD OVER A HUNDRED YEARS AGO.

The following are the productions of an Eisteddfod which was held on Ascension Day, 1743, in a Public House at Glynceiriog :—

ADDRESSES BY THE BARDS WHO WERE PRESENT AT THE MEETING.

Eisteddwch ceisiwch eich cân—llu claear,
   Lle clywir ymddiddan ;
Gosodiad fel gwe sidan,
Cu, rwym glos, Cymru glân.
                HENRI PARRY.

Ai Hector neu flaenor iawn flys—yw Hari,
   O'i berwydd 'rwy'n drwblys ;
Y gwr uchaf a'r gair iachus,
Ddiwad o nwyf, a ddoi di'n is.
           SION AB EDWARD.

Cymdeithion dawn union di nag—swn afiaeth
   Sy'n yfed melyn-frag ;
Os yw'r fulen yn folwag,
Mae to brwyn ar y ty brag.   ARTHUR JONES.

Eisteddfod dda nôd ddi nag—yw hon
   A henwyd brun bynag :
Mae rhyw opiniwn yn y rhai penwag,
Gael tiwnio o'u bron yn y ty brag.
             SION PARRY.

Trafaeliais ni fethais i fawr—yn ifanc
   Iawn afiaeth sy ddirfawr ;
'Rwy'n naturiol, er tair awr,
Was da o lwydd i eiste' i lawr.
            PETER JONES.

One of the subjects was "Ascension Day."

Dydd perffaith, mwynwaith Emanuel,—a chyfion
   Dderchafiad oen Israel ;
Am nawdd iach i'r Nefoedd nehel,
Ei gywir Sant a agorai'r sêl.   SION PARRY.

Dderchafel, ddydd uchel iach,—Icsu
   O isod fyd afiach ;
Ne' glaerwen yn eglurach,
A ranwyd byth i'r enaid bach.
            ARTHUR JONES.

Dydd Iau dyrchafu'n dra chyfion—oen Icsu
   O 'nysoedd Iddewon ;
A'i ddiddig friwedig fron,
Erchyllwaith, yn archollion.   SION EDWARD.

Dydd Jupiter, llawnder wellhâd,—Icsu gwyn,
   Esgynodd o gariad ;
Ar law gre' dehe' ei dad,
Mi wn, yn eiste' mae'n wastad.   PETER JONES.

Canwn a seiniwn yn siwr—Dderchafael,
   A chofio'n Pryniawdwr ;
Sydd yn eiste', gore' gwr,
Duw da lwydd a dadleuwr.   HARI AB HARI.

The chief subject for competition was "Glyn Ceiriog Valley."

Eiste' mewn gole'n y Glyn—le cynar
   Ail Canaan o ddyffryn ;
Cerddoriaeth cywir ddirwyn,
Brith iawn gae y brethyn gwyn.

Glyn dolydd a Glyn deiliog—Glyn hylwydd,
   Glyn haela'. Glyn heulog ;
Glyn cu arwydd, Glyn Ceiriog,
Glyn orau llwydd, Glyn aur y llog.
            ARTHUR JONES.

Glyn Ceiriog, luosog le—Glyn coediog,
   Glyn cadarn gynheddfe ;
Glyn nerthol a glân wrthie,
Noddiad y gân, o nyddiad gwe.
           PETER JONES.

Dyffrynlwys glân ciwrus Glyn Ceiriog—llwyn adar,
   Lle nodir cerdd blethog ;
Lle cynar, glaear glog,
Gloew aberoedd gwlybyrog.
           SION AB EDWARD.

Glyn Ceiriog luosog lwysedd—lle cynar.
   Lle cynwys gwir fawredd ;
Bri gwenith a bro Gwynedd,
Gorau man am gwrw a medd.   SION PARRY.

The adjudicator of the Eisteddfod was John Prys, Philomath, of Bryn Eglwys-in-Yale, a composer and publisher of Welsh Almanacks. He addressed the chair bard, Arthur Jones, Gyldini, near Moelfre Pool, who also was parish clerk of Llangadwaladr, with the following impromptu :—

   Arthur heb wâd yw athro'r beirdd,
      Gan hwn y cawn gynghanedd cerdd ;
   Dowch blant yn bendant i'r bwrdd,
      I godi hwn i'w Gadair hardd.

It is related that Arthur Jones was taken very ill as he was returning home from Oswestry market, and that he died the same night at Gyldini. Jonathan Hughes the poet speaks very highly of him as a

   "Gwladwr doeth, gwiw lediwr dysg."

Harri Parry, the second bard, was a native of Craig-y-Gath, Llanfihangel, and died in very narrow circumstances at Llanfyllin, aged ninety years, and was buried at Llanfihangel. He was a great enemy to the Quakers, who had a chapel at Dolobran, Meifod.

The celebrated Gwallter Mechain composed the following pathetic and descriptive englynion in commemoration of poor Harri :—

   Yma, ddu oera ddaiaren—mae nyth
      Mwyn ieithydd dysgywen ;
   "Harri bach," nid hir ei ben,
      A'i ddiniwaid ddawn awen.

   A'i wefusau a'i fysedd—dilafar,
      Dylifai cynghanedd ;
   Yna deuai yn y diwedd
      Englyn cain mal glain mewn gwledd.

   A'i ni wnai anglod—i feirddion
      O fawr-ddysg fyfyrdod ;
   Ei ddull yn gwau clymau clod,
      Hir a fydd yn rhyfeddod.

   Clera'n fynycha' a wuai—yn benllwyd,
      Heb unlle na roddai ;
   Carolion ceinion canai
      A'i lais mwyn fel Eos Mai.

The third bard was John Edwards of Glynceiriog, a translator of the "Pilgrim's Progress" into Welsh. He was great grandfather to the late Rev. Abel Jones, Baptist Minister, Merthyr.

The fourth bard was John Parry of Corwen, who was very intimate with Doctor Edward Samuel of Llangar, who composed the biography of the celebrated Huw Morus, Pontymeibion.

The fifth bard, Peter Jones, thirteen years of age, who composed englynion as well as the best at the eisteddfod, was the son of Arthur Jones, the parish clerk. He enlisted in the army, and nothing was heard of him afterwards.   LLYWARCH HEN.

NOTES.

THE FIRST SHREWSBURY NEWSPAPER.

The first newspaper printed in Shrewsbury appears to have been a small fly-sheet, not much larger than an ordinary half-foolscap, of two pages only, having the following title and imprint :—

"A Collection of all the material news."

"Printed and sold by Thomas Jones at his house in Hill's Lane (?), near Mardol. Price 1d."

The number which I saw bore the date "16[-]1"; there was an erasure of the figure, here indicated within brackets. I had an impression that the whole date was tampered with ; and according to a note written by some hand, this seventeenth century date was false, and that it was printed in "1704." The following news paragraph which it gave may serve to help out its date—"His Grace the Duke of Marlborough is gone to Woodstock to give his last instructions about building his palace, being to go immediately to Holland on the French army's moving on the Rhine." It is some years since it came under my observation, and I recollect that I was under the impression that this was the first issue ; and having no note made of any "No." on it, I still retain that impression. The news it contained, if my memory serves me correctly, were merely gleanings from London papers, rather than local news. Perhaps some of your readers can give fuller particulars, with perhaps more of its meagre contents.

T. W. HANCOCK.

THE OLD WELSH ALMANACKS.
(May 11, 1881.)

For the four years, 1820—1823, there were *five* issues, and within the covers I find the following lines :—

1821—Cadwed Duw ni os gwel e'n dda,
    Na ddel i'n plith na haint na'r plâ.

Er ini ofni terfysg, i'n mysg mewn garwaf wedd,
Os gwelir gwell disgwyliad, i'n bwriad wrth ein bodd ;
Gochelwn rhag i n pechod, i ddwyn rhyw gawod gerth,
Rhag ofn i'n hamser ddarfod, heb wybod am ei werth.

Er cael ein bygwth beunydd a llawer cerydd llym,
Gochelwn fod yn aros ryw achos mawr ei rym ;
Duw'n ddiau biau'n bywyd, gall synud drygfyd draw,
Ac attal yn arbedol ei ddialeddol law.

In the first issue for 1822 are these verses on—"Enwau y Deuddeng Arwydd :"—

Dosperthir cyfseryddiad sy'n rhediad cylch yr haul,
Bu'r hen Seryddion dwysgu i'w drefnu drwy fawr draul,
Mae'r enwau'n adnabyddus, yn drefnus iawn eu drych,
Gosodiad trefn y *Sidydd*, wrth ddeuddeg arwydd Gwych.

Y lle mae'r Haul disgleirwyn y Gwanwyn yn ei g'wrdd
Yw'r *Tarw* a'r *Gefsilliaid*, a'u rhediad gyda'r *Hwrdd ;*
Mae'n arwydd a thueddrwydd i'n gwneud yn ddedwydd iawn,
Sef cynydd diadelloedd, ar diroedd, oreu dawn.

Yr Haul i'r *Crange* sydd etto i fyn'd drwyddo, 'nol y drefn,
Pan ele'r hirddydd heibio, a chilio'n ol drachefn ;
Y *Forwyn* sy'n dwyn bendith, a'i hysgub wenith wiw,
Yn awydd o'r cynhaua, i drefnu bara i'r byw.

Y *Fantol* ydyw'r nesaf, mi dd'wedaf yn ddi os,
Mae'n dangos hyd cyfartal anwadal dydd a nos;
A hithau'r *Sarph* dwyllodrus, arswydus, arw ei sail,
Arwydda hin wenwynig adwythig cwppiad dail.

Y nawfed ydyw'r *Saethydd*, was celfydd, megis cawr,
Sy'n dangos tymp helwriaeth, gan gael gorfodaeth fawr,
A'r *Afr*, wrth ddringo'r gelltydd, yw'r arwydd uniawn r'ol,
O'r haul, pan fo'r dydd byra, yn awr dyrchafa 'n ol.

Y *Dyfrwr* ydyw'r nesaf, annheccaf, yn fy nhyb,
Dyuoda hwn ddyfodiad i'n gwlad y tymor gwlyb :—
Arddangos pryd pysgotta, 'mhob parthau mae y *Pysg*,
A dyna'r cyfseryddiad, ar dd'wediad gwyr o ddysg.

In the *second* issue for the same year (1822) there are only these lines :—

Er ini dreulio'r bywyd yn ynfyd ac yn iach,
Rhaid myn'd yn wael ein hagwedd, i'r bedd 'mhen gronyn bach,
. Am hynny, dwys ystyriwn, mai fel y byddwn byw,
Y cawn ein barnu hefyd â dedryd gyfiawn Duw.

In my next I will give the title pages themselves.

E.G.S.

MONTGOMERYSHIRE WEIGHTS AND MEASURES.—Davies's *Agricultural Survey of North Wales* gives the following information connected with the old local weights and measures of this county :—" A cylindrical vessel containing twenty quarts is called a *hoop*, two of such hoops make a strike or measure, and two strikes or measures make a bushel of eighty quarts, equal to a Denbighshire *hobed*. A bushel of oats in Welshpool is seven hoops, or half strikes heaped ; a bushel of malt is nine-tenths of the corn-measure." I copy the foregoing from a note to paper on Welshpool, in *Mont : Coll ;* p. 203. V. 14.   NEMO.

STONE-WORSHIP.—No superstition has been more general among savage races everywhere than the Fetichism which considers that almost any natural object, certain stones especially, may be the temporary or permanent abode of the spirit which it worships. Till recently on the West coast of Ireland peasants have been known to keep smooth round stones carefully wrapped in flannel, which were from time to time exposed to the adoration of the faithful of that "cultus." There are pretty clear indications that such Fetichism was the religion of the unconverted among the Cymry and Gael as late as the 6th or 7th century. (Skene's *Celtic Scotland* II. 112 et passim). At St. David's was a celebrated stone called "Llechlafar" or the speaking stone, "of whose name, size and quality we have treated in our Prophetic History" says Giraldus. (*Itin.* II. 7.) When Henry II. visited that holy place an old Welsh woman whose complaint was not at once attended to by the King on the spot, appealed to the stone, "vindicate us this day, Lechlafar, revenge us and the nation in this man !" At Llanllyfni, in Carnarvonshire, there was a stone, part of the church or churchyard wall, I forget which, that used to be called "Y garreg atteb o'r mur"=the stone that answers from the wall.   CYNWYL.

QUERIES.

D'ISRAELI AT SHREWSBURY.—On the occasion of the election at Shrewsbury in 1841, I remember that Mr. D'Israeli did not arrive in time to address a meeting at which it had been announced he would speak. This non-appearance gave rise to an election song, set to the tune of "The Misletoe Bough", the refrain to each verse being "O where, O where is the wonderful boy." Could any one contribute a copy of this song?   ELGO.

AN OSWESTRY GUILD.—It is a fact not generally known that there was formerly at least one Trade Guild in Oswestry, viz., the *Corvisors Company.* I have before me the original book in which the rules are recorded, and entries made, as early as 1587. A local society of three centuries ago is deserving a fuller record than a stray paragraph now and then in *Bye-gones,* so I purpose putting the manuscript at the disposal of the *Shropshire Archæological Society.* Meanwhile I give your readers the benefit of a specimen of the contents :—

Memorandum that upon the eighteenth day of June in the first year of our Solvraign Lord King James the 2d, by the Grace of God, of England, Scotland, france, and Ireland, defender of the faith, &c., being Corpus Christi day, Agreed then by the consent of the wardens, four sitters, with the maior parte of the Company of Cord-wainors alias Corvisors that at ye Special Request of Nicholas Jones an Ancient freeman of the aforesaid Company and in consideration of his Voluntary oath and Attestation before the abovesaid two wardens four sitters the maior parte of the Company That his son ffranciss Jones hath duely and truely served him as an apprentice for the compleat term of Seaven years and upward They the above said wardens and four sitters with the maior parte of the aforesaid Company doe Allow of the said Nicholas Jones his oath & doe admitt of his son as free-man and Coebrother of the Company of Corvizors Anno Dom. 1685

Signed by

William Piggott	
The marke of	} Wardens.
John IP. Parrey	
Edward Jones	
John Muccleston	
Richard Lloyd	} fower sitors.
The marke of	
John IT. Twisingham	

The last name occurs in an entry of 1691 as "John Tussingham," but there was no rule as to spelling of names—of persons or places—in those days. The book contains names of Oswestry residents unknown to this generation, such as Longman, Michiner, Calthorpe, Tom-kins, Boodle, Blodwell, Moody, Bromhead, Boulton. Baynes, &c., all of which appear in the eighteenth century; and under date 1746 I find an "Edward Pain" a warden. Is there any connection between the "Pains" of the present day and the "Paynes" whose tokens have been mentioned in *Bye-gones* as being current coin in Oswestry at the end of the seventeenth century?

                                        JARCO.

REPLIES.

NEW WALES (April 6, 1881).—Pennsylvania be-came very early a city of refuge whereunto Welsh Friends fled for very life's sake. The first Governor of Pennsylvania was Thomas Lloyd of Dolobran near Meivod,Montgomery-shire,he having removed thence soon after its settlement as a province, and was of great service to that State in its infant days. Having joined William Penn in the settle-ment of Pennsylvania,Thomas Lloyd drew after him to the banks of the Delaware the persecuted Friends of his native land. Hence we find the Thomas Owenses,the Lloyds, the Ellises,of Montgomeryshire and Merioneth, numerously re-presented there,whilst the familiar names of their old Cymric homes are perpetuated in the names of flourishing stations on the Pennsylvania Rail road. The Governor Lloyd's resting place in the south west corner of the Friends'burial ground, Philadelphia, became a sacred and dear spot to Welsh Friends,and many a persecuted Merionethshire and Montgomeryshire Quaker found quiet and rest near the grave of their trusted and true friend, Thomas Lloyd of Dolobran.   FRIEND.

THE POOR CURATE OF FORD (April 27, 1881). Poor curates do not usually indulge in the risks of authorship, but I presume the pamphlet paid or we should not find Mr. Matthews rushing into print again within a few months of his first publication. I have be-fore me "Serio-comic observations on the Hoax and Humbug of Planetary Influence and Judicial Astrology, &c." This was published by Messrs. Eddowes of Shrews-bury in 1801, and on the title page bears as the name of its author "James Matthews, M.A., Curate of Ford, Salop,

and author of Thoughts on Scarcity lately published." In the course of the pamphlet he again styles himself "The Poor Curate of Ford," and the object of the work is to show up the folly of paying any attention to the hierogly-phics of *Moore's Almanack*. At the date of writing, as your readers are aware, the nation was in a twitter about Napoleon and his meditated descent on our shores. Old Moore of course framed his predictions to suit the popular feeling and some of Mr. Matthews's friends seem to have been so much alarmed, that he published the little book before me, in the form of a letter to one of them, and by being alternately grave and gay, lively and severe, sought to show up the astrologers to the satisfaction of the most timid. The gist of his argument is that astrologers assign to certain planets power over persons and things, and have so monopolized every part of the human frame and every mineral, that now that a new planet [Uranus, discovered 1781] has made its appearance, they, having no use for it, " have shuffled it out of the pack!" The hieroglyphic for 1801 that moves the parson to write represented "John Bull prostrate on the cold earth: his tongue most barbarously cut out; his once comely legs and graceful horns now cruelly knocked off; his noble back most ignominiously stamped with those execrable *fleurs de lis*; and the poor cows in the back ground lifting up their mournful heads to heaven, and moaning his departure." The imaginary "friend" to whom the pamphlet-letter is supposed to be written, is addressed as "one of those whose *faith* is gigantic, and whose *reason* is yet in swaddling clothes." The author thinks he has a right to affirm this, because he has heard him "solemnly declare his firm belief in every syllable of *Milton's Paradise Lost*: a book, most sublime in sentiment, improbable in incident, and surely, in-credible in subject—*War in heaven*!" The "Poor Curate of Ford" was evidently a character. The copy of his little book in my possession once belonged to Mr. Pidgeon of Shrewsbury, and contains some MS. corrections in the author's autograph.   N.W.S.

CURRENT NOTES.

The *Athenæum* of May 21, in recording the meeting of the Society of Antiquaries of the 12th, says :—"Mr. J. P. Harrison exhibited a piece of slate, with scratchings on it, and other remains from Towyn, in Merionethshire. Mr. Harrison had persuaded himself that the scratchings in question were representations of arms, celts, hatchets, baskets, tunics, and other articles." Our readers will remember that we published something about this dis-covery on May 11th.

The following are the heights above the level of the sea, according to the official measurements of the Ordnance Survey now being made in Shropshire, of the undermen-tioned hills :—Brown Clee (Abdon), 1,778ft. ; Stiperstones, 1,759ft. ; Titterstone Clee, 1,754ft. ; Longmynd, 1,679ft. The heights of the neighbouring hills in Wales are :—Corn-don (Montgomeryshire), 1,685ft. ; Radnor Forest, 2,166ft. ; Black Mountain, 2,136ft. It is stated that the ships at Liverpool are clearly distinguishable from the top of the Brown Clee, whilst they can be seen also from scaffolding raised on the top of the Wrekin.

We are told in the newspapers this week, that "Mrs. Mollie Utz, of New Albany, Ind., a little over a year ago noticed a numbness in her fingers. Since then her hands and arms nearly to the elbows have become appa-rently solid bone. Her physicians say that ossification will continue until some vital part is reached, when death will ensue. A case somewhat of the same nature (accord-ing to the *Gents: Mag :*) occurred at Shrewsbury in 1806.

On the 17 May that year died, at the age of 44, the Rev. John W. Harrison, M.A., Rector of St. Clement's, Shrewsbury (sic) and a Minor Canon of Worcester. "He had suffered for years from pains in the head, and in compliance with his wish Mr. Cole made an examination after death, and found the membranes that surrounded and divided the brain ossified ; from which it was deemed almost miraculous that Mr. Harrison lived so long."

Mr. Charles Hanmer of Rhyl has issued the following notice to about two hundred landowners in Flintshire, claiming rent for the land they hold in the manor of Englefield :—"I, the undersigned, Charles James Hanmer, of Rhyl, in the parish of Rhuddlan, in the county of Flint, this 27th day of April, do hereby give you notice that I, being Lord of the Manor of Englefield, am entitled to the fee simple of the soil and materials of and under the whole of this said lordship of Englefield, in the county of Flint, and do hereby claim from and after the above date the rent heretofore paid by you to any person whom you acknowledged to be the owner heretofore."

SHREWSBURY SCHOOL.—The medal which is annually given by the Earl of Powis for the best poem in Latin hexameter verse, composed by an undergraduate in the University of Cambridge, who has resided not less than two terms, has (as we stated last week) t is year been awarded to Mr. J. C. Moss, Scholar of St. John's College, and late a pupil at Shrewsbury School, and younger brother of the Head Master. The subject of the poem is "Colonia Agrippina."

MONMOUTHSHIRE.—In the House of Commons on Thursday Mr. Hussey Vivian asked the Attorney-General whether the definition "Wales" in an Act of Parliament would be legally held to include Monmouthshire. The Attorney-General had no difficulty in answering the question in the negative. The Reform and Boundary Act had treated the Monmouthshire boroughs as being boroughs in England. He was afraid that the hon. member must give up all hope of claiming Monmouthshire as a Welsh county. Lady Llanover writes to the Daily News to urge that Monmouthshire should be included in the operation of the Sunday Closing Bill for Wales. "The county of Monmouth is, in fact, one of the thirteen counties of Wales, and a clerical blunder has been the cause of a fiction having been gradually impressed on the minds of the public, the continuation of which has often given rise to an absolute absurdity, which, however ludicrous in itself, is now likely to entail serious consequences." Lady Llanover enters into an historical statement to show that Monmouthshire is part of Wales and was accidentally excluded from it by Henry VIII.

SIMNEL CAKES.—Confound simnel cake ! The allusion to it last week has brought upon us an enormous number of letters, one of which I now quote :—"Tell your correspondent that 'simnel bread' was the finest form of white bread eaten by the 'upper crust' (as bread should be) of the thirteenth and fourteenth centuries, when it was likewise called 'pain demayn,' or bread of our Lord, from the figure of our Saviour or the Virgin which was stamped upon the loaf. Add further that 'simnel cakes' are to this day made at Shrewsbury and other places thereabouts for Lent and Easter—being raised cakes with a crust made of fine flour and water, with saffron enough to give it a rich yellow colour, and the inside stuffed with the makings of a rich plum cake, candid lemon-peel ad lib., &c. Make very stiff, tie in a cloth, boil for several hours, then brush over with egg, and bake. The crust is as hard as wood when quite ready. The biggest cost as much as half a guinea or a guinea. And Herrick has an epigram which shews that at Gloucester, century

seventeenth, the young people made presents to their mammas of 'simnel cakes' on Mid-Lent ('Mothering') Sunday. Some say they are called after the father of Lambert Simnel the Pretender, in that being a baker he invented them ; and then that an old pair called Simon and Nelly, being of a saving turn, fell to making a cake out of their scraps at the end of Lent. They began with the unleavened dough, and threw in the remains of an old plum pudding. Then Sim proposed to boil and Nell to bake it. Then they went in at each other with the broom and the stool, and had a free fight, which ended in a compromise, viz., that the cake should be boiled first and baked afterwards. So they set on the big pot, and broke up the broom and stool for fuel, and shied some eggs, which they had smashed in the row, over the outside to give it a shine. And when it was done they called it a Simnell cake."
—World.

ST. JOHN'S CHURCH TOWER, CHESTER.—Mr. John Douglas, architect, of Chester, has reported to a Committee upon the condition of the tower and porch of St. John's Church, Chester. His report states that in his opinion any restoration of the existing ruin is impossible ; he adds that the belfry stage of the tower has shown symptoms of cracking during the last few days, and this, unfortunately, in the corner of the buttress which overhangs the church. In order to prevent possible disaster to the latter, the committee have, under his advice, reluctantly given orders that the upper portion of the tower should be taken down without delay ; this will accordingly be done as far as the belfry floor. The work of removing the debris has been commenced, and many interesting stones of a date older than the tower have been discovered amongst it. The porch wall which remains is so far shaken that it must be taken down, and the porch entirely rebuilt. The committee have some hope that the bells can be rehung in that portion of the tower which they may be able to preserve. The committee also hope shortly to issue a definite appeal for funds to enable them to complete the work entrusted to them in a satisfactory manner. The cost of rebuilding the porch and placing everything in a satisfactory state of repair will necessitate a considerable sum.

PROPOSED REVISION OF THE WELSH NEW TESTAMENT.

On May 17 the revised version of the New Testament in English was presented in Convocation. In the Lower House of Convocation on the 18th a petition was presented on behalf of the Welsh-speaking people of Great Britain, urging that steps should be taken to obtain a revision of the Welsh Scriptures. On the same day Chancellor Briscoe gave notice that on an early day he would move "That the Bishops of Bangor, St. Asaph, St. David's, and Llandaff be requested to consider whether it be desirable that the Welsh New Testament should be revised according to the text adopted by the revisers of the English New Testament, and, if it be considered by them desirable and practicable, to adopt measures for carrying such a revision into effect." A gravamen was on the same occasion brought forward by Rev. D. Walter Thomas (Bangor), which was carried up by the prolocutor to the Upper House on the following day. In response to an address from Welsh members attending Convocation to the four Welsh bishops, their lordships received a deputation of the same in the Bishops' Robing-room, House f Lords, on Friday the 20th, the Bishop of Bangor in the chair. The subject was fully and ably introduced by Chancellor Briscoe, seconded by the Dean of Bangor, and supported by other members of the deputation. The Bishop of Llandaff said a letter had been addressed to him on the subject by the syndics and delegates of the University presses both of Oxford and Cambridge, requesting his advice as to the expediency of undertaking a new version of the Welsh Testament. In consequence, there had been a conference of Welsh bishops that morning with a deputation of the Welsh clergy, and the following resolution was passed :—"At a meeting of the Welsh bishops and the deputation appointed for the purpose of bringing before them the question of the desirableness of revising the Welsh version of the New Testament, it was resolved, on the motion of the Bishop of Llandaff, seconded by the Bishop of St. Asaph, ' that a committee be appointed for the purpose of considering the expediency of undertaking a revision of the Welsh version of the New Testament according to the text adopted in the revision of the English version, and that they report to the Welsh bishops on this matter as soon as they can after due consideration, stating at the same time the grounds upon which their opinion is founded.'" In accordance with this resolution, the members of the deputation subsequently met, and appointed the following committee, as representing the several dioceses :—For Bangor : The Dean, Chancellor Briscoe, D. Walter Thomas, vicar, St. Ann s, Proctor. For St. Asaph : Canon Wynne Edwards, Canon Richardson, D, R. Thomas, vicar, Meifod, Proctor. For St. David's : Archdeacon North, Canon D. Williams, vicar, Llanelly ; Joseph Hughes, vicar, Cwmdu. For Landaff : Archdeacon Griffiths, Canon Powell Jones, vicar, Llantrisant ; John Griffiths, rector of Merthyr. The committee will meet on an early day, and it is expected that the report will be in the hands of the Welsh bishops in the course of three weeks or a month. The Rev. D. R. Thomas, Meifod Vicarage, Welshpool, will act as secretary pro tem., and will receive communications on the subject, which will be treated on the principles and method of the English version.

JUNE 1, 1881.

NOTES.

ROBERT OWEN.—In a second-hand copy of " The Life of Robert Owen written by himself " (1857) there is the following presentation inscription, apparently in the handwriting of the author :—"Presented to His Excellency the Saxon Ambassador to Great Britain, by the Author, who has written these works with a view to open a new Book of Life to Man, and a greatly superior Existence to the Human Race. Sevenoaks Park, Sevenoaks, 20th April, 1858."

DICK SPOT.—In Bye-gones for Mar. 27, 1878, a memoir of this local celebrity was quoted, which gave an account of his death in 1793, and burial at Oswestry. According to that account he died in his bed, and surrounded by friends ; but in the little book by the "Poor Curate of Ford," which was published in 1801 (see Bye-gones, May 25,) there is the following passage :—

A Shropshire conjuror, vulgarly called Dick Spot, could do great matters—tell a wench her fortune; when she was to be married ; whether the young one would be boy or girl ; discover a stray sheep ; or a stolen cock ; and all by the *planets* : yet, with all this great knowledge into futurity, his hap was to die in a ditch.—Poor Dicky ! I sincerely wish the Doctor a better fate ; but the knowing ones are sometimes taken in.

By " the Doctor " Mr. Matthews means the compiler of " Moore's Almanack :"—the object of his pamphlet being to shew up its astrological absurdities. His illustration respecting Dick Spot seems to have been unfortunate ; and if true, it was scarcely one to prove his case. Astrology may be true, and yet its professors sometimes die in ditches !   N.W.S.

ROODDEE.—Is not this name a corruption of Rhyd-ddu—the ford of the Ddu or Dee?   ELGO.

QUAKERS IN WALES.—I shall be much indebted for information as to the members of the Society of Friends formerly existing in the neighbourhood of Llwyngwril. Is the body now extinct ? Where are the records of the members to be found ?   NEWO.

THE WELSH FLANNEL TRADE.—I gather from the newspapers of 1839 that during the autumn of that year the Flannel Market was removed from Newtown and Llanidloes to Shrewsbury ; the first market in the latter town being held on the 15 Oct. Are we to understand that the Welsh towns voluntarily transferred their market to the Shropshire capital ?   H.B.

REPLIES.

Y GOFITTY (May 4, 1881).—May not this be a corruption of Gofid-dy, or Ty-'r-gofid, (i.e.) the house of trouble ?   F.S.A.
Brecon.

SEVENTEENTH CENTURY TOKENS (May 11, 1881).—The initial letters upon the tokens are those of the issuers and their wives, it being the custom when the issuer was married to join his wife's initials with his own. I have a few hundred examples in which all the initials are so placed.   LANDWOR.

Doubtless the middle letter in the initials mentioned represented the better half of the tradesmen, who in those primitive times materially assisted in the business of the shop. If TELL is a married man he will probably see the same plan adopted on his silver spoons !   TOLD.

The third initial letter on the field of the 17th Century tokens is that of the wife of the issuer, and the initial of the surname is generally placed over those of the christian names of the issuer and his wife, thus—

M.
W. L.

as on No. 2 of my Shropshire list, but for convenience of printing the initials are placed in line.
                                   JAMES W. LLOYD.

VOLUNTEER ARMY OF 1803-4 (May 18, 1881).—In addition to the Oswestry Rangers (Cavalry), and the Oswestry Artillery ; there was a local troop connected with the county infantry commanded by Mr. John Kynaston-Powell. The latter afterwards were formed into a militia company. When I first remember them the local captains were the Hon. Thomas Kenyon of Pradoe, and Mr. Parker of Sweeney. Mr. John Croxon was also an officer. The band met opposite the Wynnstay Arms on Sunday evenings, and then marched to Maesyllan, but I don't remember to which of the companies the band belonged.

The names of the players, as far as I remember them, were as follows :—Mr. Eyeley, painter, First Clarionet ; William Hughes, shoemaker, second ditto ; Samuel Jones, painter, ditto ditto ; Mr. Edwards, Unicorn, French Horn ; Henry Evans, bricklayer, Horn ; George Roe, hatter, Serpent ; Thomas Cureton, shoemaker, Bassoon ; Thomas Cash, slater, Tambourine ; William Roberts, cooper, Cymbals ; John Temkies, Big Drum ; Benjamin Rogers (" Ben Starch,") Trumpeter ; Thomas Thomas and Alec. Gilmore, Fifers ; Richard Hughes, Drummer.

The companies met on week days, sometimes in Maesyllan, sometimes in Greenfields. John Jones of Croeswylan was Sergeant in the Artillery, under Captain Bradbridge. The captain belonged to Llanymynech, and some years after I heard of some of his family being in Liverpool. This company assembled by the Coach and Dogs, and their field was called Fox's Croft, and was situated behind the Barley Mow in Salop Road.

There were also two other sergeants connected with one or other of the companies, whom I very well remember—Samuel Mitchener, shoemaker, Willow Street (who was leader of the singing in the Old Chapel), and John Lloyd, bricklayer. There were also Pioneers belonging to one of the companies; I remember two—Dick Burnett and Ned Richards, Whittington.　　　　W. Thomas.

Penylan Lane, Oswestry.

[There were three Croxons connected with the local companies in 1803, as officers, viz., Richard, John, and Edward. We have before us the list of officers of Colonel Kynaston-Powell's county company, under date of Oct. 1804, and the name of Mr. Parker does not appear in it, so he must have joined later. In 1802 he was major of the Brimtree Loyal Legion, a Shropshire Corps, which included Shifnal, near to which town Mr. Parker then resided. We have no evidence of the fact, but, as the "Brimtree" does not figure in the List of 1804, it is probable the corps was disbanded after the Peace of 1802.—Ed.]

LORD HILL'S SWORD (Mar. 17, 1880.)—*Sir J. B. Williams's Banquet.*—The following Jeu d' Esprit followed this event :—

(*For the Salopian Journal.*)

Blame not my muse, should she essay
To weave an unambitious lay,
　A lofty theme to sing,
To celebrate a festival
Late held within the new Town Hall,
　Oh, 'twas a splendid thing !

Bold is th' attempt, yet I would fain,
Since other poets still refrain,
　Tell feast and feasters o'er :
And first and foremost in the Chair,
The worthy and lamented Mayor,
　Who fills that place no more.

And he not Mayor alone, but Knight,
In all his new-born honours bright,
　Receiv'd the Corporation
With dignified and courtly grace,
Befitting both the time and place
　And his exalted station.

His was the feast—he gave the feed,
Fish, flesh, and fowl, and all, indeed,
　That throng'd the loaded table ;
And Mrs. Peters, of the Crown,
She roasted, boil'd, and stew'd them down,
　As well as she was able.

The Mayor's own cellar wine supplied,
Both port, and white, and what beside ?
　Why, only think—Champagne !
Pray *Chronic'e* th' astounding fact,
The guests not once the liquor lack'd,
　Nor ever call'd in vain.

Some ne'er had drank Champagne before,
And swallow'd glasses half a score,
　Altho' 'twas not in ice,
Omissions could not matter then,
For Shrewsbury Common Council men
　Were never over nice.

Twas pleasant to behold the Mayor
Presiding o'er the viands rare,
　With triumph all elate ;
A real Lord, too, by his side,
No wonder that he felt much pride
　In such a novel state.

The Queen, and usual toasts being o'er,
The Mayor arose, amid the roar
　Of cheering loud and hearty,
And said, " No language can express
" My boundless joy and happiness
　" At heading such a party ;—

" Your hearts, I'm sure, respond to mine,
" Pledge then each man his glass of wine,
　" And fill up to the brim :—
" We drink our County's boast and pride,
" The Noble Hero at my side,
　" Long life and health to him ! !

" A humble individual I,
" Yet think how great my destiny,
　" For I in Courts have been :
" And I, who now before you stand,
" At my *illustrious friend's* command
　" Have knelt before the Queen !

" The Royal Sussex saw in me
" Claims that no other man could see
　" That I should be advanced ;
" And when the facts I shall have shown
" Of how 'twas done, you all will own
　" The honour much enhanc'd :

" For as in rev'rence due and meet,
" I knelt at our young Sov'reign's feet,
　" And scarcely dar'd to breathe,
" Oh, think what soft ecstatic thrill
" O'erpower'd me when I saw Lord Hill
　" His shining blade unsheathe :

" Yes, hear, my friends ! the wond'rous truth,
" And tell it to your rising youth,
　" And spread it forth to fame ! —
" The sword that gleam'd at Waterloo
" O'er this poor breast the Hero drew,
　" To give me Knightly name !

" No wonder I was overpower'd,
" When honours such as these were shower'd
　" On my unworthy head :
" Think what distinction on me shone,
" I went plain 'Squire—came back Sir John
　" What lustre's o'er me spread !"

Long had the silence been unbroken,
The Mayor, *benighted*, would have spoken,
　But sounds of approbation
Arose so vehement and strong,
He could not possibly prolong
　His eloquent oration.

My Lord gave thanks, and pledg'd Sir John,
Who much in civic worth had shone,
　And still would shine as Knight ;
And many years he hop'd would bear
The honours all acknowledg'd there
　As spotless and as bright.

Another Knight they toasted then,
One of our Warrior race of men,
　Who said, as thanks he gave,
Still was he at his country's call
For battle, or for banquet hall,
　Like all men truly brave.

　　*　　*　　*　　*　　*

Next came the worshipful Recorder,
Promoter of good will and order,
　With just and due applause,
Who hop'd, with very slight evasion,
To try them ne'er to have occasion
　For any breach of laws.

But time forbids that I should write
All that was done that festive night
　In honour of their host :
How quick the gen'rous wine was pour'd,
How some grew bright, and some were floor'd,
　As toast succeeded toast.

The hours sped fast, my Lord retir'd,
So did the Mayor, but first desir'd
  Cooper the chair to take,
Which till had disappeared the swipes,
The wine, the spirits, and the pipes,
  He'd doubtless ne'er forsake.

Unworthy do I own my song
To celebrate the feast and throng
  That grac'd the joyous scene,
But I have sung, and Watton said,
And when the two accounts you've read
  You'll wish you there had been.

                          ANON.

JUNE 8, 1881.

NOTES.

LIMITED ARITHMETIC.—Competent authorities have maintained that Welshmen have much aptitude in Mathematics—natives of Carmarthenshire, according to the late Principal of Jesus College, Oxford being specially distinguished. If so extremes meet. Some 20 years ago there lived at Brunant in this county a servant man who could count no higher than five. Any greater number than this he could only indicate indefinitely. It is well known that many savage races cannot count beyond five. The aborigines of Australia can only say "one, two, three, great many." We know that both in the human and animal stock there is an occasional instance of nature harking back to some primitive and forgotten type, and perhaps the faithful old servant of Brunant was such.
                      CYNWYL.

PARLIAMENT OF ENGLAND (Apr. 20, 1881). *Montgomeryshire*, County and Borough. The first named under each date was the representative of the County, and the other of the Borough :—

1541-2	Jacobus Leche, armiger.	Willielmus Herbert
1552-3	Edwardus Herbert, armiger.	Ricardus Herbert, generosus
1553	Ditto.	Johannes ap Edmunde, generosus.
1554	Ditto.	Riccardus Lloyd, generosus.
1557	Ditto.	Willielmus Herbert, sen., armiger.
1558-9	Edward Herbert, Esq.	John Man, Esq.
1562-3	Ditto.	John Price, Esq.
1572	John Price, Esq., of New Town.	Rowland Pugh, Esq.
1584	Richard Harbert, gent. of Montgomery.	Richard Harbert, gent. of Gray's Inn.
1586	Oliver Lloid, Esq.	Matthew Harbert, gent.
1588-9	Edward Herberte, Esq.	Rowland Pughe, Esq.
1592-3	Reginald Williams, Esq.	Richard Morgan, gent.
1597	William Herbert, Esq.	Thomas Jucks, Esq.
1601	Edward Herberte, Esq.	John Harries, Esq.
1603-4	No Returns found. (1)	
1614	No Returns found. (2)	
1620-1	Sir William Herbert, Knight of the Bath.	Edward Herbert, Esq.
1623-4	Ditto.	George Herbert, gent.
1625	Sir William Herberte, Knt.	George Herberte, Esq.
1625-6	Ditto.	Sir Henry Herbert, Knt.
1627-8	Ditto.	Richard Lloyd, gent.
1640	Edward Herbert, Esq.	Sir Richard Lloyd, Knt.

(1) A List compiled by Mr. E. R. Morris in *Mont : Coll:* Vol. 2, supplies this blank with the names of Sir William Herbert, Knight, and Edward Whittingham. This list differs in two or three instances with the official one we quote.
(2) Sir W. Herbert, Knight, and Edward Herbert *(Ibid)*
5

1640	Sir John Price, bart.	Richard Herbert, Esq. of Montgomery.
		Edward Vaughan, Esq. (3) George Devereux, Esq. (4)
1654	Sir .... bart.	Charles .... (5)
1656	No returns found (6)	
1658-9	No returns found (7)	
1660	John Purcell, Esq.	[Thom]as Myddleton, Esq.
1661	Edward Vaughan (8).	John Purcell, Esq.
1678-9	Edward Vaughan, Esq.	Matthew Price, Esq. (9)
1679	Ditto	Matthew Price, Esq.
1680-1	Ditto	Matthew Price, Esq.
1685	Ditto	William Williams, Esq.
1688-9	Edward Vaughan, Esq., of Llandiarth *(sic.)*, county Montgomery. Charles Herbert, Esq., of Aston.	
1689-90	Ditto.	Ditto. (10)
1695	Ditto.	Price Devereux, Esq,
1698	Ditto.	Ditto.
1700-1	Ditto.	John Vaughan, Esq.
1701	Ditto.	Ditto.
1702	Ditto.	Ditto. (11)

           (To be continued.)

QUERIES.

TROSPON.—How has this village of Osbaston, near Oswestry, come to be corrupted into "Tross-pun," and do educated people, when they speak of Osbaston, place the accent on the first or second syllable? Are there any other names of places in the Oswestry district contracted or corrupted?   NEMO.

PRISON BASE.—In these days of Cricket and Football we scarcely hear of the old games of our boyhood; and one has just been revived in my memory by the perusal of a paragraph in the *Oswestry Herald* of Sep. 19, 1820, to the effect that on the 12th of the preceding month "a Game of Prison Base was played between the young men of Overton and those of Hanmer, which was decided in favour of the former; they gaining eleven ticks, while the Hanmer men gained only five." Lord Kenyon awarded Two pounds to the winners. "Prison Bars" or "Prisoners Base" was a popular school game when I was a boy, but this is the only instance I have met with of a match being played between rival villages. Was this at all a usual practice?   JARCO.

ST. ALKMOND'S GHOST.—Who was Mr. Joseph Williams, the author of "a Visionary Poem" called *St. Alkmond's Ghost*? We are led to believe in a collected edition of his works (published after his death, by T. Wood, Shrewsbury) that, under the signature of "Clio," his productions became so favourably known that

(3) This was the "Long Parliament." Vaughan was elected vice Price "disabled to sit."
(4) Devereux was elected for the Borough vice Herbert "disabled to sit."
(5) In this case the official Return is torn. *Mont: Coll:* gives Sir John Price and Charles Lloyd.
(6) Hugh Price and Charles Lloyd *(Ibid)*
(7) Edward Vaughan and Charles Lloyd *(Ibid)*
(8) Andrew Newport, Esq., on the decease of Vaughan, was elected 25 Oct. 1661.
(9) Double return of the same date; that by which Edward Lloyd, Esq., was returned, was declared void by order of the House, dated Apr. 1, 1679. (Commons Journals.)
(10) Price Devereux, Esq., of Vaynor, elected 18 Nov. 1691, vice Ch. Herbert, deceased.
(11) Up to this date the member is described as representing "Montgomery Borough." He is now member for "Montgomery, Llanidloes, Pool, and Llanfylling *(sic)* Borough."
                34

it was anticipated the collection would "deserve to be added to the productions of our other celebrated English Poets," therefore the little book was "printed in the Size of *Mr. Bell's British Poets*," and was "intended as a Volume to be added to that Work." That is. of course, "intended" by the friends of the deceased. Where did "Clio" make his mark as a poet? The date of the collected pieces is 1786, but it is stated in the preface that some of them had been previously published, and one is dated as early as 1774. The volume is introduced by an "Elegiac Poem" on the death of the author, by "E. T.," Salop, Sept. 28, 1785." Who was he? And to revert to the "Poem" that gives a heading to my query; was it written as a compliment or as a satire on the Rev. Mr. De Courcey? What is its history? R.D.

REPLIES.

D'ISRAELI AT SHREWSBURY (May 25, 1881). I cannot answer ELGO's query, but I would inform him that he would have violently to distort the air of the 'Misletoe Bough," to fit in the "refrain" he quotes! MUSICIANER.

DR. BELL'S AMANUENSIS (May 18, 1881).— There are three or four sons of the daughters of Mr. Davies, "Dr. Bell's Amanuensis" and the friend of Southey, residing in the parish of Oswestry. Mr. T. Owen, bookseller, is one, and Mr. T. Roberts, Cambrian House, another. OSWALD.

REMARKABLE TREES (May 11, 1881).—The last vol. of the *Collections* of the Powysland Club refers, on page 426, to the oak tree in Glyn Valley, and gives some dimensions of Montgomeryshire oaks that formerly grew in Vaynor Park, of still greater size. Of 26 trees cut down between the years 1793 and 1796, the smallest contained 1,018 feet of timber and ,the largest 2,501 feet. *Mont: Coll:* also stated that there is still a growing oak tree in Powis Castle Park measuring 24 feet in circumference three feet from the ground; at the height of about thirty feet it divides into three branches, each of which is of the size of a large tree. M.P.C.

SEVENTEENTH CENTURY TOKENS (June 1, 1881).—The following notes relate to Oswestry :—

No. 48. Hugh Edwards, shoemaker, is named as a Town Councillor of Oswestry in the Charter of Charles II., dated 1673.

No. 50. Phillip Ellis, mercer, was elected a Town Councillor of Oswestry in 1681. He was probably the tradesman who issued the token, for it is usual, even to the present day, for mercers to be also grocers and tobacconists. He was Mayor in 1686.

No. 52. There was a Richard Payne, Alderman of Oswestry, who was Mayor in 1721, and died in 1747; and others of the same family who seem to have been leading tradesmen. One was a glover.

No. 55. Arther Ward was one of seven witnesses (including the two bailiffs of the town) to the declaration of Mr. Payne on his re-appointment as Head Master of Oswestry School in 1660. JARCO.

[We should be glad to send a copy of the List of Shropshire Tokens we published in *Bye-gones* to any party who would take the trouble to glean any information about the Tradesmen who issued them. Eventually we hope to see the list, and a goodly number of notes, published in the *Transactions* of the Shrop : Arch : Society.—ED.]

CHURCH LEWN AT OSWESTRY (May 11, 1881).—"Lowns and Taxes" is a proverbial expression amongst the illiterate on the Welsh border; and when I was a child at Llandysilio the former was usually the

term applied to the "allowance" made by the parish to paupers. 'Lowance we called ,it; a word easily further curtailed into Lowns! R.M.

Miss Jackson in her work on "Shropshire Archaic and Provincial Words" derives "Lewu" from *Anglo Saxon*, loen, a loan, and defines it to be a church-rate, but I think it was also applied to poor and other parochial assessments, it is a word common very recently in Mont. gomeryshire, and doubtless is yet used. BOOKWORM.

I have heard this word applied in this County so as to represent a layer—such as the quantity of straw put on a stack as thatching—that is so much as a man does at one time from bottom to top of stack. "John! come to dinner." "I will, as soon as I finish this Lewn." MONTGOMERY.

CAMBRIAN INSTITUTIONS (Nov. 10, 1880).— At the annual meeting of the *Gwyneddigion*, held in London on Dec. 11, 1820, Mr. Parry, editor of the "Welsh Melodies," presided, and there was much singing after dinner. "The Great Master of the Mimic Art, *Munden*, kept the table in a roar with his inimitable comic singing. On re-. turning thanks after his health had been given, he observed, 'I love the Welsh, for generally speaking, they are good and loyal subjects—besides, I have passed many of my youthful days in Chester, and on the borders of the Principality, where I always experienced the greatest kindness and friendship.'"

Welsh Manuscript Society. From a paragraph I have seen in the papers of May 1838, I should imagine that this Society was formed about that time; under the title of "Society for the Publication of Ancient Welsh Manuscripts." Its object was the transcribing and printing of Bardic and Historical remains, still extant in the Principality and other parts of the world, and so save from decay matter of interest and importance in a literary point of view. It was stated that an attempt had been made to form the Society in 1837, with King William the Fourth as patron, but his Majesty's death delayed proceedings. The Queen consented to become patron. The foundation stone of the *Royal Institution of South Wales* was laid in Swansea on the 24 Aug.,|1838, by L. W. Dilwyn, |Esq., F.R.S., at the command of the Queen. The building was for the purposes of a Philosophical and Literary Institution. In a cavity of the stone the two annual reports of the Society were deposited. CYMRO.

JUNE 15, 1881.

NOTES.

SHREWSBURY SCHOOL.—*Playing at Soldiers.* In 1803, when every other man you met was either a real or an amateur soldier, we can readily believe that the rising generation caught the infection. Boys have always been Jingoes. In the papers we are told that, with the approbation of Dr. Butler, the young gentlemen of Shrewsbury School formed themselves into two companies; the "Dismounted Cavalry," under the command of Captain Evans; and the "Infantry," under Captain Gilby. Colours were presented to these juvenile companies—with much ceremony—on Sep. 26, 1803; Miss Evans, a young Warwickshire lady, made the presentation to,the cavalry, and Miss Kynnersley to the infantry. The Cornet and the Ensign who, respectively, received the colours from their Captains, were sons of W. Oakeley, Esq., of Tanybwlch, and Valentine Vickers, Esq., of Cranmere. I presume these youthful heroes were never gazetted, for their names and their companies, are not mentioned in the War Office list published twelve months later. J.?.R.

THE REV. PETER ROBERTS.—Southey, no
doubt through his close intimacy with Mr. Charles
Williams Wynn, had a pretty good knowledge of the
merits of Welsh literary men, and in a letter to his friend,
dated July 22, 1819, he thus refers to the death of the
author of Price's *History of Oswestry* :—

Peter Roberts is a great loss. I begin to despair of ever seeing
more of the Mabinogion. And yet if some competent Welshman
could be found to edit it carefully, with as literal a version as
possible, I am sure it might be made worth his while by a subscription, printing a small edition at a high price, perhaps 200,
at £5 5s. I myself would gladly subscribe at that price per
volume for such an edition of the whole of your genuine remains
in prose and verse. Till some such collection is made, the
"gentlemen of Wales" ought to be prohibited from wearing a
leek ; aye, and interdicted from toasted cheese also. Your bards
would have met with better usage if they had been Scotchmen.

Some interesting details connected with the Rev. Peter
Roberts' connection with Oswestry will be found in *Bye-
gones* Sep. 1, 1880.   N.W.S.

NONCONFORMITY IN SHROPSHIRE.—*Ruyton-of-the-Eleven-Towns.* In a little book on *Congregationalism in Shropshire*, compiled by the Rev. D. D.
Evans of Bridgnorth in 1872, it is stated that "a chapel
was built and a minister was settled" at this place in
1833. Amongst the Old Chapel papers in Oswestry, of
Dr. Williams's time, there is the following :—

SHROPSHIRE.

At the General Quarter Sessions of the Peace of our Sovereign
Lord the King held at the Guildhall in Shrewsbury in and for
the county of Salop on Tuesday in the week next after the
Translation of Saint Thomas the Martyr to wit the twelfth day
of July in the twenty-fifth year of the Reign of our Sovereign
Lord George the third by the Grace of God of Great Britain
France and Ireland King Defender of the Faith and so forth
and in the Year of our Lord one thousand seven hundred and
eighty-five Before Edward Pemberton, John Gardner, John
Kynaston Esquires and others theire Fellow Justices assigned
to keep the Peace in the County aforesaid and also to hear and
determine divers Felonies Trespasses and other Misdemeanours
in the same County done and Committed.

ROBERT MORE Esquire Sheriff

Ordered that the Dwelling House of Richard Richards at
Ruyton in this County be recorded as a place of religious Wor-
ship for his Majesty's Protestant subjects dissenting from the
Church of England and it is hereby ordered accordingly.

By the Court
J. LOXDALE, D.G.C.P.

This refers, I presume, to Ruyton-of-the-Eleven-Towns?
The other places in the county with similar names are
spelt Ryton.   JARCO.

QUERIES.

FOLK LORE.—DUCKS.—Ducks hatched in May
turn on their backs and die. So one of my servants says,
who is a native of Cardiganshire. Is this a common
superstition?   T. H. ROATH.

BAILEY CLOCK, OSWESTRY. — I believe
Cathrall does not mention it, but I have often been told,
in my younger days, that the first clock placed on what is
now the Powis Hall, was presented to the town by Mr.
Charles Stanton, the lessee of the theatre. A clock existed
as early as 1815, when Price's History was published, but
in those days the theatre was situated in Lower Brook-
street. Was Mr. Stanton connected with that one? The
Theatre in Willow-st. was opened Sep. 27, 1819, by Mr.
Stanton's company. What is the date of the original
clock?   FITZALAN.

SHROPSHIRE HOUSES IN LONDON.—Are
there any Shropshire Houses of Entertainment in
London now-a-days? Years ago there were three or four

either kept by Shropshire men, or cultivating the support
of Salopians. There was one not far from the Waterloo
railway station, kept by Mr. Price, who hailed from St.
Martins, near Oswestry ; and another also kept by a Mr.
Price, in Villier St., Strand. I believe he was related to
the Salter family of Oswestry. Dolly's Chop House in
P. N. Row, too, was once managed by an Oswestrian, one
of the Howell family. Probably other Shropshire towns
were equally favoured.   OLD OSWESTRY.

A DENBIGHSHIRE WORTHY.—The *Salopian
Journal* of Sep. 28, 1796, records the death of the Rev.
GEORGE HAMPTON, A.M., a native of Wrexham, who died
at the age of 79, on the 22nd of September of that year.
The *Journal* says, "Mr. Hampton took his degree in the
University of Glasgow. He was at the head of a Dissenting Congregation at Banbury for 56 years, where he did
honour to the character of the scholar, the gentleman, and
the divine. He distinguished himself by a Treatise in
support of the Doctrine of the Atonement, in opposition
to the late Dr. Taylor, and in later years to Dr. Priestley,
who acknowledged him amongst the most candid of his
opponents. He was respected by all who knew him ; by
the clergy of all denominations, and by none more than by
those of the Establishment, some of whom have borne
testimony to his candour, by reading in the same desk, and
preaching from the same pulpit, for the last six years of
his life, during the rebuilding of the parish church."
Hampton is not a usual name in Wrexham ; but from the
foregoing we may assume that 160 years ago there was a
family of the name residing there. Are any descendants
still living there?   PURITAN.

REPLIES.

SHROPSHIRE SCHOOLS (Apr. 27, 1881.)—The
Salopian Journal of Dec. 23, 1839, states that the Rev. Wilson
Evans, Senior Fellow and late Tutor of Trin. Coll., Camb.,
has placed at the disposal of Dr. Kennedy, Head Master
of *Shrewsbury* School, a Prize of Twenty Guineas, "for
the best Latin Elegiac composition on the following subject :—*Desiderium Samuelis Episcopi Lichfieldiensis.*" Mr.
Evans was the rector of Tarvin, and had been examining
chaplain to the late Bishop of Lichfield. He was himself
an "old boy" of the Shrewsbury School.
SCROBBES BYRIG.

REMARKABLE TREES (June 8, 1881.)—In
your last number a correspondent quotes a record
of some huge oak trees cut down in Vaynor Park
between 1793 and 1796, varying from 1,018 to one, measuring no less than 2,501 feet. This is not the first occasion
that I have heard of this record ; but the dimensions are
so startling that I should be much obliged if any of your
correspondents could inform me of an oak tree now standing in any part of the kingdom which is computed by competent judges to contain 1,500 feet of timber. The
largest oaks I believe to be in Windsor Park, Bagot's
Park in Staffordshire, Thoresby Park (part of old
Sherwood Forest), where the oaks were reported in the
reign of Charles the 2nd, to be too much decayed for use in
the Royal Navy, and in Stoneleigh Park in Warwickshire. The finest specimens of sound timber are probably
in the last-named ; but I do not believe that in any one
of these parks is there an oak tree measuring anything
near 1,500 feet of timber.   A DOUBTER.

SHROPSHIRE BORDER WORDS (Jan. 12,
1881).—Has the word "Twayke" ever been recorded? It
is often used on the Montgomeryshire side of Oswestry,
and signifies "to sponge." "O yo bin cum twayking again
bin'ne?" Another word of the same district I have re-

cently heard, I refer to "Oss," meaning progress, get on. "How does your new servant oss?" "Yore trees dunna oss like ourn, they binna getting on; perhaps yome coulder than we bin." Mr. Hartshorne does not record these words, and Miss Jackson has not yet arrived at them. I note, too, that Mr. Hartshorne omits "Tan-dowy," a word signifying a loutish, mealy-mouthed, oily, and somewhat sycophantish fellow.   R.P.M.

[Mr. Halliwell gives "Oss" as a Cheshire word, signifying "to help," and Mr. Hamer in his glossary of words in use at Llanidloes (*Mont. Coll*,, vol. 10, p. 300), says the word is there used as "to start on a journey." When a person leaves home he will say, "I am going to oss now." Mr. Hamer thinks the word is derived from the Welsh *osio*—to offer to do, to essay.—ED.]

CURRENT NOTES.

In an address at the recent Conference of the Monmouthshire Baptist Association, held at Ebbw Vale, the Rev. J. A. Jones of Blaenau, said—"The Welsh Bible deserves a few words from us. Its history can be briefly told. The pioneer in the work of translation was the immortal W. Salesbury, a layman, who may be said to be both the Wickliffe and Tyndal of Wales. He published the Gospels and Epistles in 1551, and the entire New Testament in 1567. He was assisted by Dr. R. Davies of St. David's, and the Rev. T. Huet. Dr. Morgan of St. Asaph published a translation of the whole Bible in 1588, and was assisted by Dr. J. Davies of Mallwyd, Dr. D. Powell of Ruabon, and probably by a few others. Dr. R. Parry of St. Asaph published a revised edition of this Bible in 1620. This is the present Welsh Bible, and occupies the same position as King James's version does in England. It is a singular fact that all these men were natives of Denbighshire, except Dr. Morgan, who was a native of the neighbouring county of Carnarvon; and Thomas Huet, whose native place is not known. The Welsh version occupies a position very similar in all respects to the English. It is the greatest Welsh classic, and the standard of modern Welsh."

ANTIQUITIES AT TOWYN.—On page 233 of *Bye-gones* will be found an account of a so-called antiquarian discovery at Towyn, which the *Athenæum* (as will be seen on page 244) has since questioned. The same paper of May 28 contains a letter from Mr. J. Park Harrison, stating that the slate tablet in question, and which is covered with figures, was found nearly two years ago, and that, when shown at the meeting of the Society of Antiquaries at Burlington House a few weeks back, there were but few present competent to report on the subject, and it met with scant attention. He states that the slate was to be submitted to a meeting of the Royal Archæological Institution. At the meeting of the Archæological Institute on the 2nd of June Mr. J. Park Harrison read a paper "On Incised Figures upon Slate and other Remains from Towyn, Merionethshire." The incised slate was sent to the author for examination and exhibition by Mr. R. Williams, of Celynog, Newtown, who obtained possession of it in the autumn of last year. The figures upon it were conclusively shown to be engraved, and not to be mere surface markings, and it was evident to the meeting that they had a meaning, and were of great interest. Mr. Harrison believed that the work was Irish, and he showed from the writings of Sir W. Wilde and Sullivan, who minutely describe the dress and arms of the ancient Irish, that the figures on the slate were very similar in form, the resemblance of some of the outlines to Irish axes being very marked. To the same meeting Mr. Harrison sent a collection of antiquities, some as late as the seventeenth century, from Towyn.

THE REV D. R. THOMAS OF MEIFOD.—We are glad to hear that the Bishop of St. Asaph has conferred the non-residentiary canonry in St. Asaph Cathedral, vacant through the death of Canon Williams, of Rhydycroesau, upon the Rev. D. R. Thomas, Vicar of Meifod, in recognition of his well-known work, "The History of the Diocese of St. Asaph." The Society of Antiquaries have also recently elected Mr. Thomas a Fellow of their body.

DEATH OF MR. L. R. MORGAN.—The death is announced, after a lingering illness, at Rhyl, of Mr. Lewis Richards Morgan, High Bailiff of the North-Wales circuit of County Courts. The deceased was in his 48th year. He was a man widely known. The office of high bailiff, worth about £700 a year, dies out, and, according to a recent Act, the duties and fees pass to the various registrars in the North Wales district.

WILL OF THE LATE BARON HANMER.—The will (dated August 7, 1879) of the Right Hon. John, Baron Hanmer, late of Bettisfield Park, Flintshire, who died on March 8 last at Knotley Hall, Leigh, Kent, was proved on the 13th May by the Hon. George Thomas Kenyon, and the Rev. Henry Hanmer, the brother, the executors, the personal estate being sworn under £35,000. The testator, in addition to all other provision made for her by settlement or otherwise, leaves to his wife £1,000, and his house in Eaton-place, with the furniture and effects, and an annuity of £1,000 for life; at her death he gives his books, pictures, furniture, peer's robes, journals of the House of Lords, and patent as a baron to the person who succeeds to the mansion house of Bettisfield Park; to his executors, £500 each; and the residue of the personalty to his brother Wyndham Edward Hanmer; all his real estate in the parish of St. Giles he devises to the said Rev. Henry Hanmer; and the residue of his real estate is directed to be settled so that it is entailed on the lineal issue of his late father, Lieutenant-Colonel Thomas Hanmer.

AN INFANT'S EPITAPH.

Mr. Francis Turner Palgrave has written the following graceful epitaph, which is inscribed on the tomb of Violet, the infant daughter of Sir Robert and Lady Cunliffe in Wrexham Cemetery :—

Roses are for summer,
Violets bloom in spring,
Prophesying gladness
For the year they bring ;
But this July Violet
Coming out of date,
In her baby spring-time
Left us desolate.

Thou wast more to us, love,
More than words can tell ;
All our happy sunshine
Went with one farewell.
Only this can comfort ;
Safe from earthly harms,
Christ the Saviour holds thee
In His loving arms.

Spring eternal round Him
Flowers ever fair :—
Will His mercy set us
All beside thee there ?
Will her kisses greet us
At the golden gate ?
—Wait a little, darling !
We must also wait.

REVISION OF THE WELSH NEW TESTAMENT.

(From the *Oswestry Advertizer*, June 15.)

The Committee appointed to report on the desirableness of a new version of the Welsh Testament met at Shrewsbury on Thursday, and agreed, we believe, to recommend that the work should be carried out. We publish to-day a letter from the Rev. D. R. THOMAS, explaining the constitution of the preliminary committee ; the more delicate and important task of selecting the Company of Revisers has now to be performed, and we have no doubt that care will be taken to obtain the services of the best Welsh as well as the most erudite Greek scholars, and to appoint a body of men who will enjoy the confidence of all sections of the Protestant Church.

SIR,—There appears to be considerable misapprehension as to the appointment and duties of the committee recently formed on this subject. At the meeting of the Welsh Bishops and the deputation of the Welsh members of Convocation on the 20th of May, the Bishops passed a resolution "That a committee be appointed for the purpose of considering the expediency of undertaking a revision of the Welsh version of the New Testament, according to the text adopted in the revision of the English version, and that they report to the Welsh Bishops on this matter, as soon as they can after due consideration, stating at the same time the grounds upon which their opinion is founded." The members of this committee were appointed subsequently, at the request of the Bishops, by the deputation, who, having fixed on the number of three from each diocese, chose to that number from the representatives present or supplemented them with the additional names. The committee, therefore, are in no way the nominees of the Bishops ; and as they met in Shrewsbury on Thursday, the 9th instant, and agreed upon their report, their work is done, and the Bishops are quite free as to the selection of men for the actual revision. This will explain the composition of the committee and will remove the doubts as to its competency for the more important work of the revision.—I am, &c.,

Meifod Vicarage,   D. R. THOMAS, Sec.

THE LATE LORD JUSTICE JAMES.

The *Times* says of the late Lord Justice James, who died last week, "like so many eminent judges he was a Welshman, having been born at Merthyr Tydfil in 1807. When first called to the Bar he went the great Welsh Sessions, and he thus dealt with both law and equity in the Principality. He was a Liberal in politics and one of the earliest members of the Reform Club, and he twice contested Derby unsuccessfully. He was a Judge of the highest order, of rare ability and supreme integrity." On Mar. 2 last, we published an account of the Jameses of Merthyr—Mr. Christopher James, first a wine merchant there, and afterwards engaged in business of various kinds, by which he realized a competence, and then retired to Swansea, and his three sons, Mr. D. W. James, Mr. Job James, and the late Lord Justice. (See page 201.)

Lord Justice James, whose death will cause profound sorrow amongst Chancery lawyers, is a victim to his determination to work to the last. Being ill, he still attended to his legal duties ; and the want of rest at the proper moment killed him. He was the burliest of the judges. When he was a counsel, and there were several other Jameses not easily distinguished from one another, he was called "fat James" by the members of the bar. He was a sound lawyer, and sometimes won applause by

the brilliancy of his earlier speeches. His knowledge of ecclesiastical law was so wide that he would have been a better judge of the Court of Arches than Lord Penzance. A Welshman by descent, a Scotsman by education, and an Englishman by long residence, he was shrewd, persistent, and, those who knew him well say, genial. He has been Lord Justice for eleven years, and judge of Chancery for more than thirteen. For fifteen years previously he was Vice-Chancellor of the County Palatine. Sir Charles Hall is likely to succeed him as Lord Justice, but it will be difficult to. find a successor to Sir Charles Hall.—*Liverpool Mercury*.

A London Correspondent says that "an old Salopian, whose father sat at the feet of Rowland Hill, has purchased the pulpit and communion table belonging to Surrey Chapel (now marked out for sale as building material), and taken them to his home in Canada."

VICAR OF LLANRHAIADR.—It is with much regret that we record the sudden death of the Rev. E. Jones, M.A., vicar of Llanrhaiadr-yn-Mochnant and Llanarmon Mynydd Mawr. A correspondent writes:—"He it was who first collected the works of the eminent Welsh poet, Goronwy Owen, under the title of Gronovians, with a preface in the shape of a critical essay on the genius and works of the poet. This of itself stamped the young writer as an accomplished Welsh essayist and critic, and is considered a model of elegance and chasteness. He was himself a writer of verses of no mean order, although we are not aware that he has published many of his effusions. His grave is adjacent to that of one of his predecessors, the accomplished Gwallter Mechain."

JUNE 22, 1881.

NOTES.

CHURCHES IN THE RHYL DISTRICT.

LLANRHAIADR-IN-CINMERCH CHURCH.

During a short stay at Rhyl I made an excursion to Llanrhaiadr Church, four miles beyond Denbigh, situate on an eminence overlooking the beautiful and well-wooded Vale of Clwyd, bounded by Moel Vammau on the east. My principal object in going there was to see the "Jesse window," of which only one other example exists in the kingdom, at St. Mary's Church, Shrewsbury. The glass fills a large late perpendicular window of five lights, at the east end of the present nave. It is said to have been brought from Basingwerk Abbey at the Dissolution, and to have been preserved for about three centuries in a large black oak chest, which is now placed near the window. This oak chest is in itself a great curiosity, being about three yards long, and one yard broad and deep, and copiously banded with ironwork. On the top, from the centre of the front, arises a pillar poor-box about one foot high, and square in form, guarded by three iron locks, the slit for offerings being on the upper part. The Jesse glass is of coarse and clumsy design and execution compared with the elegant and artistic window of earlier date at St. Mary's, Shrewsbury. Nevertheless the colours are very deep and rich, and well and carefully harmonized. The date of its execution is preserved at the south corner of the base of the window in the glass itself. It is mᵒ. ccccᵒ. ' xxxiij. (1533)

The masonry of Llanrhaiadr Church is externally of a very Cyclopean character, especially in the lower and older portions of the walls, huge stones of all sizes being imbedded in copious mortar, without any regularity of layers or strata. In the upper portions the layers are more regular and uniform. Like many other Welsh churches it has two adjacent aisles or portions of equal length and breadth, the northern one being used as a nave and the southern one as a chancel. Originally the edifice was Norman, a round-headed door now blocked up existing on the south side of the east window of the present nave. The north walls, the tower, and the west and north doors are of decorated æra. The present nave probably formed the earlier church, and the south aisle or present chancel is separated from the former by four broad arches springing from octagonal pillars with plain filleted imposts. The two east windows and the entire south wall are of perpendicular style. A square, narrow, and tall tower, with diagonal buttresses, of two storeys, terminates the west end, and internally opens to the nave by a very rudely constructed archway or door, the arch-stones of which are very narrow, and very similar to the masonry of Dolbadarn Castle, in the pass of Llanberis. This tower contains two bells, one of which, I was informed, was about 200 years old, on which the clock strikes, and has certainly a very fine, shrill tone. Before the north door, which is the principal entrance to the church, is a very large and beautifully carved wooden porch, with a foliated niche and other ornamentation on the front, and embattled cornices, showing it to be of the time of Henry VII. The east window of the chancel is of perpendicular architecture, similar to that of the nave. The roof of this portion is coved and adorned with beautiful carvings in wood, and rests on projecting corbels of angels holding books and shields. The lower and intermediate string-courses are broad and adorned with grapes and vines. From these spring upwards two series of parallel oblong panels, the upper portions of which are ornamented with wheels, canopies, and various other devices. The other portions of the roofs of chancel and nave are of strong open timber-work. On the south side there is a square-headed window of four lights with trefoiled heads containing modern stained glass, representing actions of our Saviour's life and four acts of mercy, to the memory of Margaret, wife of Thomas Hughes of Ystrad, 1854. Westwards is another large depressed window of four lights with trefoil heads, in which is modern stained glass to James Vaughan Horne, 1848. The west window of the nave and all the windows on the north side are restorations, but evidently carefully copied from the original decorated windows. On the north of the altar in the east wall is a large square locker or aumbrey, and in the churchyard are several fine yew trees, under one of which lies a round stone water-stoup, no doubt removed from the north porch. The font is modern, of blackish marble.

On the whole we may gather that there was originally a Norman church, which was reconstructed in the decorated age of the Edwards, and again reconstructed and enlarged in the latter end of Henry VII's. reign, and in that of his successor, Henry VIII.

West of the Church is an almshouse, and eastwards is the Hall.

In the churchyard is a fine old altar tomb of the time of Charles I., on which is this inscription in capitals :—

IOHN . AP . ROBERT . OF . PONT .
AP . DAVID . AP . GRVFFETH .
AP . DAVID . VAVGHAN . AP . BLETHYN .
AP . GRVFFITH . AP . MEREDITH .
AP . JERWORTH . AP . LLEWELYN .
AP . JEROOH . AP . HELLIN . AP .
COVRYD . AP . CADVAN . AP .
ALTAWGWR . AP . CADELL . THE
KING . OF . POWYS . XX . MARCH .
1642 . AGED . XCV.

On another slab in the churchyard is in capitals :—

HIC . IACET . CORPVS .
SAMVELIS . EDDOW .
FIL . THO . EDDOW .
SEPVLT . 5 .
FEBRVARII .
ANNO .
DOMINI .
1648.

FILIVS . HIC . SITVS . EST . CHARA
SSIMO . PATRE . DOLENDVM .
CVIVS . IN . HOC . TVMVLO .
. . . . OSSA . CVBANT .
. . . . FVIT .
NRS . LITERA . CŒLI .
HODVNS . SIC . REDIT .
. . . LIBET . . . ANDE . FVIT.

This portion of the inscription is much rubbed and worn down and nearly illegible.

Around the verge is :—

. . . . .. CORPVS . ANNÆ . VXORIS . THO . EDDOW . DE .
TYBROVGHTON . . . . . NAT . FIL . DE . . . . . .
GVLHILL . VICAR . DE . LLANERHAYD'R . SEPVLT . 27 . DEC .
. . . . . .

Round the verge of another slab in capitals is :—

CORPVS . IOHANNIS . LLOYD . DE . PENTRE . GENEROSI .
SEPVLTI . DECIMO . TERTIO . DECEMBRIS . ANNO . DOMINI .
1650.

And on the face also in capitals :—

PVLVERIS . IN . LECTO . IACEO . MODO . MOXQ . RESVRGAM .
CHRIST . VIGORE . TVO . CARNE . VIDERE . DEVM .
IAM . TERRENVS . ERAM . MODO . SVM . CŒLESTIS . IESV .
MORTVVS . AC . VIVVS . SVM . MANEOQ . TVVS .
A . ME . DISCE . MORI . LECTOR . QVO . VIVERE . POSSIS .
MORS . FVIT . IN . ME . HODIE . CRAS . TIBI . FORSAN . ERIT .
HIC . IACET . CORPVS . EDVARDI . LLOYD . DE . LLECH .
GEN . QVI . MORTEM . OBIIT .

A marble tablet on south wall of chancel records :—
John Lloyd of Brynthyrto Esq. s. & h. of John Lloyd of Brynthyrto Esq. & Katharine eld. d. of John Foulkes of Vaynol. co. Flint Esq. He marrd. Mary d. & h. of Gabriel Jones of Keetla co. Merioneth gent. by whom he had issue John Foulk, Watkin, Katharine, Anne & Mary. He died 5 April 1723.
Arms or 3 lions passant in pale sa. and on an escutcheon arg. lion rampant gardant gu.

On Brass in north wall of nave :
Robert Lloyd of Llwyn gent. & Elizabeth his wife. He died 1766, aged 55. She died 1771, aged 69.

On south wall of chancel.
Henry Meredith Mostyn, R,N. of Segrwyd & Lleweny co. Denbigh. 1840.

On Slabs in the floor.
John Roberts of Pen-y-coed, 1743.

John Wynne s. of John W. of Llewesog by Margaret his wife, 1770.
Robert s. of above Surgeon of Liverpool, 1832.

Robert Wynne s. of John W. of Llewesog by Margaret his wife, 1766.
John Wynne the father, 1798.

Walter Edwards Wynne esq. of Llwyn "last existing heir of Gwydir" 1796.
Anna Maria his widow. 1828.

Elizabeth Wynne wife of John Wynne of Greengen d. of Wm. Salisbury of Llewenni Gent. 1657, aged 83.

On Slabs in the Churchyard.
Mary Wynne, 1639.
Elizabeth eld. d. of Robert Wynne of Llwyn Esq.

Edward s. of Edward Williams of Pent-y-Gwyddel Esq. by Mary 2d d. of Edward Wynne of Astrad Esq.
Arms a chevron between 3 boars' heads couped.

Captain Edward Wynne 4th s. of Edward Wynne who died in defence of Denbigh Castle besieged by Oliver Cromwell.
Also Owen Wynne of Kilchen Esq. 3d s. of Edwd. W. marrd. Lady Mostyn relict of Sir Thos. M. Bt. & died s. p.

Edward Wynne of Astrad Esq. only s. of Maurice W. of Gwydir Esq. by Catharine Tudor of Leven. They had 4s. & 7 d. 1640.
Robert Wynne of Llwyn esq. s. of Edwd. W. had 5 s. & 2d. by the heiress of Llwyn.
Owen Wynne of Llwyn esq. & s. of Robt. W. 1701
Watkin Edwd. Wynne eld. s. of Owen W. esq. of Llwyn 1796 aged 42.

Blanch wife of Edwd. Wynne of Astrad Esq. d. of John Vaughan of Blanycwm co. Carnarvon Esq.

Thomas Wynne of Denbigh s. of Edwd. W. of Astrad esq. 1623.
John 4th s. of Robt. W. of Llwyn Esq. 1716.

Large marble monument with recumbent figure, leaning on his arm, in full court dress and full bottomed flowing wig.
Maurice Jones of Llanrhaiadyr esq. s. of Humphrey Jones of Ddol esq. by Jane his wife d. of Eubull Thelwall of Nantclwyd Esq. He marrd. Jane d. of Sir Walter Bagot of Staffordshire Bart. and died 1702.
Arms:—gu. 3 chevrons arg. impaling erm. 2 chevrons az.

Margaret wife of Thos. Roberts of Astrad Issa Gent. 1812.
Also Johanna his 2d w. 1832.
Thos. R. died in 71st yr of his age.

Ambrose Price, 1853.

James Vaughan Horne, 1808.
Also Elizth. d. of John Price esq. of Denbigh & widow of J. V. Horne. 1880.

John Griffith Price Major 2nd Dragoon Guards eld. s. of John & Harriet P. of Llanrhaiadr Hall, 1858.
Also Harriet w. of John Price 1850 sister of George Griffith of Garn.
Also John Price 1872. W.A.L.

QUERIES.

YE LEGEND OF YE WREKIN.—Where was the ballad with the above title originally published and who was the author? Was it by Mr. Barham? It is not in the Ingoldsby collectiou. The following lines are in the ballad :—

Not that in Wales,
They talk of their ales,
But spell it, as though 'twere on purpose to trouble you
With a C and a W,—R and a W.
A word to pronounce which you'd have some ado,
But the nearest approach to the sound is cooroo;
For to learn the Welsh language if e'er you should choose
You'll W have to pronounce like two U's.

The ballad is clever; is the legend on which it was founded ancient? H.B.

MILLS IN OSWESTRY.—I fancy some reference to both the queries I am about to put have appeared in *Bye-gones*, but there have certainly not been any replies or I should have remembered them. I have been told that the house now occupied by Mr. Blaikie in Church-street was formerly a mill turned by water power, and that the mill pond was situated at the back of the house now occupied by Dr. Beresford; the stream crossing the street. Was this before "New Gate" was demolished, or did it remain afterwards? Then there was a snuff mill, I am told, in Beatrice-street, by the stream that ran past the Beatrice Gate. Was it ever worked, and when? FITZALAN.

SONGS BY A GENTLEMAN AT SALOP.—A little book was published by J. Pridden, at the Feathers in Fleet-street, London, in 1760, called *The Muse's Delight*. Its contents are rubbish, and the only reason for noticing it in these columns is that it contains three or four songs by "a Gentleman at Salop." On the strength of this, I suppose there are the names of two Shrewsbury booksellers on the title-page, viz., "J. Eddows (sic) and S. Price (sic) at Salop" The pieces referred to are called, respectively, "Damon and Salvia," "The Disappointment," and "On the May." There is also another song, headed "The Salopian," by which one would gather that the chief occupation of our countrymen in those days was to drink;—punch and wine if they could get it; "nuty brown ale" if they couldn't. Whether this effusion emanated from a genuine Salopian or not, we are not informed. Probably not, or the following line would scarcely appear :—"To all our good friends round the raken so high." This sounds like the old Shropshire Toast at a distance, and a good distance too! Who was the "Gentleman at Salop," whose songs warranted the publisher in parading a couple of Salopian publishers? I may observe that the names of a Bristol, and a Darlington bookseller, also appear on the title-page. R.D.

OWEN RICHARDS OF MERIONETHSHIRE. Information is requested, for purposes of genealogical interest, regarding the family history, date of emigration, &c. of Owen Richards, of Merionethshire, Wales, who came to Pennsylvania, U.S.A. some time previous to 1718, locating on 300 acres of land within 40 miles of Philadelphia. He married in 1727 Elizabeth Baker, but had previously married in Wales. His sons James and William, and perhaps his first wife and other children, accompanied him to America. Please address
LOUIS RICHARDS, Attorney-at Law,
Reading, Berks County, Penna., U.S.A.

OLD FOLKS (Dec. 22, 1880). — June, 1812. Died, of a cancer in her breast, in her 104th year, Eliz. Beech, of Market Drayton. She was born in the 6th year of the reign of Queen Anne, and fully remembered the coronation of Geo. 1, which happened when she was about 6 years old. She disliked broth, tea, and all kind of slops, and partook of the coarsest food, such as potatoes and bacon, &c., on which she fed heartily. Of late she abstained from cheese. She possessed her memory and eyesight till within the last year or two unimpared.

Died at Whitchurch, Salop, Feb. 1812, aged 102, Mrs. Wood, "who for the last 50 years drank no other beverage than water." *(Gents : Mag :)* Query ; if the good lady restricted herself to one beverage, what other one was there besides water that she could have lived upon ?

Died, at Meole Brace, Salop, Apr. 1812, in his 99th year, Mr. Vaughan. He has left a widow now in her 100th year, to whom he had been married more than 76 years. She died a few weeks later.

Died, May 1812, at Croeswen, near Margam Copper Works, Glamorgan, aged 109, Morgan Corslett.
                                                         DUBIOUS.

CURRENT NOTES.

Among the illustrations in the current number of the *British Architect* is the Congregational Church built by Mr. Thomas Barnes at The Quinta, which makes a very pretty picture. The same paper, continuing its " Visits to Great Industries," gives an illustrated account of the Coalbrookdale Iron Works.

Last week a chapel of ease and burial ground were consecrated at Penrhyncoch, Aberystwyth, by the Right Rev. Charles Alford, late bishop of Victoria. The building, which has been erected by Messrs. R. Williams and Son. of Aberystwyth, with Mr. R. J. Withers of London as architect, has cost £1,500, a large proportion of which sum, together with the site, has been given by Sir Pryse Pryse, Bart. The architecture is of the old English style, and the building consists of a nave, chancel, organ chamber and robing room. The opening services were well attended and the bishop preached a sermon.

JUNE 29, 1881.

NOTES.

ABERYSTWYTH IN 1833.—Amongst the latest arrivals at this fashionable watering-place (say the papers of Sep. 1833) were the Duke and Duchess of St. Albans, who have patronized the theatres, balls, &c.; also the Duke of Newcastle and family, who remain here some time previous to his grace taking possession of his princely seat, Havod, which he has lately purchased.   G.G.

QUERIES.

ANCIENT BREEDS OF WELSH CATTLE.— Some of the Welsh Cattle in the 10th century are described as being "white, with red ears," resembling the wild cattle of Chillingham Castle. An early record speaks of a hundred white cows with red ears being demanded as a compensation for certain offences against the Princes both of North and South Wales. Was this the usual colour of the ancient breed of Welsh Cattle, or was it a rare variety ? Is it represented by any breed now extant ? If the cattle were of a dark or black colour 150 were to be presented instead of 100. What are the characteristics of the Montgomeryshire breed of cattle ? Are they not dark or black ?
                                                         Z.

MR. DONNE AND MR. MARSAN.—The following letter, without note or comment, appears in the *Salopian Journal* of May 5, 1802 :—

A letter from Mr. Donne to Mr. Marsan.

DEAR SIR,—I was very much pleased to hear that you had at length heard from your friends, and had received such pleasant accounts concerning them. We could not help at the same time regretting, that you are come to, a resolution to leave this country. But since that resolution is formed, I cannot help being sensible of the handsome way in which you do all you can to accommodate me, by continuing to attend here till Midsummer next.

I would sooner have answered your letter, had I not been prevented partly by indisposition, and partly by the business which always crouds upon me at this time of the year. I am angry with myself for not having sooner answered you, lest you should have said anything to induce your friend the Chevalier, to relinquish his present situation. I own to you, it does not appear to me, that a gentleman, most of whose life has been spent in the army, is likely to be an active or successful teacher of any language. I therefore feel very strong objections against employing your friend in a department, which has hitherto been filled with so much ability and diligence.

We shall be glad to see you on the 14th instant.—Your pupils as well as myself, will feel no small regret that we are to have your company only for another half year,
            I remain, Dear Sir, Your faithful
                          and humble servant,
Oswestry, 9th Feb. 1802.   JAS. DONNE.

There is little difficulty in understanding the purport of this letter. No doubt Mr. Marsan was French teacher at the Oswestry School, of which Mr. (afterwards Dr.) Donne was at that time master. But if Mr. Marsan was leaving the country what was his object in publishing the letter? It was not one calculated to get his "friend the Chevalier " a situation as a teacher of languages ; and could be of no possible benefit to himself. Who was the Chevalier ? and can any one say why the letter was published?   OSWALD.

REPLIES.

THE LATE CANON WILLIAMS (May 4, 1881). I was in error when I stated that the first appearance of the song on *Aberconwy* was under the auspices of the Cymmrodorion Society. I was led astray by a somewhat ambiguous statement on the title page of the first edition of *Eminent Welshmen.* And, touching the latter work--which, as I stated, was the enlargement of a prize paper, I find amongst the notices to correspondents inside the cover of the *Cam : Quar : Mag :* for October, 1831, the following announcement:—"We intended to publish, under authority of the Cymmrodorion, ' The Biographical Memoirs of Eminent Welshmen since the Reformation,' but, on an attentive perusal, we have ascertained that however high its qualifications may be as a manuscript prize paper, it is not adapted for publication in our magazine."   A.R.

EVELINA'S SARCOPHAGUS (Jan. 5, 1881).— Mr. TEWK, at this date asked who Mr. J. H. Wynne was who wrote a poem with this title in 1774. He will find in Williams's *Eminent Welshmen* that John Huddlestone Wynne was born of respectable Welsh parents in 1743. By trade he was a printer in London, but afterwards obtained a commission in the army, and when he laid down his sword, turned author. His principal works were "A General History of the British Empire in America," and a "History of Ireland." Mr. Williams does not allude to his having been a poet. He died in 1788. His uncle, Richard Wynne, M.A., of All Souls' Coll : Oxford, was rector of St. Alphege, London, and of Ayot St. Lawrence, Hertfordshire. This uncle published a New Testament in English, collated with the Greek. He died in 1799.   ANON.

JULY 6, 1881.

NOTES.

THE OLD WELSH ALMANACKS.

(May 25, 1881.)

The one for 1820 is called "Cyfaill Cyfrinachol," was printed at Dublin, price sixpence, and it has the following verses on its title page :—

1 Fy hên gyfeillion di-ddrwg,
　O Fôn i fro Morganwg ;
　'Rwy'n d'od i'ch mysg, yn fawr
　　fy nhrael,
　Heb ofni cael eich cilwg,

2 Fe ddichon rhai'n ddiachaws,
　Ragfarnu mewn ofer-naws,
　Naill ai o *gynfigen* lem,
　Neu ryw *uchel-drem* chwyl-
　　draws.

3 Mae lle, chwe' mis yn ddian,
　Na welir Heulwên oleu ;
　A'r chwe' mis eraill, yn 'r un
　　fan,
　Heb gyrhaedd dan ei gaerau.

4 Y Byd, fel pêl, sy'n treiglo,

Rhai sy'n dyrchafu ynddo ;
A *llawer* sydd, er maint eu
　cwyn,
Yn cael eu dwyn o dano.

5 Er dynion heirdd, â doniau,
Cywir-ddysg yn ein *Cyrddau* ;
Trais, llid, a balchder, yn ein
　tir,
Sy'n lledu'n wir *Fanerau.*

6 May GOD preserve our King-
　dom
According to His *wisdom,*
That we may run our earthly
　race,
To th'end in *Peace* and *Free-
　dom.*

The one for 1821 is called "Cyfaill Gwyladd," was published at Dublin, price sixpence, and has the following verses on title page :—

1 Trwy'ch cenad Gymry mwyn-
　　ion,
　Wnai goelio mrodyr gwaelion,
　Myfi 'ch dyddanaf oll os câf,
　Hyderaf gwnaf yn dirion.

2 Adwaenir fy lleferydd
　Pan gludir fi drwy'r gwledydd,
　Ac fe'm derbynir yn ddi stwr ;
　Gan lawer gwr cyfarwydd.

3 Fy rhai sy'n byw'n gyfanedd,
　Ar gyfer y gyhydedd,
　Wrth y Planedau'n fwy di dôr,
　Cant chwaneg o'r gwirionedd.

4 Mae rhai o'n cenedl ninau,
　Er pelled ein trigfanau,

Yn deall diffyg nos neu ddydd,
Wedd lwyr, a'r newydd loerau.

5 Er glewed yw plant *Gomer,*
A lliwgu deulu Lloegr,
Mae llawer cymmal, braich, a
　glin,
Yn well am yr hin o'r haner.

6 We ought to observe our
　duty,
And thanks for peace and
　plenty,
And let us always loudly sing,
And pray for King and
　country.

The *first* issue for 1822 is called "Cyfaill Hyglod," was printed in Dublin, price sixpence, and has the following lines on title page :—

1 Fy hen Gyfeillion hoyw,
　Iselaidd, deilwch sylw,
　Er d'od rhai gwaelach, dylach
　　dawn
　Yn fynych iawn yn f' enw.

2 Mae'r breiniawg lu wybrenol,
　A'u nodau'n dra dirnadol,
　Yn dangos trefniad, llywiad
　　llwyr,
　I'r rhai a wyr eu rheol.

3 I radd mae llaw geryddol,
　Duw IOR ar ddyn daearol,
　Yn wyneb *tremser,* loywber,
　　lefn
　Yn tori o'n trefn naturiol.

4 Llu'r wybren a'r llawr obry,
　Ond dyn, maent yn cyd-tynu,
　I gadw eu deddfau i gyd heb
　　goll,
　Er pelled, oll heb ballu.

5 Mae amser yn diflanu,
　Fel cysgod haul o'n deutu,
　A thrag'wyddoldeb, yn ddi os,
　O ddydd i nos yn nesu.

6 Let every soul consider
The most important matter,
This irrevocable *day* when
　past
May be the *last* for ever.

The second issue for 1822, printed at Dublin, is called "Cyfaill Cyfeillgar," no price named, the following being the verses on the title page :—

1 Fy hen gyfeillion dibrin,
　O *Gybi* hyd *Gaerfyrddin,*
　Rwy'n d'od ger bron eich
　　wynebpryd,
　Er fod yn enbyd erwin.

2 Gwyr gonest *De* a Gwynedd,
　Y Calan, ddo'nt i'm coledd,
5

Er maint yw llid a gofid
　gweilch
Anhaw'gar, beilch eu hag-
　wedd.

3 Geill mawrion gyraedd *llyfr-
　yn,*
I nodi peb munudyn ;

Ond holl gyffredin bobl y wlad,
Am *Gyfaill* rhad sy'n gofyn .

4 Medd rhai mai *ser* aneglur,
Fel　*Sadwrn,　Mawrth,* a
　Mercher,
Sydd â llywodraeth ar bob
　dyn
Anhydyn yn ei natur.

5 Gwirionedd di-amheuol,
Fod graddau pechod gwreidd-
　iol,
A had llygredig, fyth y'nglyn,
Yn enaid dyn anianol.

6 May God protect our country,
Lest malice, pride and envy,
Should be the *ruin* of us all,
'Tis time to call for mercy.

The one for 1823 is called "Cyfaill Buddiol," was printed at Dublin, but has no price mentioned. These are the lines upon the title page :—

1 GYFEILLION union, enwog,
　Hael, hynaws, a chalonog,
　O Ynys Fôn hyfrydlon fryd,
　Sy i'm chwenych, hyd Frych-
　　einiog.

2 Eleni 'rwy'n ddylynol,
　O fwriad, fel arferol,
　I chwi drachefn, yn nhrefn y
　　rhod,
　Gael pob rhyfeddod fuddiol.

3 Hen Awdwr y Planedau,
　A nododd eu trefniadau ;
　A'r holl arwyddion, wiwlon
　　wedd,
　I ymarwedd y Tymhorau.

4 Rhyw gywrain waith rhagorol
I ddynion, er mor ddoniol,
Yw dyall deddfau nodau'r nef
I'w haddef yn gyboeddol.

5 Ond er pob dealldwriaeth,
O'r deg-wedd Greadigaeth ;
Llafuriwn oll o foreu i nawn,
Heb oedi, am IAWN wybod-
　aeth.

6 JEHOVAH reigns triumphant,
His ways, both light and dor-
　mant,
Display his wisdom, Power,
　and Praise
His Glory, and Grace abun-
　dant.

E.G.S.

PARLIAMENT OF ENGLAND (June 8, 1881).

Members for *Montgomeryshire,* concluded.　The first name under each date refers to the County, and the second to the Boroughs.

1705	Edward Vaughan, esq., of Llwydiarth, co. Montgomery.　Charles Mason, esq.	
1708	Ditto.　　　John Pugh, esq.	
1710	Ditto.　　　　　　Ditto.	
1713	Ditto.　　　　　　Ditto.	
1714-5	Ditto.　(1)　　　Ditto.	
1722	Pryce Devereux, esq.　John Pughe, esq.	
1727	Ditto.　　William Corbet, esq.　(2)	
1734	Ditto.　(3)　　　Ditto.	
1741	Sir Watkin Williams Wynn, bart., of Llwydiarth　(4).　James Cholmondeley, esq.	
1747	Edward Kynaston, esq.　Henry Herbert, esq.　(5)	
1754	Ditto.　　William Bodvell, esq.　(6)	
1761	Ditto.　　　Richard Clive, esq.	
1768	Ditto.　(7)　　　Ditto.　(8)	
1774	William Owen, esq.　Whitshed Keene, esq.　　(9)	

(1) Jan. 9, 1718-19 ; Price Devereux, Esq., elected, *vice* Edward Vaughan, Esq., deceased.

(2) Double return.　The indenture by which Robert Williams, Esq., was returned was taken off the file by order of the House, dated 16 Apr. 1728.—*Blue Book.*　The Contributing boroughs of Llanidloes. Machynlleth, Llanfyllin, and Welshpool, were disfranchised, and right of election declared by Committee of Privileges, to be in the Burgesses of Montgomery only.—*Mont. Coll.*

(3) Robert Williams, Esq., elected 12 Dec. 1740, *vice* Price Devereux, Esq., called to the Upper House as Lord Viscount Hereford.

(4) Robert Williams, Esq., elected 2 Apr. 1742, *vice* Sir Watkin who elected to serve for the county of Denbigh.

(5) Francis Herbert, Esq., elected 16 Apr. 1748, *vice* Henry Herbert, deceased.　In *Mont : Coll :* "William" instead of "Francis" Herbert is given.

(6) Richard Clive, Esq., elected 21 Nov. 1759, *vice* William Bodvill, Esq., deceased.

(7) Watkin Williams, Esq., elected 9 June, 1772, *vice* Edward Kynaston, Esq., deceased.

(8) Frederick Cornewa'll, Esq., elected 15 June, 1771, *vice* Richard Clive, Esq., deceased.

(9) Re-elected 4 July, 1777, after accepting Chiltern Hundreds. Ditto 1 Jan. 1779, after appointment as Surveyer General of Works.

1780	William Owen, esq.	Whitshed Keene, esq.	(10)
1784	Ditto.	Ditto.	
1790	Ditto. (11)	Ditto.	
1796	Francis Lloyd. (12)	Ditto.	
1802	C. W. W. Wynn, esq. of Llwydiarth, co. Montgomery.	Whitshed Keene.	
1806	C. W. W. Wynn, esq. of Pentrefgoe, co. Montgomery.	Whitshed Keene.	
1807	C. W. W. Wynn, esq. of Penhggoe, co. Montgomery.	Whitshed Keene.	
1812	Ditto.	Ditto.	
1818	Ditto.	Henry Clive, esq.	(13)
1820	Ditto. (14)	Ditto.	
1826	Ditto.	Ditto.	
1830	Ditto. (15)	Ditto.	
1831	Ditto.	Ditto.	

·For return of Members from the passing of the Reform Bill up to 1880, see *Bye-gones*, Apr. 7, 1880.

CHURCHES IN THE RHYL DISTRICT.

(June 22, 1881.)

HENLLAN CHURCH.

Hênllan is a considerable village, two and a half miles north-west of Denbigh, situate in a hollow, the commencement of a large and finely-wooded valley. The parish is of great extent. The prominent feature of the village is the Parish Church, originally erected in the decorated or Edwardian æra, with insertions in the perpendicular period. The edifice is of one pace, without any break or distinction of nave and chancel, and of very great and disproportionate width, and has a plain coved wooden roof. The east window is large, of five lights and minor upper divisions, and of perpendicular architecture. There are four decorated plain windows on the north and south and two decorated windows at the west end. The north and south doors are also plain decorated, with a porch before the south one. The font is modern, 1854. The altar is a fine old carved oak table, and in the south wall is a piscina. Near the south door is the octagonal shaft of a cross, the head gone, and in the churchyard are three fine yew trees. The graves are entirely on the south side. At the north-east end of the churchyard, and about thirty yards distant from the Church, is a plain square embattled tower of two storeys, without buttresses, the entrance door being on the east side, to which a flight of stone stairs outside leads. In it are two bells, re-cast 1853, one now cracked. The reason given for the tower being detached is that the parishioners wished to build on the solid limestone rock and on an eminence, so that the bells may be heard in the deep-distant valley below. The building has been restored about 1853, but the original features have been carefully preserved and copied throughout.

At south corner of east end of chancel is a good deal of long and short work, which may be Saxon and a relic of some very early church.

(10) Re-elected 16 Apr. 1783, after appointment as one of the Lords Commissioners of the Admiralty.—*Blue Book.* Brother-in-law of the Earl of Dartmouth.—*Mont. Coll.*
(11) The *Blue Book* describes him as of Bryngwyn, co. Montgomery. *Mont. Coll.* as William Mostyn Owen. Francis Lloyd, Esq., of Dongay, elected 4 Apr. 1795, *vice* Owen, deceased.
. (12) Charles Watkin Williams Wynn, Esq., of Glasceed Hall, co. Montgomery, elected 14 Mar. 1799, *vice* Lloyd, deceased.
(13) *Mont. Coll.* gives 1820 as the first return of Mr. Henry Clive.
(14) Re-elected 13 Feb. 1822, after appointment as First Commissioner for the Affairs of India.
(15) Re-elected 15 Dec. 1830, after appointment as Secretary at War.

Against west wall is a marble tablet to John Jones of Galltvaynan in this parish and of Penaner in parish of Cerigydruidion Esq. M.B. who died 25 Feby. 1778 aged 76.

Also Elizabeth his wife the heir of Edward Salusbury of Galltvaynan Esq. who died 26 March 1758 aged 63.

Also Edward Salusbury Jones their eldest son of Lincolns Inn Esq. Barrister at law who died 31 Aug. 1769 aged 36.

Also Elizabeth their eld. daughter died 10 Feb. 1760 aged 28.

In All Saints' Church Cambridge, lies Salusbury Jones youngest son of said John and Elizth. M.A. Fellow of St. John's College and Chaplain to Dr. Lyttelton Bishop of Carlisle who died 20 May 1760 aged 28.

Erected by Margaret only surviving child 1780 who herself died 23 March 1791 aged 58.

Arms at top, but obliterated.

On stone tablet :—
Hugh Peake of Perthewig in this parish gent. died 28 Jan. 1767 aged 60.

Margaret his wife died 9 Oct. 1788 aged 77.

Margaret their child died 18 May 1796 aged 56.

On another stone tablet adjoining :—Hugh Peake Gent. lies here interred. He dyd at Perthewig May 17, 1697, leaving no issue.

Arms :—Quarterly : 1st chequy *or & gu* over all an Andrew cross *erm.* 2d. *sa* a spread eagle with 2 heads *or,* on a canton *az* a bird *or.* 3d. A fox tripping regardant with a branch in his mouth *or.* 4th. *arg* 6 bees or flies. 3. 2 & 1. *sa.*

Against north wall.
Thomas Peake died 26 May 1811 aged 78.
Martha his wife died 3 May 1818 aged 64.

On a Brass fixed in the splay of a small window in north wall.
Thomas Peake of Perthewig, Serjeant at law, born 1770 ob. 1837, leaving numerous posterity. His family possessed Perthewig since Edward I.

In the adjacent window on stained glass are the arms of intermarriages. 1. Done Atkinton. 2. Salusbury, Maesmynan 1569. 3. Hanmer Fenns 1593. 4. Wynne Voelas Throgmorton 1618. 5. Mostyn Caldecote 1678. 6. Lloyd Goodman 1687.

On marble tablet, north wall of chancel.
Richard Augustus Griffiths, Esq., of Garn in this parish died 28 Sept., 1831, aged 34.

On marble tablet, north wall of chancel.
Heaton Lloyd Williams, M.D., H.E.I.S., 2d son of Richard Lloyd Williams, M.D. F.R.C.S.L., of Denbigh, and of Georgina his wife, daughter of Major C. M. Barrow, H.E.I.C.S., who died of cholera 30 Aug., 1862.

Stained glass in south wall of chancel.
Crucifixion and Resurrection and heads of 4 Evangelists, to the memory of Dorothy Roberts, spinster, of Plas-yngreen, 1863.

Stained glass, south nave.
Christ and Nathaniel, to memory of John Heaton.

Marble slab, south nave.
Catharine Greatrex, who died at Dolhon, 1837, aged 51, daughter of Samuel Proud, Esq., of Bilston, Staffordshire, and wife of Alfred Greatrex, Esq.

Stained glass, south nave.
Dorcas and Cornelius, to the memory of John Powell
Ffoulkes, and Caroline Mary his wife, of Eriviatt in this
parish, 1878.

In the churchyard on a slab under east window, round
the verge, in capitals :—
Hic jacet Hugo Peke, Gent., tumulatus qui obiit mortem
vigesimo quarto die Martii Anno Domini, 1691.
On face :—
John Peak of Perthewig, Gen., 1727, aged 70.
Margaret, his wife, 1734, aged 56.

On stone slab adjacent, in capitals.
HIC IACET CORPVS
GVLIELMI VAVGHAN
GENEROSI QVI SEPVL
TVS FVIT VICESIMO
PRIMO DIE MENSIS IVLII.
ANNO DOMINI 1661.
by consent of Hugh Peake.

On a stone slab fixed in east wall are four shields of arms
sculptured.
1st. Peake.   2. Lion rampant.   3. Fox tripping with
branch in his mouth.   4. Three halberts.
Round verge of slab underneath, in capitals.
Hic jacet Agnes Peake contumulata quæ obiit mortem
sexto die Augusti Anno Do : 1618.
There is also an inscription on the face which is
illegible.   W.A.L.

QUERIES.

MOUNT SION.—Can any one give the derivation
of this name which is found near the Hên ddinas [Old
Oswestry]. Sion House at Isleworth is said to be so
named from a Nunnery of Bridgetines that was formerly
there. At Hanmer there was a Nunnery in Saxon times,
and there is still a Mount Sion.   M.H.L.

RESURRECTIONISTS AT SHREWSBURY.—
Mr. R. Salter of Oswestry published, more than half a
century ago, a pamphlet called :—
The RESURRECTION, a POEM ; the style in imitation of
Hudibras ; being a ludicrous Description of an Attack made on
the Graves of Two Felons, executed at Shrewsbury, Aug. 17,
1817.
The poem is poor enough, and the author apologises for it,
pleading the "extreme hurry in which the lines were
written—three hundred having been completed in one
day." From the contents I gather that the culprits had
been hung for sheep-stealing, and buried in the precincts
of the county gaol. Two doctors, whom the author calls
Brooke and Villars, bribe two of the warders of the gaol
(called Peter and Cerberus) to unearth the bodies and
convey them to Brooke's lodgings. They are interrupted
by a spy (called Castles) who lays an information. The
news spreads, and Brooke's house is speedily surrounded
by a howling mob. The governor of the gaol sends a cart
(strongly guarded) to fetch the bodies, and they are re-
buried, and all becomes quiet. Perhaps some reader of
this will be able to tell us more about the circumstance,
and how the pamphlet came to be printed in Oswestry?
Were either of the doctors Oswestry men, and who was
the author?   H.B.

REPLIES.

MR. DONNE AND MR. MARSAN (June, 29,
1881).—The "Chevalier" referred to was no doubt Mr.
Martinet, a French royalist gentleman, who served in the
Vendean War, and when it ended, had to take refuge in
England. He had lost all his property, and had to
support himself by teaching French. He lived in
Oswestry for many years, very much respected and liked,
and visiting with the families in and around it. At the
peace in 1814 he went to France to pay his respects to
Louis the 18th, from whom he received some mark of
honour, either knighthood or the Cross of the Legion.
When he returned to Oswestry, which he did, for some
time, he was designated "the Chevalier Martinet." He
finally went to live in his native place in Franche Comté.
                                                   C.T.L.
[It would appear from this that Dr. Donne thought better of
his resolve not to have a soldier as a teacher ; and was rewarded
in so doing.—ED.]

SHROPSHIRE BORDER WORDS (June 15,
1881.).—"R.P.M." says that Hartshorne does not record
the word OSS, but if he will refer to page 309 of Salopia
Antiqua, he will find the following, "Ause, oss, v. to try,
essay, attempt, promise favourably. Ex. 'He auses well
saying as how he's a young un.' 'Ause at it.' It has
been conjectured to spring out of the Lat. audeo ; ausus."
LIVERY, an adjective used in the border parish of Worthen.
Potatoes which, when cooked, are the reverse of "mealy,"
are said to be "livery."   R.E.D.
Shrewsbury.

SALOPIAN LITERATURE (Jan. 26, 1881).—In
the "Select Poetry" of the Gents : Mag : for Mar. 1817,
there is an Ode "On seeing the old withered Yew-tree by
the side of Oswald's Well ;" signed "W.E.," and a Prologue by Mr. Dovaston, written for a performance at
Shrewsbury Theatre on the 10th of the same month. The
play was for the benefit of the poor, and acted by a private
company ; Mr. Dovaston spoke the Prologue in the character of Prospero. The receipts were £113 11s. 8d. This
is a digression. What I want to know is who was
"W.E."?   TELL.

BAILEY CLOCK, OSWESTRY (June 15, 1881).
Your correspondent is certainly wrong in saying that Mr.
Stanton erected the first clock on the Town Hall, for, (as
we were told in the report of the Oswestry Advertizer when
the Market Hall extension was opened) the Powis family
paid nearly £20 for repairs of the clock on the Town Hall,
in 1803 : the clock being at that period their property.
Stanton's Company performed in the Brook Street Theatre
twenty years before the one in Willow-street was built.
In 1802 it was advertised as "The New Theatre," and in
1807, I think, Mr. Stanton introduced Young Rosius on
its boards.   JARCO.

REMARKABLE TREES (June 22, 1881.)—One of
your correspondents doubts whether there is any oak now
standing which would yield 1,500 feet of wood. Allow me
to say that there is now a magnificent tree, which I have
frequently seen, in Croft Castle Park, the seat of the Rev
Keville Davies, near Leominster, Herefordshire. A
friend of mine, residing in the parish, informs me that it
was accurately measured and valued by the builder of his
house some years ago. He valued it at 2s. 6d. the cubic foot,
or £240, which would represent a measurement of 1,920
feet. Since then several large branches have been broken
off. I have also seen two enormous oak trees, called the
King's and Abbot's Oaks, in Lord Bagot's Park, in
Staffordshire, a part of old Needwood Forest. These trees
appeared to me to be quite as large as, if not larger than,
the one in Herefordshire.   J.W.M.
[We are asked to remind A DOUBTER (who wrote on June 22)
that the record of the dimensions of the Vaynor Oaks is taken
from the sale account, in the handwriting of the late Mr. Lyon-
Winder.—ED.]

CURRENT NOTES.

A white marble memorial of the late Duchess of Westminster, by Mr. J. E. Boehm, A.R.A., is now in an advanced state of completion. The statue, which is life size, is intended for erection at Eaton.

Mr. Allsopp of Hindlip Hall, Worcester, is preparing a Dictionary of "Public School Words and Phrases," dealing amongst other schools with Shrewsbury, and invites communications.

Mr. J. Roland Phillips, author of "Memoirs of the Civil War in Wales and the Marches," has been appointed by the Queen stipendiary magistrate for West Ham, Essex, a new police district formed under the recent statute.

Dr. Hicks has recently discovered some interesting plant-remains in Penyglôg Quarry, near Corwen. The fossils include carbonaceous fragments having the characteristic structure of the plant which Mr. Carruthers has named nematophycus, and which he regards as an anomalous form of alga.

The library of the late eminent ornithologist, Mr. J. C. Eyton, of Eyton, Salop, was sold by auction at the rooms of Messrs. Sotheby, Wilkinson, and Hodge on the 20th June, and produced £1,793 10s. It was rich in works of natural history, especially in publications on birds of all climates. "Eyton's Shropshire" fetched £20.

We are glad to learn that the Rev. W. A. Leighton has in preparation a *Catalogue Raisonnée* of the antiquities in the Museum of the Shropshire Archæological Society. This will shortly be published in the Transactions of the Society, also in separate form for the use of visitors to the Museum.

The public memorial erected in memory of the late Sir Richard Bulkeley is a massive obelisk, 100 feet high, which occupies the site of an old tower on Tower Hill, above Beaumaris, and is plainly visible from the Carnarvonshire side of the Menai Straits. The work has been carried out by Messrs. Hughes and Owen, contractors, Wrexham, the original contract of £1,154 being supplemented by £200 to meet the additional expenditure incurred through a portion of the obelisk giving way after a storm.

We are glad to understand that the National Eisteddfod Association is receiving the support of some of our leading men. The list of subscribers is rapidly increasing. Among recent additions may be mentioned the Duke of Westminster, K.G., £10, Mr. Hussey Vivian, M.P., 5 guineas, Earl of Powis, Lord Penrhyn, Lord Aberdare, Lord Richard Grosvenor, M.P., Sir E. J. Reed, K.C.B., M.P., Mr. S. Pope, Q.C., £5 each, the Right Hon. G. Osborne Morgan, 3 guineas, Mr. Stuart Rendel, M.P., the Hon. F. Hanbury Tracy, 2 guineas each, Mr. John Corbet, M.P., Mr. L. H. Thomas, the Earl of Denbigh, &c., &c., 1 guinea each. It is confidently anticipated that the Welsh people generally will co-operate with their representatives and aid the work of the Association by becoming members.

It has been reported for some time past that the Governors of the Welsh Charity School at Ashford have had under their consideration a scheme, drawn up we believe by Mr. Stanley Leighton, M.P., the hon. treasurer, for the re-construction of the Institution as a middle-class school for girls. For some years past the applications for admission by charity children eligible for election had fallen much below the number that could be accommodated; consequently a certain number of pay scholars were admitted under new conditions. This again failed to bring about the desired success, and the position of the schools became a matter of some anxiety. A change of constitution was thought by some to be necessary; hence the formulation of Mr. Leighton's scheme. This was more than twelve months ago. Now it is reported that the House Committee, at its meeting on Wednesday last, agreed to shelve this scheme for the present, and that a sub-committee has been appointed to frame a scheme to be submitted to the House Committee on a future occasion. Meanwhile it behoves the Welsh public, whose charity it is, to take a more active interest in the subject.

Two stained glass windows have been placed in Bodelwyddan Church by Sir W. Grenville Williams and his brothers and sisters, in memory of their mother, Lady Williams of Bodelwyddan Castle; and by the relatives of Lady Willoughby de Broke.

RARE BIRDS. I hear a solan goose or gannet was caught near Llanyblodwel last week. The bird was in a very weak state when captured and died shortly afterwards. So I take it the Wild Birds Act was not infringed. What it was doing there at this time of year I do not know. These birds are very common all along the West Coast of Scotland, and it is a grand sight to watch them diving after herrings and other fish, sometimes from a great height, the compressed air in their breasts preventing any injury from concussion.—TANTARA.

HUW MORUS AND EDWARD MORUS.

These celebrated Welsh poets flourished about two hundred years ago. They were not relations, but were intimate friends. Pont-y-Meibion is situated in the parish of Llansilin, and Perthi Llwydion in the parish of Cerrigydrudion. Huw was an old bachelor residing with his brother, and Edward was a cattle dealer residing most of his time on his farm. Edward Morus died in Essex in 1689, about twenty years before Huw Morus. Huw composed a very pathetic elegy to his memory, in which he alludes to Edward's interment in a strange place, in the following couplet:—

> Ai clai Sais yw'r cloiau sydd
> Ar wyneb yr awenydd.

Several Welsh bards were noted for their impromptu utterances, especially if they happened to meet each other on the road or on the summit of the Welsh mountains. For example, the following was a dialogue between two poets, who happened to meet each other in the neighbourhood of Selattyn:—

> 1st Bard—I b'le mae'r daith hirfaith hon?
> 2nd Bard—I geisio mawn, goesau meinion.
> 1st Bard—Oes lety i'w gael yn Slatyn?
> 2nd Bard—Oes, main ei goes, mwy nag un.

Huw and Edward Morus saw each other first at a fair at Chirk, when Huw was selling oxen for his brother. The old people used to call the ox that trod the furrow when ploughing "rhychawr," and the other that trod on the grass "gwelltawr." Edward Morus knew that Huw was at the fair, and he walked about amongst the cattle uttering :—

> Duw ar yr ychain—p'run ydyw y rhychawr?

When he came near Huw's oxen, Huw answered :—

> Peidiwch a gwylltio, hwn yw y gwelltawr

The two poets afterwards repaired to the village inn—

> Where nut-brown draughts inspired,
> Where grey-beard mirth, and smiling toil, retired ;
> Where village statesmen talk'd with looks profound,
> And news much older than their ale went round.

Huw Morus, according to the account given by the old people, was a very tall person, with long pale face, marked by

smallpox. He was going one Sunday morning to Llansilin
Church, on a white horse, looking very serious, when some
one said to his friend "That is Huw Morus." "Who! that
ram?" exclaimed the other. The poet heard their conversation, and said—

> Dyn wyf fi, nid wy ti hwrdd,
> Gan fy hun nac w; hardd ;
> Dywed ti i fi os wyt ti fardd,
> Lle mae colofnau cangau cerdd !

The two poets were once together spending Christmas
at Brogyntyn, and quaffing strong old beer of twenty years'
standing. The family of Brogyntyn were warm patrons
of the Welsh bards in by-gone days, and Huw Morus was
often invited there. He recited there at one time a string
of epigrams in the way of an address to Dr. Lloyd, the
learned Bishop of St. Asaph. The two poets afterwards
started together in the evening for Plas Newydd, Llansilin,
to finish their strolling rounds. On reaching the summit
of the racecourse they could not go any further, on account
of the effects of the beer they had had, and they were obliged
to lie down. Edward Morus wished that some one would
bring a horse to meet them, and exclaimed—

> Archa Dduw mai march a ddel,

when Huw answered—

> Archa Iesu am farch isel.

However, no horse was sent to meet them, and after sleeping on the moss for some hours, Edward Morus awoke, and,
hearing a cockerel crowing somewhere, he said to Huw—

> Y ceiliog ! ffei o'n c'wilydd !
> Gyhoedd dôn, sy'n gwaeddi—dydd !

Huw Morus, being weary unwilling to get up, answered—

> Y ceiliog ! ni chân ond celwydd,
> Brân a edwyn derfyn dydd.

Before long the crows commenced to caw, and Edward
Morus, beginning to lose his temper, said—

> A glywch chwi dd——l y gl^rch ddydd ?

Huw replied in a twinkling—

> Dyn â maen a dyno'l menydd.

Some of the old bards, no doubt, were often considered
to be tiplers. Ellis Wynn, the Sleeping Bard, mentions
seven of his neighbours, who were always thirsty, viz.,
Tinker, Dyer, Smith, Sweep, Miner, Poet, and Parson—

> A'r goreu o'r rhai'n am gwrw rhudd
> Offeiriedyn a phrydydd.

Huw Morus was a moral and sober character, as there are
ample testimonies in his works. Public houses in his days
were not numerous, and the opportunities of getting drink
were comparatively scarce. There was but one house
named Ty'nyllan, or the Church Inn, for each parish, and
this was one result of the influence of the Book of Sports.
To return to the old poets, Huw and Edward Morus
were sleeping together, and about an hour or more before
getting up, Edward addressed the cockerel in the following englyn :—

> Y ceiliog llaes glog edn llwyd—cais godi,
> Cysgadur ymysgwyd ;
> Cria ynglyn mewn cronglwyd,
> Cynar i glâf—cân o'r glwyd.

He soon had his wish, and thanked the bird for his kindness in the following manner :—

> Cenaist, ti'm llonaïst, lliw union—glaslwyd,
> Glân oslef hyfrydion ;
> Iechyd hir am dy iach dòn,
> Fyth geiliog—f'o i'th galon.

He asked Huw Morus if he was listening to what was
going on. Huw answered, and said—

> Clywn lais, nid gwaglais, ond gwiwgloch—y borau,
> Beraidd iawn blygeingloch ;
> Awch o benglog, chwiban-gloch,
> Mab iar, fawl clauar fel cloch.

Afterwards the two poets heard churning going on in the
kitchen, when Huw exclaimed :—

> Trwst a gordd, trystio dugell—dycbryn-gwsg,
> Trwm trwblgwsg, trem treblgell ;
> Twrw plethglwm—trip o laethgell.
> Twrw naw cawr, taranau cell.

Then Edward Morus answered—

> Dip-dap, lip-lap, gip-gap gwpan—cabl abl,
> Oera' nabl ar drebl driban ;
> Croch och wchw—garw twrw taran,
> Gwaedd goedd gwydd—gwedd giaidd gan.

There is not a spark of poetry in the last two verses, only
something to imitate sound. When Huw Morus was on
his deathbed, a friend asked him how he was. The poet
answered him in the following englyn :—

> Mynd i'w ail adail ar redeg—yr wyf,
> Lle ceir oes ychwaneg ;
> I Baradwys bur wiwdeg,
> Yn enw Duw—yn union deg.

Which is rendered thus into English by George Borrow in
his "Wild Wales":—

> Now to my rest I hurry away,
> To the world which lasts for ever and aye,
> To Paradise, the beautiful place,
> Trusting alone in the Lord of Grace.

LLYWARCH HEN.

THE LAKE LEGENDS OF WALES.

On Wednesday evening Professor Rhys of Oxford read
a paper before the Cymmrodorion Society at the Freemasons'
Tavern on "The Lake Legends of Wales." The chair
was taken by Mr. Howel W. Lloyd, M.A., who briefly introduced the speaker to the audience.

Professor Rhys said a few years ago he had begun to
collect the lake legends of Wales. To some people such
legends might appear childish and frivolous, but they might
rest assured that they bore on questions which themselves
could be called neither childish nor frivolous. So, however
silly they might think a legend, let them communicate it
to somebody who would place it on record ; they would
then probably find out that it had more meaning and interest than they had anticipated. The first legend treated
by Professor Rhys was the Myddvai Legend of the Little
Van Lake and its variants. These included the versions
of Mr. Rees of Tonn, written down from the oral recita-
tions of John Evans of Myddvai, David Williams, Morva
Myddvai, and Elizabeth Morgan of Henllys, Llandovery,
Mr. Wirt Sikes's versions in British Goblins, &c. Coming
to North Wales, we had similar legends relating to the
lakes of Geirionydd and Quellyn, and Llyn du'r Arddu, with
their variants at Bettws Garmon and Waenfawr, of which
the Rev. Owen Davies (Eos Llechyd) had supplied several,
and Mr. Hugh Derfel Hughes, a local antiquarian of
great industry and zeal, who is responsible for interesting
tales connected with the Corwrion Lake, in Upper
Arllechwedd, Carnarvonshire. In respect of these several
important linguistic points were touched upon by the
speaker. The whole matter will be exhaustively treated
by Professor Rhys in the forthcoming numbers of the
Cymmrodor.

Mr. Howel W. Lloyd mentioned several of his own recollections, &c., on the subject, principally connected with
Merionethshire and other North Wales lakes. Mr.
Phillemon referred to a parallel in connection with a
custom at Conwil Caio, Carmarthen, where offerings of
food, &c., were placed under a stone to procure, as it was
supposed, the return of lost cattle, &c. Mr. Hancock referred to the Llyn Barfog Legend. A few remarks from
the Rev. John Davies, M.A., Dr. Isambard Owen, M.A.,
and the Rev. J. Morgan, closed the proceedings.

MONMOUTH AND WALES.

Up to the twenty-seventh year of Henry VIII, there were no statutory enactments as to the division of Wales into Counties. At that time there were eight shires "of ancient and long time," viz.:—Glamorgan, Caermarthen, Pembroke, Cardigan, Flint, Caernarvon, Anglesea, and Merioneth. In that year a statute was passed which affected not the counties above enumerated, but that part of Wales which was then known as "The Marches." These "marches" are described in that Act as "Lordship Marchers within the said Country or Dominion of Wales, lying between the Shires of England and the Shires of the said Country or Dominion of Wales." Be it understood that the territory above alluded to was part of the dominion of Wales, but was that eastern portion of the Principality of Wales which lay next to England, the sea being the boundary of Wales on the west.

The object of the Act is declared to be that certain of these Lordship Marchers should be annexed to English Counties, certain others to Welsh Counties, and "that all the residue of the said Lordship Marchers, within the said country or dominion of Wales, shall be severed and divided into certain particular Counties or Shires, that is to say, the County or Shire of Monmouth, the County or Shire of Brecknock, the County or Shire of Radnor, the County or Shire of Montgomery, and the County or Shire of Denbigh."

The only other Act of Henry VIII. in any way affecting the constitution of the Welsh Counties, is that of the thirty-fourth and thirty-fifth year of Henry VIII., which recites the Act of the twenty-seventh year of that King as having created additional divisions in Wales, "that is to say, the Shires of Radnor, Brecknock, Montgomery, and Denbigh, over and besides the Shire of Monmouth." This is the last Act of Henry VIII. with regard to Wales. It is beyond all argument undeniable from these Acts, that the County of Monmouth was legally defined by the Act of twenty-seventh year of Henry VIII., out of territory expressly stated to be part of the Dominion of Wales, and was by that Act merely created a County in the territory of Wales, as were also at the same time the Counties of Brecknock, Radnor, Montgomery, and Denbigh; and this view is confirmed by the fact that the regulations as to the administration of justice, and the issuing of writs from Westminster, which were enacted by the Act, creating the five new divisions of the Principality above described were, within a very few years, extended by a subsequent Act (1. Edward VI., c 10) to the eight older Counties of Wales.

That any certain exceptional legal enactment may have at any time been applied (or not) to any borough in the county of Monmouth is totally irrelevant, and in no way affects the question, inasmuch as no application of a law can alter a territory or destroy a race. Wales is the part of Great Britain still inhabited by the aboriginal race, and has been so acknowledged and so treated ever since the ancient Britons confined themselves especially to that part of the Kingdom yclept historically and legally Wales, and to attempt to alienate any portion of it is to rob and insult the whole Principality. The above legal statements are extracted from the statute book, and the few remarks appended are for the purpose of rendering the facts clear and distinct to unprofessional readers—so that no one need plead ignorance of the law because they do not belong to the legal profession, or timidly shrink from forming individually an independent opinion through inability to detect the skilful suppression of those points, which the professional advocate of a political party might find it on certain occasions his duty to ignore. JUSTINIAN.

ENID AND THE MABINOGION.

One of the most interesting illustrations of Mr. Tennyson's method of dealing with his raw material is to be found in *Enid*. Here we can follow him step by step; here we can study in detail the distinctive features of his art. The story itself is to be found in the *Mabinogion*. That charming collection of tales was translated in 1838 by Lady Charlotte Guest, and it is of Lady Guest's translation that Mr. Tennyson has availed himself. To give something of an allegorical significance to the character of Geraint, and to make the story bear on the main action of his epic, Mr. Tennyson assigns the departure of Geraint from Arthur's Court, not to any anxiety on the part of the young man to return to

his aged father and his troubled realm, but to a desire to sever Enid from communion with Guinevere, whose guilty love for Launcelot was now beginning to be suspected.

And many there were who accompanied Geraint, and never was there seen a fairer host journeying towards the Severn. And for a long time he abode at home, and he began to shut himself up in the chamber of his wife, and he took no delight in anything besides, insomuch that he gave up the friendship of his nobles together with his hunting and his amusements.

In Mr. Tennyson's versification of this the effect of the five repetitions of the word "forgetful"—

> Forgetful of the falcon and the hunt;
> Forgetful of the tilt and tournament;
> Forgetful, &c. —

has often been deservedly admired. We may notice, however, that it would seem to be an echo from a similarly effective iteration in Keats's *Isabel* :

> And she *forgot* the stars and moon and sun,
> And she *forgot* the blue above the trees,
> And she *forgot* the dells where waters run,
> And she *forgot* the chilly autumn breeze.

And there was murmuring and scoffing concerning him among the inhabitants of the palace on account of his relinquishing so completely their companionship for the love of his wife. And when Erlin heard these things he spoke unto Enid, and inquired of her whether it was she that had caused Geraint to act thus. "Not I," said she, "there is nothing more hateful to me than this." And she was very sorrowful.

> And by and by the people when they met
> In twos and threes, or fuller companies,
> Began to scoff and gear and babble of him
> As of a prince whose manhood was all gone,
> And molten down in mere uxoriousness.
> This too the women who attired her head,
> To please her dwelling on his boundless love,
> Told Enid, and they saddened her the more.

This last is one of those delicate and thoughtful touches which Mr. Tennyson seldom misses an opportunity of introducing.—*From* "*A New Study of Tennyson*," *in the* "*Cornhill Magazine*" *for July.*

A PEEP INTO SNOWDONIA, VIA THE GLYN TRAMWAY.

How many old Oswestrians, I wonder, are there who know that within a dozen miles of the town they can enjoy a scene of natural beauty which includes the mountains of Snowdonia, and for extent and variety is scarcely surpassed in Wales? If I said to one of them some fine afternoon in June, "let us refresh ourselves with a glimpse of these a and the Snowdonian mountains before the sun sets," I should be told the sea was forty miles away as the crow flies, and Snowdon fifty, that there were countless hills to intercept the view, and that nobody who knew the neighbourhood talked of seeing either from anywhere near Oswestry. But if I could persuade my friend to try the experiment, a brisk walk of three hours or a little more would bring him within sight of the mountain, and in thirty minutes more he would be revelling in a view of the sea. We will reach the place by an easier mode of locomotion. The Great Western carries us to Chirk in twenty minutes, and in ten more we have walked down into the Ceiriog Valley, to the primitive little station at Pontfaen, where the Glyn Tramway has its present terminus. For the next six miles—an hour's journey—our way lies up the valley, by the side of the joyous river, and if the sun shines we shall agree that it is a journey worth taking, though it would be still more delightful if the company could afford to provide cars constructed to allow an uninterrupted view. The tram-car runs in places between hedges brilliant with wild roses, which we can almost pluck as we pass along, and the Ceiriog, close by on our left, hurrying towards the Dee, makes a pretty picture amongst the trees. The valley is full of quiet beauty and grateful repose. The hills are not lofty or grand, but here they are clothed with woods, there a pleasant contrast is supplied by slopes of green or brown on which no trees have grown, and, as we drive along after the patient horse, it is interesting to trace the countless roadways over the heights and to think of the fresh beauties they would lead us to. The driver blows his horn and we pull up at our first station, Castle Mill, where Offa's Dyke, running on up into Chirk Castle Park, is intercepted by the tramway. Driving on, signs are not wanting that in winter time the valley sometimes presents a very different scene from that which charms us now. In a few hours the waters burst their banks, tear up trees by the roots, and deluge the line and the fields; and then as quickly return again to their natural course, leaving behind signs of their force and fury, like the tree which is now lying in mid-stream, telling of a recent flood. At the next station, Pontfadog, the little inn, the Swan, looks clean and cozy, and fishermen hang about the door, for this is an anglers' house, frequented by visitors from distant towns, who can freely fish—and actually catch trout!—from here upwards. Near by, on our right, over the farm of Cilcychwyn, we see the branches of a famous tree, an oak of monstrous girth, in which, they say, a few years ago, a bull was lost for two whole days. The animal ran into the tree but could not back out again, and there, after two days' search, it was found, and rescued from its involuntary retirement. The horn is blown again at Dolywern, where we cross the stream, and stop for a moment or two before the Queen's Head; then on again, past the flannel mills, looking strange and out of place in this remote Welsh valley, to our terminus at Llansantffraidglyn-Ceiriog, a populous village, but rather under a cloud now, for something like two hundred and fifty workmen have lost employment by the closing of the Slate works; and though the flannel industry shows signs of increasing, it cannot make up for the stoppage of the quarries. If our expedition ends at Glyn, we find several inns ready to welcome us; and the valley here has grown more picturesque. We are encompassed by the hills, which below sweep round a great basin of green, and higher up, where the road runs on towards Llanarmon, contract into a wooded ravine. An excursion to Glyn by rail and tram is well worth taking for its own sake, and the pedestrian who does not care to extend his travels can find his way back to Oswestry, if he is so inclined, by a mountain road which will bring him home past Cern-y-bwch; or a pleasant afternoon may be spent in following the Ceiriog up towards Llanarmon, past Pandy-melin-deirw to Pontymeibion (two miles from Glyn), classic ground to Welshmen, as the dwelling place of Huw Morris the poet. Our way lies upwards, past the plain village church, perched high enough to try the piety of the villagers by the waterside, along the Llangollen road until the summit is reached, and the hills on the other side of the Vale of Llangollen come in view—the quaint Eglwyseg rocks, with Castell Dinas Bran standing out in front, Moel-y-Gamelyn, Moel Morfydd, and others, a group of great beauty of colour and contour. Here, by a farm-house which stands some 1,300 feet or so above the sea—one of the highest farmhouses in the kingdom, I should think—we turn to the left, and another turn, to the right, in a few yards, and again to the left almost immediately, puts us in a cart track across the hill which leads towards a shooting box plainly seen, apparently close at hand, but in reality a mile and a half away. When we reach the building—which is just two miles from the Glyn, and 1,715 feet high, or, say a thousand feet above the village—the

doubts of my sceptical friend are set at rest. Looking north-west by west, Snowdon rises in all his grandeur between two low-lying hills, with a shoulder of Moel Siabod on his right. The cairn-marked summit is plain enough through a glass, or even to a pair of good eyes, the point of Crib-y-Ddysgyl rises to the right, and to the left it is possible to discern the ridge of Lliwedd. But if we are to see a still more delightful scene the hill which rises beyond us must be our goal; say half-an-hour away for a good walker. We reach it through the heather, finding a path if we are fortunate, and admiring as we go along the stag-horn moss which lies in beautiful green patches here and there. The summit, when we have reached it, is found to be 2,000 feet high or so, and the prospect is enchanting. To the right of Snowdon now we see Siabod; the Glyders with their stony summits; Y Garn, the mountain which rises above the village of old Llanberis; the rocky pinnacles of Tryfaen; Foel Goch, at the entrance to Nant Francon; Carnedd Davydd, Carnedd Llewelyn, Foel Fras, and the hills stretching down almost to Penmaenmawr. The sunlight streams between the mountains which rise round Llyn Ogwen, Snowdon rises against a sky of silver-grey, and the scene is one never to be forgotten. Further to the right the sea, with here and there a sail, comes into View, the houses at Rhyl are visible, Moel Fammau with its commemorative tower is a conspicuous object, and then, carrying the eye round the horizon, we see the Cheshire hills, Hawkstone, Grinshill, the Wrekin, the Caradoc, the Stiperstones, the Breidden, and close at hand the highest summits of the Berwyn, on a spur of which we stand. We descend towards the Dee, following as our guide the fence which runs to our right as we face the Berwyns. Presently a road is reached, and keeping Snowdonia in sight until we are half way down, we pass from these majestic views to the softer beauties of the Vale of Llangollen. The road which the owner of Plas-yn-Vivod, the mansion passed on our right, has beautified with flowers and shrubs, rapidly descends, the Dee comes in sight below us, and turning to the right we soon reach the prettiest railway station in Wales—Berwyn, on the Great Western; and over against us is Mr. Newbery's delightful little inn, where Mr. Mallock would never have asked us whether life was worth living. E.

June, 1881.

NOTES.

THE OLD WELSH ALMANACKS.

(July 6, 1881.)

The following are the title pages of the Almanacks for the four years 1824—1827, all printed at Dublin :—

The one for 1824 is called "Cyfaill Deallus." The price is not marked :—

1 Fy hen Gyfeillion heini,
Dilynais etto leni,
I ddyfod attoch yr un wedd
A'r llynedd er eich lloni.

2 Heb lewyrch byddai lawer
O honoch mwy na haner,
Pe llwyr ddiflannai golau
gwych
Y CYFAILL od-wych, cofler.

3 Rhodfau Planedau nodir,
Lloer, Haulwen, oll rheolir;
A rhyw hyfforddiant, er y
ffael,
O'r hin sy' i'w gael os gwelir.

4 Er hynny oll, rhyw Hunan,
Swn drwg a gwg a gogan,
Y sydd ar droed, erioed gan
rai,
Heb achos, am fai bychan.

5 Yn Eden, gynt niweidiwyd
Ein hanian,—hi wenwynwyd
A galar, fyth, o goelio'r fall,
Pob rhinwedd gall a gollwyd.

6 The chain of Superstition
Dissolves, when Education
First penetrates into the
mind;
It cannot find protection.

The one for 1825 is called "Cyfaill Amserol," and has no price mentioned :—

1 GYFEILLION, dynion doniol,
Drwy Wynedd, fro dirionol,
'Rwy'n d'od i'ch plith 'ran da
drwy'ch plaid,
Omeriaid, yn dymmorol.

2 Chwe' Sir Deheudir hwdiwch
Y CYFAILL newydd ;—cofiwch
Ei·fod, yn rhwydd, ar sicr-
wydd sail
Hen arfer,—ail gynnerfwch.

3 Gall ambell un gael llawn-
barch,
Na haeddo ei gofio a'i gy-
farch,
Lle na cha'r llall, un diwall
da,
Er dim a wna ond ammarch.

4 Ond dyma ffordd plant dynion,
O digiant wrth gym'dogion,
Un nodau, bron, hwy wnant
brad,
A'r lleill sy'n ngwlad 'r ellyll-
o'r.

5 Gwrthodwn rhag gwarth
hudol,
Hen agwedd anghrist'nogol;
A cheisiwn oll am ddigoll
ddawn,
Fudd uniawn, yn feddiannol.

6 The Heavenly Orbs in union,
Display through all Creation,
Th' Almighty's wisdom in His
ways
And never cease in motion.

The one for 1826 is called "Cyfaill Cymeradwy," and the selling price sixpence :—

1 Fy hen Gyfeillion hynod,
Mae gobaith i'ch' gael gwybod
Am d_refn y Rhôd, bod nôd, yn
wir,
Yn ol hen ddifyr ddefod.

2 Ymdrechu, felly yw f'wyllys,
I'ch donio yn wych a dawnus,
Drwy olrhain Cylchau, llwy-
brau llon,
Yn nosparth Newton hyspys.

3 Y dull sy'n hardd a deallus
I'w drin gan yr oedranus ;
Câr pawb, o Fôn i gyrion Gwy,
Ei wedd yn fwy nwyddus.

4 Yr *agerdd-longau rwygant,
Y weilgi, am Gybi gwibiant ;
O'r †Ynys fawr i Ynys Fôn,
Gyfeillion ddigon ddygant.

5 Os d'wedir gwir rhagorol,
A hynny yn lled wahanol
I'r byn a dybir,—meddir mai
Ynfydrwydd—bal anfeidrol.

6 May God, the source of mercy,
Protect our King and country,
And may we subjects, and our
King,
Suppress the sting of envy.

*Steam Packets. †Ywerddon.

The one for 1827 is called "Cyfaill Cymwynasgar." The price sixpence :—

1 GYFEILLION tiriou, tyrwch
Y'nghyd, i gyd,—nag oedwch,
I brynu'r Cyfaill yn ddi nam,
Heb addysg pa'm y bydd-
wch.

2 Mae són o Fôn i'r Fenni,
Am dano'n gwneud daioni ;
A gwyr y wlad a gâr ei lwydd,
Heb wyddynt arwydd oeri.

3 Yr Haul a'r Lloer sy'n rheoli
Y dyfroedd oll mewn difri ;
A'r holl Blanedau, moddau
mâd,
A luniodd Tad goleuni.

4 Y Ser, i'w gyfer, cofiant
Eu gwiw-per, a chyd ganant
Ei fawl a'i glôd,—ufelawg lef,
Yn nenawr nef ennynant.

5 Ond er y nifer nefol,
Sy'n gym'mwys yn ei gan'mol,
Rhyfedd ! mae wedi hoffi ei
hun,
Ddawn diriaid ddyn daearol !

6 May God, who is Almighty,
From Malice, Fraud, and
Envy,
Protect the Person of our
King
And our loving country.

Within the cover of the Almanack for 1825 I find :—

Symmud yr achos ymaith,
O bob nych, gwych yw y gwaith.

And in the one for 1826:—

Y leni, O ! moliannwn ddaioni yr hwn a ro'es
Ein lluniaeth, a'n llawenydd, bob nos a dydd hyd oes ;
Ac hefyd rhaid yw cofio, tra'n rhodio ts y Rhôd
Am fyw yn addas iddo heblaw cryg-leisio ei glôd.

E.G.S.

THE LATE LORD HANMER (June 15, 1881).—It is stated in the Gents : Mag : for 1818, that on Nov. 5 of that year the eldest son of Sir Thomas Hanmer of Bettisfield Park died at the age of 38, in consequence of the accidental discharge of a fowling-piece, which he had placed alongside of his arm while in a vehicle, in a shoot-ing excursion. Before his elevation to the peerage the late Lord Hanmer was a baronet, but according to the obituary notice of him in Bye-gones he was the son of Lieut.-Col. Thomas Hanmer. When did he become a baronet ? TELL.

MONTGOMERYSHIRE HIGHWAYMEN.—As recently as 1835, it would seem some parts of Wales were not free from highwaymen ; and prudent travellers, un-attended, went armed. On the 18th of Feb. in the year just named, the High Sheriff of Montgomeryshire, H. D. Griffith, Esq., was passing over the Berwyn chain of mountains on his way from his residence at Caer-rhyn, in Carnarvonshire, to Llechweddgarth Hall, his seat in Montgomeryshire, in a pony carriage, unattended, when a brace of ruffians, armed with bludgeons, appeared on the scene and stopped the carriage. Mr. Griffith, however, was equal to the occasion, for he immediately presented a couple of pistols, on which they made off. The same fellows were said to have robbed several parties about the time. Were they ever captured ? BLACKPOOL.

MRS. CORNWALL BARRY WILSON.—How was this lady interested in Welsh affairs ? On Mar. 2, 1881, "G. G." gave your readers the benefit of an ode she wrote for the children to sing at the St. David's Dinner in London in 1838 ; and ten years later, viz., on Mar. 1, 1848, we are told that, after the banquet, the children belonging to the charity were ushered in and sang "the following beautiful ode, written by the late Mrs. Cornwall Barry Wilson "—

Again when the banquet of Cambria is spread,
Our steps, as our hearts, are by gratitude led ;
Again shall our Patrons with blessings be hail'd
To that fountain of mercy which never has fail'd.

GIRLS.

In the pathway of life, render'd thornless by you,
To the shrine of fair virtue our road we'll pursue ;
For the highest rewards of benevolent deeds,
Is to know that the labour of kindness succeeds.

BOYS.

In the fields, on the wave, like true Welshmen we'll show,
We've a heart for each friend, and an arm for each foe ;
What our voices now promise, our actions shall prove,
And the deeds of the man, show the boy's honest love.

Here we are told that "all the children sang soft, accom-panied by the harp " :—

Yet o'er this bright scene of which Wallia is proud,
One mournful regret casts its shaddowing cloud ;
For the sadness of grief sits on Cambria's fair brow,
For the Patriot she hallows in memory now.

This was in allusion to the Earl of Powis, who had died in the month of January previous ; so the death of Mrs. Wilson must have been very shortly before the Ancient Britons met. N.W.S.

[In July, 1876, "D. L." of Shrewsbury, in Salopian Shreds and Patches, incidentally alluded to Mrs. Wilson as "our gifted towns woman ;" on which Mr. Salisbury wrote to that publica-tion for its "authority" but received no reply.—ED.]

LONDON MISSIONARY SOCIETY (Sep. 15, 1880).—At this date I gave some particulars of a local nature relative to the first commencement of the London Missionary Society, and the connection of the Rev. John Whitridge of Oswestry with it. I have just had a letter from the Rev. M. Wilks of London to Mr. Whitridge placed in my hands, which is interesting as giving an account of the early doings of the society, following the preliminary meeting at London, which Mr. Whitridge attended. The letter is as follows :—

My dear Mr. Whitridge,

The Directors of the Missionary Society have authorized me to make their acknowledgments to your associated Brethren for their readiness to unite with us in forming a society to carry to the Ends of the Earth that Gospel which is the joy and rejoicing of their Hearts. We trust that we shall find the great advantage of having the assistance of so respectable a Body of Ministers and Churches not only from their pecuniary aid but also from their advice, their prayers, and from the consecration of some of their services, moral and experimental members, to the important Embassy.'

I suppose you will feel gratified by a general account of our proceedings since you left London.

The Committee of Examination sit frequently. We have accepted several and some of him (sic) have afforded us a pleasure that has more than compensated for our past toil. One of the Candidates is an approved classical scholar, one a bricklayer, one a carpenter, one a cooper, &c.; one a soldier in the Train was a taylor (a fine fellow), one a pocket-book maker—he was brought up to husbandry; and one a whitesmith, but fear he has not missionary abilities. We want a good weaver—smith—shipwright—gardener : a man of musical knowledge; and perhaps a collier or miner might be of service. Will you look out for such, and try to stir up a missionary spirit. The Cause wants it, Jesus is worthy of it, the salvation of souls requires it. I trust when the Churches understand that all our Missionaries need not be preachers or scholars, they will furnish a number sufficient for the work.

We have at present £3,000 at least in hand or subscribed. The Churches who fav'r us in Town are busy, and so I hear many are in the Country. Kingsbury has sent us £273 . 17 . 3 and £33 annual. I hope you are neither inactive nor unsuccessful. A *Collecting Journey*, and that soon, w'd serve us materially. Will you make it ? Burder and Moody will in their neighbourhood.—If it be impracticable for you w'd you advise any Director or Member of the Society to undertake it in y'r county ? We think something more must be done in the outset than can be expected in subsequent years. We have but a short time to work and shall have a long time to rest. Work while it is called to-day, but—stop—I need not get into the imperative mood till you have the indicative.

We have some enemies to our cause.—Aldridge and Huntington have preached against us.—Let them alone; we are ab't a great work.—Jesus must reign till every nation call him blessed, and every Tongue confess him. For our great encouragement we have friends in a quarter where essential help can be rendered to us. Suffice it to say we are promised a freight for our ship, and protection to our sailors, all of whom are to be professors at least.

The Committee of Provisions and Conveyance have made a report on conveyance, and Mr. Hawies in an excellent memoir upon a Mission to Africa. Both lie on the table.

It is necessary to unite with us in the Direction one of y'r Association. Whoever y'r Brethren shall nominate shall be the object of our confidence, and through him we shall communicate with your Association upon the particular business of the Society.

I have sent you a number of letters unsealed, and beg you will fill up the blank of each with the substance of this letter, and such hints of y'r own as may tend to gratify y'r Brethren and forward the interests of the Society.

Probably you will request them to read y'e letter to their People, and have also read the Minutes of the Conference out of the Magazine with pleasing effect. If you want plans you may have as many as you please.

Directors send Christian love to all y'e Brethren ; and accept the same for them and y'rself from Dr. Bro.

　　　　　　　　　　　　　Y'rs in our Dear Lord
London, Oct. 31. 95.　　　　　　　　　　M. WILKS.

The letters are from Shropshire and Cheshire and part of Wales, the limits of y'r Association—and others in y'r county not of it. Send to Baptists, they may help. Have sent Boden for Staffordshire, perhaps you had better correspond.

Such was the small beginning of a Society whose annual income sometimes reaches £100,000.　　　　　J.?.R.

5

CURRENT NOTES.

Lord Sudeley of Gregynog and the Chevalier Lloyd of Clochfaen have each sent £5 to the National Eisteddfod Association.

The first Temperance Society in Wales is said to have been established at Mold in May, 1835. There was a choice of three pledges—1. Total abstinence from intoxicating drinks. 2. Total abstinence from spirituous liquors. 3. An undertaking not to get drunk.

Mr William Jones of Glandwr, Dolgelley, the oldest member of the London Court of Common Council, to which he has been elected fifty-one times by the ward of Bishopsgate, has become disqualified by non-attendance for six months, and a new writ has been issued by the Council.

Mr Wirt Sikes, whose new book "Studies of Assassination" has just appeared, is engaged in revising the proof sheets of a new and important work entitled "Rambles and Studies in South Wales," which will be illustrated. The work will shortly be published by Messrs. Sampson, Low, & Co.

Sir T. Erskine, in response to representations from Mr. Rathbone, M.P., who waited upon him with an introduction from Mr. Osborne Morgan, has signified his willingness to transfer the lease of Conway Castle to the Corporation of that town, on condition that they will devote the income to the maintenance of the structure, and see that if the old custodian of the castle had any family they are provided for. The Council intend to avail themselves of the offer.

THE OSWESTRY AND WELSHPOOL NATURALISTS' FIELD CLUB.

A member of the Naturalists' Field Club has kindly sent us the following interesting account of their visit to Harlech :—

A few of the members of this Club made an extended excursion to Harlech from July 5th to the 9th. The party that met at the Castle Hotel, Harlech, on Tuesday the 5th, comprised the following members and friends :— Major and Mrs. Barnes, Mr. Harold Barnes, Mr. Theodore Gwyther, the Rev. G. G. Monck, and Rev. O. M. Feilden, the energetic secretary of the Club, to whose exertions the success of the expedition was mainly due. The party started on Wednesday morning, and, driving through the picturesque village of Llanbedr, left their carriage at Pen-y-bont, and immediately ascended over the mountain to the pass of Drws Ardudwy. After leaving the lonely farm—Maes-y-Garnedd, famous for once having been the home of Col. Jones, the Regicide, Cromwell's brother-in-law—the solitude and dreariness of this pass became extreme, the more so as heavy black clouds were hanging about the peaks and crags of Rhinog-fawr. The top of the pass was at last reached, and after a short halt for lunch, the party crossed over the moorland, and soon entered the narrow pass of Bwlch Tyddiad, through which a track runs from Trawsfynydd to Harlech. There seems to be very little doubt that the wonderful causeway, with its parapet walls, and flights of steps, was made by Romans, and it is still in marvellous preservation, carrying the traveller along an easy path, amidst some of the wildest and weirdest scenery to be found in North Wales. The narrowness of the pass, the height of the mountains, the luxuriant vegetation in the crevices of the rocks, the huge masses piled up on either side, all tend to fascinate by their strange mixture of awfulness and beauty. The descent to Cwm Bychan was soon made, and the carriage found at the farm below the lake, after a walk of some eleven miles, rough and swampy. The botanists were rewarded by finding sundews, marsh pimpernel, blue butterwort, bog asphodel, beech and mountain fern, viper's bugloss. After dinner Harlech Castle was visited, more especially for the sake of seeing the sun set from the walls. The castle is a large square building in a good position on the rock, and in the days of old was almost invincible except by famine. It held out nine years for the Lancastrians, and it was this siege that evoked the melody of the famous "March of the Men of Harlech." The castle was also the longest to hold out for King Charles. On a clear summer's evening, after a long walk among mountains and llyns, we can think of nothing more soothing than to sit on the walls of Harlech Castle, and from time to time, as we turn over the pages of some old stories of knights and sieges and fair ladies, to lift the eyes across the bay and see the sun sinking behind Yr Eifl and lighting up all the peaks of Snowdonia with its parting rays.

On Thursday, the 7th, an excursion was made by train to Pwllheli, and thence by carriage to the village of Llithfaen at the foot of Yr Eifl. An easy ascent of about an hour brought the party through the walls and up the causeway to the gate of the strange old British Camp called Tre'r Ceiri. This camp, on the hill top, covers about five acres of ground within the boundary wall, and dotted all about are the remains of the circular houses of the ancients, the walls in places still being five to six feet high. The view from the top of the camp over land and sea is very lovely. After lunch the party walked round the north shoulder of Yr Eifl to a romantic little dingle, running down to the sea, called Nant Gwrtheyrn, where the mount of Vortigern's Castle is still to be seen. This prince, the story goes, finding that his policy of calling in the Saxons to drive out the Picts and Scots in 450 only resulted in himself and his people being driven out too, retired to this lonely spot and built a castle for himself, but the memory of former years was too much for him; and so one day he climbed the mountain above his castle, and from a rocky promontory hurled himself into the sea, and the point is still called Vortigern's Leap, a worthy memorial of a statesman with a policy—so disastrous. The view of the dingle below, and the mountain above from this spot, and of all the coast line and country as far as Nevin, is one not easily forgotten, and this little-known country is well worth exploring by those who care for historical remains amidst pleasant coast scenery. The descent to Llanaelhaiarn was made in rather over an hour; here the carriage was again picked up, and the return journey to Pwllheli and Harlech was accomplished. The chief interest of the excursion lay in the historical remains, but the botanists found a profusion of Butterfly Orchis. After dinner some of the party went to visit the wreck that lies embedded in the sand, about two miles from Harlech. About six years ago, a fine three-masted sailing ship ran aground on the sands on a dark night; her captain thought he was making Liverpool; and in spite of all efforts made to tug her off, she had to be abandoned to the mercy of wind, and wave, and sand; and there she lies, a sad monument of the vicissitudes of a life on the ocean wave.

Friday morning found the unwearied naturalists again abroad driving to Festiniog, and paying a visit to the water-falls on the way, but this part of the day was spoilt by a heavy downpour of rain for nearly an hour. The botanists, however, found some good specimens of ferns, spleenworts, lastrea spinulosa, polystichum aculeatum, and beech fern in abundance. The carriage was taken on again at Festiniog to Diffwys to see the Welsh Slate Company's Quarry. This quarry is somewhat peculiar, and well worth a visit, on account of the galleries having been run far under the mountain, like a series of immense caves, intersected by tunnels and lines at various levels. Mr. Jones, the manager of one of the Diffwys quarries, kindly took charge of the party and showed them all the different workings. The thunder of the blasting, the clouds of smoke issuing from the dark cavernous mouths, the constant splash of water, and crash of slates, all went to make up a busy, and somewhat startling scene to the uninitiated, and especially to the quiet-loving students of peaceful solitudes and ancient ruins; but perhaps the climax of all was reached, when, after groping their way down a long dark passage with ominous sounds of trucks behind and water before, the party were placed on a platform with a truck of slates and suddenly raised up to daylight and air again by an hydraulic lift. At Diffwys the party separated for their various homes on Friday evening. The thanks of all were given to Mr. and Mrs. Lovegrove of the Castle Hotel, Harlech, who made the party so comfortable and provided them with an excellent table, and every attention at a reasonable rate. The affability of the landlord, the comfort of the hotel within, and the lovely view without, will long remain as some of the most pleasant reminiscences of this club.

NOTES.

POWYS-LAND MUSEUM PORTRAITS.

(Apr. 27, 1881.)

The following additions have been made to the collection previously enumerated :—

35. Sir J h Conroy, Baronet, painted by H. W. Pickersgill, R.A. Engraved b R. T. Ryall. Published 1st June, 1840, by E. G. Moony

36. John Naylor, Esq., Leighton Hall, "from the picture presented to Mrs. Naylor, at Brynllowarch, 1858." Painted by Francis Grant, R.A. Engraved by George Sanders.

37. Mrs. Naylor, Leighton Hall, "from the picture presented at Leighton Hall to John Naylor, Esq., 1858." Painted and engraved by the same Artists as the last.

38. "Sr Hugh Myddleton Knight and Baronet [inscribed] "The famous aquæduct called the New River was perform'd at his charge (notwithstanding many natural difficulties and the envious opposition he met with) A.D. 1613. He also caus'd to be wrought the Silver Mines in Wales to the great advantage of the crown and of the public."

"Dij Tibi Divitias dederant Artemq : fruendi.

"Ad Tabulum Cornelij Janssonij jam penes illustris. Comitem Oxoniensem Georgius Vertue Sculpsit A.D. 1722."

This portrait was presented by the Rev. H. T. Ellacombe, Clyst St. George Topsham—a descendant of the family and the present owner of the original copper-plate.

The following portraits, which have been published, are still lacking in the collection.

The Hon. General Sir Percy Herbert, K.B.

The Dean of Hereford.

The Hon. R. H. Clive.

David Pugh, Esq., at one time M.P. for Montgomery Boroughs.

Panton Corbett, Esq.

Thomas Jones, Esq., formerly of Trinity College, Cambridge.

Richard Wilson, R.A. (born in Penegoes.)

John Bill Pryce, Esq., and many other modern portraits. Any person having any of the above portraits and being willing to present them or to sell them at a moderate price are invited to communicate with the Hon. Curator, Powysland Museum, Welshpool.

CHURCHES IN THE RHYL DISTRICT.

(July 6, 1881.)

WHITCHURCH OR WHITE CHURCH.

Whitchurch, or *White Church*, so called because the exterior has been plastered over and whitewashed, is the original Parish Church of Denbigh, and dedicated to St. Marcellus, from which it is distant about one mile east. Like so many other Welsh churches, it has two parallel portions of equal length and width, the northern portion as chancel, the southern as nave. Originally there must have been a Norman church, judging from the existing Norman priest's door, and also a singular door on the north, with a straight-sided triangular head cut out of one great stone, and which may possibly be even of Saxon date. The present church has been entirely constructed in the Perpendicular style of Henry VII.'s time, with certain insertions and modifications of a later Tudor or Elizabethan age. The western tower is very plain, square, embattled, and of four storeys, with diagonal buttresses, its lower west window of two lights and plain round heads of Elizabethan date is rather striking from its mullion and dripstones ending in grotesque heads. There is a low-pointed arch, now blocked up, at west end of nave, which must have been the original entrance. That is now on the south with a modern porch before it, on a stone in which are indicated some reparations of the edifice.

RR <> RE . WARDENS 1722.

TGE <> RR Wardens, Repd., 1853.

On the south side are three over fine Henry VII. windows of three lights, with minor divisions in the head; their dripstones terminate in fine sculptured corbels, representing foliage, a head, fleur de lis, and Tudor roses. The east window of the nave is perpendicular, very large and finely proportioned, of five lights and minor upper divisions, in which are slight remains of stained glass. The east window of the chancel is similar, broader, and more dumpy, and not so well proportioned. On the north side is an Elizabethan window of three lights, five-foiled, without dripstone, and another of same date, square headed, of two lights, five-foiled, the bold dripstone terminating in heads as corbels. Above the triangular headed door before mentioned, the masonry is of thin or narrow layers, indicating early work. The nave and chancel are separated by five Henry VII. arches, with beautiful mouldings springing from octagonal pillars with plain filleted capitals. Font octagonal, 1640. The roofs of both chancel and nave are of fine, bold, open timber work, the hammer beams springing from stone corbels resting on the pillars representing angels with shields of arms and various animals. A portion at west end of chancel has the peculiar embattled work of Henry VII.'s time indicating the date of both roofs. A curious hollow cornice runs round both chancel and nave just below roof, filled with Tudor roses, heads, flowers, and various animals, amongst which the elephant is repeatedly conspicuous. A portion of the carved roodscreen is adapted as entrance to the vestry, and other parts are scattered about reading desk and altar.

In the porch is a large Brass engraved with figures of a man and woman kneeling opposite each other before prayer desks on which are open books; behind the man kneel 9 sons, behind the woman 7 daughters. Above in clouds some Hebrew letters.

On a shield above the prayer desks are these arms :—Quarterly : 1. & 4 *sa.* a bend *vert* with 3 foxes or wolves' heads erased *arg.* 2. *vert* a chevron *arg.* between 3 foxes or wolves' heads *arg.* 3. *Quarterly* : 1. & 4 *gu* a bend *or* with 3 boars passant *sa.* 2. & 3. Two birds. Impaling *sa* two fawns or deer back to back.

On a shield over the man :—
Quarterly : 1 & 4 *sa* a bend *vert* with 3 foxes or wolves' heads erased *arg.* 2. & 3. *vert* a chevron *arg.* between 3 foxes' heads *arg.*

On a shield over the woman :—
sa. 2 fawns or deer back to back.

Below is this inscription :—

In vayne the brage and boaste of bloode, in vayne of sinne the vaunte

Syth fleashe and blood must lodge at last where nature us did graunte

To where he lyeth that lyved of late, with love and favoure muche

To fynde his ffriend, to feele his foes, his Countrey skante had suche

Whose lyff doyth well reporte his death, whose death his lyff doyth trye

And poyntes with fynger what he was, that here in claye doyth lye.

His vertues shall enroll his acts, his Tombe shall tell his name

His sonnes and dawghters lefte behynd, shall blase on earth his fame

Look under feete and you shall fynd, upon the stone yow stand,

The Race he ranne, the lyff he lead, eatch with an upright hand.

She dyed last of Decembr. 1565 etatis sue 40.
He dyed the viij of February 1575 etatis sue 67.

There is no name mentioned, but this Brass is said to commemorate Richard (Governor of Denbigh Castle temp. Ed. VI., Mary and Eliz.) the father of Sir Hugh Myddelton and Jane Dryhurst his wife daughter of an alderman of Denbigh. On the north side of the church in the churchyard is a large burial place of the Myddelton family.

(To be continued.)

QUERIES.

SEALS IN THE SHROPSHIRE MUSEUM.—In the Museum of the Shropshire Archæological and Natural History Society are the following seals, about which information is requested.

1. Bronze Matrix and Counter Seal of Monastery of St. Peter (of 15th century), found in Radnor Castle, inscribed "Sigillum Fraternitatis Sci Petri," with a figure of St. Peter in sacerdotal vestments, in his left hand a key, his right upraised in blessing according to the Greek use. Counter Seal inscribed "Portio mea Domine," and a chalice into which a dove is descending.

2. Impression of Seal of Lady Hawis, heiress of Powisland, 1320 (of 14th century), found in foundation of a house at Oswestry. A lady in flowing robes standing, in her right hand a shield of arms, a lion rampant, and in her left a shield of arms, two lions passant in pale. Inscribed " * S'. Hawisie. Dne. de. keveoloc."

3. Impression of a Silver Seal of 14th century, found 1834, at a British Camp near Hendomen, co. Montgomery. Inscribed " * Volo. quodvis. et. volo. quovis."

W.A.L.

REPLIES.

SEVENTEENTH CENTURY TOKENS.—(June 8, 1881.)—I have been favoured with the following interesting notes on the Shrewsbury tokens Nos. 73, 75 and 77, by Mr. Charles Golding, author of "The Coinage of Suffolk." "The issuers of these tokens were Quakers and frequent sufferers for their opinions.

"John Millington and Owen Roberts on 6th day of 10 mo. 1660 were committed to prison and lay there 15 weeks for meeting together as Quakers and refusing to swear.

"Constantine Overton and Humphrey Overton were sufferers for not paying Church, or as they termed them 'Steeple House,' rates.

"Constantine Overton was again committed to prison on 26th, 12 month 1663, for attending a meeting of Quakers. Again Constantine Overton, a Freeman of the Corporation of Shrewsbury, was disfranchised and denied all privileges he was entitled to because he had meetings of 'Friends' at his house in 1665, and also for refusing to swear."   JAMES W. LLOYD.
Kington.

ANCIENT BREEDS OF WELCH CATTLE (June 29, 1881).—Upwards of a century ago, when dairy farming was by no means a principal object in this county (Montgomery), the colour of the cows most generally preferred was a *blood red with smoky faces*, called the Montgomeryshire breed of cattle. The smoky faced breed which occupied a good position in the county at one time, has given way within the last half century to breeds requiring less time to attain maturity, and consequently affording quicker and more profitable returns to the producer. This breed was, until late years, tenaciously clung to by some of its more ardent admirers; but it is now all but extinct, and its rapid extermination must be attributed to the fact that, for crossing with the finer breeds, more especially the Hereford, it was found invaluable, nothing was ever known to excel the cross-breed for its rapid growth, development, and production of the finest quality of beef in the same climate and on the same condiment of food; its chief features being its extraordinary proportion of excellent lean flesh. It is questionable if the old smoky-faced cattle would not answer well yet to breed specially for the purpose of " crossing." Some of this " distinct breed" can be seen at Crosswood, near Welshpool, the seat of Colonel Heyward, and it will be observed that "Montgomeryshire smoky faces" are to be exhibited at the forthcoming show of the Shropshire and West Midland Agricultural Society to be held at Welshpool this month.   G.B.

Your correspondent quoting word for word on the above subject from *The Pictorial Museum of Animated Nature* enquires, "What are the characteristics of the Montgomeryshire breed of cattle?" I am not able to inform him. but there are here and there to be seen white cattle with red muzzles and red inside their ears, also white cattle with black muzzles and black inside their ears at the present day in some parts of South Wales.
Brecon.   J.J.

CURRENT NOTES.

The whole of the Principality of Wales now has a population of 1,359,895 persons, being an increase of 142,760 upon the enumeration of 1871; of these 677,028 are males, and 682,867 are females, or rather less than 101 females to every 100 males. This disparity is very slight, and is probably accounted for by the large number of males engaged in mining operations, and the comparative absence of domestic servants. In England the proportion of females is 106 to 100 males. In the counties comprising South Wales the population is 879,841, showing an increase of 115,502. This population is spread as follows:—

Counties.	1871.	1881.	Increase.	Decrease.
Brecknock	59,901	57,735	—	2,166
Cardigan	73,441	70,226	—	3,215
Carmarthen	115,710	124,861	9,151	—
Glamorgan	397,859	511,672	113,813	—
Pembroke	91,998	91,808	—	190
Radnor	25,430	23,599	—	1,891
Totals	764,339	879,841	122,964	7,462

It will thus be seen that in only two of the six counties was there an increase, but that in Glamorganshire the increase was very large, whereas in the other four there was a declining population, varying from 4·4 per cent. in Cardiganshire to 0·2 per cent. in Pembrokeshire.

THE CARADOC FIELD CLUB'S VISIT TO THE NORTH SHROPSHIRE MERES.

We have been favoured by one of the party with the following interesting account of the visit of the Caradoc Club to the Shropshire meres :—

A remarkable change in the appearance of the water of some of the North Shropshire Meres usually, if not invariably, occurs in the summer, giving rise to various conjectures as to the cause which produces it, but as yet it is not fully explained. The change consists in the water assuming a very turbid appearance owing to the existence of a vast quantity of dark green matter being diffused throughout the whole body, but often more abundantly on the surface, forming a conspicuous scum. Those who have been in the habit of fishing in these meres have observed that as soon as this change appears, all chances of sport vanish, and the fish are said to become " sick." The name given to this condition of the water by those who reside in the vicinity of the meres is the " breaking of the meres "; in some other parts of Shropshire, where a similar change has been observed in large pools, the water is said to be " curdled," and the cause assigned for it is the dissemination over the water of the seeds of the abundant vegetation clothing the sides of the meres. The author of a well-known book, " Mountain, Meadow, and Mere," threw out the supposition that it arose from the growth of the American weed (Anacharis alsinastrum) which has extended with such rapidity through the canals, rivers, and lakes of this country, but as that plant is said, on the best authority, to have been introduced into England not earlier than 1841, though known to be in Ireland five years earlier, and the " breaking " of the meres was observed long prior to that date, this explanation utterly fails to account for it. The investigation of this subject falling strictly within the province of a body of naturalists such as compose the Caradoc Field Club, attention was called to it by one of the members in a paper read before the Club last autumn, in the course of which the author said that the true cause of the turbidity of the water was the extremely rapid growth of very minute plants known to Botanists as *Algæ*, which make their appearance at a certain time of the year with the same regularity as that observed by higher vegetation. Owing to these plants being so excessively minute, several thousand specimens occupying a space that may be covered by a sixpenny piece, a good microscope is required for their examination as well as some skill in the handling of it. The author further stated that though one particular species caused the breaking in Ellesmere mere, an entirely different species caused the change in the condition of the water in a pool at Hawkstone, and suggested that further observation may reveal the fact that different bodies of water may owe the change produced in them to different species of these microscopic plants. The Club, deeming this subject one of great interest and considering that comparatively little was known about the number of meres and pools in the county presenting this remarkable condition, or the particular species of Algæ producing it, appointed a committee, consisting of Messrs. T. P. Blunt, W. E. Beckwith, and W. Phillips, to collect all the information that could be gained, and to report to the Club the result at the final meeting of the season. Several members of the Club having expressed a desire to witness the breaking of the meres, the present excursion was arranged. It must not be supposed this "breaking" is confined to the North Shropshire Meres, or is an uncommon phenomenon. Botanical literature abounds with instances of both large and small bodies of water becoming coloured by an abundant growth of Algæ. A striking instance, for example, is recorded in Greville's "Scottish Cryptogamic Flora" (tab. 303) of Loch Haining, in Selkirkshire, being coloured of a rich purple tint by the diffusion of *Lyngbya prolifica Grev.* Nor is the discolouration of water by Algæ confined merely to fresh water, the sea having been observed to be coloured for many miles by the presence of *Trichodesmium erythræum*, Ehr, and other species of Algæ, while some authorities affirm that the Red Sea has acquired its name from the presence of these plants. After this brief explanation of the phenomenon under investigation by the members of the Caradoc Field Club, we proceed to give a short account of the day's excursion.

The party proceeded to Wem by rail on Friday last, whence they were conveyed by carriage to the pretty little church standing on a gentle elevation near the eastern shore of Colemere Mere, and there they dismounted to begin their perambulations. This mere is beautifully situated, and being well wooded on all sides except that where the church stands, forms a most picturesque object, indeed it only needed a background of lofty hills to convey the impression that we had dropped down by the side of one of the Cumberland lakes. Although this mere is said to "break" several times in the year, we found it perfectly clear; but as it is noted for another curious circumstance, namely, the prodution of what the people in the neighbourhood call "urchins" or "hedgehogs," a search was made for them, not without success, for a few specimens were discovered rolled up a few feet from the shore. These curious productions do not as their name would imply, belong to the animal kingdom, being composed of a loosely compacted mass of dead larch leaves, popularly known as needles, standing all out over the surface, and presenting a remarkable similarity to a hedgehog when rolled up for protection as is the habit of this animal when assailed by an enemy. They are generally round, sometimes slightly oblong, varying in size from a goose egg to a man's head. Several of these were opened, but no core or nucleus could be detected, the needles standing at all possible angles showed no uniformity of direction, and the question naturally arose how the "hedgehogs" could have been formed in the first instance, and what held the larch needles together? One gentleman of the party suggested the following as the most probable way of accounting for the formation of these curious bodies :—The larch leaves falling from the trees that line the shore become waterlogged, fall to the bottom of the mere, forming a layer, on which the gelatinous balls, known to science as *Ophridium versatile*, which are colonies of an *Infusorium*, varying in size from a pea to a swan's egg, are formed; these being rolled to and fro by under-currents over the bed of larch leaves become pierced by them in all directions, gathering them up and holding them together.

The party now proceeded under the guidance of Mr. Beckwith, through the wood skirting the northern side of the mere, obtaining beautiful peeps between the foliage, the mere glistening like a mirror under the bright sunshine. Several interesting plants were observed on the way, amongst which may be mentioned Yellow Loose-strife (*Lysimachia vulgaris*), Twayblade (*Listera ovata*), Lily of the Valley (*convallaria majalis*). This locality is also noted in our county for the growth of *Carex elongata*. Before quitting this charming mere we were provided, by the thoughtfulness of our guide, with a timely luncheon. The party then proceeded along the Ellesmere canal to the Kettlemere and Blackmere, permission to walk round which was kindly granted by the proprietor. These two little meres lie in deep hollows embosomed in trees, very near to each other, supposed by some to be connected by a subterranean channel. Kettlemere is believed to have no bottom, and Blackmere is said to be the deepest of the two—at least our facetious guide informed us that such is the opinion held by the natives hard by. We had the good fortune to find Kettlemere in the very act of breaking, while the adjoining mere was perfectly transparent. This fact goes far to prove there can be no actual connection between them. The Blackmere is said never to break. The effect we witnessed here was very remarkable; a floating scum of a yellowish dirty-white colour covered the surface of the water, and the particles of which it was composed were diffused throughout the whole mass of the water as deep down as we were able to see. Specimens of the water were procured for microscopic examination, and the temperature was noted, which doubtless has much to do in promoting the growth of the Algæ composing the scum. Attention was now drawn to the very rare and beautiful Least Water Lily (*Nuphar pumila*) which grew side by side with the much commoner White Water Lily (*Nymphæa alba*), this being the only English locality known for it. Though rare this plant cannot be compared for a moment for beauty with our two more generally distributed Water Lilies. Passing through the shady woods round Kettlemere and Blackmere the party gained the Canal and here being divided, part going on to Ellesmere, while the more ardently scientific wended their way to Whitemere to witness the breaking just then at its height. The scum on this was, if anything, more abundant and dense than on the one just quitted, and of a more decidedly yellow tinge. If several tons weight of mustard had been tilted into this mere a similar appearance might have been produced, and it must be confessed that pretty as this mere is its beauty was by no means enhanced by this discolouration. Having procured specimens of the water and tested the temperature, the steps of the party were now turned towards Ellesmere. On arriving at this mere, decidedly the most beautiful of all the North Shropshire meres, much satisfaction was felt in finding that this also was in the full course of breaking. Unlike all the others, however, there was no unsightly scum floating on the surface, but the water appeared of a dark verdigris green colour from surface to bottom, and when the sun shone through the water small spherical bodies could be seen with the naked eye floating in great quantity, which in fact gave rise to the colour. When looked at with a common pocket lense, these bodies were seen to be composed of a little globule of green jelly, from the centre of which radiated a great number of slender threads, each thread tapering outwards towards its extremity. These starshaped bodies were so nearly the same specific gravity as that of the water that they floated at all depths, not more of them near the surface than beneath. The name of this pretty little Alga is *Echinella articulata*, and it is a totally different species from that which causes the breaking of the other meres visited. Specimens having been collected, and the temperature having been ascertained, the party assembled at the Red Lion Hotel, where an excellent dinner was provided by the landlord, Mr. Sparrow, all being by this time fully capable of doing it justice. After dinner some of the rarer plants that had been collected were handed round for inspection, amongst which should be mentioned the very pretty Bladder-wort *(Utricularia vulgaris)*, the Hornwort *(Ceratophyllum demursum)*, the Frog-bit *(Hydrocharis Morsus-Ranæ)*, the Shore-weed *(Litorella lacustris)*, the Needle-rush *(Elocharis acicularis)*, the carnivorous long-leaved Sun-dew *(Drosera Anglica)*, the Crowberry *(Empetrum nigrum)*, the Cranberry *(Oxycoceus palustris)*, Marsh Andromeda *(Andromeda polifolia)*.

The President, the Rev. J. D. La Touche, having thanked Mr. Beckwith on behalf of the Club for his able guidance, the party returned in the break to Rednal station, en route for Shrewsbury, whence they dispersed for their homes, all expressing themselves highly gratified with the day's excursion. W. P.

THE LIVERPOOL WATERWORKS.

LAYING THE FIRST STONE.

The first stone of the great embankment which is to dam up the waters of the Verniew for the use of Liverpool was laid on Thursday by the Earl of Powis with appropriate ceremonial, and in the presence of a thoroughly representative gathering.

VERNIEW WATERWORKS

The Lake Verniew will be formed by the construction of a masonry embankment across the south eastern end of the Upper Verniew Valley.

Length of the Lake ....4½ Miles
Area of the Lake ....1,115 Acres
Contents of the Lake above the level at which the water will be drawn for the supply of Liverpool.......................11,900,000,000 Gallons
Available drainage area contributing to the Lake ..22,000 Acres
Length of masonry embankment, from rock to rock ..1,255 Feet
Height of masonry embankment, from lowest part of rock foundation to coping of parapet...............139 Feet
Height of masonry embankment from river level to coping of parapet.............................98 Feet
Length of contributing tunnel, from River Marchnant to Lake, about ....1½ Mile
Length of contributing tunnel from River Cowny to Lake, about ....1¼ Mile

AQUEDUCT WORKS.

Length of Aqueduct, from the intended Lake Verniew to the Reservoirs of the Liverpool Corporation at Prescot ....67 Miles
The Aqueduct consists of a triple line of pipes, and of the following three tunnels :—
The Hirnant Tunnel, in length about ....2¼ Miles
The Morda Tunnel, in length about....................¾ Mile
The Oswestry Tunnel, in length about ....¾ Mile
On the line of Aqueduct there will be Filter Beds, and several minor Reservoirs.
Estimated daily supply, including compensation—52 Million Gallons.

This is an age of Water-schemes—wholesale, retail, and for exportation. Our nation possesses thirteen teetotal mayors ; men who have the courage of their opinions, and who, to judge by their likenesses in one of the picturepapers, do credit to their beverage. The British Public too often rests content with its "pure water contaminated," so has sought in medicated adulterations to correct the evil. And these adulterations known as soda, seltzer, potash, magnesia, and the like, getting too common to be appreciated, we have sought for healing streams abroad, and have bottled Apollinaris, Friedrichshall, Gerolstein, Hunyadi-jános, and the like, for the benefit of suffering humanity. But still we are not happy. We know that what we buy away from home must necessarily be better than what we get at our own doors—for commodities, like prophets, lack honour in their own country. We know, too, that the higher sounding or more unpronounceable the name is, the better the article to be swallowed ; and yet we crave for a simpler water than that we get in bottles, and one somewhat cheaper, too, and less pronounced in the mouth. Happy Liverpool has succeeded in meeting all the requirements of the modern Englishman. It has tapped for water a river so fed by other streams that its correct cognomen cannot be ascertained : to do so it has sent its spies to a place the very name of which they cannot pronounce, and to a district hitherto a terra incognita to them ; and it has found water pure and cheap, free from taint and brim full of health. What more can it want?

"It is not often," says the Vicar of Llanwddyn (the happy valley to be swallowed by Liverpool), "we can meet with a parish in England or Wales having so great a number of streams originating or terminating within its own boundaries as Llanwddyn. But it has one main river into which all the others flow, the correct name of which it is difficult to make out." Most people speak of it as the Verniew, and no doubt the Liverpool people have been told that it is the Verniew water they are to have. But we have seen it is a mixture. If we wish to imbibe the German waters we have previously referred to, we have to pay for each separately ; here we have one grand amalgamation, that will beat all Prussia hollow in appellations, as it will in purity. A few of the chief names must suffice. The river is chiefly fed by eight streams, and thus are they denominated :—" Hirddydd fach and Hirddydd fawr, Eunant fach and Eunant fawr, Iddew fawr and Iddew fach, Nadroedd fawr and Nadroedd fach." Fancy all these mixed in one draught ! But this is not all, for these glad streams are subdivided into Nant Llwynto and Afon Trafaeliau—two small water-courses, so subtle that when conjoined they become Nantcwmlloi. The main river has also poured into it " a numerous family of affluents, each one bearing a distinct name," such as Nantrhydyrhydd, Nantyfrithgraigwen, Nantblaenycaeau, &c., &c., &c., the waters of which, amalgamated, Liverpool will, it is to be hoped, be able very shortly to enjoy and appreciate.

All these streams rush into a valley which seems formed by nature for a grand lake or reservoir. The vale is contracted, at some points not being more than two chains across, and there are well-wooded hills on either side. Beyond, in the direction of Bala, may be seen, towering above the rest, one of the shoulders of Arran mountain. The average width of the vale is about three quarters of a mile, and its extent about six miles. The surface is a dead level of marsh. The river flows out of it like liquid from the neck of a bottle, and this neck is to be corked up, and the water dammed back until the vale is full ; the surplus water to run over the 'corking' in the form of a waterfall, and the reservoir tapped at the side by a tunnel. Thus a new and beautiful lake will be formed, which, like Llynclys, will have (if not a palace) a village in its depths !

Llanwddyn, ague notwithstanding, must be a healthy place, for we read of people living there to fabulous ages ; and if a new Llanwddyn springs up on the side of the hills there is no reason why it should not become a health resort for the denizens of smoky cities. Such a situation would be lovely, and if a tramway (which will perhaps be wanted in order to complete the Liverpool scheme) was made permanent, a goodly traffic along the line might be realized. In the paper we have quoted (*Mont : Coll :* vol. 6) we are told that the agricultural produce of the parish is scanty, and that upwards of £1,000 is paid annually by the inhabitants to provision dealers for flour only. One reason assigned for the absence of wheat crops is that the season for ripening and harvesting white crops is so late, short, and uncertain; grazing is found less expensive. The expense, too, for the conveyance of lime, is an item that seriously interferes with the agricultural development of the district.

A tramway would benefit in every way the conveyance of cattle, crops, lime, produce and people, and if grain can be grown elsewhere amongst the mountains, why, the weather is much the same in one valley as another. We leave the subject for our Liverpool speculators to ponder over.

Llanwddyn is said to owe its name to a giant named Wddyn. In Nicholas Carlisle's "Topographical History of Wales" we read that "there is a place on the hills called Gwely Wddyn, i.e., the bed of Wddyn, where the country people say great treasures are hidden, but that every attempt to discover them has been frustrated by tremendous storms of hail and thunder. Others, however, with more reason, say that Owddyn was an anchorite, and his cell in the rocks is still called Gwely, or the Bed. His path when he paid visits to his neighbour, St. Monacella, at Pen Nant Melangell, being divided only by a mountain five miles over, is still traced and called by his name. If Owddyn was contemporary with Monacella, he lived in the seventh century. The superstitious tradition that vast treasures are concealed about this hermit's cell caused Hennings, a German miner (who superintended Lord Powis's mines at Llangynog, and who had an annual allowance of £100 to make new trials for or ore) to spend his last £100 at the bed of Owddyn, but, as might be expected, without success." As the church of Llanwddyn (which is dedicated to St. John the Baptist and formerly belonged to the Knights Templars) will have to be swept away, a new church and churchyard will be provided by the Liverpool Corporation. In order to make temporary provision for burials, the Corporation, about six months ago, caused a vault to be constructed for the reception of bodies, but not a single death has occurred in the parish since that time. Mr Joseph Parry, C.E., the assistant water engineer of Liverpool, in an interesting and lucid description of the intended works, says that at Llanwddyn the valley attains a width of over half a mile, and then following the course of the river, becomes narrower, until at a distance of two and a-half miles below the village its width, at the narrowest part, is not more than about 300 yards. Across this gorge, through which the Verniew runs, the Corporation intend to construct the embankment, the first stone of which was laid on Thursday. Its total length will be 418 yards, and the top of which, measured to the water line, will be about 84 feet above the present valley bottom. The effect of erecting this short embankment will be to dam back the river so as, without any further enclosure than the natural valley sides, to form a lake which will be four and three-quarter miles long, with a water area at the surface of about 1,115 acres. The surface area of Bala Lake is 1,100 acres. The contents of Lake Verniew, above the level at which water will be drawn off for Liverpool, will be about 12,000,000,000 gallons, which is ½ more than the storage capacity of the Loch Katrine works of the Glasgow

Corporation. The embankment is to be built of masonry, and will be the largest work of the kind in this country. The excavation of a trench for the foundation has been commenced, and it has been ascertained by trial holes that a solid rock bottom will be obtained at a depth which, in the centre of the valley, does not exceed 41 feet below the natural surface. The total height from the bottom of the foundation to the top water line of the embankment will therefore be about 121 feet. This will be spanned by arches carrying a road and footways, having a total width of 17 feet between the parapet walls, the height from the water-line of the dam to the top of the parapet walls being 14 feet. Any overflow from the lake will pass through the central series of arches, and down the outer face of the wall. Thus the costly and troublesome weirs and byewashes of ordinary earth embankments will be dispensed with. The greatest width of the embankment at the base will be over 100 feet. For the discharge of the compensation water which the Corporation are bound to supply to the river, there will be two tunnel outlets, with necessary sluices and appliances through the embankment. Mr. Parry states that the area of the watershed from which water would naturally flow into Lake Verniew is 17,583 acres, and it is from this area only that it is proposed to collect and impound water in the first instance, but, as the demands in Liverpool increase, additional water will be brought into the lake from two streams called the Cowny and Marchnant, which now fall into the Verniew below the proposed embankment. These streams will be brought into the lake by tunnels respectively 1¼ and 1⅝ miles in length. The Cowny and Marchnant will give an additional contributing area of 4,417 acres, making the total watershed of the lake, when all the works contemplated by the Act have been carried out, 22,300 acres. The water to be thus collected will be of the usual excellent quality derived from the Welsh hills. Previous to the application to Parliament for the Water Act of last session the water was analysed under various conditions of flood and drought by Dr. Frankland, Dr. Tidy, and Dr. Brown. Their reports were of the most favourable character, though chemical evidence is scarcely necessary where, as in this case, the watershed is so admirably adapted for the collection of water in the purest and best possible condition for potable purposes. There is probably no district in Great Britain of equal area that is so thinly populated. There are no mines or mineral workings, and the only dwellings remaining will be a few scattered sheep farms. The hills are precipitous and sterile, and the slate rocks of which they are composed throw off the rainfall with great facility. The Verniew has long been celebrated for the excellence, variety, and abundance of its fish. Pennant wrote that the river merited the title of Piscosus Amnis as much as any he knew. The aqueduct for conveying the water from Lake Verniew to Liverpool will be formed partly by tunnelling and partly by cast-iron pipes. Where the aqueduct is in tunnel it will be made of sufficient capacity to convey as much water to Liverpool as the lake will be capable of yielding, but where pipes are to be used it is intended to lay, in the first instance, only one pipe, which will be large enough to deliver about one-third of the calculated total yield available for Liverpool from the watershed. The aqueduct will commence at the lake by a tunnel about seven feet in diameter and two and a quarter miles in length, starting from the north side of the Verniew Valley and terminating in the Hirnant Valley. From the outlet of the tunnel a cast-iron pipe of about 42 inches internal diameter will be laid through the Hirnant Valley across the river Tanat, and to the north of

the village of Llanrhaiadr-yn-Mochnant, near which place
the first section of the pipe line will terminate in a small
reservoir or relieving tank to be constructed at Parc Uchaf.
Thence it will be laid through the parish of Llansilin to
the valley of Cynynion, on the borders of Denbigh and
Salop counties, whence a tunnel of about one mile in
length will be driven to the west side of the Morda
Valley. There will be a raised aqueduct over the Morda
river, and from the east side a second tunnel of one mile
long, terminating in a reservoir to be formed on elevated
ground, about a mile to the west of Oswestry, in front of
Oerley Hall. At this point filter beds are to be made, if
filtration should be required. From Oswestry the cast-iron
main proceeds in a north-easterly direction, through the
parishes of Whittington and Ellesmere, Hanmer and
Malpas. In Malpas there will be another relieving
tank on Oat-hill. Thence the pipe will
be continued through Bunbury and Beeston, passing at
about a mile to the east of Tarporley, to a relieving tank
on Luddington-hill; thence through Delamere Forest, and
under the river Weaver, near Kingsley ford, through
Aston, to a tower to be erected at Norton. From the
Norton water-tower the main takes a northerly direction
to the Mersey, which it crosses at a point two and three-
quarter miles to the east of the Runcorn viaduct. After
crossing the Mersey the pipe follows an almost straight
line through Farnworth and Rainhill to the existing
reservoirs of the Corporation at Prescot, near Liverpool.
The total length of the aqueduct from the Verniew to
Prescot is 67 miles, but the distance from the Verniew to
Liverpool in a direct line is only 46 miles. The Corporation have already entered into contracts with Messrs.
Cochrane, Grove, and Co., Dudley, and Messrs.
D. Y. Stewart and Co., Glasgow, for the supply of
about 27 miles of pipes, and pipelaying has been commenced at Hirnant by the Corporation workmen.
The river Verniew is at present subject to great fluctua-
tions in flow. During heavy floods the discharge at the
point of proposed interception exceeds 700 million gallons
per day, while in seasons of drought the discharge falls
below two million gallons per day. After the lake has been
made, the Corporation will have to send down the river the
statutory supply of compensation water, which, being delivered in a steady, regular, and constant stream, instead
of the present irregular flow, will be a great improvement
to the river, and a great advantage to the residents on its
banks. The total estimated yield of Lake Verniew watershed, including the compensation water, is estimated at
52 million gallons per day. The estimated cost of the first
section of the works is about a million and a quarter. With
regard to the time of completion, it is, of course, impossible to foresee all the difficulties that may arise in
the execution of such an undertaking, but it is confidently anticipated that the whole of the operations connected with the first instalment will
be so far completed as to enable the water to
be delivered into Liverpool in the year 1885.
The engineers for the works are Mr. Thomas Hawksley,
of London, and Mr. George F. Deacon, of Liverpool, under whose superintendence the drawings and specifications
are to be made and the works to be carried out, Mr. Deacon having been relieved of all responsibility for the existing Rivington and Liverpool works in order that he may
devote the whole of his time to this large undertaking.
When the works now being inaugurated have been
finished, Liverpool will possess the finest supply of water
of any city in the world. In the Rivington and Verniew
watersheds and the new red sandstone wells the Corporation have the means of supplying a population of more
than 2,300,000 with a constant supply of unexceptionable

water. The population at present supplied by the Corporation, according to the recent census, is 720,000. If it
continues to increase as it has done during the last decade
the population will, at the end of the present century,
amount to more than a million. In addition to this the
Corporation have agreed to supply water to the towns of
St. Helens, Widnes, Warrington, and Oswestry as soon
as the Verniew water reaches Liverpool. The total
estimated cost of the work is £3,250,000.

JULY 27, 1881.

NOTES.

STONE COFFIN-LID AT LLANFIHANGEL.
There is built up into the mantel-piece of the heating apparatus in the vestry of Llanfihangel Church, together
with other carved slabs, which possibly formed part of a
tomb or shrine, a stone coffin-lid, bearing, in slight relief,
a foliated cross, with a dagger beneath the sinister arm,
and a border and inscription (the last all but obliterated)
around. The coffin-lid appears to be either of 13th or
early 14th century workmanship. It possibly belonged
to an ancestor of the Vaughans of Llwydiarth, and may
even have marked the resting place and covered the remains of Celynin himself. Both coffin-lid and slabs were,
I believe, found when the church was re-built. It is to
be hoped that they will be moved to some part of the
church, where they will be less liable to damage and can
be better seen.　　　　　C.J.D.

NONCONFORMITY IN SHROPSHIRE.—(June
15, 1881.)—*Ellesmere.* The following is copied from a
document amongst the Oswestry Old Chapel papers of
the time that Dr. Williams was Minister —:
  "SHROPSHIRE.
  "At the General Quarter Sessions of the Peace of our
Sovereign Lord the King holden at the Guildhall in
Shrewsbury in and for the County of Salop on Tuesday in
the Week next after the Close of Easter (to wit) the ninth
Day of April in the twenty-second year of the Reign of our
Sovereign Lord George the third by the Grace of God of
Great Britain France and Ireland King Defender of the
Faith and so forth and in the year of our Lord one
thousand seven hundred and eighty two Before Edward
Pemberton and Robert Corbett Esquires and others their
fellow Justices assigned to keep the Peace in the County
aforesaid and also to hear and determine divers Felonies
Trespasses and other Misdemeanors in the same County
done and committed
  "*Ordered* that the Building lately altered and fitted up
belonging to a House commonly known by the name of
the White House in the Town of *Ellesmere* in the County
of Salop be recorded as a Place of Religious Worship for
His Majesty's Protestant Subjects dissenting from the
Church of England and it is hereby ordered accordingly
                "By the Court
                  "WINGFIELD, C.C."
The Centenary of Congregationalism at Ellesmere being
so near some further records of its early history would be
acceptable in *Bye-gones.*　　　　　JARCO.

QUERIES.

NANTGARW CHINA is sufficiently well known
to, and prized by collectors and connoisseurs to warrant
one in making a little enquiry as to the manufacturer. His
name appears to be quite lost in the fame of his ware.
Who was he? and what is known of him?　　　D.J.

HORSE CAMPBELL.—In a letter from Southey to Wynn, written from Keswick in 1808, he speaks of having received a letter from "Horse Campbell," attempting to convert him to the Calvinist faith, and inviting him to Shrewsbury. In a note we are told that "Horse" was a Westminster nick name, and that the writer made ineffectual enquiries about Campbell at Shrewsbury. Can any reader say who this Campbell was?   N.W.S.

KING JOHN IN GLAMORGANSHIRE.—In Woodward's *History of Wales* mention is made of a ballad at page 359-60 thus :—"A not ungraceful ballad-legend tells how King John had divorced his faithful wife Isabella, daughter of the Lord of Glamorgan, and how, when the barons rose up against him and transferred their allegiance to his mortal enemy, he was sheltered and protected by her at Boverton Place (her father's halls to which she had retired) for half a year, under the assumed name of Gerald Fitzalan, and that afterwards he went out and met his fate and dying as is known, at Swinestead Abbey." I have not been able to meet with this ballad, and if any of your readers can help me to it I should feel obliged.   D.J.

COLERIDGE AT WREXHAM.—Mr. E. Meredith Jones has unearthed a letter of Coleridge's, dated July 22, 1794, in which he records a tour in North Wales, in the course of which he passes through Wrexham. He says :—

It had entirely escaped my memory that Wrexham was the residence of a Miss E. Evans, a young lady with whom, in happier days, I had been in habits of fraternal correspondence: she lives with her grandmother. As I was standing at the window of the inn she passed by, and with her, to my utter astonishment, her sister, Mary Evans, *quam afflictum et perdité amabam*, yea, even to anguish. They both startled and gave a short cry, almost a faint shriek. I sickened, and well nigh fainted, but instantly retired. Had I appeared to recognize her, my fortitude would not have supported me.

The lady must have been one that the poet had been very much in love with, for, he adds, "Her image is in the sanctuary of my bosom, and never can it be torn from thence but with the strings that grapple my heart to life." On sight of the ladies he retired from the window, but it appears they passed and re-passed, as if they thought themselves "deceived by some face somewhat like" his. The letter was published in 1836, in the *New Monthly Magazine*. Mr. E. M. Jones. on perusing it, sent a copy to Lord Coleridge, who, in acknowledging it, says: although he knew of S. T. Coleridge's affection for the lady, he had never before heard of the visit to Wrexham. Mr. Jones, in sending a full transcript of the letter to the *Wrexham Advertiser*, asks "Who was Mary Evans, and what became of her ?"   NEMO.

TROSPON (June 8, 1881.)—In reference to this let me suggest "Trosban from Osbaldiston" ; the process, I fancy, has been the work of the Welsh-speaking people : —first, Osbaldiston has been compressed into Osban—then with a question "Where are you going?" "I am going to Yr (pronounced err) Osban"; then "To yr Osban" would become "Trospan."   J.E.

MRS. CORNWALL BARRY WILSON (July 13, 1881).—The reason why "D.L.", in *Shreds and Patches*, alluded to this lady as a native of Shrewsbury, was because he had met with a piece of poetry of hers entitled "My Native Town : Written in Shrewsbury Quarry." Probably the reason why Mr Salisbury was not answered when he sought to glean further particulars was, that "D.L." had nothing further to communicate, although it would manifestly have been better had he at least said

5

from what publication he copied the lines. I presume Mr. Salisbury failed to glean information from any quarter, as he has not introduced the name amongst his *Border Counties Worthies*. Chambers does not mention "D.L.'s" "gifted towns-woman" in his *Cyclopædia of English Literature*.   G.
Wem, Salop.

WILLIAM OWEN PUGHE (Apr. 27, 1881).— As I expected, I find the letter referred to at the above date, in the Correspondence of Southey published by Mr. Warter. It is dated Jan. 3, 1823, and the passage runs as follows :—

I am very incredulous concerning what is said of the "Welsh Paradise Lost." My old acquaintance William Owen [Pughe] was one of Joanna Southcott's four and twenty elders; full of Welsh information certainly he was, but a muddier minded man I never met with. There is abundant proof in his "Dictionary" how loose and inaccurate his knowledge of his own language is; and I could almost as soon believe in Joanna Southcott myself, as be persuaded that he has well translated a book which I am very sure he does not understand.

It will be remembered that, in 1804, Southey was "delighted" with the way in which the "Mabinogion" were translated by Pughe. This was shown in his letter to Coleridge I quoted on Apr. 27. On June 16, 1804, he also says, in a letter to Mr. Wynn, "I did not see you after I had read three tales of the Mabinogion. Owen has translated them admirably, in so Welsh a syntax and idiom, that they convey the full manner of the original." But earlier than this I find Southey dissatisfied with William Owen Pughe's work. On Aug. 29, 1801, writing to Mr. Wynn, he says—

It is a serious evil that no man of adequate talents will take the Welsh antiquities in hand, and that no encouragement is given those who do. Owen has translated "Llywarc Hen" badly, that is evident ; yet his version is better than none, and eminently useful to all who want information either in old history or our old manners.

In the same letter Southey expresses a wish—if he ever does have a settled home, that it should be "on the South side of some Welsh mountain." Once in his life, it is said, he was very near finding a home in the Valley of Neath, only being then a Radical in politics, the Tory squire who owned the property declined having him as a tenant. (See *Bye-gones*, Apr. 28, 1875, quoting Sampson's *History of Advertising*, p. 253.)   N W.S.

The second excursion of the Menai Society for the season included a visit to the Arch of Caligula, and the neighbouring caves, on the coast of Anglesey, not far from the Valley Station. A promontory of white rock juts out into the sea, and through this there is a passage some 30 or 40 feet high. Most of the party walked over the arch.

Mr. Theed has just completed a fine bust of the late Field Marshal Viscount Combermere, in the uniform of the 1st Life Guards, of which he was colonel 31 years, showing his many orders and decorations. This work of art is to be presented by his widow, Lady Combermere, to be placed in the officers' messroom of Hyde Park barracks.

Two fresh schemes have been proposed in connection with the Welsh Charity School at Ashford, one framed by a sub-committee, of which Mr. Stanley Leighton, M.P., the treasurer of the Society, is chairman, and the other proposed by the Vice-Treasurer, the Rev. H. W. P. Richards, the vicar of Isleworth. The sub-committee recommend that the present system of admission be abandoned, that the standard of education imparted in

37

the schools be raised, that gradually the schools be converted into a girls' school—preference being given to orphans—to be managed in a manner somewhat similar to the Howell's Schools at Denbigh and Llandaff, and that the scholars be of three classes, viz.: "Foundationers," "half-pay," and "full-pay." In the alternative scheme proposed by him Mr. Richards suggests that the school should be continued as a mixed one for boys and girls, and that the conditions of admission, so far as age of child and nationality of parent are concerned, should remain the same, save that children be in future admitted if they be only of Welsh descent. Mr. Richards, however, proposes one radical change, namely, that each child shall pay £12 per annum to the funds of the Society. A meeting of Governors to consider them will be held at the offices of the Society on the 2nd of August.

The *Graphic* contains a sketch of the ceremony of the stone-laying at Llanwddyn. The portrait of Lord Powis would serve equally well for almost anybody else, and the Welsh women with high crowned hats, who are placed in a conspicuous position, are entirely the creation of the artist's imagination.

On the recommendation of the Prime Minister, her Majesty has graciously conferred the honour of knighthood upon Mr. Hugh Owen for his distinguished and life-long service in the cause of education. A lively satisfaction is felt among London Welshmen owing to the honour conferred on one of their number, a feeling that will be reciprocated by Welshmen generally, in whose educational progress Sir Hugh Owen has ever taken the highest interest.

A NEW INDUSTRY.—A correspondent says:—"Passing through Chester Station on Thursday I observed, in a prominent situation, a large wardiau case filled with beautiful flowers, at which a young lady was busily engaged in making up bouquets and selling them to passengers by the trains. Whether this is a private speculation, or for the benefit of some charity, I did not learn, but a porter told me the stall had only been in existence a few days."

AUGUST 3, 1881.

NOTES.

OLD WELSH ALMANACKS.

(July 13, 1881.)

For the four years 1828-1831 there were seven issues of the Dublin Welsh Almanack. They were all printed at Dublin, and, with the exception of the one for 1828, are all priced at sixpence each. The one for 1828 is called "Cyfaill Diffuant," and these are the verses on the title page:—

1 Fy hen Gyfeillion heini,
  Dilynais etto, 'leni,
  I ddyfod attoch yn ddiffael—
  Gwych genyf gael eich gweini.

2 Fe all mai'r *gau Gyfeillion*
  A gerir gan rai gwirion,
  Yn oreu heunydd, er eu bod,
  Yn gosod *trefn a'nghyson.*

3 Os weithian y mae sothach,
  Gan eraill yn gynarach,
  Da gwyr y wlad o *Gaer i Lyn,*
  Fod y llynedd *un* yn llawnach.

4 Yn hyf, *eleni*, hefyd,

Y gwir a wnaf agoryd,
Un fodd a *Moore*—ni fydd un meth,
Ond ambell beth diembyd.

5 Syr Newton sy' oreu'n atteb,
  Er un-dyn, am gywreindeb;
  Goleuo'r byd wnai ef heb wad
  A th'wyniad ei ddoethineb.

6 The Beast and the false Prophet,
  Though nearly related,
  Their Crusades, and their Grecian Wars
  Rebound the bars of Tophet.

The first issue for 1829 hath the following verses on title page, and is called "Cyfaill Cyfarwydd":—

1 GYFEILLION, dynion doniol,
  Drwy *Wynedd,* fro dirionol,
  'Rwy'n teimlo serch i'ch annerch chwi,
  Eleni, yn ddylynol.

2 Ardaloedd *Gwent* a *Dyfed,*
  Y Gwyliau, ddo'nti'm gweled,
  Y'nghyd a *Phowys*—y'mhob ffair,
  Llu gair yn llaw-agored.

3 Mae'n addas i'm weinyddu,
  Yn llon, Gyfeillion felly ;
  A maddeu i bawb y modd bo'nt
  O'r rhai na ddo'nt i 'mhrynu.

4 Tremau'r Planedau nodaf,
  Chwiliad y Lloer ni chelaf ;
  Codiad, machludiad, tyniad hon,
  Yn eigion dwfr, mynegaf.

5 Lle'r Haulwen, a'r Lloer hylwydd,
  Heb wyro, y'mhob arwydd,
  A'u diffygiadau'n orau wnaf—
  Ond tawaf am y tywydd.

6 Beware lest Popish Erin,
  And Rome, contrive to ruin ;
  The Church and State—the great and grand
  Laws of the land we live in.

The *Second* issue for 1829 is called "Cyfaill Gwladol," and has these verses on the title page:—

1 Fy hen Gyfeillion hoywedd,
  Dywedaf iwch'yn brydwedd ;
  Bydd 'leni lu o'm brodyr gau
  Yn llenwi ffau ac annedd.

2 Y llynedd d'wedais i chwi,
  Bod Seren wib am wgu ;
  Bydd felly erchyll foreu wawr
  Gan Rwssia Fawr ar Dwrci.

3 Wrth sôn am bob rhyw ddyfais,
  Sy o brydi bryd mewn urddas,
  Mae'n dwyn i'm côf eleni'n lân.
  Am *gerbyd tân Elias.*

4 Cenfigen, rhagfarn, athrod,
  Prif blaäu daear isod ;
  Maleis-ddrwg frä'i i enw da
  Fydd 'leni yn dra hynod.

5 Ond 'Fengyl hedd el llafar,
  Sydd yn ein hoes yn trydar,
  O ddwyrain i orllewin wawl
  O bawl i bawl o'r ddaear.

6 Let's all unite together,
  To pray with one another ;
  That Britain with her OAK train
  May rule the MAIN for ever.

The *First* issue for 1830 is called "Cyfaill Cyflawn ;" and it has these verses on the title page :—

1 GYFEILLION teg, fy ewyllys,
  Eleni, yn haelionus,
  Wrth geisio'ch boddio, yw gaddo'r gwir,
  I'n deuddeg Sir nodweddus.

2 O Fôn i ffaen Sir Fynwy,
  Gwlad odiaeth o glodadwy,
  'Does undyn sy'n ymboeni a'r byd,
  A wrthyd fy nghynorthwy.

3 Rheolau—pob rhyw alwad—
  Iawn ystum blwyddyn wastad
  A geir ar waith, o'r goreu erioed,
  A *lle* ac *oed* y lleuad.

4 Er hyny tra mae'r *hinon,*
  'Ân siomi doniau dynion,
  Aml un a ddengys fys at faiFe allai hên Gyfeillion.

5 Mor wych yw llewych lluoedd
  Y Bod a wnaeth y bydoedd,
  A'u rhodau'n gwau ar edyn gwynt,—
  Ufhr ydynt ei weithredoedd !

6 True Christians all are wailing,
  Lest, for our double dealing,
  The Lord will suffer us to see
  Carlisle and T—prevailing.

(To be Continued.) E.G.S.

CHURCHES IN THE RHYL DISTRICT.

(July 20, 1881.)

WHITECHURCH.—*(Concluded.)*

At the east end of the nave is a large alabaster altar tomb with recumbent effigies on top—male with curled hair, moustache, and broad-peaked beard vesting on helmet with crest, in plated armour with collar of mail and apron of mail below, the rings sewed upright to linen or leather, chains and straps gilt, ruffed collar round neck, hands conjoined in prayer. Gauntlets, and a sort of closed fan by legs, feet resting on a lion. Sword on left side, and fan, dagger, and writing pen on right.

The lady with coif and weeper behind, and close cap resting on tasselled cushion, large ruff round neck, close robe with chain and promander, mantle fastened by two tasselled cords undulating to feet, hands in prayer with rings on first and fourth fingers, painted and gilded.

Round ledge in old English :—Here lieth the bodies of Sir Ihon Salusbury of Lleweny in the Countie of De'bigh knight who deceassed the xviijth of March in the yere of

Our Lord God 1578 and Dame Jane his wief daughter and co heire to David Midleton esquier Alderma' of Westchester wch. Jane in Ao. 1588 at her charges fully erected this tombe or monument & died the . . . . of . . . . in Ao. 15 . . . .

Arms at head :—Under woman—sa. a bend vert. with three erased foxes' heads arg. with motto around : To God att onlye geve the prayse. Under man : gu. a lion rampant between three crescents arg. Motto around : Post funera virtus vivit.

Arms at foot :—1. Arms as under man ; 2. gu. a saracen's head ppr. ; 3. sa., a bend arg. with three pheons sa., on a chief arg. a bugle horn sa. ; 4. arg. three roses in pale gu. ; 5. sa., a lion passant or. ; 6. arg., a cross fleury engrailed between four birds sa. ; 7. gu., three lions passant gardant or. ; 8. or. on a bend az., three stags' heads caboshed or. above on a chief quarterly 1. and 4. arg. . . . . . . 2. and 3. . . . . . . impaling quarterly 1. Arms as under woman : 2. vert., a chevron arg. between three foxes' heads erased arg. ; 3. gu., on a bend or., three boars passant sa. ; 4. arg., three birds 2. and 1. sa.

Motto :—To theym that feare God att are wroght to the best.

Arms on south side :—Man's as before, impaling woman's as before. Virtue liveth after death.

Arms on north side :—Man's as before, impaling vert., a chevron between three foxes' heads erased arg. En Dieu je espoiere—In God is our hope.

Weepers on north side—Two females robed, and two chrysom children.

Weepers on south side :—1. Knight in gilt armour. 2. Civilian in black dress and gown. 3. Three knights in armour with swords. 4. One knight without sword. 5. Two knights in armour with swords. 6. One knight without sword.

—————

Broken Slab in floor, capitals.

. . . OYD . OF . LANBEDER . GENT . WHO . DYED . IN . THE . 39 . YEAR . OF . HIS . AG . . .

CATHERINE MYDDLETON . 1692.

Robert son of Rev. John Williams and Mary his wife, 19 Oct., 1789, aged 5.

Rev. John Williams, Vicar of Llanasaph, May 7, 1798, aged 45.

Robert, Elizabeth, Mary, and Thomas, their children.

—————

On a Brass.

Thomas Davies of Denbigh Mercer June 15, 1705 aged 81. Anne his wife Aug. 16, 1744 aged 84.

—————

Large marble monumental slab with arms 1715 to memory of family of Salusbury of Lleweni. Inscription in Latin difficult to see on account of situation.

—————

On tablets.

Mary Drihurst daughter and heir of Hugh Drihurst of Denbigh Gent. She married John Roberts of Denbigh Mason by whom she had John, Thomas, Anne, and Margaret, died 7 January 1692.

Arms :—arg. a fesse az. with three torteaux arg. between 3 foxes' heads couped sa.

—————

Mrs. Ann Lloyd wife to Robert Lloyd of Plannog Gent. daughter and heir of Edward Davies of Denbigh Gent. ob. 21 Jan. 1686 aged 23 leaving one son. Mors ultima linea rerum est.

Arms :—Quarterly. 1. gu. a' chevron erm. between 3 boars arg. 2. arg. cross flenry engrailed between 4 birds sa. 3. paly of 8 arg. & sa. 4. paly of 6 arg. & gu. with a bordure or. impaling quarterly : 1 arg. a chevron erminois between 3 boars' heads sa. 2 gu. a chevron erm. between 3 saracens' heads arg. hair or. 3 vert. a stag arg. antlers or. 4 gu. a saracen's head arg. Over all a crescent for difference.

—————

Recent marble tablets.

Thomas Twiston of Henllan Place and Elizabeth his wife. He died 1833 aged 85. She died 1837 aged 86. Erected by their daughter Anna Maria Davies of Glanaber.

—————

Lieut. Thos. Lewis Twiston of 63 or West Suffolk Regt. 24 Aug. 1859 aged 23.

—————

John Twiston Esq. of Henllan Place Denbigh 12 Jan. 1853 aged 67. Al o Maria, Barbara and Adelaide Fanny infant daughters of John Twiston and Margaret his wife.

—————

Slabs in floor of Chancel.

John Davies son of Fowke Davies of Denbigh Apothecary 1670.

—————

David son of Robt. Roberts of Denbigh 1690 aged 81.

—————

Johne Roberts son of Robt. Roberts mercer in Denbigh 1661.

—————

John Parry of Denbigh mercer 1653.   Mercers' arms.

—————

Hic jacet Margareta Mitton uxor. . . . .

—————

Hic jacet Johannes Hughes qui obiit mortem 14 Julii Ann. Dom. 1604.

—————

Marble Tablets in Chancel.

Robt. Salusbury Esq. of Cotton House 1774 aged 50 and Gwen his wife 1787 aged 54. John their son 1791 aged 33 and Katherine infant daughter.

Thos. Salusbury of Denbigh Esq. 1831 aged 70.

Also Sarah his relict 1850 aged 93.

—————

A singular looking stone monument representing a man in Spanish costume kneeling at prayer-desk under arches. Arms obliterated. An inscription in capitals underneath, but very imperfect from the stone shelling off.

Humfrey Lloyd M. of Arts . . . . a worthy wight . . . . took to wife Barbara 2nd sister to . . . . . . Lord Lumle . . . .

—————

Thos. Shaw Gent. Recorder of Denbigh (illegible).

—————

Richd. Heaton of Plas Heaton Esq. 1791 aged 53. Elizth. his eldest daughter 1849.

—————

Sarah relict of Richd. Heaton 1844 aged 54.

—————

Richard Clough of Glanwern eldest surviving son and heir of Hugh Clough of Plas Clough and Catherine his wife only daughter and heir of . . . . . Powell Esq. of Glanywern. Also Patty his wife 2nd daughter and heir of James Butler Esq. of Warminghurst Park, Sussex, 1838 aged 76.   W.A.L.

PRYCE SHIELD IN LLANWNOG CHURCH.

This emblazoned stone shield, which was erected after the death of John Pryce of Park, Esq., the father of Matthew Pryce of Park, Esq., M.P. for the Montgomery Boroughs from 1678 to 1685, is placed against the South wall of Llanwnog Church, within the altar rails and is particularly interesting as being, in fact, a stone substitute for the more modern hatchment. It is much to be regretted that the hand of time and other causes have done much to render the heraldic colours indistinct, faint, and difficult to read. A full description of the shield and the nine quarterings thereof will be found, if I remember rightly, in the first volume of the *Cambrian Quarterly Magazine.*　　　　　　　　　　　　　C.J.D.

QUERIES.

JOHN ROWLAND OF MACHYNLLETH.— In the *Blodeugerdd*, published in the year 1759, there are some poems by "John Rowland o Fachynlleth." Can anyone give me some account of this writer? DEINIOL.

PRINCE LLEWELYN'S REPUTED RESI- DENCE.—A board over the shop door of a bookseller at Beddgelert bears the above inscription, with a picture painted above it of the Prince discovering his child after he has slain the dog. What authority is there for supposing that the cottage in question was ever the residence of Llewelyn? I do not find anything about it in the *Gossiping Guide to Wales*, which I presume I should do was there any foundation for the supposition.　　　H.B.

REPLIES.

SEALS IN THE SHROPSHIRE MUSEUM (July 20, 1881).—In 1868 the late John Gough Nicholls wrote a review of Mr. Morris Jones's *Feudal Barons of Powys*, in which he referred to one of the seals mentioned by "W.A.L." The paper was reprinted in the second volume of the *Montgomeryshire Collections*, accompanied by a facsimile of the seal. It is stated to be the seal of Hawise, Lady of Keveleoc. The silver matrix was there said to have been found at Oswestry shortly before 1850, and a reference is given to *Notes and Queries* 4 s., v. 4, p. 343. Anyone who has access to this volume, which was issued, I think, in 1869, would be doing good service by transcribing what is said for the benefit of your readers.　　JARCO.

NEW WALES (May 25, 1881).— FRIEND in his reply to the query of April 6, states that Thomas Lloyd of Dolobran, near Meifod, Montgomeryshire, was the first Governor of Pennsylvania. In the report of the "Bureau of Statistics of Labour and Agriculture for the State of Pennsylvania, years 1872-3," at page 106, a list of Governors under the Dutch, Swedish, English, and Proprietary Rule is given. "In 1681, King Charles II., in liquidation of a debt of £16,000 due to the estates of Admiral Penn, conveyed to his son William the Province Pennsylvania. The name was given to it by the King, in honour of the Admiral, and against the consent of the grantee, then only known as a Quaker preacher. William Penn made two visits to this country of about two years each, and was then the actual Governor of the Province," *ibid.* pp. 93-94. The list as given is—William Markham, Deputy from June, 1681, to Oct. 24, 1682; William Penn, Governor from Oct. 24, 1682, to Aug. 12, 1684; Thomas Lloyd, President of Council, from June, 1684, to December, 1686; five Commissioners appointed by Penn from 1686 to 1688; John Blackwall, Deputy Governor from 1688 to 1690; Thomas Lloyd, President of Council from 1690 to 1691; Thomas Lloyd, Deputy Governor from 1691 to 1693. At this point, William Penn's "suspected inti-

macy with the deposed King James" caused William and Mary to forfeit his patent, and order Benjamin Fletcher, Governor of New York, to assume for the Crown the Province of Pennsylvania. In August, 1694, however, being satisfied of the injustice done him, William Penn was reinstated "in all his rights," when he appointed William Markham Deputy Governor.　　BOOKWORM.

TOMEN-Y-MUR (Sept. 22, 1880; Mar. 16, 1881). A second visit has not enabled me to decide whether the Inscribed Stone at Tomen-y-Mur is or is not a relic of historical importance. It is oblong with three faces, on two of which occur the marks which have puzzled me. They have been cut either by nature or by the hand of man, but as the letter M is quite plain we must believe that they are not the work of nature. They are not runic. There are no marks on the third face of the stone. I took a rubbing, but as the wind was blowing, and we were some hundreds of feet above the level of the sea, it was not satisfactory. I brought away a few fragments of Samian ware, and a portion of a tile with reticulated patterns on the reverse side. No coins have been found, at least within the memory of the present tenant. It is a very interesting spot, and would amply repay a visit. The scenery is of the grandest kind, Snowdon and Cader Idris, about equidistant, the one north the other due south. The Roman roads in three or four directions need accurate survey. An antiquary or two would find very good accommodation at Trawsfynydd, and profitable occupation for a fortnight at least. The conglomerate rock west of the Churchyard is quite unique.　　BOILEAU.

CURRENT NOTES.

A cat at Horton in Cheshire having been deprived of all her kittens but one, has secured a rabbit as a companion for the remaining one, and is now nursing both.

It is proposed to remove the Beaumaris Grammar School to Holyhead, under the new scheme which has been framed for the management of David Hughes's charity.

In speaking at Llandovery College on Friday, Professor Rhys said the recent education commission inquiry had shown that Government aid was indispensable for Welsh Grammar Schools, and good reasons were obtainable why the Government should treat Wales as liberally as other portions of the kingdom. University education was desired in Wales among the people, who, if they were Englishmen and lived in England, would never dream of such things. Although the commissioners only sought the good of Wales, yet so liable were good men to be misunderstood that he did not doubt some people would wish to stone them a month or two hence.

The *Pall Mall Gazette* says—The gentleman who has transferred to the Corporation of Conway without any pecuniary condition his interest in the historic ruins of the Castle of Conway has set an example which may be judiciously followed by other proprietors. Most of the owners of these relics of antiquity show a commendable liberality in opening them for the enjoyment of the world at large, but until these sites are vested in a public body there is always a danger lest such privileges should be withdrawn. The private owner who does not retain such possessions for his own personal enjoyment or the gratification of his friends alone naturally imposes upon the public the payment of a small fee for the privilege of entering, and this often has the effect of keeping outside the very class which would most of all be benefited by the right of admission. When such buildings are kept up by the rates they are open to all and the sense of proprietorship comes home to everyone.

THE CENSUS.

The results of the Census taken last April have been published by the Registrar-General, and although the totals are subject to revision, the alterations to be made will, in all probability, be exceedingly slight. The population of England and Wales is 25,968.286, and of this total 12,624,754 are males and 13,343,532 are females ; an increase altogether of 3,256,020, or of 14·3 per cent., the highest rate since 1831-41, when it was 14·5. In round figures England and Wales has added to its population a total not far from that of London, while London in its turn has added to its population a total not far from that of Liverpool. In the past ten years the births have exceeded the deaths by 3,425,982, and as the actual increase of population has been 3,256,020, it follows that the difference of 169,962 represents the disturbing influences of emigration and immigration ; so little is the growth of large populations affected by these causes. The different rates of increase in the counties are seen in the following table :

Increasing Populations.

	Per cent.		Per cent.
Surrey	31·5	Worcestershire	12·2
Glamorganshire	28·6	Northamptonshire	11·7
Durham	26·6	Berkshire	11·2
Essex	23·5	Hampshire	9·0
Nottinghamshire	22·6	Monmouthshire	8·1
Lancashire	22·5	Carmarthenshire	7·9
Derbyshire	21·5	Lincolnshire	7·6
Leicestershire	19·2	Gloucestershire	7·1
Yorkshire	18·5	Hertfordshire	5·6
Merionethshire	17·6	Flintshire	5·3
Sussex	17·5	Denbighshire	3·6
Warwickshire	16·2	Suffolk	2·3
Kent	15·2	Bedfordshire	2·2
Middlesex	14·9	Norfolk	1·4
Cheshire	14·6	Somersetshire	1·2
Staffordshire	14·3	Oxfordshire	0·9
Cumberland	13·8	Wiltshire	0·7
Northumberland	12·3	Devonshire	0·5
Carnarvonshire	12·3	Buckinghamshire	0·2

Decreasing Populations.

	Per cent.		Per cent.
Cornwall	9·1	Montgomeryshire	2·7
Radnorshire	7·4	Dorsetshire	2·4
Huntingdonshire	6·4	Westmoreland	1·3
Cardiganshire	4·4	Cambridgeshire	0·8
Brecknockshire	3·6	Pembrokeshire	0·2
Herefordshire	3·5	Anglesey	0·1
Rutlandshire	2·9	Shropshire	0·05

The population of London has doubled itself in the course of 41 years, whereas it has taken the rest of England and Wales 57 years. It further appears that the proportion of females to males has been steadily increasing since 1851, the figures being 104·2, 105·4, and 105·7, and as the marriage rate continues greatly depressed the matrimonial prospects of women do not seem very encouraging.

In Shropshire there were 247,993 inhabitants in April last, a decrease of 118 in the ten years. Of the total 124,016 were males, and 123,977 females. There were 50,756 inhabited houses, 3,393 uninhabited, and 208 were being built. For Montgomeryshire the population is 65,798, namely, 33,024 males, and 32,774 females, the total shewing a decline of 1,825 for ten years. Shropshire is divided into 11 districts or unions for poorlaw purposes, and Montgomeryshire into 4. These are set out in the following table, together with Denbighshire and Merionethshire :—

Districts.	Population 1871.	Population 1881.	Increase.	Decrease.
SALOP—				
Ludlow	18,078	18,584	506	—
Clun	10,801	10,166	—	635
Church Stretton	6,343	5,663	—	680
Cleobury Mortimer	8,317	7,967	—	350
Bridgnorth	15,448	15,270	—	178
Shifnal	12,787	12,821	34	—
Madeley	30,364	27,313	—	3,051
Atcham	45,565	48,640	3,075	—
Oswestry	26,848	27,077	229	—
Ellesmere	14,465	13,716	—	749
Wem	10,879	10,565	—	314
MONTGOMERYSHIRE—				
Machynlleth	13,317	12,576	—	741
Newtown	24,554	25,440	886	—
Forden	18,858	18,274	—	584
Llanfyllin	21,671	19,955	—	1,716
DENBIGHSHIRE—				
Wrexham	48,837	55,172	6,335	—
Ruthin	15,399	14,215	—	1,184
St. Asaph	27,878	29,456	1,578	—
Llanrwst	13,050	14,109	1,059	—
MERIONETHSHIRE—				
Corwen	16,451	16,829	378	—
Bala	6,604	6,740	136	—
Dolgelley	14,311	15,108	797	—
Festiniog	24,141	29,528	5,387	—

We also give the fuller statistics :—

Sub-Districts.	Inhabited Houses.		Population Enumerated.		Increase or Decrease of Population between 1871 and 1881.	
	1871.	1881.	1871.	1881.	Increase.	Decrease.
OSWESTRY—						
Knockin	924	874	4,408	4,134	—	274
Llansilin	849	793	4,136	3,919	—	217
Oswestry	2,405	2,441	11,652	11,927	275	—
St. Martins	1,362	1,460	6,652	7,097	445	—
ELLESMERE—						
Overton	384	335	1,720	1,469	—	251
Hanmer	511	506	2,428	2,372	—	56
Ellesmere	1,372	1,277	6,716	6,256	—	460
Baschurch	746	745	3,601	3,619	18	—
WEM—						
Wem	1,531	1,498	7,414	7,215	—	199
Prees	741	718	3,465	3,350	—	115
W'CHURCH—						
Whitchurch	1,670	1,623	7,912	7,826	—	86
Malpas	727	698	3,512	3,420	—	92
MACHYNTH—						
Machynlleth	979	918	4,624	4,307	—	317
Pennal	1,062	1,083	4,730	4,772	42	—
Darowen	813	762	3,963	3,497	—	466
NEWTOWN—						
Upper						
Llanidloes	806	789	4,184	3,897	—	287
Lower						
Llanidloes	799	882	4,207	4,470	263	—
Llanwnog	871	887	4,894	4,721	—	173
Kerry	494	495	2,619	2,601	—	18
Newtown	1,397	1,513	5,886	7,170	1,284	—
Tregynon	539	500	2,764	2,581	—	183
FORDEN—						
Montgomery	1,240	1,187	5,914	5,721	—	193
Chirbury	1,166	1,146	5,921	5,707	—	214
Welshpool	1,488	1,462	7,023	6,846	—	177
LLANFYLLIN						
Llanfair	1,249	1,158	6,100	5,587	—	513
Llans'tffraid	2,200	2,055	10,447	9,582	—	865
Llanrhaiadr	1,097	1,072	5,124	4,786	—	338
WREXHAM—						
Holt	1,405	1,375	6,760	6,615	—	145
Ruabon	3,463	3,378	15,494	15,501	7	—
Wrexham	5,329	6,433	26,583	33,056	6,473	—

The following are the totals for the counties of North Wales :—

COUNTIES AND PARLIAMENTARY DIVISIONS OF COUNTIES.	Including Represented Cities and Boroughs.				Excluding Rep. Cities & Boroughs.	
	1871.		1881.		1881.	
	Inhab. Houses.	Pop.	Inhab. Houses.	Pop.	Inhab. Houses.	Pop.
NORTH WALES.						
Anglesey	12,170	51,040	11,965	50,964	8,773	36,722
Carnarvonshire	23,298	106,121	26,100	119,195	19,685	90,500
Denbighshire	22,500	105,102	22,944	108,931	18,426	88,100
Flintshire............	16,636	76,312	17,271	80,373	11,767	55,153
Merionethshire	10,006	46,598	11,621	54,798	11,621	54,798
Montgomeryshire	13,911	67,623	13,631	65,798	9,241	45,756

The following are the statistics for various urban sanitary districts :—

Urban Sanitary District.	Inhabited Houses.		Population Enumerated.		Increase or Decrease of Population between 1871 and 1881.	
	1871.	1881.	1871.	1881.	Increase.	Decrease.
Ellesmere..	390	374	2,013	1,875	—	138
Llangollen..	599	700	2,798	3,124	326	—
Llanidloes..	737	775	3,428	3,421	—	7
Newtown & Llanllwch'rn	1,397	1,513	5,886	7,170	1,284	—
Oswestry ..	1,483	1,593	7,306	7,851	545	—
Shrewsbury	4,811	5,300	23,406	26,478	3,072	—
Welshpool	1,531	1,515	7,199	7,090	—	109
Whitchurch & Dodington	810	808	3,696	3,756	60	—
Wrexham ..	1,631	2,046	8,576	10,928	2,352	—

OSWESTRY.

THE LATE MR. WEAVER.—In the death of our respected townsman, Mr. Weaver, in his 92nd year, and not his 88th, as reported last week, we have lost one of our oldest inhabitants, for he had resided in the borough since about the year 1820, and it may be recorded as an instance of the longevity of his family that five years ago Mr. Weaver had three sisters living, all older than himself. He was descended from an old Herefordshire family, being the youngest son of the late Francis Watkin Weaver, Doctor of Medicine, of Hereford, which city his ancestors represented in Parliament for several generations, and were at the time of Cromwell made custodians of the city on behalf of the Commonwealth, there being still in the city the "Weaver's Almshouses," founded by one Richard Weaver some hundred years ago. Mr. Weaver, like his ancestors, was a staunch Liberal in politics, and although surrounded by Conservative friends, he was never afraid to express and maintain his convictions. Starting life with a good constitution, and being always a most moderate man in eating and drinking, he may reasonably have expected great freedom of the ills that flesh is heir to, but for the last forty years he was at intervals a terrible sufferer from gout, of which he would sometimes jokingly remark that it was the necessary result of having ancestors who had evidently been fond of the good things of this life. He never went in for municipal honours, but during the mayoralty of his late friend, Mr. Hales, he was, unknown to himself, elected a member of the Town Council, but with this exception, he never came prominently before the public. Many years ago a conscription took place for the army, when many of the inhabitants of Oswestry formed themselves into a Society to procure substitutes, if necessary, for each other, and Mr. Weaver was one of the first to be drawn by ballot, when of course the Society, which we believe held its meetings at the Three Tuns Inn, procured and paid for a substitute in his place. For some years past, although retaining all his faculties up to a few days of his decease, he had become very infirm in body, and seldom left his residence, consequently he was but little known to the members of the present generation. There are, however, some old townsmen, competitors in the race of life with Mr. Weaver, from whom his death will call forth a feeling of kindly sympathy and regret.

GRAMMAR SCHOOL.

At the annual distribution of prizes held last week, Mr. Longueville told an amusing story of the prizes for meritorious conduct which were occasionally given in his time at Oswestry School. A few days before he left Buxton, he met with an old schoolfellow, of the name of Longfield, of Longueville, near Mallow, which place he for some years represented in Parliament. They had not met each other for more than sixty years, and they naturally began to talk over their old school days. Another of their class fellows was Mr. Verschoyle, who afterwards became Bishop of Kilmore. Just as Verschoyle was leaving Ireland for school, an uncle kindly gave him £5. On his father hearing of this, he requested Dr. Donne to take the £5 from his son, and to give it him back in small instalments. The Doctor accordingly told Verschoyle of the letter he had received from his father, and desired him to give him the £5. He had only been at school a few days, and to the Doctor's astonishment he was told that the money was all gone. The Doctor therefore asked him to give the particulars of the way in which the money had been spent. The first item was "£1 to Pat Longfield for walking through the pool with his clothes on." (Laughter.) This pool was nearly six feet deep in one part. The remaining items were pretty much of the same description. The Doctor therefore dismissed his young friend after giving him many wise counsels as to his profitable investments.

We are at liberty to give another amusing story which Mr. Longueville told Sir Watkin of his old friend when at School, and which the latter had recalled to his recollection. On Sir Watkin's birth Dr. Donne promised to give the boys a holiday if they would each write some verses on the occasion. The following were Mr. Longfield's verses, and to understand them it is necessary to state that two grand dinners were given on the occasion, one at the Wynnstay Arms, of which Mr. Leigh was then proprietor, and the tickets for which were a guinea each, the other at the Queen's Head, for which the tickets were 5s. each. Mr. Longfield thought a great deal more of the dinner than of the birth of the worthy baronet, and accordingly these were his Verses :—

Sir Watkin Wynn has got a son and heir,
For which event I feel nor joy nor care.
The guinea dinner is too much for me,
The meaner one I do not wish to see.
A guest with empty pockets suits not Mr. Leigh.

Major Wingfield, the introducer of lawn tennis, who is well known in Montgomeryshire, has been presented with a handsome gold watch, a pair of embossed raised platinum bats, beautifully executed, together with an elaborate platinum and gold chain, and a purse of 200 guineas.

It is said that salmon fishermen on the river Dee with draught and trammel nets have never experienced such good sport as they are now enjoying. Salmon have been coming up the Dee in shoals, and men have caught as many as five at one haul of the net. One boatman caught 75 salmon in one day. Immense quantities are being sent away to London, Manchester, Liverpool, and Birmingham markets. Salmon are being hawked about Chester at 9½d. per lb.

A meeting of the Welsh Dialect Section of the Cymmrodorion Society was recently held at the residence of Dr. Isambard Owen in London, and attended, amongst others, by Prince Louis-Lucien Bonaparte and Mr. Howel Lloyd. The general prospectus or scheme of the work of the section was submitted in draft, and after discussion and revision was adopted. After stating that the section has been founded in connection with the Cymmrodorion Society to carry out a systematic investigation of the varieties of spoken Welsh, the committee proceed to point out the heads under which the peculiarities of dialect may be arranged. The first division comprises local words, phrases, and idioms ; under the second head are grouped peculiarities of grammar and syntax ; in the third place come peculiar place-names, and names embodying a record of historical events, &c.; the fourth division consists of local names of animals, plants, and minerals, while under the fifth head is placed the mode of pronunciation prevailing in different districts.

DEAN STANLEY'S WELSH DESCENT.—"Decanus Cambrensis" writes in the *Times* :—"It may interest many of your readers to know that the late Dean, so widely loved for his many-sided virtues, was wont to attribute some of his great gifts to the mixture of Saxon and Cymric blood in his veins. Two years ago, at the annual dinner of the Westminster scholars, I had the honour of enjoying the well-known charms of his conversation. In the course of the evening he playfully remarked, 'I am glad to meet a Welshman, for if there is any brilliancy and vivacity in my family I attribute it to the fact that my grandfather, a Cheshire squire, had the good sense to marry a bright, mercurial Welshwoman, from whom we have inherited a share of the Celtic fire.' The Dean's grandmother, wife of Sir John Thomas Stanley of Alderley, was Mary, daughter and heiress of Mr. Hugh Owen, of Penrhyn and Penrhos, in Anglesey. The Dean's Christian names seem both due to this descent—his first derived from the British hero, and his second from the old family seat, 'Penrhyn,' near Holyhead."—The name of Dean Stanley's grandmother, we believe, was "Margaret," not "Mary." One of her daughters, Louisa-Margaret, was married, in 1802, to Sir Baldwin Leighton, grandfather of the present baronet. The grandmother of Sir Baldwyn and Mr. Stanley Leighton therefore was sister to Dean Stanley's father, the late Bishop of Norwich.

DEATH OF MR. GEORGE BORROW.—Mr. George Borrow, author of "Wild Wales," the "Bible in Spain," "Lavengro," "Romany Rye," and other books, died a few days ago at Oulton, near Lowestoft. He was the son of an officer in the army, and was born at East Dereham, Norfolk, in 1803. In his sixteenth year, after being educated at the High School of Edinburgh, he was articled to a solicitor in Norwich, but soon afterwards abandoned the law, came to London, and turned his attention to literature. Even at this early period, it would seem, he had begun to take interest in the Gipsies, a number of whom were encamped near Norwich while he lived in that city. In 1833 he became an agent of the British and Foreign Bible Society,

and in this capacity was sent to St. Petersburg. Here, among other work, he edited the New Testament in Manchu. Migrating to Spain, he lived for some time with the Zincali, whose language he found to bear a marked resemblance to Romany, and translated the whole of St. Luke for their benefit. He also attempted to circulate the Bible in the vernacular. By doing so, of course, he exposed himself to a good deal of inconvenience, if not positive danger. He was twice put under arrest, and at one time, in order to save himself from the fury of the fanatical populace, was compelled to take refuge in the woods in disguise. In 1839, severing his connexion with the Society, he returned to England, and two years afterwards brought out "The Zincali, or an Account of the Gipsies of Spain." In 1844 he visited the South east of Europe, where he mixed with the Gipsies, and in the year following his return "Lavengro" and "Romany Rye" were published.

GHOST STORIES FROM WALES.

THE PRINCES OF POWYS FADOG, by J. Y. W. Lloyd of Clochfaen, Esq., M.A., K.S.G. (London : T, Richards, 37, Great Queen-street.)

This is a book for the antiquary and the lover of what, without any disrespect, we may call literary hotch-potch, for the Chevalier Lloyd sets before us a dish composed of the most varied materials. If one reader has no taste for genealogy, he has only to turn over a few pages to have his hair set on end by stories of ghosts and apparitions ; if another has a fancy for the study of curious rites and ceremonies, he will find them here ; if he delights in theology, the writer is ready, in a liberal, though a reverent, and, as some would think, a credulous spirit, to discuss the problems of the other world. And through it all the handiwork of a good man is so plain, that, however much we may differ with him in opinion, it is impossible not to admire his spirit. The title of the work—"The History of the Princes, the Lords Marcher, and the Ancient Nobility of Powys Fadog, and the Ancient Lords of Arwystli, Cedewen, and Meirionydd (Vol. I)" is sufficient to explain its scope. An immense amount of pains must have been expended upon this labour of love. We do not pretend to test the accuracy of the mass of facts which the Chevalier Lloyd, with so much patience, has collected. Perhaps his genial and amiable temper leads him to accept statements with too much readiness. That question must be left to critics who have a sufficient acquaintance with the subject, if such there are, but we may express our regret that the results of the Chevalier's labour should not have been presented in a more convenient form. If the history of Powys Fadog had been given as a connected whole, with fuller explanations in some parts, and without the breaks and divisions which now puzzle the ordinary reader, the book would have gained in interest and value. Such descriptions as that of "Serpent Mounds and Cairns," which occupies pp. 31—37, and which is full of interest, should have been relegated to an appendix, together with the sections devoted to "Our Future Home," "Apparitions," "Second Sight," &c., which extend to eighty pages or so in the body of the work. It is possible that in another volume the Chevalier may see his way to some such alterations as those which we have ventured to suggest. The majority of our readers, we know, will prefer a ghost story to a piece of historical criticism, and we intend to gratify them. From the numerous tales which the writer has collected we shall select three that are local and of recent date. In the first case the name of the place is disguised, but the disguise is easily pierced. The narrator is the Chevalier himself—

About four years ago I was staying on a visit with the Rev.
G. G., at Llan . . . . g, in North Wales. Mrs. G. was accustomed to have an afternoon tea in the drawing-room. In one
of the corners of this room, between the door and the fireplace,
was a bracket of three shelves, with various ornaments upon
them. Among them was the couchant figure of a greyhound,
beautifully executed in white Parian china. We were all sitting
round the table, when suddenly we heard something fall and
break. Mrs. G. immediately went to the spot, to see what had
happened, and found that the figure of the greyhound had fallen,
and was broken to pieces. The good lady was much distressed
at what had occurred, as the ornament was the parting gift
of her oldest and dearest friend, whom she had left behind her,
in the Isle of M., when she came to Llan . . . . . g. For some
reason or another, some one happened to look at his watch, and
found that it was just half-past four. The next morning Mrs.
G. got a letter to say that her friend had died at that very time
the previous afternoon. What, then, was the power that
lifted the inanimate figure of the dog from its place in the centre
of the second shelf of the bracket, and then let it fall and break?
—apparently, too, at the very time when the spirit of the lady
had just freed itself from its body in the city of C——, in
England.

Upon this, the comment is obvious, that, of a thousand
articles which fall from some unexplained cause—the
movement of a mouse, perhaps, or the vibration of a chord
of music—one is possibly associated in a wonderful way
with such an event as is recorded in this story. Whether
the rare coincidence will bear the interpretation put upon
it, each reader must decide for himself.. But here is a
more remarkable narrative, in which, it is important to
observe, the Chevalier is not a witness :—

During the latter part of the month of October, 1880, a Mr.
de C. was spending a short time in the parish of Llangurig. On
the night of Monday the 25th, he had the following dream or
vision. He observed that he was in bed, as usual, and that the
corpse of a tall man, whom he did not know, with nothing on
but a flannel shirt, was stretched out on the outside of the quilt
alongside of him. He looked at it with great attention for
some time, when presently the corpse appeared to be lying in a
coffin with no lid on, so that the naked body was as visible as
before. After a short time, it appeared as if a pall had been placed
over it, the edge of which came down to the counterpane. Whilst
Mr. de C. was looking at this, he observed his mother, who died in
1856, enter the room, apparently through the side wall, at the
opposite corner, and stand in the middle of the apartment.
Although she died when about seventy, she did not appear to
be more than thirty years of age. Mr. de C., perceiving his
mother was in the room, got out of bed, went up to her, and
asked why that strange corpse should be placed on his bed. His
mother replied, "It is my wish that it should be done," and then
vanished. Mr. de C. then returned to bed, and, after looking
for some time at the coffin and its sable covering, lying beside
him, he went to sleep. The next morning (Tuesday), Mr. de C.
told his servant of the extraordinary dream he had had. The
man said that it must have been caused by indigestion, and Mr.
de C., concurring in this view of the matter, thought no more
about it. About three o'clock that afternoon, Mr. de C.'s servant came to tell him that a young man from Llanidloes, named
Dafydd R., wanted particularly to see him, as his father had
died on the previous afternoon. The young man, Dafydd R. . s
was admitted, and told Mr. de C. that his father had died of inflammation of the lungs, at two o'clock on the previous day ; but
just before he died he called his son to him, and told him that
as soon as he was dead, he was to go to Mr. de C., and tell him
that he was the nearest relation that Mr. de C. had in Llanidloes. Dafydd, as soon as his father was dead, instead of going
up to Mr. de C., as his father had told him, went to an undertaker, to order a shroud and coffin for his father, but he was
refused both unless he brought ready money with him. This
he could not do, for there was no ready money in the house. So
the father had to lie the next night and the next day without
anything on but his flannel shirt, exactly as he appeared on that
identical night to Mr. de C. On Tuesday morning Dafydd went
to those farmers in the neighbourhood who owed him money, but
could not get one sixpence. He then, half-broken hearted, went
to Mr. de C., and told his story, and his poor father's body was
decently buried in Llanidloes churchyard. Knowing that his
son had not gone to Llangurig to see Mr. de C., the father of
Dafydd went himself in the night, to show Mr. de C. the state

his body was lying in. This man's mother was Eleanor Owen,
one of the family of Owen, who once owned Llwyn Gwyn and
Glyn Gynwydd, mentioned in the *History of Llangurig.*

But our third selection is by far the most marvellous of
all :—

In the month of August, 1843, I (the Chevalier) was staying
at Clochtaen, in the parish of Llangurig, in Arwystli Uwch y
Coed, and one morning I received a letter from my mother, who
was at that time living at the Castle House, now the College, at
Aberystwyth, desiring me to come there immediately, as my
sister Julia had been taken suddenly ill. I therefore went down
to the village, and waited at a little inn called the Blue Bell,
kept by a worthy, excellent old lady, named Mrs. Jenny Bennett.
On entering the house, I told her that I was come there to wait
for the mail, which at that time ran from Gloucester to Aberystwyth, as I was obliged to go home on account of the illness
of my poor sister. It happened that that morning, a young
woman from Pembrokeshire, a niece of Mrs. Jenny Bennett's,
had arrived at Llangurig, from Aberystwyth. As soon as I left,
this young woman asked her aunt who that gentleman was. Her
aunt only replied that she should not ask questions about gentlemen. "O, aunt," the girl replied, "I do not mean anything
of that sort ; but did he not say that there was a young lady,
his sister, who was very ill." "Yes," replied the aunt, "he did,
but what can that matter to you, who know nothing whatever
about her ; and besides that, you should never ask questions
about what concerns the old ancient families ; you should only
listen, and not ask questions about them." "Well, aunt," replied the young woman (who, by-the-bye, had never been to Llangurig before, and this was the first time that her aunt had ever
seen her), "I cannot tell what is the cause, but the moment that
gentleman said that his sister was ill, a heavy sorrow fell on my
heart, as if my heart would break, and I feel for her as if she
was my own sister, and I am wretched and miserable." Upon
hearing this, Mrs. Bennett thought that her niece must be out
of her mind, so, trying to cheer her up, she took her up with
her into the hayfield, where the people were working, and where
she could enjoy the bright sunshine, and the cool mountain
breezes. However, instead of getting better, she got more
melancholy and depressed than ever, and they had to take her
into the house, and put her to bed. During the two or three
days that she kept her bed, she was continually saying, "Oh,
aunt, what can be the reason of this? I feel, and I know for a
certainty, notwithstanding all that you say to the contrary, that
I am a relation of that young lady's ;" and her aunt as constantly
told her to drive all such presumptuous thoughts out of her
head. On the third night she got so much worse, that to soothe
her mind, and thinking she might not live, her aunt said to her,
"Well, my dear, I will now tell you, that all that you believed
to be the cause of your illness is perfectly true. The young
lady is your seventh cousin." After hearing this, she appeared
to be greatly relieved, and fell off to sleep. The next morning
she awoke about five o'clock, and told her aunt that the young
lady was then dying, and that she would not be buried at Rhiw-
abon, but that her body would be brought to Llangurig, for
during the night she had seen the Drycholaeth, i.e., the funeral
procession. She then minutely described the funeral, the number of persons that would come with it, and one gentleman in
particular she described by a certain spot or mark on his face,
the late M. Davies Williams, Esq., of Cwm Cynfelyn. About a
few hours afterwards a messenger arrived at Llangurig, to order
the passing bell to toll, as my poor sister had just departed.
My sister, who was born at Plâs Madog, died on the 11th of
August, in the above-named year, and was buried at Llangurig,
as the young woman said she would be, and all happened exactly as she saw and described it.

We must add that this collection of ghost stories
includes the story of Mrs. Veal, which, the
Chevalier does not seem to know, was Defoe's mas-
terpiece of fiction, composed to push the sale of "Drelincourt on Death." The ghost of Mrs. Veal recommends
"Drelincourt," just as patent medicines are now recommended by fictitious personages in the advertisements in
the newspapers, and the story was an immortal puff,
that is all. One other mistake, which it is necessary to
point out, must be put down, we should think, to the
printer—

The soul's dark cottage, battered and *betrayed,*
Lets in *fresh* light through chinks that time has made—

should of course have "decayed" substituted for "betrayed," while "fresh," should be " new." The quotation with which the book closes is characteristic of the writer, and of the discursive way in which he treats his subject : it leaves us in excellent good humour with him after all his wanderings—

> When ocean-waves of wealth aɪ ouɴd thee roll,
> 　Be calm amid their noise ;
> Nor warp thro' care the freedom of thy soul.
> Life's barque is ever battered by the shocks
> 　Of storm-winds lacking poise,
> And drives from side to side and wildly rocks.
> 　But righteousness stands fast amid the strife ;
> Nought else there is that buoys
> 　The soul in safety through the seas of life.

AUGUST 10, 1881.

NOTES.

OSWESTRY MAGISTRATES.—More than one reference has been made in *Bye-Gones* to the method of appointing Magistrates for Oswestry. It would appear from the Corporation Records that when the late R. J. Venables, Esq., and E. Wright, Esq., were appointed in 1854, they were first consulted whether they would accept office, and were then nominated by the Town Council. This was done at a meeting held May 26, 1854.

JARCO.

THE OLD WELSH ALMANACKS.
(July 27, 1881.)

The *second* issue for 1830 is called " Cyfaill Crwydrol," and hath these verses on the title page :—

1 Fy hen gyfeillion doniol,
　Rhai dawnus, call, a dynol ;
　Rwy'n d'od i'ch plith heb ffug
　　na phall,
　Dan enw cyfaill crwydrol

2 Rhyw dywydd gwyllt anhoywedd,
　Fu'n farn am flwydd gyfannedd,
　Ond tremau'r sêr sy'n dyweud
　　o bell,　　　　　[edd.
　Bydd 'leni yn well na'r llyn-

3 Wrth fwrw golwg sybur,
　Ar feithder mawr yr wybur ;
　Nid ydyw dosbarth fawl yr
　　haul
　Ond difyn, sail difesur.

4 Er deunaw miliwn cyfan,
　O'r haul hyd at y *Georgian* ;
　Can miliwn mwy o weithiau'n
　　faith
　Sy at *Sirius* laith ei helfen.

5 Wrth ddeddfau pwys a thyniad,
　A gorchwyl cyd-dueddiad ;
　Mae bydoedd y ffurfafen faith
　Yn gwneud eu taith, rwy'n
　　tybied.

6 May God protect Britannia,
　'Gainst foes from *Gaul* to
　　India;
　True supplicitous may be told
　For peace to old Hibernia.

The *first* issue for 1831 is called "Cyfaill Tymhorol," and has these verses on the title page :—

1 GYFEILLION dynion doniol,
　Sy'n barnu'n llais i'n llesol ;
　Dois at eich gorchwyl etto, os
　　caf,
　Hyderaf byddaf fuddiol.

2 Mae ambell WR dysgedig,
　Yn adwaen fy nghalennig ;
　Nid hoffi tôn *Cyfeillion* gau,
　O waith hen arfau benthyg.

3 'Waeth ini un bwygilydd,
　Braidd dewi a sön am dywydd,
　Mae hen gymalau wrth deimlo eu clwy,
　'N cyfeirio'n fwy cyfarwydd.

4 Mae'r ddaear gron yn ymdro
　I'r Dwyrain, fel maen llifo,
　Dros ddeg can' milltir mewn
　　un awr,—
　A rhai heb fawr ystyrio.

5 A throi'mewn modd mwy araf,
　I beri bâf a gauaf ;
　Ystyriwn, cadwn yn ein co'—
　Daeth brön y tro diweddaf.

6 I wish an happy year
　To every honest Ranger ;
　In Summer, Autumn, Winter,
　And always getting better.

·The *second* issue for 1831 is called "Cyfaill Cwynfanus," and has the following lines on the title page :—

---

1 GYFEILLION o bob enwa',
　Yn waela gwych 'rhyd *Walia ;*
　Gobeithiaf na chewch 'leni wg
　Nag unrhyw gilwg gartra.

2 Mae methu'r hin rai gweithiau
　Trwy dremau y planedau,
　A barn ar dro trwy drefn y
　　ne',
　Yn gwneud o'u lle y llyfrau.

3 Mae 'nawr yr enw crefydd,
　Yn glodus 'rhyd y gwledydd ;
　Ond gresyn gweled cynnydd,
　　clyw
　Ar haid sy'n byw yn benrhydd.

4 Nid yw ein planed odiaeth,
　Na'n byd i gyd sy'n brydferth ;
　Ond difyn lleiaf dan y Ne',
　Mewn maint i'r Greadigaeth.

5 Pe llin y taflym doner,
　Gan ryw ryferthwy 'sgeler ;
　Mewn pedwar diwrnod, pym-
　　theg awr,
　Doe'n lloer i lawr i'r ddaear.

6 Britannia has lost her dear,
　Good Sov'reign, great and
　　clever ;　　　　　[fame
　O may our gracious William's
　Resound the same for ever.

Within the inner pages of the Almanack for 1828 I find these lines opposite the "signs":—

Yr *Hwrdd* reola'n gymen y pen
　a'r wyneb hy ;
A sêr y *Tarw* sarug drwy'r gwddf
　a'r sefnyg sy' ;
Ar osgo'r 'fraich a'r ysgwydd
　Gefeilliad hylwydd fydd ;
A'r *Crane*, un fodd, reola y fron
　a'r cylla cudd,
Y *Llew* cadarn-ddull, êon,drwy'r
　cefn a'r galon gu ;
A'r *Forwyn* fwyn yn fanol i drall
　y bôl a dry ;

Y lwynau i'r *Fantol* union, a
　fyddlon yn ei phwys ;
Ac felly'r *Sarph* i'r arffed ordeinied mewn modd dwys.
Y *Saethydd,* drwy naws ethol,
　gelynol, i'r ddwy glu!' :
I'r gliniau *Gafr* a gyf'rwyd, hi
　benwyd i bob un ;
Y *Dyfrwr,* arwydd difrad, hardd
　gydiad, i'r ddwy goes ;
I'r *Pysg,* y ddeu-droed, buan yn
　rhan, yr ION a'u rho'cs.

In the *first* issue for 1829 are these lines :—

> O ! Frydain, fan hyfryda, na hir freuddwydia'n hwy,
> Rhag ofn i'r Bwystfil Pabaidd ro'i iti glafaidd glwy.

In the *second* issue for the same year by MIDDLETON :—

> Dyfroedd, moroedd mawrion—rhuadwy
> 　Y rhedant y feisdon ;
> Llanw a thrai o'u lle ni thron'
> A ordeiniwyd er dynion.

Within the *second* issue for 1830 is the following "Englyn y Deuddeg Arwydd":—

> Yr Hwrdd trwy gyffwrdd—Tarw—Gefaill—
> 　Yn llaw Cranc—
> Llew—Morwyn ddiall—
> Mantol—Sarff—Saethydd—Saithvel
> Gafr—Defrwr—Pysg o for pell.*

In the *second* issue for 1831 I find these lines :—

> O Frydain cefaist alar a thrydar i dy ran,
> Am George dy ben, a noddaid i'w ddeiliaid yn mhob man ;
> O rhoddad Brenin Seion yn dirion eto rôdd,
> I'w anwyl ddilyniedydd fod beunydd wrth ei fodd.

* The *signs* are given in the original.

E.G.S.

A SUMMER STORM.—The Shrewsbury papers of Aug. 1839 contain reports of a storm of unusual severity, that burst over the country on the 31st July.　At Oswestry there was such a flood as never was known.　In Willow-street some of the gardens at the backs of the houses were completely covered with water, so that only the tops of the gooseberry trees were visible ; and a house building in the vicinity was washed away.　The roads to Maesbury and Felton were for many hours impassable. From Llanidloes to Buttington, and from Llanymynech to Melverley, the Severn and Verniew swept the valleys in their course with irresistible fury "carrying along nearly all the severed produce of the soil ; and when the united torrents poured into the fertile plain of Melverley, the soil itself gave way before the inundation ; and corn, hay, grass, and everything movable, was floated down the stream, and deposited in many cases several hundred yards from the bed of the river, while the produce of the rich valleys adjoining the Severn in its lower course, was swept off, and

5　　　　　　　　　　　　　　　　　　　　　　　　38

carried out to sea." The Teme, at Ludlow, was much in the same state as the Severn, and so deep were the floods that in one case the mail coach had to be lashed to a tree, and the bags conveyed in a boat to higher ground.
                                              SCROBBES BYRIG.

QUERIES.

GROUSE SHOOTING IN WALES.—We are told by the papers that in Aug., 1839, Mr. Daniel Whittle Harvey arrived at Bala, with a large retinue; rumour says, " to insist on his rights of sporting over the whole of the Crown lands in Wales." On what grounds was the claim made, and was any action taken in it?
                                              TWELFTH.

THE WREKIN, A POEM.—Was the poem on the Wrekin, by the Rev. Richard Corfield, rector of Pitchford, ever published in extenso? The following geographical extract is given by Hulbert:—

The Summit gain'd, the weary toil's repaid,
By prospects varied, mountain, wood, and glade;
O'er Salop's plains with beauteous verdure drest,
The Cambrian mountains stretch along the West.
Turn to the North, and Hawkstone Hills you see,
With Cheshire prospects reaching to the Dee.
When to the East you bend the admiring gaze,
The barren Peak your startl'd thoughts amaze!
More Eastward still, you ken in distant view
Edge-hill, where Charles his faithful follow'rs drew.
This fairy circle let us onward trace
O'er Brecon's beacons, Radnor's forest chase.
And as the outline may be further known,
So past its limits may our love be shewn—
Love to our Country—and, to all held dear
By ties of kindred, friendship's off'ring bear—
Love to our Country—and to all friends round
The Wrekin's circle, may our love resound—
Such wishes there all Shropshire hearts inspire,
In social converse round the winter's fire.
                                              H.B.

GENEALOGICAL ENQUIRY.—Can any of your readers give me a reliable account of the descendants of Hughes of Clwt, Montgomeryshire? Hugh Hughes married Grasi Davies on the 23rd of June, 1660, and they had issue, 1, JOHN, born 14th April, 1661; 2, THOMAS (whose birthday is uncertain); 3, ELLIS (whose birthday is also uncertain); 4, CHARLES, born 8th February, 1665; 5, ROWLAND, born 14th of May, 1666; and 6, MARY, born 29th January, 1669. Some of their descendants emigrated to Pennsylvania before the close of the seventeenth century, but they are supposed to have been in the line of Thomas, or of Ellis, and I wish to know if anyone can render help in making this plain.   GENEALOGIST.

REPLIES.

RESURRECTIONISTS AT SHREWSBURY (July 6, 1881).—The author of the Poem was Mr. Charles Jones of Oswestry, well known in his day as "Jones the Critic," a name given him, I believe, some years later than the publication of "The Resurrection" in consequence of his writing dramatic criticisms on the performances of Stanton's Company for the Oswestry Herald. I happen to possess an interleaved copy of "The Resurrection," with some MS. Notes entered, in the autograph of the author. He seems to have quarrelled with his printer, because the latter tampered with the MS. He says:—

This little address I got Printed in Shrewsbury, when I found that my Oswestry Printer had introduced 50 of the Most Gross Blunders the effects of Vanity and Pedantry. Note, his blunders were not accidental, and further, that I have corrected many of them.

The corrections are made in the copy before me, but they do not materially alter the text. What the author refers to as "this little address" which he had printed in Shrewsbury, it is impossible to say, for he omits to add the text of it in his annotations. The following lengthy note is written on the blank leaves inside the cover :—

The following are some observations intended as an apology for the errors in Style, &c., of "The Resurrection." This affair was first known to the public on Monday, and it being an occurrence unprecedented in Shrewsbury, it created much interest, and was almost the sole topic of conversation among all ranks; I became acquainted with the particulars, upon which it occurred to me that the affair would make a good farce; and on Tuesday morning I commenced a first attempt at Dramatic writing. I soon found that without great additions it was no subject for this sort of effect; and I believe that the Shrewsbury folks would in this respect have so great a regard for truth that they would be better pleased with a strict Description, however dull, than with any flights of Poetic Fiction : I also considered that though I have no objections to jest with such a subject, the more sober minded people would (and perhaps justly) condemn such proceeding. I wrote 2 scenes of a Farce, and then placed it, together with the Idea of continuing it, in the fire;—after Dinner commenced writing the Piece of descriptive Dogrel which I have sent for your perusal : by 6 o'clock I had completed 100 Lines, when I went out for the purpose of collecting further information : I wrote some lines, perhaps 30 before I went to Bed, and on the next Day completed it being 440 Lines.—I certainly do not mean this as an ostentatious display of the quickness of my fingers (for it depended as much on my fingers as my head), I merely mean to state to you that the Rhyming is the work of a day and half, and should be read as such, and not as the studied composition of a greater length of time. Some persons have told me there was no necessity for hurry : my answer was that I knew the subject was so trifling, that it could not maintain its interest in the minds of people many days; I therefore knew that if my poem was published when the affair had become a dead subject, I should have the copies on hand, and the expense to pay, as the reward of my labour.—You will thus understand that if a Rhyme were tolerable, I let it pass, well knowing that were it ever so good it must shortly with its subject sink into oblivion.—If I had any idea that it would act with any person as an augmentation to my credit, I should of course have put my name to it, but I was far from being of opinion that literary fame was to be acquired by the unconsidered nonsense of a few leisure hours spent upon a Subject which though much talked of at the time was trifling and insignificant in the extreme.——You may perhaps form an idea of my opinion of my own writing from the following Lines: They are taken from my Preface to Shrewsbury Show:—

The next thing I would have you note
Is that I've learnt to steal and quote,
And though most Plagiarists are asses
I Maxims learn of Hudibrasses;
One of which I'll most strictly follow,
But that I mean to beat it hollow :
He thinks that each for Sense and Rhyme
One Line sufficient at one Time;
But I who have not Butler's noddle,
Must Rhyme and Sense and nonsense cobble;
And if my Muse in Lines twice four,
Give one of sense, I'll ask no more,
But think my Stars have kindly fated
That I should be genteely treated, &c., &c.

These "observations," he tells a Mr. Taylor (of Whitchurch?) in a letter he forwards with a copy of the book, were intended for an Aunt, but he afterwards decided not to trouble her with Rhyme or notes. Can any one say whether the "Shrewsbury Show" mentioned and quoted was ever published?   JARCO.

CURRENT NOTES.

It is said that there are now living in the town of Mold a man and wife who have 11 children, 45 grandchildren, and 25 great grandchildren, making a total of 81 descendants, all of whom are now living.

The Bishop of Oxford and his family, and Dr. Thring, head master of Uppingham School, have been staying at Borth, to which it will be remembered Uppingham School was removed during an outbreak of fever at Uppingham in 1876 and 1877. Aberystwyth, Borth, Towyn, Barmouth, and the West coast of Wales watering places are exceptionally full. The Cambrian Railway train arrangements have resulted in a great influx of visitors from all parts of the United Kingdom.

The members of the Liverpool Geological Association paid a holiday visit last week to the Wrekin, for the purpose of observing the bedded pre-Cambrian lavas and other igneous rocks, of which the hill is principally composed. It was explained that the Wrekin has within the last few years been shown to contain the oldest volcanic deposits in Great Britain; it also possesses the remains of a subsequent volcanic outburst in the form of basaltic dykes traversing the more ancient lavas. Some distance from the summit there occurs a bare mass of basalt and agglomerate, which spot in all probability marks the place where the vent of the latter volcano existed. The quarry in Ercal Hill was visited, a red granitoid rock being found there containing an intrusive mass of Wrekin rhyolite, and the Quarry in Lawrence Hill, where there are to be observed altered basaltic dykes which have intruded into and disrupted the ancient pre-Cambrian bedded tuffs.

The little parish church of Cwm, in Flintshire, about four miles from St. Asaph, was opened by the Bishop of St. Asaph, after reparation, on Tuesday, Aug. 2. The church, which is a plain structure, dedicated to St. Mael and St. Sulien, is said to date from the fifth or sixth century. The parish contains 100 houses, and 418 inhabitants. The Bishop preached for an hour in Welsh, and at a subsequent luncheon his lordship said that nothing was a greater drawback to the Church than the old pew system, and he was delighted to see a change effected in their church. They should remember that the Church was the Church of the people. Of all places on earth, the church was that where rich and poor should meet on equal terms. The Bishop afterwards spoke of the great value of the connection of the Church with the State, and said he hoped, on the ground of religious liberty, that they would never be separated. Religious liberty would die if they separated the Church from the State. In the afternoon there was English service sung by the choir of St. Asaph's Cathedral. The preacher was the Rev. S. Gladstone. There was evening service in Welsh, with a sermon by the Rev. D. Williams.

CAMBRIAN ARCHÆOLOGICAL SOCIETY.

MEETING AT CHURCH STRETTON.

MONDAY, AUGUST 1.

Weather permitting, the Cambrian Archæologists have an attractive week before them, and if rain falls to-morrow (as some who profess to be weather-wise say it will), we have had such a glorious peep of the hills to-day, and sunshine tempered with balmy breezes, that it will go far to compensate for one wet day; so let us hope for the best, and prognosticate defeat to the croakers.

By the way, those who are familiar with Church Stretton know that Thursday is an unlucky day in that charming little town; a monument over the remains of one of its natives tells us that—

> On a Thursday she was born,
> On a Thursday made a bride,
> On a Thursday her leg was broke,
> On a Thursday she died.

So if we are to have rain at all, it will of course come down heavily that day.

Church Stretton is of course rather out of the boundary of the Society's operations; but Ludlow (to be visited on Wednesday) and Shrewsbury (down for to-morrow's programme) have played such prominent parts in Welsh history, that but a small stretch of the imagination is required to make us believe that Lawley, Caradoc, and The Longmynd are really Welsh mountains.

The mention of Caer Caradoc—so prominent an object from the valley—reminds us that it is the scene of one of the modern battle-fields of "Historic Doubts." The local Guide Books naturally incline to the opinion—though they don't enforce it—that on its heights took place the last battle of Caractacus; but, like the story of the birth of the Prince of Wales in the Eagle Tower at Carnarvon, and the Parliament House of Owen Glyndwr at Dolgelley, the theory is now pretty well exploded, and a hill, nearer to Wales (The Breidden) holds its own as the lofty battle-field.

Everything looks as if the Society were going to have a successful gathering. A strong local committee has been formed to welcome its members. The chairman of this committee is Mr. Ralph A. Benson of Lutwyche Hall, and the Rev. W. Allport Leighton of Shrewsbury the vice-chairman. Mr. Richd. Wilding of Church Stretton is the indefatigable local secretary; and Mr. Windsor, bookseller, of the Post Office, has a register of lodgings, and a book in which to enter the names and temporary residences of visitors.

Amongst the arrivals, whose names appear in Mr. Windsor's register, are—Professor Babington, the Rev. E. L. Barnwell, Mr. Howel W. Lloyd, Rev. R. W. Pritchard, Mr. Arthur Gore, Rev. R. Trevor Owen, Mr. Charles Wilkins, Miss Darkin, Mr. R. Kyrke Penson, Mr. G. E. Robinson, Mr. James Davies, Mr. R. V. Kyrke, Mr. W. G. Smith, Mr. Askew Roberts, Mr. R. Drane, and more are expected to-morrow.

The annual meeting took place in the Town Hall, soon after 9 o'clock in the evening. There was quite a goodly gathering of ladies and gentlemen of the district. On the platform were Mr. Ralph Benson, Sir Charles Rouse-Boughton, Professor Babington, the Rev. E. L. Barnwell, Mr. Howel W. Lloyd, and the Rev. R. Trevor Owen. On the motion of Mr. Kyrke Penson, seconded by Mr. R. V. Kyrke, Mr. Barnwell took the chair, in the absence of the president of last year—Mr. Philipps of Picton Castle. This occupation lasted but a few moments, when the President-elect, Professor Babington, was voted to the post.

Mr. Babington first read a letter he had received from Mr. Philipps, explaining his absence, and apologizing for it, and then proceeded to say that he intended to depart from the usual custom observed in inaugural addresses, and devote himself to one subject—that of Camps, and other primeval fortifications which abounded in Wales and other hilly districts. These seemed to be of all ages; some of the earliest perhaps, formed merely as a defence from wild beasts; later ones for temporary occupation, and a shelter from enemies. Their construction was various, so much so that it might reasonably be supposed they were formed by successive races. These remains Mr. Babington arranged under four heads, viz., Simple Earthworks; Earthworks with external stone supports; Drystone Walls; and Simple Earthworks again. Most of the hill-camps belonged to the first class. The second class consisted of more elaborate works, and had the appearance of having been occupied by garrisons, and were often provided with water. An example of one of these was to be found at Dinas Dinorwig, near Llanberis, which had been described in *Arch: Camb*. In Anglesey there were also examples in Din Sylwy and Lligwy, both of some-what later construction. The third class, which shewed a considerable advance in constructive power, was exhibited on Penmaenmawr, and still more perfectly at Tre 'r Ceiri, on Yr Eifl. Works of this class were by far the grandest and most interesting forts remaining in Britain, which were anterior to the Roman period. The examples he alluded to had been described in their Journal. Mr. Babington then went on to describe Carn Goch, Llandovery, Castell Cawr (he had recently written about in *Arch. Camb.*) Castell Caer Helen, Caer Drewyn, Corwen, &c., and he concluded with the mention of a couple of remarkable illustrations of class four in the immediate district, viz., Caer Caradoc and Bedbury Ring.

This is a most meagre and imperfect outline of an exhaustive and interesting paper, and one, I venture to hope, that will find its way into *Bye-Gones*, as well as into the Journal of the Cambrian Society. In the course of the reading of the paper it was to be remarked that the learned Professor spoke of Caer Car-rád-doc. In Church Stretton "Hodge" would call it "Querdock," and "His Master" would say "Cár-adoc" both of which are equally wrong.

Mr. BENSON, in proposing a vote of thanks to Mr. Babington, and giving a welcome to the Cambrians, gave a glowing description of the district to be visited. He gave a little slap at the Peace-preserving Government so humorously, that Liberals could laugh as heartily as Tories at the joke, and called Taffy a Thief so cheerily, that the satire took the form of a compliment.

Sir C. ROUSE-BOUGHTON, in seconding the vote, also referred to several objects of interest in the locality, in a lengthy speech that was warmly appreciated by the audience. He, too, had his joke with the Welshman, and remarked that when Offa's Dyke was constructed, any Welshman crossing the line was liable to lose his right arm. Their Cambrian visitors might have noticed some formidable looking cleavers in the butchers' shops, but he could assure them these were only intended for the slaughter of Saxon beeves for the use of the invaders !

The PRESIDENT, in returning thanks for the welcome the Society had received, remarked that he had just been informed that the gentleman holding the distinguished position of High Sheriff of the county (Mr Jasper More) was amongst the audience. Had the Society known this, of course he would have been asked to take part in doing what had been so gracefully done by the distinguished local gentlemen who had addressed them. This announcement was received with loud cheers.

The SECRETARY then read the report as follows :—

In 1852 the Society met in this part of the Welsh Marches, when the sixth annual meeting took place at Ludlow, under the presidency of the Honourable R. H. Clive, M.P. On that occasion the general secretary, the Rev W. Basil Jones, now Bishop of St, David's, congratulated the meeting on the prosperous termination of the first five years of the existence of the Society. The first meeting was held at Aberystwyth in 1847, at which the Society was established in a qualified sense, one of the rules being that no pecuniary subscription should be required. The *Archæologia Cambrensis*, however, had existed for nearly two years before this meeting, the first number having been issued in January, 1846, but it was not the *Journal of the Association* as at present, but the private property of the Rev H. Longueville Jones, who subsequently organized and, so to speak, established the Society. At the end of its fourth year Mr Jones gave up the *Journal*, making over the remaining copies to Mr J. Russell Smith, of Soho-square, These four volumes constitute the first series of the *Archæologia Cambrensis*. In the year 1850 an important alteration was made in the constitution and administration of the Society. In the report of the committee, read at the fourth annual meeting, held at Dolgelley, mention is made of the meeting at Gloucester in the preceding March, at which various important changes were made, the most im-portant of which was "the establishment of a system of sub-scription on a settled plan as a security for the permanence of the *Archæologia Cambrensis*, and through it of the Society itself." A new series of the *Journal* was then commenced, arrangements having been made with Mr Mason of Tenby, which made him the sole proprietor of the *Journal*, the Society purchasing copies for its subscribing members, and making grants for suitable illustrations. Thus the Society was put on a new and in some respects more satisfactory basis. This arrangement, however, lasted only five years, as Mr. Basil Jones, who principally conducted the business of the Association, was obliged to resign owing to new official duties at Oxford, which resignation was announced at the special meeting held at the close of the Ruthin meeting in 1854. The Society was then placed on a new footing. The arrangement with Mr. Mason was given up, and the Society undertook the expense of printing and publishing for itself. A new series of the *Archæologia Cambrensis* was commenced in 1855 and continued until 1869, when, owing to the difficulty new members had in procuring complete sets, the volumes of 1855 and 1856 having become out of print, a fourth series, namely, the present one, was commenced. The important change made in 1855 would probably not have been attempted, much less carried out, but for the action of four or five members, who agreed to support each other in carrying on the work of the Association, and particularly of taking part in the Council meetings. Of these members, two alone survive, one of them being Professor Babington, who has so kindly consented to the request of the Society to act as president on this occasion, and your Committee therefore heartily congratulate the members on being presided over by a gentleman distinguished no less for his extensive and accurate knowledge than for his courteous manner and .... d .... in communicating to others any information sought .... iness

It is with great regret that your Committee records the removal of so many valuable friends of the Association since the meeting at Pembroke, the first of whom was Mrs. Stackhouse Acton, of Acton Scott, who died on the 24th of January, in her eighty-seventh year. She assisted at the Ludlow meeting in 1852, where she exhibited an illustrated MS. account of Stokesay Castle, which splendid work deservedly attracted great attention. Had her life been spared and her strength permitted, she had promised to render all the assistance in her power towards the success of the present meeting. Another valuable member was Edwin Guest, Esq., LL.D., F.R.S., late master of Caius College, who died Nov. 23rd, 1880, at his seat, Sandford Park, Oxfordshire. His only distinct work was a *History of English Rhythm*, a work now become exceedingly scarce. But in the long series of volumes of the Royal Archæological Institute there are most valuable essays on the history of Britain from the departure of the Roman armies to the establishment of the Saxons, of which we know so little that the smallest contribution from Dr. Guest's pen is of the greatest value. His love of accuracy was so great that many of his researches as to ancient landmarks were usually attended with considerable labour as a pedestrian. His view of the Stonehenge question has not been replaced by any other more probable. Full obituary notices of two others from among the most valued members of our Association have appeared so recently that it is only needful to mention their names here—The Rev. Canon Williams, a contributor to our pages from the very first number of the *Journal*, and Mr. Breese, F.S.A., Local Secretary for Merionethshire.

The first volume of the History of the Princes, the Lord Marchers, and the Ancient Nobility of Powys Fadog, by J. Y. W. Lloyd of Clochfaen, Esq., M.A., K.S.G., has lately been issued to the subscribers. It is a substantial volume of more than 400 pages, and contains much curious and supplemental information, in addition to the genealogical portions, of which much has already appeared in the *Journal*. This is one more addition to our local histories, and one which but for the existence of the Cambrian Archæological Association, would probably have never been published. There are several useful illustrations, and, what is still more valuable, a copious index. It is to be hoped that the learned author will soon be able to present to his supporters the second volume.

It was stated in the last report that the Rev. Canon D. R. Thomas, F.S.A., intended to bring out a supplementary volume to his invaluable History of the Diocese of St. Asaph; and it is hoped that this desirable object will before long be accomplished. Professor Rhys is also engaged on a History of the Breton Celts, a history that has been long desired ; while the Rev. D. Silvan Evans has undertaken a Welsh dictionary, the value of which may be considered guaranteed as far as careful accuracy and thorough knowledge of the language can secure success. It will be remembered that subsequently to the last meeting of the Society at Carnarvon a proposal was carried to print the Chronicle of the famous Clerke, Peter Roberts, called Cwtta Cyfarwydd, being a chronicle of births, deaths, and marriages, and of the principal local events in the Vale of Clwyd, and other parts of Flintshire and Denbighshire. The late Mr Breese, who was the owner of this interesting document, had it transcribed, and printed a specimen page of the work. Since his death his executor, after repeated researches and enquiries, has not been able to find it. All that has been discovered is a copy of a small part of the transcript with corrections in Mr Breese's hand-writing ; at present there does not appear to be much chance of its recovery. Your committee regret to make this announcement, and if, after further delay, there is no prospect of finding either transcript or the original, the subscriptions that have been advanced will be returned.

Those who attended the Pembroke meeting will remember the kind exertions of the president, Mr Philipps of Picton Castle, in promoting the success of that very pleasant and interesting meeting. Your committee would, therefore, suggest a hearty vote of thanks, and that his name should be added to the list of vice-presidents, and also those of the Hon. and Rev. Canon G. T. Orlando Bridgeman and the Hon. F. H. Tracy, M.P. The retiring members of the committee are R. H. Wood, Esq., F.S.A., D. H. Lloyd, Esq., M.A., and J. Y. W. Lloyd, Esq., M.A., K.S G. and are recommended for re-election ; and in place of the Hon. and Rev. Canon Bridgeman (appointed vice-chairman) and the Rev. Walter Evans (withdrawn) the names are proposed of the Rev. Canon D. R. Thomas and the Rev. Professor Edmondes. Your Committee also propose that the following local secretaries be appointed :—Evan Parry Jones, Esq., for Merionethshire ; Rev. E. Tudor Owen for Flintshire ; Rev. Charles Chidlow for Carmarthenshire.

Since the last meeting the following have joined the Association, and await confirmation of their election :—*North Wales*: Miss Light, Plas Llewelyn, Festiniog, the Rev. J. S. Lewis, Guilsfield Vicarage, Welshpool, the Rev. D. Jones, Llanfechain Rectory, the Rev.T. Meredith, Rhyl, Henry Leslie, Esq., Bryntanat, Llansaintffraid,A. N. Palmer, Esq.,Ar-y-bryn-terrace, Wrexham. *South Wales*: W. Hulm, Esq., Pembroke, C. E. G. Philipps, Esq., Picton Castle, Haverfordwest. *Shropshire*: The Rev. W. A. Leighton, F.L.S., Shrewsbury ; Col. Buckle, Shakenhurst, Cleobury Mortimer.

TUESDAY, AUGUST 2.

The weather-wise were otherwise for once, and the party assembled at the railway station with faces as bright as the sunshine, and imaginations as flowery as the speech of the President of the Local Committee on the previous evening ! A start was made for Shrewsbury at 9.15, and the county-town was reached by 10 o'clock, where we were met by the friends of and other members of the Shropshire Society :—Rev. W. Allport Leighton, Canon Butler, Canon Lloyd, Mr. W. Phillips, Mr. Callcott, Captain Stanton, Rev. T. Auden, Rev. C. H. Drinkwater, Mr. J. P. Smith, Mr. Jebb, Mr. W.Hughes, Mr. J. P. White, Mr. Beacall, Mr. Arthur Sparrow, Mr Pryce ; also by the Rev. Canon D. R. Thomas, Mr. Lloyd Griffith, Mr. Palmer, and other members of the Cambrian Society. There were also several ladies present. A start was at once made (under the guidance of Mr. Leighton) to the Castle, the grounds of which were inspected and enjoyed, and the interior explored. The next object of interest was The Schools, and here Canon Lloyd was the chief exponent. Two statements, by the way, that fell from his lips, did not altogether jump with the humour of all his audience ; to judge by sundry demurs uttered in under tones. When he said that the statues and coat of arms on the front were to be removed to the new buildings, there was more than one expression of opinion that they should remain where they were ; and when he said that the pictures in the Library would probably be removed to the head-master's private residence fears were expressed that they might thus in time be claimed as the master's private property ; and if not so, at

any rate would be lost to the public. One opinion of Canon Lloyd's was heartily approved, viz., that the School buildings should be converted into a county museum and library, and it is to be hoped the Shropshire Society will keep the idea prominently in view. Again the party moved on, and entered St. Mary's Church where Canon Lloyd pointed out in an instructive and most interesting style the various features of interest. Canon Lloyd also took much pains to explain the figures in the very beautiful window (in the north wall of the chancel) the glass of which is supposed to be the work of Albert Durer. From this interesting church a move was made to Old St. Chad's where Mr. Worthington Smith, at the request of Mr. Barnwell, made a sketch of the remarkable pulpit with the representation of a Bible (in wood) carved in the front. From Old St. Chad's the party proceeded to The Abbey, Mr. Leighton acting as guide. In the evening both Societies—the Cambrian, and the Shropshire—dined together at the George. After dinner the Rev. C. H. Drinkwater read a paper on "The Inner Wall of Shrewsbury," and also exhibited a rubbing of an Inscribed Stone he had written about in the *Bye-Gones* column of the *Oswestry Advertizer* on Sep. 22, 1880 ; and to which Mr. Askew Roberts referred in *Arch : Cam :* for July. Such of your readers as possess the reprint of *Bye-Gones* will find a reference to the query of Mr. Drinkwater (from the pen of the Rev. W. A. Leighton) in the issue of Mar. 16, 1881. Another reference to the stone appears in the *Advertizer* this week (Aug. 3). The Cambrians left Shrewsbury in the evening for their quarters at Church Stretton ; and held a night meeting, at which the President combated some of the conclusions of Canon Lloyd, who had expressed an opinion that the arches dividing the nave from the side aisles of St. Mary's Church had been completely renewed by an architect or builder, by being underpinned. That might be true, but there was another theory ; that the whole of the masonry had not been touched, and that, instead of taking out all the lower parts, they had simply cut off the outside (as at Winchester) of the Norman columns, and carved them in such a way as to make them look like the columns of a later day. The President then, in a short and interesting address, reviewed, generally, the proceedings of the day. A paper was read by the Rev. J. D. La Touche on "Stokesay Castle," and one on "Ancient Plough Marks on the Hills," by Mr. J. D. Dyke. The latter gave rise to some discussion.

WEDNESDAY, AUGUST 3.

This morning there was every prospect of a continued rain, and a repetition of the Welshpool weather of two years ago, but happily the showers proved to be merely "the pride of the morning," as a Salopian would say. After a visit to Stretton Church, and to the old Manor House, now the Buck's Head Hotel, the party proceeded by train to Craven Arms, from whence they had a pleasant walk to Stokesay Castle, which Mr. La Touche described. An elaborate paper (very well illustrated) from his pen, will be found in the first volume of the *Transactions* of the Shropshire Archæological Society. Returning to Craven Arms, train was taken to Ludlow, where the archæological hunt included the Church and Castle, the scent being rather crossed by an unexpected lunch at The Feathers. There was no meeting on Wednesday night.

THURSDAY, AUGUST 4.

Again we had a fine day, and Wenlock was the goal. The Mayor (Mr. Thursfield) in the absence of Mr. W. P. Brookes, met the party and escorted it to the Town Hall, where the "Stocks" were duly inspected, and a few mild regrets expressed that such an instrument of parish torture was not in vogue now-a-days, when drunkards' wives answered for their husbands before the magistrates, and scraped out of their own hard earnings .to pay the fine! The Corporation Records were also glanced at, and hopes were expressed that they would find their way into the *Transactions* of the Shropshire Society. Then the Church was visited, and last, but not least, the Abbey. At the latter place the party was welcomed by Mr. Gaskell. After the party got back to home quarters an evening meeting was held, at which a paper was read by Mr. Banks on "The Borders of Shropshire in Saxon Times;" and hearty thanks were voted to the local committee on the motion of Mr. Barnwell, seconded by Mr. Howel W. Lloyd.

FRIDAY, AUGUST 5.

This was the last day, and it was spent at Wroxeter, Haughmond, Atcham, and Shrewsbury.

The Cambrian Society is to be congratulated on so successful a week, and on so indefatigable an honorary secretary as the Rev. Trevor Owen. Everything passed off without a hitch, which says much for the foresight of the "Welcoming Committee" of Salopians. If there is one thing we might suggest it would be that on these occasions the matter of lunch should have its place in the programme. Archæologists, like ordinary mortals, have a knack of getting hungry, and it was found that at Shrewsbury on Tuesday, and Ludlow on Wednesday, the party got divided in consequence of some going to seek after provender in one place and some in another, and others not at all.

In addition to the names of members and visitors already given as attending the Shropshire meeting, may be given the following :—Professor Edmondes, Rev. Prebendary Davies, Lady Goodriche, Mr Lister, Rev. W, Elliott, Dr. Cranage, Rev. Donald Carr, Rev. Holland Sandford, Mrs Auden, Rev. A. T. Pelham, Mrs and Miss Penson, and several other ladies whose names were not entered in the visitors' book.

It has been arranged to hold next year's meeting at Llanrwst, a capital centre both for rail and road.

AUGUST 17, 1881.

NOTES.

SHROPSHIRE CHINA ABROAD.—We are told by the newspapers that on Nov. 11, 1801, three very elegant services of Coalbrook Dale China, finished in a most superb style, with rich burnished gold, were completed for the Marquis Cornwallis. This was the first British china introduced into France.   N.W.S.

TOURISTS' RHYMES.—At different times there have been a variety of specimens of the rhymes written by Tourists in Hotel Books transcribed into *Bye-Gones*, and I would suggest to such of your readers who are travelling this season in Wales that they should run their eyes over the books of the houses they stop at, and glean the best specimens they can find for the amusement of your readers. Here are a couple culled last week at the Saracen's Head, Beddgelert :—

The winter passed, the spring time came, the summer sun
   shone bright;
A green grave lies beneath the shade of Snowdon's kingly
   height;
And many a tear I shed for her, who lies in death so low,
Lost Nancy Jones of Llanfairpwllgwyngylltysilio.

As usual the lines are followed by very free criticism, and

somewhat personal remarks ; and one writer asks " Where is Llanfair &c. &c. &c. ?" to which another replies, " You will find out if you consult the *Gossiping Guide*."

Another Tourist writes as follows his opinion of his brother rhyming Tourists :—

How doth the busy British T.
   In scribbling take delight
He sweats and suffers all the day
   And gushes here at night.

This of course does not pass unchallenged, but the best emendation is the one in which the writer for "And gushes here at night" substitutes "And lushes here all night !"

FOOTPAD.

SHROPSHIRE PAROCHIAL REGISTERS.—Parish Registers owe their commencement to one of the general injunctions to the clergy, by Thomas Cromwell, in the year 1538. It was enjoined, in the King's name (Henry VIII.), that "every parson, vicar, or curate, shall for every church keep one book or register, wherein he shall write the day and year of every wedding, christening, and burying," and the book was to be provided at the expense of the parishes out of their common charges.

Six parishes, of the county of Salop, have registers dating as far back as 1538, but they are mostly defective.

OSWESTRY.—The following books of Registers exist, for this parish, in the possession of the Vicar, or should be so, according to notes furnished me :—I. Contains Baptisms, Burials, and Marriages for the years 1558—1609, 1612—1640, 1653—1668 ; ii. Baptisms and Marriages, 1669—1727 ; Burials, 1669—1678 ; iii. Burials, 1678—1750 ; iv. v. Baptisms, 1727—1779 ; Marriages, 1727—1754 ; vi. Baptisms, 1780—1812 ; vii. viii. Burials, 1751—1812 ; ix.— xii. Marriages, 1755—1812. These include entries for Aston, and Baptisms and Burials for the House of Industry, 1783—1789.

Another week I will give a list of the dates at which the Registers commence at all the Shropshire parishes.

T.W.HANCOCK.

THE PRINCE OF WALES AND THE WELSH. When the "Ancient Britons" waited upon the Prince of Wales last year [1772] he continued for several days after to talk of "his people." He boasted continually before his brothers and sisters about "his people," and the whole nursery, in short, echoed with nothing else. These suspicious omens of patriotism gave the alarm, and it was resolved from that time that he and "his people" should not meet again till he is better able to receive them. The magnanimity and spirit of the Prince on the above occasion deserve to be applauded as it shows his ardent desire, though very young, to be beloved, especially by those brave spirited and loyal Britons, from whence he derives his title.—*Wood's British Gazetteer* and *Shrewsbury Chronicle*, March 6, 1773.—The Prince of Wales here referred to was George Augustus Frederick, afterwards King George IV. He was born 12th of August, 1762, and consequently at the interview in question, was only in the 11th year of his age.   T.W.H.

[Extracts from the *Annual Register* were given in *Bye-Gones* of Feb. and Mar. 1878, referring to the audiences granted to the Welsh Society by the Prince, the first of which took place, in 1765, when he was scarcely three years old ! On St David's Day, 1772, after the audience, the Society was informed that future applications would be discountenanced. The paper quoted by "T.W.H." gives a novel reason for this ! It would appear that, although the usual hundred guineas donation was not discontinued, and, as will be seen in *Bye-Gones*, Mar. 13, 1878, in the year 1776 the Welshmen were received to Royal favour.—ED.]

QUERIES.

"MINSHULL THE PRINTER."—You have ever and anon had specimens of this man's wit and wisdom. Here is one which doubtless satirizes somebody or some event. Can any reader say who or what?

"*Notis.* Hon Tewsdi next, in Sall up Rode, Hodges.tree, the Kummittee hintendd haffing, has yushull, the Gim Nas Stik Xercisez, Ho-Limpyc Gaymes, hand Ethennyun Sportes, purvyded the Nebbors hand Gentl Folks pey thur Subbskrippshuns to the Stewheart in Sall up Rode, for byin the Prizzis, &cettra. Hawgust 16, 1830_4_."

The handbill, of which this is a copy, was surmounted by a rude engraving of a bear dancing to the sound of a tabor, and bore the imprint "Minshull, Printer, Oswestry."

H.B.

THE SALOPIAN ZEALOT.—I have before me a small-octavo tract, entitled "The Salopian Zealot; or, The Good Vicar in a Bad Mood. By John the Dipper." It is dated 1778, and was sold by booksellers in Bristol, Swansey, and Shrewsbury. From the Introduction I gather that there was a controversy on the Baptist question in Shrewsbury, in which Mr. Medley and Mr. De Courcey took the leading parts. The names of Turner, Sandys, and Phillips are also referred to. The printers seem to have had plenty of employment arising out of the dispute, one "rejoinder" on the part of Mr. De Courcey having comprised a Three-shilling volume. "The Salopian Zealot" is a "satirical poem." Who was the author, how many parties were engaged in the controversy, and how many pamphlets were published? Was Mr. Medley a Baptist Minister in Shrewsbury? He seems to have preached a sermon on Immersion, a portion of which was retailed to Mr. De Courcey, who replied to it in an Eighteen-penny pamphlet, which set the presses going!

R.D.

REPLIES.

A CAERNARVONSHIRE MARTYR (May 18, 1881).—I am greatly obliged to "F.S.A." and Scrobbes Byrig for their communications of the 2nd March and 18th May respectively in reply to my query on the 19th January last, under the title of "A Shropshire Martyr," who appears, however, to be more properly entitled to the appellation of "A Caernarvonshire Martyr," notwithstanding some discrepancies in the two accounts, the date being identical in both. In the "Early Chronicles of Shrewsbury," his surname (spelt Joanes) only is given; he is called a Shropshyrman; and the place of his execution, "Sainct Mary Watterings"; whereas Bishop Challoner, who follows three contemporary authorities, calls him "John Jones, alias Buckley, Priest. O.S.F.," and states that "on the 12th of July in the forenoon, Mr. Jones was drawn to St. Thomas's Waterings, the place designed for his execution," and that "his body afterwards was bowelled and quartered, and his quarters were set up on poles in the ways to Newington and Lambeth, and his head in Southwark." All this would seem to point to the conclusion that Father Jones was executed in London, as does also Dr. C's observation that "the execution is mentioned by Mr. Stow in his Chronicle," although I have been unable to discover in the Liber Ecclesiasticus or the Clergy List the mention of any such locality in it as St. Mary or St. Thomas' Waterings. We learn also from the account in "Missionary Priests" (v. 1, p. 360, Derby Reprint) that "John Jones was born of a gentleman's family, in the parish of Clenock (Clynog Fawr) in the County of Caernarvon. At what place he had his education, or where he

was made priest I have not yet found; only I have seen a list of priests, prisoners in Wisbeach castle, 1587, in which I met with his name, with a note that at that time he was a secular priest. How, or when he got out of Wisbeach castle I cannot tell; but certain it is that after this time he was received into the Order of St. Francis, either at Rome, or at Pontoise. . . . . Returning into England about 1593, he laboured there for three years with great fruit, and then fell again into the hands of the persecutors, and was kept in prison for about two years more, where many resorting to him received great benefit to their souls from his conversation, till Topcliffe, the arch persecutor, caused him to be arraigned (together with Mr. Barnet and Mrs. Wiseman, who had been aiding and assisting to him) in the beginning of July, 1598. Father Jones pleaded that he had never been guilty of any treason against his Queen or country; and desired that his case should rather be referred to the conscience of the judges than to an ignorant jury. Judge Clinch told him they were sensible he was no plotter against the queen, but that he was a Romish priest, and, being such, had returned into England, contrary to the statute of Elizabeth 27, which was high treason by the laws. 'If this be a crime,' said the confessor, 'I must own myself guilty; for I am a priest, and came over into England to gain as many souls as I could to Christ.' Upon this he was condemned, and when sentence was pronounced upon him, according to the usual form, as in cases of high treason, falling upon his knees, with a loud voice, he gave thanks to God. Mr. Barnet and Mrs. Wiseman were also condemned to die; but were not executed." . . . . "Being taken off the sled, and set up into the cart, he declared that he had never spoken a word or entertained a thought, in his whole life, against the Queen or his country, but daily prayed for their welfare. He stood there for about an hour (for it seems that the hangman had forgot to bring the rope with him) sometimes speaking to God in prayer; sometimes preaching to the people; till at length a rope being brought and fitted to his neck, the cart was drawn away, and he was permitted to hang till he was quite dead." Truly a worthy disciple of St. Francis! The fuller account given by Bishop Challoner clearly explains what was intended when the Government of Elizabeth caused it to be circulated that he, and men like him, "studd stowtely against the Queene's Mts proceedings," and what was the nature and object of such proceedings.

Challoner does not state precisely what part of England was the scene of his labours, but it may be conjectured to have been London from the circumstance that he was executed there after a lapse of three years only from his first arrival. The error that he was a Shropshireman may possibly have arisen from a more intimate connexion that may have existed at some time between him and the Franciscan Monastery of St. Julian's at Shrewsbury, and thus have procured him a niche in the 'Early Chronicles' of that city. Otherwise it is to be inferred that the Government of the day took special care to cause intelligence of their ghastly proceedings to be distributed throughout the kingdom, in order to strike the greater terror into the hearts of those who, through good report and ill report, had still the courage to adhere to the ancient Faith.

Why St. Thomas' Waterings was selected for the scene of his martyrdom does not clearly appear, but that this, as well as Tyburn and Tower Hill, was at that day used as a place of execution of persons sentenced to death for high treason, is shown by the fact that John Penry (Martin Marprelate) was executed there some years before, and the Rev. John Fybush (or Pibush) in 1601, solely for being a Catholic priest.

Nicholas Otterden, a priest, is mentioned by Collier as having been executed together with Anne Askew and another for denying the First of Henry VIIIth's six Articles, which affirmed the corporal presence of Christ in the Holy Eucharist, but nothing is said by him as to his antecedents, or of his being a Shropshireman. H. W. L.

SOUTHEY AND HEBER AT LLANGEDWYN.
(May 18, 1881.)

The interesting paper on this subject, from the pen of the Vicar of Meifod, was largely quoted on the above-named date by a Reviewer in the *Oswestry Advertizer*, who questioned Mr. Thomas's dates, and asked if any of your readers could give an account of Southey's earliest visit to this district. Since the paper appeared I have been looking over Warter's *Selections from the Letters of Robert Southey*, published in 1856, and there I find several references to the poem *Madoc*, and the methods employed by the author to glean information. On Sep. 24, 1799, writing to Mr. C. W. Williams Wynn, Southey says: "I want sadly to see your country, and, if it were a study that promised any success, to understand your language that I might get at the hidden treasures. You Welshmen do so little for us! Is there not nationality enough among you to give us poor Englishmen Taliessin and the long list of his followers down to Owen Glendower's time? or are they left untranslated, lest by stripping them of their Welsh dress you should expose their nakedness?" Again on Oct. 10, 1799, he writes, "How comes it that Wales has produced no great man? We take Taliessin upon trust, probably much to his advantage; but since they learnt to speak English your countrymen have never said anything to be remembered. . . Did I tell you three months ago that I had finished the outline of 'Madoc'? I much wish you to see it, and would send it if I could trust my only copy to the chance of carriage." Again on April 30, 1801, he writes from Lisbon, "On my return I shall soon leave Bristol, to pass through Wales to the Lakes, there to pass the autumn, and perhaps the winter. My Welsh abode and excursions you may regulate. The History will be my employment, to that I shall devote myself, relieving labour by the correction of 'Madoc.' . . As 'Madoc' must be my monument I am anxious to erect it in my lifetime."

On June 26, 1801, Southey writes thus to John May, Esq.:—"In the autumn it is possible that I shall pass a few weeks with Wynn, in Wales, and take my long intended journey in the steps of 'Madoc.'" On Aug. 20, 1801, he writes to Mr. Wynn from Bristol, and says:—

In the Welsh books (the Odyssey part of "Madoc,") I design to introduce old Giraldus excommunicating Owen Cyveilioc (as he did) for not going to the Crusade, and to remove the interview with Llewellyn to the island of Bardsey, which I wish to visit. He shall also take a dog, which is to be found in Giraldus, with him. The poor beast watched his master's corpse for eight days. I can make him useful; and he ought to have his fame—only how to Christen him? Have you any decent dog-names in Wales? for the *propria quæ canibus* of England are vile.

In Sep. 1801, Southey visits Wales, and writes a long letter to his wife, dated "Bangor; which, on another occasion, may be worth transcribing for the *Oswestry Advertizer*. Mr. Charles Wynn seems to have accompanied him on his ramble. The start is made from Wynnstay, from whence they visit Llangollen, Corwen, Llanrwst, Conway, &c., and he concludes his letter by stating that he hopes to arrive at Llangedwyn on the following Saturday.

I find no further letter to Mr. C. Williams Wynn until 1803; and then there is one from Keswick, dated Oct. 28, in which he enters very fully into his plans about "Madoc." He says:—

What was the dress of the Welsh? I have given Ririd at a venture a shirt of fine linen, a tunic, an embroidered girdle, a mantle bordered with fur, and a fur cap, and he looks very well in it. Supposing that they had assimilated to Saxon decency, I would have given him breeches; but neither breeches, smallclothes, indescribable pantaloons, nor galligaskins could be put in English verse. Stockings may have been in use then, but could not when the King had a *pedifer* to chafe his feet as he sat at table.

I am going to carry Madoc to Bardsey, if you have Powell or Warrington at hand to tell me which of the old Kings were buried there. Owen Gwynedd and his father Gryffith were buried at Bangor. I could make a swelling and sonorous passage about the old gentlemen and their worthinesses, if I knew them. The extracts which I made at Wynnstay from the *Royal Tribes* and the *Gwydir History* are becoming very useful. It was unfortunate that we did not visit Bardsey; I feel it now. This Welsh part of the poem will be very Odyssey-like. I am weaving into it all the collectable circumstances of the time and manners of the people in this order:—Journey to Mathraval; the Hirlas Horn; the Grave of Iorwerth at Pennant Melangle; the Meeting of the Bards; Dinevawr and the Embassy of Gwgan of Caer Einion from the *Royal Tribes*. Thus far is done. Then come Bardsey and Llewelyn; the Child of Hoel; the Excommunication of Owen Cyveilioc at Bangor for not crusading; and the Priest directed by Madoc in digging a hole from his father's grave through into the churchyard to eject his body, he having died under the censure of the Church (from Giraldus and your friend Mr. Yorke). This will tell well; and Madoc shall carry over the bones of Owen to America. I shall then try my strength with Camoens and Valerius Flaccus (who was a man of far more genius) in the embarkation scene. I can find a place for only one picture, and that will be taken from the Llanberris scenery—about the village, not the lake. Dinevawr is such mere English scenery that I have but hinted at it, to contrast it with glens and mountains; but the 'Tivey' had beavers in the days of Giraldus; and I have shown Madoc one poor hermit,—one to put him in mind of his own countrymen. I wish your brother would colonise the Dee with some of the old Welshmen. There is something to me very affecting in the extirpation of so interesting an animal.

So much for the preparation of *Madoc*. In Nov. 1804 Mr. Southey informs Mr. Wynn that it was "beyond the reach of accident," as the whole poem was printed, and he was daily expecting proofs of the notes. In Jan. 1805 he complains that "the printer lags with the notes." However, it very shortly makes its appearance, and in a letter of May 11, 1805, to Miss Barker, Southey says, "My great book, Wynn tells me, is almost as universally admired as he could wish, and that, he says, is as much as I can desire." Nevertheless, his friend had suggestions to make, which are thus referred to in a letter to him on Oct. 3, 1805, "Dear Wynn; I shall take your advice respecting 'Madoc,' and confine myself to correcting the parts as they are. About the catastrophe, when my thoughts acquire anything like a definite form, you shall be consulted."

How *Madoc* fared at the hands of the Reviewers, and how it failed to put money in the purse of its author, is no part of my purpose to relate here:—one extract from a letter to Charles Darwen, Esq., dated May 13, 1806, will reveal as much as our readers will care to know, and with that I will dismiss the subject:—

In examining my accounts in the Row, I find that my profits upon "Madoc" amount to three pounds, seventeen shillings, and one penny. There remain about 180 copies on hand, each of which, when sold, will produce me fifteen shillings; but it will be long before they drop off, if ever they do during my life. However, we shall print a small edition in two volumes without loss of time, in which there will be no alterations, that the quarto may retain its full value, in which case it will still find some purchasers who like to pay for good margins and fill quarto shelves.

In all this correspondence not one word is said of Heber. He comes into the story (as we shall see) at a much later date. Writing to Henry Taylor, Esq., on July 10, 1830, Southey says:—

Few persons took so much interest in my writings [as Heber] which may partly have arisen from the almost entire coincidence in our opinions and ways of thinking upon all momentous subjects; the Catholic question alone excepted. Mrs. Heber told me that I have had no little influence in directing his thoughts and desires towards India; and I have no doubt that some lines in "Joan of Arc" set him upon the scheme of his poem on the death of King Arthur. My personal acquaintance with him was but little; but we knew a great deal of each other through Charles Wynn.

Ten years earlier Southey and Heber had been guests together at Llangedwyn, then the residence of Mr. Charles Watkin Williams Wynn; and a few years after Heber's death Southey referred to this visit in the following lines from the poem "On the Portrait of Bishop Heber,"—

Ten years have held their course
Since last I looked upon
That loving countenance,
When on Llangedwin's terraces we paced
Together to and fro,
Partaking there its hospitality,
We with its honoured master spent,
Well-pleased the social hours;
His friend and mine, . . my earliest friend, whom I
Have ever, thro' all changes, found the same,
From boyhood to grey hairs,
In goodness, and in worth and warmth of heart.
Together there we traced
The grass-grown site, where armed feet once trod
The threshold of Glendower's embattled hall;
Together sought Melangel's lonely Church,
Saw the dark yews, majestic in decay,
Which in their flowering strength
Cyveilioc might have seen;
Letter by letter traced the lines
On Iorwerth's fabled tomb;
And curiously observed what vestiges
Mouldering and mutilate,
Of Monacella's legend there are left,
A tale humane, itself
Well nigh forgotten now.

This was written in 1830, and not in 1820, as some editions of Southey's poems state. The visit to the quaint old Church of Pennant Melangell he refers to in a letter (you quoted in May) dated "Shrewsbury, April 25, 1820," addressed to "Edith May Southey":—

Having nothing else to do for a dismal hour or two, I sit down to write to you, in such rhymes as may ensue, be they many be they few, according to the cue which I happen to pursue. I was obliged to stay at Llangedwin till to-day; though I wished to come away, Wynn would make me delay my departure yesterday, in order that he and I might go and see a place whereof he once sent a drawing to me.

And now I'll tell you why it was proper that I should go thither to espy the place with my own eye. 'Tis a church in a vale, whereby hangs a tale, how a hare being pressed by the dogs and much distressed, the hunters coming nigh and the dogs in full cry, looked about for someone to defend her, and saw just in time, as it now comes pat in rhyme, a saint of the feminine gender.

The saint was buried there, and a figure carved with care, in the churchyard is shewn, as being her own; but 'tis used for a whetstone (like a stone at our backdoor), till the pity is the more, (I should say the more's the pity, if it suited with my ditty), it is whetted half away—lack-a-day, lack-a-day!

They show a mammoth's rib (was there ever such a fib?) as belonging to the saint Melangel. It was no use to wrangle, and tell the simple people, that if this had been her bone, she must certainly have grown, to be three times as tall as the steeple.

Moreover there is shown a monumental stone, as being the tomb of Yorwerth Drwndwn (w, you must know, serves in Welsh for long o). In the portfolio there are drawings of their tombs, and of the church also. This Yorwerth was killed six hundred years ago. Nevertheless, as perhaps you may guess, he happened to be an acquaintance of mine, and therefore I always have had a design to pay him a visit whenever I could, and now the intention is at last made good.

5

These later letters I extract from *Southey's Life and Correspondence*, edited by his son, and published in 1850. The poet's visits to Powysland and letters to the Hon. Charles Williams Wynn, have, on three or four occasions, been noticed in *Bye-gones*, and there is ample material for future papers.   N.W.S.

CURRENT NOTES.

Last week the pupils of the St. Asaph Grammar School re-assembled after the midsummer holidays in the new buildings, which have been erected at a cost of £5,000.

The *United Irishman*, a Fenian organ printed in New York, claims that the fire at the Shirehall, Shrewsbury, was of Fenian origin.

Presentations have been made to the Rev. W. P. Whittington, by the masters and the boys of the Reading School on his leaving for the head mastership of Ruthin School.

The Chester Town Council on Wednesday accepted a portrait of the late Mr. Henry Brown, sent by Miss N. Brown, niece of the deceased gentleman, to be placed in the Town-hall, and the thanks of the Council were accorded to Miss Brown for her gift.

Some new and commodious school buildings were opened on Monday, at Rhyl, having been built at a cost of £4,500, by Miss Evans, sister of Mr. Joseph Evans, Haydock, Lancashire, and presented to the trustees for the use of the Nonconformist children of Rhyl.

The Rev. John Pryce, who has held the vicarage of Bangor since 1863, and has recently been preferred to the rectory of Trefdraeth, Anglesey, was on Thursday presented by the parishioners of Bangor with his portrait, a purse of 100 guineas, and an address in album form.

The parish church of Llangoed, near Beaumaris, which has been rebuilt from the designs of Mr Kennedy, architect, Bangor, was re-opened on Wednesday. The Bishop of Bangor preached at the morning service, and consecrated an addition to the burial ground. The Rev. D. Lloyd James, D.D., rector of Pontrobert, was one of the preachers at the Welsh services.

There was a large muster of Governors of the Honourable Society of Ancient Britons at the Special General Meeting, recently held at the Society's Offices, St. James's. The object of the meeting was to consider a scheme prepared by the sub-committee, viz., Mr. Stanley Leighton, M.P., Sir Theodore Martin, K.G., Sir Alexander Wood, Mr. Hugh Owen, the Rev. M. Brownrigg, and the Rev. H. W. P. Richards, for the reconstruction and development of the Welsh Charity Schools at Ashford, together with an alternative scheme proposed by the Rev. H. W. P. Richards. The scheme brought forward by the sub-committee was adopted by a large majority. This scheme provides (a) That no more scholars be admitted under the present system (b) That a higher education be given in the school (c) That the school shall ultimately be one for girls exclusively (preference being given to orphans), after the design generally of the Howell's Schools at Denbigh and Llandaff, but with such modifications as may be deemed expedient (d) That a portion of the scholars be foundationers, a portion half-pay, and a portion full pay scholars. The carrying out of this scheme, which will necessarily involve a considerable alteration of the existing system, has been entrusted to the sub-committee already named, who will at once proceed with the work of reconstruction.

The Society for the Preservation of the Irish Language state in their report just issued that the Irish language now holds a prominent place on the curricula of the three great systems of national education in Ireland. In America, we are told, the study is being pursued with great enthusiasm. Irish-American newspapers devote their columns to the publishing of Irish literature in the Irish character; and a sister Society in New York has recently brought out a handsome cheap edition of Dr. MacHale's Irish version of Moore's Melodies. In Germany Dr. Windisch of the University of Leipzic has published an Irish grammar with Irish texts for advanced students. Dr. Limmer, who came over from Berlin to preside at some of the council meetings of the Society last year, still continues his Irish class in the University of Berlin, and in Australia a flourishing branch of the Society has been formed. One of the four vice-presidents of the Society is Marshal MacMahon, "ex-president of the French Republic."

WELSH COLONISTS IN SOUTH AMERICA.—The *Buenos Ayres Standard* of June 14 says:—"A large batch of Welsh colonists having arrived, the Government has ordered an Argentine war steamer to carry them down to Chubut, and as the colony down there is now so large that more lands are required, the Government is about to give a large tract of territory on the Rio Negro for the newly-arrived colonists. To each Welsh family the Government gives free one hundred hectares of land, and the right to buy 250 more, at a very low price and at long time, adjoining each farm. The Welsh colonists at the Chubut are to name a committee to select the land, which is at once to be surveyed by the Government surveyor, and the farms to be marked out."

OSWESTRY AND WELSHPOOL NATURALISTS' FIELD CLUB.

This Club made its third excursion on Aug. 9, when the members, to the number of twenty-one, met at Montgomery Station, and drove through Church Stoke to Symond's Castle, where they left the carriages. Symond's Castle is an old earthwork without any vestige of a castle remaining on it, if there ever was one; it stands in a fine position, overlooking the valley of the Camlad towards Clun Forest. Leaving the Castle, the party proceeded to ascend Corndon, visiting on the way a distinctly marked castle ring. They paused for lunch in a secluded valley by a little stream and old copper mine. the latter covered with moss. After lunch they proceeded to the top of Corndon (1,685 feet), where they had a magnificent view, including the Brecon Beacons, Plinlimmon, and Cader Idris, but not Snowdon, which can only be seen in exceptionally fine weather. On the mountains they found plenty of Oak and Parsley Fern, and Bilberries. The descent was made past Mitchell's Fold, a circle of stones, some upright and some fallen, to Chirbury. The church at Chirbury is very old, and was nicely restored about ten years ago under the direction of Mr. E. Haycocks. It is curious on account of the pillars on both sides of the nave being considerably out of the perpendicular; the new mural decoration at the east end is very good, and the altar cloth one of the handsomest to be seen. At Chirbury the carriages were resumed, and the party drove back to Montgomery. By the kindness of the Rector, the Rev. F. W. Parker, the Club were invited in to tea, which they were well prepared to appreciate after the brisk air of the mountain and their long walk. The principal plants found were naked-stalked Teesdalia, Mountain Cudweed, Procumbent Marshwort, and others less rare.

NOTES.

CHURCHES IN THE RHYL DISTRICT.
(Aug. 3, 1881.)
RHUDDLAN CHURCH.

Rhuddlan Church, the original Parish Church of Rhyl, is distant about 2½ miles nearly south from that place. As usual, the chancel and nave are parallel and of equal length and width. The edifice has been restored throughout, but if the original features have been preserved and copied, it would appear to have been erected in the early English style with subsequent reconstructions in the Decorated and Perpendicular and Tudor æras. All the three windows on the south side are double lancets, and there is a pointed priest's door. The east window of the south nave is a triple lancet, and in a square recess or niche above is a figure of some female saint. The east window of the north chancel is of five lights and of Decorated architecture. The windows on north side of chancel are a Tudor window of three three-foiled lights; a double lancet; a decorated of two lights three-foiled; a double lancet and a square window of three lights, now blocked up. The west windows of both nave and chancel are triple lancets. On the north side of chancel is a pointed door blocked up. A square embattled tower of two storeys, with buttresses diagonal and straight, and north door blocked up, is at west end of chancel. There is a porch at south door with some carving from the roodloft. Internally the chancel and nave are separated by six perpendicular arches springing from octagonal plain pillars with filleted capitals. There is a plain pointed arch from the tower to the chancel. The roofs are of modern open timber work; and the font is also modern. There are seven bells in the tower, but modern. The living is a Rectory of about £600 per annum. Church dedicated to St. Mary. The nave must once have been shorter than at present, as in south wall, about two-thirds of present length, are a piscina and aumbrey.

On north wall of chancel are monuments to William Davis Shipley M.A. of Bodryddan, Dean and Chancellor of St. Asaph, born October 16, 1745 d. 1826.

Penelope relict of Ellis Yonge of Brynyorkin Esq. eldest daughter and co-heiress of James Russell Stapleton Col. of His Majesty's Guards and Penelope his wife daughter of Sir John Conway of Bodryddan Bart. 1788 aged 56.

Penelope wife of Very Rev. W. D. Shipley Dean of St. Asaph eldest daughter and co-heiress of the above Ellis and Penelope Yonge 1789, aged 31.

Mordaunt James second son of Dean Shipley 1806, aged 25.

Conway, Post Captain in R.N., his third son 1808 aged 25.

Robert John, Lieut. R.E. his fifth son 1812 aged 22.

William, Lieut. Col. M.P. for Flint his eldest son 1820 aged 41 and his wife Charlotte second daughter of Sir W. W. Wynne 1855.

W. D. Shipley Dean son of Rt. Rev. Jonathan Shipley Bishop of St. Asaph 1826 aged 80.

Charles of Twyford Hants and Rector of Mappowder Dorsetshire his fourth son 1834 aged 50.

Barbara Yonge only sister of Penelope Shipley 1837 aged 77.

Wm. Shipley Conway 1869 aged 61.

Honble Charlotte Rowley 1871 aged 60.

In the east window is stained glass of our Lord's Life to memory of Wm. Shipley Conway.

Against south wall of chancel—marble tablet.
Elizabeth and Frances Stapleton third and fourth
daughters and co-heiresses of James Russell Stapleton and
Penelope his wife. One married Watkin Williams Esq. of
Penbedw and the other Sir Robert Cotton Salusbury of
Combermere—aged 76 and 85.

Tablet east end of nave.
Mary Jones of Brynywall 1848 aged 68 and Richard
Jones 1858 aged 81.

Stained glass of Acts of Mercy in east window of nave,
given by Hon. Mrs. Rowley.

Tablet east end of nave.
D . MMA . I . MAE . YN .
GORWEDD . CORPH .
THOMAS . JONES .
A . GLADDWYD . 14 .
O . FEH . 1676 .
OH . NA . BAENT . DDO .
ETHION . NA . DDEALL .
ENT . HYN . NAD . YS .
TYRIENT . I . DIWEDD
DEVT . 32 . 29 .

Stained glass in window of south nave representing
Samuel and Virgin Mary and Child, in memory of Wm.
Eric Watkin Rowley Conway, 1874, aged 3, and Glyn
Richard Leveson Rowley Conway, 1874, aged 2.

Two stone tablets illegible from their height in wall.

Stained glass. Salutation of B. V. M.

Stained glass in west window of nave—Our Lord's Life,

Slabs in floor.
Relict of Henry Lloyd Rhydarddwy Gent 1731 aged 71.

Mark Edward . . . .
1684 . . . .
Llewellyn . . . .

In the churchyard.
I . H .
ANNO DOM'I
1674

WILLIAM . PRICHARD 20 Dec. 1602.

WILLIAM . PARRY . 1691.

On a raised altar tomb—round the verge.
HERE . LYETH . THE . BODY . OF . DAVID . EDWARDS . OF .
STANSTY . IN . THE . COVNTY . OF . DENBIGH . GENT . WHO .
WAS . BVRIED . THE . FIFTEENTH . DAY . OF . MARCH .
ANNO . DOMINI . 1685 .
Arms on a shield :—a cross fleury between 4 birds.
AGED . 63.

HENRY . LLOYD , OF . RHYDARDDWY , GENT . 1705
aged 59.
Arms on a shield :—2 fesses wavy charged with 3 legless
birds on each.

IOHN . CONWAY . OF . HIL . GENT . 1700 . aged 73.
Arms on a shield :—a bend charged with 2 annulets and
a rose, on either side a bendlet *erm.* impaling a broken
cross, a crescent for difference.

THOMAS . MORRIS . 1664.
THOMAS . AP . THOMAS . MORRIS. 1695 aged 91.

In the churchyard are three broken sculptured tombs
of ecclesiastics, and two sculptured cross slabs, probably
brought from the adjoining Abbey, where are many
similiar sculptures, described and figured in *Archæologia
Cambrensis*, and in lowering the floor, which was three
feet above present level, a stone coffin was found.
W.A.L.

BRIEF FOR OSWESTRY.—Extract from the
Registers of the parish of Hedon, Yorkshire, 1676 :—
"Collected for & towards y'e repair of y'e parish church
of Oswestree in y'e county of Salop, August y'e twentieth
1676, the summe of six shillings sevenpence three farthings." Was the church then destroyed by fire?
P.B.M,
[The Brief of 1675 was granted towards the cost of repairs,
estimated at £1,500, damage done during the Civil Wars. There
was a Brief in 1691, on account of a great fire in Oswestry; but
its church was never injured by fire. The good folks of Hedon
seem to have been more liberal than most places (so far as we
have information) in their subscriptions to the Brief of 1675.—
ED.]

SYMONDS AND MITCHELL. — I went up
Corndon with the Field Club the other day, but
none of them could tell me who the Symonds or
the Mitchell was whose castle and fold we visited.
Perhaps some archæological reader of your paper can help
us by their history, or an explanation as to why these
names got attached to these localities. Symonds-yat and
Mitcheldean occur not far apart in the Wye country.
CUCULLUS.

AMPHITHEATRE AT SHREWSBURY.—"Are
there any remains at Shrewsbury of the Amphitheatre
which in Elizabeth's reign had been made there in an old
quarry between the city walls and the Severn? Church.
yard the poet (a Shrewsbury man) describes it as holding
ten thousand spectators ; the area served for bear-baiting,
wrestling, &c., and on better occasions your school predecessors acted plays there ; certainly in a more classical
theatre than the Dormitory at Westminster. Sir Philip
Sydney and his friend and biographer Lord Brook, entered
that school on the same day ; and it was then in as high
estimation as any public school in England."—Letter from
Southey to J. W. Warter, Esq., June 9, 1830. NEMO.

PRINCE LLEWELYN'S REPUTED RESI-
DENCE (Aug. 3, 1881).—There is not a particle of evidence to show that Prince Llewelyn ab Iorwerth was ever
at Beddgelert, to say nothing of his having a residence
there. The shopkeeper who put up the sign-board mentioned by "H.B." is evidently wise in his generation.
CELERT.

NANTGARW CHINA (July 27, 1881).—Nant-
garw is a village 6 miles north of Cardiff—a pottery is
still there—the original maker of the china was named
Pardoe, his descendants still carry on the pottery.
Canton, Cardiff. R.J.Y.

The Nantgarw Porcelain Works were established
by Billingsley and Walker in 1813. Billingsley was
apprenticed to Mr. Duesbury of Derby, for five years,
from Sept. 1774, where he remained until 1785. In 1811
he was engaged by Flight and Barr of Worcester, until
1813, when he left their employ, and in conjunction with
his son-in-law, Walker, started the Nantgarw factory,

which was purchased about 1820 by Mr. John Rose of Coalport, who removed the plant to Coalbrookdale, and took Billingsley and Walker into his service. Billingsley died in 1828, and Walker went to America to establish a pottery there. LANDWOR.
Wrexham.

Billingsley was apprenticed at Derby, and was there from Sept. 1774 (16 years old, at 5s. a week, and ultimately at 40s.) to 1796; from 1796 to 1800 at Pinxton; from 1800 to 1804 at Mansfield, then for about four years at Torksey, then for about three years at Wirksworth. In 1811 he went to "Flight and Barr at Worcester, and left in 1813 for Nantgarw." In 1814 he commenced for Dillwyn of Swansea, but soon returned to Nantgarw about 1816, and there made china till 1821, when Messrs. J. Rose of Coalport bought everything of the Nantgarw and Swansea China Works, and removed them to Coalport. Billingsley also went there, and died at Coalport in 1827 or 8. He was the founder of the Nantgarw Works, and was assisted by his son-in-law, Geo. Walker. W.D.
Crockherbtown.

BELL LEGENDS (May 4, 1881.)—The Bishop in question was Arthur Bulkeley, Bishop of Bangor, consecrated Dec. 20, 1541. Besides alienating much of the lands of the Church, he sold the bells of his Cathedral, and it is certainly reported that going to the seaside to see them shipped, he had not set three steps on his way homeward, before he was stricken with blindness, so that he never saw afterwards. (Catalogue of English Bishops. By Francis Godwin. 1615.) Another authority (Strype) speaks of Bulkeley as Bishop from the year 1541 to 1555, that is in three Princes' reigns, and that he was blind some time before his death, "being suddenly struck blind, as though it had been some judgment upon him for sacrilege." T.P.
Washington D.C.

CURRENT NOTES.

A work of very great antiquarian and artistic value has lately been obtained by Mr. Bennett, old bookseller, Mardol, Shrewsbury, and purchased from him by Mr. Samuel Caswell, Meole Brace. It is the private collection of etchings, water colour, sepia, and pencil drawings, of old streets and buildings in the town of Shrewsbury, made at the beginning of the present century by the late Archdeacon Owen, the historian of Shrewsbury, and his son, the Rev. E. Pryce Owen. The work consists of three large quarto volumes, and contains all the original drawings for the illustration of Owen and Blakeway's History, and a vast number which have never been published. The total number of drawings and sketches is upwards of four hundred.

From the tenth annual report of the Chester Society of Natural Science, it appears that the Society is in a very satisfactory condition. It now numbers 561 members, and its financial position is sound. The Botanical Garden in the Grosvenor Park was last year stocked with representative plants of many of the principal natural orders. The number of books in the Library of the Society has been considerably augmented, and many cases have been added to the Museum. The botany and chemistry classes have been well attended. The Committee express their great regret at the loss of one of their first honorary members, Sir Philip de Malpas Grey Egerton, Bart., who took a deep and lively interest in the Society, and who "amidst all his public duties found time to cultivate a branch of geological science, which had previously been little studied, and of which he has left a lasting memorial in his vast collection of fossil fish."

THE CAMBRIAN ARCHÆOLOGICAL SOCIETY AT CHURCH STRETTON.
(From *The Academy*.)

Under happy auspices, the Cambrian Society transferred its place of meeting this year to the English side of the border, and made closer acquaintance with the roads and hills, baronial halls and feudal strongholds, of South Shropshire, the camps and castles which environ the heights of the Wrekin, the Longmynd, and Caer Caradoc. Church Stretton, by its name, betokens its proximity to Watling Street, which here runs up the valley on its course from Magna or Kenchester to Uriconium or Wroxeter. Whatever is left of intelligence, esprit de corps, or enthusiasm as to earlier history centres in the dwellers round about this thoroughfare of the past; and hither, night after night, when the day's excursions were over, trooped natives and foreigners to compare notes with each other.

The evening meetings were well chosen and appropriate. Mr. Drinkwater, at Shrewsbury, where the club dined with a local Society, read an erudite paper on "The Inner Wall of Shrewsbury;" and no small life was thrown into the history of the church of St. Mary, a puzzle of architecture of cruciform shape, and containing nave, sideaisles, chancel, transept, and two chantry chapels. Beside the Norman semi-circular arches here, and those leading from the aisles to the transept, there is much to study in the judicious restoration of the fine old Abbey-church; to say nothing of that problem which occupied archaeologists on Tuesday last—the stone pulpit in the garden overlooking the street, designed for a local brother to address his fellows from (similarly to the use adopted of old at Tintern, in Monmouthshire) while the brethren were at meals. These were but a prelude to those rare old houses, gates, and doorways—of which a prominent one was that of Mr. Lloyd—the Whitehall, and Rowley's mansion of the fourteenth century, with its original chestnut roof. In the front of the court-yard of the Whitehall is a sylvan giant of ample girth, a walnut, 15ft. 7½in. in measurement, we believe, at 4 inches from the ground, and with a spread of branches over 40 yards: the only notable sylvan phenomenon we recollect on the present campaign, if we except a curious case of an inosculated oak near Leebotwood station, visited at Leebotwood station on the Thursday, where the orifice formed by the inosculating branches started asunder near the ground, and might have admitted a grown man's body passed through them. Such features in a landscape serve to fix particular points in the memory, and worthily occupy the attention of the "Draughtsman of the Cambrian Society." But to explore the timbers of Salop you must not parcel yourself for churches, names, roofs, &c., but go in for one or other. So, dinner done, we went back to Stretton, where, at the evening meeting, the veteran Rev. J. D. Latouche read a lucid and learned paper from Mrs. Stackhouse Acton's notes on Stokesay Castle, which was to be visited on the morrow, *en route* for Ludlow—a paper which both described one of the finest examples in England of a castellated mansion of the thirteenth century, and also let the hearers into the touching devotion of the Earl of Craven for the Princess of Bohemia. It was at Stokesay, too, that was slain Sir William Crofts, in the words of Vicars "the best headpiece and the activest man in that country slain in the place." Tradition tells that the men of Luston, whom he led to the fight, basely abandoned him in the hour of danger, and their descendants were taunted with their cowardice for successive generations. Much of the interior of the castle betokens some refinement of architecture, notably its principal apartment, with elaborate mantelpiece and wainscoted chamber, by some held not earlier than the second Charles. The gate-tower of the tower is an example of grotesque carving; and the church has two old carved pews, like those at Rhug Chapel, in Merionethshire.

The next day was given up to tracing the road of the Wenlock edge to the quaintly placed fabric of the priory of Milburgh, granddaughter of Mercian Kings, and the relic of her quondam seat and nunnery. Time will not permit our delaying over it; and, truth to tell, a feeling of xĕnĕlasia prevents many who have the possession of abbey-churches or priories from greeting enthusiastic strangers to shrines which they can best make their own by throwing open to the stranger's eye. The move from Wenlock was a hurried retreat, though to our thinking the parish church of mixt style from Norman to Decorated, and the Guildhall, a timber building with a piazza, and the council chamber of which contains some very interesting and antique carved oak, were thrown open to view in a spirit more liberal and laudable than the crowning ruins of the Priory. For a resume of the features and measurements of the stately ruin, the Minster of which more than equals Hereford, and exceeds Rochester, among our old cathedrals, it may suffice in this place to point to the lamented Mackenzie E. Walcott's "Four Minsters round the Wrekin"—three of which, viz., Wenlock, Buildwas, and Haughmond Abbey, are exactly and minutely described and illustrated in his work, published by Adnitt and Naunton, Shrewsbury, in 1877, the 4th Minster, Lilleshall Abbey, lying too far off the Cambrian Programe for 1881 to be visited. On from thence the archæologists went (by rail) to the Cistertian monastery or "alluvial flat" of Buildwas, where the proportions of the building are ample and noble, and where there was every disposition to suffer liberal and intelligent admission to the chapter-house, the choir, and the rest of the interesting remains. Among these were the abbot's house, the ambulatory, the chapel, and a large hall of the thirteenth century with interesting doorways and carved stones. After making their way to Wenlock, and so to Acton Burnell to see the building where Edward I. held his first Parliament in 1283, the party got back by Leebotwood Station for Church Stretton, girding themselves up for a final excursion to Haughmond Abbey and Uriconium. Of the former, it is only necessary to say that it is still in its ruins a very charming old sanctuary of the Augustine canons, whose amply proportioned guest-hall (eighty-one feet long) and other striking features are enhanced by a striking view of the Breidden and Montgomeryshire hills. To have agreed to the inclusion of Uriconium and its treasures in the day's march, we take to have been flat slaughter of two birds with one stone, for which reason we shall forbear any description of the discoveries or researches of the day till some other occasion.

Some of the evening papers were exceptionally good, to wit, a paper by the Rev. J. D. Latouche on Stokesay; one by Mr R. W. Banks, of Ridgebourne near Kington, on the "Relations of Herefordshire with the Welsh in the Saxon Times," and one by Mr Dyke, "On Early Hill Ploughing," which elicited a good deal of discussion and more or less co-operation. The Rev. W. Allport Leighton did the honours of the Shrewsbury Museum, which he has re-arranged, on the Uriconium plan.

JAMES DAVIES.

At the last meeting of the Cambrian Archæological Society, held at Church Stretton on Friday, Aug. 5, Mr. Richard Williams of Newtown exhibited the Inscribed Slate discovered at Towyn, and which had already been "discussed" by the Society of Antiquaries, as stated in recent issues of Bye-gones. Mr. Williams stated that Mr. Park Harrison was so impressed with the curious nature

of the stone that they together spent several days in excavating the ground where the slate was found; the result being that extensive ruins were discovered of what are supposed to have been dwellings of Irish settlers, or marauders, in the fourth or fifth century; as well as numerous stone and iron implements, bits of pottery, and animal and human bones. A full account of these discoveries, Mr. Williams stated, was in preparation by Mr. Harrison; and at the request of the Committee Mr. Worthington Smith was permitted to make an exact drawing of the slate and its inscriptions.

We wonder (says the *Guardian*), how many scholars in our elementary, or second grade, or public schools, could give the name of a town in Great Britain beginning with Y and ending with g, and having more than 50,000 inhabitants. Many must have been taken by surprise in learning from a Parliamentary return, quoted in the papers, that Ystradyvodwg was one of the four largest "urban sanitary districts" in the kingdom unrepresented in Parliament. situated in Glamorganshire, it has 9,193 houses, with 56,617 inhabitants. The only three larger districts in the list are West Ham, Croydon, and St. Helens (Liverpool.) Such well-known names as Accrington, Barrow-in-Furness, Southport, and (disfranchised) Yarmouth are along way below it. Is it the difficulty of spelling or of pronouncing ten consonants and two vowels that has kept Ystradyvodwg in the background? It is not to be found in two modern gazetteers that we have at hand, and the official *Postal Guide* does not know it. In the *Clergy List* it is mentioned only, as is too often the case, to be referred to another page. Under Llantrisant we find it mentioned as a district under a vicar and six curates with 17,777 inhabitants (its number in 1871), in the patronage of the vicar of Llantrisant, who, with four curates had charge of a population of 8,086, both these places having Pontypridd for a post town.

In an article on "Kings as Bishopmakers," the *Pall Mall Gazette* gives the following story:—"James I. was a scholar, and promoted scholars, though occasionally moved in the disposal of benefices by less exalted motives than a desire to encourage learning. There is an anecdote told of him which is a good illustration of what personal government of the genial kind may mean. The King was out hunting, and lost his way. By-and-by he came to an inn, and, feeling hungry, asked if there was anything to eat. Nothing ready, except what the parson and his curate had ordered for their dinner. This, however, was no lenten fare, and the King (who was incognito) asked to be allowed to join them. His request was acceded to, and the meal was a merry one, for James could talk well. Came the moment of reckoning, when the stranger guest, without the least embarrassment, observed that he had no money. Whereat the parson spoke his mind frankly—that is to say rudely; but the curate declared he had been so entertained by the new comer's discourse that he would joyfully pay for him. At this moment a gentleman of the King's suite entered, and, at the sight of James fell on his knees. Soon as the parson heard the word 'Majesty,' he quaked exceedingly, and besought the King to pardon him. 'Have no fear,' said James, 'I shall not deprive you of your living; but my friend the curate I shall make a canon of Windsor.' One only hopes a Stuart kept his word for once." We believe this version of the story hails from Maidenhead, and may be found in Murray's *Handbook to Berkshire*. A far more interesting version takes its rise in Cheshire, where it has given rise to the proverbial expression, "Higgledy Piggledy, Malpas Shot." (See *Bye-gones*, Feb. 17, 1875; also *Cheshire Sheaf*, Feb. 2, 1881.)

On Friday evening, Mr Mundella placed the report of the Departmental Committee on Higher and Intermediate Education in Wales, which had that day been presented to the Education Department, on the table of the House of Commons. The report, however, has not yet been gazetted, and three or four days must elapse before it will be issued to the public. Meanwhile, the following summary may be relied upon. Dealing with the present state of education in Wales, the report shows that the existing aggregate of endowments is £19,300; £12,800 of which belongs to schools for boys. The number of boys receiving education in Welsh Intermediate Schools is said to be 4,036, divided as follows: 2,287 belonging to private schools, 1,540 to endowed grammar schools, and 209 to proprietary schools. Taking the population of Wales and Monmouth to be 1,570,000, it is opined that intermediate schools should be provided for 15,700 boys. At present, the accommodation is limited, as far as public schools are concerned, to 3,000 boys. The report proceeds in detail with the history of the University College of Wales, and states that the education of the 57 students in the College costs £53 per annum each, the fees being only £10. It is also noted that the impartial and independent attitude of the College towards all denominations would be better secured were the Principal a layman. The report recommends the extension of the Charter of St. David's College. It further recommends that the power of conferring degrees should be transferred to a Board or Syndicate composed in equal proportions of members of the governing bodies of St. David's, Aberystwyth, and any other college, being a place of advanced secular instruction which may be affiliated for the purpose. While recommending the establishment of another college for the Glamorganshire district, the report lays great importance on the necessity of providing adequate intermediate education before proceeding with any other provincial colleges. To the colleges already named they recommend a Parliamentary grant of £4,000 a year. The grant for building, &c., is left in abeyance, the Committee expressing an opinion that local subscriptions should be raised. They recommend that the teaching should be unsectarian, and that women should be allowed to participate in the educational advantages thus provided. The present system of the Welsh schools at Ashford is condemned, but this, as we have before pointed out, is to undergo immediate modification. No special recommendation is made as to Jesus College, Oxford. The schemes presented by Sir Hugh Owen, Mr. Marchant Williams, and Mr. Gee, are embodied in the report. Mr. Henry Richard, M.P., disagrees so far as to object to the giving of religious instruction in State-aided schools.

RARA AVIS.—On Wednesday a gentleman, after many attempts, succeeded in killing, near Llanymynech, a bird that bore very strongly the appearance of a white sparrow. Its white body had spots of a brownish tinge upon it.

MATHEWS (THE ELDER?) IN COURT.—A good story of Mathews and Judge Park is told, as follows:—Charles Mathews, once on a visit to Shropshire, went to the court of justice at Shrewsbury. He had not been there (in court) two minutes before the judge was seen making courteous signs to some one in the thick of the crowd, beckoning to him to come up and occupy the vacant seat by his side. Mathews, though he perceived that the judge's eye looked and his finger pointed in his direction, felt assured that the summons could not be meant for him, as he had not the honour of knowing the great functionary; therefore he looked behind him, to notify to any more probable person he might see that he was signalled to. The judge (the excellent James Allan Park), hopeless of making himself understood, scribbled on a small piece of paper these words, "Judge Park hopes Mr. Mathews will come and sit by him." He then folded it up, put it into the notch of the long rod of one of the ushers, and ordered it to be delivered to its address. On opening it Mathews told me that he felt himself blush like a maiden at the compliment thus suddenly paid him. That he, a poor player, should be singled out for such distinction by one of the judges of the land, and one known to be of strict piety and blameless life, gave him more intense gratification than the notice of his Sovereign. Threading his way through an obsequious multitude, he mounted the judgment seat, and humbly yet proudly took the place awarded to him. The judge shook him cordially by the hand, as if he had been an old friend, put a list of the cases for trial before him, directing his special attention to one, which he said would prove of painful and pathetic interest, and completing his civilities by placing a packet of sandwiches by his side. Two or three years after this memorable visit to Shropshire, he went into Monmouthshire, to stay with his friend, Mr. Rolls. While he and his host were over their wine and walnuts, the latter, looking up to the ceiling, and trying to recall some incident which had escaped his memory, said, as if speaking to himself, "Who was it? Who on earth was it that was here some time ago, and was talking of you? I cannot think who it could have been. Oh, yes; I remember now. It was Judge Park. Did not you and he meet somewhere or other?"—"Ah," said Mathews, "I'm proud to say we did. What a fascinating person he is! I think I never saw a man of such sterling benevolence and such captivating manners." By this time Mr. Rolls had recalled the circumstances that had slipped his recollection; so that when Mathews began to indulge in a glowing eulogium on Park, he could not repress a smile. This his thin-skinned guest was not slow to perceive; and his withers began to wince. "Pray," said he, "did the good judge say anything about me, then, eh?"—"Well," returned Rolls, "if you will not be offended, I will tell you the truth. When he was here he said to me, 'I think, Rolls, you are a friend of Mathews, the actor—a man, I hear, with a dreadful propensity for taking people off. Conceive, then, my consternation, two years ago, at Shrewsbury, on seeing him directly in front of me, evidently with the intention of studying me and showing me up! Well, what do you think I did? Knowing that I should not be able to attend to my notes while the fellow was there, I sent a civil message to him, and invited him to come and sit by me; and this, I trust, propitiated him, so that he will now have too much good feeling, I should think, ever to introduce me into his gallery of legal portraits.'"

MRS. VEAL.

To the Editor of the Oswestry Advertizer.

SIR,—Your Reviewer, in his notice of Chevalier Lloyd's new book, assumes that the author was not aware that the *Apparition of Mrs. Veal* was only an advertising trick. I need scarcely say that a gentleman of the reading and culture of the Chevalier would be perfectly conversant with Sir Walter Scott's "historic doubts" in the matter; and, by ignoring all mention of his criticism, has some reason for believing in the genuineness of the story. It would be interesting to know "the other side" of the subject; the side that does not reject the bonâ fides of the narrative.—I am, &c., A.R.O.

P.S.—With your Reviewer I regret that the supernatural portion of *The History of Powys Fadog* was not relegated to an appendix; but nothing can take away from the stirring worth of the book to all Antiquaries; and in this belief I know the Reviewer will agree with me.

NEGLECTED BIOGRAPHIES.

Under this heading an article appears this month in *Our Times*, a new shilling monthly that bids fair to become successful. The lives include those of

WILLIAM SALESBURY AND WILLIAM MORGAN.

Just at this moment, when our thoughts are occupied with the revised edition of the New Testament, and Convocation has considered the expediency of having the Welsh version of the same Book revised, it will not be thought amiss if we call attention to the honoured names of two very eminent Welshmen whose Biographies are but little known to English readers. We allude to William Salesbury, who translated, and afterwards published in 1567, the New Testament in Welsh, and William Morgan, who in 1588 did the same service for the entire Bible.

William Salesbury* was born at Plas-Issa (the Lower Hall) Llanrwst, Denbighshire, in the early part of the sixteenth century, being the second son of his parents, and a descendant of the distinguished family of Salusburie of Lleweni on his father's side, and of the equally distinguished families of Puleston and Vaughan on the maternal one. He was educated at Oxford, and upon leaving that seat of learning, he proceeded to Thavies Inn, London, to study the law; but upon the death of his elder brother, and his consequently becoming trustee and guardian to his daughters, and having married Miss Prys of Plas-Iolyn, with whom he acquired an estate called Cae-du Llansannan, he returned to his native country, and dwelt there during some years of his early manhood.

He was a very learned and accomplished scholar, being well versed in seven languages, in addition to English and Welsh; and being an ardent reformer in religion, it fell to his lot to introduce, in the mother tongue, to his countrymen, various useful printed works, and, indeed, in that particular, he may be called the father of Welsh literature. The very first book printed in the Welsh language was the production of his pen. It was a mere compilation of the Calendar, the Creeds, the Lord's Prayer, the Ten Commandments, the seven Sacraments, Litanies, and some Prayers. But it was much needed, and both its issue and the year 1546, in which this was done, will be for ever marked in Cambrian history. In 1547 he published "A Dictionary in Englyshe and Welshe, moste necessary to alle suche Welshemen as will spedily learn the Englyshe tongue;" and in 1550 "A brief and plain introduction, teaching how to pronounce the letters in the British tongue, now commonly called Welsh;" and also in the same year "Battery of the Pope's botterculx, commonly called the High Altar." In 1551 appeared a translation of the Epistles and Gospels for the whole year; and, thenceforth, we may presume he gave himself up wholly to the greatest of his labours—the translation of the New Testament.

All these early Welsh works are scarce, and very few of them are now met with in a perfect condition; but there is a beautiful copy of the Testament in the Cambrian Library at Glan Aber, Chester, which book contains 800 pages, printed in black letter, in a small quarto. Dr. Richard Davies and Thomas Huet, respectively Bishop and Precentor of St. David's, at the time, rendered Mr. Salesbury some assistance, but the bulk of the translation was his own, and therefore it is called to this day "Testament William Salesbury." In many respects Mr Salesbury possessed unequalled advantages for furthering his literary projects, for his family name had long been honoured in

*The family name has from a very early date been spelt in various ways—the father using one form, the son another very often—such as, Salusburie, Salesburie, Salusbury, Salesbury, and Salisbury.

the Principality, and divers members of it had rendered good service to King Henry the Seventh, and afterwards to his son, the Eighth Henry. He had some share of Tudor blood in his veins, and some of the younger branches of the Lleweni house were attached to the Court; but when Queen Mary came to the throne, all these things counted for nothing, for William Salesbury was not only a heretic in faith, but he was a daring and earnest worker for the reformation in religion. He was in hiding for a long time in her reign, being concealed in a small chamber, curiously built, and accessible only by climbing to it up the chimney: but he had three sure defenders at his back, namely, the love and affection of his countrymen; the lonesomeness of his abode in the midst of the great Denbighshire mountain fastnesses; and his trust in the sure mercies of his God: and thus was his valuable life preserved to render to his nation the greatest service any man could bestow upon it. He died, it is supposed, about 1591, but innumerable Welsh antiquaries have searched in vain for the records of his death, or the place of his burial. The impression is that he died at Cae-du, and that his hallowed remains were interred in the Llansannan Churchyard. For close upon three hundred years, his name has been reverenced in every Welsh household; and in remote country places where it is mentioned in connection with the "Testament," the humble Cambrian peasant will doff his hat, and say in the full fervour of his religious faith, "Aye, sure, he was one of God's Saints on Earth." And no doubt he was, for he did a right saintly work, and so long as the Welsh language continues, so long will his name be honoured by the sons and daughters of the Principality.

William Morgan was the son of John Morgan, of Gwibernant, in the parish of Penmachno, Carnarvonshire, and had descended from Ednyfed Hardd, the founder of the Sixth Noble Tribe of North Wales. According to an old MS., he was born at the ancient house of his family, about 1530, but the general impression is that he was born in 1539. At all events, he proceeded to St. John's, Cambridge, for his education, and having chosen the Church for a profession, he was instituted in 1575, to the Vicarage of Welshpool in Montgomeryshire, and three years later, to that of Llanrhaiadr yn Mochnant in the same county, "where he *finished* his great undertaking of translating the Bible into the Welsh language." When or where he *commenced* the work we know not, but, it is said, his original design was to translate the Pentateuch only, and that he undertook the greater work of finishing the Old Testament, at the solicitation of Archbishop Whitgift, who had been so much impressed with his holy and devout conduct, his scholarship, and his attachment to his mother tongue, that he pressed him to continue the work he had so well begun, and, in further earnest of his favour, he appointed him to be his Chaplain. We know from undoubted authority that in 1587 he had completed his undertaking, and had also "corrected" Salesbury's Testament, and thereby had made it his own, as part of the Bible. We meet with him in that year, at the Deanery, Westminster, as the guest of Dean Goodman, and engaged in superintending his great work as it proceeded through the press. In 1588 it was published in a handsome folio volume, a fine copy of which is carefully preserved in the Glan Aber Library. It is of most excellent workmanship, and is a model of scholarship, that will always secure high and just praise.

The heads of the Church were not unmindful of his claims to preferment, and hence he is recorded in the annals of the Church as the happy possessor of divers Welsh livings, which he held until 1595, when, by the express command of Queen Elizabeth, he was rewarded with the Bishopric of Llandaff. There he remained for six years, when (in 1601) he was translated to the see of St. Asaph. Three years later, there on the 10th of September, he died at his post, full of years and of honours, leaving behind him a good name, and some trusty sons to continue his ancient line in his country.

But it is strange and painful to relate that no one can tell the spot where his remains were buried in the yard attached to the Cathedral Church of St. Asaph; and this is all the more remarkable, when we know that his successor, Bishop Richard Parry, was a very dear friend of his, and that his own son, Evan Morgan, was at the time of his father's death a resident clergyman within the city, and then, or shortly afterwards, a Canon of this very Church. Thus we have the two names most dear to Welshmen—William Salesbury and William Morgan—unrecorded upon stone or brass, and their very sepulchres unmarked to mortal eye. Their works do follow them it is true, and there is not a child in the Northern division of the Principality who is ignorant of their fame; the service they rendered to their nation is unquestioned, and they are acknowledged to have been the prime instruments in God's hands for bringing their countrymen to a knowledge of the truth—but there the matter ends. May we not say that it so ends in a lasting disgrace to a people who were so greatly indebted to them, and that the time has now come when Welsh Churchmen and Welsh Nonconformists should unite their forces to emblazon these honoured names upon marble within the walls of the great Church of St. Peter's, Westminster, as a fitting tribute of a nation's indebtedness to their sacred memory.

The strange and eventful circumstances which ever surround us in this old country of ours have brought to pass a singular co-mingling of the blood of these two men. Mr. Salisbury of Glan Aber, Chester, a lineal descendant of William Salesbury, married Sarah, the youngest daughter of the Rev. Arthur Jones, D.D., a lineal descendant of William Morgan, and in their son the two lines have met.†
The law has kept its hold upon one of the two from William Salesbury's day down to the present, as the Gospel has kept hers upon the other line from William Morgan's time to our own, and as the two great men we have mentioned had evinced their attachment to their native language, and to Welsh literature, so, in the very house where their two valuable works are religiously preserved, may be found the best and largest collection of Cambrian literature known in the world.

ENGLISHMEN AND WELSHMEN.
(From the Pall Mall Gazette.)

As one walks along the streets of a quiet little Welsh town during this tourist season, it is somewhat curious to observe the singular difficulty one finds in distinguishing by sight between the visitors and the natives, especially when both belong to corresponding classes, and are dressed in much the same way. An English observer in almost any continental country—say in France or Germany—is constantly struck by the large number of faces belonging to types wholly different from those which he is accustomed to see at home. In Germany, the greater part are fairer, flatter, and rounder-headed; in France, the greater part are darker, and have the distinctive Gallic modification of the typical semi Celtic physique; but in Wales the mass of the people might be everyday Englishmen of the ordinary London type for aught that one can see to the contrary in their features, their build, or their manner. It is

† The late Reverend Sir Charles Salusbury, of Llanwern, County Monmouth, Baronet, was another representative of this old Welsh family.

almost startling at times to hear a group of such thorough English-looking people standing in the street and talking to one another in a foreign language. You scan them as you pass from head to foot, and you say to yourself in your heart they must be English. To be sure there are a few more very dark-haired and dark-eyed people proportionately than in some parts of eastern England, though hardly more than in Dorset, in Lancashire, or even in Suffolk; but with this slight exception, the average physique differs in no appreciable way from the average physique of that very heterogeneous ethnical compound—the born Londoner. The slight difference is merely one of varying proportions in the elements, not of totally different elements themselves. The man who goes from Normandy to Pau or to Provence feels that he is practically among another race; the man who goes from any part of England to Wales feels that he is still among essentially the same people accidentally speaking a different tongue.

This almost absolute identity of physical appearance, extending as it does even to those more measurable anatomical peculiarities which are capable of objective statement, such as the size and relative proportions of the skull, seems to afford a useful hint as to the ethnical composition of most Englishmen at the present day. If it were true that the early English in their conquest of Britain absolutely exterminated the native Britons, then it would be hard to understand the wide divergence of the modern English from the usual Teutonic or Scandinavian type, or their close approximation to the ancient British type. Some people talk as though the ancient Briton were an extinct animal, only to be recovered from a few very misleading remarks of Cæsar's, or from the bronze utensils and mouldy skulls in Mr. Evans's collection and the British Museum. But of course the real fact is that we can find the Ancient Briton still in our midst, in his unmixed purity, from Anglesey to Cornwall, and hear him speaking the ancient British language intact in Merioneth or Carnarvonshire. All talk about Britons and Anglo-Saxons tends to mask the simple truth that we are dealing from the first with Englishmen and Welshmen: it belongs to the same exploded school of thought as "the ancients" and "the moderns." Looking at the question as a simple matter of observation, most inhabitants of England at the present day possess many anatomical traits in common with the undoubted Celts of Wales and Cornwall, which traits are demonstrably wanting to the modern Germans and Scandinavians, and some of which were demonstrably wanting to the early English invaders whose bones we find in barrows of the heathen English age. The inference seems pretty clear that most inhabitants of England now have at least some fraction of Celtic blood in their veins. This Celtic blood is doubtless due in many cases to comparatively modern intermarriages with the numerous Welsh, Cornish, Scotch, and Irish families which have migrated eastward and southward for three centuries past; but it is probably also due in part to the survival of certain Britons, more or less, at the date of the English conquest.

People generally forget, indeed, how small is the distance, measured by generations, which separates us from heathen British or heathen English times. Only 50 lives divide the existing Welsh farmer whom we meet in our mountain rambles from the levies which withstood Caius Cæsar upon the shore at Pevensey. The number of generations between Hengist or Horsa and the modern Kentish men is not greater than the number of generations between an Arab horse in the reign of Charles II. and a Derby winner in our own day. To the Scandinavians we stand even nearer; for a man could raise in his own lifetime nearly thrice as many generations of peas as those which separate modern Yorkshiremen from the companions of Ragnar and Halfdan. Indeed, the aphides on our rosetrees in a conservatory will crowd the same number of lives into three years. All these proportions are calculated, too, on the ordinary reckoning of 33 years to a generation; but if we take exceptional instances, there must probably be some Englishman now living who are divided by only 20 or 25 ancestors from the heathen English conquerors of Sussex and Wessex, or by only 15 or 18 from the heathen Danish conquerors of East Anglia and Northumbria. It is no wonder, under these circumstances, as Karl Vogt suggests, that an occasional "recrudescence of barbarism" should still produce a Zulu war or a Judenhetze amid the modern civilisation of England or Germany. But it would be very wonderful indeed if so short a number of generations should suffice to alter those persistent racial features of skull and skeleton which seem to be the most lasting elements in human varieties. The boldest evolutionist would hesitate before suggesting that 20 or 30 lifetimes could turn brachycephalic Jutes and Saxons into dolichocephalic Britons, or could make the type of East Anglians and Dalesmen so closely approximate to the ordinary Welsh and Cornish physique. This would indeed be heredity plus modification with a vengeance.

AUGUST 31, 1881.

CONTRIBUTORS TO BYE-GONES.— In the April part of *Montgomeryshire Collections* a record is given of the planting of three elm trees in Powis Castle Park more than a century ago. One of these was planted by Mr. Edmund Edye, whose son, Mr. Thomas Edye, the narrative states, "is still flourishing at the age of ninety." Mr. Edmund Edye died in 1849, at the age of ninety-two years and three weeks, and on Thursday last, Aug. 25, Mr. T. Edye entered on his 91st year, so, as he reminds us in a letter we received from him last week, "Father and son have run their course for 124 years and 8 months, not perhaps unprecedented, but not a very common event." As we stated recently, an engraved portrait of Mr. Edye, senior, is preserved in the Powys-land Museum at Welshpool. With one exception Mr. Thomas Edye is the oldest contributor we have had to our *Bye-gones* column, and as we have also one of thirteen years, there is a difference of seventy-seven years between the ages of our oldest and our youngest correspondent! The one older than Mr. Edye, we refer to, is the late Mr. Downes Rider, who died at Westbury, Salop, in Oct. 1876, at the age of 93.

NOTES.

SPORTING LAST CENTURY.—On Aug. 29, 1798, the *Salopian Journal* reported partridges to be numerous and forward. Moor fowl scarce because of the dry season when their eggs were hatched. "On a moderate calculation few gentlemen shoot their own partridges at less than five shillings a piece, or moor game at so little as three times that sum. Hares may be killed from a guinea a brace, upwards; but your full grown fox is by far the dearest game! N.B. We reckon nothing for hand labour." SCROBBES BYRIG.

IMPROVEMENTS AT ABERYSTWYTH, 1835. A Bill is now in Parliament to enable the inhabitants to procure a supply of delicious water and great abundance by means of pipes from the hills; instead of that great nuisance, conveying it in carts from the river. The Bill also includes the lighting of the town with gas, establishment of police, and removal of nuisances by the Commissioners. Several new lodging houses have been built since last season, and a mail coach from London, through Worcester, through Leominster, and Kington has commenced running, which arrives every evening at eight o'clock, by which means letters can be obtained at the

post-office twelve hours earlier than heretofore. A splendid organ, purchased by subscription, built by Robson and Son, has been placed in the new church, and a highly talented young man, Mr. Williams, nephew to Mr. Ree, the celebrated organist of Ludlow, has been appointed to the situation. The works of the new harbour have commenced, under the superintendence of Mr. Bushe, the engineer appointed to carry out the other improvements.—*Vide* Newspaper of the time.   G.G.

OLD WELSH ALMANACKS.

(Aug. 10, 1881.)

In the four years—1832-1835—there were double issues each year; in the latter one, indeed a triplet, but as one of these will require a separate notice I reserve it for my final letter. I shall now content myself with giving the lines upon the eight title pages to be dealt with, reserving the inner ones for another notice.

The *first* issue for 1832 is called "Cyfaill Diwigiadol." It was printed at Dublin, and the price was sixpence :—

1 Fy hen GYFEILLION heini,
  Eich annerch wnaf eleni;
  Gan lwyr obeithio yn ddinam
  Na ddêl un drwg-lam i chwi.

2 Ni welwyd dyn mor ddoniol,
  A gallu plesio'n hollol;
  Na chwaith yr un er maint ei
    fai,
  Na chlywir rhai'n ei ganmol.

3 I'r rhai sy'n honni beunydd,
  Y lluniont *hun-symudydd*[*]
  Y rhoddwn gynghor yn ddi-
    sen,
  I rwymo pen di-fenydd.

4 Yr *Eurfaen*[†] yn ein goror,
  A geisid lawer tymhor;
  Yr Eurfaen gwir, diwydrwydd
    yw,
  A dry bob rhyw yn drysor.

5 Mae moroedd a mynyddau,
  A rhai creaduriaid weithiau,
  Yn dangos tywydd (lawer
    gwell),
  Na lloniaid cell o lyfrau.

6 Britannia strive for ever,
  Keep Peace within thy power,
  May WILLIAM, nor good
    Adelaide,
  Be ne'er afraid of danger.

    * *Perpetual motion.*   † *Philosopher's stone.*

The *second* issue for 1832 is called "Cyfaill Gorchwiliol;" printed at Dublin, price sixpence, and has the following lines on the title page :—

1 Fy hen GYFEILLION diball,
  Llangciau, gwyr, ac eraill,
  Foreu-ddydd ffair, yn bur ddi-
    ffael,
  Ow! cofiwch gael y CYFAILL.

2 Trafaelio wnes i'n ddichlyn,
  Y diffrwyth dir a'r dyffryn,
  Dois yma ddoe, yn hwyr bryd-
    nawn,
  Yn ddiblog iawn o *Ddublin.*

3 'Rwy'n awr, wrth hir drafaelio
  Heb lonydd, wedi blino;
  A ro'wch chwi o'ch gras a'ch
    synwyr gre'
  I'm ffasiwn le i orphwyso?

4 Mi fyddaf yn ufuddol,
  Un fwriad ag arferol,
  I ddangos newid, ffair, a'r
    llawn,
  Yn fedrus iawn anfeidrol.

5 Ond am yr hin a'i rhansu,
  Mae'r nef yn gwgu weithiau;
  Fe allai farn am wail di feth,
  In siomi peth a'r lyfrau.

6 The Britons altogether,
  Let God be their defender;
  And let them all, as near they
    can,
  Agree with one another.

The *first* issue for 1833 is called "Cyfaill Buddugawl;" printed in Dublin, price sixpence, and has the following lines on the title page :—

1 Fy hen GYFEILLION mwynion
  O Dde a Gwynedd dirion;
  Boed iwch eleni fi wyddyn dda
  A llawn gynhaua ffrwythlon.

2 Ein dyddiau sy'n myn'd heibio
  Fel cysgod hwyraidd didro;
  Da fyddai cilfach deg ei glan,
  Fod yn ein rhan cyn huno.

3 Rhyw fydoedd dirifedi,
  O'n hamgylch sydd yn troelli;
  Ac ambell *seren wibiog* ddrwg
  Sy'n bygwth cilwg ini.

4 *Diwygiad* gwych ei urddas,

Sy dda mewn gwlad a theyr-
    nas;
  Da eto pe ceid conglau'r *Ty*
  Yn lân o lu'r hen *Suddas.*

5 Ni roid yn 'rhen flynyddau,
  Awch tân i rwyddo llongau;
  Ond nawr mae *agerdd,* hynod
    ddrych,
  Yn gyru gwych gerbydau.

6 Rule rule Britannia ever,
  Shew firm thy active power;
  That foreign foes may bend
    the knee
  And brought by thee too d .

The *second* issue for 1833 is called " Cyfaill Puraidd ;" printed in Dublin, price sixpence, and has the following lines on title page :—

1 Hyd atoch hen GYFEILLION;   Nid ofn y *Geri marwol** ;
Dichenwyr a Gwyneddion,   Nid dim ond doniau Ysbryd
Rwy' eto'n dyfod mal bob tro,   DUW
Yn wir o gywir galon.   Wna ddyn i fyw yn dduwiol.

2 Yn mhlith proffeswyr ffurfiol,   5 Och ! iasau tra echryslon
Ni wnaethpwyd gwrthiau   Drywanodd drwy'n cyfeillion ;
nerthol,   Pechasom ninnau ; awn i'r
Ond y rhai *cleifion* yn eu plith   llwch
A brofodd fendith nefol.   Mewn edifeirwch calon.

3 Y galon galed gyfan   6 Pour down thou fount of
Yw hoff eisteddle Satan,   mercy,
Ac nid oes dim rydd iddi friw   Thy blessings on our country ;
Ond gallu DUW ei hunan.   Remove Oh ! far remove thy
   rod,
4 Nid taerni dynion doniol,   Insulted GOD of Glory.

       * *Cholera Morbus.*

    (To be Continued.)   E.G.S.

QUERIES.

FFYNON ELIAN.—The *Gossiping Guide* tells us of a cursing well, Ffynon Elian, at Llanelian, near Colwyn ; Cliffe, in his *Book of North Wales*, tells of Ffynon Elian, at Llanelian in Anglesey. Into the latter, Cliffe says, people entered and tried to turn round. If they could do so they would live " until their time came"; if they could not they would die within the year. Are there two " Ffynon Elians," or is one of the guides in error ?   W.E.

ST. MARY'S CHURCH, WELSHPOOL.—When the Camb: Arch: Association visited Welshpool, the vicar kindly gave some details about the parish church. He referred to architectural discoveries made during the restoration a few years ago. Remains of the 13th century had been found and portions of later periods. They also found traces of decorated work, which he said had been taken out of the old church. What is here spoken of as the "old church"? In the Powysland Museum is a photograph of a wood-cut copy of an old church, which stood near the Old Queen's Head, now the site of Terrace Buildings, and stated to have been erected in 1587, and burnt down in 1659. There must have been a church anterior to the latter. It would be interesting to know something of this old church, and why the site was changed. Can any one give this information ?   POLA.

REPLIES.

EDWARD MEREDITH (June 30, July 28, 1880).—"E.M.J.," at the earlier date spoke of Meredith as a public singer in Liverpool in 1790. At the latter date, LANDWOR, quoting a recent *North Wales Chronicle*, refers to his having been a cooper whose voice attracted Sir Watkin Will ams Wynn seventy years ago, and says that Sir Watkini had him trained. It will be seen that there is a discrepancy of dates here. There is a reference to Meredith in *Bye-gones*, Dec. 29,1875, that seems to have been overlooked in the recent query and reply ; and it is taken from Colman's *Random Records*. In this there is the copy of a Wynnstay Play Bill, of the date of 1780, and one of the characters is sustained by "Meredith." The author adds that Meredith "had been a cooper, and was a bass singer of some celebrity." At what date he attained celebrity we are not informed : the book was published in 1830, but the date of the Wynnstay performance shows that the authority quoted by LANDWOR was in error.   N.W.S.

TOURISTS' RHYMES (Aug. 17, 1881).—A tourist staying at the Royal Ship Hotel, Dolgelley, singing the praises of the house and hostess in the Visitors' Book, adds—

   "Those who read this book well know
     That rhymes are made as jokes,
   So don't suppose that I came here
     In love with Mrs. Stokes."

Another writer in the same book, referring to the old legend, says :—

   "'Tis said that by sleeping on Cader
     A man a poet or madder
   Than when he went up will arise ;
   But for making of poets or madmen, I wis
   This ' Ship' can compare with Cader Id-ris
   As the verse in this book testifies."

Out of a mass of rubbish in the same book the following has redeeming qualities :—

   " Bright weather, wholesome fare,
     Pure invigorating air,
     Good ponies, trusty Guide,
     Grand scenery on every side ;
   I strongly recommend a trip
     To quaint Dolgelley's ' Royal Ship.' "

           R.A.

COFFIN PLATES ON CHURCH WALLS (Apr. 27, 1881).—Joseph Cradock, in his account of Dolgelley, published in 1777, describing the Church, says, " The next morning being Sunday, I went to eight o'clock prayers here ; the area of the church is spacious, and the pews neat ; there is a coving roof of wood, which is necessary to aid the voice, as the floor is only clay covered with deep rushes." He says nothing about coffin-plates on the walls ; but the Rev. J. Evans, whose *Tour* was published in 1800, says, "The church is a decent edifice of limestone, consisting of a handsome tower, and a large nave. The seats are forms, and the floor is paved with limestone flags, a circumstance extraordinary for Wales. The desire for perpetuating the remembrance of departed friends is expressed in a whimsical way ; the coffin plates, exhibiting the name, age, &c., of the deceased, are placed as *memento moris* against the walls, and other conspicuous parts of the church."   G.G.

QUAKERS IN WALES (June 1, 1881).—*Friends' Burial Ground at Llwyngwril.*—This burial ground is not used at present by the Quakers. There is an iron plate on the gate with the date 1646. There are no Quakers in the neighbourhood. They used to worship in former times at the farm Llwyn-du, which is close by. It is now used by the Wesleyans, but how it came into their possession I could not ascertain. There are many graves on the ground, but no tombstones, with the exception of four or five, which have been placed there quite recently.   T.Ll.L.W.
Whittington.

CURRENT NOTES.

The *Whitehall Review* says :—Extremes meet. In the Market-square of Northampton, where the free and independents meet to protest against the "illegal exclusion" of their junior member from the House of Commons, is an ancient house, and over one of the windows the Welsh motto : " Heb Dyw, Heb Dym. Dwye Digon." (" Without God, without everything. God and enough.") Even the stones are not silent.—Your contemporary is shaky in his Welsh, but it is not for that I quote him. What I want to know is how the motto comes to be on a house at Northampton ?—TAFFY.

The Right Rev. Alfred Ollivant, D.D., Bishop of Llandaff, was born at Manchester on August 16, 1798, and thus completed his eighty-third year on Tuesday, Aug. 23. His lordship was consecrated Bishop of Llandaff in 1849, and is the oldest prelate on the Episcopal bench.

The designs for a memorial window to be placed in the west transept of Bangor Cathedral by the relatives of the late Colonel Holt, Gorphwysfa, were on Wednesday submitted to a meeting of the chapter. An oaken reredos is also about to be placed in the Cathedral as a family memorial of the late Colonel.

The Government, having received an intimation that a private manufacture of infernal machines was being carried on near Buckley, Flintshire, a few miles from the residence of the Premier, by an unknown person, for a firm at Birmingham, put themselves in communication with the heads of the police in Cheshire, who, in turn, communicated with the Chief Constable of Flintshire. The result was that a detective was sent down from Scotland-yard and returned on Wednesday, having ascertained that the article manufactured at the works was not only not used in the construction of infernal machines, but had actually received the patronage of Mr. Gladstone. It appears that the police at headquarters received their instructions from Birmingham, whither portions of the article had been sent in a rather mysterious manner. The suspected manufacture was no other than that of a " patent, newly-invented and indispensable adjustable and reversible toasting-fork." The secrecy of the inventor in sending the portions of his apparatus to and fro between Birmingham and Buckley previous to its being patented had given rise to the suspicions which were so ludicrously mistaken.

The Boston (U.S.) Journal says :—A band of gipsies has appeared each summer for many years past at Elmwood, a small village near East Orange, N.J. Five years ago, when the band appeared on its regular annual round, Dr. Bishop, rector of Christ Church, was called to attend one of the men, who was dying. This man confided to Dr. Bishop that he was Uriah Wharton, a native of Shropshire, England, and that years before he had deserted his home for the love of a beautiful woman in the tribe, whom he married, and that thereafter he had led the vagrant life of his adopted people, and was made king of the tribe. On Sunday Dr. Bishop was called upon by a number of the same band to unite the daughter of Uriah Wharton to the new king of the company. The girl was a beautiful girl of nineteen, and the marriage was performed after the ritual of the Protestant Episcopal Church, in the presence of the whole company of gipsies. The bridegroom, Henry Lee, is a lineal descendant of Oak Lee, who was the recognized king of all English gipsies sixty years ago.

A chapel for the use of the inmates of St. Clare's Convent and Orphanage, Pantasaph, near Holywell, founded some years ago by the Order of the Sisters of Charity of St. Vincent de Paul, was opened on Wednesday. The chapel is a beautiful structure of the Early English style, designed by Mr. Edmund Kirby of Liverpool, the architect of the conventual buildings. One of the principal features of the church is the handsomely carved altar and reredos of Caen stone, with polished marble and alabaster columns introduced, the gift of Mr. and Mrs. Payne, Liverpool. The nave windows, which are simple lancet, will all be filled with stained glass, presented by different contributors. There was a celebration of High Mass, and a sermon was preached by the Right Rev. Dr. Knight, Bishop Auxiliary of Shrewsbury. The Sisters afterwards entertained the Bishop and visitors to luncheon. Among those present were the Earl and Countess of Denbigh, Lady Clare Feilding, Lady Edith Feilding, Lady Mostyn and Miss Mostyn. In the afternoon the Bishop confirmed 35 of the inmates of the Convent and Orphanage. There are now 50 girls in the Convent and 130 in the Orphanage.

A portrait of the late Mr. Thomas Hughes, chairman of the Denbighshire Quarter Sessions, has been placed in Denbigh council chamber, having been presented to the borough by his son, Major H. R. Hughes, Ystrad, who made the gift in preference to its being provided by public subscription. The deceased gentleman was the first mayor of Denbigh, and long and intimately connected with all the institutions in the borough.

UNIVERSITY COLLEGE OF WALES.—Mr. F. R. Rudler, curator of the Museum of Practical Geology, London, and formerly a Professor at this College, has presented the library with twenty-eight volumes of valuable new books on scientific subjects. Mr. A. E. Richards of Begelley, Pembrokeshire, has presented several valuable ancient coins to the museum, in addition to the large collection previously presented.

SIR HUGH OWEN.—Sir Hugh Owen of Voel, Hornseylane, Middlesex, formerly of the Poor Law Board, is the son of the late Mr. Owen Owen of Voel, Anglesey, by his marriage with Mary, daughter of Mr. Owen Jones of Quirt, in that county, and was born in 1804. He has been for many years actively engaged in work connected with education in Wales, among which may be mentioned the formation of the Cambrian Society for the education of the deaf and dumb, the establishment of British schools and of colleges for the training of teachers, and the promotion of higher education, especially in connection with the University College of Wales. Sir Hugh Owen is one of the oldest members of the British and Foreign School Society, and has been for many years treasurer of the National Temperance League. He was for nearly 40 years an officer of the Poor Law Board, and for upwards of 20 years honorary secretary to the London Fever Hospital, a position which he recently resigned on being elected a vice-president of that institution. He is also one of the representatives of Finsbury on the London School Board. Sir Hugh Owen married, in 1829, Ann, daughter of Mr. Richard Wade.

THE OSWESTRY AND WELSHPOOL NATURALISTS' FIELD CLUB.

EXCURSION TO LLANWDDYN.

Amidst the pouring rain of the morning of August 23rd the Secretary of the Club rallied his members and friends for an excursion to the Liverpool waterworks at Llanwddyn. After picking up contingents at Gobowen and Preesgweene the party went on by rail to Bala, nothing daunted, apparently, by the dismal weather. Their perseverance was rewarded, for before they reached Bala the clouds opened and the rain ceased, and the sun came out just in time to make the twelve miles drive over the mountains to Llanwddyn most agreeable. The road passes by the pretty hamlet and church of Rhos-y-Gwaliau and along the valley of the Hirnant, every turn and slope of which is a new picture of loveliness. After Aber Hirnant, where there is a shooting-box belonging to Sir Edmund Buckley, the road becomes fearfully rough and steep in places, passing through streams and hanging on the slope of the mountain in a manner rather alarming to some of the ladies of the party, who were not altogether reassured of the safety of the road by the driver gaily pointing out the spot where horse and carriage and all had lately rolled some sixty yards down the precipitous slopes, resulting in the death of the horse, the smashing up of the carriage, and the marvellous escape of the driver. A two mile walk up, and a very sharp descent down brought them to Rhiw-argor, where a lovely view of the whole length of the Llanwddyn valley breaks upon the sight. Passing along the left hand side of the valley, they get a glimpse of Pistyll Rhyd-y-maingcau, and Eunant, and soon reach the village of Llanwddyn. The carriages were left at the inn, and the party went on foot to see the works at the end of the valley, about two miles from the village, where the dam is to be made to block up the water in the lake. After inspecting the stone laid by the Corporation in the rock where one end of the dam will spring from, they were fortunate enough to fall in with one of the sub-engineers, who very kindly explained the works as far as they had gone at present. They were chiefly employed in making a new bed for the river, so that they might excavate down to the rock and get a firm foundation for the dam. In some places they would have to go very deep, and there was always the difficulty of keeping the water out of the workings. If the winters were favourable, and the work could be carried on by electric light at night, as well as day, it was expected to be finished in five or six years. Unfortunately, any further exploration of the works was prevented by the ominous sounds of thunder, which warned the party to be making their way back, but the storm was too quick for them, and caught them before they could find shelter. It rained and thundered and lightened as it only can in mountainous places, and wetted most of them through ; but if their clothes were damped their spirits were not, and after a refreshing tea at the inn they started in a steady rain and thunderstorm for Bala, to catch the last train. The thunder, however, passed away before the open mountain was reached, and the rain grew lighter, in fact, at one time, a gleam of sunshine shot out, and lit up all the peaks with a glow of golden light, circled by a brilliant rainbow. With this above, and the dark muddy waters of the Hirnant below, and with the light mist hanging over the trees, one of the most lovely evening scenes imaginable was formed. Bala was reached in good time, and in spite of their wetting, all agreed they had had a very successful day. The two carriages were supplied from the White Lion Hotel, and great credit is due to the drivers for the way they manipulated their horses over a road that most coachmen would have pronounced impassable. It is undoubtedly the finest approach to Llanwddyn to go from Bala, the road from beginning to end being full of interest and beauty. Botanists will find the following without much trouble :— Climbing Corydalis, Yellow Mountain Pansy, Spiræa Salicifolia, Saxifragia Stellaris, Rough-leaved Hawkweed, Golden-wort. Campanula Hederacee, and Beech Fern, Sun-dews, White Heather, &c.

GHOST STORIES FROM WALES.
(Aug. 3, 1881.)

The Llangurig Ghost Stories are interesting, and their recital recals one of *Powis Castle* which is recorded in the Autobiography of the grandfather of the late Mr. Thomas Wright, the well-known Shropshire antiquary. Mr. Wright, sen., was a Methodist, and in the early days of that body the belief in apparitions was not uncommon amongst its members. The story was told to Mr. Wright in 1780, at the house, in Yorkshire, of Miss Bosanquet (afterwards the wife of Fletcher of Madeley), by Mr. John Hampson, sen., a well-known preacher amongst the Methodists, who had just arrived from Wales. The following is the narrative :—

It had been for some time reported in the neighbourhood that a poor unmarried woman, who was a member of the Methodist Society, and had become serious under their ministry, had seen and conversed with the apparition of a gentleman, who had made a strange discovery to her. Mr. Hampson being desirous to ascertain if there was any truth in the story, sent for the woman, and desired her to give him an exact relation of the whole affair from her own mouth, and as near the truth as she possibly could. She said she was a poor woman who got her living by spinning hemp and line ; that it was customary for the farmers and gentlemen of that neighbourhood to grow a little hemp or line in a corner of their fields, for their own home consumption, and as she had a good hand at spinning the materials, she used to go from house to house to enquire for work ; that her method was, where they employed her, during her stay to have meat, and drink, and lodging (if she had occasion to sleep with them), for her work, and what they pleased to give her besides. That, among other places, she happened to call in one day at the Welsh Earl Powis's country seat, called Redcastle, to inquire for work, as she usually had done before. The quality were at this time in London, and had left the steward and his wife, with other servants, as usual, to take care of their country residence in their absence. The steward's wife set her to work, and in the evening told her that she must stay all night with them, as they had more work for her to do next day. When bedtime arrived, two or three of the servants in company, with each a lighted candle in her hand, conducted her to her lodging. They led her to a ground room, with a boarded floor and two sash windows. The room was grandly furnished and had a genteel bed in one corner of it. They had made her a good fire, and had placed her a chair and a table before it, and a large lighted candle upon the table. They told her that was her bedroom, and she might go to sleep when she pleased : they then wished her a good night, and withdrew altogether, pulling the door quickly after them, so as to hasp the spring-sneck in the brass look that was upon it. When they were gone, she gazed awhile at the fine furniture, under no small astonishment that they should put such a poor person as her in so grand a room and bed, with all the apparatus of fire, chair, table, and candle. She was also surprised at the circumstance of the servants coming so many together, with each of them a candle ; however, after gazing about her some little time, she sat down and took a small Welsh Bible out of her pocket, which she always carried about with her, and in which she usually read a chapter—chiefly in the New Testament—before she said her prayers and went to bed. While she was reading her head, saw a gentleman enter in a gold-laced hat and waistcoat, and the rest of his dress corresponding therewith. (I think she was very particular in describing the rest of his dress to Mr. Hampson, and he to me at the time, but I have now forgot the other particulars.) He walked down by the sash-window to the corner of the room, and then returned. When he came at the first window in his return (the bottom of which was nearly breast-high) he rested his elbow on the bottom of the window, and the side of his face upon the palm of his hand, and stood in that leaning posture for some time, with his side partly towards her. She looked at him earnestly to see if she knew him, but though, from her frequent intercourse with them, she had a personal knowledge of all the present family, he appeared a stranger to her. She supposed afterwards, that he stood in this manner to encourage her to speak ; but as she did not, after some little time he walked off, pulling the door after him, pulling the door after him as the servants had done before. She began now to be much alarmed, concluding it to be an apparition, and that they had put her there on purpose. This was really the case. The room, it seems, had been disturbed for a long time so that nobody could sleep peaceably in it, and as she passed for a very serious woman, the servants took it in their heads to put the Methodist and spirit together, to see what they would make of it. Startled at this thought, she rose from her chair, and kneeled down by the bedside to say her prayers. While she was praying he came in again, walked round the room, and came close behind her. She had it on her mind to speak, but when she attempted it she was so very much agitated, that she could not utter a word. He walked out of the room again, pulling the door after him as before. She begged that God would strengthen her, and not suffer her to be tried beyond what she was able to bear; she recovered her spirits, and thought she felt more confidence and resolution, and determined if he came in again she would speak to him if possible. He presently came in again, walked round, and came behind her as before; she turned her head and said, "Pray, sir, who are you, and what do you want?" He put up his finger, and said, "Take up the candle and follow me, and I will tell you." She got up, took up the candle, and followed him out of the room. He led her through a long boarded passage, till they came to the door of another room, which he opened and went in; it was a small room, or what might be called a large closet. "As the room was small, and I believed him to be a spirit," said she, "I stopped at the door; he turned and said, 'Walk in; I will not hurt you;' so I walked in. He said 'Observe what I do;' I said 'I will.' He stooped, and tore up one of the boards of the floor, and there appeared under it a box with an iron handle in the lid. He said, 'Do you see that box?' I said, 'Yes, I do.' He then stepped to one side of the room and showed me a crevice in the wall, where, he said, a key was hid that would open it. 'This box and key must be taken out, and sent to the earl in London' (naming the earl and his place of residence in the city). He said, 'Will you see it done?' I said, 'I will do my best to get it done;' he said, 'Do, and I will trouble the house no more.' He then walked out of the room and left me. (He seems to have been a very civil spirit, and to have been very careful to affright her as little as possible.) I stepped to the room-door, and set up a shout. The steward and his wife, with the other servants, came to me immediately; all clung together, with a number of lights in their hands. It seems they had all been waiting to see the issue of the interview betwixt me and the apparition. They asked me what was the matter? I told them the foregoing circumstances, and showed them the box. The steward durst not meddle with it, but his wife had more courage, and, with the help of the other servants, tugged it out, and found the key. She said by their lifting it appeared to be pretty heavy, but that she did not see it opened, and therefore did not know what it contained;—perhaps money, or writings of consequence to the family, or both." They took it away with them, and she then went to bed and slept peaceably till the morning. It appeared afterwards that they sent the box to the earl, in London, with an account of the manner of its discovery, and by whom; as the earl sent down orders immediately to his steward to inform the poor woman who had been the occasion of the discovery, that if she would come and reside in his family, she should be comfortably provided for the remainder of her days; or, if she did not choose to reside constantly with them, if she would let them know when she wanted assistance, she should be liberally supplied at his lordship's expense, as long as he lived. And Mr. Hampson said it was a known fact in the neighbourhood, that she had been so supplied from his lordship's family from the time the affair was said to have happened.

SUPRA-CENTENARIAN.—BOILEAU writes:—"In Trawsfynydd Churchyard I noticed the following—*which the Rector said was unquestionably true*—' In memory of Edmund Morgan of Dôl-y-mynech, who died on the 6th day of February, 1817, aged 113 years.'" We should be glad of the Rector's "proofs." In our issues for 1879 this old gentleman was discussed, and a descendant told us that at the time of Mr. Morgan's death he was supposed to be " only 111," and that age was engraved on the coffin plate, and cut on the tombstone; but afterwards it was discovered that he really had attained 113 years! This was challenged in *Bye-gones* Feb. 13, 1879, but from that day to this we have heard no more of the matter.

NOTES.

EARLY PRINTERS IN WALES, &c.—Under this heading a series of notes appeared in *Bye-gones* of 1878. In turning over the file of the paper the other day, I came across the 'notes' in question and observed the name of Rhys Thomas, who was a printer at Cowbridge from 1771 to 1781. From a contemporary record I can throw one ray of light into Mr. Thomas's printing office, and show how matters stood there on two days in May 1777. Your readers would, I fancy, have welcomed the little I have to say had I offered it them three years ago: I hope it is not too late to be of use now.

The extract I am about to make is from a school-boy's diary kept in the years 1777-1778. The lad's name was Daniel Walters, and he was the second son of the Rev. John Walters, rector of Landough, but who is better known to the majority of Welshmen from his labours as a lexicographer. Let me mention that Landough is within an easy walk of Cowbridge. And now for the words of the diarist:—

"May 13th (1777). The bailiffs came to the printers to seize their goods. Mrs. Thomas, after sending Caleb backwards and forwards many times, came with tears in her eyes to intreat my father to come to Cowbridge." The entry is carried on without a break into the division for May 14th, where it reads: "He went; and the goods being appraised he bought them."

The diary is of a very fragmentary character; a few leaves only having been preserved, and are by no means consecutive. I can guarantee their authenticity, for they came into the hands of the elderly lady who now owns them direct from the Walters family upon the death of its last but one surviving representative.

There are two other items in the diary which it may be of interest to quote. Early in January, 1778, Mr. Walters had some work which was passing through the press. I imagine it to be a portion of his Dictionary, but I cannot say what it could have been. There is this entry under January 3rd:—"Caleb brings the revise to be corrected; my father and I correct it." Again, on April 15 following, there is "Go to Cowbridge; bring home 90 numbers," and this I take to be some serial work in course of publication. In Williams's *Eminent Welshmen* it is stated that the Dictionary was completed in 1794, but no date is given as that on which it was begun.

Does the reader feel any interest in Caleb, who, I suppose, was Rhys Thomas's son? Young Walters, on Friday, January 9th, 1778, goes at night with his brother Henry to Cowbridge, and "Call to see Caleb, who on Tuesday last was hoisted up by the rope of the bell and vastly bruised"—a sorry ending to the poor fellow's Christmas merry making.

Daniel Walters, the diarist, was a youth of great promise—a promise which was fulfilled as far as his early manhood permitted, for he became Master of the Cowbridge Free Grammar School when in his twenty-second year. He held that position just long enough to show how rich his attainments were, and then sunk into a premature grave when but little more than twenty-five years of age. D.J.

CRUDE-DITTIES.—Besides the *Royal Tribes of Wales*, and the *Tracts of Powys*, a volume of 34 pp. in 4to. was printed by the late Philip Yorke, Esq., of Erthig, in 1802, entitled *Crude-Ditties*, and containing some two dozen short poems, mostly humorous. The following, "to Abergele," penned, probably, during a sea-side visit, is a specimen :—

ABERGELE.

Abergele entreats
You would print her receipts,*
And give her a chance,
In this maritime dance,
With Parkgate and Hylake (sic)
They very great cry make,
When their Sea's but a fool,
To our wider pool :
Here, whenever you strip,
At all times, you may dip ;
There, like oyster or crab,
As a cockle, or dab,
Your mouth open'd wide,
You gasp for the tide.
'Tis true that in Peers,
We may find some arrears,
But of Ladies we boast,
As fine, as your coast :
Here, Neptune each morn,
Embraces Miss Horn,
Miss Evans, Miss Sutton,
Miss Barret, Miss Button,
Mistress Ridgway, and York,
And six Ladies from Cork,
Mistress Roberts and Daughter,
All toasts of our water :
Of 'Squires the best sort,
We have to report,
Messieurs Leche, Evans, Phrys, (qu. Rhys ?)
And neither a Quiz.
In able Divines,
Our shore also shines ;
With Wingfield and Jackson,
One Welsh, one a Saxon.
To finish our bill,
A Physician† of skill,
Who joins to his art,
Much goodness of heart,
And to this situation,
Gives recommendation. H.W.L.

QUERIES.

CAMBRIAN ARCHÆOLOGICAL SOCIETY.— I have been looking over the list of names published in *Arch. Camb.* for Oct., 1846, of the parties who had signified their intention of forming a Cambrian Archæological Association ; and of the ninety names there given I only find two who appear in the list of members for 1880. These are Lord Penrhyn (in 1846 Hon. D. Pennant) and Professor Westwood. Who were the active promoters of the Society ? I see by the Secretary's report at the Church Stretton meeting, Aug. 1881, that it was formally inaugurated at Aberystwyth in 1847. The first suggestion of a Society was made in *Arch. Camb.*, pt. 3, vol. 1, issued in 1846, by "A Welsh Antiquary." Who was he ? N.W.S.

* Arrivals at Abergele. † Dr. Thackeray.

BURGESSES OF HOLT, DENBIGHSHIRE.— I read in a newspaper for July 25, 1820, that "On Friday week another batch of Burgesses was made at Holt, the whole of them it is said in the interest of Mrs. Biddulph." What does this mean ? WREXHAMITE.

REPLIES.

SHROPSHIRE BORDER WORDS (July 6, 1881). I heard a new application of a word the other day— that is, new to me :—to others I believe it is not a novelty. A poor woman speaking with reluctance of her family troubles, said,—"I am not one to speak of my *Pedigrees*."

Topmost. I also heard this word used the other day in, what was to me, a new sense. A woman from the Welshpool side of Oswestry met me in the road as she was coming to market. I did not at first recognize her, so she said "Ime the *topmost* now, sir." I presume she meant that she "had the advantage of me," in remembering me when I did not recollect her face. Miss Jackson, in her admirable *Shropshire Word Book*, has no reference to this use of the word, neither Mr. Halliwell in his Dictionary. Nor does Mr. Hamer notice it in his gleaning of words used in Montgomeryshire, which appeared in *Mont : Coll :* Vol 10. JARCO.

REMARKABLE TREES (June 29, 1881).—Your correspondent, "J.W.M.," in answering my letter of the 21st June last, in which I expressed my doubts of any oak tree in England measuring 1,500 cubic feet of timber, says he has been informed that one standing in Croft Castle Park has been measured by a builder at 1,920 feet ; but he adds that the well-known King's and Abbot's Oak in Bagot's Park may be larger now. Though I believe these to be among the greatest in England, I cannot admit them to contain 1,500 feet. Since "J.W.M.'s" letter appeared, through the kindness of a friend, I have obtained the measurements of thirteen of the largest trees at Stoneleigh, and of these only two exceed 1,000 feet, one being 1,125, the other 1,170. These were measured by a professional authority without knowing the object of the inquiry. The circumference of one at one foot from the ground being 31 feet, the other 31 feet 2 inches. Until I have more direct and definite information, shall I be considered very perverse if I still sign myself A DOUBTER.

WHITECHURCH (Aug. 3, 1881.)—The Salusbury memorials in the old White-Church, near Denbigh (and to which your correspondent W.A.L. has called attention,) are (although *early ones* in our estimation) comparatively, but modern records of the dead members of the very ancient family hailing from Lleweni. I should be glad to know if any of your correspondents can give us some reliable account of the burial places of the progenitors of the particular Sir John Salusbury, who died in 1578, and whose remains lie buried under the "large alabaster altar tomb" at the end of the nave of the old Church in question. According to *Burke*, one Thomas Salusbury, founded the Carmelite Priory at Denbigh ; and the late Sir Charles Salusbury of Llanwern, Monmouthshire, in a letter now before me says,—" his son John who married Katherine Seymour, died in 1289, and was buried within the grounds attached to the Priory." I read in another account that John's great grandson Ralph Salusbury "died in 1405 and was buried at Lleweni Chapel," but the writer does not say if this was a chapel attached to Lleweni, or some church near to it. The grandson of Ralph—the well known Thomas Salusbury *hen* of Lleweni, and who was grandfather to the Sir John mentioned by your correspondent, is supposed to have been buried at Tremeirchion, where a painted window is said to have been put up to his memory, but whether it remains there to this day or not I am unable to say. Several members of the Salusbury family were buried at Bodfarry, others at Llanrhaiadr, and others, I believe, at Henllan; but most, if not all, of the last three branches were probably descendants of old Thomas in the lines of the Bachegraig, Llanrhaiadr, and Galltfaenan descendants of the parent stock of Lleweni. The clergymen of the respective parishes I have mentioned might be able to throw some light upon the matter; as it is, we have no records in existence that I am aware of, which will enable us to fill up the gaps between 1289—1405— and 1578, and yet the Salusburies continued at Lleweni from the earliest of these dates, in lineal succession, down to Hester Salusbury, who married Sir Robert Cotton of Combermere, and so carried the estates of Lleweni and Berain to that family. The late Lord Combermere was a lineal descendant of Sir Robert Cotton, and in the *Cambrian Quarterly Magazine* for May 1832, there is a letter of his published in which he says "I am very proud to say that Lleweni, the residence of my forefathers, the Salusburies, in Denbighshire, is my birthplace;" and thus, after all, the "Cheshire Hero" we have read so much about, was a Welshman both by birth and by descent.

CAMBRO-BRITON.

CURRENT NOTES.

According to a story current in New York last month Mr. Bennett was about to make the Hon. Francis Lawley, uncle of the present Lord Wenlock, managing editor of the *New York Herald*. Mr. Lawley, who was Richmond correspondent of the *Times*, sat for Beverley from 1852 to 1854.

There was exhibited last week in the window of Mr. Thomas Heywood, jeweller and watchmaker, of Wrexham, a very handsome silver teapot, bearing the following inscription:—" Presented by Sir W. W. Wynn, Bart., M.P., to Miss Lewis, Llwynnottia, for the best young fox hound, 1881."

Last week the workmen engaged in removing the floor of Market Drayton parish church discovered several hitherto unknown vaults. Over one vault was found a large alabaster slab, the incription on which, with the exception of three words, is entirely worn away, but the style of the lettering indicates that it belongs to the four-teenth century.

A somewhat novel Court sat at Chester Castle on Saturday relative to the property of Hannah Wright, Peploe street, Bishopsfields, Chester, who has died without a will or devising her property. Under the circumstances the Crown claimed the property, amounting, it is calculated, to more than one thousand pounds, and appointed Commissioners to inquire into the matter. A special jury was accordingly empanelled, and witnesses having been called as required by law, the Court ordered the property to revert to the Crown.

In the report of the Local Government Board, it is stated that an appeal was made by the Overseers of a South Wales hamlet against the disallowance of an item in their account for rewards paid for killing foxes. A formal resolution had been come to by the vestry to pay a guinea a head for every full-grown fox killed in the hamlet. Half-a-crown was also offered for each dead raven. The appeal was of course unsuccessful, " no ingenuity," as the report states, " being able to connect the slaughter of foxes with the repairs of the highways." From the same fund in other localities rewards had been paid to mole-catchers and sparrow clubs.

DR. ERASMUS DARWIN, elder brother of Mr. Charles Darwin, died on Friday, Aug. 26, at the age of 77.

A correspondent writes :—In *Bye-gones*—Current Notes —Feb. 23, 1881, it is said that " Miss Rhoda Broughton, the well known novelist, is one of the Broughtons of Broughton *in Cheshire*." This is a mistake. Broughton is in Staffordshire, about six miles N.W. of Eccleshall, a beautiful old "black and white" mansion full of *ghosts*, which, with its neighbouring church (a "donative" in the patronage of Sir H. D. Broughton), is described in Miss Broughton's novel, "Cometh up as a flower." Doddington, the principal seat of the Broughton family, *is* in Cheshire. It came to them by marriage with the heiress of the Delveses of Doddington (particulars will be found in Burke's *Landed Gentry*), but the present Sir Henry Delves Broughton lives entirely in London, and does not inhabit either of his country houses.

THE SHROPSHIRE WORD BOOK.

We have from time to time said so much about Miss Jackson's *Shropshire Word Book* during the course of its publication that now the work appears as a whole little is left for us to do further than to say that every fresh examination of the book only the further impresses us with the faithfulness and value of Miss Jackson's labours. A work that has received the substantial recognition of two opposing Governments, and that has met with the approval of the greatest authorities of the day, surely needs no praise from us to recommend it to the Shropshire public. All who were interested in the preservation of the old words in use when their fathers were young, must have felt that Mr. Hartshorne's book, valuable certainly, was but an imperfect work ; and yet *Salopia Antiqua*—originally published at 16s—will now sometimes fetch a couple of pounds in the market ! So it will no doubt be with Miss Jackson's far more valuable and exhaustive *Shropshire Word Book*. It may be secured now for a guinea and a half ; in a year or two copies will probably realize three or four pounds ; for our readers must remember that in a work of this nature—appealing only to an educated class—the number put through the press is limited. Therefore we would again urge on all those who are interested in the subject, at once to secure this most interesting and valuable dictionary.

To present our readers with anything like a complete review of the work would be labour thrown away, because it is the examination of the book for themselves that will form the charm to the possessor who appreciates it ; and we can well imagine its perusal—although " only a dictionary"—whiling away many an hour at the fire-side during the coming winter. As our object at present is to recommend the book, we only purpose noting one or two words ; leaving it for our *Bye-gones* contributors to do, as they have so often done, criticise and illustrate words and phrases as these may strike them.

In giving the name of Haughmond, as pronounced by the local people, Miss Jackson has not favoured us with the whimsical tradition of "A-men, the battle's won ;" perhaps we shall have that in the "Folk Lore" section, handed over to the editorship of Miss Burne ; although she does give us, under Dudleston, the couplet that tells us there the devil was starved to death.

Another word Miss Jackson gives that we do not often hear now-a-days. We refer to "Raught"—reached. In a "Narrative of the Fires in the Parish of Whitchurch," written by the Rev. J. Evans in 1832, one of the witnesses at the trial uses the word thus :—"I seed him before he *wrought* to the gate ;" a form in which the word was very commonly used in years gone by. In the Appendix

Miss Jackson has "Antelute"—a tea party at a cottage, got up for the benefit of the goodwife. This is stated to be used in Ellesmere. In such a connection the word is quite new to us; but on the Borders many years ago "Anterlutes" or "Interludes" were by no means uncommon; they were, we believe, chiefly what we may call stage plays on Bible subjects; something akin to the Miracle plays which have of late attracted so much attention at Ober Amergau. In the list of names of Shropshire places not pronounced by the natives as spelt, Miss Jackson gives "Caradoc," commonly called "Cwerdoc." She might have given another illustration in this case; for not only do the vulgar mispronounce the name, but their "betters" do likewise. As our correspondent who accompanied the Cambrian Archæological Society in the Church Stretton district the other day pointed out, Professor Babington, in his inaugural address was careful to say "Kar-rád-dock;" whereas the most educated inhabitant of South Shropshire would erroneously say "Kár-adock."

There are but few words, and these very limited in their use, that Miss Jackson omits. Of these we may instance, Tandowry, a smooth and oily, and sometimes loutish person; Twake, to sponge, &c. But all these are probably very local, and parties possessing the work, by ordering their binders either to interleave the book, or add blank paper at the end, can add at pleasure the (we are sure they will be but few) words omitted.

In conclusion we may say that the work can be supplied by Woodall and Venables, Oswestry; Adnitt and Naunton, Shrewsbury; or Minshull and Hughes, Chester. A new work is in preparation, but we regret to say that Miss Jackson's health will not allow of her completing it. We allude to the *Shropshire Folk Lore*, which Miss Jackson has handed over to Miss Burne, Pyebirch, Eccleshall, who will gladly receive from such of our readers as will take the trouble to communicate with her, any well-accredited Dreams, Ghost Stories, Charms, Old Customs, &c., that are strictly connected with the county.

THE LATE BISHOP THIRLWALL.

The following letter from Professor Rhys has been published :—"3rd Aug., 1881. Dear——, I have read the late Bishop of St. David's sermons, and, as to the Welsh in which they are written, I may say that it struck me as vigorous and classical, but at the same time thoroughly intelligible. Here and there the author failed to hit the genuine Welsh idiom; but most Welshmen could not help wondering, as I was forced to do, that he had learnt the language with such remarkable success, rather than dwell on an occasional sentence which might be improved. I fancy those who mostly do the latter are men who themselves revel in that sort of macaronic and poverty-stricken Welsh of the newspapers which makes me sometimes wish the language dead to escape degradation. Believe me, yours very truly, JOHN RHYS." The following is an interesting passage from a letter by Bishop Thirlwall dated April 22, 1865. "I feel highly flattered by your determination to let me pass as a Celt. The fact is I am a hybrid. It would be vain for me to disclaim all Saxon descent, as my name speaks of a time when some of my forefathers were thirling their way with might and main through the old 'wall' which was the scene of so many hard-fought battles. But on the female side I have reason to believe that I share whatever Welsh blood flows in Radnorshire, where we had family connections, which, when I was a boy were kept up by periodical visits to a house called Stapleton Castle, near pleasant Presteign, of which, though at the time I saw it not, I used to hear a great deal, as well as of the terrific mountains in the neighbour-

hood—among others Water-break-its-neck—which inspired me with deep longing, not to be gratified until I became a bishop, when I visited the castle, then become a mere, though very picturesque, ruin. It has now very likely disappeared, or made way for a more modern building. But the old hill, over which I rode with great interest, still continues to break the neck of the same little rill, which forms a tiny cascade, stupendous to the untravelled eyes of former generations, but not now commonly producing any very deep sense of awe."

TO OUR CONTRIBUTORS.—Communications from Mr. James W. Lloyd, C.J.D., Edromo, T.W H., Norman, D.J., Landwor, W.T.P., and others, have been delayed in consequence of the pressure on our space caused by the publication of the Rhyl Churches, and Old Welsh Almanacks.

NOTES.

A SALOPIAN MONUMENT AT SALISBURY.

We are told in the *Gents: Mag:* for April 1817, that a splendid monument was erected by Mr. Carline, sculptor, Shrewsbury, in Salisbury Cathedral, in memory of Edward Poore, Esq., who died in 1780, a descendant of the Bishop of the See and founder of the Cathedral in 1222. The monument was designed by the Rev. Hugh Owen of Shrewsbury, one of the Prebendaries of the cathedral, and was pronounced to be "one of the most perfect specimens of florid Gothic in the kingdom." NEMO.

CHURCHES IN THE RHYL DISTRICT.
(Aug. 3, 1881.)

MELIDEN AND GWAUNYSCOR.

Meliden is a mining village one-and-a-half mile south of Prestatyn. The Church is small, miserable, and dilapidated, plastered all over externally, of one pace, with a nondescript ruinous bell-turret and one bell at west, porch on the south, and a coved roof inside, all modern. There are no architectural characteristics to indicate what the building originally was. The east window, in which are a few fragments of stained glass, has been a good perpendicular one, but the mullions and tracery are all gone, and a plain one built inside the original arch. There is a good Tudor window of three lights on the south. The rest of the windows are square-headed, without dripstones, of two, three, and four lights of Tudor age. A pointed door on the north is blocked up. There are no old gravestones in the churchyard of note. The interior has several modern coffin plates affixed to the walls, and there is a marble tablet to Edward Parry, Esq., 1825, aged 65.

A rough scramble over the high limestone mountain, Coed-yr-Egob, on which there is a small round tumulus, brought me to

GWAUNYSCOR,

A retired agricultural village on the edge of a valley bounded by Coed-yr-Esgob on north-west, and Gop on the south-east. This latter has a large and lofty tumulus on its summit, which in early ages probably formed the base of a mountain fortress. The Church is of one pace, small and without distinction of nave and chancel. The walls externally upright are internally curved outwards. The reason and meaning of this peculiar construction are explained in Mr. J. H. Parker of Oxford's paper in the *Antiquary*, Vol. 3, pp. 152-3, with other similar ones in English churches. The curious triangular-headed south door, and also the blocked-up northern one, indicate the edifice to be of early Saxon or rather British period.

At the west is a good open bell turret with one bell, but no window. On the south is a modern porch and square-headed window of three trefoiled lights, but no dripstone. On the south of chancel is a similar window of two lights. The east window is exceedingly good and beautiful, a Henry VII. depressed perpendicular window of three lights, trefoiled with six upper divisions also trefoiled. On north side of chancel is a small square loop-holed window, and also a square one without dripstone of two lights, the heads being depressed without cusping. The north door is pointed, but now blocked up—the keystones of the arch of alternately long and short narrow stones. The triangular head of the south door is ornamented with rude depressions of dots, loops, crosses, &c. Internally over the south door is a sepulchral floriated cross, with a sword, built into the wall. The roof is coved, of open timber work.

On the south wall are five modern coffin plates, and on the north wall is a marble tablet to Walter Jones, sixth son of Wm. Gresley Jones, Esq., and Elizabeth his wife, 1873, aged 8. Near this is a large hatchment of arms, quarterly, 1. *gu.*, a chevron *erm.* between three saracens' heads *proper*; 2, *arg.* a chevron between three boars' heads *sa.* ; 3, *arg.*, a pelican feeding her young from her breast *sa.* ; 4, *az.*, a lion passant *arg.* Over all an escutcheon of pretence bearing *arg.*, a cross indented between four birds *sa.* and a chief *az.* with boar's head *arg.* impaling *arg.* a heart *gu.* and a chief *az.* bearing three stars of five points *arg.* Over the first quartering is a crest, a saracen's head *ppr.* Over the second a dove *ppr*, and over the female a boar passant under a tree, both *pp'er*.

Motto :—Heb Dduw, heb ddim ; Duw a Digon.

Slabs in floor.

Thomas Morgan of Gronant 7 June 1771 aged 36.

Thomas Kirk of Gwaniscor August 1743 aged 47—both in capitals.

Slabs in the churchyard in capitals.

Robert Owen son of William Owen Rector of Gwaynyscor 12 February 1672 and his relict.

. . . . . Owen, Rector 1646.

Catharine, wife of Robert of Gw. . . . . . 1641.

Pillar dialstone 1663 RE . PE .

No Interment on north side.

Population, 220. Register, a thin 8vo. volume, begins 1538, and is the oldest existing register in the Diocese.
W.A.L.

ARTHUR BLAYNEY'S FUNERAL.—*Arthur Blayney of Gregynog, Esq.*, who was Baptized on the 11th February, 1716, died on Oct. 1, 1795, and was buried at Tregynon on the 6th of the same month, left the following singular

DIRECTIONS FOR MY FUNERAL.

It is usual for people in this Country (out of a pretended respect but rather from an Impertinent Curiosity) to desire to see persons after they are dead. It is my earnest request that no person upon any pretence whatever may be permitted to see my Corpse but those who unavoidably must.

I desire to be buried in the North side of the Church-Yard of Tregunon, somewhere about the Centre, my Coffin to be made in the most plain and simple manner, without the usual Fantastical Decorations, and the more perishable the Material the better.

5

I desire that no Undertaker or professed performer of Funerals may be employed ; But that I may be conveyed to the Church-Yard in some Country Herse, which may be hired for the Occasion : And my Corpse to be carried from the Herse to the Grave immediately, without going into the Church, by six of the Chief Tregunon Tenants, to whom I give 2 Guineas each for their Trouble. It is my Earnest request & desire to have no upper Bearers, or any persons whatever invited to my Funeral which I desire may be at so early an Hour as will best prevent a Concourse of People from collecting together, The better sort I presume will not Intrude as there is no Invitation.

I have been present at the Funerals of three of my Unkles at Morvil. I was pleased with the privacy and decency, with which all Things were conducted, no strangers attended. All was done by the servants of the Family. It is my Earnest desire to follow these examples however unpopular, and that no Coach, no Escutcheon & no pomp of any kind may appear. I trust that my Executor will be well Justified against the clamor and obloquy of Mercenary people, when he acts in performance of the last request of a dying Friend ; who solemnly adjures him in the name of God punctually to observe these directions.   AR: BLAYNEY.

I likewise give to all my Servants five Guineas each in lieu of all Mourning, which it is my desire no person may use on my account.

These "Directions" are in the handwriting of Arthur Blayney.

The uncles referred to were members of the family of *Weaver* of Morville near Bridgnorth, Arthur Blayney's mother being Ann, daughter of John and Ann Weaver of Morville. It was through an alliance with the Weaver family, namely, the marriage of Henry, 8th Viscount Tracy, with *Miss Weaver* (cousin of Arthur Blayney), that the estates of Arthur Blayney came into possession of the Tracy family ; and from that family, by marriage of Henrietta-Susanna, only daughter of Henry, 8th Viscount Tracy, and Ann Weaver, with Charles Hanbury, Esq., who assumed the additional surname and arms of Tracy, and was raised to the peerage in 1838 as Baron Sudeley, it has descended to the present noble lord, formerly member for the Montgomery Boroughs.   EDROMO.

QUERIES.

OSWESTRY GRAMMAR SCHOOL. — In the earliest schedule of School lands I can find, all the property was situated in the Manor of Duparts, which included Maesbury, Sweeney, Treflach, Crickheath, &c. And in one of the earliest Table of Fees for Education, the boys of the parish of St. Martins had equal privileges with those of Oswestry. What I should like to know is why St. Martins was so favoured, while the parishes in which the school lands were situated, were not? And when did St. Martins cease to be able to send its youth at reduced fees? Also, I find as early as the reign of Elizabeth, a sum of £2 per annum was paid to the School by the Crown. When was this discontinued, and when was it first granted? In 1773 there was an item in the School Revenue "Bounty Money, £1 3s. 4d.," and at the end of the century "Debenture out of the Exchequer, £1 13s. 4d." In the report of the Commissioners of 1830, the sum of £1 12s. 0d. is mentioned as received from "the receiver of Crown rents, in respect of a sum of £2, charged on the land revenues." These items all refer to the same fund, I presume?   J.?.R.

CORONATION OF GEORGE IV.—On July 19, 1821, the Coronation of George IV was celebrated all over the country, and I hope some day to give short records of the local celebrations of this, and other coronations, in *Bye-gones*. My purpose in referring to the subject now is to note that the Mayor and Corporation of Oswestry on the celebration of 1821, wore (as did other parties in the procession), "Coronation Medals," also that the "eloquent sermon" preached on the occasion by the Vicar, the Rev.

41

J. W. Bourke, was so popular that a request was made that it should be printed. Was it ever printed, and if so is there a copy in existence? And are there any of the Medals preserved? JARCO.

REPLIES.

AMPHITHEATRE AT SHREWSBURY (Aug. 24, 1881).—The remains of the Amphitheatre mentioned by Southey still exist on the west side of The Quarry, immediately above the Austin Friars; but the greatest portion has been covered by the Claremont Buildings and Claremont Mews. It was never "an old quarry." See "Early Chronicles of Shrewsbury," in Shrop. Arch. *Trans.* vol. 3. W.A.L.

COFFIN PLATES IN CHURCHES (Aug. 31, 1881).—*Penmorfa.*—This Church will repay careful examination. There are some fine monuments in the yard with long Latin inscriptions. As the key is kept at Tremadoc, the interior was inaccessible. Looking through the windows I observed the north wall and the gallery front covered with coffin plates and hatchments. I counted 43 of the former. I could not see the font. I should have expected a very old and handsome one. The cross on the bell turret at the W. end outside has the upper limb carved into the representation of a human head. The people think it is meant for St. Beuno, the patron saint. In the village I saw this announcement—Robert Griffiths, licensed to sell Tea, Coffee, Tobacco, and Temperance. The use of the last word is remarkable. Elsewhere you see "Temperance, &c." BOILEAU.

TOURISTS' RHYMES (Aug. 31, 1881). — *The Grave of Gelert.* Most tourists to Beddgelert I suppose go to see the so-called grave of the hound, and a goodly number seem to record their impressions in the Visitors' books of the hotel they stop at. The other day I had occasion to make my temporary abode at that very comfortable house the Saracen's Head, and in looking over the book in the Coffee room I found the following :—

I came to weep at Gelert's grave, but found the skies before
Had washed it so, I feared myself to wash it any more ;
Ah! 'lucky dog !' if such the state of sweet Beddgelert's weather,
I fancy you are ne'er unwept for many hours together !

Another tourist also records his impressions in a verse to the following effect :—

Under the shadow of Moel Hebog
Lies buried Llewelyn's faithful dog
In a fit of anger one day he stuck it
For he fancied his child had kicked the bucket
So he reverently buried the bones
And to show he repented put up these stones.

I am not aware that history records that the Goat hotel was erected on the site where Llewelyn's child was eventually buried, but a more recent tourist has added to the verse just quoted the following—

P.S.—And they put up the 'Goat' where they buried the 'Kid.' G.G.

CURRENT NOTES.

At the meeting of the British Association Professor Mc K. Hughes submitted the result of his examination with Mr. A. Williams Wynn of the deposits in the caves of Cefn, near St. Asaph. Glaciated stones had been found there, together with signs of the existence of man, but his investigation proved, as he maintained, conclusively that these deposits were long post glacial, and were even subse-

quent to the period of marine elevation following the glacial deposit. He attributed the deposits to the re-arrangement of the boulder clay. Professor Prestwich in this case felt rather inclined to doubt whether these deposits might not be pre-glacial or inter-glacial. This was one of those questions which he would put to their suspense account.

At Denbigh on Thursday the presentation of a portrait of Dr. Pierce, painted by Major Mercier of London, took place. The portrait, which cost about £300, is life-size, and is a striking likeness of the doctor in mayor's robes. It was accompanied by a beautifully-illuminated address and list of subscribers in Album form, by Mr. Orr Marples of Liverpool. The Mayor (Mr. E. T. Jones) made the presentation, and, in addressing Dr. Pierce, alluded to his long and philanthropic career, his exertions on behalf of the poor, his labours as a physician when the town was stricken with cholera in furnishing and keeping open for the poor a hospital at great cost, to his great efforts for the promotion of the Sunday School, as well as to his services as mayor for five years and coroner for 33 years. The portrait was unveiled amid cordial demonstrations on the part of the audience. Dr. Pierce, in returning thanks, alluded to his long connection with the borough and the great kindness he had always received, and related some of the events of his career and his escapes from death. "Upon two occasions," he said, "I have had encounters with lunatics, one of whom shot at me with a revolver, at a distance of only a yard. Nine times my carriages have been brought home in a cart, and upon one occasion a gentleman who was driving with me during one of these accidents was killed on the spot; and six of my horses have been accidentally killed." The painting bears an inscription stating that it was publicly subscribed for, to be placed in the council chamber, to commemorate a notable and philanthropic career.

The *Pall Mall Gazette*, in an article on the Eisteddfod, says—"It is quite manifest that all the year round nearly everybody in Wales—man, woman, and child, miners, clerks, postmasters, bankers, even clergy—devote every leisure hour to drilling in choirs, in brass bands, and on the harp, to writing Welsh poems and novels, to painting in oil, or to researches and original Welsh composition in history and political economy, with the view of achieving gain or glory or both at the Eisteddfod. A mild Bedlamite tint, generated by the Eisteddfod, suffuses the whole state of things in the Principality, yet it is not without preponderating compensations. Probably an immense mass of nonsense is annually produced, and unsatisfactory characteristics of personal and social conceit engendered ; but there must also be a vast amount of intellectual and artistic energy and sympathy rescued from the ruin of vacuity, sloth, and vice, and a great development of pure and strengthening enjoyment in connection with that genuinely redemptive process. The Member of Parliament and the Baptist Minister who charged the Eisteddfod with demoralizing Wales have a difficult paradox to substantiate, and seem legitimately exposed to the criticism of the Rector of Merthyr, who vouches for the improvement of its morals under Eisteddfodic influences. The advocates of the Eisteddfod claim that it has created a better popular amusement than 'climbing greasy poles, eating hot puddings, or grinning through horse collars at a fair.' It is a pity to play Pecksniff over the 'greasy pole,' for which, too, something may be said ; but it is certainly better for a Welsh miner to spend his spare time in writing thousands of verses on 'Life' or 'Love,' however far behind Pope or Anacreon, than in drinking gin and beating his wife. There is profit as well as entertainment to be had out of the Eisteddfod." The Welsh people will take this as very kind, coming from the superior English critic; but when the critic asks, as he does, "who was Thomas Stephens," his ignorance is somewhat startling, for even Englishmen who pretend to be educated ought to have heard of Stephens of Merthyr.

GWYDDELWERN CHURCH.

It was highly desirable that when the restoration of Gwyddelwern Church, which dates in part from the twelfth century, was contemplated, the work should be put in the hands of a gentleman who would appreciate and preserve the beauties and peculiarities of the building. The Hon. C. H. Wynn took up the matter with great zest, and at once accepted all the responsibility of the undertaking, placing the work under the direction of Mr. Henry Kennedy, architect, of Bangor and London, while the contract fell to Mr. W. E. Samuel of Market-street, Wrexham, who ably carried it out, without the assistance of a clerk of the works. The contract amounted to £2,600, of which about £400 now remains uncollected. Previously to its restoration we may say that the church consisted of a nave, chancel, and south porch, but was without any spire. It had, however, a small bell turret on the west gable. The chancel, being the older portion of the church, had grown into a state of considerable dilapidation, and it was necessary entirely to rebuild it, but the walls of the nave being of more modern construction were retained. In the chancel the whole of the windows have been re-dressed, and amongst others the north and south windows, which are of first pointed date—twelfth century. The roof, which is entirely composed of the fine old oak of which it was originally made, and which certainly belongs to the perpendicular period, has been bolted at the joints, and scraped, and now presents a very good appearance. The oaken roof over the chancel, which was formerly covered with plaster, has been laid bare and cleaned. The roof over the communion table has a canopy of carved oak which was formerly buried in plaster, but which has also been laid bare and cleaned. The chancel is divided from the nave by an oak screen, the design of which is of ancient date. The upper portion of the screen is new, and has been designed by Mr. Kennedy as nearly as possible in character with the old one, the lower portion of the screen being still the "old original." The screen belongs to the same period as the east window, that is the Perpendicular, third pointed, or Tudor period. The chancel arch is a curiosity, inasmuch as it lacks abutments, and to avoid the introduction of buttresses it is "tied" by the top beam of the screen. The stalls, prayer desk, and pulpit are of oak, and some curious little buttresses of very old oak, supposed to have adorned the front of the gallery, have been introduced into the elaboration of the pulpit. At present not more than one half of the church has fixed seats (open), the seating accommodation now being for 120, including the chancel. There is ample space, as necessity arises, for increasing the seats, in order to accommodate ultimately about three hundred people. So much of the floor not occupied by the open sittings is laid with encaustic tiles. Mr. Kennedy has also utilised a qu.ntity of old oak as pannelling, and adjoining the west entrance there is a partitioned apartment which is used as a vestry. Externally the principal addition has been that of an elegant tower and spire which are both entirely new. The tower is built in three stages, the lower one being used as a porch or entrance to the church, the second floor as a ringing chamber, and the third as a belfry—in which there are at present two bells, but where space is reserved for a peal of bells—attained by a winding stone staircase.

The spire is built of rubble work filling, with angles of Eyarth and Denbigh limestone. The spire is decorated with several gablets and string-courses, and it is surmounted with a gilt cross. The church is protected by two lightning conductors, one at the east end, and one on the spire, both being connected on Newhall's principle. In addition to the other work the church has been entirely re-slated with green slates.

SEPTEMBER 21, 1881.

NOTES.

THE OLD WELSH ALMANACKS.
(Aug. 31, 1881.)

The *first* issue for the year 1834 is called "Cyfaill Cywiraf," was printed at Dublin, price sixpence, and has the following verses on title page :—

1 Fy hen GYFEILLION heini,
　Haelionus cyn eleni;
　Mi dreiaf eto fy holl ddawn
　I geisio'ch llawn foddloni.

2 Pwy bynag a'm derbynio,
　Dymunaf lwyddiant iddo;
　A'rsawl a'drycho arna' i'n gas,
　Boed iddo ras i beidio.

3 Er bod y ser ar unwaith
　Yn fil a miloedd eilwaith;
　Ni ddichon undyn, os daw chwant,
　Byth rifo cant 'run noswaith.

4 Y Ddaear sy'n amgylchu
　Yr Haulw n fawr o bob tu,

Pan bo un wlad yn doriad dydd,
Gwlad arall fydd yn t'wyllu.

5 Duw sydd yn hwyllo 'n helaeth,
　Olwynion mawr rhaglun-iaeth;
　Dybenion pur ei wg a'i wên,
　Yw tynu 'th hen elyniaeth.

6 May GOD in his great mercy
　Preserve our King and country;
　May William's throne for ever be
　Unmoved, and free from envy.

The *second* issue for 1834, printed at Dublin, price sixpence, is called "Cyfaill Ebrwydd," and has the following lines on the title page :—

1 Fy hen gyfeillion tyner,
　Rwy'n d'od yn ol fy arfer;
　O wlad i wlad, o dre i dre,
　I 'mofyn lle dros amser.

2 Y byd yn awr sy'n 'smala,
　Ni wadt pwy ol neu flaena';
　A dalo'i ffordd neu dwyllo'r wlad,
　Onid oes brâd yn rhywle.

3 Er maint sydd o bregethu,
　Trwy râd 'rhyd gonglau Cymru;
　Mae 'balchder câs mor fyw 'mhob gradd,
　A'r llang a gadd eu llyncu.

4 Mae rhai yn fawr eu dwnad,
　Yn siriol deg wrth siarad;
　Ond yn y cefn ni bydd naws boen
　Sôn am y croen a'r bared.

5 Wrth drofa'r ddaear beunydd,
　Yn deg ar ei phegynydd;
　Daw dydd a nos; ond blwydd-yn deg,
　Rhaid troi trwy'r deuddeg arwydd.

6 Peace be restored to *Holland*,
　As well to noble *Ireland*;
　And may our *Heroes* of reform
　Stem every storm from *England*.

The *first* issue for the year 1835 is called "Cyfaill Manteisiol." It was printed at Dublin; and the author's name is for the first time announced upon the title page, thus:—"Gan Robert Roberts, awdwr Seryddiaeth," &c. The price is sixpence, and these are the verses which appeared upon it :—

1 GYFEILLION, dynion doniol,
　'Wyllysiant *Gyfaill* llesol;
　'Chewch odid un mor lawn o stôr,
　I'ch t'wyso mor *fanteisiol*.

2 Y Lloer a'r Ser fesuraf,
　A'u newidiadau d'wedaf,
　Ac am y *Clups* pa awr y bydd,
　A'r tywydd—pa'm y tawaf?

3 Am farn y Dysgedigion,
　Neu rôdd yr hên Seryddion;
　Mae rhai yn awr, am drefn y sêr
　I'w galw'n ofer-goelion.

4 Boed hyny fel y byddo,

Cewch gant o bethau i'w gowntio;
Y *Terms*, â ffeiriau'n ddigon pell,
Bydd sicr i'r Cyfaill gofio.

5 'Does unrhyw ddyn mor ddoniol,
　A foddia bawb yn fuddiol;
　Ac er bod arno fynych fai
　Bydd llawer rhai'n ei ganmol

6 May God preserve our country
　From discord, strife, or envy;
　From famine, sore afflicting rod,
　Let's pray to God for mercy.

The *second* issue for 1835 is simply called "Almanack," compiled by R. Roberts. Printed at Dublin, by Patrick O'Conell; price sixpence. The verses on the title page being:—

1 Gyfeillion, haelion, holir,
Am danaf, drwy'r Deheudir;
A gwyr y Gogledd (mawr eu chwant),
A garant Gyfaill geirwir.

Mae'n wasanaethgar drwyddo;
Cewch werth eich arian, a pheth mwy,
Am hyn; Pwy fyddai hebddo?

2 Y Lloer a'r Sêr fesuraf,
A'i newidiadau d'wedaf;
Aq am y *clip*, pa awr y bydd,
Odid am y tywydd tawaf.

5 'Does unrhyw ddyn mor ddoniol,
A foddia bawb yn fuddiol;
Ac er bod arno fynych fai,
Bydd llawer rhai'n ei gannol.

3 Am farn y dysgedigion,
Neu rodd yr hên seryddion,
Mae rhai yn awr am drefn y sêr,
I'w galw'n ofergoelion.

6 'Does achos imi heddyw,
Yn 'anrⁱgeᵘu f' enw;
Na chael fy erlid gan walch blin,
Fe droes yr hin ar hwnw.

4 Boed hynny mal y byddo,

E.G.S.

QUERIES.

SOUTHEY AND DENBIGHSHIRE.—In a letter to Mr. C. Williams Wynn, dated Sep. 5, 1815, Southey says :—

I will try at an inscription as soon as I can find out how to set about it. *Lapidary* inscriptions I have never written, and know not how to write, never having been able to discover any principle upon which they are composed. But what can be done in verse, with the county of Denbigh and Sir W. W. W.? Your resolutions may, perhaps, put something into my head. We have had a bonfire on Skiddaw for the Battle of Waterloo, &c. Follow the example on Snowdon, and you will have a feeling of sublimity which is certainly not to be obtained in a lower region. I wish you had been with us. Wordsworth was there, and Boswell.

For what purpose was "an inscription" wanted? At the date in question Sir Watkin was a hero in Wales, being newly returned from the wars; and there was a grand presentation to him at Ruthin of a silver vase. On this were engraved English, Welsh, and Latin inscriptions. Was it to supply one of these that Southey was solicited?

N.W.S.

PERILS OF A BISHOP IN WALES.—In 1739, Archbishop Hering, who was also Bishop of Bangor, wrote thus to a friend :—

Kensington, September 11, 1739.

Dear Sir,—I met your letter here, on my return from *Wales*. I bless God for it, I am come home quite well, after a very romantic, and, upon looking back, I think it a most perilous journey. It was the year of my primary visitation, and I determined to see every part of my diocese, to which purpose I mounted my horse, and rode intrepidly, but slowly, through *North Wales* to *Shrewsbury*.

I am a little afraid, if I should be particular in my description, you would think I am playing the traveller upon you : but indeed I will stick religiously to truth ; and because a little journal of my expedition may be some minutes' amusement, I will take the liberty to give it you. I remember, on my last year's picture of *North Wales*, you complimented me with somewhat of a poetical fancy. That, I am confident, you will not now ; for a man may as well expect poetical fire at *Copenhagen*, as amidst the dreary rocks of *Merionethshire*. You find by this intimation that my landscapes are likely to be something different from what they were before, for I talk somewhat in the style of *Othello* :—

"——— of antres vast, and desert wide,
Rough quarries, rocks, and hills whose heads touch heaven."

I set upon this adventurous journey on a Monday morning, accompanied, (as bishops usually are) by my chancellor, my chaplain, secretary, two or three friends, and our servants. The first part of our road lay across the foot of a long ridge of rocks, and was over a dreary morass, with here and there a small dark cottage, a few sheep, and more goats, in view, but not a bird to be seen, save, now and then, a solitary heron watching for frogs. At the end of three miles we got to a small village, where the view of things mended a little, and the road and the time were beguiled by travelling for three miles alongside of a fine lake, full of fish, and transparent as glass.

That pleasure over, our work became very arduous, for we were to mount a rock, and, in many places of the road, over natural stairs of stone. I submitted to this, which they told me was but a taste of the country, and to prepare me for worse things to come. However, worse things did not come that morning, for we dined soon after out of our own wallet, and though our inn stood in a place of most frightful solitude, and the best formed for the habitation of monks (who once possessed it) in the world, yet we made a cheerful meal. The novelty of the thing gave me spirits, and the air gave me appetite much keener than the knife I ate with. We had our music too, for there came in a harper, who soon drew about us a group of figures that Hogarth would give any price for. The harper was in his true place and attitude ; a man and a woman stood before him, singing to his instrument wildly, but not disagreeably ; a little child was playing with the bottom of the harp ; a woman, in a sick night-cap, hanging over the stairs ; a boy with crutches fixed in a staring attention ; and a girl carding wool in the chimney, and rocking a cradle with her naked feet, interrupted in her business by the charms of the music ; all ragged and dirty, and all silently attentive.

These figures gave us a most entertaining picture, and would please you, or any man of observation ; and one reflection gave me particular comfort,—that the assembly before us demonstrated that, even here, the influential sun warmed poor mortals, and inspired them with the love of music.

When we had despatched our meals, and had taken a view of an old church, very large for that country, we remounted, and my guide pointed to a narrow pass between two rocks, through which, he said, our road lay. It did so, and in a little time we came to it. The inhabitants call it in their language "the road of kindness." It was made by the *Romans* on their passage to *Carnarvon*. It is just broad enough for a horse, paved with large flat stones, and is not level, but rises and falls with the rocks at whose feet it lies.

It is half a mile long. On the right hand, a vast rock hangs almost over you ; on the left, close to the path, is a precipice, at the bottom of which rolls an impetuous torrent, bounded on the other side, not by a shore, but by a rock, as bare, not so smooth, as a whetstone, which rises half a mile in perpendicular height. Here we all dismounted, not only from reasons to justify fear, but that I might be in leisure to contemplate in pleasure, mixed with horror, this stupendous mark of the Creator's power. Having passed over a noble bridge of stone, we found ourselves upon a fine sand, then left by the sea, which have indents upon the country, and arrived in the evening, passing over more rough country, at our destined inn. The accommodations there were better than we expected, for we had good beds and a friendly hostess, and I slept well, though by the number of beds in the room, I could have fancied myself in an hospital. The next morning, I confirmed at the church, and after dinner set out for the metropolis of the country, called *Dolgelle*. There I staid, and did business the next day, and the scene was much mended. The country I had hitherto passed through was like one not made by the Father of the Creation, but in the wrath of power ; but here were inhabitants, a town and church, a river, and fine meadows. However, on the Thursday I had one more iron mountain of two miles to pass, and then was entertained with the green hills of *Montgomeryshire*, high indeed, but turfed up to the top, and productive of the finest sheep ; and from this time the country and the prospects gradually mended, and indeed the whole economy of nature, as we approached the sun ; and you cannot conceive what an air of cheerfulness it gave us, to compare the desolations of *North Wales* with the fine valleys and hills of *Montgomeryshire*, and the fruitful green fields of fair *Warwickshire*, for I made myself amends in the following part of my journey, directing my course through *Shrewsbury*, *Wolverhampton*, *Birmingham*, *Warwick*, and *Oxford*, some of the finest towns and counties in the island. But I must stop, and not use you so unmercifully.—I am, &c., Thomas Bangor.

I copy the above from an old issue of the *Shrewsbury Chronicle*. Perhaps some of your readers can tell where it originally appeared, and supply the earlier communication referred to, giving the previous visit of the Bishop to his diocese.

A.W.H.

REPLIES.

MORE VARIETIES OF WEATHER (May 18, 1881).—At the end of Jan., 1761, several flocks of swallows, and other summer birds, were seen at Swansea, in South Wales: the weather was very mild, but a sudden frost came and killed many of them. Great thunderstorms all over the country in July, 1766; several casualties reported from Cheshire. In Nov. the same year the floods destroyed much property on the banks of the Usk, and at Newcastle in Cardiganshire a bridge and three or four houses were destroyed. "The memory of man cannot recollect such quantities of snow to have fallen" as was witnessed in the neighbourhood of Holywell, in Jan., 1773: in a house three stories high, the owner was "scarce secure in his garret." Men, women, and children "found their tombs in the snow." Moel Vamma was convulsed with something like an earthquake, and people at Ruthin were buried in the drift. The *Annual Register* says that people trying to escape from St. Asaph rushed into the sea and were drowned! In Jan., 1790, the Severn at Shrewsbury rose higher than had been known for twenty years. In Dec. of the same year there was a violent storm of hail and lightning in various parts of the country: "the drivers of the mails had the greatest difficulty in keeping their horses together; church spires, and trees, and chimnies were blown down, or struck. The driver of the Liverpool stage-coach was terribly scorched by the lightning, and the accounts from North Wales are full of melancholy events." In May, 1806, "the elements seemed to be in a perfect blaze" at Monmouth, and the tempest was violent. The severity of the frost in Jan., 1814, was said to be more violent in Shropshire than had been known for many years. The Severn was frozen over and "the vicinity of Shrewsbury covered with skaters." In Sep., 1818, there were tremendous gales of wind, heavy rain and floods in Cardiganshire. J.?.R.

CURRENT NOTES.

The Late Rev. Robert W. Eyton.

The Rev. Robert W. Eyton, the distinguished antiquary and author of "The Antiquities of Shropshire" and other works, who died recently at Winchfield House, Hants, was the son of the Rev. John Eyton, vicar of Wellington, and Eyton, Salop, by his marriage with Anna Maria, only child of Edmond Plowden of Plowden, Salop, and was born December 21, 1815. He was educated at Rugby and at Christchurch, Oxford, where he obtained a second class in classics and graduated in 1839. He was rector of Ryton, Salop, from 1841 to 1863, during which time he composed his great work, "The Antiquities of Shropshire." The minuteness and extent of his researches into the history of his native county will be appreciated when it is stated that, although he has not carried his history further down than the reign of Edward I., the work extends over twelve volumes. Unlike most county histories, which deal almost entirely with genealogical and local questions, Mr. Eyton's work is a valuable contribution to the history of the feudal and judicial systems of the country for the first two centuries following the Norman Conquest. Mr. Eyton was also the author of "Digests of the Domesday of Dorset, Somerset, and Staffordshire," and of the "Itinerary of King Henry II." His latest work has been the editing of the "Pipe Rolls," and early charters of Staffordshire for the William Salt Archæological Society. In Mr. Eyton the country has lost an antiquary who for accuracy and fulness of research could hardly be surpassed.

THE "CARREG CADFAN."

I have been requested by a distinguished antiquary, one well-versed in Welsh antiquities, who recently visited Towyn, to draw the attention of such persons as are interested in the subject, to the perilous position of one of the most ancient of Welsh inscribed-stones—the "Carreg Cadfan,"(Anglice, the "Stone of (Saint) Cadfan,") which was formerly placed on a raised step in Towyn church, but which is now lying amongst the débris, with which the sacred edifice is at present crowded. It must be immediately manifest that, in its present position, runs a very great risk of being accidentally defaced and damaged by the workmen employed on the restoration of the church. It is much to be desired that, if local archæologists take no interest in the matter, some of those really interested in Welsh, and, more especially, in Welsh ecclesiastical archæology should come forward and take steps for the immediate removal of this truly national antiquity to a place of safety, where it could remain until, the restoration of the church ended, it could with safety be restored to its former position in the church. And, while engaged in preserving the "Carreg Cadfan," it would be well that the font, mural monuments, and other antiquities of local interest were consigned to a place of greater safety, by the same hands, as will, it is to be hoped, remove the "Carreg Cadfan." C.J.D.

SEPTEMBER 28, 1881.

NOTES.

CHURCHES IN THE RHYL DISTRICT.
(Sep. 14, 1881.)
DISERTH.

Diserth is a small village distant about four miles south-east from Rhyl. The situation is a romantic and sequestered one at the base of several hills on the east. The little Church lies on the east bank of the brook or rivulet which, rising in the noted spring or well, Ffynon Asaph, about two miles eastwards, flows to the village, there forming the celebrated cascade, and thence going westwards, falls into the river Elwy. The Church is a restored edifice, and it is difficult to say what were its original features or date of erection, but judging from the sepulchral crosses in the interior, one of which has letters of 14th century, and especially from the fine erect cross in the churchyard figured in Westwood's *Lapidarium Walliæ*, it must originally have been of very early date,8th or 9th Century. All we can say of it now is that the restored windows are of early plain decorated æra,with alterations in the perpendicular and Tudor ages. At the west end is a simple bell turret and one bell, a modern porch on the south; the nave and chancel of one pace with a slight break. There is a kind of aisle or chantry chapel on north of chancel and a similar one on the north of the nave, both separated by a pointed decorated arch. The great feature of the Church is the perpendicular east window of five lights and minor upper divisions. In this is stained glass which, by the old English letters used in the inscriptions, is of 16th century work, but there is no date. It is called a Jesse window, but it appears rather to represent our Lord's genealogy from the kings of Judah. There is ample room at the base for a recumbent figure of Jesse, but this is now filled by a patchwork of broken fragments. The central figures of each light are crowned and gorgeously robed kings seated, and figures of ancestors of our Lord on either side. In the central light is a king and Joseph at his side, above David playing on his harp,and above him the B.V.M. holding the Saviour and surrounded by an aureola of glory. The colours are exceedingly deep and rich, and the design and execution are much more artistic than the window of similar date (1533) at Llanrhaiadr-in-Cinmerch Church.

At the restoration of this church the slabs of the floor were cut and made to fit into the present pavement. Consequently very many old stones have been mutilated and destroyed either entirely or partially. The most ancient are five sepulchral cross-slabs with floriated ornamentation and a sword on each, no doubt, the memorials of ancient inhabitants of the adjacent ruinous castle, and probably great warriors in their time.

In the chancel floor is a slab which had an inscription in capitals round the verge, now illegible, and on the face—

DOROTHY . RELICT . OF . WILLIAM . MOSTYN . ESQVIER . OBIIT . I NOVR. 1681.

Another slab with the verge inscription illegible, in which the word MOSTYN can be alone deciphered, and on the face a portion of another imperfect inscription.

. . . .
EPISCOPI . ASAPHEN . SEPVLTVS . FVIT . VICESIMO . TERTIO . FEBRVARII . ANNO . DOM . 1637.

On a shield below is a lion rampant sculptured, and below that (in capitals)—

William Mostyn of Rhyd esqr.　died 6 November 1678 aged 26.

In the vestry floor.

MARIA . VX . WILLM . AP . EVAN . FVIT . SEPVLT . 17 . DIE . MAII . ANNO . D'NI . 1609.

E.　Ω　C.

On slabs in the churchyard in capitals.

Hic jacet Thomas ap Edward ap David ap Robert qui obiit mortem 21 Januarii 1589.

Dymma . lle . y . daiarwyd . corph . Edward . Jones . yr . hwn . a . fu . farw . y . 23 . o . dachwedd . 1636 . ag . a . adawodd . i . dlodion . y . ddisserth . 2l . per . annum . admundi . finem .

Hic jacet Edwardus
The rest broken off.

Harry Lloyd of Rhyd Gent　25 June 1638

Hugh Lloyd　4 October 1664.

Henry Lloyd of Rhyd gent.　2 March 1688.

Robert Hughes of Rhydissa Gent.　30 September 1720 aged 47.

Inscription illegible 1580.
Aue Lloyd daughter of Hugh Lloyd of Rhyd Gent. 6 December 1665.

Mary Lloyd daughter of Henry of Rhyd Gent. 1703.

Robert Hughes 1721.

Edward Jones of Comb. 1676.

William Hughes of Llewerllyd Gent. 17 March 1635

William Lloyd Gent. 25 July 1691 second brother of John Lloyd of Gwrych in county Denbigh.

In the churchyard are three old yews, under which are two old altar tombs with a rounded cove or arch over, said to be those of Lloyd of Gwrych. The stone is of a very shaly nature, and so all inscriptions have perished. At the end of one is a shield of many quarterings, but all nearly broken away except the first quartering, which is two lions passant in pale with a rose for difference. This would indicate a Hanmer, a descendant of a seventh son.　　　　W.A.L.

QUERIES.

SUPRA-CENTENARIAN (Sep. 7, 1881).—Why should there be so much incredulity in this question of longevity? People are permitted to die at the ages of 96, 97, 98, but if they go over the century doubts are at once cast upon the dates of their birth. I copied yesterday the following from a Latin cross over a grave in Leighton Churchyard, below Shrewsbury :—"In memory of Stephen Davies who was born at Leighton & died February 1837. Aged one hundred and two." The Rector of Trawsfynydd will no doubt take the trouble to prove the statement on the gravestone over the body of Mr. Edmunds, else it will incur the remark made concerning a loftier memorial. 'Twill be said that it " lifts its *short* head and lies."
　　　　　　　　　　　　　　　　　BOILEAU.

LEG STREET, OSWESTRY.—A correspondent of the *Shrewsbury Chronicle* of Nov. 17, 1820, stated that the street in Oswestry known as Leg-street, derived its name " from the sign of the *Three Legs of Man*, which formerly distinguished a public-house in that street "! The accomplished antiquary who wrote this might as well have said that the horse carved in stone on the front of the New Gate in Church-street, was called after the White Horse public-house which was the next house to the gateway ! But has it ever been ascertained why Leg-street was so called ? And what were its limits ?
　　　　　　　　　　　　　　　　　AN OSWESTRIAN.

REPLIES.

WELL AT WOOLSTON (Oct. 27, 1880).—You have published more than one theory about this well, all more or less guess work. According to Eyton *Antiq. of Shrop.* v. 10, p. 318, the place is associated with S. Oswald. He says, "The village of Woolston, though it stands four miles distant from the scene of Oswald's death, probably got its name from some connection with him or his line of march. It was originally called *Oswald's-stane* or *Oswald's-tun*, and it was still called *Osulvestune* in the eleventh century." Mr. Eyton accepts the theory that Oswald was slain without the precincts of modern Oswestry ; others, however, suppose Maesbury or Maesbrook to have been the " Maeshir" where the battle was fought. Now these places are much nearer to Woolston than to modern Oswestry. Who knows but at Woolston we have the real *Oswald's Well* !　　　　FITZALAN.

CAMBRIAN INSTITUTIONS (June 8, 1881).—The *Welsh Charity School.* Died, Nov. 13, 1809, aged 57, Mr. John Thomas, upwards of 30 years secretary of the Welsh Charity School in Gray's Inn Road, London.

The Britons' Society.—" On Monday last (says the *Merthyr Tydvil Guardian* of Oct. 4, 1834), a meeting of this Society was held at the house of Mr. William Teague, the Swan Inn, Dowlas, near Merthyr Tydfil, under the presidency of Mr. Daniel Thomas of Merthyr. The objects of this respectable meeting were the recital of pieces of composition on the following subjects :—1, The excellency of the unity of the Mind ; 2, The Orphan's Complaint ; 3, The Deceitful Man ; 4, Nathan's parable of the ewe lamb to David :—and singing, with pennillion singing to the harp, in the manner of North Wales. The chair was taken about eight o'clock by the President, under whose able and conciliating management the harmony and amusement of the evening was greatly promoted. Several pieces of considerable merit were recited, on the different subjects, and among them one by Thomas Powell of Dowlas, who was present wearing the medal which he won at Cardiff Eisteddfod. We cannot but greatly applaud the meritorious objects of such meetings as this, where the improvement of the mind is combined with the charms of music, and the pleasures of neighbourly and social intercourse." By being held at "The Swan," I presume this Feast of Reason was accompanied by a Flow of Beer?

TAFFY.

NONCONFORMITY IN SHROPSHIRE (July

27, 1881).—*Ruyton-of-the-Eleven-Towns.* On June 15, JARCO gave a copy of the License from the Quarter Sessions of Salop in 1785, of a house at this place for preaching. Since the note was published I have been favoured with some extracts from the private diary of the Rev. T. W. Jenkyn, minister of the Old Chapel, Oswestry (1827-35), in which there is much connected with the progress of Nonconformity in the neighbouring villages when he was resident in the county. On M··r. 25, 1832, he says,

Immediately after the morning service Mr. Lacon drove me to Ruyton, where I had an engagement to preach in the afternoon. When Dr. Edward Williams had the 'Academy' at Oswestry the students used to preach at Ruyton, but ever since then—now nearly 50 years—there has been no preaching there, except a few attempts made by the 'Ranters' who have been repeatedly drummed out the village. I had long made enquiries for a place to preach in, and at last a publican allowed me to preach on the bailey before his door: "The Admiral Benbow," kept by Mr. Benbow. I approached Ruyton with some feeling of anxiety, and anticipation of disturbance, especially as hitherto the rabble has been encouraged in such outrages by . . . . . . and more particularly by . . . . . . : of . . . . . . , a descendant of an illustrious Nonconformist. *Et tu Brute!* At the public house I found some people drinking who had been at church in the morning, and were there to hear me. The publican, Mr. Benbow, was very civil. When the time was up I turned the gig into a pulpit, and gave out a hymn which was sung by the people from Grinpo and Dovaston, whom I had invited there for this purpose. During the singing the people gathered together, whereas before they were straggling and keeping at a respectable distance. Some dandified young shopkeepers and farmers made their appearance, who seemed somewhat giggling, but were quiet. During the prayer a very respectful silence prevailed. In the sermon from Rom. 8, 33, all were exceedingly attentive. The congregation became larger and larger to the end of the sermon. I was determined to finish before three o'clock, the Church service time, so as to avoid all unnecessary occasion of offence. In all the course of my out-door preaching I never had a more respectable and respectful audience. At the close enquiries went through the crowd whether I was coming again, and one came to ask me. I then mounted the gig and announced that on this day three weeks I would preach there again.

This was Mr. Jenkyn's first service at Ruyton, to be followed by many others, at which sometimes there was a show of opposition amongst the crowd, but usually respectful attention. At times he left Oswestry so early on Sunday morning as to be able to preach at Ruyton and be back again for his service at the Old Chapel at a quarter to eleven! There is much in the Diary connected with the progress of Nonconformity in the village, which at some future time it may be interesting to publish. In 1833 Mr. Jenkyn had the satisfaction of seeing a new chapel—he had been the means of erecting—opened ; the ground on which it was built having been given by Mr. Bickerton of Sandford. The opening services (on Good Friday, Ap. 5) were conducted by the Revs. Dr. Ross of Kidderminster, Thomas Weaver of Shrewsbury, J. Jones of Bryncastle, J. Griffiths of Pant, Mr. D. Harris (the Carmarthen student appointed to be minister at Ruyton), and Mr. Jenkyn himself.

T.

REMARKABLE TREES (September 7, 1881).— In reply to your correspondent, who doubts the alleged bulk of certain oak trees, allow me to say that a friend, living in the parish, has been kind enough to measure for me the large oak I mentioned as standing in Croft Castle Park, Herefordshire. At 3 feet from the ground he found its girth to be 35 feet 4 inches ; at 16 feet from the ground, 28 feet 9 inches. The spring of the first branch, itself in girth equal to a considerable sized tree, was about 25 feet from the ground. He could not give me the height of the tree, which would require trigonometrical measurement, but from what I well remember of it, I feel confident this oak is from 80 to 90 feet to its topmost bough.

J. W. M.

CURRENT NOTES.

A stained glass window in memory of the late Mr. Whitehall Dod of Llanerch Park, has been placed in Trefnant Church, near Denbigh.

Amongst forthcoming publications are "The Boy's Mabinogion," being the original Welsh legends of King Arthur, with an introduction by Sidney Laurier (Messrs. Low and Co.), and a cheap edition of "Bishop Selwyn's Life," by the Rev. W. H. Tucker (Wells, Gardner, Darton, and Co.)

In the course of the alterations at the house occupied by Mr. Roberts, fishmonger, Wyle-cop, Shrewsbury, who was about to place a new window in his shop, the workmen, on removing a quantity of plaster, came upon a beautiful carved oak window frame, said to date from the beginning of the 16th century. The window is to be "restored," with a suitable inscription recording its discovery, and the armorial bearings of the House of Berrington, which, according to Owen and Blakeway's History, are supposed to have been formerly inscribed on this ancient house, where, it is conjectured, Henry VII. slept on his way to Bosworth field.

THE LATE VISCOUNT COMBERMERE.—The marble bust of the late Field-Marshall Viscount Combermere, executed by Mr. Theed, and presented to the Household Cavalry Brigade by his widow, has been placed in the mess room of the Knightsbridge Barracks. It is admirably executed. The Viscount is represented in uniform, and on the marble pedestal are enumerated the principal battles and actions in which he was engaged, as follows :— —" Flanders—1793 ; Cape of Good Hope, Malavelly, Seringapatam, Douro, Talavera, Busaco, Sevia, Villa Garcia, Fuentes d'Honor, El Bodon, Castrejon, Salamanca, Orthes, Toulouse, and Bhurtpore—1826."

THE "CARREG CADFAN."

Allow me to corroborate the statement of "C. J. D." as to the present condition of this interesting stone. During the week I have visited Towyn, and have seen the "Carreg Cadfan" lying at the west end of the north aisle of the Church among a heap of rubbish and broken stones. Besides this stone, there are in the Church an ancient font and a curious old alms-box, both of which are in imminent danger of being destroyed. Surely, sir, some one with a knowledge of the value of these things to archæology ought to take the matter up—if the authorities of the Church will not do so—and see that these interesting objects are preserved.

R. B.

OPENING OF THE EYE, EAR, AND THROAT HOSPITAL FOR SHROPSHIRE AND WALES.

The fine building which has been erected in a commanding position at Shrewsbury, overlooking the Severn and facing the Grammar School on Kingsland, was opened on Wednesday by the Countess of Bradford, the wife of the Lord Lieutenant of the county, in the presence of a large gathering of all classes of society.

It is over sixty years ago since the first Eye Dispensary was established for Shrewsbury and the county of Salop, and the first president was Sir John Hill, Bart. The institution, which was opened in Castle-street, was afterwards removed to Dogpole, where, for many years it did excellent service, not to Shrewsbury or Shropshire only, but to an extensive district reaching far into Wales. From 1819 to 1866 the total number of patients treated amounted to 9,704; from 1867 to 1880 there were 14,473; and last year 120 in-patients and 1,400 out-patients enjoyed the benefits of the hospital. The necessity for providing more capacious premises had long been felt and often urged, when, at length, the energy and enterprise of Dr. Andrew, who is the life and soul of the institution, were successful in bringing about the erection of the handsome building at Murivance, which has been built from plans prepared by Mr. C. O. Ellison of Liverpool and London. The foundation stone was laid by the Earl of Powis on September 9th, 1879, and the work has been carried out in a most satisfactory manner by Messrs. Treasure and Son, builders, of Shrewsbury.

As a correspondent pointed out in these columns a fortnight ago, this admirable institution appeals to a far wider class than "Shrewsbury and the surrounding neighbourhood," although we observe one of the speakers implied by his remarks that such was the scope of its operations. All Central Wales, and much of the north and south, has largely benefited by its operations, and, now that greater space is acquired, will benefit to a greater degree. The Earl of Powis—as he always does—put the case comprehensively when he pointed out how convenient the new building was for the Principality; and, we are glad to say, several of our contemporaries in Wales have recently called attention to the subject. The result of all this, let us hope, will be an accession of Welsh names on the list of subscribers.

In carrying out the plans the architect has had the advantage of the advice of the honorary surgeon, Dr. Edwyn Andrew, who has been untiring in his devotion to the work. The site, as we have said, is a commanding one, but unfortunately it is somewhat limited, and the beauty of the building is seen to less advantage than it would have been in a more open situation. In regard to the internal arrangements the first great point aimed at was the absolute separation of the out-door and in-door patients, and to effect this object the out-door patients' apartments are placed at one end of the building, and have special doors for entrance and exit, the only communication with the rest of the interior being by means of a private door. The out-door patients' department consists of a large general waiting-room, with windows and skylight, and two consulting rooms—carefully arranged as to light, and each with its own special ophthalmoscopic or dark room—entered direct from the waiting-room. Having been attended to by the surgeon, the patients pass from these to a smaller waiting-room, where they receive the medicines prescribed directly from the dispensary, and being supplied they pass out by a special exit in the front of the building, and without again passing through the general waiting-room. This is regarded as an invaluable arrangement, and it will, no doubt, tend very largely to facilitate the practical working of this department, especially when the demands upon it are heavier than usual. There is also a special consulting-room attached to the two others, for use by the surgeons in special cases. The other part of the building has a very handsome central entrance, and is occupied by rooms for the staff, and separate day rooms for male and female patients. The wards, occupying the first floor, the men one wing and women the other, each ward having windows on three sides, and the corridor windows all along one side, so securing that through current and free circulation of air so necessary in good hospitals; and, as to this one, it may indeed be said that there is not even a corner in which light and air are not abundant. The upper floor is occupied in the west wing by kitchen and domestic apartments, the east wing by the operating theatre, and special wards for those requiring attention therein. The operating room, or "theatre," has a splendid north light, which enters through a very large sheet of glass (one of the largest in the town) placed at an angle to the walls so as to be due north. On the same floor there is another novel feature—a good yard, or airing court, provided by roofing over the ward below with concrete arches and girders, in addition to the covered airing courts beneath. The arrangements as to the necessary conveniences are unique and perfect in their isolation from the main building, any passage of foul air therefrom to the wards being a simple impossibility, the conveniences being in a separate block and connected with the main building by means of bridges, each ventilated its entire length. The warming and ventilation of the new building are effected by the system of Messrs. John King and Co. (Limited), Liverpool, known as "the small tube (registered) hot water heating apparatus." By means of this system fireplaces are to a great extent dispensed with, and in this respect a vast amount of labour is avoided—indeed, all over the building the object has been to reduce the necessity for manual labour as far as it was possible and practicable to do so, and with this aim in view lifts are provided to raise the food from the kitchens direct to the serving-room which adjoins the dining-room, and all cooking will be done by gas, and telephones, speaking tubes, and electric bells are freely used. The centre of the building is occupied by a bold and effective staircase, open from the entrance-hall to the upper floor, and having large front windows filled in with stained glass from the works of Forrest and Son, Liverpool; and the glass in the various wards was specially made of a blue tint, as used for spectacles, and gives a delightfully cool effect to the interior of the apartments. The exterior is timber work, blending with brick and terra-cotta, and the over-hanging gables and verandas give it a picturesque appearance. The Ruabon red brick and terra-cotta are from the works of Mr. Edwards of Trefynant, which is a guarantee of their excellent quality. Mr. Edwards presented the beautiful tiling at the entrance, and the architect gave a decorated figure panel representing Christ restoring sight to the blind. The building has cost upwards of £10,000, and of that sum no less than £8,000 was subscribed without any special appeal being needed.

OCTOBER 5, 1881.

THE BLAYNEY FAMILY (Sep. 14, 1881).—LEGO, writing respecting a steel engraving by Hardy of a portrait by Beechey, A.R.A., of Arthur Blayney, Esq., asks where the original picture is preserved? EDROMO informs us that these engravings are well known in Montgomeryshire, and that he believes the painting is at Gregynog, or possibly at Teddington.

NOTES.

SEVENTEENTH CENTURY TOKENS.
(June 8, 1881.)
NORTH AND SOUTH WALES.

The tokens of the Principality are a small but interesting series. About half the number issued in North Wales are pennies, while among those of South Wales there is only one recorded, and this one is, I expect, wrongly described and should be included in North Wales. In the large proportion of pennies North Wales resembles its border counties of Chester and Salop, for among them are more tokens of this value than in all the English counties besides. Several of the Welsh pennies are no larger than the ordinary halfpenny or farthing tokens. It is also worthy of note that the *first* penny token issued in the following century, of which we are hearing a good deal of late, was a Welsh one, viz., the Anglesey or Druid penny of 1787.

Aberconway.
B. 1. Ob. HENRY . HVGHES . 1663—The Grocers' Arms
　　　Re. IN . ABERCONWAY—1D.　　　　1D.
　2. A variety without date
B. 3. Ob. ELIZABETH . IONES—Detrited
　　　Re. OF . CONWAY . 1668—1D.　　　1D.

Abergele.
3a. Ob. IOHN . HVMPHREYS—The Mercers' Arms
　　Re. OF . ABERGELEY . 1668—1D.　　1D.
A specimen of this hitherto undescribed token has been recently found in Wrexham and is in the possession of Mr. Edward Rowland of Bryn Offa, who has kindly furnished me with the description.

Bala.
4. Ob. ROBERT . THOMAS—R. T. 1D.
　Re. OF . BALLA . 1667—R. T. 1D.　　1D.

Beaumaris.
B. 5. Ob. RICE . BOLD . 1669—HIS . PENY
　　　Re. IN . BEWMARISS—R . B.　　　1D.
B. 6. Ob. IOHN . DAVIS . HIS . PENY—A castle
　　　Re. OF . BEWMARIS . 1669—I . D with an interlaced flower.　　1D.
　7. Ob. BEN . IONES . IOHN . WORSLEY—Arms of England and France.
　　　Re. IN . BEWMARIS—A ship with arms on shield. 3 lions passant.
　8. A variety smaller in size (probably a farthing and 7 a halfpenny).

Brecon.
B. 9. Ob. THE . ARMES . OF . BRECKNOCK—The arms of Brecon, a Mantle.
　　　Re. A . BRECKNOCK . FARTHING — B . B . 1670 (Large).　　¼
" The arms of the Borough of Brecon are thus given by Guillim: " Luna, A mantle of Estate Mars, doubled Ermine, ouched Sol, garnished with strings fastened thereunto Fretways dependant and Tasselled of the same." •

B. 10. Ob. THOMAS . IVXSON . GLOVER—A pair of shears and a glove.
　　　Re. IN . BRECKNOCK . 1669—HIS . HALF . PENY (Octagonal).　　½

Caerwys.
B. 11. Ob. IAMES . HVGHES—A fox.
　　　Re. IN . CAROVSE . 1669—I . I . H. 1D.　　1D.
　12. Ob. THOMAS . WYNNE . OF . CARWIS—T . M . W . 1D.
　　　Re. CHYRVRGEON . HIS . PENY . 68—A fan-shaped forceps on one side a tooth with three fangs, on the other a tooth with two fangs; above an ordinary pair of forceps.　　1D.
Since publication of the first portion of my Welsh list I have been informed by Mr. H. S. Gill of Tiverton of a variety of No. 12, Caerwys, dated '69, and with a slightly different design on field of reverse.

Cardiff.
B. 13. Ob. IAMES . HVGHES—A fox.
　　　Re. IN . CARDIFF . 1669—I . I . H. 1D.　　1D.
This token is no doubt incorrectly described by Boyne and really the same as No. 11 of Caerwys.

Carmarthen.
B. 14. Ob. ABRAHAM . HEELY . OF—A spread eagle.
　　　Re. CARMARTHEN . MERCER—HIS . HALF PENY　½
B. 15. Ob. IOHN . HVGHES . IVNIOR—The Mercers' Arms.
　　　Re. OF . CARMARTHEN . MERCER—I . S . H .　¼
　16. Ob. THOMAS . NEWSHAM—HIS . HALF PENY
　　　Re. IN . CARMARTHEN . 1668—T . K . N .　½
B. 17. Ob. THOMAS . NEWSHAM—1666
　　　Re. OF . CARMARTHEN—T . R . N .
　18. Ob. IOHN . WEBB . SOPE . BOYLER—Three Doves (part of Chandlers' Arm.)
　　　Re. IN . CARMARTHEN . 1669—HIS . HALF PENY　½
B. 19. Ob. ELIZABETH . WILLIAMS.—A castle.
　　　Re. IN . CARMARTHEN . 1663—E . W .　¼
B. 20. Ob. IOHN . WILLSON . GROCER—The Tallow Chandlers' Arms.
　　　Re. IN . CARMARTHEN . 1669—HIS . HALF PENY　½

Carnarvon.
　21. Ob. ELLIS . IONES . 1664—A bird.
　　　Re. IN . CARNARVAN—1D.　　1D.
　22. There is a variety of this token from a different die.
　23. Ob. THOMAS . KNIGHT—A roll of Tobacco.
　　　Re. OF . CARNARVAN . 1667—1D.　　1D.
B. 24. Ob. GRIFFITH . WYNN—1D.
　　　Re. OF . CARNARVON '69·—A castle.　　1D.

Corwen.
B. 25. Ob. ROBERT . WYNNE . OF . 1669.—(Detrited)
　　　Re. CORWEN . MERCER . HIS . PENY—E . W. 1D.　1D.

Cowbridge.
B. 26. Ob. WILL . BASSETT . MERCER.—HIS . HALFE . PENY
　　　Re. IN . COWBRIDGE . 1669.—W . K . B .　½

Denbigh.
　27. Ob. THOMAS . SHAW . 1666—A Goat.
　　　Re. IN . DENBEIGHE . GLOVER—1D.　　1 ·.

42

The Goat or Buck on the obv. of this token is a part of the Leathersellers' Arms, viz, three bucks trippant regardant.

The Shaws were among the most celebrated of the Denbigh Glovers of those times.

One of this ancient and respectable family went by the name of "*London Shaw*" from the fact that in 1665 he set out for the metropolis as a plague doctor, carrying with him a cart load of wormwood, as an antidote for the pestilence, by which he rendered himself the laughing stock of the town ever afterwards.

His Skinnery occupied the site of the present residence of Dr. Lloyd Williams.

He seems to have been of a rather covetous disposition, from the following record of the Council in 1671:—"That Thos Shaw, the elder, glover, be sum'oned to appre here next meeting day, &c., to shew cause why he erected a new building over agt his house in Henllan-street, to ye annoyance of ye publick. And to appear also to produce such writings as he pretends to have for the erecting of his new house upon the com'ons." However, we find him expiating for such encroachments upon public rights by bequeathing at his death a meadow called *Lavaria*, in the outskirts of the town, to the poor of Denbigh for ever. (Williams's *Ancient and Modern Denbigh.*)

In the "Records of Denbigh and its Lordship" it is stated that at the election of Aldermen, 1651, Jany. 9th, Thomas Shaw, tanner, vice Sir William Myddleton, deceased, was elected. Also in the same, that on a monumental tablet at Whitchurch it is stated that Thomas Shaw, gentleman, who died in 1717, was for many years Recorder of the Lordship and Town of Denbigh. This was probably a son of Thomas Shaw the tanner and glover.

I am indebted to Mr. Edward Rowland of Bryn Offa, Wrexham, for these interesting extracts.

Haverfordwest.

B. 28. Ob. HENRY . BOWER . 1666—The Mercers' Arms.
Re. OF HAVERFORD . WEST—H . K . B . ½

B. 29. Ob. THO . BOWTON . OF—Arms; on a bend between two fleurs-de-lys, three heads, a star for a difference. Crest; on a helmet, an arm holding an arrow.
Re. HAVERFORD . WEST—T . B . ¼

B. 30. Ob. RICE . IONES . 1667—HIS . HALFE . PENNY.
Re. OF . HAVERFORDWEST—R . A . I . ½

B. 31. Ob. IANE . SPARKE . 1667—The Mercers' Arms.
Re. OF . HAVERFORD . WEST—I . S . ¼

Hay.

B. 32. Ob. MATTHEW . PARRY . 1663—OB.
Re. MERCER . IN . THE . HAY—M . P . ½

This Matthew Parry was decended from a younger branch of the family of Parry of Poston, in the Golden Vale, co. Hereford. Blanche Parry, one of the maids of honour to Queen Elizabeth, being descended from the elder branch of the same family. "Matthew Parry of Hay, Mercer, married Priscilla Watkins of Llanigon, co. Brecon."—Jones' *History of Breconshire*, Pedigree of the Parry family, vol. II., p. 557, 8 & 9.

Holyhead.

B. 33. Ob. HVGH . DAVIS . 1666—Three books clasped.
Re. IN . HOLY . HEAD—HIS 1D 1D.

Kidwelly.

B. 34 Ob. MORRIS . HOWELL—A Church.
Re. A KIDWELLY . FARTHING—A Castle. ¼

B. 35 Ob. EDWARD . LLOYD . OF KIDWELLIE—HIS. HALFE . PENY.
Re. Arms; A lion rampant crowned, within a border of nine cinquefoils. ½

B. 36. Ob. Same as the last.
Re. QVID . LEONE . FORTIVS—Arms as last, with crest, on a helmet a lion's head erased. ½

Both these tokens are engraved in Boyne's Work.

Knighton.

37. Ob. IAMES . MASON . MERCER . OF—The Mercers' Arms.
Re. KNIGHTON . HIS . HALFPENY—1668 ½

B. 38. Ob. IOHN . MASON . HIS . HALFE . PENNY . 1668. (In five lines.)
Re. IN . KNIGHTON . PLAINE . DEALING . I.S.M. (In five lines.) ½
Engraved in Boyne's Work.

I have been favoured with the following extracts from the Parish Register of Knighton, relating to the Mason family, through the courtesy of the Vicar—the Rev. Martin H. Ricketts:—

1668.—Baptizati.
Johan'es filius Walteri Mason et Eleanoræ uxoris. Novemb. 16
Brigeta filia Jacobi Mason et Elenoræ uxoris feb 15

Boyne questions whether the latter token rightly belongs to Knighton, Radnorshire, but the above extracts are sufficient to prove they are both correctly placed.

Lantwit Major.

B. 39. Ob. LEWIS . MADOCKS . OF—The Grocers' Arms.
Re. LANTWIT . MAIOR—L.M. ¼

Llanidloes.

B. 40. Ob. IENKIN . THOMAS . OF—The Mercers' Arms.
Re. LLANNIDLOES . 1669—HIS . HALF PENY . I.T. ½
Engraved in Boyne's Work.

Llanrwst.

B. 41. Ob. IOHN . DAVIES . 1667—The Mercers' Arms.
Re. LLANROOST . PENCE—I . D 1D.
Engraved in Boyne's work.

Llanvyllin.

B. 42. Ob. WALTER . GRIFFITHES . OF—A goat.
Re. LLANVILLINGE . HIS ½ PENY—W . M . G . ½

Boyne incorrectly assigns this token to Llanvihangel, co Radnor.

Machynlleth.

43. Ob. ISACK . PVGH . 1660—A rose.
Re. OF . MATHENLETH—I . P . ¼

Mold.

B. 44. Ob. IOHN . RICHARDSON
Re. OF . MOVLD 1669—(Incomplete description)

B. 45. Ob. EDWARD . WILLIAMS—1D.
Re. GROCER . IN . MOVLD . 1666—E.W. 1D.
Engraved in Boyne's work.

Narberth.

46. Ob. ALLEX . BATEMAN—A shield of arms (probably the Mercers')
Re. OF . NORBERTH . 1667—A dove standing ¼

I am indebted to the Rev. B. W. Adams of Santry, Dublin, for description and sketch of this token.

Neath.

B. 47. Ob. THOMAS . LOVE—The Mercers' Arms
Re. OF . NEATH . MERCER—T . B . L . ¼
Engraved in Boyne's work.

Northop.

B. 48. Ob. RICHARD . WILLIAMS—A dog
Re. OF . NORTHAPP . 1668—HIS . PENNY 1D.

Overton Madoc.

49. Ob. IAMES . OWENS . 1667—HIS . HALF PENY.
Re. OF . OVERTON . MADOCK—I . A . O . An uncertain
object below. ½

Presteign.

B. 50. Ob. IOHN CONWAY—An Angel.
Re. IN PRESTEIGNE, 1665—HIS . HALF . PENY. ½
Engraved in Boyne's Work.

John Conway was a mercer. The following entries relating
to the Conway family during the 17th century, are from the
Presteign parish registers:—
Jane the daughter of John Conway by Margaret his wife was
baptized the xxviiith day of March 1641.
Jane the daughter of John Conway was buried the vth of
May 1641.
John Conway buried the 31st (sic) day of August in Templo
1652.
Tnomas the sonne of John Conway was buried the fifteenth
day of ffebruary in Templo (1666)
John the sonne of John Conway mercer was baptized the 11th
day of August 1669
Thomas the sonne of John Conway was baptized the 30th day
of August 1669
Samuell the sonne of John Conway was baptized the 28th day
of July 1672
Edward the sonne of John Conway was baptized the seaventh
day of December 1675
Anne the wife of John Conway was buried the 27th day of
August in Templo 1676
Edward the sonne of John Conway was buried the third day
of October 1676
Burials 1689 feb 6. John Conway

51. Ob. IOSEPH . GRONNOVS . IN . —The Grocers'
Arms.
Re. PRESTEEN . COVNTY . RADNOR—HIS HALF .
PENY

. The Gronnous or Gronous families were numerous here and
in the neighbouring town of Kington, where two members of the
family issued tokens (see Herefordshire list). The name, although it continued in the above form until the beginning of the
present century, seems to have passed into the more euphonious one of "Greenhouse."
It would appear the family originally belonged to Radnorshire,
some members migrating into the adjoining county of Hereford,
this Joseph probably for one, as his name does not occur after
1673 in the Presteign registers, while in the registers of Kington
(see under Kington in the Herefordshire list), the name appears first in 1676 and ends with his death in 1696.
The following entries are from the Presteign Registers—
Mathew the sonne of Richard Gronouse gent. by Anne his
wife was baptized the ffirst of January 1646
James the sonne of Richard Gronouse gent. by Anne his wife
was baptized the 19th of Aprill 1648
Edward the sonne of Richard Gronouse gent. by Anne his
wife was baptized the third day of July 1657.
Cellion (?) the wife of John Gronous was buried the 27th day
of November, in Templo—1660
1661—James the sonne of John Gronouse the younger was baptized the 14th day of July.
Elinor the daughter of John Gronnose Chanler was baptized
the 17th day of January 1663.
1664—William Knight of Lyngen Tanner and Margerett Gronouse
were married the third day of February by licence.
1665—Elizabeth the daughter of Hugh Gronouse was baptized
the 7th day of August.
Joseph the sonne of John Gronouse Chanler was baptized the
seaventh day of July 1667.
1667—Richard Beddoes and Johan Gronouse were married the
8th day of October by Lycence
1668—Richard Gronouse of Stapleton was buried the ffirst day
of November, in Templo. (This was probably the father of the
issuer of the token also of the two Kington issuers.)
1669—Katherine the daughter of John Gronouse Chanler was
baptized the 16th day of Aprill.
Anne the daughter of Joseph Gronouse was baptized the
second day of May 1669.

John Gronouse chanler was buried the 19th day of Aprill 1670
Joseph the sonne of Joseph Gronouse was baptized the 13th
day of August, 1671
Beniamine the sonne of Joseph Gronouse was baptized the
14th day of January 1673
Richard Whetnall and Jane Gronouse were married the 9th
day of ffebruary 1673.
Richard the sonne of Mathew Gronouse by Anne his wife was
baptized the 31th of July 1676
fridayesweed (?) the daughter of Mathew Gronouse gent wa
buried the 19th day of June in Templo 1679.
Edward Gronouse and Margaret Warberton were married
second day of June by Lycence 1680
Margaret the daughter of Mathew Gronouse was buried the
26th day of June in Templo 1680
John Bent and Jane Gronouse were married the 4th day o
January by Lycence 1681
Richard the sonne of Mathew Gronouse of Kinsau was buried
the ffirst day of ffebruary in Templo 1682.
1685—May 12. Thomas ye son of Thomas Gronouse by Anne
his wife
Burials for 1685—Aug 6 John Gronouse
1695—Feby 14 Hugh *Greenhouse*
1697—July 5 Catherine Greenouse one of ye poor
ffeby 26 Matthew Greenouse in ye little
chancel
1690—Sep 19. Mary ye daughter of Hugh Gronouse Baker by
Sibil his wife
1692—June 8. Mary ye daughter of Joseph Grinoos by Martha
his wife
1698—January 11th. Elizabeth ye daughter of Hugh Greenouse
Baker by Sibill his wife
1700—December ye 1st. Elizabeth Greenouse one of ye poor
On a table tomb near the south porch of Presteign Church is
the following—"Howard Gronous the last of the numerous
offspring of Gilbert and Elizabeth Gronous died on the 10th day
of March in the year 1819 Aged 80 years." Other portions of
the inscription are illegible through peeling of the stone.

Pwllheli.

B. 52. Ob. RICHARD . PREECE—A double-headed eagle
displayed.
Re. OF . PORTHELLIE . 1666—R . P . 1D. 1D.
Boyne describes this token under Porthelly, Cornwall, but
there is no doubt it belongs to Pwllheli, the pronunciation of
which agrees with the spelling of the place of issue on the
token.

B. 53. Ob. WILLIAM . REYNOLDS —The Mercers' Arms
Re. OF . PVLL . HELY . 1667—1D. 1D.
Engraved in Boyne's work.

Ruthin.

54. Ob. DAVID . VAVGHAN . 1668—The Mercers' Arms
Re. OF . RVTHIN . MERCER—D . V . 1D. 1D.

B. 55. Ob. BASIL . WOOD . APOTHECARY—The Apothe
caries' Arms
Re. IN . RVTHIN . HIS . PENCE . 65—1D. 1D.
Engraved in Boyne's work.

Swansea.

56. Ob. ISAAC . AFTER—I . A . between two roses
Re. IN . SWANSEY—I . A . between two roses ½
Engraved in Boyne's work, but incorrectly described by him.

R. 57. Ob. MATHEW . DAVIES . IN—The Mercers's Arms
Re. SWANZEY . MERCER . 1666—HIS . HALFE . PENY ½
Engraved in Boyne's work.

Tenby.

58. Ob. IOHN . SAVES . MERCER—I . O . S . in monogram
Re. OF . TEMBY. 1668—I . O . S . in monogram ¼

Welshpool.

B. 59. Ob. RICH . DAVIES . FELTMAKER—A lion rampant.
        Re. IN . WELCH . POOLE . 1667—HIS . HALF . PENY ½
B. 60. Ob. HVMPHRY . DRAPER—Arms of the Draper
        family ; bendy of eight, over all three
        fleurs de lys.
        Re. OF . WELCH . POOLE—HIS . HALF . PENY   ½
B. 61. Ob. THOMAS . FARMER . MERCER—A griffin pas-
        sant : in chief three lions' heads erased.
        Re. IN . WELCH . POOLE . 1670—HIS . HALF . PENY
        (Octagonal.)   ½
              Engraved in Boyne's Work.
B. 62. Ob. SAMVELL . WOLLASTON—HIS . HALFE . PENNY.
        Re. IN . WELCH . POOLE . 1667—S.W.   ½

——

Wrexham.

B. 63. Ob. GEORG . BVTTALL . HIS . HALPENY—G . G . B .
        Re. IN . WRIXHAM . IRONMONGER— 1664.   The
              Ironmongers' Arms.   ½
    64. A variety with date, 1668.
B. 65. Ob. EDWARD . DAVIES . 1666 (in three lines.)
        Re. IN . WREXHAM—HIS . HALF . PENY   ½
B. 66. Ob. ROBERT . IACKSON—Arms ; three lions' heads
        erased.
        Re. IN . WREXHAM—R . I .   ¾
B. 67. Ob. EVAN . IONES . OF—A pair of scales.
        Re. WRIXHAM . 1666—HIS . HALF . PENY   ½
B. 68. Ob. WILLIAM . LEWIS . 1666—The Cordwainers'
        Arms. W . A . L.
        Re. IN . WRIXHAM—HIS . HALF . PENY.   ¾
              Engraved in Boyne's Work.
    69. Ob. IOHN . PERRY . 1667—HIS . HALFE . PENNY.
        Re. IN . WREXHAM—I . (?) P.   ½
My thanks are rendered to Mr. Edward Rowland of Bryn
Offa, Wrexham, for the description of this token lately found in
Wrexham, and now in Mr Rowland's possession.
B. 70. THOMAS . PLATT—HIS . HALF . PENY.
        Re. IN . WREXHAM . 1666—T . M . P .   ½

Boyne describes among his uncertain tokens one which
no doubt belongs to Wales, and I shall be glad if any
reader of *Bye-gones* can localize the token, of which following is description —   :
        Ob. OWEN . WILLIAMS—A lion rampant.
        Re. HIS . HALFE . PENNY—O . I . W. 1666.
Kington.   JAMES W. LLOYD.

———

QUERIES.

THE FIGARO IN WALES.—A trial for libel was
heard at the Salop Assizes July 1836, in which Mr. Jones,
a mining agent for T. Assheton Smith, Esq., M.P., sought
to recover damages from another Jones, a printer and beerhouse keeper at Bangor, Carnarvonshire, who issued a
publication called *The Figaro in Wales.* Damages one
farthing. It was stated that at the Merionethshire
assizes defendant was not so fortunate in a libel case in the
same publication. Was this a periodical publication, or
only a single issue?   TAFFY.

PONTCYSYLLTE AQUEDUCT.—In a notice
of this structure, published in Price's *History of Oswestry*
(1816), we are told that "A fine view of the Aqueduct
is publishing by subscription, by Mr. G. Yates of Oswestry." Was this the Mr. Yates who, as a land-surveyor,
had an office in Church-street thirty years ago? And was
the picture published   OSWALD.

REPLIES.

WHITECHURCH (Sep. 7, 1881).—The earliest
entry in the Parish Registers of Bodfari bears the date of
1571, and is as follows :—" Roger and Catherine vh Evan
were married [a word illegible] ye feast day of ye
nativitie of our Lord God in the [word illegible]." There
are several entries of Births, Marriages and Deaths of
members of the Salusbury family in subsequent years.
                                                 H.W.L.

SUPRA-CENTENARIAN (Sep. 28, 1881).—
BOILEAU says "people are permitted to die at 98," but
when they live over the century "doubts are raised as to
the date of their births." He cannot see why there
should be so much incredulity about it. The reason I
suppose is because in so many cases when a test is applied
the ages are disproved. BOILEAU asks if 98 is allowed why
not 100? But why make any limit? If 100, why not 101,
and so on to, at the least, Old Parr's modest 152? I wait
anxiously the Rector's proof in the Trawsfynydd case.
                                                 DUBIOUS.

Mr. Edmund Morgan's death, in 1817, at the age of
113 years, has been more than once referred to in *Bye-gones.*
Here is something about him when living, taken from
The Cambrian of Sep. 23, 1815 :—" A man named Ed.
Morgan is now living in good health and spirits at Daly-
munech, parish of Trawsfynydd on a farm belonging to
Sir W. W. Wynn, Bart., turned 111 years of age. He
never lost a tooth out of his head, can crack nuts, and eat
the hardest bread in the house. His hearing is perfect,
and his sight equally so : reads small print without the
aid of spectacles ; walks to church almost every Sunday,
a distance of three miles ; he stands near six feet high, and
his person is quite erect ; he can walk as well without a
stick as with ; and when he likes he can fuddle more ale,
glass for glass, than his two young sons, who are not much
more than 80 years of age."   D.J.

CURRENT NOTES.

Intelligence has been received that Mr. W. H. Cornewall Lyttelton (nephew of the late Lord Lyttelton, and
grandson of the late Mr. F. H. Cornewall of Delbury
Hall, Salop) was murdered by one of the natives of the
island of New Britain in May last.

The fine art and industrial exhibition at Cardiff, which
has been opened for the past two months, and has been
visited by some 120,000 persons, was brought to a close
on Wednesday. By this exhibition £3,000 has been raised
towards the furnishing and decoration of the local museum
and science and art schools, and the formation of an art
gallery in the town.

THE WYNNE MEMORIAL CHURCH.—The foundation stone
of a church to be erected at Bryncrug in memory of the
late Mr. W. E. Wynne of Peniarth, was laid by Lady
Harlech, in the presence of a number of the friends of the
late gentleman and a large concourse of people from the
surrounding district, on Monday, September the 26th.
The Marquess of Londonderry, Lord Harlech, and the
Vicars of Towyn and Llanfihangel, spoke of the many excellent qualities of the late Mr. Wynne, and especially of
his great acquirements as an antiquary, and his devotion
to Wales, the Church, and his neighbours. The memorial
church is to be built on a beautiful site on the bank of the
river Matthew, which runs through a part of the village of
Bryncrug. One of the last of the many acts of good will
which Mr. Wynne did towards the Church of England
was to grant a site and approve of the plans of the new
church, which the committee have decided shall now be
his memorial church.

The first part of Stephens's "Gododin" has been issued by the Cymmrodorion Society. The present instalment consists of the Life of Aneurin and a portion of the introduction to the Poem, which is one of the oldest compositions in the Welsh language. We reserve a longer notice of this interesting publication of the Cymmrodorion Society until its completion, but may here remark that it is impossible to open the book without being struck by the pains which the writer took to avoid the common snare of statements made without sufficient authority by previous writers. He examines those statements by the light of such facts as are available, and then gives us the conclusions at which he himself has arrived. The late Mr. Stephens, though the *Pall Mall Gazette* recently wrote of him as an unknown man, was one of the most trustworthy of Celtic students.

A LITERARY LADY IN WALES.—The *Cornhill Magazine* for October contains an interesting account of "Orinda," a lady born in London, who married Mr. Philips of Cardigan Priory, and afterwards became celebrated in literary society. "The matchless Orinda seems to have adopted the melodious pseudonym by which she has become known to posterity in 1651. It would appear that among her friends and associates in and near Cardigan she instituted a Society of Friendship, to which male and female members were admitted, and in which poetry, religion, and the human heart were to form the subjects of discussion. This society, chiefly, no doubt, owing to the activity of Mrs. Philips, became widely known, and an object of interest to contemporaries. Jeremy Taylor recognized it from afar, and Cowley paid it elaborate compliments. In the eyes of Orinda it took an exaggerated importance.

> Nations will own us now to be
> A temple of divinity ;
> And pilgrims shall ten ages hence
> Approach our tombs with reverence,

a prophecy which still waits to be fulfilled. On December 28, 1651, Miss Anne Owen, a young lady of Llanshipping, entered the Society under the name of Lucasia, it being absolutely necessary that each member should be known by a fancy name. The husband of the poetess, for instance, is never mentioned in her poems or her correspondence, except as Antenor. Lucasia was the chief ornament of the Society, and the affection of Orinda was laid at her feet for nearly thirteen years in a style of the most unbounded and vivacious eulogy. It is very delightful to contemplate the little fat, ruddy cockney lady, full of business and animation, now bustling the whole parish by the ears, now rousing her rather sluggish husband to ambition, now languishing in platonic sentiment at the feet of the young Welsh beauty who accepted all her raptures so calmly and smilingly. In Miss Owen Mrs. Philips saw all that can be seen in the rarest altitudes of human character.

> Nor can morality itself reclaim
> The apostate world like my Lucasia's name :
> .   .   . Lucasia, whose harmonicus state
> The Spheres and Muses only imitate.
> .   .   . So to acknowledge such vast eminence,
> Imperfect wonder is our eloquence,
> No pen Lucasia's glories can relate.

Nor is Lucasia the only member of her little provincial quorum of whom she predicates such brave things. There is Ardelia, whose real name neglectful posterity has forgotten to preserve ; there is Miss Mary Aubrey, who becomes Mrs. Montague as time goes on, and whose poetical name is

Rosania ; there is Regina, 'that Queen of Inconstancy,' Mrs. John Collier ; later on Lady Anne Boyle begins to figure as 'adored Valeria,' and Lady Mary Cavendish as 'dazzling Polycrite.' The gentlemen have very appropriate names also, though propriety prevents Orinda, in their cases, from celebrating friendship in terms of so florid an eloquence. The 'excellent Palæmon' was Francis Finch, originally, but the name was transferred, as the 'noble Palæmon,' to Jeremy Taylor ; the 'noble Silvander,' Sir Edward Dering, was more fortunate in preserving his name of honour ; and last, but not least, the elegant Sir Charles Cotterel achieved a sort of immortality as Orinda's greatest friend, under the name of Poliarchus."

THE CARADOC FIELD CLUB.—THE BREAKING
OF THE MERES.

The last meeting of the Club for the season was held at Cause Castle on Friday, Sept. 23. The members were received, and entertained to luncheon by Mr. J. E. Severne, M.P., the owner of the Castle, of which an account was given by the Rev. W. A. Leighton. Cause Castle, though now in complete ruin, yet affords in its natural position—one of commanding strength—and in the traces of its extensive buildings still plainly discernible, ample indication of what must have been once its great importance as a Border stronghold and fortress. Few places appear to have played a more considerable part in the history of the country from its foundation, in the early days of the Norman Conquest, down to the very date of its demolition at the close of the Great Civil War. Illustrating his remarks by reference to some private papers kindly lent for the occasion by Mr. Severne, Mr. Leighton passed in brief review the former history of this most interesting place. Founded by Robert Corbet, a Norman nobleman, and companion of Roger de Montgomery, from whom he received the grant of the manor, and named by him after his own Castle in the Pays de Caux of Normandy, it continued in the possession of his family for many generations. It was made forfeit by King John on account of the part taken by its then owner with the insurgent Barons, but was restored on the submission of the latter. The same king granted a charter for a weekly market to be held there. Subsequently the castle and manor passed into the hands of the family of Stafford, afterwards ennobled by the title of Buckingham. And being sold by a descendant of this family to Sir Rowland Hayward, a wealthy merchant and Lord Mayor of London, in 1613, it was given by him to his daughter, who married Sir John Thynne, an ancestor of the present Marquis of Bath. At the conclusion of Mr Leighton's address, for which a vote of thanks was at once tendered, Mr. Elliott mentioned, as a somewhat curious fact, that it was Sir John Hayward, a half-brother of the Lady Thynne referred to, who, in 1620, sold the manors of Cardington and Lydley to Edward Corbett, Esq., of Longnor, a descendant, as were others of the same name, from the original Corbet of Caus. The annual dinner was afterwards held at the George Hotel. Mr. W. Phillips read the report of the committee which had been appointed to investigate the Phenomenon of "The Breaking of the Meres," of which we gave an account at the time the Club visited Ellesmere.

Mr. PHILLIPS reported that some five or six meres had been visited and experimented on, including the pools at Berrington. The dates on which each had "broken" were carefully registered, occurring about the middle of July. Water from each had been subjected to microscopical examination, with the result that the turbidity of the water had been ascertained to be due to the presence of what' in his opinion, were four distinct species of fresh water alga. Each pool seemed to have its own particular algæ. Of these he handed for inspection some beautifully executed drawings. Much, he said, remained to be done for the full elucidation of this question, towards which, it was to be hoped, the co-operation of naturalists residing in the vicinity of the respective meres would be obtained.

Mr. BLUNT ventured to suggest a probable explanation of the occurrence of this phenomenon at the particular and invariable time of year at which it did occur. He thought the algæ were nourished by the carbon to be found in the carbonic acid given off at that period of the year from decaying vegetation in the lakes. The algæ would perform thus a useful economic function in neutralizing the carbonic acid so deleterious to animal life.

The Rev. Canon BUTLER remarked on what he considered the beautiful circle of life and death, sketched out in Mr. Blunt's theory.

OSWESTRY AND WELSHPOOL NATURALISTS' FIELD CLUB' —The last excursion for the season was made on Monday, September 26, by the following members—Major Barnes (president), Mrs., and Mr. Harold Barnes, Miss Chapman, Mr. J. Dovaston, Mr. and Miss Dovaston, Mr. W. Oswell, and the Revs. O. M. Feilden, W. L. Martin, G. G. Monck, and T. S. Raffles. Assembling at Shrewsbury, they proceeded by train to Longville, between Church Stretton and Much Wenlock, and walked thence to the "Ditches," an ancient fortification near Lutwyche Hall (the seat of Mr. Benson). On their way some of the party searched a quarry for the fossils which abound in the Wenlock shale, others sought for wild flowers, and found goat's beard (Tragopogan), field gentian (gentiana campestris), yellow wort (chlora perfoliata), and a violet in bloom. Shortly after crossing a field which abounded in the mauve blossoms of the meadow saffron, they arrived at the "Ditches," a huge circular space about 200 yards in diameter, surrounded with a triple or quadruple series of ramparts and ditches, the latter increasing in depth and the former in steepness towards the interior of the inclosure. No tradition attaches to this remarkable site, but the history of the neighbourhood may suggest that it dates from the time of the Roman occupation. After luncheon the party proceeded to Cardington Church, which consists of nave, chancel, and west tower, of Norman and later work, with a timber porch dated 1639. Here the chief object of interest was the tomb of Judge Leighton (anno 1607 obiit), with a full coloured life sized effigy of that worthy, recumbent under a canopy, with attendant effigies of his wife and children. The oldest of the bells was dated 1633, the latest (1742) having the legend, "Fear God, honour the King." After the Vicar had kindly refreshed the members with tea at the Vicarage, he conducted them to Caer Caradoc, which they ascended to the top. The traces of its volcanic origin and affinities were observed, as was also the difference between its contour and that of some neighbouring hills, composed entirely of Wenlock Shale. The faultless weather enabled the party to enjoy fully the fine views on all sides, and to note all the important summits which could be seen. On returning to Church Stretton some of the members paid a hasty visit to the church, which was lighted for divine service. They found there a quantity of interesting carved oak of the Caroline period, framed into a lining for the sanctuary, with a not very happy effect. But it was too late to examine the church in detail, so the party returned home. All were well pleased with the excursion, the unbotanical un-geological member not less than the skilled and scientific.

SERIOUS LAND SLIP AT BROSELEY.

An extensive land slip has occurred on the side of the river Severn, at Broseley. One of the hills which border the river at this point has recently given way, falling towards the river, and carrying with it the Severn Valley Railway, which runs through the hill. Within a short period the railway has been lowered by the slip to the extent of five yards, thereby necessitating continual attention and expense on the part of the Great Western Railway Company in keeping up the level. The slip has now assumed a serious aspect, and at one point, near Jackfield, the river has been so narrowed by the fall of earth as to be scarcely navigable. The fall continues daily, and is placing in jeopardy the buildings upon the hill. With the view of taking immediate measures for preventing loss of life, or any further damage to property, a trial shaft has been sunk for the purpose of ascertaining the depth of the slip, and it is thought probable that a scheme may be adopted to prevent the slipping of the hill. It is believed that the cause of the slip is a stratum of blue clay at the foot of the hill and near the bed of the river, which the perpetual current of the river washes away, thus bringing down the hill. The slip is 100 yards in breadth, and upon the land affected there is a church, as well as other buildings.

OCTOBER 12, 1881.

NOTES.

DAME DOROTHY JEFFREYS.
(Apr. 19, 26, 1876).

Much curiosity has been expressed about this Lady, who is deservedly remembered as the founder of several charities in Wrexham and the adjoining parishes, She died in 1729, having survived her husband Sir Griffith Jeffreys of Acton for a long period, and her will was printed in *Bye-gones* for April 1876. Her maiden name is omitted in the notice of Sir Griffith in Le Neve's *Knights*, and is not given in the *Cae Ceiriog Book*. Questions as to her family have been asked frequently but have never, I believe, been answered.

I have now before me a copy of Sir Griffith's will which effectually clears up this uncertainty about "Dame Dorothy." I send it as likely to be interesting to many of those who read *Bye-gones*. And the following short statement of her parentage, for which I am indebted to the kindness of a friend, will shew exactly who she was and explain several portions of both wills :—

Robert Pleydell of=	Elizabeth dau. of		
Holyrood Amney,	John Saunders, M.D.,		
Co. Gloucester, Esq.	Provost of Oriel		
	College, Oxon.		

Elizabeth wife of Charles Hughes of Trostry, Co. Monmouth, Esq.	Dorothy wife of Sir Griffith Jeffreys of Acton, Co. Denbigh, Kt.	Robert Pleydell= only son and heir	Sarah dau.
		Justice ot the	of Philip
		Peace and D.L.	Shephard
		Co. Monmouth.	of Minching
Ob. anno 1675, ætat: 53			Hampton, Co. Gloucester, Esq.

I may add that this branch of the widely-spread family of Pleydell is now represented by Lord Downe. The Brother of Lady Dorothy Jeffreys was succeeded at Amney Holyrood by his only son, who was also Robert ; and Charlotte Louisa, daughter and heir of this Robert Pleydell, married in 1721 John Dawnay, eldest son of the

2nd Viscount Downe. Henry Pleydell Dawnay, and John Dawnay, the sons of this marriage, were successively 3rd and 4th Viscounts; and the title still continues in the family of the latter.

"Pledwell," the spelling of the name in Sir Griffith's will, is most probably the mistake of a lawyer or his clerk.

W.T.P.

Extracted from the Principal Registry of the Probate, Divorce and Admiralty Division of the High Court of Justice.

In the Prerogative Court of Canterbury.

"In the Name of God Amen this ninth day of March Anno Domini One thousand six hundred and ninety four and in the seventh yeare of the reigne of our sovereigne Lord King William over England &c. I Griffith Jeffryes of Acton in the County of Denbigh Knight being weake in body but of perfect memory (thankes bee to God) Doe make this my last Will and Testament revoking all other Wills heretofore by mee made First I bequeath my soul into the hands of Almighty God my heavenly Father by whom of his meere grace I trust to bee saved through the meritts and death of my only Saviour and Redeemer Jesus Christ And my body to be buried in Christian buriall att the discretion of my overseers and Trustees hereafter named and touching the disposition of my worldly estate with which it hath pleased God to bless me I dispose thereof in manner following My debts and funerall expenses being first paid and deducted And first whereas by certain marriage articles bearing date the twenty sixth day of July in the thirty fifth yeare of the reigne of our late Sovereign King Charles the Second Anno Domini one thousand six hundred eighty three I covenanted agreed and promised to make a Settlement of Four hundred pounds per ann. if the said Marriage took effect cleare and free from all taxes and impositions whatsoever (public taxes only and always excepted) upon 'Dorathy Pledwell' (sic) my then intended wife which said marriage was afterwards compleated and whereas by the said Settlement accordingly made it is menton'd and declared that the intent and meaning thereof is only for the setling and securing to my deare Wife the yearly rent of Three hundred and fifty pounds per annum during her life in lew and recompense of her dower joynture and meaning faithfully to fulfil keep and perform the said Articles I doe hereby will devise and bequeath unto my said dear Wife Fifty pounds yearly out of such part of my estate as is unsettled to be clearly and yearly paid her during her life as a rent charge by my executor hereafter named (publick taxes only excepted) to the intent that the said Articles may bee fully compleated and performed Item I give and bequeath unto my three daughters Elizabeth Margaret and Frances or if more bee living at the time of my decease the sum of six thousand pounds to be equally divided among them and two or more survivors of them or in case there happen to bee but one daughter then my will is that shee have the sum of Five thousand pounds only paid her And touching the time of payment of the said pore'ons my will is that my Executor doe pay the said portons to my said daughter or daughters as they shall respectively attaine the age of eighteen years or at the day of marriage which shall first happen Provided always that such marriage shall bee contracted by and with the consent of their Guardians hereafter named or the major part of them And as touching my said daughters my will is that immediately from and after my decease toward_s their present maintenance and education my said executor shall pay yearly and every yeare the sum of Fifty pounds per ann. to each of them till such time as the pore'ons before mentioned shall be paid and my further will is that if my said Executor shall

marry without the consent of his Guardians hereafter named and the major part of them that then he shall stand charged with the payment of Ten thousand pounds porc'on for my said daughters or daughter to bee payable to and devided among them as aforesaid and the better to enable my executor hereafter named to pay my debts discharge my funeral expenses and the legacyes hereby bequeathed (or which shall bee mentioned and expressed in a schedule or codicil to this my Will annexed and subscribed with my hand) I doe hereby give grant devise and bequeathe to my said executor all the Rest and Residue of my estate reall or personall within doores or without (other than such part of my estate as by the said articles or settlement are already disposed of) whether it bee houses lands tenements hereditaments leases mortgages rents arrearages of rent estates of inheritance or purchased in the County of Denbigh or Elsewhere and all my household goods chattells and Cattell Whatsoever and all bills bonds and debts due to mee by law and equity from any person or persons whatsoever To have and to hold all the said houses lands tenements and hereditaments and other the premises to my said executor and the heires males of his body lawfully begotten and for want of such issue the remainder thereof to my right heirs for ever Item I give devise and bequeath to my Cosen Thomas Gardner late Fellow of All Souls Colledge in Oxon the sum of Twenty pounds yearly dureing his life to bee paid by my executor desireing him Joyntly with my Wife to take care of the tuic'on education and government of him dureing his minority Item I bequeath to Mr. John Price Vicar of Wrexham the sum of twenty pounds Item I give and bequeath to my mother and to Dr. Jeffreyes's Widow and her son each of them Ten pounds to buy them mourning Item I give devise and bequeath to Mrs. Judith Matthews of Acton the yearly sum of Twenty pounds during her life if she live wth my children after mine and my wife's decease or else but ten pounds per annum And I doe hereby nominate and appoint my son Robert Jefferyes sole Executor of this my last Will and Testament And I doe make order and ordaine my said Wife and my brother in law Robert Pledwell (sic) of Holyrood Amney in the County of Gloucester Esqr Doctor Jonathan Edwards] Principall of Jesus Colledge Oxon Peter Ellis of Crosnewydd in the County of Denbigh Esqr and the said Thomas Gardner Trustees of this my Will And I nominate my said Wife together with the said Peter Ellis Esqr and the said Thomas Gardner to be guardians to my said Executor Robert Jeffreys and to my said daughters Elizabeth Margaret and Frances until they severally attaine the age of one and twenty yeares or bee married In witness whereof o have to this my last Will sett my hand and seal the Iay and year first above written

Griffith Jeffreys

Signed sealed and published in presence of us

Tho Bradshaw—William Beavan

Jonath Stanton—Edward Williams

Tricesimo die mensis Maii an'o dom' mill'mo sexcemno nonagesimo sexto emanavit Com'o Dnoe Dorotheœ Jeffreys viduœ Petro Ellis Armiger et Thomœ Gardner Gen. gardianis sive tutoribus Testamentariis in Testemno nominatis Dni Griffith Jeffreys Militis defuncti habentis &c Ad administrand bona jura et credita dioti defuncti juxta tenorem et effectum Testmi ipsius defci in usum et beneficium et donec et quosque Robtus Jeffrevs Ar minor filius dioti defuncti et Executor in d'c'o Testamento nominatus vicesimum primum oetatis suœ ann compleverit de bene et fideliter administrando eadem ad Sancta Dei evangelici (vigore Comconis juratis)"

FARTHINGS.—How is it that farthings are not used to any extent—if indeed at all—in our district? I saw a couple of years ago in the newspapers that in a midland town a tradesman had been robbed of a bag containing £3 worth of them, bright from the mint, which it is supposed the rogues mistook for sovereigns! This was in a town rather smaller than Oswestry. And we know that in larger places, and in other counties, farthings are quite a common currency. Are they ever used on the borders?
H. B.

WORMWOOD IN MONTGOMERYSHIRE.— In the Rev. J. Evans's Welsh Tour, published in 1800, which was mainly a botanical trip. the author says, speaking of *Buttington*, " By the roadside grows in great abundance the Artemisia Absinthium. It is used by the country people instead of hops, and has the peculiar property of destroying acesency in beer, grown hard for want of them. A property mentioned by Dr. Stokes, renders this a valuable plant. The leaves steeped in boiling water, and repeatedly applied to a recent bruise, remove the pain, and prevent the swelling and discoloration of the part." The use of " wormwood tea," I believe, was once rather popular with old ladies ; do the good folks of Buttington still use it for the stronger beverage? TELL.

AN ORIGINAL CADER IDRIS GUIDE (May 26, 1880).—The *Cambrian* newspaper of the period publishes the following :—" Dec., 1810 ; died Robert Edwards, the eccentric old guide from Dolgelley to Cader Idris ; aged 90." D.J.

LLANRHAIADR-IN-CINMERCH CHURCH (June 22, 1881).—I, some time back, copied the following epitaph from a MS. Book containing inscriptions in some of the Churches in the Mold and Denbigh district :—

Here lyeth the body of Ambrose Thelwall, ninth son of Sir John Thelwall, the second of that name at Bathafern Park, born the 7th of Ja'r 1571. He was Yeoman of the Robes to Kg. James, in pension to Kg. Charles and againe Yeoman of the Robes to Prince Charles till yielding to age and troublesome times he retired to the place of his birth where having ever beene a greate lover and supporter of his family He dyed the 5th of August A° Dn'i ; 1653, and enjoys the blessing he much desired to be buried in the sepulchre of his fathers.

Your correspondent " W.A.L." does not include this inscription in the list he published. NEMO.

PORTMADOC EMBANKMENT (Mar. 23, 1881)· The following is from *The Cambrian* of Feb. 29, 1812 :— " Mr. Madocks, M.P., who has enclosed a tract of land from the sea at Tremadoc, in the county of Carnarvon, is about to try a question of great importance to the landed interest, viz., whether land so inclosed is liable to the payment of tithe? By some of the first legal authorities he is supported in his own opinion that such land, time immemorial, having had no mark of boundary at high water, must of necessity have been extra parochial, and therefore tithe free." D. J.

In two of the most popular serials there are contributions of a local interest to Oswestry readers this month. We refer to "A Wind Song," in the *Leisure Hour*, from the pen of the Rev. Alfred Norris, once resident in the town ; and "A Flower of the Field," by A. Matheson, a native of Oswestry, and the daughter of a former minister of the Old Chapel.

It is proposed to establish an Owen scholarship in connection with the University College of Wales, to celebrate the knighting of Sir Hugh Owen.

Mr. Gladstone has forwarded à letter, enclosing a gratuity of £200, to Mr. Robert Parry (Robin Ddu Eryri), the well-known Welsh bard and lecturer, in recognition of his literary services.

Mr. Morgan Owen, H. M. Inspector, has been examining the school-management papers of students at the end of their second year's training. On the whole he is very well pleased, but some of our future school teachers at present supply more entertainment than instruction as the result of their studies. For example, Mr. Owen says—"On healing a case of faintness one student wrote, 'the children are to be kept *aloft ;*' another was of opinion that ' opening of doors, windows, and ventilators, with application of water, would cause the child to *survive* ;' others suggested, ' ease the clothing,' '*plash* water over the face,' ' carry child into draft and then open coat and vest,' ' a stimulant,' ' spirits and water,' ' brandy and water,' ' brandy,' ' aromatic vinegar,' ' tickling the feet, " wine,' ' vinegar,' ' salvolatile,' ' salts of ammonia,' ' hartshorn,' ' Eau de Cologne,' ' vinaigrette,' ' quinine,' ' take a mouthful of water *inwardly*,' 'put his feet in hot water,' ' the lines of the forehead should be stroked with a camel's hair brush, dipped in water.' One student wrote, 'a volcano generally being a mountain ;' another, ' tides were just water trying to fall to the moon.' One student compared the teacher to ' a light in the *valley*,' (not on the hill-top) ; another sagely observed, 'To ordinary people, to say that a teacher should be honest, truthful, appears superfluous.' All that I can say to that is, 'would that it were so.' Another stated that the pupil imitated the teacher because what is 'sauce for the goose is sauce for the gander ;' and another said that he did so because 'as the old cock crows the young one learns ;' he further described this remark as ' a good old weighty Scotch proverb.'"

A WELSH SCULPTOR.—We understand that Mr. James Milo Griffiths, the successful designer and sculptor of the memorial drinking fountain to the late Mr. Henry Whitmore, which Lord Forester has kindly consented to unveil at Bridgnorth on Thursday, the 20th of October, at half-past two o'clock in the afternoon, is a native of Wales, and speaks the ancient language of his country. The figure of "Sabrina," which stands on a pedestal above the fountain, is said by those who have seen it to be of great merit as a work of art. Mr. J. Milo Griffiths's medallion portrait of the late Mr. Henry Whitmore, which will appear on the fountain, is said to be an admirable likeness. Many will no doubt be interested to attend the unveiling of this memorial, which, for artistic value, originality, and beauty of design, will probably not be surpassed by any drinking fountain in England.

THE WYNNE MEMORIAL CHURCH.—A week ago we recorded the ceremony of laying the foundation of the new church to be erected at Bryncrug, in memory of the late Mr. W. W. E. Wynne of Peniarth ; and this week we give a complete list of the subscriptions received up to the present time. As we have more than once reminded our readers, it was the earnest wish of the deceased gentleman that a church should be erected at Bryncrug, and shortly before his death he had inspected and approved plans for the building. The whole sum required is not a very large one—as sums go in church building and restoration now-a-days—but the district is poor, and the funds must come from well-wishers of the Church elsewhere, and the late Mr. Wynne's friends and admirers. These make up a very large class, for wherever Mr. Wynne was known he was respected and loved. A sovereign given now will be worth more than two at a future period, for, as one deeply interested in the good work very truly says, in a letter lying before us as we write :—"There are many little improvements that might be made when building, which cannot be done afterwards." In the list of subscribers we see some life-long friends of Mr. Wynne's, but there are also many who knew him whose names, so far, are not included. None need hesitate to send a subscription because they can only afford a small one; for sums as low as 10s. are acknowledged; and, we doubt not, it is only the want of a direct appeal that has hitherto prevented many names being added to the list of donors. Amongst the latest amounts acknowledged are the profits of the Machynlleth Bazaar, £322 15s. 7d., which included £100, the proceeds of the stall of Sarah Lady Harlech.—*Oswestry Advertizer.*

The new instalment of the *Montgomeryshire Collections* of the Powysland Club—which forms the second part of the fourteenth volume—contains much that will interest the subscribers; and one paper, we are glad to say, others besides members will be able to secure at a moderate cost. We refer to one entitled "Description of the Armorial Insignia of the Vaughans of Llwydiarth," illustrated by some eighteen pages of arms, the history of which is interesting. They formerly surrounded the family pew in Llanfihangel Church, but of late years have been stowed away, until, in 1870 Sir Watkin Williams Wynn sent them for exhibition to the annual meeting of the Powys-land Club. They were arranged and set in order by Mr. Morris C. Jones, F.S.A., and the Rev. W. V. Lloyd, chaplain to the Duke of Edinburgh (the hon. secs. of the Club), and afterwards found a permanent resting place in the Wynnstay Chapel. These panels have been carefully copied by Mr. T. W. Hancock, and lithographed for the *Collections*, and an interesting paper by Mr. Lloyd accompanies them. A limited number of the paper and pictures has been printed, the profits arising from the sale of which will be devoted to an "Illustration Fund." Copies of the work, 5s. each, may be had from the hon. secs., or from Woodall and Venables, Oswestry.

BREAKING OF THE MERES.—Our columns have on several occasions contained reports and opinions on this subject. The latest contribution to the question is the following from the pen of Mr. Townshend Mainwaring of Galltfaenan :— As the phenomenon of the "Breaking of the Meres" is attracting attention in the minds of scientific men, will you allow me, no scientific man, to suggest a solution. Some weeks ago, whilst searching for medicinal waters not far from Corwen, a farmer took me to a spring at which he and his labourers had drunk during the harvest, and were all violently purged. I sent a two-gallon jar of the water to an eminent firm of chemists in Liverpool, and received the analysis of their analyst. I ought to state that the water had been detained for some days at a goods station, so that when it reached the analytical chemist it was fetid. He accordingly reported, "This sample of water is slightly turbid, and has a most disgusting smell of sewage," &c. As it was totally impossible that any sewage could have got into the water, I asked a learned geological professor for his opinion, which was that the water came off vegetable matter, and that, as it had been corked up for some days, carburetted hydrogen had been generated, as it would be, he said, if the water of Ellesmere Mere, in the "flowering" season, was corked up for some days. I beg to suggest to the Caradoc Field Club to make the experiment.

5

THE POWYS-LAND CLUB.

The fourteenth annual meeting of the members of the Powys-Land Club was held at their Museum, Welshpool, on Thursday afternoon.

The chair was taken by the Earl of Powis, the President of the Club, and amongst those present were—Mr. and Mrs. Lewis Lewis and family, Newtown Hall, Mr. T. Sturkey, Rev. Joshua Biggs, Welshpool, Rev. R. Smith, Llanymynech, Rev. D. P. Lewis, Llandrinio, Rev. A. Field, Pool Quay, Miss Rownson, Mr. P. A. Beck, Mr. and Mrs. A. Howell, Mr. Chas. E. Howell, Mr. M. W. Howell, Mr. J. Williams, Buttington, Mr. Edward Jones, Town Clerk, Welshpool, Rev. D. R. Thomas, Meifod, Rev. Edward Robinson, Penrhos, Mr. Chas. W. Williams Wynn, Coedymaen, Mr. R. J. Harrison, Caerhowell, Captain Mytton, Misses Mytton, Captain J. Jones, R.N., Hon. Colonel William Herbert and Mrs. Herbert, Mr. Hugh Montgomery and Lady Charlotte and Misses Montgomery, Rev. R. J. Roberts, Buttington, Captain Pryce, Cyfronydd, Mr. A. H. Pryce, Cyfronydd, Mrs. Lovell and Misses Johnson, Llanerchydol, Mr. and Mrs. William Parker, Welshpool, Miss Nona Roberts, Cheltenham, Mr. William Fisher, Maesfron, Mr. D. P. Owen, Welshpool, Mr. Thos. Savin, Oswestry, Mr. W. H. G. Weaver, Oswestry, Rev. J. Lewis, Ford, Rev. J. Mackintosh, Llanerfyl, Mr. M. P. Jones and Mrs. M. P. Jones, Liverpool, Mr. T. Simpson Jones, London, Mr. Morris C. Jones, Hon. Sec., Mrs. and Miss Morris C. Jones, Gungrog.

The CHAIRMAN, in opening the proceedings, said—I will now request the Secretary to read the report for the year.

The report was then read as follows :—

The Committee, although they have little that is new to communicate, have pleasure in reporting the continued prosperity of the club. The number of members, notwithstanding the depression of the times, has been maintained. Four members have been removed by death and five have resigned, but on the other hand ten new members have joined the club including an important public library in London, and a gentleman in Washington, both of whom have taken complete sets of the Montgomeryshire Collections. The Committee have to deplore the loss by death of the following members, viz : Edward Breese, Esq., F.S.A., Miss Jane Davies, John Sides Davies, Esq., and the Rev. Canon Robert Williams, of Culmington. The balance in the hands of the Honorary Treasurer has increased from £42 9s. 3d to £104 2s. 6d. The new room added to the Museum has provided considerable additional accommodation. This has enabled much progress to be made in the re-arrangement of the objects in the Museum. The resolutions passed at the last annual meeting of the Club were communicated to the Cambrian Archæological Association, but no definite reply has been received from that Society. The literary work of the Club has proceeded satisfactorily. The principal feature of the last part of the "Montgomeryshire Collections" is the numerous plates with which it is illustrated. A large proportion of these illustrations have been provided at the cost of members of the Club interested in the articles illustrated, and the thanks of the Club are due to them for their generosity and public spirit. The scheme, which has long been in contemplation, for reprinting the portion of Lewys Dwnn's Heraldic Visitations relating to Montgomeryshire, is again occupying attention and will, it is hoped, soon be commenced. The collections of books and objects of antiquity and natural history are constantly receiving additions, and are becoming of an importance which is recognized and appreciated by all strangers who visit the museum. Still the institution is only in its infancy and it is hoped that it will ultimately become of more extensive interest. The aid o members of the Club is earnestly invited to forward the attainment o that result.

43

His Lordship said he would next request Mr. Beck, the Treasurer, to read an abstract of the financial report.

Mr. P. A. Beck said that the accounts for the year ending October 1st showed a balance in hand at the beginning of the year of £24 9s. 3d., receipts £236 9s. 9d., payments £174 16s. 7d., balance in hand £104 2s. 5d.

The Chairman then said : Ladies and Gentlemen, I will now move that the report which has just been read, together with the statement of accounts, be approved and adopted. In the present year we have not had anything of so stirring a character to record as the visit in recent years of the Cambrian Archæological Association, though that visit, by keeping us in communication with the larger body, will have had its advantages in making Welshmen in the distant parts of the Principality take an interest in and become better acquainted with our local history, and the increasing collection which we have in a few years gathered together in this building. If we look abroad this year, we find that one very remarkable antiquarian discovery has taken place. I refer to those tombs of ancient Egyptian kings recently discovered in Egypt. The inscriptions which have been found on the mummies which have been for us, after the lapse of two thousand years, again brought to light, have already been partially deciphered, and promise to afford very great and interesting additions to our knowledge of the various and bewildering dynasties of Egyptian kings, some of these inscriptions already showing that they date from the time when the Israelites were in Egypt, or even from still earlier periods. I am afraid that our antiquarian knowledge is in that case, as in many others, purchased at the expense of not regarding much the quiet of the tomb, though perhaps the remains of those Egyptian kings and of those inscriptions will be more likely to preserve their immortality in the British Museum than in the hands of the plunderers of those tombs. But in general, I fear, we antiquaries are as likely to be trusted among the tombs as a juvenile vivisectionist is with a lap dog. (Laughter.) If, passing from those greater antiquities, we may come to resuscitate the relics of an era which is modern as compared with that era of Egypt—although as Cambrians we are bound to consider it old—you will see in the last number of the *Montgomeryshire Collections* an interesting account of the foundations and dimensions of an ancient church or cell at Meifod, which has been discovered when they were digging earth for foundations for a chapel. I hope the fact of the chapel rising on the ruins of the church is not symbolic of speedy Disestablishment. (Laughter.) The Library referred to in the report as having taken a complete set of our publications is that of the learned Society of the Inner Temple, which shows that the lawyers there are interested in keeping up information as to the historical changes which have taken place both in Society and territorially within the kingdom. For the continued prosperity of this Society we are very much indebted to our worthy Secretary, Mr. Morris Jones, who takes the greatest interest and the greatest share in its practical management. (Cheers.) In addition to his achievements in persuading donors to give a large number of interesting objects which we see around us, and to the fact that he has been busily engaged during the last few years in gradually extending the size of the Museum, we may point to the achievements of our ancestors which he has recorded on the upper part of the wall. (Hear, hear.) I beg to move that the report and balance sheet be approved and adopted, and that it be printed and circulated amongst the members.

This was seconded by Mr. C. W. Williams Wynn and carried. Other speeches followed.

NOTES.

"BYE-GONES."—The *Globe* of Oct. 10 takes us to task for so spelling the title of our column. It says, "Why is 'By-gones' spelt with an 'e'? It ought to be known that the final 'e' is misplaced here as it is in 'by-the-by,' 'by-law,' and 'by-way.' It is retained in 'Good bye,' as this is a contraction of 'God be with ye.'" We are fully aware of the force of what the writer says, and when we first adopted the title—ten years ago—did not do so without consideration. But it appeared to us that *Bye-gones* was not inappropriate for a column that published chiefly matters of an age when such a spelling of the word was common ; besides, on a Title-page it unquestionably looks better than the modern spelling *By-gones* would do !—Ed.

QUERIES.

ANTIQUITIES AT CONDOVER HALL.—The *Annual Register* for 1767, says, under its June Chronicle : —"As some workmen were employed in pulling down part of Condover Hall, near Shrewsbury, they found, in removing some stones in the vault, an iron box of about 20 in. long, and 14 in. broad, in which were contained several very curious ancient medals, together with a brass statue, about 16 in. high, which is supposed to be the statue of some heathen god." Is this statue still in existence, and what did it turn out to be? Nemo.

SKEANES.—In Leycester's *Civill Warres* of England there is the following passage :—" The Lord Byron having a strong and potent Army, marched up to the Nantwich, and besieged it, the which the noble Sir William Brereton understanding the greatness of his strength sent to Sir Thomas Fairfax for help to raise the siege, which noble Sir Thomas did no sooner heare of, but did hasten up to Sir William Brereton, who when they were joyned, marched up to the Lord Byron, and suddenly fell upon him, and after a hot fight raised the siege and routed him, took 152 Knights and Gentlemen, 126 Commanders, 160 common soldiers, 120 Irish women with long skeanes. Feb. 14th, 1644." What implement of war was the "long skeane" with which these amazons were armed? Norman.

[Skeen, A. S., Sword.—Ed.]

REPLIES.

OSWESTRY CORPORATION PLATE (Feb. 17, 1875.)—In *Bye-gones*, Nov. 11, 1874, I gave a list of the plate, &c., belonging to the Corporation, and which is handed over year by year into the custody of each succeeding mayor. Amongst the articles enumerated were "Two Silver gilt Maces." By a Corporation account I find that the Mayor of 1722, Mr. Richard Maurice, charged the Corporation with no less a sum than £8 10s. 0d. for "makeing and beautyfying the maces, with tenn ounces of additional silver ;" and on account of which he got into trouble, as I intend in a future contribution to show. In looking over the Corporation Books (which, thanks to Mr. Stanley Leighton, have now been put in order and rendered easy for reference), I have come across other entries in connection with the "Insignia." One of the Corporation belongings is a set of "Four Silver Candlesticks ; in a mahogany box ; crest a griffin." Whose gift this was the list did not inform us, but under date of Oct. 2, 1795, when Arthur Davies, Esq., was mayor, and Richard Morrice, Esq., his deputy, there is the following entry of a resolution passed by the Council :—

"It being this day reported that George Venables of Liverpool Esquire hath made a present of two pair of very handsome Silver Candlesticks to the Corporation.

"Resolved that the thanks of this Common Hall be given to Mr. Venables and a copy of this Resolution signed by the Town Clerk transmitted to him."

The minutes are signed by Arthur Davies, mayor, James Edwards, coroner (i.e. Ex-Mayor), Richard Jones, Richard Morrice, John Lloyd, E. W. Evans, Thomas Howell, Richard Salisbury, Lewis Jones, John Gibbons, W. V. Morris, Thomas Lovett, Richard Bickerton, and John Croxon.

Another gift in the list was that of a "Silver Punch Ladle by the Honour'd Sir Watkin Williams Wynn, in 1740." In the "Burgess Book" amongst the entries of election is introduced the following receipt :—

"Rec'd 5th Sep. 1740 of the Hon'd Watkin Williams Wynn, Esq., the sum of Five Pounds, two shillings and Ten pence halfpenny for a Silver punch Ladle, p'r me C. WICKSTEAD."

I presume Oswestry Tradesmen were not asked to give "discount" in those days, as the account was paid to the uttermost farthing ! Mr. Wickstead has been mentioned in this column (May 19, 1880), as a Watchmaker in the town, who was made a burgess in 1732. It will be observed that the "Honoured Watkin Williams Wynn," is titled "Esquire" in the document just quoted. When Dr. Tomkies (the mayor of 1740) rendered the financial account of his stewardship, he enters into his account, "To Sir Watkin Williams's man that brought the punch Ladle given to the Corporation, 5s." It was during that year the first "Sir Watkin" got his title, and he inherited it from his father Sir William Williams of Llanvorda, the son of the Speaker. He was more often called "Sir Watkin Williams" than Sir Watkin Williams Wynn."

Another entry in the list was that of a "Silver Tureen, the gift of Noel Hill, Esq." This was really a race cup won by a horse of Mr. Hill's ; the prize being the gift of Sir Watkin in 1777. Mr. Noel Hill was not elected Mayor until 1779, but the gift to the Corporation was probably made on account of his election as a Burgess in 1777, although he was not sworn into office until he became a Town Councillor a year later. His election as Burgess is thus recorded :—

"At an Assembly of a full House this fifth day of July 1777, Noel Hill of Tern in the county of Salop Esquire was unanimously elected a Burgess of the said Town provided the Lord of the Manor approves of such Election."

A further entry records the thanks of the Corporation for the gift, thus :—

"Resolved that the thanks of the Body Corporate be given to Noel Hill, Esq., for his magnificent present of a silver cup given to this Corporation ; and that ffra's Chambre, Esq., Mayor, William Griffiths, Esq., coroner [i.e., ex-mayor], Robert Lloyd, Esq., William Griffiths, and John Edwards, gentlemen ; aldermen of the said Town Do wait of Mr. Hill to know where he will be pleased to receive an address of thanks.—HERBERT."

"Herbert," the Town Clerk of the period, was a "Barrister at Law."

I hope to compile a more complete list of Corporation officers than that given in *Bye-gones*, 1874; and publish several interesting items from the Corporation Books ; but before doing so await the completion of Mr. Stanley Leighton's interesting documents in the *Transactions* of the Shropshire Archæological Society.　　　　JARCO.

CURRENT NOTES.

Mr. John Rhys, Professor of Celtic at Oxford, has been elected Fellow of Jesus College.

THE TOWYN SLATE TABLET.—Mr. Park Harrison has finished his "Descriptive Account of the Towyn Slate Tablet," with plates, and Mr. Quaritch will publish it. A number of identifications are given of the figures incised upon the relic.

DEATH OF THE ROMAN CATHOLIC BISHOP OF SHREWS-BURY.—The Right Rev. James Brown, D.D., Roman Catholic Bishop of Shrewsbury, died on Friday afternoon. He had been in failing health for some time, although only within the last few days had he been confined to his house. The deceased bishop was highly respected by both Protestants and Roman Catholics. He had held the bishopric for over a quarter of a century.

OPENING OF A NEW CHURCH AT LLAWRYGLYN.

The Bishop of Bangor opened a new church at Llawryglyn on Thursday, and the event attracted a large number of visitors from various parts of the county to the secluded spot in the valley of the Traunon known by this name. The following is the architect's description of the building :—The church consists of nave 43.0 x 20.0, chancel 17.0 x 20.0, with vestry at S.E. corner 10.0 x 9.0; and porch 7.6 x 7.6, with tower over N.E. corner. It is built on a site given by Mr. Nicholas Bennett of Glan'rafon (who also is one of the largest subscribers, and has taken a great interest in its erection) of local grey stone, with Cefn freestone dressings to the angles, windows, and coping, forming a good contrast with the native stone. The roof is open timbered, and covered with Machynlleth slates ; the seats are of pitch pine varnished. The aisle and chancel are laid with ornamental encaustic tiles. The tower is of three stages—porch, ringing chamber, and belfry, the last is surmounted with handsome open oak tracery framing, with ornamental weather louvres, capped with gilded vane. The pulpit, which is old oak, has carved tracery panels, and is much admired, was the gift of Mrs. Joseph Barrows of Birmingham, who has been a liberal subscriber besides. The style of the church is late decorated Gothic, and forms quite a feature in the valley. The east window is of three lights, with the side ones filled with Cathedral tinted glass, in seven tints. The architects are Messrs. Jones and Parke of Newtown ; the builder is Mr. E. Williams of Newtown.

We have been requested to publish the following englyn :—

Diwrnod i wneuthur dernyn—o waith da,
　Bendith Duw a'i canlyn ;
　Heddyw codir i Dduw-ddyn
　Allor gwlad yn Llawryglyn.　　　　CEIRIOG.

THE LATE REV. KNYVETT LEIGHTON.—The Rev. Francis Knyvett Leighton, D.D., Warden of All Souls, Oxford, who died at his residence on Thursday last, after a long illness, was the only surviving son of the late Col. Francis Knyvett Leighton of Bauseley, Montgomeryshire, by the Hon. Louisa Anne, fourth daughter of St. Leger, 1st Viscount Doneraile. He was born in 1806, succeeded to the Bauseley estate in 1834, married in 1843, Catherine, second daughter of the Hon. and Rev. James St. Leger, who survives him, and by whom he had, with other issue, Charles Arthur Baldwin Knyvett, born in 1854. The deceased gentleman was educated at Rugby and Magdalen College, Oxon, afterwards Fellow of All Souls. In 1835, he was appointed Vicar of St. Chad's, Shrewsbury, in 1836, Vicar of Great Ilford, Essex, and in 1841, Rector of

Harpsden, Oxon. In 1858, he was elected Warden of All Souls in succession to Mr. Sneyd, and became at the same time Rector of Lockinge, which preferment has hitherto been annexed to the Wardenship, but is in future to be separated from it. In 1868, he was appointed to a Residentiary Canonry at Westminster, which preferment is rendered vacant at his demise. He was Vice-Chancellor of the University from 1866-70, in which position he was distinguished by his courtesy and hospitality. The labours of the office brought on a severe illness, from which, we believe, he never completely recovered. Dr. Leighton was an intimate friend of Bishop Wilberforce, and his house was that Bishop's head-quarters in Oxford. Dr. Leighton was distinguished by an amiable and refined, but genial courtesy. He was a good scholar of the old-fashioned type, enjoyed a quotation from a classical author, and appreciated the scholarship of others.

UNIVERSITY HONOURS.—Mr. Percy Ewing Matheson, B.A., scholar of Balliol College, son of the late Rev. James Matheson, at one time minister of the Old Chapel, Oswestry, has been elected to the vacant open fellowship at New College, Oxford, out of twelve candidates, whose examination commenced on Oct. the 4th. The election is made subject to the usual conditions imposed by the Commissioners. Mr. Matheson obtained a first-class at the first public Classical Examination in 1878, and a first at the final Classical Examination in 1881.

THE CONNECTION OF THE BROGYNTYN
FAMILY WITH OSWESTRY.

Lord Harlech—in his address of thanks to the Oswestry deputation last week, who went to Brogyntyn with congratulatory messages on the marriage of the son and heir—sketched very briefly the connection of his family with the town from the time of Oeni de Porkinton, who owned Castell Brogyntyn in the twelfth century, down to Major Ormsby Gore, who represented North Shropshire from 1835 to 1857. The subject just now being of more than usual interest, I will endeavour, as briefly as possible, to narrate sundry details connected with the relationships that have for many long years existed between the family of Porkington, or (as it is now properly called) Brogyntyn, and the Borough of Oswestry.

In 1673 Charles the Second granted Oswestry a new charter, under the provisions of which we had Mayors instead of Bailiffs. A new charter was deemed necessary on the ground that Oswestry during the late wars had suffered greatly from the "usurping powers," and (as Mr. Stanley Leighton has told us in the Shrop. Arch. Trans.) the petition asked that the "popularitie be excluded from the election of Mayor, Aldermen, and Common Council for the prevention of blood shedding and other great disorders." Amongst the "names of countrey gent' p'sons of note and qualitie" petitioning and aiding by their purse, is given the name of "William Owen, Esq.," of Porkington. He never seems to have become a member of the Council; indeed he did not live more than four or five years after it was first elected; but almost as soon as the new Corporation had entered into its teens we find it congratulating itself on the acquisition of the son of William Owen, and head of the house of Porkington, as its chief officer. Here is the entry—which I copy from the original—recording the fact:—

"Octob' the j't 1686. This Day the worthy S'r Robert Owen was unanimously Elected & chosen May'r of this Towne & Borough for the yeare ensueinge."

Sir Robert Owen came from a famous stock. His grandfather, Colonel Sir John Owen, Knight, was the well known defender of Conway Castle when attacked by the Roundheads, and to whom Lord Capel the day before he was executed presented his sword, knowing that in such custody it would be worn with honour. This sword, which for many years was kept at Porkington Cottage, is now at Brogyntyn. Sir Robert served the office of Mayor of Oswestry a second time, and died soon after, and was buried at Selattyn where a monument thus records his virtues:—

H. S. E.
Robertus Owen de Porkington, Eques auratus;
Ex antiquo Hwfæ ap Cynddelw, et Regio Oeni
Gwyneth stemmate oriundus.
Probitate et fortitudine clarus,
Nulli infestus,
Plurimis amicus,
Bonis omnibus carus.
Dum vixit amatus,
Desideratus dum obiit,
3tito Calendarum Aprilis
MDCXCVIII

Sir Robert was married to the eldest daughter and heiress of Owen Wynne of Glyn, Co. Merioneth, and they had issue several children, one of whom, William Owen, the heir, became Mayor of Oswestry in 1730. In those days it was usual for the retiring Mayor to "return" the names of three of the Council from which to choose his successor in office, and the one that obtained the "majority of voices" was elected. The parties "returned" in Oct. 1730, were "William Owen, Esq., Edward Williams, Esq., and John Owen, Esq." The latter was a younger brother of the one chosen. He had been elected a town councillor a year or two earlier, as I find by the following entry:—

"John Owen of Porkington, Esq'r was the sworne common councell of y'e Towne of Oswestry.—PARRY, Town Clerk."

This entry is dated 3 Oct. 1729, and at the same meeting "Charles Lloyd, Esq., of Drenewith" was elected Mayor. Mr. John Owen never occupied the chief office, and died, unmarried, in 1732, at the age of 40. Mr. William Owen, elected Mayor in 1730, appointed Alderman Thomas Tomkies, surgeon (who had been Mayor in 1708-9) as his deputy, so he probably did not attend to municipal matters very much himself. This, we may say, was the usual course: a deputy was always chosen when the Mayor was a country gentleman.

William Owen, Esq., died in 1768, at the age of 79, and was succeeded at Porkington by Robert Godolphin Owen. This member of the family was elected Mayor of Oswestry in 1772, and appointed John Edwards, mercer (who had been Mayor in 1763), as his deputy. Mr. R. G. Owen became Alderman in 1789. He died unmarried 1792, aged 59, and was buried at Llangollen. He was the last of the Owens, and his sister, who by his death became the heiress, married Owen Ormsby of Willow Brook, Co. Sligo, Esq.

The Owens first became acquainted with Porkington in the sixteenth century by the marriage of John Owen with the heiress Ellen Maurice, granddaughter of Sir William Maurice of Clenenney—the friend of James the First's—of whom much has appeared in Bye-gones, from the Brogyntyn MSS. She was married secondly to the Hon. Sir Francis Eure, Lord President of the Marches, and died in 1626. By her will she founded the Alms Houses in Willow-street, Oswestry.

The name of Owen Ormsby has been handed down to us in a military as well as a civic connection in our local institutions. He was elected to the office of Common Councillor in 1793, and sworn Mayor in 1796. Alderman Richard Morrice was at the same time appointed his Deputy. I am not quite sure who the latter was: he more than once served as Deputy Mayor, and was probably the same man who was mayor in 1767. In his military capacity Mr. Ormsby succeeded John Mytton of Halston, Esq., in command of the Oswestry Rangers, and on November 14, 1799, entertained the company to a banquet at Porkington to inaugurate the event. He died in 1804, leaving an only child—a daughter—who became the wife of William Gore, Esq., who descended from a common ancestor with the Earls of Arran and Earls of Ross. He took the additional surname of Ormsby, and was the last of the Porkington family who served the office of Mayor of Oswestry—being elected in 1823; ten years before the passing of the Municipal Corporations Bill, since which time our Mayors have all been men more intimately connected with the Borough.

I am aware that my sketch is bald and prosy, but my object has been to supply details, not to pass eulogiums. Such a course would be quite superfluous after the enthusiastic proceedings of last week. "The words of Mercury are harsh after the songs of Apollo."　　　　Jarco.

OCTOBER 26, 1881.

NOTES.

LLANSANFRAYDE GLAN KEIRIOG (June 2, 1880.)—The following is a further record from the old parish books :—

Att a vestree for the said parish the 5 day of October 1741.

Ordered that all the Glass windows about and belonging to the said Church be put in sufficient repaire, on or before the last day of this month.

That a new common prayer booke be bought forthwith for the use of the Church, and the old one sold to the best bidder.

That a x x (Lewne—loan—sume?) of three pence in the pound be rast and levied towards repareing the Church and other necessaries thereunto belonging.

Hereafter ordered that every parishioner shall forfeit six pence for a forfeit upon any dog or dogs of such parishioner as shall be found in the church at divine service and the sexton upon Sunday next to give due notice hereof to the parishioners such forfeit to be given to the poore.·

Noe fforreigner to be admitted to partake of the holy sarvauce (service?) without 2d paid to the use of the poore.

Edward Maurice, Cler :
The mark of H I Howel Jones Churchwarden
The mark of D H David ab Hugh
John Humphreys
John Jones
Peter Maurice.
The Glyn.　　　　　　　　　　　　　　T.A.H.

QUERIES.

ELIJAH WARING was the author of *Recollections of Iolo Morganwg*. Who was Mr. Waring, and when and where did he die?　　　　　　　　　　　　D.J.

TLWS OWAIN CYVEILIOG.—Edward Lhuid, in the *Philosophical Transactions*, 1720, speaks of some crystals, cut like a lottery-ball, and perforated, of which our ancestors made themselves beads, for want of more precious stones. "One of them," he adds, "was lately given me (set in copper with a little handle to it) by the name of Tlws Owen Kyveiliog, i.e., Owen of Cyveiliog's Jewel; so called because found in an old *Crig* (Crug?) or barrow." Is this crystal ball known to be still in existence? And if so, where is it to be seen?　　　　　　H.W.L.

FFYNON ELIAN (Aug. 31, 1881).—Mr. Cliffe—usually so well informed—was certainly wrong in placing the "cursing well" at Llanelian in Anglesey; or in describing people as "turning round" in one anywhere. It was a "semi-circular box, 6ft. long, 3ft. wide, and 4ft. high," in the cloister of the church, in which people used to decide their fate by attempting to turn. The well there was only used to bathe in to ensure blessings—but these blessings were not secured unless after the bath a sum of money was deposited in St. Elian's Chest within the church. The Llanelian in question is two miles from Amlwch.　　　　　　　　　　　　　　　　J.?.R.

THE YOUNG ROSCIUS (July 9, 1879).—This precocious juvenile—who lived to be ninety—has many times figured in your pages, but I think you have never stated that he took his final leave of the stage on July 4, 1808, in the character of Young Norval, at Stratford-on-Avon. The authority for which is the *Gents: Mag:* of the period.　　　　　　　　　　　　　　　　Nemo.

A RUABON CONJUROR (Mar. 19, 1879).—At this date "J.?.R." called attention to a Chap book called *The Conjuror of Rhuabon*. The following notice of his death was published in the *Sporting Magazine* of Oct. 1806 :—Lately died in the parish of Rhuabon, in Wales, at an advanced age, John Roberts, better known by the appellation of Mochyn-y-Nant, or Pig of the Brook. Mochyn was conjuror and fortune-teller to a great part of the Principality, and his fame extended far into Cheshire and Shropshire. He professed to have attained his science in Egypt, though he was never beyond his parish bounds. He was continually resorted to for the recovery of strayed linen, poultry, hatchets, and asses; even his name served to make rogues observe the rules of honesty. When he could not mark out infallibly the offender, he still was able to afflict him with any infirmity or disease the injured party should like : agues, rheumatism, and St. Vitus's dance were entirely at his command, and dealt out by him in the most liberal manner. In fortune telling he no less excelled : no swain or maiden ever applied in vain ; he could not only create love in the human breast, but also chill it with aversion and disdain. For these purposes he gave, or rather sold, charms couched in hieroglyphic characters, which were also in request to insure success in any enterprize—a boat race or a cock fight. Such was the Pig of the Brook. Rogues will rejoice in his death, whilst the credulous and superstitious will lament until his place is supplied by some one equally gifted and imposing.
　　　　　　　　　　　　　　　　　　　　　D.J.

CURRENT NOTES.

At the height of the gale on the 14th a number of swallows were seen flying about the trees on the Trefonen Road, near Oswestry.

The memorial in honour of the late Mr. H. Whitmore, M.P., of Bridgnorth, was unveiled on Thursday in the presence of a large concourse of spectators. The memorial, which we have already described in our columns, consists of a drinking fountain, the base of which is of Yorkshire stone. It is situated at the junction of Station Road, West Castle Street, and Castle Hill. The medallion portrait, in front of the fountain, is regarded as an excellent likeness. At half-past two o'clock the procession started from the Town Hall, headed by the constables, followed by the Mayor, accompanied by Lord Forester, Mr. W. H. Foster, M.P., the Town Council, the County and Borough Magistracy, Mr. Hubert Smith (secretary to the Memorial Committee), &c. Upon reaching the memorial, Lord Forester and the Mayor took their seats upon a raised dais prepared for them at the side of the memorial. Lord Forester unveiled the monument, and Mr. Hubert Smith then presented it to the Mayor and Corporation and their successors in perpetuity, as a token of sincere friendship and regard for the late Mr. Whitmore.

A History of Nantwich is about to be published by Mr James Hall of Willaston, who has been collecting materials for some years, and has had the Wilbraham MS. Diary placed at his disposal.

Mr. Stanford has published a reprint of a rare and curious book by a Welshman, Jenkin Lewis, a servant of the Duke of Gloucester, son of Princess, afterwards Queen, Anne. The book is a memoir of the little Duke, who died at the age of eleven. Only 250 copies are printed.

On Friday there was buried at Wrexham one of the oldest inhabitants of that town, Charles Davies, a man of some note in local annals. Mr. Davies, who died at the age of 84, was the oldest surviving member of the set of ten Wrexham ringers who, when the Earl of Powis came of age, spent a week at Welshpool to celebrate the event on the church bells. Davies was a devoted musician. When a boy he played the fife in the militia band, and there were, it is said, few musical instruments which he did not learn to play. When very young he was apprenticed to a confectioner in Hope-street, named Roberts, who went to live to Oswestry, and took Davies with him. At this time there were a number of French prisoners in Oswestry on parole. Amongst these Davies, owing to his musical talents and military taste, soon made an extensive acquaintance. The parole of the prisoners extended about a mile along the different roads outside the town, and one day one of Davies's intimate French friends had a strong desire to go and see Oswestry races, the race course lying considerably beyond the limits of parole. Young Davies saw many difficulties in the way of his friend going as far as the racecourse. The Frenchman saw none. It appears that the words of the warning were that the French prisoners were not to "pass the post;" and on arriving at this limit the Frenchman said "I'll not pass it," and at once wrested it from the ground, and carried it on his shoulders till he returned to the spot, when he coolly replaced it, having seen the whole of the races without "passing the post." On the day of Davies's death and on that of his burial, peals were rung in honour of his memory.

A DREAM IN WALES.—The Rev. T. W. Trevor writes from Penmon Vicarage, Beaumaris, to the *Spectator* :— What explanation can be suggested for the following dream, and its attendant circumstances? I was staying with a friend, a clergyman, in south Carnarvonshire, in March, 1877, I think, and dreamt that I was one of a shooting party. One of the company shot a woodcock. When I awoke I was impressed with a very vivid recollection of my dream, and its locality, which, as it appeared to me, I had never seen before. I had no occasion to mention the dream until the evening, when the following circumstances occurred. Returning with my friend from a long walk in the neighbourhood of Madryn Park, we chanced to fall in with the squire's gamekeeper, carrying his gun on his shoulder. My friend and the keeper walked on some fifty or sixty yards in advance of me. They presently turned off the road at right angles, and disappeared from my view. When I came to the spot where they had left the road, I saw them following a path through a dingle. Though I had never been in the neighbourhood before, I felt the scene was familiar to me. I

stopped to collect my thoughts, and endeavour to reconcile the inconsistency. In a moment it flashed upon me that this was the scene of my last night's dream. I had a strange feeling of expectation ; the identity of the scene became every moment clearer and clearer ; my eyes fell on the exact spot where the woodcock of my dream had risen. I was certain the event of my dream would inevitably be re-enacted. I felt I must speak, and that there was not a moment to lose. I shouted to my friend,—"Look out ! I dreamt I shot a woodcock here last night !" My friend turned and replied,—"Did you ?" The words were hardly out of his mouth and the gun off the keeper's shoulder, I was still intently gazing on the very foot of ground, when up gets a woodcock, the woodcock of my dream, and falls to the keeper's gun, a capital snap shot. We were all not a little astonished, the keeper, moreover, remarking that he thought all the woodcocks had left the country some weeks before.

LORD HARLECH'S SPEECH AT BROGYNTYN.

Lord Harlech delivered a speech at Brogyntyn the other day, which, in its way, was a model of good speaking, and led the reader to regret there is not more of it. He referred to the early connection of the renowned Welsh chieftain, Owen Brogyntyn, with the historic house of Porkington, a fact fairly well attested, although the event took place more than six hundred years ago. The late Mr. Wynne of Peniarth, in one of his invaluable notes to Lewis Dwnn, says :—"He resided at Porkington, in Shropshire, in Welsh Brogyntyn, and (was) the owner of that place, from whence doubtless he derived his name." He was not legally entitled to bear his reputed father's name, for he was base born ; but so brave a man was he that under any name his fame would make him a commendable personage, and he had very much to do in making Porkington historic, just as the name of the place had in making him so. Bleddyn, his second son, who married Maud, daughter of Gwyn ap Gruffydd, succeeded Owen in possession, I imagine, and after him, his son, Owen ab Bleddyn, and he, we may suppose, was father to Gruffydd, who married Elin Ingram, and by whom he had a son, John Grufydd. The long stretch between this John Grufydd, and Sir John Wynn Lacon, Constable of Oswestry Castle in the reign of Henry VIII., should, if possible, be bridged over, and no one could do this better than Lord Harlech himself, if we could but induce him to turn his attention to the matter. It is becoming more and more needful that we should try to perfect the records of the period intervening between Edward I. and the close of Henry VII.'s reign, for the Anglo-British story of the epoch is full of interest, inasmuch as it was the period in which both England and Wales had in their respective ways to grow into the perfect state of independence whereby the two peoples had to secure their religious liberties.

In old records Porkington is known to be rich. The present head of the house has just given us an insight into his antiquarian turn of mind, and hence I am justified in asking Lord Harlech to perfect the Porkington story he so well commenced the other day, for it is the story of border growth and also of border fame. Even Wynnstay, in all its glory, falls far short of Brogyntyn, the home of the chief of that name, and I am persuaded that we have very much more to learn about the great owner of that place, than has, as yet, been conveyed to us in our so-called "histories."　　　　　　　　　　　　GLYNDWFRDWY.

THE BATTLE OF TRAFALGAR.

Colonel Lloyd of Aston has been kind enough to supply
s with the following letter, describing the battle of
rafalgar, of which Friday last was the 76th anniversary.
he writer was Sir Eliab Harvey, K.C.B. (afterwards
dmiral Harvey), who commanded the Téméraire, under
elson, at Trafalgar.   Sir Eliab Harvey of Rolls Park,
ssex, was the father of the late Mrs. Lloyd of Aston,
d grandfather of Colonel Lloyd, to whom Rolls Park
us descended.   The letter is addressed to the writer's
ife, "The Right Honble. Lady Louisa Harvey, Chigwell,
ssex, to be forwarded without loss of time :"

23rd October, 1805.

Téméraire in her way to Gibraltar after the action
of the 21st October, 1805.

You will, my dear, rejoice at the important events which
I am about to relate, and particularly so, as our country
ill have the greatest reason to triumph, and that I am
safe.   For two days previous to the battle our frigates and
the intermediate ships from them to the fleet had informed us of the enemy's combined force having put to
sea.   We, of course, were all anxiety and expectation.
The winds were light, and from the westward.   Lord
Nelson with his fleet made sail for Gibraltar straight, and
arrived within sight of Cape Trafalgar soon after daylight
the 20th, under the apprehension that they would have
availed themselves of the opportunity which we gave them
of passing the Gut, and proceeding to Carthagena or
Toulon.   What was our delight on seeing the signal for
the enemy to the northward, and afterwards the signal
for their being forty sail.   During the whole of the day
repeated signals were made shewing their bearing, &c., &c.,
and during the night we saw their lights, rocketts, and
false fires.   As soon as the day appeared, the 21st, we
saw their fleet, which proved to be thirty-three sail of
the line, French and Spanish ; the rest frigates, or smaller
vessels, and although we had the advantage of the wind,
and they shewed no disposition to avoid our attack, it was
noon before the action commenced, which was done according to the instructions given to us by Lord Nelson.   The
first ship in action was the Royal Sovereign, with Vice-
Admiral Collingwood's flag on board.   I did not see any
other ship engaged before Lord Nelson opened his fire on
the enemy, they having opened upon him, and from the
Santissima Trinidada, about ten minutes, as well as from
several other ships of theirs a-head of her.   The Téméraire at this time almost touched the stern of the Victory,
which station she had taken about a quarter of an hour
previous to the enemy having commenced their fire upon
the Victory, in consequence of a signal made from the
Victory.   You are to understand from this statement that
we bore down upon the enemy in two columns—the
weather column led by the Commander-in-Chief, the lee
one by Vice-Admiral Collingwood, which occasioned my
being a-stern instead of a-head of the Victory ; but Lord
Nelson had sent to me, and given me leave to lead and
break through the enemy's line, about the fourteenth ship
from the van, but afterwards made the signal referred to
above.   From this period, for two hours, we were so warmly
engaged that I can give you no other account of this part
of this most glorious day's work than what immediately
concerned the Victory or myself.   We were engaged with
the Santissima Trinidada and the other ships for, perhaps, twenty minutes or more, when for a minute or two
I ceased my fire, fearing that I might, from the thickness

of the smoke, be firing into the Victory ; but I soon saw
the Victory close on board a French ship of two decks, and
having the ship under command.   Notwithstanding, we
had suffered much in our masts and sails, &c., &c., I placed
the ship so as to give this Redoutable a most severe
dressing by raking of her fore and aft.   However, the
Victory fell on board of her, and she struck, and soon
after they came on board the Téméraire, so that the
Frenchman was exactly between the two ships, being upon
my larboard side.   Some time previous to this, finding I
could do nothing further with that ship, I had commenced
upon another ship with my larboard guns, and very soon
put her into so disabled a state that we fell on board
of her also.—(25th at night).   I soon forced her to strike,
and sent Lieutenant Kennedy, my first, with a party of
men, to secure this prize, and finding the Victory had got
clear from the Redoutable, I sent my second Lieutenant
to secure her, and order both these ships to be securely
lashed to Téméraire—the St. Anne, a Spanish three-
decker, having raked us all this time.   When the smoke
began to clear away I saw the Royal Sovereign nearly
in the place which I had seen the St. Anne in.   When, for
about half-an-hour or more I thought with us the battle
was at an end, and we had but to secure the captured
ships, and I had made a signal for a frigate to take us in
tow, when, behold, I was informed some of the enemy's
ships were coming up astern of us.   They proved to be
four French ships, apparently in good order, their intention to escape to the southward.   When they were
about three-quarters of a mile to windward they opened
their guns upon Téméraire and her prizes, and for
some time I could return no guns, but when those we
could fight with were brought to bear upon the enemy the
gentlemen thought proper to haul to a more respectable
distance, and thus towards evening with me ended this
most glorious action, and perhaps never was a ship so
circumstanced as mine, to have for more than three hours
two of the enemy's line of battle ships lashed to her, one
upon each side, in one of, if not the, most decided actions
ever fought.   Soon after the firing ceased, the Sirius, who
had bore down in obedience to my signal, came and took
the Téméraire in tow.   The Phœbe took one of the prizes
in tow, and this is all I have from my own observation
the power to mention.   At this time our object was to go
to Gibraltar, but the wind was contrary, and with almost
constant and severe gales ever since, has prevented our
getting there since.   The state of Téméraire is so bad
we have been in constant apprehension of our lives, every
sail and yard having been destroyed, and nothing but the
lower masts left standing, the rudder head almost shot off,
and is since quite gone, and lower masts all shot through and
through in many places.—(25, Saturday.)   Since Monday
we have had severe S. and S.S.W. winds, and are now
anchored off the enemy's coast, in the state above mentioned.   The weather having been so bad I could not
continue my journal.   The death of Lord Nelson I did
not know until yesterday by signal from the Defiance,
Captain Denham.   How much must our country
lament this gallant and valuable man.   We
have nothing like him to supply his place.
We anchored this morning at seven o'clock, and are not
more than four leagues from a part of the Spanish coast,
not far from Cadiz.   We can see in different bearings dis-
masted ships, five which are compleat, but were not in
the action, are supposed to be Admiral Lewis's squadron
from Gibraltar.   The Defence joined me yesterday,
but keeps under-weigh with the Phœbe frigate and two
English, one a three decker, at a distance.   The Sirius
kept me in tow for two days, but Admiral Collingwood
made her signal then to leave me, as the enemy ships were

attempting to cut some of our prizes. The Africa, the day after, Thursday, came near to us in the morning, and said nothing until the evening, when she informed me Admiral Collingwood had sent him to see me into port. I desired him to stay by the ship, but the good Captain Digby thought proper to take care of himself and made off in the night. The blowing up of the ship, I believe a Spanish one, was the most extraordinary and magnificent sight which can be conceived. We saw another explosion from a ship on fire upon the Wednesday evening, but from the distance which she was off, it was by no means the same thing. I know not when we shall get into port, we are all harassed to death, and when we do arrive at Gibraltar I fear our accommodations will be but bad.—(28th Oct.) An opportunity offers of sending my returns of killed and wounded—killed 47, badly wounded 31, slightly 45, in all 123. You must write to my sister's house, &c., &c., as I shall have no opportunity, the Scourge brig having no time to lose. I am quite well, safe at anchor three leagues from the coast of Spain, the winds constantly from the south to west. We can make no progress until a change of wind. The weather at present moderate, but ever since the battle it has been very bad, almost a constant gale of wind, with constant rain, shocking for our poor wounded. I have heard nothing how our poor Louisa goes on. Give my love to all the children. Adieu my love, how happy I shall be to see you all next month or December.

NOVEMBER 2, 1881.

NOTES.

A SINGULAR RACE.—"Saturday morning a singular race was run on the road between Redbarn and St. Alban's, one mile, between a labouring man and a Welsh girl in her pattens, when the girl won the match."—*Wood's British Gazetteer*, April 24, 1773.   T.W.H.

QUERIES.

TWM SION CATTI.—When did this work of fiction first appear, and where was it printed and published? Of the author, Mr. J. Llewellin Prichard, what is known? Any information respecting him would be acceptable.   D.J.

SONGOING.—There is a very peculiar word used about here in harvest time, termed "Songoing," by which gleaning is meant. Can any of your contributors explain the origin and derivation of this term? Wrexham.   LANDWOR.

[See Halliwell's dictionary of Provincial Words; Wilbraham's Cheshire Words, and Miss Jackson's new book on Shropshire Words.—ED.]

DAFYDD IONAWR.—Information is greatly desired concerning the *maternal* ancestry of this poet. The name of his mother was Catherine David, and she was married to Mr. John Richards of Glan y morfa, Towyn, about the year 1750. Any particulars of Catherine David's family will be valued.   OWAIN VEDDYG.

THE THELWALL FAMILY.—In a MS. volume of Welsh Pedigrees in the British Museum is the following paragraph:—"Richard Thelwall, Recorder of Ruthin, married Margaret daughter (the 'Cae Cyriog MS.' adds heiress) of John ab Edward Lloyd ab David ab John ab Ithel ab Robert Bakarn. This Richard Thelwall Houlds (sic) lands from Adam Vardon Baron Llanbedr." The "Cae Cyriog MS." has "John ab Richard ab Ithel," and says nothing of Robert but mentions Edward as then

living, and a son of Richard and Margaret. Will some reader of *Bye-gones* say : 1. When a Richard Thelwall was Recorder of Ruthin? 2. To which branch of the numerous family of Thelwall did he belong? 3. Of what family was his wife Margaret? The "Cae Cyriog MS.?" states that she was daughter of John ab Edward Lloyd o *Lanbedr*." 4. Who was Robert Bakarn? and 5. Who can Adam Vardon have been, and how was he "Baron Llanbedr"?   H.W.L.

REPLIES.

CHURCH LEWN AT OSWESTRY (June 8, 1881).—Miss Jackson, in the *Shropshire Word Book*, defines "Lewn" to be a Church rate, but that it meant more than this in Oswestry is shewn by the following entry from the record of the Borough Quarter Sessions in 1765 :—"Ordered that a Lewu of three pence by the pound rate be assessed & laid upon the inhabitants of the said Town to repair the Roads."   JARCO.

LODOWICK LLOYD (Apr. 1, 1874).—In the volume of "Additional MSS." in the British Museum known as "Y Melynhi" is a poem subscribed by Lodowick Lloyd entitled "The most ancient and comendable sweet sonet of Britishe Sidanen, applied by a courtier to the princelye praise of the queenes maiestie. To the wealthe not of Sidanen." As may be surmised from the title, the poem is filled with fulsome adulation of the beldame Queen.   H.W.L.

THE FIGARO IN WALES (Oct. 5, 1881).—I have a copy of this very scarce paper, which was issued in a monthly sheet of four folio pages. The first number appeared in March, 1835 ; the last in January, 1836 ; eleven numbers in all. But in February 1836 another sheet was issued, called *Philo-Figaro*, and I think no more under that title. My copy came to me from the late Dr. Owen Owen Roberts of Bangor, and he said it was perfect. He should know, for he had the principal hand in getting it up, chiefly with the View of showing up the parsons, and the way in which they were said to have neglected their public duties. Some clergymen laughed very heartily over its contents, others were very angry ; the latter predominating undoubtedly, although they might have pretended otherwise to treat the whole thing as so much nonsense. The paper was printed and published by Robert Jones at the Albion Office, Friars' Place, Bangor.   GLADWYN.

THE LATE LORD HANMER, (July 13, 1881). The question as to when Lord Hanmer became a Baronet is a very simple one, although it requires a rather categorical answer. The late Lord Hanmer succeeded his grandfather, Sir Thomas Hanmer, as third Baronet in 1828. His father, who died Nov. 1818, ten years earlier, was the Lieut. Col. Hanmer referred to. He was the heir to the Baronetcy, but dying in his father's life time, his eldest son, John (the late lord) stepped into his shoes. His (Col. Hanmer's) widow resided at Whitehall, Shrewsbury, with her family, for many years after her husband's death.   W.H. Shrewsbury.

SEVENTEENTH CENTURY TOKENS (Oct. 19, 1881).—One of the towns named by Snelling, an authority who wrote on these pieces in the year 1766, was BANGOR FAWR. Boyne, who wrote later and edited a valuable work on them, which was published in 1858, and which has ever since been looked on as an authority, remarks under Wales :—"I have not met with a token of Bangor Fawr, so did not insert it." The writer of this letter, owever, has the original token in his possession, and it is very fine one, reading very plainly :—

Ob. RICHARD . BOVLTON, 1667—in the field ; a pair of Scales & 1D.

Re. OF . BANGOR . FAWR—A Cathedral Church.

ne other that Boyne places to Bangor (Co. Down, Ireland), , I consider, incorrectly assigned, as that token reads :—

JAMES CLEALAND—A Cathedral.

OF BANGOR—An Anchor 1D.

his is engraved (Boyne plate 39, No. 3) under Ireland, ut as the churches on each are similar edifices, I attach hem to Wales. For these reasons, I ask some of your Welsh antiquaries to confirm or reject my ideas that both hese seventeenth century tokens are of *Bangor*, and should be placed in any list of Wales that professes to present the okens of the whole Principality.

Colchester. CHARLES GOLDING.

NANTGARW CHINA (Aug. 24, 1881).—I am much obliged to those correspondents who kindly replied to my enquiry, but I regret to say they have not been able to supply the information I particularly wanted, namely, some account of the man who really made Nantgarw china famous—William Weston Young—a man singularly gifted and accomplished, being at once a most ingenious scientist and a delightful artist. The development of the latter gift, and the use he made of it, was all the more remarkable inasmuch as he was of Quaker parentage, and maintained, I believe, through life his connection with the Society of Friends. But if Nature gave him rich endowments, Fortune, who often seeks to be revenged on Nature's favourites, withdrew from him even the shadow of her countenance, and the story of his life, as far as I have been able to gather particulars of it, is as sad a tale of disappointed hope and undeserved calamity as anything I have ever heard. If space permits I will touch on this a little further on.

It may be gathered from this that I know more now of Nantgarw china, and the maker of it whom I had in my mind, than I did when I penned the enquiry which appeared in this column. For this increased knowledge I am partly indebted to an historical notice of the manufacture which appeared in the *Cardiff Times* of August 13th, and partly to conversations with residents in Glamorganshire, during a recent visit to that county. The information given in each of the three replies to my enquiry being in a greater or less degree either misleading or incomplete, I venture to quote a portion of the historical notice alluded to as the readiest means of placing the subject in a clearer light than it has at present in *Bye-gones*. The writer in the *Cardiff Times* says :—

A porcelain manufactory was established at Nantgarw in 1813, by Billingsby, a celebrated flower-painter of Derby ; he served his time to Mr. Duesbury for five years from 1774 to 1779, and probably left there about 1785. He was not only a first-class painter, but he thoroughly understood the manufacture of porcelain in all its branches, and he had the advantage of a wife who was also an artist. . . . . . From 1811 to 1813 he was engaged by Messrs. Flight and Barr of Worcester. His son-in-law, Walker, was also at the Worcester works and made some great improvements—in particular the reverberating enamel kiln, already in use in London and Derby. The method of building this kiln was kept secret, Walker always working at night to complete it. In 1813 Billingsby and Walker left Worcester to establish a porcelain manufactory at Nantgarw. Here they produced some very fine porcelain of the same peculiar character as that of Pinxton, with a sort of vitreous appearance, and a granulated surface like lump sugar. The paste, being very soft, would not in all cases stand the heat of the kiln. Some of the early pieces are consequently often found cracked on the glaze or slightly warped and bent. About the year 1820, Billingsby and Walker disposed of their interest in the concern to Mr. J. Rose.

5

A manufactory of Earthenware had been established at Swansea under the style of the "Cambrian Pottery" as far back as the year 1750. In 1802 Mr. Lewis Weston Dillwyn purchased these works, and by the aid of Mr. Wm. Weston Young—the draughtsman employed by him in his works on natural history whom he had instructed in enamel painting—the opaque china becomes remarkable. After the establishment of the Nantgarw works in 1813, Young was occasionally engaged there and eventually joined Billingsby and Walker (in partnership I presume) and continued the manufactory after their departure in 1820.

With this the writer ends his notice of 'Nantgarw' and he leaves off just where the interest of the story commences : for it was under Mr. Young's management that the manufacture of the china was perfected ; it was his delicate and charming pencil which gave the china produced after 1820 its high artistic value ; and it is of him that so very little is known. No one but a 'specialist' could do the subject justice—and justice I hope will one day be done this long neglected and all but forgotten Quaker artist. For me it will suffice if I say that the works were energetically carried on for a few years : but the cost of production was too great to admit of their being carried on at a profit. If Mr. Young did not 'fail,' his withdrawal from Nantgarw was akin to failure, for the venture I believe sorely impoverished the friends who had supported him. About 1828 the stock was sold by auction (partly) and the place was shut up for years. Later the premises fell into the hands of a Mr. Pardo, and I understand that, intermittently, the potter's business has in some form been carried on there by him. I have seen common kitchen ware of a date later than 1830 marked 'Nantgarw' ; and once being in that neighbourhood (1846) I thought I would like to see the works. Permission was readily given me to see what there was to be seen : but my visit quite disenchanted me ; they made nothing there *then* but common clay tobacco pipes ! What may be made there now I cannot say ; but seeing what an attraction there would be to the public in anything which could honestly have " Nantgarw " marked upon it, the wonder is that the name is not turned to profit.

Of Mr. Young's career subsequent to the closing of the Nantgarw works I have from private sources gleaned but a few scanty particulars. He went to America, and there the industry for which he had always been distinguished added to his skill and talent, gained him many friends and yielded him so handsome a recompence that he saved money. His desires probably were modest, and his longing to return to the old country great. He set out upon his return bringing his savings with him. When within sight of the English coast a storm arose, the vessel struck upon a rock, and all on board had to be taken to the boats. Poor Young had jealously guarded the treasured savings of his toil and had it with him in a stocking. In getting into the boat, Young in his haste took up the stocking by the wrong end, and every coin of the precious hoard went rattling into the sea ! " Ah William ! " said an old Quakeress, to whom he related the sad adventure " thee'st always taken the stocking up by the wrong end ! " D.J.

CURRENT NOTES.

ORNITHOLOGY.—Mr. Samuel Ward of the Wood, Llanymynech, writes, under date October 25 :—Last evening, at about half-past four, I saw three or four chimney swallows (*hirundo rustica*) plying their vocation over the gardens in Salop-road, Oswestry. This morning I flushed a fine woodcock, but, unfortunately, failed to get a shot at it. Is not this a coincidence so unusual as to be worthy of record ?

It is reported that several wild swans have been seen on the Severn above Shrewsbury.

44

Mr. T. W. Hare writes to *The Times* from Berthddu, Llandinam :—" I have been watching for some minutes about six house martens flying at a considerable height. All the swallows had disappeared from this neighbourhood three weeks ago. Their re-appearance in a cold east wind I look upon as an ornithological phenomenon. I wonder whether Mr. Morris, or any other ornithologist, has made a similar observation? If you will kindly insert this in *The Times* some light may be thrown on the sub-ject."

As I was going towards Llanyblodwel the other day, and passing by the heap of water pipes, there happened to be a flock of geese flying over head at the time. The pipes had somewhat the appearance of a black or blue sheet of water, and the geese seemingly wish-ful to have a duck or a swim, descended right on to the pipes. Two or three of the workmen, who were at their dinner in a little hut close by, startled by such an unusual sound, appeared to think that some evil demons were coming to them in the shape of geese. Two of the birds were hurt and could not rise ; the rest got away safe.
JOHN ROBERTS, Welsh Harper.

THE GREAT STORM OF 1839.

When the Great Storm swept over the country on the 14th October the "Great Storm of 1839" was referred to by many who have a vivid recollection of its ravages. In *Bye-gones* Aug. 11, 1880 one singular circumstance con-nected with that storm was narrated, viz.:—That in Os-westry there was a " white incrustation on the windows" of several of the houses facing west. This was confirmed a week later by another correspondent, who, as a boy, had been shown by his father a similar deposit of salt at Welsh-pool. The following notes concerning the storm have been supplied to us :—

Jan. 6, 1839. A hurricane blew down the chimney of the dining room at Mr. Jones's, Brook-street, Oswestry. A very high engine stack at Aston, and one at Sweeney New Colliery were also blown down. Five hundred trees were destroyed at Clungunford, and at Oteley Park, Elles-mere, several of the windows were broken. The damage by gales on the coasts was said at Lloyd's to amount to half a million.
JARCO.

A search in the newspapers of 1839 would reveal some curious records of the great storm of the night of January 6, in that year. I have only recently met with the follow-ing, which was written by an official in the Chester post-office :—When Mr. John Lloyd, grandfather to our worthy Recorder, and the popular Prothonotary of that day, called at the post-office the following morning, I asked how he fared during the night, at his exposed residence at the Mount, in Boughton? He said, "I lay quiet in bed until my bedroom window was blown in, and the pic-tures began to fly about the room, when I thought it was time to get up!" The writer also states that he saw a man with a three-legged table on his head, crossing the street at an early hour, who had adopted that means to save his head from the slates flying off the roofs in Foregate street.
H.B.

A statement made in your *Bye-gones* column some months back, and corroborated, I believe, by more than one writer, informed us of a very remarkable salt deposit on some of the windows at Oswestry and other places after the storm of January, 1839. It would appear by a letter to the *Shrewsbury Chronicle* last week,—written by Mr. W. N. Thursfield of Shrewsbury—that a similar in-crustation was found after the recent gales. He says : " On Saturday last (Oct. 22), after the last gale, I noticed that the upper windows on one side of my house presented a frosted appearance, evidently from some kind of white deposit upon the outside. I had this deposit carefully removed from six panes with a clean sponge and distilled water, and on analysing the solution thus obtained, I found it to contain, in addition to the atmospheric dust at all times more or less present on windows, five and a half grains of saline chlorides, such as are found in sea water, chiefly common salt. I do not think it possible that such a de-posit can have come from any other source than sea spray carried inland by the wind. Apart from the interest of this evidence of direct sea breeze so far inland, it is a note-worthy instance of one of the great distributing forces of nature, as five and a half grains of salt deposited upon a few feet of partially sheltered vertical glass must repre-sent many thousands of tons distributed over the general surface of the country, doubtless with benefit to the land."
NEMO.

I have somewhere read an account of this storm, but now I want to refer to it am unable to do so. I remember it well, having been out in it from about half past one till ten a.m. It took place on the night of Sunday the 6th and morning of the 7th of January, 1839. I had been at home about a mile from Birmingham for my Christmas holiday, and so far as I remember the storm began to rise after dark on the Sunday night from the north-west, and blew a hurricane by the early hours of the morning. I left my father's house about half-past one to take the mail coach in Birmingham to return to Oswestry, the chimney-pots and bricks, &c., falling around most dan-gerously. In Birmingham the wind affected not only the chimneys, &c., but shop shutters were wrenched off the windows and were literally dancing about the streets. I was the only passenger inside the mail coach, and only the coachman and guard outside. At Tettenhall, about a couple of miles on this side of Wolverhampton, an im-mense oak tree fell across the road just the moment after the coach passed, and so near that the branches almost touched the guard in the dickey (his seat behind). We were often blown to a standstill. As I don't remember much more until daylight, I fancy I must have slept, but as daylight dawned, some little way beyond Haygate, near Wellington, the storm having considerably abated, I got outside on the box seat of the coach, and then wit-nessed the devastation—houses wholly unroofed, stacks of hay, &c., completely carried away, and immense trees, with tons of soil adhering to their roots, torn up and strewed everywhere, often impeding the progress of the coach. By the time I got to Oswestry (from nine to ten o'clock) it had completely subsided. At that date there was a high chimney at the pits at Croeswylan, nearly as high, I fancy, as the present Gasworks chimney. This, among others, was blown down. In Chirk Castle park and at Erddig, near Wrexham, many fine old oak trees were torn up. In my Diary of that date the only obser-vation I find is, "A terrible hurricane," and which it truly was. I believe the wind pressure was something like 70lbs. to the foot. I have heard—but you must take it for what it is worth—that the minute hand of St. Mary's clock at Shrewsbury, about six feet long, was blown off, and was found at or near Wolverhampton (about thirty miles off). I remember that the wind blew at the rate of about 120 miles an hour, so that I look upon such an event as not impossible. I remember reading of an aged noble-man (I think it was Lord Rolle, who at the Queen's Coro-nation, some eighteen months before, stumbled and fell whilst doing homage, when her Majesty, with that natural good feeling which has always characterized her, regard-less of State etiquette and ceremony, rose, and descended from the throne and raised him up), who, on going to the indow to watch the storm, was killed by the window lowing in on him. This hurricane was general throughut the kingdom, and was attended with great loss of life nd of property, but whether it extended further I do not t present remember. W. I. BULL.

THE PRINCE OF WALES AT SWANSEA.—A NOVEL ARCH. A novel arch was erected at Swansea on the occasion of ιe visit of the Prince and Princess of Wales, by Messrs. . P. Parry (of Oswestry) and Rocke, well-known as anutacturers of Welsh stocking yarns. The arch, which as erected across High-street, the principal thoroughfare ι the town, had the form of a castellated gateway of three rches, one over each pathway and one over the road ; the wo piers were built of bales of compressed wool, painted hocolate colour, with gilded hoops. The bales, forming he piers, were kept in place by wooden uprights, which 'ere covered with raw wool bound with spirals of coloured arns, and enriched with a line of evergreens between hem and the bales. The bridge across had a parapet of trellis work, and in the centre, on each side of the arch, was surmounted by a huge Prince of Wales plume, worked entirely of raw wool and coloured yarns. The top of each pier in a level with the bridge was decorated with large ornamental geometric designs in the form of a star, extending the whole width of the pier, formed of hanks of yarn of the richest colours and striking contrasts, giving quite an oriental appearance to the whole structure. A pair of curtains formed of fleece wool and fringed with yarns depended from the bridεe on each side of the central arch, and were looped up at the top by festoons of yarns, and gathered up beneath the arch under the shields by massive ropes of entwined yarns formed into graceful knots, and terminating in huge scarlet tassels. The whole was surmounted by three làrge flags, the Royal Standard in the centre, supported by the Royal and Danish Ensigns, and besides 100 smaller staves gracefully arranged carrying streamers of coloured yarns. On the bridge when the Royal procession passed, sat four Welsh women in the national costume, knitting ; on the approach of the Prince and Princess they rose and made their curtsey, evidently much to the amusement of the Royal pair. Engravings of the arch appear in the *Graphic* and the *Illustrated London News.*

NOVEMBER 9, 1881.

NOTES.

THE SPANISH INVASION, 1588.—An abstract of the Numbers of every sort of the armed men in the Marches of Wales, and the English shires is annexed :—

Counties.	Able men.	Armed.	Trained.	Untrained.	Pioneers.	Launces.	Light Horse.	Petronels.
Salop	— ..	1200 ..	600 ..	600 ..	700 ..	88 ..	70 ..	—
Denbigh ..	1200 ..	600 ..	400 ..	200 ..	160 ..	— ..	30 ..	100
Flintshire.	— ..	300 ..	200 ..	100 ..	200 ..	— ..	3 ..	30
Carmarthen	— ..	704 ..	300 ..	400 ..	300 ..	— ..	15 ..	10
Radnor ..	1500 ..	400 ..	200 ..	200 ..	100 ..	— ..	14 ..	—
Anglesea..	1120 ..	112 ..	— ..	— ..	100 ..	— ..	17 ..	—
Worcester.	— ..	— ..	600 ..	— ..	100 ..	17 ..	83 ..	10
Montgomery	— ..	600 ..	300 ..	300 ..	50 ..	1 ..	19 ..	30
Pembroke.	— ..	800 ..	800 ..	800 ..	896 ..	— ..	— ..	30

The following Welsh Counties were not certified :— Carnarvon, Merioneth, Cardigan, Glamorgan, and Brecon.

The following were the rates of entertainment of the officers of Companies appointed for the service in the year 1588 :—The Lieut.-Gen. of the Army per day, £6 0s. 0d. ; the Captain General of the Launces, £1 0s. 0d. ; Lieutenant, 10s. 0d. ; Surgeon, 1s. 6d. ; Halberdier, 8d. The Colonel of the Footmen, £2 0s. 0d. ; Lieutenant, 10s. 0d. ; Sergeant-Major, 10s. 0d. ; Corporals, 4s. 0d. ; Halberdier, 8d.— (From the *Annual Register, 1760.*) M.N.

THE OLD WELSH ALMANACKS.

(Sept. 21, 1881.)

I said in my last letter that there remained a *third* issue of a Dublin Welsh Almanack for the year 1835 ; and as I have to make some remarks upon that one, I propose inserting the title page of it just as it is printed :—

Y CYFAILL, SEF ALMANAC
CAERGYBI AM 1835.
1 Fy hen Gyfeillion heini
'Rwy'n dyfod o GAERGYBI ;
Eleni'n *rhydd* heb ofni sgrech
Y *Giwaid* frech fu'n gwaeddi.

2 *Blynyddoedd* anesmwythder
Fu ini mewn *Cyfyngder ;*
Gwaith anhawdd iawn oedd cario pwn
Ac ofni **hwn* bob amser.

3 Mae pedair rhan y flwyddyn
Yn darfod bob yn ronyn ;
Ac *felly* mae pob dydd o'n taith,
Nid maith yr erys undyn.

4 Pa fodd y darfuch wario
Y flwyddyn a aeth heibio ?
'Nawr ystyriwch, sobrwch chwi,
Ni welwch mo'ni etto.

5 Rheolwr mawr y bydoedd
A eilw farn ar gyboedd,
A bydd trigolion yr *holl fyd*
Dan *farn* am gydweithred-oedd.

6 We did, but not at random,
Procure our *Rights,* through wisdom ;
And our advantages to possess
The PRINTER'S PRESS in *Freedom.*

* *Cyfaill.*

DUBLIN :—Argraffwyd am y flwyddyn 1835. DROS ROBERT ROBERTS. *Gwerth Chwe' Cheiniog.*

The *monopoly*—ugly word in the vocabulary of a so-called "free country"—in the publication of Almanacks in England and Wales, had compelled Mr. Roberts to get his printed in Ireland, and with a view of evading the law, he gave each a distinctive name, as we have seen, not daring to call them "Almanacks ;" but in 1835, as he says above, the "Press" was free, and thus he calls this one *Almanac Caergybi,* and openly proclaims himself as its author. That is the last of the Almanacks I have in my possession with the DUBLIN imprint upon it ; but I have one for the same year with this title page :—

AMSERONI ; neu ALMANAC, AM y FLWYDDYN O OEDRAN EIN HARGLWYDD 1835, yr hon yw y drydedd ar ol Blwyddyn y Naid, ar y 5ed o deyrnasiad ei Fawrhydi William IV., Brenin Prydain Fawr a'r Ywerddon ; yn cynwys—Answedd y Flwyddyn, y Calendar, Tremiadau y Planedau, y Diffygiau, Codiad a Machludiad yr Haul, Lloer, &c., hefyd Ffeiriau Cymru, &c., &c.

Y Prif .... 12 Rhif y Cyfarwyddiad 8
Yr Epact .... 1 Llythyren Sul .... D
Cylch yr Haul........ 24 O'r Cyfrif Newydd .. 85

Gan ROBERT ROBERTS, CAERGYBI, awdwr y Daearyddiaeth, &c. Y cyntaf gwedi Dileu y Doll. BRYNGWRAN, ger Caergybi, argraffwyd gan ROBERT ROBERTS. *Gwerth Chwe' Cheiniog.*

It has always struck me as being curious, that although it is stated on the face of the page that this was printed *the first year after the abolition of the duty,* the price should have been continued at sixpence. The Welsh Almanacks became common enough soon afterwards ; for competition in their production set in, and thenceforth their peculiar history may be said to have ceased altogether, and I do not think it necessary, therefore, to follow the story of the Almanacks beyond the year 1835. The Dublin ones were peculiar, and therefore noteworthy, and the one printed at Bryngwran is noticeable as the *first* issued by Mr. Roberts, and printed by him in his native land. It only remains for me, in conclusion, to give an account of verses printed *within* the covers of the Almanacks noticed in this and my preceding letter, and I shall then have fulfilled the object I had in view when I first undertook to send these communications to the press.

No. 1, 1832.

Dihun, dihun, Frytannia, ac na phetrusa'n hwy,
Rhag it wrth wag ymferwi, gael profi dirfawr glwy' ;
Ymostwng 'nawr yn effro ; pwy wyr nad gwrando fydd,
It 'feddu tangnef cryno, 'i'th nos droi eto'n ddydd.

No. 2, 1832.

Niferoedd roed yn feirw trwy'r *geri* groyw gri,
Nid am fod eu pechod yn fwy na'n pechod ni ;
Gwnawn ninau edifarhâu 'te cawn ein claddu a'n cloi,
Medd geiriau gwir y Beibl, heb le na sail i 'sgoi.
Cyflawnder Nef sy'n gwaeddi, Ior hwythau 'leni i lawr ! ! !
Na gad hwy flwyddyn etto, medd yr Eiriolwr mawr,
'Rhof iddynt dail o dalent 'r Efengyl, warrant wir,
Os na wnant ffrwytho wedi, ti gei eu torri o'r tir.

No. 2, 1833.

Hwyra dial Duw,
Llwyra dial, dial Duw.

Fe wawria dyddiau rhyfedd,—nid y'nt yn neppell iawn,
Na welwyd eu cyffelyb—pob bro o dwrf yn llawn :
Na *all* ein teyrnas sefyll—hi gwymp yn chwiffriw mân,
Ofnadwy fydd y gawod—dychrynllyd fydd y tân.

O Frydain ! cais, dihuna, cyn dêl y gawod gref,
Nid oes a dry hon heibio ond gallu brenin Nef ;
Gweddia am arbediad—mae gweddi'n fawr ei grym,
Efalla cei dy guddio rhag y digofaint llym.

No. 1, 1834.

CYNGOR I'R DERBYNWYR.

Gochelwch gau Gyfeillion,
Na phrynwch sothach Arfon ;
Ffowch ! ffowch rhag surdoes *Shôn* Llanrwst,
Ar ffrwst i *Gybi* dirion.*

Magna est veritas.

Fe wawria dyddiau rhyfedd, nid y'nt yn nepell iawn, &c., &c.

[Same as in No. 2, 1833, already given.]

No. 1, 1835.

"Ond cysur Cristion fydd o hyd,
Mai 'i Frawd sy'n llywodraethu'r byd."

No. 2, 1835.

[The above lines repeated] also :—

ATTEB I'R GOFYNIAD YN 1833.

Atteb eich gofyniad,
A d'wedyd rhi' eich amser chwi,
Sef blwyddau'r oed ar rediad, fu fwriad genyf fi,
Eich oed oedd ddeg o flwyddi,
A chwe' mis llawn, a'i wneud yn iawn ;
A hi'n dri deg i'w chyfri, tri haner gwedi a gawn,
A charu saith o flwyddi maith,
A thair a haner, wîw-ber waith ;
A hyn, a'u gwneud i fynu,
Sy'n dweud i ni eich oedran chwi ;
Does eisiau ond eu cysylltu.
Ceir felly ar hyny eu rhi'.
Yn awr 'r y'ch un ar hugain llawn,
Mewn gemau serch yn gymmwys iawn :
A hithau'n ddwy a deugain,
Mewn oedran gwych, yn awr heb nych ;
Boed i chwi'n gariad gywrain,
Fu'n drwyad fain ei drych.

And finally we have this one verse in No. 3, 1835 :—

Myn'd heibio mae'n *Blynyddoedd* 'run modd a'n *Misoedd* maith,
Cyd nesu mae *Wythnosau* a *Dyddiau* pen ein taith ;
Mae'r *awr* ddiwedda'n dyfod ; gwyn fyd y parod rai,
Sy a'u pwys ar Iesu prydferth, heb geisio Aberth llai.

E.G.S.

* A sure proof that poor old Roberts's craft was in danger.

SOUTHEY AND WELSH WOMEN.—In a letter to Mrs. Southey, from Bwlch, Breconshire, dated Oct. 14, 1798, Mr. Southey says, " I much like the appearance of the Welch women ; they all have a character in their countenances, an intelligence which is very pleasant. Their round shrewd national physiognomy is certainly better than that of the English peasantry, and we have uniformly met with civility. There is none of the insolence and brutality which characterise our colliers and milk-women."
N.W.S.

QUERIES.

OSWESTRY TOWN CLERK.—Previous to the passing of the Municipal Corporations Act the Town Clerk was appointed by the Lord of the Manor, the Earl of Powis. In a note on the Oswestry Corporation Plate, Oct. 19, JARCO stated that "Herbert, Councillor at Law," was Town Clerk in 1777. Was he any connection of the Powis family ?
TELL.

PHILIP HENRY'S RIDDLE.—In the *Life of Philip Henry*, p. 273, is inserted a letter written by Mr. H. to his friend the Rev. Francis Tallents in which the following words occur :—" A line is better than nothing, if it be only to wish you a happy new year, and to present you with a new year's gift, which is, a half moon, the body of the sun, and the fourth part of a star, which, when you have put it together you will find me always yours, &c., P. H." The author speaks of the above as a quaint riddle, which the reader will not probably find a very great puzzle to unriddle. For my own part I cannot make it out, nor have I met with any one who can. Can any of your correspondents help me out of the difficulty ?
T.T.

[Our correspondent has not read all the letter, or he would have found the reply. Mr. Henry concludes with " Your CORdial Brother," &c., in which we have the riddle, such as it is, unriddled !—ED.]

THE HARLECH EXHALATIONS (Nov. 24, 1880).—In a memorandum of a table of contents to a volume of the *Philosophical Transactions* is the following:—" Mr. Lhuyd of Locusts lately observed in Wales, and of a fiery exhalation or damp, which burnt several hayricks in Merionethshire—*Phil. Trans.* n. 208, 213." After considerable search in the abridgement I have failed to discover the full account of the circumstances referred to. They may prove interesting if some contributor to *Byegones* should be able to supply them.
H.W.L.

DISERTH CHURCH (Sep. 28, 1881).—William Hughes, Bishop of St. Asaph, who died in October, 1600, was in some way connected with Diserth and Rhyd. His daughter and heiress, Anne, married Thomas, the youngest son of Sir Thomas Mostyn, from whom the Mostyns of Rhyd are descended. It is probable that the slab with the word "Mostyn" upon it (and to which your correspondent "W.A.L." refers) may cover her remains ; and that William Mostyn, who died in 1678, was her grandson ; the Dorothy who died in 1681 being his wife. Catherine Mostyn, daughter of the Thomas and Anne above mentioned, married Thomas Hanmer, and that match will most likely account for the quartering upon the shield which your correspondent mentions. Some antiquary could, with a little trouble, make out the descents from Thomas Mostyn and Anne his wife to the Lloyds, and thus perfect another of the many broken Welsh pedigrees that cause so much perplexity to the students of genealogy. Will some one do it ?
RHYD.

THE GALLTFAENAN FAMILY (July 6, 1881). The Henllan Church record, as given by "W.A.L.," has revived an enquiry which was made some years ago, as to the owners and occupiers of that house in the early days of the last century. *Edward Salusbury*, whose name is now given, was clearly the father of *Elizabeth*, who married John Jones of Penaner, M.B. She died, it appears, in 1758, aged 63, and would be born therefore in 1695, and, as her husband did not die until 1778, we may conclude that between 1695 and 1778 the estate was held by Edward Salusbury and his son-in-law, John Jones. Of their children Salusbury and Elizabeth died in 1760, aged respectively 28, and they would therefore be born in 1732. Edward Salnsbury Jones died in 1769, aged 36, and the surviving sister, Margaret, died 1791, aged 58, and, strangely enough, therefore, they must have been born in the same year—1733. The record reads as if the then race had died out with her, and I should be glad to know who succeeded her in possession, and how the new possessor acquired the name of the old family who had been there aforetime ; also, whose son Edward Salusbury was.
ANTIQUARY.

GWEDDI'R FORWYN (May 11, 1881.)—The following is the full text of the "Gweddi'r Forwyn," which under the title of "Breuddwyd Mair" was published by the late Dr. Pughe of Aberdovey in the volume of *Archæologia Cambrensis* for 1865. As several versions of it are said to exist in different parts of the country, any variations in the text would be acceptable if forwarded to *Bye-gones*. I am not aware whether it is extant or not in any other European language. The idea is very beautiful. The Infant Jesus is introduced as questioning His Blessed Mother respecting a dream put forth by Himself forecasting the sufferings to be undergone by Him in His Passion. The last stanza concludes with a prayer that no one who repeats it thrice by heart, ere going to sleep, may be lost eternally ; and with an expression of confidence that none who do so will be harmed by evil dreams.

"Mam wen Mair, wyt ti yn huno?"
"Ydwyf, fy anwyl fab, yr wyf yn breuddwydio."
"Mam wen, beth a weli yn dy freuddwyd?"
"Gwelaf y'th ymlid, a'th ddilyn, a'th ddal, a'th roi ar y Groes ;
A hoelio dy draed, a'th ddwylo.
Gwr du dall, wedi'r fall ei dwyllo,
A phig el ffon dy biga di dan dy fron ddethau,
A'th holl waed bendigedig yn colli."

"O dros fynydd, ac oer fynydd,
Gwelwn Fair, a'i phen ar obenydd ;
Yn tirio lle rhwng pob enaid ac uffern.
Tir uffern byth nas cerddo
Y sawl a'i medro, ac a'i dywedo
Dairgwaith cyn huno ;
Byth wnaiff breuddwyd drwg niwed iddo."

TRANSLATION.

"Mary, blessed Mother, art thou sleeping ?"
"Yes, my dear Son, I am dreaming."
"Blessed Mother, what seest thou in thy dream ?"
"I see Thee pursued, followed, taken, and laid upon the Cross ;
And nailed Thine hands and Thy feet.
A black blind man, after being deceived by the Devil,
With the point of his spear is piercing Thee under Thy right breast,
And all Thy blessed blood is being shed."

"From over a mountain, and a cold mountain,
We see Mary with her head on a pillow,
Traversing the space between every soul and hell.
The region of Hell may he never travel,
Whoever has learnt and said this
Three times before he sleeps,
Never shall a bad dream do him harm." H.W.L.

CYMRU FU.

The following was printed on a card by Mr. Salter, printer, Oswestry, inviting the Rev. Thomas Richards, Rector of Darowen, to the Llanrwst Eisteddfod, which was held June 14 and 15, 1791 :—

Yn Llanrwst y llunir eistedd—o feirdd,
Fo urddas cynghanedd ;
Cu hyfrydwch cyfrodedd,
Dwy ochr y wlad dowch i'r wledd.

Gwledd Helicon, llon fydd llais—y delyn,
A dilwfr a'i hymgais ;
Dawn odiau diniweidlais,
Dull y swydd nis deall Sais.

Clio's alarm doth pierce the skies,
Invites the bardic race ;
For to attempt the golden prize,
At the Olympic Chase.
Ut tua fuerit oratio, ita tibi respondebitur.

Owen Gruffydd of Llanystumdwy, who died in 1730, was very much against using coffins for burial. He gave strict orders that he should himself be buried in a linen shroud, giving the following reason :—

O ffei ! gwaith ffiaidd o'i go—wneud eirch ;
Nid archiad Duw mo'no ;
Mewn llian, graian a gro,
Bu gorff Iesu'n gorphwyso.

Goronwy Owen was obliged to leave his native Anglesey in search of a curacy at Oswestry, where he remained for three years. On leaving his native parish in 1746, where he had been for a short time Curate for the salary of £20 a year, to make room for one John Ellis, "a young ciergyman of a very good fortune," whom Dr. Hutton, the Bishop of Bangor, had promised to promote, Goronwy composed the following stanza :—

Hynt croes fu i'm hoes o hyd—echrysawl,
A chroesach o'm mebyd ;
Bawaidd fu hyn o'm bywyd,
Ond am a dda w—baw i'r byd.

The same lines were rendered into English by an enthusiastic Welshman, and appeared in the *Carnarvon Herald* for September 17, 1853 :—

Adverse and bitter winds have marred my course
Through life, and hard the hurricane has hurled ;
Henceforth I fear not but defy its force,
And wage a war unwearied with the world.

The late Cynddelw lived, when seventeen years of age, as servant at a farmhouse near Chirk Castle. The young poet had scarcely anything to eat at his meals, but whey, and that continually night and morning, which made him quit his situation in disgust, satirizing it in the following stanzas :—

Ces nawpryd wanfyd o wynfaidd—yn bawr
O beiriau y mallfaidd ;
Cawn arfer ciniaw oerfaidd,
Am enyd yn myd y maidd.

Enyd o flinfyd aflanaidd—a gefais,
Mi gofiaf y drygfaidd ;
Y nos, oerfwyd oedd surfaidd,
A'r oror yn fôr o faidd.

LLYWARCH HEN.

CURRENT NOTES.

A plaster cast of the Towyn Incised Stone, and a number of archæological remains lately found at Towyn, have been placed in the museum of the University College of Wales.

The Committee of the Welsh Dialect Section of the Cymmrodorion Society met at 40, Gloucester Gardens, last week, and held a long sitting to receive the preliminary scheme for the phonetic representation of the Welsh dialects. There were present, Prince Louis Lucien Buonaparte, Mr. John Davies, M.A., Messrs. Alexander Ellis (late President Philological Society), Walter D. Jeremy, Howel Lloyd, and Isambard Owen. Communications respecting the scheme had been received from Professor Silvan Evans, Professor Rhys, Professor Ellis Edwards, Bala, and Gweirydd ap Rhys.

MONTGOMERYSHIRE SWALLOWS.—Mr Cornelius Nicholson, Ventnor, writes to the *Times* :—"Your correspodent Mr. T. W. Hare, writing on the 20th October, says that the swallows of Montgomeryshire disappeared three weeks ago and had re-appeared again in an east wind ; and then he asks if any ornithologist can throw light on the phenomenon. Swallows are obedient to climatic influences, and I venture to suggest that the Montgomeryshire Hirundines very likely fled from the north-west storms which prevailed, or were impending, to the southern and south-eastern shores of England ; when, after some days, knowing their time of migration had not arrived, and the storms were tranquillized, they returned to their chosen locality."—The Rev. F. O. Morris, referring to Mr. Hare's letter, writes :—"On the 18th of September there were still many martens about here, and so on, more or fewer, till the 25th, when there were only a few left. On the 26th there was but one. On the 17th of October I saw three winging their way about, no doubt from some place further north ; and on or about the 25th one put in an appearance, flying high over my head as I was in the village. I thought I had put the exact date down, but am sorry to find I did not. It may, however, be taken as a matter of fact that there is no day in the year on which, at one place or another, a swallow or a marten has not been seen in the United Kingdom. The first I saw here this year was on the 1st of May—the swallow came earlier—and on the 7th one of the former went into its last year's nest to see what repairs it might want a little later on. I have just had a note from Torquay, signed 'G.,' in which the writer states that on the morning of the 23rd there were three 'many swallows flying about both high and low.' But it will be seen I had one here at a later date than that."

THE RECENT STORM.—The damage to timber during the great gale of October 14 was probably unprecedented as far as living memory goes. In some parts of Wales the havoc wrought was very great. At Hafodunos, in Carmarthenshire, 1,500 trees fell in a few hours. The aggregate destruction can only be approximately estimated, but we are probably rather under than over the mark in saying that at least 100,000 oaks, chesnuts, elms, beeches, poplars, firs, thorns, and other descriptions of wood, were destroyed by the hurricane. Some of these trees were of historic interest. At Eton, several of the fine old elms planted by Provost Rouse, who was Speaker of the House of Commons in the time of Charles I., and by whose influence, it is said, Cromwell was induced to spare Eton from spoliation, were blown down ; and at Stamford a famous lime tree, planted by Queen Elizabeth during one of her visits to Burghley, was demolished. The trunk of this monarch of the forest measured nearly twenty-three feet in circumference, and about seven feet from the ground it divided into four parts, each being as large as an ordinary tree. Some splendid limes, said to be 300 years old, were uprooted at Hampton Court Park ; and tourists in the Vale of Conway will miss a famous ash and birch which grew together in a hedgerow, forming one head, and which was quite a feature in the landscape, having stood at an altitude of 550 feet above the level of the Conway.

THE LANDSLIP IN SHROPSHIRE.—At a meeting of the Broseley Local Authority, on Wednesday night, an agreement was entered into between the Board and the promoters of the scheme for preventing the further slipping of the hills on the side of the Severn at Jackfield, Salop. For a distance of 300 feet of the hills along the river side barriers are being erected to prevent the continuance of the slips towards the river. The Great Western Railway Company, who are interested in the matter, owing to the fact that the Severn Valley Railway runs through the valley, has given £100 towards the sum required to defray the cost of the work. The agreement sets forth that the Local Authority shall subscribe £70 towards the cost of the work, on the understanding that the scheme prove effectual for a period of three years. Some members of the Board expressed the opinion that the slip would not be stopped by the scheme, and the Chairman (Dr. T. G. Thursfield) said he thought the falling of the higher parts of the hill might be stopped, but the slipping at the base, he was of opinion, would continue, notwithstanding the operations.

A BRAVE OSWESTRY SCHOOL BOY.—As we stated last week, Lieutenant-General Mackenzie, who died on Sunday, October 23, at Edinburgh, was educated at Oswestry School, where he was contemporary with Mr. Longueville, with whom, we believe, he kept up a life-long friendship. Lieutenant-General Mackenzie entered the army in 1826, and in 1834 served with General Lindsay's column in Coorg in all the actions which led to the conquest of Mercara. In 1841 he led the advanced guard at the forcing of the Khoord Cabul Pass. Subsequently he defended the fort of Nishan Khan, in the city of Cabul, and afterwards forced his way through the enemy's lines, bringing off the wounded, with the women and children. In January, 1842, he was given up as a hostage at the special demand of Akbar Khan. He was twice sent disguised as an Afghan to negotiate with General Pollock, and was employed as Political Chargé of Prince Shahpur during the expedition to Istalif, and took a conspicuous part in the storming of that place in September, 1842. General Mackenzie raised and commanded the 4th Sikh Light Infantry on the frontier during the Punjab campaign in 1848-49 ; and in 1853 took possession of the ceded districts of Berar. He was repeatedly thanked by Government for his services in India, and was nominated a Companion of the Order of the Bath. General Mackenzie married Miss Helen Douglas, daughter of Admiral J. E. Douglas. Lieutenant C. R. Low writes to the *Times* :—"In General Colin Mackenzie, whose death you chronicled yesterday, disappears a once conspicuous figure in our Indian military history. During the disasters of the first Afghan war no name stands out in brighter relief than that of Captain Mackenzie, who possessed in a marked degree the best qualities of the typical soldier. Brave, modest, able, generous, and gifted with great powers of endurance, he was alike beloved and respected by his brother officers and by the Wild Afghan 'Jezailchees,' or match-lockmen, who, awed by his indomitable will and high courage, alone remained faithful among their countrymen to the losing cause of England. In the operations around Cabul, so well described by his friend and comrade, the late Sir Vincent Eyre, whom he has so quickly followed to the grave, Captain Mackenzie was in the thick of the fight-ing, and appeared to lead a charmed life. Vincent Eyre describes with graphic power the scene when Mackenzie, fresh and breathless from the disastrous action of the 23rd of November, 1841, when British and native soldiers alike fled before the victorious Afghans, rushed into the wounded officers' quarters, and telling them of the disgrace to our arms, threw open his coat, out of which fell a spent bullet, proving that he at least had boldly faced the foe. Captain Mackenzie, as one of Sir William Macnaghten's political assistants, accompanied the ill-fated envoy in his last fatal interview with Mahomed Akbar Khan, on the 23rd of December, 1841, and describes the event in his graphic narrative published in Eyre's journal. Akbar Khan carried him off on his own horse, and, he says, 'finding the Ghazi bent on my slaughter, even after I had reached his stirrup, he drew his sword and laid about him right man-fully.' He was eventually released, and returned to camp only to be involved in the horrors of the retreat through the passes. After the terrible night at Boothak, Captain Mackenzie with Major Pottinger, and Captain (now Gene-ral) Sir George Lawrence, were surrendered as hostages by General Elphinstone, at the demand of Akbar Khan; as his Jezailchees were nearly all killed, 'his services,' says Major Pottinger, 'could be of little further use,' while Akbar Khan set a special value on securing his person. Kaye well says of Captain Colin Mackenzie, 'than him there was not in all the army a braver or a better soldier.' In his views regarding the policy that led to the last Afghan war the late General Colin Mackenzie was an un-compromising adherent of the late Lord Lawrence, and was an active member of the Afghan Committee." Gen. Mackenzie, we believe, paid a visit to Penylan, Oswestry, as lately as three years ago. When the General was a boy his father resided for some years at Llanvorda.

THE LATE WILLIAM LACON CHILDE, ESQ.—The death is announced of Mr. William Lacon Childe of Kinlet, one of the magistrates for Shropshire. He was the eldest son of the late William Lacon Childe, who married on August 13, 1807, Harriet, youngest daughter of William Cludde, Esq., of Orleton, and brother of the Rev. Edward George Childe. The following Sheriffs were ancestors of the de-ceased gentleman:—Rowland Lacon, Sheriff in 1571, whose son suffered much in the service of Charles I. Francis Lacon, son of Rowland, Sheriff in 1612. In 1705 Thomas Childe, second son of Sir William Childe, by the daughter and heiress of Rowland Lacon, was sheriff. The Baudewin, or Baldwyns, rank among the historical families of Staffordshire, and the name occurs in the roll of Battle Abbey. A member of this family represented Ludlow in the Long Parliament.

NOVEMBER 16, 1881.

NOTES.

MUNICIPAL CORPORATIONS ACT.
AN OSWESTRY SERMON.

TITLE.—The Duty of the Christian Magistrate in Things pertaining to God: being a Sermon, preached before the Mayor and Corporation of the Borough of Oswestry, on Friday, January 22, 1836. By the Rev. T. Salwey, B.D.,

vicar of Oswestry, and late Fellow of St. John's College, Cambridge. London: Printed for J. G. and F. Riving-ton, St. Paul's Church yard, and Waterloo Place, Pall Mall; Eddowes, Shrewsbury; Price, Oswestry; and Jones, Ludlow. 1836.

TEXT.—"And Gallio cared for none of these things."—*Acts* xviii. 17.

Mr. Salwey, in common with a large class, was appre-hensive of the effect of the Radical measures of the day; and the Municipal Corporations Act was one of these. The sermon opens with the character of Gallio:—as a heathen "a man of pleasing manners, the delight of every-body, free from every kind of vice," but not a Christian. Says the preacher:—

"We have fallen upon times, my brethren, when the opinions of Gallio seem to be reviving amongst us; when Christian philosophers, in poring amongst the dust and the ruins of an extinct heathen philosophy, appear to have discovered principles that are worthy of again seeing the light; and through the press, and in the senate, these principles are brought forward, and recommended as the only principles which should guide the conduct of Christian Magistrates, and influence the counsels of an enlightened Christian nation."

Mr. Salwey goes on to mourn the "open and direct attack upon principles, which, happily for this country, have so long had influence upon the minds of British senators and legislators," and points out "that whatever shall become the character of British senators, such will, in no long time, become also the character of British magistrates," so he preaches a sermon on which he "be-lieves to be those principles that should govern the conduct of a Christian Magistrate."

The principles laid down by the preacher for the guid-ance of the Christian Magistrate were two: First, "That all power and authority are derived from God," and, second, "That these are entrusted to us in order to con-duce to God's glory, and to the promotion of the Redeemer's Kingdom." Men, Mr. Salwey said, were per-mitted to choose the particular nature of their government, and constitution, but "no law of man can contravene the law of God; for the instant it does so, the obedience of the subject ceases, and he is compelled to obey God rather than man." The multitude, Mr. Salwey feared, now that they had the power of choosing how they would be governed, talked of "the sovereignty of the people" as if the Almighty were displaced from his Throne, "and man blasphemously exalted in his stead; but," he added, "woe be unto that people who shall not recognise the Lord as their God; who shall not regard Him as the author and dispenser of all power and all authority; and who, in those counsels which may result in altering the form of their constitution, make not this acknowledgment of God's sovereignty the main element in their deliberations: and woe be also unto that ruler or magistrate, who, when appointed, rules not in the fear of God. . woe be unto him if he considers himself responsible only to man, who is indeed the instrument of appointing him, and not unto God, who is the sole author of the power with which he is invested."

The Mayor, before whom the sermon was delivered, was John Croxon, Esq., the first elected under the Muni-cipal Corporations Act. It is not within the scope of *Bye-gones* to offer any opinions on political matters; but it is merely a matter of history to state that the Reform Bill, passed a year or two earlier, as well as this measure, giving, as they did, so much power to the people, troubled not a little the Tories of those days; and that many of the old Whigs shared the alarm.　　　　　JARCO.

FUNERALS IN OSWESTRY.—A question was once asked in *Bye-gones*, I think, but never answered: Why was it the custom when a funeral procession marched from Beatrice-street to the Old Church, always to go round by the Bailey Head, by which route there was a steep hill to climb and a longer distance to traverse? Funerals, in fact, followed the same line as that which divides the town into wards.   TELL.

BOOKS BY BORDERERS.—A Mrs. Phillips, who is said to have been a Borderer (but of whom we know next to nothing), published a curious book (N.D.) in the last century entitled, "An apology for the conduct of Mrs. Phillips, for her marriage with an eminent Dutch merchant." It is not a commendable book, and I do not at all wonder to find the writer of it saying upon the title page, "Such extraordinary care has been taken to intimidate the booksellers, in order to stifle the work, that Mrs. Phillips is obliged to publish it herself, and only at her house." There was a great run for the book accordingly, and the guineas which she received in exchange for it, must have made her rich in money, but the sale did not add much to her reputation. It it now very scarce and but rarely to be met with. Another scarce book, ' privately printed' at Strawbery Hill in 1758, entitled "An account of Russia as it was in 1710, by Charles, Lord Whitworth," was the production of a Borderer (born in Cheshire), but published after his death, from a manuscript which he had left behind him. And yet another very curious book, published in 1815, being "A correct statement of the circumstances that attended the last illness and death of Johanna Southcott, with an account of the appearances on dissection, and the artifices that were employed to deceive the medical attendants;" was written by Richard Reece, a Herefordian, himself a curious character, and according to the "regulars," a mere quack doctor. It would be interesting to make up lists of Borderers' books, for very many of them are quite unknown to the general run of readers.   A BOOKWORM.

BAILEY CLOCK, OSWESTRY (July 6, 1881).—At this date, and in reply to a correspondent (who asked if Mr. Stanton, Lessee of the Theatre, did not erect the first clock on the Bailey Head), I quoted a Corporation minute of 1803, at which time the clock was repaired by the Powis family at a cost of £30. I have since found an earlier memorandum, which shows that the clock was in the hands of the Corporation "19 Mar. 1762: Ordered that the Murrenger pay one Guinea yearly to a proper Person for taking care of the Bayley Clock." Earlier still; in the Corporation Accounts, under date 1680, there is an item:—"P'd John Tomley, smith, towards setting up the Clocke, £01 : 00 : 00." By "the Clocke" I presume the one on the Bailey Head is meant; and as only a portion of the amount is paid by the Corporation probably the rest was paid by the Lord of the Honour?   JARCO.

SEVENTEENTH CENTURY TOKENS (Nov. 2, 1881).—I am pleased to know that an authentic token of Bangor Fawr exists, and I feel that an explanation is due from me for omitting that city from my list. Boyne includes Bangor Fawr in his list, but gives no description of a token, merely saying that it "is one of the towns in Snelling's list : I have not met with a token of it. See Bangor, co. Down, Ireland." Under the Irish Bangor two tokens are described, viz., James Clealand (see *Bye-gones*, Nov. 2), and James Moor.

These tokens are no doubt rightly placed under Bangor' Ireland, as, before deciding to omit Bangor Fawr from my list, I wrote to the Rev. Dr. Adams of Dublin, asking if he could afford me any information about the two issuers, James Clealand and James Moor, and the following is his reply :—

The Rectory, Santry, Dublin, May 24, 1881.—I visited yesterday our Public Record Office, where I found the Hearth-roll for co. Down is not in existence, but in the Subsidy Roll, co. Down, I found the following entries :—

" Patrick Cleland de Bangor, value *iij l.* 10s "
" James Moore de Bangor,   ,,   *iij l.*

The first I presume was son to the issuer of the token (Boyne, page 540, No. 62), and the latter the issuer of the token (B. p. 540, No. 63). I suppose it was the fact of the parties being inhabitants of Bangor (Ireland) that induced Boyne to assign them to this side of the Channel, and perhaps he had in addition some local information.—Faithfully yours,   B. W. ADAMS.

This I considered ample confirmation of Boyne, and in the absence of any particulars of Snelling's for saying tokens were issued at the Welsh Bangor I had no alternative but to omit it from my list. The fact of the Church or Cathedral being the same on the two tokens may in a degree strengthen Mr. Golding's opinion, but the representation of the Cathedral in Boyne's engraving on Clealand's token does not agree with the Cathedral of Bangor, Wales, as it appeared early in the last Century.
Kington.   JAMES W. LLOYD.

The reports of the inspecting officers for the present year show a decided improvement in the attendance at the annual training of the Yeomanry Cavalry, and in most cases a marked improvement in the drill, especially in shooting. The strength of the thirty-nine regiments of Yeomanry is 14,458 of all ranks. The Northern district supplies seventeen, of which the Cheshire stands first. The Denbighshire Hussars come next, and here, again, there is evidence of healthy condition, Lieut.-Col. Leyland's four-troop regiment being as well off for officers as it apparently is for men. The Montgomeryshire regiment (Lieut.-Col. Sir W. G. Williams) is not well off for officers, there being vacancies on the establishment for one captain and five lieutenants. The Shropshire, six troops (Lieut. Col. R. Lloyd), has its full complement.

The death is announced of the Rev. George Arthur Clive, Rector of Shrawardine and Vicar of Montford, near Shrewsbury. He was a nephew of the great Lord Clive, and son of Mr. William Clive of Styche, for some time M P. for Bishop's Castle. One of his brothers was Archdeacon of Montgomery, and is now hon. canon of St. Asaph and Rector of Bymhill, and another was for some years M.P. for Ludlow. The rev. gentleman died on the 8th of this month at the age of 78. He has held the livings of Montford and Shrawardine for 41 years. The livings are in the gift of the Earl of Powis. The vicarage of Montford is returned as worth £246, with a good substantial residence built in 1842. The rectorship of Shrawardine is returned at £380 per annum.

The Princess Louise arrived at Chester on Sunday by the train leaving Euston at eleven a.m., and arriving at Chester at 3.40 p.m. Rain fell during the afternoon in Chester, but notwithstanding this, the streets and rows of the city were lined with citizens, and the precincts of the station were crowded. A special saloon had been attached to the train for the use of the Princess and her suite. In attendance upon her Royal Highness was Lady Sophia Macnamara, and she was also accompanied by Lord Walter Campell, her brother-in-law. The train was met by the Duke of Westminster and the Hon. Compton Cavendish, he Duke's son-in-law, and the royal party were conveyed a Eaton Hall in two covered carriages. As the Princess eft the station, she received a hearty ovation, which she raciously acknowledged. The visit was entirely private, nd no guests have been specially invited to meet her loyal Highness. The evening service at the cathedral as attended by the Duke and the Princess and party. After an absence from this country of three years, the Marquis of Lorne, Governor-General of Canada, arrived in the Mersey on Monday afternoon. The Princess Louise and a distinguished party proceeded down the river in the tender and met the steamer some distance beyond the Rock Light. The Marquis then left the Sardinian, and with the Princess and party were landed at Woodside, thence proceeding by the 5.10 train to Chester for Eaton Hall, Sir T. G. Frost, the mayor of Chester, and Lady Frost, received the Governor-General and the Princess on their alighting from the train, and congratulated the Marquis on his safe arrival. A landau and six horses with postilions and an outrider, with other conveyances, drove up to the Mold siding, at which the train was stopped, and the Royal party were driven away to Eaton Hall amidst hearty cheers. The streets and rows of Chester were crowded with spectators.

The foundation stone of a new church, to be built at Ffynnongroew, in the parish of Llanasa, was laid on Wednesday by the Right Hon. Lord Mostyn.

OWAIN GLYNDWR AND DOLGELLEY.—A paragraph has been going the round of the papers, and was inadvertently inserted in the *Advertizer*, stating what is exactly the opposite of the truth in connection with an old house just destroyed at Dolgelley. The paragraph in question states that the house was "known to antiquaries as the place of assembly of the last Parliament of Wales, which was convened by Owain Glyndwr in the fourteenth century." Had the paragraph said, "known to *tourists* as the Old Parliament House," it would have stated the fact: Welsh antiquaries (as may be seen by referring to *Bye-gones*, Jan., 1876, and *Arch: Camb:* later on in the same year) stigmatized the assertion that Glyndwr held a Parliament at Dolgelley as a "brand new theory." The old house was formerly known as "Cwrt Plas yn Dre," and was no doubt the residence of the murdered Baron Owen.

THE WELSH W.—Most "Saxons" have a congenital horror and dread of the Cymric tongue, which they absurdly declare to be full of consonants and absolutely unpronounceable. As a matter of fact, Welsh is far softer and more vocal than our own harsh Teutonic speech, for it lies about halfway between English and Italian, so far as the relative predominance of vowels or consonants is concerned; and lest my reader should view this parodoxical statement with suspicion, taking me for a Welshman in disguise, I hasten to add that I am not in any way connected with Wales, and that I shared all the common Saxon prejudices on this matter myself until I began to learn a smattering of Welsh for philological purposes. Almost all the terror and mystery of those awesome combinations of letters which are wont so greatly to fright'n us is removed in a moment, as soon as people have discovered the simple fact that *w* in Welsh is a vowel and not a consonant, its phonetic value being merely that of our own *oo*. Cwm and Drws look very terrible indeed, until one knows that they are pronounced exactly like Combe and Druce; while the fearsomeness of Llwch disappears entirely as soon as we recognise that it is nothing more than the Scotch Loch in an unfamiliar guise. Yet, in spite of the perfect transparency and regularity of Cymric phonetic spelling, ten thousand English tourists continue every year to talk about those jaw-breaking long Welsh names, which are utterly unpronounceable by English lips; merely because they have never taken the trouble to get up the most elementary rules of the language, as they would get up a little German before going up the Rhine, or a little Italian before trying a winter at Rome or Florence.—*From "Some English Place Names," in the "Cornhill Magazine."*

THE LATE MR. I. S. HODGSON.

A respected correspondent writes:— Mr. Isaac Scott Hodgson, who died at his residence, Sodylt Hall, on November 4th, will long be affectionately remembered by all who had the pleasure and advantage of his acquaintance. A brief notice of his life may therefore be not unacceptable at this time to the large circle of those who are now sorrowing for his loss. Mr. Hodgson was the only surviving son of the Hon. Abraham Hodgson of Huddersfield, Jamaica. He was born at Juan Fernandez, S. Mary's parish, Jamaica, on the 30th of December, 1807. He commenced his education at Shrewsbury School under Dr. Butler, and afterwards received a medical education at Edinburgh University, where he was the contemporary and great friend of Sir William Fergusson, the late eminent surgeon. Although he never practised professionally, he turned his talents to good effect amongst his poorer neighbours wherever he resided. On his marriage in 1831 he lived at Goppa, near Denbigh. On coming to reside at Sandford Hall, near Wem, he became master of the Shropshire Hounds in 1839, and the spirit and ability with which he maintained that sport is well remembered. Mr. Hodgson was a favourite amongst all sportsmen, and it may be here remarked that at one of the Champion meetings at Amesbury between "North and South," no professional judge being available, he was requested by the Committee to undertake the duty, which he discharged to the entire satisfaction of the meeting, so much so that they presented Mrs. Hodgson with an admirable full length portrait of her husband. The Sporting Editor of *Bell's Life* of that week was equally complimentary on the soundness of his judgment and his admirable horsemanship. In 1841 he joined the Shropshire Yeomanry when living at Broughton Hall. At his first appearance he had to take command of his troop at Ellesmere, and though only a Cornet, his Colonel remarked that he discharged his duty like an "Old Soldier." He remained in the Yeomanry until 1871, when feeling his health declining, he resigned in favour of younger men. He purchased Sodylt Hall in 1856, where he has lived ever since. He was also a magistrate for Shropshire. Having given these few particulars of Mr. Hodgson's varied and active life, this memoir would be deficient on a most important point, if it omitted all mention of his personal qualities, which were in all respects exemplary. The writer of this notice was intimately and almost daily in his society for about twenty years, and therefore had every opportunity for observing him. He never heard him speak ill of anyone, nay, when the conversation bordered on censoriousness, he either kept silence or adroitly turned it in another and more innocent direction. In short he was ever "wearing the white flower of a blameless life." A poor man's blessing is always valuable as ascending as a testimony to heaven; and with this he was plentifully favoured, for he was ever open-handed to the poor and needy. He made such an impression on myself that I am not ashamed to say that I am writing these lines in tears, and I have been careful to write "nil nisi verum." His mortal remains were consigned to "God's Acre" at Dudleston Chapel on the 9th November, accompanied by a weeping concourse of relations, friends, and neighbours.

5

45

ANNUAL MEETING OF THE CYMMRODORION SOCIETY.

The Honourable Society of Cymmrodorion held their annual gathering on Wednesday last at the Freemasons' Tavern, Great Queen-street. The Council met at five o'clock, under the presidency of Mr. Stephen Evans, and the annual meeting of members was afterwards held, Sir Watkin Williams Wynn, Bart., M.P., being in the chair. Proceedings commenced with the reading of the report for the year ending 9th Nov., 1881, by the Secretary, Mr. C. W. Jones. The following is a summary of it. The Council of the Honourable Society of Cymmrodorion had to congratulate its members not only on increased numbers but upon much good work which it had been the means of accomplishing during the past twelve months. As many as fifty new members had been admitted to the Society during the year, bringing the total up to 291. Mr. Alexander J. Ellis, F.R.S, late president of the Philological Society, had been added to the list of honorary members; the Rev. W. Watkins, M.A., Llanover, had been appointed additional corresponding member for South Wales, and Mr. J. C. Roberts of Utica corresponding member for the United States [of America. Another number of "Y Cymmrodor" was announced as being in the press, and the remainder of the "Gododin," which has been delayed, owing to the difficulty of supplying some missing references, is promised with all possible expedition. During the year the following meetings were held : A conversazione, including a bibliographical and antiquarian exhibition, and a select concert, contributed to by Welsh vocalists; a lecture on "Owen Glendower," by the Hon. Wirt Sykes, United States Consul for Wales; and a lecture on "The Lake Legends of Wales," by Professor Rhys, Celtic Professor at Oxford, Mr. Howel W. Lloyd, M.A., presiding. At the meetings of the Cymmrodorion Section of the Merthyr Tydvil National Eisteddfod, several important papers were read and discussed. The attendance thereat, and the general interest evinced in the proceedings, appeared to indicate that in instituting this section the Society had met a public want. As it was intended, with the sanction and co-operation of the National Eisteddfod Committee, to continue these meetings in the ensuing August at Denbigh, it was requested that members of the Society, and others who proposed to read papers there, would send early intimation thereof to the Secretary. The Committee appointed to collect materials for a new Bibliography of Welsh printed books issued before 1807, had already received certified descriptions of a large number of these books, including a complete catalogue of Prince Louis-Lucien Bonaparte's collection, compiled by Mr. Thomas W. Hancock. These had been placed in the care of the Rev. John Davies, M.A., Hampstead, who would be glad to receive descriptions of any other rare and valuable books of the period above-mentioned. Another important step had been taken by the Society in the formation of a Welsh Dialect Section, which proposed to carry out such a complete and systematic investigation of the existing varieties of spoken Welsh as was aimed at by the English Dialect Society in the case of the English language. As yet, the subject, as far as Wales was concerned, had only been studied in a fragmentary and imperfect manner. By uniting the labours of many observers in all parts of the Principality in collecting and classifying local peculiarities of speech upon a definite system, it was hoped that the section would be able to carry out the work to a satisfactory conclusion. A Committee consisting of H.I.H. Prince Louis-Lucien Bonaparte, the Rev. John Davies, M.A., Mr. Alexander J. Ellis, F.R.S., Mr. W. D. Jeremy, Mr. J. Ignatius Williams, Dr. Isambard Owen, M.A., Mr. David Lewis, and Mr. T. W. Hancock, had been formed to arrange the preliminaries in conjunction with the following gentlemen not resident in London :—Professor Silvan Evans, Llanwrin, Professor Rhys, Oxford, Mr. R. J. Price (Gweirydd ap Rhys), Holyhead, the Rev. T. C. Edwards, M.A. Principal of Aberystwyth College, Professor Ellis Edwards, Bala College, Mr. Richard Williams, Newtown, the Rev. W. James, M.A., Llandyssul, the Rev. B. Williams, Llandovery, the Rev. Elias Owen, M.A., Ruthin, the Rev. J. B. Jones, B.A., Brecon, the Rev. W. Watkins, M.A., Llanover, Mr. Llywarch Reynolds, Merthyrtydfil, Mr. Thomas Powell, M.A., Bootle, and others whose services might be secured. The Committee had nearly completed the preliminary arrangements, and the various forms &c. required for the work would shortly be issued. Members and others desirous of assisting were requested to communicate with the Committee through Mr. W. D. Jeremy, No. 10, New Square, Lincoln's Inn. The Council acknowledged the following gifts of books from Prince L. L. Bonaparte, a copy of "the Gospel of St. Matthew in the Sassarese dialect of Sardinia with preface by H.I.H. Prince L. L. Bonaparte" and a copy of "The Montgomeryshire Transactions of the Powys-Land Club," presented by Mr. M. C. Jones, Hon. Sec. For the forthcoming session papers had been promised on various subjects by the Rev. D. Jones-Davies, M.A., Mr. Alexander J. Ellis. F.R.S., Mr. David Lewis, barrister-at-law, Professor W. Boyd Dawkins, and Mr. John Owen (Owain Alaw). The Council respectfully requested members who had papers to bring before the Society to communicate with the Secretary at an early date. The dies of the Society's medal (casts of which were shewn) were being prepared in accordance with the design of Mr. Joseph Edwards by Messrs. Elkington, and Co., and were now in a fair way of completion. The cost would be somewhere about £120, and subscriptions were still needed to meet this amount. The following members of the Council retired, but were eligible for re-election, viz., Mr. Aviet Agabeg, Mr. W. D. Jeremy, Mr. W. Jones (Gwrgant), Mr. Brinley Richards, Professor Rudler, Mr. T. M. Williams, Mr. Howel Lloyd, Mr. John Thomas, Mr. Lewis Morris, and Mr. W. Hanbury Davies. The statement of accounts shewed a balance in hand at beginning of the financial year of £70 12s. 4d., subscriptions received £194 19s., money received by sale of Cymmrodor, £6 6s., making total receipts £271 17s. 4d. The expenditure amounted to £177 11s. 8d., thus leaving a balance in hand of £94 5s. 8d. The amount received on behalf of the Medal Fund was £47 3s.

The adoption of the report was moved by Mr. HOWEL W. LLOYD who remarked that the Society during last year had not only maintained its previous work but extended its sphere of operations. In some cases "too many cooks spoiled the broth," and there might be danger that some things might fail when too many were undertaken. In the case of the Society, however, he trusted that the zeal and efficiency of the Committees would guard them against such a catastrophe. Two special objects now claimed the attention of the Society; the first a bibliographical one. This meant collecting a full and complete description of Welsh printed books, so as to get a standard work on the subject. The second was a dialectic one. All known languages were apt to fall into different dialects. In a mountainous country like Wales, where formerly but little intercommunication prevailed, this was all the more likely to happen. Now that railways had to a great extent over-run the country, dialects were likely to diminish. It was, therefore, important to gather together particulars of different modes of speech while they were still in existence. It was also important to get the different pronunciations of words, and with this view Mr. A. J. Ellis had drawn up an alphabet which, with a little study, would enable friends of the movement to prosecute their enquiries in this direction. The alphabet and forms would shortly be issued.

Mr. IGNATIUS WILLIAMS seconded the motion, which was unanimously passed.

The retiring members of the Council having been reelected, the Rev. JOHN MORGAN rose to move a vote of thanks to the lecturers and others who had assisted the Society during the past year, which, being seconded by Mr. W. Davies (Mynorydd), was cordially passed.

On the motion of the Rev. JOHN EVANS (Eglwys Bach), seconded by Mr. VENNOR MORRIS, a cordial recognition was made of the services of the Council and of its President, Mr. Stephen Evans.

In acknowledging the vote, Mr. EVANS remarked that it was a real satisfaction to him to feel that the Cymmrodorion Society had now become a great established fact. After a somewhat hard struggle it had developed into the most important Society connected with Wales. The list of members was continually increasing, and in his opinion the Society was now in a better position than ever to do valuable service in the cause of the nationality they all loved so well. Knowing neither sect nor party, the Council worked together harmoniously with the one object of benefiting Wales and the Welsh people. As in the past so he hoped it would continue in the future. In conclusion he begged to move a vote of thanks to the Editors of the "Transactions," the Secretary, and Auditors.

The Rev. JOHN DAVIES, M.A., seconding the motion, pointed out that the chief editor, Mr. Thomas Powell, possessed very high qualifications for the post, especially in philological matters. Than Dr. Isambard Owen he knew no one who had more the true interests of the Society at heart. Neither was it to be denied that the present highly prosperous condition of the Society was due to the efforts of the Secretary, Mr. C. W. Jones. He felt that the Cymmrodorion were commencing to act on the public feeling of Wales, and hoped that this would have the effect not only of giving an impetus to the study of Welsh literature, but would aid in developing all the resources of Wales educationally and otherwise.

The last speaker having no knowledge of the auditors, Mr. STEPHEN EVANS pointed out the great indebtedness of the Society to Mr. E. W. Davies, and especially to Mr. Howel Thomas, who afforded most valuable assistance. The motion was then most cordially passed.

Mr. BRINLEY RICHARDS next rose to move a resolution to the effect that "The members of the Honourable Society of Cymmrodorion assembled at their annual meeting on 9th November, 1881, beg to offer to Sir Hugh Owen, treasurer of the Society, their most cordial congratulations on the distinction which has recently been conferred upon him by her Majesty. The Cymmrodorion rejoice that the valuable and disinterested services rendered by Sir Hugh Owen during the past 40 years in connection with education in Wales have been thus recognized. They believe that to his ceaseless labours in promoting and furthering every important movement for the moral and material advancement of his fellow countrymen is justly to be attributed much of the progress which Wales has made in those respects in recent times, and that the beneficial effects of his enlightened efforts will earn for him the grati-

tude of future generations, as they certainly have caused him to be regarded by the great mass of his contemporaries with an affectionate esteem accorded in like measure to no other living Welshman."

At the suggestion of the PRESIDENT, a paragraph expressing great regret at the enforced absence of Sir Hugh Owen, and an earnest hope that he would be enabled to attend the banquet at which his countrymen intend to do him honour, was added to the foregoing resolution.

Dr. ISAMBARD OWEN having briefly seconded the resolution, it was carried with acclamation.

A vote of thanks to Sir Watkin for presiding was carried with cheers, on the motion of Dr. A. WYNN WILLIAMS, Montague Square, seconded by Mr. R. H. JENKINS, Abchurch Lane.

Sir WATKIN, acknowledging the vote, regretted that he had been unable to attend the Cymmrodorion meetings at Merthyr, but doctors being arbitrary mortals he had been obliged to go to the South of France at the time those meetings were held. Referring parenthetically to the condition of Wales, he rejoiced to see there the promise of better times, while it appeared to him that the population were at present prosperous and contented.

THE DINNER.

Between fifty and sixty members sat down to dinner, Sir W. W. Wynn presiding. The worthy baronet was supported on the right by The Right Hon. The Earl of Powis, Mr. Lewis Morris, M.A., Mr. Stephen Evans, Dr. Wynn Williams, Mr. Bernard Quaritch, &c., and on the left by Mr. Brinley Richards, Mr. Howel W. Lloyd, Mr. Howel Thomas, &c. At cross tables were among others Mr. John Thomas (Pencerdd Gwalia), vice-president, the Rev. John Davies, M.A., Dr. Isambard Owen, M.A., Mr. Ignatius Williams, the Rev. John Morgan, the Rev. John Evans (Eglwys Bach), Mr. David Lewis, Mr. Lloyd Roberts, Mr. Edward Phillips, Mr. R. H. Jenkins, Mr. C. W. Jones, secretary, Mr. Rich. Roberts, B.A., Mr. Lewis H. Roberts, Mr. Simner, Mr. W. E. Davies, Mr. St. John Hancock, &c., &c.

Grace was said by the Rev. JOHN DAVIES, after which Sir WATKIN proposed the toast of "Her Majesty the Queen," who, though she preferred her comfortable home in Scotland to the beautiful scenery of Wales, reigned supreme in the loyalty and respect of the inhabitants of the Principality.

The toast was drunk with musical honours, Mr. Hirwen Jones singing the "National Anthem."

In proposing the "Prince and Princess of Wales," the PRESIDENT remarked that all Welshmen were proud of the visit of their Royal Highnesses to South Wales, and he hoped that North Wales might soon receive a like honour.

Mr. Hirwen Jones sang "God bless the Prince of Wales," accompanied by Mr. Brinley Richards.

Then came the toast of "Success to the Society of Cymmrodorion." Sir Watkin pointed out that the Society was started in 1755, resuscitated in 1820 (the year, he was sorry to say, wherein he was born), and for the third time started in 1875, chiefly through the exertions of Sir Hugh Owen, whose absence he deeply regretted, and other patriotic Welshmen. Profiting by the experiences of the previous societies, and eschewing the steps which had led to their failure, he earnestly hoped the present Cymmrodorion Society would continue to prosper. After a kind reference to "his old friend Gwrgant," one of the supporters of the old Society, Sir Watkin concluded by wishing "Llwyddiant i Gymdeithas y Cymmrodorion," coupling the toast with the name of Mr. Howel Thomas, Local Government Board.

In response, Mr. HOWEL THOMAS said the Society had been doing good and valued work in the past, and he had every faith that its usefulness would be increased in the future. Its direct object was the encouragement of literature, science, and art, more especially in connection with Wales. In point of literature, the contents of "Y Cymmrodor" kept up the fair fame of the Society. As regarded science, there was much room for improvement, so far as the Principality was concerned, and it might be well for the Society to consider whether they could do anything to encourage the establishment of science schools in Wales, where Welsh boys with an aptitude for science (of whom there were many) could be taught. Referring to the Society's publication of "Gododin Aneurin Gwawdrydd," the speaker characterized it as being a contribution to Welsh literature second only in importance to Lady Charlotte Guest's edition of the "Mabinogion."

Mr. John Griffiths having sung, the toast of "Literature, science, and art" was proposed by Mr. LEWIS MORRIS. The Welsh nature, said Mr. Morris, was thoroughly saturated with the love of literature. While going about on the Welsh Education Commission, he had been struck with the sacrifices undergone by the people in pursuit of literary knowledge. As President of Eisteddfodau he was again struck by the extraordinary enthusiasm of the people in connection with literary and musical art. With regard to science, something had been done at the meetings of the Cymmrodorion section of the Eisteddfod, but he thought special prizes ought to be given on scientific subjects at the Eisteddfod proper. The art of music was much cultivated, and Mr. Brinley Richards and Mr. John Thomas (with whose names the toast was coupled) were instances of the musical genius of the Welsh people.

Mr. BRINLEY RICHARDS, after referring to some extraordinary criticism on recent poetry that had appeared in a contemporary, dwelt with some indignation on the ignorant criticism to which Eisteddfodau were too often subjected by obscure and unknown writers.

Mr. JOHN THOMAS (Pencerdd Gwalia) made an impressive speech in favour of his scheme for a Welsh Musical Scholarship. The Eisteddfod, he pointed out, did much for Welsh music in revealing latent talent, but something more was needed with a view to its development. All other countries were before Wales in the latter respect. For himself he was indebted to the daughter of Lord Byron for his musical education, as was his friend, Mr. Brinley Richards, to the Duke of Newcastle. The Royal Academy had many scholarships, but not a single Welsh one. A sum of £1,000 was necessary to establish a scholarship. Of this amount he (Mr. Thomas) had collected £800, and hoped, with the assistance of music-loving Welshmen, to complete the work at no very distant date.

The next toast was that of "The President of the Society, Sir W. Williams Wynn," proposed by the Earl of POWIS, who humorously referred to it as being one that had been loyally drunk since the creation, if not before! He was glad to be present on this occasion to support Sir Watkin. The Wynnstay family had long been connected with public life in Wales. Many at that gathering might be old enough to remember the time when the President's uncle was the first authority on Constitutional Law in the House of Commons. For forty years, or thereabouts, Sir Watkin himself had sat in that Assembly as the representative of an important constituency. While the City of London was swimming in turtle in honour of a new Lord Mayor, and the West all ablaze with lights in honour of the Prince of Wales, it was fitting that they as Welshmen should be assembled betwixt and between in honour of the Prince *in* Wales. The Romans could honour two

Consuls, and he (the Earl of Powis) did not see that, while loyally true to the Prince whose ancestor hailed from Carnarvon, they need waver or hesitate in their allegiance to the Prince, whose banner they were proud to see floating from the towers of Wynnstay. The toast was honoured with the greatest cordiality.

Sir WATKIN, responding, said he rejoiced in the success of Wales, and of the Cymmrodorion Society. He was pleased with the improvement manifest in the Society's publications. Much, he thought, might yet be done in rescuing and re-producing old Welsh MSS. Unfortunately a fire in London and a fire at Wynnstay, had destroyed many of his MSS., but some were yet left that might be of service to the antiquary and archæologist. If so he would be happy to hold them at the disposal of the Cymmrodorion. He trusted that, in conjunction with the Eisteddfod, the Society would induce the people of Wales to search out, preserve, and re-produce many of the rare old books still existing in the country. Thanking the Earl of Powis for his support, and the company "for their good wishes to me and mine," the worthy President concluded by proposing the toast of "Cymro, Cymru, a Chymraeg," coupled with the name of the Rev. John Evans (Eglwys Bach.)

In responding, Mr. EVANS dwelt on the natural and mental resources in Wales which required development. Referring to the proposed testimonial portrait to Mr. Gladstone by the Welsh Liberals, he suggested that a Welsh artist should be employed to do the work. Rejoicing in the new era about to dawn on the Principality in respect of educational facilities, the speaker insisted that the prosperity of Wales would be ever dependent on its morality and religion, which ought to receive the support of all true patriots.

Dr. WYNN WILLIAMS proposed "The health of the Vice-President of the day," Mr. JOHN THOMAS (Pencerdd Gwalia), who briefly responded.

Sir WATKIN WILLIAMS WYNN proposed the last toast of the evening, "The Council of the Society of Cymmrodorion," coupled with the names of Mr. Stephen Evans and Dr. Isambard Owen.

Mr. Stephen Evans having left the room, Dr. OWEN responded. The programme of the Society, he explained, had undergone a gradual and essential change. Originally established with the view of binding the Welsh of London together, its aim gradually got considerably widened. It was now considered essential for a nation to illustrate its language, its literature, and its antiquities. Wales had hitherto been backward in this respect. To illustrate even a minute point was no light task, but the united work of many would accomplish much. The aim of the Cymmrodorion Society was to bring about this work of illustration. It was at present engaged in cataloguing Welsh books, and in preparing for the compilation of an accurate account of Welsh dialect forms. In the prosecution of these objects, they (the committee) had been greatly assisted by the valuable services of gentlemen eminently qualified in this direction, viz., H.I.H. Prince L. L. Bonaparte, Mr. Bernard Quaritch, and Mr. Alexander J. Ellis. Prince Lucien had commissioned him to express his regret at being unable to be present. Now, with the aims mentioned in view, it could not be too widely understood that no scrap of information, whether about some rare and prized book or about some quaint and interesting dialectic phrase, would be lost if entrusted to the care of the Society's Committee. Should these aims eventually be realized, he for one would say their labours had not been in vain.

This brought the proceedings to a close, and the company shortly afterwards separated.

NOTES.

SHROPSHIRE PAROCHIAL REGISTERS (Aug. 17, 1881).—The following compilation of the dates of the *earliest* Parish Registers in the county of Salop, I have drawn up from Reports found in the Record Office, arranging the same according to centuries, and in alphabetical order. The State Reports are of a very imperfect and statistical kind only. Many of the Registers are in a very imperfect and dilapidated condition, and many lost. The parochial districts which are designated in the reports as " Perpetual Curacies" and " Curacies," I here distinguish by an Italic Capital *V*, thus placing them according to the new Ecclesiastical nomenclature of " Vicarages."

T. W. HANCOCK.

16th Century.

Abden, R.	1554	Market Drayton, V.	1558	
Acton Bottrell, R.	1559	Middle, R.	1541	
Acton Burnell, R. (with		Morvill, V.	1562	
Langley)	1568	Moreton Corbet, R.	1530	
Alberbury, V. (with *Woollaston* and *Criggion*)	1564	Munslow, R.	1541	
		Neen Savage, V.	1575	
Albrighton, V.	1555	Neenton, R.	1558	
Alveley, V.	1561	Nestrange (or Great Ness),		
Astley Abbotts, V.	1561	V.	1589	
Berrington. R.	1559	Newport, V.	1569	
Benthall, V.	1558	Norton-in-Hales, R.	1573	
Bishops Castle. V.	1559	Norbury, V.	1560	
Bolas Magna, R.	1582	Oldbury, R.	15=3	
Briggnorth,		Onibury, R.	1577	
St. Leonard's, V.	1556	Oswestry, V.	1558	
Bromfield, V. (with *Halford*)	1559	Pitchford, R.	1558	
		Pontesbury, R. (with *Longton*).	1538	
Broseley, R. (with *Linley*)	1570			
Bucknell, V.	1598	Prees, V.	1597	
Burwarton, R.	1559	Pulverbatch, R.	1542	
Burford, R (with *Overs*).	1558	Richard's Castle, V.	1559	
Cainham, V.	1558	Rushbury, R.	1538	
Cardington, V.	1598	Selattyn, R.	1557	
Chelmarsh, V.	1558	Sibdon, V.	1580	
Chelton-Glazeley. R. (with *Deuxhill* and *Stow*)	1588	Shawbury, V.	1561	
		Shelve, R.	1583	
Chetwynd, R.	1558	Shipton, V.	1583	
Cheswardine, V.	1558	Shrewsbury,		
Child's Ercall, V.	1570	St. Alkmand, V.	1560	
Claverley, V.	1568	St. Giles and Holy Cross,		
Clungerford, R.	1559	V.	1541	
Clunbury, V.	1574	St. Julian, V.	1559	
Condover, V.	1578	St. Mary, V.	1584	
Coreley, V.	1543	Stanton Lacy, V.	1581	
Diddlesbury, V.	1583	Long Stanton, V.	1568	
Donington, R.	1556	Stockton, R.	1558	
Dowles, R	1572	Stoke-upon-Tern, R.	1538	
Ercall Magna, V.	1585	Stokesay, V.	1558	
Frodesley, R.	1547	Stow, V.	1576	
Fitz, R.	1559	Stottesden, V. (with *Fairlow*)	1565	
Ford, V.	1589			
Grinshill, R.	1592	Sutton Maddock, V.	1559	
Halesowen, V.	1559	Tasley, R.	1563	
Hanwood, R.	1559	Uffington, V.	1578	
Highley, V.	1551	Upton Magna, R.	1563	
Hope Bowdler, R.	1564	Upton Parva, R. (or *Water Upton*)	1563	
Hopton Castle, R.	1538			
Hughley, R.	1576	Whittington, R.	1591	
Ightfield, R.	1557	Wem, R.	1582	
Leebotwood, V	1547	Much Wenlock, V.	1568	
Lee Brockhurst, V.	1556	Weston -under-Redcastle,		
Longford, R.	1558	V.	1565	
Longnor, V.	1586	Wheathill, R.	1573	
Ludlow, V.	1558	Withington, V.	1591	
Lydbury North, V.	1558	Worfield, V.	1562	
Lyddam (or Ledon) R.	1596	Worthen, R.	1558	

(To be continued.)

QUERIES.

SHERIDAN AND HIS TIMES.—Who was the author of a work under this title, published by J. F. Hope of Great · Marlborough Street in 1859? On the title page he calls himself " An Octogenarian," and on page 164, vol. 2, he speaks of himself as " a mountain boy who had roamed among the Cambrian Hills with the warm enthusiasm of untrained youth, trained only in the classics by a Welsh clergyman." The author became an attached friend of the family, and was a constant visitor at the house during the last illness of Sheridan.　　G.G.

REPLIES.

THE THELWALL FAMILY (Nov. 2, 1881).— Richard Thelwall of Llanbedr, near Ruthin, was the fourth son of John Thelwall of Bathafarn Park, near Ruthin, where he was born about 1550. He acquired Llanbedr by marrying Margaret Lloyd of that place. He has the reputation of being a very learned man, and King James marked his appreciation of his good qualities by appointing him Recorder of Ruthin for life. He died in 1630. Of the Lloyds family I know nothing.

F. THELWALL.

THE WYNNES OF ASTRAD AND LLWYN (June 22, 1881).—Your correspondent " W.A.L.," under date of the 22nd of June, 1881, has given some interesting accounts of the Wynne memorials at Llanrhaiadr, near Denbigh. Any of our ancient families claiming descent from Catherine Tudor of Berain—" Mam Cymru," may be said to possess a share of her historic fame, and it is for that reason chiefly I send you this note. *Catrin o'r Berain*, had been first married to John Salisbury, eldest son of Sir John Salusbury of Lleweni, by Jane Middleton of Chester, his wife, and by him she had issue THOMAS, who was executed for his share in the Babington conspiracy ; JOHN, who afterwards succeeded to Lleweni and Berain ; and a daughter ELIZABETH, who married Owen Brereton of Bersham. She married secondly the celebrated Sir Richard Clough, by whom she had two daughters ; and thirdly Maurice Wynne of Gwydir, by whom she had an only son, EDWARD WYNNE, known as of Astrad, and who, according to your correspondent, died, and was buried at Llanrhaiadr in 1640. I have seen it stated that Edward Wynne had *four* sons, viz., Thomas (who died in 1623), Edward (who died in defence of Denbigh Castle in 1646, he being the *fourth* son according to " W.A.L."), Robert (who married the heiress of Llwyn), and Owen. Now according to the records given by " W.A.L." Owen, son of Robert Wynne of Llwyn, was buried at Llanrhaiadr in 1701 ; and Owen's eldest son, Watkin Edward, was buried in the same place in 1796, *aged 42 ;* which is manifestly impossible if his father had died in 1701, and therefore the records as given in *Bye-gones*, cannot convey to the reader an accurate history of the descents from Edward Wynne, the son of Catherine Tudor. Your correspondent of course has simply recorded the memorials as he found them ; but under the circumstances I have mentioned it would be well if possible to get a clear account of the descents from Edward Wynne through his sons Robert and Owen ; and I should feel obliged to some of your correspondents if they could do this. Archdeacon Newcome tells us in his history of Denbigh Castle that he had compiled that work " from authentic documents written at the time," and among them he mentions " Memoranda possessed by the heir of the Wynnes of Llwyn," so that we may reasonably hope my request can be complied with. According to the Archdeacon's account, Captain Wynne was *taken* (not slain) in April, 1646 ; but on page 106—quoting from the Llwyn Memoranda—he says, " Edward Wynn, 4th son of Edward Wynn, the only son of Maurice Wynne of Gwydir and Catherine of Beren, by Blanche, his wife, daughter of John Vychan of Blaen y Cwm, was captain of a company of foot in Denbigh Castle in the service of Charles the First, was wounded in a sally made by the said garrison against the be-siegers under Sir John Carter, and in three days after died of his wounds, and was interred with military honours at Llanrhaiadr," &c., thus verifying the record of his death as given by "W.A.L." Archdeacon New-come says further that Denbigh Castle was garrisoned by William Salisbury (meaning *Hosanau Gleision*) "at the expense of himself *and kindred*." The Wynnes had in-termarried with the Salisburys, and the Salisburys with the Vaughans, and thus they were spoken of as *kindred* ; old Maurice Wynne in fact being so on one side ere he married Catherine Tudor ; Blanch Vaughan being so on another side before she married Edward Wynne ; or, as it is stated in one of Richard Llwyd's genealogical notes, " It is hard to say where the links became broken, for Wynnes, Vaughans, and Salusburies were so intermixed by marriage as to constitute *a kindred* in blood and relationship of a perplexing and curious character, and yet so distinctive as to justify Col. Wynn (meaning Wynn of Marl), to say he had descended in a direct line from each." Bishop Vaughan, old Sir John of Gwydir, William Salisbury of Cae-du, William Salisbury of Rug, the Prys's of Plas Iolyn,could one and all appropriately use Richard Llwyd's language, so that thus the Wynnes of Llwyn became his-toric in Wales as descendants of the whole.

                              ANTIQUARY.

CURRENT NOTES.

St. John's Church, Portmadoc, has just been beautified by the erection of a stained glass window to the memory of two of the principal promoters of the building of the church—the late Mr. Edward Breese, F.S.A., and his sister, the wife of Dr. Roberts, of Portmadoc. The numerous friends of Mr. Breese concurred in the desire to provide some memorial of their appreciation of his worth, and a committee appointed to consider the mat-ter recommended as one portion of the proposed memorial that a large stained glass window should be placed in St. John's Church, Portmadoc, to the joint memorial of Mr. Edward Breese and his sister. A design sent in by Messrs. Burlison and Grylls, of Newman-street, Oxford-street, London, was ultimately fixed upon. The window, which is at the east end of the church is divided into three lights and contains altogether six subjects ;—the central subject is " The Ascension," in which our Saviour is represented with a golden aureole, the apostles occupying the fore-ground. The principal subjects of the side lights are respectively " The Sower " on the left hand of the congre-gation, and "The Reaper " on the right hand. The subject occupying the base of the left hand panel is "Saul at the feet of Gamaliel ; " that of the base of the centre panel, "The talents," and that of the base of the right hand panel, " Dorcas." The quatrefoils and trefoils in the upper portion of the tracery are filled in with figures of Faith, Hope, and Charity. Underneath the subjects of the bases of the panels are the respective inscriptions, "Doctor o'r gyfraith, parchedig gan yr holl bobl," " Da was, da a ffyddlawn," and " Hon oedd yn llawn o weith-redoedd da." Occupying the base of the three lights runs the inscription, "Er cof am Edward Breese, F.S.A., Morfa Lodge, a'i chwaer, Jane Elizabeth Roberts, Tu-hwnti'rbwlch, y ddau o'r dref hon, O.C. 1881." There yet re-mains a sum of about £400 to be devoted to the "Breese Scholarship," which it is intended to establish in connec-tion with the Portmadoc Board Schools.

The present Mayor of Ruthin, Edward Roberts, Esq., is the 600th mayor of that borough, which was incor-porated in 1282. The Corporation plate includes pieces presented by Bishop Goodman in 1638 ; and one of the names on the plate is that of a man who was tried for felony at Wrexham, and on his way home murdered his gaoler, for which he was hung.

Death of Sir Hugh Owen.

Our readers in Wales will hear with regret of the death of one of the best known of Welshmen, Sir Hugh Owen. The deceased gentleman had been in feeble health for some weeks, and for this reason a complimentary dinner to celebrate his knighthood had been postponed till the spring, but his decease was unexpected. He was ordered to winter in the south of Europe, and had travelled with his daughters to Mentone, where he died on Sunday morn-ing in his 78th year. He appears to have taken cold on the journey, and medical advice was called in, but on the Tuesday preceding his death intelligence was received in England that his health was improving. A relapse must have followed, and the melancholy news which reached London on Sunday occasioned considerable sensation and great regret amongst the Welsh inhabitants of the metro-polis.

Sir Hugh Owen was born in January, 1804, at Voel, in the parish of Llangeinwen, Anglesea, came to London in 1825, and in 1836 entered the office of the Poor Law Com-mission, Somerset House, where he was soon promoted to a position of responsibility, and eventually appointed chief clerk of the Poor Law Board, which post he resigned in 1872 to devote himself exclusively to educational work, with which he had been closely connected from an early period. He was one of the founders of the Bangor Normal College for the training of teachers, and also of the University College of Wales. To the latter institu-tion he has devoted his whole attention and energy, for many years acting as honorary secretary, and latterly as treasurer. The appointment of the Departmental Com-mittee last Session to inquire into the condition of educa-tion in Wales was in great part brought about by his labours, and to the production of evidence to lay before the committee and the formulation of a scheme which would meet the educational wants of the Principality he devoted many months. He was also mainly instrumental in introducing the British School system into Wales, and in establishing the Cambrian Association for the Educa-tion of the Deaf and Dumb, and more recently he took an active part in the revival of the Honourable Cymmro-dorion Society, the National Eisteddfod Association, and the Social Science Section of the National Eisteddfod. He held the post of hon. secretary to the London Fever Hospital for 23 years, and has since been one of the vice-presidents of the hospital. For 28 years he was a member of the British and Foreign Schools Society, and for many years the chairman of the Committee of the National Tem-perance League, and its treasurer at the time of his death. Sir Hugh Owen succeeded Mr. W. M. Torrens, M.P., in the representation of the Finsbury division of the London School Board, but he found it necessary, owing to the pressure of other educational work, to retire from the Board at the end of three years. A knighthood was con-ferred upon him only a few months ago, in recognition of his services to the cause of education in Wales, and this was regarded by all classes in the Principality as a national compliment.

Nov., 1881. BYE-GONES. 339

WINTER SWALLOWS.—Mr. W. E. Beckwith, the author of "Shropshire Birds," under date, Ellesmere, Nov. 19th, writes to us as follows:—A swallow (Hirundo rustica) was flying quite briskly round Ellesmere Church this morning.

BALA GRAMMAR SCHOOL.—Mr. J. C. Evans, B.A., late Powis Exhibitioner and Scholar of Jesus College, Oxford, and at present an assistant master at Christ College, Brecon, has been appointed Head-master of Bala Grammar School. There were over forty candidates for the post.

The first part of the fifth volume of the *Transactions* of the Shropshire Archæological Society, which is now ready for issue, contains a history of the Oswestry Grammar School, illustrated by a picture of the Chapel and School, and portrait of Dr. Donne the famous head-master of three quarters of a century ago. Some curious episodes in the School's history are for the first time brought to light, and some notices of masters given whose names do not occur in the scanty outlines of school matters published in our local histories. The paper also contains an account of the career of several of the "Old Boys," and other matters that will make it especially interesting to Oswestrians. We are glad to be able to state that this paper (which extends to 88 octavo pages) will be incorporated in a book to be called *Contributions to Oswestry History*, which will be issued at Christmas; the other subjects being, Oswestry Old Church, New Church, Old Chapel, The Hon. T. Kenyon, high-steward, The Death of King Oswald, &c. To return to Pt. 1 of Vol. 5, we may add that the other papers it contains include an account of Uppington Church, by the Rev. W. A. Leighton; The Connection of Amy, Countess of Leicester, with Shropshire, by Mr. H. F. J. Vaughan, &c. In the second Part, to be published in Feb. next, there will be another instalment of Oswestry Records by Mr. Stanley Leighton.

In a former reference to Part 2, of Vol. 14, of the *Montgomeryshire Collections* of the Powys-land Club, we only mentioned one paper. The number contains several. First we may note the continuation of the very interesting historical sketches of Welshpool by Mr. Morris Jones, F.S.A. (whom we congratulate on his appointment as a Justice of the Peace for his native county). These records will interest everybody, for they contain little of the archæological nut element, so hard for most people to crack! Then there is an interesting relation, by our correspondent CYFFIN, of the discovery of the foundation of S. Gwyddfarch's Church, Meifod, in digging the foundations of an Independent Chapel. Our readers will remember the happy thought of the Earl of Powis at the annual meeting of the Club, when he hoped this contemplated erection was "not significant of speedy disestablishment!" The Rev. G. Sandford gives a very large number of "Incidents in Montgomeryshire" of the time of the Civil War (in which, by the way, he omits one or two names in his list of "Compounders"), and Mr. Vaughan continues his paper on the family of Jones of Chilton. Mr. R. Williams contributes a List of Solicitors, 33 in number, who practised in Montgomeryshire in 1837, only one of whom (Alderman Minshall of Oswestry) is now living. There are two or three other papers we have not mentioned, that are quite up to the standard, and help to make a capital volume. Since the foregoing was in type the supplementary part, completing the volume, has been issued; and with it is given what will be exceedingly useful, a complete index to the fourteen volumes published. This should be bound at the end of vol. 14, to ensure its safety.

THE CYMMRODORION.

The London Committee of the Welsh Dialect Section founded in connection with the Society of Cymmrodorion in order to carry out a complete and systematic investigation of the existing varieties of spoken Welsh, met again last week at 41, Gloucester Gardens. The following members were present:—Prince Louis-Lucien Bonaparte, the Rev. John Davies, M.A., Mr. Alexander J. Ellis, F.R.S., Mr. Howel Lloyd, M.A., Mr. W. D. Jeremy, Mr. T. W. Hancock, Mr. David Lewis, and Dr. Isambard Owen, M.A. The business of the meeting was the further revision of the forms required to enable the Committee to carry out the collection and classification of all local peculiarities of speech. These peculiarities are in the first instance arranged under the following heads, viz., (1) local words, phrases and idioms; (2) grammatical peculiarities, including peculiarities of construction of sentences, of use of pronouns, prepositions, conjunctions, and particles, of inflection of verbs, of feminine forms, of plural forms of adjectives, of gender of nouns, and of mutations; (3) peculiar place names, including names of unknown or doubtful meaning, of names seemingly inconsistent with the features of the place they designate or applied in unusual senses, of names embodying rare words or unusual proper names of persons, or embodying local words or a record of historical or quasi-historical events; (4) local names of animals, plants, and minerals, zoologically, botanically, and mineralogically classified, according to competent authorities; (5) the mode of pronunciation prevailing in different districts.

It is laid down that these various peculiarities should be expressed phonetically, as well as in the ordinary orthography. To carry this out a scheme for the phonetic representation of Welsh Dialects is under consideration. This scheme will shortly be submitted to the full Committee, which, as announced in my report of the Cymmrodorion banquet, includes the names of Professor Silvan Evans, Professor Rhys, Principal Edwards, Aberystwyth College, Gweirydd ap Rhys, Mr. Richard Williams, Newtown, Rev. Elias Owen, M.A., Ruthin, and many other Welsh scholars.

In the scheme referred to, the sounds of standard literary Welsh are first of all defined according to the best authorities, and characters as nearly as possible identical with those in ordinary use assigned to represent them. In writing diphthongal sounds the writer is enjoined not to employ the combinations of letters used in ordinary orthography unless fully satisfied that they represent the real elements of the diphthong, which is the exception rather than the rule in the dialects. To represent shades of sound not found in literary Welsh or in the scheme, the writer must use the standard sound nearest to the one intended, italicizing the word and defining the shade of sound thereby intended. Words ordinarily run together in speech are to be run together also in writing, but for convenience should be separated by a hyphen. The position of the stress is to be indicated by a turned period immediately following the vowel. Finally, it is to be kept clearly in mind that what is required is the actual sound of words and phrases as heard from people's mouths, and not the sound which theoretically should be heard. Then follows the definition of Welsh vowel and consonant sounds which must needs be well studied by those who intend to give practical assistance.

As I have already notified, the Cymmrodorion have in view the formation of a complete Welsh Bibliography. Curiously enough, at the present time Mr. John Pryse of Llanidloes is announcing a cheap re-issue of Rowlands's *Llyfryddiaeth y Cymry*, hitherto the only work of importance on the subject. In the face of Mr. Lewis Morris's statement that the Welsh as a nation are saturated with love for literature, it is painful to have to admit that Welsh publishers seldom if ever succeed by publishing Welsh books. The publisher of the Cambrian Bibliography lost at least £150 over this one Welsh venture, and is now broken in health, and in urgent need of rest, appealing to patriotic Welshmen to assist him to pay off the debt yet remaining on account of the work. It is to be hoped, for the honour of Welsh literature, that he will not be allowed to appeal in vain. The Bibliography projected by the Cymmrodorion Society will necessarily take many years for its accomplishment. Meanwhile prominent members of the Society are giving Rowlands's Bibliography a helping hand.

NOVEMBER 30, 1881.

NOTES.

SHROPSHIRE PARISH REGISTERS (Nov. 23, 1881).—I this week complete the list, with the Parishes whose Registers commence with the seventeenth and eighteenth, and present centuries.   T.W.H.

17th Century.

Acton Burnell, V.	1651	Kinnerley, V.	1677
Acton Scott, R.	1690	Kinlet, V.	1657
Adderley, R.	1692	Knockin, R.	1672
Albrighton, V.	1649	Leighton, V.	1662
Ashford Bowdler, V.	1609	Littleshall, V.	1656
Aston-under-Edgmond (or		Longdon-upon-Tern, V.	1692
Church Aston,) V.	1621	Loppington, V.	1654
Astley, V.	1630	Ludford, V.	1643
Atcham, V.	1621	Llanfair Waterdine, V.	1606
Badger, R.	1662	Llanyblodwel, V.	1695
Baschurch, V. (with *Little*		Llanymynech, R.	1668
Ness)	1600	Madeley, V.	1645
Battlefield, V. (Shrews-		Mainstone, R.	1604
bury)	1663	Meole Brace, V. (or *Brace*	
Beckbury, R.	1661	*Meole)*	1681
Bettws, V.	1662	Mindtown, R.	1607
Bitterley, R.	1657	Milson, V.	1678
Bonninghall, V.	1698	Monkhopton, V.	1603
Bridgnorth, St. Mary Mag		Montford, V.	1661
dalen, V.	1610	Neen Solars, V.	1678
Buildwas, V.	1659	Petton, V.	1677
Calver Hall (or *Carver*		Preston, V.	1691
Chapel) in Prees p, V.	1668	Preston Gubbalds, V.	1602
Chirbury, V.	1629	Quatt, V.	1672
Church Preen V.	1680	Quatford, V.	1687
Church Stretton, R.	1662	Rodington, R.	1678
Clive, V.	1611	Ryton, R.	1659
Clunn, V.	1653	Shrewsbury,	
Clee, St. Margaret, V.	1634	St. Chad, V.	1616
Cleobury Mortimer, V.	1603	Shifnal, V. (with *Priors*	
Cleobury North, R.	1680	*Lee)*	1678
Cold Weston, R.	1600	Shrawardine, R.	1641
Cound, R.	1608	Smethcote, R	1612
Dawley, V.	1666	Stanton-upon-Hineheath,	
Deuxhill and Glazeley, V.	1655	V.	1655
Detton Priors, V.	1673	Stapleton, R.	1630
Dudleston, V.	1693	Stoke St. Milborough, V.	
Easthope, R.	1624	(with *Heath Chapel).*	1654
Eaton, V.	1688	St. Martin, V.	1601
Eaton Constantine, R.	1684	Tong, V.	1620
Edgmond, R.	1680	Uppington, V.	1650
Ellesmere, V.	1653	Wellington, V.	1626
Eyton, R.	1698	Wentnor, R.	1662
West Felton, R.	1628	Little Wenlock, R.	1690
Habberley, R.	1670	Westbury, R. (with *Mins-*	
Halston, V.	1686	*terley)*	1637
Hinstock, R.	1695	Willey, R.	1644
Holgate, V.	1669	Winstanton, R.	1687
Hopesay, R.	1676	Woolstanton, R.	1601
Hordley, V.	1686	Wroxeter, V.	1613
Kemberton, R.	1659	Whitchurch, R. (with *Til-*	
Kinley, V.	1682	*stock)*	1633
Kinnersley, R.	1691		

18th Century.

Ashford Carbonell, V.	1721	Middleton Scriven, R.	1728
Barrow, V.	1727	Newtown (in *Wem* p.)	1780
Bedstone, R.	1719	Ratlinghope, R.	1702
Billingsley, R.	1739	Ruyton, V.	1719
Broughton, V.	1714	St. Kenelm's (in *Hales*	
Cardiston, R.	1706	*Owen* p.) V.	1736
Cockshutt, V.	1772	Sheinton, R.	1711
Cresage, V.	1722	Sidbury, R.	1731
Edgton, V.	1722	Silvington, V.	1716
Edstanton, V.	1712	Stirchley, R.	1718
Greet, R.	1728	Tibberton, V.	1710
Hadnal, V.	1721	Tugford, R.	1754
Harley, R.	1745	Upton Cressett, R.	1755
Hodnet, R.	1700	Welch Hampton, V.	1772
Hope Baggott, R.	1754	Whixall, V.	1753
Hope Wafers, R.	1729	Wormbridge, V.	1721
Melverley, V.	1723		

19th Century.

Hopton Cangford, V.	1812	St. George, V. (in *Don-*	
Sutton, R.	1814	*nington Wood)*	1806

CHESTER CORPORATION MANUSCRIPTS.—I am somewhat surprised the Free Library Committee of Chester do not follow the example of their brethren at Liverpool, and take the necessary steps to get some of their Corporate MSS. printed, for they must contain many very curious scraps of information. The following I have extracted from the report of the Historical MS. Commissioners is proof of this :—

"March 1593. Letter from the Earl of Derby to the Mayor of Chester, written on information of a serious fray in the same city between Owen Salusburie, and the writers son in law, John Salusburie, in which the former combatant had been grievously, it not mortally wounded. It is ordered that the best surgical aid may be procured for Owen Salusburie, and that in case of his death an inquest may be had for the cause thereof. Rec. 1 April 1593."

"9 August 1593. Letter from the Earl of Derby to the Mayor of Chester recommending that Richard Wright may be reinstated in the position of an innkeeper of the City of Chester, from which occupation he is very properly detained for his misconduct in ' suffering Owen Salusburie to bee conveyed out of his howse notwithstanding your commandment to him to the contrarie.'"

The Earl of Derby's "son-in-law" was Sir John Salusburie of Lleweni ; and Owen Salusburie was his cousin, of Rûg, a daring Welshman "who possessed a readie tongue, and a sharp sworde, and who could use both with equal skill when required to doe soe."   RAPHO.

PARLIAMENT OF ENGLAND (July 6, 1881).—Members for *Flintshire*. The first name under each date refers to the County, and the second to the Boroughs :—

1552-3	Thomas Hanmer. Edwardus Stanley, de Flynt, armiger.
1553	Robertus Massye. Edwardus Stanley, armiger.
1554	Willielmus Moston, miles (1). Robertus Salesbury, armiger.
1554	Ditto. Robertus Massy, armiger.
1555	Robertus Massye. Edwardus Stanley, armiger.
1557-8	Johannes Conwey, armiger. Petrus Moston, armiger.
1558-9	John Gruffyth, esq. John Hanmer, esq.
1562-3	George Raynscrofte, esq. John Conwey, esq.
1572	William Mosten, esq, of Mosten. Humphrey Hanmer, gent.
1584	John Hope, esq. Richard Lloyde, esq.
1586	William Ravenscrofte, esq. Michael Doughtye, gent.
1588-9	Roger Puleston (2). John Edwards (2).

(1) Return defaced.
(2) Returned by one Indenture.

592-3	Thomas Hanmer, esq.	Thomas Gruff, gent
597	William Ravenscrofte, esq.	Edward Morgan, jun. gent
601	Ditto.	John Price (1)
603-4	Roger Puleston, esq.	Roger Brereton, esq.
614	No Return found.	
620-1	Ditto.	William Ravenscroft, esq.
623-4	Sir John Hanmer, bart. (3).	William Ravenscrofte, esq.
625	Sir John Trevor, jun. Knight.	Ditto
625-6	John Salisbury, esq.	Ditto.
627-8	Robert Jones, esq.	Ditto (4)
640	John Mostyn, esq.	Sir Thomas Hanmer, bart
640	Ditto. (5)	John Salisburie, jun. esq (6)
654	John Trevor.	Andrew Ellice
656	No Returns found (7)	
658-9	Ditto.	
660	Kenrick Eyton, esq.	Roger Whitley, esq.
661	Sir Henry Conwey, bart. (8)	Ditto.
678-9	Mutton Davies, esq.	Ditto.
679	Ditto, of Gwrsaney.	Ditto, sen.
680-1	Sir John Hanmer, Knight and bart.	Thomas Whittley, esq
1685	Sir John Conwey, bart. of Potwthan.	Sir John Hanmer, Knight and bart
1688-9	Sir Roger Puleston, Knight.	Ditto
1690	Roger Puleston of Emerall, county Flint.	Thomas Whitley, esq.
1695	Sir John Conwey, bart.	Sir Roger Puleston, bart. (9)
1698	Sir John Conway, bart.	Thomas Mostyn, esq.
1701	Ditto.	Ditto
1701	Sir Roger Mostyn, bart.	Sir Thomas Hanmer, bart. (10)
1702	Sir Thomas Hanmer, bart.	Sir Roger Mostyn, bart. (11)
1705	Sir John Conway, bart.	Sir Roger Mostyn, bart.
1708	Sir Roger Mostyn, bart.	Sir John Conway, bart.
1710	Ditto (12)	Ditto
1713	Sir John Conway, bart.	Sir Roger Mostyn, bart.
1714-5	Sir Roger Mostyn, bart.	Sir John Conway, bart. (13)
1722	Ditto	Thomas Eyton, esq.
1727	Ditto	Salusbury Lloyd, esq. (14)

(3) Sir John Trevor, jun., Knight, returned vice Sir John Hanmer, bart., deceased, 6 Dec., 1624.
(4) Peter Wynne, gent., returned vice William Ravenscrofte, deceased, 1 Dec., 1628.
(5) John Trevor, esq., returned vice John Mostyn, esq., disabled to sit, 7 Dec., 1640.
(6) Thomas Midleton, esq., returned vice John Salisbury, jun., esq., disabled to sit, 7 Dec., 1640.
(7) John Glynne, Chief Justice, was elected to serve for Carnarvon county, but elected to serve for county Flint.
(8) Sir Thomas Hanmer, bart., returned vice Sir Henry Conwey, deceased, 1 Nov., 1669. Mutton Davies, returned vice Sir Thomas Hanmer, deceased, 18 Nov., 1678.
(9) Thomas Ravenscroft, esq., returned vice Sir Roger Puleston, deceased, 8 April, 1697.
(10) Sir John Conway, bart, returned vice Sir Thomas Hanmer, who elected to serve for Thetford, co. Norfolk, 2 Feb., 1701-2.
(11) Thomas Mostyn, esq., returned vice Sir Roger Mostyn, who elected to serve for the county of Chester, 2 Dec., 1702.
(12) Sir Roger Mostyn, re-elected 30 Dec. 1711, after appointment to an office of profit by the Crown.
(13) Thomas Eyton, esq. elected vice Sir John Conway deceased, 10 June 1721.
(14) Salusbury Lloyd, esq. and George Wynne, esq., were returned by separate Indentures, but by Order of the House dated 21 May 1728, both Indentures were taken off the file, and a new Return was ordered to be made.
5

1734	Thomas Mostyn, esq. of Mostyn.	Sir George Wynne, bart.
1741	Sir John Glyn, bart. of Broad-lane.	Richard Williams, esq.
1747	Sir Thomas Mostyn, bart.	Kyffin Williams, esq. (15)
1754	Ditto (16)	Sir John Glynne, bart.
1761	Sir Roger Mostyn, bart.	Ditto
1768	Ditto	Ditto
1774	Ditto	Ditto (17)
1780	Ditto	Watkin Williams, esq. of Penbedw
1784	Ditto	Ditto
1790	Ditto	Ditto
1796	Ditto (18)	Ditto (19)
1802	Ditto	Ditto
1806	Ditto	Sir Edward Pryce Lloyd, bart.
1807	Ditto	William Shipley, esq.
1812	Ditto	Sir E. P. Lloyd, bart.
1818	Ditto	Ditto
1820	Ditto	Ditto
1826	Ditto	Ditto
1830	Ditto	Ditto
1831	Edward Mostyn Lloyd Mostyn, esq.	Ditto (20)

For return of Members from the passing of the Reform Bill, up to 1880, see Bye-gones, Apr. 7, 1880.

QUERIES.

JOHN JONES OF GLANGORS.—This Welshman lived in London for many years and died there in 1821. He obtained considerable celebrity as the writer of popular songs. In a short biographical notice of him which appeared at the time of his death he is said to have been a prolific song writer, and his "Dic Sion Dafydd," and "Siencin Morgan's wedding," were said to be well known. I should like to know something more of the man than the date of his death, and more of his songs than their mere names? Let me add that I have made diligent search in the Library of the British Museum and elsewhere for any trace of the man and his productions, but beyond the obituary notice to which I have alluded have found nothing. I hope I shall not appeal in vain in Bye-gones for all the information I want, and at the same time secure some notice for a name, which, for aught I know, may have sunk into undeserved oblivion.　　D.J.

REPLIES.

LLANRHAIADR IN CINMERCH—(Oct. 12, 1881).—The inscription on the tomb of Ambrose Thelwall raises some interesting questions. From the title at the head of NEMO'S remarks I somewhat hastily concluded that the tomb had been placed in Llanrhaiadr Church, which can scarcely be supposed to contain the "sepulchre

(15) Sir John Glynne, bart. elected vice Kyffin Williams, esq. deceased, 28 Nov. 1753.
(16) Sir Roger Mostyn, bart., elected vice Sir Thomas Mostyn deceased, 26 April 1758
(17) Watkin Williams, esq. elected vice Sir John Glynne deceased, 26 June 1777.
(18) John Lloyd, esq., of Tyddyn, elected 8 Nov. 1796, vice Sir Roger Mostyn, bart., deceased. Sir Thomas Mostyn, bart., elected 8 Nov. 1799 vice John Lloyd, esq., who accepted the Chiltern Hundreds.
(19) Watkin Williams, esq., re-elected 17 Mar. 1799.
(20) Henry Glynne, esq., elected 22 Sep. 1831, vice Lloyd, called to the Upper House as Baron Mostyn. Sir Stephen Richard Glynne, bart., elected 25 Feb. 1832, vice Henry Glynne, who accepted the Chiltern Hundreds.

46

of his fathers," as the several branches of his family inhabited other neighbouring parishes, but not, as far as I know, Llanrhaiadr. But, on further examination, I find that the inscription is copied by the writer, not from that in the Church itself, but from a MS. containing some from other Churches also. Hence I infer that " W.A.L." did not include it in his list because he failed to find it there. By the pedigree given of his family in Add. MSS. 9,865, an Ambrose Thelwall was one of the nine sons of Edward Thelwall, the second son of John Wynn Thelwall of Llanrudd (i.e. Bathavarn Park ?), son of John Thelwall by his wife Margaret, dau. of John, son of David, son of Meredydd of Bachegraig. Whose son, then, was the Sir John Thelwall of the inscription ? His tombstone would probably, therefore, be found in the Church of Llanrudd, where there are monuments to other members of the Thelwall family, copies of which, it is greatly to be desired, may shortly appear in *Bye-gones.*   H.W.L.

OSWESTRY TOWN CLERK (Nov. 9, 1881).—I cannot answer TELL's query, but for the information of your readers I may state that "Thomas Herbert, Esq., Councillor at Law" succeeded Humphrey Parry in the office of Town Clerk in Nov. 1759. Richard Davies was appointed Deputy-Clerk, about the same time. On Oct. 23, 1761, Davies was sworn Town Clerk in the place of Herbert, but in 1775, and down to 1782, we have the name of Herbert again attached to the records of Corporation meetings. For a short time between the dates of Parry and Herbert, one "Simon" signs the books, but there is no record that he was ever appointed Town Clerk. In 1783 "John Probert, Esquire" produced his appointment by Lord Powis, and was sworn. In 1791 he was made Mayor, and "Lewis Jones, gent." was appointed Town Clerk.   JARCO.

THE CYMMRODORION (Oct. 6, 1880).—The correspondent who has enquired the reason why this Society is called Honourable will scarcely find a direct solution of his query in the account given of its original institution in the Society's transactions. But the explanation appears to be in the fact that the Society was founded under the patronage and auspices of the Prince of Wales, who was actually a member. And I am informed that the etiquette in such matters is that to Societies of which the Sovereign is a member is accorded the distinctive epithet of "Royal" as a part of the title, and of "Honourable" to those who have been honoured by the membership of any one of the Royal Family not actually the Sovereign. Hence the distinction between the "Royal Society," the "Royal Academy," &c., and the Honourable Societies of Lincoln's Inn, Gray's Inn, and others, the titles of which will readily be accounted for in a similar manner.   H.W.L.

CURRENT NOTES.

The *University College of Wales Magazine* (published at the College, Aberystwyth) has made its first appearance for the new session. The contents are varied, the most interesting, perhaps, being "Shakspeare's Hypocrites," an extract from an essay for which, as we understand, Mr. J. J. Waller, one of the students of the College, won the prize of the new Shakspeare Society. Dr. Humpidge contributes a paper on "Wasted Energy in Wales," in which he says—"We often hear outcries that the great source of energy in our coal-fields is rapidly becoming exhausted, and that in not many years we shall be without any cheap and easily available source of energy. I do not think we have much to fear on this score. People talk of the waste of coal, but forget the waste of water and wind power. Should our coal-fields become exhausted, more than sufficient energy for all man's needs can always

be obtained from the falling water and the moving air—sources of energy which can never be exhausted as long as the sun shines, or as long as life is possible on our globe." Dr. Humpidge's contribution leads us to ask whether the pages of the magazine could not be devoted more than they are to local subjects, such as the history, natural history, geology, and archæology of Wales, mountaineering papers, and so on. This would give the publication a special character, and make it far more valuable and interesting. If one of the students would carefully study, say, one of the parishes near Aberystwyth, and bring out the main features of its physical formation, and read for us the story which the ancient glaciers have written on the surface of the earth ; if another would bring the history on by the light of archæological remains ; and a third would carry it forward in historic times ; how good the results might be for the students of the College, and how interesting for the readers of the Magazine.

The *Tablet,* in an article on "Old English Devotion," professes its belief in the restoration of Winefride to life, at the intercession of Beuno, after her head had been cut off. "Having vowed her virginity to God, she was slain by Caradoc while in flight to the church to escape insult. The severed head of the martyr rolled into the church, where it was raised by St. Beuno, who was saying Mass. As the tradition tells us, he covered her body with his cloak, returned to finish the Mass, and then called upon the people to unite with him in prayer ; and Gwenfrewi (Winefride) arose as if she had been sleeping, only a mark upon her neck tracing where the sword had cut its way. The blood-red marks upon the stones are still shown, the moss is still famed for what has been called its ' odour of frankincense,' the perfect clearness of the stream is still a marvel, and with such force does it fill the well itself that there, at the source, it would be impossible to keep a footing where the water rises. Many cures well attested are to be found in every account of Holywell ; still more are within the memory of all who live near ; the useless crutches have long been numberless in the sight of those visiting the well ; and the healing of lameness, blindness, and painful and humanly incurable diseases, is only the exterior sign of greater invisible favours. Knightly and even royal names have been recorded as pilgrims to Holywell in the old days of faith. But we believe that it adds still more interest to the holy spot to remind our readers that, after the shrine had been ruthlessly plundered and left desolate as the wrecking Reformation swept over the land, pilgrim Catholics and disguised priests still made their way thither to pray to St. Winefride, where their forefathers had prayed. Those who were afterwards to share the glory of martyrdom trod the paths of Holywell, and bathed in the water flowing from the martyr's well. Father John Gerard came there in pilgrimage, and there Father Oldcorne was restored to health, only to preserve it for his Master's sake until he was 'butchered alive' at Worcester. On his way thither he had been cured of a cancer in the mouth by the touch of a stone from the well ; and Challoner tells us that, before bathing in the waters, labour and austerities had so exhausted him that he was scarcely able to stand."

Mr. John Owen Griffith (Ioan Arfon) of Carnarvon, one of the best known bards in the Principality, died on Tuesday, Nov. 22. Mr. Griffith, who was fifty-three years of age, was born at Waenfawr in 1828. In 1865 he carried off the chair prize at the Bethesda Eisteddfod, and won many prizes and medals at other Eisteddfodau in the Principality and in Australia. Of late years, however, he was best known as an able and impartial adjudicator in these competitions. Mr. Griffith was an active and zealous supporter of the Liberal cause in his native county. His funeral took place on Saturday in the burial ground at Brynrodyn, near Carnarvon, and was attended by a great number of persons. The chief mourners were his widow; Mr. Robert Griffith and Mr. Owen Griffith, sons; his four daughters; and his two brothers. Some twenty private carriages closed the procession. Before leaving the house prayer was offered by the Rev. E. Herber Evans; the Rev. J. Jones, Groeslon, officiated in the Chapel, and the service at the grave was conducted by the Rev. J. Alun Roberts. A committee has been formed with the object of erecting a public memorial upon the grave.

The old parish church of Eglwysfach, near Conway, was re-opened on Tuesday, Nov. 15, after restoration. The preachers were the Bishop of St. Asaph, Canon Hugh Jones, and the Rev. D. Evans, rector of Abergele. At the luncheon in the National School, after the opening service, the Bishop of St. Asaph, in replying to the toast of his health, spoke hopefully of the future of the Church of England, and remarked that if the Church was disestablished there was nothing in existence to stand between them and the corrupt communion of the Church of Rome.

Mr. A. Strahan, M.A., F.G.S., of her Majesty's Geological Survey, gave a very interesting lecture last week, on "The Denudations of North Wales," at a meeting of the Chester Society of Natural Science, on Thursday evening. In the course of his lecture he traced the geological history of the district from the earliest rocks (the Bala Beds), the deposition of which was characterized by great volcanic activity. At the close of the Lower Silurian period the great volcanic outbursts ceased, and it was not possible to recognize in all North Wales a fragment of any volcanic crater. In conclusion Mr. Strahan gave a description of the way in which the river Alyn had cut its way into the gravel of the gracial drift, and spread that gravel over many acres of the almost level ground at Rossett to the depth of some ten feet. In many other cases the rivers flowed in channels contained almost wholly in the glacial drift which thus formed a protective covering to the rock beneath. When this had been removed, and they had regained their pre-glacial channels in the solid rock the deepening of the old valleys, probably often before interrupted, would be continued until the next great change placed North Wales once more beneath the waters of the ocean.

SIR WATKIN WILLIAMS WYNN, BART., M.P., is about to present the Rev. Arthur Robins with some carved oak choir stalls for the Parish Church of Holy Trinity, Windsor, in memory of his nephew, Mr. Wynn, of the Scots Guards, who was accidentally drowned at Windsor last year.

DAVID COX, THE ARTIST, REPAIRING THE SIGNBOARD. Cox had promised the landlord that some fine day, when he should have nothing better to do, he would "touch it up" and restore its faded charms. Accordingly, one day he procured a ladder, and with palette on thumb and a handful of brushes, he set vigorously to work. He had not been long thus occupied, dabbling away with plenty of pigment, the forest monarch putting forth new foliage of most verdant hue, and the herbage at foot springing into life and beauty at every touch, when it suddenly occurred to him that his position at that moment was not a dignified one for an artist of reputation, and that should any one pass who knew him a story might be circulated not greatly to his advantage. But he comforted himself with the reflection that possibly he might get through his task unobserved, or that, if noticed at all by any passing tra-veller, he would be taken to be the legitimate sign painter of the district, who had been engaged to do the job. Before long he heard the sound of a carriage approaching. "Now," thought he, "I'm caught." Still he kept his place on the ladder, and painted away, never looking around to ascertain who or what was coming. Greatly to his dismay the vehicle stopped at the very foot of the ladder, the carriage door was opened, the steps were let down, and presently he perceived a sweet female face peeping at him from below. "Why, it is Mr. Cox, I declare!" greeted his ear, and made him almost drop to the ground. "You are not painting for fame, sir, now!" Looking down he discovered that the lady was an old London pupil who had recently been married, and was then travelling through Wales with her husband.—*Biography of David Cox.*

The Baroness Willoughby D'Eresby has subscribed £500 towards the new church at Dolwyddelan.

FUNERAL OF SIR HUGH OWEN.

On Saturday the remains of the late Sir Hugh Owen, which were brought from Mentone on the previous Thursday, were interred at the Abney Park Cemetery. The details of the procession had been settled at a committee (made up of those who had taken a prominent part in the proposed banquet) held at Lonsdale Chambers on Friday evening, by whom the control of the arrangements was delegated to Messrs. Howel Thomas and Solomon Owen. The procession started from the Voel, Hornsey Lane, in the following order. An open carriage bore the coffin, which was covered with wreaths of flowers. The members of the family of the late Sir Hugh Owen followed in four carriages. The first contained his sons, Mr. Hugh Owen and Mr. William Owen, his brother, Mr. William Owen, Voel, Anglesea, and his son-in-law, Mr. Hugh Pugh, Carnarvon; the second had Mr. Henry Burt, Mr. Covey Wright, and Mr. Dix Lewis, sons-in-law, and Mr. Squire; the third and fourth brought Mr. R. K. Burt and grandsons of the deceased. At the committee meeting above mentioned, precedence in the procession had been voted to the representatives of the University College of Wales, with whose establishment and existence the late Sir Hugh had been so intimately associated. Four carriages bore the following representatives of the institution, viz., the Rev. T. C. Edwards, M.A., Principal, Mr. Lewis Morris M.A., Dr. Evans, secretary, Mr. T. J. Thomas, C.C., Queen Victoria-street, Professor Rhys, Mr. Thomas Gee, Mr. W. Rowlands, Manchester, Mr. T. M. Williams, B.A., Mr. John Hughes, C.C., Mr. Simner. The British and Foreign School Society was represented by Messrs. J. Marriage, J. C. Curtis, A. F. Smith, A. Bourne, and W. Prydderch Williams. The National Temperance League, of which the deceased was honorary treasurer, by Mr. John Taylor, Chairman, Mr. R. Rae, Secretary, Messrs. W. Walker and M. Young, Dr. Scutliff, Lieut.-Col. Young, Dr. Williams, and Mr. T. E. Minshall, Oswestry. The Honorable Society of Cymmrodorion by Mr. Stephen Evans, Chairman of Council, Mr. Brinley Richards, Mr. Evan Evans, and Mr. C. W. Jones, Secretary. The National Eisteddfod Association, which the late Sir Hugh was the principal means of founding, by Mr. Joseph Edwards, sculptor, and Mr. Howel Thomas, Local Government Board. The North Wales Scholarship Association, by Mr. W. C. Davies, Bangor, and Mr. H. Lloyd Roberts, Temple; and the Borough of Finsbury, with which the deceased gentleman was educationally and politically connected during many years, by Messrs. Dethridge, Pickburn, and Poley. Following these came a large number of private carriages

containing or representing Mr. Henry Richard, M.P.,
Mr. W. McCullagh Torrens, M.P., Mr. J. H. Puleson,
M.P., the Ven. Archdeacon Griffith, Mr. Ellis Jones,
Hounslow, Rev. John Evans (W), Captain Verney, Alder-
man T. J. Williams, Denbigh, Mr. Betjemann, Mr. and
Mrs. W. Lewis, Mrs. Dr. Hannay, Mr. and Mrs. Drew,
Dr. Glover, Mr. L. H. and Mr. R. Roberts, Canonbury,
Major Blunkley, Dr. Luke, &c., &c.

At the entrance to the cemetery the procession was
headed by a choir who, led by Mr. W. Davies (Mynorydd),
sang to the tune of "Bangor" the old Welsh hymn

Mor ddedwydd yw y rhai, twy ffydd
Sy'n myn'd o blith y byw.

At the grave, portions of the Church of England service
for the dead were impressively read alternately in English
and Welsh, by the Ven. Archdeacon Griffith of Llandaff,
the Rev. John Evans (Eglwysbach), minister of the Welsh
Wesleyan Circuit of London, offering up prayer and pronouncing the benediction. Some more Welsh hymns and
the English one commencing

There is a land of pure delight
Where saints immortal reign,

were also sung.

Owing to the inclemency of the weather and the large
attendance, it was deemed desirable to adjourn from the
cemetery to the Abney Congregational Chapel, opposite
the Church-street entrance, for the purpose of delivering
the funeral addresses.

DECEMBER 7, 1881.

NOTES.

MONUMENT TO MATTHEW PRYCE, M.P.
The handsome 17th century mural monument to the
memory of Matthew Pryce, of Park, M.P., is placed
against the E. wall of Llanwnog church, on the S. E.
side of the communion-table, and consists of a large marble
slab (the inscription upon which is subjoined), surmounted
by a pediment above which is placed, supported by two
cherubs, an armorial shield bearing, dexter, gules, a lion
rampant reguardant, or, and sinister, gules, a fess or,
between three boars' heads argent, (the emblazonry of
the arms sinister both here and below is much faded).
The slab is flanked by two pillars having on their respective bases shields bearing arms as dexter and sinister above.
The lower part of the whole is ornamented with a death's
head, etc. The inscription, which is a remarkably good
specimen of the ornate and elaborate style of the age, is
as follows :—

Here lieth interr'd the Body of Mathew Pryce of Park-pen
price in the County of Montgomery Esqr who was Eldest Son
of John Pryce of Park aforesaid Esqr (by Mary, Daughter of
William Read of Castle Bromshill in the County of Gloucester
Esqr) who was only Son of Mathew Pryce of Park Esqr (by
Catherine Eldest daughter of Lewis Gwynne of Llanidloes Esqr)
who was second Son of John Pryce of Newtown Hall in ye
County of Montgomery Esqr.

As He had the Happiness to be descended from an Antient
& Worshipfull Family, so he took Care to improve ye Advantages
of his Birth & Fortune, that He might be able to distinguish
himself No less by his own personal Worth & Merits than by
the Dignity and lustre of his Ancestors. His known Abilities
& Integrity recommended him to the Service of his Prince &
Country. In several Imployments and Important Trusts At ye
Barr an Able & Learned Councellour, on ye Bench an Upright
and Vigilant Justice of ye Peace. In ye Militia A Loyal &
Active Deputy Lieutenant & Captain of ye County Troop. And
in Parliament where He had the Honour to serve as Burgess for
Montgomery, In ye two last Parliaments of King Charles ye
Second's Reign. He shew'd himself a good Patriot & True
Lover of his Country In all these Honourable Trusts He

acquitted himself with Inviolable Fidelity to his Prince with
eminent Care & zeal for ye good and Prosperity of his Country
& With Singular Duty and observance to his Mother ye Church
of England, of which he always approved himself A True &
obedient Son & A zealous and steady Defender of her Rights &
Constitution. Nor was He less Exemplary in ye Vertues that
adorn a private Life in respect of which He Worthily sustain'd
ye Character of A Wise and truly Honest Man & of A Sincere &
Hearty Christian.

He married Hester Thelwall ye Twelfth Daughter of John
Thelwall of Bathavern Park in ye County of Denbigh Esqr, who
surviving Him and desireous to transmitt His deserved Character
to Posterity at her sole Charge Erected this Monument as well
to be A Publick & lasting Mark of that true Love & Affection
She had for him when alive. as for ye Respect & Veneration
She retains for the memory of her deceas'd Husband.

He died ye 23rd of Jan. A.D. 1699. Annoque Ætat futæ 60.

C.J.D.

OSWESTRY CHURCH NOTES.

In the list of Oswestry Vicars given in our local histories
the appointment of Mr. Guild is dated 1694 : Corporation
documents show it should be 1691. Following this we
have Mr. Thomas Jones as appointed in 1697. This, too,
is an error : a Corporation minute says, that "Thomas
Jones, vicar and schoolmaster," was made a burgess "in
the time of David Lloyd, Mayor." Mr. Lloyd was
Mayor in 1694. So if we put the appointment of Jones
back three years it will tally with the other minute
referred to which states that Guild was "recommended
to the office of vicar" in 1691.

Our Vicars seem to have been made burgesses pretty
soon after their appointments. Early in 1716 Mr. Parry
(who was instituted vicar in 1713-4) was elected a burgess,
"gratis," provided he could "have the High Steward's
approbation."

In connection with the new Church I find that in 1863,
Bishop Short supported an application for "Gally Knight
benefaction," £400, towards erection of Trinity Parsonage,
and promised £100 himself. Other subscriptions were
notified, viz :—the Earl of Powis £200, Mr. T. L. Longueville [£100, Mrs. Lloyd, Aston, £50, Mrs. Ormsby
Gore £25, &c.

In a paper on Oswestry Ecclesiastical History I published in the third vol. of the Shropshire Archæological
Society's *Transactions*, I gave an entry from the Oswestry
Corporation records showing that lead had been purchased previous to 1549 from Langley of Salop for the church
and presumed some building work must have been on
hand about that time. In connection with this subject I
find by the will of Richard Staney, executed in 1542, that
"fyve poundes" was left for "reparacon and buylding
of the churche" and "fyve poundes" for "buylding of a
new scole within the churche yarde." A clause in the
will of Robert ap Howell, 1541, is as follows :—"Item
my will is that my executor doe bestowe after my decease
a lode of Leade towardes the coveringe of the Roffe of
thalteries of the Roode and saint Katherin within the paryshe
Churche of Oswestrie aforesaide and the same to be de-
lyveride at the tyme the foresaide Roffe be reddye to
receve coveringe."

In a paper on Old Chapel history (Vol. 4. *Trans.* S. A.S.)
it was stated that "Rowland Nevett of Weston, *clerk*"
was one of the "newly-appointed Burgesses" sworn after
the Charter of Charles II was granted. In another Corporation entry I find that "Rowland Nevett of Weston,
gent." was one of the ancient burgesses who made his
claim in 1674, and "Richard Edwards, vicar," was
another. Mr. Nevett's having been deposed by the Act
of Uniformity was the reason of the substitution of
"gent." for "clerk" in the entry I suppose, but as he
had been legally ordained this was not warranted. A.R.

HIGHWAY ROBBERY NEAR SHELTON.—
Sometime during the spring of 1835, John Phillips, a smith
residing in the Queen's Head Yard, Oswestry, was attacked on his way home from Shrewsbury, near Shelton,
by three men, who robbed him and threw him over the
hedge—more dead than alive. When the poor fellow recovered sufficiently he managed to crawl to the road
again, and was brought home by The Accommodation
coach. He was never well again, and died early the next
year. At the time of his death it was said that two of
the villains were known in Shrewsbury. Was the case
ever investigated ? SCROBBES BYRIG.

DISERTH CHURCH (Nov. 9, 1881).—From the following genealogical table, taken from a MS. in the British
Museum, it will appear that Dorothy, wife of William
Moston, Esquire, was daughter to John Langford, Esquire,
of Trevalyn, Co. Flint, and that, in all probability, the
gaps in another inscription are to be partly filled by the
words RICARDUS . . . . . . EPISCOPI. ASAPHEN. FILIUS.
The table is remarkable for the numerous cross-marriages
it displays with the family of Bishop Parry, and as showing that the Rhyd property was carried twice by the marriage of an heiress into the family of Mostyn of Mostyn.
H.W.L.

Moston (or Mostyn)
of Rhyd.

Harl. MS., 1481.

1st Wife.
Anne, dau. and heir =Thomas Moston of Rhyd, = Gwen, dau. to John Wyn ab Rhys
to Thomas Hughes, son of Sir Roger of Llwyn Ynn, widow of Richard
Bishop of St. Asaph. Moston, Knight. Parry, Bishop of St. Asaph.

2nd Wife.

2nd Son.
William Moston=Anne, dau. to Richard Thomas Moston. 1. Lucy=William Conway, eldest son
of Rhyd. Parry, Bishop of St. Asaph. of Sir John Conway.

2. Mary=Richard, son to Richard Parry,
Thomas Moston=Margaret, dau. to William Bishop of St. Asaph. [Appears
of Rhyd. Llwyd of Halton. by the inscription on his tomb
at Diserth to have been buried
there on 23rd February, 1637.]

Eldest Son. 2. Not named. 1. Beatrice.
William Moston=Dorothy, dau. to John 3. Richard, 2. Lucy.
of Rhyd. Oblit, Langford of Trevalyn. drowned,
6th Nov., 1678, Oblit, 1st Nov., 1681. issueless.
Aged 26.[Inscrip- [Inscription on Tombstone
tion on Tomb- at Dyserth.]
stone at Dyserth]

1. Margaret=Thomas Moston of Rhyd, 2nd son of Sir Thomas Moston of Moston, Bart., by his wife, Bridget,
2. Elizabeth. dau. and heir to Darcy Savage of Langton, Co. Chester, and brother of Sir Roger
Moston, who married Lady Essex Finch, dau. of Daniel, Earl of Nottingham.

THE YOUNG ROSCIUS (Oct. 26, 1881).—Yet
another word about this precocious Shropshire prodigy. At
one time his life was despaired of, in consequence, it is
said, of his having taken poison. It would appear from
the Salopian Journal of Nov. 28, 1804, that grave fears
were entertained lest the avarice of his friends, who
worked him night and day, "and at places so distant from
each other as to occasion much fatigue in travelling"
would cut off his career prematurely ; and an awful
example is given in the fate of a boy Parker, who had
some time before exhibited at Covent Garden as a Musical
genius. Young Betty, however, seems to have had more
calibre, for, as stated already, he lived to be nearly
ninety ; and at the time the charge of avarice was made
the father repudiated it. BUSKIN.

THE FIRST OSWESTRY NEWSPAPER (Dec.
29, 1880).—At this date I made some extracts from the
original prospectus of the Oswestry Herald, a paper that
was issued in our borough for nearly three years, and was
then "swamped by excessive taxation." In the Book of
Quarter Sessions, amongst the Corporation Records, I find
the following, under the proceedings of 1820 :—

"WILLIAM CATHRALL of Oswestry as Publisher of a
Newspaper entitled the Oswestry Herald appeared per-
sonally before me one of his Majesty's Justices of the
Peace in and for the Town of Oswestry and entered into
Recognizances himself in the sum of Two hundred Pounds,
And James Williams and John Prynallt his Sureties also

appeared personally before me and entered into Recognizances in the sum of Two hundred Pounds in due form as
a Penalty payable to his Majesty his Heirs and Successors
that is to say James Williams in the sum of one hundred
and ninety Pounds and John Prynallt in the sum of Ten
Pounds of lawful British money on the condition mentioned in the eighth section of an Act of Parliament
passed in the sixtieth year of his late Majesty George the
third, Chapter the ninth, acknowledged by the Within
named William Cathrall, James Williams and John
Prynallt respectively this Twentieth day of March One
thousand eight hundred and twenty.
" Before me————————"
" Town of Oswestry.
"I WILLIAM CATHRALL do hereby give notice that I
have a printing press and types which I purpose to use for
printing in a House situate in Cross Street, Oswestry,
which I require to be entered pursuant to an Act passed
in the 39th year of George the third entitled ' An Act for
the more effectual Suppression of Societies established for
treasonable purposes and for better preventing treasonable
and seditious practices !'
" Witness :————————
" To the Clerk of the Peace at
Oswestry, 20th March, 1820."
The entry is evidently only a copy of the original document, for it contains no signatures. The first No. of this
paper was published the day following the above date.
JARCO.

CURRENT NOTES.

There is a movement on foot among the artists resident in Wales—especially in the neighbourhood of Bettws-y-Coed—to establish a Society of Arts for the Principality. Though a Royal Academy has existed in England many years, and the Scottish and Hibernian Academies are old institutions, yet Wales has had no society of this kind. It is felt that the time has arrived when a "Cambrian Academy of Arts" should be brought into existence, and most of the artists, resident in Wales, and those connected with the Principality, have agreed to form themselves into a society with the object of holding annual summer exhibitions at Llandudno. An executive council and officers have been elected. This list of members will be definitely closed on or before the 1st of February next, after which successful applicants for admission will be placed on the associates' list.

The Hon. Evelyn Ashley, M.P., the second son of the Earl of Shaftesbury, and one of the proprietors of Palmerston Quarry at Festiniog, addressed a large meeting of quarrymen and others at Festiniog last week. In the course of his speech he said that his old friend, Mr. Morgan Lloyd, had offered to give him lessons in Welsh. Speaking of Mr. Lloyd reminded him of a good story which was related of that gentleman when he (Mr. Ashley) was at the bar. He would not vouch for its accuracy, but he would tell it as he heard it. Mr. Lloyd was defending a prisoner against whom it was evident the judge would sum up strongly. He asked permission to address the jury in Welsh, and on its being granted cautioned the jury in the strongest terms against paying any attention to that old woman on the Bench if he should attempt to interfere, as he knew nothing whatever about the subject. Naturally, after this the judge's charge was received with suspicion, and the prisoner was let off.

CWTTA CYFARWYDD.—Some of our readers will remember that it was stated in the last annual report of the Cambrian Archæological Society, that the late Mr. Breese's transcript of the "Cwtta Cyfarwydd" had been mislaid. It now transpires that the MS. has been all the time at the printers' in London, where Mr. Breese left it only a day or two before his lamented death. It will be published as soon as a sufficient number of subscribers, at 6s. 6d., have sent in their names.

THE LATE MR. WYNN.—The beautifully-carved oak choir stalls presented by Sir Watkin Wynn in memory of his nephew, who was accidentally drowned at Windsor last year, designed and executed by Mr. Kendall, have been fixed in Holy Trinity parish church, Windsor. They display the carver's art in the highest perfection, and are equal to the best work contributed by Mr. Kendall to the House of Lords. They were fixed by Saturday last, when a sermon appropriate to the occasion was preached by the rector, the Rev. Arthur Robins.

THE CYMMRODORION SOCIETY.—The committee of the Welsh dialect section of the Cymmrodorion Society met on Saturday, Nov. 26, at Gloucester Gardens. There were present—Prince Louis-Lucien Bonaparte, Messrs. Alexr. J. Ellis, Howel Lloyd, Thos. W. Hancock, Henry Sweet, vice-president Philological Society, David Lewis, barrister, and Dr. Isambard Owen. Communications were received from Professor Silvan Evans, Gweirydd ap Rhys, the Rev. W. Watkins, Llanover, and the Rev. B. Williams, Llandovery. The Committee sat nearly four hours finally revising the phonetic scheme which Mr. Ellis has recast. Proofs had been submitted to all members in Wales and England. After further verbal revision the scheme will be approved, printed, and issued.

DECEMBER 14, 1881,

NOTES.

COLLECTORS OF LOCAL BOOKS.—The collectors of local books were few and far between when I first began to pick up Cambrian and Border Counties Works, but of late they are common enough, and they compete with each other for any old local books that are advertised in London, or in Provincial Catalogues. At times purchasers are sadly taken in by the incorrect description of such works; and at other times they miss many a needed book by the carelessness of authors and of printers. I have a small duo volume of *thirty nine pages* entitled "The Stranger's Companion In Chester; being a familiar Guide to its Public Buildings, Institutions, and other places remarkable either for their Curiosity or Antiquity. London : Printed by C. Kerwood, John Street, Edgware Road, for G. Batenham, at the North Gate, Chester, 1821." I had occasion the other day to look over a parcel of old cuttings once the property of Richard Llwyd (The Bard of Snowdon), when I found a loose copy of the above book in sheets, but upon examining it I found it contained *seventy one pages*, and forthwith I compared it with the former one. The two titles were exactly alike except in this particular—the smaller one was printed by Kerwood "for G. Batenham," the larger one by the same printer "for the Author," and then a more careful examination shewed me they were two distinct works; printed in a different type though upon the same sized paper, and each in the year 1821. If the printer had said *enlarged edition*, or, a *new edition*, the distinction would have been made plain ; as it is I find one friend who insists the "Stranger's Companion" of 1821 has but 39 pages, whilst another friend is equally sure it has 71 pages ; the fact being that neither of them knew of the two separate editions which had appeared in the same year ! I could give other instances in proof of my contention, but this one will suffice to show how necessary it is that more care should be taken in describing local books.   A BOOKWORM.

A WELSHMAN'S "IF."—The following anecdote of the ancient house of Plas Coch, Anglesey, appears in *The Cambrian* newspaper for March 11, 1800 :—

Hugh Hughes of this house was Queen Elizabeth's Attorney in N. Wales : a lawyer and reputed a great oppressor : therefore upon his building Plas Coch a certain poet made this Englyn :

> Plâsau, Parlyrau, pur loywon—dyrau
> A Difrad fendithion,
> Os gwyrwyd aid y gwirion,
> A sai tai yn y sut hon ?

The poet was sued in the Star Chamber by the said H. H. for libel, but saved himself by the dubitative conjunction *os*. The following is a translation of the Englyn by the Revd. E. Evans, Prydydd Hir :

> " Ye stately palaces and princely towers,
> And all the wealth that luxury devours,
> If by the poor man's sweat and wrongs you rise,
> Can you last long and Heaven not hear his cries?"
>   D.J.

QUERIES.

LEG STREET, OSWESTRY (Sep. 28, 1881).—The writer in the *Shrewsbury Chronicle* of Nov. 17, 1820, who gave so absurd an origin for the name of this street, seems to have been corrected the following week, as I gather from a third communication published in the *Chronicle* of Dec. 1st that year. The writer there says—"On the attainder of Richard, Earl of Arundel, in the

·eign of Richard II., the Manor of Oswestry was granted o Lord Scrope, King of Man, the armorial bearing of hich Island is well-known to be the Three Legs of Man the very form of the above street." The communication as signed "L.M.O." Commenting on this statement, N.W.S." in *Bye-gones*, Feb. 23, 1876, quoted Price's *istory of Oswestry* for the fact that the street was called eg-street at an earlier date, and it will be seen by hose of your readers who are subscribers for the publica-lons of the Shropshire Archæological Society that Mr. tanley Leighton refers in one of his papers to a Grant .8 Edw. II., 1324) by the Earl of Arundell to the Bur-esses of Oswestry of two shops "in the row which is alled Legge streete, betwixt the shops of Richard the ·ranger and William son of William the baker." In ·oking over the Oswestry Corporation books I have found n entry, under the date 1687—when James Felton was uringer—of an account "P'd Edward Morris for mend-ng y'e bridges in Newgate & Legg streete gate." This is he only entry I have found where the Black Gate is so alled ; and it plainly indicates where one of the "legs" stretched out. The other two branched (from the 'seat' in the open space near the Cross Keys) to the Cross in one direction and the top of Beatrice-street in the other. Can any reader say where the old hostel called "The Three Legs of Man" was situated? JARCO.

REPLIES.

PARLIAMENT OF ENGLAND (Nov. 30, 1881). In the history of Oswestry Grammar School, published in the new number of the Shropshire Archæological Society *Transactions*, it is stated that there were probably two David Holbache's who were local members of Parliament early in the fifteenth century, but that they wer e never in Parliament at the same time. In looking over the list of Shropshire members in *Bye-gones* (Mar. 24, 1880,) I find under the year 1413, that David Holbach is returned both for the County of Salop and Borough of Shrewsbury. How is this discrepancy to be explained? ARGUS.

[We are obliged to ARGUS for giving us the opportunity of explaining. According to the new " Blue Book" there were two elections in 1413, the one for a Parliament summoned to meet at Westminster 14 May, 1413, and the other to meet at Leicester 29 Jan., 1413-14. A David Holbache is given as representing the county town in the former, and the county in the latter ; though it should be observed that no return for the county town is given for the latter date, so it may be after all the fact that two David Holbache's sat in the same Parliament.—ED.]

SHROPSHIRE BORDER WORDS (Sep. 7, 1881). In looking over an old Table of Tolls taken at the Oswes-try Gates in 1673, I have found a few terms I cannot quite comprehend, and should be glad to have elucidated. I give the entries in full, with the words I am in doubt about in italics :—

ffor ev'y horse load of *spills* ½ penny
ffor ev'y horse load of yarn to make *mapps* a penny
ffor ev'y pack of *moulds* a penny
ffor a Pedlar or *Shempsters* box a penny
ffor ev'y horse load of wooden *canns* a penny.
JARCO.

Joram.—Hartshorne, writing in 1841, says that this word means "a large dish," but Miss Jackson, forty years later, gives the meaning as "a large quantity of good ·eatables or drinkables." Doubtless the one is the ori-ginal, and the other the secondary, signification. In the ·ourse of time the name has been transferred from the vessel itself to its contents. This seems to be an instance ·f the change which Archbishop Trench thus notices, in his *English, Past and Present*. "Sometimes a word does ·not thus merely narrow or extend its meaning, but alto-gether changes it, and this in more ways than one. Thus a secondary figurative sense will occasionally quite put out of use and extinguish the literal, until in the entire pre-dominance of that it is altogether forgotten that it ever possessed this."

Nurse-tender.—I do not find this word in either of our county glossaries, but it is perhaps sufficiently peculiar to be worth notice here. It simply means one who nurses or tends the sick and dying, and is a specimen of that Salopian love of duplicated terms which gives rise to such expressions as a "double couple" for twins, and which led a woman to say of a drunkard that " he soon brought his end to a speedy close." R.E.D.
Shrewsbury.

[" Nurse-Tending" was mentioned in *Bye-gones* Sep. 6, 1876.]

TWM SION CATTI (Nov. 2, 1881).—I was for-tunate enough the other day to pick up an original edi-tion of this work. It was published at Aberystwyth by John Cox in 1828, by whom it is stated to have been " printed for the author." The second edition,of which I also possess a copy, was printed and published at Cow-bridge by 'J. T. Jones for E. Pool : there is no date on the title page but the special preface to this edition is dated " Builth, Breconshire, August 1839." The second edition differs considerably from the first ; several scenes are changed ; fresh characters are introduced ; and there is perhaps as much as fifty or sixty pages of additional incident. On the fly leaf of this latter volume the follow-ing announcement is made —

Works ready and preparing for the press,
By the Author of Twm Sion Catty.

1.—A Tale of the Times of Terror, and specimens of an un-published work to be entitled the Worthies of Wales with National Songs and Scenic Sonnets.
2.—The Points and Poetry of the Welsh Watering places and other Cambrian haunts of pleasure.
3.—The Dolorous Doings and Merry Mishaps of Dick Shon Davydd,the Welshman who forgot his mother tongue.
4.—The life and adventures of Will y Tee-Heer (Will o'r Ty Hir) the Welsh Smuggler.

Whether any of these works actually were published I cannot say : I suspect they never appeared, for I have sought for them in several public libraries and have not found them. Mr. Prichard was a ready and versatile writer ; his poem of "Cantref y Gwailod, or, the Land beneath the Sea," deserves to be better known than it is. There are selections from it given in that dainty little volume of poetry relating to Wales, compiled by him, called the "Cambrian Wreath." Then he wrote a biographical work entitled " Heroines of Welsh History," dedicated, I believe, to Lady Llanover—which, though it may be complete as far as it goes, was not carried as far as its author intended. A "Guide to Aberystwyth," which went through several editions, is the only other work with which I know his name to be connected. While in Swansea this summer I made enquiries respecting the latter days of this sadly neglected Welsh author, and I was told I would find all I wanted to know in " Gam-well's Guide to Swansea." I procured the book, but I am sorry to say the information there given (p. 104) is but meagre. All it says is that " he lived for some time in Swansea, where he was derided by the vulgar on account of his artificial wax nose, which was kept in its place by his spectacles. He fell asleep over his books in his poor lodging at Thomas-street and his death was accelerated by, if not the result of, the burns he received from his clothes and papers taking fire." From other sources I learnt that for several years before his death he was in deep poverty, private charity only interposing itself betwixt him and the workhouse, his best

friend I believe being a patriotic innkeeper in the town. I did hear the name of this Good Samaritan, but not having made a note of it at the time, I cannot at this moment recollect it, or I would mention it.   The date of Mr. Prichard's death I could not learn ; one of whom I asked thought it was sometime in 1874-5, but that he was buried at the 'Tabernacle,' where a record of the event would be found.   His literary executor is a gentleman residing at Page Street, Swansea, and the quantity of MS. which has come into his possession is said to be very considerable.
                                                                AP THOMAS.

CURRENT NOTES.

Sir James Picton, in a speech at Liverpool last week, said that according to the Directory that city contained 444 John Joneses.

A public meeting was held last week at Pwllheli in connection with the proposed restoration of the parish church. About £1,000 was promised in the room.

The restoration of Market Drayton Parish Church is said to be making steady progress.   The pillars of the north arcade have been completed, and the building of the arcade itself is being proceeded with.

The Rev. Thomas Ragg, vicar of Lawley, lately died at an advanced age. Mr. Ragg, who was highly esteemed by his parishioners, was the author of " Creation's Testimony to its God," a work which at the time of its publication excited some attention.

The Dean of Lichfield has received a letter from Mr. A. P. Heywood-Lonsdale offering £4,000 towards the £10,000 which the Dean is endeavouring to raise for the completion of the restoration of the west front.   The sum of £3,000 is now needed.

A committee has been formed at Penmaenmawr for the purpose of obtaining funds for the completion of the tower of St. Seiriol's Church and of endowing the Church. The corner stone of the Church was laid by Mrs. W. E. Gladstone in 1867, and the Prime Minister has promised, when the tower is finished, to give a bell.

MR. BRIGHT AT LLANDUDNO.

(From the *Oswestry Advertizer*.)

On Thursday Mr. Bright laid the first stones of the new Board Schools at Llandudno. The right hon. gentleman had a most enthusiastic reception. In the evening a public meeting was held in St. George's Hall, which was crowded to excess, and a great number of persons were unable to obtain admission. Mr. Rathbone, M.P., presided. An address was presented to Mr. Bright thanking him for the interest he had taken for so many years in the prosperity of Llandudno, and claiming at the hands of Parliament a system of Higher Education for the Principality. Mr. Bright, in replying to the address, spoke at some length on education and kindred topics. We were at last, he said, beginning to awake to the importance of properly training the youth of the country, though even now, if we travelled through the country,the great public buildings which were to be seen were poor houses and prisons—memorials and proofs of the unwisdom of past Governments and to some extent of the charity of the public. The right hon. gentleman afterwards referred at some length to the wars carried on by England at various times, in all parts of the world, and to the taxes which had now to be raised to cover the interest of the debts contracted to carry them on, and said that this system of foreign wars had made pauperism, and had a great bearing upon the existence of so much ignorance as we know now

exists among the great bulk of the population. Mr. Bright next turned to the "new and better system" which we had begun, and after contrasting the cost of education and the appliances of education a generation since with what they were to day, went on to speak of the changes that had taken place in our political system since 1832, and said : The whole state of things political is greatly changed educationally, changed because what would be a more dire calamity than the extension of political rights to hundreds of thousands of people who had no knowledge whatever of how to exercise those rights? We might be made the victims of corruption on the one hand or of wild and impossible schemes on the other. It is as essential for the people that they should know something of politics as that they should have the political weapon of the vote in their hands. Mr. Bright concluded by expressing his belief that if the children in our schools were taught self-respect, respect of their playmates, respect of their parents, kindness to animals, a love of truth, a love of industry, and an idea of what is meant by prudence, " looking to our home affairs, we may expect that, with regard to our legislation, we may have greater justice done between class and class, and that the terms class and class may in time be almost obliterated by the fact of our becoming a united people and nation. With regard to our foreign affairs, may we not hope as to that, looking back to the past, the page of glory, false glory, of glory based on misery and bloodshed, may be closed, and that there shall be a new chapter, and that the history of the future shall record in it the policy of our children and our children's children, that we have come to a time of higher civilization, and a time of a higher and purer national morality ?"

Mr. W. Rathbone, M.P., has subscribed £25 ; and Dr. Nicol and Mr. Woodcock, chairman of the School Board, £20 each, towards the fund of £500 which is being raised for the establishment of a scholarship to commemorate Mr. Bright's visit to Llandudno.

We have already quoted a long passage from Mr. BRIGHT's speech at Llandudno, and here can only give a summary of the interesting sentences in which he referred to three celebrated Welshmen. The first of these was GIBSON the sculptor—the son of a gardener at Conway—who, when Mr. BRIGHT met him at Rome twenty-one years ago, told the story of his life. PENRHYN WILLIAMS the painter, another of the men Mr. BRIGHT saw at Rome, was the second ; and the third was Mr. WILLIAMS, the translator of the Greek Testament. Mr. BRIGHT, in his walks about Llandudno, had conversed, through an interpreter, with Mr. WILLIAMS'S father, a blacksmith, in what Mr. BRIGHT's children called " the windmill village." The boy was taught at the little school near Llanrhos church, and showing capacity, was helped on by the MOSTYN family in higher instruction, until he finally became a good Greek scholar, and was minister at Newtown, where, at rather an early age, he died. "But he lived long enough to translate the New Testament from the original Greek into the Welsh language—I have been told, for I am no judge either of Greek or Welsh, something better or more correct than the translation which you have, and which, I suppose, has been taken from the authorised English version. That then, is a case in point. (Cheers.) Only yesterday, or the day before, I learned that an advertisement had appeared in some Welsh newspaper announcing that a new edition of that translation of the New Testament is about to be published. I mention it to show there is one individual case in which in what we call a common school, a Board school, we may have a boy to whom nature has given brains and genius, who, with the opportunity for study, is able to achieve a great purpose.

DISPERSAL OF THE LIBRARY OF THE LATE CANON WILLIAMS OF RHYDYCROESAU.

A correspondent writes—This collection, the work of half a century or upwards, as well as the remainders of several works compiled and edited by the late Canon Williams, was sold during the last month by Messrs. Puttick and Simpson of 47, Leicester Square, who also have just completed the marvellous sale of the Sunderland Collection up to Letter B., and which has realized upwards of £19,000. Not observing any notice of Canon Williams's sale in the *Oswestry Advertizer*, it has occurred to the writer, who attended both days' sale, one of very few, if not the only, Welshman, that notes of the prices which some of the books realized might interest the readers of the *Advertizer* as well as Welsh book collectors generally.

Canon Williams's collection numbered 669 lots, and the sale opened with two copies of the History of Aberconwy, a work well known to your readers; this lot realized 12s. Lot 2. a similar number, 10s. Several other lots of tens and twenties realized about the same price. Ancient Laws, and Institutes of Wales, 2 vols., 26s.: Archæologia Cambrensis Magazine (imperfect copy, 31 vols. only), £20 10s.; Sir W. Betham's the "Gael and the Cymbri," 11s. (Ridler) ; 2 Welsh Bibles, 1718, 1752, 7s. (Quaritch) ; ten Bibles, English, Welsh, and Spanish, 4s. (Stevens) ; two copies Biographical Dictionary of Eminent Welshmen, by Canon Williams, 8s.; three other copies, 11s. (Stevens); four others, 16s.; ten others, 35s.; ten others, 40s.; The Cambro Briton, 32s.; Cambrian Register, £3; Davies's Celtic Researches, 13s.; Davies's Mythology and Relics of the British Druids, 12s.; The Mabinogion (original edition), 3 vols., 55s.; Y Gwyliedydd, 7 vols., 33s.; The Gwyneddion, or an account of Denbigh Eisteddfod, 1828, and other books 10s. History of Llangurig by E. Hamer, 10s. (Quaritch). Hartshorne's Salopia Antiqua, 27s. Yr Haul, various numbers, 9s. Homiliau, Dolgellau, 1817, ditto, 1817, and other Welsh Theological Works, 20 vols. in all, 13s. Jones's Welsh Dictionary, 1688, and 2 others, modern, 6s. (Quaritch). Armstrong's Gaelic Dictionary, 21s. Calendars of the Ancient Charters of the Welsh and Scottish Rolls, 5s. Carlisle's Topographical Dictionary of Wales, 2s. Coxe's Tour in Monmouthshire, 1801, 36s. Davies's Antiquæ Linguæ Britannicæ, etc., (imperfect), 1632, Ed : 20s. Dictionarium Scoto-Celticum, 46s. (Sotheran). Evans's specimens of the Poetry of the Ancient Welsh Bards (1764), and one other 6s. (Hindley). Fenton's Pembrokeshire, 40s., (Quaritch). Jones (Owen), Cymru : yn Hanesyddol, Parthedigol a Bywgraphyddol, maps and plates, 2 vols., 1875, 15s. Jones and Freeman's History and Antiquities of St. Davids, 12s. Kalendars of Gwynedd, 12s. Llwyd's History of Wales, reprint 1811, 20s. Llwyd (A), History of the Island of Mona, 21s. Welsh Bible, 1620, ditto 1620, ditto 1620, all imperfect, £4 2s. 6d. (Quaritch). Borlase (W), Antiquities of Cornwall, 1769, 32s. (Gray). Chaucer's Works (much damaged), 1593, 39s. 2 Welsh Common Prayers and Welsh Bibles, all imperfect, 34s. Enderbie's Cambria Trium-

phans, reprint, 1810, 32s. (Ridler). Llyfr yr Homiliau and other Welsh Books, 18 vols. 9s. (Quaritch). Manx Bible, Welsh Testament, 1850, and other Welsh Bibles and Prayer Books (modern) 21s. (Quaritch). 2 parcels Miscellaneous Welsh Magazines, 35s. 15 parcels Miscellaneous Theological and other books, 55s. Montgomeryshire Collections, 9 vols. only, £6 5s. The Myfyrian Archæology of Wales, 3 vols. Imp. 8vo, 1801, £5 5s. (Quaritch). Ditto Gee's Edition, 21s. O'Brien's Irish-English Dictionary, 21s. Pennant's Tours in Wales, 3 vols., 32s. Price's Hanes Cymru, 14s. Pritchard's Welsh Minstrelsy, Dovaston's poems, Sayer's poems, and Northern Mythology, 23s. (Quaritch). Prifannau sanctaidd neu lawlyfr o Weddiau (1658). Llwybr Hyfordd i'r Nefoedd, 1682. and Flores Poetorum Britannicorum, 1710, 31s. (Quaritch). Pughe's Welsh Dictionary, 5 vols. Denbigh, 1832, 42s. (Harley) ; do. 2 vols. Denbigh, 1832, 13s. (Quaritch). Rees's Welsh Saints, 19s. (Quaritch). Roscoe's Wanderings in Wales, 28s. (Rymer). Rowland's Cambrian Bibliography, 6s. "Y Seint Greal," Edited by Canon Williams, 1 copy, 6s., do. 7s., do. 5s., do. 6s. ; 3 copies, 8s., do. 10s. ; 17 copies, 20s. Stephens's Literature of the Kymry, 6s. (Edwards); ditto Prof. Silvan Evans's Edition, 8s. (Reeves). Thomas's History of St. Asaph, 19s. Thomas's Owen Glyndwr, 7s. Six vols. Welsh MSS. Society's publications (being all published except Dwnn's Welsh pedigrees), £4. Wright's History of Ludlow, 21s. Reynolds's Display of Heraldry, 1739, and two other books, 23s. Rowland's Mona Antiqua Restaurata (Ed. 1766) 25s. Williams's Cornish Lexicon, 18s. ; do. 20s. Williams's History of Monmouthshire, 47s. Wynne's History of the Gwydir Family (Askew Roberts's Edition, a presentation copy in Morocco), 27s. Yorke's Tribes, 29s. Jones (Edward) Musical and Poetical Relics of the Welsh Bards, 1784 and 1794 editions, 27s. Llwyd Archæologia Britannica (1707), 50s. Monumenta Historica Britannica, 1 vol. (all published), 52s. Tanner's Notitia Monastica, 21s. Wottonus (G) Leges Wallicæ, 11s. These are some of the lots sold. The books were badly arranged, and Mr. Simpson, who occupied the rostrum, though an exceedingly clever and highly honourable salesman, unfortunately had no knowledge of Welsh, and could not therefore point out in some cases the value of the parcels he was submitting. On the whole the books realized bad prices, and will figure at very different rates when they appear in the second hand booksellers' catalogues. There were none of the late Canon's manuscripts offered at this sale. Very few persons attended on either of the days, but almost all present were buyers. To this we may add that the sale was so imperfectly advertised in this district, that probably the foregoing account will be the first intimation that many book-buyers in Wales have had that the sale has taken place.

DECEMBER 21, 1881.

NOTES.

A BORN WELSHMAN !—Southey writing to Wynn, Oct. 11, 1806, announces the birth of a son, a "long-bespoken godson" of Mr. Wynn's, and who is to be called "Herbert." Mr. Southey adds, "I shall be heartily glad when you can communicate to me the like good tidings. Will you not carpet your bedroom with turfs from Wales, that your son may be born upon Welsh ground; baptize him in water from the Dee ; and, if he is to have any other food than what nature provides expressly for his use, choose for him such a wet-nurse as Jupiter himself had ?" N.W.S.

SHROPSHIRE BORDER WORDS (Dec. 14, 1881.)—*Again*. This is a common word enough, but uncommonly used by many. For instance, I wrote to a friend near Oswestry the other day asking him to send me certain articles. This he did, all but a book, and he wrote : "The book shall be sent again." I have the impression that I once saw a similar use of the word in *Byegones*, where the writer gave the copy of an old Welsh document, and added, "The translation you shall have again." How is it that Welshmen so often say " again" when they mean, "some other time," or " by and by."
FAR AWAY.

TWM SION CATTI (Dec. 14, 1881).—T. J. Llewelyn Prichard was born in the parish of Trallong, co. Brecon, and died in the Swansea Union Workhouse. I cannot lay my hands upon the 1st of three editions of the above work, but, if my memory correctly serves me, it was published by John Cox. Aberystwyth. I saw Prichard perform at the Brecon Theatre in 1841.
Brecon. F.S.A.

DAVID HOLBACHE (Mar. 24, 1880).—Some light may possibly be thrown upon the connection of this worthy with Oswestry, and the motives which prompted him to found a free school in the town, from consideration of his genealogical tree, and its surrounding circumstances. David Holbache was of the Noble Tribe of the Marches, the reputed founder of which was Tudor Trevor, who, as we learn from the *History of Powys Vadog* by the Chevalier Lloyd, was not only sovereign prince of Gloucester, Hereford, Erging, and Ewias in right of his mother Rhiengar, grand-daughter of Caradoc Vreichvras (of the Brawny Arm), but also inherited, at the commencement of the 10th century, the Lordships of the two Maelors, Chirk, Whittington, Oswestry, and Nantheudwy, from his father, Ynyr ab Cadvarch, who is said to have built the old Castle of Whittington, and dwelt there. These possessions he divided among his three sons, Goronwy, Lluddoccaf, and Dingad, the second of whom took all the northern territory (Maelor Uchaf excepted, which fell to Dingad), inclusive of Whittington, and Oswestry, and transmitted them to three descendants in succession, Llywarch Gam, Ednyved ab Llywarch, and Rhys Sais ab Ednyved. The latter died in 1070, leaving three sons, the eldest of whom, Tudur ab Rhys Sais, succeeded to the Lordships of Chirk, Whittington, Nantheudwy, and the English Maelor ; Elidur became Lord of Eyton Isaf, Erlisham, Borasham, Sutton and Ruyton, while Iddon, the third son, is stated to have inherited only Dudleston and *part of Oswestry*. What became of the remaining part of Oswestry the historian has omitted to state, but it is to be presumed that ere this it had fallen into Norman hands, and become lost for ever to the Tribe of the Marches. So far the *History of Powys Vadog*. Now, from the paper entitled Dudleston in *Archæologia Cambrensis*, 1873, p. 255, we learn further that " the Lordship of Oswestry comprises also that part of the parish of Ellesmere which contains the townships of Upper and Lower Dudleston : that David Holbeche of Dudleston was Deputy Steward of Bromfield and Yale in 1409, and that he belonged to the family of Heilin of Pentre Heilin descended from Iddon, from whose posterity it may readily be conceived that he devoted the portion of land in Oswestry which he devoted to the foundation of a free school. This he could do the more freely, as he died without issue male, whence the bulk of his property fell to his uncles Einion Goch of Pant y Bursli, and Madoc Goch. This will more clearly appear from the following

continuation of his pedigree, the more interesting from its connexion with the ancestry of two such well-known modern families as those of Morrall of Plas Iolyn, and Edwardes (Baronets) of Shrewsbury, who take their descent from Cadivor, the second son of Trahaiarn.

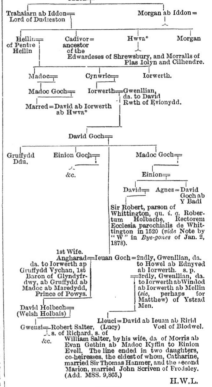

CURRENT NOTES.

A census has been taken of the attendance at public worship in Nantwich on a Sunday, with the following result :—At morning service, 1,759 ; evening, 2,421. The population is 7,450. There are eleven places of worship in the town, and the Wesleyan Chapel heads the list with a total morning and evening attendance of 1,275, the Parish Church being next with 1,266.

RELIGIOUS CENSUS IN WREXHAM.

On Sunday, Dec. 4, a census of attendance at all the places of worship in the Parliamentary Borough was taken by the *Wrexham Advertiser*. The first Sunday in he month was fixed upon as best, it being Communion Sunday with most of the Churches, and enumerators were engaged who carried out the work voluntarily and efficiently. The following was the result :—

PLACES OF WORSHIP.	Accommodation provided.	Attendances. Morn. ing.	Even. ing.	Total.
St. Giles's Parish Church	1209	503	755	1258
St. Mark's Church	700	403	219	622
St. James's Church, Rhosddu	250	212	215	427
Iron Church, Hightown	200	93	121	214
Welsh Church, Savings Bank	100		55	55
Baptist Chapel, Chester-street	350	102	144	246
Congregational Chapel, Penybryn	200	84	156	240
Congregational Chapel, Chester-street	550	177	163	340
Church of Christ, meeting in King-street	120	38	40	78
Mission Chapel, Beast Market	80		39	39
Presbyterian Chapel, Hill-street	320	103	137	240
Primitive Methodist Chapel, Talbot-road	200	105	148	253
United Methodist Free Church, Rhosddu	160	39	23	62
Welsh Baptist Chapel, Temperance Hall	250	25	81	106
Welsh Calvinistic Chapel, Regent-street	740	165	236	401
Welsh Calvinistic Ebenezer, Rhosddu	150	84	115	199
Welsh Independent, Queen-street	500	95	163	258
Welsh Wesleyan Chapel, Brook-street	168	66	93	162
Wesleyan Chapel, Brynyffynnon	520	208	278	486
St. Mary's Catholic Church	400	*460	183	643
Salvation Army, Public Hall	1200	467	1455	1922
	8358	3429	4819	8243

* The morning attendance is the number of those present at three successive services, held at 8, 9, and 10 30 a.m.

The population of the parliamentary borough, according to the census taken this year, is 12,333. That of the municipal borough is 10,903. The three places outside the latter are St. James's Church, United Methodist Free Church, and Welsh Ebenezer, which are all in Rhosddu.

On Wednesday the Council of the Cymmrodorion Society met at Chancery-lane, the Rev. John Davies, M.A., occupying the chair pro tem. On the motion of Mr. Howel W. Lloyd, M.A., seconded by the Rev. John Morgan, a vote of condolence with the family of the late Sir Hugh Owen was passed in silence. Proceeding to the election of officers for the ensuing year, the Council unanimously re-elected Mr. Stephen Evans as their Chairman. Dr. Isambard Owen, M.A., proposed, "That the thanks of the Council be given to Mr. Stephen Evans for the very faithful and able manner in which he had furthered the interests of the Society during past years." The vote of thanks was most cordially passed. Mr. Evans, in acknowledgment, said he felt honoured by the confidence of the Council. His great desire was to see the Society thoroughly successful, and productive of great and lasting benefits to the Principality and its people. On the motion of Mr. T. M. Williams, seconded by Mr. Howel Thomas, Mr. H. Lloyd Roberts was appointed honorary treasurer, vice Sir Hugh Owen, deceased. Mr. C. W. Jones then an-

nounced the arrangements for forthcoming lectures. These will be delivered one each month as far as practicable. The Rev. D. Jones Davies, M.A., will lead with a paper on an educational subject ; Mr. David Lewis. of the South Wales Circuit, comes next, with "The Welshmen of Modern Literature." Mr. John Owen (Owain Alaw), Chester, will treat of "Welsh Music," of which musical illustrations will be given by Welsh singers. Professor W. Boyd Dawkins promises a paper on "The Arcient Ethnology of Wales," and Mr. W. St. John Hancock one on "Celtic Dwellings and their Inhabitants," while the well-known philologist, Mr. Alexander J. Ellis, F.R.S., will speak on "The delimitation of the Welsh and English languages." A number of *Y Cymmrodor* is announced to be nearly ready for issue. Dr. Owen called attention to the generous offer of Sir Watkin Williams Wynn, at the annual dinner, to place the Wynnstay MSS. at the disposal of the Society. On the motion of Mr. Howel Lloyd, seconded by Mr. Stephen Evans, the hearty thanks of the Cymmrodorion Society were accorded to Sir Watkin for his offer, and Dr. Isambard Owen was empowered to open communication, with a view to secure for the members the advantages of these most valuable manuscripts.

Her Majesty has been pleased to grant £50 a year to the Rev. J. Jones (Idrisyn), vicar of Llandysilio, Cardiganshire, out of the Civil List fund, in recognition of his valuable services to Welsh literature. The rev. gentleman, in addition to numerous sermons, pamphlets, and contributions to the Welsh press, is the author of a popular Welsh commentary on the Bible, in five volumes, which has passed through several editions. Over 40,000 copies of this work have been sold, a sale almost unprecedented in the history of Welsh books. Mr. Jones had the honour of being appointed a few years ago to translate into Welsh her Majesty's "Journal of our Life in the Highlands."

DECEMBER 28, 1881.

NOTES.

WELSHMEN IN ROYAL LIVERY. – Under this heading, in Dec. 1873, there appeared a query and reply in *Bye-gones*, concerning a Welshman who was once state coachman. It was stated that his name was Thomas Roberts, and that he "served King George and King William, and the present Queen as long as he lived." He was first cousin to Mrs. Davies of St. Martins, who before the Oswestry Market Halls were built had a "standing" in Bailey-street for the sale of meat. There is a reference to Roberts in *Fifty Years of My Life*, by the Earl of Albemarle, published by Macmillan in 1876. On p. 291, v. 2, after narrating the adventures of a Royal Footman in the time of William IV., the writer goes on to say :—

Another of the royal servants figured indirectly in the history of this time. Mr Roberts, the little portly state coachman, whose carriage was ordered so suddenly on the memorable 22nd of August, 1831, when the King dissolved Parliament in person on the defeat of the Reform Bill.

Every one knows the story as graphically told by my father's old friend, Harriet Martineau—how the King resolved to go down instantly and dissolve Parliament with his own voice — how he refused to wait for the royal carriages, and called for a hackney coach – how Lord Durham drove off in the Lord Chancellor's carriage to the Master of the Horse, and startled him in the middle of his late breakfast : all this is now a matter of history. "Lord Albemarle," says Miss Martineau, "started up on the entrance of Lord Durham, asking what was the matter. 'You must have the King's carriage ready instantly.' 'Very well, I will just finish my breakfast.' 'Not you ; you must not lose a moment. The King ought to be in the House.'

'Lord bless me! is there a revolution?' 'Not at this moment, but there will be if you stay to finish your breakfast.' So the tea and roll were left, and the royal carriages drove up to the palace in an incredibly short time. The King was ready and impatient, and walked with an unusually brisk step. And so did the royal horses in their passage through the streets, as was observed by the curious and anxious gazers."

Concerning the excited state of the royal horses, I know more than even Miss Martineau. As the carriage containing the King and his Master of the Horse was passing the guard of honour, the Ensign in charge of the colours lowered them to the Sovereign, according to the established formula. The usually impassive "cream-colours" took umbrage at this act of homage, swerved, and broke into an undignified trot. Mr Roberts, the coachman, whose mind and body were alike thrown off their balance by the unwonted hurry of the morning, and by the insubordination of his steeds, proceeded, in utter forgetfulness of the royal presence, loudly to anathematize the guard of honour generally, and the standard-bearer in particular. Before the procession had reached the Horse Guards, the opprobrious epithets had winged their flight to the officials within the building. The consequence was, that Mr Roberts, who had played so important a part in the morning pageant, was compelled to make a public apology to the offended guard of honour before it was marched off to its private parade.

N.W.S

VOLUNTEER ARMY OF 1803-4 (Aug. 25, 1880).

Our list this week relates to *Carmarthenshire* :—

CARMARTHEN CAVALRY.

Captains : George Lord Dynevor, James Howell (no dates) ; William Davies—31 Oct, 1803.
Lieutenants : —— Jones — 31 Oct. 1803 ; George Davies (no date) ; Robert Waters—20 Aug. 1803.
Cornet : Edward Davies—31 Oct. 1803.

CARMARTHEN, First Battalion.

Lt. Col. Comm : George Lord Dynevor—21 Oct. 1803.
Majors : D. Williams, Morgan Lloyd—21 Oct. 1803.
Captains : Edward Jones, J. Dela Chambre Smith, William Davies, J. Reese Bishop, Lewis Lloyd Bowen, William Jones, Henry Irwin—21 Oct. 1803.
Lieutenants : Thomas Bishop, David Thomas, Thomas Price, Thomas Thomas, David Jones Llewis, William Jones—21 Oct. 1803.
Ensigns : Edward Jones, Thomas Morgan, William Morgan, Joseph Yeamans, Evan Jones, Thomas Williams—21 Oct. 1803.
Adjutant : Henry Irvin—21 Oct. 1803.
Quarter Master : Surgeon : John Yeoman.

CARMARTHEN, Second Battalion.

Lt. Col : Lord Robert Seymour—21 Oct 1803.
Majors : J. G. Phillips, Richard Gardner—21 Oct. 1803.
Captains : Howell Price, Jenkin Davies, William Evans, Griffith Phillips, Charles Bowen, Lewis Evans—21 Oct. 1803.
Lieutenants : John Hoptinshall, Thomas Rees, David Griffiths, Richard Hughes—21 Oct. 1803 ; Thomas Lewis, John Mapleton (no date).
Ensigns : Thomas Thomas, John Morgan, John Bishop, John Evans, John Francis, Richard Morris—21 Oct. 1803.
Adjutant : Thomas Edwards (no date).
Quarter Master : Surgeon : Thomas Thomas—21 Oct. 1803.

CARMARTHEN, Third Battalion.

Lt. Coll : Sir William Paxton—21 Oct. 1803.
Major : —— Paggott—21 Oct. 1803.
Captains : John Morgan, jun., Thomas Morris, John Brown, John Williams, David Davies—21 Oct. 1803.
Lieutenants : William Hughes, John Davies, David Thomas, David Howell - 21 Oct. 1803 ; John Baile (no date).

Ensigns : George Knott, Walter Bowen, Thomas Collins Pritham—21 Oct. 1803 ; John Bagnall, William B. Taylor (no date).
Adjutant : Francis Wilkinson.
Quarter-Master : Surgeon : John Jenkins.

CARMARTHEN, Fourth Battalion.

Lt. Col : Walter Williams—21 Oct. 1803.
Majors : John Bowen—21 Oct. 1803 ; Richard Isaac Starke (no date).
Captains : John Bushell, William Thomas, Griffith Lloyd, Joseph Waters—21 Oct. 1803 ; David Hughes, Thomas Benyon.
Lieutenants : Seth Lewis, John Griffiths—21 Oct. 1803 ; Nathaniel Rowlands, William Higgon, John Williams, J. Howells.
Ensigns : Thomas Rees Thomas, Thomas Jones, David Morgan, Walter Hughes, James Lewis, Thomas Thomas.
Adjutant : John Bushell.
Quarter Master : John Hughes.
Surgeon : Thomas Bowen.

CARMARTHEN, Fifth Brigade.

Lt. Coll : J. W. Hughes.
Majors : W. M. Cleary—21 Oct. 1803 ; David Pugh.
Captains : Thomas Edwards, David Parry, John Rees, J. H. Bevan, William Hopkins, John Williams—21 Oct. 1803.
Lieutenants : John Humphrys, William Child, William Davies, William Phillips, Rees Harries—21 Oct. 1803 ; David Painter.
Ensigns : Thomas Humphrys, William Hopkins, jun.— 21 Oct. 1803 ; Hugh Evans, Thomas Howell.
Adjutant : John Lewis.

[From the War Office List, Oct. 1804.]

MERTHYR TYDVILL IN 1800.—The *Gentleman's Magazine* of Dec. 1806, contains the following statistics :—

In 1800 or 1801, a woman was living at Merthyr Tydvill in Wales, aged 94, who remembered when there were only 25 inhabitants in the parish. In the above year a very intelligent gentleman took pains to ascertain the population of that place, and found it to be, 13,680. The increase was owing to the very great iron works set up there. So crowded is the place, that 12 men and one woman lived in one room of 12 square feet, which served them "For parlour for kitchen and all.' The men worked in the mines, 6 by day and 6 by night. Three beds supplied them all. Thus the room was constantly occupied by 7 persons. One would almost suppose that Morton had seen this paragraph before he wrote his amusing farce of *Box and Cox.* The writer goes on to say —

The rectory was no more than £80 a year, but the present incumbent has greatly increased it by obtaining an Act to let his glebe (14 acres) on building leases for 99 years ; he lets it at 3d. a square yard. He has also got rid of a modus which was claimed at 4d. for each farm ; but if a farm was divided into 2 or 10 parts, each part paid 4d., which was held to make it uncertain.

R.D.

GAS AND IRON IN 1816.—In these days when the electric light threatens to put gas in the shade, and we are told our coal fields may some day, when we are not aware of it, fail us, it is curious to read the opinions of our grandfathers in the age when gas was beginning to attract attention, and railways were unknown. In the autumn of 1816 a contributor to the *Shrewsbury Chronicle* recommended the lighting of the great public roads with gas ; and gave as a reason—over and above the convenience it would be to the travelling public—the fact that it would require tens of thousands of tons of iron, and give employment to thousands of men. The expense he suggested should be met by additional tolls at the turnpike gates, assisted by general and local subscriptions, and parochial aid. H.B.

QUERIES.

OSWESTRY SCHOOL (Sep. 14, 1881).—In all authorities that give a list of the Head Masters of Oswestry School, the one elected in 1772 is called " Charles Anson Tisdale." I have just met with his signature, several times repeated, during the years 1774-8, and in each case he spells his surname " Tisdall." Before coming to Oswestry he was master of Wrexham Grammar School. Perhaps some one can say how his name appears in the Wrexham annals? JARCO.

A WELSH HOAX ON SOUTHEY.—From the notes that have appeared in the last series of *Bye-gones*, it has been shewn what an interest Southey took in Wales and Welshmen. In his correspondence, published by his son-in-law, we have a reference to a hoax once practised upon him in connection with a promising young man of the Principality. On Aug. 19, 1814, he writes thus to Mr. C. W. Williams Wynn:—

" You know that there prevails an unlucky opinion in the world respecting Wales, that it never produced a man of genius; as if nature, having bestowed great care in bringing the mutton of the Principality to perfection, left the men thereof in a very unfinished state. I have more than once been driven to a nonplus in opposing this wicked opinion, not having been able to produce any greater men than Sir Henry Morgan the Buccaneer, and his namesake, the great heresiarch, Pelagius. Your friends the Catholics, however, hold that miracles have not ceased in Wales, and St. Winifred is at this time in full odour. But if a man of genius should peradventure be found there, look you, Mr. Charles Williams, it may be a miracle; I dare not deny that; but, as a good Protestant and a staunch No-Popery man, I defy Dr. Milner to prove that St. Winefred has anything to do with it.

" As you may well suppose, I receive plenty of letters from poets aspirant, more especially since my promotion to a dignity which they regard as curates do the archiepiscopal see of Canterbury. This evening, however, I have had a letter which is very remarkable for its good sense; and, more remarkable still, this letter is from a Welsh herdman in the Vale of Clwyd.

" He tells me that his father died when he was seven years of age, leaving him nothing to depend upon but a knowledge of reading, writing, and the principles of grammar, which must needs have been little enough; that for nine years and a half he tended the herds of a farmer between Ruthin and Denbigh; that through the indulgence of a neighbouring gentleman (whom he has not named) he possesses many advantages; and he requests permission to send one specimen of his compositions in prose and verse, that I may advise him whether to submit them to public notice, or let them rest in peace! The most remarkable part of the letter is, that he seems to be perfectly contented. He says that his situation is comfortable; that he has no wish to change it; and that his highest ambition is the acquaintance of learned men. Whether he will prove poet or not, remains to be seen; but he is certainly an extraordinary man, and seems to possess that wisdom which is more rare, and far more valuable, than any brilliancy of talents.

" He sent his letter by an acquaintance to Manchester, and requested an answer through the same channel; but I am apprehensive, from the date and the time alloted for

his friend's stay there, that that answer may arrive too late, and lie in the Manchester Post Office. So I wrote a second reply in the hope that you may direct it so as to find him. And I have told him to direct his specimens under cover to you, giving him a proper caution as to the weight. Greeton Evans is his name, and he dates from Llynn Aledd (which is between Ruthin and Denbigh, he says; you perhaps will know to what post-town it had better be addressed). Would it not have surprised you to find a herdman reading " Madoc" in the Vale of Clwyd? I send my letter unsealed, that you may see in what manner I have answered him. Should his writings possess any merits of their own, his lot may be bettered by them, without changing it; and whatever their merit may be, there is something so happy in the man's state of mind that whenever I set foot in Wales again, I will find him out. If he prove to be a Welsh Bloomfield, I bespeak you for his patron. His letter is so well, I might well say so beautifully, written, that it is the admiration of every person to whom I have as yet shewn it. If he writes under cover to you, open the enclosure and judge for yourself."

Mr. Wynn interested himself in attempting to discover the hidden poet, without success; and the letter to Manchester was returned unopened! No such person as Greeton Evans existed, as far as could be discovered; and the affair, as Mr. Southey says in a letter dated Dec, 15, 1814, " must have been a trick, and never was a more witless one, for in what was the jest to end?" Was the hoax ever acknowledged? N.W.S.

REPLIES.

SHROPSHIRE SCHOOLS (June 15, 1881).—The following records are not very important, but will interest some :—

1835. Edward Justice Edwards, Esq., B.A., of Balliol College, Oxford, formerly of *Shrewsbury* School, is elected Kennicot Hebrew Scholar of that University.

1835. James Coley, Esq., commoner of Christ Church College, Oxford, and son of J. M. Coley, Esq., surgeon, of Bridgnorth, has been the successful candidate for one of the highest of Fell's Exhibitions at that College. Mr. Coley was educated at *Bridgnorth* School. H. B.

OSWESTRY TOWN CLERK (Nov. 30, 1881.)— I stated about 1775 Mr. Herbert resumed his duties as Town Clerk of Oswestry. In the contemporary Quarter Sessions book I find the last time Davies signed the minutes of proceedings was in Jan. 1774. There is no signature appended to the April Sessions, but to the proceedings of July 15th the same year, there is the name of " Herbert." On the same page is the following entry:—

Aug. 12th, 1774.

Mr. John Lloyd, Attorney, was this day sworn Deputy Town Clerk for the said Town, before us

EDWARD THOMAS
JOHN EDWARDS.

Mr. Thomas and Mr. Edwards were respectively mayor and ex-mayor. In those days the Lord of the Manor appointed the Town Clerk, and he acted at Quarter Sessions as well as in the Council Chamber. And, speaking of Town Clerks, at the beginning of the 18th century one Roger Green filled the office, but becoming Mayor in 1703, he was succeeded by Roger Green, jun. I saw the other day in the *Cambrian News*, that among the presentments to the Court at Aberystwyth in 1711, is the name of " Roger Green of Oswestry" as burgess. Why this burgessship was sought is not stated, whether as agent of the Lord of the Manor, or as a resident of Oswestry. JARCO.

ELIJAH WARING (Oct. 26, 1881.)—Mr. Waring was, I have been informed, a native of Wiltshire. At one time he was a miller and flour merchant of Neath, but he left, and was appointed manager of a branch of the West of England and South Wales District Bank at Cardiff in 1836. From Cardiff he went to Clifton, where he lived for some years; he returned to Neath. He married the eldest daughter of Mr. Peter Price of Neath Abbey. Mr. Waring's son, Mr. C. H. Waring, resides at 2, St. John's-terrace, Clifton. Mr. Waring at one time was a local preacher with the Wesleyans. He was born in the year 1786, and died 29th March, 1857, and was buried at Friends' Meeting House, Neath. IOLO MORGANWG was a frequent visitor at his house at Neath. F.S.A. Brecon.

CAMBRIAN INSTITUTIONS (Sep. 28, 1881.)—The anniversary meeting of the *Cambro-British Members of Jesus College, Oxford*, was held at Aberystwyth in Aug. 1820. At three o'clock in the afternoon, those productions to which prizes had been awarded, were read by the Rev. D. Evans, Fellow of the before-mentioned College. The premiums of £20 for the best Welsh essay on the works of Taliesin, " Eu Hiaith a gadwant;" and that of £2 for the best six Englynion on the following subject, " Llwyddiant i Goleg yr Iesu," were given in favour of the Rev. J. Jones, B.A. (Ioan Tegyd), of Jesus College. Mr. Thomas Davies, of the same College, was pronounced entitled to the prize of £10 for the best translation of a sermon in the Welsh language.

The *Gwyneddigion Society* in London held its fifty-eighth anniversary dinner on Dec. 9, 1828, at the Woolpack Tavern, Cornhill; Mr. Parry in the chair, and Mr. Williams vice-president. The National Anthem was sung, with the following additional stanza:—

May heav'n protect the throne,
And make the cause our own,
Of George our King!
From danger e'er defend
Old Cambria's prince and friend,
And blessings on him send;
Long live the King!

The health of the Duke of Wellington, as a descendant of Tudor Trevor, was drunk. The same compliment was paid to Lord Kenyon. TAFFY.

DISERTH CHURCH (Nov. 9, Dec. 7, 1881.)—Some corrections may be supplied from other documents to some statements in the interesting pedigree of the Mostyns of Rhyd in *Harl. MS.*, 4,181. The following entry occurs in an extract made by the late Mr. Edward Breese from the " Cwtta Cyfarwydd " of Peter Roberts: " Rhûd. mem. that upon Friday being the 23rd day of February, 1637, Edward Parry (youngest son of Bishop Parry, deceased) was buried at Diserth." So that to Edward (not Richard, the eldest son) is the inscription on the tombstone to be referred. In *Harl. MS.*, 2,180 (or 2,129) is a copy of "The Order of Funerall of Richard Parry of Cwm, Esqre., where he dyed, and [was] buried at S. Asaph Church, July, 1644.—50 poore in white cotes wth his name R.P. before and behind carriage p'eells.— Randle Holme junr.—Robert Wyn the penon of Armes, Evan David the helme & creste, Mr Hugh Thomas [probably of Coed Helen] the cote of Arms, Mr Evans the precher, Mr Edwards Parsson of Cwm, the corpes carried by Gent. Mr Willm Marguns [qu. for Morgan] of Golden Grove, Mr Robt Greene, the gentlemen of blood &c. Mr John Parry alone chief mourner." He was his nephew

and succeeded as his heir, there being no issue of Richard Parry. It seems doubtful, however, whether the above date is correct, as the chalice, presented by Richard Parry to his parish church at Cwm bears the date of 1647, while another statement gives 6th July, 1649, as the date of his death. On a tablet in Wrexham Church Lucy is stated to have been the daughter of Edward (not William Lloyd) of Halghton, and to have died in 1732, aged 72. The first William Mostyn of Rhyd, father of Thomas, is said in *Montgomeryshire Collections* (Sheriffs of Montgomeryshire, vol. v., p. 494) to have had a daughter, Anne, married to John Pugh, Esq., of Mathavarn. She was buried at Llanwryn on 8th June, 1676. GWENNA.

DAVID HOLBACHE'S WILL (Dec. 21, 1881.)—In default of the discovery of David Holbache's will, the curiosity of JARCO to learn " what was meant four centuries ago by a Free School" may perhaps be partially satisfied by the following extract from a work entitled *Christian Schools and Scholars* (Longmans, 1867), vol. ii., p. 258:—

The close of the xivth century witnessed the establishment in England of two new schools, the importance of which caused them to be regarded as models for all subsequent foundations of a similar kind in this country. These were William of Wykeham's twin colleges at Oxford and Winchester, the first of which, opened in 1386, may be said to have perfected the collegiate system of our Universities, while the second, which was not completed till seven years later, laid the foundation of another system, more peculiarly national—that of our English public schools. The object of these two institutions was to furnish a complete course of free education to 200 scholars, who were to be led from the lowest class of grammatical learning to the highest degrees of the various faculties. And at the same time that their intellectual training was thus amply provided for, they were subjected to a strict rule of discipline, and the religious element of education was given a much larger development than it had received in any collegiate foundation that had yet appeared. Chapels had, indeed, in some cases been attached to colleges before the time of Wykeham, though they do not seem to have been regarded as any essential portion of such institutions; but now the choral office and the magnificent celebration of ecclesiastical rites were provided for with no less scrupulous care than the advancement of studies; and thus the founder set his seal to one great principle of the earlier monastic education, namely, that habits of devotion, and those too of a certain liturgical character, ought to be infused into the training which is given to the children of Holy Church. H.W.L.

CHURCH BELLS (Feb. 16, 1881.)—On the bells of *St. Alkmond's Shrewsbury*, on Aug. 6, 1839, a Junior Band performed for the first time, Mr. Holt's peal of Grandsire Tripples, "containing 5,040 changes, with 190 bobs and 50 singles, and completely brought round in 3 hours and 5 minutes." Weight of tenor 14cwt. The following were the ringers engaged :—John Byolin, treble; William Bull, second; William Micklewright third; Daniel Ellidge, fourth; Henry Moore, fifth; Richard Micklewright, sixth; John Scholes, seventh; William Gee, tenor. Conducted by Richard Micklewright.

Llansantffraid-yn-Mechain. — Your correspondent CYFFIN, in a paper on the Parochial History of Llansantffraid he contributed to *Mont: Coll:* in 1871, says that eighty years ago the roads of that district were so neglected that all traffic had to be carried on horseback, and he adds that "it is related that 'the great bell' in the church steeple was originally intended for Llanfechain church," but all the united strength of the horses of the parish were not sufficient to move it further than a point on the road side near The Foel, where it remained for a long period, and was then placed in Llansantffraid church. G.G.

CURRENT NOTES.

ST. DAVID'S COLLEGE, LAMPETER.—The Rev. Charles Lett Feltoe, B.A., Fellow of Clare College, Cambridge, has been appointed to the vacant professorship of Latin at St. David's College, Lampeter.

DEATH OF DR. HENRY JOHNSON.—The death is announced of Dr. Henry Johnson, formerly of the Old House, Dogpole, Shrewsbury. He was a son of the Rev. John Johnson, of Bashall House, Yorkshire, and brother of the Rev. G. H. Sacheverell Johnson, Dean of Wells, whom he survived only seven weeks. Dr. Henry Johnson was appointed Physician in Ordinary to the Salop Infirmary June 9, 1835. He performed the duties of that office for nearly thirty years, and on his resignation was unanimously elected Physician Extraordinary. Dr. Johnson was virtually the founder of the Shropshire and North Wales Natural History and Antiquarian Society. He died on Tuesday, December 27, at the age of seventy-eight, at Marychurch, near Torquay, to which place he had gone for the benefit of his health.

Mr. Falconer, the late judge of County Courts in Wales, was appointed (says *Truth*) by Lord Truro, after he had made himself very popular in the Principality by heading an agitation against franchise gaols, which were a disgusting relic of feudal times. Until they were swept away by an Act of Parliament, mainly through Mr. Falconer's efforts, the Duke of Beaufort could keep a debtor in Swansea Gaol as long as he liked, without cost to himself; and if the unlucky wretch had no relatives to support him in his confinement he might die of starvation, and yet no proceedings could be taken against the Duke, who, as feudal lord, was permitted by law to do as he pleased in this respect.

The parish church of Wrockwardine, which is one of the oldest churches in Shropshire, was re-opened after restoration on Wednesday. The work was taken in hand by the Vicar, the Rev. A. P. Salisbury, the Hon. R. C. Herbert, patron of the living, Mr. H. H. F. Hayhurst, and other gentlemen. In consequence of the crushing of one of the piers of the chancel arch, it was found necessary to rebuild a portion of the south wall of the nave and the whole of the west wall of the north transept, and to effect this it was necessary to shore up the tower on two sides by great balks of timber. The new walls are built up from the solid rock with stone matching in colour and appearance the other portion of the church. A new window has taken the place of an old one on the south side of the nave, the old one in the north transept being refilled. The old plaster ceiling of the tower has been renewed, the old oak beams being cleaned and others added, so as to form a handsome panelled ceiling. The roof of the nave roof, which was very defective, has been re-covered with Broseley tiles. The bells were in a dangerous state from wear of the working parts, and from the great age of the bell frame, and they have been rehung by Messrs. Taylor and Sons of Loughborough. The restoration was placed in the hands of Mr. Pountney Smith of Shrewsbury, who entrusted the carrying out of the work to Messrs. Bowdler and Co. of the same town. Other works are still needed, but the restoration funds do not admit of more being attempted at present. The sermon at the re-opening service was preached by the Rev. G. W. Pigott, R.D.

The Council of the University College of Wales met on Wednesday at Lonsdale Chambers, Chancery Lane, the Rt. Hon. Lord Aberdare in the chair. The following members were present, viz., the Right Hon. G. Osborne Morgan, M.P., Mr. Henry Richard, M.P., Mr. Morgan Lloyd, M.P., Mr. Stephen Evans, Chislehurst, Mr. J. F. Roberts, Manchester, Principal Edwards, Aberystwyth, Mr. Lewis Angell, Mr. A. C. Humphreys-Owen, Dr. Evans, hon. sec., Mr. Ellis Jones, Queen Victoria-street, and Mr. John Hughes, C. C. Finsbury. The principal business of the sitting was the election of a treasurer in place of the late Sir Hugh Owen. The choice fell on Mr. Stephen Evans. Several members of the Council made feeling reference to the great loss sustained by Wales, and especially by the University College of Wales in the removal of Sir Hugh Owen. It was resolved to express the sympathy of the meeting with the family of Sir Hugh under their recent bereavement in a letter of condolence, which will be drawn up by Lord Aberdare.

We have to record the death of Miss Charlotte Clive, which took place at her residence, Elmhurst, on Wednesday, after a protracted illness, at the ripe age of 88 years. Miss Clive was the daughter of Mr. William Clive of Styche, near Market Drayton, who represented Bishop's Castle in Parliament before its disfranchisement by the Reform Acts, and he was the brother of Robert Lord Clive, the founder of our Indian Empire. Miss Clive came to reside in Welshpool when her brother, Archdeacon Clive, was presented to the Vicarage of Welshpool in 1820, and she has resided in the town ever since. It is a little remarkable that Miss Clive should have lived so many years after the death of her uncle, Lord Clive, which took place 108 years ago. The same remark applies to Archdeacon Clive, who survives his sister. Miss Clive was a sincere and kind friend to those with whom she was acquainted, and it may be truly said that her charity was as unobtrusive as it was liberal. Her loss will be felt by the poor of the town, to whom her usual charity of useful clothing was distributed on the day of her death (St. Thomas's day), which was her custom while living for many years past.

The Committee of the Ashford Welsh Charity Schools met last week under the presidency of the Hon. Treasurer, Mr. Stanley Leighton, M.P. The following members were present, viz., Sir Alexander Wood, General Brownrigg, Rev. Mr. Richards, Mr. T. Marchant Williams, B.A., Dr. Jones, and Mr. J. Davies of the treasury department. It will be in the recollection of our readers that the late Sir Hugh Owen, in company with the Rev. Mr. Brownrigg, had elaborated a scheme for the conversion of the schools, which, under the present system, have been a comparative failure, into a middle-class school for girls, some of whom are to be admitted on the foundation, others on part payment, and the remainder on full payment of moderate fees. This scheme was again brought before the notice of the Committee, and it was resolved to proceed without any further delay with the arrangements necessary to carry it out. When structural and other arrangements are complete, qualified teachers of good standing are to be engaged for the work of the school, which is to be organized and carried on in accordance with the best and most approved methods.

Bye-gones

RELATING TO WALES AND THE BORDERS

PUBLISHED every week in the *Oswestry Advertizer*, and reprinted in quarterly parts. Only one hundred and fifty copies issued. Price to subscribers, 5s, per annum, post free.

☞ The Reprint for 1878-9; forming a complete quarto volume of 350 pages, double columns, may still be had, price 10s. 6d. free by post. *This volume forms a distinct series*, and is not numbered, or in any way marked as one of a set. The volume for 1880-1 also forms a distinct series, and at the same price.

*** All communications for the *Bye-Gones* column to be addressed ASKEW ROBERTS, Croeswylan, Oswestry, and orders for the Reprint to WOODALL AND VENABLES, Oswestry.